TWELFTH EDITION

criminology:

THEORIES, PATTERNS, AND TYPOLOGIES

LARRY J. SIEGEL

University of Massachusetts, Lowell

CENGAGE
Learning

Australia • Brazil • Mexico • Singapore • United Kingdom • United States

Criminology: Theories, Patterns, and Typologies, **Twelfth Edition**
Larry J. Siegel

Product Director: Marta Lee-Perriard

Senior Product Manager: Carolyn Henderson Meier

Senior Content Developer: Shelley Murphy

Product Assistant: Stephen Lagos

Media Developer: Ting Jian Yap

Senior Marketing Manager: Kara Kindstrom

Senior Content Project Manager: Christy Frame

Art Director: Brenda Carmichael, Lumina Datamatics

Senior Manufacturing Planner: Judy Inouye

Production Service: Linda Jupiter Productions

Photo Development: Kim Adams Fox

Photo Researcher: Dhanalakshmi Singaravelu, Lumina Datamatics

Text Researcher: Kavitha Balasundaram, Lumina Datamatics

Copy Editor: Lunaea Weatherstone

Proofreader: Mary Kanable

Indexer: Janet Perlman

Text and Cover Designer: Brenda Carmichael, Lumina Datamatics

Cover Image: Diana Ong/Getty Images

Composition: Integra

> For product information and technology assistance, contact us at
> **Cengage Learning Customer & Sales Support, 1-800-354-9706.**
> For permission to use material from this text or product,
> submit all requests online at **www.cengage.com/permissions.**
> Further permissions questions can be e-mailed to
> **permissionrequest@cengage.com.**

Library of Congress Control Number: 2014940077

ISBN: 978-1-305-26109-9

Cengage Learning
20 Channel Center Street
Boston, MA 02210
USA

Cengage Learning is a leading provider of customized learning solutions with office locations around the globe, including Singapore, the United Kingdom, Australia, Mexico, Brazil, and Japan. Locate your local office at **www.cengage.com/global**.

Cengage Learning products are represented in Canada by Nelson Education, Ltd.

To learn more about Cengage Learning Solutions, visit **www.cengage.com**.

Purchase any of our products at your local college store or at our preferred online store **www.cengagebrain.com**.

Unless otherwise noted, all content is © 2016 Cengage Learning.

Printed in the United States of America
Print Number: 01   Print Year: 2014

This book is dedicated to my kids, Eric, Andrew, Julie, and Rachel, and to my grandkids, Jack, Kayla, and Brooke. It is also dedicated to Jason Macy (thanks for marrying Rachel) and Therese J. Libby (thanks for marrying me).

ABOUT THE AUTHOR

LARRY J. SIEGEL was born in the Bronx in 1947. While living on Jerome Avenue and attending City College of New York in the 1960s, he was swept up in the social and political currents of the time. He became intrigued with the influence contemporary culture had on individual behavior: Did people shape society or did society shape people? He applied his interest in social forces and human behavior to the study of crime and justice. After graduating CCNY, he attended the newly opened program in criminal justice at the State University of New York at Albany, earning both his M.A. and Ph.D. degrees there. After completing his graduate work, Dr. Siegel began his teaching career at Northeastern University, where he was a faculty member for nine years. After leaving Northeastern, he held teaching positions at the University of Nebraska–Omaha and Saint Anselm College in New Hampshire. He is currently a professor at the University of Massachusetts, Lowell. Dr. Siegel has written extensively in the area of crime and justice, including books on juvenile law, delinquency, criminology, criminal justice, and criminal procedure. He is a court certified expert on police conduct and has testified in numerous legal cases. The father of four and grandfather of three, Larry Siegel and his wife, Terry, reside with their two dogs, Watson and Cody.

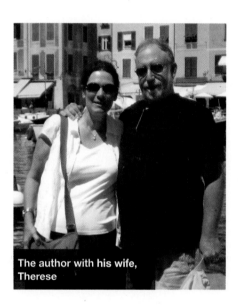

The author with his wife, Therese

BRIEF CONTENTS

FEATURES

profiles in crime

CONTENTS

CHAPTER 6

SOCIAL STRUCTURE THEORIES   179

CHAPTER 7

SOCIAL PROCESS THEORIES: SOCIALIZATION AND SOCIETY   221

CHAPTER 8

CRITICAL CRIMINOLOGY AND RESTORATIVE JUSTICE   257

CHAPTER 9

DEVELOPMENTAL THEORIES: LIFE
COURSE, LATENT TRAIT, AND
TRAJECTORY   289

PART **THREE**
CRIME TYPOLOGIES   325

CHAPTER 10

INTERPERSONAL VIOLENCE   327

CHAPTER 11

POLITICAL CRIME AND
TERRORISM 373

CHAPTER 12

PROPERTY CRIME 411

CHAPTER 13

ENTERPRISE CRIME: WHITE-COLLAR,
GREEN, AND TRANSNATIONAL
ORGANIZED CRIME 441

CHAPTER **14**

PUBLIC ORDER CRIME: SEX AND
SUBSTANCE ABUSE   481

CHAPTER **15**

CRIMES OF THE NEW MILLENNIUM:
CYBERCRIME   525

About 8 P.M. on May 5, 1993, the West Memphis, Arkansas, police department received a call from John Mark Byers reporting that his 8-year-old son, Christopher Byers, was missing. The police soon received two more calls from worried parents, Dana Moore and Pamela Hobbs, whose

Jessie Misskelley, Jason Baldwin, and Damien Echols

AP Photo/Commercial Appeal

young sons were also missing. An all-out search began for the children, and the next day police found the three boys in a drainage creek; they were naked, hogtied, and sexually mutilated. A local waitress named Vicki Hutcheson brought the police tales of devil worshipping gangs operating in the area. Her son Aaron told police he had seen three local youths, Jessie Misskelley, Damien Echols, and Jason Baldwin participating in satanic rituals. The police already had their eye on Echols, a 17-year-old dropout with a history of psychiatric problems, including major depression; besides he was a "Goth" who described himself as a Wiccan. At one time he had been admitted to a psychiatric ward and placed under suicide watch. The boys were interrogated in exhausting sessions and Misskelley gave a confession which was inconsistent with the known facts of the case. The three were brought to trial and convicted, despite the fact there was no direct evidence linking them to the crimes. Experts gave testimony on satanic rituals which may have helped sway the jury—Echols was sentenced to death, and the other two received life in prison. The three languished in prison for nearly two decades. Then a documentary film about the killings, *West of Memphis*, shown on HBO implied that Terry Hobbs, stepfather of one of the boys, Stevie Branch, was the real killer, that DNA found at the scene matched his DNA, and that a hair found on a tree stump near where the bodies were found matched that of David Jacoby, one of his friends. Other films, including *Paradise Lost: The Child Murders at Robin Hood Hills*, *Paradise Lost 2: Revelations*, and *Paradise Lost 3: Purgatory*, directed by Joe Berlinger and Bruce Sinofsky, and books, including *Blood of Innocents*, by

Guy Reel, and *The Last Pentacle of the Sun: Writings in Support of the West Memphis Three*, edited by Brett Alexander Savory and M. W. Anderson, brought attention to the case. Eventually, the Arkansas Supreme Court reviewed newly produced DNA evidence which eventually resulted in the release of the West Memphis Three on August 9, 2011. The identity of the real killers has never been determined. A new film on the case, *The Devil's Knot*, starring Colin Firth and Reese Witherspoon, was released in 2014.

The West Memphis Three case with its focus on devil worship, child killing, and rush to judgment, aptly shows the impact that crime has on a community and the nation as a whole. Here the pressure on police to solve a horrendous crime resulted in their putting the blame on three youths who fit the profile of satanic killers despite the fact there was no physical evidence or witnesses to put them at the scene. It also shows that crime and criminality are a social construct: the West Memphis Three were considered killers because people believed them to be and labeled them as such. It demonstrates the power of media to influence both public perception and the operations of the justice system. The three might still be in prison had not Hollywood taken on the case. It also illustrates the dangers of the death penalty: Damien Echols might have been executed for a crime he did not commit.

The general public is greatly concerned by acts such as the West Memphis Three murders. I share their concern. For more than 40 years, I have been able to channel my personal interest into a career as a professor of criminology. My goal in writing this text is to help students generate the same curiosity about issues of crime and justice. What could be more important or fascinating than a field of study that deals with such wide-ranging topics as the effects of violent media on young people, sex trafficking, drug abuse, and transnational organized crime? Criminology is a dynamic field, changing constantly with the release of major research studies, Supreme Court rulings, and government policy. Its dynamism and diversity make it an important and engrossing area of study.

Because interest in crime and justice is so great and so timely, this text is designed to review these ongoing issues and cover the field of criminology in an organized and comprehensive manner. It is meant as a broad overview of the field, intended to whet the reader's appetite and encourage further and more in-depth exploration. Several major themes recur throughout the book.

- **Competing Viewpoints:** In every chapter, an effort is made to introduce students to the diversity of thought that characterizes this academic discipline. One reason that the study of criminology is so important is that debates continue over the nature and extent of crime and the causes and prevention of criminality. Some experts view criminal offenders as society's victims, unfortunate people who are forced to violate the law because they lack hope for legitimate opportunity; criminals are a "product of their environment." Others view antisocial behavior as a product of mental and physical abnormalities, present at birth or soon after, which are stable over the life course; is it possible that criminals are "born and not made"? Still another view is that crime is a rational choice of greedy, selfish people who can only be deterred through the threat of harsh punishments; therefore, if "you do the crime, you do the time." We will explore these and other views of crime causation. And to help students understand these competing viewpoints, I have designed Concept Summary boxes that synthesize the main points and outlook of each theoretical model, along with its strengths and weaknesses.
- **Critical Thinking:** It is important for students to think critically about law and justice and to develop a critical perspective toward the social institutions and legal institutions entrusted with crime control. Throughout the book, students are asked to critique research highlighted in boxed material and to think outside the box. To aid in this task, a feature called "Thinking Like a Criminologist | An Ethical Dilemma" can be found throughout the text, which presents a scenario that can be analyzed with the help of material found in the chapter.
- **Diversity:** Diversity is a key issue in criminology, and the text attempts to integrate issues of racial, ethnic, gender, and cultural diversity throughout. The book includes material on international issues, such as the use of the death penalty abroad, as well as gender issues such as the rising rate of female criminality. To help with the coverage of diversity issues, Race, Culture, Gender, and Criminology boxes address key issues such as race and income inequality.
- **Currency and Immediacy:** Throughout the book, every attempt is made to use the most current research and to cover the most immediate topics. The idea is to show students the major trends in criminological research

and justice policy. Most people who use the book have told me that this is one of its strongest features. I have attempted to present current research in a balanced fashion, though this sometimes can be frustrating to students. For example, while some experts find that biological traits and conditions promote crime, other criminologists conclude this research is spurious and that biology and crime are unrelated. Which position is correct? While it is comforting to reach a definite conclusion about an important topic, sometimes that is simply not possible. In an effort to be objective and fair, each side of important criminological debates is presented in full. Throughout the text, new to this edition, Criminology in Action boxes review important research in criminology. For example, in Chapter 2, a box called "Factors that Influence Crime Trends" discusses research that helps explain why crime rates rise and fall.

- **Social Policy:** There is a focus on social policy throughout the book so that students can see how criminological theory has been translated into crime prevention programs. Because of this theme, Policy and Practice in Criminology boxes are included throughout the text. These show how criminological ideas and research can be put into action. For example, in Chapter 3, a Policy and Practice in Criminology feature entitled "Toward a Better Way to Interview Child Victims of Sexual Abuse" looks at methods being developed to improve on a child's recollection of a sexual abuse incident so that they can better testify in court.

In sum, the primary goals in writing this text are as follows:

1. To provide students with a thorough knowledge of criminology and show its diversity and intellectual content.
2. To be as thorough and up to date as possible.
3. To be objective and unbiased.
4. To describe current theories, crime types, and methods of social control, and analyze their strengths and weaknesses.
5. To show how criminological thought has influenced social policy.

TOPIC AREAS

The 12th edition has been thoroughly revised and updated. Chapter 13 has been retitled "Enterprise Crime: White-Collar, Green, and Transnational Organized Crime" and includes extensive coverage of crimes involving criminal enterprise ranging from pump and dump security scams to gangs that operate global sex trafficking schemes. Similarly, Chapter 15, "Crimes of the New Millennium: Cybercrime," covers newly emerging areas of criminality made possible by the Internet and instant communication. Crime is going global and so too is criminology.

The text is divided into three main sections or topic areas.

Part One provides a framework for studying criminology. The first chapter defines the field and discusses its most basic concepts: the definition of crime, the component areas of criminology, the concept of criminal law, and the ethical issues that confront the field. Chapter 2 covers criminological data collection methods and the nature, extent, and patterns of crime. Chapter 3 is devoted to the concept of victimization, including the nature of victims, theories of victimization, and programs designed to help crime victims.

Part Two contains six chapters that cover criminological theory: Why do people behave the way they do? Why do they commit crimes? These views focus on choice (Chapter 4), biological and psychological traits (Chapter 5), social structure and culture (Chapter 6), social process and socialization (Chapter 7), critical criminology and restorative justice (Chapter 8), and human development (Chapter 9).

Part Three is devoted to the major forms of criminal behavior. The chapters in this section cover violent crime (Chapter 10); political crime and terrorism (Chapter 11); common theft offenses (Chapter 12); enterprise crimes, including white-collar, green, and transnational organized crime (Chapter 13); public order crimes, including sex offenses and substance abuse (Chapter 14); and cybercrime, which includes cybertheft, cybervandalism, and cyberwar (Chapter 15).

GOALS AND OBJECTIVES

The 12th edition has been carefully structured to cover relevant material in a comprehensive, balanced, and objective fashion. Every attempt has been made to make the presentation of material interesting and contemporary. No single political or theoretical position dominates the text; instead, the many diverse views that are contained within criminology and characterize its interdisciplinary nature are presented in an unbiased and even-handed fashion. While the text includes analysis of the most important scholarly works and scientific research reports, it also includes a great deal of topical information on recent cases and events, ranging from cyberscams to the violence of the Zeta gang, the "muscle" formed to protect Mexican drug cartels.

WHAT IS NEW IN THIS EDITION

- We have added a new feature entitled **Criminology in Action**. These boxed inserts review important issues in criminology and reflect the major subareas of the field, measuring crime, creating theory, crime typologies,

legal theory, and penology. For example, in Chapter 1, a Criminology in Action box on "Measuring the Effect of Deviant Peers" covers research by criminologists Ray Paternoster, Jean Marie McGloin, Holly Nguyen, and Kyle J. Thomas, who conducted an interesting and informative experiment to measure whether peers influence behavior choices.

- **Cybercrime:** We now dedicate an entire chapter to this important topic, expanding coverage of the three major forms of cybercrime: cybertheft, cybervandalism, and cyberwar.

- **Famous Criminologists** are new chapter inserts that spotlight some of the key thinkers and criminological theorists (past and present) in the discipline, showing their individual contributions to the field of criminology.

Chapter-by-Chapter Changes in the 12th Edition

- **Chapter 1 (Crime and Criminology)** revisits the crimes of Dzhokhar and Tamerlan Tsarnaev, who set off bombs at the finish line of the Boston Marathon, killing three people, and maiming and injuring many more. As mentioned, a new Criminology in Action feature, "Measuring the Effect of Deviant Peers," covers an experiment to measure whether peers influence behavior choices. There are new and revised sections on the nature of criminal law, including the concept of intent and action in defining the elements of a crime.

- **Chapter 2 (The Nature and Extent of Crime)** begins with a new vignette on Aaron Alexis, who used a shotgun and a Beretta handgun to kill 12 victims and wound 4 others before he was shot and killed by law enforcement officers in the Washington Navy Yard. The newly expanded definition of rape, which was changed in 2012, is set out. And all of the data have been updated to reflect the most recent trends and patterns in crime.

- **Chapter 3 (Victims and Victimization)** begins with analysis of the Steubenville High School rape case, an incident involving the sexual assault of a 16-year-old girl who was "substantially impaired" after a night of partying and drinking. We review the different methods that have been developed to measure and calculate the cost of victimization to American society. New research on the long-term effects of childhood victimization finds that victims are more susceptible to a number of physical and mental health issues in adulthood. There is a new exhibit on state victim compensation programs. As mentioned, there is a new Policy and Practice in Criminology feature entitled "Toward a Better Way to Interview Child Victims of Sexual Abuse," which covers how abuse prosecutions can rest on a child's recollection of the alleged incident and discusses how to create mechanisms to elicit accurate information from children.

The data on patterns and trends in victimization have been updated to reflect the most recent findings of the National Criminal Victimization Survey.

- **Chapter 4 (Rational Choice Theory)** begins with the case of James "Doug" Cassity and five of his associates who were sentenced to federal prison for their role in a Ponzi-like prepaid funeral scheme that victimized some 97,000 customers in 16 states and caused more than $450 million in losses. A new section, "Is Hate Rational?" reviews studies that examine the characteristics of hate crimes and find that they indeed have a rational basis. We look at Ronald Clarke's CRAVED model of theft, which suggests that the appropriation of property is most likely to occur when six independent conditions are present. We also review how the installation of closed-circuit television (CCTV) surveillance cameras and improved street lighting techniques are currently being used around the world. A new section entitled "Can Police Add to the Certainty of Punishment?" looks at the question of whether adding cops reduces crime. A Policy and Practice in Criminology feature, "Deterring Domestic Violence," reviews the studies on whether domestic violence can be reduced by changing justice system policies. There is new material on the effect of incarceration, as well as an attempt to explain why the crime rate has dropped while the prison population has boomed.
- **Chapter 5 (Trait Theories)** An opening vignette looks at the life and crime of Adam Lanza, who first shot his mother and then traveled to the Sandy Hook Elementary School, where he shot and killed 20 students between the ages of 5 and 10 and six adult teachers. There is a new section on "Individual Vulnerability vs. Differential Susceptibility," which looks at how trait theorists today recognize that crime-producing interactions involve both personal traits and environmental factors. There is a new section on three forms of evolutionary theory, which suggests that the competition for scarce resources has influenced and shaped the human species. New research looks at the association between mental disorder and violence and shows that when compared to the mentally sound, people suffering mental illness were significantly more likely to engage in subsequent violent episodes. A Policy and Practice in Criminology feature entitled "Trait Theory and Crime Prevention" reviews treatment programs that consider biological and psychological traits and conditions in their approach.
- **Chapter 6 (Social Structure Theories)** begins with a vignette on MS-13, considered one of the most fearsome gangs in the United States. There are sections on the development of sociological criminology and how it replaced biological positivism as the main focus of criminology. There is an interesting new discussion on how social forces in disadvantaged areas may be so powerful that they overwhelm individual traits. New data on poverty are covered, including the newest trends in child poverty and minority group poverty. A Race, Culture, Gender, and

Criminology feature, "More than Just Race," reviews the work of William Julius Wilson, one of the nation's most prominent sociologists, including his most recent book, *More than Just Race: Being Black and Poor in the Inner City*. There is a new section on poverty concentration, a phenomenon that occurs when working- and middle-class families flee inner-city poverty areas, resulting in having the most disadvantaged population become consolidated in the most disorganized urban neighborhoods.

- **Chapter 7 (Social Process Theories: Socialization and Society)** begins with the story of Ethan Couch, a boy who defended himself from charges of vehicular manslaughter by arguing he suffered from "affluenza," being too rich and spoiled. Research studies now show that the more often a child is physically disciplined and the harsher the discipline, the more likely they will engage in antisocial behaviors. Another new research effort finds that kids who were abused are less likely to graduate from high school, hold a job, and be happily married; they are more likely to have juvenile and adult arrests. Other new research studies focus on high school dropouts, children born into high-risk families, and kids with delinquent peers. There is a new section, "Damaged Identity," which discusses what happens to people who are assigned deviant labels and become notorious public figures. There are efforts to reduce stigma even if someone has been charged, convicted, and even sent to prison, a topic discussed in a new Policy and Practice in Criminology feature, "Second Chance for Ex-Offenders Act."
- **Chapter 8 (Critical Criminology and Restorative Justice)** begins with a focus on the unrest in the Ukraine and the Russian seizure of the Crimea. A new section on "Failing Social Institutions" shows how critical thinkers focus on contemporary social institutions to show how they operate as instruments of class and racial oppression. Another new section covers "Illegal Domestic Surveillance" in general and the Edward Snowden case in particular. A section called "State-Organized Crime and War" shows how critical criminologists link state-organized crime to attacks on other nations. A new section on "Race and Justice" shows that racial bias is present in the justice system beginning with police contact, arrest, prosecution, and sentencing. There is a new section on "Left Realism and Incarceration" covering the use of mass incarceration as a crime control device. A new Criminology in Action feature entitled "Left Realism and Terrorism" applies the basic concepts to explain the motivation for terrorist activity. There is a new section on "Queer Criminology," covering the treatment of lesbian, gay, bisexual, transgender, and queer (LGBTQ) populations by society in general and the justice system in particular.
- **Chapter 9 (Developmental Theories: Life Course, Latent Trait, and Trajectory)** now begins with the story of the murder of Jennifer, Michaela, and Hayley Petit during a home invasion in Cheshire, Connecticut, by two career criminals, Steven Hayes and Joshua

Komisarjevsky, who were sentenced to death for their terrible crime. A new section on "Population Heterogeneity vs. State Dependence" asks the question, "Are people truly different, or are we more or less all the same but shaped by our different experiences?" A new research study shows that youth who join gangs are 30 percent less likely to graduate from high school and 58 percent less likely to earn a four-year degree than youths of similar background who do not become gang members. A new section on "Persistence and Desistance" shows how life course theorists are particularly interested in why one person persists in crime and develops a criminal career while another is able to reduce their criminal involvement and eventually desist. Another new section on "Cumulative Disadvantage" shows how according to age-graded theory some people experience repeated and varied social problems that weigh down their life chances. The material on "The Marriage Factor" has been updated and there is now a new section called "What Happens When It Ends?" that asks the question of what happens when people break up, which happens in an estimated 40 to 50 percent of first marriages, 67 percent of second marriages, and 74 percent of third marriages. And another new section, "What Causes Impulsivity to Develop?" traces the root cause of poor self-control. Recent research by Alex Piquero, Wesley Jennings, and David Farrington looks at the different trajectories of chronic offenders.

- **Chapter 10 (Interpersonal Violence)** begins with a new opening vignette that covers the case of South African athlete Oscar Pistorius, who made headlines around the world after being charged with the murder of his beautiful model girlfriend, Reeva Steenkamp. There is new coverage of the work of Harvard psychologist Steven Pinker, who has conducted pioneering research on the historical basis of violence. There is an expanded section on the cycle of violence, a theory that holds that physical abuse by parents or caregivers is a direct cause of subsequent violent behavior among youth, who grow up to be abusers themselves. A new Criminology in Action boxed feature, "American Homicide," looks at the work of social historian Randolph Roth, who has followed changes in the homicide rate in the United States from colonial times to the present. A new section discusses "Rape on Campus," an important topic since between 15 to 30 percent of all college women are victims of rape or attempted rape during their school experience. Another new section, "Rape by Deception," looks at crimes in which a rapist uses fraud or trickery to convince the victim to engage in sex, or impersonates someone with whom the victim has been intimate. The section on "Degrees of Murder" has been expanded. There is a new section on "Sexually Based Murders." A new Criminology in Action feature looks at "Myths About Serial Killers." And another new section investigates "The Calculating Robber."

- **Chapter 11 (Political Crime and Terrorism)** starts with a vignette on the Edward Snowden case. There is a new Profiles in Crime feature, "Kwame Kilpatrick: Betraying the Public's Trust," which tells the tale of the former mayor of Detroit who was sent to prison for political corruption. The sad case of former Congressman Jesse L. Jackson, Jr., sentenced to 30 months in prison for conspiring to defraud his reelection campaign funds, is also covered. There are new sections on the extent of the terrorism threat and the Department of Homeland Security. And a new Criminology in Action feature looks at lone-actor terrorists.

- **Chapter 12 (Property Crime)** now begins with the story of Sameh Khaled Danhach, whose shoplifting ring stole an estimated $10 million worth of products *every year* from 2008 to 2012. A new exhibit looks at "Check Fraud Schemes and Techniques." The chapter covers the five most stolen vehicles in the United States. A new Race, Culture, Gender, and Criminology on sexual burglary looks at how some burglaries have a sexual motivation while others involve sexual attacks, though unplanned, that occur when the burglar finds the residence unexpectedly occupied.

- **Chapter 13 (Enterprise Crime: White-Collar, Green, and Transnational Organized Crime)** has been significantly changed and now contains extensive material on transnational gangs. There is the story of Robert Allen Stanford, a financier who lived like a king on the tropical island of Antigua before being prosecuted and incarcerated for investment fraud. A new Profiles in Crime feature, "Criminal Criminal Defense Attorney," tells the story of attorney Paul Bergrin, who was convicted on 23 criminal counts and sentenced to life in prison. The section on the "Nature and Extent of White-Collar Crime" has been completely updated. Another new Profiles in Crime feature, "Take No Quarter: The Case of the Parking Meter Thief," tells of the crimes of James Bagarozzo, of Buffalo, New York, who was convicted of stealing $210,000 from the city's parking meters. A new section on the harms perspective shows how green criminologists typically conceptualize crime and deviance. A new Criminology in Action feature entitled "Is Chicken Farming Foul?" discusses legal practices that green criminologists consider illegal because they damage people and hurt animals. And a new section on citizen groups and their efforts to control green crime has been developed for this chapter.

- **Chapter 14 (Public Order Crime: Sex and Substance Abuse)** begins with a new vignette on the Underground Gangster Crips (UGC), whose members pleaded guilty to various federal charges related to a sex trafficking conspiracy. The case of former Congressman Anthony Weiner is covered. You might remember that he was forced to resign from office after compromising photos he "tweeted" to young women were posted on the Internet. A Race, Culture, Gender, and Criminology feature, "The Sex Trade in Contemporary Society," reviews a major study by Meredith Dank and her colleagues at the Urban Institute that focused on prostitution in on eight U.S. cities—Atlanta, Dallas, Denver, Kansas City, Miami, Seattle, San Diego, and Washington, D.C. There is a new section on the law and child pornography; kiddie porn is now a separate legal category. The section "How Much Drug Use Is There Today?" is updated with data from the National Survey on Drug Use and Health (NSDUH) and other sources. A Criminology in Action feature entitled "Substance Abuse and Psychosis" finds that people diagnosed with mood or anxiety disorders are about twice as likely as the general population to also suffer from a substance use disorder.

- **Chapter 15 (Crimes of the New Millennium: Cybercrime)** is now solely devoted to all forms of cybercrime: cybertheft, cybervandalism, and cyberwar. It begins with a vignette on WikiLeaks, an international organization that publishes classified and secret documents that are submitted by unnamed and anonymous sources. There is information on cyber attacks on computers, such as the SpyEye program that infected more than 1.4 million computers. There is information on recent trends in computer frauds. About 60 percent of U.S. companies report being hit by computer network attacks each year. The chapter covers the use of the Internet to disseminate pornography, including "typosquatting," and adds a new section on "Prosecuting Internet Pornography." A Profiles in Crime feature tells the story of Christopher Gunn, the cyberstalker who carried out an online sextortion scheme that spanned the globe. The chapter also covers international efforts to breach computer systems by terrorists and to conduct espionage.

FEATURES

This text contains different kinds of pedagogy that help students analyze material in greater depth and also link it to other material in the book:

- **Criminology in Action** (NEW TO THIS EDITION) features are boxed inserts that review important issues in criminology and reflect the major subareas of the field, measuring crime, creating theory, crime typologies, legal theory, and penology. For example, in Chapter 10 the research of social historian Randolph Roth that charts changes in the homicide rate in the United States from colonial times to the present, is reviewed and in Chapter 12, a Criminology in Action covers sexual burglary, crimes that have a sexual motivation or involve an unplanned sexual attacks that occur during the commission of a burglary.
- **Profiles in Crime** boxed features present students with case studies of actual criminals and crimes to help

illustrate the position or views within the chapter. By popular demand, we have expanded the feature for this edition, presenting even more real-life "from the headlines" criminal cases throughout the text. For example, in Chapter 11, the case of former Detroit mayor Kwame Kilpatrick, jailed for political fraud, is set out in some detail.

- **Famous Criminologists** (NEW TO THIS EDITION) inserts in Part II introduce students to some key thinkers and criminological theorists (past and present), showing their individual contributions to the field of criminology.
- **Policy and Practice in Criminology** boxes show how criminological ideas and research can be put into action through policies and practices of the criminal justice system. For example, in Chapter 8, the Policy and Practice feature discusses the Victim Offender Reconciliation Program, designed in response to a summer of violence in the metropolitan Denver area.
- **Race, Culture, Gender, and Criminology** boxes cover issues of racial, sexual, and cultural diversity. In Chapter 2, for example, a feature entitled "On the Run" looks at the life of inner-city kids who spend their time avoiding the police.
- **Connections** are short inserts that help link the material to other areas covered in the book. For example, a Connections box in Chapter 14 links media violence to the material discussed in Chapter 5 on behavioral theory.
- **Thinking Like a Criminologist | An Ethical Dilemma** boxes present challenging questions or issues for which students must use their criminological knowledge to answer or confront ethical dilemmas. Applying the information learned in the text will help students begin to "think like criminologists."
- **Chapter Outlines** provide a roadmap to coverage and serve as a useful review tool.
- **Learning Objectives** spell out what students should learn in each chapter. And the chapter **Summary** is geared to these objectives.
- Each chapter ends with **Critical Thinking Questions** to help develop students' critical thinking skills, as well as a list of **Key Terms**.

ANCILLARY MATERIALS

A number of supplements are provided by Cengage Learning to help instructors use *Criminology: Theories, Patterns, and Typologies* in their courses and to aid students in preparing for exams. Supplements are available to qualified adopters. Please consult your local sales representative for details.

To access additional course materials, please visit **www.cengagebrain.com**. At the CengageBrain.com home page, search for the ISBN of your title (from the back cover of your book), using the search box at the top of the page. This will take you to the product page where these resources can be found.

CENGAGE brain.com

To get access, visit CengageBrain.com

MindTap for *Criminology: Theories, Patterns, and Typologies*

MindTap from Cengage Learning represents a new approach to a highly personalized, online learning platform. A fully online learning solution, MindTap combines all of a student's learning tools—readings, multimedia, activities, and assessments—into a singular Learning Path that guides the student through the curriculum. Instructors personalize the experience by customizing the presentation of these learning tools for their students, allowing instructors to seamlessly introduce their own content into the Learning Path via "apps" that integrate into the MindTap platform. Additionally, MindTap provides interoperability with major Learning Management Systems (LMS) via support for open industry standards and fosters partnerships with third-party educational application providers to provide a highly collaborative, engaging, and personalized learning experience.

Online Instructor's Resource Manual and Lesson Plans for *Criminology: Theories, Patterns, and Typologies*

(Revised for the 12th Edition by Tina Freiburger of University of Wisconsin–Milwaukee.) This material includes learning objectives, key terms, a detailed chapter outline, a chapter summary, lesson plans, discussion topics, student activities, "What If" scenarios, media tools, a sample syllabus, and an expanded test bank with 30 percent more questions than the prior edition. The learning objectives are correlated with the discussion topics, student activities, and media tools.

Online Test Bank for *Criminology: Theories, Patterns, and Typologies*

(Revised for the 12th Edition by Keith Bell of West Liberty University.) Each chapter of the test bank contains questions in multiple-choice, true/false, completion, essay, and new critical thinking formats, with a full answer key. The test bank is coded to the learning objectives that appear in the main text, and includes the section in the main text where the answers can be found. Finally, each question in the test bank has been carefully reviewed by experienced criminal justice instructors for quality, accuracy, and content coverage so instructors can be sure they are working with an assessment and grading resource of the highest caliber.

Cengage Learning Testing Powered by Cognero

This assessment software is a flexible, online system that allows you to import, edit, and manipulate test bank content from the *Criminology: Theories, Patterns, and Typologies* test bank or elsewhere, including your own favorite test questions; create multiple test versions in an instant; and deliver tests from your LMS, your classroom, or wherever you want.

PowerPoint Lectures for Criminology: Theories, Patterns, and Typologies

Helping you make your lectures more engaging while effectively reaching your visually oriented students, these handy Microsoft PowerPoint® slides, developed by Tina Freiburger of University of Wisconsin–Milwaukee, outline the chapters of the main text in a classroom-ready presentation. The PowerPoint slides are updated to reflect the content and organization of the new edition of the text, are tagged by chapter learning objective, and feature some additional examples and real-world cases for application and discussion.

ACKNOWLEDGMENTS

The preparation of this text would not have been possible without the aid of my colleagues who helped by reviewing the previous editions and giving me important suggestions for improvement. Reviewers for the 12th edition are:

Ivy Yarckow-Brown, Missouri State University
James Kenny, Fairleigh Dickinson University
Collin Lau, Chaminade University of Honolulu
Patricia O'Brien, Elgin Community College
Gina Robertiello, Northampton Community College
Gerald Titchener, Des Moines Area Community College

My colleagues at Cengage did their typically outstanding job of aiding me in the preparation of the text and gave me counseling and support. Carolyn Henderson Meier, editor extraordinaire, is the backbone of the book. The fantastic Shelley Murphy is a terrifically superb content developer who is always there for me; I really could not do another edition without her. Kim Adams Fox, the photo editor, did her thoroughly professional job in photo research. I have worked with Linda Jupiter, the book's production editor, many times and she is always great, terrific, a close friend and confidant. Lunaea Weatherstone is the copy editor supreme and an unofficial coauthor. The fabulous Christy Frame somehow pulls everything together as production manager, and Kara Kindstrom is the marketing manager with heart. All in all, a terrific team!

Larry Siegel

PART
ONE

CONCEPTS OF CRIME, LAW, AND CRIMINOLOGY

Concern about crime and justice has been an important part of the human condition for more than 5,000 years, since the first criminal codes were set down in the Middle East. Although criminology—the scientific study of crime—is considered a modern science, it has existed for more than 200 years. The first section of the text covers some of the basic questions in criminology: How is crime defined? How much crime is there, and what are the trends and patterns in the crime rate? How many people fall victim to crime, and who is likely to become a crime victim? How did our system of criminal law develop, and what are the basic elements of crimes? What is the science of criminology all about?

These are some of the core issues that will be addressed in the first three chapters of this text. Chapter 1 introduces students to the field of criminology: its nature, area of study, methodologies, and its historical development. Chapter 2 focuses on the acquisition of crime data, crime rate trends, and observable patterns within the crime rate. Chapter 3 is devoted to victims and victimization. Topics include the effects of victimization, the cause of victimization, and efforts to help crime victims.

CHAPTER **1**
CRIME AND CRIMINOLOGY

CHAPTER **2**
THE NATURE AND EXTENT OF CRIME

CHAPTER **3**
VICTIMS AND VICTIMIZATION

Tamerlan Tsarnaev (top) and Dzhokhar Tsarnaev

1

CRIME AND CRIMINOLOGY

those of us who live in New England will never forget the terrible events of April 15, 2013, when two men, Dzhokhar and Tamerlan Tsarnaev, set off bombs at the finish line of the Boston Marathon, killing three people, and maiming and injuring many more. The two had conspired for many months to use improvised explosive devices (IEDs) to harm and kill people in the crowds of spectators who were cheering the runners on toward the marathon finish line. The IEDs were constructed from pressure cookers, explosive powder, shrapnel, adhesives, and other items and were designed to shred skin, shatter bone, and cause extreme pain and suffering, as well as death.[1]

After carefully poring over footage from surveillance cameras and other sources, on April 18, 2013, the FBI released photographs to the media of the Tsarnaevs, identifying them as suspects in the marathon bombings. These photographs were widely disseminated on television and elsewhere, and the brothers must have realized their identification and arrest were imminent. Soon after, the Tsarnaevs, armed with five IEDs, a Ruger P95 semi-automatic handgun, ammunition, a machete, and a hunting knife, drove to the MIT campus, where they shot police officer Sean Collier in an attempt to steal his service weapon. After killing Officer Collier, the brothers carjacked a Mercedes, kidnapped the driver, and forced him to drive to a gas station, robbing him of $800 along the way. After the driver managed to escape, the brothers drove the vehicle to Watertown, Massachusetts, where city police officers located the pair and a gunfight ensued. Attempting to escape, Dzhokhar Tsarnaev reentered the carjacked vehicle and drove it directly at the officers, running over and killing his brother, who had already been injured in the shootout. Gravely wounded, Tsarnaev hid in a dry-docked boat in a Watertown backyard until he was spotted and taken into custody by police.

Who were these killers? Tamerlan Tsarnaev was born in the Kalmyk Autonomous Soviet Socialist Republic, North Caucasus; Dzhokhar in Kyrgyzstan. Because their father was a Chechen, they identified themselves as being of Chechen descent. Though the family prospered in the United States and Dzhokhar attended a state university, the brothers clung to radical Islamic views and blamed the U.S. government for conducting a war against Islam in Iraq and Afghanistan. The brothers viewed the bombing victims as "collateral damage" in their war against the West. Their actions were disavowed by Islamic, Chechen, and other groups, all of whom quickly distanced themselves from the atrocity.

the Boston Marathon bombing and other high-profile criminal incidents have spurred interest in **criminology**, an academic discipline that uses the scientific method to study the nature, extent, cause, and control of criminal behavior. The subject matter of criminology ranges from explaining and understanding terrorist activity such as the Boston bombing to preventing white-collar fraud, from drug legalization to cyberbullying. Regardless of which areas of human behavior they study, criminologists, unlike political figures and media commentators—whose opinions about crime may be colored by personal experiences, biases, and election concerns—remain objective, unbiased, and impartial about the behaviors they study, even if it involves horrendous acts such as the marathon bombing.[2]

This text analyzes criminology and its major subareas of inquiry. It focuses on the nature and extent of crime, the causes of crime, and patterns of criminal behavior. This chapter introduces and defines criminology: What are its goals? How do criminologists define crime? How do they conduct research? What ethical issues face those wishing to conduct criminological research?

WHAT IS CRIMINOLOGY?

LO1 Explain what is meant by the term *criminology*

Criminology is the scientific approach to studying criminal behavior. In their classic definition, preeminent criminologists Edwin Sutherland and Donald Cressey state:

> Criminology is the body of knowledge regarding crime as a social phenomenon. It includes within its scope the processes of making laws, of breaking laws, and of reacting toward the breaking of laws.... The objective of criminology is the development of a body of general

and verified principles and of other types of knowledge regarding this process of law, crime, and treatment.[3]

Sutherland and Cressey's definition includes some of the most important areas of interest to criminologists:

- *Crime is a social phenomenon.* Although some criminologists believe that individual traits and characteristics may play some role in the cause of criminals' antisocial behavior, most believe that social factors are at the root cause of crime. Even the most disturbed people are influenced by their environment and their social interactions and personal relationships.
- *The processes of making laws.* Sutherland and Cressey's definition recognizes the association between crime and the criminal law and shows how the law defines crime. How and why laws are created and why some are strengthened and others eliminated is of great interest to criminologists.
- *Breaking laws and reacting toward the breaking of laws.* At its core, the purpose of criminology is to understand both the onset of crime and the most effective methods for its elimination. Why do people commit illegal acts, and what can be done to convince them—and others who are contemplating crime—that it is in their best interests to turn their back on criminality? These concepts are naturally bound together: it is impossible to effectively control crime unless we understand its cause.
- *Development of a body of general and verified principles.* Sutherland and Cressey recognize that criminology is a social science and criminologists must use the **scientific method** when conducting research. Criminologists are required to employ valid and reliable experimental designs and sophisticated data analysis techniques or else lose standing in the academic community.

Sutherland and Cressey's definition reflects the fact that for most of the twentieth century, criminology's primary orientation was sociological and crime was considered a social issue. Today, criminology takes a more integrated approach to the study of criminal behavior; it has become a multidisciplinary science. **Criminologists** hold degrees in a variety of diverse fields, most commonly sociology, but also criminal justice, political science, psychology, public policy, economics, and the natural sciences. It is not uncommon to see criminologists holding a degree in biology or psychology and conducting research on the genetic basis of crime or the relationship between personality and criminal activity.

How this field developed, its major components, and its relationship to crime law and deviance are some of the topics discussed in this chapter.

Criminology and Criminal Justice

Although the terms criminology and **criminal justice** may seem similar, and people often confuse the two or lump them together, there are major differences between these

---

criminology The scientific study of the nature, extent, cause, and control of criminal behavior.

scientific method Using verifiable principles and procedures for the systematic acquisition of knowledge; typically involves formulating a problem, creating a hypothesis, and collecting data through observation and experiment to verify the hypothesis.

Criminologists Researchers who use scientific methods to study the nature, extent, cause, and control of criminal behavior.

criminal justice The field of study that focuses on law enforcement, the legal system, corrections, and other agencies of justice involved in the apprehension, prosecution, defense, sentencing, incarceration, and supervision of those suspected of or charged with criminal offenses.

fields of study. Criminology explains the etiology (origin), extent, and nature of crime in society, whereas criminal justice refers to the study of the agencies of social control—police, courts, and corrections—that arrest, prosecute, convict, and treat criminal offenders. While criminologists are mainly concerned with identifying the suspected cause of *crime*, criminal justice scholars spend their time identifying effective methods of *crime control*.

Since both fields are crime-related, they do overlap. Some criminologists devote their research to **justice** and social control and their research focuses on how the agencies of justice operate, how they influence crime and criminals, and how justice policies shape crime rates and trends. Conversely, criminal justice experts often want to design effective programs of crime prevention or rehabilitation and to do so must develop an understanding of the nature of crime and its causation. It

The line that separates deviant behavior from the conventional is often quite blurry. Vincent Graham, a center manager, helps Mark Paquette, a patient, at the River Rock Medical Marijuana Center in Denver, Colorado. When Colorado legalized the sale of marijuana, a former deviant behavior that had become criminal was now quite normative. Colorado has experienced a spurt in tax revenue as people are buying weed in droves.

Matthew Staver/New York Times/Redux

is common, therefore, for criminal justice programs to feature courses on criminology and for criminology courses to evaluate the agencies of justice.

Criminology and the Sociology of Deviance

LO2 Identify the difference between crime and deviance

Criminology is also related to the study of **deviant behaviors**—those actions that depart from social norms, values, and beliefs. Included within the broad spectrum of deviant acts are behaviors ranging from violent crimes to joining a nudist colony. The two fields of study are independent because significant distinctions can be made between crime and deviance. However, they also overlap, because many crimes are not unusual or deviant, and many deviant acts are neither illegal nor criminal.

Take, for instance, substance abuse. Selling and/or possessing recreational drugs, such as marijuana, may be illegal in most states and in the federal criminal code, but can it actually be considered deviant? A significant percentage of the population have used or are using drugs; more than half of all high school students have tried drugs before they graduate, and a number of states have legalized the sale and possession of marijuana.[4] Therefore, it is erroneous to argue that all crimes are deviant behaviors that depart from the norms of society.

Similarly, many deviant acts are not criminal even though they may be both disturbing and shocking to the conscience. Suppose a passerby witnesses someone floundering in the ocean and makes no rescue attempt. Most people would condemn the onlooker's coldhearted behavior as callous, immoral, and deviant. However, no legal action could be taken since a private citizen is not required by law to risk his or her own life to save another's. There is no legal requirement that a person rush into a burning building, brave a flood, or jump into the ocean to save someone from harm. They may be deviant and not share commonly held values, but according to the law, they are not criminals.

In sum, criminologists are concerned with the concept of deviance and its relationship to criminality, whereas those sociologists who study deviant behaviors often want to understand and/or identify the line that separates criminal from merely unusual behaviors. The shifting definition of deviant behavior is closely associated with our concepts of crime. The relationships among criminology, criminal justice, and the sociology of deviance are illustrated in Concept Summary 1.1.

justice The quality of being fair under the law. Justice is defined by the relationship that exists between the individual and the state; justice demands that the state treat every person as equally as possible without regard to their gender, religion, race, or any other personal status.

deviant behavior Behavior that departs from the social norm.

The principal purpose of the Office on National Drug Control Policy (ONDCP) is to establish policies, priorities, and objectives for the nation's drug control program, the goals of which are to reduce illicit drug use, manufacturing, and trafficking; reduce drug-related crime and violence; and reduce drug-related health consequences. For more information about the United States' program for controlling drugs, visit the ONDCP website at **http://www.whitehouse.gov/ondcp.**

A number of states have now legalized marijuana for personal or medical use. Compare the laws of states such as Colorado and California that allow personal use with those such as Kansas and Alabama where it remains illegal to use or possess.

WHAT CRIMINOLOGISTS DO: CRIMINOLOGY IN ACTION

LO3 Recognize what is meant by the concept of "criminology in action"

Regardless of their theoretical orientation, criminologists are devoted to the study of crime and criminal behavior. As two noted criminologists, Marvin Wolfgang and Franco Ferracuti, put it: "A criminologist is one whose professional training, occupational role, and pecuniary reward are primarily concentrated on a scientific approach to, and study and analysis of, the phenomenon of crime and criminal behavior."[5]

"Criminology in action" refers to the efforts of criminologists to use their insight, training, and experience to understand human behavior and predict its occurrence. Because criminologists have been trained in diverse fields, several subareas reflecting different orientations and perspectives are now contained within the broader arena of criminology. Criminologists may specialize in a subarea in the same way that psychologists might specialize in a subfield of psychology, such as cognition, development, perception, personality, psychopathology, or sexuality. What are some of the specific goals and areas of study that criminologists focus their attention?

Criminal Statistics and Crime Measurement

The subarea of criminal statistics and crime measurement involves devising valid and reliable measures designed to calculate the amount and trends of criminal activity: How much crime occurs annually? Who commits it? When and where does it occur? Which crimes are the most serious? Criminologists:

- Formulate techniques for collecting and analyzing institutional (police, court, and correctional agency) records and data.
- Develop survey instruments to measure criminal activity not reported to the police by victims. These instruments can by used to estimate the percentage of people who commit crimes but escape detection by the justice system.
- Identify the victims of crime and create surveys designed to have victims report loss and injury that may not have been reported to the police.
- Develop data that can be used to test crime theory. For example, measuring community-level crime rates can help prove whether ecological factors, such as neighborhood poverty and unemployment rates, are related to crime rates.

Those criminologists who devote themselves to criminal statistics engage in a number of different tasks, including:

- Devising accurate methods of collecting crime data
- Using these tested methods to measure the amount and trends of criminal activity

- Using valid crime data to determine who commits crime and where it occurs
- Measuring the effect of social policy and social trends on crime rate changes
- Using crime data to design crime prevention programs and then measuring their effectiveness

The media love to sensationalize crime and report on lurid cases of murder and rape. The general public is influenced by these stories, becoming fearful and altering their behavior to avoid victimization.[6] These news accounts, proclaiming crime waves, are often driven by the need to sell newspapers or increase TV viewership. There is nothing like an impending crime wave or serial killer on the loose to boost readership or viewership. Media accounts therefore can be biased and inaccurate, and it is up to criminologists to set the record straight. That fact is that fewer than 10 million crimes were reported in 2013, a drop of more than 4 million reported crimes since the 1991 peak, and this despite a boost of about 50 million in the general population. A far cry from what the media would have us believe.

Criminologists try to create valid and reliable measurements of criminal behavior. They create techniques to access the records of police and court agencies and use sophisticated statistical methods to understand underlying patterns and trends. They develop survey instruments and then use them with large samples to determine the actual number of crimes being committed and the number of victims who suffer criminal violations: how many people are victims of crime, and what percentage reports the crime to police.

Criminologists are also interested in helping agents of the criminal justice system develop effective crime control policies that rely on accurate measurement of crime rates. By using advanced statistical techniques to calculate where crime will take place, police departments can allocate patrol officers based on these predictions.[7]

The development of valid methods to measure crime and the accuracy of crime data are crucial aspects of criminology in action. Without valid and reliable crime data sources, efforts to conduct research on crime and create criminological theories would be futile. It is also important to determine why crime rates vary across and within regions in order to gauge the association between social and economic forces and criminal activity.

Sociology of Law, Law and Society, Socio-Legal Studies

The sociology of law, also referred to as the study of law and society, is a subarea of criminology concerned with the role social forces play in shaping criminal law and, concomitantly, the role of criminal law in shaping society. Criminologists interested in studying the social aspects of law focus on such topics as:

- The history of legal thought
- How social forces shape the definition and content of the law
- The impact of legal change on society
- The relationship between law and social control
- The effect of criminalization/legalization on behaviors

Some criminologists who study law and society consider the role of law in the context of criminological theory. They try to understand how legal decision making influences individuals, groups, and the criminal justice system. Others try to identify alternatives to traditional legal process—for example, by designing nonpunitive methods of dispute resolution. Some seek to describe the legal system and identify and explain patterns of behavior that guide its operation. Others use the operations of law as a perspective for understanding culture and social life.[8]

Because the law is constantly evolving, criminologists are often asked to determine whether legal change is required and what shape it should take. Criminologists may use their research skills to assess the effects of a proposed legal change. Take for instance the crime of obscenity. Typically, there is no uniform standard of what is considered obscene; material that to some people is lewd and offensive may be considered a work of art by others. How far should the law go in curbing "adult films" and literature? Criminologists might conduct research aimed at determining the effect the proposed law will have on curbing access to obscene material such as child pornography. Other relevant research issues might include analysis of the harmful effects of viewing pornography: Are people who view pornography more likely to commit violent crime than non-watchers? And what about the effect of virtual porn? Is viewing computer-generated sexual imagery the same as viewing live actors? The answers may one day shape the direction of legislation controlling sexual content on the Internet.

Computer fraud, file sharing, ATM theft, and cyberstalking did not exist when the nation was founded. Consequently, the law must be revised to reflect cultural, societal, and technological changes. In fact, the Supreme Court has often considered empirical research supplied by criminologists on such topics as racial discrimination in the death penalty before it renders an opinion.[9] The research conducted by criminologists then helps shape the direction of their legal decision making. Might the research discussed in the accompanying Policy and Practice in Criminology box influence the shape of the criminal law and how it is applied?

Theory Construction and Testing

Social theory can be defined as a systematic set of interrelated statements or principles that explain some aspect of social life. At their core, theories should serve as models or frameworks for understanding human behavior and the forces that shape its content and direction.

Because, ideally, theories are based on verified *social facts*—readily observed phenomena that can be consistently

ARE SEX OFFENDER REGISTRATION LAWS EFFECTIVE?

Criminologists interested in legal studies also evaluate the impact new laws have on society after they have been in effect for a while. Take for instance the practice of sex offender registration, which requires convicted sex offenders to register with local law enforcement agencies when they move into a community. These are often called Megan's Laws in memory of 7-year-old Megan Kanka, killed in 1994 by sex offender Jesse Timmendequas, who had moved unannounced into her New Jersey neighborhood. Megan's Laws require law enforcement authorities to make information available to the public regarding registered sex offenders, including the offender's name, picture, address, incarceration date, and nature of crime. The information can be published in newspapers or put on a sex offender website.

In *Connecticut Dept. of Public Safety v. Doe* (2003), the U.S. Supreme Court upheld the legality of sex offender registration when it ruled that persons convicted of sexual offenses may be required to register with a state's Department of Public Safety and then be listed on a sex offender registry on the Internet containing registrants' names, addresses, photographs, and descriptions. In a 9–0 opinion upholding the plan, the Court reasoned that, because the law was based on the fact that a defendant had been convicted of a sex offense, disclosing their names on the registry without a hearing did not violate due process.

But while sex offender registration laws may be constitutional and pervasive (they are used in all 50 states), appeal to politicians who may be swayed by media crusades against child molesters (i.e., "To Catch a Predator" on *Dateline NBC*), and appease the public's desire to "do some-thing" about child predators, do they actually work? Does registration deter future sex offenses and reduce the incidence of predatory acts against children?

To answer this question, criminologists Kristen Zgoba and Karen Bachar conducted an in-depth study of the effectiveness of New Jersey's registration law and found that while expensive to maintain, the system did not produce effective results. On the one hand, sex offense rates in New Jersey were in a steep decline before the system was installed and the rate of decline actually slowed down after 1995 when the law took effect. Zgoba and Bachar's data show that the greatest rate of decline in sex offending occurred prior to the passage and implementation of Megan's Law. On the other hand, passage and implementation of Megan's Law did not reduce the number of rearrests for sex offenses, nor did it have any demonstrable effect on the time between when sex offenders were released from prison and the time they were rearrested for any new offense, such as a drug, theft, or another sex offense.

Sex offender registration also has little effect on the recidivism rates of parolees. Jill Levenson and her associates investigated the relationship between failure to register (FTR) as a sex offender and subsequent recidivism with a sample of 3,000 people convicted of sexually related crimes. Levenson found that there was no significant difference in the proportion of sexual recidivists and non-recidivists with registration violations nor did FTR predict sexual recidivism. And when there was recidivism, there was no significant difference in time to recidivism when comparing those who failed to register (2.9 years) with compliant registrants (2.8 years).

These results challenge the effectiveness of sex offender registration laws. Rather than deter crime, sex offender laws may merely cause sex offenders to be more cautious while giving parents a false sense of security. Offenders may target victims in other states or communities where they are not registered and parents are less cautious. And many of these laws restrict where offenders can live, pushing them into rural areas where social services are meager, thereby disrupting their chances of treatment and rehabilitation.

Critical Thinking

1. Considering the findings of Zgoba and Bachar, would you advocate abandoning sex offender registration laws because they are ineffective? Or might there be other reasons to keep them active?

2. What other laws do you think should be the topic of careful scientific inquiry to see if they actually work as advertised?

SOURCES: Kelly Socia, "The Policy Implications of Residency Restrictions on Sex Offender Housing in Upstate New York," *Criminology and Public Policy* 10 (2011): 351–389; Wesley Jennings, Kristen Zgoba, and Richard Tewksbury, "Comparative Longitudinal Analysis of Recidivism Trajectories and Collateral Consequences for Sex and Non-Sex Offenders Released Since the Implementation of Sex Offender Registration and Community Notification," *Journal of Crime and Justice* 35 (2012): 356–364; Jill Levenson, Elizabeth Letourneau, Kevin Armstrong, and Kristen Zgoba, "Failure to Register as a Sex Offender: Is It Associated with Recidivism?" *Justice Quarterly* 27 (2010): 305–331; *Connecticut Dept. of Public Safety v. Doe*, 538 U.S. 1 (2003); Kristen Zgoba and Karen Bachar, "Sex Offender Registration and Notification: Research Finds Limited Effects in New Jersey," National Institute of Justice, April 2009, http://www.ncjrs.gov/pdffiles1/nij/225402.pdf (accessed March 2014).

quantified and measured—criminological theorists use the scientific method to test their theories. They gather data, derive *hypotheses*—testable expectations of behavior that can be derived from the theory—and then test them using valid empirical research methods. For example, social learning theory (see Chapter 7) states that people learn behavior by observing how other people act. Adolescent behavior is controlled by the influence of parents, peers, and neighbors.

If this statement is accurate, then logically there should be a significant association between peer influence and behavior.

To test this theory, criminologists might conduct an experiment to see if peers who engage in and espouse deviant attitudes actually influence behavior. The Criminology in Action feature describes one such experiment.

Criminal Behavior Systems and Crime Typologies

Criminologists who study criminal behavior systems and crime typologies focus their research on specific criminal types and patterns: violent crime, theft crime, public order crime, and organized crime. Numerous attempts have been made to describe and understand particular crime types. Marvin Wolfgang's famous 1958 study, *Patterns in Criminal Homicide*—considered a landmark analysis of the nature of homicide and the relationship between victim and offender—found that victims often precipitate the incident that results in their death.[10] Edwin Sutherland's analysis of business-related offenses helped coin a new phrase—white-collar crime—to describe economic crime activities.

Criminologists also conduct research on the links between different types of crime and criminals. This is known as a **crime typology**. Some typologies focus on the criminal, suggesting the existence of offender groups, such as professional criminals, psychotic criminals, amateur criminals, and so on. Others focus on the crimes, clustering them into categories such as property crimes, sex crimes, and so on. While 50 years ago they might have focused their attention on rape, murder, and burglary, they now may be looking at stalking, cybercrime, terrorism, and hate crimes. For example, a number of criminologists are now doing research on terrorism, trying to determine if there is such a thing as a "terrorist personality." Among the findings:

- Mental illness is not a critical factor in explaining terrorist behavior. Also, most terrorists are not "psychopaths."
- There is no "terrorist personality," nor is there any accurate profile—psychologically or otherwise—of the terrorist.
- Histories of childhood abuse and trauma and themes of perceived injustice and humiliation often are prominent in terrorist biographies, but do not really help to explain terrorism.[11]

Research on criminal behavior systems and crime types is important because it enables criminologists to understand why people commit specific sorts of crime, and using this information, gives them the tools to devise crime reduction strategies.

Punishment, Penology, and Social Control

Criminologists also are involved in creating effective crime policies, developing methods of social control, and the correction and control of known criminal offenders; it is this segment of criminology that overlaps criminal justice.

Criminologists conduct research that is designed to evaluate justice initiatives in order to determine their efficiency, effectiveness, and impact. For example, should capital punishment continue to be employed or is its use simply too risky? To explore this issue, Samuel Gross and his colleagues looked at death row inmates who were later found to be innocent. The sample of 340 death row inmates (327 men and 13 women), exonerated after having served years in prison, indicated that about half (144 people) were cleared by DNA evidence. Collectively, they had spent more than 3,400 years in prison for crimes they did not commit—an average of more than 10 years each. Gross and his colleagues found that exonerations from death row are more than 25 times more frequent than exonerations for other prisoners convicted of murder, and more than 100 times more frequent than for all imprisoned felons.[12] How many wrongful convictions might be uncovered if all criminal convictions were given the same degree of scrutiny as death penalty cases? The Gross research illustrates how important it is to evaluate penal measures in order to determine their effectiveness and reliability.

Victimology: Victims and Victimization

In two classic criminological studies, one by Hans von Hentig and the other by Stephen Schafer, the critical role of the victim in the criminal process was first identified. These authors were the first to suggest that victim behavior is often a key determinant of crime and that victims' actions may actually precipitate crime. Both men believe that the study of crime is not complete unless the victim's role is considered.[13] For those studying the role of the victim in crime, these areas are of particular interest:

- Using victim surveys to measure the nature and extent of criminal behavior not reported to the police
- Calculating the actual costs of crime to victims
- Measuring the factors that increase the likelihood of becoming a crime victim
- Studying the role of the victim in causing or precipitating crime
- Designing services for the victims of crime, such as counseling and compensation programs

The study of victims and victimization has uncovered some startling results. For one thing, criminals have been found to be at greater risk for victimization than

crime typology The study of criminal behavior involving research on the links between different types of crime and criminals. Because people often disagree about types of crimes and criminal motivation, no standard exists within the field. Some typologies focus on the criminal, suggesting the existence of offender groups, such as professional criminals, psychotic criminals, occasional criminals, and so on. Others focus on the crimes, clustering them into categories such as property crimes, sex crimes, and so on.

MEASURING THE EFFECT OF DEVIANT PEERS

recently, criminologists Ray Paternoster, Jean Marie McGloin, Holly Nguyen, and Kyle J. Thomas conducted an interesting and informative experiment to measure whether peers influence behavior choices. They set up an experiment at a local university that was allegedly designed to measure short-term memory. The experimenter read a list of 20 words, which the subjects would be asked to recall at the end of the experiment; they were told they would receive $1 for each word they recalled correctly, for a maximum possible payment of $20. The participants were also asked to complete a short online survey, about their background (demographic information), self-perceived memory ability, and other factors. Participants were told that they had eight minutes to answer the survey questions on the computer and that if they finished before then, they should simply sit quietly and wait so that every person waited the same amount of time before recalling the words. The experimenter left the room, and when he returned he told the subjects how to enter the words online. The experimenter then appeared to be shocked as he noticed four "junk web links" located at the bottom of the recall page. The experimenter clicked on the links and announced that they opened up lists of the words to be recalled (i.e., each of the four links opened a page of 5 words, giving participants access to all 20 words).

The experimenter said the presence of the links was a software error and the participants should ignore the links when recalling the words. He then told the participants that he was going to leave the room to speak with a technician about removing the links. All subjects were well aware that there was an opportunity to cheat on this task.

Unknown to the participants, a hired actor was also in the room who looked and acted like the other students (he was a student at another university). In some cases, the peer confederate completed

Research shows that if people see their peers or friends committing crime or engaging in deviance, they are more likely to join in themselves.

Joel Gordon/Peer Pressure

the memory task without cheating and said nothing. In the experimental condition, once the experimenter left the room to talk to the technician, the peer confederate addressed the other subjects in the room using the following script:

> That guy was right—you can totally see the words if you click the links. Screw it. I'm using the lists. I thought we were guaranteed the 20 dollars—now we have to remember all the words? That's ridiculous. I am doing it.

The confederate then openly and clearly cheated on the task by clicking on all four links and using them to fill in the word recall list.

When the experimenter came back, he told the group that because of the need to fix the software glitch, there was no time to count the number of correct words for each subject in order to determine payment, so everyone would receive the $20 compensation.

Despite the fact the peer deviance was committed by a stranger offering a verbal intention and justification for cheating that lasted less than 15 seconds, his behavior significantly increased the probability of subjects engaging in deviance. While

none of the control subjects cheated, 38 percent of the participants exposed to the cheating peer chose to do so!

This experiment lends significant support to both the influence of peers and the theory of differential association: people exposed to positive attitudes toward deviant behavior are more likely to adapt similar behaviors themselves. And remember, the actor was merely a peer and not a close friend. Had a best friend approved cheating, for a longer duration than 15 seconds, we can only imagine what the outcome would have been.

Critical Thinking

Would you be influenced by someone loudly proclaiming it is okay to cheat on a test if an instructor left the room? Be honest now, would another student whom you hardly knew influence your behavior? What if everyone around you started to cheat?

SOURCE: Ray Paternoster, Jean Marie McGloin, Holly Nguyen, and Kyle J. Thomas, "The Causal Impact of Exposure to Deviant Peers: An Experimental Investigation," *Journal of Research in Crime and Delinquency* 50 (2013): 476–503.

noncriminals.[14] Rather than being the passive receptors of criminal acts who are in the "wrong place at the wrong time," crime victims may engage in high-risk lifestyles that increase their own chance of victimization and make them highly vulnerable to crime.

The various elements of criminology in action are summarized in Concept Summary 1.2.

CONNECTIONS

In recent years, criminologists have devoted ever-increasing attention to the victim's role in the criminal process. It has been suggested that a person's lifestyle and behavior may actually increase the risk that he or she will become a crime victim. Some have suggested that living in a high-crime neighborhood increases risk; others point at the problems caused by associating with dangerous peers and companions. For a discussion of victimization risk, see Chapter 3.

Ask Yourself ...

Does living in a college environment increase victimization risk? What can be done to make it safer? Are there places in your hometown that you avoid to reduce the risk of becoming a crime victim? Do you believe that crime victims are people in "the wrong place at the wrong time"?

CRIMINOLOGY IN ACTION

1.2

concept summary

These subareas constitute the discipline of criminology:

CRIMINAL STATISTICS AND RESEARCH METHODOLOGY
Gathering valid crime data. Devising new research methods; measuring crime patterns and trends.

THE SOCIOLOGY OF LAW/LAW AND SOCIETY
Determining the origin of law. Measuring the forces that can change laws and society.

THEORY CONSTRUCTION AND TESTING
Predicting individual behavior. Understanding the cause of crime rates and trends.

CRIMINAL BEHAVIOR SYSTEMS AND CRIME TYPOLOGIES
Determining the nature and cause of specific crime patterns. Studying violence, theft, organized, white-collar, and public order crimes.

PENOLOGY AND SOCIAL CONTROL
Studying the correction and control of criminal behavior. Using scientific methods to assess the effectiveness of crime control and offender treatment programs.

VICTIMOLOGY/VICTIMS AND VICTIMIZATION
Studying the nature and cause of victimization. Aiding crime victims; understanding the nature and extent of victimization; developing theories of victimization risk.

HOW CRIMINOLOGISTS VIEW CRIME

 LO4 Discuss the three most prominent views of the meaning of "crime"

Professional criminologists usually align themselves with one of several schools of thought or perspectives in their field. Each perspective maintains its own view of what constitutes criminal behavior and what causes people to engage in criminality. This diversity of thought is not unique to criminology; biologists, psychologists, sociologists, historians, economists, and natural scientists disagree among themselves about critical issues in their fields. Considering the multidisciplinary nature of the field of criminology, fundamental issues such as the nature and definition of crime itself are cause for disagreement among criminologists.

A criminologist's choice of orientation or perspective depends, in part, on his or her definition of crime. This section discusses the three most common concepts of crime used by criminologists.

The Consensus View of Crime

According to the **consensus view**, crimes are behaviors believed to be repugnant to all elements of society. The substantive criminal law, which is the written code that defines crimes and their punishments, reflects the values, beliefs, and opinions of society's mainstream. The term *consensus* is used because it implies that there is general agreement among a majority of citizens on what behaviors should be outlawed by the criminal law and henceforth viewed as crimes. As the eminent criminologists Edwin Sutherland and Donald Cressey put it:

> Criminal behavior is behavior in violation of the criminal law.... [I]t is not a crime unless it is prohibited by the criminal law [which] is defined conventionally as a body of specific rules regarding human conduct which have been promulgated by political authority, which apply uniformly to all members of the classes to which the rules refer, and which are enforced by punishment administered by the state.[15]

This approach to crime implies that it is a function of the beliefs, morality, and rules established by the existing legal power structure. According to Sutherland and

consensus view The belief that the majority of citizens in a society share common ideals and work toward a common good and that crimes are acts that are outlawed because they conflict with the rules of the majority and are harmful to society.

Cressey's statement, criminal law is applied "uniformly to all members of the classes to which the rules refer." This statement reveals the authors' faith in the concept of an "ideal legal system" that deals adequately with all classes and types of people. Laws prohibiting theft and violence may be directed at the neediest members of society, whereas laws that sanction economic acts such as insider trading, embezzlement, and corporate price-fixing are aimed at controlling the wealthiest. The reach of the criminal law is not restricted to any single element of society.

Social Harm   The consensus view of crime links illegal behavior to the concept of **social harm**. Though people generally enjoy a great deal of latitude in their behavior, it is agreed that behaviors that are harmful to other people and society in general must be controlled. Social harm is what sets strange, unusual, or deviant behavior—or any other action that departs from social norms—apart from criminal behaviors.[16]

This position is not without controversy. Although it is clear that rape, robbery, and murder are inherently harmful and their control justified, behaviors such as drug use and prostitution are more problematic because the harm they inflict is only on those who are willing participants. According to the consensus view, society is justified in controlling these so-called victimless crimes because public opinion holds that they undermine the social fabric and threaten the general well-being of society. Society has a duty to protect all its members—even those who choose to engage in high-risk behaviors.

The Conflict View of Crime

The **conflict view** depicts society as a collection of diverse groups—business owners, workers, professionals, students—who are in constant and continuing conflict. Groups able to assert their political power use the law and the criminal justice system to advance their economic and social position. Criminal laws, therefore, are viewed as acts created to protect the haves from the have-nots. Critical criminologists often compare and contrast the harsh penalties exacted on the poor for their "street crimes" (burglary, robbery, and larceny) with the minor penalties the wealthy

CONNECTIONS

The associations among crime, social harm, and morality are best illustrated in efforts to criminalize acts considered dangerous to the public welfare because they involve behaviors that offend existing social values. These so-called public order crimes include pornography, prostitution, and drug use. Though "victims" are often willing participants, some people believe it is society's duty to save them from themselves. To read more about crime, morality, and social harm, see Chapter 14.

Ask Yourself ...

Should victimless crimes such as drug abuse be decriminalized? Or would that simply lead to more people using drugs on a regular basis like they do with cigarettes and alcohol now?

receive for their white-collar crimes (securities violations and other illegal business practices), though the latter may cause considerably more social harm. While the poor go to prison for minor law violations, the wealthy are given lenient sentences for even the most serious breaches of law. Rather than being class neutral, criminal law reflects and protects established economic, racial, gendered, and political power and privilege.

Crime, according to this definition, is a political concept designed to protect the power and position of the upper classes at the expense of the poor. Even crimes prohibiting violent acts, such as armed robbery, rape, and murder, may have political undertones. Banning violent acts ensures domestic tranquility and guarantees that the anger of the poor and disenfranchised classes will not be directed at their wealthy capitalist exploiters. According to this conflict view of crime, "real" crimes would include the following acts:

- Violations of human rights due to racism, sexism, and imperialism
- Unsafe working conditions
- Inadequate child care
- Inadequate opportunities for employment and education
- Substandard housing and medical care
- Crimes of economic and political domination
- Pollution of the environment
- Price-fixing
- Police brutality
- Assassinations and war-making
- Violations of human dignity
- Denial of physical needs and necessities, and impediments to self-determination
- Deprivation of adequate food
- Blocked opportunities to participate in political decision making

The Interactionist View of Crime

The **interactionist view** of crime traces its antecedents to the symbolic interaction school of sociology, first popularized by pioneering sociologists George Herbert Mead, Charles Horton Cooley, and W. I. Thomas.[17] This position holds that (a) people act according to their own interpretations of reality, through which they assign meaning to things; (b) they observe the way others react, either positively or negatively; and (c) they reevaluate and interpret their own behavior according to the meaning and symbols they have learned from others.

According to this perspective, there is no objective reality. People, institutions, and events are viewed subjectively and labeled either good or evil according to the interpretation of the evaluator. The hit film *The Wolf of Wall Street* illustrates how the definition of crime is subjective: what some consider clever business practices, others define as fraud. The same interactions help define crime:

According to the interactionist view of crime, the definition of criminality is created by those holding social and economic power, so-called moral entrepreneurs. Leonardo DiCaprio starred in the 2013 film *The Wolf of Wall Street*, which focused on the greed and illegal behavior of stock market guru Jordan Belfort, who went to prison for his shady deals. His behavior was defined as criminal by those in power; he saw himself as a savvy businessman.

- The content of the criminal law and consequently the definition of crime often depend on human interaction and perceptions. Marijuana is now legal in some jurisdictions (Colorado for one) and illegal in others. It could easily be the other way around. Gay marriage is legal in some jurisdictions, illegal in others.
- Deciding whether an individual act is considered a crime is also a function of interaction and labeling. When an argument results in the death of one of the participants, a jury may be asked to decide whether the act was murder, self-defense, or merely an accidental fatality. Each person on the jury may have his or her own interpretation of what took place, and whether the act is labeled a crime, and the actor a criminal, depends on the juror's interpretation of events.

The process in which people are defined or labeled as criminal is also subjective. One person is viewed as an unrepentant hardcore offender and sent to a maximum security prison. Another, who has committed essentially the same crime, is considered remorseful and repentant and given probation in the community. Though their acts are similar, the treatment they receive is quite different. In a classic statement, sociologist Howard Becker argued, "The deviant is one to whom that label has successfully been applied; deviant behavior is behavior people so labeled."[18] According to the interactionist view, the definition of crime reflects the preferences and opinions of people who hold social power in a particular legal jurisdiction. These **moral entrepreneurs** wage campaigns (*moral crusades*) to control behaviors they view as immoral and wrong (e.g., abortion) or, conversely, to legalize behaviors they consider harmless social eccentricities (e.g., carrying a handgun for self-protection; smoking pot). Because drug use offends their moral sense, it is currently illegal to purchase cocaine and hashish, while liquor and cigarettes are sold openly, even though far more people die of alcoholism and smoking than from drug abuse each year.[19] Even the definition of serious violent offenses, such as rape and murder, depends on the prevailing moral values of those who shape the content of the criminal law. For example, Florida has implemented a "stand your ground law" that legalizes killing in self defense even if the attacker was unarmed; in other states, shooting an unarmed person might be considered murder. Fifty years ago, a man could not be prosecuted for raping his wife; today, every state criminalizes marital rape. In sum, the definition of crime is more reflective of prevailing moral values than of any objective standard of right and wrong.

interactionist view The view that one's perception of reality is significantly influenced by one's interpretations of the reactions of others to similar events and stimuli.

moral entrepreneurs Interest groups that attempt to control social life and the legal order in such a way as to promote their own personal set of moral values. People who use their influence to shape the legal process in ways they see fit.

The interactionist view of crime is similar to the conflict perspective; both suggest that behavior is outlawed and considered criminal when it offends people who hold social, economic, and political power. However, unlike the conflict view, the interactionist perspective does not attribute capitalist economic and political motives to the process of defining crime. Laws against pornography, prostitution, and drugs are believed to be motivated more by moral crusades than by economic values.

The three main views of crime are summarized in Concept Summary 1.3.

Defining Crime

It is possible to take elements from each school of thought to formulate an integrated definition of crime, such as this one:

> Crime is a violation of societal rules of behavior as interpreted and expressed by a criminal legal code created by people holding social and political power. Individuals who violate these rules are subject to sanctions by state authority, social stigma, and loss of status.

This definition combines the consensus position that the criminal law defines crimes with the conflict perspective's emphasis on political power and control and the interactionist concept of labeling and stigma. Thus crime, as defined here, is a political, social, and economic function of modern life.

THE DEFINITION OF CRIME — 1.3

concept summary

The definition of crime affects how criminologists view the cause and control of illegal behavior and shapes their research orientation.

CONFLICT VIEW
- The law is a tool of the ruling class.
- Crime is a politically defined concept.
- "Real crimes" are not outlawed.
- The law is used to control the underclass.

CONSENSUS VIEW
- The law defines crime.
- The law reflects public opinion.
- Agreement exists on outlawed behavior.
- Laws apply to all citizens equally.

INTERACTIONIST VIEW
- Moral entrepreneurs define crime.
- Crimes are illegal because society defines them that way.
- The definition of crime evolves according to the moral standards of those in power.

CRIME AND THE LAW

No matter which definition of crime we embrace, criminal behavior is tied to the law. It is therefore important for all criminologists to have some understanding of the development of law, its objectives, its elements, and how it has evolved.

A Brief History of the Law

L05 Outline the development of criminal law

The concept of criminal law has been recognized for more than 3,000 years. Hammurabi (1792–1750 BCE), the sixth king of Babylon, created the most famous set of written laws of the ancient world, known today as the Code of Hammurabi. Preserved on basalt rock columns, the code established a system of crime and punishment based on physical retaliation ("an eye for an eye"). The severity of punishment depended on class standing: if convicted of an unprovoked assault, a slave would be killed, whereas a freeman might lose a limb.

More familiar is the Mosaic Code of the Israelites (1200 BCE). According to tradition, God entered into a covenant or contract with the tribes of Israel in which they agreed to obey his law (the 613 laws of the Old Testament, including the Ten Commandments), as presented to them by Moses, in return for God's special care and protection. The Mosaic Code is not only the foundation of Judeo-Christian moral teachings but also a basis for the U.S. legal system. Prohibitions against murder, theft, and perjury preceded by several thousand years the same laws found in the modern United States.

Though ancient formal legal codes were lost during the Dark Ages, early German and Anglo-Saxon societies developed legal systems featuring monetary compensation for criminal violations. Guilt was determined by two methods. One was *compurgation*, in which the accused person swore an oath of innocence with the backing of 12 to 25 oath helpers, who would attest to his or her character and claims of innocence. The second was trial by ordeal, which was based on the principle that divine forces would not allow an innocent person to be harmed. It involved such measures as having the accused place his or her hand in boiling water or hold a hot iron. If the wound healed, the person was found innocent; if the wound did not heal, the accused was deemed guilty. Another version, trial by combat, allowed the accused to challenge his accuser to a duel, with the outcome determining the legitimacy of the accusation. Punishments included public flogging, branding, beheading, and burning.

Common Law

After the Norman conquest of England in 1066, royal judges began to travel throughout the land, holding court in each shire several times a year. When court was in session, the royal administrator, or judge, would summon a number of citizens who would, on their oath, tell of the crimes and serious breaches of the peace that had occurred since the judge's last visit. The royal judge would then decide what to do in each case, using local custom and rules of conduct as his guide. Courts were bound to follow the law established in previous cases unless a higher authority, such as the king or the pope, overruled the law.

The present English system of law came into existence during the reign of Henry II (1154–1189), when royal judges began to publish their decisions in local cases. Judges began to use these written decisions as a basis for their decision making, and eventually a fixed body of legal rules and principles was established. If a new rule was successfully applied in a number of different cases, it would become a precedent. These precedents would then be commonly applied in all similar cases—hence the term **common law**. Crimes such as murder, burglary, arson, and rape are common-law crimes whose elements were initially defined by judges. They are referred to as *mala in se*, inherently evil and depraved. When the situation required it, the English Parliament enacted legislation to supplement the judge-made common law. These were referred to as statutory or *mala prohibitum* crimes, which reflected existing social conditions. English common law evolved constantly to fit specific incidents that the judges encountered. For example, in the *Carriers* case (1473), an English court ruled that a merchant who had been hired to transport merchandise was guilty of larceny (theft) if he kept the goods for his own purposes.[20] Before the *Carriers* case, it was not considered a crime under the common law when people kept something that was voluntarily placed in their possession, even if the rightful owner had only given them temporary custody of the merchandise. Breaking with legal tradition, the court acknowledged that the commercial system could not be maintained unless the laws of theft were expanded. The definition of larceny was altered in order to meet the needs of a growing free enterprise economic system. Larceny now included the taking of goods not only by force or stealth but also by embezzlement and fraud.

The Law in Contemporary Society

LO6 **Analyze the different categories of law**

In contemporary U.S. society, the law governs almost all phases of human enterprise, including commerce, family life, property transfer, and the regulation of interpersonal conflict. It contains elements that control personal relationships between individuals and public relationships between individuals and the government. The former is known as *civil law*, and the latter is called *criminal law*. The law then can generally be divided into four broad categories:

- *Substantive criminal law.* The branch of the law that defines crimes and their punishment is known as

substantive criminal law. It involves such issues as the mental and physical elements of crime, crime categories, and criminal defenses.
- *Procedural criminal law.* Those laws that set out the basic rules of practice in the criminal justice system are **procedural criminal laws**. Some elements of the law of criminal procedure are the rules of evidence, the law of arrest, the law of search and seizure, questions of appeal, jury selection, and the right to counsel.
- *Civil law.* The set of rules governing relations between private parties, including both individuals and organizations (such as business enterprises or corporations), is known as **civil law**. The civil law is used to resolve, control, and shape such personal interactions as contracts, wills and trusts, property ownership, and commerce. Contained within the civil law is tort law, discussed in Exhibit 1.1.
- *Public or administrative law.* The branch of law that deals with the government and its relationships with individuals or other governments is known as **public law**. It governs the administration and regulation of city, county, state, and federal government agencies.

common law Early English law, developed by judges, that incorporated Anglo-Saxon tribal custom, feudal rules and practices, and the everyday rules of behavior of local villages. Common law became the standardized law of the land in England and eventually formed the basis of the criminal law in the United States.

mala in se Acts that are outlawed because they violate basic moral values, such as rape, murder, assault, and robbery.

mala prohibitum Acts that are outlawed because they clash with current norms and public opinion, such as tax, traffic, and drug laws.

substantive criminal law The branch of the law that defines crimes and their punishment. It involves such issues as the mental and physical elements of crime, crime categories, and criminal defenses.

procedural criminal laws Those laws that set out the basic rules of practice in the criminal justice system. Some elements of the law of criminal procedure are the rules of evidence, the law of arrest, the law of search and seizure, questions of appeal, jury selection, and the right to counsel.

civil law The set of rules governing relations between private parties, including both individuals and organizations (such as business enterprises and/or corporations). The civil law is used to resolve, control, and shape such personal interactions as contracts, wills and trusts, property ownership, and commerce.

public (or administrative) law The branch of law that deals with the government and its relationships with individuals or other governments. It governs the administration and regulation of city, county, state, and federal government agencies.

The four categories of the law can be interrelated. A crime victim may file a tort action against a criminal defendant and sue for damages in a civil court. Under tort law, a crime victim may sue even if the defendant is found not guilty because the evidentiary standard in a civil action is less than is needed for a criminal conviction (preponderance of the evidence versus beyond a reasonable doubt). In some instances, the government has the option to pursue a legal matter through the criminal process, file a tort action, or bring the matter before an administrative court. White-collar crimes often involve criminal, administrative, and civil penalties.

Shaping the Criminal Law

Before the American Revolution, the colonies, then under British rule, were subject to the common law. After the colonies won their independence, state legislatures standardized common-law crimes such as murder, burglary, arson, and rape by putting them into statutory form in criminal codes. As in England, whenever common law proved inadequate to deal with changing social and moral issues, the states and Congress supplemented it with legislative statutes. Similarly, statutes prohibiting such offenses as the sale and possession of narcotics or the pirating of DVDs have been passed to control human behavior unknown at the time the common law was formulated. Today, criminal behavior is defined primarily by statute. With few exceptions, crimes are removed, added, or modified by the legislature of a particular jurisdiction.

The content of the law may also be shaped by judicial decision making. A criminal statute may be no longer enforceable when an appellate judge rules that it is vague, deals with an act no longer of interest to the public, or is an unfair exercise of state control over an individual. Conversely, a judicial ruling may expand the scope of an existing criminal law, thereby allowing control over behaviors that heretofore were beyond its reach. In a famous 1990 case, 2 Live Crew (made up of Luther Campbell, Christopher Wong Won, Mark Ross, and David Hobbs), a prominent rap group, found its sales restricted in Florida as police began arresting children under 18 for purchasing the band's sexually explicit CD *As Nasty as They Want to Be*. The hit single "Me So Horny" was banned from local radio stations. Prosecutors tried but failed to get a conviction after group members were arrested at a concert. If members of the Crew had in fact been found guilty and the conviction had been upheld by the state's highest appellate court, obscenity laws would have been expanded to cover people singing (or rapping) objectionable music lyrics.

LO7 Articulate the relationship between the criminal law and the U.S. Constitution

Constitutional Limits Regardless of its source, all criminal law in the United States must conform to the rules and dictates of the U.S. Constitution.[21] Any criminal law that even appears to conflict with the various provisions and articles of the Constitution must reflect a compelling need to protect public safety or morals.[22]

Criminal laws have been interpreted as violating constitutional principles if they are too vague or too broad to give clear meaning of their intent. A law forbidding adults to engage in "immoral behavior" could not be enforced because it does not use clear and precise language or give adequate notice as to which conduct is forbidden.[23] The Constitution also prohibits laws that make a person's status a crime. Becoming or being a heroin addict is not a crime, although laws can forbid the sale, possession, and manufacture of heroin.

The Constitution limits laws that are overly cruel and/or capricious. Whereas the use of the death penalty may be constitutionally approved, capital punishment would be forbidden if it were used for lesser crimes such as rape or employed in a random, haphazard fashion.[24] Cruel ways of executing criminals that cause excessive pain are likewise forbidden. One method used to avoid "cruelty" is lethal injection. In the 2008 case *Baze and Bowling v. Rees*, the Court upheld the use of lethal injection unless there is a "substantial risk of serious harm" that the drugs will not work effectively.[25]

The Substantive Criminal Law

LO8 Synthesize the different purposes of criminal law

The substantive criminal law defines crime and punishment. Each state and the federal government have their own substantive criminal code, developed over many generations and incorporating moral beliefs, social values, and political, economic, and other societal concerns.

Criminal laws are divided into felonies and misdemeanors. The distinction is based on seriousness: a **felony**

felony A serious offense, such as rape, murder, robbery, or burglary, that is punishable by a prison sentence or, in the case of first-degree murder, by capital punishment.

is a serious offense; a **misdemeanor** is a minor or petty crime. Crimes such as murder, rape, and burglary are felonies; they are punished with long prison sentences or even death. Crimes such as unarmed assault and battery, petty larceny, and disturbing the peace are misdemeanors; they are punished with a fine or a period of incarceration in a county jail.

Regardless of their classification, acts prohibited by the criminal law constitute behaviors considered unacceptable and impermissible by those in power. People who engage in these acts are eligible for severe sanctions. By outlawing these behaviors, the government expects to achieve a number of social goals:

- *Enforcing social control.* Those who hold political power rely on criminal law to formally prohibit behaviors believed to threaten societal well-being or to challenge their authority. For example, U.S. criminal law incorporates centuries-old prohibitions against the following behaviors harmful to others: taking another person's possessions, physically harming another person, damaging another person's property, and cheating another person out of his or her possessions. Similarly, the law prohibits actions that challenge the legitimacy of the government, such as planning its overthrow, collaborating with its enemies, and so on.

- *Discouraging revenge.* By punishing people who infringe on the rights, property, and freedom of others, the law shifts the burden of revenge from the individual to the state. As famed jurist and Supreme Court Judge Oliver Wendell Holmes stated, this prevents "the greater evil of private retribution."[26] Although state retaliation may offend the sensibilities of many citizens, it is greatly preferable to a system in which people would have to seek justice for themselves.

- *Expressing public opinion and morality.* Criminal law reflects constantly changing public opinions and moral values. *Mala in se* crimes, such as murder and forcible rape, are almost universally prohibited; however, the prohibition of legislatively created *mala prohibitum* crimes, such as traffic offenses and gambling violations, changes according to social conditions and attitudes. Criminal law is used to codify these changes.

- *Deterring criminal behavior.* Criminal law has a social control function. It can control, restrain, and direct human behavior through its sanctioning power. The threat of punishment associated with violating the law is designed to prevent crimes before they occur. During the Middle Ages, public executions drove this point

The substantive criminal law defines crimes and sets out their punishment. Aaron Schaffhausen, who killed his three daughters in an act of revenge against his ex-wife, is led from a St. Croix County Courtroom after being sentenced to three consecutive life terms in prison on July 15, 2013, in Hudson, Wisconsin.

AP Images/*Star Tribune*/Elizabeth Flores

home. Today criminal law's impact is felt through news accounts of long prison sentences and an occasional execution.

- *Punishing wrongdoing.* The deterrent power of criminal law is tied to the authority it gives the state to sanction or punish offenders. Those who violate criminal law are subject to physical coercion and punishment.

- *Maintaining social order.* All legal systems are designed to support and maintain the boundaries of the social system they serve. In medieval England, the law protected the feudal system by defining an orderly system of property transfer and ownership. Laws in some socialist nations protect the primacy of the state by strictly curtailing profiteering and individual enterprise. Our own capitalist system is also supported and sustained by criminal law. In a sense, the content of criminal law is more a reflection of the needs of those who control the existing economic and political system than a representation of some idealized moral code.

- *Providing restoration.* Victims deserve restitution or compensation for their pain and loss. The criminal law can be used to restore to victims what they have lost. Because we believe in equity and justice, it is only fair that the guilty help repair the harm they have caused others by their crimes. Punishments such as fines, forfeiture, and restitution are connected to this legal goal.

misdemeanor A minor or petty crime, typically punished by a fine, community sentence, or a jail term.

The Elements of Criminal Law

 LO9 Compare and contrast the elements of the criminal law

Although each state and the federal government have unique methods of defining crime, there are significant uniformities and similarities that shape the essence of almost all criminal law codes. Although the laws of California, Texas, and Maine may all be somewhat different, the underlying concepts that guide and shape their legal systems are universal. The question remains: regardless of jurisdictional boundaries, what is the legal definition of a crime and how does the criminal law deal with it?

Legal Definition of a Crime   Today, in all jurisdictions, the legal definition of a crime involves the elements of the criminal acts that must be proven in a court of law if the defendant is to be found guilty.[27] For the most part, common criminal acts have both mental and physical elements, both of which must be present if the act is to be considered a legal crime. In order for a crime to occur, the state must show that the accused committed the guilty act, or *actus reus*, and had the *mens rea*, or criminal intent, to commit the act. The *actus reus* may be an aggressive act, such as taking someone's money, burning a building, or shooting someone; or it may be a failure to act when there is a legal duty to do so, such as a parent neglecting to seek medical attention for a sick child. The *mens rea* (guilty mind) refers to an individual's state of mind at the time of the act or, more specifically, the person's intent to commit the crime.

Actus Reus   To satisfy the requirements of *actus reus*, guilty actions must be voluntary. Even though an act may cause harm or damage, it is not considered a crime if it was done by accident or was an involuntary act. It would not be a crime if a motorist obeying all the traffic laws hit a child who ran into the street. If the same motorist were drinking or speeding, then his action would be considered a vehicular crime because it was a product of negligence. Similarly, it would not be considered a crime if a babysitter accidentally dropped a child and the child died. However, it would be considered manslaughter if the sitter threw the child down in anger or frustration and the blow caused the child's death. In some circumstances of *actus reus*, the use of words is considered criminal. In the crime of sedition, the words of disloyalty constitute the *actus reus*. If a person falsely yells "fire" in a crowded theater and people are injured in the rush to exit, that person is held responsible for the injuries, because the use of the word in that situation constitutes an illegal act.

Typically, the law does not require people to aid others in distress, such as entering a burning building to rescue people trapped by a fire. However, failure to act is considered a crime in certain instances:

- *Relationship of the parties based on status.* Some people are bound by relationship to give aid. These relationships include parent/child and husband/wife. If a husband finds his wife unconscious because she took an overdose of sleeping pills, he is obligated to save her life by seeking medical aid. If he fails to do so and she dies, he can be held responsible for her death.
- *Imposition by statute.* Some states have passed laws requiring people to give aid. For example, a person who observes a broken-down automobile in the desert but fails to stop and help the other parties involved may be committing a crime.
- *Contractual relationships.* These relationships include lifeguard and swimmer, doctor and patient, and babysitter or au pair and child. Because lifeguards have been hired to ensure the safety of swimmers, they have a legal duty to come to the aid of drowning persons. If a lifeguard knows a swimmer is in danger and does nothing about it and the swimmer drowns, the lifeguard is legally responsible for the swimmer's death.

Mens Rea   In most situations, for an act to constitute a crime, it must be done with criminal intent, or *mens rea* (guilty mind). Intent, in the legal sense, can mean carrying out an act intentionally, knowingly, and willingly. However, the definition also encompasses situations in which recklessness or negligence establishes the required criminal intent. For example, criminal intent exists if the results of an action, although originally unintended, are certain to occur. When Timothy McVeigh planted a bomb in front of the Murrah Federal Building in Oklahoma City, he did not intend to kill any particular person in the building. Yet the law would hold that McVeigh or any other person would be substantially certain that people in the building would be killed in the blast, and McVeigh therefore had the criminal intent to commit murder.

Strict Liability   Though common-law crimes require that both the *actus reus* and the *mens rea* must be present before a person can be convicted of a crime, several crimes defined by statute do not require *mens rea*. In these cases, the person accused is guilty simply by doing what the statute prohibits; intent does not enter the picture. These strict liability crimes, or public welfare offenses, include violations of health and safety regulations, traffic laws, and narcotic control laws. For example, a person stopped for speeding is guilty of breaking the traffic laws regardless of whether he or she intended to go over the speed limit or did it by accident. The underlying purpose of these laws is to protect the public; therefore, intent is not required.

Criminal Defenses

When people defend themselves against criminal charges, they must refute one or more of the elements of the crime of which they have been accused. A number of different approaches can be taken to create this defense.

First, defendants may deny the *actus reus* by arguing that they were falsely accused and that the real culprit has yet to be identified. Second, defendants may claim that although they engaged in the criminal act of which they are accused, they lacked the *mens rea* (intent) needed to be found guilty of the crime.

If a person whose mental state is impaired commits a criminal act, it is possible for the person to excuse his or her criminal actions by claiming that he or she lacked the capacity to form sufficient intent to be held criminally responsible. Insanity, intoxication, and ignorance are types of excuse defenses. A defendant might argue that because he suffered from a mental impairment that prevented him from understanding the harmfulness of his acts, he lacked sufficient *mens rea* to be found guilty as charged.

Another type of defense is justification. Here the individual usually admits committing the criminal act but maintains that he or she should not be held criminally liable because the act was justified. Among the justification defenses are necessity, duress, self-defense, and entrapment. A battered wife who kills her mate might argue that she acted out of duress; her crime was committed to save her own life.

Persons standing trial for criminal offenses may thus defend themselves by claiming that they did not commit the act in question, that their actions were justified under the circumstances, or that their behavior can be excused by their lack of *mens rea*. If either the physical or mental elements of a crime cannot be proven, then the defendant cannot be convicted.

The Evolution of Criminal Law

The criminal law is constantly evolving in an effort to reflect social and economic conditions. Sometimes legal changes are prompted by highly publicized cases that generate fear and concern. A number of highly publicized cases of celebrity stalking, including Robert John Bardo's fatal shooting of actress Rebecca Schaeffer on July 18, 1989, prompted more than 25 states to enact **stalking statutes** that prohibit "the willful, malicious, and repeated following and harassing of another person."[28] California's sexual predator law, which took effect on January 1, 1996, allows people convicted of sexually violent crimes against two or more victims to be committed to a mental institution after their prison terms have been served.[29]

The criminal law may also change because of shifts in culture and social conventions, reflecting a newfound tolerance of behavior condemned only a few years before. In an important 2003 case, *Lawrence v. Texas*, the Supreme Court declared that laws banning sodomy were unconstitutional because they violated the due process rights of citizens because of their sexual orientation. In its decision, the Court said:

> Although the laws involved … here … do not more than prohibit a particular sexual act, their penalties and purposes have more far-reaching consequences, touching upon the most private human conduct, sexual behavior, and in the most private of places, the home. They seek to control a personal relationship that, whether or not entitled to formal recognition in the law, is within the liberty of persons to choose without being punished as criminals. The liberty protected by the Constitution allows homosexual persons the right to choose to enter upon relationships in the confines of their homes and their own private lives and still retain their dignity as free persons.

As a result of the decision, sodomy laws in the United States are now unconstitutional and therefore unenforceable.[30]

What are some of the new laws that are being created and old ones that have been eliminated?

Stalking Laws More than 25 states have enacted stalking statutes, which prohibit and punish acts described typically as "the willful, malicious, and repeated following and harassing of another person."[31] Stalking laws were originally formulated to protect women terrorized by former husbands and boyfriends, although celebrities are often plagued by stalkers as well. In celebrity cases, these laws often apply to stalkers who are strangers or casual acquaintances of their victims.

Prohibiting Assisted Suicide Some laws are created when public opinion turns against a previously legal practice. Physician-assisted suicide became the subject of a national debate when Dr. Jack Kevorkian began practicing what he called *obitiatry*, helping people take their own lives.[32] In an attempt to stop Kevorkian, Michigan passed a statutory ban on assisted suicide, reflecting what lawmakers believed to be prevailing public opinion.[33] Kevorkian was paroled on June 1, 2007, and died in 2011. Forty-four states now disallow assisted suicide either by statute or common law, including Michigan.[34]

Registering Sex Offenders Some legal changes have been prompted by public outrage over a particularly heinous crime, such as the murder of Megan Kanka (Megan's Law):

- *Sex offender registration.* A revision of the 1994 Jacob Wetterling Act, which had required the states to register individuals convicted of sex crimes against children, also established a community notification system.
- *Community notification.* States were compelled to make private and personal information on registered sex offenders available to the public.

---

stalking statutes Laws that prohibit "the willful, malicious, and repeated following and harassing of another person."

Variations of Megan's Law have been adopted by all 50 states. Although civil libertarians have expressed concern that notification laws may interfere with an offender's postrelease privacy rights, recent research indicates that registered offenders find value in Megan's Law because it helps deter future abuse. When DNA collection is included in the law, it helps reduce false accusations and convictions.[35]

Clarifying Rape Sometimes laws are changed to clarify the definition of crime and to quell public debate over the boundaries of the law. When does bad behavior cross the line into criminality, and when does it remain merely bad behavior? An example of the former can be found in changes to the law of rape. In a number of states, including California, it is now considered rape if the victim consents to sex, the sex act begins, the victim changes his/her mind during the act and tells his/her partner to stop, and the partner refuses and continues. The fact that the victim initially consented to and participated in a sexual act does not bar him/her from withdrawing that consent. However, the victim must communicate the withdrawal of consent in such a manner that the accused knew or reasonably should have known that the consent was withdrawn. Before the legal change, such a circumstance was not considered rape but merely aggressive sex.[36]

Controlling Technology Changing technology and the ever-increasing role of technology in people's daily lives will require modifications of the criminal law. Such technologies as automatic teller machines and cellular phones have already spawned a new generation of criminal acts involving theft of access numbers and software piracy. For example, a modification to Virginia's Computer Crimes Act that took effect in 2005 makes *phishing*—sending out bulk email messages designed to trick consumers into revealing bank account passwords, Social Security numbers, and other personal information—a felony. Those convicted of selling the data or using the data to commit another crime, such as identity theft, now face twice the prison time.

Rape is a common-law crime whose elements were initially defined by judges but are now part of the statutory law. They are referred to as *mala in se*, inherently evil and depraved. Self-proclaimed pimp and accused killer Ammar Harris listens while prosecutor Lisa Luzaich (right) speaks during sentencing in Clark County District Court on February 26, 2014. District Judge Kathleen Delaney sentenced Harris to 16 years to life in Nevada state prison in a rape and robbery case.

Protecting the Environment In response to the concerns of environmentalists, the federal government has passed numerous acts designed to protect the nation's well-being. The Environmental Protection Agency has successfully prosecuted significant violations of these and other new laws, including data fraud cases (e.g., private laboratories submitting false environmental data to state and federal environmental agencies); indiscriminate hazardous waste dumping that resulted in serious injuries and death; industrywide ocean dumping by cruise ships; oil spills that caused significant damage to waterways, wetlands, and beaches; and illegal handling of hazardous substances such as pesticides and asbestos that exposed children, the poor, and other especially vulnerable groups to potentially serious illness.[37]

Legalizing Marijuana A number of states are now exploring the legalization of marijuana for medical purposes. New Jersey Senate Bill 119, signed into law on January 18, 2010, is typical of changes in the law. The bill protects "patients who use marijuana to alleviate suffering from debilitating medical conditions, as well as their physicians, primary caregivers, and those who are authorized to produce marijuana for medical purposes" from "arrest, prosecution, property forfeiture, and criminal and other penalties." It also provides for the creation of alternative treatment centers, "at least two each in the northern, central, and southern regions of the state. The first two centers issued a permit in each region shall be nonprofit entities, and centers subsequently issued permits may be nonprofit or for-profit entities." The bill allows marijuana to be prescribed for a variety of illnesses ranging from severe chronic pain, nausea, and vomiting to terminal illnesses such as cancer. Physicians determine how much marijuana a patient needs and give written instructions to be presented to an alternative treatment center. The maximum amount for a 30-day period is two ounces.[38] According to the Drug Policy Alliance, Alaska, California, Hawaii, Maine, Michigan, Montana, Nevada, New Mexico, Oregon, Rhode Island, Vermont, and Washington have created laws that effectively remove state-level criminal penalties for growing and/or possessing medical marijuana. Another ten states, plus the District of Columbia, have symbolic medical marijuana laws (laws that support medical marijuana but do not provide patients with legal protection under state law).[39] Some states such as Colorado have legalized marijuana for personal use.

While providing medical marijuana has strong public support, the federal government still criminalizes any use of marijuana, and federal agents can arrest users even if they have prescriptions from doctors in states where medical marijuana is legal. The Supreme Court ruled in 2005 in *Gonzales v. Raich* that the federal government can prosecute medical marijuana patients, even in states with compassionate use laws.[40] The Court ruled that under the Commerce Clause of the United States Constitution, which allows the United States Congress "To regulate Commerce ... among the several States," Congress may ban the use of cannabis even where states approve its use for medicinal purposes. The reasoning: because of high demand, marijuana grown for medical reasons would find its way into the hands of ordinary drug users. So while the law may change on a local or state level, federal rules take precedent.

Responding to Terrorism   The criminal law has also undergone extensive change in both substance and procedure in the aftermath of the September 11, 2001, terrorist attacks.

The future direction of U.S. criminal law remains unclear. Certain actions, such as crimes by corporations and political corruption, will be labeled as criminal and given more attention. Other offenses, such as recreational drug use, may be reduced in importance or removed entirely from the criminal law system.

ETHICAL ISSUES IN CRIMINOLOGY

LO10   Summarize the main ethical issues in criminology

A critical issue facing students of criminology involves recognizing the field's political and social consequences. All too often, criminologists forget the social responsibility they bear as experts in the area of crime and justice. When government agencies request their views of issues, their pronouncements and opinions become the basis for sweeping social policy. The lives of millions of people can be influenced by criminological research data.

Debates over gun control, capital punishment, and mandatory sentences are ongoing and contentious. Some criminologists have successfully argued for social service, treatment, and rehabilitation programs to reduce the crime rate, but others consider them a waste of time, suggesting instead that a massive prison construction program coupled with tough criminal sentences can bring the crime rate down. By accepting their roles as experts on law-violating behavior, criminologists place themselves in a position of power; the potential consequences of their actions are enormous. Therefore, they must be aware of the ethics of their profession and be prepared to defend their work in the light of public scrutiny. Major ethical issues include these:

- What to study?
- Whom to study?
- How to study?

What to Study?

Under ideal circumstances, when criminologists choose a subject for study, they are guided by their own scholarly interests, pressing social needs, the availability of accurate data, and other similar concerns. Nonetheless, in recent years, a great influx of government and institutional funding has influenced the direction of criminological inquiry. Major sources of monetary support include the Justice Department's National Institute of Justice, the National Science Foundation, and the National Institute of Mental Health. Private foundations, such as the Edna McConnell Clark Foundation, have also played an important role in supporting criminological research.

Though the availability of research money has spurred criminological inquiry, it has also influenced the direction research has taken. State and federal governments provide a significant percentage of available research funds, and they may also dictate the areas that can be studied. In recent years, for example, the federal government has spent millions of dollars funding long-term cohort studies of criminal careers. Consequently, academic research has recently focused on criminal careers. Other areas of inquiry may be ignored because there is simply not enough funding to pay for or sponsor the research.

A potential conflict of interest may arise when the institution funding research is itself one of the principal subjects of the research project. Governments may be reluctant to fund research on fraud and abuse of power by government officials. They may also exert a not-so-subtle influence on the criminologists seeking research funding: if criminologists are too critical of the government's efforts to reduce or counteract crime, perhaps they will be barred from receiving further financial help. This situation is even more acute when we consider that criminologists typically work for universities or public agencies and are under pressure to bring in a steady flow of research funds or to maintain the continued viability of their agency. Even when criminologists maintain discretion of choice, the direction of their efforts may not be truly objective. The objectivity of research may be questioned if studies are funded by organizations that have a vested interest in the outcome of the research. For example, a study on the effectiveness of the defensive use of handguns to stop crime may be tainted if the funding for the project comes from a gun manufacturer whose sales may be affected by the research findings. Efforts to show that private prisons are more effective than state correctional facilities might be tainted if the researchers received a research grant from a corporation that maintains private prisons.

Whom to Study?

A second major ethical issue in criminology concerns who will be the subject of inquiries and study. Too often, criminologists focus their attention on the poor and minorities while ignoring the middle-class criminal who may be committing white-collar crime, organized crime, or government crime. Critics have charged that by "unmasking" the poor and desperate, criminologists have justified any harsh measures taken against them. For example, a few social scientists have suggested that criminals have lower intelligence quotients than the average citizen, and that because minority group members have lower than average IQ scores, their crime rates are high.[41] This was the conclusion reached in *The Bell Curve*, a popular though highly controversial book written by Richard Herrnstein and Charles Murray.[42] Although such research is often methodologically unsound, it brings to light the tendency of criminologists to focus on one element of the community while ignoring others. The question that remains is whether it is ethical for criminologists to publish biased or subjective research findings, paving the way for injustice.

How to Study?

Ethics are once again questioned in cases where subjects are misled about the purpose of the research. When white and African American individuals are asked to participate in a survey of their behavior or an IQ test, they are rarely told in advance that the data they provide may later be used to prove the existence of significant racial differences in their self-reported crime rates. Should subjects be told about the true purpose of a survey? Would such disclosures make meaningful research impossible? How far should criminologists go when collecting data? Is it ever permissible to deceive subjects to collect data? Criminologists must take extreme care when they select subjects for their research studies to ensure that they are selected in an unbiased and random manner.[43]

When criminological research efforts involve experimentation and treatment, care must be taken to protect those subjects who have been chosen for experimental and control groups. For example, it may be unethical to provide a special treatment program for one group while depriving others of the same opportunity. Conversely, criminologists must be careful to protect subjects from experiments that may actually cause them harm. An examination of the highly publicized Scared Straight program, which brought youngsters into contact with hardcore prison inmates who gave them graphic insights into prison life (to scare them out of a life of crime), discovered that the young subjects may have been harmed by their experience. Rather than being frightened into conformity, subjects actually increased their criminal behavior.[44]

SUMMARY

LO1 Explain what is meant by the term *criminology*

Criminology is the scientific approach to the study of criminal behavior and society's reaction to law violations and violators. It is an academic discipline that uses the scientific method to study the nature, extent, cause, and control of criminal behavior. Criminology is an interdisciplinary science. Criminologists hold degrees in a variety of fields, most commonly sociology, but also criminal justice, political science, psychology, economics, engineering, and the natural sciences. Criminology is a fascinating field, encompassing a wide variety of topics that have both practical application and theoretical importance.

LO2 Identify the difference between crime and deviance

Criminologists devote themselves to measuring, understanding, and controlling crime and deviance. Deviance includes a broad spectrum of behaviors that differ from the norm, ranging from the most socially harmful to the relatively inoffensive. Criminologists are often concerned with the concept of deviance and its relationship to criminality.

LO3 Recognize what is meant by the concept of "criminology in action"

The various subareas included within the scholarly discipline of criminology, taken as a whole, define the field of study. The subarea of criminal statistics/crime measurement involves calculating the amount of, and trends in, criminal activity. Sociology of law/law and society/socio-legal studies is a subarea of criminology concerned with the role that social forces play in shaping criminal law and the role of criminal law in shaping society. Criminologists also explore the causes of crime. Another subarea of criminology involves research on specific criminal types and patterns: violent crime, theft crime, public order crime, organized crime, and so on. The study of penology, correction, and sentencing involves the treatment of known criminal offenders. Criminologists recognize that the victim plays a critical role in the criminal process and that the victim's behavior is often a key determinant of crime.

LO4 Discuss the three most prominent views of the meaning of "crime"

According to the consensus view, crimes are behaviors that all elements of society consider repugnant. This view holds that the majority of citizens in a society share common values and agree on what behaviors should be defined as criminal. The conflict view depicts criminal behavior as being defined by those in power to protect and advance their own self-interest. According to the interactionist view, those with social power are able to impose their values on society as a whole, and these values then define criminal behavior.

LO5 Outline the development of criminal law

The criminal law used in U.S. jurisdictions traces its origin to the English system. At first the law of precedent was used to decide conflicts on a case-by-case basis during the middle ages. Judges began to use these written decisions as a basis for their decision making, and eventually a fixed body of legal rules and principles was established. If a new rule was successfully applied in a number of different cases, it would become a precedent. These precedents would then be commonly applied in all similar cases—hence the term *common law*. In the U.S. legal system, lawmakers have codified common-law crimes into state and federal penal codes.

LO6 Analyze the different categories of law

Substantive criminal law involves such issues as the mental and physical elements of crime, crime categories, and criminal defenses. Procedural criminal law sets out the basic rules of practice in the criminal justice system. It includes the rules of evidence, the law of arrest, the law of search and seizure, questions of appeal, jury selection, and the right to counsel. The civil law governs relations between private parties, including both individuals and organizations (such as business enterprises and/or corporations), and is used to resolve, control, and shape such personal interactions as contracts, wills and trusts, property ownership, personal disputes (torts), and commerce. Administrative laws are enforced by governmental agencies such as the IRS or EPA.

LO7 Articulate the relationship between the criminal law and the U.S. Constitution

All criminal law in the United States must conform to the rules and dictates of the U.S. Constitution. Criminal laws have been interpreted as violating constitutional principles if they are too vague or too broad to give clear meaning of their intent. The Constitution also prohibits laws that make a person's status a crime. The Constitution limits laws that are overly cruel or capricious.

LO8 Synthesize the different purposes of criminal law

The criminal law serves several important purposes. It represents public opinion and moral values. It enforces social controls. It deters criminal behavior and wrongdoing. It punishes transgressors. It creates equity and abrogates the need for private retribution.

LO9 Compare and contrast the elements of the criminal law

The criminal law contains two main elements: the criminal act (*actus reas*) and the mental intent to commit that act (*mens rea*). In most instances, both must be present before an act can be considered a crime. A criminal defense can be either (a) to deny the act took place or to claim that the accused did not commit the act, or (b) to deny intent, claiming the act was justified because, for example, it was committed in self-defense or should be excused because it was a product of mental illness or intoxication. Some crimes are strict liability—they do not require intent; the mere act is sufficient to be considered criminal.

LO10 Summarize the main ethical issues in criminology

Ethical issues arise when information-gathering methods appear biased or exclusionary. These issues may cause serious consequences because research findings can significantly affect individuals and groups. Criminologists must be concerned about the topics they study. Another ethical issue in criminology revolves around the selection of research subjects. A third area of concern involves the methods used in conducting research.

CRITICAL THINKING QUESTIONS

1. Some criminologists believe that the threat of punishment is sufficient to control crime. Are there other forms of social control? Aside from the threat of legal punishments, what else controls your own behavior?
2. Would it be ethical for a criminologist to observe a teenage gang by "hanging" with them, drinking, and watching as they steal cars? Should he or she report that behavior to the police?
3. Can you identify behaviors that are deviant but not criminal? What about crimes that are illegal but not deviant?
4. Do you agree that some of the most damaging acts in society are not punished as crimes? If so, what are they?
5. Should the concept of *mens rea* or the "guilty mind" be eliminated from the criminal law and replaced with a strict liability standard? (If you do the crime, you do the time, regardless of what you were thinking at the time.)
6. If you could change the criminal law, what behaviors would you legalize? What would you criminalize? For example, would you want to legalize drug use? What might be the consequences of your actions? In other words, are there any hidden drawbacks or benefits?

KEY TERMS

criminology (4)
scientific method (4)
criminologists (4)
criminal justice (4)
justice (5)
deviant behavior (5)

crime typology (9)
consensus view (11)
social harm (12)
conflict view (12)
interactionist view (13)
moral entrepreneurs (13)

common law (15)
mala in se (15)
mala prohibitum (15)
substantive criminal law (15)
procedural criminal laws (15)
civil law (15)

public law (15)
felony (16)
misdemeanor (17)
stalking statutes (19)

NOTES

1. United States Department of Justice, "Federal Grand Jury Returns 30-Count Indictment Related to Boston Marathon Explosions and Murder of MIT Police Officer Sean Collier," June 27, 2013, http://www.fbi.gov/boston/press-releases/2013/federal-grand-jury-returns-30-count-indictment-related-to-boston-marathon-explosions-and-murder-of-mit-police-officer-sean-collier (accessed March 2014).
2. John Hagan and Alberto Palloni, "Sociological Criminology and the Mythology of Hispanic Immigration and Crime," *Social Problems* 46 (1999): 617–632.
3. Edwin Sutherland and Donald Cressey, *Principles of Criminology*, 6th ed. (Philadelphia: J. B. Lippincott, 1960), p. 3.
4. Monitoring the Future, "Teen Marijuana Use Tilts Up, While Some Drugs Decline in Use," December 14, 2009, http://monitoringthefuture.org/pressreleases/09drugpr_complete.pdf (accessed March 2014).
5. Marvin Wolfgang and Franco Ferracuti, *The Subculture of Violence* (London: Social Science Paperbacks, 1967), p. 20.
6. Mirka Smolej and Janne Kivivuori, "The Relation Between Crime News and Fear of Violence," *Journal of Scandinavian Studies in Criminology and Crime Prevention* 7 (2006): 211–227.
7. Jacqueline Cohen, Wilpen Gorr, and Andreas Olligschlaeger, "Leading Indicators and Spatial Interactions: A Crime-Forecasting Model for Proactive Police Deployment," *Geographical Analysis* 39 (2007): 105–127.
8. The Sociology of Law Section of the American Sociological Association, http://www.departments.bucknell.edu/soc_anthro/soclaw/textfiles/Purpose_soclaw.txt (accessed March 2014).
9. Rosemary Erickson and Rita Simon, *The Use of Social Science Data in Supreme Court Decisions* (Champaign, IL: University of Illinois Press, 1998).
10. Marvin Wolfgang, *Patterns in Criminal Homicide* (Philadelphia: University of Pennsylvania Press, 1958).
11. Randy Borum, *Psychology of Terrorism* (Tampa: University of South Florida, 2004). Available at http://www.ncjrs.gov/pdffiles1/nij/grants/208552.pdf (accessed March 2014).
12. Samuel Gross, Kristen Jacoby, Daniel Matheson, Nicholas Montgomery, and Sujata Patil, "Exonerations in the United States, 1989 through 2003," *Journal of Criminal Law and Criminology* 95 (2005): 523–559.
13. Hans von Hentig, *The Criminal and His Victim* (New Haven: Yale University Press, 1948); Stephen Schafer, *The Victim and His Criminal* (New York: Random House, 1968).
14. Linda Teplin, Gary McClelland, Karen Abram, and Darinka Mileusnic, "Early Violent Death Among Delinquent Youth: A Prospective Longitudinal Study," *Pediatrics* 115 (2005): 1586–1593.
15. Sutherland and Cressey, *Criminology*, 6th ed., p. 8.
16. Charles McCaghy, *Deviant Behavior* (New York: Macmillan, 1976), pp. 2–3.
17. See Herbert Blumer, *Symbolic Interactionism* (Englewood Cliffs, NJ: Prentice Hall, 1969).
18. Howard Becker, *Outsiders: Studies in the Sociology of Deviance* (New York: Free Press, 1963), p. 9.
19. The National Council on Alcoholism and Drug Dependence, http://www.ncadd.org (accessed March 2014).
20. *Carriers* case, 13 Edward IV 9.pL.5 (1473).
21. See John Weaver, *Warren—The Man, the Court, the Era* (Boston: Little, Brown, 1967); see also "We the People," *Time*, July 6, 1987, p. 6.
22. *Kansas v. Hendricks*, 117 S.Ct. 2072 (1997); *Chicago v. Morales*, 119 S.Ct. 246 (1999).
23. *City of Chicago v. Morales et al.*, 527 U.S. 41 (1999).
24. Daniel Suleiman, "The Capital Punishment Exception: A Case for Constitutionalizing the Substantive Criminal Law," *Columbia Law Review* 104 (2004): 426–458.

25. *Baze and Bowling v. Rees*, 553 U.S. _____ (2008).

26. Oliver Wendell Holmes, *The Common Law*, ed. Mark De Wolf (Boston: Little, Brown, 1881), p. 36.

27. The following is based on Joshua Dressler, *Cases and Materials on Criminal Law* (American Casebook Series) (Eagan, MN: West Publishing, 2003); Joel Samaha, *Criminal Law* (Belmont, CA: Wadsworth Publishing, 2001).

28. National Institute of Justice, *Project to Develop a Model Anti-Stalking Statute* (Washington, DC: National Institute of Justice, 1994).

29. Associated Press, "Judge Upholds State's Sexual Predator Law," *Bakersfield Californian*, October 2, 1996.

30. *Lawrence et al. v. Texas*, No. 02-102. June 26, 2003.

31. National Institute of Justice, *Project to Develop a Model Anti-Stalking Statute*.

32. Marvin Zalman, John Strate, Denis Hunter, and James Sellars, "Michigan Assisted Suicide Three Ring Circus: The Intersection of Law and Politics," *Ohio Northern Law Review* 23 (1997): 863–903.

33. 1992 P.A. 270, as amended by 1993 P.A.3, M.C. L. ss. 752.1021 to 752. 1027.

34. Michigan Code of Criminal Procedure, "Assisting a Suicide," Section 750.329a.

35. Sarah Welchans, "Megan's Law: Evaluations of Sexual Offender Registries," *Criminal Justice Policy Review* 16 (2005): 123–140.

36. Matthew Lyon, "No Means No? Withdrawal of Consent During Intercourse and the Continuing Evolution of the Definition of Rape," *Journal of Criminal Law and Criminology* 95 (2004): 277–314.

37. Environmental Protection Agency, Criminal Enforcement Division, http://www.epa.gov/compliance/criminal/ (accessed March 2014).

38. State of New Jersey 213th Legislature, Senate Bill 119, http://medicalmarijuana.procon.org/sourcefiles/NJS119.pdf (accessed March 2014).

39. Drug Policy Alliance Network, Medical Marijuana, http://www.drugpolicy.org/marijuana/medical/ (accessed March 2014)

40. *Gonzales v. Raich*, 545 U.S. 1, 2005.

41. See, for example, Michael Hindelang and Travis Hirschi, "Intelligence and Delinquency: A Revisionist Review," *American Sociological Review* 42 (1977): 471–486.

42. Richard Herrnstein and Charles Murray, *The Bell Curve* (New York: Free Press, 1994).

43. Victor Boruch, Timothy Victor, and Joe Cecil, "Resolving Ethical and Legal Problems in Randomized Experiments," *Crime and Delinquency* 46 (2000): 330–353.

44. Anthony Petrosino, Carolyn Turpin-Petrosino, and James Finckenauer, "Well-Meaning Programs Can Have Harmful Effects! Lessons from Experiments of Programs Such as Scared Straight," *Crime and Delinquency* 46 (2000): 354–379.

AP Images/FBI

THE NATURE AND EXTENT OF CRIME

aron Alexis, 34, was employed as a contractor for a private information technology firm. Alexis was assigned to a project at the Washington Navy Yard and arrived in the Washington, D.C., area on August 25, 2013. On September 14, Alexis purchased a Remington 870 shotgun and ammunition at a gun shop in northern Virginia. Two days later at the Washington Navy Yard, he used the shotgun and a Beretta handgun to kill 12 victims and wound 4 others before he was shot and killed by law enforcement officers. The shotgun had been altered with a sawed-off barrel and stock. Etched into the barrel were the words "End to the torment!" "Not what yall say!" "Better off this way!" and "My ELF weapon!" ELF referred to his delusional belief that he was being controlled or influenced by extremely low frequency electromagnetic waves. On his computer, law enforcement agents found the statement that "Ultra low frequency attack is what I've been subject to for the last 3 months, and to be perfectly honest that is what has driven me to this."[1] The company that employed Alexis had withdrawn his access to classified material for two days earlier that month when mental health problems became evident, but restored it quickly and never told the Navy about the incident.

W

hen stories such as the Navy Yard killings are splashed across the media and rehashed on nightly talk shows, they help convince most Americans that we live in a violent society. If a delusional man can buy high-powered weapons and bring them to his place of work, is anyone safe? When people read headlines about a violent crime spree, they begin to fear crime and take steps to protect themselves, perhaps avoiding public places and staying at home in the evening. More than one-third of Americans say they are afraid to walk alone in their neighborhood at night. Even though the crime rate has dropped considerably, more than two-thirds of Americans believe it is more dangerous today than a year ago.[2]

Are Americans justified in their fear of violent crime? Should they barricade themselves behind armed guards? Are crime rates actually rising or falling? Where do most crimes occur and who commits them? To answer these and similar questions, criminologists have devised elaborate methods of crime data collection and analysis. Without accurate data on the nature and extent of crime, it would not be possible to formulate theories that explain the onset of crime or to devise social policies that facilitate its control or elimination. Accurate data collection is also critical in assessing the nature and extent of crime, tracking changes in the crime rate, and measuring the individual and social factors that may influence criminality.

In this chapter, we review how crime data are collected on criminal offenders and offenses and what this information tells us about crime patterns and trends. We also examine the concept of criminal careers and discover what available crime data can tell us about the onset, continuation, and termination of criminality.

PRIMARY SOURCES OF CRIME DATA

LO1 Compare and contrast the most widely used forms of crime data collection

There are primary sources of crime data routinely used by criminologists around the globe, including official records and national surveys collected, compiled, and analyzed

Uniform Crime Report (UCR) Large database, compiled by the Federal Bureau of Investigation, of crimes reported and arrests made each year throughout the United States.

index crimes The eight crimes that, because of their seriousness and frequency, the FBI reports the incidence of in the annual Uniform Crime Report. Index crimes include murder, rape, assault, robbery, burglary, arson, larceny, and motor vehicle theft.

Part I crimes Another term for index crimes; eight categories of serious, frequent crimes.

by government agencies such as the federal government's Bureau of Justice Statistics and the Federal Bureau of Investigation (FBI). Criminologists use these techniques to measure the nature and extent of criminal behavior and the personality, attitudes, and background of criminal offenders. It is important to understand how these data are collected to gain insight into how professional criminologists approach various problems and questions in their field. What are these primary sources, how are they collected, and how valid are their findings?

Official Records: The Uniform Crime Report

In order to understand more about the nature and extent of crime, criminologists use the records of government agencies such as police departments, prisons, and courts. Official record data can be used to examine crime rates and trends. They can also be analyzed to uncover the individual and social forces that affect crime: to study the relationship between crime and poverty, for example, criminologists might use income and family data from the United States Census Bureau and then cross-reference this information with crime data collected by local police departments. The most important crime record data are collected from local law enforcement agencies by the Federal Bureau of Investigation (FBI) and published yearly in their **Uniform Crime Report (UCR)**.

 The Bureau of Justice Statistics website is one of the most important sources of crime data. Become familiar with their annual collections on law enforcement, court processing, and correctional populations, among other topics. Access the BJS site at **http://www.bjs.gov/**.
   As an exercise, find out how many local police departments there are in the United States.

The UCR includes both crimes reported to local law enforcement departments and the number of arrests made by police agencies. The UCR is the best known and most widely cited source of official criminal statistics.[3] The FBI receives and compiles records from more than 17,000 police departments serving a majority of the U.S. population. Its major unit of analysis involves **index crimes** or **Part I crimes**: murder and nonnegligent manslaughter, forcible rape, robbery, aggravated assault, burglary, larceny, arson, and motor vehicle theft. Exhibit 2.1 defines these crimes; note that the definition of rape was changed in 2012. The revised definition now includes any gender of victim or perpetrator, and includes instances in which the victim is incapable of giving consent because of temporary or permanent mental or physical incapacity, including due to the influence of drugs or alcohol or because of age. The ability of the victim to give consent must be determined in accordance with state statute. Physical resistance from the victim is not required to demonstrate lack of consent.[4]

EXHIBIT 2.1

Part I (Index) Crime Offenses

Criminal Homicide

Murder and Nonnegligent Manslaughter The willful (non-negligent) killing of one human being by another. Deaths caused by negligence, attempts to kill, assaults to kill, suicides, accidental deaths, and justifiable homicides are excluded. Justifiable homicides are limited to (a) the killing of a felon by a law enforcement officer in the line of duty and (b) the killing of a felon, during the commission of a felony, by a private citizen.

Manslaughter by Negligence The killing of another person through gross negligence. Traffic fatalities are excluded. Although manslaughter by negligence is a Part I crime, it is not included in the crime index.

Forcible Rape

The carnal knowledge of a female forcibly and against her will. Included are rapes by force and attempts or assaults to rape. Statutory offenses (no force used—victim under age of consent) are excluded. This definition was changed in 2012 and since 2013 the FBI has used: "The penetration, no matter how slight, of the vagina or anus with any body part or object, or oral penetration by a sex organ of another person, without the consent of the victim."

Robbery

The taking or attempting to take anything of value from the care, custody, or control of a person or persons by force or threat of force or violence and/or by putting the victim in fear.

Aggravated Assault

An unlawful attack by one person upon another for the purpose of inflicting severe or aggravated bodily injury. This type of assault usually is accompanied by the use of a weapon or by means likely to produce death or great bodily harm. Simple assaults are excluded.

Burglary/Breaking or Entering

The unlawful entry of a structure to commit a felony or a theft. Attempted forcible entry is included.

Larceny/Theft (Except Motor Vehicle Theft)

The unlawful taking, carrying, leading, or riding away of property from the possession or constructive possession of another. Examples are thefts of bicycles or automobile accessories, shoplifting, pocket picking, or the stealing of any property or article that is not taken by force and violence or by fraud. Attempted larcenies are included. Embezzlement, con games, forgery, worthless checks, and so on are excluded.

Motor Vehicle Theft

The theft or attempted theft of a motor vehicle. A motor vehicle is self-propelled and runs on the surface and not on rails. Specifically excluded from this category are motorboats, construction equipment, airplanes, and farming equipment.

Arson

Any willful or malicious burning or attempt to burn, with or without intent to defraud, a dwelling house, public building, motor vehicle, or aircraft, personal property of another, or the like.

SOURCE: FBI, *Uniform Crime Report, Crime in the United States, 2012.*

The FBI tallies and annually publishes the number of reported offenses by city, county, standard metropolitan statistical area, and geographical divisions of the United States. In addition to recording crimes reported to the police, the UCR also collects data on the number and characteristics (age, race, and gender) of individuals who have been arrested for committing a crime. Included in the arrest data are people who have committed Part I crimes and people who have been arrested for all other crimes, known collectively as **Part II crimes**. This latter group includes such criminal acts as sex crimes, drug trafficking, and vandalism.

Compiling the Uniform Crime Report

 LO2 Articulate the problems associated with collecting the official crime data

The methods used to compile the UCR are quite complex. Each month law enforcement agencies report the number of index crimes known to them. These data are collected from records of all crime complaints that victims, officers who discovered the infractions, or other sources reported to these agencies.

Whenever criminal complaints are found through investigation to be unfounded or false, they are eliminated from the actual count. However, the number of actual offenses known is reported to the FBI whether or not anyone is arrested for the crime, the stolen property is recovered, or prosecution ensues.

The UCR uses three methods to express crime data. First, the number of crimes reported to the police is expressed as raw figures. In 2012, an estimated 1,214,462 violent crimes occurred nationwide. Second, crime rates

Part II crimes All crimes other than index and minor traffic offenses. The FBI records annual arrest information for Part II offenses.

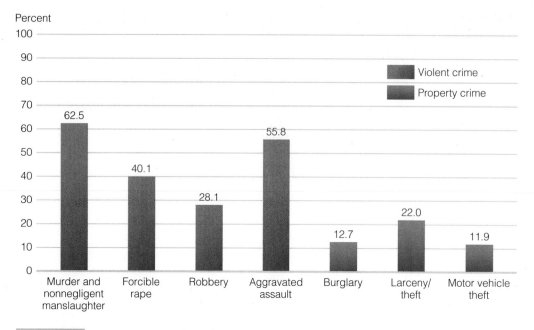

Percent

FIGURE 2.1 Crimes Cleared by Arrest

SOURCE: FBI, *Crime in the United States, 2012*, http://www.fbi.gov/about-us/cjis/ucr/crime-in-the-u.s/2012/crime-in-the-u.s.-2012/offenses-known-to-law-enforcement/clearances (accessed March 2014).

per 100,000 people are computed. There were an estimated 386.9 violent crimes per 100,000 inhabitants in 2012. This is the equation used:

$$\frac{\text{Number of Reported Crimes}}{\text{Total U.S. Population}} \times 100,000 = \text{Rate per } 100,000$$

Third, the FBI computes changes in rate of crime over time. Preliminary 2013 data show that violent crime declined 5 percent below the 2012 numbers.[5]

Clearance Rates In addition, each month law enforcement agencies also report how many crimes were **cleared**. Crimes are cleared in two ways: (1) when at least one person is arrested, charged, and turned over to the court for prosecution; or (2) by exceptional means, when some element beyond police control precludes the physical arrest of an offender (i.e., the offender leaves the country). Data on the number of clearances involving the arrest of only juvenile offenders, data on the value of property stolen and recovered in connection with Part I

cleared crimes Crimes are cleared in two ways: when at least one person is arrested, charged, and turned over to the court for prosecution; or by exceptional means, when some element beyond police control precludes the physical arrest of an offender (for example, the offender leaves the country).

offenses, and detailed information pertaining to criminal homicide are also reported.

Traditionally, more than 20 percent of all reported index crimes are cleared by arrest each year, including slightly less than half of all violent crimes and about 20 percent of property crimes. Not surprisingly, as Figure 2.1 shows, the most serious crimes such as murder and rape are cleared at much higher rates than less serious property crimes such as larceny. What factors account for this clearance rate differential?

- The media gives more attention to serious violent crimes, and as a result local and state police departments are more likely to devote time and spend more resources in their investigations.
- There is more likely to be a prior association between victims of violent/serious crimes and their attackers, a fact that aids police investigations.
- Even if they did not know one another beforehand, violent crime victims and offenders interact so that identification is facilitated.
- Serious violent crimes often produce physical evidence—blood, body fluids, fingerprints—that can be used to identify suspects.

Are the Uniform Crime Reports Valid?

Despite criminologists' continued reliance on the UCR, its accuracy has been suspect. The three main areas of concern are reporting practices, law enforcement practices, and methodological problems.

Reporting Practices   Less than half of all violent crimes and only one-third of property crimes are reported to the police.[6] The reasons for not reporting vary. Some victims do not trust the police or have confidence in their ability to solve crimes. Others do not have property insurance and therefore believe it is useless to report theft. Some victims fear reprisals from an offender's friends or family or, in the case of family violence, from their spouse, boyfriend, or girlfriend.[7] Others justify not reporting by stating that the incident was "a private matter," that "nothing could be done," or that the victimization was "not important enough." People who are themselves involved in criminal activities and have "dirty hands" are less likely to report crime than those whose "hands are clean." The dirty hands may not be related to criminal activity: people who cheat on their spouse, drink excessively, or have other skeletons in the closet are less likely to call the police than their less deviant peers.

Because less than half of all crimes are reported to police it is evident that the UCR significantly underreports the actual total number of annual criminal events. Some of the reasons crime victims decide to report crime are set out in Exhibit 2.2.

Law Enforcement Practices   The way police departments record and report criminal and delinquent activity also affects the validity of UCR statistics. Some police departments define crimes loosely—reporting a trespass as a burglary or an assault on a woman as an attempted rape—whereas others pay strict attention to FBI guidelines. These reporting practices may help explain interjurisdictional differences in crime.[8] Changes in reporting can shape the crime trends reported in the UCR.[9] So what may be viewed as a significant change in crime rates may in fact represent a change in victims' behavior more than in criminals' behavior. Arson is seriously underreported because many fire departments do not report to the FBI, and those that do define many fires that may well have been set by arsonists as "accidental" or "spontaneous."[10]

Some local police departments make systematic errors in UCR reporting. They may count an arrest only after a formal booking procedure, although the UCR requires arrests to be counted if the suspect is released without a formal charge.

More serious allegations claim that in some cases police officials may deliberately alter reported crimes to improve their department's public image. Police administrators interested in lowering the crime rate may falsify crime reports by classifying a burglary as a nonreportable trespass. John Eterno and Eli Silverman studied reporting practices in New York City and found that police commanders, under intense pressure to reduce crime by hard-charging police commissioners, manipulated crime statistics in order to show success.[11] How did they cheat? One method was to check eBay and other websites to find prices for items that had been reported stolen that were actually lower than the value provided by the crime victim. They would then use the lower values to reduce felony grand larcenies (crimes that are in the UCR) to misdemeanor petit larcenies that go unrecorded. Some commanders reported sending officers to crime scenes to persuade victims not to file complaints or to alter crimes so they did not have to be reported to the FBI. While it is possible that the New York police administrators were under more pressure to reduce crime than their counterparts around the country, the fact that members of the largest police department in the United States may have fudged UCR data is disturbing.

Crime rates also may be altered based on the way law enforcement agencies process UCR data. As the number of employees assigned to dispatching, record keeping, and criminal incident reporting increases, so too will national crime rates. What appears to be a rising crime rate may be simply an artifact of improved police record-keeping ability.

Methodological Issues   Methodological issues also contribute to questions pertaining to the UCR's validity. The most frequent issues include the following:

- No federal crimes are reported.
- Reports are voluntary and vary in accuracy and completeness.
- Not all police departments submit reports.
- The FBI uses estimates in its total crime projections.
- According to the "Hierarchy Rule," in a multiple-offense incident, only the most serious crime is counted. Thus if an armed bank robber commits a robbery, assaults a patron as he flees, steals a car to get away, and damages property during a police chase, only the robbery

---

EXHIBIT 2.2

Why Do Victims Report Crime?

- *Seriousness.* The more serious the crime, the more likely it is to be reported. How do victims judge seriousness? If they are injured, especially if a weapon was involved, they are more likely to consider the incident serious and report it to the police. If the crime was completed, and the criminal got away with their wallet, purse, car, or package, reporting is more likely to occur.
- *Social support.* The more support victims have from family, friends, and social service agencies, the more likely they are to report crime.
- *Victim–offender relationship.* Crimes involving strangers are more likely to be reported than those involving friends and relatives. One exception to this rule: if the crime was committed by an ex-husband or ex-wife, the police are more likely to be called than if it was committed by a stranger.

SOURCE: Andrew Karmen, *Crime Victims: An Introduction to Victimology* (Belmont, CA: Cengage, 2012).

is reported because it is the most serious offense. Consequently, many lesser crimes go unreported.

- Each act is listed as a single offense for some crimes but not for others. If a man robbed six people in a bar, the offense is listed as one robbery, but if he assaulted or murdered them, it would be listed as six assaults or six murders.
- Incomplete acts are lumped together with completed ones.
- Important differences exist between the FBI's definition of certain crimes and those used in a number of states.

In addition to these issues, the complex scoring procedure used in the UCR program means that many serious crimes are not counted. If during an armed bank robbery the robber strikes a teller with the butt of a handgun, then runs from the bank and steals an automobile at the curb, he has technically committed robbery, aggravated assault, and motor vehicle theft, which are three Part I offenses. However, because only the most serious crime is reported, the robbery would be the only one recorded in the UCR.[12]

The National Incident-Based Reporting System (NIBRS)

Clearly there must be a more reliable source for crime statistics than the UCR as it stands today. Beginning in 1982, a five-year redesign effort was undertaken to provide more comprehensive and detailed crime statistics. The effort resulted in the **National Incident-Based Reporting System (NIBRS)**, a program that collects data on each reported crime incident. Instead of submitting statements of the kinds of crime that individual citizens report to the police and summary statements of resulting arrests, the new program requires local police agencies to provide at least a brief account of each incident and arrest, including the incident, victim, and offender information. Under NIBRS, law enforcement authorities provide information to the FBI on each criminal incident involving one or more of 46 specific offenses, including the 8 Part I crimes, that occur in their jurisdiction; arrest information on the

46 offenses plus 11 lesser offenses is also provided in NIBRS. These expanded crime categories include numerous additional crimes, such as blackmail, embezzlement, drug offenses, and bribery; this allows a national database on the nature of crime, victims, and criminals to be developed. Other collected information includes statistics gathered by federal law enforcement agencies, as well as data on hate or bias crimes. When fully implemented, NIBRS will provide:

- Expansion of the number of offense categories included
- Detail on individual crime incidents (offenses, offenders, victims, property, and arrests)
- Linkage between arrests and clearances to specific incidents or offenses
- Inclusion of all offenses in an incident rather than only the most serious offense
- The ability to distinguish between attempted and completed crimes
- Linkages between offense, offender, victim, property, and arrestee variables that permit examination of interrelationships[13]

About one-third of all the police agencies that contribute data to the UCR are now part of the NIBRS program.[14] When fully implemented and adopted across the nation, NIBRS should bring about greater uniformity in cross-jurisdictional reporting and improve the accuracy of official crime data. Whether it can capture cases missing in the UCR remains to be seen.[15]

For more information about NIBRS, visit http://www.bjs.gov/index.cfm?ty=dcdetail&iid=301.
In what ways would knowledge and information about individual crimes help criminologists?

Survey Research

The second primary source of crime/victimization measurement is through surveys in which people are asked about their attitudes, beliefs, values, and characteristics, as well as their experiences with crime and victimization. Surveys typically involve **sampling**, which refers to the process of selecting for study a limited number of subjects who are representative of entire groups sharing similar characteristics, called the **population**. To understand the social forces that produce crime, a criminologist might interview a sample of 3,000 prison inmates drawn from the population of more than 2 million inmates in the United States; in this case, the sample represents the entire population of U.S. inmates. It is assumed that the characteristics of people or events in a carefully selected sample will be quite similar to those of the population at large. If the sampling was done correctly, the responses of the 3,000 inmates should represent the entire population of inmates.

National Incident-Based Reporting System (NIBRS) A program that requires local police agencies to provide a brief account of each incident and arrest within 22 crime patterns, including incident, victim, and offender information.

sampling Selecting a limited number of people for study as representative of a larger group.

population All people who share a particular personal characteristic, such as all high school students or all police officers.

In some circumstances, criminologists may want the survey to be representative of all members of society; this is referred to as a **cross-sectional survey**. A survey of all students who attend the local public high school would be considered a cross-sectional survey since all members of the community, both rich and poor, male and female, go to high school. Cross-sectional surveys are a useful and cost-effective technique for measuring the characteristics of large numbers of people:

- Because questions and methods are standardized for all subjects, uniformity is unaffected by the perceptions or biases of the person gathering the data.
- Carefully drawn samples enable researchers to generalize their findings from small groups to large populations.
- Though surveys measure subjects at a single point in their life span, questions can elicit information on subjects' past behavior as well as expectations of future behaviors.[16]

 A number of academic institutes are devoted to survey research, including the Princeton University Survey Research Center (SRC). Visit it at **http://www.princeton.edu/~psrc/**.

Do a self-report survey in class: By a show of hands, how many students have *never* committed a crime—never taken drugs, gambled, shoplifted, engaged in underage drinking? What does this tell you about the true amount of crime in society?

The National Crime Victimization Survey (NCVS)

Because more than half of all victims do not report their experiences to the police, the UCR cannot measure all the annual criminal activity. To address the nonreporting issue, the federal government's Bureau of Justice Statistics sponsors the **National Crime Victimization Survey (NCVS)**, a comprehensive, nationwide survey of victimization in the United States. Begun in 1973, the NCVS provides a detailed picture of crime incidents, victims, and trends.[17] It provides information about victims (age, sex, race, ethnicity, marital status, income, and educational level), offenders (sex, race, approximate age, and victim–offender relationship), and the crimes (time and place of occurrence, use of weapons, nature of injury, and economic consequences). Questions also cover the experiences of victims with the criminal justice system, self-protective measures used by victims, and possible substance abuse by offenders. Supplements are added periodically to the survey to obtain detailed information on topics such as school crime.

How the NCVS Is Conducted   The NCVS is administered to persons age 12 or older from a nationally representative sample of households, defined as a group of members who all reside at a sampled address. Persons are

CONNECTIONS

Victim surveys provide information not only about criminal incidents that have occurred, but also about the individuals who are most at risk of falling victim to crime, and where and when they are most likely to become victimized. Data from recent NCVS surveys will be used in Chapter 3 to draw a portrait of the nature and extent of victimization in the United States.

Ask Yourself ...
If you were contacted by the NCVS, would you be willing to share information on your personal victimizations?

considered household members when the sampled address is their usual place of residence at the time of the interview and when they have no usual place of residence elsewhere. Once selected, households remain in the sample for three years, and eligible persons in these households are interviewed every six months either in person or over the phone for a total of seven interviews. In the most recent survey, about 92,000 households were selected and more than 160,000 persons age 12 or older were interviewed for the NCVS. Each household was interviewed twice during the year. The response rate was 87 percent for households and 87 percent for eligible persons. Since the NCVS relies on a sample rather than a census of the entire U.S. population, the data is weighted to reflect population totals and to compensate for survey nonresponse and other aspects of the sample design.

Since its inception, the survey has undergone a number of significant modifications. In 1993, it was redesigned to provide detailed information on the frequency and nature of the crimes of rape, sexual assault, personal robbery, aggravated and simple assault, household burglary, theft, and motor vehicle theft. In 2006, significant methodological changes were made, including a new sampling method, a change in the method of handling first-time interviews with households, and a change in the method

cross-sectional survey Survey data derived from all age, race, gender, and income segments of the population measured simultaneously. Because people from every age group are represented, age-specific crime rates can be determined. Proponents believe this is a sufficient substitute for the more expensive longitudinal approach that follows a group of subjects over time to measure crime rate changes.

National Crime Victimization Survey (NCVS) The ongoing victimization study conducted jointly by the Justice Department and the U.S. Census Bureau that surveys victims about their experiences with law violation.

of interviewing. Some selected areas were dropped from the sample while others were added. Finally, computer-assisted personal interviewing (CAPI) replaced paper and pencil interviewing (PAPI).

NCVS: Advantages and Problems The greatest advantage of the NCVS over official data sources such as the UCR is that it can estimate the total amount of annual crimes and not only those that are reported to police, which means that the NCVS data provide a more complete picture of the nation's crime problem. Also, because some crimes are significantly underreported, the NCVS is an indispensable measure of their occurrence. Take for example the crimes of rape and sexual assault, crimes which are traditionally underreported. The UCR shows that in 2012 slightly more than 84,000 rapes occurred, as compared to the 346,000 rapes and sexual assaults found by the NCVS. In addition, the NCVS helps us understand why crimes are not reported to police and whether the type and nature of the criminal event influence whether the police will ever know it occurred. With the crime of rape, research shows that victims are much more likely to report rape if it is accompanied by another crime such as robbery than they are if it is a stand-alone event. Official data alone cannot provide that type of information.[18]

While its utility and importance are unquestioned, the NCVS may suffer from some methodological problems. As a result, its findings must be interpreted with caution. Among the potential problems are the following:

- Overreporting due to victims' misinterpretation of events. A lost wallet may be reported as stolen, or an open door may be viewed as a burglary attempt.
- Underreporting due to the embarrassment of reporting crime to interviewers, fear of getting in trouble, or simply forgetting an incident.
- Inability to record the personal criminal activity of those interviewed, such as drug use or gambling; murder is also not included, for obvious reasons.
- Sampling errors, which produce a group of respondents who do not represent the nation as a whole.
- Inadequate question format that invalidates responses. Some groups, such as adolescents, may be particularly susceptible to error because of question format.[19]

While these issues are critical, there is no substitute available that provides national information on crime and victimization with extensive detail on victims and the social context of the criminal event.

self-report surveys A research approach that requires subjects to reveal their own participation in delinquent or criminal acts.

Self-Report Surveys

While the NCVS is designed to measure victimization directly and criminal activity indirectly, participants in **self-report surveys** are asked to describe, in detail, their recent and lifetime participation in criminal activity. Self-reports are generally given anonymously in groups, so that the people being surveyed are assured that their responses will remain private and confidential. Secrecy and anonymity are essential to maintain the honesty and validity of responses. Self-report survey questions might ask:

- How many times in the past year have you taken something worth more than $50?
- How many times in the past year did you hurt someone so badly that they needed medical care?
- How many times in the past year did you vandalize or damage school property?
- How many times in the past year did you use marijuana?

While most self-report studies have focused on juvenile delinquency and youth crime, they can also be used to examine the offense histories of select groups such as prison inmates, drug users, and even police officers.[20]

In addition to crime-related items, most self-report surveys contain questions about attitudes, values, and behaviors. There may be questions about participants' substance abuse history, arrest history, and their family relations, such as "Did your parents ever strike you with a stick or a belt?" By correlating the responses, criminologists are able to analyze the relationship between personal factors and criminal behaviors. Statistical analysis of the responses can be used to determine whether people who report being abused as children are also more likely to use drugs as adults.

One of the most important sources of self-report data is the Monitoring the Future (MTF) study, which researchers at the University of Michigan Institute for Social Research (ISR) have been conducting annually since 1978. This national survey typically involves more than 2,500 high school seniors.[21] The MTF is considered the national standard to measure substance abuse trends among American teens.

Visit the Monitoring the Future website, **http://www .monitoringthefuture.org/.**
Do you believe that people answering self-report studies are truthful? Are you concerned that they fail to report their criminal activity or that the teenage subjects exaggerate in order to be "cool"?

The MTF data indicate that the number of people who break the law is far greater than the number projected by official statistics. Almost everyone questioned is found to have violated a law at some time, including truancy, alcohol abuse, false ID use, shoplifting or larceny under $50, fighting, marijuana use, or damage to the property of others. Furthermore, self-reports dispute the notion that criminals and delinquents specialize in one type of crime or another; offenders seem to engage in a mixed bag of crime and deviance.[22]

Validity of Self-Reports Critics of self-report studies frequently suggest that it is unreasonable to expect people to candidly admit illegal acts. This is especially true of those with official records, who may be engaging in the most criminality. At the same time, some people may exaggerate their criminal acts, forget some of them, or be confused about what is being asked. Some surveys contain an overabundance of trivial offenses, such as shoplifting small items or using false identification to obtain alcohol, often lumped together with serious crimes to form a total crime index. Consequently, comparisons between groups can be highly misleading.

The "missing cases" phenomenon is also a concern. Even if 90 percent of a school population voluntarily participate in a self-report study, researchers can never be sure whether the few who refuse to participate or are absent that day comprise a significant portion of the school's population of persistent high-rate offenders. Research indicates that offenders with the most extensive prior criminality are also the most likely "to be poor historians of their own crime commission rates."[23] It is also unlikely that the most serious chronic offenders in the teenage population are willing to cooperate with criminologists administering self-report tests.[24] Institutionalized youths, who are not generally represented in the self-report surveys, are not only more delinquent than the general youth population but are also considerably more misbehaving than the most delinquent youths identified in the typical self-report survey.[25] Consequently, self-reports may measure only nonserious, occasional delinquents while ignoring hardcore chronic offenders who may be institutionalized and unavailable for self-reports.

There is also evidence that reporting accuracy differs among racial, ethnic, and gender groups. It is possible that some groups are more worried about image than others and less willing to report crime, deviance, and/or victimization for fear that it would make them or their group look bad. Take these cases, for instance:

- Research shows that girls are usually more willing than boys to disclose drug use, with the exception of Latino girls, who significantly underreport their drug usage. Such gender- and ethnic-based differences in reporting might provide a skewed and inaccurate portrait of criminal and/or delinquent activity—in this case, the self-report data would falsely show that Latino girls use fewer drugs than other females.[26]
- African Americans have been found to be less willing to report traffic stops than Caucasians, a phenomenon that prevents accurate assessments of **racial profiling** by police. Because of this reluctance to report stops that have occurred, it is possible that the "driving while black" phenomenon is actually more frequent than research surveys indicate.[27]

Self-reports also contain other problems that cloud their validity. Asking subjects about their past behavior

Self-report surveys can be used to assess the "dark figures of crime," offenses that would never otherwise be counted in the official crime data. Self-reports have been used to measure trends and patterns in teen substance abuse, something that official data would never be able to assess.

Ace Stock Limited/Alamy

CONNECTIONS

Criminologists suspect that a few high-rate offenders are responsible for a disproportionate share of all serious crime. Results would be badly skewed if even a few of these chronic offenders were absent or refused to participate in school-wide self-report surveys. For more on chronic offenders, see the sections at the end of this chapter. Self-report data are used to track the development of criminal careers, a topic that is discussed in great detail in Chapter 9.

Ask Yourself ...

How might errors in self-reporting skew perceptions of the nature and extent of delinquent involvement?

racial profiling Selecting suspects on the basis of their ethnic or racial background.

may capture more serious crimes but miss minor criminal acts—that is, people remember armed robberies and rapes better than they do minor assaults and altercations.[28] In addition, some classes of offenders, such as substance abusers, may have a tough time accounting for their prior misbehavior.[29]

Evaluating the Primary Sources of Crime Data

The UCR, NCVS, and self-reports are the standard sources of data used by criminologists to track trends and patterns in the crime rate. Each has its own strengths and weaknesses.

- The UCR contains information on the number and characteristics of people arrested, information that the other data sources lack; it also provides unique data on homicide rates and trends.[30] However, UCR data omit many criminal incidents victims choose not to report to police, and it is subject to the reporting caprices of individual police departments.
- The NCVS includes unreported crime and important information on the personal characteristics of victims. While highly important, NCVS data consist of estimates made from relatively limited samples of the total U.S. population, so that even narrow fluctuations in the rates of some crimes can have a major impact on findings. It also relies on personal recollections that may be inaccurate. The NCVS does not include data on important crime patterns, including murder and drug abuse.
- Self-report surveys provide unique information on the personal characteristics of offenders—such as their attitudes, values, beliefs, personal history, and psychological profiles—that is unavailable from any other source. Yet, at their core, self-reports rely on the honesty of criminal offenders and drug abusers, a population not generally known for accuracy and integrity.

Although their tallies of crimes are certainly not in synch, the crime patterns and trends the three sources provide are often quite similar (see Concept Summary 2.1).[31] Each of the sources of crime data agree about the personal characteristics of serious criminals (age and gender) and where and when crime occurs (urban areas, nighttime, and summer months). In addition, the problems inherent in each source are consistent over time. Therefore, even if the data sources are incapable of providing an exact, precise, and valid count of crime at any given time, they are reliable indicators of changes and fluctuations in yearly crime rates.

cohort A sample of subjects whose behavior is followed over a period of time.

DATA COLLECTION METHODS 2.1

concept summary

UNIFORM CRIME REPORT

- Data are collected from records from police departments across the nation, crimes reported to police, and arrests.
- Strengths of the UCR are that it measures homicides and arrests, and it is a consistent, national sample.
- Weaknesses of the UCR are that it omits crimes not reported to police, omits most drug usage, and contains reporting errors.

NATIONAL CRIME VICTIMIZATION SURVEY

- Data are collected from a large national survey.
- Strengths of the NCVS are that it includes crimes not reported to the police, uses careful sampling techniques, and is a yearly survey.
- Weaknesses of the NCVS are that it relies on victims' memory and honesty, and it omits substance abuse.

SELF-REPORT SURVEYS

- Data are collected from local surveys.
- Strengths of self-report surveys are that they include unreported crimes, they can be used to measure substance abuse, and they often include questions that can assess an offender's personal history information, values, attitudes, and beliefs.
- Weaknesses of self-report surveys are that they rely on the honesty of offenders and they omit offenders who refuse or are unable to participate and who may be the most deviant.

SECONDARY SOURCES OF CRIME DATA

In addition to these main sources of crime data, a number of other techniques are used by criminologists to gather data on specific crime problems and trends, to examine the lives of criminal offenders, and to assess the effectiveness of crime control efforts.

Cohort Research

Cohort research involves observing a group of people who share a like characteristic over time. Researchers might select all girls born in Albany, New York, in 1970 and then follow their behavior patterns for 20 years. The research data might include their school experiences, arrests, hospitalizations, and information about their family life (divorces, parental relations). The subjects might be given repeated intelligence and physical exams; their diets might be monitored.

Data may be collected directly from the subjects during interviews and meetings with family members. Criminologists might also examine records of social organizations, such as hospitals, schools, welfare departments, courts, police departments, and prisons. School records contain data on students' academic performance, attendance, intelligence, disciplinary problems, and teacher ratings. Hospitals record incidents of drug use and suspicious wounds, which may be indicative of child abuse. Police files contain reports of criminal activity, arrest data, personal information on suspects, victim reports, and actions taken by police officers. Court records enable researchers to compare the personal characteristics of offenders with the outcomes of their court appearances, conviction rates, and types of sentence. Prison records contain information on inmates' personal characteristics, adjustment problems, disciplinary records, rehabilitation efforts, and length of sentence served. If the cohort is carefully drawn, it may be possible to determine which life experiences produce criminal careers.

Because it is extremely difficult, expensive, and time-consuming to follow a cohort over time, another approach is to take an intact cohort from the past and collect data from their educational, family, police, and hospital records. This format is known as a **retrospective cohort study**.[32] For example, a cohort of girls who were in grade school in 1970 could be selected from school attendance records. A criminologist might then acquire their police and court records over the following four decades to determine (a) which ones developed a criminal record and (b) whether school achievement predicts adult criminality.

Experimental Research

Sometimes criminologists are able to conduct controlled experiments to collect data on the cause of crime. They may wish to directly test whether (a) watching a violent TV show will (b) cause viewers to act aggressively. This test requires experimental research. To conduct experimental research, criminologists manipulate or intervene in the lives of their subjects to see the outcome or the effect of the intervention. True experiments usually have three elements: (1) random selection of subjects, (2) a control or comparison group, and (3) an experimental condition. Using this approach to find out the effects of viewing violent media content, a criminologist might have one group of randomly chosen subjects watch an extremely violent and gory film (*Resident Evil* or *World War Z*) while another randomly selected group viewed something more mellow (*The Lego Movie* or *Toy Story*). If the subjects who watched the violent film were significantly more aggressive than those who watched the nonviolent film, an association between media content and behavior would be supported. The fact that both groups were randomly selected would prevent some preexisting condition from invalidating the results of the experiment.

Quasi-experiments Because it is sometimes impossible to randomly select subjects or manipulate conditions, criminologists may be forced to rely on what is known as a *quasi-experimental design*. A criminologist may want to measure whether kids who were abused as children are more likely to become violent as adults. Of course, it is impossible to randomly select youth, assign them to two independent groups, and then purposely abuse members of one group in order to gauge their reactions. To get around this dilemma, a criminologist may select a group of adults who years earlier had been identified by school or medical authorities as being abused and then compare them with a control group, who though similar in every other respect, were never so identified. Even if a difference could be found in current behavior, it would still be impossible to know for certain the earlier child abuse was the source of adult violence or whether some other factor was the actual cause. For example, it's possible that child abuse victims self-medicate with drugs and alcohol, and it's substance abuse and not child abuse that is the true cause of future antisocial behavior.

Despite the need for them, true criminological experiments using all the elements of the scientific method are relatively rare because they are difficult and expensive to conduct; they involve manipulating subjects' lives, which can cause ethical and legal roadblocks; and they require long follow-up periods to verify results.

Observational and Interview Research

Sometimes criminologists focus their research on relatively few subjects, interviewing them in depth or observing them as they go about their activities. This research often results

CONNECTIONS

Some critical criminological research has been based on cohort studies, such as the important research conducted by University of Pennsylvania criminologist Marvin Wolfgang and his colleagues. Their findings have been instrumental in developing an understanding about the onset and development of a criminal career. Wolfgang's cohort research, which is discussed later in this chapter, helped identify the chronic criminal offender. Other research that relies on cohort data can be found in Chapter 9, which focuses on the development of delinquent and criminal careers.

Ask Yourself ...

Would a cohort study that follows people over time provide much more accurate information than a survey that asks people what they did in the past, what they are doing in the present, and what they plan to do in the future?

retrospective cohort study A study that uses an intact cohort of known offenders and looks back into their early life experiences by checking their educational, family, police, and hospital records.

In Chapter 1, an experiment designed to measure whether peers influence behavior choices was described. As you may recall, it involved having a hired actor try to influence kids involved in an experiment to engage in cheating. Such experiments are relatively rare but not unknown in criminology. One area, however, that has received a significant amount of experimental research is the effect of media violence on behavior, a topic that is discussed in greater detail in Chapter 5. As you can imagine, many studies are structured as described above, having one group of subjects watch violent films while a control group observes family fare and then comparing post-viewing differences in behavior and attitudes.

Ask Yourself ...

Are there areas of criminological study for which experiments are impossible to conduct, such as the behavioral effects of taking drugs? If so, how else might you measure that association?

in the kind of in-depth data absent in large-scale surveys. In one such effort, Claire Sterk-Elifson focused on the lives of middle-class female drug abusers.[33] The 34 interviews she conducted provide insight into a group whose behavior might not be captured in a large-scale survey. Sterk-Elifson found that these women were introduced to cocaine at first "just for fun": "I do drugs," one 34-year-old lawyer told her, "because I like the feeling. I would never let drugs take over my life."[34] Unfortunately, many of these subjects succumbed to the power of drugs and suffered both emotional and financial stress.

Another common criminological method is to observe criminals first-hand to gain insight into their motives and activities. This may involve going into the field and participating in group activities; this was done in sociologist William Whyte's famous study of a Bos-

ton gang, *Street Corner Society*.[35] Other observers conduct field studies but remain in the background, observing but not being part of the ongoing activity.[36]

Meta-Analysis and Systematic Review

Meta-analysis involves gathering data from a number of previous studies. Compatible information and data are extracted and pooled together. When analyzed, the grouped data from several different studies provide a more powerful and valid indicator of relationships than the results provided from a single study. A **systematic review** is another widely accepted means of evaluating the effectiveness of public policy interventions. It involves collecting the findings from previously conducted scientific studies that address a particular problem, appraising and synthesizing the evidence, and using the collective evidence to address a particular scientific question.

Through these well-proven techniques, criminologists can identify what is known and what is not known about a particular problem and use the findings as a first step for carrying out new research. Criminologists David Farrington and Brandon Welsh used a systematic review and a meta-analysis to study the effects of street lighting on crime.[37] After identifying and analyzing 13 relevant studies, Farrington and Welsh found evidence showing that neighborhoods that improve their street lighting do in fact experi-

meta-analysis A research technique that uses the grouped data from several different studies.

systematic review A research technique that involves collecting the findings from previously conducted studies, appraising and synthesizing the evidence, and using the collective evidence to address a particular scientific question.

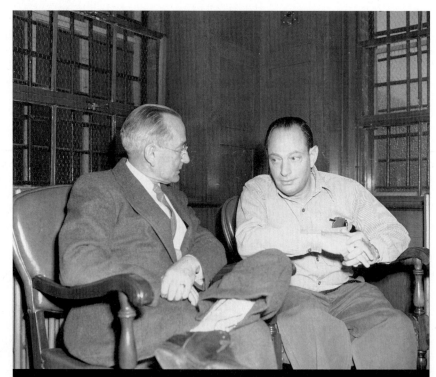

Criminologists have been conducting observational and interview studies for many years. Here, Nathan Leopold (right), a thrill-slayer who served 28 years in prison for the 1924 murder of a 14-year-old boy, talks with Professor William Byron, Northwestern University sociologist and criminologist, a few months before Leopold was granted parole from the Stateville Penitentiary in Joliet, Illinois, March 13, 1953.

AP Images/Ed Maloney

ence a reduction in crime rates. Their findings should come as no great surprise: it seems logical that well-lit streets would have fewer robberies and thefts because (a) criminals could not conceal their efforts under the cover of darkness, and (b) potential victims could take evasive action if they saw a suspicious-looking person lurking about. The meta-analysis produced an unusual finding: improving lighting caused the crime rate to go down during the day just as much as it did during the night! Obviously, the crime-reducing effect of streetlights had little to do with illuminating the streets. Farrington and Welsh speculate that improved street lighting increases community pride and solidarity, and the result of this newfound community solidarity is a lowered crime rate, during both the day and evening.

Data Mining

A relatively new criminological technique, data mining, uses multiple advanced computational methods, including artificial intelligence (the use of computers to perform logical functions), to analyze large data sets usually involving one or more data sources. The goal is to identify significant and recognizable patterns, trends, and relationships that are not easily detected through traditional analytical techniques alone.[38] Criminologists then use this information for various purposes, such as the prediction of future events or behaviors.

Data mining might be employed to help a police department allocate resources to combat crime based on offense patterns. To determine if such a pattern exists, a criminologist might employ data mining techniques with a variety of sources, including calls for service data, crime or incident reports, witness statements, suspect interviews, tip information, telephone toll analysis, or Internet activity.

Data mining permits proactive or "risk-based" deployment of police resources, a procedure that can increase public safety by optimizing the allocation of resources. For example, Richmond, Virginia, has experienced frequent random gunfire on New Year's Eve that has long presented a challenge to local law enforcement agencies. Through the use of data mining, the Richmond Police Department identified and targeted locations associated with increased random gunfire during the previous New Year's Eve holiday and deployed additional police resources to these areas. The results were extremely positive: there was a 49 percent reduction in the number of random gunfire complaints, with a concomitant increase in seized weapons of 246 percent. Using data mining to target resources, the Richmond Police Department required fewer police personnel than originally anticipated, which permitted the release of approximately 50 sworn employees. Data mining yielded a cost savings of approximately $15,000 during the eight-hour initiative. The Richmond Police Department's initiative demonstrated the ability to do more with less through the use of data mining and risk-based deployment strategies in the public safety arena.[39]

Crime Mapping

Criminologists are now using crime maps to create graphic representations of the spatial geography of crime. Computerized crime maps allow criminologists to analyze and correlate a wide array of data to create immediate, detailed visuals of crime patterns. The most simple maps display crime locations or concentrations and can be used, for example, to help law enforcement agencies increase the effectiveness of their patrol efforts. More complex maps can be used to chart trends in criminal activity. For example, criminologists might be able to determine if certain neighborhoods in a city have significantly higher crime

THE CATCH PROGRAM

One innovative mapping program, CATCH—the Crime Analysis Tactical Clearing House—supports local law enforcement agencies in analyzing crime series and patterns. CATCH staff use a number of crime mapping and analysis software applications and techniques to help agencies analyze identified crime series. CATCH is based on next-event forecasting, which differs from geographic profiling. Geographic profiling analyzes the locations of a series of crimes to determine where the offender most likely resides. Next-event forecasting looks at where previous crimes occurred to predict where the next crime will happen. So far CATCH has had several successes. In one case, the Savannah-Chatham, Georgia, police department was baffled by a series of nine kidnappings and rapes. CATCH staff mapped the crime locations along with other variables and created a timeline. Because the victims were kidnapped and then taken to isolated locations and assaulted, the mapping was complex. Using movement-analysis techniques, CATCH team members projected probable locations where the offender had targeted the victims and provided a list of recommendations for disrupting the series. These forecasts and recommendations backed up conclusions by the Savannah authorities, who initiated a public awareness campaign about the crimes. The Savannah-Chatham Police Department arrested the offender following an attack in an area targeted for increased surveillance.

Critical Thinking

Do you believe it is possible to predict where crime will take place in the future? It sounds like the film *Minority Report*, using computers. Is there a downside to this type of prediction?

SOURCE: *TechBeat*, National Law Enforcement and Corrections Technology Center, "A Good Catch," https://www.justnet.org/pdf/AGoodCatch.pdf (accessed March 2014).

policy and practice in criminology

FIGURE 2.2 Police Crime Map: Providence, RI

SOURCE: © Cengage Learning®

rates than others—so-called hot spots of crime.[40] Figure 2.2 illustrates a crime map generated in Providence, Rhode Island. How mapping is used by police is the topic of the Policy and Practice in Criminology feature which appears on page 39.

CRIME TRENDS

LO3 Identify recent trends in the crime rate

Crime is not new to this century.[41] Studies have indicated that a gradual increase in the crime rate, especially in violent crime, occurred from 1830 to 1860.

Following the Civil War, this rate increased significantly for about 15 years. Then, from 1880 up to the time of the first World War, with the possible exception of the years immediately preceding and following the war, the number of reported crimes decreased. After a period of readjustment, the crime rate steadily declined until the Depression (about 1930), when another crime wave was recorded. As measured by the UCR, crime rates increased gradually following the 1930s until the 1960s, when the growth rate became much greater. The homicide rate, which had actually declined from the 1930s to the 1960s, also began a sharp increase that continued through the 1970s.

Official Crime Trends

By 1991, police recorded about 14.6 million crimes. Since then, the number of crimes has been in decline; in 2012, about 10 million crimes were reported to the police, a drop of more than 4 million recorded crimes from the peak despite an increasing national population. Preliminary 2013 data indicate that the crime drop is continuing: both property and violent crimes declined about 5 percent between 2012 and 2013.

As Table 2.1 and Table 2.2 show, the number and rate of violent and property crimes has declined significantly during the past two decades despite the fact that the population has increased by more than 50 million people!

Victimization Trends

During the same period, the number of victimizations reported to the NCVS also showed a significant downturn. For example, in 2012, the NCVS recorded about 7 million violent crimes (rapes or sexual assaults, robberies, aggravated assaults, and simple assaults) and 20 million property crimes (burglaries, motor vehicle thefts, and household thefts).[42] This number has dropped by half since 1991, when 43 million crimes were reported, including more than 10 million violent crimes. The victimization rate for violence was more than 50 incidents per 1,000 population, while today it is less than 30; in 1991, victims reported

TABLE 2.1

Number of Violent Crimes and Violence Rates

Year	Population	Number of violent crimes	Rate per 100,000
1992	255,029,699	1,932,274	757.7
2000	281,421,906	1,425,486	506.5
2004	293,656,842	1,360,088	463.2
2009	307,006,550	1,318,398	429.4
2012	312,780,968	1,214,462	386.9

SOURCE: FBI, *Uniform Crime Reports, 2012.*

TABLE 2.2

Number of Property Crimes and Property Crime Rates

Year	Population	Number of property crimes	Rate per 100,000
1992	255,029,699	12,505,917	2,903.7
2000	281,421,906	10,182,584	3,618.3
2004	293,656,842	10,319,386	3,514.1
2009	307,006,550	9,320,971	3,036.1
2012	312,780,968	8,975,438	2,859

SOURCE: FBI, *Uniform Crime Reports, 2012.*

more than 300 incidents of property crime per 1,000 population, while today it is about 150.[43]

Will this downward trend in the crime rate continue? According to the most recent NCVS data, the number and rate of victimizations ticked upward in the past year. Whether these recent increases mean an end to the crime drop in America remains to be seen since the official crime rate has maintained its downward trend.

Trends in Self-Reporting

Self-report results appear to be more stable than the UCR and NCVS data indicate. When the results of recent self-report surveys are compared with various studies conducted over a 20-year period, a uniform pattern emerges. The use of drugs and alcohol increased markedly in the 1970s, leveled off in the 1980s, increased until the mid-1990s, and has been in decline ever since. Theft, violence, and damage-related crimes seem more stable. Although a self-reported crime wave has not occurred, neither has there been any visible reduction in self-reported criminality.

The most recent MTF survey shows that a surprising number of teenagers report involvement in serious criminal behavior.[44] About 11 percent reported hurting someone badly enough that the victim needed medical care (6 percent said they did it more than once). About 24 percent reported stealing something worth less than $50, and another 9 percent stole something worth more than $50; 25 percent reported shoplifting one or more times; 11 percent damaged school property, half more than once. (See Table 2.3.)

If the MTF data are accurate, the crime problem is much greater than official statistics would lead us to believe. There are approximately 40 million youths between the ages of 10 and 18. Extrapolating from the MTF findings, this group accounts for more than 100 percent of all the theft offenses reported in the UCR. About 4 percent of high school students said they had used force to steal (which is the legal definition of a robbery). Half the high school students who reported forcing someone to hand over cash said they committed this crime more than once in a year. At this rate, high school students alone commit more than 1.6 million robberies per year. In comparison, the UCR now tallies about 354,000 robberies for all age groups yearly. While official data show that the overall crime rate is in decline, the MTF surveys indicate that, with a few exceptions, self-reported participation in theft, violence, and damage-related crimes seems to be more stable than the trends reported in the UCR arrest data.

International Crime Trends

While making international comparisons is often difficult because the legal definitions of crime vary from country to country, it appears that while there has been a marked decline in U.S. crime rates, international crime rates are on the increase.[45] There are of course international differences

TABLE 2.3

Survey of Criminal Activity of High School Seniors, Percentage Engaging in Offenses

Crime	Committed at least once	Committed more than once
Set fire on purpose	2	2
Damaged school property	6	5
Damaged work property	2	3
Auto theft	3	3
Auto part theft	2	2
Break and enter	12	11
Theft, less than $50	11	13
Theft, more than $50	4	5
Shoplift	11	14
Gang fight	9	8
Hurt someone badly enough to require medical care	5	6
Used force or a weapon to steal	2	2
Hit teacher or supervisor	1	2
Participated in serious fight in school or at work	7	5

SOURCE: *Monitoring the Future, 2012* (Ann Arbor, MI: Institute for Social Research, 2013).

in crime rate trends. Today, the lowest rates are found in Spain, Japan, Hungary, and Portugal; cities in developed countries with the lowest crime rates are Hong Kong, Lisbon, Budapest, Athens, and Madrid. In contrast, many nations, especially those experiencing social or economic upheaval, have crime rates much higher than the United States.

The United Nations global tabulation of homicide indicates that more than 450,000 people each year are killed. More than a third (36 percent) of those are estimated to have occurred in Africa, 31 percent in the Americas, 27 percent in Asia, 5 percent in Europe, and 1 percent in Oceania. When controlling for population, the homicide rate in Africa and the Americas (at 17 and 16 per 100,000 population, respectively) is more than double the global average (6.9 per 100,000), whereas in Asia, Europe, and Oceania (between 3 and 4 per 100,000) it is roughly half. At one extreme, where homicide rates are high and firearms and organized crime in the form of drug trafficking play a substantial role, 1 in 50 men aged 20 will be murdered before they reach the age of 31; at the other, the probability being killed is up to 400 times lower.

Since 1995, the homicide rate has decreased in many countries, mainly in Asia, Europe, and Northern America, but has risen dramatically in Africa, Central America, and South America. Colombia, Venezuela, and Brazil now have much higher murder rates than the United States. Even though Colombia's murder rate has declined in recent years, it is still six times greater than the United States, a phenomenon linked to drug trafficking, gang feuds, vigilantism, and

disputes over trivial matters, in which young, unmarried, uneducated males are involved.[46]

Women and children are particularly vulnerable. Each year more than 50,000 children under 15 years of age are murdered. The homicide rates for children aged 0 to 4 years are over twice as high as rates among children aged 5 to 14 years. Many more children are subjected to nonfatal abuse and neglect; 8 percent of male and 25 percent of female children up to age 18 experience sexual abuse of some kind.

Attacks against women are also on the rise in some nations. Well-publicized rape-murder cases in India have received media attention around the globe. The most well-known case occurred in Delhi in 2012, when a highly educated 23-year-old female was beaten and gang-raped by six men when she and a companion boarded what they thought was a privately operated bus. Horribly injured, the woman died from her injuries 13 days later while undergoing emergency treatment in Singapore. The five adults who raped her were sentenced to death, while the most violent among them was treated as a juvenile offender.[47] Violence against women is often related to economic hardship and the social status of women. Rates are high in poor nations in which women are oppressed. Where women are more emancipated, the rates of violence against women are lower. In some nations, more than 40 percent of adolescent women and 20 percent of adolescent men report sexual coercion at the hands of family members, teachers, boyfriends, or strangers.

What the Future Holds

LO4 Discuss the factors that influence crime rate trends

It is risky to speculate about the future of crime trends because current conditions can change rapidly. It's possible that crime rates may rise in the future if the unemployment rate remains high for a prolonged period of time and the current generation of teens lose hope of ever gaining legitimate employment. Gang membership may increase and those involved in gangs may remain in them longer. However, as economist Steven Levitt comments, if teens commit more crime in the future, their contribution may be offset by the aging of the population, which will produce a large number of senior citizens and elderly, a group with a relatively low crime rate.[48] The immigrant population is also increasing, another factor that may reduce crime rates.

Such prognostications are reassuring, but there is, of course, no telling what changes are in store that may influence crime rates. Technological developments such as e-commerce on the Internet have created new classes of crime that are not recorded by any of the traditional methods of crime measurement. It's possible that some crimes such as fraud, larceny, prostitution, obscenity, vandalism, stalking, and harassment have increased over the Internet while falling under the radar of official crime data. For example, the number of people arrested for prostitution has declined almost 20 percent during the past decade. It's possible that (a) there are simply fewer prostitutes, (b) police are less likely to arrest prostitutes than they were a decade ago, or (c) prostitution is booming, but because clients now can arrange dates via the Internet, prostitutes are now better able to avoid detection.

What factors influence these trends, either causing an upward spiral or a downtrend? This topic is the subject of the Criminology in Action feature beginning on page 44.

CRIME PATTERNS

Criminologists look for stable crime rate patterns to gain insight into the nature of crime. The cause of crime may be better understood by examining the rate. If, for example, criminal statistics consistently show that crime rates are higher in poor neighborhoods in large urban areas, then the cause of crime may be related to poverty and neighborhood decline. If, in contrast, crime rates are spread evenly across society, and rates are equal in poor and affluent neighborhoods, this would provide little evidence that crime has an economic basis. Instead, crime might be linked to socialization, personality, intelligence, or some other trait unrelated to class position or income. In this section, we examine traits and patterns that may influence the crime rate.

The Ecology of Crime

LO5 Assess how crime rates reflect different ecological conditions

Patterns in the crime rate seem to be linked to temporal and ecological factors. Some of the most important of these are discussed here.

Day, Season, and Climate Most reported crimes occur during the warm summer months of July and August. During the summer, teenagers, who usually have the highest crime levels, are out of school and have greater opportunity to commit crime. People spend more time outdoors during warm weather, making themselves easier targets. Similarly, homes are left vacant more often during the summer, making them more vulnerable to property crimes. Two exceptions to this trend are murders and robberies, which occur frequently in December and January (although rates are also

Crime is more common in some areas at certain times of the year. While crime rates decline in the winter, crime does not disappear when it gets cold outside. Here, a man stands in front of an Electromania store in Newark, New Jersey, after it was hit during an early morning robbery on January 3, 2014. The thieves, according to Mohammed Mallouk, son of the owner, used a pickup truck to ram through the entrance of the store before taking off with merchandise in a snowstorm. It wasn't the first time the store had been robbed in such fashion—last year a robber did the same thing during another snowstorm.

AP Images/Julio Cortez

high during the summer). One reason: robberies are more likely to take place when it gets dark out, something that occurs earlier in these winter months (in the United States and Europe, at least).[49]

Crime rates also may be higher on the first day of the month than at any other time. Government welfare and Social Security checks arrive at this time, and with them come increases in such activities as breaking into mailboxes and accosting recipients on the streets. Also, people may have more disposable income at this time, and the availability of extra money may relate to behaviors associated with crime such as drinking, partying, gambling, and so on.[50]

Temperature Weather effects (such as temperature swings) may have an impact on violent crime rates. Traditionally, the association between temperature and crime was thought to resemble an inverted U-shaped curve: crime rates increase with rising temperatures and then begin to decline at some point (85 degrees) when it may be too hot for any physical exertion.[51] However, criminologists continue to debate this issue:

- Some believe that crime rates rise with temperature (i.e., the hotter the day, the higher the crime rate).[52]
- Others have found evidence that the curvilinear model is correct.[53]
- Some research shows that a rising temperature will cause some crimes to continually increase (e.g., domestic assault), while others (e.g., rape) will decline after temperatures rise to an extremely high level.[54]

FACTORS THAT INFLUENCE CRIME TRENDS

Crime experts have identified a variety of social, economic, personal, and demographic factors that influence crime rate trends. Although crime experts are still uncertain about how these factors impact these trends, directional change seems to be associated with changes in crime rates.

Age Structure

As a general rule, the crime rate follows the proportion of teens in the population: more kids, more crime! Crime rates skyrocketed in the 1960s when the baby boomers became teens and the 13 to 19 population grew rapidly. Crime rate drops since 1993 can be explained in part by an aging society: the elderly commit relatively few crimes. However, the age–crime relationship may be mitigated by social factors: areas where youth are alienated and disengaged have higher crime rates than communities whose youth population are involved with prosocial institutions such as school or church. So while young people are more likely to get in trouble with the law than their elders, not all do and those who don't are the ones who have successful involvement with supportive social institutions.

Immigration

Immigration has a suppressor effect on crime. Research shows that immigrants are less crime prone than the general population, so that as the number of immigrants increases per capita crime rates decline. During the past two decades, cities with the largest increases in immigration have experienced the largest decreases in crime rates, especially homicides and robberies. However, this effect may be short-lived: by the second generation, children of immigrants have begun to catch up and their crime rates begin to resemble that of the native-born population.

Economy

The general public believes that crime rates increase as the economy turns down and unemployment rises. However, there is little correlation between these indicators of economic prosperity and crime rates. Unemployed people do not suddenly join gangs or commit armed robberies. Criminals are usually unemployed or underemployed and therefore not affected by short-term economic conditions.

Crime rates may, however, be influenced by other types of economic factors. The decline in the burglary rate over the past decade may be explained in part by the abundance and subsequent decline in price of commonly stolen merchandise such as iPads, laptops, cell phones, flat screen TVs, and digital cameras. On the other hand, new targets may increase crime rates; subway crime increased in New York when thieves began targeting people carrying iPads and expensive cell phones such as the iPhone.

Abortion

There is evidence that the recent drop in the crime rate is linked to the availability of legalized abortion. In 1973, *Roe v. Wade* legalized abortion nationwide, and the drop in the crime rate began approximately 18 years later, in 1991. Crime rates began to decline when the first groups of potential offenders affected by the abortion decision began reaching the peak age of criminal activity. It is possible that the link between crime rates and abortion is the result of two mechanisms: (1) selective abortion on the part of women most at risk to have children who would engage in criminal activity, and (2) improved child rearing or environmental circumstances caused by better maternal, familial, or fetal care because women are having fewer children.

Gun Availability

The availability of firearms may influence the crime rate: as the number of guns in the population increases, so do violent crime rates. Handguns are especially dangerous if they fall into the hands of teens. Surveys of high school students indicate that between 6 and 10 percent carry guns at least some of the time. Guns also cause escalation in the seriousness of crime. As the number of gun-toting students increases, so too does the seriousness of violent crime as a schoolyard fight turns into murder.

Gangs

Another factor that affects crime rates is the explosive growth in teenage gangs. There are about 800,000 gang members in the United States. Data collected by the National Youth Gang Center show that gang members are responsible for a large proportion of all violent offenses committed during the adolescent years.

Boys who are members of gangs are far more likely to possess guns than nongang members; criminal activity increases when kids join gangs. Gangs involved in the urban drug trade recruit juveniles because they work cheaply, are immune from heavy criminal penalties, and are daring and willing to take risks. Arming themselves for protection, these drug-dealing children present a menace to their community, which persuades nongang-affiliated neighborhood adolescents to arm themselves for protection. The result is an arms race that produces an increasing spiral of violence. As gangs become more organized, so too does their level of violence and drug dealing. Without gang influence, the crime rate might be much lower.

Drug Use

Some experts tie increases in the violent crime rate between 1985 and 1993 to the crack epidemic, which swept the nation's largest cities, and to drug-trafficking gangs that fought over drug turf. These well-armed gangs did not hesitate to use violence to control territory, intimidate rivals, and increase market share. As the crack epidemic subsided, so too did the violence rates in New York City and other metropolitan areas where crack use was rampant. A sudden increase in drug use, on the other hand, may be a harbinger of future increases in the crime rate, especially if guns are easily obtained and fall into the hands of gang members.

Media

Some experts argue that violent media can influence the direction of crime rates. As the availability of media with a violent theme skyrocketed with the introduction of home video players, DVDs, cable TV, computer and video games, and so on, so too did teen violence rates. Efforts to curb violence on TV may help account for a declining crime rate.

Medical Technology

The presence and quality of health care can have a significant impact on murder rates. Murder rates might be up to five times higher than they are today without medical breakthroughs in treating victims of violence developed over the past 40 years. The big breakthrough occurred in the 1970s when technology developed to treat injured soldiers in Vietnam was applied to trauma care in the nation's hospitals. Since then, fluctuations in the murder rate can be linked to the level and availability of emergency medical services.

Justice Policy

Law enforcement experts have suggested that a reduction in crime rates may be attributed to adding large numbers of police officers and using them in aggressive police practices that target "quality of life" crimes such as panhandling, graffiti, petty drug dealing, and loitering. By showing that even the smallest infractions will be dealt with seriously, aggressive police departments may be able to discourage potential criminals from committing more serious crimes. Cities employing aggressive, focused police work may be able to lower homicide rates in the area.

It is also possible that tough laws imposing lengthy prison terms on drug dealers and repeat offenders can affect crime rates. The fear of punishment may inhibit some would-be criminals and place a significant number of potentially high-rate offenders behind bars, lowering crime rates. As the nation's prison population expanded, the crime rate has fallen.

However, justice policy can sometimes backfire and actually lift crime rates. Take for instance the long-term effect of incarceration. The imprisonment boom has resulted in more than 2 million people behind bars. While this policy may take some dangerous offenders off the street, eventually most get out. About 600,000 inmates are now being released each year, and many return to their communities without marketable skills or resources. The number of releasees will rise for the foreseeable future as more and more sentences bestowed during the high crime rate of the 1990s are completed. The recidivism rate of paroled inmates is quite high, averaging about 40 percent for those released from federal penitentiaries and 67 percent for those released from state custody. Inmates reentering society may have a significant effect on local crime rates.

Social and Cultural Change

International scholar Martin Kilias notes that crime trends can be influenced by sudden "breaches"—that is, new opportunities for offending that open as a result of changes in the technological or social environment. As an example he shows that violence among men has decreased since 1850 in some countries because the concept of "honor" has lost most of its importance. There is evidence, he finds, that it was common in the past for a small argument to end in a duel or at least a brawl if a person's personal or family honor was impugned or questioned. Today, honor-based killings can still be found, such as areas of Turkey where any critical remark about a person's reputation is dealt with by aggression against the source of "rumors."

While maintaining honor and saving face are still important factors in contemporary society, other cultural macro-level conditions such as the number of single-parent families, high school dropout rates, racial conflict, and the prevalence of teen pregnancies also exert a powerful influence on crime rates. High levels of race- and ethnicity-based income inequality have been shown to have an impact on crime rates. Areas where there is both within and between group inequality experience more violent crimes than neighborhoods in which most residents are doing equally well.

Critical Thinking

While crime rates have been declining in the United States, they have been increasing in Europe. Is it possible that factors that correlate with crime rate changes in the United States have little utility in predicting changes in other cultures? What other factors may increase or reduce crime rates?

SOURCES: Bianca E. Bersani, "A Game of Catch-Up? The Offending Experience of Second-Generation Immigrants," *Crime and Delinquency*, first published online October 1, 2013; Patricia L. McCall, Kenneth Land, Cindy Brooks Dollar, and Karen F. Parker, "The Age Structure-Crime Rate Relationship: Solving a Long-Standing Puzzle," *Journal of Quantitative Criminology* 29 (2013): 167–190; Tim Wadsworth, "Is Immigration Responsible for the Crime Drop? An Assessment of the Influence of Immigration on Changes in Violent Crime Between 1990 and 2000," *Social Science Quarterly* 91 (2010): 531–553; Amy Anderson and Lorine Hughes, "Exposure to Situations Conducive to Delinquent Behavior: The Effects of Time Use, Income, and Transportation," *Journal of Research in Crime and Delinquency* 46 (2009): 5–34; Ramiro Martinez, Jr., and Matthew Amie Nielsen, "Local Context and Determinants of Drug Violence in Miami and San Diego: Does Ethnicity and Immigration Matter?" *International Migration Review* 38 (2004): 131–157; Richard Rosenfeld, Robert Fornango, and Andres Rengifo, "The Impact of Order-Maintenance Policing on New York City Homicide and Robbery Rates: 1988–2001," *Criminology* 45 (2007): 355–384; National Youth Gang Center, "What Proportion of Serious and Violent Crime Is Attributable to Gang Members," http://www.nationalgangcenter.gov/About/FAQ#R50 (accessed March 2014); Martin Killias, "The Opening and Closing of Breaches: A Theory on Crime Waves, Law Creation and Crime Prevention," *European Journal of Criminology* 3 (2006): 11–31; Alfred Blumstein, "The Crime Drop in America: An Exploration of Some Recent Crime Trends," *Journal of Scandinavian Studies in Criminology and Crime Prevention* 7 (2006): 17–35; Brad Bushman and Craig Anderson, "Media Violence and the American Public," *American Psychologist* 56 (2001): 477–489; John J. Donohue and Steven D. Levitt, "The Impact of Legalized Abortion on Crime," *Quarterly Journal of Economics* 116 (2001): 379–420.

If in fact there is an association between temperature and crime, how can it be explained? The relationship may be due to the stress and tension caused by extreme temperatures. The human body generates stress hormones (adrenaline and testosterone) in response to excessive heat; hormonal activity has been linked to aggression.[55] One way to combat the temperature–crime association: turn off your air conditioner! James Rotton and Ellen Cohn found that assaults in air-conditioned settings increased as the temperature rose; assaults in non-air-conditioned settings declined after peaking at moderately high temperatures.[56]

Regional Differences Large urban areas have by far the highest violence rates; rural areas have the lowest per capita crime rates. Exceptions to this trend are low population resort areas with large transient or seasonal populations, typically have higher crime rates than the norm; this phenomenon has been observed in the United States and abroad.[57] Typically, the western and southern states have had consistently higher crime rates than the Midwest and Northeast. This pattern has convinced some criminologists that regional cultural values influence crime rates; others believe that regional differences can be explained by economic differences.

Use of Firearms

Firearms play a dominant role in criminal activity. According to the UCR, about two-thirds of all murders and 40 percent of robberies involve firearms; most of these weapons are handguns.

Because of these findings, there is an ongoing debate over gun control. Internationally respected criminologists Franklin Zimring and Gordon Hawkins believe the proliferation of handguns and the high rate of lethal violence they cause are the most significant factors separating the crime problem in the United States from the rest of the developed world.[58] Differences between the United States and Europe in nonlethal crimes are only modest at best—and getting smaller over time.[59]

In contrast, some criminologists believe that personal gun use can actually be a deterrent to crime. In a classic study, Gary Kleck and Marc Gertz claimed that as many as 400,000 people per year use guns in situations in which they later claim that the guns "almost certainly" saved lives. Even if these estimates are off by a factor of 10, it means that armed citizens may save 40,000 lives annually.

instrumental crimes Offenses designed to improve the financial or social position of the criminal.

expressive crimes Crimes that have no purpose except to accomplish the behavior at hand, such as shooting someone.

Although Kleck and Gertz recognize that guns are involved in murders, suicides, and accidents, which claim more than 30,000 lives per year, they believe their benefit as a crime prevention device should not be overlooked.[60]

Social Class, Socioeconomic Conditions, and Crime

LO6 Debate the association between social class and crime

It makes sense that crime is inherently a lower-class phenomenon. After all, people at the lowest rungs of the social structure have the greatest incentive to commit crimes, and people who are undergoing financial difficulties are the ones most likely to become their targets.[61] It seems logical that people who are outside the economic mainstream and therefore are unable to obtain desired goods and services legally will resort to illegal activities—such as selling narcotics—to obtain a share of the "American Dream": if you can't afford a car, steal it; if you cannot afford designer clothes, become a drug dealer. **Instrumental crimes** are those committed by indigent people to compensate for the lack of legitimate economic opportunity. People living in poverty are also believed to engage in disproportionate amounts of **expressive crimes**, such as rape and assault, as a result of their anger and frustration against society, a condition fueled by alcohol and drug abuse, common in impoverished areas.[62]

When measured with UCR data, official statistics indicate that crime rates in inner-city, high-poverty areas are generally higher than those in suburban or wealthier areas.[63] Surveys of prison inmates consistently show that prisoners were members of the lower class and unemployed or underemployed in the years before their incarceration. These are empirical indicators of a class–crime connection.

While the association between class and crime seems logical, it is not accepted by all criminologists. An alternative explanation is that the relationship between official crime and social class is a function of law enforcement practices, not actual criminal behavior patterns. Police may devote more resources to poor areas, and consequently apprehension rates may be higher there. Similarly, police may be more likely to formally arrest and prosecute lower-class citizens, especially racial and ethnic minorities, while giving those in the middle and upper classes more lenient treatment, such as handling their law violations with a warning. Police behavior and not actual behavior may account for the lower class's overrepresentation in official statistics and the prison population. This explanation is supported by self-report data that do not find a direct relationship between social class and crime.[64] The conclusion: if the poor have more extensive criminal records than the wealthy, this difference is attributable to differential law enforcement and not to class-based behavior differences. That is, police may be more likely to arrest lower-class offenders and treat the affluent more leniently.[65]

Evaluating the Class–Crime Association While the true relationship between class and crime is difficult to determine, the weight of recent evidence seems to suggest that serious, official crime such as rape, murder, and burglary is more prevalent among the lower classes and that lower-class communities have higher crime rates than more affluent neighborhoods; less serious and self-reported crime is spread more evenly throughout the social structure.[66] Neighborhoods experiencing income inequality and resource deprivation have crime rates significantly higher than those that can provide equal or more economic opportunities to their citizens.[67]

Crime and Unemployment It stands to reason that if there is a relationship between crime and socioeconomic status, then crime rates should correlate with unemployment rates, peaking during tough economic times when people are out of work and the poor are hard-pressed to find jobs.

While this association seems logical, there is a great deal of conflicting research, some of which shows that aggregate crime rates and aggregate unemployment rates are only weakly related: crime rates sometimes rise during periods of economic prosperity and fall during periods of economic decline.[68] In contrast, other research links unemployment rates to higher rates of economic crimes, especially when the state does not provide sufficient economic support such as welfare and unemployment benefits.[69]

There are four diverging views on the association between the economy and crime rates:

- *Bad economy means higher crime rates.* When the economy turns down, people who are underemployed or unemployed will become motivated to commit property crimes to obtain desperately needed resources.
- *Good economy means higher crime rates.* A good economy requires that more people be hired, including teens. Unfortunately, kids with after-school jobs are more likely to engage in antisocial activities. Since teens typically commit more crimes than adults, high teenage employment will actually increase the overall crime rate.[70] A good economy means that people can buy valuable goods which make tempting targets. When people perceive that the economy is doing well, and there is positive consumer sentiment, the rate of property crimes such as burglary, larceny, and motor vehicle theft declines; why steal when you can get a good job and buy what you need without the risk of crime?[71]

The association between class and crime is not clear: most poor people are not criminals and some very rich people break the law. Nonetheless, crime rates are higher in lower-class communities and people may be influenced by their environment. Here, Reggy Colby, age 30 and a recovering heroin addict, digs through the trash looking for food on August 21, 2013, in Camden, New Jersey. Colby got out of jail two days before, where he was forced to get clean while serving a 30-day sentence for stealing food. Colby says he grew up in a *Leave It to Beaver* home in Cherry Hill, an affluent city nearby, and studied architecture in college before dropping out. After leaving school he moved to Florida, where he married and had a daughter. He joined the army in 2007, trained as a field artillery specialist, and served in Afghanistan in 2009 through 2010, until he was injured by an improvised explosive device, which peppered his body with shrapnel. It was while recovering from his injuries that he became addicted to heroin, a drug he had also tried as a teen. Since becoming addicted, he has been dishonorably discharged from the army, divorced, estranged from his daughter, and has become homeless in Camden. "As a kid I was terrified to come to Camden. I was so scared—I never thought I would be out here, never … it's just like, what … happened."

- *Bad economy means lower crime rate.* During an economic downturn, unemployed parents are at home to supervise children and guard their possessions. When people are unemployed, they have less money on hand and purchase fewer things worth stealing. They may even sell their valuables to raise cash, reducing suitable targets for burglars and thieves.
- *Crime and the economy are unrelated.* It is also possible that the state of the economy and crime rates are unrelated. It seems unlikely that middle-class workers will suddenly join gangs or become bank robbers when they lose their jobs. Unemployed people are neither likely to stick up gas stations, banks, and drug stores, nor are they more likely to engage in nonviolent property crimes, including shoplifting, residential burglary, theft of motor vehicle parts, and theft of automobiles, trucks, and motorcycles.[72]

One reason for all this confusion may simply be methodological: measuring the associations among variables such as jobs, the economy, and crime is often quite difficult.

There are significant economic differences at the state, county, community, and neighborhood level. While people in one area of the city are doing quite well, their neighbors living in another part of town may be suffering unemployment. Crime rates may even vary by street, an association that is difficult to detect.

Long-Term Trends It is also possible that the association between crime and the economy is not immediate. Just because unemployment is high does not mean that crime rates are also on the increase. Criminologist Shawn Bushway has recently shown that crime rates go up and down in long, slow trajectories that vary considerably from period to period. These trajectories may be influenced by changes in the economic structure of society. Since 1960, women have joined the workforce in large numbers, union influence has shrunk, manufacturing has moved overseas, and computers and the Internet have changed the way that resources are created and distributed. As manufacturing has moved overseas, less-educated, untrained male workers have been frozen out of the job market. These workers may find themselves competing in illegal markets: selling drugs may be more profitable than working in a fast-food restaurant. Similarly, people may find prostitution and/or sex work more lucrative relative to minimum-wage jobs in the legitimate market. When the economy turns, drug dealers do not suddenly quit the trade and get a job with GE or IBM. Hence, argues Bushway, labor markets, rather than unemployment rates, are the economic engine that shapes the crime rate and creates incentives for individuals to participate in illegal activities.[73]

So the association between economic factors and crime is quite complex and cannot be explained with a simple linear relationship (i.e., the higher the unemployment rate, the more crime).[74] Class and economic conditions may affect some crimes and some people differently than they affect others. Some subgroups in the population (e.g., women, African Americans) seem more deeply influenced by economic factors than others (e.g., men, whites).[75]

Age and Crime

There is general agreement that age is inversely related to criminality. Criminologists Travis Hirschi and Michael Gottfredson state, "Age is everywhere correlated with crime. Its effects on crime do not depend on other demographic correlates of crime."[76] Regardless of economic status, marital status, race, sex, and so on, younger people commit crime more often than their older peers. Research shows that on average, kids who are persistent offenders begin committing crime in their childhood, rapidly increase their offending activities in late adolescence, and then begin a slowdown in adulthood. Early starters tend to commit more crime and are more likely to continue to be involved in criminality over a longer period of time.[77] While it has been long assumed that most kids commit crime in groups, and that peer support encourages offending in adolescence, the most recent research disputes the "co-offending" hypothesis and suggests the great bulk of youth crime is a solo act.[78] Kids who assume an outlaw persona find that their antisocial acts bring them increased social status among peers who admire their risk-taking behaviors. Young criminals may be looking for an avenue of behavior that improves their peer group standing.[79] Hence, they commit more crime in adolescence.

The elderly are particularly resistant to the temptations of crime; they make up more than 14 percent of the population and less than 1 percent of arrests. Elderly males 65 and over are predominantly arrested for alcohol-related matters (e.g., public drunkenness and drunk driving) and elderly females for larceny (e.g., shoplifting). The elderly crime rate has remained stable for the past 20 years, but because the over-65 population is increasing and will continue to increase as the baby boomers come of age, the number of elderly involved with the criminal justice system will surely follow suit.[80]

CONNECTIONS

If class and crime are related, then crime is primarily a lower-class phenomenon. This view is discussed in Chapter 6. If, however, crime and economic conditions are unrelated, then the causes of crime must be found in factors experienced by members of all social classes—psychological impairment, family conflict, peer pressure, school failure, and so on. Theories that view crime as a function of problems experienced by individuals in all social classes are reviewed in Chapters 4 and 5. And theories that combine both individual and social causes are discussed in Chapter 9.

Ask Yourself ...
Before reading further, what is your take on crime? Is it a social problem, an individual problem, or a combination of both?

CONNECTIONS

Hirschi and Gottfredson have used their views on the age–crime relationship as a basis for their General Theory of Crime. This important theory holds that the factors that produce crime change little after birth and that the association between crime and age is constant. For more on this view, see the section on the General Theory of Crime in Chapter 9.

Ask Yourself ...
Why do you think crime rates drop with age? Isn't it true that the economic, social, and emotional problems that cause crime in adolescence are still present in adulthood?

LO7 Clarify what is meant by the term *aging-out process*

Aging Out of Crime Most kids who commit crime as teens discontinue their illegal activities as they mature. Aging out of crime may be a function of the natural history of the human life cycle.[81] Deviance in adolescence is fueled by the need for money and sex and reinforced by close relationships with peers who defy conventional morality. At the same time, teenagers are becoming independent from parents and other adults who enforce conventional standards of morality and behavior. They have a new sense of energy and strength and are involved with peers who are similarly vigorous and frustrated.

In adulthood, people strengthen their ability to delay gratification and forgo the immediate gains that law violations bring. They also start wanting to take responsibility for their behavior and to adhere to conventional mores.[82] Getting married, raising a family, and creating long-term family ties provide the stability that helps people desist from crime.[83]

For many years the official statistics told us that young people are arrested at a disproportionate rate to their numbers in the population. However, in recent years the teen arrest rate has plummeted so today the difference between adult and juvenile crime rates has diminished. According to the most recent UCR data, the arrest rate for teens dropped 37 percent since 2003, while adult arrests dropped only 3 percent, evening out the gap between adult and teen official crime rates. If these trends continue, the rates will eventually converge and the age–crime connection reevaluated.

Gender and Crime

LO8 Describe the gender and racial patterns in crime

Male crime rates are much higher than those of females. Victims report that their assailant was male in more than 80 percent of all violent personal crimes. The most recent Uniform Crime Report arrest statistics indicate that males account for about 80 percent of all arrests for serious violent crimes and 65 percent of the arrests for serious property crimes; murder arrests are 7 males to 1 female. MTF data also show that young men commit more serious crimes, such as robbery, assault, and burglary, than their female peers.

Even though gender differences in the crime rate have persisted over time, there seems little question that females are now involved in more crime than ever before and that there are more similarities than differences between male and female offenders.[84]

Explaining Gender Differences in the Crime Rate Early criminologists pointed to emotional, physical, and psychological differences between males and females to explain the differences in crime rates. Cesare Lombroso's 1895 book *The Female Offender* argued that a small group of female criminals lacked "typical" female traits of "piety, maternity, undeveloped intelligence, and weakness."[85] In physical appearance as well as in their emotional makeup, delinquent females appeared closer to men than to other women. Lombroso's theory became known as the **masculinity hypothesis**; in essence, a few "masculine" females were responsible for the handful of crimes women commit.

Another early view of female crime focused on the supposed dynamics of sexual relationships. Female criminals were viewed as either sexually controlling or sexually naive, either manipulating men for profit or being manipulated by them. The female's criminality was often masked because criminal justice authorities were reluctant to take action against a woman.[86] This perspective is known as the **chivalry hypothesis**, which holds that much female criminality is hidden because of the culture's generally protective and benevolent attitude toward women.[87] In other words, police are less likely to arrest, juries are less likely to convict, and judges are less likely to incarcerate female offenders.

Although these early writings are no longer taken seriously, some criminologists still believe that gender-based traits are a key determinant of crime rate differences. Among the suspected differences include physical strength and hormonal influences. According to this view, male sex

CONNECTIONS

Gender differences in the crime rate have been linked to hormones that cause areas of the brain to become less sensitive to environmental stimuli. Gender differences in biochemical makeup result in males being more likely to seek high levels of stimulation and to tolerate more pain in the process. Chapter 5 discusses the biosocial causes of crime and reviews this issue in greater detail.

Ask Yourself ...
Why do you think males are more involved in criminal activity than females?

---

aging out The process by which individuals reduce the frequency of their offending behavior as they age. It is also known as spontaneous remission, because people are believed to spontaneously reduce the rate of their criminal behavior as they mature. Aging out is thought to occur among all groups of offenders.

masculinity hypothesis The view that women who commit crimes have biological and psychological traits similar to those of men.

chivalry hypothesis The idea that low female crime and delinquency rates are a reflection of the leniency with which police treat female offenders.

hormones (androgens) account for more aggressive male behavior, and gender-related hormonal differences explain the gender gap in the crime rate.[88]

Socialization and Development   Although there are few gender-based differences in aggression during the first few years of life, girls are socialized to be less aggressive than boys and are supervised more closely by parents.[89] Differences in aggression become noticeable between ages 3 and 6 when children are first socialized into organized peer groups such as the day care center or school. Males are more likely to display physical aggression while girls display relational aggression—excluding disliked peers from playgroups, gossiping, and interfering with social relationships.

Males are taught to be more aggressive and assertive and are less likely to form attachments to others. They often view their aggression as a gender-appropriate means to gain status and power, either by joining deviant groups and gangs or engaging in sports. Even in the middle-class suburbs, they may seek approval by knocking down or running through peers on the playing field, while females literally cheer them on. The male search for social approval through aggressive behavior may make them more susceptible to criminality, especially when the chosen form of aggression is antisocial or illegal. Recent research by Jean Bottcher found that young boys perceive their roles as being more dominant than young girls.[90] Male perceptions of power, their ability to have freedom and hang with their friends, helped explain the gender differences in crime and delinquency.

In contrast, girls are encouraged to care about other people and avoid harming them; their need for sensitivity and understanding may help counterbalance the effects of poverty and family problems. And because they are more verbally proficient, many females may develop social skills that help them deal with conflict without resorting to violence. Females are taught to be less aggressive and to view belligerence as a lack of self-control—a conclusion that is unlikely to be reached by a male.

Girls are usually taught—directly or indirectly—to respond to provocation by feeling anxious and depressed, whereas boys are encouraged to retaliate. Overall, when they are provoked, females are much more likely to feel distressed than males—experiencing sadness, anxiety, and uneasiness. Although females may get angry as often as males, many have been taught to blame themselves for harboring such negative feelings. Females are therefore much

more likely than males to respond to anger with feelings of depression, anxiety, fear, and shame. Although females are socialized to fear that their anger will harm valued relationships, males react with "moral outrage," looking to blame others for their discomfort.[91]

Cognitive Differences   Psychologists note significant cognitive differences between boys and girls that may impact on their antisocial behaviors. Girls have been found to be superior to boys in verbal ability, while boys test higher in visual-spatial performance. Girls acquire language faster, learning to speak earlier and faster with better pronunciation. Girls are far less likely to have reading problems than boys, while boys do much better on standardized math tests. (This difference is attributed by some experts to boys receiving more attention from math teachers.) In most cases these cognitive differences are small, narrowing, and usually attributed to cultural expectations. When given training, girls demonstrate an ability to increase their visual-spatial skills to the point where their abilities become indistinguishable from the ability of boys.

Cognitive differences may contribute to behavioral variations. Even at an early age, girls are found to be more empathic than boys—that is, more capable of understanding and relating to the feelings of others.[92] Empathy for others may help shield girls from antisocial acts because they are more likely to understand a victim's suffering. Girls are more concerned with relationship and feeling issues, and they are less interested than boys are in competing for material success. Boys who are not tough and aggressive are labeled sissies and cry babies. In contrast, girls are given different messages; they are expected to form closer bonds with their friends and share feelings. Their superior verbal skills may allow girls to talk rather than fight. When faced with conflict, women might be more likely to attempt to negotiate, rather than to either respond passively or to physically resist, especially when they perceive increased threat of harm or death.[93]

Feminist Views   In the 1970s, **liberal feminist theory** focused attention on the social and economic role of women in society and its relationship to female crime rates.[94] This view suggested that the traditionally lower crime rate for women could be explained by their "second-class" economic and social position. As women's social roles changed and their lifestyles became more like men's, it was believed that their crime rates would converge. Criminologists, responding to this research, began to refer to the "new female criminal." The rapid increase in the female crime rate, especially in what had traditionally been male-oriented crimes (such as burglary and larceny), supports the feminist view. In addition, self-report studies seem to indicate that (a) the pattern of female criminality, if not its frequency, is quite similar to that of male criminality, and (b) the factors that predispose male criminals to crime have an equal impact on female criminals.[95]

liberal feminist theory Theory suggesting that the traditionally lower crime rate for women can be explained by their second-class economic and social position. As women's social roles have changed and their lifestyles have become more like those of men, it is believed that their crime rates will converge.

CONNECTIONS

Critical criminologists view gender inequality as stemming from the unequal power of men and women in a capitalist society and the exploitation of females by fathers and husbands. This perspective is considered more fully in Chapter 8.

Ask Yourself ...

As gender differences in socialization evaporate, should crime rate differences also disappear? Or do you think gender differences in crime and violence are a function of biological and not social factors?

Race and Crime

Official crime data indicate that minority group members are involved in a disproportionate share of criminal activity. African Americans make up about 12 percent of the general population, yet they account for almost 38 percent of Part I violent crime arrests and 29 percent of property crime arrests. They also are responsible for a disproportionate number of Part II arrests (except for alcohol-related arrests for crimes such as DWI).

Are these data a reflection of true racial differences in the crime rate, or do they reflect racial bias in the justice process? We can evaluate this issue by comparing racial differences in self-report data with those found in official delinquency records. Charges of racial discrimination in the justice process would be substantiated if whites and blacks self-reported equal numbers of crimes, but minorities were arrested and prosecuted far more often.

Early efforts by noted criminologists found virtually no relationship between race and self-reported delinquency, a finding that supported racial bias in the arrest decision process.[96] Other, more recent self-report studies that use large national samples of youths have also found little evidence of racial disparity in self-reported crimes committed.[97] These and other self-report studies seem to indicate that the delinquent behavior rates of black and white teenagers are generally similar and that differences in arrest statistics may indicate a differential selection policy by

police.[98] Suspects who are poor, minority, or male are more likely to be formally arrested than suspects who are white, affluent, or female.[99]

Evidence of racial bias in the arrest process can be found in the use of racial profiling to stop African Americans and search their cars without probable cause or reasonable suspicion.[100] Police officers, some social commentators note, have created a new form of traffic offense called DWB, "driving while black."[101] National surveys of driving practices show that young black and Latino males are more likely to be stopped by police and suffer citations, searches, and arrests, as well as be the target of force even though they are no more likely to be in the possession of illegal contraband than white drivers.[102]

Although the official statistics, such as UCR arrest data, may reflect discriminatory justice system practices, African Americans are arrested for a disproportionate amount of serious violent crime, such as robbery and murder, and some criminologists find it improbable that police discretion and/or bias *alone* could account for these proportions. It is doubtful that police routinely release white killers, robbers, and rapists while arresting violent black offenders who commit the same offenses.[103] If these racial differences in serious crimes exist how can they be explained?

System Bias Race-based differences in the crime rate can be explained in part as an effect of unequal or biased treatment by the justice system. One reason, known as

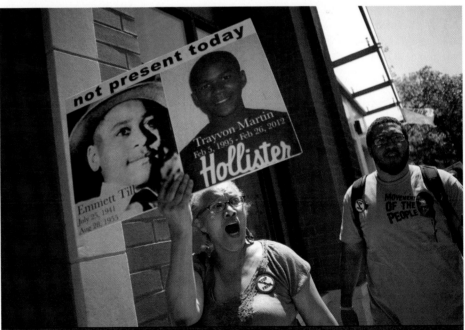

The association between race and crime is highly controversial. Police are often accused of racially profiling minority group members because of race-based suspicion. Here, protesters take part in a rally against the NYPD's stop-and-frisk policy in the Bronx borough of New York, May 13, 2012. New York police conducted more than 200,000 frisk searches in the first three months of 2012—a 10 percent increase from the same period in 2011.

race, culture, gender, and criminology

When sociologist Alice Goffman was an undergraduate at the University of Pennsylvania, she tutored a high school student named Aisha. She later met Aisha's brother Ronny, age 15, when he came home from a juvenile detention center, and Ronny introduced her to Mike, who was 21, and then Mike's best friend Chuck, age 18, who also came home from county jail. Chuck, Mike, and Ronny were part of a loose group of about 15 young men who grew up around 6th Street in Philadelphia, most of whom were unemployed and trying to make it outside of the formal economy. Some worked as low-level crack dealers; others sold marijuana, "wet" (PCP and/or embalming fluid), or pills like Xanax. Some of the men occasionally made money by robbing other drug dealers. One earned his keep by exotic dancing and offering sex to women.

Through her connections to these young people, Goffman was able to draw an understanding of life in the Philadelphia underclass, the burdens faced by the urban poor, and the role of law enforcement in everyday life. On 6th Street, the constant threat of arrest and incarceration shaped behavior and

values and became an integral part of everyday behavior.

In these neighborhoods, children learn at an early age to watch out for the police and to prepare to run when they see them in the neighborhood. The first topic of the day focused on who had been taken into custody the night before and who had outrun the cops and gotten away. The young men discussed how the police identified and located the people they were looking for, what the charges were likely to be, what physical harm had been done to the man as he was caught and arrested, and what property the police had taken and what had been wrecked or lost during the chase.

In the 6th Street neighborhood, a significant portion of the young men were "on the run," some because they were suspects in actual street crimes, but most because there were outstanding arrest warrants for minor infractions such as shoplifting or possession of recreational drugs. Young men were constantly worried that they would be picked up by the police and taken into custody even when they did not have a warrant out for their arrest. Those on probation or parole, on house arrest, or going through a trial expressed concern that they would soon be picked up and

taken into custody for some violation that would "come up in the system." People on the run made a concerted effort to thwart their discovery and apprehension.

Goffman found that once a man finds that he may be stopped by the police and taken into custody, he discovers that people, places, and relations he formerly relied on, and that are integral to maintaining a respectable identity, get redefined as paths to confinement. Public places and institutions are seen as threatening. When Alex and his girlfriend, Donna, both age 22, drove to the hospital for the birth of their son, two police officers came into the room and arrested Alex for violating parole. After Alex was arrested, other young men expressed hesitation to go to the hospital when their babies were born. Equally scary was a job in the legitimate economy where the police knew your schedule in advance and traps could be set, resulting in arrest and confinement.

People learn to avoid calling upon the justice system for help, especially if they have a criminal record. Goffman noted numerous instances in which members of the group contacted the police when they were injured, robbed, or threatened. These men were either

---

the **racial threat hypothesis** states that as the percentage of minorities in the population increases, so too does the amount of social control that police direct at minority group members.[104] The source of racial threat begins when residents overestimate the proportion of minorities living in their neighborhood, a circumstance that leads to heightened false perceptions of disorder.[105] When fear

grips an area, police are more likely to aggressively patrol minority areas; suspect, search, and arrest minority group members; and make arrests for minor infractions, helping to raise the minority crime rate.[106] As perceptions of racial threat increases, so too does the demand for greater law enforcement protection.[107] The result is a stepped-up effort to control and punish minority citizens, which segregates minorities from the economic mainstream and reinforces the physical and social isolation of the barrio.[108]

The "racial threat" effect is not the only evidence of system bias. There are some indications that the justice system treats minority defendants differently from members of the white majority. Black, Latino, and American Indian youth are treated more severely in juvenile court than their white

> **racial threat hypothesis** The belief that as the percentage of minorities in the population increases, so too does the amount of social control that police direct at minority group members.

in good standing with the courts or had no pending legal constraints. She did not observe any person with a warrant call the police or voluntarily make use of the courts during the six years she spent there. Young men with warrants seemed to see the authorities only as a threat to their safety. This has two important implications:

- Because they steer clear of the law, young men with criminal records are vulnerable to criminals looking for an easy score.
- Because they cannot call the police, wanted people are more likely to use violence to protect themselves or to get back at others. This kind of self-help crime is typically carried out when the police and the courts are unavailable because people have warrants out for their arrest and may be held in custody if they contact the authorities.

Like going to the hospital or using the police and the courts, even more intimate relations—friends, family, and romantic partners—may pose a threat and thus have to be avoided or at least carefully navigated. In some instances, the police are used as agents of social control and as a form of direct retaliation. When Michelle, age 16, got pregnant, she claimed that 17-year-old Reggie was the father. Reggie denied he had gotten her pregnant until he was in jail and was forced to admit he was the father in order to buy the silence of Michelle and her aunt.

While family members, partners, or friends of a wanted man occasionally call the police on him to control his behavior or to punish him for a perceived wrong, close kin or girlfriends also link young men to the police because the police compel them to do so. It is common practice for the police to put pressure on friends, girlfriends, and family members to provide information, particularly when these people have their own warrants, are serving probation or parole, or have a pending trial. Family members and friends who are not themselves caught up in the justice system may be threatened with eviction or with having their children taken away.

In this world, maintaining a secret and unpredictable routine decreases the chance of arrest: it is easier for the police to find a person through his last known address if he comes home at around the same time to the same house every day. Finding a person at work is easier if he works a regular shift in the same place every day. Cultivating secrecy and unpredictability, then, serves as a general strategy to avoid confinement. The "secret life" also provides an excuse for failure: "I could not lead a respectable life because it would lead me to jail." This explains social and economic failure in a culturally acceptable manner.

The presence of the criminal justice system in the lives of the poor, Goffman found, cannot simply be measured by the number of people sent to prison or the number who return home with felony convictions. The recent rise in imprisonment has fostered a climate of fear and suspicion in poor communities—a climate in which family members and friends are pressured to inform on one another and young men live as suspects and fugitives, with the daily fear of confinement. One strategy for coping with these risks is to avoid dangerous places, people, and interactions entirely. A young man thus does not attend the birth of his child or seek medical help when he is badly beaten. He avoids the police and the courts, even if it means using violence when he is injured or becoming the target of others who are looking for someone to rob. A second strategy is to cultivate unpredictability—to remain secretive and to work outside the economic mainstream. To ensure that those close to him will not inform on him, a young man comes and goes in irregular and unpredictable ways, remaining elusive and untrusting, sleeping in different beds, and deceiving those close to him about his life. Considering this burden, is it surprising that young men raised in this environment find themselves on the run and outside the law?

Critical Thinking

Goffman paints a pretty bleak picture of underclass life and the social forces that shape its existence. Should the United States intervene in other countries in attempts at "nation building" or to develop democracy abroad in third-world nations when there are so many problems here at home?

SOURCE: Alice Goffman, "On the Run: Wanted Men in a Philadelphia Ghetto," *American Sociological Review* 74 (2009): 339–357.

counterparts. They may be more likely to be detained, have formal charges (petitions) filed, and be removed from their homes and placed in secure confinement.[109] The Race, Culture, Gender and Criminology feature discusses the associations between the threat of arrest, incarceration, poverty, and culture in the minority community.

As adults, minority group members, especially those who are indigent or unemployed, continue to receive disparate treatment. Black and Latino adults are less likely to receive bail in violent crime cases than whites, and consequently more likely to be kept in detention pending trial.[110] They also receive longer prison sentences than whites who commit similar crimes and have similar criminal histories. Take for instance the use of habitual offender statutes that provide very long sentences for a second or third conviction ("three strikes and you're out"). Matthew Crow and Kathrine Johnson looked at the use of habitual sentencing practices in Florida and reached the conclusion that race and ethnicity still matter: minority drug and violent offenders are viewed as particular threats to dominant, mainstream values and are more likely to be charged as habitual offenders than are European Americans.[111] Nor is this solely a state court problem. After reviewing sentences in the federal court system, Jill Doerner and Stephen Demuth found that particularly harsh punishments are focused disproportionately on the youngest Hispanic and black male defendants. Young Hispanic male defendants have the highest odds of incarceration, and young black male defendants receive the longest sentences.[112] Yet when African Americans are victims of crime, their predicaments receive less public concern and media attention than that afforded white victims.[113] Murders involving whites (and females) are much more likely to be punished with death than those whose victims are black males, a fact not lost on the minority population.[114]

Disparities in justice policy result in the widely disproportionate makeup of the prison population. The percentage of minority men and women who are behind bars is far higher than the percentage of European Americans. It is not surprising that African Americans of all social classes hold negative attitudes toward the justice system and view it as an arbitrary and unfair institution.[115]

Cultural Bias

Another explanation of racial differences in the crime rate rests on the legacy of racial discrimination based on personality and behavior.[116] The fact that U.S. culture influences African American crime rates is underscored by the fact that black violence rates are much lower in other nations—both those that are predominantly white, such as Canada, and those that are predominantly black, such as Nigeria.[117]

Some criminologists view black crime as a function of socialization in a society where the black family was torn apart and black culture destroyed in such a way that recovery has proven impossible. Early experiences, beginning with slavery, have left a wound that has been deepened by racism and lack of opportunity.[118] Children of the slave society were thrust into a system of forced dependency and ambivalence and antagonism toward one's self and group.

In an important work, *All God's Children: The Bosket Family and the American Tradition of Violence,* crime reporter Fox Butterfield chronicles the history of the Boskets, a black family, through five generations.[119] He focuses on Willie Bosket, who is charming, captivating, and brilliant. He is also one of the worst criminals in the New York State penal system. By the time he was in his teens, he had committed more than 200 armed robberies and 25 stabbings. Butterfield shows how the early struggles in the South, with its violent slave culture, led directly to Willie Bosket's rage and violence on the streets of New York City. Beginning in South Carolina in the 1700s, the southern slave society was a place where white notions of honor demanded immediate retaliation for the smallest slight. According to Butterfield, contemporary black violence is a tradition inherited from white southern violence. The need for respect has turned into a cultural mandate that can provoke retaliation at the slightest hint of insult.

Economic and Social Disparity

Racial and ethnic differentials in crime rates may also be tied to economic and social disparity. Racial and ethnic minorities are often forced to live in high-crime areas where the risk of victimization is significant. People who witness violent crime and are victimized may themselves engage in violence.[120]

Racial and ethnic minorities face a greater degree of social isolation and economic deprivation than the white majority, a condition that has been linked by empirical research to high violence rates.[121] Not helping the situation is the fact that during tough economic times, blacks and whites may find themselves competing for shrinking job opportunities. As economic competition between the races grows, interracial homicides do likewise; economic and political rivalries lead to greater levels of interracial violence.[122]

Even during times of economic growth, lower-class African Americans are left out of the economic mainstream, a fact that meets with a growing sense of frustration and failure.[123] As a result of being shut out of educational and economic opportunities enjoyed by the rest of society, this population may be prone to the lure of illegitimate gain and criminality. African Americans living in lower-class inner-city areas may be disproportionately violent because they are exposed to more violence in their daily lives than other racial and economic groups.[124] Many black youths are forced to attend essentially segregated schools that are underfunded and deteriorated, a condition that elevates the likelihood of their being incarcerated in adulthood.[125]

Family Dissolution Family dissolution in the minority community may be tied to low employment rates among African American males, which places a strain on marriages. The relatively large number of single-female-headed households in these communities may be tied to the high mortality rate among African American males, caused by disease and violence.[126] When families are weakened or disrupted, their social control is compromised. It is not surprising, then, that divorce and separation rates are significantly associated with homicide rates in the African American community.[127]

Is Convergence Possible? Race differences in family structure, economic status, education achievement, and other social factors persist. Does that mean that racial differences in the crime rate will persist, or is convergence possible? One argument is that if and when economic conditions improve in the minority community, differences in crime rates will eventually disappear.[128] Another view is that the trend toward residential integration, under way since 1980,

CONNECTIONS

The concept of relative deprivation refers to the fact that people compare their success to those with whom they are in immediate contact. Even if conditions improve, they still may feel as if they are falling behind. A sense of relative deprivation, discussed in Chapter 6, may lead to criminal activity.

Ask Yourself ...

Which do you think has a greater impact on behavior, actual or relative deprivation?

may also help reduce crime rate differentials.[129] An important study by Gary LaFree and his associates tracked race-specific homicide arrest differences in 80 large U.S. cities from 1960 to 2000, and found substantial convergence in black/white homicide arrest rates over time.[130]

Homicide rate differences narrowed in cities with a growing black population and also where there was little race-based difference in the number of intact families. In other words, where the percentage of families led by a single parent were equal in the black and white communities, crime rates went down. Conversely, homicide ratios expanded in cities where African Americans were involved in more drug-related crimes than whites. This finding indicates that crime rate convergence may be linked to social factors. Positive factors, such as equality in family structure, will reduce race-based differences; negative factors, such as drug use differentials, will enhance race-based differences. In sum, the weight of the evidence shows that although there is little difference in the self-reported crime rates of racial groups, Hispanics and African Americans are more likely to be arrested for serious violent crimes. The causes of minority crime have been linked to poverty, racism, hopelessness, lack of opportunity, and urban problems experienced by all too many African American citizens.

Immigration and Crime

There is a prevailing view that illegal immigrants are dangerous and violent people and that areas that house illegal immigrants experience a spike in their crime rates. This view culminated in the passage in Arizona of a new law—the Support Our Law Enforcement and Safe Neighborhoods Act—that created new crimes and enabled police officers to stop, detain, and arrest people for what they perceive as immigration violation, a reasonable suspicion that they are in the country without documentation.[131] This law made it a crime to lack immigration papers and required police to determine whether people they encounter are in the country illegally.[132] In June 2012, the U.S. Supreme Court upheld the provision requiring immigration status checks during law enforcement stops, but struck down other provisions as violations of the U.S. Constitution.[133]

The Arizona law remains highly controversial, and lawsuits have been filed to prevent its application; nonetheless, it represents the belief that immigrants are crime prone and represent a social threat. How true is this perception? In reality, immigrants are far less likely than the average U.S. native to commit crime. Significantly lower rates of incarceration and institutionalization among foreign-born adults suggest that long-standing fears of immigration as a threat to public safety are unjustified. One study in California found:

- People born outside the United States make up about 35 percent of California's adult population but represent about 17 percent of the state prison population.

- U.S.-born adult men are incarcerated in state prisons at rates up to 3.3 times higher than foreign-born men.
- Among men ages 18 to 40—the age group most likely to commit crime—those born in the United States are 10 times more likely than immigrants to be in county jail or state prison.
- Noncitizen men from Mexico ages 18 to 40—a group disproportionately likely to have entered the United States illegally—are more than 8 times *less* likely than U.S.-born men in the same age group to be in a correctional setting (0.48 percent versus 4.2 percent).[134]

The findings are striking because immigrants in California are more likely than the U.S.-born to be young and male and to have low levels of education—all characteristics associated with higher rates of crime and incarceration. Yet the report shows that institutionalization rates of young male immigrants with less than a high school diploma are extremely low, particularly when compared with U.S.-born men with low levels of education.

The California report is not unique. A number of research studies have concluded that immigrants have lower crime rates than the norm. For example, a recent examination by Ramiro Martinez of homicide rates in Texas found that counties on the Mexican border have significantly *lower* homicide rates than non-border counties, and Texas counties with *higher* levels of immigration concentration had lower levels of homicide. Not only are Latino homicide rates lower in these areas, so are those of non-Latino whites and blacks. No compelling support was found for the claim that border areas are more violent due to proximity or immigration.[135]

The low rates of criminal involvement by immigrants may be due in part to current U.S. immigration policy, which screens immigrants for criminal history and assigns extra penalties to noncitizens who commit crimes.

Chronic Offenders/Criminal Careers

LO9 Describe the pioneering research on chronic offending by Wolfgang, Figlio, and Sellin

Crime data show that most offenders commit a single criminal act and upon arrest discontinue their antisocial activity. Others commit a few less serious crimes. A small group of criminal offenders, however, account for a majority of all criminal offenses. These persistent offenders are referred to as **career criminals** or **chronic offenders**. The concept of

career criminals A person who repeatedly violates the law and organizes his or her lifestyle around criminality.

chronic offenders According to Wolfgang, a delinquent offender who is arrested five or more times before he or she is 18 stands a good chance of becoming an adult criminal; such offenders are responsible for more than half of all serious crimes.

the chronic or career offender is most closely associated with the research efforts of Marvin Wolfgang, Robert Figlio, and Thorsten Sellin.[136] In their landmark 1972 study, *Delinquency in a Birth Cohort*, they used official records to follow the criminal careers of a cohort of 9,945 boys born in Philadelphia in 1945 from the time of their birth until they reached 18 years of age in 1963. Official police records were used to identify delinquents. About one-third of the boys (3,475) had some police contact. The remaining two-thirds (6,470) had none. Each delinquent was given a seriousness weight score for every delinquent act.[137] The weighting of delinquent acts allowed the researchers to differentiate between a simple assault requiring no medical attention for the victim and serious battery in which the victim needed hospitalization. The best-known discovery of Wolfgang and his associates was that of the so-called chronic offender. The cohort data indicated that 54 percent (1,862) of the sample's delinquent youths were repeat offenders, whereas the remaining 46 percent (1,613) were one-time offenders. The repeaters could be further categorized as nonchronic recidivists and chronic recidivists. The former consisted of 1,235 youths who had been arrested more than once but fewer than five times and who made up 35.6 percent of all delinquents. The latter were a group of 627 boys arrested five times or more, who accounted for 18 percent of the delinquents and 6 percent of the total sample of 9,945. (See Figure 2.3.)

The chronic offenders (known today as "the chronic 6 percent") were involved in the most dramatic amounts of delinquent behavior: they were responsible for 5,305 offenses, or 51.9 percent of all the offenses committed by the cohort. Even more striking was the involvement of chronic offenders in serious criminal acts. Of the entire sample, the chronic 6 percent committed 71 percent of the homicides, 73 percent of the rapes, 82 percent of the robberies, and 69 percent of the aggravated assaults.

Wolfgang and his associates found that arrests and court experience did little to deter the chronic offender. In fact, punishment was inversely related to chronic offending: the more stringent the sanction chronic offenders received, the more likely they would be to engage in repeated criminal behavior.

In a second cohort study, Wolfgang and his associates selected a new, larger birth cohort, born in Philadelphia in 1958, which contained both male and female subjects.[138] Although the proportion of delinquent youths was about the same as that in the 1945 cohort, they again found a similar pattern of chronic offending. Chronic female delinquency was relatively rare—only 1 percent of the females in the survey were chronic offenders. Wolfgang's pioneering effort to identify the chronic career offender has been replicated

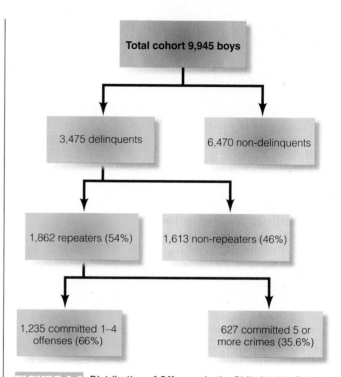

FIGURE 2.3 Distribution of Offenses in the Philadelphia Cohort

SOURCE: Marvin Wolfgang, Robert Figlio, and Thorsten Sellin, *Delinquency in a Birth Cohort* (Chicago: University of Chicago Press, 1972). Reprinted with permission of University of Chicago Press.

by a number of other researchers in a variety of locations in the United States.[139] The chronic offender has also been found abroad.[140]

LO10 Evaluate the suspected causes of chronicity

What Causes Chronicity? As might be expected, kids who have been exposed to a variety of personal and social problems at an early age are the most at risk to repeat offending, a concept referred to as **early onset**. One important study of delinquent offenders in Orange County, California, conducted by Michael Schumacher and Gwen Kurz, found several factors (see Exhibit 2.3) that characterized the chronic offender, including problems in the home and at school.[141] Other research studies have found that early involvement in criminal activity (getting arrested before age 15), relatively low intellectual development, and parental drug involvement were key predictive factors for chronicity.[142] Offenders who accumulate large debts, use drugs, and resort to violence are more likely to persist.[143] In contrast, those who spend time in a juvenile facility and later in an adult prison are more likely to desist.[144]

Persistence: The Continuity of Crime One of the most important findings from the cohort studies is that persistent juvenile offenders are the ones most likely to continue their criminal careers into adulthood.[145] Paul Tracy and Kimberly Kempf-Leonard followed up all subjects in the second 1958 cohort and found that two-thirds of delinquent offenders

early onset A term that refers to the assumption that a criminal career begins early in life and that people who are deviant at a very young age are the ones most likely to persist in crime.

EXHIBIT 2.3

Characteristics that Predict Chronic Offending

School Behavior/Performance Factors

- Attendance problems (truancy or a pattern of skipping school)
- Behavior problems (recent suspensions or expulsion)
- Poor grades (failing two or more classes)

Family Problem Factors

- Poor parental supervision and control
- Significant family problems (illness, substance abuse, discord)
- Criminal family members
- Documented child abuse, neglect, or family violence

Substance Abuse Factor

- Alcohol or drug use (by minors in any way but experimentation)

Delinquency Factors

- Stealing pattern of behavior
- Runaway pattern of behavior
- Gang member or associate

SOURCE: Michael Schumacher and Gwen Kurz, *The 8% Solution: Preventing Serious Repeat Juvenile Crime* (Thousand Oaks, CA: Sage, 1999).

---

desisted from crime, but those who started their delinquent careers early and who committed serious violent crimes throughout adolescence were the most likely to persist as adults.[146] This phenomenon is referred to as **persistence** or the **continuity of crime**.[147]

Children who are found to be disruptive and antisocial as early as age 5 or 6 are the most likely to exhibit stable, long-term patterns of disruptive behavior throughout adolescence.[148] They have measurable behavior problems in areas such as learning and motor skills, cognitive abilities, family relations, and other areas of social, psychological, and physical functioning.[149] Youthful offenders who persist are more likely to abuse alcohol, get into trouble while in military service, become economically dependent, have lower aspirations, get divorced or separated, and have a weak employment record. They do not specialize in one

CONNECTIONS

It is evident that chronic offenders suffer from a profusion of social problems. Some criminologists believe that accumulating a significant variety of these social deficits is the key to understanding criminal development. For more on this topic, see the discussion on problem behavior syndrome in Chapter 9.

Ask Yourself …

Make a list of all the social problems that you believe contribute to crime and then compare what you wrote to other students in class.

AN ETHICAL DILEMMA

DOES TOUGH LOVE WORK?

The planning director for the State Department of Juvenile Justice has asked for your advice on how to reduce the threat of chronic offenders. Some of the more conservative members of her staff seem to believe that these kids need a strict dose of rough justice if they are to be turned away from a life of crime. They believe juvenile delinquents who are punished harshly are less likely to recidivate than youths who receive lesser punishments, such as community corrections or probation. In addition, they believe that hardcore, violent offenders deserve to be punished; excessive concern for offenders and not their acts ignores the rights of victims and society in general.

The planning director is unsure whether such an approach is ethical. Is it ethical to use tough punishment with kids, as it may produce deviant identities that lock kids into a criminal way of life? She is concerned that a strategy stressing punishment is not only unethical, but it will have relatively little impact on chronic offenders and, if anything, may cause escalation in serious criminal behaviors.

The director has asked you for your professional advice on this ethical dilemma. Write a two-page memorandum: On the one hand, the system must be sensitive to the adverse effects of stigma and labeling. On the other hand, the need for control and deterrence must not be ignored. Is it possible to reconcile these two opposing views?

thinking like a criminologist

---

type of crime; rather, they engage in a variety of criminal acts, including theft, use of drugs, and violent offenses.

Implications of the Chronic Offender Concept The findings of the cohort studies and the discovery of the chronic offender have revitalized criminological theory. If relatively few offenders become chronic, persistent criminals, then perhaps they possess some individual trait that is responsible for their behavior. Most people exposed to troublesome social conditions, such as poverty, do not become chronic offenders, so it is unlikely that social conditions alone can cause chronic offending. Traditional theories of criminal behavior have failed to distinguish between chronic and occasional offenders. They concentrate more

persistence The idea that those who started their delinquent careers early and who committed serious violent crimes throughout adolescence are the most likely to persist as adults.

continuity of crime The view that crime begins early in life and continues throughout the life course. Thus, the best predictor of future criminality is past criminality.

on explaining why people begin to commit crime and pay scant attention to why people stop offending. The discovery of the chronic offender 30 years ago forced criminologists to consider such issues as persistence and desistance in their explanations of crime; more recent theories account for not only the onset of criminality but also its termination.

The chronic offender has become a central focus of crime control policy. Apprehension and punishment seem to have little effect on the offending behavior of chronic offenders, and most repeat their criminal acts after their correctional release. Because chronic offenders rarely learn from their mistakes, sentencing policies designed to incapacitate chronic offenders for long periods of time without hope of probation or parole have been established. Incapacitation rather than rehabilitation is the goal. Among the policies spurred by the chronic offender concept are mandatory sentences for violent or drug-related crimes, "**three strikes**" policies, which require people convicted of a third felony offense to serve a mandatory life sentence, and "truth in sentencing" policies, which require that convicted felons spend a significant portion of their sentence behind bars. Whether such policies can reduce crime rates or are merely "get tough" measures designed to placate conservative voters remains to be seen.

three strikes Policies whereby people convicted of three felony offenses receive a mandatory life sentence.

SUMMARY

LO1 Compare and contrast the most widely used forms of crime data collection

The Federal Bureau of Investigation collects data from local law enforcement agencies and publishes that information yearly in its Uniform Crime Report (UCR). The National Incident-Based Reporting System (NIBRS) is a program that collects data on each reported crime incident. The National Crime Victimization Survey (NCVS) is a nationwide survey of victimization in the United States. Self-report surveys ask people to describe, in detail, their recent and lifetime participation in criminal activity. Other forms of crime data come from mapping, data mining, experiments, and examining records from hospitals and schools.

LO2 Articulate the problems associated with collecting the official crime data

Many serious crimes are not reported to police and therefore are not counted by the UCR. Police may misrepresent crimes to lower or raise crime rates. There are also unintentional mistakes. Methodological issues such as counting only the most serious crime can invalidate counts.

LO3 Identify recent trends in the crime rate

Official crime rates peaked in 1991 when police recorded almost 15 million crimes. Since then, the number of crimes has been in decline. About 10 million crimes were reported in 2012, a drop of 4 million reported crimes since the 1991 peak, despite an increase of about 50 million in the general population. NCVS data show that criminal victimizations have declined significantly during the past 30 years. Self-report trends are more stable.

LO4 Discuss the factors that influence crime rate trends

The age composition of the population, the number of immigrants, the availability of legalized abortion, the number of guns, drug use, availability of emergency medical services, numbers of police officers, the state of the economy, cultural change, and criminal opportunities all influence crime rates.

LO5 Assess how crime rates reflect different ecological conditions

Patterns in the crime rate seem to be linked to temporal and ecological factors. Most reported crimes occur during July and August. Large urban areas have by far the highest rates of violent crimes, and rural areas have the lowest per capita.

LO6 Debate the association between social class and crime

People living in poverty engage in disproportionate amounts of expressive crimes, such as rape and assault. Crime rates in inner-city, high-poverty areas are generally higher than those in suburban or wealthier areas. However, the association between unemployment and crime is less clear.

LO7 Clarify what is meant by the term *aging-out process*

Regardless of economic status, marital status, race, sex, and other factors, people tend to commit less crime as they age, and this relationship has been stable over time. Changes in biological and social factors help explain the aging-out process.

LO8 Describe the gender and racial patterns in crime

Male crime rates are higher than those of females, especially violent crime rates. Gender differences in the crime rate have persisted over time, but there is little question that females are now involved in more crime than ever before and that there are more similarities than differences between male and female offenders. Official crime data indicate that minority group members are involved in a disproportionate share of criminal activity. Racial and ethnic differentials in crime rates may be tied to economic and social disparity, institutional and structural racism, and other factors.

LO9 Describe the pioneering research on chronic offending by Wolfgang, Figlio, and Sellin

The concept of the chronic or career offender is most closely associated with the research efforts of Marvin Wolfgang, Robert Figlio, and Thorsten Sellin. Chronic offenders are involved in significant amounts of delinquent behavior and tend later to become adult criminals. Unlike most offenders, they do not age out of crime.

LO10 Evaluate the suspected causes of chronicity

Kids who have been exposed to a variety of personal and social problems at an early age are the most at risk to repeat offending. Chronic offenders often have problems in the home and at school, relatively low intellectual development, and parental drug involvement.

CRITICAL THINKING QUESTIONS

1. Would you answer honestly if a national crime survey asked you about your criminal behavior, including drinking and drug use? If not, why not? If you would not answer honestly, do you question the accuracy of self-report surveys?

2. How would you explain gender differences in the crime rate? Why do you think males are more violent than females?

3. Assuming that males are more violent than females, does that mean crime has a biological rather than a social basis (because males and females share a similar environment)?

4. The UCR reports that crime rates are higher in large cities than in small towns. What does that tell us about the effects of violent TV and films and rap music on teenage behavior?

5. What social and environmental factors do you believe influence the crime rate? Do you think a national emergency would increase or decrease crime rates?

KEY TERMS

Uniform Crime Report (UCR) (28)
index crimes (28)
Part I crimes (28)
Part II crimes (29)
cleared crimes (30)
National Incident-Based Reporting System (NIBRS) (32)

sampling (32)
population (32)
cross-sectional survey (33)
National Crime Victimization Survey (NCVS) (33)
self-report surveys (34)
racial profiling (35)
cohort (36)

retrospective cohort study (37)
meta-analysis (38)
systematic review (38)
instrumental crimes (46)
expressive crimes (46)
aging out (49)
masculinity hypothesis (49)
chivalry hypothesis (49)

liberal feminist theory (50)
racial threat hypothesis (52)
career criminals (55)
chronic offenders (55)
early onset (56)
persistence (57)
continuity of crime (57)
three strikes (58)

NOTES

1. Federal Bureau of Investigation, "Law Enforcement Shares Findings of the Investigation into the Washington Navy Yard Shootings," September 25, 2013, http://www.fbi.gov/washingtondc/press-releases/2013/law-enforcement-shares-findings-of-the-investigation-into-the-washington-navy-yard-shootings (accessed April 2014).

2. Sourcebook of Criminal Justice Statistics, 2014, http://www.albany.edu/sourcebook/pdf/t2332011.pdf (accessed April 2014).

3. Federal Bureau of Investigation, *Crime in the United States, 2012* (Washington, DC: U.S. Government Printing Office, 2013), http://www.fbi.gov/about-us/cjis/ucr/crime-in-the-u.s/2012/crime-in-the-u.s.-2012 (accessed April 2014).

4. FBI, "U.S. Department of Justice Attorney General Eric Holder Announces Revisions to the Uniform Crime Report's Definition of Rape; Data Reported on Rape Will Better Reflect State Criminal Codes, Victim Experiences," January 6, 2012, http://www.fbi.gov/news/pressrel/press-releases/attorney-general-eric-holder-announces-revisions-to-the-uniform-crime-reports-definition-of-rape (accessed April 2014).

5. FBI, *Preliminary Semiannual Uniform Crime Report*, January–June 2013, http://www.fbi.gov/about-us/cjis/ucr/crime-in-the-u.s/2013/preliminary-semiannual-uniform-crime-report-january-june-2013/tables/table_1_january_to_june_2012-2013_percent_change_by_population_group.xls (accessed April 2014).

6. Jennifer Truman, Lynn Langton, and Michael Planty, *Criminal Victimization, 2012* (Washington, DC: Bureau of Justice Statistics, 2013), http://www.bjs.gov/content/pub/pdf/cv12.pdf (accessed April 2014).

7. Richard Felson, Steven Messner, Anthony Hoskin, and Glenn Deane, "Reasons for Reporting and Not Reporting Domestic Violence to the Police," *Criminology* 40 (2002): 617–648.

8. Duncan Chappell, Gilbert Geis, Stephen Schafer, and Larry Siegel, "Forcible Rape: A Comparative Study of Offenses Known to the Police in Boston and Los Angeles," in *Studies in the Sociology of Sex*, ed. James Henslin (New York: Appleton Century Crofts, 1971), pp. 169–193.

9. Eric Baumer and Janet Lauritsen, "Reporting Crime to the Police, 1973–2005: A Multivariate Analysis of Long-Term Trends in the National Crime Survey (NCVS)," *Criminology* 48 (2010): 131–185.

10. Patrick Jackson, "Assessing the Validity of Official Data on Arson," *Criminology* 26 (1988): 181–195.

11. John Eterno and Eli B. Silverman, *The Crime Numbers Game: Management by Manipulation* (Boca Raton, FL: CRC Press, 2012).

12. FBI, *UCR Handbook* (Washington, DC: U.S. Government Printing Office, 1998), p. 33.

13. National Archive of Criminal Justice Data, *National Incident-Based Reporting System Resource Guide*, http://www.icpsr.umich.edu/NACJD/NIBRS/ (accessed April 2014).

14. FBI, "A Word About NIBRS," 2013, http://www.fbi.gov/about-us/cjis/ucr/nibrs/2012 (accessed April 2014).

15. Lynn Addington, "The Effect of NIBRS Reporting on Item Missing Data in Murder Cases," *Homicide Studies* 8 (2004): 193–213.

16. Michael Gottfredson and Travis Hirschi, "The Methodological Adequacy of Longitudinal Research on Crime," *Criminology* 25 (1987): 581–614.

17. Bureau of Justice Statistics, "The Nation's Two Crime Measures," http://bjs.ojp.usdoj.gov/content/pub/pdf/ntcm.pdf (accessed April 2014).

18. Lynn A. Addington and Callie Marie Rennison, "Rape Co-occurrence: Do Additional Crimes Affect Victim Reporting and Police Clearance of Rape?" *Journal of Quantitative Criminology* 24 (2008): 205–226.

19. L. Edward Wells and Joseph Rankin, "Juvenile Victimization: Convergent Validation of Alternative Measurements," *Journal of Research in Crime and Delinquency* 32 (1995): 287–307.

20. Saul Kassin, Richard Leo, Christian Meissner, Kimberly Richman, Lori Colwell, Amy-May Leach, and Dana La Fon, "Police Interviewing and Interrogation: A Self-Report Survey of Police Practices and Beliefs," *Law and Human Behavior* 31 (2007): 381–400.

21. Lloyd Johnston, Patrick O'Malley, and Jerald Bachman, *Monitoring the Future, 2006* (Ann Arbor, MI: Institute for Social Research, 2006).

22. D. Wayne Osgood, Lloyd Johnston, Patrick O'Malley, and Jerald Bachman, "The Generality of Deviance in Late Adolescence and Early Adulthood," *American Sociological Review* 53 (1988): 81–93.

23. Leonore Simon, "Validity and Reliability of Violent Juveniles: A Comparison of Juvenile Self-Reports with Adult Self-Reports Incarcerated in Adult Prisons," paper presented at the annual meeting of the American Society of Criminology, Boston, November 1995, p. 26.

24. Stephen Cernkovich, Peggy Giordano, and Meredith Pugh, "Chronic Offenders: The Missing Cases in Self-Report Delinquency Research," *Journal of Criminal Law and Criminology* 76 (1985): 705–732.

25. Terence Thornberry, Beth Bjerregaard, and William Miles, "The Consequences of Respondent Attrition in Panel Studies: A Simulation Based on the Rochester Youth Development Study," *Journal of Quantitative Criminology* 9 (1993): 127–158.

26. Julia Yun Soo Kim, Michael Fendrich, and Joseph S. Wislar, "The Validity of Juvenile Arrestees' Drug Use Reporting: A Gender Comparison," *Journal of Research in Crime and Delinquency* 37 (2000): 419–432.

27. Donald Tomaskovic-Devey, Cynthia Pfaff Wright, Ronald Czaja, and Kirk Miller, "Self-Reports of Police Speeding Stops by Race: Results from the North Carolina Reverse Record Check Survey," *Journal of Quantitative Criminology* 22 (2006): 279–297.

28. Jennifer Roberts, Edward Mulvey, Julie Horney, John Lewis, and Michael Arter, "A Test of Two Methods of Recall for Violent Events," *Journal of Quantitative Criminology* 21 (2005): 175–193.

29. Lila Kazemian and David Farrington, "Comparing the Validity of Prospective, Retrospective, and Official Onset for Different Offending Categories," *Journal of Quantitative Criminology* 21 (2005): 127–147.

30. Barbara Warner and Brandi Wilson Coomer, "Neighborhood Drug Arrest Rates: Are They a Meaningful Indicator of Drug Activity? A Research Note," *Journal of Research in Crime and Delinquency* 40 (2003): 123–139.

31. Alfred Blumstein, Jacqueline Cohen, and Richard Rosenfeld, "Trend and Deviation in Crime Rates: A Comparison of UCR and NCVS Data for Burglary and Robbery," *Criminology* 29 (1991): 237–248. See also Michael Hindelang, Travis Hirschi, and Joseph Weis, *Measuring Delinquency* (Beverly Hills: Sage, 1981).

32. See, generally, David Farrington, Lloyd Ohlin, and James Q. Wilson, *Understanding and Controlling Crime* (New York: Springer-Verlag, 1986), pp. 11–18.

33. Claire Sterk-Elifson, "Just for Fun? Cocaine Use among Middle-Class Women," *Journal of Drug Issues* 26 (1996): 63–76.

34. Ibid., p. 63.

35. William F. Whyte, *Street Corner Society* (Chicago: University of Chicago Press, 1955).

36. Herman Schwendinger and Julia Schwendinger, *Adolescent Subcultures and Delinquency* (New York: Praeger, 1985).

37. David Farrington and Brandon Welsh, "Improved Street Lighting and Crime Prevention," *Justice Quarterly* 19 (2002): 313–343.

38. Colleen McCue, Emily Stone, and Teresa Gooch, "Data Mining and Value-Added Analysis," *FBI Law Enforcement Bulletin* 72 (2003): 1–6.

39. Colleen McCue, "Using Data Mining to Predict and Prevent Violent Crimes," presentation made to SPSS Incorporated, 2004.

40. Jerry Ratcliffe, "Aoristic Signatures and the Spatio-Temporal Analysis of High Volume Crime Patterns," *Journal of Quantitative Criminology* 18 (2002): 23–43.

41. Clarence Schrag, *Crime and Justice: American Style* (Washington, DC: U.S. Government Printing Office, 1971), p. 17.

42. Lynn Langton, Michael Planty, and Jennifer Truman, *Criminal Victimization, 2012* (Washington, DC: Bureau of Justice Statistics, 2013). Victim data in this chapter come from this source.

43. Kathleen Maguire and Ann Pastore, *Sourcebook of Criminal Justice Statistics, 1995* (Albany, NY: Hindelang Research Center, 1996), http://www.druglibrary.org/schaffer/govpubs/sourcebook/1995/ (accessed April 2014).

44. Lloyd Johnston, Patrick O'Malley, and Jerald Bachman, *Monitoring the Future, 8* (Ann Arbor, MI: Institute for Social Research, 2012), http://www.monitoringthefuture.org (accessed April 2014); Lloyd Johnston, Patrick O'Malley, Jerald Bachman, and John Schulenberg, "Teen Smoking Continues to Decline in 2013," University of Michigan News Service, Ann Arbor, 2013.

45. Jan van Dijk, John van Kesteren, and Paul Smit, "Criminal Victimisation in International Perspective: Key Findings from the 2004–2005 ICVS and EU ICS, 2008,"

http://unicri.us/services/library_
documentation/publications/icvs/
publications/ICVS2004_05report.pdf
(accessed April 2014).

46. United Nations Office on Drugs and Crime, *Global Study on Homicide 2011*, Vienna, Austria, 2011, http://www.unodc.org/documents/data-and-analysis/statistics/Homicide/Globa_study_on_homicide_2011_web.pdf (accessed April 2014).

47. Gardiner Harris, "Murder Charges Are Filed Against 5 Men in New Delhi Gang Rape" *New York Times*. January 3, 2013, http://www.nytimes.com/2013/01/04/world/asia/murder-charges-filed-against-5-men-in-india-gang-rape.html (accessed April 2014).

48. Steven Levitt, "The Limited Role of Changing Age Structure in Explaining Aggregate Crime Rates," *Criminology* 37 (1999): 581–599.

49. Lisa Tompson and Kate Bowers, "A Stab in the Dark? A Research Note on Temporal Patterns of Street Robbery," *Journal of Research in Crime and Delinquency* 50 (2013): 616–631.

50. Ellen Cohn, "The Effect of Weather and Temporal Variations on Calls for Police Service," *American Journal of Police* 15 (1996): 23–43.

51. R. A. Baron, "Aggression as a Function of Ambient Temperature and Prior Anger Arousal," *Journal of Personality and Social Psychology* 21 (1972): 183–189.

52. Brad Bushman, Morgan Wang, and Craig Anderson, "Is the Curve Relating Temperature to Aggression Linear or Curvilinear? Assaults and Temperature in Minneapolis Reexamined," *Journal of Personality and Social Psychology* 89 (2005): 62–66.

53. Paul Bell, "Reanalysis and Perspective in the Heat-Aggression Debate," *Journal of Personality and Social Psychology* 89 (2005): 71–73.

54. Ellen Cohn, "The Prediction of Police Calls for Service: The Influence of Weather and Temporal Variables on Rape and Domestic Violence," *Journal of Environmental Psychology* 13 (1993): 71–83.

55. John Simister and Cary Cooper, "Thermal Stress in the U.S.A.: Effects on Violence and on Employee Behaviour," *Stress and Health* 21 (2005): 3–15.

56. James Rotton and Ellen Cohn, "Outdoor Temperature, Climate Control, and Criminal Assault," *Environment and Behavior* 36 (2004): 276–306.

57. Daniel Montolio and Simón Planells-Struse, "Does Tourism Boost Criminal Activity? Evidence from a Top Touristic Country," *Crime and Delinquency*, first published online October 28, 2013.

58. Franklin Zimring and Gordon Hawkins, *Crime Is Not the Problem: Lethal Violence in America* (New York: Oxford University Press, 1997).

59. Ibid., p. 36.

60. Gary Kleck and Marc Gertz, "Armed Resistance to Crime: The Prevalence and Nature of Self-Defense with a Gun," *Journal of Criminal Law and Criminology* 86 (1995): 219–249; Gary Kleck and Jongyeon Tark, "Resisting Crime: The Effects of Victim Action on the Outcomes of Crimes," *Criminology* 42 (2005): 861–909.

61. Felipe Estrada and Anders Nilsson, "Segregation and Victimization: Neighbourhood Resources, Individual Risk Factors and Exposure to Property Crime," *European Journal of Criminology* 5 (2008): 193–216.

62. Robert Nash Parker, "Bringing 'Booze' Back In: The Relationship Between Alcohol and Homicide," *Journal of Research in Crime and Delinquency* 32 (1995): 3–38.

63. Victoria Brewer and M. Dwayne Smith, "Gender Inequality and Rates of Female Homicide Victimization Across U.S. Cities," *Journal of Research in Crime and Delinquency* 32 (1995): 175–190.

64. James Short and F. Ivan Nye, "Extent of Unrecorded Juvenile Delinquency, Tentative Conclusions," *Journal of Criminal Law, Criminology, and Police Science* 49 (1958): 296–302.

65. Charles Tittle, Wayne Villemez, and Douglas Smith, "The Myth of Social Class and Criminality: An Empirical Assessment of the Empirical Evidence," *American Sociological Review* 43 (1978): 643–656.

66. Judith Blau and Peter Blau, "The Cost of Inequality: Metropolitan Structure and Violent Crime," *American Sociological Review* 147 (1982): 114–129; Richard Block, "Community Environment and Violent Crime," *Criminology* 17 (1979): 46–57; Robert Sampson, "Structural Sources of Variation in Race-Age-Specific Rates of Offending across Major U.S. Cities," *Criminology* 23 (1985): 647–673.

67. John R. Hipp and Adam Boessen, "Egohoods as Waves Washing Across the City: A New Measure of Neighborhoods," *Criminology* 51 (2013): 287–327; Ramiro Martinez, Jacob Stowell, and Jeffrey Cancino, "A Tale of Two Border Cities: Community Context, Ethnicity, and Homicide," *Social Science Quarterly* 89 (2008): 1–16.

68. Steven Messner, Lawrence Raffalovich, and Richard McMillan, "Economic Deprivation and Changes in Homicide Arrest Rates for White and Black Youths, 1967–1998: A National Time Series Analysis," *Criminology* 39 (2001): 591–614.

69. Mikko Aaltonen, John M. Macdonald, Pekka Martikainen, and Janne Kivivuor, "Examining the Generality of the Unemployment–Crime Association," *Criminology* 51 (2013): 561–594.

70. Robert Apel, Shawn Bushway, Robert Brame, Amelia M. Haviland, Daniel S. Nagin, and Ray Paternoster, "Unpacking the Relationship Between Adolescent Employment and Antisocial Behavior: A Matched Samples Comparison," *Criminology* 45 (2007): 67–97.

71. Richard Rosenfeld and Robert Fornango, "The Impact of Economic Conditions on Robbery and Property Crime: The Role of Consumer Sentiment," *Criminology* 45 (2007): 735–769.

72. Gary Kleck and Ted Chiricos, "Unemployment and Property Crime: A Target-Specific Assessment of Opportunity and Motivation as Mediating Factors," *Criminology* 40 (2002): 649–680.

73. Shawn Bushway, "Economy and Crime," *The Criminologist* 35 (2010): 1–5.

74. Douglas Smith and Laura Davidson, "Interfacing Indicators and Constructs in Criminological Research: A Note on the Comparability of Self-Report Violence Data for Race and Sex Groups," *Criminology* 24 (1986): 473–488.

75. R. Gregory Dunaway, Francis Cullen, Velmer Burton, and T. David Evans, "The Myth of Social Class and Crime Revisited: An Examination of Class and Adult Criminality," *Criminology* 38 (2000): 589–632.

76. Travis Hirschi and Michael Gottfredson, "Age and the Explanation of Crime," *American Journal of Sociology* 89 (1983): 552–584, at 581.

77. Misaki Natsuaki, Xiaojia Ge, and Ernst Wenk, "Continuity and Changes in the Developmental Trajectories of Criminal Career: Examining the Roles of Timing of First Arrest and High School Graduation," *Journal of Youth and Adolescence* 37 (2008): 431–444.

78. Lisa Stolzenberg and Stewart D'Alessio, "Co-offending and the Age-Crime Curve," *Journal of Research in Crime and Delinquency* 45 (2008): 65–86.

79. Derek Kreager, "When It's Good to Be 'Bad': Violence and Adolescent Peer Acceptance," *Criminology* 45 (2007): 893–923.

80. Ronald Aday and Jennifer Krabill, "Aging Offenders in the Criminal Justice System," *Marquette Elder's Advisor* 7 (2006): 237–258.

81. James Q. Wilson and Richard Herrnstein, *Crime and Human Nature* (New York: Simon and Schuster, 1985), pp. 126–147.

82. Ibid., p. 219.

83. Ryan King, Michael Massoglia, and Ross MacMillan, "The Context of Marriage and Crime: Gender, the Propensity to Marry, and Offending in Early Adulthood," *Criminology* 45 (2007): 33–65.

84. Paul Tracy, Kimberly Kempf-Leonard, and Stephanie Abramoske-James, "Gender

Differences in Delinquency and Juvenile Justice Processing: Evidence from National Data," *Crime and Delinquency* 55 (2009): 171–215.

85. Cesare Lombroso, *The Female Offender* (New York: Appleton, 1920), p. 122.

86. Otto Pollack, *The Criminality of Women* (Philadelphia: University of Pennsylvania, 1950).

87. For a review of this issue, see Darrell Steffensmeier, "Assessing the Impact of the Women's Movement on Sex-Based Differences in the Handling of Adult Criminal Defendants," *Crime and Delinquency* 26 (1980): 344–357.

88. Alan Booth and D. Wayne Osgood, "The Influence of Testosterone on Deviance in Adulthood: Assessing and Explaining the Relationship," *Criminology* 31 (1993): 93–118.

89. This section relies on the following sources: Kristen Kling, Janet Shibley Hyde, Carolin Showers, and Brenda Buswell, "Gender Differences in Self-Esteem: A Meta Analysis," *Psychological Bulletin* 125 (1999): 470–500; Anne Campbell, *Men, Women and Aggression* (New York: Basic Books, 1993); Ann Beutel and Margaret Mooney Marini, "Gender and Values," *American Sociological Review* 60 (1995): 436–448; John Gibbs, Velmer Burton, Francis Cullen, T. David Evans, Leanne Fiftal Alarid, and R. Gregory Dunaway, "Gender, Self-Control, and Crime," *Journal of Research in Crime and Delinquency* 35 (1998): 123–147.

90. Jean Bottcher, "Social Practices of Gender: How Gender Relates to Delinquency in the Everyday Lives of High-Risk Youths," *Criminology* 39 (2001): 893–932.

91. Daniel Mears, Matthew Ploeger, and Mark Warr, "Explaining the Gender Gap in Delinquency: Peer Influence and Moral Evaluations of Behavior," *Journal of Research in Crime and Delinquency* 35 (1998): 251–266.

92. Lisa Broidy, Elizabeth Cauffman, and Dorothy Espelage, "Sex Differences in Empathy and Its Relation to Juvenile Offending," *Violence and Victims* 18 (2003): 503–516.

93. Debra Kaysen, Miranda Morris, Shireen Rizvi, and Patricia Resick, "Peritraumatic Responses and Their Relationship to Perceptions of Threat in Female Crime Victims," *Violence Against Women* 11 (2005): 1515–1535.

94. Freda Adler, *Sisters in Crime* (New York: McGraw-Hill, 1975); Rita James Simon, *The Contemporary Woman and Crime* (Washington, DC: U.S. Government Printing Office, 1975).

95. David Rowe, Alexander Vazsonyi, and Daniel Flannery, "Sex Differences in Crime: Do Means and Within-Sex Variation Have Similar Causes?" *Journal of Research in Crime and Delinquency* 32 (1995): 84–100; Michael Hindelang, "Age, Sex, and the Versatility of Delinquency Involvements," *Social Forces* 14 (1971): 525–534; Martin Gold, *Delinquent Behavior in an American City* (Belmont, CA: Brooks/Cole, 1970); Gary Jensen and Raymond Eve, "Sex Differences in Delinquency: An Examination of Popular Sociological Explanations," *Criminology* 13 (1976): 427–448.

96. Leroy Gould, "Who Defines Delinquency: A Comparison of Self-Report and Officially Reported Indices of Delinquency for Three Racial Groups," *Social Problems* 16 (1969): 325–336; Harwin Voss, "Ethnic Differentials in Delinquency in Honolulu," *Journal of Criminal Law, Criminology, and Police Science* 54 (1963): 322–327; Ronald Akers, Marvin Krohn, Marcia Radosevich, and Lonn Lanza-Kaduce, "Social Characteristics and Self-Reported Delinquency," in *Sociology of Delinquency*, ed. Gary Jensen (Beverly Hills: Sage, 1981), pp. 48–62.

97. David Huizinga and Delbert Elliott, "Juvenile Offenders: Prevalence, Offender Incidence, and Arrest Rates by Race," *Crime and Delinquency* 33 (1987): 206–223. See also Dale Dannefer and Russell Schutt, "Race and Juvenile Justice Processing in Court and Police Agencies," *American Journal of Sociology* 87 (1982): 1113–1132.

98. Paul Tracy, "Race and Class Differences in Official and Self-Reported Delinquency," in *From Boy to Man, from Delinquency to Crime*, ed. Marvin Wolfgang, Terence Thornberry, and Robert Figlio (Chicago: University of Chicago Press, 1987), p. 120.

99. Miriam Sealock and Sally Simpson, "Unraveling Bias in Arrest Decisions: The Role of Juvenile Offender Type-Scripts," *Justice Quarterly* 15 (1998): 427–457.

100. Billy Close and Patrick L. Mason, "Searching for Efficient Enforcement: Officer Characteristics and Racially Biased Policing," *Review of Law and Economics* 3 (2007): 263–321.

101. Nicola Persico and Petra Todd, "The Hit Rates Test for Racial Bias in Motor-Vehicle Searches," *Justice Quarterly* 25 (2008): 37–53.

102. Robin Shepard Engel and Jennifer Calnon, "Examining the Influence of Drivers' Characteristics During Traffic Stops with Police: Results from a National Survey," *Justice Quarterly* 21 (2004): 49–90.

103. Robert Sampson, "Race and Criminal Violence: A Demographically Disaggregated Analysis of Urban Homicide," *Crime and Delinquency* 31 (1985): 47–82.

104. Hubert Blalock, Jr., *Toward a Theory of Minority-Group Relations* (New York: Capricorn Books, 1967).

105. Rebecca Wickes, John R. Hipp, Renee Zahnow, and Lorraine Mazerolle, "'Seeing' Minorities and Perceptions of Disorder: Explicating the Mediating and Moderating Mechanisms of Social Cohesion," *Criminology* 51 (2013): 519–560.

106. Engel and Calnon, "Examining the Influence of Drivers' Characteristics During Traffic Stops with Police."

107. Malcolm Holmes, Brad Smith, Adrienne Freng, and Ed Muñoz, "Minority Threat, Crime Control, and Police Resource Allocation in the Southwestern United States," *Crime and Delinquency* 54 (2008): 128–152.

108. Bradley Keen and David Jacobs, "Racial Threat, Partisan Politics, and Racial Disparities in Prison Admissions," *Criminology* 47 (2009): 209–238.

109. Nancy Rodriguez, "Outcomes and Why Preadjudication Detention Matters: The Cumulative Effect of Race and Ethnicity in Juvenile Court," *Journal of Research in Crime and Delinquency* 47 (2010): 391–413, http://jrc.sagepub.com/content/47/3/391.abstract (accessed April 2014).

110. Michael Leiber and Kristan Fox, "Race and the Impact of Detention on Juvenile Justice Decision Making," *Crime and Delinquency* 51 (2005): 470–497; Traci Schlesinger, "Racial and Ethnic Disparity in Pretrial Criminal Processing," *Justice Quarterly* 22 (2005): 170–192.

111. Matthew Crow and Kathrine Johnson, "Race, Ethnicity, and Habitual-Offender Sentencing: A Multilevel Analysis of Individual and Contextual Threat," *Criminal Justice Policy Review* 19 (2008): 63–83.

112. Jill Doerner and Stephen Demuth, "The Independent and Joint Effects of Race/Ethnicity, Gender, and Age on Sentencing Outcomes in U.S. Federal Courts," *Justice Quarterly* 27 (2010): 1–27.

113. Alexander Weiss and Steven Chermak, "The News Value of African-American Victims: An Examination of the Media's Presentation of Homicide," *Journal of Crime and Justice* 21 (1998): 71–84.

114. Jefferson Holcomb, Marian Williams, and Stephen Demuth, "White Female Victims and Death Penalty Disparity Research," *Justice Quarterly* 21 (2004): 877–902.

115. Ronald Weitzer and Steven Tuch, "Race, Class, and Perceptions of Discrimination by the Police," *Crime and Delinquency* 45 (1999): 494–507.

116. Barry Sample and Michael Philip, "Perspectives on Race and Crime in Research and Planning," in *The Criminal*

Justice System and Blacks, ed. Daniel Georges-Abeyie (New York: Clark Boardman Callaghan, 1984), pp. 21–36.

117. Ruth Peterson, Lauren Krivo, and Mark Harris, "Disadvantage and Neighborhood Violent Crime: Do Local Institutions Matter?" *Journal of Research in Crime and Delinquency* 37 (2000): 31–63.

118. James Comer, "Black Violence and Public Policy," in *American Violence and Public Policy*, ed. Lynn Curtis (New Haven, CT: Yale University Press, 1985), pp. 63–86.

119. Fox Butterfield, *All God's Children: The Bosket Family and the American Tradition of Violence* (New York: Avon, 1996).

120. Joanne Kaufman, "Explaining the Race/Ethnicity–Violence Relationship: Neighborhood Context and Social Psychological Processes," *Justice Quarterly* 22 (2005): 224–251.

121. Karen Parker and Patricia McCall, "Structural Conditions and Racial Homicide Patterns: A Look at the Multiple Disadvantages in Urban Areas," *Criminology* 37 (1999): 447–469.

122. David Jacobs and Katherine Woods, "Interracial Conflict and Interracial Homicide: Do Political and Economic Rivalries Explain White Killings of Blacks or Black Killings of Whites?" *American Journal of Sociology* 105 (1999): 157–190.

123. Melvin Thomas, "Race, Class and Personal Income: An Empirical Test of the Declining Significance of Race Thesis, 1968–1988," *Social Problems* 40 (1993): 328–339.

124. Mallie Paschall, Robert Flewelling, and Susan Ennett, "Racial Differences in Violent Behavior Among Young Adults: Moderating and Confounding Effects," *Journal of Research in Crime and Delinquency* 35 (1998): 148–165.

125. Gary LaFree and Richard Arum, "The Impact of Racially Inclusive Schooling on Adult Incarceration Rates Among U.S. Cohorts of African Americans and Whites Since 1930," *Criminology* 44 (2006): 73–103.

126. R. Kelly Raley, "A Shortage of Marriageable Men? A Note on the Role of Cohabitation in Black–White Differences in Marriage Rates," *American Sociological Review* 61 (1996): 973–983.

127. Julie Phillips, "Variation in African-American Homicide Rates: An Assessment of Potential Explanations," *Criminology* 35 (1997): 527–559.

128. Roy Austin, "Progress Toward Racial Equality and Reduction of Black Criminal Violence," *Journal of Criminal Justice* 15 (1987): 437–459.

129. Reynolds Farley and William Frey, "Changes in the Segregation of Whites from Blacks During the 1980s: Small Steps Toward a More Integrated Society," *American Sociological Review* 59 (1994): 23–45.

130. Gary LaFree, Eric Baumer, and Robert O'Brien, "Still Separate and Unequal? A City-Level Analysis of the Black–White Gap in Homicide Arrests Since 1960," *American Sociological Review* 75 (2010): 75–100.

131. Arizona SB 1070, §1 (2010).

132. Ramiro Martínez, Jr., "Crime and Immigration," *The Criminologist* 35 (2010): 16–17.

133. *Arizona v. United States*, 567 U.S. ___ (2012).

134. Kristin F. Butcher and Anne Morrison Piehl, "Crime, Corrections, and California: What Does Immigration Have to Do with It?" Public Policy Institute of California, 2008, http://www.ppic.org/main/publication .asp?i=776 (accessed April 2014).

135. Martínez, Jr. "Crime and Immigration."

136. Marvin Wolfgang, Robert Figlio, and Thorsten Sellin, *Delinquency in a Birth Cohort* (Chicago: University of Chicago Press, 1972).

137. See Thorsten Sellin and Marvin Wolfgang, *The Measurement of Delinquency* (New York: Wiley, 1964), p. 120.

138. Marvin Wolfgang, "Delinquency in Two Birth Cohorts," in *Perspective Studies of Crime and Delinquency*, ed. Katherine

Teilmann van Dusen and Sarnoff Mednick (Boston: Kluwer-Nijhoff, 1983), pp. 7–17.

139. Lyle Shannon, *Criminal Career Opportunity* (New York: Human Sciences Press, 1988).

140. D. J. West and David P. Farrington, *The Delinquent Way of Life* (London: Hienemann, 1977).

141. Michael Schumacher and Gwen Kurz, *The 8% Solution: Preventing Serious Repeat Juvenile Crime* (Thousand Oaks, CA: Sage, 1999).

142. Peter Jones, Philip Harris, James Fader, and Lori Grubstein, "Identifying Chronic Juvenile Offenders," *Justice Quarterly* 18 (2001): 478–507.

143. Lila Kazemian and Marc LeBlanc, "Differential Cost Avoidance and Successful Criminal Careers," *Crime and Delinquency* 53 (2007): 38–63.

144. Rudy Haapanen, Lee Britton, and Tim Croisdale, "Persistent Criminality and Career Length," *Crime and Delinquency* 53 (2007): 133–155.

145. See, generally, Wolfgang, Thornberry, and Figlio, eds., *From Boy to Man, from Delinquency to Crime*.

146. Paul Tracy and Kimberly Kempf-Leonard, *Continuity and Discontinuity in Criminal Careers* (New York: Plenum Press, 1996).

147. Kimberly Kempf-Leonard, Paul Tracy, and James Howell, "Serious, Violent, and Chronic Juvenile Offenders: The Relationship of Delinquency Career Types to Adult Criminality," *Justice Quarterly* 18 (2001): 449–478.

148. R. Tremblay, R. Loeber, C. Gagnon, P. Charlebois, S. Larivee, and M. LeBlanc, "Disruptive Boys with Stable and Unstable High Fighting Behavior Patterns During Junior Elementary School," *Journal of Abnormal Child Psychology* 19 (1991): 285–300.

149. Jennifer White, Terrie Moffitt, Felton Earls, Lee Robins, and Phil Silva, "How Early Can We Tell? Predictors of Childhood Conduct Disorder and Adolescent Delinquency," *Criminology* 28 (1990): 507–535.

VICTIMS AND VICTIMIZATION

In a case that made national headlines, two members of the champion Steubenville High School football team, Trent Mays (17, left) and Ma'lik Richmond (16, right) were found to be juvenile delinquents for an incident involving the sexual assault of a 16-year-old girl who was "substantially impaired" after a night of partying and drinking. The victim later told police she remembered holding Mays's hand as she left a party with him, Richmond, and others. The next thing she remembered was waking up in the morning naked on a couch in an unfamiliar house. At trial, the defense claimed the sex was consensual and employed expert witnesses who testified that even when drunk, people can engage in consensual sex.[1] In the end, the prosecution proved their case by showing videos, posted on the Internet, of the unconscious young woman being mocked by kids at the party, and also produced emails from people who knew what was going on but did nothing to stop the attack. The prosecution was also aided by captured screenshots off the Web, including one showing Mays and Richmond carrying the naked victim. Other evidence—including scores of text messages, pictures, and videos—indicated the girl was barely conscious during much of the time the attacks occurred. Texts also showed that Mays had attempted to cover up his actions after police became aware of the attack.

On March 17, 2013, Judge Thomas Lipps found Mays and Richmond delinquent and ordered their detention in a juvenile facility. But the convictions did not end the case. Shortly after the verdict, was in, prosecutors said they would convene a grand jury to determine if further charges should be filed against witnesses who failed to report the rape and against adults who might have been aware of the rape and covered it up. On October 8, 2013, the grand jury indicted William Rhinaman, the IT director for Steubenville City Schools, on obstruction of justice and evidence tampering charges. And on November 25, 2013, elementary school principal Lynnett Gorman, 40, and a strength coach, Seth Fluharty, 26, were charged with failing to report possible child abuse. In the course of the investigation evidence was uncovered that Steubenville City Schools superintendent Michael McVey had interfered in another rape case involving a minor, and he was subsequently charged with obstructing justice, tampering with evidence, obstructing official business, and falsification.[2]

The Steubenville rape case is one of a slew of recent incidents during which an inebriated minor female is sexually assaulted, and photos are taken and then put on the Internet. In more than one of these cases, the young victim later took her own life. In 2013, Rehtaeh Parsons, a 17-year-old Canadian girl committed suicide 18 months after she was sexually assaulted by four boys and photos taken of the assault were posted on the Internet. Audrie Pott, a student at Saratoga High School in Silicon Valley, hanged herself on September 10, 2012, after passing out drunk at a party where boys she had known for years took off her clothes, sexually assaulted her, and took photos of the attack with their phones.[3]

Why do people become victims, the targets of predatory criminals? Is it simply bad luck, being in the wrong place at the wrong time, or do victims somehow contribute to their own mistreatment? Did the young victim in Steubenville precipitate her attack by staying out late at night, drinking, and being alone with teenage boys? Or is this a matter of unfairly "blaming the victim"? After all, many of the young women were attacked by people they considered friends and schoolmates, people they trusted. Is it fair to blame someone who is preyed upon by a trusted friend? And once an attack does occur, what can be done to help people such as Audrie Pott and Rehtaeh Parsons recover and avoid the devastating effects of an attack?

Criminologists who focus their attention on crime victims refer to themselves as **victimologists**. This chapter examines victims and their relationship to the criminal process. We begin with discussion of the problems of victims and the costs of victimization. The nature and extent of **victimization** and the relationship between victims and criminal offenders are then reviewed. Finally, the various theories of victimization and how society has responded to the needs of victims are covered in some detail.

PROBLEMS OF CRIME VICTIMS

LO1 Discuss the greatest problems faced by crime victims

The National Crime Victimization Survey (NCVS) indicates that more than 25 million theft and violence victimizations occur each year.[4] And while this number has declined considerably during the past 20 years, it still means that close to *20 percent of all the households in America experience theft or violent crime sometime during the year.* These data are especially disturbing considering that becoming a victim of crimes such as rape, robbery, or assault can not

only be immediately devastating but also have considerable long-term consequences and costs, ranging from damaged property to mental anguish.[5] What are the main effects of victimization?

Economic Costs

Victimization brings with it a bevy of economic costs (see Exhibit 3.1). When the costs of goods taken during property crimes is added to productivity losses caused by injury, pain, and emotional trauma, the cost of victimization is estimated to be in the hundreds of billions of dollars.

A number of different methods have been developed to measure the cost of victimization to American society and how that cost influences the average American. Kathryn McCollister and her associates employed complex statistical analysis to determine how much an individual crime might cost society; their calculations included intangible, tangible, criminal justice system, and other costs. The crimes they could put a figure on included:

- Murder: $8,982,907 (range = $4,144,677 to $11,350,687)
- Rape/sexual assault: $240,776 (range = $80,403 to $369,739)
- Robbery: $42,310 (range = $18,591 to $280,237)
- Household burglary: $6,462 (range = $1,974 to $30,197)
- Stolen property: $7,974 (range = $151 to $22,739)

EXHIBIT 3.1

Costs Associated with Victimization

Victim Costs

Personal economic losses, including medical care costs, lost earnings, and property loss/damage.

Criminal Justice System Costs

Local, state, and federal government funds spent on police protection and investigations, legal and adjudication services, such as prosecution, public defenders, and trial costs, and the cost of both community and secure corrections programs, including counseling and other programs.

Crime Career Costs

Opportunity costs associated with the criminal's choice to engage in illegal rather than legal and productive activities, including funds spent on supporting their families.

Intangible Costs

Indirect losses suffered by crime victims, including pain and suffering, decreased quality of life, and psychological distress.

SOURCE: Kathryn McCollister, Michael T. French, and Hai Fang, "The Cost of Crime to Society: New Crime-Specific Estimates for Policy and Program Evaluation," *Drug and Alcohol Dependence* 108 (2010): 98–109.

---

victimologists People who study the victim's role in criminal transactions.

victimization by the justice system While the crime is still fresh in their minds, victims may find that the police interrogation following the crime is handled callously, with innuendos or insinuations that they were somehow at fault. Victims have difficulty learning what is going on in the case; property is often kept for a long time as evidence and may never be returned. Some rape victims report that the treatment they receive from legal, medical, and mental health services is so destructive that they cannot help but feel "re-raped."

According to McCollister, the cost to society of an average murder is almost $9 million. Considering that about 15,000 Americans are the victims of murder each year, murder alone has costs of about $135,000,000,000.[6]

Total Impact Another way of gauging the cost of victimization is to measure the total impact all crimes have on the economic well-being of society. Economist David Anderson estimates that the annual cost of crime increased from $2.4 trillion in the mid-1990s to more than $3 trillion today, despite the fact that crime has undergone a significant drop. The total cost of crime during the past decade is what the government spent on both the wars in Afghanistan and Iraq, plus American military aid to Pakistan!

Driving the price of crime up are such costs as lost productivity, the value of items taken from victims, private security, fences, alarm systems, computer security software, safe deposit boxes, insurance, safety lighting, lethal and nonlethal weapons, martial arts courses, and other goods and services. The per capita cost for every American citizen is approximately $5,300 per year.

Some crimes are particularly costly. While murder may be the most costly crime, rape adds $20 billion to the total. Heroin abuse costs the nation another $20 billion per year, including the medical complications of heroin addiction, primarily treatment for HIV/AIDS and psychiatric care, as well as paying for incarceration, policing, legal adjudication, and the cost to crime victims. There is also the cost of lost productivity—heroin addicts are less than half as likely to have a full-time job as compared with the national average—and the treatment of heroin addiction in clinics and hospitals.[7]

Individual Costs

In addition to these societal costs, victims may suffer long-term losses in earnings and occupational attainment. Some victims are physically disabled as a result of serious wounds sustained during episodes of random violence, including a growing number who suffer paralyzing spinal cord injuries. If victims have no insurance, the long-term effects of the crime may have devastating financial as well as emotional and physical consequences.[8]

Suffering Stress Victims may suffer stress and anxiety long after the incident is over and the justice process has been completed.

Posttraumatic stress disorder (PTSD)—a condition whose symptoms include depression, anxiety, and self-destructive behavior—is a common problem, especially when the victim does not receive adequate support from family and friends.[9] To shield themselves, some victims deny the attack occurred or question whether they were "really raped." But denial only goes so far and does not shield victims from the long-term effects of sexual assault.[10]

Men may be particularly susceptible to post-rape PTSD, believing that their situation is both unique and somehow "unmanly." Knowing the effect of a sexual assault on men, rape has become an interrogation tool in some theaters of war; sexual assault was routinely used during the civil war in Yugoslavia to terrorize male prisoners.[11]

Adolescent Stress Younger victims are also more prone to suffer stress and PTSD.[12] Kids who have either witnessed child abuse at home or personally experienced abuse are the most likely to experience negative personal outcomes.[13] People who have traumatic sexual experiences in childhood later suffer psychological deficits.[14] A history of childhood trauma, including rape and molestation, is significantly associated with visual, auditory, and tactile hallucinations.[15]

Many young victims run away to escape their environment, which puts them at risk for juvenile arrest and involvement with the justice system.[16] Others suffer posttraumatic mental problems, including acute stress disorders, depression, eating disorders, nightmares, anxiety, suicidal ideation, and other psychological problems.[17]

Victimization in childhood has long-term consequences: it may lead to despair, depression, and even homelessness in adulthood. Children who are psychologically, sexually, or physically abused are more likely to suffer low self-esteem and be more suicidal as adults.[18] They are also placed at greater risk to be reabused as adults than those who escaped childhood victimization.[19] The reabused carry higher risks for psychological and physical problems, ranging from sexual promiscuity to increased HIV infection rates.[20]

Leana Bouffard and Maria Koeppel studied the long-term effects of childhood victimization and found that individuals who are victimized before the age of 12, especially those who experienced repeated bullying, are more susceptible to a number of physical and mental health issues, such as negative perceptions of physical and mental health, smoking, subsequent victimization experiences, and homelessness.[21] Another study of homeless women found that they were much more likely than other women to report childhood physical abuse, childhood sexual abuse, adult physical assault, previous sexual assault in adulthood, and a history of mental health problems.[22]

Relationship Stress The stress encountered in childhood endures into adulthood, especially for those who are the victim of intimate partner violence (IPV). Numerous research efforts show that people who suffer IPV experience an extremely high prevalence of psychological problems, including but not limited to depression, generalized anxiety disorder (GAD), panic disorder, substance use disorders, borderline personality disorder, antisocial personality

> **posttraumatic stress disorder (PTSD)** Psychological reaction to a highly stressful event; symptoms may include depression, anxiety, flashbacks, and recurring nightmares.

disorder, posttraumatic stress disorder, anxiety disorder, and **obsessive-compulsive disorder** (an extreme preoccupation with certain thoughts and compulsive performance of certain behaviors).[23] One reason may be that abusive partners are as likely to mistreat their victims psychologically with threats and intimidation as they are to use physical force; psychological abuse can lead to depression and other long-term disabilities.[24]

Fear   Many people fear crime, especially the elderly, the poor, and minority group members.[25] Their fear is escalated by lurid news accounts of crime and violence.[26] While hearing about crime causes fear, those who experience it are even more likely to be fearful and change their behaviors.[27] Victims of violent crime are the most deeply affected, fearing a repeat of their attack. Many go through a fundamental life change, viewing the world more suspiciously and as a less safe, controllable, and meaningful place. Some develop a generalized fear of crime and worry about being revictimized.

Those who experience one type of crime may fear another: if they have been assaulted, they may develop fears that their house will be burglarized.[28] These people are more likely to suffer psychological stress for extended periods of time.[29] In a moving book, *Aftermath: Violence and the Remaking of a Self*, rape victim Susan Brison recounts the difficult time she had recovering from her ordeal. The trauma disrupted her memory, cutting off events that happened before the rape from those that occurred afterward, and eliminated her ability to conceive of a happy or productive future. Although sympathizers encouraged her to forget the past, she found that confronting it could be therapeutic.[30]

In some instances fear can be a good thing. Research shows that people who experience victimization and fear its consequences are less likely to engage in criminal activity. In contrast, those experiencing violence and surviving its consequences may embolden some victims and contribute to their perception that offending is not dangerous; this group is the one most likely to engage in violence themselves.[31]

Vicarious Fear   Even if people are not personally victimized, those who observe or are exposed to violence on a routine basis become fearful.[32] Hearing about another's victimization may make people timid and cautious.[33] If they don't fear for themselves,

they become concerned for others—their wives or husbands, children, elderly parents, and siblings.[34] Not only are people likely to move out of their neighborhood if they become crime victims, but they are also likely to relocate if they hear that a friend or neighbor has suffered a break-in or burglary.[35]

Vicarious fear is escalated by lurid news accounts of crime and violence.[36] For example, news stories about serial killers on a rampage can cause a chill felt throughout the city. People who read or hear about serial killers experience an increase in their fear of crime that prompts them to protect themselves and their family by implementing some sort of protective measure, such as carrying mace or pepper spray or adding a security device to their home.[37]

Victims experience fear and anxiety long after the criminal incident occurred. Sometimes the support of others can help the healing experience begin. Kristina Ponischil is shown here in 2012 on the campus of the University of Washington in Seattle, where she works as a researcher. For months after Ponischil was raped at a party in her off-campus apartment, her life at Western Washington University was hell. Police wouldn't act. Despite a restraining order, she kept running into her assailant on campus, prompting panic attacks. But if the criminal justice system let Ponischil down, Western Washington did not, offering her the support she needed and suspending her assailant, removing him from campus until she graduated in 2009. "I was able to start healing," she said. "When I was constantly afraid, there was no healing. It was just constant fear."

AP Images/Elaine Thompson

obsessive-compulsive disorder An extreme preoccupation with certain thoughts and compulsive performance of certain behaviors.

The Cycle of Violence

LO2 Clarify the term *cycle of violence*

Victimization also increases the chance of getting involved in antisocial behavior; violence begets violence.[38] According to the **cycle of violence** phenomenon, people who are the victims of violence and abuse in adolescence are more likely to later engage in violent behavior as adults; victims of sexual abuse may often grow up to be sexual offenders themselves.[39] They are also more likely to smoke, drink, and take drugs than nonabused youth.[40] As adults, people who are the victims of violence are also quite likely to later become perpetrators.[41]

LO3 Analyze the victim's role in the crime process

The Link Between Victimization and Crime Given the evidence pointing to a link between victimization and crime, how can the association be explained?

- *Victimization causes social problems.* People who are crime victims experience long-term social problems, including issues with unemployment and developing personal relationships, factors related to criminality. Some young victims may run away from home, taking to the streets and increasing their risk of becoming a crime victim again.[42]
- *Victimization causes stress and anger.* Victimization may produce anger, stress, and strain. Known offenders report significant amounts of posttraumatic stress disorder as a result of prior victimization, which may in part explain their violent and criminal behaviors.[43] Victims, especially those who lack self-control, may try to cope with this stress by self-medicating, drinking, or taking drugs, a form of behavior highly correlated with future criminality.[44]
- *Victimization prompts revenge.* Victims may seek revenge against the people who harmed them or whom they believe are at fault for their problems. In some cases, these feelings become generalized to others who share the same characteristics of their attackers

(e.g., men, Hispanics).[45] As a result, their reactions become displaced, and they may lash out at people who are not their attackers. They may take drastic measures, fearing revictimization, and arm themselves for self-protection.[46] In some cultures, retaliation is an expected and accepted response to victimization.[47]

- *Spurious association.* It is also possible that the association between victimization and crime is spurious and that victims and criminals are actually two separate groups. The personal traits that produce violent criminals, such as impulsive personality, may not be the same ones that produce victims.[48] There may appear to be a connection because both criminals and victims tend to have the same lifestyle and live in the same neighborhoods, making it seem they are one and the same.

THE NATURE OF VICTIMIZATION

How many crime victims are there in the United States, and what are the trends and patterns in victimization? As noted earlier, 25 million criminal victimizations now occur each year.[49] While this total is significant, it represents almost a 20-year decline in criminal victimization from a peak of more than 40 million reported victimizations in 1995.

While the number and rate of victimization have declined, patterns in the victimization survey findings are stable and repetitive, suggesting that victimization is not random but is a function of personal and ecological factors. The stability of these patterns allows us to make judgments about the nature of victimization; policies can then be created in an effort to reduce the victimization rate. Who are victims? Where does victimization take place? What is the relationship between victims and criminals? The following sections discuss some of the most important victimization patterns and trends.

The Social Ecology of Victimization

LO4 Assess the ecology of victimization risk

The NCVS shows that violent crimes are more likely to take place in an open, public area (such as a street, a park, or a field), in a school building, or at a commercial establishment such as a tavern during the daytime or early evening hours than in a private home during the morning or late

The mission of the National Center for Victims of Crime is to help victims of crime rebuild their lives: "We are dedicated to serving individuals, families, and communities harmed by crime." The NCVC released *Taking Action: An Advocate's Guide to Assisting Victims of Financial Fraud* to provide those who serve the more than 30 million Americans who are victims of financial fraud every year with an important tool to aid their clients. Learn more by visiting **http://www .victimsofcrime.org/**.

Should people who make foolish investments be compensated or should "the buyer beware"?

cycle of violence The idea that victims of crime, especially childhood abuse, are more likely to commit crimes themselves.

evening hours. The more serious violent crimes, such as rape and aggravated assault, typically take place after 6 P.M. Approximately two-thirds of rapes and sexual assaults occur at night—6 P.M. to 6 A.M. Less serious forms of violence, such as unarmed robberies and personal larcenies like purse snatching, are more likely to occur during the daytime. Neighborhood characteristics affect the chances of victimization. Those living in the central city have significantly higher rates of theft and violence than suburbanites; people living in rural areas have a victimization rate almost half that of city dwellers. The risk of murder for both men and women is significantly higher in disorganized inner-city areas where gangs flourish and drug trafficking is commonplace.

School Victimization Schools, unfortunately, are the locale of a great deal of victimization because they are populated by one of the most dangerous segments of society, teenage males. During before- and after-school activities, adult supervision is minimal, and hallways and locker rooms are typically left unattended. Kids who participate in school sports may leave their valuables in locker rooms that make attractive targets; others may congregate in unguarded places, making them attractive targets for predators who come on school grounds.[50] The latest data from the National Center for Educational Statistics find that there were more than 1.2 million victimizations at school during the current year, including 648,600 thefts and 597,500 violent victimizations. The number of school crimes increased significantly from the prior year: the total crime victimization rate of students ages 12 to 18 at school increased from 35 victimizations per 1,000 students in 2010 to 49 victimizations per 1,000 students in 2011. Despite this recent uptick, the rate of school crime, on and off campus, is far lower today than 20 years ago.[51]

- At last count, students ages 12 to 18 were victims of about 1,246,000 nonfatal victimizations at school, including 648,600 thefts and 597,500 violent victimizations.
- About 85 percent of public schools record one or more crime incidents take place at school each year. This translates to a rate of 40 crimes per 1,000 public school students enrolled.
- About 60 percent of public schools reported a crime incident that occurred at school to the police, amounting to 689,000 crimes—or 15 crimes per 1,000 public school students enrolled.
- Each year, almost 40 percent of public schools (about 32,300 schools)

take at least one serious disciplinary action against a student for specific offenses. Of these 74 percent were suspensions for five days or more, 20 percent were transfers to specialized schools, and 6 percent were removals with no services for the remainder of the school year.

- While for most people and most crimes summer is the most dangerous season, adolescent victimization actually peaks in the fall when the school year begins. Overall risk for violence is significantly lower during the summer. An adolescent's risk of violent victimization decreases after the school year ends.[52]
- About 30 student, staff, and nonstudent school-associated violent deaths occur each year, including 25 homicides and 6 suicides.

The Victim's Household

LO5 Describe the victim's household

The NCVS tells us that within the United States, larger homes, African American homes, urban homes, and those in the West are the most vulnerable to crime. In contrast, rural homes, white homes, and those in the Northeast are the least likely to contain crime victims or be the target of theft offenses, such as burglary or larceny. People who own their homes are less vulnerable than renters.

Recent population movement and changes may account for decreases in crime victimization. U.S. residents have

Unfortunately, schools are the location of a great deal of crime, including tragic incidents of school shootings, the most deadly being the killings at Sandy Hook Elementary School in Newtown, Connecticut, on December 14, 2012. Here, a young girl is given a blanket after being evacuated from the site of that school shooting. Twenty-six teachers, workers, and children were killed when a young man named Adam Lanza opened fire at the school. Lanza committed suicide as police closed in.

Michelle Mcloughlin/Reuters/Landov

become extremely mobile, moving from urban areas to suburban and rural areas. In addition, family size has been reduced; more people than ever before are living in single-person homes (about one-quarter of the population). It is possible that the decline in household victimization rates during the past decades can be explained by the fact that smaller households in less populated areas have a lower victimization risk.

Victim Characteristics

LO6 Categorize the most dominant victim characteristics

Social and demographic characteristics also distinguish victims and nonvictims. The most important of these factors are gender, age, social status, and race.

Gender   Gender affects victimization risk. Except for the crimes of rape and sexual assault, males are more likely than females to be the victims of violent crime. Men are almost twice as likely as women to experience robbery. Women, however, are six times more likely than men to be victims of rape, domestic violence, and sexual assault. Although males are more likely to be victimized than females, the gender differences in the victimization rate have narrowed significantly over time.

When men are the aggressors, injuries are more severe. Female aggressors tend to engage in verbal rather than physical abuse. Violence is more severe when perpetrated by males versus females as indicated by higher injury rates and greater victim fear.[53]

One significant gender difference is that women are much more likely to be victimized by someone they know or with whom they live. Of those offenders victimizing females, about two-thirds are someone the victim knew or was related to. In contrast, fewer than half of male victims were attacked by a friend, relative, or acquaintance.

While women are more likely to be the target of domestic assaults, intimate partner violence seems to be declining. One reason may be an increasing amount of economic and political opportunities for women: research shows that economic inequality is significantly related to female victimization rates. As more laws or acts favorable to women are passed and more economic opportunities become available, the lower their rates of violent victimization.[54]

Age   Victim data reveal that young people face a much greater victimization risk than do older persons. Even the youngest kids are not immune and are as likely to experience serious child abuse as their older siblings.[55]

Victim risk diminishes rapidly after age 25: teens 16 to 19 suffer 45 violent crimes per 1,000, whereas people over 65 experience only 2 per 1,000. Teens and young adults experience the highest rates of violent crime. Violent crime rates declined in recent years for most age groups.

The New York State Office of Victim Services (OVS) helps people in a number of ways to cope with victimization from a crime. Go to their website at **http://www.ovs.ny.gov/** and read "A Guide to Crime Victim Compensation in New York State," "Frequently Asked Questions," and "Our Claim Application and Instructions."

Elderly Victims   Although the elderly are less likely to become crime victims than the young, they are most often the victims of a narrow band of criminal activities from which the young are more immune. Frauds and scams, purse snatching, pocket picking, stealing checks from the mail, and committing crimes in long-term care settings claim more older than younger victims. The elderly are especially susceptible to fraud schemes because they have insurance, pension plans, proceeds from the sale of homes, and money from Social Security and savings that make them attractive financial targets. Because many elderly live by themselves and are lonely, they remain more susceptible to telephone and mail fraud. Unfortunately, once victimized, the elderly have more limited opportunities either to recover their lost money or to earn enough to replace what they have lost.[56]

Elder abuse is a particularly important issue because of shifts in the U.S. population. Currently there are about 40 million people in the United States over age 65 and the Bureau of the Census predicts that by 2030 the population over age 65 will reach 70 million people, and older people will make up more than 20 percent of the population (up from 12 percent in 1990). The saliency of elder abuse is underscored by reports from the National Center on Elder Abuse that between 7.6 and 10 percent of elderly people experience abuse each year and, despite the fact that an overwhelming number of cases of abuse, neglect, and exploitation go undetected and untreated each year, there is still an increasing trend in the reporting of elder abuse. Another growing problem: financial exploitation which may be higher than rates of emotional, physical, and sexual abuse or neglect.[57]

What causes people to abuse the elderly? Some of the most significant views of elderly abuse are set out in Exhibit 3.2

Social Status   The poorest Americans are also the most likely victims of violent and property crime. For example, homeless people, who are among the poorest individuals in America, suffer very high rates of assault.[58] This association occurs across all gender, age, and racial groups. Although the poor are more likely to suffer violent crimes, the wealthy

elder abuse A disturbing form of domestic violence by children and other relatives with whom elderly people live.

EXHIBIT 3.2

What Causes Elder Abuse?

- The *caregiver stress view* asserts that parents experiencing stress are more likely to maltreat their children. In the context of elder maltreatment, maltreatment occurs when family members caring for an impaired older adult are unable to adequately manage their caregiving responsibilities. The elderly victim is typically described as highly dependent on the caregiver, who becomes overwhelmed, frustrated, and abusive because of the continuous caretaking demands posed by the elderly person.

- The *social learning view* holds that elder abuse results from the abusive individual learning to use violence to either resolve conflicts or obtain a desired outcome.

- The *social exchange view* is rooted in psychology and economics. It conceptualizes social behavior as involving negotiated exchanges of material and nonmaterial goods and services. When the sociodynamic balance in a relationship is upset or perceived to have been upset, the disadvantaged party will use violence to restore balance. People who abuse elders perceive themselves as not receiving their fair share from their relationship with the elderly person or other family members, and their resort to violence is an effort to restore or obtain deserved equilibrium.

- The *background-situational view* asserts that relationship discord results from a combination of contextual factors (e.g., a history of family violence) and situational factors (e.g., a lack of relationship satisfaction), which primes a person's acceptance of violence as a conflict resolution strategy. Elder abuse occurs when the abusive individual is the spouse or intimate partner of the victim, but it might also apply when the abusive individual is a codependent adult child or caregiver of the elderly person.

- The *power and control view* highlights an abusive individual's use of a pattern of coercive tactics to gain and maintain power and control during the course of a relationship with another person. It has been used to explain spousal abuse among elderly couples, although it could be applied as well when such traits describe an adult child or caregiver who has assumed, perhaps grudgingly, responsibility for the elderly person.

- The *ecological model* explains human behavior by including a range of potential influences on this process, including the impact of individual, relationship, community, and societal influences.

- In the *biopsychosocial model*, elder maltreatment can be attributed to the characteristics of both the elderly person and the abusive individual, both of whom are embedded in a larger sociocultural context (family and friends); their status inequality, relationship type, and power and exchange dynamics all help explain the outcome of their interactions.

SOURCE: Shelley Jackson and Thomas Hafemeister, *Understanding Elderly Abuse*, National Institute of Justice, 2013, https://www.ncjrs.gov/pdffiles1/nij/241731.pdf (accessed April 2014).

are more likely targets of personal theft crimes such as pocket picking and purse snatching. Perhaps the affluent—sporting more expensive attire and driving better cars—attract the attention of thieves.

CONNECTIONS

The association between age and victimization is undoubtedly tied to lifestyle: adolescents often stay out late at night, go to public places, and hang out with other kids who have a high risk of criminal involvement. Later in this chapter we will discuss lifestyle theories of victimization. People may control their own destiny: living on a farm in Kansas is a lot safer than being a party person in Tampa or clubbing in New York.

Marital Status Marital status influences victimization risk and vice versa. Never-married males and females are victimized more often than married people. Widows and widowers have the lowest victimization risk. This association between marital status and victimization is probably influenced by age, gender, and lifestyle:

- Adolescents and teens, who have the highest victimization risk, are too young to have been married.
- Young single people go out in public more often and sometimes interact with high-risk peers, increasing their exposure to victimization.
- Widows and widowers suffer much lower victimization rates because they are older, interact with older people, and are more likely to stay home at night and to avoid public places.

Not only is victimization influenced by marital status, it is also possible that victimization status influences the likelihood of marriage. Danielle Kuhl and her associates found that kids who were the victims of violent street crime were also the ones most likely to marry at an early age.[59] Why victimization spurs marriage is hard to determine. It is possible that those scarred by street violence seek stable relationships to provide a sense of security and tranquility in their lives. However, youthful marriage may also bring with it unwanted turmoil. Early marriage is positively associated with divorce, and divorced persons have lower levels of psychological and economic well-being.[60] So while victimization may cause people to seek the stability of marriage in the short run, it may not bring "happily ever after" for all.

Race and Ethnicity African Americans and ethnic minorities are more likely than whites to be victims of violent crime. Why do these discrepancies exist? Because of income inequality, racial and minority group members are often forced to live in deteriorated urban areas beset by alcohol and drug abuse, poverty, racial discrimination, and violence. Consequently, their lifestyle places them in the most at-risk population group. The rate of black victimization has been in steep decline, and the racial gap in victimization rates seems to be narrowing.

Repeat Victimization Individuals who have been crime victims have a significantly higher chance of future victimization than people who have not been victims.[61] For example, when Marie Skubak Tillyer and her associates studied repeat sexual assault victimization among a high school sample they found that repeat victimization was normative, and that impulsive kids, who hang out with antisocial peers, and who are involved in unsupervised social activities, are the ones most at risk for repeat victimization.[62]

Not only are individuals at risk for repeat victimization, so too are households. Those that have experienced victimization in the past are the ones most likely to experience it again in the future.[63]

What factors predict **chronic victimization**? Most repeat victimizations occur soon after a previous crime has occurred, suggesting that repeat victims share some personal characteristic that makes them a magnet for predators.[64] Predators have specific targets: children who are shy, physically weak, or socially isolated may be prone to being bullied in the schoolyard.[65] David Finkelhor and Nancy Asigian have found that three specific types of characteristics increase the potential for victimization:

- *Target vulnerability.* The victims' physical weakness or psychological distress renders them incapable of resisting or deterring crime and makes them easy targets.
- *Target gratifiability.* Some victims have some quality, possession, skill, or attribute that an offender wants to obtain, use, have access to, or manipulate. Having attractive possessions such as a leather coat may make one vulnerable to predatory crime.
- *Target antagonism.* Some characteristics increase risk because they arouse anger, jealousy, or destructive impulses in potential offenders. Being gay or effeminate, for example, may bring on undeserved attacks in the street; being argumentative and alcoholic may provoke barroom assaults.[66]

Repeat victimization may occur when the victim does not take defensive action. If an abusive husband finds out that his battered wife will not call the police, he repeatedly victimizes her; if a hate crime is committed and the police do not respond to reported offenses, the perpetrators learn they have little to fear from the law.[67] Women who fight back and/or use self-protective action during the first incident of sexual battering reduce their likelihood of being a recurrent victim.[68]

Of course, not all victims are repeaters. Some take defensive measures to lessen their chance of future victimizations. Some may change their lifestyle, take fewer risks, and cut back on associating with dangerous people; once burnt, twice shy.[69]

Victims and Their Criminals

The victim data also tell us something about the relationship between victims and criminals. Males are more likely to be violently victimized by a stranger, and females are more likely to be victimized by a friend, an acquaintance, or an intimate.

Victims report that most crimes are committed by a single offender over age 20. Crime tends to be intraracial: black offenders victimize blacks, and whites victimize whites. However, because the country's population is predominantly white, it stands to reason that criminals of all races will be more likely to target white victims. Victims report that substance abuse is involved in about one-third of violent crime incidents.[70]

Although many violent crimes are committed by strangers, a surprising number of violent crimes are committed by relatives or acquaintances of the victims. In fact, more than half of all nonfatal personal crimes are committed by people who are described as being known to the victim. Women are especially vulnerable to people they know.

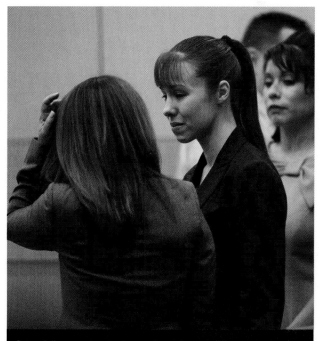

One of the most notorious crimes in recent memory involved Jodi Arias, shown standing in court, who murdered her boyfriend, Travis Alexander. It is more common in murder cases for criminals and victims to know one another rather than to be complete strangers.

Reuters/Pool/Landov

chronic victimization Those who have been crime victims maintain a significantly higher chance of future victimization than people who have remained nonvictims. Most repeat victimizations occur soon after a previous crime has occurred, suggesting that repeat victims share some personal characteristic that makes them a magnet for predators.

More than 60 percent of rape or sexual assault victims state the offender was an intimate, a relative, a friend, or an acquaintance. Women are more likely than men to be robbed by a friend or acquaintance; most males report that the people who robbed them were strangers.

THEORIES OF VICTIMIZATION

LO8 Compare and contrast the most important theories of victimization

For many years, criminological theory focused on the actions of the criminal offender; the role of the victim was virtually ignored. But more than 50 years ago, scholars began to realize that the victim is not a passive target in crime, but someone whose behavior can influence his or her own fate, someone who "shapes and molds the criminal."[71] These early works helped focus attention on the role of the victim in the crime problem and led to further research efforts that have sharpened the image of the crime victim. Today a number of different theories attempt to explain the causes of victimization; the most important are discussed below.

Victim Precipitation Theory

According to **victim precipitation theory**, some people may actually initiate the confrontation that eventually leads to their injury or death. Victim precipitation can be either active or passive.

Active precipitation occurs when victims act provocatively, use threats or fighting words, or even attack first.[72] In 1971, Menachem Amir suggested that female rape victims often contribute to their attacks by dressing provocatively or pursuing a relationship with the rapist.[73] Although Amir's findings are controversial, courts have continued to return not-guilty verdicts in rape cases if a victim's actions can in any way be construed as consenting to sexual intimacy.[74]

Passive precipitation occurs when the victim exhibits some personal characteristic that unknowingly either threatens or encourages the attacker. Although the victim may never have met the attacker or even know of his or her existence, the attacker feels menaced and acts accordingly.[75] In some instances, the crime can occur because of personal conflict—for example, when two people compete over a job, promotion, love interest, or some other scarce and coveted commodity. A woman may become the target of domestic violence when she increases her job status and her success results in a backlash from a jealous spouse or partner.[76]

Passive precipitation may also occur when the victim belongs to a group whose mere presence threatens the attacker's reputation, status, or economic well-being. For example, hate-crime violence may be precipitated by immigrant group members arriving in the community to compete for jobs and housing. Research indicates that passive precipitation is related to power: if the target group can establish themselves economically or gain political power in the community, their vulnerability will diminish. They are still a potential threat, but they become too formidable a target to attack; they are no longer passive precipitators.[77] By implication, economic power reduces victimization risk.

Victim Impulsivity Perhaps there is something about victims' personality traits that incite attacks. A number of research efforts have found that both male and female victims have an impulsive personality that might render them abrasive and obnoxious, characteristics that might incite victimization.[78] People who are impulsive and lack self-control are less likely to have a high tolerance for frustration and a physical rather than mental orientation; they are less likely to practice risk avoidance. It is possible that impulsive people are not only antagonistic and therefore more likely to become targets, but they also are risk takers who get involved in dangerous situations and fail to take precautions.[79]

Lifestyle Theory

Some criminologists believe people may become crime victims because their lifestyle increases their exposure to criminal offenders. Victimization risk is increased by such behaviors as associating with young men, going out in public places late at night, and living in an urban area. Conversely, one's chances of victimization can be reduced by staying home at night, moving to a rural area, staying out of public places, earning more money, and getting married. The basis of **lifestyle theory** is that victimization is not a random occurrence but rather a function of the victim's lifestyle. For example, due to their lifestyle and demographic makeup, college campuses contain large concentrations of young women who may be at greater risk for rape and other forms of sexual assault than women in the general population. Single women who drink frequently and have a prior

victim precipitation theory The idea that the victim's behavior was the spark that ignited the subsequent offense, as when the victim abused the offender verbally or physically.

active precipitation The view that the source of many criminal incidents is the aggressive or provocative behavior of victims.

passive precipitation The view that some people become victims because of personal and social characteristics that make them attractive targets for predatory criminals.

lifestyle theory People may become crime victims because their lifestyle increases their exposure to criminal offenders.

history of being sexually assaulted are most likely to be assaulted on campus.[80]

People who belong to groups that have an extremely risky life—homeless, runaways, drug users—are at high risk for victimization; the more time they are exposed to street life, the greater their risk of becoming crime victims.[81] When Kimberly Tyler and Morgan Beal interviewed more than 100 homeless youth in midwestern cities, they found that personal and behavioral characteristics helped put them in danger for physical and sexual abuse. Those who ran away at an earlier age, slept on the street, panhandled, and hung out with deviant peers rather than protective family members were the ones most likely to suffer physical victimization. Sexual victimization risk was elevated if the homeless youth was a female, had an unkempt and disheveled appearance, and had friends who were willing to trade sex for money.[82] Tyler and Beal's research shows that lifestyle promotes victimization.

Others are exposed to risk because of their status. Teenage males have an extremely high victimization risk because their lifestyle places them at risk both at school and once they leave the school grounds.[83] They spend a great deal of time hanging out with friends and pursuing recreational fun.[84] Their friends may give them a false ID so they can go drinking in the neighborhood bar, or they may hang out in taverns at night, which places them at risk because many fights and assaults occur in places that serve liquor.

College Lifestyle College students maintain a high-risk lifestyle—partying, taking recreational drugs—that makes them victimization prone.[85] Bonnie Fisher and her colleagues surveyed thousands of college students and found that college women face the risk of sexual assault at a higher rate than women in the general population.[86] Fisher and her colleagues found that 90 percent of the victims knew the person who sexually victimized them. Most often this was a boyfriend, ex-boyfriend, classmate, friend, acquaintance, or coworker; college professors were not identified as committing any rapes or sexual coercions. The vast majority of sexual victimizations occurred in the evening (after 6 P.M.), typically (60 percent) in the students' living quarters; many were connected to drinking. Other common crime scenes were other living quarters on campus and fraternity houses (about 10 percent). Off-campus sexual victimizations, especially rapes, also occurred in residences. Incidents where women were threatened or touched also took place in settings such as bars, dance clubs or nightclubs, and work settings. Research confirms that young women who involve themselves in substance abuse and come into contact with men who are also substance abusers increase the likelihood that they will be sexual assault victims.[87]

Criminal Lifestyle Not surprisingly, getting involved in criminality also increases the chance of victimization. The perils of a deviant lifestyle do not end in adolescence and haunt risk takers through their life. Kids with a history

of family violence and involvement in crime increase their chances of becoming the victims of homicide as adults.[88] Kids who take drugs and carry weapons in their adolescence maintain a greater chance of being shot and killed as adults.[89]

Take for instance gang boys, a group at high risk for victimization. The gang lifestyle—engaging in serious crime and delinquency, carrying guns, selling drugs, retaliating against perceived slights or disrespect—typifies behaviors that significantly increase the chances of becoming the victim of violent crimes. Protecting the gang's turf and engaging in retaliatory vendettas to maintain the gang's reputation also increase the risk of personal victimization.[90] Gang boys are much more likely to own guns and associate with violent peers than nonmembers.[91] Those who choose aggressive or violent friends are more likely to begin engaging in antisocial behavior themselves and suffer psychological deficits.[92] Experiencing victimization brings on retaliation, creating a never-ending cycle of violence begetting even more violence.[93]

The association between victimization and criminal lifestyle may be more one of risk than propensity: people who are involved in crime are constantly exposed to dangerous people who elevate their victimization risk. Considering the risk criminals take and the likelihood they will become victims themselves, what impact does victimization have on a criminal career? Does it encourage more crime and bloody retaliation or does it result in rethinking the dangers of a criminal way of life?

Deviant Place Theory

According to **deviant place theory**, the greater their exposure to dangerous places, the more likely people will become victims of crime and violence.[94] Victims do not encourage

deviant place theory People become victims because they reside in socially disorganized, high-crime areas where they have the greatest risk of coming into contact with criminal offenders.

crime, but are victim prone because they reside in socially disorganized high-crime areas where they have the greatest risk of coming into contact with criminal offenders, irrespective of their own behavior or lifestyle.[95] The more often victims visit dangerous places, the more likely they will be exposed to crime and violence.[96] Neighborhood crime levels, then, may be more important for determining the chances of victimization than individual characteristics. Consequently, there may be little reason for residents in lower-class areas to alter their lifestyle or take safety precautions because personal behavior choices do not influence the likelihood of victimization.[97]

Deviant places are poor, densely populated, highly transient neighborhoods in which commercial and residential property exist side by side.[98] The commercial property provides criminals with easy targets for theft crimes, such as shoplifting and larceny. Successful people stay out of these stigmatized areas; they are homes for "demoralized kinds of people" who are easy targets for crime: the homeless, the addicted, the retarded, and the elderly poor.[99] People who live in more affluent areas and take safety precautions significantly lower their chances of becoming crime victims; the effect of safety precautions is less pronounced in poor areas. Residents of poor areas have a much greater risk of becoming victims because they live near many motivated offenders. Sociologist William Julius Wilson has described how people who can afford to leave dangerous areas do so. He suggests that affluent people realize that criminal victimization can be avoided by moving to an area with greater law enforcement and lower crime rates. Because there are significant interracial income differences, white residents are able to flee inner-city high-crime areas, leaving members of racial minorities behind to suffer high victimization rates.[100]

Routine Activities Theory

Routine activities theory was first articulated in a series of papers by Lawrence Cohen and Marcus Felson.[101] They concluded that the volume and distribution of preda-

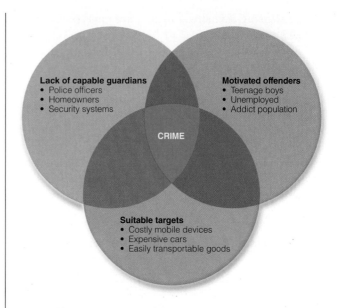

FIGURE 3.1 Routine Activities Theory: The Interaction of Three Factors

SOURCE: © Cengage Learning®

tory crime (violent crimes against a person and crimes in which an offender attempts to steal an object directly) are closely related to the interaction of three variables that reflect the routine activities of the typical American lifestyle (see Figure 3.1):

- The availability of **suitable targets**, such as homes containing easily salable goods
- The absence of **capable guardians**, such as police, homeowners, neighbors, friends, and relatives
- The presence of **motivated offenders**, such as a large number of unemployed teenagers

The presence of these components increases the likelihood that a predatory crime will take place. Targets are more likely to be victimized if they are poorly guarded and exposed to a large group of motivated offenders, such as teenage boys.[102] As targets increase in value and availability, so too should crime rates. Conversely, as the resale value of formerly pricey goods such as iPods and cell phones declines, so too should burglary rates.[103]

Increasing the number of motivated offenders and placing them in close proximity to valuable goods will increase victimization levels. Even after-school programs, designed to reduce criminal activity, may produce higher crime rates because they lump together motivated offenders—teen boys—with vulnerable victims (other teen boys).[104] Young women who drink to excess in bars and frat houses may elevate their risk of date rape because (a) they are perceived as easy targets, and (b) their attackers can rationalize the attack because they view intoxication as a sign of immorality ("She's loose, so I didn't think she'd care").[105] Conversely, people

routine activities theory The view that the volume and distribution of predatory crime are closely related to the interaction of suitable targets, motivated offenders, and capable guardians.

suitable targets According to routine activities theory, a target for crime that is relatively valuable, easily transportable, and not capably guarded.

capable guardians Effective deterrents to crime, such as police or watchful neighbors.

motivated offenders The potential offenders in a population. According to rational choice theory, crime rates will vary according to the number of motivated offenders.

can reduce their chances of victimization if they adopt a lifestyle that limits their exposure to danger: by getting married, having children, and moving to a small town.[106]

Guardianship   Even the most motivated offenders may ignore valuable targets if they are well guarded. Despite containing valuable commodities, private homes and/ or public businesses may be considered off-limits by seasoned criminals if they are well protected by capable guardians and efficient security systems.[107]

Criminals are also aware of police guardianship. In order to convince them that crime does not pay, more cops can be put on the street. Proactive, aggressive law enforcement officers who quickly get to the scene of the crime help deter criminal activities.[108]

Hot Spots   Motivated people—such as teenage males, drug users, and unemployed adults—are the ones most likely to commit crime. If they congregate in a particular neighborhood, it becomes a "hot spot" for crime and violence. People who live in these hot spots elevate their chances of victimization. For example, people who live in public housing projects may have high victimization rates because their fellow residents, mostly indigent, are extremely motivated to commit crime.[109] Yet motivated criminals must have the opportunity to find suitable undefended targets before they commit crime. Even the most desperate criminal might hesitate to attack a well-defended target, whereas a group of teens might rip off an unoccupied home on the spur of the moment.[110] In hot spots for crime, therefore, an undefended yet attractive target becomes an irresistible objective for motivated criminals. Given these principles, it is not surprising that people who (a) live in high-crime areas and (b) go out late at night (c) carrying valuables such as an expensive watch and (d) engage in risky behavior such as drinking alcohol, (e) without friends or family to watch or help them have a significant chance of becoming crime victims.[111]

Support for Routine Activities Theory   Research supports many facets of routine activities theory (see the Criminology in Action feature). Cohen and Felson themselves found that crime rates increased between 1960 and 1980 because the number of adult caretakers at home during the day (guardians) decreased as a result of increased female participation in the workforce. While mothers are at work and children in day care, homes are left unguarded. Similarly, with the growth of suburbia and the decline of the

According to routine activities theory, if a motivated criminal encounters a vulnerable unguarded target a crime may occur. Here, in a frame from video provided by the Detroit Police, a man is seen viciously punching a 70-year-old woman before robbing her in a Detroit apartment building hallway on June 29, 2011. The surveillance video shows the man punching the woman at least twice in the face. The man walked away with personal items and cash.

AP Images/Detroit Police

traditional neighborhood, the number of such familiar guardians as family, neighbors, and friends diminished.[112] Steven Messner and his associates found that as adult unemployment rates *increase*, juvenile homicide arrest rates *decrease*. One possible reason for this phenomenon: it is possible that juvenile arrests decrease because unemployed adults are at home to supervise their children and make sure they do not get in trouble or join gangs.[113] The availability and cost of easily transportable goods has also been shown to influence victimization rates: as the costs of goods such as mobile phones and camcorders declined, so too did burglary rates.[114]

Routine Activities and Lifestyle   Routine activities theory and the lifestyle approach have a number of similarities. They both assume that a person's living arrangements can affect victim risk and that people who live in unguarded areas are at the mercy of motivated offenders. These two theories both rely on four basic concepts: (1) proximity to criminals, (2) time of exposure to criminals, (3) target attractiveness, and (4) guardianship.[115]

Based on the same basic concepts, these theories share five predictions: People increase their victimization risk if they (1) live in high-crime areas, (2) go out late at night, (3) carry valuables such as an expensive watch, (4) engage in risky behavior such as drinking alcohol, and (5) are without friends or family to watch or help them.[116]

The various theories of victimization are summarized in Concept Summary 3.1.

according to Marcus Felson, crime began to increase in the United States as the country changed from a nation of small villages and towns to one of large urban environments. Because metropolitan areas provide a critical population mass, predatory criminals are better able to hide and evade apprehension. After committing crime, criminals can blend into the crowd, disperse their loot, and make a quick escape using the public transportation system.

As the population became more urban, the middle class, fearing criminal victimization, fled to the suburbs. Rather than being safe from crime, the suburbs produced a unique set of routine activities that promote victimization risk. In many families, both parents are likely to commute to work, leaving teens unsupervised. Affluent kids own or drive cars, date, and socialize with peers in unsupervised settings, all behaviors that are related to both crime and victimization.

The downtown shopping district was replaced by the suburban shopping mall. Here, strangers converge in large numbers and youths hang out. The interior is filled with people, so drug deals can be concealed in the pedestrian flow. Stores have

attractively displayed goods, encouraging shoplifting and employee pilferage. Substantial numbers of cars are parked in areas that make larceny and car theft virtually undetectable. Cars that carry away stolen merchandise have an undistinguished appearance: who notices people placing items in a car in a shopping mall lot? Also, shoppers can be attacked in parking lots as they walk in isolation to and from their cars. As car ownership increases, teens have greater access to transportation outside parental control. So while victimization rates in urban areas are still higher, routine activities in the suburbs may also produce the risk of victimization. Felson has set out the factors that increase the likelihood of victimization as the features of metropolitan living have spread to the suburbs:

- It has become more difficult to protect people from criminal entry because homes have been dispersed over larger areas, huge parking lots have been created, and building heights lowered.
- By spreading people and vehicles over larger areas as they travel and park, people are more exposed to attack.

- There are fewer people in each household and consequently less interpersonal and intrafamily supervision.
- As shopping, work, and socializing are spread further from home, people are forced to leave their immediate neighborhood, and, as strangers, they become more vulnerable to attack.
- By spreading vast quantities of retail goods throughout huge stores and malls, with fewer employees to watch over them, the divergent metropolis creates a retail environment that invites people of all ages to shoplift.
- Commuting to the inner city for work requires that millions of dollars' worth of vehicles be left in parking lots without supervision.

Critical Thinking

Does routine activities theory merely describe why people become victims rather than get at the heart of the matter? Why are there motivated offenders? If people are motivated to commit crime, where does their motivation come from?

SOURCE: Marcus Felson and Rachel Boba, *Crime and Everyday Life: Insights and Implications for Society*, 4th ed. (Thousand Oaks, CA: Sage, 2009).

CARING FOR THE VICTIM

 LO9 Assess programs dedicated to caring for the victim

National victim surveys indicate that almost every American age 12 and over will one day become the victim of a common-law crime, such as larceny or burglary, and in the aftermath suffer financial problems, mental stress, and physical hardship.[117] Surveys show that more than 75 percent of the general public has been victimized by crime at least once in their life; as many as 25 percent of the victims develop posttraumatic stress disorder, and their symptoms last for

more than a decade after the crime occurred.[118] The long-term effects of sexual victimization can include years of problem avoidance, social withdrawal, and self-criticism. Helping these victims adjust and improve their coping techniques can be essential to their recovery.[119] Law enforcement agencies, courts, and correctional and human service systems have come to realize that due process and human rights exist for both the defendant and the victim of criminal behavior.

The Government's Response to Victimization

Because of public concern over violent personal crime, President Ronald Reagan created a Task Force on Victims of Crime in 1982.[120] This group suggested that a balance be

	Major Premise	Strengths of the Theory	Research Focus of the Theory
Victim precipitation	The major premise of victim precipitation theory is that victims trigger criminal acts by their provocative behavior. Active precipitation involves fighting words or gestures. Passive precipitation occurs when victims unknowingly threaten their attacker.	The strength of the theory is that it explains multiple victimizations: if people precipitate crime, it follows that they will become repeat victims if their behavior persists over time.	The research focuses of the theory are the victim's role, crime provocation, and the victim–offender relationship.
Lifestyle	The major premise of lifestyle theory is that victimization risk is increased when people have a high-risk lifestyle. Placing oneself at risk by going out to dangerous places results in increased victimization.	The strength of the theory is that it explains victimization patterns in the social structure. Males, young people, and the poor have high victimization rates because they have a higher-risk lifestyle than females, the elderly, and the affluent.	The research focuses of the theory are personal activities, peer relations, place of crime, and type of crime.
Deviant place	The major premise of deviant place theory is that victims do not encourage crime but are victim prone because they reside in socially disorganized high-crime areas where they have the greatest risk of coming into contact with criminal offenders, irrespective of their own behavior or lifestyle.	The strength of the theory is that it shows why people with conventional lifestyles become crime victims in high-risk areas. Victimization is a function of place and location, not lifestyle and risk taking.	The research focus of the theory is victimization in high-crime, disorganized neighborhoods.
Routine activities	The major premise of routine activities theory is that crime rates can be explained by the availability of suitable targets, the absence of capable guardians, and the presence of motivated offenders.	The strengths of the theory are that it can explain crime rates and trends, it shows how victim behavior can influence criminal opportunity, and it suggests that victimization risk can be reduced by increasing guardianship and/or reducing target vulnerability.	The research focuses of the theory are opportunity to commit crime, effect of police and guardians, population shifts, and crime rates.

achieved between recognizing the victim's rights and providing the defendant with due process. Recommendations included providing witnesses and victims with protection from intimidation, requiring restitution in criminal cases, developing guidelines for fair treatment of crime victims and witnesses, and expanding programs of victim compensation.[121] Consequently, the Omnibus Victim and Witness Protection Act was passed, which required the use of victim impact statements at sentencing in federal criminal cases, greater protection for witnesses, more stringent bail laws, and the use of restitution in criminal cases.

In 1984, the Comprehensive Crime Control Act and the Victims of Crime Act authorized federal funding for state victim compensation and assistance projects.[122] With these acts, the federal government began to address the plight of the victim and make victim assistance an even greater concern of the public and the justice system. In 2004, the Justice for All Act modified existing federal law and created a new set of rights for victims. Part of this act, the Crime Victims' Rights Act, sets out these rights, including the right to be protected from the accused in their case and to be informed of their release (see Exhibit 3.3).[123]

Due to this recognition of the needs of victims, an estimated 2,000 **victim-witness assistance programs** have developed around the United States.[124] Victim-witness assistance programs are organized on a variety of governmental levels

victim-witness assistance programs Government programs that help crime victims and witnesses; may include compensation, court services, and/or crisis intervention.

and serve a variety of clients. We will look at the most prominent forms of victim services operating in the United States.[125]

Victim Compensation In order to help victims survive their ordeal, state governments have set up **victim compensation** programs to help pay for damages associated with the crime. Rarely are two compensation schemes alike, however, and many state programs suffer from lack of both adequate funding and proper organization within the criminal justice system. Compensation may be made for medical bills, loss of wages, loss of future earnings, and counseling. In the case of death, the victim's survivors can receive burial expenses and aid for loss of support.[126] Awards are typically in the $100 to $15,000 range. Occasionally programs will provide emergency assistance to indigent victims until com-

pensation is available. Emergency assistance may come in the form of food vouchers or replacement of prescription medicines. Three typical victim compensation programs are described in Exhibit 3.4.

In 1984, the federal government created the Victims of Crime Act (VOCA), which grants money to state compensation boards derived from fines and penalties imposed on federal offenders. The money is distributed each year to the states to fund both their crime victim compensation programs and their victim assistance programs, such as rape crisis centers and domestic violence shelters. Victims of child abuse and victims of domestic violence receive most of the funds. VOCA money goes to support victims' medical expenses, gives them economic support for lost wages, helps to compensate for the death of loved ones, and provides mental health counseling.[127] At this time the House Appropriations Committee has proposed increasing the VOCA funding from $730 million to $745 million while the Senate Appropriations Committee would set the cap at $765 million; the 2013 funding was about $425 million.[128]

victim compensation The victim ordinarily receives compensation from the state to pay for damages associated with the crime. Rarely are two compensation schemes alike, however, and many state programs suffer from lack of both adequate funding and proper organization within the criminal justice system. Compensation may be made for medical bills, loss of wages, loss of future earnings, and counseling. In the case of death, the victim's survivors can receive burial expenses and aid for loss of support.

Debra Rabideau-Stevens is seen in her home near Ashland, Wisconsin. On a June night in 2007, she tried to break up a fight between two women at a northern Wisconsin tavern. The husband of one of the women grabbed her wrist, snapping it in two places. Four surgeries later, she has racked up more than $31,000 in medical bills. With no insurance and no job, the former cook turned to Wisconsin's crime victim compensation fund. But the cash-strapped program has covered less than half of her expenses, leaving her to fend off as many as eight creditor calls a day. Should the government do more to help victims?

Victim Advocates   Ensuring victims' rights can involve an eclectic group of advocacy groups, some independent, others government sponsored, and some self-help. Advocates can be especially helpful when victims need to interact with the agencies of justice. Advocates lobby police departments to keep investigations open as well as request the return of recovered stolen property. They also work closely with police when victims are interviewed about violent crimes, helping them to deal with reliving traumatic events.

Police departments are now instituting training designed to prepare officers to work more effectively with victim advocates.[129] They can demand from prosecutors and judges protection from harassment and reprisals by, for example, making "no contact" a condition of bail. They can help victims make statements during sentencing hearings as well as probation and parole revocation procedures. Victim advocates can also interact with news media, making sure that reporting is accurate and that victim privacy is not violated. Victim advocates can be part of an independent agency similar to a legal aid society. If successful, top-notch advocates may eventually open private offices, similar to attorneys, private investigators, or jury consultants.

Some programs assign advocates to help victims understand the operations of the justice system and guide them through the process. Victims of sexual assault may be assigned the assistance of a rape victim advocate to stand by their side as they negotiate the legal and medical systems that must process their case. Research shows that rape survivors who had the assistance of an advocate were significantly more likely to have police reports taken, were less likely to be treated negatively by police officers, and reported less distress from their medical contact experiences.[130]

Court advocates prepare victims and witnesses by explaining court procedures: how to be a witness, how bail works, and what to do if the defendant makes a threat. Lack of such knowledge can cause confusion and fear, making some victims reluctant to testify in court procedures.

Helping Child Abuse Victims   One of the most significant problems court advocates must deal with is helping the victim of child abuse navigate a court hearing. Children get confused and frightened and may change their testimony. Much controversy has arisen over the accuracy of children's reports of physical and sexual abuse, resulting in hung juries. Prosecutors and experts have been accused of misleading children or eliciting incriminating testimony.

State jurisdictions have enacted legislation allowing videotaped statements or interviews with child witnesses to be admissible in court in order to spare child witnesses the trauma of testifying in open court. Most of the states now allow a child's testimony to be given on closed-circuit television (CCTV). The child can view the judge and attorneys, and the courtroom participants can observe the child. In addition to innovative methods of testimony, children in sexual abuse cases have been allowed to use anatomically correct dolls to demonstrate happenings that they cannot describe verbally. The Victims of Child Abuse Act of 1990 allows children to use these dolls when testifying in federal courts; at least eight states have passed similar legislation.[131] Other programs are designed to help very young children remember what happened and be able to tell authorities about their victimization. The Policy and Practice in Criminology feature discusses one program that has been a success.

Many victim programs also provide transportation to and from court, and advocates may remain in the courtroom during hearings to explain procedures and provide support. Court escorts are particularly important for elderly and disabled victims, victims of child abuse and assault, and victims who have been intimidated by friends or relatives of the defendant. These types of services may be having a positive effect since recent research shows that victims may now be less traumatized by a court hearing than previously believed.[132]

Public Education   More than half of all victim programs include public education to help familiarize the general public with their services and with other agencies that assist crime victims. In some instances, these are primary education programs, which teach methods of dealing with conflict without resorting to violence. For example, school-based programs present information on spousal and dating abuse followed by discussions of how to reduce violent incidents.[133]

TOWARD A BETTER WAY TO INTERVIEW CHILD VICTIMS OF SEXUAL ABUSE

Child abuse prosecutions can hang on a child's recollection of the alleged incident. One way to help avoid false accusations and ensure justice in these cases is to create mechanisms to elicit accurate information from children. The quality of forensic interviewing practices is of utmost importance if child victims are to be protected at the same time as the rights of innocent suspects are to be upheld.

Considerable knowledge has been gained in the last two decades about child development, memory, and cognition, and researchers have developed several techniques for improving the way child victims of sexual abuse are interviewed. One technique that shows promise in a laboratory has now been tested in the field in Utah's criminal justice system. According to Margaret-Ellen Pipe, a member of the team that has developed and tested the protocol, "In the '80s people started recognizing children could provide reliable evidence. There had been real skepticism prior to that whether you would believe children."

A team of researchers led by Pipe investigated how the protocol might affect prosecution outcomes. Their findings make it clear that the training and protocol elicit more information from possible victims. The findings cannot, of course, determine whether the information is more accurate—that is, the findings cannot definitively confirm details of what happened. But it is clear that after the protocol was introduced, prosecutors accepted more cases, and more cases that went to trial resulted in conviction than before the protocol was introduced.

The Protocol

The techniques employed by the protocol were designed to integrate advances in scientific understanding about memory and children's linguistic and cognitive development. The interview protocol includes three phases:

- Introductory
- Rapport-building
- Substantive or free recall

At the beginning of the conversation, the child and the interviewer discuss expectations and set ground rules: this is the introductory phase. Interviewers then ask children to talk about events unrelated to the suspected abuse; the idea is to encourage the child to be comfortable leading the conversation by developing this rapport. In this phase, the children learn the conversational rules, because they are different from many conversations in which children take part.

Later, interviewers encourage children to recall the target incident and talk about it in a narrative stream, as opposed to answering directed questions about it, one after another. Evidence indicates open-ended prompts draw out more accurate information than ones that simply elicit a child's recognition. The techniques discourage suggestive leads or questions with yes/no or either/or answers: "Where were his clothes?" for example, is preferred over "Were his clothes on the floor?"

Nearly a decade of research confirms that when interviewers follow the guidelines outlined in the protocol, children give both more and higher-quality information. Their narrative accounts reveal greater detail when the protocol is implemented.

A recent study examined the outcomes of cases before and after police detectives were trained on the Investigative Interview Protocol. Eleven detectives in the study performed forensic interviews at the Salt Lake County Children's Justice Center (CJC), an arm of the Utah Attorney General's Office. The study involved 1,280 sexual abuse cases between 1994 and 2000 that were referred to authorities in Salt Lake County, Utah, and investigated by the 11 detectives. Of the total sample, these detectives conducted 551 interviews

before receiving training on the NICHD protocol and 729 after they had implemented the protocol. The same detectives, prosecutors, and judges who handled the cases were used throughout the study period. Among the cases of alleged abuse nearly 60 percent involved improper touching and 5 percent were characterized by exposure; penetration was alleged in 35 percent of the cases reviewed. Detectives interviewed children between the ages of 2 and 14 and then presented their evidence to the district attorney, who decided whether or not to prosecute. After the protocol was used, the percentage of investigated cases in which charges were filed rose from 45 percent to over 54 percent. Furthermore, these cases held up as they progressed through the system. More than 90 percent of those prosecuted after implementation of the protocol resulted in conviction compared with 54 percent before its introduction. The impact of the protocol was strongest in cases in which the children were between 7 and 9 years old. For children in this age group, the rate at which prosecutors filed charges rose from 42 percent before to 64 percent after detectives were trained.

Critical Thinking

Is there a danger of coaching children during interviews to give damaging testimony? What can be done to make sure these proceedings are totally impartial, considering the damage a false accusation can cause?

SOURCES: Sara Harris, "Toward a Better Way to Interview Child Victims of Sexual Abuse," *NIJ Journal* 267 (Winter 2010), http://www.nij.gov/journals/267/pages/child-victim-interview.aspx (accessed April 2014); Margaret-Ellen Pipe, Yael Orbach, Michael Lamb, Craig B. Abbott, and Heather Stewart, *Do Best Practice Interviews with Child Abuse Victims Influence Case Outcomes?* Final report for the National Institute of Justice (Washington, DC: National Institute of Justice, November 2008), https://www.ncjrs.gov/pdffiles1/nij/grants/224524.pdf (accessed April 2014).

policy and practice in criminology

Crisis Intervention Most victim programs refer victims to specific services to help them recover from their ordeal, referred to as **crisis intervention**. Clients are commonly referred to the local network of public and private social service agencies that provide emergency and long-term assistance with transportation, medical care, shelter, food, and clothing. In addition, more than half of all victim programs provide crisis intervention for victims who feel isolated, vulnerable, and in need of immediate services. Some programs counsel at their offices; others visit victims in their homes, at the crime scene, or in the hospital. For example, the Good Samaritans program in Mobile County, Alabama, unites law enforcement and faith-based and community organizations to train and mobilize volunteers who can help crime victims. Good Samaritan volunteers provide services such as:

- Making repairs to a home after a break-in
- Conducting home safety inspections to prevent revictimization
- Accompanying victims to court
- Supplying "victim care kits" or other support[134]

Victim–Offender Reconciliation Programs

Victim–offender reconciliation programs (VORPs) use mediators to facilitate face-to-face encounters between victims and their attackers. The aim is to engage in direct negotiations that lead to **restitution agreements** and, possibly, reconciliation between the two parties involved.[135] Hundreds of programs are currently in operation, and they handle thousands of cases per year. Designed at first to address routine misdemeanors such as petty theft and vandalism, programs now commonly hammer out restitution agreements in more serious incidents such as residential burglary and even attempted murder.

 Since 1982, the Victim Offender Reconciliation Program (VORP) has been bringing victims and offenders together in safe mediation or family group conference settings to permit the offender to take responsibility for his or her actions, to make things as right as possible with the victim, and to be clear about future intentions. VORP follows up to ensure that agreements are kept. Read about their history, programs, and training assistance at **http://www.vorp.org/**.

CONNECTIONS

Reconciliation programs are based on the concept of restorative justice, which rejects punitive correctional measures in favor of viewing crimes of violence and theft as interpersonal conflicts that need to be settled in the community through noncoercive means. See Chapter 8 for more on this approach.

Victim Impact Statements Every state jurisdiction allows victims to make an impact statement before the sentencing judge. Victim impact information is part of the Federal Crime Act of 1994, in which Congress gave federal victims of violent crime or sexual assault the right to speak at sentencing. Through the Child Protection Act of 1990, child victims of federal crimes are allowed to submit victim impact statements that are "commensurate with their age and cognitive development," which can include drawings, models, etc.[136]

This gives the victim an opportunity to tell of his or her experiences and describe the ordeal. In the case of a murder trial, the surviving family can recount the effect the crime has had on their lives and well-being.[137]

The effect of victim impact statements on sentencing has been the topic of some debate. Some research finds that victim statements result in a higher rate of incarceration, but others find that the statements are insignificant.[138] One recent study by Joel Caplan found that the use of victim statements at parole hearings had little influence on the decision process, and inmate release was based more on factors such as measures of institutional behavior, crime severity, and criminal history.[139]

Those who favor the use of impact statements argue that because the victim is harmed by the crime, he or she has the right to influence the outcome of the case. After all, the public prosecutor is allowed to make sentencing recommendations because the public has been harmed by the crime. Logically, the harm suffered by the victim legitimizes his or her right to make sentencing recommendations.[140]

Community Organization

Citizens have been working independently and in cooperation with local police agencies in neighborhood patrol and block watch programs. These programs organize local citizens in urban areas to patrol neighborhoods, watch for suspicious people, help secure the neighborhood, lobby for improvements (such as increased lighting), report crime to police, put out community newsletters, conduct home security surveys, and serve as a source for crime information or tips.[141] Although such programs are welcome additions to police services, there is little evidence that they appreciably

crisis intervention Emergency counseling for crime victims.

restitution agreements Conditions of probation in which the offenders repay society or the victims of crime for the trouble the offenders caused. Monetary restitution involves a direct payment to the victim as a form of compensation. Community service restitution may be used in victimless crimes and involves work in the community in lieu of more severe criminal penalties.

affect the crime rate. There is also concern that their effectiveness is spottier in low-income, high-crime areas, which need the most crime prevention assistance.[142] Block watches and neighborhood patrols seem more successful when they are part of general-purpose or multi-issue community groups rather than when they focus directly on crime problems.[143]

Victims and Self-Protection

Although the general public mostly approves of the police, fear of crime and concern about community safety have prompted some to become their own "police force," taking an active role in community protection and citizen crime control groups.[144] The more crime in an area, the greater the amount of fear and the more likely residents will be to engage in self-protective measures.[145]

Research indicates that a significant number of crimes may not be reported to police simply because victims prefer to take matters into their own hands.[146] One manifestation of this trend is the concept of **target hardening**, or making one's home and business crime-proof through locks, bars, alarms, and other devices.[147] Other commonly used crime prevention techniques include a fence or barricade at the entrance; a doorkeeper, guard, or receptionist in an apartment building; an intercom or phone to gain access to the building; surveillance cameras; window bars; warning signs; and dogs chosen for their ability to guard the house. The use of these measures is inversely proportional to perception of neighborhood safety: people who fear crime are more likely to use crime prevention techniques. Although the true relationship is still unclear, there is mounting evidence that people who protect their homes are less likely to be victimized by property crimes.[148] One study conducted in the Philadelphia area found that people who install burglar alarms are less likely to suffer burglary than those who forgo similar preventive measures.[149]

Fighting Back   Some people take self-protection to its ultimate end by preparing to fight back when criminals attack them. How successful are victims when they resist? Research indicates that victims who fight back often frustrate their attackers but also face increased odds of being physically harmed during the attack.[150] In some cases, fighting back decreases the odds of a crime being completed but increases the victim's chances of injury.[151] Resistance may draw the attention of bystanders and make a violent crime physically difficult to complete, but it can also cause offenders to escalate their violence.[152]

target hardening Making one's home or business crime proof through the use of locks, bars, alarms, and other devices.

What about the use of firearms for self-protection? Again, there is no clear-cut answer. Each year, 2.5 million times, victims use guns for defensive purposes, a number that is not surprising considering that about one-third of U.S. households contain guns.[153] Gary Kleck has estimated that armed victims kill between 1,500 and 2,800 potential felons each year and wound between 8,700 and 16,000. Kleck's research shows, ironically, that by fighting back victims kill far more criminals than the estimated 250 to 1,000 killed annually by police.[154] Kleck has found that the risk of collateral injury is relatively rare and that potential victims should be encouraged to fight back.[155] In a recent study conducted with colleague Jongyeon Tark, Kleck reviewed more than 27,000 contact crime incidents and found that when compared to nonresistance, self-protection significantly

AN ETHICAL DILEMMA

STAND YOUR GROUND

The governor's council is sponsoring an open house debate on a proposed "stand your ground" law. About 15 states have passed laws that allow crime victims to use deadly force in certain situations in which they might have formerly been charged with a crime, some allowing the use of deadly force when a person reasonably believes it necessary to prevent the commission of a "forcible felony," including carjacking, robbery, or assault, and the governor's council wants to follow suit.

The traditional "castle doctrine" requires that people could only use deadly force in their own home when they reasonably believed that their lives were in danger. The new law being proposed allows the average citizen to use deadly force when they reasonably believe that their homes or vehicles have been illegally invaded. Furthermore, under the new law, a person has no duty to retreat and can meet force with force; they are granted immunity from prosecution if they can prove they were the target of a crime and feared that their life was in danger.

A number of controversial cases have put the "stand your ground" law under a legal microscope. Most notable was the killing of Trayvon Martin by George Zimmerman, who was acquitted after convincing a Florida jury that he feared for his life despite the fact that Martin was an unarmed teen. There is a question of ethics: is it appropriate to allow someone to take a life for committing a crime that would not be subject to capital punishment? Why should someone be allowed to take a life if the state cannot?

 Divide the class into two groups and have each prepare a "talking points" paper, one supporting the ethical value of the "stand your ground" concept and the other pointing out its flaws and limitations.

thinking like a criminologist

reduced the likelihood of property loss and injury and that the most forceful tactics, including resistance with a gun, appear to have the strongest effects in reducing the risk of injury. Importantly, the research indicated that resistance did not contribute to injury in any meaningful way. The conclusion: it is better to fight than flee.[156]

Victims' Rights

LO10 Articulate why there is a need for victims' rights

More than 30 years ago, legal scholar Frank Carrington suggested that crime victims have legal rights that should assure them of basic services from the government.[157] According to Carrington, just as the defendant has the right to counsel and a fair trial, society is also obliged to ensure basic rights for law-abiding citizens. These rights range from adequate protection from violent crimes to victim compensation and assistance from the criminal justice system.

Because of the influence of victims' rights advocates, every state now has a set of legal rights for crime victims in its code of laws, often called a Victims' Bill of Rights.[158] These generally include the right:

- To be notified of proceedings and the status of the defendant
- To be present at criminal justice proceedings
- To make a statement at sentencing and to receive restitution from a convicted offender
- To be consulted before a case is dismissed or a plea agreement entered
- To a speedy trial
- To keep the victim's contact information confidential

JESSE TIMMENDEQUAS AND MEGAN'S LAW

profiles in crime

Richard and Maureen Kanka thought that their 7-year-old daughter Megan was safe in their quiet, suburban neighborhood in Hamilton Township, New Jersey. Then, on July 29, 1994, their lives were shattered when Megan went missing. Maureen Kanka searched the neighborhood and met 33-year-old Jesse Timmendequas, who lived across the street. Timmendequas told her that he had seen Megan earlier that evening while he was working on his car. The police were called in and soon focused their attention on Timmendequas's house when they learned that he and two other residents were convicted sex offenders who had met at a treatment center and decided to live together upon their release. Timmendequas, who appeared extremely nervous when questioned, was asked to accompany police back to their headquarters, where he confessed to luring Megan into his home by inviting her to see a puppy, then raping her and strangling her to death.

Timmendequas had served six years in prison for aggravated assault and attempted sexual assault on another child. The fact that a known sex offender was living anonymously in the Kankas' neighborhood turned Megan's death into a national crusade to develop laws that require sex offenders to register

with local police when they move into a neighborhood and require local authorities to provide community notification of the sex offender's presence. New York State's Sex Offender Registration Act is typical of these efforts, commonly known as Megan's Law. Becoming effective on January 21, 1996, the statute requires that sex offenders in New York are classified by the risk of reoffense. A court determines whether an offender is a level 1 (low risk), 2 (moderate risk), or 3 (high risk). The court also determines whether an offender should be given the designation of a sexual predator, sexually violent offender, or predicate sex offender. Offenders are required to be registered for 20 years or life. Level 1 offenders with no designation must register for 20 years. Level 1 offenders with a designation, as well as level 2 and level 3 offenders regardless of whether they have a designation, must register for life. Local law enforcement agencies are notified whenever a sex offender moves into their jurisdiction. That agency may notify schools and other "entities with vulnerable populations" about the presence of a level 2 or level 3 offender if the offender poses a threat to public safety. The act established a toll-free telephone information line that citizens can call to inquire whether a person is listed in the registry and access

information on sex offenders living in their neighborhoods. On the federal level, the Jacob Wetterling Crimes Against Children Law, passed in May 1996, requires states to pass some version of Megan's Law or lose federal aid. At least 47 states plus the District of Columbia have complied. Jesse Timmendequas was sentenced to death on June 20, 1997; his sentence was commuted to life without parole when New Jersey abolished the death penalty in 2007.

Critical Thinking

The case of Megan Kanka illustrates both the risk children face from sexual predators and the efforts being made by the justice system to limit that risk. To some civil liberty groups, such as the American Civil Liberties Union, registration laws go too far because they will not prevent sex offenders from committing crimes and because they victimize rehabilitated ex-offenders and their families. Should the rights of the victim take precedent over the privacy of the offender?

SOURCE: New York State Sex Offender Registry and the Sex Offender Registration Act (SORA), http://criminaljustice.state.ny.us/nsor/ (accessed April 2014), New York State Correction Law Article 6-C (Section 168 et seq.).

Not only has the victims' rights movement caught on in the United States, it has also had an impact in Europe. The European Union member nations have agreed in principle to a set of rules that creates minimum standards for the protection of victims of crime. These guarantee that all victims should:

- Be treated with respect
- Have their entitlement to a real and appropriate role in criminal proceedings recognized
- Have the right to be heard during proceedings and to supply evidence
- Receive information on: the type of support available; where and how to report an offence; criminal proceedings and their role in them; access to protection and advice; entitlement to compensation; and, if they wish, the outcomes of their complaints, including sentencing and release of the offender
- Have communication safeguards: that is, member states should take measures to minimize communication difficulties in criminal proceedings
- Have access to free legal advice concerning their role in the proceedings and, where appropriate, legal aid

- Receive payment of expenses incurred as a result of participation in criminal proceedings
- Receive reasonable protection, including protection of privacy
- Receive compensation in the course of criminal proceedings
- Receive penal mediation in the course of criminal proceedings where appropriate
- Benefit from various measures to minimize the difficulties faced where victims are resident in another member state, especially when organizing criminal proceedings[159]

A final, albeit controversial, element of the victims' rights movement is the development of offender registration laws that require that the name and sometimes addresses of known sex offenders be posted by law enforcement agencies. Today almost every state has adopted sex offender laws, and the federal government runs a National Sex Offender Public Registry with links to every state.[160] Sex offender registration is indelibly linked to the death of Megan Kanka, an incident described in the Profiles in Crime feature "Jesse Timmendequas and Megan's Law."

SUMMARY

LO1 Discuss the greatest problems faced by crime victims

The costs of victimization can include such things as damaged property, pain and suffering to victims, and the involvement of the police and other agencies of the justice system. The pain and suffering inflicted on an individual can result in the need for long-term medical care and counseling, the loss of wages from not being able to go to work, and reduced quality of life from debilitating injuries and/or fear of being victimized again.

LO2 Clarify the term *cycle of violence*

People who are crime victims may be more likely to commit crime themselves. Some may seek revenge against the people who harmed them. The abuse–crime phenomenon is referred to as the cycle of violence.

LO3 Analyze the victim's role in the crime process

There is an association between crime and victimization, but the linkage is a matter of some debate. One view is that the people who are crime victims experience long-term negative consequences that lead them to commit crime. It is also possible that victimization may produce anger, stress, and strain that results in their involvement in antisocial behavior. Victims may seek revenge against the people who harmed them or whom they believe are at fault for their problems. It is also possible that both criminals and victims tend to have the same lifestyle and live in the same neighborhoods, making it seem they are one and the same.

LO4 Assess the ecology of victimization risk

Victimization is more likely to take place in an open, public area, such as a street, a park, or a field. The more serious violent crimes, such as rape and aggravated assault, typically take place after 6 P.M. Those living in the central city have significantly higher rates of theft and violence victimizations than suburbanites; people living in rural areas have a victimization rate almost half that of city dwellers. Schools unfortunately are the site of a great deal of victimization because they are populated by one of the most dangerous segments of society, teenage males.

LO5 Describe the victim's household

The NCVS tells us that within the United States, larger, African American, western, and urban homes are the most vulnerable to crime. In contrast, rural, European American homes in the Northeast are the least likely to contain crime victims or be the target of theft offenses, such as burglary and larceny. People who own their homes are less vulnerable than renters.

LO6 Categorize the most dominant victim characteristics

Except for the crimes of rape and sexual assault, males are more likely than females to be the victims of violent crime. Victim data reveal that young people face a much greater victimization risk than older persons. The poorest Americans are the most likely to be victims of violent and property crime. This association occurs across all gender, age, and racial groups. African Americans are about twice as likely as European Americans to be victims of violent crime. Never-married males and females are victimized more often than married people.

LO7 Explain the concept of repeat victimization

Individuals who have been crime victims have a significantly higher chance of future victimization than people who have remained nonvictims. Households that have experienced victimization in the past are the ones most likely to experience it again in the future. One reason: some victims' physical weakness or psychological distress renders them incapable of resisting or deterring crime and makes them easy targets.

LO8 Compare and contrast the most important theories of victimization

According to victim precipitation theory, some people may actually initiate the confrontation that eventually leads to their injury or death. Victim precipitation can be either active or passive. Some criminologists believe that people may become crime victims because their lifestyle increases their exposure to criminal offenders. People who have high-risk lifestyles—drinking, taking drugs, getting involved in crime—have a much greater chance of victimization. According to deviant place theory, the greater their exposure to dangerous places, the more likely people are to become victims of crime and violence. Deviant places are poor, densely populated, highly transient neighborhoods in which commercial and residential properties exist side by side. Routine activities theory links victimization to the availability of suitable targets, the absence of capable guardians, and the presence of motivated offenders.

LO9 Assess programs dedicated to caring for the victim

Victim-witness assistance programs are government programs that help crime victims and witnesses; they may include compensation, court services, and/or crisis intervention. Such programs often include victim compensation—financial aid awarded to crime victims to repay them for their loss and injuries; this assistance may cover medical bills, loss of wages, loss of future earnings, and/or counseling. Some programs assign counselors to victims to serve as advocates to help them understand the operation of the justice system and guide them through the process. Every state jurisdiction allows victims to make an impact statement before the sentencing judge. Most victim programs refer victims to specific services to help them recover from their ordeal.

LO10 Articulate why there is a need for victims' rights

Every state now has a set of legal rights for crime victims in its code of laws, often called a Victims' Bill of Rights. These generally include the victim's right to be notified of proceedings and the status of the defendant, to be present at criminal justice proceedings and to make statements at trials, to receive restitution from a convicted offender, and to be consulted about trial procedures, such as when a plea is offered.

CRITICAL THINKING QUESTIONS

1. Considering what you learned in this chapter about crime victimization, what measures can you take to better protect yourself from crime?
2. Do you agree with the assessment that schools are some of the most dangerous locations in the community? Did you find your high school to be a dangerous environment?
3. Does a person bear some of the responsibility for his or her victimization if the person maintains a lifestyle that contributes to the chances of becoming a crime victim? In other words, should we "blame the victim"?
4. Have you ever experienced someone "precipitating" crime? If so, did you do anything to help the situation?
5. Are potential victims justified in using deadly force if they believe their life is in danger even if their assailant is unarmed?

KEY TERMS

victimologists (66)
victimization by the justice system (66)
posttraumatic stress disorder (PTSD) (67)
obsessive-compulsive disorder (68)

cycle of violence (69)
elder abuse (71)
chronic victimization (73)
victim precipitation theory (74)
active precipitation (74)
passive precipitation (74)

lifestyle theory (74)
deviant place theory (75)
routine activities theory (76)
suitable targets (76)
capable guardians (76)
motivated offenders (76)

victim-witness assistance programs (79)
victim compensation (80)
crisis intervention (83)
restitution agreements (83)
target hardening (84)

1. *Plain Dealer staff*, "Steubenville Rape Case: Defense Expert Says Teen Girl Could Have Made Decisions Even After Heavy Drinking," *Cleveland Plain Dealer*, March 16, 2013, http://www.cleveland.com/steubenville-rape-case/index.ssf/2013/03/steubenville_rape_case_defense.html (accessed April 2014).

2. Michael Muskal, "School Superintendent, 3 Others Charged in Steubenville Rape Case," *Los Angeles Times*, November 25, 2013, http://www.latimes.com/nation/nationnow/la-na-nn-steubenville-rape-indictments-20131125-story.html (accessed June 2014).

3. Beth Stebner, "Audrie Pott Suicide: Details of Online Chats Emerge a Year After Teen Killed Herself Following Alleged Assault and Cyberbullying," *New York Daily News*, September 18, 2013, http://www.nydailynews.com/news/national/new-details-revealed-audrie-pott-cyber-bullying-suicide-article-1.1459904 (accessed April 2014); CTV News, "Police Warn Against Vigilantism in Rehtaeh Parsons Case," http://atlantic.ctvnews.ca/police-warn-against-vigilantism-in-rehtaeh-parsons-case-1.1234199 (accessed April 2014).

4. Jennifer Truman, Lynn Langton, and Michael Planty, *Criminal Victimization, 2012* (Washington, DC: Bureau of Justice Statistics, 2013), http://www.bjs.gov/content/pub/pdf/cv12.pdf (accessed April 2014).

5. Arthur Lurigio, "Are All Victims Alike? The Adverse, Generalized, and Differential Impact of Crime," *Crime and Delinquency* 33 (1987): 452–467.

6. Kathryn McCollister, Michael T. French, and Hai Fang, "The Cost of Crime to Society: New Crime-Specific Estimates for Policy and Program Evaluation," *Drug and Alcohol Dependence* 108 (2010): 98–109.

7. National Institute of Drug Abuse, "Heroin," http://drugabuse.gov/ResearchReports/heroin/heroin.html (accessed April 2014).

8. James Anderson, Terry Grandison, and Laronistine Dyson, "Victims of Random Violence and the Public Health Implication: A Health Care or Criminal Justice Issue?" *Journal of Criminal Justice* 24 (1996): 379–393.

9. Angela Scarpa, Sara Chiara Haden, and Jimmy Hurley, "Community Violence Victimization and Symptoms of Posttraumatic Stress Disorder: The Moderating Effects of Coping and Social Support," *Journal of Interpersonal Violence* 21 (2006): 446–469.

10. Heather Littleton and Craig Henderson, "If She Is Not a Victim, Does That Mean She Was Not Traumatized? Evaluation of Predictors of PTSD Symptomatology Among College Rape Victims," *Violence Against Women* 15 (2009): 148–167.

11. Mladen Loncar, Neven Henigsberg, and Pero Hrabac, "Mental Health Consequences in Men Exposed to Sexual Abuse During the War in Croatia and Bosnia," *Journal of Interpersonal Violence* 25 (2010): 191–203.

12. David Finkelhor, Heather Turner, and Richard Ormrod, "Kid's Stuff: The Nature and Impact of Peer and Sibling Violence on Younger and Older Children," *Child Abuse and Neglect* 30 (2006): 1401–1421; Dean Kilpatrick, Benjamin Saunders, and Daniel Smith, *Youth Victimization: Prevalence and Implications* (Washington, DC: National Institute of Justice, 2003); Catherine Grus, "Child Abuse: Correlations with Hostile Attributions," *Journal of Developmental and Behavioral Pediatrics* 24 (2003): 296–298.

13. Noora Ilonen, Minna Piispa, Kirsi Peltonen, and Mikko Oranen, "Exposure to Parental Violence and Outcomes of Child Psychosocial Adjustment," *Violence and Victims* 28 (2013): 3–15.

14. Kim Logio, "Gender, Race, Childhood Abuse, and Body Image Among Adolescents," *Violence Against Women* 9 (2003): 931–955.

15. Mark Shevlin, Martin Dorahy, and Gary Adamson, "Childhood Traumas and Hallucinations: An Analysis of the National Comorbidity Survey," *Journal of Psychiatric Research* 41 (2007): 222–228.

16. Jeanne Kaufman and Cathy Spatz Widom, "Childhood Victimization, Running Away, and Delinquency," *Journal of Research in Crime and Delinquency* 36 (1999): 347–370.

17. N. N. Sarkar and Rina Sarkar, "Sexual Assault on Woman: Its Impact on Her Life and Living in Society," *Sexual and Relationship Therapy* 20 (2005): 407–419.

18. Michael Wiederman, Randy Sansone, and Lori Sansone, "History of Trauma and Attempted Suicide Among Women in a Primary Care Setting," *Violence and Victims* 13 (1998): 3–11; Susan Leslie Bryant and Lillian Range, "Suicidality in College Women Who Were Sexually and Physically Abused and Physically Punished by Parents," *Violence and Victims* 10 (1995): 195–215; William Downs and Brenda Miller, "Relationships Between Experiences of Parental Violence During Childhood and Women's Self-Esteem," *Violence and Victims* 13 (1998): 63–78; Sally Davies-Netley, Michael Hurlburt, and Richard Hough, "Childhood Abuse as a Precursor to Homelessness for Homeless Women with Severe Mental Illness," *Violence and Victims* 11 (1996): 129–142.

19. Jane Siegel and Linda Williams, "Risk Factors for Sexual Victimization of Women," *Violence Against Women* 9 (2003): 902–930.

20. Michael Miner, Jill Klotz Flitter, and Beatrice Robinson, "Association of Sexual Revictimization with Sexuality and Psychological Function," *Journal of Interpersonal Violence* 21 (2006): 503–524.

21. Leana Bouffard and Maria Koeppel, "Understanding the Potential Long-term Physical and Mental Health Consequences of Early Experiences of Victimization," *Justice Quarterly*, first published online October 22, 2012.

22. Lana Stermac and Emily Paradis, "Homeless Women and Victimization: Abuse and Mental Health History Among Homeless Rape Survivors," *Resources for Feminist Research* 28 (2001): 65–81.

23. Gregory Stuart, Todd M. Moore, Kristina Coop Gordon, Susan Ramsey, and Christopher Kahler, "Psychopathology in Women Arrested for Domestic Violence," *Journal of Interpersonal Violence* 21 (2006): 376–389; Caron Zlotnick, Dawn Johnson, and Robert Kohn, "Intimate Partner Violence and Long-Term Psychosocial Functioning in a National Sample of American Women," *Journal of Interpersonal Violence* 21 (2006): 262–275.

24. K. Daniel O'Leary, "Psychological Abuse: A Variable Deserving Critical Attention in Domestic Violence," *Violence and Victims* 14 (1999): 1–21.

25. Ron Acierno, Alyssa Rheingold, Heidi Resnick, and Dean Kilpatrick, "Predictors of Fear of Crime in Older Adults," *Journal of Anxiety Disorders* 18 (2004): 385–396.

26. Mirka Smolej and Janne Kivivuori, "The Relation Between Crime News and Fear of Violence," *Journal of Scandinavian Studies in Criminology and Crime Prevention* 7 (2006): 211–227.

27. Fawn T. Ngo and Raymond Paternoster, "Toward an Understanding of the Emotional and Behavioral Reactions to Stalking: A Partial Test of General Strain Theory," *Crime and Delinquency*, first published online November 7, 2013.

28. Pamela Wilcox Rountree, "A Reexamination of the Crime–Fear Linkage," *Journal of Research in Crime and Delinquency* 35 (1998): 341–372.

29. Robert Davis, Bruce Taylor, and Arthur Lurigio, "Adjusting to Criminal Victimization: The Correlates of Postcrime Distress," *Violence and Victimization* 11 (1996): 21–34.

30. Susan Brison, *Aftermath: Violence and the Remaking of a Self* (Princeton, NJ: Princeton University Press, 2001).

31. Tyler Frederick, Bill McCarthy, and John Hagan, "Perceived Danger and Offending: Exploring the Links Between Violent Victimization and Street Crime," *Violence and Victims* 28 (2013): 16–35.

32. Chris Gibson, Zara Morris, and Kevin Beaver, "Secondary Exposure to Violence During Childhood and Adolescence: Does Neighborhood Context Matter?" *Justice Quarterly* 26 (2009): 30–57.

33. Susan Popkin, Victoria Gwlasda, Dennis Rosenbaum, Jean Amendolla, Wendell Johnson, and Lynn Olson, "Combating Crime in Public Housing: A Qualitative and Quantitative Longitudinal Analysis of the Chicago Housing Authority's Anti-Drug Initiative," *Justice Quarterly* 16 (1999): 519–557.

34. Karen Snedker, "Altruistic and Vicarious Fear of Crime: Fear for Others and Gendered Social Roles," *Sociological Forum* 21 (2006): 163–195.

35. Min Xie and David McDowall, "Escaping Crime: The Effects of Direct and Indirect Victimization on Moving," *Criminology* 46 (2008): 809–840.

36. Smolej and Kivivuori, "The Relation Between Crime News and Fear of Violence."

37. Matthew Lee and Erica DeHart, "The Influence of a Serial Killer on Changes in Fear of Crime and the Use of Protective Measures: A Survey-Based Case Study of Baton Rouge," *Deviant Behavior* 28 (2007): 1–28.

38. Alex R. Piquero, John MacDonald, Adam Dobrin, Leah E. Daigle, and Francis T. Cullen, "Self-Control, Violent Offending, and Homicide Victimization: Assessing the General Theory of Crime," *Journal of Quantitative Criminology* 25 (2005): 55–71.

39. Cathy Spatz Widom, *The Cycle of Violence* (Washington, DC: National Institute of Justice, 1992), p. 1; Amy Reckdenwald, Christina Mancini, and Eric Beauregard, "The Cycle of Violence: Examining the Impact of Maltreatment Early in Life on Adult Offending," *Violence and Victims* 28 (2013): 466–482.

40. Timothy Ireland and Cathy Spatz Widom, *Childhood Victimization and Risk for Alcohol and Drug Arrests* (Washington, DC: National Institute of Justice, 1995).

41. Marie Skubak Tillyer, and Emily M. Wright, "Intimate Partner Violence and the Victim-Offender Overlap" *Journal of Research in Crime and Delinquency*, first published online April 29, 2013.

42. Min Jung Kim, Emiko Tajima, Todd I. Herrenkohl, and Bu Huang, "Early Child Maltreatment, Runaway Youths, and Risk of Delinquency and Victimization in Adolescence: A Mediational Model," *Social Work Research* 33 (2009): 19–28.

43. Brigette Erwin, Elana Newman, Robert McMackin, Carlo Morrissey, and Danny Kaloupek, "PTSD, Malevolent Environment, and Criminality Among Criminally Involved Male Adolescents," *Criminal Justice and Behavior* 27 (2000): 196–215.

44. Jillian J. Turanovic and Travis C. Pratt, "The Consequences of Maladaptive Coping: Integrating General Strain and Self-Control Theories to Specify a Causal Pathway Between Victimization and Offending," *Journal of Quantitative Criminology* 29 (2013): 321–345.

45. Ulrich Orth, Leo Montada, and Andreas Maercker, "Feelings of Revenge, Retaliation Motive, and Posttraumatic Stress Reactions in Crime Victims," *Journal of Interpersonal Violence* 21 (2006): 229–243.

46. Chris Melde, Finn-Aage Esbensen, and Terrance Taylor, "'May Piece Be with You': A Typological Examination of the Fear and Victimization Hypothesis of Adolescent Weapon Carrying," *Justice Quarterly* 26 (2009): 348–376.

47. Charis Kubrin and Ronald Weitzer, "Retaliatory Homicide: Concentrated Disadvantage and Neighborhood Culture," *Social Problems* 50 (2003): 157–180.

48. Christopher Schreck, Eric Stewart, and D. Wayne Osgood, "A Reappraisal of the Overlap of Violent Offenders and Victims," *Criminology* 46 (2008): 872–906.

49. Truman, Langton, and Planty, *Criminal Victimization, 2012.*

50. Pamela Wilcox, Marie Skubak Tillyer, and Bonnie S. Fisher, "Gendered Opportunity? School-Based Adolescent Victimization," *Journal of Research in Crime and Delinquency* 46 (2009): 245–269.

51. Simone Robers, Jana Kemp, Jennifer Truman, and Thomas D. Snyder, *Indicators of School Crime and Safety: 2012*, National Center for Educational Statistics, http://www.bjs.gov/content/pub/pdf/iscs12.pdf (accessed April 2014).

52. Kristin Carbone-Lopez and Janet Lauritsen, "Seasonal Variation in Violent Victimization: Opportunity and the Annual Rhythm of the School Calendar," *Journal of Quantitative Criminology* 29 (2013): 399–422.

53. Sherry Hamby, David Finkelhor, and Heather Turner, "Perpetrator and Victim Gender Patterns for 21 Forms of Youth Victimization in the National Survey of Children's Exposure to Violence," *Violence and Victims* 28 (2013): 915–939.

54. Victoria Titterington, "A Retrospective Investigation of Gender Inequality and Female Homicide Victimization," *Sociological Spectrum* 26 (2006): 205–231.

55. David Finkelhor, Heather Turner, and Richard Ormrod, "Kid's Stuff: The Nature and Impact of Peer and Sibling Violence on Younger and Older Children," *Child Abuse and Neglect* 30 (2006): 1401–1421.

56. Lamar Jordan, "Law Enforcement and the Elderly: A Concern for the 21st Century," *FBI Law Enforcement Bulletin* 71 (2002): 20–24.

57. Data from the National Center for Elder Abuse, 2014, http://www.ncea.aoa.gov/Library/Data/index.aspx#population (accessed April 2014).

58. Tracy Dietz and James Wright, "Age and Gender Differences and Predictors of Victimization of the Older Homeless," *Journal of Elder Abuse and Neglect* 17 (2005): 37–59.

59. Danielle Kuhl, David Warner, and Andrew Wilczak, "Adolescent Violent Victimization and Precocious Union Formation," *Criminology* 50 (2012): 1089–1127.

60. Danielle Kuhl, David Warner, and Andrew Wilczak, "Adolescent Violent Victimization and Precocious Union Formation," *Criminology* 50 (2012): 1089–1127.

61. Karin Wittebrood and Paul Nieuwbeerta, "Criminal Victimization During One's Life Course: The Effects of Previous Victimization and Patterns of Routine Activities," *Journal of Research in Crime and Delinquency* 37 (2000): 91–122; Janet Lauritsen and Kenna Davis Quinet, "Repeat Victimizations Among Adolescents and Young Adults," *Journal of Quantitative Criminology* 11 (1995): 143–163.

62. Marie Skubak Tillyer, Brooke Miller Gialopsos, and Pamela Wilcox, "The Short-Term Repeat Sexual Victimization of Adolescents in School," *Crime and Delinquency*, first published online September 9, 2013.

63. Denise Osborn, Dan Ellingworth, Tim Hope, and Alan Trickett, "Are Repeatedly Victimized Households Different?" *Journal of Quantitative Criminology* 12 (1996): 223–245.

64. Graham Farrell, "Predicting and Preventing Revictimization," in *Crime and Justice: An Annual Review of Research*, Vol. 20, ed. Michael Tonry and David Farrington (Chicago: University of Chicago Press, 1995), pp. 61–126.

65. Ibid., p. 61.

66. David Finkelhor and Nancy Asigian, "Risk Factors for Youth Victimization: Beyond a Lifestyles/Routine Activities Theory Approach," *Violence and Victimization* 11 (1996): 3–19.

67. Graham Farrell, Coretta Phillips, and Ken Pease, "Like Taking Candy: Why Does Repeat Victimization Occur?" *British Journal of Criminology* 35 (1995): 384–399.

68. Bonnie S. Fisher, Leah E. Daigle, and Francis T. Cullen, "What Distinguishes Single from Recurrent Sexual Victims? The Role of Lifestyle-Routine Activities and First-Incident Characteristics," *Justice Quarterly* 27 (2010): 102–129.

69. Graham C. Ousey, Pamela Wilcox, and Bonnie S. Fisher, "Something Old, Something New: Revisiting Competing Hypotheses of the Victimization–Offending Relationship Among Adolescents," *Journal of Quantitative Criminology*, published online July 2010.

70. Christopher Innes and Lawrence Greenfeld, *Violent State Prisoners and Their Victims* (Washington, DC: Bureau of Justice Statistics, 1990).

71. Hans von Hentig, *The Criminal and His Victim: Studies in the Sociobiology of Crime* (New Haven: Yale University Press, 1948), p. 384.

72. Marvin Wolfgang, *Patterns of Criminal Homicide* (Philadelphia: University of Pennsylvania Press, 1958).

73. Menachem Amir, *Patterns in Forcible Rape* (Chicago: University of Chicago Press, 1971).

74. Susan Estrich, *Real Rape* (Cambridge, MA: Harvard University Press, 1987).

75. Martin Daly and Margo Wilson, *Homicide* (New York: Aldine de Gruyter, 1988).

76. Edem Avakame, "Female's Labor Force Participation and Intimate Femicide: An Empirical Assessment of the Backlash Hypothesis," *Violence and Victim* 14 (1999): 277–283.

77. Rosemary Gartner and Bill McCarthy, "The Social Distribution of Femicide in Urban Canada, 1921–1988," *Law and Society Review* 25 (1991): 287–311.

78. Wilcox, Tillyer, and Fisher, "Gendered Opportunity?"

79. Christopher Schreck, Eric Stewart, and Bonnie Fisher, "Self-Control, Victimization, and Their Influence on Risky Lifestyles: A Longitudinal Analysis Using Panel Data," *Journal of Quantitative Criminology* 22 (2006): 319–340.

80. Bonnie Fisher, Francis Cullen, and Michael Turner, *The Sexual Victimization of College Women* (Washington, DC: National Institute of Justice, 2001).

81. Dan Hoyt, Kimberly Ryan, and Mari Cauce, "Personal Victimization in a High-Risk Environment: Homeless and Runaway Adolescents," *Journal of Research in Crime and Delinquency* 36 (1999): 371–392.

82. Kimberly Tyler and Morgan Beal, "The High-Risk Environment of Homeless Young Adults: Consequences for Physical and Sexual Victimization," *Violence and Victims* 25 (2010): 101–115.

83. See, generally, Gary Gottfredson and Denise Gottfredson, *Victimization in Schools* (New York: Plenum Press, 1985).

84. Gary Jensen and David Brownfield, "Gender, Lifestyles, and Victimization: Beyond Routine Activity Theory," *Violence and Victims* 1 (1986): 85–99.

85. Bonnie Fisher, John Sloan, Francis Cullen, and Chunmeng Lu, "Crime in the Ivory Tower: The Level and Sources of Student Victimization," *Criminology* 36 (1998): 671–710.

86. Fisher, Cullen, and Turner, *The Sexual Victimization of College Women.*

87. Elizabeth Reed, Hortensia Amaro, Atsushi Matsumoto, and Debra Kaysen, "The Relation Between Interpersonal Violence and Substance Use Among a Sample of University Students: Examination of the Role of Victim and Perpetrator Substance Use," *Addictive Behaviors* 34 (2009): 316–318.

88. Michael Ezell and Emily Tanner-Smith, "Examining the Role of Lifestyle and Criminal History Variables on the Risk of Homicide Victimization," *Homicide Studies* 13 (2009): 144–173; Rolf Loeber, Mary DeLamatre, George Tita, Jacqueline Cohen, Magda Stouthamer-Loeber, and David Farrington, "Gun Injury and Mortality: The Delinquent Backgrounds of Juvenile Offenders," *Violence and Victim* 14 (1999): 339–351; Adam Dobrin, "The Risk of Offending on Homicide Victimization: A Case Control Study," *Journal of Research in Crime and Delinquency* 38 (2001): 154–173.

89. Loeber et al., "Gun Injury and Mortality"; Dobrin, "The Risk of Offending on Homicide Victimization."

90. James Howell, "Youth Gang Homicides: A Literature Review," *Crime and Delinquency* 45 (1999): 208–241.

91. Alan Lizotte and David Sheppard, *Gun Use by Male Juveniles* (Washington, DC: Office of Juvenile Justice and Delinquency Prevention, 2001); Daneen Deptula and Robert Cohen, "Aggressive, Rejected, and Delinquent Children and Adolescents: A Comparison of Their Friendships," *Aggression and Violent Behavior* 9 (2004): 75–104.

92. Sylvie Mrug, Betsy Hoza, and William Bukowski, "Choosing or Being Chosen by Aggressive-Disruptive Peers: Do They Contribute to Children's Externalizing and Internalizing Problems?" *Journal of Abnormal Child Psychology* 32 (2004): 53–66.

93. Daniel Neller, Robert Denney, Christina Pietz, and R. Paul Thomlinson, "Testing the Trauma Model of Violence," *Journal of Family Violence* 20 (2005): 151–159.

94. Maryse Richards, Reed Larson, and Bobbi Viegas Miller, "Risky and Protective Contexts and Exposure to Violence in Urban African American Young Adolescents," *Journal of Clinical Child and Adolescent Psychology* 33 (2004): 138–148.

95. James Garofalo, "Reassessing the Lifestyle Model of Criminal Victimization," in *Positive Criminology*, ed. Michael Gottfredson and Travis Hirschi (Newbury Park, CA: Sage, 1987), pp. 23–42.

96. Richards, Larson, and Miller, "Risky and Protective Contexts and Exposure to Violence in Urban African American Young Adolescents."

97. Terance Miethe and David McDowall, "Contextual Effects in Models of Criminal Victimization," *Social Forces* 71 (1993): 741–759.

98. Rodney Stark, "Deviant Places: A Theory of the Ecology of Crime," *Criminology* 25 (1987): 893–911.

99. Ibid., p. 902.

100. William Julius Wilson, *The Truly Disadvantaged* (Chicago: University of Chicago Press, 1990); see also Allen Liska and Paul Bellair, "Violent-Crime Rates and Racial Composition: Convergence Over Time," *American Journal of Sociology* 101 (1995): 578–610.

101. Lawrence Cohen and Marcus Felson, "Social Change and Crime Rate Trends: A Routine Activities Approach," *American Sociological Review* 44 (1979): 588–608.

102. Teresa LaGrange, "The Impact of Neighborhoods, Schools, and Malls on the Spatial Distribution of Property Damage," *Journal of Research in Crime and Delinquency* 36 (1999): 393–422.

103. Melanie Wellsmith and Amy Burrell, "The Influence of Purchase Price and Ownership Levels on Theft Targets: The Example of Domestic Burglary," *British Journal of Criminology* 45 (2005): 741–764.

104. Denise Gottfredson and David Soulé, "The Timing of Property Crime, Violent Crime, and Substance Use Among Juveniles," *Journal of Research in Crime and Delinquency* 42 (2005): 110–120.

105. Georgina Hammock and Deborah Richardson, "Perceptions of Rape: The Influence of Closeness of Relationship, Intoxication, and Sex of Participant," *Violence and Victimization* 12 (1997): 237–247.

106. Wittebrood and Nieuwbeerta, "Criminal Victimization during One's Life Course," pp. 112–113.

107. Brandon Welsh and David Farrington, "Surveillance for Crime Prevention in Public Space: Results and Policy Choices in Britain and America," *Criminology and Public Policy* 3 (2004): 701–730.

108. Richard Timothy Coupe and Laurence Blake, "The Effects of Patrol Workloads and Response Strength on Arrests at Burglary Emergencies," *Journal of Criminal Justice* 33 (2005): 239–255.

109. Don Weatherburn, Bronwyn Lind, and Simon Ku, "'Hotbeds of Crime?' Crime and Public Housing in Urban Sydney," *Crime and Delinquency* 45 (1999): 256–271.

110. Andy Hochstetler, "Opportunities and Decisions: Interactional Dynamics in Robbery and Burglary Groups," *Criminology* 39 (2001): 737–763.

111. Richard Felson, "Routine Activities and Involvement in Violence as Actor, Witness, or Target," *Violence and Victimization* 12 (1997): 209–223.

112. Lawrence Cohen, Marcus Felson, and Kenneth Land, "Property Crime Rates in the United States: A Macrodynamic Analysis, 1947–1977, with Ex-ante Forecasts for the Mid-1980s," *American Journal of Sociology* 86 (1980): 90–118.

113. Steven Messner, Lawrence Raffalovich, and Richard McMillan, "Economic Deprivation and Changes in Homicide Arrest Rates for White and Black Youths, 1967–1998: A National Time Series Analysis," *Criminology* 39 (2001): 591–614.

114. Melanie Wellsmith and Amy Burrell, "The Influence of Purchase Price and Ownership Levels on Theft Targets: The Example of Domestic Burglary," *British Journal of Criminology* 45 (2005): 741–764.

115. Terance Miethe and Robert Meier, *Crime and Its Social Context: Toward an Integrated Theory of Offenders, Victims, and Situations* (Albany, NY: State University of New York Press, 1994).

116. Felson, "Routine Activities and Involvement in Violence as Actor, Witness, or Target."

117. Patricia Resnick, "Psychological Effects of Victimization: Implications for the Criminal Justice System," *Crime and Delinquency* 33 (1987): 468–478.

118. Dean Kilpatrick, Benjamin Saunders, Lois Veronen, Connie Best, and Judith Von, "Criminal Victimization: Lifetime Prevalence, Reporting to Police, and Psychological Impact," *Crime and Delinquency* 33 (1987): 479–489.

119. Cassidy Gutner, Shireen Rizvi, Candice Monson, and Patricia Resick, "Changes in Coping Strategies, Relationship to the Perpetrator, and Posttraumatic Distress in Female Crime Victims," *Journal of Traumatic Stress* 19 (2006): 813–823.

120. U.S. Department of Justice, *Report of the President's Task Force on Victims of Crime* (Washington, DC: U.S. Government Printing Office, 1983).

121. Ibid., pp. 2–10; "Review on Victims/ Witnesses of Crime," *Massachusetts Lawyers Weekly*, April 25, 1983, p. 26.

122. Robert Davis, *Crime Victims: Learning How to Help Them* (Washington, DC: National Institute of Justice, 1987).

123. Michael M. O'Hear, "Punishment, Democracy, and Victims," *Federal Sentencing Reporter* 19 (2006): 1.

124. Peter Finn and Beverly Lee, *Establishing a Victim-Witness Assistance Program* (Washington, DC: U.S. Government Printing Office, 1988).

125. This section leans heavily on Albert Roberts, "Delivery of Services to Crime Victims: A National Survey," *American Journal of Orthopsychiatry* 6 (1991): 128–137; see also Albert Roberts, *Helping Crime Victims: Research, Policy, and Practice* (Newbury Park, CA: Sage, 1990).

126. This section leans heavily on Albert Roberts, "Delivery of Services to Crime Victims: A National Survey," *American Journal of Orthopsychiatry* 6 (1991): 128–137; see also Albert Roberts, *Helping Crime Victims: Research, Policy, and Practice* (Newbury Park, CA: Sage, 1990).

127. National Association of Crime Victim Compensation Boards, http://www.nacvcb .org (accessed April 2014).

128. National Association of VOCA Assistance Administrators, VOCA Funding, 2014, http:// navaa.org/budget/ (accessed April 2014).

129. Karen Rich and Patrick Seffrin, "Police Officers' Collaboration with Rape Victim Advocates: Barriers and Facilitators," *Violence and Victims* 28 (2013): 681–696.

130. Rebecca Campbell, "Rape Survivors' Experiences with the Legal and Medical Systems: Do Rape Victim Advocates Make a Difference?" *Violence Against Women* 12 (2006): 30–45.

131. Debra Whitcomb, *When the Victim Is a Child* (Washington, DC: National Institute of Justice, 1992), p. 33.

132. Ulrich Orth and Andreas Maercker, "Do Trials of Perpetrators Retraumatize Crime Victims?" *Journal of Interpersonal Violence* 19 (2004): 212–228.

133. Pater Jaffe, Marlies Sudermann, Deborah Reitzel, and Steve Killip, "An Evaluation of a Secondary School Primary Prevention Program on Violence in Intimate Relationships," *Violence and Victims* 7 (1992): 129–145.

134. Good Samaritans Program, http://www.ojp .usdoj.gov/ovc/publications/infores/ Good_Samaritans/ (accessed April 2014).

135. Andrew Karmen, "Victim–Offender Reconciliation Programs: Pro and Con," *Perspectives of the American Probation and Parole Association* 20 (1996): 11–14.

136. Information provided by the National Center for Victims of Crime, http://www .victimsofcrime.org/ (accessed April 2014).

137. Rachelle Hong, "Nothing to Fear: Establishing an Equality of Rights for Crime Victims Through the Victims' Rights Amendment," *Notre Dame Journal of Legal Ethics and Public Policy* (2002): 207–225; see also *Payne v. Tennessee*, 111 S.Ct. 2597, 115 L.Ed.2d 720 (1991)

138. Robert Davis and Barbara Smith, "The Effects of Victim Impact Statements on Sentencing Decisions: A Test in an Urban Setting," *Justice Quarterly* 11 (1994): 453–469; Edna Erez and Pamela Tontodonato, "The Effect of Victim Participation in Sentencing on Sentence Outcome," *Criminology* 28 (1990): 451–474.

139. Joel Caplan, "Parole Release Decisions: Impact of Positive and Negative Victim and Nonvictim Input on a Representative Sample of Parole-Eligible Inmates," *Violence and Victims* 25 (2010): 224–242.

140. Douglas E. Beloof, "Constitutional Implications of Crime Victims as Participants," *Cornell Law Review* 88 (2003): 282–305.

141. James Garofalo and Maureen McLeod, *Improving the Use and Effectiveness of Neighborhood Watch Programs* (Washington, DC: National Institute of Justice, 1988).

142. Peter Finn, *Block Watches Help Crime Victims in Philadelphia* (Washington, DC: National Institute of Justice, 1986).

143. Peter Finn, *Block Watches Help Crime Victims in Philadelphia* (Washington, DC: National Institute of Justice, 1986).

144. Sara Flaherty and Austin Flaherty, *Victims and Victims' Risk* (New York: Chelsea House, 1998).

145. Pamela Wilcox Rountree and Kenneth Land, "Burglary Victimization, Perceptions of Crime Risk, and Routine Activities: A Multilevel Analysis Across Seattle Neighborhoods and Census Tracts," *Journal of Research in Crime and Delinquency* 33 (1996): 1147–1180.

146. Leslie Kennedy, "Going It Alone: Unreported Crime and Individual Self-Help," *Journal of Criminal Justice* 16 (1988): 403–413.

147. Ronald Clarke, "Situational Crime Prevention: Its Theoretical Basis and Practical Scope," in *Annual Review of Criminal Justice Research*, ed. Michael Tonry and Norval Morris (Chicago: University of Chicago Press, 1983).

148. See, generally, Dennis P. Rosenbaum, Arthur J. Lurigio, and Robert C. Davis, *The Prevention of Crime: Social and Situational Strategies* (Belmont, CA: Wadsworth, 1998).

149. Andrew Buck, Simon Hakim, and George Rengert, "Burglar Alarms and the Choice Behavior of Burglars," *Journal of Criminal Justice* 21 (1993): 497–507; for an opposing view, see James Lynch and David Cantor, "Ecological and Behavioral Influences on Property Victimization at Home: Implications for Opportunity Theory," *Journal of Research in Crime and Delinquency* 29 (1992): 335–362.

150. Alan Lizotte, "Determinants of Completing Rape and Assault," *Journal of Quantitative Criminology* 2 (1986): 213–217.

151. Polly Marchbanks, Kung-Jong Lui, and James Mercy, "Risk of Injury from Resisting Rape," *American Journal of Epidemiology* 132 (1990): 540–549.

152. Caroline Wolf Harlow, *Robbery Victims* (Washington, DC: Bureau of Justice Statistics, 1987).

153. Gary Kleck, "Guns and Violence: An Interpretive Review of the Field," *Social Pathology* 1 (1995): 12–45, at 17.

154. Gary Kleck, "Guns and Violence: An Interpretive Review of the Field," *Social Pathology* 1 (1995): 12–45, at 17.

155. Gary Kleck, "Rape and Resistance," *Social Problems* 37 (1990): 149–162.

156. Jongyeon Tark and Gary Kleck, "Resisting Crime: The Effects of Victim Action on the Outcomes of Crimes," *Criminology* 42 (2004): 861–909.

157. See Frank Carrington, "Victim's Rights Litigation: A Wave of the Future," in *Perspectives on Crime Victims*, ed. Burt Galaway and Joe Hudson (St. Louis: Mosby, 1981).

158. National Center for Victims of Crime, http://www.victimsofcrime.org/ (accessed April 2014).

159. "Council Framework Decision of 15 March 2001 on the Standing of Victims in Criminal Proceedings," http://eur-lex .europa.eu/LexUriServ/LexUriServ.do?uri= OJ:L:2001:082:0001:0004:EN:PDF (accessed April 2014); "Proposal for a Council Directive on Compensation to Crime Victims," http://ec.europa.eu/ civiljustice/comp_crime_victim/comp_ crime_victim_ec_en.htm (accessed April 2014).

160. U.S. Department of Justice, Dru Sjodin National Sex Offender Public Registry, http://www.nsopr.gov (accessed April 2014).

THEORIES OF CRIME CAUSATION

An important goal of criminologists is to create valid and accurate theories of crime causation. A theory can be defined as an abstract statement that explains why certain phenomena or things do (or do not) happen. A valid theory must (a) have the ability to predict future occurrences or observations of the phenomenon in question and (b) have the ability to be validated or tested through experiment or some other form of empirical observation. So, for example, if a theory states that watching violent TV shows leads to aggressive behavior, it can be considered valid only if careful and empirically sound tests can prove that kids who watch a lot of violent TV in the present will become violent in the future.

Criminologists have sought to collect vital facts about crime and interpret them in a scientifically meaningful fashion. By developing empirically verifiable statements, or hypotheses, and organizing them into theories of crime causation, they hope to identify the causes of crime.

Since the late nineteenth century, criminological theory has pointed to various underlying causes of crime. The earliest theories generally attributed crime to a single underlying cause: atypical body build, genetic abnormality, insanity, physical anomalies, socialization, or poverty. More recent theoretical efforts are more dynamic, incorporating multiple personal and social factors into a complex web to explain the onset, continuation, and eventual desistance from a criminal career.

In this section, theories of crime causation are grouped into six chapters. Chapters 4 and 5 focus on theories that view crime as based on individual traits. They hold that crime is either a free will choice made by an individual, a function of personal psychological or biological abnormality, or both. Chapters 6, 7, and 8 investigate theories based in sociology and political economy. These theories portray crime as a function of the structure, process, and conflicts of social living. Chapter 9 is devoted to theories that combine or integrate a number of concepts that explain criminal behavior over the life course, otherwise known as developmental views of crime.

RATIONAL CHOICE THEORY

4

I n 2013, James "Doug" Cassity (pictured arriving at federal court) and five of his associates were sentenced to federal prison for their role in a Ponzi-like prepaid funeral scheme that victimized some 97,000 customers in at least 16 states. The scheme caused more than $450 million in losses, smaller or nonexistent death benefits for families at their most vulnerable, and huge profits that lined the pockets of the defendants.

While there are laws to help ensure that these advance payments are available when they're needed, protections vary widely from state to state, sometimes providing a window of opportunity for unscrupulous operators. Taking advantage of this, Cassity and his Missouri-based company National Prearranged Services Inc. (NPS) devised and ran a scheme to defraud purchasers of prearranged funeral contracts.

How did they pull off their scheme? After discussing what the customer wanted, a price would be agreed upon and payment accepted. NPS would make arrangements with the customer-designated funeral home. In accordance with state law, the funds would be placed with a third party—a financial institution that would put the funds into a trust that could be only used for safe investments (like government-backed securities) or a life insurance company that would put the funds into a life insurance policy in the name of the customer. However, Cassity and his co-conspirators didn't put all of the funds from customers into a trust or life insurance policy, but instead altered application documents, for example by changing deposit amounts, naming themselves as a beneficiary, or converting whole life insurance policies to term life. They then used the money for unauthorized purposes such as risky investments, payments for existing funeral claims, and personal enrichment.

The complex case—investigated by three federal agencies, a number of state regulatory agencies, and the Department of Justice—began in 2008 and ended five years later in November 2013, when Cassity and his co-conspirators were finally brought to justice.[1]

While some crimes seem impulsive and spontaneous, others involve law violators such as Cassity who carefully plan their activities, buy the proper equipment, try to avoid detection, and then attempt to squirrel away their criminal profits in some hidden bank account. Their calculated actions suggest that the choice to commit crime involves rational and detailed planning and decision making, designed to maximize personal gain and avoid capture and punishment. Some criminologists go as far as suggesting that the source of all criminal violations—even those that seem at first glance unplanned and spontaneous, such as vandalizing property or getting involved in a brawl—rests upon at least some sort of rational decision making with a clear motivation: greed, revenge, need, anger, lust, jealousy, thrill-seeking, or vanity. But the final decision to commit a crime is only made after the potential offender carefully weighs the potential benefits and consequences of their planned action and decides that the benefits of crime are greater than its consequences:

- The jealous suitor concludes that the risk of punishment is worth the satisfaction of punching a rival in the nose.
- The greedy shopper considers the chance of apprehension by store detectives so small that she takes a "five-finger discount" on a new sweater.
- The drug dealer concludes that the huge profit from a single shipment of cocaine far outweighs the possible costs of apprehension.
- The schoolyard bully carefully selects his next victim—someone who is weak, unpopular, and probably won't fight back.
- The college student downloads a program that allows her to illegally copy music onto her iPod.

But can all crimes be a function of planning and calculation? While we can easily assume that white-collar criminals such as James Cassity and organized crime figures use planning, organization, and rational decision making to commit their crimes, can we also assume that such common crimes as theft, fraud, and even murder are a function of detailed planning and decision making? Before the college students take music off the Web, they must first not only acquire expertise and skill, but also decide that the money they save is worth the risk of detection. But what about the drunken college student who gets into a bar fight? Are his actions calculated and shrewd or random and senseless? Even if inebriated, would he have assaulted someone much larger and muscular who would fight back and injure him severely? Or is the decision to fight only made after calculating the costs and benefits of the attack? Some criminologists would answer that they believe all criminal behavior, no matter how destructive or seemingly irresponsible, is actually a matter of thought and decision making. As a group, they are referred to as rational choice theorists.

This chapter reviews the philosophical underpinnings of rational choice theory, tracing it back to the classical school of criminology. We then turn to more recent theoretical models that flow from the concept of choice. These models hold that because criminals are rational, their behavior can be controlled or deterred by the fear of punishment; desistance can then be explained by a growing and intense fear of criminal sanctions. These views include situational crime control, general deterrence theory, specific deterrence theory, and incapacitation. Finally, the chapter briefly reviews how choice theory has influenced criminal justice policy.

THE DEVELOPMENT OF RATIONAL CHOICE

During the early Middle Ages (1200–1400), superstition and fear of satanic possession dominated thinking. People who violated social norms or religious practices were believed to be witches or possessed by demons and not rational decision makers. St. Thomas Aquinas (1225–1274) argued that there was a God-given "natural law" that was based on people's natural tendency to do good. People who were evil were manifesting original sin and a fall from grace, similar to that experienced by Adam and Eve when they were expelled from the Garden of Eden.

The prescribed method for dealing with the possessed was burning at the stake, a practice that survived into the seventeenth century. Beginning in the mid-thirteenth century, the jurisdiction of central governments reached a significantly broader range of social behaviors. Human problems and conflicts began to be dealt with in a formalized and legal manner.[2] Nonetheless, superstition and harsh punishments did not end quickly. The authorities were on guard against Satan's offspring, who engaged in acts ranging from witchcraft to robbery. Between 1581 and 1590, Nicholas Remy, head of the Inquisition in the French province of Lorraine, ordered 900 sorcerers and witches burned to death; likewise, Peter Binsfield, the bishop of the German city of Trier, ordered the death of 6,500 people. An estimated 100,000 people were prosecuted throughout Europe for witchcraft during the sixteenth and seventeenth centuries. It was also commonly believed that some families produced offspring who were unsound or unstable and that social misfits were inherently damaged by reason of their "inferior blood."[3] It was common practice to use cruel tortures to extract confessions, and those convicted of violent or theft crimes suffered extremely harsh penalties, including whipping, branding, maiming, and execution. Almost all felons were punished with death; the law made little distinction between thieves and murderers.

This rather fantastical vision of deviant behavior and its control began to wane as new insights were developed about human nature and behavior during the Renaissance.

One influential authority, philosopher Thomas Hobbes (1588–1678), suggested the existence of a "social contract" between people and the state: people naturally pursue their own self-interests but are rational enough to realize that selfishness will produce social chaos, so they agree to give up their own selfish interests as long as everyone else does the same thing. Not all agree to the social contract, and therefore the state became empowered with the right to use force to maintain the contract.

Development of Classical Criminology

LO1 Describe the development of rational choice theory

During the eighteenth century **Enlightenment** period, social philosophers such as Jeremy Bentham (1748–1833) began to embrace the view that human behavior was a result of rational thought processes.

According to Bentham's "utilitarian calculus," people choose to act when, after weighing costs and benefits, they believe that their actions will bring them an increase in pleasure and a reduction of pain. It stands to reason that criminal behavior could be eliminated or controlled if would-be law violators could be convinced that the pain of punishment exceeds the benefits of crime.[4] The purpose of law is to produce and support the total happiness of the community it serves. Because punishment is in itself harmful, its existence is justified only if it promises to prevent greater evil than it creates. Punishment, therefore, has four main objectives:

1. To prevent all criminal offenses
2. When it cannot prevent a crime, to convince the offender to commit a less serious crime
3. To ensure that a criminal uses no more force than is necessary
4. To prevent crime as cheaply as possible[5]

Cesare Beccaria

The development of rational classical criminology is most closely identified with the thoughts of Italian social philosopher Cesare Beccaria (1738–1794) and his famous treatise "On Crimes and Punishment" in which he called for fair and certain punishment to deter crime. Beccaria believed people are egotistical and self-centered, and therefore they must be motivated by the fear of punishment, which provides a tangible motive for them to obey the law and suppress the "despotic spirit" that resides in every person.[6] He suggested that (a) people choose all behavior, including criminal behavior; (b) their choices are designed to bring them pleasure and reduce pain; (c) criminal choices can be controlled by fear of punishment; and (d) the *more severe, certain, and swift the punishment*, the greater its ability to control criminal behavior.

According to Beccaria, punishment must be proportional to the seriousness of crime; if not, people would be encouraged to commit more serious offenses. For example, if robbery, rape, and murder were all punished by death, robbers or rapists would have little reason to refrain from killing their victims to eliminate them as witnesses to the crime. Today, this is referred to as the concept of **marginal deterrence**—if petty offenses were subject to the same punishment as more serious crimes, offenders would choose the more serious crime because the resulting punishment would be about the same.[7]

Beccaria also suggested that the extremely harsh punishments of the day and routine use of torture were inappropriate and excessive. To deter crime, the pain of punishment must be administered in a fair, balanced, and proportionate amount, just enough to counterbalance the pleasure obtained from crime. Beccaria stated his famous theorem like this:

> In order for punishment not to be in every instance, an act of violence of one or many against a private citizen, it must be essentially public, prompt, necessary, the least possible in the given circumstances, proportionate to the crimes, and dictated by the laws.[8]

To read more about Beccaria, go to **http://www.iep .utm.edu/beccaria/**.
How have Beccaria's ideas influenced contemporary criminal law in the United States?

Classical Criminology

The writings of Beccaria and his followers form the core of what today is referred to as **classical criminology**. As originally conceived in the eighteenth century, classical criminology theory had several basic elements:

- In every society, people have free will to choose criminal or lawful solutions to meet their needs or settle their problems.
- Criminal solutions can be very attractive because for little effort they hold the promise of a huge payoff.

Enlightenment A philosophical, intellectual, and cultural movement of the seventeenth and eighteenth centuries that stressed reason, logic, criticism, education, and freedom of thought over dogma and superstition.

marginal deterrence The concept that a penalty for a crime may prompt commission of a marginally more severe crime because that crime receives the same magnitude of punishment as the original one.

classical criminology Eighteenth-century social thinkers believed that criminals choose to commit crime and that crime can be controlled by judicious punishment.

- A person will choose not to commit crime only if he or she believes that the pain of expected punishment is greater than the promise of reward. This is the principle of deterrence.
- In order to be an effective crime deterrent, punishment must be severe, certain, and swift enough to convince potential criminals that "crime does not pay."

This classical perspective influenced penal practices for more than 200 years. The law was made proportionate to crime so that the most serious offenses earned the harshest punishments. Executions were still widely used but slowly began to be employed for only the most serious crimes. The catchphrase was "let the punishment fit the crime."

Beccaria's ideas and writings inspired social thinkers to believe that criminals choose to commit crime and that crime can be controlled by judicious punishment. His vision was widely accepted throughout Europe and the United States.[9]

This vision was embraced by France's post-revolutionary Constituent Assembly (1789) in its Declaration of the Rights of Man:

> [T]he law has the right to prohibit only actions harmful to society.... The law shall inflict only such punishments as are strictly and clearly necessary ... no person shall be punished except by virtue of a law enacted and promulgated previous to the crime and applicable to its terms.

Similarly, a prohibition against cruel and unusual punishment was incorporated in the Eighth Amendment to the U.S. Constitution.

Beccaria's writings have been credited as the basis of the elimination of torture and severe punishment in the nineteenth century. The practice of incarcerating criminals and structuring prison sentences to fit the severity of crime was a reflection of his classical criminology.

By the end of the nineteenth century, the popularity of the classical approach began to decline, and by the middle of the twentieth century, this perspective was neglected by mainstream criminologists. During this period, criminologists focused on internal and external factors—poverty, IQ, education, home life—which were believed to be the true causes of criminality. Because these conditions could not be easily manipulated, the concept of punishing people for behaviors beyond their control seemed both foolish and cruel. Although classical principles still controlled the way police, courts, and correctional agencies operated, most criminologists rejected classical criminology as an explanation of criminal behavior.

Contemporary Choice Theory Emerges

Beginning in the mid-1970s, there was renewed interest in the classical approach to crime. First, the rehabilitation of known criminals came under attack. According to liberal criminology, if crime was caused by some social or psychological problem, such as poverty, then crime rates could be reduced by providing good jobs and economic opportunities. Despite some notable efforts to provide

CLASSICAL THEORY

famous criminologists

ORIGIN About 1764

FOUNDERS Cesare Beccaria, Jeremy Bentham

MOST IMPORTANT WORKS Beccaria, *On Crimes and Punishments* (1764); Bentham, *Moral Calculus* (1789)

CORE IDEAS People choose to commit crime after weighing the benefits and costs of their actions. Crime can be deterred by certain, severe, and swift punishment.

MODERN OUTGROWTHS Rational choice theory, routine activities theory, general deterrence theory, specific deterrence, incapacitation

Portrait of Cesare Bonesana Beccaria by Eliseo Sala/Pinacoteca Ambrosiana, Milan, Italy/De Agostini Picture Library/© Veneranda Biblioteca Ambrosiana - Milano/Bridgeman Art Library

DEI DELITTI
E
DELLE PENE

EDIZIONE SESTA
Di nuovo corretta ed accresciuta

In rebus quibuscumque difficilioribus non expectandum, ut quis simul & serat, & metat, sed praeparatione opus est, ut per gradus maturescant. Bacon Serm. fidel nu XLV.

HARLEM
MDCCLXVI.

Universal Images Group/Art Resource, NY

The title page of the treatise *Dei delitti e delle pene* (*On Crimes and Punishments*, 6th edition, 1766), by Italian jurist, philosopher, and politician Cesare Beccaria (1738–1794).

such opportunities, a number of national surveys (the best known being Robert Martinson's "What Works?") failed to find examples of rehabilitation programs that prevented future criminal activity.[10] A well-publicized book, *Beyond Probation*, by Charles Murray and Louis Cox, went as far as suggesting that punishment-oriented programs could suppress future criminality much more effectively than those that relied on rehabilitation and treatment efforts.[11]

A significant increase in the reported crime rate, as well as serious disturbances in the nation's prisons, frightened the general public. The media depicted criminals as callous and dangerous rather than as needy people deserving of public sympathy. Some criminologists began to suggest that it made more sense to frighten these cold calculators with severe punishments than to waste public funds by futilely trying to improve entrenched social conditions linked to crime, such as poverty.[12]

Thinking About Crime

In the 1970s, a number of criminologists began producing books and monographs expounding the theme that criminals are rational actors who plan their crimes, fear punishment, and deserve to be penalized for their misdeeds. In a 1975 book that came to symbolize renewed interest in classical views, *Thinking about Crime*, political scientist James Q. Wilson debunked the view that crime was a function of external forces, such as poverty, that could be altered by government programs. Instead, he argued, efforts should be made to reduce criminal opportunity by deterring would-be offenders and incarcerating known criminals. People who are likely to commit crime, he maintained, lack inhibition against misconduct, value the excitement and thrills of breaking the law, have a low stake in conformity, and are willing to take greater chances than the average person. If they could be convinced that their actions will bring severe punishment, only the totally irrational would be willing to engage in crime.[13] Wilson made this famous observation:

Wicked people exist. Nothing avails except to set them apart from innocent people. And many people, neither wicked nor innocent, but watchful, dissembling, and calculating of their chances, ponder our reaction to wickedness as a clue to what they might profitably do.[14]

Here Wilson is saying that unless we react forcefully to crime, those "sitting on the fence" will get a clear message—crime pays.

To read a famous talk given by James Wilson, "Two Nations," the 1997 Francis Boyer lecture delivered at the annual dinner of the American Enterprise Institute, visit **http://www.aei.org/article/society-and-culture/two-nations-speech/**.

Wilson says "Religion, independent of social class, reduces deviance." Do you agree?

Impact on Crime Control Wilson's book was part of the conservative shift in U.S. crime control policy in the 1980s that led to tough new laws creating mandatory prison sentences for many different crimes, including drug dealing. There was a prison construction boom and the nation's prison population skyrocketed.[15] A disproportionate number of young minority men were locked up for drug law violations; more than half of the prison population is now African American or Hispanic.[16] The "get tough" attitude was buoyed by the fact that as the prison population grew to new heights, the crime rate has been in a steep decline. To some this meant that a "lock 'em up" correctional policy can produce markedly lower crime rates. To others, it was an abandonment of the liberal rehabilitation and treatment philosophy.[17]

Even if the death penalty were an effective deterrent, some critics believe it presents ethical problems that make its use morally dubious. For more information about what the American Civil Liberties Union has to say, visit **https://www.aclu.org/capital-punishment**.

Do you agree with the ACLU positions on capital punishment?

THE CONCEPTS OF RATIONAL CHOICE

LO2 Discuss the most important concepts of rational choice theory

From these roots, a more contemporary version of classical theory has evolved, referred to as **rational choice theory**. It is based on the premise that criminal decision making is rational and coherent, not spontaneous or impulsive.[18] The decision to commit crime is shaped by human emotions and thought processes, influenced by social relationships, individual traits and capabilities, and environmental characteristics. So this new version of rational choice theory assumes that human behavior is both "willful and determined."[19]

According to the contemporary rational choice approach, law-violating behavior occurs when an offender decides to risk breaking the law after considering both personal factors (i.e., the need for money, revenge, thrills, and entertainment) and situational factors (i.e., how well a target is protected and the efficiency of the local police force). People who believe that the risks of crime outweigh the rewards may decide to go straight. If they think they are

rational choice theory The view that crime is a function of a decision-making process in which the potential offender weighs the potential costs and benefits of an illegal act.

likely to be arrested and punished, they are more likely to seek treatment and turn their lives around than risk criminal activities.[20]

Why Crime?

The core premise of rational choice theory is that people choose crime if the circumstances are right. Though the consequences can be painful, costly, and embarrassing, for some people choosing crime is actually an easy decision to make. Take adolescents, who regularly violate the law. The criminal lifestyle fits well with this group, whose membership routinely organize their life around risk taking and partying. Crimes can provide money for drugs and alcohol and serve as an ideal method for displaying courage and fearlessness to one's running mates. Rather than create overwhelming social problems, a criminal way of life can be extremely beneficial, helping kids overcome the problems and stress they face in their daily lives.

Crime also can help some people, especially teens, achieve a sense of control or mastery over their environment. Adolescents in particular may find themselves feeling out of control because society limits their opportunities and resources.[21] Antisocial behavior gives them the opportunity to exert control over their own lives and destinies by helping them avoid situations they find uncomfortable or repellant (e.g., running away from an abusive home) and can help them obtain resources for desired activities and commodities (e.g., stealing or selling drugs to buy stylish outfits).[22] Crime may also help them boost their self-esteem by attacking perceived enemies (e.g., they vandalize the property of an adult who has called the cops on them). Drinking and drug taking may help some kids ward off depression and compensate for a lack of positive experiences; they learn how to self-medicate themselves. Some, angry at their mistreatment, may turn to violence to satisfy a desire for revenge or retaliation.[23]

Engaging in risky behavior helps some people feel alive and competent. Some turn to substance abuse to increase their sense of personal power, to become more assertive, and reduce tension and anxiety.[24] Others embrace a deviant lifestyle to compensate for their feelings of powerlessness or ordinariness. There is also evidence that antisocial acts can provide positive solutions to problems. Violent kids, for example, may have learned that being aggressive with others is a good means to control the situation

and get what they want; counterattacks may be one means of controlling people who are treating them poorly.[25] So while most of us see crime as a poor choice that can result in many unhappy and unwanted consequences, for some people choosing crime can bring desired social, economic, and psychic benefits; it can be a good choice despite its consequences.

Choosing Crime

Even those who decide to enter a criminal way of life do not commit crime all the time. People who commit crime go to school, church, or work, they have family time, engage in romances, play sports, and go to movies. Why do they choose to commit a particular crime at a particular time?

Before choosing to commit a crime, **reasoning criminals** evaluate the risk of apprehension, the seriousness of expected punishment, the potential value of the criminal enterprise, and their immediate need for criminal gain; their behavior is systematic and selective. For example, burglars choose targets based on their value, novelty, and resale potential. A piece of electronic gear such as the newest iPhone or iPad may be a prime target, because it has not yet saturated the market and still retains high value.[26]

Risk evaluations may cover a wide range of topics: What's the chance of getting caught? How difficult will it be to commit the crime? Is the profit worth the effort? Should I risk committing crime in my own neighborhood where I know the territory, or is it worth traveling to a strange place in order to increase my profits?[27]

People who decide to get involved in crime weigh up the chances of arrest (based on their past experiences), plus the subjective psychic rewards of crime including the excitement and social status it brings and perceived opportunities for easy gains. If the rewards are great, the perceived risk small, and the excitement high, the likelihood of committing additional crimes increases.[28] Successful thieves say they will do it again in the future; past experience has taught them the rewards of illegal behavior.[29]

Criminals, then, are people who share the same ambitions as conventional citizens but have decided to cut corners and use illegal means to achieve their goals. Many criminal offenders retain conventional American values of striving for success, material attainment, and hard work.[30] Even drug dealers express motivations not dissimilar from the average citizen: they are upwardly mobile, scrambling around to obtain their "piece of the pie."[31] If they commit crime, it is because they have chosen an illegal path to obtain the goals that might otherwise have been out of reach.

Choosing Noncrime Considering its benefits, why do most at-risk people choose not to commit crime? While crime may provide short-run solutions that are appealing to adolescents, it becomes less attractive as a long-term answer to personal problems. The decision to forgo crime and seek

reasoning criminals According to the rational choice approach, law-violating behavior occurs when an offender decides to risk breaking the law after considering both personal factors (such as the need for money, revenge, thrills, and entertainment) and situational factors (how well a target is protected and the efficiency of the local police force).

other means to solve problems may occur when those who contemplate crime realize that risks outweigh rewards:

- They stand a good chance of being caught and punished.
- They begin to fear the consequences of punishment.
- They learn that crime rarely pays as well as they thought.
- They risk losing the respect of their peers, damaging their reputations, and experiencing feelings of guilt or shame.[32]
- They grasp the fact that the risk of apprehension outweighs the profit and/or pleasure of crime.[33]

These issues escalate as people mature and begin to appreciate the dangers of using crime to solve problems.[34] Going to a drunken frat party may sound appealing to sophomores who want to improve their social life, but the risks involved to safety and reputation make such parties off limits as people grow older. As people mature, their thinking extends farther into the future, and risky behavior is a threat to long-range plans.

Offense and Offender

Rational choice theorists view crime as both offense- and offender-specific.[35] That a crime is **offense-specific** means that offenders will react selectively to the characteristics of an individual criminal act. Take for instance the decision to commit a burglary. The thought process might include:

- Evaluating the target yield
- Probability of security devices
- Police patrol effectiveness
- Ease of escape
- Effort needed to dispose of stolen merchandise
- Presence of occupants
- Neighbors who might notice a break-in
- Presence of guard dogs
- Presence of escape routes
- Entry points and exits

The fact that a crime is **offender-specific** means that criminals are not robots who engage in unthinking, unplanned random acts of antisocial behavior. Before deciding to commit crime, individuals must decide whether they have the prerequisites to commit a successful criminal act. These might include evaluation of:

- Whether they possess the necessary skills to commit the crime
- Their immediate need for money or other valuables
- Whether legitimate financial alternatives to crime exist, such as a high-paying job
- Whether they have available resources to commit the crime
- Their fear of expected apprehension and punishment
- Availability of alternative criminal acts, such as selling drugs
- Physical ability, including health, strength, and dexterity

Note the distinction made here between crime and criminality.[36] Crime is an event; **criminality** is a personal trait. Professional criminals do not commit crime all the time, and even ordinary citizens may, on occasion, violate the law. Some people considered high risk because they are indigent or disturbed may never violate the law, whereas others who are seemingly affluent and well adjusted may risk criminal behavior given enough provocation and/or opportunity. What conditions promote crime and enhance criminality?

Structuring Criminality

LO3 Analyze the process in which offenders structure criminality

The decision to commit crime is shaped by both personal factors and situational conditions. Time, place, audience, guardianship, and other factors all play a role in criminal decision making.

Analysis of the situational factors that draw people into criminal events have identified peers and guardianship, thrills and excitement, economic opportunity, learning and experience, and knowledge of criminal techniques as being among the most important.

Peers and Guardianship Guardianship plays an important role in criminal decision making. Monitoring by parents reduces the likelihood kids will commit crime; hanging out with adolescent friends increases the risk.[37] Kids are more likely to choose crime when they are drinking with their buddies, in a public space, without adult supervision. In the absence of peer support and the presence of adult supervision, that choice is less likely to occur.[38]

Differences in guardianship and peer relations help explain gender differences in the crime rate. Adolescent girls are more likely to experience direct and indirect supervision in their social activities, including their parents insisting on knowing where they are, with whom they are socializing, and where and how the socializing is taking place—for example, a friend's parents must be home. Adolescent boys are given more freedom to socialize as they wish.[39] Because of this control, young girls are more likely to socialize at home than their male peers, a restriction that limits their opportunities for deviance. Because they are less likely to be monitored, adolescent males are free to roam public places where they find more opportunities to engage in delinquent

offense-specific crime The idea that offenders react selectively to the characteristics of particular crimes.

offender-specific crime The idea that offenders evaluate their skills, motives, needs, and fears before deciding to commit crime.

criminality A personal trait of the individual as distinct from a "crime," which is an event.

Rational choice theorists view the offense and offenders as separate elements in a criminal event. Under some circumstances anyone may commit crime and in others even highly motivated offenders will refrain from criminal acts. Why does someone like Alexis Wright, 30, here leaving the Cumberland County Courthouse, a Zumba fitness instructor in Portland, Maine, engage in prostitution? Was there another path she might have traveled? Why people choose crime is a question that rational choice theorists seek to answer.

AP Images/Robert F. Bukaty

fear of apprehension and punishment. In fact, some offenders will deliberately seek out especially risky situations because of the added "thrill." The need for excitement is a significant predictor of criminal choice.[41]

Economic Opportunity Perceptions of economic opportunity influence the decision to commit crime. Some people may engage in criminal activity simply because they need the money to support their lifestyle and perceive few other potential income sources. Sociologists Melissa Thompson and Christopher Uggen found that people who begin taking hard drugs also increase their involvement in crime, taking in from $500 to $700 per month. Once they become cocaine and heroin users, the benefits of other criminal enterprises become overwhelmingly attractive: how else can a drug user earn enough to support his or her habit?[42]

Crime also becomes attractive when an individual becomes convinced that it will result in excessive profits with few costs. Criminals are motivated to commit crime when they know people who have made big scores and begin to believe they can gain economically via crime.[43] They are likely to desist if they begin to believe that their future criminal earnings will be relatively low and that attractive and legal opportunities to generate income are available.[44]

How much do you have to earn before crime is considered an economically viable alternative? Thompson and Uggen found that the typical drug dealer earned less than $800 profit per month; those committing predatory offenses such as burglary and robbery earned an average of $1,087. The real winners were criminals who sold drugs and also committed predatory crimes; they averaged $1,723 per month from illegal sources.[45] But even the most "successful" criminals earned less than $24,000. This is not enough to justify the risks of the dangers of a criminal career; it's not surprising then that most criminals eventually desist from crime—it just does not pay (enough).

behavior. When girls do go out, they tend to gather in places like shopping malls, where there are security guards and cameras that monitor behavior and limit criminal choice.[40]

Excitement and Thrills Some criminal offenders may engage in illegal behavior because they love the excitement and thrills that crime can provide. In his highly influential work *Seductions of Crime*, sociologist Jack Katz argues that there are immediate benefits to criminality that "seduce" people into a life of crime. For some people, shoplifting and vandalism are attractive because getting away with crime is a thrilling demonstration of personal competence; Katz calls this "sneaky thrills." The need for excitement may counter

CONNECTIONS

The role of economic needs in the motivation of white-collar criminals is discussed in Chapter 13. Research shows that even consistently law-abiding people may turn to criminal solutions when faced with overwhelming economic needs. They make the rational decision to commit crimes to solve some economic crisis.

Learning and Experience   Learning and experience may be important elements in structuring the choice of crime.[46] Career criminals may learn the limitations of their powers; they know when to take a chance and when to be cautious. Experienced criminals may turn from a life of crime when they develop a belief that the risk of crime is greater than its potential profit.[47] Patricia Morgan and Karen Ann Joe's three-city study (San Francisco, San Diego, and Honolulu) of female drug abusers found that experience helped dealers avoid detection. One dealer, earning $50,000 per year, explained her strategy this way:

> I stayed within my goals, basically … I don't go around doing stupid things. I don't walk around telling people I have drugs for sale. I don't have people sitting out in front of my house. I don't have traffic in and out of my house … I control the people I sell to.[48]

Here we see how experience in the profession shapes criminal decision making.

Knowledge of Criminal Techniques   Criminals report learning techniques that help them avoid detection, a sure sign of rational thinking and planning. Some are specialists, who learn to be professional car thieves or bad-check artists. Others are generalists who sell drugs one day and commit burglaries the next. In his studies of drug dealers, criminologist Bruce Jacobs found that crack dealers learn how to stash crack cocaine in some undisclosed location so they are not forced to carry large amounts of product on their persons. Dealers carefully evaluate the security of their sales area before setting up shop.[49] Most consider the middle of a long block the best place for drug deals because they can see everything in both directions; police raids can be spotted before they develop.[50] If a buyer seems dangerous or unreliable, the dealer requires that they do business in spaces between apartment buildings or in back lots. Although dealers lose the tactical edge of being on a public street, they gain a measure of protection because their associates can watch over the deal and come to the rescue if the buyer tries to "pull something."[51]

When Jacobs, along with Jody Miller, studied female crack dealers, they discovered a variety of defensive moves used by the dealers to avoid detection.[52] One of these techniques, called stashing, involved learning how to hide drugs on their person, in the street, or at home. One dealer told Jacobs and Miller how she hid drugs in the empty shaft of a curtain rod; another wore hollow earmuffs to hide crack. Because only female officers may conduct body cavity searches on women, the dealers often had time to get rid of their drugs before they got to the station house. Dealers are aware of legal definitions of possession. One said she stashed her drugs 250 feet from her home because that was beyond the distance (150 feet) police considered a person legally to be in "constructive possession" of drugs.

Criminals who learn the proper techniques may be able to prolong their criminal careers. Jacobs found that

CONNECTIONS

Rational choice theory dovetails with routine activities theory, which you learned about in Chapter 3. Although not identical, these approaches both claim that crime rates are a normal product of criminal opportunity. Both suggest that criminals consider such elements as guardianship and target attractiveness before they decide to commit crimes. The routine activities and rational choice views also agree that criminal opportunity is a key element in the criminal process. The overlap between these two viewpoints may help criminologists suggest means for effective crime control.

these offenders use specific techniques to avoid being apprehended by police. They play what they call the "peep game" before dealing drugs, scoping out the territory to make sure the turf is free from anything out of place that could be a potential threat (such as police officers or rival gang members).[53] One crack dealer told Jacobs:

> There was this red Pontiac sittin' on the corner one day with two white guys inside. They was just sittin' there for an hour, not doin' nothin'. Another day, diff'rent people be walkin' up and down the street you don't really recognize. You think they might be kin of someone but then you be askin' around and they [neighbors] ain't never seen them before neither. When ya' see strange things like that, you think somethin' be goin' on [and you don't deal].[54]

Drug dealers told Jacobs that they also carefully consider whether they should deal alone or in groups; large groups draw more attention from police but can offer more protection. Drug-dealing gangs and groups can help divert the attention of police: if their drug dealing is noticed by detectives, a dealer can slyly walk away or dispose of evidence while confederates distract the cops.[55]

Structuring Crime

LO4   Depict in your own words how criminals structure crime

Criminal decision making is not only based on an assessment of personal needs and capabilities but also on a rational assessment of the criminal event. Decisions must be made about what, where, when, and whom to target.

Choosing the Type of Crime   The choice of crime may be dictated by market conditions. Generalists may alter their criminal behavior according to shifting opportunity structures: they may rob the elderly on the first of the month when they know that Social Security checks have been cashed, switch over to shoplifting if a new fence moves into the neighborhood, and, if a supply becomes available, sell a truckload of hijacked cigarettes to neighborhood convenience stores. Crack users choose robbery over burglary: they need to make quick cash to purchase drugs and are in no position to plan a burglary and take the time to sell their loot; hitting someone with a lead pipe and taking their wallet is faster providing instant funds.[56]

Choosing the Time and Place of Crime   There is also evidence that criminal choice is structured by the time and place. Interviews with burglars show that they prefer "working" between 9 A.M. and 11 A.M. and in mid-afternoon, when parents are either at work or dropping off or picking up kids at school.[57] Burglars avoid Saturdays because most families are at home; Sunday morning during church hours is considered a prime time for weekend burglaries.[58] Some find out which families have star high school athletes because those that do are sure to be at the weekend game, leaving their houses unguarded.[59]

The place of crime is also carefully chosen. Because criminals often go on foot or use public transportation, they are unlikely to travel long distances to commit crimes and are more likely to drift toward the center of a city than to move toward outlying areas.[60] Some may occasionally commute to distant locations to commit crimes if they believe the payoff is greater, but most prefer to stay in their own neighborhood where they are familiar with the terrain.[61] They will only travel to unfamiliar areas if they believe the new location contains a worthy target and lax law enforcement. They may be encouraged to travel when the police are cracking down in their own neighborhood and the "heat is on."[62] Predatory criminals are in fact aware of law enforcement capabilities and consider them closely before deciding to commit crimes. Communities with the reputation of employing aggressive crime-fighting cops are less likely to attract potential offenders than areas perceived to have passive law enforcers.[63]

Selecting the Target of Crime   Criminals may also be well aware of target vulnerability. When they choose targets, they may shy off if they sense danger. In a series of interviews with career property offenders, Kenneth Tunnell found that burglars avoid targets if they feel there are police in the area or if "nosy neighbors" might be suspicious and cause trouble.[64] Paul Bellair found that robbery levels are relatively low in neighborhoods where residents keep a watchful eye on their neighbors' property.[65]

Predatory criminals seek out easy targets who can't or won't fight back and avoid those who seem menacing and dangerous. Not surprisingly, they tend to shy away from potential victims whom they believe are armed and dangerous.[66] The search for suitable victims may bring them in contact with people who themselves engage in deviant or antisocial behaviors.[67] Perhaps predatory criminals sense that people with "dirty hands" make suitable targets because they are unlikely to want to call the police or get entangled with the law.

In some instances, however, targets are chosen in order to send a message rather than to generate capital. Bruce Jacobs and Richard Wright used in-depth interviews with street robbers who target drug dealers and found that their crimes are a response to one of three types of violations:[68]

- *Market-related* violations emerge from "professional" disputes over territory.
- *Status-based* violations involve violence that starts when someone challenges the robber's character or manhood.
- *Personalistic* violations occur when the robber believes someone is acting like a punk and needs to be taught a lesson.

Robbery in this instance is an instrument used to settle scores, display dominance, and stifle potential rivals. Retaliation certainly is rational in the sense that actors who lack legitimate access to the law and who prize respect above everything else will often choose to resolve their grievances through a rough and ready brand of self-help.

IS CRIME RATIONAL?

LO5   Clarify the arguments that crime is rational

It is relatively easy to show that some crimes are the product of rational, objective thought, especially when they involve an ongoing criminal conspiracy centered on economic gain. When prominent bankers in the savings and loan industry were indicted for criminal fraud, their elaborate financial schemes exhibited not only signs of rationality but brilliant, though flawed, financial expertise.[69] The stock market manipulations of Wall Street executives, the drug dealings of international cartels, and the gambling operations of organized crime bosses all demonstrate a reasoned analysis of market conditions, interests, and risks. Even small-time wheeler-dealers, such as the female drug dealers discussed earlier in the chapter, are guided by their rational assessment of the likelihood of apprehension and take pains to avoid detection. But what about common crimes of theft and violence? Are these rational acts or unplanned, haphazard, and spontaneous?

Is Theft Rational?

Some common theft-related crimes—larcenies, shoplifting, purse snatchings—seem more likely to be random acts of criminal opportunity than well-thought-out conspiracies. However, there is evidence that even these seemingly unplanned events may be the product of careful risk assessment, including environmental, social, and structural factors.

Professional shoplifters, referred to as **boosters**, use complex methods in order to avoid detection. They steal with the intention of reselling stolen merchandise online or reselling it to professional fences, another group of criminals who use cunning and rational decision making in their daily activities. Fences may buy the stolen goods and then resell them to the merchants who were the original target of the professional shoplifters!

Another group of criminals, professional burglars, seem to carefully choose the neighborhood location of their crimes.[70] They seem to avoid areas where residents protect their homes with alarms, locks, and other methods of "target hardening" or where residents watch out for one another and try to control unrest or instability in their communities.[71] Most burglars prefer to commit crimes in **permeable neighborhoods**, those with a greater than usual number of access streets from traffic arteries into the neighborhood.[72] These areas are chosen for theft and break-ins because they are familiar and well traveled, they appear more open and vulnerable, and they offer more potential escape routes.[73] Burglars appear to monitor car and pedestrian traffic and avoid selecting targets on heavily traveled streets.[74] Corner homes, usually near traffic lights or stop signs, are the ones most likely to be burglarized: stop signs give criminals a legitimate reason to stop their cars and look for an attractive target.[75] Secluded homes, such as those at the end of a cul-de-sac or surrounded by wooded areas, also make suitable targets.[76]

Burglars are choosy when they select targets. They avoid freestanding buildings because they can more easily be surrounded by police; they like to select targets that are known to do a primarily cash business, such as bars, supermarkets, and restaurants.[77] Burglars also seem to know the market and target goods that are in demand.

Is Drug Use Rational?

Did Oscar-winning actor Philip Seymour Hoffman make an objective, rational choice to OD on heroin? Did rising young star Heath Ledger make a rational choice when he abused prescription drugs to the point that it killed him? And what about British singer Amy Winehouse, did she choose to drink herself to death? Or Michael Jackson, who died of acute propofol and benzodiazepine intoxication on June 25, 2009? Is it possible that these and other drug users, a group not usually associated with clear thinking, make rational choices?

Research does in fact show that from its onset drug use is controlled by rational decision making. Users report that they begin taking drugs when they believe that the benefits of substance abuse outweigh its costs (e.g., they believe that drugs will provide a fun, exciting, thrilling experience). Their entry into substance abuse is facilitated by their perception that valued friends and family members endorse and encourage drug use and abuse substances themselves.[78]

In adulthood, heavy drug users and dealers show signs of rationality and cunning in their daily activity, approaching drug dealing as a business proposition. Research conducted by Leanne Fiftal Alarid and her partners shows that women drawn into dealing drugs learn the trade in a businesslike manner. One young dealer told them how she learned the techniques of the trade from an older male partner:

> He taught me how to "recon" [reconstitute] cocaine, cutting and repacking a brick from 91 proof to 50 proof, just like a business. He treats me like an equal partner, and many of the friends are business associates. I am a catalyst.... I even get guys turned on to drugs.[79]

Note the business terminology used. This coke dealer could be talking about an IT training course at a major corporation! Nor are Alarid's research findings unique. When James Densley studied drug-dealing gangs in London, he found that they evolved from nonviolent, noncriminal peer groups into organized criminal enterprises.[80] Nothing was left to chance, one gang member, street name "Wolverine," explained to Denlsey:

> We was committing crimes so we sat down together, it was like a meeting, I suppose and we just gave each other names and it started like that. Because it was not like socializing, it was actually going out to commit crime and do stuff. We was premeditating what we was doing before it happened. Planning it up.

Densley found that that drug dealers learn special skills—how to seize territory, how to use violence, how to maintain secrecy, how to obtain intelligence—that enable them to successfully regulate and control the production and distribution of illegal drugs while maximizing their profits.

Is Violence Rational?

Is it possible that violent acts, through which the offender gains little material benefit, are the product of reasoned decision making? Yes, it is. There are a number of indicators that suggest violence has rational elements. When Trevor Bennett and Fiona Brookman conducted interviews with offenders with a history of violence, they found that some motivations were cultural, such as maintaining one's status and honor, and others might be visceral, such as excitement and getting a buzz from dangerous pursuits. However, there were also rational elements to violent acts, such as calculating whether they could win the battle. Put another way, violent repeaters don't start something they can't finish: if the target looks tough, they look for someone else to attack.[81]

---

boosters Professional shoplifters who steal with the intention of reselling stolen merchandise.

permeable neighborhoods Areas with a greater than usual number of access streets from traffic arteries into the neighborhood.

Crime expert Richard Felson argues that violence is a matter of choice and serves specific goals:

- *Control.* The violent person may want to control his or her victim's behavior and life.
- *Retribution.* The perpetrator may want to punish someone without calling the police or using the justice system to address his or her grievances. The person takes the law into his or her own hands.
- *Deterrence.* The attacker may want to stop someone from repeating acts that he or she considers hostile or provocative.
- *Reputation.* An attack may be motivated by the need to enhance reputation and create self-importance in the eyes of others.

Felson also recognizes that the violent act may have multiple goals. But in any case, even violence may be a product of rational decision making.[82]

Violence can be rational, for example, when someone attacks another person to get revenge for a prior bad deed. Andre Dickerson Jr. pleaded guilty to assault and was sentenced to six years in prison after he and another man and his daughter took part in the beating of Miguel Esteban Cruz, who had raped the young woman. Cruz was struck 15 or more times, suffered skull fractures, large cuts to his scalp that required more than two dozen staples, a lung injury, a mangled ear, missing teeth, and several broken bones. Do you agree that such a revenge attack is "rational"?

Rational Robbers Street robbers also are likely to choose victims who are vulnerable, have low coercive power, and do not pose any threat.[83] In their survey of violent felons, James Wright and Peter Rossi found that robbers avoid victims who may be armed and dangerous. About three-fifths of all felons interviewed were more afraid of armed victims than of police, about two-fifths had avoided a victim because they believed the victim was armed, and almost one-third reported that they had been scared off, wounded, or captured by armed victims.[84] It comes as no surprise that cities with higher than average gun-carrying rates generally have lower rates of unarmed robbery.[85]

Robbers also tend to pick the time and day of crimes carefully. When they rob a commercial establishment, they choose the time when there is the most cash on hand to increase their take from the crime. For example, robbery rates increase in the winter partly because the Christmas shopping season means more money in the cash registers of potential targets.[86] Targets are generally found close to robbers' homes or in areas in which they routinely travel. Familiarity with the area gives them ready knowledge of escape routes; this is referred to as their "awareness space."[87] A familiar location allows them to blend in, not look out of place, and not get lost when returning home with their loot.[88]

Rational Killers? Hollywood likes to portray deranged people killing innocent victims at random, but people who carry guns and are ready to use them typically do so for more rational reasons. They may perceive that they live in a dangerous environment and carry a weapon for self-protection. Some are involved in dangerous illegal activities such as drug dealing and carry weapons as part of the job.[89] Even in apparently senseless killings among strangers, the conscious motive is typically revenge for a prior dispute or disagreement among the parties involved or their families.[90] Many homicides are motivated by offenders' desire to avoid retaliation from a victim they assaulted or to avoid future prosecutions by getting rid of witnesses.[91] Although some killings are the result of anger and aggression, others are the result of rational planning.

Even serial murderers, outwardly the most irrational of all offenders, tend to pick their targets with care. Most choose victims who are defenseless or who cannot count on police protection: prostitutes, gay men, hitchhikers, children, hospital patients, the elderly, and the homeless. Rarely do serial killers target weightlifters, martial arts experts, or any other potentially powerful group.[92]

Rational Sex Criminals? One might think that sex crimes are highly irrational, motivated by emotions and psychological maladies that defy rational planning. But sex criminals report using rational thought and planning when carrying out their crimes. Serial rapists rationally choose their targets. They travel, on average, three miles from their homes to commit their crimes in order to avoid victims who might recognize them later. The desire to avoid detection supersedes the wish to obtain a victim with little effort. Younger sex offenders create *scripts* that guide their interactions with victims. If they follow the script, they can commit their crimes and avoid detection. Before committing their crimes, the young sex offender will go through a series of steps, first locating their victims in institutional, domestic, or public locations, gaining their victims' trust, and then formulating strategies to proceed to the best location for sexual contact. For that purpose, offenders will usually promise rewards or give inducements such as money, or even threaten or use violence to get their way.[93]

Child molesters/rapists report that they volunteer or seek employment in day care centers and other venues where victims can be found. They use their status to gain the trust of children and to be seen as nonthreatening to the child. Within the context of this work environment they can then use subtle strategies of manipulation, such as giving love and attention to suitable targets (e.g., spending a lot of time with them), so they can gradually desensitize the children and gain their cooperation in sexual activity (e.g., through nonsexual touching).[94] These efforts obviously display planning and rationality.

Is Hate Rational? Can hate crimes possibly be rational? Hard to believe, but when Ryan King and Gretchen Sutto examined the characteristics of an outbreak of hate crimes they found that three factors seem to trigger these events: an antecedent incident that leaves one group with a grievance against another, a definable target group held responsible for the deed, and publicity sufficient to make the event known to a broad public; all these are signs of rationality.[95] A lethal, highly publicized terror attack such as the bombing at the Boston Marathon in April 2013 might ignite a spate of hate crimes aimed at the Muslim community, which increase almost immediately after the incident and then deescalate at an equally rapid pace. When anger and prejudice drive retaliatory hate crimes they dissipate quickly. Hate crimes, then, are not merely the product of a disturbed mind, but rather a calculated response to a concrete event whose impact is often fanned and inflamed by the media.

ELIMINATING CRIME

For many people, crime is attractive; it brings rewards, excitement, prestige, or other desirable outcomes without lengthy work or effort.[96] Whether the motive is economic gain, revenge, or hedonism, crime has an allure that some people cannot resist.[97] Some law violators describe the adrenaline rush that comes from successfully executing illegal activities in dangerous situations as **edgework**, the "exhilarating, momentary integration of danger, risk, and skill" that motivates people to try a variety of dangerous criminal and noncriminal behaviors.[98] Crime is not some random act, but a means that can provide both pleasure and solutions to vexing personal problems. As Michael Gottfredson and Travis Hirschi put it, these criminals derive satisfaction from "money without work, sex without courtship, revenge without court delays."[99]

Considering its allure, how can crime be prevented or eliminated? It seems logical that if crime is rational and people choose to commit crime after weighing its rewards and benefits and factoring in their needs and abilities, then it can be controlled or eradicated by convincing potential offenders that:

- Crime is a poor choice that will not bring them rewards, but instead lead to hardship and deprivation.
- Crime is not worth the effort. It is easier to work at a legitimate job than to evade police, outwit alarms, and avoid security.
- Crime brings pain that is not easily forgotten. People who experience the pains of punishment will not readily commit more crimes.

The following sections discuss each of these crime reduction or control strategies in some detail.

SITUATIONAL CRIME PREVENTION

Desperate people may contemplate crime, but only the truly irrational would attack a well-defended, inaccessible target and risk strict punishment. Crime prevention can be achieved by reducing the opportunities people have to commit particular crimes, a practice known as **situational crime prevention**. According to this concept, in order to reduce criminal activity, planners must be aware of the characteristics of sites and situations that are at risk to crime; the things that draw or push people toward these sites and situations; what equips potential criminals to take advantage of illegal opportunities offered by these sites and situations; and what constitutes the immediate triggers for criminal actions.[100] Criminal acts will be avoided if (a) potential targets are

edgework The excitement or exhilaration of successfully executing illegal activities in dangerous situations.

situational crime prevention A method of crime prevention that stresses tactics and strategies to eliminate or reduce particular crimes in narrow settings, such as reducing burglaries in a housing project by increasing lighting and installing security alarms.

guarded securely, (b) the means to commit crime are controlled, and (c) potential offenders are carefully monitored.

Situational crime prevention was first popularized in the United States in the early 1970s by Oscar Newman, who coined the term **defensible space**. This term signifies that crime can be prevented or displaced through the use of residential architectural designs that reduce criminal opportunity, such as well-lit housing projects that maximize surveillance.[101] C. Ray Jeffery wrote *Crime Prevention through Environmental Design*, which extended Newman's concepts and applied them to nonresidential areas, such as schools and factories.[102] According to this view, mechanisms such as security systems, deadbolt locks, high-intensity street lighting, and neighborhood watch patrols should reduce criminal opportunity.[103]

LO6 Identify the elements of the CRAVED model of crime choice

In 1992, Ronald Clarke published *Situational Crime Prevention*, which compiled the best-known strategies and tactics to reduce criminal incidents.[104] Clarke later formulated the CRAVED model of theft, which suggests that the appropriation of property is most likely to occur when the target is:

- *Concealable.* Merchandise that is easily hidden is more vulnerable to shoplifters than bulkier items. Things that are difficult to identify after being stolen are desirable. While it might be possible to identify a diamond ring, commodities such as copper tubing is easily concealable.
- *Removable.* Mobile items such as cars or bikes are desirable. A laptop makes a more appealing target than a desktop. Jewelry, cash, drugs, and the like are easy to carry and quite valuable on resale. Refrigerators may cost more, but you would need three people and a truck to remove them from a home.
- *Available.* Desirable objects that are widely available and easy to find are at high risk for theft. Cars actually become at greater risk as they get older, because similar models need parts and car thieves can bring them to chop shops to be stripped. Older cars are also owned by people living in disorganized neighborhoods with motivated offenders and limited security.
- *Valuable.* Thieves will generally choose more expensive, in-demand goods that are easily sold. Some may want to keep valuable goods for themselves and target goods that will confer status, such as a Rolex.
- *Enjoyable.* Hot products tend to be enjoyable things to own or consume, such as the newest electronic gadget or flashy bling.

- *Disposable.* Thieves tend to target items that are easy to sell. Cartons of cigarettes can be resold at a discount to a convenience store. While more valuable, it's tougher to sell a Picasso print.[105]

Based on this research, criminologists have suggested using a number of situational crime prevention efforts that might reduce crime rates. One approach is not to target a specific crime but to create an environment that can reduce the overall crime rate by limiting the access to tempting targets for a highly motivated offender group (such as high school students).[106]

Targeting Specific Crimes

Situational crime prevention can also involve developing tactics to reduce or eliminate a specific crime problem (such as shoplifting in an urban mall or street-level drug dealing). Typically situational crime prevention efforts are divided into a number of strategies:[107]

- Increase the effort needed to commit crime
- Reduce the opportunity to commit crime
- Increase the risks of committing crime
- Reduce the rewards for committing crime
- Reduce provocation/induce guilt or shame for committing crime
- Reduce excuses for committing crime

Increase Effort   The harder it is to attack a target, the less likely it will be attacked! Some of the tactics to increase effort include target-hardening techniques such as putting unbreakable glass on storefronts, locking gates, and fencing yards. Some people go as far as living in gated communities, protected by guards and fences. Does it work? Research by Lynn Addington and Callie Marie Rennison shows that living in a gated community actually reduces the risk of being targeted by burglars.[108]

Technological advances can make it more difficult to commit crimes; for example, having an owner's photo on credit cards should reduce the use of stolen cards. The development of new products, such as steering locks on cars, can make it more difficult to commit crimes. Empirical evidence indicates that steering locks have helped reduce car theft in the United States, Britain, and Germany.[109] Installing a locking device on cars that prevents inebriated drivers from starting the vehicle (breath-analyzed ignition interlock device) significantly reduces drunk-driving rates among people with a history of driving while intoxicated.[110] Removing visibility-blocking signs from store windows, installing brighter lights, and instituting a pay-first policy can help reduce thefts from gas stations and convenience stores.[111]

Reduce Opportunities   Another way to increase effort is to reduce opportunities for criminal activity. At least 30 states and thousands of municipalities have passed laws

defensible space The principle that crime prevention can be achieved through modifying the physical environment to reduce the opportunity individuals have to commit crime.

preventing registered sex offenders from residing within a specific distance of schools, parks, day care centers, school bus stops, or other places commonly frequented by children; buffer zones typically range from 500 to 2,500 feet between the offender's home and designated locations. While aimed at reducing sex offending and reducing recidivism, there is scant evidence that such measures can be effective.[112]

Many cities have established curfew laws in an effort to limit the opportunity juveniles have to engage in antisocial behavior.[113] However, curfew laws have not met with universal success.[114] So another approach has been to involve kids in after-school programs that take up their time and reduce their opportunity to get in trouble. An example of this type of program is the Doorsteps Neighbourhood Program in Toronto, Ontario, which is designed to help children in high-risk areas complete their schoolwork as well as providing them with playtime that helps improve their literacy and communication skills. Children who are part of this program enter into routines that increase the effort they must make if they want to get involved in after-school crime and nuisance activities.[115]

Reduce Rewards Target reduction strategies are designed to reduce the value of crime to the potential criminal. These include making car radios removable so they can be kept in the home at night, marking property so it is more difficult to sell when stolen, and having gender-neutral phone listings to discourage obscene phone calls. Tracking systems, such as those made by the LoJack Corporation, help police locate and return stolen vehicles.

Increase Risk If criminals believe that committing crime is very risky, only the most foolhardy would attempt to commit criminal acts. Managing crime falls into the hands of people Marcus Felson calls **crime discouragers**.[116] These discouragers can be grouped into three categories:

guardians, who monitor targets (such as store security guards); handlers, who monitor potential offenders (such as parole officers and parents); and managers, who monitor places (such as homeowners and doorway attendants). If crime discouragers do their job correctly, the potential criminal will be convinced that the risk of crime outweighs any potential gains.[117]

Crime discouragers have different levels of responsibility, ranging from highly personal involvement, such as the homeowner protecting her house and the parent controlling his children, to the most impersonal general involvement, such as a stranger who stops someone from shoplifting in the mall (see Exhibit 4.1).

Research indicates that crime discouragers can have an impact on crime rates. An evaluation of a police initiative in Oakland, California, found that an active working partnership with residents and businesspeople who have a stake in maintaining order in their places of work or residences can reduce levels of drug dealing while at the same time increasing civil behavior. Collective action and cooperation in solving problems were effective in controlling crime, whereas individual action (such as calling 911) seemed to have little effect.[118]

It may also be possible to raise the risks of committing crime by creating mechanical devices that increase the likelihood that a criminal will be observed and captured.

> **crime discouragers** Discouragers can be grouped into three categories: guardians, who monitor targets (such as store security guards); handlers, who monitor potential offenders (such as parole officers and parents); and managers, who monitor places (such as homeowners and doorway attendants).

EXHIBIT 4.1

Crime Discouragers

Level of responsibility	Types of Supervisors and Objects of Supervision		
	Guardians (monitoring suitable targets)	Handlers (monitoring likely offenders)	Managers (monitoring amenable places)
Personal (owners, family, friends)	Student keeps eye on own laptop	Parent makes sure child gets home from school	Homeowner monitors house
Assigned (employees with specific assignment)	Store clerk monitors iPhones	Police officer sends kids back to school	Concierge protects building
Diffuse (employees with general assignment)	Accountant notes shoplifting	School clerk discourages truancy	Hotel maid impairs trespasser
General (strangers, other citizens)	Bystander reports shoplifter	Stranger questions teens at mall	Customer observes parking garage

SOURCE: Adapted from *Crime and Place*, ed. John E. Eck and David Weisburd (Boulder, CO: Lynne Rienner Publishers, 2010).

One prominent approach is the installation of closed-circuit television (CCTV) surveillance cameras and improved street lighting, techniques that are currently being used around the world. CCTV can deter would-be criminals who fear detection and apprehension while aiding police in the detection and apprehension of suspects, aid in the prosecution of alleged offenders, improve police officer safety and compliance with the law (cameras mounted on the dashboard of police cruisers to record police stops, searches, and so on), and aid in the detection and prevention of terrorist activities. Nowhere is the popularity of CCTV more apparent than in Great Britain, where an estimated 4.2 million CCTV cameras, or 1 for every 14 citizens, are in operation. Some cities in the United States have large numbers of security cameras: New York City has more than 4,000 cameras in Manhattan alone; Chicago's linked public and private security cameras number around 10,000.[119] Research shows that CCTV interventions (a) have a small but significant desirable effect on crime, (b) are most effective in reducing crime in car parks (parking lots), (c) are most effective in reducing vehicle crimes, and (d) are more effective in reducing crime in the United Kingdom than in other countries.[120]

Increase Shame Crime may be reduced or prevented if we can communicate to people the wrongfulness of their behavior and how it is harmful to society. We may tell them to "say no to drugs" or that "users are losers." By making people aware of the shamefulness of their actions we hope to prevent their criminal activities even if chances of detection and punishment are slight.

Another method is to order people convicted of socially unacceptable crimes to advertise their guilt in the hope that they will be too ashamed to recidivate. "John lists" have been published to shame men involved in hiring prostitutes or other sex offenses.

Other methods of inducing guilt or shame might include such techniques as posting signs or warnings to embarrass potential offenders or creating mechanisms to identify perpetrators and/or publicize their crimes.[121] Megan's Laws require sex offender registration and notification systems. While these systems have been used for nearly two decades, there is little evidence that they reduce sex crimes: research shows that sex offender registration does not have a statistically significant effect on the number of rapes reported at the state level.[122] One reason may be that instead of deterring crime, public disclosure resulting from community notification laws negatively impacts an offender's efforts at rehabilitation, resulting in further offending.[123]

diffusion of benefits Efforts to prevent one crime help prevent another; in other instances, crime control efforts in one locale reduce crime in another area.

Reduce Provocation Some crimes are the result of extreme provocation—for example, road rage. It might be possible to reduce provocation by creating programs that reduce conflict. Posting guards outside of schools at recess might prevent childish taunts from escalating into full-blown brawls. Antibullying programs that have been implemented in schools are another method of reducing provocation.

Alcohol may act as a fuel that fans the flames, turning a disagreement into an assault. One way to reduce this sort of crime is to raise the price of beer, wine, and hard liquor through taxation, which has been shown to be effective.[124] Another approach: mandating an early closing time in local bars and pubs might limit assaults that result from late-night drinking and conflicts in pubs at closing time.

Remove Excuses Crime may be reduced by making it difficult for people to excuse their criminal behavior by saying things like "I did not know that was illegal" or "I had no choice." Some municipalities have set up roadside displays that electronically flash cars' speed rates as they drive by, so that when stopped by police, drivers cannot say they did not know how fast they were going. Litter boxes, brightly displayed, can eliminate the claim that "I just did not know where to throw my trash." Reducing or eliminating excuses also makes it physically easy for people to comply with laws and regulations, thereby reducing the likelihood they will choose crime.

Situational Crime Prevention: Costs and Benefits

LO7 Assess the validity of situational crime prevention techniques for reducing crime

Some attempts at situational crime prevention have proven highly successful while others have not met their goals. However, it is now apparent that the approach brings with it certain nontransparent or hidden costs and benefits that can either increase effectiveness or undermine success. Before the overall success of this approach can be evaluated, these costs and benefits must be considered. Among the hidden benefits of situational crime control efforts are:

- *Diffusion.* Sometimes efforts to prevent one crime help prevent another; in other instances, crime control efforts in one locale reduce crime in surrounding areas.[125] This effect is referred to as **diffusion of benefits**. Diffusion may be produced by two independent effects: We can see the effect of diffusion when video cameras set up in a mall to reduce shoplifting can also reduce vandalism. Police surveillance teams whose aim is to control trafficking in a known drug zone unintentionally reduce the incidence of prostitution and other public order crimes by scaring off would-be clients (drug users).[126] Intensive police patrols designed to target teen gangs in one area of town have been shown to help reduce crime in neighboring areas as well.[127]

- *Discouragement.* When protection efforts become effective potential criminals may become discouraged. **Discouragement** may cause them to either leave the area or seek other methods of gaining financial rewards. While there are hidden benefits to situational crime prevention, there may also be costs that limit their effectiveness:

- *Displacement.* A program that seems successful because it helps lower crime rates at specific locations or neighborhoods may simply be redirecting offenders to alternative targets; this is known as **displacement**, as crime is not prevented but deflected or displaced.[128] Beefed-up police patrols in one area may shift crimes to a more vulnerable neighborhood.[129]

- *Extinction.* Sometimes crime reduction programs may produce a short-term positive effect, but benefits dissipate as criminals adjust to new conditions. Would-be criminals learn to dismantle alarms or avoid patrols; they may try new offenses they had previously avoided. And elimination of one crime may encourage commission of another: if every residence in a neighborhood has a foolproof burglar alarm system, motivated offenders may be forced to turn to armed robbery, a riskier and more violent crime. A recent analysis of a program in Philadelphia that made use of foot patrols to lower crime rates in areas with high violence rates found that while the program produced statistically significantly less violent crime at first, the deterrent effects began to quickly slow down and eventually became extinct. It is possible that at first offenders may have overestimated the risk of apprehension but as time went on began to realize their mistake and resumed illegal activities; positive results were relatively short lived.[130]

- *Encouragement.* Crime reduction programs may boomerang and increase rather than decrease the potentiality for crime. Some situational efforts rely on increasing the risk of crime by installing street lighting, assuming that rational criminals will avoid areas where their criminal activities are more visible. Take for instance street lighting: many people believe that criminals will avoid a well-lit street. Such plans may backfire. Well-lit areas may bring a greater number of potential victims and potential offenders into the same physical space; increased visibility may allow potential offenders to make better judgments of target vulnerability and attractiveness (e.g., they can spot people with jewelry and other valuables). Increased illumination may make it easier for offenders to commit crimes and to escape.[131]

Before the effectiveness of situational crime prevention can be accepted, these hidden costs and benefits must be weighed and balanced.

GENERAL DETERRENCE

LO8 Categorize the elements of general deterrence

According to the rational choice view, motivated, rational people will violate the law if left free and unrestricted. **General deterrence** theory holds that crime can be controlled by the threat and/or application of criminal punishment. If people fear being apprehended and punished, being locked up in a harsh prison, or even sentenced to death, they will not risk breaking the law. An inverse relationship should then exist between crime rates and legal sanctions. If the punishment for a crime is increased and the effectiveness and efficiency of the criminal justice system improved, then the number of people willing to risk committing crime should decline.

The severity, certainty, and speed of punishment are interrelated. If a particular crime—say, robbery—is punished severely, but few robbers are ever caught or punished, the severity of punishment for robbery will probably not deter people from robbing. However, if the certainty of apprehension and conviction is increased by modern technology, more efficient police work, or some other factor, then even minor punishment might deter the potential robber.

The certainty of punishment seems to have a greater impact than its severity or speed. People will more likely be deterred from crime if they believe that they will get caught; what happens to them after apprehension seems to have less impact.[132] Nonetheless, all three elements of the deterrence equation are important, and it would be a mistake to emphasize one at the expense of the others. For example, if all resources were given to police agencies to increase the probability of arrest, crime rates might increase because there were insufficient funds for swift prosecution and effective correction.[133]

The Perception of Punishment/ Perceptual Deterrence

The *perception of punishment* plays a major role in producing crime deterrence.[134] People who feel threatened, who believe they will get caught and punished, will be deterred

discouragement Crime control efforts targeting a particular locale help reduce crime in surrounding areas and populations.

displacement A program that helps lower crime rates at specific locations or neighborhoods may be redirecting offenders to alternative targets.

general deterrence A crime control policy that depends on the fear of criminal penalties. General deterrence measures, such as long prison sentences for violent crimes, are aimed at convincing the potential law violator that the pains associated with crime outweigh its benefits.

Police sergeant Troy Redd performs a business checkup with Bryon Gans, owner of Shoe Kings, during an on-street training session with the newly hired Camden County (New Jersey) police officers in the Whitman Park neighborhood of Camden on December 20, 2013. Crime rates have been dropping in Camden: adding new police officers seems to have deterred crime.

The perception of deterrence works for some people and some crimes more than others; deterrence is rarely an all or nothing proposition.[139] The most significant deterrent effects can be achieved on minor petty criminals, whereas more serious offenders such as murderers are harder to discourage.[140] People who have already experienced punishment in the past are more likely to overestimate the likelihood of future punishments.[141] People "learn from their mistakes," and those who are caught and punished will perceive greater risk than those who have escaped detection.[142]

Certainty of Punishment and Deterrence

According to **deterrence theory**, crime and punishment are inversely related: as the probability of legal sanction increases, crime rates decline. If punishment were both certain and imminent, even the most motivated criminal would desist because the risks of crime outweigh its rewards.[143]

Unfortunately, punishment is not very certain. Only 10 percent of all serious offenses result in apprehension (half go unreported, and police make arrests in about 20 percent of reported crimes). As offenders are processed through all the stages of the criminal justice system, the odds of their receiving serious punishment diminishes. As a result, some believe they will not be severely punished for their acts and consequently have little regard for the law's deterrent power. If, however, the certainty of punishment could be increased to a critical level, the so-called **tipping point**, then the deterrent effect would kick in and crime rates decline.[144]

One way of reaching the tipping point is to add police officers. As the number of active, aggressive, crime-fighting cops increases, so too do arrests and convictions, convincing would-be criminals that the risk of apprehension outweighs the benefits they can gain from crime.[145]

Can Police Add to the Certainty of Punishment? While adding cops seems a logical way of reducing crime, this assumption has been questioned ever since a famous experiment was conducted by the Kansas City, Missouri, Police Department that showed crime rates were unaffected by merely increasing (or decreasing) the number of police on patrol.[146] The disappointing results of the Kansas City

from committing crime even if the true likelihood of detection and punishment is insignificant; this is referred to as **perceptual deterrence**.[135] Conversely, the *actual likelihood* of punishment will have little effect if potential criminals perceive or believe they can escape detection.[136]

What can be done to increase the perception of punishment? Hiring more police officers and allocating them in ways that increase their visibility have been shown to deter potential offenders.[137] Even the most committed offenders (e.g., gang members, domestic terrorists) who fear legal punishments will forego or reduce criminal activities if they believe they will be apprehended and punished.[138]

perceptual deterrence The theory that the perceived certainty, severity, and celerity of punishment are inversely related to the decisions by would-be offenders to commit crime, regardless of the actual likelihood of being apprehended and punished. People who believe they will be punished will be deterred even if the actual likelihood of punishment is insignificant.

deterrence theory The view that if the probability of arrest, conviction, and sanctioning increases, crime rates should decline

tipping point The minimum amount of expected punishment necessary to produce a significant reduction in crime rates.

experiment shaped attitudes toward the deterrent effect of police patrol for more than 40 years. However, there has been some recent evidence indicating that adding to police patrol forces does in fact help reduce crime rates.[147] Perhaps the findings of the Kansas City study were a "rush to judgment"?

The deterrent effect of police may be aided by the tactics they use to control crime. Focused crime-fighting initiatives, targeting specific crimes such as murder or robbery, are more effective than routine patrol.[148] Some police departments have instituted **crackdowns**—sudden changes in police activity designed to increase the communicated threat or actual certainty of punishment. One approach is to create a specialized police task force that targets street-level narcotics dealers by using undercover agents and surveillance cameras in known drug-dealing locales. Evaluations of the deterrent effect of crackdowns have met with mixed reviews.[149] Lawrence Sherman found that while crackdowns initially deterred crime, crime rates returned to earlier levels once the crackdown ended.[150] Other research efforts have also found that while at first successful as a crime suppression technique, the initial effect of the crackdown soon wore off after high-intensity police activity ended.[151] While these evaluations provided little evidence that crackdowns can deter crime, there is some support for an approach where police departments combine crackdowns with aggressive problem-solving and community improvement techniques, such as increasing lighting and cleaning vacant lots.[152] Merely saturating an area with police may not deter crime, but focusing efforts on a particular problem area has a deterrent effect.

Severity of Punishment and Deterrence

According to general deterrence theory, as the severity of punishment increases, crime rates should decrease. Does this equation hold water? The evidence is decidedly mixed. While some studies have found that increasing sanction levels can control common criminal behaviors, others have not achieved a positive result.[153]

Take the case of enhancing punishment in order to discourage people from using handguns. In this instance a state might add five years to a criminal sentence if a handgun was used during the commission of a crime. When Daniel Kessler and Steven Levitt evaluated the deterrent effect of California's sentencing enhancement act, they found that it did in fact lower crime rates.[154] However, other research efforts found that gun crimes went down in other states, even those that did not enhance or increase their sentences![155] The apparent deterrent effect was actually spurious, because gun crime dropped all over, even in jurisdictions that did not enhance punishments.

It stands to reason that if severity of punishment can deter crime, then fear of the death penalty, the ultimate legal deterrent, should significantly reduce murder rates. What

does the evidence show? Because this topic is so important, it is featured in the accompanying Criminology in Action.

Shame and Humiliation Fear of shame and embarrassment can be a powerful deterrent to crime. Those who fear being rejected by family and peers are reluctant to engage in deviant behavior.[156] These factors manifest themselves in two ways: (1) personal shame over violating the law and (2) the fear of public humiliation if the deviant behavior becomes public knowledge. People who say that their involvement in crime would cause them to feel ashamed are less likely to offend than people who deny fears of embarrassment.[157]

People who are afraid that significant others—such as parents, peers, neighbors, and teachers—will disapprove of their behavior are less likely to commit crime. The fear of exposure and consequent shaming also may vary according to the cohesiveness of community structure and the type of crime. **Informal sanctions** may be most effective in highly unified areas where everyone knows one another and the crime cannot be hidden from public view. The threat of informal sanctions seems to have the greatest influence on instrumental crimes, which involve planning, and not on impulsive or expressive criminal behaviors or those associated with substance abuse.[158]

While shame can be a potent deterrent, offenders also seem to be influenced by forgiveness and acceptance. They are less likely to repeat their criminal activity if victims are willing to grant them forgiveness.[159]

crackdowns The concentration of police resources on particular problem areas, such as street-level drug dealing, to eradicate or displace criminal activity.

Informal sanctions Disapproval, stigma, or anger directed toward an offender by significant others (parents, peers, neighbors, teachers), resulting in shame, embarrassment, and loss of respect.

THE DETERRENT EFFECT OF CAPITAL PUNISHMENT

according to deterrence theory, the death penalty—the ultimate punishment—should deter murder—the ultimate crime. Most Americans approve of the death penalty, even convicted criminals who are currently behind bars. But is the public's approval warranted? Is the death penalty an effective deterrent to murder or should the policy and practice of capital punishment be ended once and for all?

Empirical research on the association between capital punishment and murder can be divided into three types: immediate impact studies, comparative research, and time-series analysis.

Immediate Impact

If capital punishment is a deterrent, the reasoning goes, then its impact should be greatest after a well-publicized execution. Robert Dann began testing this assumption in 1935 when he chose five highly publicized executions of convicted murderers in different years and determined the number of homicides in the 60 days before and after each execution. Each 120-day period had approximately the same number of homicides, as well as the same number of days on which homicides occurred. Dann's study revealed that an average of 4.4 more homicides occurred during the 60 days following an execution than during those preceding it, suggesting that executions might actually increase the incidence of homicide. Since Dann's pioneering effort, a number of research efforts have found that even when executions were highly publicized in the local press, they still had little influence on the murder rate.

Comparative Research

Another type of research compares the murder rates in jurisdictions that have abolished the death penalty with the rates of those that employ the death penalty. Studies using this approach have found little difference in the murder rates of adjacent states, regardless of their use of the death penalty; capital punishment did not appear to influence the reported rate of homicide. Research conducted in nations around the world found little evidence that countries with a death penalty have lower violence rates than those without; homicide rates actually decline after capital punishment is abolished, a direct contradiction to its supposed deterrent effect.

Time-Series Studies

Time-series studies look at the long-term association between capital sentencing and murder. If capital punishment is a deterrent, then periods that have an upswing in executions should also experience a downturn in violent crime and murder. Most research efforts have failed to show such a relationship.

The Death Penalty and Deterrence

An overwhelming majority of criminologists believe that capital punishment has little if any deterrent effect. Murder

Speed (Celerity) of Punishment and Deterrence

The third leg of Becarria's model of deterrence involves the celerity or speed of punishment: the faster punishment is applied and the more closely it is linked to the crime, the more likely it will serve as a deterrent.[160] Research indicates that the value of a given criminal sanction steadily decreases as the lag between crime and punishment lengthens. Because criminals discount punishments that trail behind their crimes, how and when punishment is applied can alter its effect. A criminal who is apprehended, tried, and convicted soon after committing a crime will be more deeply affected than one who experiences a significant delay between crime and punishment.[161]

Unfortunately, the American justice system is handcuffed by delaying tactics by trial lawyers. It is routine to request postponements for trial preparation, in the hope that delaying the trial will benefit their client: evidence may be lost, victims relocate, police officers retire, key witnesses die or change their minds about testifying. As a result, the criminal process can be delayed to a point where the connection between crime and punishment is broken. Take for instance how the death penalty is employed. More than 10 years typically elapse between the time a criminal is convicted for murder and his or her execution. Delay in its application may mitigate or neutralize the potential deterrent effect of capital punishment.

Not unexpectedly, the most experienced offenders, those who know the ins and outs of the system, are the hardest to deter: they know that crimes provide immediate gratification, whereas the threat of punishment is far in the future.[162] The threat of punishment may also be neutralized by the belief that even if caught criminals can avoid severe punishment by having a smart lawyer who can either get them off or reduce their sentence through plea negotiations.[163]

Restrictive/Partial Deterrence Deterrence measures may not eliminate crime but reduce or restrict its occurrence.

is often an expressive "crime of passion" involving people who know each other and who may be under the influence of drugs and alcohol. Those who choose to take a life may be less influenced by the threat of punishment, even death, than those who commit crime for economic gain. There are also moral questions about the use of the death penalty, not the least of which is that it's used in a racially biased manner. There also remains the fear that an innocent person may be executed because of system error. During the past 30 years, more than 100 people have been wrongfully convicted and sentenced to death in the United States. A majority of death penalty convictions have been overturned, many due to "serious, reversible error," including egregiously incompetent defense counsel, suppression of exculpatory evidence, false confessions, racial manipulation of the jury, "snitch" and accomplice testimony, and faulty jury instructions. Moral thinkers believe that not executing those who have committed capital crimes demonstrates mercy, a practice that is morally preferable to execution.

In sum, the majority of research efforts on the effectiveness of capital punishment have found little deterrent effect. While there are a few criminologists who believe that the death penalty can save lives and should continue to be employed, they are in the minority.

Critical Thinking

1. Even if effective, there is no question the death penalty can cause problems. For example, when Geoffrey Rapp studied the effect of the death penalty on the safety of police officers, he found that the introduction of capital punishment actually created an extremely dangerous environment for law enforcement officers. Because the death penalty does not have a deterrent effect, criminals are more likely to kill police officers when the death penalty is in place. Tragically, the death penalty may lull officers into a false sense of security, causing them to let down their guard—killing fewer citizens but getting killed more often themselves. Given Rapp's findings, should we still maintain the death penalty?

2. Is it possible that the insignificant effects of the death penalty on murder rates is a function in the legal delays that prolong the sentence from being carried out, leaving killers on death row for many years, even decades, before they are executed? Would you recommend that the process be accelerated and executions carried out soon after guilt is established? Or is there a real purpose to delaying executions so that people on death row can exercise every avenue of appeal, making sure an innocent person is not wrongfully executed?

SOURCES: C. F. Manski and J. V. Pepper, "Deterrence and the Death Penalty: Partial Identification Analysis Using Repeated Cross Sections," *Journal of Quantitative Criminology* 29 (2013): 123–141; Steven Durlauf, Chao Fu, and Salvador Navarro, "Capital Punishment and Deterrence: Understanding Disparate Results," *Journal of Quantitative Criminology* 29 (2013): 103–121; Michael Radelet and Traci Lacock, "Do Executions Lower Homicide Rates? The Views of Leading Criminologists," *Journal of Criminal Law and Criminology* 99 (2009): 489–508; Bradley Wilson, "Justice with Mercy: An Argument Against Capital Punishment," *International Journal of Applied Philosophy* 26 (2012): 119–135; Meredith Martin Rountree, "'I'll Make Them Shoot Me': Accounts of Death Row Prisoners Advocating for Execution," *Law and Society Review* 46 (2012): 589–622; David Baldus, Catherine Grosso, George Woodworth, and Richard Newell, "Racial Discrimination in the Administration of the Death Penalty: The Experience of the United States Armed Forces (1984–2005)," *Journal of Criminal Law and Criminology* 101 (2011): 1227–1335; Pew Foundation, "Death Penalty," http://www.pewtrusts.org/our_work_detail.aspx?id=322 (accessed April 2014); Joanna Shepherd, "Deterrence versus Brutalization: Capital Punishment's Differing Impacts Among States," *Michigan Law Review* 104 (2005): 203–253; Geoffrey Rapp, "The Economics of Shootouts: Does the Passage of Capital Punishment Laws Protect or Endanger Police Officers?" *Albany Law Review* 65 (2002): 1051–1084; Robert Dann, "The Deterrent Effect of Capital Punishment," *Friends Social Service Series* 29 (1935).

Deterrence measures may not totally convince criminals that crime does not pay, but might help increase their sensitivity to the risks involved in crime and thereby alter or shape their decision making.

Criminologist Bruce Jacobs has identified the concept of **restrictive deterrence**, a phenomenon that occurs when deterrence measures convince would-be criminals that the risk of committing a particular crime is just too great. Potential criminals then find ways to adapt to this perceived threat:

- The offender reduces the number of crimes he or she commits during a particular period of time.
- The offender commits less serious crimes, assuming that even if he or she is apprehended, the punishment will not be as severe for a more minor infraction (thus, an offender shoplifts a $100 pair of jeans instead of robbing a convenience store for the same monetary reward).
- The offender takes actions to reduce the chance that he or she will be caught and to increase the chance that the

contemplated offense will be undertaken without risk of detection (e.g., wearing a disguise to avoid being identified by the victim).
- Recognizing danger, the offender commits the same crime at a different place or time.[164]

Analyzing General Deterrence

Some experts believe that the true purpose of the law and justice system is to create a "threat system."[165] That is, the threat of legal punishment should, on the face of it, deter lawbreakers through fear. Nonetheless, as we have already discussed, the relationship between crime rates

restrictive deterrence Convincing criminals that committing a serious crime is too risky and that other less-dangerous crimes or actions might be a better choice.

and deterrent measures is far less clear than choice theorists might expect. Despite efforts to punish criminals and make them fear crime, there is little evidence that the fear of apprehension and punishment alone can reduce crime rates. How can this discrepancy be explained?

Rationality   Deterrence theory assumes a rational offender who weighs the costs and benefits of a criminal act before deciding on a course of action. In many instances, criminals are desperate people who suffer from personality disorders that impair their judgment and render them incapable of making truly rational decisions.[166] It is doubtful that any deterrent measure could have influenced an irrational Jared Loughner when he attempted to assassinate U.S. Representative Gabrielle Giffords or Adam Lanza when he killed children in a Newtown, Connecticut, school. Some criminals may be deranged, impulsive, and imprudent rather than reasoning and calculating.

Compulsion   We know that a relatively small group of chronic offenders commits a significant percentage of all serious crimes. Some psychologists believe this select group suffers from an innate or inherited emotional state that renders them both incapable of fearing punishment and less likely to appreciate the consequences of crime.[167] Their compulsive behavior and heightened emotional state negate the deterrent effect of the law.[168]

Need   Many offenders are members of the underclass—people cut off from society, lacking the education and skills they need to be in demand in the modern economy.[169] Such desperate people may not be deterred from crime by fear of punishment because, in reality, they have few other options for success. Among poor, high-risk groups, such as teens living in economically depressed neighborhoods, the threat of formal sanctions is irrelevant.[170] Young people in these areas have less to lose because their opportunities are few, and they have little attachment to social institutions such as school or family. In their environment, they see many people who appear relatively well off (the neighborhood drug dealer) committing crimes without getting caught or punished.[171]

Greed   Some may be immune to deterrent effects because they believe the profits from crime are worth the risk of punishment; it may be their only significant chance for gain and profit. The lure of criminal gains outweighs the fear of capture and punishment. Perceived risk of punishment may deter some potential and active criminal offenders, but only if they doubt that they can make a "big score" from committing a crime.[172]

Greed may encourage some law violators to overestimate the rewards of crime that in reality are often quite meager. When Steven Levitt and Sudhir Alladi Venkatesh studied the financial rewards of being in a drug gang, they found that despite enormous risks to health, life, and freedom, average gang members earned only slightly more than what they could in the legitimate labor market (currently, the minimum wage is typically between $7.25 and $8 per hour, depending on state law).[173] Why then did they stay in the gang? Members believed that there was a strong potential for future riches if they stayed in the drug business and earned a "management" position (i.e., gang leaders earned a lot more). Deterrence is neutralized because the gang boys' greed causes them to overestimate the potential for future criminal gain versus the probability of apprehension and punishment.[174]

SPECIFIC DETERRENCE

LO9   Articulate the basic concepts of specific deterrence

The theory of **specific deterrence** (also called special or particular deterrence) holds that after experiencing criminal sanctions that are swift, sure, and powerful, known criminals will never dare repeat their criminal acts. While general deterrence relies on the perception of future punishments, specific deterrence relies on its application:

- The drunk driver whose sentence is a substantial fine and a week in the county jail should be convinced that the price to be paid for drinking and driving is too great to consider future violations.
- The burglar who spends five years in a tough maximum security prison will find his enthusiasm for theft dampened.
- The tax cheat who is assessed triple damages will think twice before filing a false return.

In principle, punishment works if a connection can be established between the planned action and memories of its consequence; if these recollections are adequately intense, the action will be unlikely to occur again.[175] Yet the connection between experiencing punishment and fearing future punishment is not always as strong as expected.[176]

At first glance, specific deterrence does not seem to work because a majority of known criminals are not deterred by their punishment. Arrest and punishment seem to have little effect on experienced criminals and may even increase the likelihood that first-time offenders will commit new crimes.[177] A sentence to a juvenile justice facility does little to deter a persistent delinquent from becoming an adult criminal.[178] Most prison inmates had prior records of arrest and conviction before their current

specific deterrence The view that if experienced punishment is severe enough, convicted offenders will be deterred from repeating their criminal activity.

offenses.[179] About two-thirds of all convicted felons are rearrested within three years of their release from prison, and those who have been punished in the past are the most likely to recidivate.[180] Incarceration may sometimes slow down or delay recidivism in the short term, but the overall probability of rearrest does not change following incarceration.[181]

According to the theory of specific deterrence, the harsher the punishment, the less likely the chances of recidivism. But research shows that this is not always the case. Offenders sentenced to prison do not have lower rates of recidivism than those receiving more lenient community sentences for similar crimes. The effect of incarceration on rearrest appears to be minimal.[182] White-collar offenders who receive prison sentences are as likely to recidivate as those who receive community-based sanctions.[183]

Can Punishment Produce More Crime?

In some instances, rather than reducing the frequency of crime, severe punishments may actually increase reoffending rates.[184] Some states are now employing high-security "supermax" prisons that use bare minimum treatment and 23-hours-a-day lockdown. Certainly such a harsh regimen should deter future criminality. But a recent study in the state of Washington showed that upon release supermax prisoners had significantly higher felony recidivism rates when compared to a matched sample of traditional

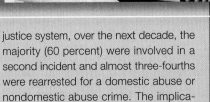

DETERRING DOMESTIC VIOLENCE

One of the most famous efforts to determine the specific deterrent effect of punishment was the classic study by Lawrence Sherman and Richard Berk on the effects of arrest on domestic violence. Sherman and Berk had police officers in Minneapolis randomly assign one of three outcomes to domestic assault cases they encountered on their beats:

- Advice and mediation only
- Remove the assailant from the home for a period of eight hours
- Formally arrest the assailant

According to specific deterrence theory, a formal arrest should have a greater impact than advice and mediation, and in this case it did. Sherman and Berk found that when police took formal action (arrest), the chance of recidivism was substantially less than when less punitive measures, such as warning offenders or ordering offenders out of the house for a cooling-off period, were used. A six-month follow-up found that only 10 percent of those who were arrested repeated their violent behavior, while 19 percent of those advised and 24 percent of those sent away repeated their offenses. Sherman and Berk concluded that a formal arrest was the most effective means of controlling domestic violence, regardless of what happened to the offender in court, and the specific deterrent effect of arrest produced positive long-term outcomes.

The Minneapolis experiment deeply affected police operations around the nation. Atlanta, Chicago, Dallas, Denver, Detroit, New York, Miami, San Francisco, and Seattle, among other large cities, adopted policies encouraging arrests in domestic violence cases. A number of states adopted legislation mandating that police either take formal action in domestic abuse cases or explain in writing their failure to act. Nonetheless, replicating the Minneapolis experiment in five other locales—including Omaha, Nebraska, and Charlotte, North Carolina—failed to duplicate the original results. In these locales, formal arrest was not a greater deterrent to domestic abuse than warning or advising the assailant.

Subsequent efforts to link punishment and deterrence in domestic violence cases have also produced inconclusive results. Andrew Klein and Terri Tobin found that batterers in a Massachusetts district court were undeterred by arrest, prosecution, probation supervision, incarceration, and treatment. Although only a minority of the men in the study reabused (32 percent) or were arrested for any crime (43 percent) within a year of their first involvement with the justice system, over the next decade, the majority (60 percent) were involved in a second incident and almost three-fourths were rearrested for a domestic abuse or nondomestic abuse crime. The implications of the domestic violence research is that even if punishment can produce a short-term specific deterrent effect, it fails to produce longer-term behavior change.

Critical Thinking

If the effect of arrest on spouse abuse is only short term, what else can be done to convince men not to batter? Is treatment rather than punishment a better approach? Or would arrest work if it were backed up by mandatory prison sentences? Maybe getting tough is still not tough enough.

SOURCES: Frank Sloan, Alyssa Platt, Lindsey Chepke, and Claire Blevins, "Deterring Domestic Violence: Do Criminal Sanctions Reduce Repeat Offenses?" *Journal of Risk and Uncertainty* 46 (2013): 51–80; Lawrence Sherman and Richard Berk, "The Specific Deterrent Effects of Arrest for Domestic Assault," *American Sociological Review* 49 (1984): 261–272; J. David Hirschel, Ira Hutchison, and Charles Dean, "The Failure of Arrest to Deter Spouse Abuse," *Journal of Research in Crime and Delinquency* 29 (1992): 7–33; Franklyn Dunford, David Huizinga, and Delbert Elliott, "The Role of Arrest in Domestic Assault: The Omaha Experiment," *Criminology* 28 (1990): 183–206. Andrew Klein and Terri Tobin, "A Longitudinal Study of Arrested Batterers, 1995–2005: Career Criminals," *Violence Against Women* 14 (2008): 136–157.

policy and practice in criminology

inmates.[185] There are a number of factors that might help explain why severe punishments promote rather than restrict criminality:

- Offenders may believe they have learned from their experiences, and now know how to beat the system and get away with crime.[186]
- Severely punished offenders may represent the "worst of the worst," who will offend again no matter what punishments they experience.[187]
- Punishment may bring defiance rather than deterrence. People who are harshly treated may want to show that they cannot be broken by the system. Punishment might be perceived to be capricious, unjust, or unfair, which causes sanctioned offenders to commit additional crimes as a way to lash out and retaliate.
- Harsh treatment labels and stigmatizes offenders, locking them into a criminal career.
- Criminals who are punished may also believe that the likelihood of getting caught twice for the same type of crime is remote: "Lightning never strikes twice in the same spot," they may reason; no one is that unlucky.[188]

incapacitation effect The idea that keeping offenders in confinement will eliminate the risk of their committing further offenses.

One crime that is notorious for involving repeat incidents is domestic violence. Can punishment reduce repeat offending? This topic is discussed in the Policy and Practice in Criminology feature on the previous page.

INCAPACITATION

LO10 Critique the incapacitation strategy to reduce crime

It stands to reason that if more criminals are sent to prison, the crime rate should go down. Because most people age out of crime, the duration of a criminal career is limited. Placing offenders behind bars during their prime crime years should lessen their lifetime opportunity to commit crime. The shorter the span of opportunity, the fewer offenses they can commit during their lives; hence crime is reduced. This theory, known as the **incapacitation effect**, seems logical, but does it work? The most recent data indicate that nationwide about 1.5 million people are in prison and another 750,000 are incarcerated in local jails.[189] Because the number of American adults is about 230 million, this means that one in every 100 adults is behind bars.[190] Advocates of incapacitation suggest that this growth in the prison/jail population is directly responsible for the decade-long decline in the crime rate: by putting dangerous felons under lock and key for longer periods of time, the opportunity they have to commit crime is significantly reduced and so too is the crime rate.

Belief that a strict incarceration policy can shape criminal choice and reduce crime rates has encouraged states to adopt tough sentencing laws such as the "three strikes and you're out" policy. This sentencing model mandates that people convicted of three felony offenses serve a mandatory life term without parole. Other states employ habitual offender laws that provide long (or life) sentences for repeat offenders. Those who advocate for these tough laws credit them with producing the two-decade crime drop in America.[191]

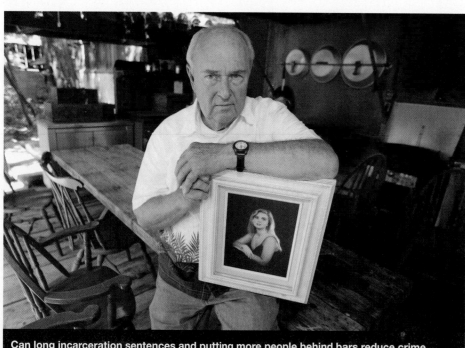

Can long incarceration sentences and putting more people behind bars reduce crime rates? Pictured here is Mike Reynolds, author of California's 1994 voter-approved three-strikes law, which requires those convicted of a third felony to serve a minimum of 25 years in prison. Reynolds wrote and campaigned to pass the three-strikes initiative after his daughter Kimber, 18, was killed during a 1992 purse snatching. While skeptics question whether incarceration can reduce crime rates, advocates point to the fact that as the prison population swelled, crime rates in the United States dropped.

AP Images/Rich Pedroncelli

Does Incarceration Control Crime?

The fact that crime rates have dropped while the prison population has boomed supports incapacitation as an effective crime control policy. This assumption seems logical considering how much crime chronic offenders commit each year and the fact that criminal opportunities are ended once they are behind bars.

While it is difficult to measure precisely, there is at least some evidence that crime rates and incarceration rates are interrelated. Economist Steven Levitt concludes that each person put behind bars results in a decrease of 15 serious crimes per year. The social benefits associated with crime reduction equal or exceed the social and financial costs of incarceration.[192] Benjamin Meade and his associates found that inmates serving long sentences (five years or more) are less likely to recidivate once released than those serving shorter sentences, suggesting that incarceration can reduce crime rates.[193]

The downside of an incarceration policy: inmates at Chino State Prison, which houses 5,500 inmates, sleep on double and triple bunk beds in a gymnasium that was modified to house 213 prisoners. A federal court ruled that the California state prison system would have to release 40,000 prisoners to cope with overcrowding so severe that it violated their human rights; in 2011 that decision was upheld by the Supreme Court. Nonetheless, despite reforms, there are today more than 120,000 inmates currently incarcerated in prisons that were designed to hold about 80,000.

Kevork Djansezian/Getty Images News/Getty Images

While these findings are supportive, there are also factors that limit the deterrent effect of incarceration:

- There is little evidence that incapacitating criminals will deter them from future criminality and even more reason to believe they may be more inclined to commit crimes upon release. The more prior incarceration experiences inmates have, the more likely they are to recidivate (and return to prison) within 12 months of their release.[194]
- By its nature, the prison experience exposes young, first-time offenders to higher-risk, more experienced inmates who can influence their lifestyle and help shape their attitudes. Novice inmates also run an increased risk of becoming infected with AIDS and other health hazards, and that exposure reduces their life chances after release.[195] The short-term crime reduction effect of incapacitating criminals is negated if the prison experience has the long-term effect of escalating frequency of criminal behavior upon release.
- The economics of crime suggest that if money can be made from criminal activity, there will always be someone to take the place of the incarcerated offender. New criminals will be recruited and trained, offsetting any benefit accrued by incarceration. Imprisoning established offenders may likewise open new opportunities for competitors who were suppressed by more experienced criminals. Incarcerating gang members or organized crime figures may open crime and illegal drug markets to new groups and gangs who are even hungrier and more aggressive than the gangs they replaced.
- Most criminal offenses are committed by teens and very young adult offenders who are unlikely to be sent to prison for a single felony conviction. Aging criminals are already past the age when they are likely to commit crime. As a result, a strict incarceration policy may keep people in prison beyond the time they are a threat to society while a new cohort of high-risk adolescents is on the street.[196]

CONNECTIONS

Chapter 2 discussed the factors that control crime rates. What appears to be an incapacitation effect may actually reflect the effect of some other legal phenomena and not the incarceration of so many criminals. If, for example, the crime rate drops as more people are sent to prison, it would appear that incapacitation works. However, crime rates may really be dropping because potential criminals now fear punishment and are being deterred from crime. What appears to be an incapacitation effect may actually be an effect of general deterrence. Similarly, people may be willing to build new prisons because the economy is robust. If the crime rate drops, it may be because of economic effects and not because of prison construction.

- Incapacitating criminals only produces modest benefits and is not a cost-effective strategy.[197] One reason is that the recidivism rate is quite high. Serving a prison sentence and suffering postrelease personal and financial problems may cause people to commit more crimes than they might have had they not been sentenced to prison. The crimes that are "saved" while they serve time in prison are more than made up for after they are released.[198]

- Even if incarceration could reduce the crime rate, the costs would be enormous. Are U.S. taxpayers willing to spend billions more on new prison construction and annual maintenance fees? A strict incarceration policy would result in a growing number of elderly inmates whose maintenance costs are far higher than that of younger inmates. The numbers of elderly inmates are already skyrocketing: there are now 240,000 elderly inmates behind bars, costing states about $70,000 per inmate annually to care for and maintain.[199]

- Relying on incapacitation as a crime control mechanism has resulted in an ever-expanding prison population. Eventually most inmates return to society in a process referred to as reentry. In most states, prison inmates, especially those convicted of drug crimes, have come from comparatively few urban inner-city areas. Their return may contribute to family disruption, undermine social institutions, and create community disorganization. Rather than act as a crime suppressant, incarceration may have the long-term effect of accelerating crime rates.[200]

While the debate over the effectiveness of incapacitating criminals to reduce the crime rate rages on, there is no doubt that U.S. sentencing policies have embraced the practice of putting lots of people behind bars for very long periods of time. Prison sentences in the United States today are frequently two to three times the length for similar offenses in the United Kingdom, the Netherlands, France, and other industrialized nations.[201]

Concept Summary 4.1 outlines the various methods of crime control and their effects.

CONNECTIONS

Inmates may recidivate due to lack of economic opportunities once they are released. The association between crime and economic status is reviewed in Chapter 6.

Ask Yourself ...
What can be done to help inmates adjust? Should they be given jobs even though millions of law-abiding citizens are unemployed? And if former inmates cannot find work, how can we expect them to "go straight"?

thinking like a criminologist

© iStockphoto.com/ssharick

NO FRILLS

The governor is running on a law and order plank. He claims that prisons don't work because they are too lenient. He proposes ending hot meals, education programs, counseling, and phone privileges. Television and other recreation would be curtailed, as well as visitation. His reasoning is that if prison were just an awful experience, few inmates would risk returning and therefore would be afraid to commit new crimes.

Write a brief position paper giving your take on the plan. Would it work? Even if it did, are there ethical issues with the governor's proposed "no frills" approach? To paraphrase the decision in *Bell v. Wolfish*, prisons are places for punishment, but should they be punishing places? Is it more ethical to try to rehabilitate inmates to help them in the future rather than to punish them for what they did in the past?

PUBLIC POLICY IMPLICATIONS OF CHOICE THEORY

From the origins of classical theory to the development of modern rational choice views, the belief that criminals choose to commit crime has influenced the relationships among law, punishment, and crime. Although research on the core principles of choice theory and deterrence theories produces mixed results, these models have had an important impact on crime prevention strategies.

When police patrol in well-marked cars, it is assumed that their presence will deter would-be criminals. When the harsh realities of prison life are portrayed in movies and TV shows, the lesson is not lost on potential criminals. Nowhere is the idea that the threat of punishment can control crime more evident than in the implementation of tough mandatory criminal sentences to control violent crime and drug trafficking.

The fact that punishment may deter criminals from committing crime has shaped sentencing policy. A number of states have adopted draconian sentencing policies that require mandatory prison terms for specific crimes such as drug trafficking or the use of a firearm while committing crime. Another deterrence strategy is the "three strikes and you're out" laws, which require the state courts to hand down mandatory periods of incarceration of up to life in prison to persons who have been convicted of a serious criminal offense on three or more separate occasions. While a policy of placing people convicted of a third felony behind bars for life is politically compelling, many criminologists believe these laws are ineffective and will create a growing population of expensive to maintain elderly inmates who committed relatively minor crimes.[202]

And despite the ongoing debate about the deterrent effect of the death penalty, it is still employed in a majority of states and by the federal government. Some advocates argue that the death penalty can effectively restrict criminality; at least it ensures that convicted criminals never again get the opportunity to kill. Many observers are dismayed because people who are convicted of murder sometimes kill again when released on parole. About 9 percent of all inmates on death row have had prior convictions for homicide. Death penalty advocates argue that if these criminals had been executed for their first offenses, hundreds of people would be alive today.[203] And the recent evidence indicating that if used a lot capital punishment can reduce a state's murder rate has encouraged some members of the moral and legal community to suggest that capital punishment is justified because it is a life-saving social policy. Writing in the *Stanford Law Review*, Cass Sunstein and Adrian Vermeule conclude that "a government that settles upon a package of crime control policies that does *not* include capital punishment might well seem, at least prima facie, to be both violating the rights and reducing the welfare of its citizens—just as would a state that failed to enact simple environmental measures promising to save a great many lives."[204]

Just Desert

The concept of criminal choice has also prompted the creation of justice policies referred to as **just desert**. In his classic book *Doing Justice*, legal expert Andrew Von Hirsch suggests that punishment, commensurate with the seriousness of the crime, is needed to preserve the social equity disturbed by crime.[205] As he puts it, those who violate others' rights deserve to be punished, but, to be fair, since punishment makes those punished suffer, it should only be sufficient to prevent more misery than it inflicts—no more,

just desert The philosophy of justice that asserts that those who violate the rights of others deserve to be punished. The severity of punishment should be commensurate with the seriousness of the crime.

no less.[206] Punishing someone to deter others is wrong and unfair and so is punishing someone so they won't commit crime in the future, since the future is impossible to predict. People should be punished simply because they deserve to be; they are **blameworthy**.

According to legal scholar Richard Frase, two basic elements determine an offender's degree of blameworthiness: the nature and seriousness of the harm caused or threatened by the crime and the offender's degree of fault in committing the crime.[207] If an offender is blameworthy for what they did in the present, their punishment should only reflect the character of their present offense; people deserve to be punished for what they did, not for what others may do or what they may do in the future.

Assigning Blame   How do we determine how much punishment is fitting for a particular crime? In other words, how do we assess blame? According to Frase, in contemporary society, fault is measured by a number of factors: the offender's intent (e.g., deliberate wrongdoing is considered

more serious than criminal negligence); his or her capacity to obey the law (e.g., blameworthiness is tempered by such conditions as mental disease or defect, chemical dependency, or situational factors such as threats or other strong inducements to commit the crime); the offender's motives for committing the crime (which may mitigate or aggravate culpability); and, for multidefendant crimes, the defendant's role in the offense as instigator, leader, follower, primary actor, or minor player.[208] According to Frase, fairness is brought to the justice process by assessing blame in a fair and even-handed manner: fairness to the victim and the victim's family (i.e., otherwise they might seek vengeance on their own), fairness to law-abiding persons (who refrained from committing this offense), and fairness to the defendant (who has a right to be punished in proportion to his blameworthiness).

In sum, the just desert model suggests that retribution justifies punishment because people deserve what they get for past deeds. Punishment based on deterrence or incapacitation is wrong because it involves an offender's future actions, which cannot accurately be predicted. Punishment should be the same for all people who commit the same crime. Criminal sentences based on individual needs or characteristics are inherently unfair because all people are equally blameworthy for their misdeeds. The influence of Von Hirsch's views can be seen in sentencing models that give the same punishment to all people who commit the same type of crime.

blameworthy Basing punishment solely on whether a person is responsible for wrongdoing and deserving of censure or blame.

SUMMARY

LO1 Describe the development of rational choice theory

Rational choice theory has its roots in the classical school of criminology developed by the eighteenth-century Italian social thinker Cesare Beccaria. James Q. Wilson observed that people who are likely to commit crime are unafraid of breaking the law because they value the excitement and thrills of crime, have a low stake in conformity, and are willing to take greater chances than the average person.

LO2 Discuss the most important concepts of rational choice theory

Law-violating behavior is the product of careful thought and planning. People who commit crime believe that the rewards of crime outweigh the risks. If they think they are likely to get arrested and punished, people will not risk criminal activities. Before choosing to commit a crime, reasoning criminals carefully select targets, and their behavior is systematic and selective. Rational choice theorists view crime as both offense- and offender-specific.

LO3 Analyze the process in which offenders structure criminality

Criminals consider their needs and capabilities before committing crimes. One important decision that is made before

someone enters a life of crime is the need for money. Personal experience may be an important element in structuring criminality. Before committing crimes, criminals report, they actually learn techniques to help them avoid detection while making profits.

LO4 Depict in your own words how criminals structure crime

Criminals carefully choose where they will commit their crime. Evidence of rational choice may be found in the way criminals locate their targets. Rational choice involves both shaping criminality and structuring crime. If a target appears dangerous, they will choose another.

LO5 Clarify the arguments that crime is rational

There is evidence that theft-related crimes are the product of careful risk assessment, including environmental, social, and structural factors. Target selection seems highly rational. Even drug use is controlled by rational decision making. Users report that they begin taking drugs when they believe the benefits of substance abuse outweigh its costs. Evidence confirms that even violent criminals select suitable targets by picking people who are vulnerable and lack adequate defenses. In some instances, targets are chosen in order to send a message rather than to generate capital.

LO6 Identify the elements of the CRAVED model of crime choice

According to the CRAVED model of crime choice, the elements that encourage crime are targets that are easily hidden, portable, widely available and easy to find, valuable, enjoyable to own, and easy to sell.

LO7 Assess the validity of situational crime prevention techniques for reducing crime

Situational crime prevention involves developing tactics to reduce or eliminate a specific crime problem. These include tactics to increase the effort required to commit crime, such as putting unbreakable glass on storefronts, locking gates, and fencing yards. It can also involve increasing the risks of crime through better security efforts. Reducing the rewards of crime is designed to lessen the value of crime to the potential criminal. Crime may be reduced or prevented if we can communicate to people the wrongfulness of their behavior and how it is harmful to society. Crime may be reduced by making it difficult for people to excuse their criminal behavior by saying things like "I didn't know that was illegal" or "I had no choice."

LO8 Categorize the elements of general deterrence

As the fear of punishment increases, crime rates decrease. If the certainty of arrest, conviction, and sanctioning increases, crime rates should decline. The threat of severe punishment should also bring the crime rate down. The faster punishment is applied and the more closely it is linked to the crime, the more likely it will serve as a deterrent. Not only does the actual chance of punishment influence criminality, so too does the perception of punishment. People who perceive they will be punished for crimes will avoid doing those crimes.

LO9 Articulate the basic concepts of specific deterrence

The theory of specific deterrence holds that criminal sanctions should be so powerful that known criminals will never repeat their criminal acts. Research on specific deterrence does not provide any clear-cut evidence that punishing criminals is an effective means of stopping them from committing future crimes. Punishment may bring defiance rather than deterrence. People who are harshly treated may want to show that they cannot be broken by the system. The stigma of harsh treatment labels people and helps lock offenders into a criminal career instead of convincing them to avoid one.

LO10 Critique the incapacitation strategy to reduce crime

The more criminals are sent to prison, the more the crime rate should go down. Placing offenders behind bars during their prime crime years should reduce their lifetime opportunity to commit crime. The shorter the span of opportunity, the fewer offenses they can commit during their lives; hence, crime is reduced. However, there is little evidence that incapacitating criminals will deter them from future criminality and reason to believe they may be more inclined to commit even more crimes upon release.

CRITICAL THINKING QUESTIONS

1. Are criminals rational decision makers, or are they motivated by uncontrollable psychological and emotional drives?
2. Would you want to live in a society where crime rates are low because criminals are subjected to extremely harsh punishments, such as flogging?
3. If you were caught by the police while shoplifting, which would you be more afraid of: receiving criminal punishment or being ashamed to face your friends or relatives?
4. Is it possible to create a method of capital punishment that would actually deter murder—for example, by televising executions? What might be some of the negative consequences of such a policy?

KEY TERMS

Enlightenment (97)
marginal deterrence (97)
classical criminology (97)
rational choice theory (99)
reasoning criminals (100)
offense-specific crime (101)
offender-specific crime (101)
criminality (101)
boosters (105)
permeable neighborhoods (105)

edgework (107)
situational crime prevention (107)
defensible space (108)
crime discouragers (109)
diffusion of benefits (110)
discouragement (111)
displacement (111)
general deterrence (111)
perceptual deterrence (112)
deterrence theory (112)

tipping point (112)
crackdowns (113)
informal sanctions (113)
restrictive deterrence (115)
specific deterrence (116)
incapacitation effect (118)
just desert (121)
blameworthy (122)

1. Federal Bureau of Investigation, "Prepaid Funeral Scam," January 17, 2014, http://www.fbi.gov/news/stories/2014/january/prepaid-funeral-scam (accessed April 2014).

2. Alan Harding, *Medieval Law and the Foundations of the State* (New York: Oxford University Press, 2002).

3. Eugen Weber, *A Modern History of Europe* (New York: W. W. Norton, 1971), p. 398.

4. Jeremy Bentham, *A Fragment on Government and an Introduction to the Principle of Morals and Legislation* (1776), ed. Wilfred Harrison (Oxford: Basil Blackwell, 1967).

5. Ibid., p. xi.

6. Ibid.

7. George J. Stigler, "The Optimum Enforcement of Laws," *Journal of Political Economy* 78 (1970): 526–528.

8. Marvin Wolfgang, *Patterns in Criminal Homicide* (Philadelphia: University of Pennsylvania Press, 1958).

9. Bob Roshier, *Controlling Crime* (Chicago: Lyceum Books, 1989), p. 10.

10. Robert Martinson, "What Works? Questions and Answers about Prison Reform," *Public Interest* 35 (1974): 22–54.

11. Charles Murray and Louis Cox, *Beyond Probation* (Beverly Hills: Sage, 1979).

12. Ronald Bayer, "Crime, Punishment, and the Decline of Liberal Optimism," *Crime and Delinquency* 27 (1981): 190.

13. James Q. Wilson, *Thinking about Crime*, rev. ed. (New York: Vintage Books, 1983), p. 260.

14. Ibid., p. 128.

15. Michael Tonry, *Malign Neglect: Race, Crime and Punishment in America* (New York: Oxford University Press, 1995).

16. Ann Carson and Daniela Golinelli, *Prisoners in 2012—Advance Counts* (Washington, DC: Bureau of Justice Statistics, 2013), http://www.bjs.gov/content/pub/ascii/p12ac.txt (accessed April 2014).

17. John Irwin and James Austin, *It's About Time: America's Imprisonment Binge* (Belmont, CA: Wadsworth, 1997).

18. See, generally, Derek Cornish and Ronald Clarke, eds., *The Reasoning Criminal: Rational Choice Perspectives on Offending* (New York: Springer Verlag, 1986); and Morgan Reynolds, *Crime by Choice: An Economic Analysis* (Dallas: Fisher Institute, 1985).

19. David A. Ward, Mark C. Stafford, and Louis N. Gray, "Rational Choice, Deterrence, and Theoretical Integration," *Journal of Applied Social Psychology* 36 (2006): 571–585.

20. Hung-en Sung and Linda Richter, "Rational Choice and Environmental Deterrence in the Retention of Mandated Drug Abuse Treatment Clients," *International Journal of Offender Therapy and Comparative Criminology* 51 (2007): 686–702.

21. Timothy Brezina, "Delinquent Problem-Solving: An Interpretive Framework for Criminological Theory and Research," *Journal of Research in Crime and Delinquency* 37 (2000): 3–30.

22. Bill McCarthy and John Hagan, "Mean Streets: The Theoretical Significance of Situational Delinquency Among Homeless Youths," *American Journal of Sociology* 3 (1992): 597–627.

23. Andy Hochstetler, "Opportunities and Decisions: Interactional Dynamics in Robbery and Burglary Groups," *Criminology* 39 (2001): 737–763.

24. Jeff Ferrell, "Criminological Verstehen: Inside the Immediacy of Crime," *Justice Quarterly* 14 (1997): 3–23.

25. Peter Wood, Walter Gove, James Wilson, and John Cochran, "Nonsocial Reinforcement and Habitual Criminal Conduct: An Extension of Learning," *Criminology* 35 (1997): 335–366.

26. Melanie Wellsmith and Amy Burrell, "The Influence of Purchase Price and Ownership Levels on Theft Targets: The Example of Domestic Burglary," *British Journal of Criminology* 45 (2005): 741–764.

27. Carlo Morselli and Marie-Noële Royer, "Criminal Mobility and Criminal Achievement," *Journal of Research in Crime and Delinquency* 45 (2008): 4–21.

28. Ross Matsueda, Derek Kreager, and David Huizinga, "Deterring Delinquents: A Rational Choice Model of Theft and Violence," *American Sociological Review* 71 (2006): 95–122.

29. Jeffrey Bouffard, "Predicting Differences in the Perceived Relevance of Crime's Costs and Benefits in a Test of Rational Choice Theory," *International Journal of Offender Therapy and Comparative Criminology* 51 (2007): 461–485.

30. Christopher Uggen and Melissa Thompson, "The Socioeconomic Determinants of Ill-Gotten Gains: Within-Person Changes in Drug Use and Illegal Earnings," *American Journal of Sociology* 109 (2003): 146–187.

31. Philippe Bourgois, *In Search of Respect: Selling Crack in El Barrio* (Cambridge: Cambridge University Press, 1995), p. 326.

32. Bouffard, "Predicting Differences in the Perceived Relevance of Crime's Costs and Benefits in a Test of Rational Choice Theory."

33. George Rengert and John Wasilchick, *Suburban Burglary: A Time and Place for Everything* (Springfield, IL: Charles C Thomas, 1985).

34. Christopher Birkbeck and Gary LaFree, "The Situational Analysis of Crime and Deviance," *American Review of Sociology* 19 (1993): 113–137.

35. Derek Cornish and Ronald Clarke, "Understanding Crime Displacement: An Application of Rational Choice Theory," *Criminology* 25 (1987): 933–947.

36. Michael Gottfredson and Travis Hirschi, *A General Theory of Crime* (Stanford, CA: Stanford University Press, 1990).

37. D. Wayne Osgood, and Amy Anderson, "Unstructured Socializing and Rates of Delinquency," *Criminology* 42 (2004): 519–550.

38. Wim Bernasco, Stijn Ruiter, Gerben Bruinsma, Lieven Pauwels, and Frank Weerman, "Situational Causes of Offending: A Fixed-Effects Analysis of Space–Time Budget Data," *Criminology* 51 (2013): 895–926.

39. Megan Bears Augustyn and Jean Marie McGloin, "The Risk of Informal Socializing with Peers: Considering Gender Differences Across Predatory Delinquency and Substance Use," *Justice Quarterly* 30 (2013): 117–143.

40. Ibid.

41. Holly Nguyen and Jean Marie McGloin, "Does Economic Adversity Breed Criminal Cooperation? Considering the Motivation Behind Group Crime," *Criminology* 51 (2013): 833–870.

42. Uggen and Thompson, "The Socioeconomic Determinants of Ill-Gotten Gains."

43. Pierre Tremblay and Carlo Morselli, "Patterns in Criminal Achievement: Wilson and Abrahamse Revisited," *Criminology* 38 (2000): 633–660.

44. Liliana Pezzin, "Earnings Prospects, Matching Effects, and the Decision to Terminate a Criminal Career," *Journal of Quantitative Criminology* 11 (1995): 29–50.

45. Melissa Thompson and Christopher Uggen, "Dealers, Thieves, and the Common Determinants of Drug and Nondrug Illegal Earnings," *Criminology* 59 (2012): 1057–1087.

46. Ronald Akers, "Rational Choice, Deterrence, and Social Learning Theory in Criminology: The Path Not Taken," *Journal of Criminal Law and Criminology* 81 (1990): 653–676.

47. Neal Shover, *Aging Criminals* (Beverly Hills: Sage, 1985).

48. Patricia Morgan and Karen Ann Joe, "Citizens and Outlaws: The Private Lives and Public Lifestyles of Women in the Illicit Drug Economy," *Journal of Drug Issues* 26 (1996): 125–142, at 132.

49. Bruce Jacobs, "Crack Dealers' Apprehension Avoidance Techniques: A Case of Restrictive Deterrence," *Justice Quarterly* 13 (1996): 359–381.

50. Ibid., p. 367.

51. Ibid., p. 372.

52. Bruce Jacobs and Jody Miller, "Crack Dealing, Gender, and Arrest Avoidance," *Social Problems* 45 (1998): 550–566.

53. Jacobs, "Crack Dealers' Apprehension Avoidance Techniques."

54. Ibid., p. 367.

55. Ibid., p. 368.

56. Eric Baumer, Janet Lauritsen, Richard Rosenfeld, and Richard Wright, "The Influence of Crack Cocaine on Robbery, Burglary, and Homicide Rates: A Cross-City, Longitudinal Analysis," *Journal of Research in Crime and Delinquency* 35 (1998): 316–340.

57. George Rengert and John Wasilchick, *Space, Time, and Crime: Ethnographic Insights into Residential Burglary* (Washington, DC: National Institute of Justice, 1989); see also Rengert and Wasilchick, *Suburban Burglary*.

58. Paul Cromwell, James Olson, and D'Aunn Wester Avary, *Breaking and Entering, an Ethnographic Analysis of Burglary* (Newbury Park, CA: Sage, 1989), pp. 30–32.

59. Ibid., p. 24.

60. Michael Costanzo, William Halperin, and Nathan Gale, "Criminal Mobility and the Directional Component in Journeys to Crime," in *Metropolitan Crime Patterns*, ed. Robert Figlio, Simon Hakim, and George Rengert (Monsey, NY: Criminal Justice Press, 1986), pp. 73–95.

61. Morselli and Royer, "Criminal Mobility and Criminal Achievement."

62. Joseph Deutsch and Gil Epstein, "Changing a Decision Taken Under Uncertainty: The Case of the Criminal's Location Choice," *Urban Studies* 35 (1998): 1335–1344.

63. Robert Sampson and Jacqueline Cohen, "Deterrent Effects of the Police on Crime: A Replication and Theoretical Extension," *Law and Society Review* 22 (1988): 163–188.

64. Kenneth Tunnell, *Choosing Crime* (Chicago: Nelson-Hall, 1992), p. 105.

65. Paul Bellair, "Informal Surveillance and Street Crime: A Complex Relationship," *Criminology* 38 (2000): 137–167.

66. Gary Kleck and Don Kates, *Armed: New Perspectives on Guns* (Amherst, NY: Prometheus Books, 2001).

67. Elizabeth Ehrhardt Mustaine and Richard Tewksbury, "Predicting Risks of Larceny Theft Victimization: A Routine Activity Analysis Using Refined Lifestyle Measures," *Criminology* 36 (1998): 829–858.

68. Bruce A. Jacobs and Richard Wright, "Researching Drug Robbery," *Crime and Delinquency* 54 (2008): 511–531.

69. Associated Press, "Thrift Hearings Resume Today in Senate," *Boston Globe*, January 2, 1991, p. 10.

70. Ralph Taylor and Stephen Gottfredson, "Environmental Design, Crime, and Prevention: An Examination of Community Dynamics," in *Communities and Crime*, ed. Albert Reiss and Michael Tonry (Chicago: University of Chicago Press, 1986), pp. 387–416.

71. Pamela Wilcox, Tamara Madensen, and Marie Skubak Tillyer, "Guardianship in Context: Implications for Burglary Victimization Risk and Prevention," *Criminology* 45 (2007): 771–803.

72. Garland White, "Neighborhood Permeability and Burglary Rates," *Justice Quarterly* 7 (1990): 57–67.

73. Ibid., p. 65.

74. Matthew Robinson, "Lifestyles, Routine Activities, and Residential Burglary Victimization," *Journal of Criminal Justice* 22 (1999): 27–52.

75. Cromwell, Olson, and Avary, *Breaking and Entering*.

76. Andrew Buck, Simon Hakim, and George Rengert, "Burglar Alarms and the Choice Behavior of Burglars: A Suburban Phenomenon," *Journal of Criminal Justice* 21 (1993): 497–507.

77. John Gibbs and Peggy Shelly, "Life in the Fast Lane: A Retrospective View by Commercial Thieves," *Journal of Research in Crime and Delinquency* 19 (1982): 229–230.

78. John Petraitis, Brian Flay, and Todd Miller, "Reviewing Theories of Adolescent Substance Use: Organizing Pieces in the Puzzle," *Psychological Bulletin* 117 (1995): 67–86.

79. Leanne Fiftal Alarid, James Marquart, Velmer Burton, Francis Cullen, and Steven Cuvelier, "Women's Roles in Serious Offenses: A Study of Adult Felons," *Justice Quarterly* 13 (1996): 431–454, at 448.

80. James A. Densley, "It's Gang Life, but Not as We Know It: The Evolution of Gang Business," *Crime and Delinquency*, first published April 4, 2012.

81. Trevor Bennett and Fiona Brookman, "The Role of Violence in Street Crime: A Qualitative Study of Violent Offenders," *International Journal of Offender Therapy and Comparative Criminology* 53 (2009): 617–633.

82. Richard B. Felson, *Violence and Gender Reexamined* (Washington, DC: American Psychological Association, 2002).

83. Richard Felson and Steven Messner, "To Kill or Not to Kill? Lethal Outcomes in Injurious Attacks," *Criminology* 34 (1996): 519–545, at 541.

84. James Wright and Peter Rossi, *Armed and Considered Dangerous: A Survey of Felons and Their Firearms* (Hawthorne, NY: Aldine de Gruyter, 1983), pp. 141–159.

85. Gary Kleck and Marc Gertz, "Carry Guns for Protection: Results from the National Self-Defense Survey," *Journal of Research in Crime and Delinquency* 35 (1998): 193–224.

86. Peter van Koppen and Robert Jansen, "The Time to Rob: Variations in Time and Number of Commercial Robberies," *Journal of Research in Crime and Delinquency* 36 (1999): 7–29.

87. William Smith, Sharon Glave Frazee, and Elizabeth Davison, "Furthering the Integration of Routine Activity and Social Disorganization Theories: Small Units of Analysis and the Study of Street Robbery as a Diffusion Process," *Criminology* 38 (2000): 489–521.

88. Wim Bernasco and Paul Nieuwbeerta, "How Do Residential Burglars Select Target Areas? A New Approach to the Analysis of Criminal Location Choice," *British Journal of Criminology* 45 (2005): 296–315.

89. Alan Lizotte, Marvin Krohn, James Howell, Kimberly Tobin, and Gregory Howard, "Factors Influencing Gun Carrying Among Young Urban Males over the Adolescent–Young Adult Life Course," *Criminology* 38 (2000): 811–834.

90. Scott Decker, "Deviant Homicide: A New Look at the Role of Motives and Victim–Offender Relationships," *Journal of Research in Crime and Delinquency* 33 (1996): 427–449.

91. Felson and Messner, "To Kill or Not to Kill?"

92. Eric Hickey, *Serial Murderers and Their Victims* (Pacific Grove, CA: Brooks/Cole, 1991), p. 84.

93. Benoit Leclerc, Richard Wortley, and Stephen Smallbone, "Getting into the Script of Adult Child Sex Offenders and Mapping out Situational Prevention Measures," *Journal of Research in Crime and Delinquency* 48 (2011): 209–237.

94. Benoit Leclerc, Jean Proulx, and André McKibben, "Modus Operandi of Sexual Offenders Working or Doing Voluntary Work with Children and Adolescents," *Journal of Sexual Aggression* 11 (2005): 187–195.

95. Ryan King and Gretchen Sutto, "High Times for Hate Crimes: Explaining the Temporal Clustering of Hate-Motivated Offending," *Criminology* 51 (2013): 871–894.

96. Christopher Birkbeck and Gary LaFree, "The Situational Analysis of Crime and Deviance," *American Review of Sociology* 19 (1993): 113–137; Karen Heimer and Ross Matsueda, "Role-Taking, Role Commitment, and Delinquency: A Theory of Differential Social Control," *American Sociological Review* 59 (1994): 400–437.

97. Peter Wood, Walter Gove, James Wilson, and John Cochran, "Nonsocial Reinforcement and Habitual Criminal Conduct: An Extension of Learning," *Criminology* 35 (1997): 335–366.

98. Ferrell, "Criminological Verstehen," p. 12.

99. Gottfredson and Hirschi, *A General Theory of Crime*.

100. Patricia Brantingham, Paul Brantingham, and Wendy Taylor, "Situational Crime Prevention as a Key Component in Embedded Crime Prevention," *Canadian Journal of Criminology and Criminal Justice* 47 (2005): 271–292.

101. Oscar Newman, *Defensible Space: Crime Prevention Through Urban Design* (New York: Macmillan, 1973).

102. C. Ray Jeffery, *Crime Prevention Through Environmental Design* (Beverly Hills: Sage, 1971).

103. See also Pochara Theerathorn, "Architectural Style, Aesthetic Landscaping, Home Value, and Crime Prevention," *International Journal of Comparative and Applied Criminal Justice* 12 (1988): 269–277.

104. Ronald Clarke, *Situational Crime Prevention: Successful Case Studies* (Albany, NY: Harrow and Heston, 1992).

105. Gohar A. Petrossian and Ronald V. Clarke, "Explaining and Controlling Illegal Commercial Fishing, An Application of the CRAVED Theft Model," *British Journal of Criminology* 54 (2014): 73–90; Ronald Clarke, Rick Kemper and Laura Wyckoff, "Controlling Cell Phone Fraud in the U.S.," *Security Journal* 14 (2001): 7–22.

106. Marcus Felson, "Routine Activities and Crime Prevention," in *National Council for Crime Prevention, Studies on Crime and Crime Prevention, Annual Review*, Vol. 1 (Stockholm: Scandinavian University Press, 1992), pp. 30–34.

107. Derek Cornish and Ronald Clarke, "Opportunities, Precipitators and Criminal Decisions: A Reply to Wortley's Critique of Situational Crime Prevention," *Crime Prevention Studies* 16 (2003): 41–96; Ronald Clarke and Ross Homel, "A Revised Classification of Situational Prevention Techniques," in *Crime Prevention at a Crossroads*, ed. Steven P. Lab (Cincinnati: Anderson Publishing, 1997).

108. Lynn A. Addington and Callie Marie Rennison, "Keeping the Barbarians Outside the Gate? Comparing Burglary Victimization in Gated and Non-Gated Communities," *Justice Quarterly*, first published online February 4, 2013.

109. Barry Webb, "Steering Column Locks and Motor Vehicle Theft: Evaluations for Three Countries," in *Crime Prevention Studies*, Vol. 2, ed. Ronald Clarke (Monsey, NY: Criminal Justice Press, 1994), pp. 71–89.

110. Barbara Morse and Delbert Elliott, "Effects of Ignition Interlock Devices on DUI Recidivism: Findings from a Longitudinal Study in Hamilton County, Ohio," *Crime and Delinquency* 38 (1992): 131–157.

111. Nancy LaVigne, "Gasoline Drive-Offs: Designing a Less Convenient Environment," in *Crime Prevention Studies*, Vol. 2, ed. Clarke, pp. 91–114.

112. Matt Nobles, Jill Levenson, and Tasha Youstin, "Effectiveness of Residence Restrictions in Preventing Sex Offense Recidivism," *Crime and Delinquency* 58 (2012): 491–513.

113. Eric Fritsch, Tory Caeti, and Robert Taylor, "Gang Suppression Through Saturation Patrol, Aggressive Curfew, and Truancy Enforcement: A Quasi-Experimental Test of the Dallas Anti-Gang Initiative," *Crime and Delinquency* 45 (1999): 122–139.

114. Kenneth Adams, "The Effectiveness of Juvenile Curfews at Crime Prevention," *Annals of the American Academy of Political and Social Science* 587 (May 2003): 136–159.

115. Brantingham, Brantingham, and Taylor, "Situational Crime Prevention as a Key Component in Embedded Crime Prevention."

116. Marcus Felson, "Those Who Discourage Crime," in *Crime and Place, Crime Prevention Studies*, Vol. 4, ed. John Eck and David Weisburd (New York: Criminal Justice Press, 1995), pp. 53–66; John Eck, "Drug Markets and Drug Places: A Case-Control Study of the Spatial Structure of Illicit Drug Dealing," Ph.D. dissertation, University of Maryland, College Park, 1994.

117. Eck, "Drug Markets and Drug Places," p. 29.

118. Lorraine Green Mazerolle, Colleen Kadleck, and Jan Roehl, "Controlling Drug and Disorder Problems: The Role of Place Managers," *Criminology* 36 (1998): 371–404.

119. Keith Proctor, "The Great Surveillance Boom," *CNN News*, April 26, 2013, http://management.fortune.cnn.com/2013/04/26/video-surveillance-boston-bombings/ (accessed April 2014).

120. Brandon C. Welsh and David P. Farrington, *Making Public Places Safer: Surveillance and Crime Prevention* (New York: Oxford University Press, 2008).

121. Ronald Clarke, "Deterring Obscene Phone Callers: The New Jersey Experience," *Situational Crime Prevention*, ed. Ronald Clarke (Albany, NY: Harrow and Heston, 1992), pp. 124–132.

122. Bob Edward Vásquez, Sean Maddan, and Jeffery T. Walker, "The Influence of Sex Offender Registration and Notification Laws in the United States: A Time-Series Analysis," *Crime and Delinquency* 54 (2008): 175–192.

123. Naomi J. Freeman, "The Public Safety Impact of Community Notification Laws: Rearrest of Convicted Sex Offenders," *Crime and Delinquency* 58 (2012): 539–564.

124. Philip Cook and Jens Ludwig, "The Economist's Guide to Crime Busting," *NIJ Journal* 270 (2012), http://nij.gov/nij/journals/270/economists-guide.htm (accessed April 2014).

125. Ronald Clarke and David Weisburd, "Diffusion of Crime Control Benefits: Observations of the Reverse of Displacement," in *Crime Prevention Studies*, Vol. 2, ed. Clarke.

126. David Weisburd and Lorraine Green, "Policing Drug Hot Spots: The Jersey City Drug Market Analysis Experiment," *Justice Quarterly* 12 (1995): 711–734.

127. Anthony Braga, Andrew Papachristos, and David M. Hureau, "The Effects of Hot Spots Policing on Crime: An Updated Systematic Review and Meta-Analysis," *Justice Quarterly*, first published online May 16, 2012.

128. Robert Barr and Ken Pease, "Crime Placement, Displacement, and Deflection," in *Crime and Justice, A Review of Research*, Vol. 12, ed. Michael Tonry and Norval Morris (Chicago: University of Chicago Press, 1990), pp. 277–319.

129. Bruce Taylor, Christopher Koper, and Daniel Woods, "A Randomized Control Trial of Different Policing Strategies at Hot Spots of Violent Crime," *Journal of Experimental Criminology* 7 (2011): 149–181.

130. Evan Sorg, Cory Haberman, Jerry Ratcliffe, and Elizabeth Groff, "Foot Patrol in Violent Crime Hot Spots: The Longitudinal Impact of Deterrence and Posttreatment Effects of Displacement," *Criminology* 51 (2013): 65–101.

131. Brandon Welsh and David Farrington, "Crime Prevention and Hard Technology: The Case of CCTV and Improved Street Lighting," in *The New Technology of Crime, Law, and Social Control*, ed. James Byrne and Donald Rebovich (Monsey, NY: Criminal Justice Press, 2007).

132. Daniel Nagin and Greg Pogarsky, "An Experimental Investigation of Deterrence: Cheating, Self-Serving Bias, and Impulsivity," *Criminology* 41 (2003): 167–195.

133. Silvia Mendes, "Certainty, Severity, and Their Relative Deterrent Effects: Questioning the Implications of the Role of Risk in Criminal Deterrence Policy," *Policy Studies Journal* 32 (2004): 59–74.

134. Robert Apel, Greg Pogarsky, and Leigh Bates, "The Sanctions–Perceptions Link in a Model of School-Based Deterrence," *Journal of Quantitative Criminology* 25 (2009): 201–226.

135. Etienne Blais and Jean-Luc Bacher, "Situational Deterrence and Claim Padding: Results from a Randomized Field Experiment," *Journal of Experimental Criminology* 3 (2007): 337–352.

136. Robert Bursik, Harold Grasmick, and Mitchell Chamlin, "The Effect of Longitudinal Arrest Patterns on the Development of Robbery Trends at the Neighborhood Level," *Criminology* 28 (1990): 431–450.

137. Steven Durlauf and Daniel Nagin, "Imprisonment and Crime: Can Both Be Reduced?" *Criminology and Public Policy* 10 (2011): 13–54.

138. Jennifer Varriale Carson, "Counterterrorism and Radical Eco-Groups: A Context for Exploring the Series Hazard Model," *Journal of Quantitative Criminology*, first published online October 2013; Cheryl L. Maxson, Kristy N. Matsuda, and Karen Hennigan, "Deterrability Among Gang and Nongang Juvenile Offenders: Are Gang Members More (or Less) Deterrable than Other Juvenile Offenders?" *Crime and Delinquency* 57 (2011): 516–543.

139. Greg Pogarsky, "Identifying 'Deterrable' Offenders: Implications for Deterrence Research," *Justice Quarterly* 19 (2002): 431–452.

140. Dieter Dolling, Horst Entorf, Dieter Hermann, and Thomas Rupp, "Deterrence Effective? Results of a Meta-Analysis of Punishment," *European Journal on Criminal Policy and Research* 15 (2009): 201–224.

141. Thomas Loughran, Alex Piquero, Jeffrey Fagan, and Edward Mulvey, "Differential Deterrence: Studying Heterogeneity and Changes in Perceptual Deterrence Among Serious Youthful Offenders," *Crime and Delinquency* 58 (2012): 3–27.

142. Shamena Anwar and Thomas Loughran, "Testing a Bayesian Learning Theory of Deterrence Among Serious Juvenile Offenders," *Criminology* 49 (2011): 667–698.

143. R. Steven Daniels, Lorin Baumhover, William Formby, and Carolyn Clark-Daniels, "Police Discretion and Elder Mistreatment: A Nested Model of Observation, Reporting, and Satisfaction," *Journal of Criminal Justice* 27 (1999): 209–225.

144. Charles Tittle and Alan Rowe, "Certainty of Arrest and Crime Rates: A Further Test of the Deterrence Hypothesis," *Social Forces* 52 (1974): 455–462.

145. David Bayley, *Policing for the Future* (New York: Oxford University Press, 1994).

146. George Kelling, Tony Pate, Duane Dieckman, and Charles Brown, *The Kansas City Preventive Patrol Experiment: A Summary Report* (Washington, DC: Police Foundation, 1974).

147. John Worrall and Tomislav Kovandzic, "Police Levels and Crime Rates: An Instrumental Variables Approach," *Social Science Research* 39 (2010): 506–516.

148. Michael White, James Fyfe, Suzanne Campbell, and John Goldkamp, "The Police Role in Preventing Homicide: Considering the Impact of Problem-Oriented Policing on the Prevalence of Murder," *Journal of Research in Crime and Delinquency* 40 (2003): 194–226.

149. Kenneth Novak, Jennifer Hartman, Alexander Holsinger, and Michael Turner, "The Effects of Aggressive Policing of Disorder on Serious Crime," *Policing* 22 (1999): 171–190.

150. Lawrence Sherman, "Police Crackdowns," *NIJ Reports* (March/April 1990): 2–6, at 2.

151. Jacqueline Cohen, Wilpen Gorr, and Piyusha Singh, "Estimating Intervention Effects in Varying Risk Settings: Do Police Raids Reduce Illegal Drug Dealing at Nuisance Bars?" *Criminology* 42 (2003): 257–292.

152. Anthony Braga, David Weisburd, Elin Waring, Lorraine Green Mazerolle, William Spelman, and Francis Gajewski, "Problem-Oriented Policing in Violent Crime Places: A Randomized Controlled Experiment," *Criminology* 37 (1999): 541–580.

153. Nagin and Pogarsky, "Integrating Celerity, Impulsivity, and Extralegal Sanction Threats into a Model of General Deterrence," pp. 884–885.

154. Daniel Kessler and Steven D. Levitt, "Using Sentence Enhancements to Distinguish Between Deterrence and Incapacitation," *Journal of Law and Economics* 42 (1999): 343–363.

155. Cheryl Marie Webster, Anthony Doob, and Franklin Zimring, "Proposition 8 and Crime Rates in California: The Case of the Disappearing Deterrent," *Criminology and Public Policy* 5 (2006): 417–448.

156. Donald Green, "Past Behavior as a Measure of Actual Future Behavior: An Unresolved Issue in Perceptual Deterrence Research," *Journal of Criminal Law and Criminology* 80 (1989): 781–804, at 803; Matthew Silberman, "Toward a Theory of Criminal Deterrence," *American Sociological Review* 41 (1976): 442–461; Linda Anderson, Theodore Chiricos, and Gordon Waldo, "Formal and Informal Sanctions: A Comparison of Deterrent Effects," *Social Problems* 25 (1977): 103–114. See also Maynard Erickson and Jack Gibbs, "Objective and Perceptual Properties of Legal Punishment and Deterrence Doctrine," *Social Problems* 25 (1978): 253–264; and Daniel Nagin and Raymond Paternoster, "Enduring Individual Differences and Rational Choice Theories of Crime," *Law and Society Review* 27 (1993): 467–485.

157. Harold Grasmick and Robert Bursik, "Conscience, Significant Others, and Rational Choices: Extending the Deterrence Model," *Law and Society Review* 24 (1990): 837–861, at 854.

158. Thomas Peete, Trudie Milner, and Michael Welch, "Levels of Social Integration in Group Contexts and the Effects of Informal Sanction Threat on Deviance," *Criminology* 32 (1994): 85–105.

159. Harry Wallace, Julie Juola Exline, and Roy Baumeister, "Interpersonal Consequences of Forgiveness: Does Forgiveness Deter or Encourage Repeat Offenses?" *Journal of Experimental Social Psychology* 44 (2008): 453–460.

160. Richard D. Clark, "Celerity and Specific Deterrence: A Look at the Evidence," *Canadian Journal of Criminology* 30 (1988): 109–122.

161. Yair Listokin, "Crime and (with a Lag) Punishment: The Implications of Discounting for Equitable Sentencing," *American Criminal Law Review* 44 (2007): 115–140.

162. Greg Pogarsky, KiDeuk Kim, and Ray Paternoster, "Perceptual Change in the National Youth Survey: Lessons for Deterrence Theory and Offender Decision-Making," *Justice Quarterly* 22 (2005): 1–29.

163. Charles N. W. Keckler, "*Life v. Death*: Who Should Capital Punishment Marginally Deter?" *Journal of Law, Economics and Policy* 2 (2006): 101–161.

164. Bruce A. Jacobs, "Deterrence and Deterrability," *Criminology* 48 (2010): 417–442.

165. Ernest van Den Haag, "The Criminal Law as a Threat System," *Journal of Criminal Law and Criminology* 73 (1982): 709–785.

166. James A. Swartz and Arthur J. Lurigio, "Serious Mental Illness and Arrest: The Generalized Mediating Effect of Substance Use," *Crime and Delinquency* 53 (2007): 581–604.

167. David Lykken, "Psychopathy, Sociopathy, and Crime," *Society* 34 (1996): 30–38.

168. George Lowenstein, Daniel Nagin, and Raymond Paternoster, "The Effect of Sexual Arousal on Expectations of Sexual Forcefulness," *Journal of Research in Crime and Delinquency* 34 (1997): 443–473.

169. Ken Auletta, *The Under Class* (New York: Random House, 1982).

170. Foglia, "Perceptual Deterrence and the Mediating Effect of Internalized Norms Among Inner-City Teenagers"; Paternoster, "Decisions to Participate in and Desist from Four Types of Common Delinquency"; Raymond Paternoster, "Examining Three-Wave Deterrence Models: A Question of Temporal Order and Specification," *Journal of Criminal Law and Criminology* 79 (1988): 135–163; Raymond Paternoster, Linda Saltzman, Gordon Waldo, and Theodore Chiricos, "Estimating Perceptual Stability and Deterrent Effects: The Role of Perceived Legal Punishment in the Inhibition of Criminal Involvement," *Journal of Criminal Law and Criminology* 74 (1983): 270–297; M. William Minor and Joseph Harry, "Deterrent and Experiential Effects in Perceptual Deterrence Research: A Replication and Extension," *Journal of Research in Crime and Delinquency* 19 (1982): 190–203; Lonn Lanza-Kaduce, "Perceptual Deterrence and Drinking and Driving Among College Students," *Criminology* 26 (1988): 321–341.

171. Foglia, "Perceptual Deterrence and the Mediating Effect of Internalized Norms Among Inner-City Teenagers," pp. 419–443.

172. Alex Piquero and George Rengert, "Studying Deterrence with Active Residential Burglars," *Justice Quarterly* 16 (1999): 451–462.

173. Steven Levitt and Sudhir Alladi Venkatesh, "An Economic Analysis of a Drug-Selling Gang's Finances," NBER Working Papers 6592 (Cambridge, MA: National Bureau of Economic Research, Inc., 1998).

174. Bill McCarthy, "New Economics of Sociological Criminology," *Annual Review of Sociology* (2002): 417–442.

175. James Q. Wilson and Richard Herrnstein, *Crime and Human Nature* (New York: Simon & Schuster, 1985), p. 494.

176. Alicia Sitren and Brandon Applegate, "Testing the Deterrent Effects of Personal and Vicarious Experience with Punishment and Punishment Avoidance," *Deviant Behavior* 28 (2007): 29–55.

177. Christina Dejong, "Survival Analysis and Specific Deterrence: Integrating Theoretical and Empirical Models of Recidivism," *Criminology* 35 (1997): 561–576.

178. Paul Tracy and Kimberly Kempf-Leonard, *Continuity and Discontinuity in Criminal Careers* (New York: Plenum Press, 1996).

179. Lawrence Greenfeld, *Examining Recidivism* (Washington, DC: U.S. Government Printing Office, 1985).

180. Allen Beck and Bernard Shipley, *Recidivism of Prisoners Released in 1983* (Washington, DC: Bureau of Justice Statistics, 1989).

181. Dejong, "Survival Analysis and Specific Deterrence," p. 573.

182. Daniel Nagin and G. Matthew Snodgrass, "The Effect of Incarceration on Re-Offending: Evidence from a Natural Experiment in Pennsylvania," *Journal of Quantitative Criminology* December 29 (2013): 601–642.

183. David Weisburd, Elin Waring, and Ellen Chayet, "Specific Deterrence in a Sample of Offenders Convicted of White-Collar Crimes," *Criminology* 33 (1995): 587–607.

184. Dejong, "Survival Analysis and Specific Deterrence"; Raymond Paternoster and Alex Piquero, "Reconceptualizing Deterrence: An Empirical Test of Personal and Vicarious Experiences," *Journal of Research in Crime and Delinquency* 32 (1995): 251–258.

185. David Lovell, L. Clark Johnson, and Kevin Cain, "Recidivism of Supermax Prisoners in Washington State," *Crime and Delinquency* 53 (2007): 633–656.

186. Peter Wood, "Exploring the Positive Punishment Effect Among Incarcerated Adult Offenders," *American Journal of Criminal Justice* 31 (2007): 8–22.

187. Jacobs, "Deterrence and Deterrability."

188. Greg Pogarsky and Alex R. Piquero, "Can Punishment Encourage Offending? Investigating the 'Resetting' Effect," *Journal of Research in Crime and Delinquency* 40 (2003): 92–117.

189. Lauren Glaze and Erinn Herberman, *Correctional Populations in the United States, 2012* (Washington, DC: Bureau of Justice Statistics, 2013), http://www.bjs.gov/content/pub/pdf/cpus12.pdf (accessed May 2014).

190. Pew Charitable Trust, *One in 100: Behind Bars in America 2008* (Washington, DC: Pew Charitable Trusts, 2008), http://www.pewstates.org/uploadedFiles/PCS_Assets/2008/one%20in%20100.pdf (accessed May 2014).

191. William Spelman, "Specifying the Relationship Between Crime and Prisons," *Journal of Quantitative Criminology* 24 (2008): 149–178.

192. Steven Levitt, "Why Do Increased Arrest Rates Appear to Reduce Crime: Deterrence, Incapacitation, or Measurement Error?" *Economic Inquiry* 36 (1998): 353–372; see also Thomas Marvell and Carlisle Moody, "The Impact of Prison Growth on Homicide," *Homicide Studies* 1 (1997): 205–233.

193. Benjamin Meade, Benjamin Steiner, Matthew Makarios, and Lawrence Travis, "Estimating a Dose–Response Relationship Between Time Served in Prison and Recidivism," *Journal of Research in Crime and Delinquency* November 50 (2013): 525–550.

194. John Wallerstedt, *Returning to Prison, Bureau of Justice Statistics Special Report* (Washington, DC: U.S. Department of Justice, 1984).

195. James Marquart, Victoria Brewer, Janet Mullings, and Ben Crouch, "The Implications of Crime Control Policy on HIV/AIDS-Related Risk Among Women Prisoners," *Crime and Delinquency* 45 (1999): 82–98.

196. Jose Canela-Cacho, Alfred Blumstein, and Jacqueline Cohen, "Relationship Between the Offending Frequency of Imprisoned and Free Offenders," *Criminology* 35 (1997): 133–171.

197. Hilde Wermink, Robert Apel, Paul Nieuwbeerta, and Arjan A. J. Blokland, "The Incapacitation Effect of First-Time Imprisonment: A Matched Samples Comparison," *Journal of Quantitative Criminology* 29 (2013): 579–600.

198. Michael Ostermann and Joel Caplan, "How Much Do the Crimes Committed by Released Inmates Cost? *Crime and Delinquency*, first published November 5, 2013.

199. American Civil Liberties Union, "At America's Expense: The Mass Incarceration of the Elderly," 2012, https://www.aclu.org/criminal-law-reform/report-americas-expense-mass-incarceration-elderly (accessed May 2014).

200. James Lynch and William Sabol, "Prisoner Reentry in Perspective," Urban Institute, http://www.urban.org/publications/410213.html (accessed April 2014).

201. David Cole and Marc Mauer, "Reducing Crime by Reducing Incarceration: Longer Sentences Don't Mean Fewer Crimes," *Washington Times*, November 14, 2013, http://www.washingtontimes.com/news/2013/nov/14/cole-and-mauer-reducing-crime-by-reducing-incarcer/ (accessed April 2014).

202. Marc Mauer, testimony before the U.S. Congress, House Judiciary Committee, on "Three Strikes and You're Out," March 1, 1994.

203. James Stephan and Tracy Snell, *Capital Punishment, 1994* (Washington, DC: Bureau of Justice Statistics, 1996), p. 8.

204. Cass R. Sunstein and Adrian Vermeule, "Is Capital Punishment Morally Required? Acts, Omissions, and Life-Life Tradeoffs," *Stanford Law Review* 58 (2006): 703–750, at 749.

205. Andrew von Hirsch, *Doing Justice* (New York: Hill and Wang, 1976).

206. Ibid.

207. Richard Frase, "Punishment Purposes," *Stanford Law Review* 67 (2005): 67–85

208. Ibid.

HANDOUT/Reuters/Landov

UPI/John Angelillo/Landov

5

TRAIT THEORIES

On December 14, 2012, Adam Lanza shot his mother at her home in Newtown, Connecticut, and then took her car to the nearby Sandy Hook Elementary School, where he shot and killed 20 young students, between the ages of 5 and 10, and six adult teachers and school employees. After firing 50 to 100 shots at the children and staff, Lanza fatally shot himself in the head as first responders began arriving on scene.

What could have driven this seemingly intelligent and articulate young man to commit one of the worst crimes in American history? Adam Peter Lanza was born in Exeter, New Hampshire, on April 22, 1992. His parents, Peter and Nancy Lanza, were both wealthy and successful. He had an older brother, Ryan Lanza, six years his senior. Then in 2008, when Adam was 16 years old, his parents divorced. Soon after, his classmates began to describe his behavior as "fidgety" and "deeply troubled"; he may have suffered from Asperger's syndrome. Adam began to lose his connection to reality and developed severe mental illness. By 2010, his illness had become so severe he broke off relations with almost everyone in his life and secluded himself in his bedroom, where he spent hours playing violent video games and obsessing over mass murderers. The fact that his mother was a gun enthusiast did not help matters.

Lanza's home was filled with weapons and ammunition to which he had easy access. Lanza also had a number of books and articles on other mass killings.

Adam joined the Columbine mass murder website, *Shocked Beyond Belief,* using the screen name "Smiggles," and began to express his paranoia and his belief that society was trying to manipulate him into following an immoral value system that led to both mental and physical sickness. On December 7, 2011, he posted a note showing his disdain for society and his interest in mass murder:

When civilization exists in a form where all forms of alienation (among many other things) are rampant ... new children will end up "not well" in all sorts of ways. You don't even have to touch a topic as cryptic as mass murder to see an indication of this: you can look at a single symptom as egregious as the proliferation of antidepressants.

In Adam's worldview, children were indoctrinated from a very young age to become part of a sick society. They were manipulated to live unhealthy lives and doomed to live in a joyless world where they would be used and abused. By killing them, he'd be doing them a favor, saving them from the hell he was enduring.[1] Lanza's father said in his first public comments about the massacre that what his son did couldn't "get any more evil" and that he wished his son had never been born.

enseless tragedies such as these help convince some criminologists that the root cause of crime may be linked to mental or physical abnormality. How could a young man such as Adam Lanza engage in mass murder of innocent children unless he were suffering from some form of mental instability or collapse? And yet, while in the aftermath of the killings there seemed to be ample evidence that he was under severe psychological stress, no one was able to foresee or predict his violent actions.

To hear Adam Lanza's call-in to a radio show, go to http://www.usatoday.com/story/news/nation/2014/01/16/adam-lanza-newtown-sandy-hook-radio-program/4505649/.
Does he sound delusional or rational and calculating?

This vision is neither new nor unique. The image of a disturbed, mentally ill offender seems plausible because more than one generation of Americans has grown up on films and TV shows that portray violent criminals as mentally deranged and physically abnormal. Beginning with Alfred Hitchcock's film *Psycho*, producers have made millions depicting the ghoulish acts of people who at first seem normal and even friendly but turn out to be demented and dangerous. Lurking out there are fanatical patients (*Saw I* through *Saw VI*, plus *Saw 3D*), crazed babysitters (*The Hand that Rocks the Cradle*), frenzied airline passengers (*Red Eye, Turbulence*), deranged roommates (*Single White Female*), cracked neighbors (*Disturbia, Last House on the Left*), psychotic tenants (*Pacific Heights*), demented secretaries (*The Temp*), unhinged police (*Maniac Cop*), mad cab drivers (*The Bone Collector*), irrational fans (*The Fan, Misery*), abnormal girlfriends (*Obsessed, Fatal Attraction*) and boyfriends (*Fear*), unstable husbands (*Enough, Sleeping with the Enemy*) and wives (*Black Widow*), loony fathers (*The Stepfather*), mothers (*Mama, Friday the 13th, Part 1*), and grandmothers (*Hush*), unbalanced crime victims (*I Know What You Did Last Summer*), maniacal children (*The Good Son, Children of the Corn*), manic hotel owners (*Psycho, Hostel* and *Hostel: Part II*), lunatic high school friends (*Scream*) and college classmates (*Scream II*), possessed dolls (*Child's Play 1* through *3*) and their mates (*Bride of Chucky*), and nutsy teenaged admirers (*The Crush*). Sometimes they even try to kill each other (*Freddy vs. Jason*), and some are not even totally human. No one can ever be safe when doctors, psychologists, and psychiatrists who should be treating these disturbed people turn out to be demonic murderers themselves (*The Human Centipede, Hannibal, Silence of the Lambs*). And of course, even if they are killed they may come back as zombies (*World War Z, Evil Dead, I Am Legend*). Is it any wonder

that we respond to a particularly horrible crime by saying of the perpetrator, "That guy must be crazy" or "She is a monster!"

The view that criminals bear physical and/or mental traits that make them different and abnormal is not restricted to the movie-going public. Since the nineteenth century, criminologists have suggested that biological and psychological traits have the power to influence behavior. People develop physical or mental traits at birth or soon after that affect their social functioning over the life course and influence their behavior choices. Because these mental and physical traits are rare and occur infrequently, only a few people in any social environment embark on criminal careers. As you may recall, only a small percentage of all offenders go on to become persistent repeaters; most people age out of crime. It makes logical sense that what sets these chronic offenders apart from the "average" criminal is an abnormal biochemical makeup, brain structure, genetic constitution, or some other personal trait.[2] The fact that each of us has a unique physical makeup and personality structure explains why, when faced with the same life situations, one person commits crime and becomes a chronic offender, whereas another attends school, church, and neighborhood functions and obeys the laws of society.

To understand this view of crime causation, we begin with a brief review of the development of trait theories.

FOUNDATIONS OF TRAIT THEORY

LO1 Understand the development of trait theory

During the late nineteenth century, the scientific method was beginning to take hold in Europe. Rather than relying on pure thought and reason, scientists began to use careful observation and analysis of natural phenomena in their experiments. This movement inspired new discoveries in biology, astronomy, and chemistry. Charles Darwin's (1809–1882) discoveries on the evolution of man encouraged a nineteenth-century "cult of science." Darwin's discoveries encouraged other scholars to be certain that all human activity could be verified by scientific principles. If the scientific method could be applied to the study of the natural world, then why not use it to study human behavior?

Auguste Comte (1798–1857), considered the founder of sociology, applied scientific methods to the study of society. According to Comte, societies pass through stages that can be grouped on the basis of how people try to understand the world in which they live. People in primitive societies consider inanimate objects as having life (for example, the sun is a god); in later social stages, people embrace a rational, scientific view of the world. Comte called this final stage the positive stage, and those who followed his writings became known as positivists. As we understand it today, **positivism** has two main elements:

- All true knowledge is acquired through direct observation and not through conjecture or belief. Statements that cannot be backed up by direct observation—for instance, "all babies are born innocent"—are invalid and worthless.
- The scientific method must be used if research findings are to be considered valid. This involves such steps as identifying problems, collecting data, forming hypotheses, conducting experiments, and interpreting results (see Exhibit 5.1).

According to the positivist tradition, social processes are a product of the measurable interaction between relationships and events. Human behavior therefore is a function of a variety of forces. Some are social, such as the effect of wealth and class; others are political and historical, such as war and famine. Other forces are more personal and psychological, such as an individual's brain structure and his or her biological makeup or mental ability. Each of these influences and shapes human behavior. People are neither born "good" nor "bad," and are neither "saints" nor "sinners." They are a product of their social and psychological traits, influenced by their upbringing and environment.

Biological Positivism

The earliest "scientific" studies applying the positivist model to criminology were conducted by physiognomists, such as J. K. Lavater (1741–1801), who studied the facial features of criminals to determine whether the shape of ears, nose, and eyes and the distance between them were associated with antisocial behavior. Phrenologists, such as Franz Joseph Gall (1758–1828) and Johann K. Spurzheim (1776–1832),

EXHIBIT 5.1
Elements of the Scientific Method

Observation

Identify problem and collect data and facts.

Hypothesis

Develop a reasonable explanation to account for or predict the data observed and the facts collected.

Test Hypothesis

Test hypothesis using control groups and experimental methods.

Interpretation

Analyze data using accepted statistical techniques.

Conclusion

Interpret data and verify or disprove accuracy of hypothesis.

SOURCE: © Cengage Learning®

studied the shape of the skull and bumps on the head to determine whether these physical attributes were linked to criminal behavior. Phrenologists believed that external cranial characteristics dictate which areas of the brain control physical activity. The brain, they suggested, has 30 different areas or faculties that control behavior. The size of a brain could be determined by inspecting the contours of the skull—the larger the organ, the more active it was. The relative size of brain organs could be increased or decreased through exercise and self-discipline.[3] Though phrenology techniques and methods are no longer practiced or taken seriously, these efforts were an early attempt to use a "scientific" method to study crime.

By the early nineteenth century, abnormality in the human mind was being linked to criminal behavior patterns.[4] Philippe Pinel (1745–1826), one of the founders of French psychiatry, claimed that some people behave abnormally even without being mentally ill. He coined the phrase *manie sans delire* to denote what today is referred to as a **psychopathic personality**. In 1812, an American, Benjamin Rush (1745–1813), described patients with an "innate preternatural moral depravity."[5] Another early criminological pioneer, English physician Henry Maudsley (1835–1918), believed that insanity and criminal behavior were strongly linked. He stated: "Crime is a sort of outlet in which their unsound tendencies are discharged; they would go mad if they were not criminals, and they do not go mad because they are criminals."[6] These early research efforts shifted attention to brain functioning and personality as the keys to criminal behavior. When Sigmund Freud's (1856–1939) work on the unconscious gained worldwide notoriety, the psychological basis of behavior was forever established.

Cesare Lombroso

In Italy, Cesare Lombroso (1835–1909), a physician who served much of his career in the Italian army, was studying the cadavers of executed criminals in an effort to scientifically determine whether law violators were physically different from people of conventional values and behavior.[7] Lombroso believed that serious offenders—those who engaged in repeated assault- or theft-related activities—were "born criminals" who had inherited a set of primitive

positivism The branch of social science that uses the scientific method of the natural sciences and suggests that human behavior is a product of social, biological, psychological, or economic forces.

psychopathic personality A personality characterized by a lack of warmth and feeling, inappropriate behavior responses, and an inability to learn from experience. Some psychologists view psychopathy as a result of childhood trauma; others see it as a result of biological abnormality.

POSITIVIST THEORY

ORIGIN About 1810

FOUNDERS Franz Joseph Gall, Johann Spurzheim, J. K. Lavater, Cesare Lombroso, Enrico Ferri, Raffaele Garofalo, Earnest Hooton, Charles Goring

MOST IMPORTANT WORKS Lombroso, *Criminal Man* (1863); Garofalo, *Criminology* (1885); Ferri, *Criminal Sociology* (1884); Goring, *The English Convict* (1913); William Sheldon, *Varieties of Delinquent Youth* (1949)

CORE IDEAS Some people have biological and mental traits that make them crime prone. These traits are inherited and are present at birth. Mental and physical degeneracies are the cause of crime.

MODERN OUTGROWTHS Biosocial and psychological theory, cognitive theory, behavioral theory, evolutionary theory, arousal theory

Cesare Lombroso

© INTERFOTO/Alamy.

physical traits that he referred to as **atavistic anomalies**. Physically, born criminals were throwbacks to more primitive savage people. Among the crime-producing traits Lombroso identified were enormous jaws and strong canine teeth common to carnivores and savages who devour raw flesh. These criminogenic traits can be acquired through

indirect heredity, from a degenerate family whose members suffered from such ills as insanity, syphilis, and alcoholism, or *direct heredity*—being the offspring of criminal parents.

Lombroso's version of criminal anthropology was brought to the United States via articles and textbooks that adopted his ideas. He attracted a circle of followers who expanded on his vision of **biological determinism** and helped stimulate interest in what is referred to as **criminal anthropology**.[8] Ironically, Lombroso's research was more popular in the United States than it was in Europe, and by the turn of the century, American social thinkers were discussing "the science of penology" and "the science of criminology."[9]

atavistic anomalies According to Lombroso, the physical characteristics that distinguish born criminals from the general population and are throwbacks to animals or primitive people.

biological determinism A belief that criminogenic traits can be acquired through indirect heredity from a degenerate family whose members suffered from such ills as insanity, syphilis, and alcoholism, or through direct heredity—being related to a family of criminals.

criminal anthropology Early efforts to discover a biological basis of crime through measurement of physical and mental processes.

 To read an interesting analysis of Lombroso written in 1912, go to **http://scholarlycommons.law .northwestern.edu/jclc/vol2/iss5/6.**

What do you think of the concept of the "born criminal"? Is such a thing possible? Are some people "born to be bad" or are people "made to be bad"?

Lombroso's Contemporaries Lombroso was not alone in his views on the biological basis of crime. A contemporary, Raffaele Garofalo (1852–1934), shared the belief that certain physical characteristics indicate a criminal nature: "a lower degree of sensibility to physical pain, seems to be demonstrated by the readiness with which prisoners submit to the operation of tattooing."[10] Enrico Ferri (1856–1929) added a social dimension to Lombroso's work and argued that criminals should not be held personally or morally responsible for their actions because forces outside their control caused criminality.[11]

Advocates of the **inheritance school**, such as Henry Goddard, Richard Dugdale, and Arthur Estabrook, traced several generations of crime-prone families (referred to by pseudonyms such as the "Jukes" and the "Kallikaks"), finding evidence that criminal tendencies were based on genetics.[12] Their conclusion: traits deemed socially inferior could be passed down from generation to generation through inheritance. Modern scholars point out that these families lived in severe poverty so that social rather than biological factors may have been at the root of their problems.[13]

The body build or **somatotype** school, developed more than 50 years ago by William Sheldon, held that criminals manifest distinct physiques that make them susceptible to particular types of antisocial behavior. Three types of body builds were identified:

- *Mesomorphs* have well-developed muscles and an athletic appearance. They are active, aggressive, sometimes violent, and the most likely to become criminals.
- *Endomorphs* have heavy builds and are slow moving. They are known for lethargic behavior, rendering them unlikely to commit violent crime and more willing to engage in less strenuous criminal activities such as fencing stolen property.
- *Ectomorphs* are tall, thin, and less social and more intellectual than the other types. These types are the least likely to commit crime.[14]

Sheldon recognized that pure types are rare and that most people have elements of all three types. He identified a Dionysian temperament, a person who has an excess of mesomorphy with a deficiency in ectomorphic restraint, thereby rendering them impulsive and into self-gratification, a condition that would produce crime.

The Legacy of Biological Criminology

The work of Lombroso and his contemporaries is regarded today as a historical curiosity, not scientific fact. Strict biological determinism is no longer taken seriously (later in his career even Lombroso recognized that not all criminals were biological throwbacks). Early biological determinism has been discredited because it is methodologically flawed; most studies did not use control groups from the general population to compare results, a violation of the scientific method. Many of the traits assumed to be inherited are not really genetically determined but could be caused by deprivation in surroundings and diet. Even if most criminals shared some biological traits, they might be products not of heredity but of some environmental condition, such as poor nutrition or health care. Unusual appearance, and not behavior, may have prompted people to be labeled and punished by the justice system.

Because of these deficiencies the validity of a purely biological/psychological explanation of criminality became questionable and is no longer considered valid. Today, criminologists believe that environmental conditions interact with human traits and conditions to influence behavior. Hence, the term **biosocial theory** has been coined to reflect the assumed link between physical and mental traits, the social environment, and behavior.

Sociobiology

What seems no longer tenable at this juncture is any theory of human behavior which ignores biology and relies exclusively on socio-cultural learning.... Most social scientists have been wrong in their dogmatic rejection and blissful ignorance of the biological parameters of our behavior.[15]

At midcentury, sociology dominated the study of crime and scholarship and any suggestion that antisocial behavior may have an individual-level cause was treated with enmity.[16] Some criminologists label this position as **biophobia**, the view that no serious consideration should be given to biological factors when attempting to understand human nature.[17]

Then in the early 1970s, spurred by the publication of *Sociobiology*, by biologist Edmund O. Wilson, the biological basis for crime once again emerged into the limelight.[18] *Sociobiology* differs from earlier theories of behavior in that it stresses that biological and genetic conditions affect

inheritance school Advocates of this view trace the activities of several generations of families believed to have an especially large number of criminal members.

somatotype A system developed for categorizing people on the basis of their body build.

biosocial theory An approach to criminology that focuses on the interaction between biological and social factors as they relate to crime.

biophobia A view held by sociologists that no serious consideration should be given to biological factors when attempting to understand human nature.

sociobiology The scientific study of the determinants of social behavior, based on the view that such behavior is influenced by both the individual's genetic makeup and interactions with the environment.

how social behaviors are learned and perceived. These perceptions, in turn, are linked to existing environmental structures.

Sociobiologists view the gene as the ultimate unit of life that controls all human destiny. Although they believe environment and experience also have an impact on behavior, their main premise is that most actions are controlled by a person's "biological machine." Most important, people are controlled by the innate need to have their genetic material survive and dominate others. Consequently, they do everything in their power to ensure their own survival and that of others who share their gene pool (relatives, fellow citizens, and so forth). Even when they come to the aid of others, which is called **reciprocal altruism**, people are motivated by the belief that their actions will be reciprocated and that their gene survival capability will be enhanced.

Contemporary Trait Theories

The study of sociobiology revived interest in finding a biological basis for crime and delinquency. If, as it suggests, biological (genetic) makeup controls human behavior, it follows that it should also be responsible for determining whether a person chooses law-violating or conventional behavior. This view of crime causation is referred to as **trait theory**.

Linking personal traits to crime is a significant departure for mainstream criminologists who for many years maintained that social factors, such as poverty and racism, were responsible for antisocial behavior. Today that view is softening and trait theory has entered the criminological mainstream. As criminologists John Paul Wright and Francis Cullen put it:

> … the ideological dam preventing the development of biosocial perspectives is weakening and has sprung some leaks. The reality that humans are biological creatures who vary in biological traits is becoming too obvious to ignore.[19]

As a result of this newfound acceptance, more criminologists are conducting research on the individual traits related to crime, and their findings are being published in mainstream journals.

Unlike their forebears, contemporary trait theorists do not suggest that a single biological or psychological attribute adequately explains all criminality. Rather, each offender is considered physically and mentally unique, so there must be different explanations for each person's behavior. Some may have inherited criminal tendencies; others may be suffering from neurological problems; still others may have blood chemistry disorders that heighten their antisocial activity. What sometimes appears to be an effect of environment and socialization may actually be caused by genetically determined physical and/or mental traits.[20]

But no matter what that trait may be, possession of it makes the bearer at risk to antisocial behavior. Today, even the most hardcore trait theorist recognizes that the environment plays a significant role in determining behavior. While traits may cause a reaction, environmental cues trigger the response and shape its outcome. Two competing views on the interaction of traits and environment are discussed below.

Individual Vulnerability versus Differential Susceptibility
Trait theorists today recognize that crime-producing interactions involve both personal traits (such as defective intelligence, impulsive personality, and abnormal brain chemistry) and environmental factors (such as family life, educational attainment, socioeconomic status, and neighborhood conditions). People living in a disadvantaged community may be especially at risk to crime, but that risk is significantly increased if they also bear a genetic makeup that makes them vulnerable to the crime producing influences in their environment.[21]

There are actually two views on how this interaction unfolds. The **individual vulnerability model** supposes a direct link between traits and crime: some people develop physical or mental conditions at birth, or soon thereafter, that affect their social functioning no matter where they live or how they are raised.[22]

In contrast, the **differential susceptibility model** suggests that there is an indirect association between traits and crime: some people possess physical or mental traits that make them vulnerable to adverse environmental influences.[23] While a positive environment provides benefits, unfortunately those people whose genetic makeup makes them predisposed to violence manifest more aggression when their surroundings become troubled. Someone like Adam Lanza may have benefited from a supportive, therapeutic environment, but a more adverse one triggered a violent response.[24]

Regardless of whether the connection between physical and psychological traits and crime is direct or indirect, contemporary trait theories can be divided into two major subdivisions: one that stresses psychological functioning and another that stresses biological (biosocial) makeup. Although

reciprocal altruism According to sociobiology, acts that are outwardly designed to help others but that have at their core benefits to the self.

trait theory The view that criminality is a product of abnormal biological and/or psychological traits.

individual vulnerability model Assumes there is a direct link between traits and crime; some people are vulnerable to crime from birth.

differential susceptibility model The belief that there is an indirect association between traits and crime.

there is often overlap between these views (i.e., brain functioning may have a biological basis), each branch has its unique characteristics and will be discussed separately.

BIOSOCIAL THEORY

Rather than viewing the criminal as a person whose behavior is controlled solely by conditions determined at birth, most biocriminologists believe that physical, environmental, and social conditions work in concert to produce human behavior; this integrated approach is commonly referred to as biosocial theory. The following subsections will examine some of the more important schools of thought within biosocial theory.[25] First, we look at the biochemical factors that are believed to affect behavior. Then the relationship of brain function and crime will be considered, followed by an analysis of genetics and crime. Finally, evolutionary views of crime causation are evaluated.

Biosocial conditions present at birth or soon after can have long-term effects on people's lives and behavior. A study has shown that breast-fed babies grow into better behaved and more emotionally stable children than those who are bottle fed. Five-year-olds who had been breast-fed were almost a third less likely to suffer behavioral problems severe enough to disrupt family life. Those reared on bottled milk formula tended to display more troublesome traits such as neediness, anxiety, hyperactivity, lying, or stealing. The link between breast-feeding and better behavior could be explained by fatty acids in mother's milk or bonding between child and parent.

AP Images/Katie Collins/EMPPL PA Wire

Biochemical Conditions and Crime

LO2 Differentiate between the biochemical conditions that produce crime

Some trait theorists believe biochemical conditions, including both those that are genetically predetermined and those acquired through diet and environment, control and influence antisocial behavior.[26] The influence of damaging chemical and biological contaminants may begin before birth if the mother's diet either lacks or has an excess of important nutrients (such as manganese) that may later cause developmental problems in her offspring.[27] In sum, exposure to harmful chemicals and poor diet *in utero*, at birth, and beyond may then affect people throughout their life course. Some of the more important biochemical factors that have been linked to criminality are set out in detail here.

Exposure to Smoking and Drinking Maternal alcohol abuse and/or smoking during gestation have long been linked to prenatal damage and subsequent antisocial behavior in adolescence.[28] Exposure to smoke has been associated with increased psychopathology in offspring and that exposure to secondhand cigarette smoke during pregnancy predicts later conduct disorder.[29] Having a smoking parent had a greater effect on behavior than other influences, including prematurity, low birth weight, and poor parenting practices.

Research now shows that people who start drinking by the age of 14 are five times more likely to become alcoholics than people who hold off on drinking until the age of 21. It is possible that early exposure of the brain to alcohol may short-circuit the growth of brain cells, impairing the learning and memory processes that protect against addiction; adolescent drinking has a direct and harmful influence on behavior.[30]

Exposure to Chemicals and Minerals Research shows that an over- or undersupply of certain chemicals and minerals—including sodium, mercury, potassium, calcium, amino acids, monoamines, and peptides—can lead to depression, mania, cognitive problems, memory loss, and abnormal sexual activity, all of which have proved to be correlates of crime.[31] Common food additives such as calcium propionate, which is used to preserve bread, have been linked to problem behaviors.[32] Even some commonly used medicines may have detrimental side effects: research links sildenafil, more commonly known as Viagra, with aggressive and violent behavior.[33]

Excessive intake of certain metals such as mercury, iron, and manganese may be linked to neurological dysfunctions such as intellectual impairment and attention deficit hyperactivity disorder (ADHD).[34] These neurological conditions are believed to be a precursor of delinquent and criminal behaviors.[35]

Diet and Crime

If biochemical makeup can influence behavior, then it stands to reason that food intake and diet are related to crime.[36] Those biocriminologists who believe in a diet–aggression association claim that in every segment of society there are violent, aggressive, and amoral people whose improper food, vitamin, and mineral intake may be responsible for their antisocial behavior.[37] If diet could be improved, they believe, the frequency of violent behavior would be reduced.[38]

In some instances, the absence in the diet of certain chemicals and minerals—including sodium, potassium, calcium, amino acids, magnesium, monoamines, and peptides—can lead to depression, mania, cognitive problems, memory loss, and abnormal sexual activity.[39] In contrast, research shows that excessive amounts of harmful substances such as caffeine, food dyes, and artificial flavors seem to provoke hostile, impulsive, and otherwise antisocial behaviors.[40] Ingredients that are routinely used in candy and soda have been linked to elevated hyperactivity scores, a condition that has been linked to antisocial behaviors.[41]

Diet can have a long-term influence on behavior. In a famous experiment, Adrian Raine and his colleagues charted the long-term effects of a two-year diet enrichment program for 3-year-olds and found that that 20 years later the youngsters given a more nutritious diet still did better on personality tests, had greater levels of mental health, and had lower levels of self-reported crimes than the malnourished children who not been placed in the program.[42]

Sugar Intake

One area of diet that has received a great deal of attention is the association between high intakes of carbohydrates and sugar and antisocial behavior. Experiments have been conducted in which children's diets were altered so that sweet drinks were replaced with fruit juices,

hypoglycemia A condition that occurs when glucose (sugar) levels in the blood fall below the necessary level for normal and efficient brain functioning.

androgens Male sex hormones.

table sugar with honey, molasses substituted for sugar in cooking, and so on; results indicate that these changes can reduce aggression levels.[43] A British study of the long-term effects of childhood diet on adult violence found that kids aged 10 who engaged in excessive consumption of confectionary (food items that are rich in sugar such as candy and soda) were the ones most likely to be convicted for violence in adulthood.[44] Although these results are impressive, some questions remain about the actual interaction between sugar intake and violence, and not all research projects have found a significant sugar–violence effect.[45]

Glucose Metabolism/Hypoglycemia

Research shows that persistent abnormality in the way the brain metabolizes glucose (sugar) can be linked to antisocial behaviors such as substance abuse.[46] Hypoglycemia occurs when glucose in the blood falls below levels necessary for normal and efficient brain functioning. The brain is sensitive to the lack of blood sugar because it is the only organ that obtains its energy solely from the combustion of carbohydrates. Thus, when the brain is deprived of blood sugar, it has no alternate food supply to call upon, and brain metabolism slows down, impairing function. Symptoms of hypoglycemia include irritability, anxiety, depression, crying spells, headaches, and confusion.

Research studies have linked hypoglycemia to outbursts of antisocial behavior and violence.[47] Several studies have related assaults and fatal sexual offenses to hypoglycemic reactions.[48] Hypoglycemia has also been connected with a syndrome characterized by aggressive and assaultive behavior, glucose disturbance, and brain dysfunction. Some attempts have been made to measure hypoglycemia using subjects with a known history of criminal activity. Studies of jail and prison inmate populations have found a higher than normal level of hypoglycemia.[49] High levels of reactive hypoglycemia have been found in groups of habitually violent and impulsive offenders.[50]

Hormonal Influences

Criminologist James Q. Wilson, in his book *The Moral Sense,* concludes that hormones, enzymes, and neurotransmitters may be the keys to understanding human behavior. According to Wilson, they help explain gender differences in the crime rate. Males, he writes, are biologically and naturally more aggressive than females, while women are naturally more nurturing due to the fact they are the ones who bear and raise children.[51] Hormone levels also help explain the aging-out process. Levels of testosterone, the principal male steroid hormone, decline during the life cycle and may explain why violence rates diminish over time.[52]

A number of biosocial theorists are now evaluating the association between violent behavior episodes and hormone levels, and the findings suggest that abnormal levels of male sex hormones (androgens) do in fact produce aggressive behavior.[53] High androgen levels require people to seek excess stimulation and to be willing to tolerate pain in their quest for thrills. Androgens are linked to brain seizures that, under stressful conditions, can result in emotional volatility. Androgens affect the brain structure itself. They influence the left hemisphere of the **neocortex**, the part of the brain that controls sympathetic feelings toward others.[54] One area of interest has been the influence of **testosterone**, the most abundant androgen, which controls secondary sex characteristics, such as facial hair and voice timbre. Excessive levels of testosterone have been linked to violence and aggression.[55] Studies of prisoners show that testosterone levels are higher in men who commit violent crimes than in the general population.

Lee Ellis and his associates found that self-reported violent criminality was positively correlated with masculine mannerisms, masculine body appearance, physical strength, strength of sex drive, low/deep voice, upper body strength, lower body strength, and amount of body hair.[56] Other androgen-related male traits include sensation seeking, impulsivity, dominance, and lesser verbal skills; all of these androgen-related male traits are related to antisocial behaviors.[57] There is a growing body of evidence suggesting that hormonal changes are also related to mood and behavior and, concomitantly, that adolescents experience more intense mood swings, anxiety, and restlessness than their elders.[58] An association between hormonal activity and antisocial behavior is suggested because rates of both factors peak in adolescence.[59]

Hormonal differences may be a key to understanding gender differences in the crime rate. Females may be biologically protected from deviant behavior in the same way they are immune from some diseases that strike males.[60] Girls who have high levels of testosterone or are exposed to testosterone *in utero* may become more aggressive in adolescence.[61] Conversely, boys who were prenatally exposed to steroids that decrease androgen levels display decreased aggressiveness in adolescence. Gender differences in the crime rate then may be explained by the relative difference in androgens between the two sexes.

Hormonal changes may also be able to explain regional and temporal differences in the crime rate. It is possible they are due to the side effects of stress hormones such as adrenaline, which the body generates to cope with thermal heat stress. As heat rises, people get irritable, and the body produces excess hormones, which are directly related to aggression and antisocial behaviors.[62] Hence, crime rates are higher in the summer and in regions with warmer climates.

Drugs that decrease testosterone levels are now being used to treat male sex offenders.[63] The female hormones, estrogen and progesterone, have been administered to sex offenders to decrease their sexual potency.[64] The long-term side effects of this treatment and the potential danger are still unknown.[65]

Premenstrual Syndrome Hormonal research has not been limited to male offenders. The suspicion has long existed that the onset of the menstrual cycle triggers excessive amounts of the female sex hormones, which affect antisocial, aggressive behavior. This condition is commonly referred to as **premenstrual syndrome**, or **PMS**.[66] The link between PMS and delinquency was first popularized more than 40 years ago by Katharina Dalton, whose studies of English women indicated that females are more likely to commit suicide and be aggressive and otherwise antisocial just before or during menstruation.[67] Based on her findings, lawyers began using PMS as a legal criminal defense that was accepted in courts in England and the United States.[68]

Dalton's research is often cited as evidence of the link between PMS and crime, but methodological problems make it impossible to accept her findings at face value. There is still significant debate over any link between PMS and aggression. Some doubters argue that the relationship is spurious; it is equally likely that the psychological and physical stress of aggression brings on menstruation and not vice versa.[69]

Diana Fishbein, a noted expert on biosocial theory, concludes that there is in fact an association between elevated levels of female aggression and menstruation. Research efforts, she argues, show (a) that a significant number of incarcerated females committed their crimes during the premenstrual phase and (b) that at least a small percentage of women appear vulnerable to cyclical hormonal changes, which makes them more prone to anxiety and hostility.[70] While the debate is ongoing, it is important to remember that the overwhelming majority of females who do suffer anxiety reactions prior to and during menstruation do not actually engage in violent criminal behavior; so any link between PMS and crime is tenuous at best.[71]

Allergies Allergies are defined as unusual or excessive reactions of the body to foreign substances.[72] For example, hay fever is an allergic reaction caused when pollen cells enter the body and are fought or neutralized by the body's natural defenses. The result of the battle is itching, red eyes and active sinuses.

---

neocortex A part of the human brain; the left side of the neocortex controls sympathetic feelings toward others.

testosterone The principal male steroid hormone. Testosterone levels decline during the life cycle and may explain why violence rates diminish over time.

premenstrual syndrome (PMS) The stereotype that several days prior to and during menstruation females are beset by irritability and poor judgment as a result of hormonal changes.

Cerebral allergies cause an excessive reaction in the brain, whereas **neuroallergies** affect the nervous system. Neuroallergies and cerebral allergies are believed to cause the allergic person to produce enzymes that attack wholesome foods as if they were dangerous to the body.[73] They may also cause swelling of the brain and produce sensitivity in the central nervous system, conditions linked to mental, emotional, and behavioral problems. Research indicates a connection between allergies and hyperemotionality, depression, aggressiveness, and violent behavior.[74]

Neuroallergy and cerebral allergy problems have also been linked to hyperactivity in children, a condition also linked to antisocial behavior. The foods most commonly involved in producing such allergies are cow's milk, wheat, corn, chocolate, nuts, peanut butter, citrus, and eggs; however, about 300 other foods have been identified as allergens. The potential seriousness of the problem has been raised by studies linking the average consumption of one suspected cerebral allergen, corn, to cross-national homicide rates.[75]

Environmental Contaminants The Centers for Disease Control and Prevention warns that exposure to dangerous substances in the environment, including lead, copper, cadmium, mercury, polybrominated diphenyl ethers (PBDEs), polychlorinated biphenyls (PCBs), polycyclic aromatic hydrocarbons (PAHs), and inorganic gases such as chlorine and nitrogen dioxide can cause severe illness or death. These environmental contaminants can be especially harmful to the brains of babies and small children because they may affect the developing nervous system; babies can be exposed to harmful chemicals even before they are born.[76]

Among the suspected contaminants that have been linked to developmental delays and emotional problems are chemicals used in the agricultural business in insecticides and pesticides. Another suspected cause with dysfunctional behavior is phthalates, industrial chemicals widely used as solvents and ingredients in plastics. Thousands of household items, from shampoos to flooring products, contain phthalates, and research shows that exposure is related to childhood misbehavior and improper functioning.[77] One such substance, chlorpyrifos, is now banned for residential use but is still allowed for agriculture and commercial enter-prises. Virginia Rauh and her colleagues found that children exposed to large amounts of chlorpyrifos before birth maintain an increased risk for personal problems such as attention deficit hyperactivity disorder (highly exposed children were significantly more likely to score lower on measures of psychomotor and mental development).[78] These outcomes have been linked to antisocial behavior.

Lead Ingestion A number of recent research studies have suggested that lead ingestion is linked to aggressive behaviors.[79] This association is especially important because so many children suffer harmful levels of lead exposure. According to the Centers for Disease Control and Prevention, even low levels of lead in the blood have been shown to affect IQ, the ability to pay attention, and academic achievement. And effects of lead exposure cannot be corrected. Experts now use a reference level of 5 micrograms per deciliter (of blood) to identify children with blood lead levels that are much higher than most children's levels.[80] That means that about 2 million kids 18 and under have dangerously high lead levels according to CDC standards.

There is significant evidence of a lead-aggression linkage. Areas with the highest concentrations of lead also report the highest levels of homicide.[81] Examining changes in lead levels in the United States, Britain, Canada, France, Australia, Finland, Italy, West Germany, and New Zealand (lead levels changed when nations phased out lead-containing paint and gasoline), economist Rick Nevin found that long-term worldwide trends in crime levels correlate significantly with changes in environmental levels of lead. Nevin discovered that children exposed to higher levels of lead during the preschool developmental years engaged in higher rates of offending when they reached their late teens and early twenties. His conclusion: 65 to 90 percent or more of the substantial variation in violent crime in all these countries was explained by lead. In the United States, juvenile arrest rates skyrocketed in the 1960s, an increase that tracked the increase in the use of leaded gas usage after World War II. As the use of leaded gas declined, so too did crime rates.[82]

Research also shows that even limited exposure to lead can have a deleterious influence on a child's development and subsequent behavior.[83] Delinquents are almost four times more likely to have high bone lead levels than children in the general population.[84] A number of research studies have linked lead ingestion to antisocial behaviors.[85] Recent research shows that almost any elevated level of lead ingestion is related to lower IQ scores, a factor linked to aggressive behavior.[86] There is also evidence linking lead exposure to mental illnesses, such as schizophrenia, which have been linked to antisocial behaviors.[87]

Research also shows that lead effects may actually begin in the womb due to the mother's dietary consumption of foods, such as seafood, that are high in lead content.[88] Improved prenatal care may help mothers avoid the danger of lead exposure and reduce long-term crime rates.

cerebral allergies A physical condition that causes brain malfunction due to exposure to some environmental or biochemical irritant.

neuroallergies Allergies that affect the nervous system and cause the allergic person to produce enzymes that attack wholesome foods as if they were dangerous to the body. They may also cause swelling of the brain and produce sensitivity in the central nervous system—conditions that are linked to mental, emotional, and behavioral problems.

Lead ingestion can cause behavioral problems and serious health issues. Juanna Graham holds a photo of her four-year-old son, Jarnell Brown, who died of lead poisoning after swallowing part of a charm bracelet that was included with a pair of Reebok shoes. The shoes have been recalled and the state is issuing a warning about lead poisoning. On the mantle in the gold box with the cross on it are Jarnell's ashes.

ZUMA Press, Inc./Alamy

Neurophysiological Conditions and Crime

LO3 Clarify the neurophysiological conditions associated with crime

Some researchers focus their attention on **neurophysiology**, the study of brain activity.[89] Neurological and physical abnormalities are acquired as early as the fetal or prenatal stage or through birth delivery trauma, and they control behavior throughout the life span.[90]

Studies conducted in the United States and in other nations have indicated that the relationship between impairment in executive brain functions (such as abstract reasoning, problem-solving skills, and motor behavior skills) and aggressive behavior is significant.[91] Children who suffer from measurable neurological deficits at birth are believed to also suffer from a number of antisocial traits throughout their life course, ranging from habitual lying to antisocial violence.[92]

The association between neurological disorder and antisocial behaviors may take a number of different paths:

- *Direct association.* Neurological deficits may be a direct cause of antisocial behavior, including violent offending.[93] The presence of brain abnormality causes irrational and destructive behaviors. Clinical analysis of convicted murderers found that a significant number show evidence of brain abnormalities, including epilepsy, traumatic brain injury, childhood encephalitis, or meningitis causing brain damage, genetic disorders, and unspecified brain damage.[94]

- *Indirect association.* Being in possession of a neurological impairment leads to the development of personality traits that are linked to antisocial behaviors. For example, impulsivity and lack of self-control have been linked to antisocial behavior. There is now evidence that self-control may in fact be regulated and controlled by the prefrontal cortex of the brain.[95] Neurological impairment to the prefrontal cortex reduces levels of self-control, and this reduction in self-control leads to increased levels of aggression.

- *Interactive cause.* Neurological deficits may interact with another trait or social condition to produce antisocial behaviors. Take for instance the research conducted by Adrian Raine, which found that kids who had experienced birth complications indicative of neurological impairment and had also experienced maternal rejection as they matured were more likely to engage in criminal offending than boys who did not experience these symptoms.[96] The combination of neurological dysfunction and maternal rejection had a more powerful influence on behavior than either of these conditions alone.

neurophysiology The study of brain activity.

CHAPTER 5 Trait Theories **141**

Measuring Neurological Impairment There are numerous ways to measure neurological functioning, including memorization and visual awareness tests, short-term auditory memory tests, and verbal IQ tests. These tests have been found to distinguish criminal offenders from noncriminal control groups.[97]

Traditionally, the most important measure of neurophysiological functioning is the **electroencephalograph (EEG)**, which records the electrical impulses given off by the brain.[98] It represents a signal composed of various rhythms and transient electrical discharges, commonly called brain waves, which can be recorded by electrodes placed on the scalp. The frequency is given in cycles per second, measured in hertz (Hz), and usually ranges from 0.5 to 30 Hz. Studies using the EEG find that violent criminals have far higher levels of abnormal EEG recordings than nonviolent or one-time offenders. Although about 5 percent of the general population have abnormal EEG readings, about 50 to 60 percent of adolescents with known behavior disorders display abnormal recordings.[99] Behaviors highly correlated with abnormal EEG include poor impulse control, inadequate social adaptation, hostility, temper tantrums, and destructiveness.[100] Studies of adults have associated slow and bilateral brain waves with hostile, hypercritical, irritable, nonconforming, and impulsive behavior.[101]

Newer brain scanning techniques using electronic imaging such as positron emission tomography (PET), brain electrical activity mapping (BEAM), single photon emission computed tomography (SPECT), and the superconducting quantum interference device (SQUID) have made it possible to assess which areas of the brain are directly linked to antisocial behavior.[102] Some research using PET shows that domestic violence offenders have lower metabolism in the right hypothalamus and decreased correlations between cortical and subcortical brain structures than a group of control subjects.[103] Daniel Amen and his colleagues employed SPECT to test a sample of people convicted of an impulsive murder. They found that these offenders suffered from a condition that reduced blood flow to a region of the brain involved with planning and self-control. Because this area of the brain is believed to control anger management, those who suffer reduced blood flow may be limited in their self-control, planning, and understanding of future consequences when challenged or forced to concentrate.[104]

It is possible that antisocial behavior is influenced by what is referred to as prefrontal dysfunction, a condition that occurs when demands on brain activity overload the prefrontal cortex and result in a lack of control over antisocial behaviors. Because the prefrontal lobes have not fully developed in adolescence, it is not surprising that this is the time that violent behavior peaks.[105]

Studies carried out in the United States and elsewhere have shown that both violent criminals and substance abusers have impairment in the prefrontal lobes, thalamus, medial temporal lobe, and superior parietal and left angular gyrus areas of the brain.[106] Such damage may be associated with a reduction in executive functioning (EF) a condition that refers to impairment of the cognitive processes that facilitate the planning and regulation of goal-oriented behavior (such as abstract reasoning, problem solving, and motor skills). Impairments in EF have been implicated in a range of developmental disorders, including attention deficit hyperactivity disorder (ADHD), conduct disorder (CD), autism, and Tourette syndrome. EF impairments also have been implicated in a range of neuropsychiatric and medical disorders, including schizophrenia, major depression, alcoholism, structural brain disease, diabetes mellitus, and normal aging.[107]

There is a suspected link between brain dysfunction and conduct disorder (CD), which is considered a precursor of long-term chronic offending. Children with CD lie, steal, bully other children, get into fights frequently, and break schools' and parents' rules; many are callous and lack empathy and/or guilt.[108] Adolescent boys with antisocial substance disorder (ASD) repeatedly engage in risky antisocial and drug-using behaviors. Research has linked this behavior with misfiring in particular areas of the brain and suppressed neural activity.[109]

Researching the Brain Research psychiatrist Guido Frank finds that aggressive teen behavior may be linked to the amygdala, an area of the brain that processes information regarding threats and fear, and to a lessening of activity in the frontal lobe, a brain region linked to decision making and impulse control. Frank investigated why some teenagers are more prone than others to "reactive" aggression—that is, unpremeditated aggression in response to a trigger (for instance, an accidental bump from a passerby). He found that reactively aggressive adolescents—most commonly boys—frequently misinterpret their surroundings, feel threatened, and act inappropriately aggressive. They tend to strike back when being teased, blame others when getting into a fight, and overreact to accidents. Their behavior is emotionally "hot," defensive, and impulsive; teens with this behavior are at high risk for lifelong social, career, or legal problems.

Frank's research helps explain what goes on in the brains of some teenage boys who respond with inappropriate anger and aggression to perceived threats. It is possible that rather than having a social or environmental basis, such behavior is associated with brain functioning and not environment, socialization, personality, or other social and psychological functions.[110]

---

electroencephalograph (EEG) A device that can record the electronic impulses given off by the brain, commonly called brain waves.

Minimal Brain Dysfunction Minimal brain dysfunction (MBD) is related to an abnormality in cerebral structure. It has been defined as an abruptly appearing, maladaptive behavior that interrupts an individual's lifestyle and life flow. In its most serious form, MBD has been linked to serious antisocial acts, an imbalance in the urge-control mechanisms of the brain, and chemical abnormality. Included in the category of minimal brain dysfunction are several abnormal behavior patterns: dyslexia, visual perception problems, hyperactivity, poor attention span, temper tantrums, and aggressiveness. One type of minimal brain dysfunction is manifested through episodic periods of explosive rage. This form of the disorder is considered an important cause of such behavior as spouse beating, child abuse, suicide, aggressiveness, and motiveless homicide. One perplexing feature of this syndrome is that people who are afflicted with it often maintain warm and pleasant personalities between episodes of violence. Some studies measuring the presence of MBD in offender populations have found that up to 60 percent exhibit brain dysfunction on psychological tests.[111] Criminals have been characterized as having a dysfunction of the dominant hemisphere of the brain.[112] Researchers using brain wave data have predicted with 95 percent accuracy the recidivism of violent criminals.[113] More sophisticated brain scanning techniques, such as PET, have also shown that brain abnormality is linked to violent crime.[114]

Learning Disabilities One specific type of MBD that has generated considerable interest is **learning disability (LD)**, a disorder in one or more of the basic psychological processes involved in understanding or using spoken or written languages. Learning-disabled children usually exhibit poor motor coordination (for example, problems with poor hand-eye coordination, trouble climbing stairs, clumsiness), have behavior problems (lack of emotional control, hostility, cannot stay on task), and have improper auditory and vocal responses (do not seem to hear, cannot differentiate sounds and noises).[115] Though learning disabilities are quite common (approximately 10 percent of all youths have some form of learning disorders), estimates of LD among kids who engage in antisocial behavior is far higher.[116]

What is the association between learning disabilities and crime? There are two popular explanations:

- *Susceptibility rationale* argues that the link is caused by certain side effects of learning disabilities, such as impulsiveness, poor ability to learn from experience, and inability to take social cues.
- *School failure rationale* assumes that the frustration caused by the LD produces poor school performance leading to a negative self-image and acting-out behavior.

Some recent research conducted by Tomer Einat and Amela Einat in Israel might help settle this issue. They found that a far higher percentage of Israeli prison inmates (69.6 percent) were characterized as learning disabled, as opposed to an estimated 10 to 15 percent of the general Israeli population. Among the inmates, learning disabilities were correlated both with low level of education (dropping out of school at an early age) and early age of criminal onset. Their conclusion: people with learning disabilities who give up school at early stages due to their disabilities are more likely to initiate a criminal career at an early age, as compared to individuals—with or without learning disabilities—who do not leave school. Helping LD kids adjust to school may also help them avoid criminal careers.[117]

Attention Deficit Hyperactivity Disorder (ADHD) Many parents have noticed that their children do not pay attention to them—they run around and do things in their own way. Sometimes this inattention is a function of age; in other instances, it is a symptom of **attention deficit hyperactivity disorder (ADHD)**, in which a child shows a developmentally inappropriate lack of attention, impulsivity, and hyperactivity. The various symptoms of ADHD are described in Exhibit 5.2.

About 3 percent of U.S. children (most often boys, but the condition can also affect girls) are believed to suffer from this disorder, and it is the most common reason children are referred to mental health clinics. ADHD has been associated with poor school performance, grade retention, placement in special needs classes, bullying, stubbornness, and lack of response to discipline. Although the origin of ADHD is still unknown, suspected causes include neurological damage, prenatal stress, and even reactions to food additives and chemical allergies. Some psychologists believe that the syndrome is essentially a chemical problem, specifically, an impairment in the chemical system that supports rapid and efficient communication in the brain's management system.[118]

There are also ties to family turmoil: parents of ADHD children are more likely to be divorced or separated, and ADHD children are much more likely to move to new locales than non-ADHD children.[119] It may be possible, then, that emotional turmoil either produces symptoms of ADHD or, if they already exist, causes them to intensify.

minimal brain dysfunction (MBD) An abruptly appearing, maladaptive behavior that interrupts an individual's lifestyle and life flow. In its most serious form, MBD has been linked to serious antisocial acts, an imbalance in the urge-control mechanisms of the brain, and chemical abnormality.

learning disability (LD) A disorder in one or more of the basic psychological processes involved in understanding or using spoken or written languages.

attention deficit hyperactivity disorder (ADHD) A psychological disorder in which a child shows developmentally inappropriate impulsivity, hyperactivity, and lack of attention.

EXHIBIT 5.2

Symptoms of Attention Deficit Hyperactivity Disorder (ADHD)

Lack of Attention

- Frequently fails to finish projects
- Does not seem to pay attention
- Does not sustain interest in play activities
- Cannot sustain concentration on schoolwork or related tasks
- Is easily distracted

Impulsivity

- Frequently acts without thinking
- Often "calls out" in class
- Does not want to wait his or her turn in lines or games
- Shifts from activity to activity
- Cannot organize tasks or work
- Requires constant supervision

Hyperactivity

- Constantly runs around and climbs on things
- Shows excessive motor activity while asleep
- Cannot sit still; is constantly fidgeting
- Does not remain in his or her seat in class
- Is constantly on the go like a "motor"

SOURCE: Adapted from American Psychiatric Association, *Diagnostic and Statistical Manual of Mental Disorders*, 4th ed. (Washington, DC: American Psychiatric Press, 1994).

A series of research studies now links ADHD to the onset and sustenance of a criminal career. Children with ADHD are more likely than non-ADHD youths to use illicit drugs, alcohol, and cigarettes, be physically aggressive, and engage in sex offenses in adolescence. In addition to adolescent misbehavior, hyperactive or ADHD children are at greater risk for antisocial activity and drug use/abuse that persists into adulthood.[120] They are more likely to be arrested, to be charged with a felony, and to have multiple arrests.[121]

Among the many studies that have evaluated the ADHD–crime link, Jason Fletcher and Barbara Wolfe evaluated data on nearly 14,000 individuals participating in the National Longitudinal Study of Adolescent Health (also known as Add Health) and found that children with ADHD are at a heightened risk for criminality as adults.[122] Another recent study by Patricia Westmoreland and her associates, which assessed more than 300 randomly selected prison inmates, found that more than 20 percent could be diagnosed with ADHD, and these inmates were more likely to report emotional and social problems and also had higher rates of

mood, anxiety, psychotic, antisocial, and borderline personality disorders.[123]

How is ADHD treated? Today, the most typical treatment is doses of stimulants, such as Adderall and Ritalin, which ironically help control emotional and behavioral outbursts. However, treatment is not always effective. While some treated children with ADHD improve, many do not and continue to show a greater occurrence of externalizing (acting-out) behaviors and significant deficits in areas such as social skills, peer relations, and academic performance over the life course.[124]

Tumors, Lesions, Injury, and Disease The presence of brain tumors and lesions has also been linked to a wide variety of psychological problems, including personality changes, hallucinations, and psychotic episodes.[125]

Persistent criminality has been linked to lesions in the frontal and temporal regions of the brain, which play an important role in regulating and inhibiting human behavior, including formulating plans and controlling intentions.[126] Clinical evaluation of depressed and aggressive psychopathic subjects showed a significant number (more than 75 percent) had dysfunction of the temporal and frontal regions of the brain.[127]

There is evidence that people with tumors are prone to depression, irritability, temper outbursts, and even homicidal attacks. Clinical case studies of patients suffering from brain tumors indicate that previously docile people may undergo behavior changes so great that they attempt to seriously harm their families and friends. When the tumor is removed, their behavior returns to normal.[128] In addition to brain tumors, head injuries caused by

This scan compares a normal brain (left) and an ADHD brain (right). Areas of orange and white demonstrate a higher rate of metabolism, while areas of blue and green represent an abnormally low metabolic rate. Why is ADHD so prevalent in the United States today? Some experts believe that our immigrant forebears, risk takers who impulsively left their homelands for life in a new world, may have brought with them a genetic predisposition for ADHD.

Dr. Alan Zametkin/Clinical Brain Imaging, courtesy of Office of Scientific Information, NIMH accidents, such as falls or auto crashes, have been linked to personality reversals marked by outbursts of antisocial and violent behavior.[129]

A variety of central nervous system diseases have also been linked to personality changes. Associated symptoms of these diseases are memory deficiency, orientation loss, and affective (emotional) disturbances dominated by rage, anger, and increased irritability.[130]

Brain Chemistry Chemical compounds called neurotransmitters influence or activate brain functions. Those studied in relation to aggression and other antisocial behaviors include dopamine, norepinephrine, serotonin, monoamine oxidase (MAO), and gamma-aminobutryic acid (GABA).[131]

Research efforts have linked low levels of MAO to high levels of violence and property crime, as well as defiance of punishment, impulsivity, hyperactivity, poor academic performance, sensation seeking and risk taking, and recreational drug use.[132] Abnormal levels of MAO may explain both individual and group differences in the crime rate. For example, females have higher levels of MAO than males, a condition that may explain gender differences in the crime rate.[133] The effect of MAO on crime persists throughout the life span: individuals with the low-activity form of monoamine oxidase-A who are exposed to violence in youth have a greater likelihood of engaging in physical aggression later in adulthood.[134]

Because this linkage has been found, it is not uncommon for violence-prone people to be treated with antipsychotic drugs such as Haldol, Stelazine, Prolixin, and Risperdal, which help control levels of neurotransmitters; these are sometimes referred to as **chemical restraints** or **chemical straitjackets**.

Arousal Theory

It has long been suspected that obtaining thrills is a crime motivator. Adolescents may engage in crimes such as shoplifting and vandalism simply because they offer the attraction of "getting away with it"; from this perspective, delinquency is a thrilling demonstration of personal competence.

According to **arousal theory**, for a variety of genetic and environmental reasons, some people's brains function differently in response to environmental stimuli. All of us seek to maintain a preferred or optimal level of arousal: too much stimulation leaves us anxious and stressed out; too little makes us feel bored and weary. There is, however, variation in the way people's brains process sensory input. Some nearly always feel comfortable with little stimulation, whereas others require a high degree of environmental input to feel comfortable. The latter are "sensation seekers," who seek out stimulating activities, which may include aggressive, violent behavior patterns.[135]

Evidence that some people may have lower levels of arousal comes from studies on resting heart rate levels conducted by Adrian Raine and his associates, who found that antisocial children have lower resting heart rates than the general population.[136] In one recent study, Raine and his associates found that low heart rate may produce a need for stimulation that is associated with aggressive behavior patterns. Raine has also speculated that some people lack fear and are nonresponsive to the threat of punishment, a condition that allows them to feel relatively comfortable while engaging in antisocial encounters. People who have low arousal levels will seek out risky situations and become more involved with criminal behavior as an avenue toward thrill seeking. Because lack of fear and thrill-seeking behavior are characteristics of adult psychopaths, antisocial children might therefore develop into psychopaths as adults.[137]

The factors that determine a person's level of arousal are not fully determined, but suspected sources include:

- *Brain chemistry (and brain structure).* Some people have brains with many more nerve cells with receptor sites for neurotransmitters than others.
- *Heart rate.* Another view is that people with low heartbeat rates are more likely to commit crime because they seek stimulation to increase their feelings of arousal to normal levels.[138]
- *Autonomic nervous system.* Some biosocial theorists link arousal to the autonomic nervous system as measured by skin conductance response. People with abnormally exaggerated skin conductivity may react with above average negative emotional intensity to stimulus that would have little effect on the average person. As a result, provocations that some people might merely shrug off are viewed as highly confrontational, inflammatory, insulting, and deserving of an aggressive reply.[139]

In sum, brain structure, chemistry, and development are believed to exert a strong influence on human behavior.

chemical restraints or chemical straitjackets Antipsychotic drugs such as Haldol, Stelazine, Prolixin, and Risperdal, which help control levels of neurotransmitters (such as serotonin/dopamine), that are used to treat violence-prone people.

arousal theory A view of crime suggesting that people who have a high arousal level seek powerful stimuli in their environment to maintain an optimal level of arousal. These stimuli are often associated with violence and aggression. Sociopaths may need greater than average stimulation to bring them up to comfortable levels of living; this need explains their criminal tendencies.

Genetics and Crime

 LO4 Cite examples of the different research techniques used to link genetics to crime

Another biosocial theme is that the human traits associated with criminality have a genetic basis.[140] There are actually two views of the genetics of crime. According to the direct view, (1) antisocial behavior is inherited, (2) the genetic makeup of parents is passed on to children, and (3) genetic abnormality is directly linked to a variety of antisocial behaviors.[141] According to the indirect view, genes are related to some personality or physical trait which in turn is linked to antisocial behavior.[142] Genetic makeup may shape friendship patterns and orient people toward deviant peer associations which cause them to become crime prone.[143] Adolescent attachment to parents may be controlled by their genetic makeup; attachment that is weak and attenuated has been linked to criminality.[144]

Testing Genetic Theory

If criminal tendencies are inherited, then it stands to reason that the children of criminal parents should be more likely to become law violators than the offspring of conventional parents. A number of studies have found that parental criminality and deviance do, in fact, have a powerful influence on delinquent behavior.[145] One recent study of violent offending in Sweden used a variety of pairing comparisons, between spouses of siblings and half-siblings, and across consecutive spouses, and found evidence that the genetic basis for violent crime was moderate to strong.[146]

Some of the most important data on parental deviance have been gathered as part of a long-term study of English youth called the Cambridge Study in Delinquent Development (CSDD). This research followed a group of about 1,000 males from the time they were 8 years old until they reached their adulthood. The males in the study were repeatedly interviewed and their school and police records evaluated. These cohort data indicate that a significant number of delinquent youths had criminal fathers.[147] While 8 percent of the sons of noncriminal fathers eventually became chronic offenders, about 37 percent of youths with criminal fathers were multiple offenders.[148] Analysis of the data confirms that delinquent youths grow up to become the parents of antisocial children.[149] One specific form of aggressive behavior that seems to be inherited is school yard bullying: bullies have children who bully others, and these second-generation bullies grow up to become the fathers of children who are also bullies, in a never-ending cycle.[150]

The Cambridge findings are not unique. Data from the Rochester Youth Development Study (RYDS), a longitudinal analysis that has been monitoring the behavior of 1,000 upstate New York area youths since 1988, also find an intergenerational continuity in antisocial behavior.[151]

It is possible, of course, that the genetic effect of parental deviance may be exaggerated by mating practices. It appears to be a genetic transference when the child of two drug abusers becomes a drug user too. But it is also possible that this "antisocial" family consists of people who have suffered labeling and stigma, isolating them from the economic and social mainstream and increasing their chances of criminality. While it may appear that drug abusing parents produce children who are genetically predisposed to drug abuse, it is also possible that what appears to be a genetic effect is actually the product of social processes.[152]

Sibling Similarities

It stands to reason that if the cause of crime is in part genetic, then the behavior of siblings should be similar because they share genetic material. Research does show that if one sibling engages in antisocial behavior, so do his/her brothers and sisters. The effect is greatest among same-sex siblings.[153] Sibling pairs who report warm, mutual relationships and share friends are the most likely to behave in a similar fashion; those who maintain a close relationship also have similar rates of crime and drug abuse.[154]

While the similarity of siblings' behavior seems striking, what appears to be a genetic effect may also be explained by other factors:

- Siblings who live in the same environment are influenced by similar social and economic factors.
- Deviant siblings may grow closer because of shared interests.
- Younger siblings who admire their older siblings may imitate the elders' behavior.
- The deviant sibling forces or threatens the brother or sister into committing criminal acts.
- Siblings living in a similar environment may develop similar types of friends; it is peer behavior that is the critical influence. The influence of peers may negate any observed interdependence of sibling behavior.[155]

Twin Behavior

As mentioned above, because siblings are usually brought up in the same household and share common life experiences, any similarity in their antisocial behavior might be a function of environmental influences and experiences and not genetics at all. To guard against this, biosocial theorists have compared the behavior of same-sex twins and again found concordance in their behavior patterns.[156]

However, an even more rigorous test of genetic theory involves comparison of the behavior of identical monozygotic (MZ) twins with fraternal dizygotic (DZ) twins; while the former have an identical genetic makeup, the latter share only about 50 percent of their genetic combinations. Research has shown that MZ twins are significantly closer in their personal characteristics, such as intelligence, than are DZ twins.[157]

The earliest studies conducted on the behavior of twins detected a significant relationship between the criminal activities of MZ twins and a much lower association between those of DZ twins. A review of relevant studies conducted between 1929 and 1961 found that 60 percent of MZ twins shared criminal behavior patterns (if one twin was criminal, so was the other), whereas only 30 percent of DZ twin behavior was similarly related.[158] These findings may be viewed as powerful evidence that a genetic basis for criminality exists.

One famous study of twin behavior still under way is the Minnesota Twin Family Study. This research compares the behavior of MZ and DZ twin pairs who were raised together with others who were separated at birth and in some cases did not even know of each other's existence. The study shows some striking similarities in behavior and ability for twin pairs raised apart. An MZ twin reared away from a co-twin has about as good a chance of being similar to the co-twin in terms of personality, interests, and attitudes as one who has been reared with his or her co-twin. The conclusion: similarities between twins are due to genes, not the environment.[159]

Not all research efforts have found that MZ twin pairs are more closely related in their criminal behavior than DZ or ordinary sibling pairs, and some that have found an association note that it is at best "modest."[160] Even if the behavior similarities between MZ twins are greater than those between DZ twins, the association may be explained by environmental factors. MZ twins are more likely to look alike and to share physical traits than DZ twins, and they are more likely to be treated similarly. Similarities in their shared behavior patterns may therefore be a function of socialization and/or environment and not heredity.[161]

It is also possible that what appears to be a genetic effect picked up by the twin research is actually the effect of sibling influence on criminality, referred to as the **contagion effect**: genetic predispositions and early experiences make some people, including twins, susceptible to deviant behavior, which is transmitted by the presence of antisocial siblings in the household.[162]

The contagion effect may explain in part the higher concordance of deviant behaviors found in identical twins as compared to fraternal twins or mere siblings. The relationship between identical twins may be stronger and more enduring than other sibling pairs so that contagion and not genetics explains their behavioral similarities. According to Marshall Jones and Donald Jones, the contagion effect may also help explain why the behavior of twins is more similar in adulthood than in adolescence.[163] Youthful misbehavior is influenced by friends and peer group relationships. As adults, the influence of peers may wane as people marry and find employment. In contrast, twin influence is everlasting; if one twin is antisocial, it legitimizes and supports the criminal behavior in his or her co-twin. This effect may grow even stronger in adulthood because twin relations are more enduring than any other. What seems to be a genetic effect may actually be the result of sibling interaction with a brother or sister who engages in antisocial activity.

Adoption Studies One way of avoiding the pitfalls of twin studies is to focus attention on the behavior of adoptees.

It seems logical that if the behavior of adopted children is more closely aligned to that of their biological parents than to that of their adoptive parents, then the idea of a genetic basis for criminality would be supported. If, on the other hand, adoptees are more closely aligned to the behavior of their adoptive parents than their biological parents, an environmental basis for crime would seem more valid.

Several studies indicate that some relationship exists between biological parents' behavior and the behavior of their children, even when their contact has been nonexistent.[164] One analysis of Swedish adoptees also found that genetic factors are highly significant, accounting for 59 percent of the variation in their petty crime rates. Boys who had criminal parents were significantly more likely to violate the law. Environmental influences and economic status were significantly less important, explaining about 19 percent of the variance in crime. Nonetheless, having a positive environment, such as being adopted into a more affluent home, helped inhibit genetic predisposition.[165]

Evaluating Genetic Research The genes–crime relationship is controversial because it implies that the propensity to commit crime is present at birth and cannot be altered. It raises moral dilemmas: if *in utero* genetic testing could detect a gene for violence, and a violence gene was found to be present, what could be done as a precautionary measure?

Some critics suggest that available evidence provides little conclusive proof that crime is genetically predetermined. Detractors point to the inadequate research designs and weak methodologies of supporting research. The newer, better-designed research studies, critics charge, provide less support than earlier, less methodically sound studies.[166] A recent review by Callie Burt and Ronald Simons concludes that existing research on heredity and crime is hopelessly flawed; these researchers go on to suggest that this area of research be abandoned. Their reason is that the environment and genetic functioning are so interrelated that it may be impossible to separate out the true effect of each of these factors.[167]

Evolutionary Theory

LO5 Explain the evolutionary view of crime

Some criminologists believe the human traits that produce violence and aggression are produced through the long process of human evolution.[168] According to this evolutionary view, the competition for scarce resources has influenced

---

contagion effect Genetic predispositions and early experiences make some people, including twins, susceptible to deviant behavior, which is transmitted by the presence of antisocial siblings in the household.

and shaped the human species.[169] Over the course of human existence, people whose personal characteristics enable them to accumulate more than others are the most likely to breed and dominate the species. People have been shaped to engage in actions that promote their well-being and ensure the survival and reproduction of their genetic line. Males who are impulsive risk-takers may be able to father more children because they are reckless in their social relationships and have sexual encounters with numerous partners. If, according to evolutionary theories, such behavior patterns are inherited, impulsive behavior becomes intergenerational, passed down from father to son. It is not surprising, then, that human history has been marked by war, violence, and aggression.

There are a number of individual theories of evolutionary criminology, three of which are discussed in detail below.

Rushton's Theory of Race and Evolution   One of the most controversial versions of evolutionary theory was formulated by J. Philippe Rushton and first appeared in his 1995 book, *Race, Evolution and Behavior*.[170] According to Rushton, there is evidence that modern humans evolved in Africa about 200,000 years ago and then began to migrate outward to present-day Europe and Asia. He posits that the further north elements of the populations migrated, the more they encountered harsher climates, which produce the need to gather and store food, gain shelter, make clothes, and raise children successfully during prolonged winters. As these populations evolved into present-day Europeans and Asians, their brain mass increased, and they developed slower rates of maturation and lower levels of sex hormones. This physical change produced reductions in sexual potency and aggression and increases in family stability and longevity. These evolutionary changes are responsible for present-day crime rate differences between the races.

Rushton's work was received harshly by critics, who condemned his definitions of race and crime and accused him of racial bias.[171] Among the many criticisms hurled at Rushton has been his singular focus on street crimes, such as theft, while giving short shrift to white-collar and organized crimes, which are predominantly committed by whites. Rushton ignores the fact that men are much more criminal than women even though there is little evidence of significant differences in intelligence or brain size between the genders.

R/K Selection Theory   R/K selection theory holds that all organisms can be located along a continuum based upon their reproductive drives.[172] Those along the "R" end reproduce rapidly whenever they can and invest little in their offspring; those along the "K" end reproduce slowly and cautiously and take care in raising their offspring. Evolutionary theorists believe males today "lean" toward R-selection, because they can reproduce faster without the need for investing in their offspring; females are K-selected,

because they have fewer offspring but give more care and devotion to them. K-oriented people are more cooperative and sensitive to others, whereas R-oriented people are more cunning and deceptive. Males, therefore, tend to partake in more criminal behavior. In general, people who commit violent crimes seem to exhibit R-selection traits, such as a premature birth and early and frequent sexual activity. They are more likely to have been neglected as children and to have a short life expectancy.

Cheater Theory   Cheater theory suggests that a subpopulation of men has evolved with genes that incline them toward extremely low parental involvement. They are sexually aggressive and use their cunning to gain sexual conquests with as many females as possible. Because females would not willingly choose them as mates, they use stealth to gain sexual access, including such tactics as mimicking the behavior of more stable males. They use devious and illegal means to acquire resources they need for sexual domination. Their deceptive reproductive tactics spill over into other endeavors, where their talent for irresponsible, opportunistic behavior supports their antisocial activities. Deception in reproductive strategies, then, is linked to a deceitful lifestyle.

Psychologist Byron Roth notes that cheater-type males may be especially attractive to those younger, less intelligent women who begin having children at a very early age.[173] State-sponsored welfare, claims Roth, removes the need for potential mates to have the resources needed to be stable providers and family caretakers. With the state meeting their financial needs, these women are attracted to men who are physically attractive and flamboyant. Their fleeting courtship process produces children with low IQs, aggressive personalities, and little chance of proper socialization in father-absent families. Because the criminal justice system treats them leniently, argues Roth, sexually irresponsible men are free to prey on young girls. Over time, their offspring will supply an ever-expanding supply of cheaters who are both antisocial and sexually aggressive.

Violence and Evolution   In their classic book *Homicide*, Martin Daly and Margo Wilson suggest that violent offenses are often driven by evolutionary and reproductive factors. High rates of spouse abuse in modern society may be a function of aggressive men seeking to control and possess mates. When females are murdered by their spouses, the motivating factor is typically fear of infidelity and the threat of attachment to a new partner. Infidelity challenges male dominance and future reproductive rights. It comes as no surprise that in some cultures, including our own, sexual infidelity discovered in progress by the aggrieved husband is viewed legally as a provocation that justifies retaliatory killing.[174] Men who feel most threatened over the potential of losing mates to rivals are the ones most likely to engage in sexual violence. Research shows that women in common-law marriages, especially those who are much younger than their husbands, are at greater risk than older married women. Abusive males may fear the potential loss of their younger mates, especially if they are not bound by a marriage contract, and may use force for purposes of control and possession.[175] Armed robbery is another crime that may have evolutionary underpinnings. Though most robbers are caught and severely punished, it remains an alluring pursuit for men who want to both show their physical prowess and display resources with which to conquer rivals and attract mates. Violent episodes are far more common among men who are unemployed and unmarried—in other words, those who may want to demonstrate their allure to the opposite sex but who are without the benefit of position or wealth.[176]

Gender and Evolution Evolutionary concepts have been linked to gender-based differences in the crime rate. To ensure survival of the gene pool (and the species), it is beneficial for a male of any species to mate with as many suitable females as possible since each can bear his offspring. Rather than forming stable families and developing parenting skills, the most aggressive males have a strong sexual drive, a reduced ability to form strong emotional bonds, a lack of conscience, and aggressive and violent tendencies. These traits, which express themselves in instances of antisocial behavior throughout the life span, beginning in early childhood.[177] These antisocial men produce many offspring, who are prone to criminal behaviors.[178] In contrast, because of the long period of gestation, females require a secure home and a single, stable, nurturing partner to ensure their survival. Because of these differences in mating patterns, the most aggressive males mate most often and have the greatest number of offspring. Therefore, over the history of the human species, aggressive males have had the greatest impact on the gene pool. The descendants of these aggressive males now account for the disproportionate amount of male aggression and violence.[179]

Evaluation of the Biosocial Branch of Trait Theory

Contemporary biosocial theorists distinguish their views with Lombrosian, deterministic biology. Rather than suggest that there are born criminals and noncriminals, they maintain that some people carry the potential to be violent or antisocial and that environmental conditions can sometimes trigger antisocial responses.[180] This would explain why some otherwise law-abiding citizens engage in a single, seemingly unexplainable antisocial act, and conversely, why some people with long criminal careers often engage in conventional behavior. It also explains why there are geographic and temporal patterns in the crime rate: people who are predisposed to crime may simply have more opportunities to commit illegal acts in the summer in Los Angeles and Atlanta than in the winter in Bedford, New Hampshire, and Minot, North Dakota, or perhaps their hormonal levels become activated as the temperature rises.

The biosocial view is that behavior is a product of interacting biological and environmental events.[181] Physical impairments may make some people "at risk" to crime, but it is when they are linked to social and environmental problems, such as family dysfunction, that they trigger criminal acts.[182] People who possess a biological trait that makes them at risk to crime can avoid involvement in antisocial behaviors if their environment does not contain stimuli that trigger aggression and violence.[183] Biological traits, social relationships, and routine opportunities all interact to predict criminal involvement. Concept Summary 5.1 summarizes the various biosocial theories of crime.

BIOSOCIAL THEORIES OF CRIME 5.1

concept summary

BIOCHEMICAL
- The major premise of the theory is that crime, especially violence, is a function of diet, vitamin intake, hormonal imbalance, or food allergies.
- The strengths of the theory are that it explains irrational violence; it shows how the environment interacts with personal traits to influence behavior.
- The research focuses of the theory are diet, hormones, enzymes, environmental contaminants, and lead intake.

NEUROLOGICAL
- The major premise of the theory is that criminals and delinquents often suffer brain impairment, as measured by the EEG. Attention deficit hyperactivity disorder and minimal brain dysfunction are related to antisocial behavior.
- The strengths of the theory are that it explains irrational violence; it shows how the environment interacts with personal traits to influence behavior.
- The research focuses of the theory are ADD, ADHD, learning disabilities, brain injuries, and brain chemistry.

GENETIC
- The major premise of the theory is that criminal traits and predispositions are inherited. The criminality of parents can predict the delinquency of children.
- The strengths of the theory are that it explains why only a small percentage of youth in high-crime areas become chronic offenders.
- The research focuses of the theory are twin behavior, sibling behavior, and parent–child similarities.

EVOLUTIONARY
- The major premise of the theory is that as the human race evolved, traits and characteristics have become ingrained. Some of these traits make people aggressive and predisposed to commit crime.
- The strengths of the theory are that it helps explain gender differences in the crime rate.
- The research focuses of the theory are gender differences and understanding human aggression.

PSYCHOLOGICAL TRAIT THEORIES

The second branch of trait theories focuses on the psychological aspects of crime, including the associations among intelligence, personality, learning, and criminal behavior.

Psychological theories of crime have a long history. In *The English Convict*, Charles Goring (1870–1919) studied the mental characteristics of 3,000 English convicts.[184] He found little difference in the physical characteristics of criminals and noncriminals, but he uncovered a significant relationship between crime and a condition he referred to as **defective intelligence**, which involves such traits as feeblemindedness, epilepsy, insanity, and defective social instinct.[185] Goring believed criminal behavior was inherited and could, therefore, be controlled by regulating the reproduction of families who produced mentally defective children.

Gabriel Tarde (1843–1904) is the forerunner of modern-day learning theorists.[186] Tarde believed people learn from one another through a process of imitation. Tarde's ideas are similar to modern social learning theorists who believe that both interpersonal and observed behavior, such as a movie or television, can influence criminality.

Since the pioneering work of people like Tarde and Goring, psychologists, psychiatrists, and other mental health professionals have long played an active role in formulating criminological theory. In their quest to understand and treat all varieties of abnormal mental conditions, psychologists have encountered clients whose behavior falls within categories society has labeled as criminal, deviant, violent, and antisocial.

This section is organized along the lines of the predominant psychological views most closely associated with the causes of criminal behavior. Some psychologists view antisocial behavior from a **psychoanalytic** or **psychodynamic perspective**: their focus is on early childhood experience and its effect on personality. In contrast, **behaviorism** stresses social learning and behavior modeling as the keys to criminality. **Cognitive theory** analyzes human perception and how it affects behavior.

Psychodynamic Theory

 LO6 Discuss the elements of the psychodynamic perspective

Psychodynamic (or psychoanalytic) psychology was originated by Viennese psychiatrist Sigmund Freud (1856–1939) and has since remained a prominent segment of psychological theory.[187]

 For a collection of links to libraries, museums, and biographical materials related to Sigmund Freud and his works, go to http://www.freudarchives.org/.
Do you believe we are all guided by unconscious thoughts and feelings?

Freud believed that we all carry with us residue of the most significant emotional attachments of our childhood, which then guide future interpersonal relationships. Today the term *psychodynamic* refers to a broad range of theories that focus on the influence of instinctive drives and forces and the importance of developmental processes in shaping personality. Contemporary psychodynamic theory places greater emphasis on conscious experience and its interaction with the unconscious, in addition to the role that social factors play in development. Nonetheless, it still focuses on the influence of early childhood experiences on the development of personality, motivation, and drives.

Elements of Psychodynamic Theory According to the classic version of the theory, the human personality contains a three-part structure. The **id** is the primitive part of an individual's mental makeup present at birth. It represents unconscious biological drives for sex, food, and other life-sustaining necessities. The id follows the **pleasure principle**: it requires instant gratification without concern for the rights of others.

defective intelligence Traits such as feeblemindedness, epilepsy, insanity, and defective social instinct, which Goring believed had a significant relationship to criminal behavior.

psychoanalytic or psychodynamic perspective Branch of psychology holding that the human personality is controlled by unconscious mental processes developed early in childhood.

behaviorism The branch of psychology concerned with the study of observable behavior rather than unconscious motives. It focuses on the relationship between particular stimuli and people's responses to them.

cognitive theory The study of the perception of reality and of the mental processes required to understand the world in which we live.

id The primitive part of people's mental makeup, present at birth, that represents unconscious biological drives for food, sex, and other life-sustaining necessities. The id seeks instant gratification without concern for the rights of others.

pleasure principle According to Freud, a theory in which id-dominated people are driven to increase their personal pleasure without regard to consequences.

The **ego** develops early in life, when a child begins to learn that his or her wishes cannot be instantly gratified. The ego is that part of the personality that compensates for the demands of the id by helping the individual guide his or her actions to remain within the boundaries of social convention. The ego is guided by the **reality principle**: it takes into account what is practical and conventional by societal standards.

The **superego** develops as a result of incorporating within the personality the moral standards and values of parents, community, and significant others. It is the moral aspect of an individual's personality; it passes judgments on behavior. The superego is divided into two parts: **conscience** and **ego ideal**. Conscience tells what is right and wrong. It forces the ego to control the id and directs the individual into morally acceptable and responsible behaviors, which may not be pleasurable. Exhibit 5.3 summarizes Freud's model of the personality structure.

Psychosexual Stages of Human Development

The most basic human drive present at birth is **eros**, the instinct to preserve and create life. The other is the death instinct (**thanatos**), which is expressed as aggression.

Eros is expressed sexually. Consequently, very early in their development, humans experience sexuality, which is expressed by seeking pleasure through various parts of the body. During the first year of life, a child attains pleasure by sucking and biting; Freud called this the **oral stage**. During the second and third years of life, the focus of sexual attention is on the elimination of bodily wastes—the **anal stage**. The **phallic stage** occurs during the third year, when children focus their attention on their genitals. Males begin to have sexual feelings for their mothers (the **Oedipus complex**) and girls for their fathers (the **Electra complex**). **Latency** begins at age 6. During this period, feelings of sexuality are repressed until the genital stage begins at puberty; this marks the beginning of adult sexuality.

If conflicts are encountered during any of the psychosexual stages of development, a person can become **fixated** at that point. This means, as an adult, the fixated person will exhibit behavior traits characteristic of those encountered during infantile sexual development. For example, an infant who does not receive enough oral gratification during the first year of life is likely as an adult to engage in such oral behavior as smoking, drinking, or drug abuse or to be clinging and dependent in personal relationships. Thus, according to Freud, the roots of adult behavioral problems can be traced to problems developed in the earliest years of life.

The Psychodynamics of Antisocial Behavior Psychologists have long linked criminality to abnormal mental states produced by early childhood trauma. For example, Alfred Adler (1870–1937), the founder of individual psychology, coined the term **inferiority complex** to describe people who have feelings of inferiority and compensate for them with a drive for superiority. Controlling others may help reduce personal inadequacies. Erik Erikson (1902–1984) described the **identity crisis**—a period of serious personal

ego The part of the personality, developed in early childhood, that helps control the id and keep people's actions within the boundaries of social convention.

reality principle According to Freud, the ability to learn about the consequences of one's actions through experience.

superego Incorporation within the personality of the moral standards and values of parents, community, and significant others.

conscience One of two parts of the superego; it distinguishes between what is right and wrong.

ego ideal Part of the superego; directs the individual into morally acceptable and responsible behaviors, which may not be pleasurable.

eros The instinct to preserve and create life, a basic human drive present at birth.

thanatos According to Freud, the instinctual drive toward aggression and violence.

oral stage In Freud's schema, the first year of life, when a child attains pleasure by sucking and biting.

anal stage In Freud's schema, the second and third years of life, when the focus of sexual attention is on the elimination of bodily wastes.

phallic stage In Freud's schema, the third year, when children focus their attention on their genitals.

Oedipus complex A stage of development when males begin to have sexual feelings for their mothers.

Electra complex A stage of development when girls begin to have sexual feelings for their fathers.

latency A developmental stage that begins at age 6. During this period, feelings of sexuality are repressed until the genital stage begins at puberty; this marks the beginning of adult sexuality.

fixated An adult who exhibits behavior traits characteristic of those encountered during infantile sexual development.

inferiority complex People who have feelings of inferiority and compensate for them with a drive for superiority.

identity crisis A psychological state, identified by Erikson, in which youth face inner turmoil and uncertainty about life roles.

EXHIBIT 5.3

Freud's Model of the Personality Structure

Personality Structure	Guiding Principle	Description
Id	Pleasure principle	Unconscious biological drives; requires instant gratification
Ego	Reality principle	Helps the personality refine the demands of the id; helps person adapt to conventions
Superego	The conscience	The moral aspect of the personality

SOURCE: © Cengage Learning®

questioning people undertake in an effort to determine their own values and sense of direction. Adolescents undergoing an identity crisis might exhibit out-of-control behavior and experiment with drugs and other forms of deviance.

The psychoanalyst whose work is most closely associated with criminality is August Aichhorn.[188] After examining many delinquent youths, Aichhorn concluded that societal stress, though damaging, could not alone result in a life of crime unless a predisposition existed that psychologically prepared youths for antisocial acts. This mental state, which he labeled **latent delinquency**, is found in youngsters whose personality requires them to act in these ways:

- Seek immediate gratification (to act impulsively)
- Consider satisfying their personal needs more important than relating to others
- Satisfy instinctive urges without considering right and wrong (that is, they lack guilt)

The psychodynamic model of the criminal offender depicts an aggressive, frustrated person dominated by events that occurred early in childhood. Perhaps because they may have suffered unhappy experiences in childhood or had families that could not provide proper love and care, criminals suffer from weak or damaged egos that make them unable to cope with conventional society. Weak egos are associated with immaturity, poor social skills, and excessive dependence on others. People with weak egos may be easily led into crime by antisocial peers and drug abuse. Some offenders have underdeveloped superegos and consequently lack internalized representations of those behaviors that are punished in conventional society. They commit crimes because they have difficulty understanding the consequences of their actions.[189]

Offenders may suffer from a wide variety of mood and/or behavior disorders. They may be histrionic, depressed, antisocial, or narcissistic.[190] They may suffer from **conduct disorders**, which include long histories of antisocial behavior, or mood disorders characterized by disturbance in expressed emotions. Among the latter is **bipolar disorder**, in which moods alternate between periods of wild elation and deep depression.[191] Some offenders are driven by an unconscious desire to be punished for prior sins, either real or imaginary. As a result, they may violate the law to gain attention or to punish their parents.

According to this view, crime is a manifestation of feelings of oppression and people's inability to develop the proper psychological defenses and rationales to keep these feelings under control. Criminality enables troubled people to survive by producing positive psychic results: it helps them to feel free and independent, and it gives them the possibility of excitement and the chance to use their skills and imagination. Crime also provides them with the promise of positive gain; it allows them to blame others for their predicament (for example, the police), and it gives them a chance to rationalize their sense of failure ("If I hadn't gotten into trouble, I could have been a success").[192]

Attachment Theory

Attachment theory, a view most closely associated with psychologist John Bowlby, is also connected to the psychodynamic tradition. Bowlby believed that the ability to form attachments—that is, emotionally bond to another person—has important lasting psychological implications that follow people across the life span. Attachments are formed soon after birth, when infants bond with their mothers. They will become frantic, crying and clinging, to prevent separation or to reestablish contact with a missing parent. Bowlby noted that this behavior is not restricted to humans and occurs in all mammals, indicating that separation anxiety may be instinctual or evolutionary. After all, attachment figures, especially the mother, provide support and care, and without attachment an infant would be helpless and could not survive. Bowlby also challenged Freud's view of the development of the ego and superego, claiming that at birth these were bound up in the relationship with one's mother.[193]

Bowlby's most important finding was that to grow up mentally healthy, "the infant and young child should experience a warm, intimate, and continuous relationship with his mother (or permanent mother substitute) in which both find satisfaction and enjoyment."[194]

According to this view, failing to develop proper attachment may cause people to fall prey to a number of psychological disorders. Psychologists believe that children with attachment problems lack trust and respect for others. They often display many psychological symptoms, some of which resemble attention deficit hyperactivity disorder (ADHD). They may be impulsive and have difficulty concentrating, and consequently experience difficulty in school. As adults, they often have difficulty initiating and sustaining relationships with others and find it difficult to sustain romantic relationships. Criminologists have linked people having detachment problems with a variety of antisocial behaviors, including sexual assault and child abuse.[195] It has been

latent delinquency A psychological predisposition to commit antisocial acts because of an id-dominated personality that renders an individual incapable of controlling impulsive, pleasure-seeking drives.

conduct disorders A pattern of repetitive behavior in which the rights of others or social norms are violated.

bipolar disorder An emotional disturbance in which moods alternate between periods of wild elation and deep depression.

attachment theory The belief that the ability to form attachments—that is, emotionally bond to another person—has important lasting psychological implications that follow people across the life span.

suggested that boys disproportionately experience disrupted attachment and that these disruptions are causally related to disproportionate rates of male offending.[196]

Mental Disorders and Crime

According to the psychodynamic tradition, traumatic life events can bring about severe mental disorders that have been linked to the onset of crime and deviance. Mental disorders typically involve a psychological condition that disrupts thinking, feeling, and other important psychological processes. They may cause people to deviate from social expectations and impair their everyday functioning. Less severe forms are mood disorders—prolonged and intense emotional upheavals that shape and color a person's psychic life. A more severe mental disorder is referred to as psychosis and is characterized by derangement of personality and loss of contact with reality, thereby causing deterioration of normal social functioning. These are discussed more fully below.

Mood Disorders and Crime Psychologists recognize a variety of mental disorders that may be linked to antisocial behavior. Adolescents who are frequently uncooperative and hostile and who seem to be much more difficult than other children the same age may be suffering from a psychological condition known as *disruptive behavior disorder (DBD)*, which can take on two distinct forms: *oppositional defiant disorder (ODD)* and *conduct disorder (CD)*.[197] Children suffering from ODD experience an ongoing pattern of uncooperative, defiant, and hostile behavior toward authority figures that seriously interferes with the youngsters' day-to-day functioning. Symptoms of ODD may include frequent loss of temper and constant arguing with adults; defying adults or refusing adult requests or rules; deliberately annoying others; blaming others for mistakes or misbehavior; being angry and resentful; being spiteful or vindictive; swearing or using obscene language; or having low self-esteem. The person with ODD is moody and easily frustrated and may abuse drugs as a form of self-medication.[198]

CD is typically considered a more serious group of behavioral and emotional problems.[199] Children and adolescents with CD have great difficulty following rules and behaving in socially acceptable ways. They are often viewed by other children, adults, and social agencies as severely antisocial. Research shows that they are frequently involved in such activities as bullying, fighting, committing sexual assaults, and cruelty to animals.

What causes CD? Numerous biosocial and psychological factors are suspected. There is evidence, for example, that interconnections between the frontal lobes and other brain regions may influence CD. There is also research showing that levels of serotonin can influence the onset of CD and that CD has been shown to aggregate in families, suggesting a genetic basis of the disorder.[200]

ODD and CD are not the only mood disorders associated with antisocial behavior. Some people find it impossible to cope with feelings of oppression or depression. Research shows that people who are clinically depressed are more likely to engage in a variety of illegal acts.[201] Some people suffer from **alexithymia**, a deficit in emotional cognition that prevents them from being aware of their feelings or being able to understand or talk about their thoughts and emotions; they seem robotic and emotionally dead.[202] Others may suffer from eating disorders and are likely to use fasting, vomiting, and drugs to lose weight or to keep from gaining weight.[203]

Psychosis and Crime David Berkowitz (the "Son of Sam" or the "44-calibre killer"), a noted serial killer who went on a rampage from 1976 to 1977, claimed that his killing spree began when he received messages from a neighbor's dog. His symptoms made him appear to suffer from a severe form of mental illness referred to as **psychosis**, characterized by extreme impairment of a person's ability to think clearly, respond emotionally, communicate effectively, understand reality, and behave appropriately. People suffering psychosis may hear nonexistent voices, hallucinate, and make inappropriate behavioral responses. People with severe mental disorders exhibit illogical and incoherent thought processes and a lack of insight into their behavior. They may see themselves as agents of the devil, avenging angels, or the recipients of messages from animals and plants. Psychosis is brought about by a variety of mental **disorders**, including depression, manic depression, bipolar disorder, and **schizophrenia**.

There is evidence that law violators, especially those involved in violent crime, suffer from a disproportionate amount of severe mental health problems.[204] Recently,

alexithymia A deficit in emotional cognition that prevents people from being aware of their feelings or being able to understand or talk about their thoughts and emotions; they seem robotic and emotionally dead.

psychosis A mental state in which the perception of reality is distorted. People experiencing psychosis hallucinate, have paranoid or delusional beliefs, change personality, exhibit disorganized thinking, and engage in unusual or bizarre behavior.

disorders Any type of psychological problems (formerly labeled neuroses or psychoses), such as anxiety disorders, mood disorders, and conduct disorders.

schizophrenia A type of psychosis often marked by bizarre behavior, hallucinations, loss of thought control, and inappropriate emotional responses. Schizophrenic types include catatonic, which characteristically involves impairment of motor activity; paranoid, which is characterized by delusions of persecution; and hebephrenic, which is characterized by immature behavior and giddiness.

Richard Dorn and his associates examined the association between mental disorder and violence using a longitudinal sample of about 35,000 subjects. They found that when compared to the mentally sound, people suffering mental illness were significantly more likely to engage in subsequent violent episodes, especially if they abused drugs and alcohol.[205] The diagnosed mentally ill also appear in arrest and court statistics at a rate disproportionate to their presence in the population.[206] They may also be more prone to recidivism once released from prison.[207]

The association between mental health issues and crime crosses gender, age, and cultural lines.[208] Kids growing up in homes where parents suffer mental illness are much more likely to be at risk for family instability, poverty, and other factors that are related to future delinquency and crime. So not only may mental illness be a cause of crime, but its effect may be intergenerational.[209]

> The National Mental Health Association (NMHA) is the country's oldest and largest nonprofit organization addressing all aspects of mental health and mental illness. It is dedicated to improving the mental health of all individuals and achieving victory over mental illnesses. Learn more at **http://www.mentalhealthamerica.net/.**

Direct or Indirect Linkage?   It is still uncertain whether the link between mental illness and crime is direct or indirect. While it's possible that crime is a direct result of the delusions and illogical thinking associated with mental illness, it is also possible that some intervening factor associated with mental illness is the primary cause of antisocial behaviors. Suspected associations include the following:

- Mentally ill people may be more likely than the mentally sound to lack financial resources. They are thus forced to reside in deteriorated high-crime neighborhoods, a social factor that may increase involvement with criminal behavior.[210] It is also possible that a lack of resources may inhibit the mentally ill from obtaining the proper treatment, which, if made available, would result in reduced criminality.[211]
- The police may be more likely to arrest the mentally ill, which fosters the impression that they are crime prone.[212]
- Those suffering mental illness may self-medicate by using illegal substances, a practice linked to criminal behavior.[213]
- People with severe mental illness are more at risk to violent victimization than the mentally healthy. Violent victimization has been linked to increased crime rates. Ironically, efforts to deinstitutionalize the mentally ill and treat them in more humane community settings may expose them to higher rates of both victimization and criminality.[214]

AN ETHICAL DILEMMA

SOMETHING SNAPPED

The American Psychiatric Association (APA) believes a person should not be held legally responsible for a crime if his or her behavior meets the following standard developed by legal expert Richard Bonnie:

> A person charged with a criminal offense should be found not guilty by reason of insanity if it is shown that as a result of mental disease or mental retardation he was unable to appreciate the wrongfulness of his conduct at the time of the offense.

As used in this standard, the terms *mental disease* and *mental retardation* include only those severely abnormal mental conditions that grossly and demonstrably impair a person's perception or understanding of reality and that are not attributable primarily to the voluntary ingestion of alcohol or other psychoactive substances.

You are part of a research team with expertise on forensic criminology. Your team has been asked by the judge to investigate the case of Bill W., a young man who has murdered his father, and to make a written sentencing recommendation. You discover that Bill has a history of horrendous sexual and physical abuse at the hands of his father. When interviewed, Bill admits that "it is wrong to kill," but that something just "snapped" when he saw his dad with his arm around his younger brother, who also had cuts and bruises. Have one-half of the research team write a brief recommending that Bill's behavior be excused because of his prior history of mistreatment. Have the other half write an opinion supporting a criminal conviction because he fails to meet the test of insanity according to the APA definition. Have each group make an oral presentation of their findings and have the team leader choose the most persuasive argument to present to the judge.

thinking like a criminologist

Behavioral Theory

LO7   Correlate behavioral theory to crime

Psychological behavior theory maintains that human actions are developed through learning experiences. Rather than focusing on unconscious personality traits or cognitive development patterns produced early in childhood, behavior theorists are concerned with the actual behaviors people engage in during the course of their daily lives. The major premise of behavior theory is that people alter their behavior according to the reactions it receives from others. Behavior is supported by rewards and extinguished by negative reactions or punishments. With respect to criminal activity, the behaviorist views crimes, especially violent acts, as learned responses to life situations that do not necessarily represent psychologically abnormal responses.

Social Learning Theory Social learning is the branch of behavior theory most relevant to criminology.[215] Social learning theorists, most notably Albert Bandura, argue that people are not actually born with the ability to act violently, but that they learn to be aggressive through their life experiences.

To read about the life and work of Albert Bandura, visit **http://www.simplypsychology.org/bandura .html** and **http://faculty.frostburg.edu/mbradley/ psyography/albertbandura.html.**

Is your behavior altered when you observe people acting aggressively to achieve a goal and succeeding when others fail?

These experiences include personally observing others acting aggressively to achieve some goal or watching people being rewarded for violent acts on television or in movies. People learn to act aggressively when, as children, they model their behavior after the violent acts of adults. Later in life, these violent behavior patterns persist in social relationships. For example, the boy who sees his father repeatedly strike his mother with impunity is the one most likely to grow up to become a battering parent and husband.

Though social learning theorists agree that mental or physical traits may predispose a person toward violence, they believe that activating a person's violent tendencies is achieved by factors in the environment. The specific forms that aggressive behavior takes, the frequency with which it is expressed, the situations in which it is displayed, and the specific targets selected for attack are largely determined by social learning. However, people are self-aware and engage in purposeful learning. Their interpretations of behavior outcomes and situations influence the way they learn from experiences. One adolescent who spends a weekend in jail for drunk driving may find it the most awful experience of her life—one that teaches her to never drink and drive again. Another person, however, may find it an exciting experience about which he can brag to his friends.

Social Learning and Violence Social learning theorists view violence as something learned through a process called **behavior modeling**. In modern society, aggressive acts are usually modeled after three principal sources:

- *Family interaction.* Studies of family life show that aggressive children have parents who use similar tactics when dealing with others. For example, the children of wife batterers are more likely to use aggressive tactics themselves than children in the general population,

especially if the victims (their mothers) suffer psychological distress from the abuse.

- *Environmental experiences.* People who reside in areas in which violence is a daily occurrence are more likely to act violently than those who dwell in low-crime areas whose norms stress conventional behavior.
- *Mass media.* Films and television shows commonly depict violence graphically. Moreover, violence is often portrayed as an acceptable behavior, especially for heroes who never have to face legal consequences for their actions.

The Criminology in Action feature "Does Violent Media Cause Violent Crime?" has more on the effects of the media and violent behavior.

Social learning theorists have tried to determine what triggers violent acts. One position is that a direct, pain-producing physical assault will usually trigger a violent response. Yet the relationship between painful attacks and aggressive responses has been found to be inconsistent. Whether people counterattack in the face of physical attack depends, in part, on their skill in fighting and their perception of the strength of their attackers. Verbal taunts and insults have also been linked to aggressive responses. People who are predisposed to aggression by their learning experiences are likely to view insults from others as a challenge to their social status and to react with violence. Still another violence-triggering mechanism is a perceived reduction in one's life conditions. Prime examples of this phenomenon are riots and demonstrations in poverty-stricken ghetto areas. Studies have shown that discontent also produces aggression in the more successful members of lower-class groups who have been led to believe they can succeed but then have been thwarted in their aspirations. While it is still uncertain how this relationship is constructed, it is apparently complex. No matter how deprived some individuals are, they will not resort to violence. It seems evident that people's perceptions of their relative deprivation have different effects on their aggressive responses.

social learning theory The view that human behavior is modeled through observation of human social interactions, either directly from observing those who are close and from intimate contact or indirectly through the media. Interactions that are rewarded are copied, while those that are punished are avoided.

behavior modeling Process of learning behavior (notably aggression) by observing others. Aggressive models may be parents, criminals in the neighborhood, or characters on television or in video games and movies.

DOES VIOLENT MEDIA CAUSE VIOLENT CRIME?

does the media influence behavior? Does broadcast violence cause aggressive behavior in viewers? This has become a hot topic because of the persistent theme of violence on television, in video games, and in films. Critics have called for drastic measures, ranging from banning media violence to putting warning labels on video games.

If there is in fact a media–violence link, the problem is indeed alarming. Marketing research indicates that adolescents ages 11 to 14 view violent horror movies at a higher rate than any other age group. Children this age use older peers and siblings and apathetic parents to gain access to R-rated films. Most U.S. households now have either cable TV or smart TVs that can access the Internet and, coupled with devices such as Blu-ray players, can bring violent material into the home that is unavailable on broadcast networks.

There have been numerous anecdotal cases of violence linked to media. For example, in a famous incident, John Hinckley shot President Ronald Reagan due to his obsession with actress Jodie Foster, which developed after he watched her play a prostitute in the violent film *Taxi Driver*. Hinckley viewed the film at least 15 times.

While not all experts believe that media violence is a direct *cause* of violent behavior (because if it was, there would be millions of daily incidents in which viewers imitated the aggression they watched on TV or in movies), many do agree that media violence *contributes* to aggression. Developmental psychologist John Murray carefully reviewed existing research on the effect of TV violence on children and reached the conclusion that viewing media violence is related to both short- and long-term increases in aggressive attitudes, values, and behaviors; the effects of media violence are both real and strong. Similarly, Brad Bushman and Craig Anderson have found that watching violence on TV is correlated to aggressive behaviors. Recently, research by Laura Friedlander and her associates found that teens who watch violent media are the ones most likely to engage in dating violence, especially if they do not hold strong antiviolence attitudes.

There is also evidence that kids who watch violent media are more likely to persist in aggressive behavior as adults. Children who watch more than an hour of TV each day show an increase in assaults, fights, robberies, and other acts of aggression later in life and into adulthood. One reason is that observing violent media may create changes in personality and cognition that produce long-term behavioral changes. Anjana Madan and her colleagues found that even relatively brief exposure to violent movie clips increased anxiety among late adolescents, indicating that media can create personality change.

There are several explanations for the effects of television and film violence on behavior:

- Media violence can provide aggressive "scripts" that children store in memory. Repeated exposure to these scripts can increase their retention and lead to changes in attitudes.
- Children learn from what they observe. In the same way they learn cognitive and social skills from their parents and friends, children learn to be violent from television.
- Television violence increases the arousal levels of viewers and makes them more prone to act aggressively. Studies measuring the galvanic skin response of subjects—a physical indication of arousal based on the amount of electricity conducted across

---

In summary, social learning theorists have said that the following four factors may contribute to violent and/or aggressive behavior:

- *An event that heightens arousal.* Such as a person frustrating or provoking another through physical assault or verbal abuse.
- *Aggressive skills.* Learned aggressive responses picked up from observing others, either personally or through the media.
- *Expected outcomes.* The belief that aggression will somehow be rewarded. Rewards can come in the form of reducing tension or anger, gaining some financial reward, building self-esteem, or gaining the praise of others.

- *Consistency of behavior with values.* The belief, gained from observing others, that aggression is justified and appropriate, given the circumstances of the current situation.

Cognitive Theory

LO8 Articulate the cognitive processes related to crime

One area of psychology that has received increasing recognition in recent years is the cognitive school. Psychologists with a cognitive perspective focus on mental processes and how people perceive and mentally represent the world around

156 **PART TWO** Theories of Crime Causation

the palm of the hand—show that viewing violent television shows led to increased arousal levels in young children.

- Watching television violence promotes such negative attitudes as suspiciousness and the expectation that the viewer will become involved in violence. Those who watch television frequently come to view aggression and violence as common and socially acceptable behavior.
- Television violence allows aggressive youths to justify their behavior. It is possible that, instead of causing violence, television helps violent youths rationalize their behavior as a socially acceptable and common activity.
- Television violence may disinhibit aggressive behavior, which is normally controlled by other learning processes. *Disinhibition* takes place when adults are viewed as being rewarded for violence and when violence is seen as socially acceptable. This contradicts previous learning experiences in which violent behavior was viewed as wrong.

Debating the Media–Violence Link

While this research is quite persuasive, not all criminologists accept that watching TV and movies or playing violent video games actually leads to interpersonal violence. Just because kids who are exposed to violent media also engage in violent behaviors is not proof of a causal connection. It is also possible that kids who are violent later seek out violent media: What would we expect violent gang boys to watch on TV? *Harry the Bunny*? *Glee*? There is little evidence that areas that experience the highest levels of violent TV viewing also have rates of violent crime that are above the norm. Millions of children watch violence every night but do not become violent criminals. If violent TV shows did, indeed, cause interpersonal violence, then there should be few ecological and regional patterns in the crime rate, but there are many. Put another way, how can regional differences in the violence rate be explained considering the fact that people all across the nation watch the same TV shows and films? Nor can the media–violence link explain recent crime trends. Despite a rampant increase in violent TV shows, films, and video games, the violence rate among teens has been in a significant decline.

One reason for the ongoing debate may be that media violence may affect one subset of the population but have relatively little effect on others. Sociologist George Comstock has identified attributes that make some people especially prone to the effects of media violence:

- Predisposition for aggressive or antisocial behavior
- Rigid or indifferent parenting
- Unsatisfactory social relationships
- Low psychological well-being
- Having been diagnosed as suffering from disruptive behavior disorders (DBDs)

So if the impact of media on behavior is not in fact universal, it may have the greatest effect on those who are the most socially and psychologically vulnerable.

Critical Thinking

1. Should the government control the content of TV shows and limit the amount of weekly violence? How could the national news be shown if violence were omitted? What about boxing matches or hockey games?

2. How can we explain the fact that millions of kids watch violent TV shows and remain nonviolent? If there is a TV–violence link, how can we explain the fact that violence rates may have been higher in the Old West than they are today? Do you think violent gang kids stay home and watch TV shows?

SOURCES: Laura Friedlander, Jennifer Connolly, Debra Pepler, and Wendy Craig, "Extensiveness and Persistence of Aggressive Media Exposure as Longitudinal Risk Factors for Teen Dating Violence," *Psychology of Violence* 3 (2013): 310–322; Anjana Madan, Sylvie Mrug, and Rex Wright, "The Effects of Media Violence on Anxiety in Late Adolescence," *Journal of Youth and Adolescence* 43 (2014): 116–126; George Comstock, "A Sociological Perspective on Television Violence and Aggression," *American Behavioral Scientist* 51 (2008): 1184–1211; John Murray, "Media Violence: The Effects Are Both Real and Strong," *American Behavioral Scientist* 51 (2008): 1212–1230; Craig Anderson and Brad J. Bushman, "The Effects of Media Violence on Society," *Science* 295 (2002): 2377–2379.

them and solve problems. The pioneers of this school were Wilhelm Wundt (1832–1920), Edward Titchener (1867–1927), and William James (1842–1920). Today, there are several subdisciplines within the cognitive area. The **moral development** branch is concerned with the way people morally represent and reason about the world. **Humanistic psychology** stresses self-awareness and "getting in touch with feelings." The **information processing** branch focuses on the way people process, store, encode, retrieve, and manipulate information to make decisions and solve problems.

Moral and Intellectual Development Theory   The moral and intellectual development branch of cognitive psychology is perhaps the most important for criminological theory.

Jean Piaget (1896–1980), the founder of this approach, hypothesized that people's reasoning processes develop in an orderly fashion, beginning at birth and continuing into

moral development The way people morally represent and reason about the world.

humanistic psychology A branch of psychology that stresses self-awareness and "getting in touch with feelings."

information processing A branch of cognitive psychology that focuses on the way people process, store, encode, retrieve, and manipulate information to make decisions and solve problems.

their maturity.[216] At first, children respond to the environment in a simple manner, seeking interesting objects and developing their reflexes. By the fourth and final stage, the formal operations stage, they have developed into mature adults who can use logic and abstract thought.

Lawrence Kohlberg first applied the concept of moral development to issues in criminology.[217] He found that people travel through stages of moral development during which their decisions and judgments on issues of right and wrong are made for different reasons. It is possible that serious offenders have a moral orientation that differs from that of law-abiding citizens. Kohlberg classified people according to the stage on this continuum at which their moral development ceased to grow. Kohlberg and his associates conducted studies in which criminals were found to be significantly lower in their moral judgment development than noncriminals of the same social background.[218] Since his pioneering efforts, researchers have continued to show that criminal offenders are more likely to be classified in the lowest levels of moral reasoning (Stages 1 and 2), whereas noncriminals have reached a higher stage of moral development (Stages 3 and 4).[219]

The decision not to commit crimes may be influenced by one's stage of moral development. People at the lowest levels report that they are deterred from crime because of their fear of sanctions. Those in the middle consider the reactions of family and friends. Those at the highest stages refrain from crime because they believe in duty to others and universal rights.[220]

Moral development theory suggests that people who obey the law simply to avoid punishment or have outlooks mainly characterized by self-interest are more likely to commit crimes than those who view the law as something that benefits all of society. Those at higher stages of moral reasoning tend to sympathize with the rights of others and are associated with conventional behaviors, such as honesty, generosity, and nonviolence. Subsequent research has found that a significant number of noncriminals display higher stages of moral reasoning than criminals and that engaging in criminal behavior leads to reduced levels of moral reasoning, which in turn produces more delinquency in a never-ending loop.[221]

Information Processing When cognitive theorists who study information processing try to explain antisocial behavior, they do so in terms of mental perception and how people use information to understand their environment. When people make decisions, they engage in a sequence of cognitive thought processes:

1. Encode information so that it can be interpreted.
2. Search for a proper response.
3. Decide on the most appropriate action.
4. Act on the decision.[222]

Not everyone processes information in the same way, and the differences in interpretation may explain the development of radically different visions of the world. According to this cognitive approach, people who use information properly, who are better conditioned to make reasoned judgments, and who can make quick and reasoned decisions when facing emotion-laden events are the ones best able to avoid antisocial behavior choices.[223] In contrast, crime-prone people may have cognitive deficits and use information incorrectly when they make decisions.[224] Law violators may lack the ability to perform cognitive functions in a normal and orderly fashion.[225] Some may be sensation seekers who are constantly looking for novel experiences, whereas others lack deliberation and rarely think through problems. Others maintain inappropriate attitudes and beliefs; they are thrill-seeking, manipulative, callous, deceptive, and hold rule-breaking attitudes.[226] Some may give up easily, whereas others act without thinking when they get upset.[227]

People with inadequate cognitive processing perceive the world as stacked against them; they believe they have little control over the negative events in their life.[228] Chronic offenders come to believe that crime is an appropriate means to satisfy their immediate personal needs, which take precedence over more distant social needs such as obedience to the law.[229] They have a distorted view of the world that shapes their thinking and colors their judgments. Because they have difficulty making the right decision while under stress, they pursue behaviors that they perceive as beneficial and satisfying, but that turn out to be harmful and detrimental.[230] They may take aggressive action because they wrongly believe that a situation

CONNECTIONS

The deterrent effect of informal sanctions and feelings of shame discussed in Chapter 4 may hinge on the level of a person's moral development. The lower one's state of moral development, the less impact informal sanctions may have; increased moral development and informal sanctions may be better able to control crime.

Ask Yourself ...

Can a person's state of moral development be altered by life events? Or, once formed, does it remain resistant to change?

To read more about information processing theory, go to **http://www.education.com/reference/article/information-processing-theory/.**

Do you ever wonder whether you are misinterpreting cues and behavior, such as thinking that someone is standoffish and arrogant when they really are just shy?

demands forceful responses when it actually does not. They find it difficult to understand or sympathize with other people's feelings and emotions, which leads them to blame their victims for their problems.[231] Thus, the sexual offender believes his target either led him on or secretly wanted the forcible sex to occur: "She was asking for it."[232]

Shaping Perceptions To violence-prone kids, people seem more aggressive than they actually are and seem to intend them ill when there is no reason for alarm. According to information processing theory, as these children mature, they use fewer cues than most people to process information. Some use violence in a calculating fashion as a means of getting what they want; others react in an overly volatile fashion to the slightest provocation. Aggressors are more likely to be vigilant, on edge, or suspicious. When they attack victims, they may believe they are defending themselves, even though they are misreading the situation.[233]

There is evidence that delinquent boys who engage in theft are more likely to exhibit cognitive deficits than nondelinquent youth. For example, they have a poor sense of time, leaving them incapable of dealing with or solving social problems in an effective manner.[234] Information processing theory has been used to explain the occurrence of date rape. Sexually violent males believe that when their dates say no to sexual advances the women are really "playing games" and actually want to be taken forcefully.[235]

Errors in cognition and information processing have been used to explain the behavior of child abusers. Distorted thinking patterns abusers express include the following:

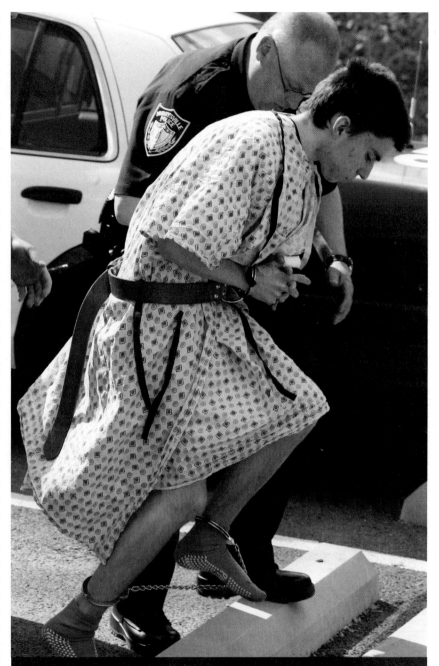

On April 9, 2014, Alex Hribal, 16, was arrested for stabbing and slashing 20 students and a security guard at Franklin Regional High School in Murrysville, Pennsylvania. Here he is shown being escorted by police to a district magistrate to be arraigned. Is it possible that Hribal's unexplained outburst was a function of a cognitive deficit that convinced him he had to retaliate against some imagined grievance? When told to drop his weapons after his rampage, he responded, "No, I am not dropping them, my work is not done. I have more people to kill."

AP Images/Keith Srakocic

- *Child as a sexual being.* Children are perceived as being able to and wanting to engage in sexual activity with adults.[236]
- *Nature of harm.* The offender perceives that sexual activity does not cause harm (and may in fact be beneficial) to the child.
- *Entitlement.* The child abuser perceives that he is superior and more important than others and hence

is able to have sex with whomever and whenever he wants.
- *Dangerous world.* An offender perceives that others are abusive and rejecting, and he must fight to be safe.
- *Uncontrollable.* The world is perceived as uncontrollable, and circumstances are outside of his control.

Cause and Treatment of Cognitive Deficits Why do some individuals develop cognitive deficits that prevent them from conforming to social expectations and adjusting properly to society? One reason may be damage to the area of the brain, the frontal lobe, that controls executive functions, attention, working memory, verbal skills, and intelligence. Such damage can occur prenatal as a result of birth trauma or maternal substance abuse, or even later in development as a result of child abuse or injury.[237]

People whose cognitive processes are skewed or faulty may be relying on mental scripts learned in childhood that tell them how to interpret events, what to expect, how they should react, and what the outcome of the interaction should be. Hostile children may have learned improper scripts by observing how others react to events; their own parents' aggressive and inappropriate behavior would have considerable impact. Some may have had early and prolonged exposure to violence (for example, child abuse), which increases their sensitivity to slights and maltreatment. Oversensitivity to rejection by their peers is a continuation of sensitivity to rejection by their parents.[238] Violent behavior responses learned in childhood become a stable behavior because the scripts that emphasize aggressive responses are repeatedly rehearsed as the child matures.[239] There is also evidence that adolescents who use violence as a coping technique with others are more likely to exhibit other social problems, such as drug and alcohol abuse.[240] Most likely there are not one but several compounding causes of impaired cognitive functioning, which encompass genetic, biological, psychological, and social influences.[241]

Treatment based on how people process information takes into account that people are more likely to respond aggressively to a provocation because thoughts tend to intensify the insult or otherwise stir feelings of anger. Cognitive therapists, during the course of treatment, attempt to teach explosive people to control aggressive impulses by viewing social provocations as problems demanding a solution rather than retaliation. Programs are aimed at teaching problem-solving skills that may include self-disclosure, role-playing, listening, following instructions, joining in, and using self-control.[242]

Therapeutic interventions designed to make people better problem solvers may involve such measures as (a) enhancing coping and problem-solving skills; (b) enhancing relationships with peers, parents, and other adults; (c) teaching conflict resolution and communication skills and methods for resisting peer pressure related to drug use and violence; (d) teaching consequential thinking and decision-making abilities; (e) modeling prosocial behaviors, including cooperation with others, self-responsibility, respecting others, and public speaking efficacy; and (f) teaching empathy.[243] Treatment interventions based on learning social skills are relatively new, but

there are some indications that this approach can have long-term benefits for reducing criminal behavior.[244] The various psychological theories of crime are set out in Concept Summary 5.2.

PSYCHOLOGICAL TRAITS AND CHARACTERISTICS

In addition to creating theories of behavior and development, psychologists also study psychological traits and characteristics that define an individual and shape how he or she functions in the world. Certain traits have become

---

concept summary 5.2

PSYCHOLOGICAL TRAIT THEORIES

PSYCHODYNAMIC
- The major premise of the theory is that the development of the unconscious personality early in childhood influences behavior for the rest of the person's life. Criminals have weak egos and damaged personalities.
- The strengths of the theory are that it explains the onset of crime and why crime and drug abuse cut across class lines.
- The research focuses of the theory are on mental disorders, personality development, and unconscious motivations and drives.

BEHAVIORAL
- The major premise of the theory is that people commit crime when they model their behavior after others they see being rewarded for similar acts. Behavior is reinforced by rewards and extinguished by punishment.
- The strengths of the theory are that it explains the role of significant others in the crime process; it shows how the media can influence crime and violence.
- The research focuses of the theory are the media and violence, as well as the effects of child abuse.

COGNITIVE
- The major premise of the theory is that individual reasoning processes influence behavior. Reasoning is influenced by the way people perceive their environment.
- The strengths of the theory are that it shows why criminal behavior patterns change over time as people mature and develop their reasoning powers. It may explain the aging-out process.
- The research focuses of the theory are perception and cognition.

associated with psychological problems and the development of antisocial behavior trends. Two of the most critical—personality and intelligence—are discussed in detail in the following sections.

Personality and Crime

 LO9 Identify the elements of personality related to crime

Personality can be defined as the reasonably stable patterns of behavior, including thoughts and emotions, that distinguish one person from another.[245] One's personality reflects a characteristic way of adapting to life's demands and problems. The way we behave is a function of how our personality enables us to interpret life events and make appropriate behavioral choices. Can the cause of crime be linked to personality?

The association between personality traits and crime has a long history. Sheldon Glueck and Eleanor Glueck identified a number of personality traits that they believe characterize antisocial youth:[246]

self-assertiveness	lack of concern for others
defiance	extroversion
feeling unappreciated	ambivalence
distrust of authority	impulsiveness
poor personal skills	narcissism
mental instability	suspicion
hostility	destructiveness
resentment	sadism

Psychologist Hans Eysenck linked personality to crime when he identified two traits that he associated with antisocial behavior: *extroversion-introversion* and *stability-instability*. Extreme introverts are overaroused and avoid sources of stimulation; in contrast, extreme extroverts are unaroused and seek sensation. Introverts are slow to learn and be conditioned; extroverts are impulsive individuals who lack the ability to examine their own motives and behaviors. Those who are unstable, a condition Eysenck calls "neuroticism," are anxious, tense, and emotionally unstable.[247] People who are both neurotic and extroverted lack self-insight and are impulsive and emotionally unstable; they are unlikely to have reasoned judgments of life events. While extrovert neurotics may act self-destructively (e.g., abusing drugs), more

stable people will be able to reason that such behavior is ultimately harmful and life threatening. Eysenck believes that personality is controlled by genetic factors and is heritable.

A large number of factors are believed to contribute to the development of a criminal personality.[248] Some are related to improper socialization, such as having a psychopathic parent, experiencing parental rejection and lack of love during childhood, and maternal cigarette smoking and receiving inconsistent discipline.[249] Others are psychological pathologies, including impulsivity, hostility, aggressiveness, and callousness.[250] These personality defects have been linked not only to aggressive antisocial behaviors such as assault and rape but also to white-collar and business crimes.[251]

According to this view, the personality is the key to understanding antisocial behavior. The more severe the disorder, the greater the likelihood that the individual will engage in serious and repeated antisocial acts.[252] Take for instance **sadistic personality disorder**, defined as a repeating pattern of cruel and demeaning behavior. People suffering from this type of extreme personality disturbance seem prone to engage in serious violent attacks, including homicides motivated by sexual sadism.[253]

The Antisocial Personality The Diagnostic and Statistical Manual of the American Psychiatric Association (APA) defines the antisocial personality as a pervasive pattern of disregard for, and violation of, the rights of others that begins in childhood or early adolescence and continues into adulthood. In addition, those suffering from this disease usually exhibit at least three of the following behaviors:

- Failure to conform to social norms with respect to lawful behaviors as indicated by repeatedly performing acts that are grounds for arrest
- Deceitfulness, as indicated by repeatedly lying, use of aliases, or conning others for personal profit or pleasure
- Impulsivity or failure to plan ahead
- Irritability and aggressiveness, as indicated by repeated physical fights or assaults
- Reckless disregard for safety of self or others
- Consistent irresponsibility, as indicated by repeated failure to sustain consistent work behavior or honor financial obligations
- Lack of remorse, as indicated by being indifferent to or rationalizing having hurt, mistreated, or stolen from another[254]

 CONNECTIONS

The Glueck research is representative of the view that antisocial people maintain a distinct set of personal traits, which makes them particularly sensitive to environmental stimuli. The section on life course theories in Chapter 9 shows how the Gluecks' views, once dismissed by mainstream criminologists, still influence contemporary criminological theory.

---

personality The reasonably stable patterns of behavior, including thoughts and emotions, that distinguish one person from another.

sadistic personality disorder A repeat pattern of cruel and demeaning behavior. People suffering from this type of extreme personality disturbance seem prone to engage in serious violent attacks, including homicides motivated by sexual sadism.

THE PSYCHOPATH

Some violent offenders may have a disturbed character structure commonly referred to as psychopathy, sociopathy, or antisocial personality. Although they may exhibit superficial charm and above-average intelligence, this often masks a disturbed personality that makes them incapable of forming enduring relationships with others and continually involves them in such deviant behaviors as violence, risk taking, substance abuse, and impulsivity. In fact, the higher psychopaths score on intelligence tests, the more likely they are to get involved in criminal activities.

From an early age, many psychopaths have had home lives that were filled with frustration, bitterness, and quarreling. Antisocial youths exhibit low levels of guilt and anxiety and persistently violate the rights of others. Their intelligence may alter their criminal career development, and render it quite different from that of nonpsychopathic criminals; high intelligence appears to enhance the destructive potential of a psychopath, while intelligence may mediate the criminality of the nonpsychopath.

As a result of this instability and frustration, these individuals developed personalities that became unreliable, unstable, demanding, and egocentric. Most psychopaths are risk-taking, sensation seekers who are constantly involved in a wide variety of antisocial behaviors. Some may become almost addicted to thrill seeking, resulting in repeated and dangerous risky behaviors. They are often described as grandiose, egocentric, manipulative, forceful, and cold-hearted, with shallow emotions and the inability to feel remorse, empathy with others, or anxiety over their misdeeds. When they commit antisocial acts, they are less likely to feel shame or empathize with their victims.

Considering these personality traits, it is not surprising that research studies show that people evaluated as psychopaths are significantly more prone to criminal and violent behavior when compared to nonpsychopathic control groups. Psychopaths tend to continue their criminal careers long after other offenders burn out or age out of crime. They are continually in trouble with the law and, therefore, are likely to wind up in penal institutions. After reviewing available data, forensic psychologist James Blair and his colleagues conclude that approximately 15 to 25 percent of U.S. prison inmates meet diagnostic criteria for psychopathy. Once they are released, former inmates who suffer from psychopathy are three times more likely to reoffend within a year of release than other prisoners, and four times more likely to reoffend violently.

The Cause of Psychopathy

Though psychologists are still not certain of the cause of psychopathy, a number of factors are believed to contribute to its development.

Traumatic Socialization Some explanations focus on family experiences, suggesting that the influence of an unstable parent, parental rejection, lack of love during childhood, and inconsistent discipline may be related to psychopathy. Children who lack the opportunity to form an attachment to a mother figure in the first three years of life, who suffer sudden separation from the mother figure, or who see changes in the mother figure are most likely to develop psychopathic personalities. According to

---

psychopath People who have an antisocial personality that is a product of a defect or aberration within themselves.

sociopath Personality disorder characterized by superficial charm and glibness, a lack of empathy for others, amoral conduct, and lack of shame, guilt, or remorse for antisocial behavior. The term may be used interchangeably with psychopath, but both terms have been replaced by antisocial behavior disorder.

Minnesota Multiphasic Personality Inventory A widely used psychological test that has subscales designed to measure many different personality traits, including psychopathic deviation (Pd scale), schizophrenia (Sc scale), and hypomania (Ma scale).

The terms **psychopath** and **sociopath** are commonly used to describe people who have an antisocial personality (though the APA considers the terms antiquated and obsolete). Though these terms are often used interchangeably, some psychologists distinguish between sociopaths and psychopaths, suggesting that the former are a product of a destructive home environment whereas the latter are a product of an inherited genetic defect.[255] This condition is discussed in the Criminology in Action feature "The Psychopath."

Research on Personality Since maintaining a deviant personality has been related to crime and delinquency, numerous attempts have been made to devise accurate measures of personality and determine whether they can predict antisocial behavior. One of the most widely used psychological tests is the **Minnesota Multiphasic Personality Inventory**, commonly called the MMPI. This

this view, the path runs from antisocial parenting to psychopathy to criminality.

Genetic Basis Psychopathic personality may be passed down genetically through the father. Psychologist David Lykken suggests that psychopaths have an inherited "low fear quotient," which inhibits their fear of punishment. All people have a natural or innate fear of certain stimuli, such as spiders, snakes, fires, or strangers. Psychopaths, as a rule, have few fears.

Neurological Disorder Psychopaths may suffer from lower than normal levels of arousal. Research studies show that psychopaths have lower skin conductance levels and fewer spontaneous responses than normal subjects. There may be a link between psychopathy and autonomic nervous system (ANS) dysfunction. The ANS mediates physiological activities associated with emotions and is manifested in such measurements as heartbeat rate, blood pressure, respiration, muscle tension, capillary size, and electrical activity of the skin (called galvanic skin resistance). Psychopaths may be less capable of regulating their activities than other people. While some people may become anxious and afraid when facing the prospect of committing a criminal act, psychopaths in the same circumstances feel no such fear. James Ogloff and Stephen Wong conclude that their reduced anxiety levels result in behaviors that are more impulsive

and inappropriate and in deviant behavior, apprehension, and incarceration.

Brain Structure Another view is that psychopathy is related to abnormal brain structures. Consequently, psychopaths may need greater than average stimulation to bring them up to comfortable levels (similar to arousal theory, discussed earlier). This may be linked to an impairment of the amygdala, that part of the brain that plays a crucial role in processing emotions. As James Blair and his colleagues suggest, amygdalae dysfunction gives rise to impairments in aversive conditioning, instrumental learning, and the processing of fearful and sad expressions. These impairments interfere with socialization; people with impaired amygdalae do not learn to avoid actions that cause harm to other individuals. Because of this deficiency, psychopaths have problems distinguishing and processing people's facial expressions. When researchers compared facial recognition ability of psychopaths with a control group, they found that the former were significantly less likely to recognize and emotionally respond to facial and other signals of distress. This inability may help explain the lack of emotional empathy observed among people with antisocial personalities.

Chronic Offending

The antisocial personality concept seems to jibe with what is known about chronic

offending. As many as 80 percent of high-end chronic offenders exhibit sociopathic behavior patterns. Though comprising about 4 percent of the total male population and less than 1 percent of the total female population, they are responsible for half of all serious felony offenses committed annually. Not all high-rate chronic offenders are sociopaths, but enough are to support a strong link between personality dysfunction and long-term criminal careers.

Critical Thinking

1. Should people diagnosed as psychopaths be separated from society and treated even if they have not yet committed a crime?
2. Should psychopathic murderers be spared the death penalty because they lack the capacity to control their behavior?

SOURCES: Ashley Hampton, Deborah Drabick, and Laurence Steinberg, "Does IQ Moderate the Relation Between Psychopathy and Juvenile Offending?" *Law and Human Behavior* 38 (2014): 23–33; Kevin Beaver, Meghan Rowland, Joseph Schwartz, and Joseph Nedelec, "The Genetic Origins of Psychopathic Traits in Adult Males and Females: Results from an Adoption-Based Study," *Journal of Criminal Justice* 39 (2011): 426–432; Rolf Holmqvist, "Psychopathy and Affect Consciousness in Young Criminal Offenders," *Journal of Interpersonal Violence* 23 (2008): 209–224; James Blair, Derek Mitchell, and Karina Blair, *The Psychopath: Emotion and the Brain* (New York: Blackwell Publishing, 2005).

test has subscales designed to measure many different personality traits, including psychopathic deviation (Pd scale), schizophrenia (Sc), and hypomania (Ma).[256] Research studies have detected an association between scores on the Pd scale and criminal involvement.[257] Another frequently administered personality test, the **California Personality Inventory (CPI)**, has also been used to distinguish deviants from nondeviant groups.[258] The **Multidimensional Personality Questionnaire (MPQ)** allows researchers to assess such personality traits as control, aggression, alienation, and well-being.[259] Evaluations using this scale indicate that adolescent offenders who are crime prone maintain "negative emotionality," a tendency to experience aversive affective states, such as anger, anxiety, and irritability. They also are predisposed to weak personal constraints, and they have difficulty controlling impulsive behavior urges. Because they are both impulsive and

aggressive, crime-prone people are quick to take action against perceived threats.

Evidence that personality traits predict crime and violence is important because it suggests that the root cause

California Personality Inventory (CPI) A frequently administered personality test used to distinguish deviant groups from nondeviant groups.

Multidimensional Personality Questionnaire (MPQ) A test that allows researchers to assess such personality traits as control, aggression, alienation, and well-being. Evaluations using this scale indicate that adolescent offenders who are crime prone maintain negative emotionality, a tendency to experience aversive affective states such as anger, anxiety, and irritability.

of crime can be found in the forces that influence human development at an early stage of life. If these results are valid, rather than focus on job creation and neighborhood improvement, crime control efforts might be better focused on helping families raise children who are reasoned and reflective and enjoy a safe environment.

Intelligence and Crime

 LO10 Discuss the controversy over the association between intelligence and crime

Intelligence refers to a person's ability to reason, think abstractly, understand complex ideas, learn from experience, and discover solutions to complex problems. It was long believed that people who maintain a below-average intelligence quotient (IQ) were at risk to criminality. According to the **nature theory**, intelligence is largely determined genetically, ancestry determines IQ, and low intelligence, as demonstrated by low IQ, is linked to criminal behavior. When the newly developed IQ tests were administered to inmates of prisons and juvenile training schools in the first decades of the twentieth century, the nature position gained support because a very large proportion of the inmates scored low on the tests. During his studies in 1920, Henry Goddard found that many institutionalized persons were what he considered "feebleminded"; he concluded that at least half of all juvenile delinquents were mental defectives.[260] In 1926, William Healy and Augusta Bronner tested groups of delinquent boys in Chicago and Boston and found that 37 percent were subnormal in intelligence. They concluded that delinquents were five to ten times more likely to be mentally deficient than normal boys.[261] These and other early studies were embraced as proof that low IQ scores identified potentially delinquent children and that a correlation existed between innate low intelligence and deviant behavior. IQ tests were believed to measure the inborn genetic makeup of individuals, and many criminologists accepted the idea that individuals with substandard IQs were predisposed toward delinquency and adult criminality.

Nurture Theory The rise of culturally sensitive explanations of human behavior in the 1930s led to the nurture school of intelligence. **Nurture theory** states that intelligence must be viewed as partly biological but primarily sociological. Because intelligence is not inherited, low-IQ parents do not necessarily produce low-IQ children.[262] Nurture theorists discredited the notion that people commit crimes because they have low IQs. Instead, they postulated that environmental stimulation from parents, relatives, social contacts, schools, peer groups, and innumerable others create a child's IQ level and that low IQs result from an environment that also encourages delinquent and criminal behavior. Thus, if low IQ scores are recorded among criminals, these scores may reflect criminals' cultural background, not their mental ability.[263]

Debating Intelligence Affects In the 1970s, Travis Hirschi and Michael Hindelang resurrected the IQ–crime debate.[264] Their examination of then-existing research data led them to the conclusion that IQ is a more important factor than race and socioeconomic class for predicting criminal involvement.[265] They proposed that low IQ increases the likelihood of criminal behavior through its effect on school performance. Kids with low IQs do poorly in school; school failure and academic incompetence are highly related to delinquency and later to adult criminality.

Because of their prominence in the field, Hirschi and Hindelang's inferences were taken quite seriously.[266] Richard Herrnstein and Charles Murray came down firmly for an IQ–crime link in their controversial book *The Bell Curve*.[267] Studies using large data sets have found a direct linkage between IQ and crime [268] Macro-level state and county data show that IQ and crime rates are associated: states and counties whose residents have higher IQs experience lower crime rates than those with less intelligent citizens.[269] On an international level, some research claims that nations whose population scores higher on IQ tests have lower crime rates than those with lower scoring populations.[270]

IQ Controversy While some studies cited above found an IQ–crime association, others suggest that IQ level has negligible influence on criminal behavior.[271] An evaluation of existing knowledge on intelligence conducted by the American Psychological Association concluded that the strength of an IQ–crime link was "very low."[272] Those who question the IQ–crime link suggest that any association may be based on spurious data and inadequate research methodologies:

- IQ tests are biased and reflect middle-class values. As a result, socially disadvantaged people do poorly on IQ tests, and members of that group are also the ones most likely to commit crime. The low IQ–crime association is spurious: people who suffer disadvantages such as poverty and limited educational resources do poorly on IQ tests and also commit crime.
- The measurement of intelligence is often varied and haphazard, and results may depend on the particular method used. The correlation between intelligence and antisocial behavior using IQ tests as a measure of

---

intelligence A person's ability to reason, think abstractly, understand complex ideas, learn from experience, and discover solutions to complex problems.

nature theory The view that intelligence is largely determined genetically and that low intelligence is linked to criminal behavior.

nurture theory The view that intelligence is not inherited but is largely a product of environment. Low IQ scores do not cause crime but may result from the same environmental factors.

aptitude is slight; it is stronger if attendance in special programs or special schools is used as an indicator of intellectual ability.[273]

- People with low IQs are stigmatized and negatively labeled by middle-class decision makers such as police officers, teachers, and guidance counselors. It is not a low IQ that causes criminal behavior but the reaction to negative labels: alienation, stigma, and resentment.
- Research using official record data may be flawed. It's possible that criminals with high IQs are better able to avoid detection and punishment than low-IQ people. Research using data from arrestees may omit the more intelligent members of the criminal subclass. And even if they are caught, high-IQ offenders are less likely to be convicted and punished. Because their favorable treatment helps higher-IQ offenders avoid the pains of criminal punishment, it lessens their chances of recidivism.
- Maintaining a low IQ may influence some criminal patterns, such as arson and sex crimes, but not others, further clouding the waters.[274]
- The association between IQ and crime is curvilinear: people with very high or very low IQs commit less crime than those who fall in the middle.[275]
- It is difficult to explain many patterns in the crime rate if low IQ is a significant cause of crime. Why do crime rates vary by region, time of year, and even weather patterns? Why does aging-out occur? IQs do not increase with age, so why should crime rates fall?

 To read all about the history of IQ testing and intelligence, go to **http://psychology.about.com/od/ psychologicaltesting/a/int-history.htm.** Are you a nature or nurture person?

PUBLIC POLICY IMPLICATIONS OF TRAIT THEORY

For the past hundred years, biological and psychological views of criminality have influenced crime control and prevention policy. The result has been front-end or **primary prevention programs** that seek to treat personal problems before they manifest themselves as crime. To this end, thousands of family therapy organizations, substance abuse clinics, and mental health associations operate throughout the United States. Teachers, employers, relatives, welfare agencies, and others make referrals to these facilities. These services are based on the premise that if a person's problems can be treated before they become overwhelming, some future crimes will be prevented. **Secondary prevention programs** provide treatment such as psychological counseling to youths and adults who are at risk for law violation. **Tertiary prevention programs** may be a requirement of a probation order, part of a diversionary sentence, or aftercare at the end of a prison sentence.

Biologically oriented therapy is also being used in the criminal justice system. Programs have altered diets, changed lighting, compensated for learning disabilities, treated allergies, and so on.[276] More controversial has been the use of mood-altering chemicals, such as lithium, pemoline, imipramine, phenytoin, and benzodiazepines, to control behavior. Another practice that has elicited concern is the use of psychosurgery (brain surgery) to control antisocial behavior. Surgical procedures have been used to alter the brain structure of convicted sex offenders in an effort to eliminate or control their sex drives. Results are still preliminary, but some critics argue that these procedures are without scientific merit.[277]

Numerous psychologically based treatment methods range from individual counseling to behavior modification. For example, treatment based on how people process information takes into account that people are more likely to respond aggressively to provocation if thoughts intensify the insult or otherwise stir feelings of anger. Cognitive therapists attempt to teach explosive people to control aggressive impulses by viewing social provocations as problems demanding a solution rather than retaliation. Therapeutic interventions designed to make people better problem solvers may involve measures that enhance:

- Coping and problem-solving skills
- Relationships with peers, parents, and other adults
- Conflict resolution and communication skills, and methods for resisting peer pressure related to drug use and violence
- Consequential thinking and decision-making abilities
- Prosocial behaviors, including cooperation with others, self-responsibility, respecting others, and public-speaking efficacy
- Empathy[278]

While it is often difficult to treat people with severe mental and personality disorders, there is evidence that positive outcomes can be achieved with the right combination of treatment modalities.[279] The findings of a recent study on biological and psychological based crime prevention efforts is discussed in the Policy and Practice in Criminology feature.

primary prevention programs Treatment programs that seek to correct or remedy personal problems before they manifest themselves as crime.

secondary prevention programs Treatment programs aimed at helping offenders after they have been identified.

tertiary prevention programs Crime control and prevention programs that may be a requirement of a probation order, part of a diversionary sentence, or aftercare at the end of a prison sentence.

TRAIT THEORY AND CRIME PREVENTION

policy and practice in criminology

recently, criminologists Michael Rocque, Brandon Welsh, and Adrian Raine reviewed treatment programs that consider biological and psychological traits and conditions in their approach. They believe that this technique might work because effective crime prevention strategies start from the premise that responding to crime after it happens is a missed opportunity; treatment and prevention must take place before a crime occurs. Crime prevention, according to their view, can be crafted in the same manner that doctors avert public health problems. Rather than identifying and treating a problem after it occurs, they use their knowledge of risk factors to provide guidance to those at risk in order to avoid illness before it occurs. Treatment based on psychological and biological traits identify at-risk people and then design plans to prevent future bouts of antisocial behaviors.

One approach has been parenting programs that are aimed at treating neuro-psychological or cognitive deficits along with a host of other risk factors, such as impulsivity. One technique is to teach mothers to avoid the hazards of smoking or ingesting narcotics during pregnancy, in an attempt to help reduce neuropsychological impairment of the infant. Some programs take place in a school setting. Enriched preschool programs are designed to provide economically disadvantaged children with stimulus that helps them develop cog-

nitively as well as provide them with enriching experiences that their parents are unlikely to provide at home. The main goal here is to develop improved cognitive skills, enhance school readiness, and encourage social and emotional development.

Other programs are aimed at the prevention of serious mental illnesses or disorders. There is strong evidence that a variety of illnesses, ranging from psychosis to anxiety disorders, can be successfully treated before their effects have an overtly negative impact. This suggests that programs designed to reduce mental illness, such as a schizotypal personality, can work and help prevent crime. Rocque and his colleagues suggest that considering the demonstrated link among cognitive deficits, brain functioning, and crime, it is perhaps not surprising that nutrition can help prevent antisocial behavior. Family/parenting programs focus on nutrition and healthy development, relying on evidence that nutritional supplements may have a large impact on behavior through cognitive functioning. Finally, a very relevant crime prevention strategy is developmental. Recognizing the interaction between the person and the environment, this approach tends to focus on identifying risk factors for children or families and seeks to improve environmental conditions in order to facilitate healthy development of the child. Some programs focus on helping at-risk kids very early in life in order to foster healthy

brain development. There is evidence that early prevention programs can improve cognitive functioning in a cumulative fashion. In cases where risk factors are heritable or genetic, programs can prevent crime through identifying environmental triggers that may increase criminal behavior. In the future, it is reasonable to assume, more programs or strategies concentrating on biological risk factors will emerge.

Research suggests that the earlier the intervention, the better. It is possible that treatment will begin during pregnancy to the first two years of life, as technology can now measure growth and maturation of cognitive functions during this period. Research has found that trauma during this period can be especially impactful, affecting brain development into adulthood. Thus, early intervention is of paramount importance in addressing the psychological and biological causes of crime.

Critical Thinking

Which approach to treatment do you believe could be most effective in curbing antisocial behaviors? Should the focus be on helping at the individual level or dealing with social problems such as unemployment and family functioning?

SOURCE: Michael Rocque, Brandon C. Welsh, and Adrian Raine, "Biosocial Criminology and Modern Crime Prevention," *Journal of Criminal Justice* 40 (2012): 306–312.

SUMMARY

LO1 Understand the development of trait theory

The view that criminals have physical or mental traits that make them different began with the Italian physician and criminologist Cesare Lombroso. Biological theory had many supporters in the early twentieth century who linked criminality to such traits as body build and the structure of the skull.

There were also early efforts to link criminality to mental illness, intelligence, and maladaptive personality. This work fell out of favor as social theories of crime were developed. In the early 1970s, spurred by the publication of *Sociobiology: The New Synthesis*, by Edmund O. Wilson, biological explanations of crime once again emerged. Trait theorists today recognize that crime-producing interactions involve both personal traits and environmental factors. If only a few offenders become persistent repeaters, what sets them apart from the rest of the criminal population may be some crime-producing trait.

LO2 Differentiate between the biochemical conditions that produce crime

Biochemical conditions are believed to influence antisocial behavior. Biocriminologists maintain that an improper diet can cause chemical and mineral imbalance and lead to cognitive and learning deficits and problems, and these factors in turn are associated with antisocial behaviors. Abnormal levels of male sex hormones (androgens) can produce aggressive behavior. Excessive amounts of testosterone, the principal male hormone, has been linked to aggressive behaviors. Exposure to lead and other environmental contaminants has been linked to emotional and behavioral disorders.

LO3 Clarify the neurophysiological conditions associated with crime

Inherited or acquired neurological abnormalities are believed to control behavior throughout the life span. Brain damage that is acquired prenatal, during birth, or soon after may lead to learning disabilities and other problems that are linked to antisocial behaviors.

LO4 Cite the different research techniques used to link genetics to crime

Another biosocial theme is that the human traits associated with criminality have a genetic basis. According to this view, (1) antisocial behavior is inherited, (2) the genetic makeup of parents is passed on to children, and (3) genetic abnormality is linked to a variety of antisocial behaviors. To test this view, criminologists have compared the behavior of siblings, adoptees, and identical twins.

LO5 Explain the evolutionary view of crime

Human traits that produce violence and aggression have been advanced by the long process of human evolution. According to evolutionary theory, males who are aggressive and violent produce the most children and these traits have dominated human society. Crime and violence are the products of millions of years of human breeding.

LO6 Discuss the elements of the psychodynamic perspective

The id is the primitive part of people's mental makeup, the ego is shaped by learning and experience, and the superego reflects the morals and values of parents and significant others. Criminals are id-driven people who suffer from weak or damaged egos. Crime is a manifestation of feelings of oppression and the inability to develop the proper psychological defenses and rationales to keep these feelings under control.

LO7 Correlate behavioral theory to crime

People are not born with the ability to act violently; rather, they learn to be aggressive through their life experiences. These experiences include personally observing others acting aggressively to achieve some goal or observing people being rewarded for violent acts. Kids who watch violent media may learn that violence is rewarded and that violence can be used as a solution to problems encountered in everyday life.

LO8 Articulate the cognitive processes related to crime

Crime-prone people may have cognitive deficits and use information incorrectly when they make decisions. They view crime as an appropriate means to satisfy their immediate personal needs, which take precedence over more distant social needs such as obedience to the law. People with cognitive deficits may misread behavioral cues and misinterpret what others are doing. They see a harmless gesture as a provocation and react accordingly.

LO9 Identify the elements of personality related to crime

Sociopathic, psychopathic, or antisocial people cannot empathize with others and are short-sighted and hedonistic. These traits make them prone to problems ranging from psychopathology to drug abuse, sexual promiscuity, and violence. Factors related to personality problems include improper socialization, having a psychopathic parent, experiencing parental rejection and lack of love during childhood, and receiving inconsistent discipline.

LO10 Discuss the controversy over the association between intelligence and crime

Proponents of nature theory argue that intelligence is largely determined genetically, that ancestry determines IQ, and that low intelligence is linked to criminal behavior. Proponents of nurture theory argue that intelligence is not inherited and that low-IQ parents do not necessarily produce low-IQ children. The IQ–criminality debate is unlikely to be settled soon. Measurement is beset by many methodological problems.

CRITICAL THINKING QUESTIONS

1. What should be done with the young children of violence-prone criminals if in fact research could show that the tendency to commit crime is inherited?

2. After considering the existing research on the subject, would you recommend that young children be forbidden from eating foods with a heavy sugar content?

3. Knowing what you do about trends and patterns in crime, how would you counteract the assertion that people who commit crime are physically or mentally abnormal? For example, how would you explain the fact that crime is more likely to occur in western and urban areas than in eastern or rural areas?

4. Aside from becoming a criminal, what other career paths are open to psychopaths?

5. Research shows that kids who watch a lot of TV in adolescence are more likely to behave aggressively in adulthood. This has led some to conclude that TV watching is responsible for adult violence. Can this relationship be explained in another way?

KEY TERMS

positivism (133)
psychopathic personality (133)
atavistic anomalies (134)
biological determinism (134)
criminal anthropology (134)
inheritance school (135)
somatotype (135)
biosocial theory (135)
biophobia (135)
sociobiology (135)
reciprocal altruism (136)
trait theory (136)
individual vulnerability model (136)
differential susceptibility model (136)
hypoglycemia (138)
androgens (138)
neocortex (139)
testosterone (139)
premenstrual syndrome (PMS) (139)
cerebral allergies (140)

neuroallergies (140)
neurophysiology (141)
electroencephalograph (EEG) (142)
minimal brain dysfunction (MBD) (143)
learning disability (LD) (143)
attention deficit hyperactivity disorder (ADHD) (143)
chemical restraints or chemical straitjackets (145)
arousal theory (145)
contagion effect (147)
defective intelligence (150)
psychoanalytic or psychodynamic perspective (150)
behaviorism (150)
cognitive theory (150)
id (150)
pleasure principle (150)
ego (151)
reality principle (151)
superego (151)

conscience (151)
ego ideal (151)
eros (151)
thanatos (151)
oral stage (151)
anal stage (151)
phallic stage (151)
Oedipus complex (151)
Electra complex (151)
latency (151)
fixated (151)
inferiority complex (151)
identity crisis (151)
latent delinquency (152)
conduct disorders (152)
bipolar disorder (152)
attachment theory (152)
alexithymia (153)
psychosis (153)
disorders (153)
schizophrenia (153)
social learning (155)
behavior modeling (155)
moral development (157)

humanistic psychology (157)
information processing (157)
personality (161)
sadistic personality disorder (161)
psychopath (162)
sociopath (162)
Minnesota Multiphasic Personality Inventory (162)
California Personality Inventory (CPI) (163)
Multidimensional Personality Questionnaire (MPQ) (163)
intelligence (164)
nature theory (164)
nurture theory (164)
primary prevention programs (165)
secondary prevention programs (165)
tertiary prevention programs (165)

NOTES

1. Matthew Lysiak, "Why Adam Lanza Did It," *Newsweek* January 17, 2014, http://www.newsweek.com/why-adam-lanza-did-it-226565 (accessed April 2014).
2. Israel Nachshon, "Neurological Bases of Crime, Psychopathy, and Aggression," in *Crime in Biological, Social and Moral Contexts*, ed. Lee Ellis and Harry Hoffman (New York: Praeger, 1990), p. 199.
3. Nicole Rafter, "The Murderous Dutch Giddler: Criminology, History and the Problem of Phrenology," *Theoretical Criminology* 9 (2005): 65–97.
4. Nicole Rafter, "The Unrepentant Horse-Slasher: Moral Insanity and the Origins of Criminological Thought," *Criminology* 42 (2004): 979–1008.
5. Described in David Lykken, "Psychopathy, Sociopathy, and Crime," *Society* 34 (1996): 29–38.
6. See Peter Scott, "Henry Maudsley," in *Pioneers in Criminology*, ed. Hermann Mannheim (Montclair, NJ: Prentice Hall, 1981).
7. To read about Lombroso, go to http://jahsonic.com/Lombroso.html (accessed April 2014).
8. Nicole Hahn Rafter, "Criminal Anthropology in the United States," *Criminology* 30 (1992): 525–547.
9. Ibid., p. 535.
10. Raffaele Garofalo, *Criminology*, trans. Robert Miller (Boston: Little, Brown, 1914), p. 92.
11. Enrico Ferri, *Criminal Sociology* (New York: D. Appleton, 1909).
12. See Richard Dugdale, *The Jukes* (New York: Putnam, 1910); Arthur Estabrook, *The Jukes in 1915* (Washington, DC: Carnegie Institute of Washington, 1916); Henry H. Goddard, *The Kallikak Family: A Study in the Heredity of Feeble-Mindedness* (New York: Macmillan, 1912).
13. Stephen Jay Gould, *The Mismeasure of Man*, rev. ed. (New York: Norton, 1996).

14. William Sheldon, *Varieties of Delinquent Youth* (New York: Harper Bros., 1949).

15. Pierre van den Berghe, "Bringing the Beast Back In: Toward a Biosocial Theory of Aggression," *American Sociological Review* 39 (1974): 779.

16. John Laub and Robert Sampson, "The **Sutherland**-Glueck Debate: On the Sociology of Criminological Knowledge," *American Journal of Sociology* 96 (1991): 1402–1440.

17. Lee Ellis, "A Discipline in Peril: Sociology's Future Hinges on Curing Biophobia," *American Sociologist* 27 (1996): 21–41.

18. Edmund O. Wilson, *Sociobiology* (Cambridge, MA: Harvard University Press, 1975).

19. John Paul Wright and Francis T. Cullen, "The Future of Biosocial Criminology: Beyond Scholars' Professional Ideology" *Journal of Contemporary Criminal Justice* 28 (2012): 237–253, at 244.

20. Bernard Rimland, *Dyslogic Syndrome: Why Today's Children Are "Hyper," Attention Disordered, Learning Disabled, Depressed, Aggressive, Defiant, or Violent—and What We Can Do About It* (London: Jessica Kingsley Publishers, 2008).

21. J. C. Barnes and Bruce Jacobs, "Genetic Risk for Violent Behavior and Environmental Exposure to Disadvantage and Violent Crime: The Case for Gene-Environment Interaction," *Journal of Interpersonal Violence* 28 (2013): 92–120.

22. Anthony Walsh, "Behavior Genetics and Anomie/Strain Theory," *Criminology* 38 (2000): 1075–1108.

23. Jay Belsky, "Variation in Susceptibility to Rearing Influences: An Evolutionary Argument," *Psychological Inquiry* 8 (1997): 182–186.

24. Ronald Simons, Man Kit Lei, Steven Beach, Gene Brody, Robert Philibert, and Frederick Gibbons, "Social Environmental Variation, Plasticity Genes, and Aggression: Evidence for the Differential Susceptibility Hypothesis," *American Sociological Review* 76 (2011): 833–912.

25. Leonard Hippchen, "Some Possible Biochemical Aspects of Criminal Behavior," *Journal of Behavioral Ecology* 2 (1981): 1–6; Sarnoff Mednick and Jan Volavka, "Biology and Crime," in *Crime and Justice*, ed. Norval Morris and Michael Tonry (Chicago: University of Chicago Press, 1980), pp. 85–159; Saleem Shah and Loren Roth, "Biological and Psychophysiological Factors in Criminality," in *Handbook of Criminology*, ed. Daniel Glazer (Chicago: Rand McNally, 1974), pp. 125–140.

26. See, generally, Adrian Raine, *The Psychopathology of Crime* (San Diego: Academic Press, 1993); see also Leonard Hippchen, *The Ecologic-Biochemical Approaches to Treatment of Delinquents and Criminals* (New York: Van Nostrand Reinhold, 1978).

27. Jonathon Ericson, Francis Crinella, K. Alison Clarke-Stewart, Virginia Allhusen, Tony Chan, and Richard T. Robertson, "Prenatal Manganese Levels Linked to Childhood Behavioral Disinhibition," *Neurotoxicology and Teratology* 29 (2007): 181–187; Joseph Hibbeln, John Davis, Colin Steer, Pauline Emmett, Imogen Rogers, Cathy Williams, and Jean Golding, "Maternal Seafood Consumption in Pregnancy and Neurodevelopmental Outcomes in Childhood (ALSPAC Study): An Observational Cohort Study," *The Lancet* 369 (2007): 578–585.

28. Lauren Wakschlag, Kate Pickett, Kristen Kasza, and Rolf Loeber, "Is Prenatal Smoking Associated with a Developmental Pattern of Conduct Problems in Young Boys?" *Journal of the American Academy of Child and Adolescent Psychiatry* 45 (2006): 461–467; "Diet and the Unborn Child: The Omega Point," *The Economist*, January 19, 2006.

29. Lisa M. Gatzke-Kopp and Theodore Beauchaine, "Direct and Passive Prenatal Nicotine Exposure and the Development of Externalizing Psychopathology," *Child Psychiatry and Human Development* 38 (2007): 255–269.

30. F. T. Crews, A. Mdzinarishvili, D. Kim, J. He, and K. Nixon, "Neurogenesis in Adolescent Brain Is Potently Inhibited by Ethanol," *Neuroscience* 137 (2006): 437–445.

31. K. Murata, P. Weihe, E. Budtz-Jorgensen, P. J. Jorgensen, and P. Grandjean, "Delayed Brainstem Auditory Evoked Potential Latencies in 14-Year-Old Children Exposed to Methylmercury," *Journal of Pediatrics* 144 (2004): 177–183; Eric Konofal, Samuele Cortese, Michel Lecendreux, Isabelle Arnulf, and Marie-Christine Mouren, "Effectiveness of Iron Supplementation in a Young Child with Attention-Deficit/Hyperactivity Disorder," *Pediatrics* 116 (2005): 732–734.

32. Sue Dengate and Alan Ruben, "Controlled Trial of Cumulative Behavioural Effects of a Common Bread Preservative," *Journal of Pediatrics and Child Health* 38 (2002): 373–376.

33. Harold Milman and Suzanne Arnold, "Neurologic, Psychological, and Aggressive Disturbances with Sildenafil," *Annals of Pharmacotherapy* 36 (2002): 1129–1134.

34. D. K. L. Cheuk and Virginia Wong, "Attention Deficit Hyperactivity Disorder and Blood Mercury Level: A Case-Control Study in Chinese Children," *Neuropediatrics* 37 (2006): 234–240.

35. Gail Wasserman, Xinhua Liu, Faruque Parvez, Habibul Ahsan, Diane Levy, Pam Factor-Litvak, Jennie Kline, Alexander van Geen, Vesna Slavkovich, Nancy J. Lolacono, Zhongqi Cheng, Yan Zheng, and Joseph Graziano, "Water Manganese Exposure and Children's Intellectual Function in Araihazar, Bangladesh," *Environmental Health Perspectives* 114 (2006): 124–129; Eric Konofal, Michel Lecendreux, Isabelle Arnulf, and Marie-Christine Mouren, "Iron Deficiency in Children with Attention-Deficit/Hyperactivity Disorder," *Archives of Pediatric and Adolescent Medicine* 158 (2004): 1113–1115; Konofal et al., "Effectiveness of Iron Supplementation in a Young Child with Attention-Deficit/Hyperactivity Disorder."

36. Alexandra Richardson and Paul Montgomery, "The Oxford-Durham Study: A Randomized Controlled Trial of Dietary Supplementation with Fatty Acids in Children with Developmental Coordination Disorder," *Pediatrics* 115 (2005): 1360–1366.

37. Ap Zaalberg, Henk Nijman, Erik Bulten, Luwe Stroosma, and Cees van der Staak, "Effects of Nutritional Supplements on Aggression, Rule-Breaking, and Psychopathology Among Young Adult Prisoners," *Aggressive Behavior* 35 (2009): 1–10.

38. Ronald Prinz and David Riddle, "Associations Between Nutrition and Behavior in 5-Year-Old Children," *Nutrition Reviews Supplement* 44 (1986): 151–158.

39. M. Mousain-Bosc, M. Roche, A. Polge, D. Pradai-Prat, J. Rapin, and J. P. Bali, "Improvement of Neurobehavioral Disorders in Children Supplemented with Magnesium-Vitamin B6, Part I, Attention Deficit Hyperactivity Disorder," *Magnesium Research* 19 (2006): 46–52.

40. A. L. Kristjansson, I. D. Sigfusdottir, S. S. Frost, and J. E. James, "Adolescent Caffeine Consumption and Self-Reported Violence and Conduct Disorder," *Journal of Youth and Adolescence* 43 (2013): 1053–1062; Karen Lau, W. Graham McLean, Dominic P. Williams, and C. Vyvyan Howard, "Synergistic Interactions Between Commonly Used Food Additives in a Developmental Neurotoxicity Test," *Toxicological Science* 90 (2006): 178–187.

41. Donna McCann, Angelina Barrett, Alison Cooper, Debbie Crumpler, Lindy Dalen, Kate Grimshaw, Elizabeth Kitchin, Kris Lok, Lucy Porteous, Emily Prince, Edmund Sonuga-Barke, John O. Warner, and Jim Stevenson, "Food Additives and Hyperactive Behaviour in 3-Year-Old and 8/9-Year-Old Children in the Community: A Randomised, Double-Blinded, Placebo-Controlled Trial," *The Lancet* 370 (2007): 1560–1567.

42. Adrian Raine, Kjetil Mellingen, Jianghong Liu, Peter Venables, and Sarnoff Mednick, "Effects of Environmental Enrichment at Age Three to Five Years on Schizotypal Personality and Antisocial Behavior at Ages Seventeen and Twenty-Three Years," *American Journal of Psychiatry* 160 (2003): 1–9.

43. Stephen Schoenthaler and Walter Doraz, "Types of Offenses Which Can Be Reduced in an Institutional Setting Using Nutritional Intervention," *International Journal of Biosocial Research* 4 (1983): 74–84.

44. Simon Moore, Lisa Carter, and Stephanie Van Goozen, "Confectionary Consumption in Childhood and Adult Violence," *British Journal of Psychiatry* 195 (2009): 366–367.

45. Mark Wolraich, Scott Lindgren, Phyllis Stumbo, Lewis Steglink, Mark Appelbaum, and Mary Kiritsy, "Effects of Diets High in Sucrose or Aspartame on the Behavior and Cognitive Performance of Children," *New England Journal of Medicine* 330 (1994): 303–306.

46. Diana Fishbein, "Neuropsychological Function, Drug Abuse, and Violence, a Conceptual Framework," *Criminal Justice and Behavior* 27 (2000): 139–159.

47. D. Hill and W. Sargent, "A Case of Matricide," *The Lancet* 244 (1943): 526–527.

48. E. Podolsky, "The Chemistry of Murder," *Pakistan Medical Journal* 15 (1964): 9–14.

49. J. A. Yaryura-Tobias and F. Neziroglu, "Violent Behavior, Brain Dysrhythmia and Glucose Dysfunction: A New Syndrome," *Journal of Orthopsychiatry* 4 (1975): 182–188.

50. Matti Virkkunen, "Reactive Hypoglycemic Tendency Among Habitually Violent Offenders," *Nutrition Reviews Supplement* 44 (1986): 94–103.

51. James Q. Wilson, *The Moral Sense* (New York: Free Press, 1993).

52. Walter Gove, "The Effect of Age and Gender on Deviant Behavior: A Biopsychosocial Perspective," in *Gender and the Life Course*, ed. A. S. Rossi (New York: Aldine, 1985), pp. 115–144.

53. Alan Booth and D. Wayne Osgood, "The Influence of Testosterone on Deviance in Adulthood: Assessing and Explaining the Relationship," *Criminology* 31 (1993): 93–118.

54. Lee Ellis, "Evolutionary and Neurochemical Causes of Sex Differences in Victimizing Behavior: Toward a Unified Theory of Criminal Behavior and Social Stratification," *Social Science Information* 28 (1989): 605–636.

55. Booth and Osgood, "The Influence of Testosterone on Deviance in Adulthood."

56. Lee Ellis, Shyamal Das, and Hasan Buker, "Androgen-Promoted Physiological Traits and Criminality: A Test of the Evolutionary Neuroandrogenic Theory," *Personality and Individual Differences* 44 (2008): 701–711.

57. Anthony Walsh, "Genetic and Cytogenetic Intersex Anomalies: Can They Help Us to Understand Gender Differences in Deviant Behavior?" *International Journal of Offender Therapy and Comparative Criminology* 39 (1995): 151–166.

58. Christy Miller Buchanan, Jacquelynne Eccles, and Jill Becker, "Are Adolescents the Victims of Raging Hormones? Evidence for Activational Effects of Hormones on Moods and Behavior at Adolescence," *Psychological Bulletin* 111 (1992): 62–107.

59. Alex Piquero and Timothy Brezina, "Testing Moffitt's Account of Adolescent-Limited Delinquency," *Criminology* 39 (2001): 353–370.

60. Walsh, "Genetic and Cytogenetic Intersex Anomalies: Can They Help Us to Understand Gender Differences in Deviant Behavior?"

61. Celina Cohen-Bendahan, Jan Buitelaar, Stephanie van Goozen, Jacob Orlebeke, and Peggy Cohen-Kettenis, "Is There an Effect of Prenatal Testosterone on Aggression and Other Behavioral Traits? A Study Comparing Same-Sex and Opposite-Sex Twin Girls," *Hormones and Behavior* 47 (2005): 230–237.

62. John Simister and Cary Cooper, "Thermal Stress in the U.S.A.: Effects on Violence and on Employee Behaviour," *Stress and Health: Journal of the International Society for the Investigation of Stress* 21 (2005): 3–15.

63. Robert Rubin, "The Neuroendocrinology and Neuro-Chemistry of Antisocial Behavior," in *The Causes of Crime, New Biological Approaches*, ed. Sarnoff Mednick, Terrie Moffitt, and Susan Stack (Cambridge: Cambridge University Press, 1987), pp. 239–262.

64. J. Money, "Influence of Hormones on Psychosexual Differentiation," *Medical Aspects of Nutrition* 30 (1976): 165.

65. Mednick and Volavka, "Biology and Crime."

66. For a review of this concept, see Anne E. Figert, "The Three Faces of PMS: The Professional, Gendered, and Scientific Structuring of a Psychiatric Disorder," *Social Problems* 42 (1995): 56–72.

67. Katharina Dalton, *The Premenstrual Syndrome* (Springfield, IL: Charles C Thomas, 1971).

68. M. S. Zeedyk and F. E. Raitt, "Biology in the Courtroom: PMS in Legal Defenses," *Psychology, Evolution and Gender* 1 (1999): 123–143.

69. Julie Horney, "Menstrual Cycles and Criminal Responsibility," *Law and Human Nature* 2 (1978): 25–36.

70. Diana Fishbein, "Selected Studies on the Biology of Antisocial Behavior," in *New Perspectives in Criminology*, ed. John Conklin (Needham Heights, MA: Allyn & Bacon, 1996), pp. 26–38.

71. Ibid.; Karen Paige, "Effects of Oral Contraceptives on Affective Fluctuations Associated with the Menstrual Cycle," *Psychosomatic Medicine* 33 (1971): 515–537.

72. H. E. Amos and J. J. P. Drake, "Problems Posed by Food Additives," *Journal of Human Nutrition* 30 (1976): 165.

73. Ray Wunderlich, "Neuroallergy as a Contributing Factor to Social Misfits: Diagnosis and Treatment," in *Ecologic-Biochemical Approaches to Treatment of Delinquents and Criminals*, ed. Leonard Hippchen (New York: Van Nostrand Reinhold, 1978), pp. 229–253.

74. See, for example, Paul Marshall, "Allergy and Depression: A Neurochemical Threshold Model of the Relation between the Illnesses," *Psychological Bulletin* 113 (1993): 23–39.

75. A. R. Mawson and K. J. Jacobs, "Corn Consumption, Tryptophan, and Cross-National Homicide Rates," *Journal of Orthomolecular Psychiatry* 7 (1978): 227–230.

76. Centers for Disease Control and Prevention, "Exposure and Risk," http://ephtracking.cdc.gov/showDevelopmentalDisabilitiesExposureRisk.action (accessed May 2014).

77. Stephanie M. Engel, Amir Miodovnik, Richard Canfield, Chenbo Zhu, Manori Silva, Antonia Calafat, and Mary Wolff, "Prenatal Phthalate Exposure Is Associated with Childhood Behavior and Executive Functioning," *Environmental Health Perspectives* 118 (2010): 565–571.

78. Virginia Rauh, Robin Garfinkel, Frederica Perera, Howard Andrews, Lori Hoepner, Dana Barr, Ralph Whitehead, Deliang Tang, and Robin Whyatt, "Impact of Prenatal Chlorpyrifos Exposure on Neurodevelopment in the First 3 Years of Life Among Inner-City Children," *Pediatrics* 118 (2006): 1845–1859.

79. Kelly P. K. Olympio, Pedro V. Oliveira, Juliana Naozuka, Maria R. A. Cardoso, Antonio F. Marques, Wanda M. R. Günther, and Etelvino J. H. Bechara, "Surface Dental Enamel Lead Levels and Antisocial Behavior in Brazilian Adolescents," *Neurotoxicology and Teratology* 32 (2010): 273–279; David C. Bellinger, "Lead," *Pediatrics* 113 (2004): 1016–1022.

80. Centers for Disease Control and Prevention, "What Do Parents Need to Know to Protect Their Children?" http://www.cdc.gov/nceh/lead/ACCLPP/blood_lead_levels.htm (accessed April 2014).

81. Paul Stretesky and Michael Lynch, "The Relationship Between Lead Exposure and Homicide," *Archives of Pediatric Adolescent Medicine* 155 (2001): 579–582.

82. Rick Nevin, "Understanding International Crime Trends: The Legacy of Preschool Lead Exposure," *Environmental Research* 104 (2007): 315–336.

83. Joel Nigg, G. Mark Knottnerus, Michelle Martel, Molly Nikolas, Kevin Cavanagh, Wilfried Karmaus, and Marsha D. Rappley, "Low Blood Lead Levels Associated with Clinically Diagnosed Attention-Deficit/Hyperactivity Disorder and Mediated by Weak, Cognitive Control," *Biological Psychiatry* 63 (2008): 325–331.

84. Jeff Evans, "Asymptomatic, High Lead Levels Tied to Delinquency," *Pediatric News* 37 (2003): 13.

85. Deborah Denno, "Considering Lead Poisoning as a Criminal Defense," *Fordham Urban Law Journal* 20 (1993): 377–400; Herbert Needleman, Christine McFarland, Roberta Ness, Stephen Fienberg, and Michael Tobin, "Bone Lead Levels in Adjudicated Delinquents: A Case Control Study," *Neurotoxicology and Teratology* 24 (2002): 711–717; Herbert Needleman, Julie Riess, Michael Tobin, Gretchen Biesecker, and Joel Greenhouse, "Bone Lead Levels and Delinquent Behavior," *Journal of the American Medical Association* 275 (1996): 363–369.

86. Todd A. Jusko, Charles R. Henderson, Jr., Bruce P. Lanphear, Deborah A. Cory-Slechta, Patrick J. Parsons, and Richard L. Canfield, "Blood Lead Concentrations <10 µg/dL and Child Intelligence at 6 Years of Age," *Environ Health Perspectives* 116 (2008): 243–248.

87. Mark Opler, Alan Brown, Joseph Graziano, Manisha Desai, Wei Zheng, Catherine Schaefer, Pamela Factor-Litvak, and Ezra S. Susser, "Prenatal Lead Exposure, [Delta]-Aminolevulinic Acid, and Schizophrenia," *Environmental Health Perspectives* 112 (2004): 548–553.

88. Emily Oken, Robert O. Wright, Ken P. Kleinman, David Bellinger, Chitra J. Amarasiriwardena, Howard Hu, Janet W. Rich-Edwards, and Matthew W. Gillman, "Maternal Fish Consumption, Hair Mercury, and Infant Cognition in a U.S. Cohort," *Environmental Health Perspectives* 113 (2005): 1376–1380.

89. Terrie Moffitt, "The Neuropsychology of Juvenile Delinquency: A Critical Review," in *Crime and Justice, An Annual Review*, Vol. 12, ed. Norval Morris and Michael Tonry (Chicago: University of Chicago Press, 1990), pp. 99–169.

90. Terrie Moffitt, Donald Lynam, and Phil Silva, "Neuropsychological Tests Predicting Persistent Male Delinquency," *Criminology* 32 (1994): 277–300; Elizabeth Kandel and Sarnoff Mednick, "Perinatal Complications Predict Violent Offending," *Criminology* 29 (1991): 519–529; Sarnoff Mednick, Ricardo Machon, Matti Virkkunen, and Douglas Bonett, "Adult Schizophrenia Following Prenatal Exposure to an Influenza Epidemic," *Archives of General Psychiatry* 44 (1987): 35–46; C. A. Fogel, S. A. Mednick, and N. Michelson, "Hyperactive Behavior and Minor Physical Anomalies," *Acta Psychiatrica Scandinavia* 72 (1985): 551–556.

91. Jean Seguin, Robert Pihl, Philip Harden, Richard Tremblay, and Bernard Boulerice, "Cognitive and Neuropsychological Characteristics of Physically Aggressive Boys," *Journal of Abnormal Psychology* 104 (1995): 614–624; Deborah Denno, "Gender, Crime and the Criminal Law Defenses," *Journal of Criminal Law and Criminology* 85 (1994): 80–180.

92. Yaling Yang, Adrian Raine, Todd Lencz, Susan Bihrle, Lori Lacasse, and Patrick Colletti, "Prefrontal White Matter in Pathological Liars," *British Journal of Psychiatry* 187 (2005): 320–325.

93. Nathaniel Pallone and James Hennessy, "Brain Dysfunction and Criminal Violence," *Society* 35 (1998): 21–27, at 25.

94. Peer Briken, Niels Habermann, Wolfgang Berner, and Andreas Hill, "The Influence of Brain Abnormalities on Psychosocial Development, Criminal History and Paraphilias in Sexual Murderers," *Journal of Forensic Sciences* 50 (2005): 1–5.

95. Kevin Beaver, John Paul Wright, and Matthew Delisi, "Self-Control as an Executive Function: Reformulating Gottfredson and Hirschi's Parental Socialization Thesis," *Criminal Justice and Behavior* 34 (2007): 1345–1361.

96. Adrian Raine, P. Brennan, and S. Mednick, "Interaction Between Birth Complications and Early Maternal Rejection in Predisposing to Adult Violence: Specificity to Serious, Early Onset Violence," *American Journal of Psychiatry* 154 (1997): 1265–1271.

97. Deborah Denno, *Biology, Crime and Violence: New Evidence* (Cambridge: Cambridge University Press, 1989).

98. Diana Fishbein and Robert Thatcher, "New Diagnostic Methods in Criminology: Assessing Organic Sources of Behavioral Disorders," *Journal of Research in Crime and Delinquency* 23 (1986): 240–267.

99. See, generally, David Rowe, *Biology and Crime* (Los Angeles: Roxbury Press, 2001).

100. R. W. Aind and T. Yamamoto, "Behavior Disorders of Childhood," *Electroencephalography and Clinical Neurophysiology* 21 (1966): 148–156.

101. See, generally, Jan Volavka, "Electroencephalogram Among Criminals," in *The Causes of Crime, New Biological Approaches*, ed. Sarnoff Mednick, Terrie Moffitt, and Susan Stack (Cambridge: Cambridge University Press, 1987), pp. 137–145; Z. A. Zayed, S. A. Lewis, and R. P. Britain, "An Encephalographic and Psychiatric Study of 32 Insane Murderers," *British Journal of Psychiatry* 115 (1969): 1115–1124.

102. Nathaniel Pallone and James Hennessy, "Brain Dysfunction and Criminal Violence," *Society* 35 (1998): 21–27; P. F. Goyer, P. J. Andreason, and W. E. Semple, "Positronic Emission Tomography and Personality Disorders," *Neuropsychopharmacology* 10 (1994): 21–28.

103. David George, Robert Rawlings, Wendol Williams, Monte Phillips, Grace Fong, Michael Kerich, Reza Momenan, John Umhau, and Daniel Hommer, "A Select Group of Perpetrators of Domestic Violence: Evidence of Decreased Metabolism in the Right Hypothalamus and Reduced Relationships Between Cortical/Subcortical Brain Structures in Positron Emission Tomography," *Psychiatry Research: Neuroimaging* 130 (2004): 11–25.

104. Daniel G. Amen, Chris Hanks, Jill Prunella, and Aisa Green, "An Analysis of Regional Cerebral Blood Flow in Impulsive Murderers Using Single Photon Emission Computed Tomography," *Journal of Neuropsychiatry and Clinical Neurosciences* 19 (2007): 304–309.

105. Adrian Raine, "The Role of Prefrontal Deficits, Low Autonomic Arousal, and Early Health Factors in the Development of Antisocial and Aggressive Behavior in Children," *Journal of Child Psychology and Psychiatry* 43 (2002): 417–434.

106. Raine, Buchsbaum, and LaCasse, "Brain Abnormalities in Murderers Indicated by Positron Emission Tomography."

107. James Ogilvie, Anna Stewart, Raymond Chan, David Shum, "Neuropsychological Measures of Executive Function and Antisocial Behavior: A Meta-Analysis," *Criminology* 49 (2011): 1063–1107.

108. Alice Jones, Kristin Laurens, Catherine Herba, Gareth Barker, and Essi Viding, "Amygdala Hypoactivity to Fearful Faces in Boys with Conduct Problems and Callous-Unemotional Traits," *American Journal of Psychiatry* 166 (2009): 95–102.

109. Thomas Crowley, Manish S. Dalwani, Susan K. Mikulich-Gilbertson, Yiping P. Du, Carl W. Lejuez, Kristen M. Raymond, and Marie T. Banich, "Risky Decisions and Their Consequences: Neural Processing by Boys with Antisocial Substance Disorder," *PLoS One* 5 (2010), http://www.ncbi.nlm.nih.gov/pmc/articles/PMC2943904/ (accessed April 2014).

110. Society for Neuroscience News Release, "Studies Identify Brain Areas and Chemicals Involved in Aggression; May Speed Development of Better Treatment," http://www.sfn.org/Press-Room/News-Release-Archives/2007/STUDIES-IDENTIFY-BRAIN (accessed April 2014).

111. D. R. Robin, R. M. Starles, T. J. Kenney, B. J. Reynolds, and F. P. Heald, "Adolescents Who Attempt Suicide," *Journal of Pediatrics* 90 (1977): 636–638.

112. R. R. Monroe, *Brain Dysfunction in Aggressive Criminals* (Lexington, MA: D.C. Heath, 1978).

113. L. T. Yeudall, *Childhood Experiences as Causes of Criminal Behavior* (Senate of Canada, Issue No. 1, Thirteenth Parliament, Ottawa, 1977).

114. Raine, Buchsbaum, and LaCasse, "Brain Abnormalities in Murderers Indicated by Positron Emission Tomography."

115. Cited in Charles Post, "The Link Between Learning Disabilities and Juvenile Delinquency: Cause, Effect, and 'Present Solutions,'" *Juvenile and Family Court Journal* 31 (1981): 59.

116. Joel Zimmerman, William Rich, Ingo Keilitz, and Paul Broder, "Some Observations on the Link Between Learning Disabilities and Juvenile Delinquency," *Journal of Criminal Justice* 9 (1981): 9–17; J. W. Podboy and W. A. Mallory, "The Diagnosis of Specific Learning Disabilities in a Juvenile Delinquent Population," *Juvenile and Family Court Journal* 30 (1978): 11–13.

117. Tomer Einat and Amela Einat, "Learning Disabilities and Delinquency: A Study of Israeli Prison Inmates," *International Journal of Offender Therapy and Comparative Criminology*, October 1, 2007, http://ijo.sagepub.com/cgi/rapidpdf/0306624X07307352v1 (accessed April 2014).

118. Thomas Brown, *Attention Deficit Disorder: The Unfocused Mind in Children and Adults* (New Haven, CT: Yale University Press, 2005).

119. Leonore Simon, "Does Criminal Offender Treatment Work?" *Applied and Preventive Psychology* (Summer 1998).

120. Russell Barkley, Mariellen Fischer, Lori Smallish, and Kenneth Fletcher, "Young Adult Follow-Up of Hyperactive Children: Antisocial Activities and Drug Use," *Journal of Child Psychology and Psychiatry* 45 (2004): 195–211; Molina Pelham, Jr., "Childhood Predictors of Adolescent Substance Use in a Longitudinal Study of Children with ADHD," *Journal of Abnormal Psychology* 112 (2003): 497–507; Peter Muris and Cor Meesters, "The Validity of Attention Deficit Hyperactivity and Hyperkinetic Disorder Symptom Domains in Nonclinical Dutch Children," *Journal of Clinical Child and Adolescent Psychology* 32 (2003): 460–466.

121. W. R. Lindsay, D. Carson, A. J. Holland, J. L. Taylor, G. O'Brien, and J. R. Wheeler, "The Impact of Known Criminogenic Factors on Offenders with Intellectual Disability: Previous Findings and New Results on ADHD," *Journal of Applied Research in Intellectual Disabilities* 26 (2013): 71–80.

122. Jason Fletcher and Barbara Wolfe, "Long-Term Consequences of Childhood ADHD on Criminal Activities," *Journal of Mental Health Policy and Economics* 12 (2009): 119–138.

123. Patricia Westmoreland, Tracy Gunter, Peggy Loveless, Jeff Allen, Bruce Sieleni, and Donald Black, "Attention Deficit Hyperactivity Disorder in Men and Women Newly Committed to Prison," *International Journal of Offender Therapy and Comparative Criminology* 54 (2010): 361–377.

124. Stephen Hinshaw, Elizabeth Owens, Nilofar Sami, and Samantha Fargeon, "Prospective Follow-Up of Girls with Attention-Deficit/Hyperactivity Disorder into Adolescence: Evidence for Continuing Cross-Domain Impairment," *Journal of Consulting and Clinical Psychology* 74 (2006): 489–499.

125. Rita Shaughnessy, "Psychopharmacotherapy of Neuropsychiatric Disorders," *Psychiatric Annals* 25 (1995): 634–640.

126. F. A. Elliott, "Neurological Aspects of Antisocial Behavior," in *The Psychopath: A Comprehensive Study of Antisocial Disorders and Behaviors*, ed. W. H. Reid (New York: Brunner/Mazel, 1978), pp. 146–189.

127. Ibid., p. 177.

128. H. K. Kletschka, "Violent Behavior Associated with Brain Tumor," *Minnesota Medicine* 49 (1966): 1853–1855.

129. V. E. Krynicki, "Cerebral Dysfunction in Repetitively Assaultive Adolescents," *Journal of Nervous and Mental Disease* 166 (1978): 59–67.

130. C. E. Lyght, ed., *The Merck Manual of Diagnosis and Therapy* (West Point, FL: Merck, 1966).

131. Ronald Simons, Man Kit Lei, Steven Beach, Gene Brody, Robert Philibert, and Frederick Gibbons, "Social Environmental Variation, Plasticity Genes, and Aggression: Evidence for the Differential Susceptibility Hypothesis," *American Sociological Review* 76 (2011): 833–912.

132. M. Skondras, M. Markianos, A. Botsis, E. Bistolaki, and G. Christodoulou, "Platelet Monoamine Oxidase Activity and Psychometric Correlates in Male Violent Offenders Imprisoned for Homicide or Other Violent Acts," *European Archives of Psychiatry and Clinical Neuroscience* 254 (2004): 380–386.

133. Lee Ellis, "Monoamine Oxidase and Criminality: Identifying an Apparent Biological Marker for Antisocial Behavior," *Journal of Research in Crime and Delinquency* 28 (1991): 227–251.

134. Rose McDermott, Chris Dawes, Elizabeth Prom-Wormley, Lindon Eaves, and Peter Hatemi, "MAOA and Aggression: A Gene–Environment Interaction in Two Populations," *Journal of Conflict Resolution* 57 (2013): 1043–1064.

135. Lee Ellis, "Arousal Theory and the Religiosity-Criminality Relationship," in *Contemporary Criminological Theory*, ed. Peter Cordella and Larry Siegel (Boston: Northeastern University, 1996), pp. 65–84.

136. Jill Portnoy, Adrian Raine, Frances Chen, Dustin Pardini, Rolf Loeber, and J. Richard Jennings, "Heart Rate and Antisocial Behavior: The Mediating Role of Impulsive Sensation Seeking," *Criminology* 52 (2014): 292–311.

137. Adrian Raine, Patricia Brennan, and Sarnoff Mednick, "The Interaction Between Birth Complications and Early Maternal Rejection in Predisposing to Adult Violence: Specificity to Serious, Early Onset Violence," *American Journal of Psychiatry* 154 (1997): 1265–1271.

138. Adrian Raine, Peter Venables, and Sarnoff Mednick, "Low Resting Heart Rate at Age 3 Years Predisposes to Aggression at Age 11 Years: Evidence from the Mauritius Child Health Project," *Journal of the American Academy of Adolescent Psychiatry* 36 (1997): 1457–1464.

139. Daniel Hart, Nancy Eisenberg, and Carlos Valiente, "Personality Change at the Intersection of Autonomic Arousal and Stress," *Psychological Science* 18 (2007): 492–497.

140. David Rowe, "As the Twig Is Bent: The Myth of Child-Rearing Influences on Personality Development," *Journal of Counseling and Development* 68 (1990): 606–611; David Rowe, Joseph Rogers, and Sylvia Meseck-Bushey, "Sibling Delinquency and the Family Environment: Shared and Unshared Influences," *Child Development* 63 (1992): 59–67; Gregory Carey and David DiLalla, "Personality and Psychopathology: Genetic Perspectives," *Journal of Abnormal Psychology* 103 (1994): 32–43.

141. Ronald L. Simons, Man Kit Lei, Eric A. Stewart, Steven R. H. Beach, Gene H. Brody, Robert A. Philibert, and Frederick X. Gibbons, "Social Adversity, Genetic Variation, Street Code, and Aggression: A Genetically Informed Model of Violent Behavior," *Youth Violence and Juvenile Justice* 10 (2012): 3–24; Anita Thapar, Kate Langley, Tom Fowler, Frances Rice, Darko Turic, Naureen Whittinger, John Aggleton, Marianne Van den Bree, Michael Owen, and Michael O'Donovan, "Catechol O-methyltransferase Gene Variant and Birth Weight Predict Early-Onset Antisocial Behavior in Children with Attention-Deficit/Hyperactivity Disorder," *Archives of General Psychiatry* 62 (2005): 1275–1278.

142. Kevin Beaver, John Paul Wright, and Matt DeLisi, "Delinquent Peer Group Formation: Evidence of a Gene X Environment Correlation," *Journal of Genetic Psychology* 169 (2008): 227–244.

143. Kevin Beaver, Chris Gibson, Michael Turner, Matt DeLisi, Michael Vaughn, and Ashleigh Holand, "Stability of Delinquent Peer Associations: A Biosocial Test of Warr's Sticky-Friends Hypothesis," *Crime and Delinquency* 57 (2011): 907–927.

144. Kevin M. Beaver, "The Effects of Genetics, the Environment, and Low Self-Control on Perceived Maternal and Paternal Socialization: Results from a Longitudinal Sample of

Twins," *Journal of Quantitative Criminology* 27 (2011): 85–105.

145. For an early review, see Barbara Wooton, *Social Science and Social Pathology* (London: Allen & Unwin, 1959); John Laub and Robert Sampson, "Unraveling Families and Delinquency: A Reanalysis of the Gluecks' Data," *Criminology* 26 (1988): 355–380.

146. Thomas Frisell, Yudi Pawitan, Niklas Långström, and Paul Lichtenstein, "Heritability, Assortative Mating and Gender Differences in Violent Crime: Results from a Total Population Sample Using Twin, Adoption, and Sibling Models," *Behavior Genetics* 42 (2012): 3–18.

147. D. J. West and D. P. Farrington, eds., "Who Becomes Delinquent?" in *The Delinquent Way of Life* (London: Heinemann, 1977); D. J. West, *Delinquency, Its Roots, Careers, and Prospects* (Cambridge, MA: Harvard University Press, 1982).

148. West, *Delinquency*, p. 114.

149. Carolyn Smit and David Farrington, "Continuities in Antisocial Behavior and Parenting Across Three Generations," *Journal of Child Psychology and Psychiatry* 45 (2004): 230–247.

150. David Farrington, "Understanding and Preventing Bullying," in *Crime and Justice*, Vol. 17, ed. Michael Tonry (Chicago: University of Chicago Press, 1993), pp. 381–457.

151. Terence Thornberry, Adrienne Freeman-Gallant, Alan Lizotte, Marvin Krohn, and Carolyn Smith, "Linked Lives: The Intergenerational Transmission of Antisocial Behavior," *Journal of Abnormal Child Psychology* 31 (2003): 171–185.

152. Smith and Farrington, "Continuities in Antisocial Behavior and Parenting Across Three Generations."

153. Abigail Fagan and Jake Najman, "Sibling Influences on Adolescent Delinquent Behaviour: An Australian Longitudinal Study," *Journal of Adolescence* 26 (2003): 547–559.

154. David Rowe and Bill Gulley, "Sibling Effects on Substance Use and Delinquency," *Criminology* 30 (1992): 217–232; see also David Rowe, Joseph Rogers, and Sylvia Meseck-Bushey, "Sibling Delinquency and the Family Environment: Shared and Unshared Influences," *Child Development* 63 (1992): 59–67.

155. Dana Haynie and Suzanne McHugh, "Sibling Deviance: In the Shadows of Mutual and Unique Friendship Effects?" *Criminology* 41 (2003): 355–393.

156. Louise Arseneault, Terrie Moffitt, Avshalom Caspi, Alan Taylor, Fruhling Rijsdijk, Sara Jaffee, Jennifer Ablow, and Jeffrey Measelle, "Strong Genetic Effects on Cross-Situational Antisocial Behaviour Among 5-Year-Old Children According to Mothers, Teachers, Examiner-Observers, and Twins'

Self-Reports," *Journal of Child Psychology and Psychiatry* 44 (2003): 832–848.

157. David Rowe, "Sibling Interaction and Self-Reported Delinquent Behavior: A Study of 265 Twin Pairs," *Criminology* 23 (1985): 223–240; Nancy Segal, "Monozygotic and Dizygotic Twins: A Comparative Analysis of Mental Ability Profiles," *Child Development* 56 (1985): 1051–1058.

158. Rowe, "Sibling Interaction and Self-Reported Delinquent Behavior."

159. Thomas Bouchard, "Genetic and Environmental Influences on Intelligence and Special Mental Abilities," *American Journal of Human Biology* 70 (1998): 253–275; some findings from the Minnesota study can be accessed from the websitehttps://mctfr .psych.umn.edu/ (accessed April 2014).

160. Gregory Carey, "Twin Imitation for Antisocial Behavior: Implications for Genetic and Family Environment Research," *Journal of Abnormal Psychology* 101 (1992): 18–25.

161. Alice Gregory, Thalia Eley, and Robert Plomin, "Exploring the Association Between Anxiety and Conduct Problems in a Large Sample of Twins Aged 2–4," *Journal of Abnormal Child Psychology* 32 (2004): 111–123.

162. Marshall Jones and Donald Jones, "The Contagious Nature of Antisocial Behavior," *Criminology* 38 (2000): 25–46.

163. Ibid., p. 31.

164. R. J. Cadoret, C. Cain, and R. R. Crowe, "Evidence for a Gene–Environment Interaction in the Development of Adolescent Antisocial Behavior," *Behavior Genetics* 13 (1983): 301–310.

165. Lawrence Cohen and Richard Machalek, "A General Theory of Expropriative Crime: An Evolutionary Ecological Approach," *American Journal of Sociology* 94 (1988): 465–501.

166. Glenn Walters, "A Meta-Analysis of the Gene–Crime Relationship," *Criminology* 30 (1992): 595–613.

167. Callie Burt and Ronald Simons, "Pulling Back the Curtain on Heritability Studies: Biosocial Criminology in the Postgenomic Era," *Criminology* 52 (2014): 223–262.

168. For a general review, see Martin Daly and Margo Wilson, "Crime and Conflict: Homicide in Evolutionary Psychological Theory," in *Crime and Justice, An Annual Edition*, ed. Michael Tonry (Chicago: University of Chicago Press, 1997), pp. 51–100.

169. Ibid.

170. J. Philippe Rushton, *Race, Evolution and Behavior*, abridged ed. (New Brunswick, NJ: Transaction Books, 1999).

171. Michael Lynch, "J. Philippe Rushton on Crime: An Examination and Critique of the Explanation of Crime and Race," *Social Pathology* 6 (2000): 228–244.

172. Lee Ellis, "Sex Differences in Criminality: An Explanation Based on the Concept of R/K Selection," *Mankind Quarterly* 30 (1990): 17–37.

173. Byron Roth, "Crime and Child Rearing," *Society* 34 (1996): 39–45.

174. Martin Daly and Margo Wilson, *Homicide* (New York: Aldine de Gruyter, 1988), p. 194.

175. Margo Wilson, Holly Johnson, and Martin Daly, "Lethal and Nonlethal Violence Against Wives," *Canadian Journal of Criminology* 37 (1995): 331–361.

176. Daly and Wilson, *Homicide*, pp. 172–173.

177. Brian Boutwell, J. C. Barnes, Raelynn Deaton, and Kevin Beaver, "On the Evolutionary Origins of Life-Course Persistent Offending: A Theoretical Scaffold for Moffitt's Developmental Taxonomy," *Journal of Theoretical Biology* 322 (2013): 72–80.

178. Joseph Nedelec and Kevin Beaver, "The Association Between Sexual Behavior and Antisocial Behavior: Insights from an Evolutionary Informed Analysis," *Journal of Contemporary Criminal Justice* 28 (2012): 329–345.

179. Ibid.

180. Deborah Denno, "Sociological and Human Developmental Explanations of Crime: Conflict or Consensus," *Criminology* 23 (1985): 711–741.

181. Israel Nachshon and Deborah Denno, "Violence and Cerebral Function," in *The Causes of Crime, New Biological Approaches*, ed. Sarnoff Mednick, Terrie Moffitt, and Susan Stack (Cambridge: Cambridge University Press, 1987), pp. 185–217.

182. Raine, Brennan, Mednick, and Mednick, "High Rates of Violence, Crime, Academic Problems, and Behavioral Problems in Males with Both Early Neuromotor Deficits and Unstable Family Environments."

183. Avshalom Caspi, Donald Lynam, Terrie Moffitt, and Phil Silva, "Unraveling Girls' Delinquency: Biological, Dispositional, and Contextual Contributions to Adolescent Misbehavior," *Developmental Psychology* 29 (1993): 283–289.

184. Charles Goring, *The English Convict: A Statistical Study, 1913* (Montclair, NJ: Patterson Smith, 1972).

185. Edwin Driver, "Charles Buckman Goring," in *Pioneers in Criminology*, ed. Hermann Mannheim (Montclair, NJ: Patterson Smith, 1970), p. 440.

186. Gabriel Tarde, *Penal Philosophy*, trans. R. Howell (Boston: Little, Brown, 1912).

187. See, generally, Donn Byrne and Kathryn Kelly, *An Introduction to Personality* (Englewood Cliffs, NJ: Prentice Hall, 1981).

188. August Aichorn, *Wayward Youth* (New York: Viking Press, 1935).

189. See, generally, D. A. Andrews and James Bonta, *The Psychology of Criminal Conduct* (Cincinnati: Anderson, 1994), pp. 72–75.

190. Paige Crosby Ouimette, "Psychopathology and Sexual Aggression in Nonincarcerated Men," *Violence and Victimization* 12 (1997): 389–397.

191. Robert Krueger, Avshalom Caspi, Phil Silva, and Rob McGee, "Personality Traits Are Differentially Linked to Mental Disorders: A Multitrait-Multidiagnosis Study of an Adolescent Birth Cohort," *Journal of Abnormal Psychology* 105 (1996): 299–312.

192. Seymour Halleck, *Psychiatry and the Dilemmas of Crime* (Berkeley: University of California Press, 1971).

193. John Bowlby, "Maternal Care and Mental Health," *World Health Organization Monograph* (WHO Monographs Series No. 2) (Geneva: World Health Organization, 1951), p. 53.

194. Ibid., p. 13.

195. Eric Wood and Shelley Riggs, "Predictors of Child Molestation: Adult Attachment, Cognitive Distortions, and Empathy," *Journal of Interpersonal Violence* 23 (2008): 259–275.

196. Karen L. Hayslett-McCall and Thomas J. Bernard, "Attachment, Masculinity, and Self-Control: A Theory of Male Crime Rates," *Theoretical Criminology* 6 (2002): 5–33.

197. Jeffrey Burke, Rolf Loeber, and Boris Birmaher, "Oppositional Defiant Disorder and Conduct Disorder: A Review of the Past 10 Years, Part II," *Journal of the American Academy of Child and Adolescent Psychiatry* 41 (2002): 1275–1294.

198. Ellen Kjelsberg, "Gender and Disorder Specific Criminal Career Profiles in Former Adolescent Psychiatric In-Patients," *Journal of Youth and Adolescence* 33 (2004): 261–270.

199. Richard Rowe, Julie Messer, Robert Goodman, and Howard Meltzer, "Conduct Disorder and Oppositional Defiant Disorder in a National Sample: Developmental Epidemiology," *Journal of Child Psychology and Psychiatry and Allied Disciplines* 45 (2004): 609–621.

200. Paul Rohde, Gregory N. Clarke, David E. Mace, Jenel S. Jorgensen, and John R. Seeley, "An Efficacy/Effectiveness Study of Cognitive-Behavioral Treatment for Adolescents with Comorbid Major Depression and Conduct Disorder," *Journal of the American Academy of Child and Adolescent Psychiatry* 43 (2004): 660–669.

201. Minna Ritakallio, Riittakerttu Kaltiala-Heino, Janne Kivivuori, Tiina Luukkaala, and Matti Rimpelä, "Delinquency and the Profile of Offences Among Depressed and Non-depressed Adolescents," *Criminal Behaviour and Mental Health* 16 (2006): 100–110.

202. Grégoire Zimmermann, "Delinquency in Male Adolescents: The Role of Alexithymia and Family Structure," *Journal of Adolescence* 29 (2006): 321–332.

203. Ching-hua Ho, J. B Kingree, and Martie Thompson, "Associations Between Juvenile Delinquency and Weight-Related Variables: Analyses from a National Sample of High School Students," *International Journal of Eating Disorders* 39 (2006): 477–483.

204. David Vinkers, Edwin Beurs, Marko Barendregt, Thomas Rinne, and Hans Hoek, "The Relationship Between Mental Disorders and Different Types of Crime," *Criminal Behaviour and Mental Health* 21 (2011): 307–320; Michael Pullmann, Jodi Kerbs, Nancy Koroloff, Ernie Veach-White, Rita Gaylor, and DeDe Sieler, "Juvenile Offenders with Mental Health Needs: Reducing Recidivism Using Wraparound," *Crime and Delinquency* 52 (2006): 375–397; Jennifer Beyers and Rolf Loeber, "Untangling Developmental Relations Between Depressed Mood and Delinquency in Male Adolescents," *Journal of Abnormal Child Psychology* 31 (2003): 247–267.

205. Richard Dorn, Jan Volavka, and Norman Johnson, "Mental Disorder and Violence: Is There a Relationship Beyond Substance Use?" *Social Psychiatry and Psychiatric Epidemiology* 47 (2012): 487–503.

206. Bruce Link, Howard Andrews, and Francis Cullen, "The Violent and Illegal Behavior of Mental Patients Reconsidered," *American Sociological Review* 57 (1992): 275–292; Ellen Hochstedler Steury, "Criminal Defendants with Psychiatric Impairment: Prevalence, Probabilities and Rates," *Journal of Criminal Law and Criminology* 84 (1993): 354–374.

207. Michael Ostermann and Jason Matejkowski. "Estimating the Impact of Mental Illness on Costs of Crimes" *Criminal Justice and Behavior* 41 (2014): 20–40.

208. Dorothy Espelage, Elizabeth Cauffman, Lisa Broidy, Alex Piquero, Paul Mazerolle, and Hans Steiner, "A Cluster-Analytic Investigation of MMPI Profiles of Serious Male and Female Juvenile Offenders," *Journal of the American Academy of Child and Adolescent Psychiatry* 42 (2003): 770–777.

209. Susan Phillips, Alaattin Erkanli, Gordon Keeler, Jane Costello, and Adrian Angold, "Disentangling the Risks: Parent Criminal Justice Involvement and Children's Exposure to Family Risks," *Criminology and Public Policy* 5 (2006): 677–702.

210. Ujunwa Anakwenze and Daniyal Zuberi, "Health and Poverty in the Inner City," *Health and Social Work* 38 (2013): 147–157; Eric Silver, "Extending Social Disorganization Theory: A Multilevel Approach to the Study of Violence Among Persons with Mental Illness," *Criminology* 38 (2000): 1043–1074.

211. Jeffrey Wanson, Randy Borum, Marvin Swartz, Virginia Hidaym, H. Ryan Wagner, and Barbara Burns, "Can Involuntary Outpatient Commitment Reduce Arrests Among Persons with Severe Mental Illness?" *Criminal Justice and Behavior* 28 (2001): 156–189.

212. Thomas O'Hare, Ce Shen, and Margaret Sherrer, "Trauma and Posttraumatic Stress Symptoms in People with Severe Mental Illness: Examining Alternative Measures of Trauma," *Journal of Traumatic Stress* 23 (2010): 255–263; Courtenay Sellers, Christopher Sullivan, Bonita Veysey, and Jon Shane, "Responding to Persons with Mental Illnesses: Police Perspectives on Specialized and Traditional Practices," *Behavioral Sciences and the Law* 23 (2005): 647–657.

213. Tamar Mendelson, Alexandria Turner, and Darius Tandon, "Violence Exposure and Depressive Symptoms Among Adolescents and Young Adults Disconnected from School and Work," *Journal of Community Psychology* 38 (2010): 607–621.

214. Tamsin B. R. Short, Stuart Thomas, Stefan Luebbers, Paul Mullen, and James Ogloff, "A Case-Linkage Study of Crime Victimisation in Schizophrenia-Spectrum Disorders over a Period of Deinstitutionalization," *BMC Psychiatry* 13 (2013): 1–9.

215. This discussion is based on three works by Albert Bandura: *Aggression: A Social Learning Analysis* (Englewood Cliffs, NJ: Prentice Hall, 1973), *Social Learning Theory* (Englewood Cliffs, NJ: Prentice Hall, 1977), and "The Social Learning Perspective: Mechanisms of Aggression," in *Psychology of Crime and Criminal Justice*, ed. Hans Toch (New York: Holt, Rinehart & Winston, 1979), pp. 198–236.

216. See, generally, Jean Piaget, *The Moral Judgment of the Child* (London: Kegan Paul, 1932).

217. Lawrence Kohlberg, *Stages in the Development of Moral Thought and Action* (New York: Holt, Rinehart & Winston, 1969).

218. L. Kohlberg, K. Kauffman, P. Scharf, and J. Hickey, *The Just Community Approach in Corrections: A Manual* (Niantic, CT: Connecticut Department of Corrections, 1973).

219. Scott Henggeler, *Delinquency in Adolescence* (Newbury Park, CA: Sage, 1989), p. 26.

220. Carol Veneziano and Louis Veneziano, "The Relationship Between Deterrence and Moral Reasoning," *Criminal Justice Review* 17 (1992): 209–216.

221. Quinten Raaijmakers, Rutger Engels, and Anne van Hoof, "Delinquency and Moral Reasoning in Adolescence and Young Adulthood," *International Journal of Behavioral*

Development 29 (2005): 247–258; Scott Henggeler, *Delinquency in Adolescence* (Newbury Park, CA: Sage, 1989), p. 26.

222. K. A. Dodge, "A Social Information Processing Model of Social Competence in Children," in *Minnesota Symposium in Child Psychology*, Vol. 18, ed. M. Perlmutter (Hillsdale, NJ: Erlbaum, 1986), pp. 77–125.

223. Adrian Raine, Peter Venables, and Mark Williams, "Better Autonomic Conditioning and Faster Electrodermal Half-Recovery Time at Age 15 Years as Possible Protective Factors Against Crime at Age 29 Years," *Developmental Psychology* 32 (1996): 624–630.

224. Jean Marie McGloin and Travis Pratt, "Cognitive Ability and Delinquent Behavior Among Inner-City Youth: A Life-Course Analysis of Main, Mediating, and Interaction Effects," *International Journal of Offender Therapy and Comparative Criminology* 47 (2003): 253–271.

225. Elizabeth Cauffman, Laurence Steinberg, and Alex Piquero, "Psychological, Neuropsychological, and Physiological Correlates of Serious Antisocial Behavior in Adolescence: The Role of Self-Control," *Criminology* 43 (2005): 133–176.

226. Glenn Walters and Matt DeLisi, "Antisocial Cognition and Crime Continuity: Cognitive Mediation of the Past Crime–Future Crime Relationship," *Journal of Criminal Justice* 41 (2013): 135–140.

227. Donald Lynam and Joshua Miller, "Personality Pathways to Impulsive Behavior and Their Relations to Deviance: Results from Three Samples," *Journal of Quantitative Criminology* 20 (2004): 319–341.

228. Shadd Maruna, "Desistance from Crime and Explanatory Style: A New Direction in the Psychology of Reform," *Journal of Contemporary Criminal Justice* 20 (2004): 184–200.

229. Tony Ward and Claire Stewart, "The Relationship Between Human Needs and Criminogenic Needs," *Psychology, Crime and Law* 9 (2003): 219–225.

230. David Ward, Mark Stafford, and Louis Gray, "Rational Choice, Deterrence, and Theoretical Integration," *Journal of Applied Social Psychology* 36 (2006): 571–585.

231. Coralijn Nas, Bram Orobio de Castro, and Willem Koops, "Social Information Processing in Delinquent Adolescents," *Psychology, Crime and Law* 11 (2005): 363–375.

232. Elizabeth Kubik and Jeffrey Hecker, "Cognitive Distortions About Sex and Sexual Offending: A Comparison of Sex Offending Girls, Delinquent Girls, and Girls from the Community," *Journal of Child Sexual Abuse* 14 (2005): 43–69.

233. J. E. Lochman, "Self and Peer Perceptions and Attributional Biases of Aggressive and Nonaggressive Boys in Dyadic Interactions," *Journal of Consulting and Clinical Psychology* 55 (1987): 404–410.

234. Leilani Greening, "Adolescent Stealers' and Nonstealers' Social Problem-Solving Skills," *Adolescence* 32 (1997): 51–56.

235. D. Lipton, E. C. McDonel, and R. McFall, "Heterosocial Perception in Rapists," *Journal of Consulting and Clinical Psychology* 55 (1987): 17–21.

236. Vincent Marziano, Tony Ward, Anthony Beech, and Philippa Pattison, "Identification of Five Fundamental Implicit Theories Underlying Cognitive Distortions in Child Abusers: A Preliminary Study," *Psychology, Crime and Law* 12 (2006): 97–105.

237. Kevin Beaver, Michael Vaughn, Matt DeLisi, and George Higgins, "The Biosocial Correlates of Neuropsychological Deficits: Results from the National Longitudinal Study of Adolescent Health," *International Journal of Offender Therapy and Comparative Criminology* 54 (2010): 878–894.

238. Rolf Loeber and Dale Hay, "Key Issues in the Development of Aggression and Violence from Childhood to Early Adulthood," *Annual Review of Psychology* 48 (1997): 371–410.

239. Judith Baer and Tina Maschi, "Random Acts of Delinquency: Trauma and Self-Destructiveness in Juvenile Offenders," *Child and Adolescent Social Work Journal* 20 (2003): 85–99.

240. Kathleen Cirillo, B. E. Pruitt, Brian Colwell, Paul M. Kingery, Robert S. Hurley, and Danny Ballard, "School Violence: Prevalence and Intervention Strategies for At-Risk Adolescents," *Adolescence* 33 (1998): 319–331.

241. Michael Rocque, Brandon C. Welsh, and Adrian Raine, "Biosocial Criminology and Modern Crime Prevention," *Journal of Criminal Justice* 40 (2012): 306–312.

242. Reiss and Roth, *Understanding and Preventing Violence*, p. 389.

243. Cirillo et al., "School Violence."

244. See, generally, Walter Mischel, *Introduction to Personality*, 4th ed. (New York: Holt, Rinehart & Winston, 1986).

245. D. A. Andrews and J. Stephen Wormith, "Personality and Crime: Knowledge and Construction in Criminology," *Justice Quarterly* 6 (1989): 289–310; Donald Gibbons, "Comment—Personality and Crime: Non-Issues, Real Issues, and a Theory and Research Agenda," *Justice Quarterly* (1989): 311–324.

246. Sheldon Glueck and Eleanor Glueck, *Unraveling Juvenile Delinquency* (Cambridge, MA: Harvard University Press, 1950).

247. See, generally, Hans Eysenck, *Personality and Crime* (London: Routledge and Kegan Paul, 1977); Hans Eysenck and M. W. Eysenck, *Personality and Individual Differences* (New York: Plenum, 1985).

248. Lykken, "Psychopathy, Sociopathy, and Crime."

249. Kevin Beaver, Matt DeLisi, and Michael Vaughn, "A Biosocial Interaction Between Prenatal Exposure to Cigarette Smoke and Family Structure in the Prediction of Psychopathy in Adolescence," *Psychiatric Quarterly* 81 (2010): 325–334.

250. Essi Viding, James Blair, Terrie Moffitt, and Robert Plomin, "Evidence for Substantial Genetic Risk for Psychopathy in 7-Year-Olds," *Journal of Child Psychology and Psychiatry* 46 (2005): 592–597.

251. Gerhard Blickle, Alexander Schlegel, Pantaleon Fassbender, and Uwe Klein, "Some Personality Correlates of Business White-Collar Crime," *Applied Psychology: An International Review* 55 (2006): 220–233.

252. Andreas Hill, Niels Habermann, Wolfgang Berner, and Peer Briken, "Sexual Sadism and Sadistic Personality Disorder in Sexual Homicide," *Journal of Personality Disorders* 20 (2006): 671–684.

253. Ibid.

254. American Psychiatric Association, *Diagnostic and Statistical Manual of Mental Disorders* (Washington, DC: American Psychiatric Association, 1994).

255. See, generally, R. Starke Hathaway and Elio Monachesi, *Analyzing and Predicting Juvenile Delinquency with the MMPI* (Minneapolis: University of Minnesota Press, 1953).

256. R. Starke Hathaway, Elio Monachesi, and Lawrence Young, "Delinquency Rates and Personality," *Journal of Criminal Law, Criminology, and Police Science* 51 (1960): 443–460; Michael Hindelang and Joseph Weis, "Personality and Self-Reported Delinquency: An Application of Cluster Analysis," *Criminology* 10 (1972): 268; Spencer Rathus and Larry Siegel, "Crime and Personality Revisited," *Criminology* 18 (1980): 245–251.

257. See, generally, Edward Megargee, *The California Psychological Inventory Handbook* (San Francisco: Jossey-Bass, 1972).

258. Avshalom Caspi, Terrie Moffitt, Phil Silva, Magda Stouthamer-Loeber, Robert Krueger, and Pamela Schmutte, "Are Some People Crime-Prone? Replications of the Personality–Crime Relationship Across Countries, Genders, Races and Methods," *Criminology* 32 (1994): 163–195.

259. Edwin Sutherland, "Mental Deficiency and Crime," in *Social Attitudes*, ed. Kimball Young (New York: Henry Holt, 1931).

260. William Healy and Augusta Bronner, *Delinquency and Criminals: Their Making and Unmaking* (New York: Macmillan, 1926).

261. Joseph Lee Rogers, H. Harrington Cleveland, Edwin van den Oord, and David

Rowe, "Resolving the Debate over Birth Order, Family Size and Intelligence," *American Psychologist* 55 (2000): 599–612.

262. John Slawson, *The Delinquent Boys* (Boston: Budget Press, 1926).

263. Edwin Sutherland, "Mental Deficiency and Crime," in *Social Attitudes*, ed. Kimball Young (New York: Henry Holt, 1931), ch. 15.

264. Travis Hirschi and Michael Hindelang, "Intelligence and Delinquency: A Revisionist Review," *American Sociological Review* 42 (1977): 471–586.

265. Ibid.

266. Donald Lynam, Terrie Moffitt, and Magda Stouthamer-Loeber, "Explaining the Relation Between IQ and Delinquency: Class, Race, Test Motivation, School Failure or Self-Control," *Journal of Abnormal Psychology* 102 (1993): 187–196.

267. Richard Herrnstein and Charles Murray, *The Bell Curve: Intelligence and Class Structure in American Life* (New York: Free Press, 1994).

268. Kevin M. Beaver, Joseph A. Schwartz, Joseph L. Nedelec, Eric J. Connolly, Brian B. Boutwell, and J. C. Barnes, "Intelligence Is Associated with Criminal Justice Processing: Arrest Through Incarceration," *Intelligence* 41 (2013): 277–288.

269. Kevin Beaver and John Paul Wright, "The Association Between County-Level IQ and County-Level Crime Rates," *Intelligence* 39 (2011): 22–26; Jared Bartels, Joseph Ryan, Lynn Urban, and Laura Glass, "Correlations Between Estimates of State IQ and FBI Crime Statistics," *Personality and Individual Differences* 48 (2010): 579–583.

270. J. Philippe Rushton and Donald I. Templer, "National Differences in Intelligence, Crime, Income, and Skin Color," *Intelligence* 37 (2009): 341–346.

271. Camilla Hagelstam and Helinä Häkkänen, "Adolescent Homicides in Finland: Offence and Offender Characteristics," *Forensic Science International* 164 (2006): 110–115.

272. Richard Herrnstein and Charles Murray, *The Bell Curve, Intelligence and Class Structure in American Life* (New York: Free Press, 1994).

273. Murray Simpson, M. K. Simpson, and J. Hogg, "Patterns of Offending Among People with Intellectual Disability: A Systematic Review Part I: Methodology and Prevalence Data," *Journal of Intellectual Disability Research* 45 (2001): 384–396.

274. Ibid.

275. Daniel Mears and Joshua Cochran, "What Is the Effect of IQ on Offending?" *Criminal Justice and Behavior* 40 (2013): 1280–1300.

276. Mark O'Callaghan and Douglas Carroll, "The Role of Psychosurgical Studies in the Control of Antisocial Behavior," in *The Causes of Crime: New Biological Approaches*, ed. Sarnoff Mednick, Terrie Moffitt, and Susan Stack (Cambridge: Cambridge University Press, 1987), pp. 312–328.

277. Reiss and Roth, *Understanding and Preventing Violence*, p. 389.

278. Cirillo, Pruitt, Colwell, Kingery, Hurley, and Ballard, "School Violence."

279. Martin Olsson, Kjell Hansson, and Marianne Cederblad, "A Long-Term Follow-Up of Conduct Disorder Adolescents into Adulthood," *Nordic Journal of Psychiatry* 60 (2006): 469–479.

learning objectives

LO1 Discuss the history of sociological criminology

LO2 Clarify the association between social structure and crime

LO3 Identify examples of the elements of social disorganization theory

LO4 Explain the views of Shaw and McKay

LO5 Differentiate between the various elements of ecological theory

LO6 Discuss the association between collective efficacy and crime

LO7 Articulate what is meant by the concepts of strain and anomie

LO8 Compare and contrast between the different elements in Merton's theory of anomie

LO9 Clarify the concept of negative affective states

LO10 Differentiate between the different forms of cultural deviance theory

SOCIAL STRUCTURE THEORIES

before they were brought to justice in 2014, Ernesto Escobar, Miguel Alvarado-Linares, Dimas Alfaro-Granados, and Jairo Reyna-Ozuna, four leaders of the Mara Salvatrucha or MS-13 gang operating in the Atlanta metro area, terrorized the community, conspiring to commit a variety of violent crimes. They lived by the doctrine of "rape, kill, control" and employed violence to enhance their reputations among fellow gang members, to protect their turf from rival gangs, or to exact revenge for a real or perceived slight.[1]

How did this fearsome MS-13 gang develop? Ironically, it was started in Los Angeles by Salvadorans fleeing a civil war. When they first arrived in L.A. they were preyed upon by preexisting Mexican gangs. The MS-13 gang was formed as a means of self-protection. The gang's name—Mara Salvatrucha—most likely comes from *mara*, slang for "army ant," and *salvatrucha*, local slang for tough, streetwise Salvadorans; the "13" is a common L.A. gang reference. Over time, the gang grew and members entered a variety of rackets, from extortion to drug trafficking. When law enforcement cracked down and deported members, the deportees quickly created outposts in El Salvador and throughout Central America.

The deportees brought L.A. gang culture with them to a country already swamped with weapons from an ongoing civil war. Now on their home turf, gang boys recruited thousands of local teenagers into their reconstituted gangs. Joining a gang gave these poor, urban teenagers a powerful sense of identity and belonging. They were also free now to show their courage and manhood by engaging in a never-ending turf war with one another. The Salvadoran government has responded by criminalizing gang membership and arresting thousands. But government efforts have not stemmed the tide of recruitment, and the gangs appear to be more popular than ever.[2]

Now a transnational phenomenon, MS-13 operates in at least 42 states and the District of Columbia and may have up to 70,000 members nationwide. MS-13 is expanding its membership through recruitment and migration. New members are recruited by experienced gang boys who glorify the gang lifestyle (often on the Internet, complete with pictures and videos) and by absorbing smaller gangs. MS-13 members supplement their illegal income by working for legitimate businesses (often by presenting false documentation). They primarily pick employers that don't scrutinize employment documents, especially in the construction, restaurant, delivery service, and landscaping industries.[3]

S-13 is part of a significant national gang population that has spread across the nation. Teen gangs have become an ever-present fixture of the American urban experience. Gang members are heavily armed, dangerous, and violent. They are about 10 times more likely to carry handguns than nongang members, and gun-toting gang members commit about 10 times more violent crimes than non-members. The most recent national survey finds that gangs exist in all levels of the social strata, from rural counties to metropolitan areas. There are now an estimated 30,000 gangs and about 800,000 gang members throughout 3,300 cities and towns. Gang homicides seem to be on an upswing; there are almost 2,000 gang-related killings each year.[4]

To criminologists it comes as no surprise that gangs such as MS-13 develop in poor, deteriorated urban neighborhoods. Many kids in these areas grow up hopeless and alienated, believing that they have little chance of being part of the American Dream.[5] Joining a gang holds the promise of economic rewards and status enhancements, which the conventional world simply cannot provide.

This association between social conditions and crime is not lost on criminologists, many of whom conclude that criminals are indigent and desperate people rather than abnormal, calculating, or evil. Raised in deteriorated parts of town, they lack the social support and economic resources available to more affluent members of society. In disadvantaged areas, residents confront crime-producing social forces—poverty, despair, social disorganization, incivility, fatalism—almost every day. It's not surprising that they adopt a "nothing to lose" attitude because the social forces they are exposed to are so powerful that it overwhelms individual choice. In contrast, middle-class adolescents, even those who maintain an antisocial personality, may find the support they need within their community that allows them to resist a delinquent way of life.[6] In sum, according to this social structure view, crime is the product of *social forces* and not individual traits.

In this chapter, we review the theoretical vision that a person's place in the social structure determines and shapes his or her behavior. We begin by tracing the development of sociological criminology.

SOCIOLOGICAL THEORY

ORIGIN 1897

FOUNDERS Émile Durkheim, Robert Ezra Park, Ernest Burgess, Clifford Shaw, Walter Reckless, Frederic Thrasher

MOST IMPORTANT WORKS Durkheim, *The Division of Labor in Society* (1893), and *Suicide: A Study in Sociology* (1897); Park, Burgess, and McKenzie, *The City* (1925); Thrasher, *The Gang* (1926); Shaw et al., *Delinquency Areas* (1925); Sutherland, *Criminology* (1924)

CORE IDEAS A person's place in the social structure determines his or her behavior. Disorganized urban areas are the breeding ground of crime. A lack of legitimate opportunities produces criminal subcultures.

MODERN OUTGROWTHS Social disorganization theory, strain theory, cultural deviance theory

Clifford Shaw

© Chicago History Museum, USA/Bridgeman Images

DEVELOPMENT OF SOCIOLOGICAL CRIMINOLOGY

LO1 Discuss the history of sociological criminology

At the same time that biological positivists were conducting their experiments, others were using social data to scientifically study the major changes that were taking place in nineteenth-century society and in so doing helping to create the field of sociology.

Sociology seemed an ideal perspective from which to study society. After thousands of years of stability, the world was undergoing a population explosion: the population estimated at 600 million in 1700 had risen to 900 million

by 1800. People were flocking to cities in ever-increasing numbers. Manchester, England, had 12,000 inhabitants in 1760 and 400,000 in 1850; during the same period, the population of Glasgow, Scotland, rose from 30,000 to 300,000.

The development of machinery such as power looms had doomed cottage industries and given rise to a factory system in which large numbers of people toiled for extremely low wages. The spread of agricultural machines increased the food supply while reducing the need for a large rural workforce; these excess laborers further swelled city populations. At the same time, political, religious, and social traditions continued to be challenged by the scientific method.

Quetelet and Durkheim

The application of sociological concepts to criminology can be traced to the works of pioneering sociologists L. A. J. (Adolphe) Quetelet (1796–1874) and (David) Émile Durkheim (1858–1917). Quetelet instigated the use of data and statistics in performing criminological research. Durkheim, considered one of the founders of sociology, defined crime as a normal and necessary social event.[7] These two perspectives have been extremely influential on modern criminology.

Quetelet was a Belgian mathematician who began (along with a Frenchman, André-Michel Guerry) what is known as the cartographic school of criminology.[8] This approach made use of social statistics that were being developed in Europe in the early nineteenth century. Statistical data provided important demographic information on the population, including density, gender, religious affiliations, and wealth.

Quetelet studied data gathered in France (called the *Comptes generaux de l'administration de la justice*) to investigate the influence of social factors on the propensity to commit crime. In addition to finding a strong influence of age and sex on crime, Quetelet also uncovered evidence that season, climate, population composition, and poverty were related to criminality. More specifically, he found that crime rates were greatest in the summer, in southern areas, among heterogeneous populations, and among the poor and uneducated. He also found crime rates to be influenced by drinking habits.[9] Quetelet identified many of the relationships between crime and social phenomena that still serve as a basis for criminology today. His findings that crime had a social basis were a direct challenge to Lombrosian biological determinism.

According to Émile Durkheim's vision of social positivism, crime is part of human nature because it has existed during periods of both poverty and prosperity.[10] Crime is *normal* because it is virtually impossible to imagine a society in which criminal behavior is totally absent. Such a society would almost demand that all people be and act exactly alike. Durkheim believed that the inevitability of

Émile Durkheim, known as the "father of sociology," linked crime to a state of anomie in which too rapid social change brings about role confusion and a breakdown of traditional norms and values. Crime, however, can be useful because it often results in social reforms to alleviate the conditions that produced its cause. In other words, an upsurge in the crime rate might motivate those in power to address its cause—for example, by reducing economic inequality.

AP Images

crime is linked to the differences (heterogeneity) within society. Since people are so different from one another and employ such a variety of methods and forms of behavior to meet their needs, it is not surprising that some will resort to criminality. Even if "real" crimes were eliminated, human weaknesses and petty vices would be elevated to the status of crimes. As long as human differences exist, then, crime is inevitable and one of the fundamental conditions of social life.

Durkheim argued that crime can even be useful and, on occasion, healthy for society. He held that the existence of crime paves the way for social change and indicates that the social structure is not rigid or inflexible. Put another way, if such differences did not exist, it would mean that everyone behaved the same way and agreed on what is right and wrong. Such universal conformity would stifle creativity and independent thinking. To illustrate this concept, Durkheim offered the example of the Greek philosopher Socrates, who was considered a criminal and put to death for corrupting the morals of youth simply because he expressed ideas that were different from what people believed at that time.

Durkheim reasoned that another benefit of crime is that it calls attention to social ills. A rising crime rate can signal the need for social change and promote a variety of programs designed to relieve the human suffering that may have caused crime in the first place. In his influential book *The Division of Labor in Society*, Durkheim described the consequences of the shift from a small, rural society, which he labeled "mechanical," to the more modern "organic" society with a large urban population, division of labor, and personal isolation.[11] From this shift flowed anomie, or norm and role confusion, a powerful sociological concept that helps describe the chaos and disarray accompanying the loss of traditional values in modern society. Durkheim's research on suicide indicated that anomic societies maintain high suicide rates; by implication, anomie might cause other forms of deviance as well.

The Chicago School and Beyond

The primacy of sociological positivism as the intellectual basis of criminology was secured by research begun in the early twentieth century by Albion W. Small (1854–1926), who organized the famed sociology department at the University of Chicago. Referred to as the Chicago School, urban sociologists such as W. I. Thomas (1863–1947), Robert Ezra Park (1864–1944), Ernest W. Burgess (1886–1966), and Louis Wirth (1897–1952) pioneered research on the

social ecology of the city. In 1915, Robert Ezra Park called for anthropological methods of description and observation to be applied to urban life.[12] He was concerned with how neighborhood structure developed, how isolated pockets of poverty formed, and what social policies could be used to alleviate urban problems. In response, Chicago School sociologists carried out an ambitious program of research and scholarship on urban topics, including criminal behavior patterns. Harvey Zorbaugh's *The Gold Coast and the Slum*, Frederick Thrasher's *The Gang*, and Louis Wirth's *The Ghetto*[13] are classic examples of objective, highly descriptive accounts of urban life. Park, with Ernest Burgess, studied the social ecology of the city and found that some neighborhoods form so-called natural areas of wealth and affluence, while others suffered poverty and disintegration.[14] Regardless of their race, religion, or ethnicity, the everyday behavior of people living in these areas was controlled by the social and ecological climate.

This body of research inspired a generation of scholars to conclude that social forces operating in urban areas create "natural areas" for crime.[15] These urban neighborhoods maintain such a high level of poverty that critical institutions of socialization and control, such as the school and the family, begin to break down. While normally these social institutions can apply the social control necessary to restrain the neighborhood youth, their weakness means that kids are now free to engage in exciting and enticing law-violating behaviors. As crime rates soar and residents are afraid to leave their homes at night, the neighborhood becomes **socially disorganized**—unable to apply social control on its residents. It can no longer muster the cohesion needed to protect its residents from crime, drug abuse, and violence. Criminal behavior is not then a function of personal traits or choice, but is linked to environmental conditions that fail to provide residents with proper human relations and development.

The Chicago School sociologists supported the view that neighborhood conditions, and not individual pathology, were the key influence on behavior and in so doing shaped the direction of crime rates. Their writings became the core of sociological criminology, and the social environment and its influence on human behavior have remained the primary focus of criminology.

CONNECTIONS

Concern about the ecological distribution of crime, the effect of social change, and the interactive nature of crime itself has made sociology the foundation of modern criminology. This chapter reviews sociological theories that emphasize the relationship between social status and criminal behavior. In Chapter 7, the focus shifts to sociological social psychology theories that emphasize socialization and its influence on crime and deviance; Chapter 8 covers theories based on the concept of social conflict.

socially disorganized Communities where social institutions are incapable of functioning as expected and as a result their ability to create social control is nullified.

SOCIOECONOMIC STRUCTURE AND CRIME

LO2 Clarify the association between social structure and crime

People in the United States live in a **stratified society**. Social strata are created by the unequal distribution of wealth, power, and prestige. Social classes are segments of the population whose members have a relatively similar portion of desirable things and who share attitudes, values, norms, and an identifiable lifestyle. In U.S. society, it is common to identify people as upper-, middle-, and lower-class citizens, with a broad range of economic variations existing within each group. Today, the middle class earns about $50,000 per household. Then there are the moderately well off: the top 5 percent of income earners have an annual household income of about $200,000; the top 1 percent earns almost $400,000 per year. The upper-upper class is reserved for a small number of exceptionally well-to-do families who maintain enormous financial and social resources. The 400 richest Americans are now worth a combined $2 trillion, or about $5 billion per person on average; each of the 400 is worth at least $1.3 billion.[16] In contrast, more than 46 million Americans now live in poverty, defined as a family of four earning about $24,000 per year.[17] Those living below the poverty line are often forced to live in inadequate housing, have poor health care, and suffer from disrupted family lives, underemployment, and despair. They are more prone to depression, less likely to have achievement motivation, and are unable to put off immediate gratification for future gain; kids living in poverty areas may drop out before graduation because the rewards for educational achievement are in the distant future.

For an analysis of wealth and power in the United States, go to **http://www2.ucsc.edu/whorulesamerica/power/wealth.html.**
Do you believe that the unequal distribution of wealth is a growing social problem and the government should do something to redistribute wealth?

The Underclass

Fifty years ago, sociologist Oscar Lewis coined the term "the **underclass**" to describe the crushing lifestyle experienced by those living in the American "**culture of poverty**," which is passed from one generation to the next.[18] Apathy, cynicism, helplessness, and mistrust of social institutions such as schools, government agencies, and the police mark the culture of poverty. Lewis's work was the first of a group that described the plight of **at-risk** children and adults. In 1970, Swedish economist Gunnar Myrdal described a worldwide underclass that was cut off from society, its members lacking the education and skills needed to be effectively in demand in modern society.[19]

Economic disparity will continually haunt members of the underclass and their children over the course of their life span. Desperate life circumstances prevent them from developing the skills, habits, and lifestyles that lead first to educational success and later to success in the workplace.[20] Their ability to maintain social ties in the neighborhood become weak and attenuated, destabilizing community cohesiveness and interfering with mechanisms of informal social control such as the school, church, and family.[21]

The poor are constantly bombarded by the media with advertisements linking material possessions to self-worth, but they are often unable to attain desired goods and services through conventional means. Though they are members of a society that extols material success above any other, they are unable to satisfactorily compete for such success with members of the upper classes. As a result, they may turn to illegal solutions to their economic plight: they may deal drugs for profit, join gangs, boost cars and sell them to "chop shops," or commit armed robbery. They may become so depressed that they take alcohol and drugs as a form of self-tranquilization.

To read more about Oscar Lewis and the culture of poverty go to **http://www.encyclopedia.com/topic/Oscar_Lewis.aspx.**
Can people break out of poverty if they really try? Or are the odds against them too great?

Child Poverty

The timing of poverty also seems to be relevant: being poor during early childhood can have an effect that is both harmful and long lasting.[22] Poor children are much more likely than wealthy children to suffer various social and physical ills, ranging from low birth weight to a limited chance of earning a college degree. Many live in substandard housing—high-rise, multiple-family dwellings—which can

stratified society Grouping according to social strata or levels. American society is considered stratified on the basis of economic class and wealth.

underclass The lowest social stratum in any country, whose members lack the education and skills needed to function successfully in modern society.

culture of poverty The view that people in the lower class of society form a separate culture with its own values and norms that are in conflict with conventional society; the culture is self-maintaining and ongoing.

at-risk Children and adults who lack the education and skills needed to be effectively in demand in modern society.

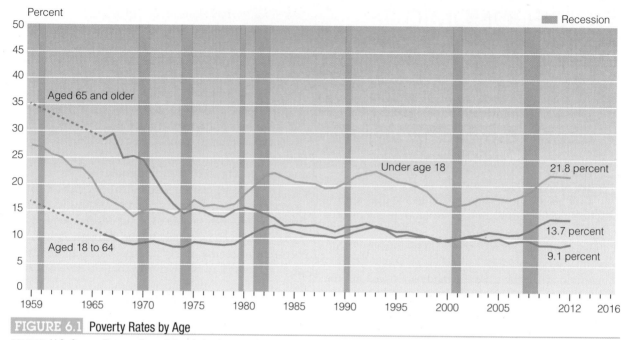

FIGURE 6.1 Poverty Rates by Age

SOURCE: U.S. Census Bureau, Current Population Survey, 1959 to 2012, Annual Social and Economic Supplements, http://www.census.gov/hhes/www/poverty/data/incpovhlth/2012/figure5.pdf.

have a negative influence on their long-term psychological health.[23] Adolescents growing up in disorganized inner-city neighborhoods share the greatest risk of dropping out of school and becoming teenage parents. As Figure 6.1 shows, children have a higher poverty rate much more than any other age group, making the damaging effects of child poverty a critical social problem.

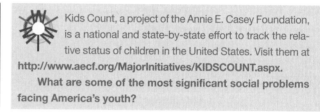

Kids Count, a project of the Annie E. Casey Foundation, is a national and state-by-state effort to track the relative status of children in the United States. Visit them at http://www.aecf.org/MajorInitiatives/KIDSCOUNT.aspx.
What are some of the most significant social problems facing America's youth?

A young girl walks by an abandoned building and lot in Camden, New Jersey. Crime rates are higher in deteriorated, disorganized neighborhoods, and minority group members are all too often forced to live in these high-risk communities.

Shannon Stapleton/Reuters/Landov

Minority Group Poverty

The burdens of underclass life are often felt most acutely by minority group members. There is real disparity in the annual income of Asian, Hispanic, and African American households.[24]

The share of young black men without jobs has climbed relentlessly, with only a slight pause during the economic peak of the late 1990s. Today, the African American unemployment rate is significantly higher than the white unemployment rate, and about 25 percent of African Americans and more than 20 percent of Hispanics live in poverty as compared to 8 percent of non-Hispanic whites and 11 percent of Asians.[25] Clearly, minority children begin life with significant social and educational deficits.

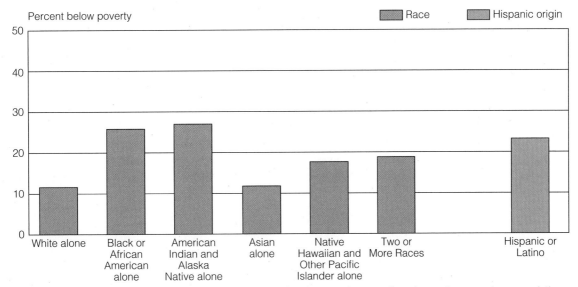

Percent below poverty

Race　Hispanic origin

Note: Persons who report only one race among the six defined categories are referred to as the race-alone population, while persons who report more than one race category are referred to as the Two or More Race population. This figure shows data using the race-alone approach. Use of the single-race population dose not imply that it is the preferred method of presenting or analyzing data. The Census Bureau uses a variety of approaches. Because Hispanics may be of any race, data in this figure for Hispanics overlap with data for race groups.

FIGURE 6.2 U.S. Poverty Rates by Race and Hispanic or Latino Origin

SOURCE: U.S. Census Bureau, 2007–2011 American Community Survey, February 2013, http://www.census.gov/prod/2013pubs/acsbr11-17.pdf.

Race-based social and economic disparity can take a terrific toll. While whites use their economic, social, and political advantages to live in sheltered gated communities protected by security guards and police, minorities are denied similar protections and privileges.[26] In contrast, a significant proportion of minority group members are relegated to living in inner-city areas, where they are hit hard by race-based disparity such as income inequality and institutional racism.[27]

There is also the perception in the minority community that the justice system is biased and racist. Minority citizens often believe that the police are overzealous in their duties when dealing with minorities, stopping them for no reason, searching them, and arresting them when they would treat Caucasians informally. And if they do commit crime, minority youth are more likely to be officially processed to the juvenile court than Caucasian youths, helping them develop an official record at an early age, an outcome that may increase their chances of incarceration as adults.[28] In the United States today, about 1 in 30 men between the ages of 20 and 34 is behind bars; for black males in that age group the figure is 1 in 9. One in 100 black women in their mid- to late-30s are incarcerated compared to 1 in 355 European American women.[29] In some neighborhoods a significant portion—up to half—of all minority males are under criminal justice system control.[30]

Interracial differences in the crime rate could be significantly reduced by improving levels of education, lowering levels of poverty, ending racial segregation in housing and neighborhood makeup, and reducing the extent of male unemployment among minority populations.[31] The issue of minority poverty is explored further in the Race, Culture, Gender, and Criminology feature "More than Just Race," which discusses the works of William Julius Wilson, one of the nation's leading experts on race and culture.

The World Wealth Report provides information on global income trends. See more at **http://www .capgemini.com/thought-leadership/world-wealth-report-2013-from-capgemini-and-rbc-wealth-management.** **The number of wealthy, high net worth individuals is growing around the world. Is that a good sign or troubling trend?**

SOCIAL STRUCTURE THEORIES

LO3 Identify examples of the elements of social disorganization theory

The problems caused by poverty and income inequality are not lost on criminologists. They recognize that the various sources of crime data show that crime rates are highest in neighborhoods characterized by poverty and social disorder. Although members of the middle and upper classes sometimes engage in crime, these are generally nonviolent acts, such as embezzlement and fraud, which present little danger to the general public. In contrast, lower-class crime is often the violent, destructive product of youth gangs and

MORE THAN JUST RACE

William Julius Wilson, one of the nation's most prominent sociologists, has produced an impressive body of work that details racial problems and racial politics in American society. He has described the plight of the lowest levels of the underclass, which he labels the truly disadvantaged. These socially isolated people live in areas in which the basic institutions of society—family, school, housing—have long since declined. Their weakening triggers similar breakdowns in the strengths of inner-city areas, including the loss of community cohesion and the ability of people living in the area to control the flow of drugs and criminal activity. In more affluent areas, neighbors might complain to parents that their children were acting out. In distressed areas, this element of informal social control may be absent because parents are under stress or all too often absent. These effects magnify the isolation of the underclass from mainstream society and promote a ghetto culture and behavior.

Because the truly disadvantaged rarely come into contact with the actual source of their oppression, they direct their anger and aggression at those with whom they are in close and intimate contact, such as neighbors, businesspeople, and landlords. Members of this group, plagued by under- or unemployment, begin to lose self-confidence, a feeling supported by the plight of kin and friendship groups who also experience extreme economic marginality. Self-doubt is a neighborhood norm, overwhelming those forced to live in areas of concentrated poverty.

In an important book, *When Work Disappears*, Wilson assesses the effect of joblessness and underemployment on residents in poor neighborhoods on Chicago's south side. He argues that for the first time since the nineteenth century, most adults in inner-city ghetto neighborhoods are not working during a typical week. He finds that inner-city life is only marginally affected by changes in the nation's economy and unaffected by technological development. Poverty in these inner-city areas is eternal and unchanging and, if anything, worsening as residents are further shut out of the economic mainstream. Growth in the manufacturing sector fueled upward mobility and provided the foundation of today's African American middle class. Those opportunities no longer exist as manufacturing plants have moved to inaccessible rural and overseas locations where the cost of doing business is lower. With manufacturing opportunities all but obsolete in the United States, service and retail establishments, which depended on blue-collar spending, have similarly disappeared, leaving behind an economy based on welfare and government supports. In less than 20 years, formerly active African American communities have become crime-infested inner-city neighborhoods.

Beyond sustaining inner-city poverty, the absence of employment opportunities has torn at the social fabric of the nation's inner-city neighborhoods. Work helps socialize young people into the wider society, instilling in them such desirable values as hard work, caring, and respect for others. When work becomes scarce, the discipline and structure it provides are absent. Community-wide underemployment destroys social cohesion, increasing the presence of neighborhood social problems ranging from drug use to educational failure. Schools in these areas are unable to teach basic skills and because desirable employment is lacking, there are few adults to serve as role models. In contrast to more affluent suburban households where daily life is organized around job and career demands, children in inner-city areas are not socialized in the workings of the mainstream economy.

Wilson finds that racism is becoming more subtle and harder to detect. Whites believe that blacks are responsible for their inferior economic status because of their cultural traits. Because even affluent whites fear corporate downsizing, they are unwilling to vote for governmental assistance to the poor because it means more taxes and lower corporate profits, a condition that threatens their jobs. Whites are continuing to be suburban dwellers, further isolating poor minorities in central cities and making their problems distant and unimportant. Wilson continues to believe that the changing marketplace, with its reliance on sophisticated computer technologies, is continually decreasing demand for low-skilled workers, which impacts African Americans more negatively than other better educated and affluent groups.

In his most recent work, *More than Just Race: Being Black and Poor in the Inner City*, Wilson shows that a law-and-order political philosophy and fear of racial conflict have led to high incarceration rates among African American males. While black women can get jobs in service industries, employers are less likely to hire black men, especially those with a criminal record. As a result, there has been a decline in the ability of black men to be providers and further stress on the stability of the African American family. Here we can see how structure and culture intertwine to produce stress in the African American community. In an era of high unemployment, the picture Wilson paints is not encouraging.

Critical Thinking

1. Is it unrealistic to assume that a government-sponsored public works program can provide needed jobs in this era of budget cutbacks?
2. What are some of the hidden costs of unemployment in a community setting?
3. How would a biocriminologist explain Wilson's findings?

SOURCES: William Julius Wilson, *More than Just Race: Being Black and Poor in the Inner City* (New York: Norton, 2009); William Julius Wilson and Richard Taub, *There Goes the Neighborhood: Racial, Ethnic, and Class Tensions in Four Chicago Neighborhoods and Their Meaning for America* (New York: Knopf, 2006); William Julius Wilson, *The Truly Disadvantaged* (Chicago: University of Chicago Press, 1987); William Julius Wilson, *When Work Disappears: The World of the Urban Poor* (New York: Knopf, 1996); William Julius Wilson, *The Bridge over the Racial Divide: Rising Inequality and Coalition Politics* (Wildavsky Forum Series, 2) (Berkeley: University of California Press, 1999).

marginally and underemployed young adults. The real crime problem is essentially a lower-class phenomenon. Recognizing this phenomenon, criminologists have formulated **social structure theories**, which as a group suggest that social and economic forces operating in disorganized lower-class areas are the key determinant of criminal behavior patterns. Social forces begin to affect people while they are relatively young and continue to influence them throughout the life course. Though not all youthful offenders become adult criminals, those who are exposed to the incivility present in deteriorated inner-city neighborhoods are the ones most likely to persist in their criminal careers.[32]

Social structure theorists challenge those who suggest that crime is an expression of some personal trait or individual choice. They argue that people living in equivalent social environments tend to behave in a similar, predictable fashion. If the environment did not influence human behavior, then crime rates would be distributed equally across the social structure, which they are not.[33] Because crime rates are higher in poor urban centers than in middle-class suburbs, social forces must be operating in these blighted inner-city areas that influence or control behavior.[34]

There are three independent yet overlapping branches within the social structure perspective—social disorganization, strain theory, and cultural deviance theory (outlined in Figure 6.3):

- **Social disorganization theory** focuses on the conditions within the urban environment that affect crime rates. A disorganized area is one in which institutions of social control—such as the family, commercial establishments, and schools—have broken down and can no longer carry out their expected or stated functions. Indicators of social disorganization include high unemployment, school dropout rates, deteriorated housing, low-income levels, and large numbers of single-parent households. Residents in these areas experience conflict and despair, and, as a result, antisocial behavior flourishes.

- **Strain theory** holds that crime is a function of the conflict between the goals people have and the means they can use to obtain them legally. Because members of the lower class are unable to achieve success through conventional means, they feel anger, frustration, and resentment, referred to as **strain**. They can either live out their days as socially responsible, if unrewarded, citizens, or they can choose an alternative means of achieving success, such as theft, violence, or drug trafficking.

social structure theory The view that disadvantaged economic class position is a primary cause of crime.

social disorganization theory Branch of social structure theory that focuses on the breakdown of institutions such as the family, school, and employment in inner-city neighborhoods.

strain theory Branch of social structure theory that sees crime as a function of the conflict between people's goals and the means available to obtain them.

strain The emotional turmoil and conflict caused when people believe they cannot achieve their desires and goals through legitimate means. Members of the lower class might feel strain because they are denied access to adequate educational opportunities and social support.

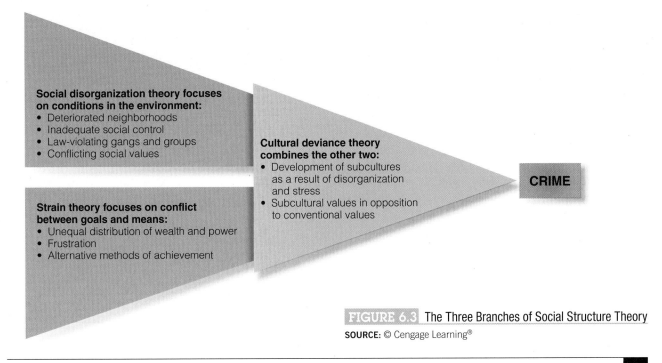

Social disorganization theory focuses on conditions in the environment:
- Deteriorated neighborhoods
- Inadequate social control
- Law-violating gangs and groups
- Conflicting social values

Strain theory focuses on conflict between goals and means:
- Unequal distribution of wealth and power
- Frustration
- Alternative methods of achievement

Cultural deviance theory combines the other two:
- Development of subcultures as a result of disorganization and stress
- Subcultural values in opposition to conventional values

CRIME

FIGURE 6.3 The Three Branches of Social Structure Theory

SOURCE: © Cengage Learning®

- **Cultural deviance theory**, the third variation of structural theory, combines elements of both strain and social disorganization: In lower-class neighborhoods a unique culture develops to help residents cope with strain. This subculture maintains a unique set of values and beliefs that are in conflict with conventional social norms. Criminal behavior is an expression of conformity to lower-class subcultural values that are handed down from one generation to the next.

Although each of these views is distinct and independent, at its core each holds the view that socially isolated people, living in disorganized neighborhoods, are the ones most likely to experience crime-producing social forces. Each branch of social structure theory will now be discussed in some detail.

Social Disorganization Theory

Social disorganization theory links crime rates to neighborhood ecological characteristics. Communities where the fabric of social life has become frayed and torn are unable to provide essential services to their residents, such as education, health care, and proper housing. Residents in these crime-ridden neighborhoods want to flee the area at the earliest opportunity. Because they want out, they become uninterested in community matters. As a result, these neighborhoods are destabilized. There is constant population turnover; people are not interested in investing in these communities. Soon streets are littered and untidy, housing becomes deteriorated, and the neighborhood is rezoned for mixed-use (i.e., residential and commercial property exist side by side).

Because the area is undergoing stress, the normal sources of *social control* common to most neighborhoods— the family, school, neighbors, business owners, the church, law enforcement, and social service agencies—become ineffective, weak, and disorganized. Personal relationships are strained because neighbors are constantly relocating to better areas. Resident turnover further weakens communication and blocks the establishment of common goals. The result: any attempt at community-level problem solving ends in frustration.[35] As social institutions become frayed or absent, law-violating youth groups and gangs form and are free to recruit neighborhood youth. Both boys and girls who feel detached and alienated from their social world are at risk to become gang members.[36] Gangs form their own subculture with unique names, slang, signs, and graffiti. There are now almost 30,000 gangs such as MS-13 in the United States, containing about 800,000 members.[37]

The problems encountered in this type of disorganized area take the form of a contagious disease, destroying the inner workings that enable neighborhoods to survive; the community becomes "hollowed out."[38] Crime and violence are like a "slow epidemic," spreading to surrounding areas and infecting them with inner-city problems.[39]

The elements of social disorganization theory are shown in Figure 6.4.

LO4 Explain the views of Shaw and McKay

Foundations of Social Disorganization Theory Social disorganization theory was first popularized by the work of two Chicago sociologists, Clifford R. Shaw and Henry D. McKay, who linked life in disorganized, transitional urban areas to neighborhood crime rates. Shaw and McKay began their pioneering work on crime in Chicago during the early 1920s while working as researchers for a state-supported social service agency.[40] They were heavily influenced by Chicago School sociologists Ernest Burgess and Robert Park, who had pioneered the ecological analysis of urban life.

Poverty
- Development of isolated lower-class areas
- Lack of conventional social opportunities
- Racial and ethnic discrimination

Social disorganization
- Breakdown of social institutions and organizations such as school and family
- Lack of informal and formal social control

Breakdown of traditional values
- Development of law-violating gangs and groups
- Deviant values replace conventional values and norms

Criminal areas
- Neighborhood becomes crime prone
- Stable pockets of crime develop
- Lack of external support and investment

Cultural transmission
Adults pass norms (focal concerns) to younger generation, creating stable lower-class culture

Criminal careers
Most youths age out of delinquency, marry, and raise families, but some remain in life of crime

FIGURE 6.4 Social Disorganization Theory

SOURCE: © Cengage Learning®

cultural deviance theory Branch of social structure theory that sees strain and social disorganization together resulting in a unique lower-class culture that conflicts with conventional social norms.

Shaw and McKay began their analysis during a period when Chicago was experiencing a rapid population expansion, fueled by a dramatic influx of foreign-born immigrants and, later, migrating southern families. Congregating in the central city, the newcomers occupied the oldest housing areas and therefore faced numerous health and environmental hazards.

Sections of the city started to physically deteriorate, prompting the city's wealthy, established citizens to become concerned about the moral fabric of Chicago society. There was concern among the moneyed classes that immigrants from Europe and the rural South were crime prone and morally dissolute. Local citizens groups called "child savers" were formed, whose stated purpose was protecting the children of poor families from succumbing to the moral decadence of their parents.[41]

Transitional Neighborhoods   While it was then popular to view crime as the property of inferior racial and ethnic groups, Shaw and McKay instead focused on the context of the changing urban environment and ecological development of the city. They saw that Chicago had developed into distinct neighborhoods (natural areas), some affluent and others wracked by extreme poverty. These poverty-ridden, **transitional neighborhoods** suffered high rates of population turnover; those who remained were incapable of defending the neighborhood against criminal groups.

The relatively low rents attracted newly arrived immigrants from Europe and the South. Children were torn between assimilating into a new culture and/or abiding by the traditional values of their parents. Informal social control mechanisms that had restrained behavior in the "old country" or rural areas were disrupted, exposing neighborhood youth to the lure of criminal gangs and groups.

In transitional areas, successive changes in the population composition, disintegration of traditional cultures, diffusion of divergent cultural standards, and gradual industrialization of the area resulted in dissolution of neighborhood culture and organization. The continuity of conventional neighborhood traditions and institutions was broken, leaving children feeling displaced and without a strong or definitive set of values. The culture of urban areas was the spawning grounds of young criminals.

Concentric Zones   Shaw and McKay identified the areas in Chicago that had excessive crime rates. Using a model of analysis pioneered by Ernest Burgess, they noted that distinct ecological areas had developed in the city, comprising a series of five concentric circles, or zones, and that there were stable and significant differences in interzone crime rates (Figure 6.5). The areas of heaviest concentration of crime appeared to be the transitional inner-city zones, where large numbers of foreign-born citizens had recently settled.[42] The zones furthest from the city's center had correspondingly lower crime rates.

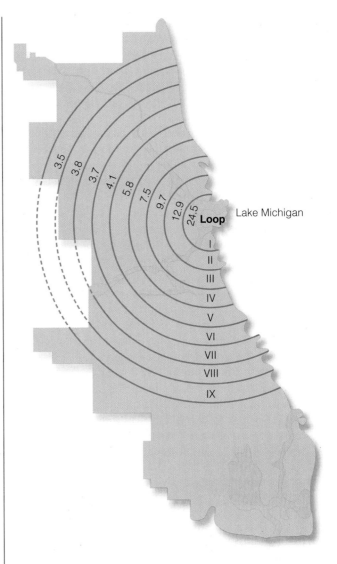

FIGURE 6.5   Shaw and McKay's Concentric Zones Map of Chicago

SOURCE: Clifford R. Shaw et al., *Delinquency Areas* (Chicago: University of Chicago Press, 1929), p. 99.
Note: Arabic numerals represent the rate of male delinquency.

Analysis of these data indicated a surprisingly stable pattern of criminal activity in the various ecological zones over a 65-year period. Shaw and McKay concluded that, in the transitional neighborhoods, multiple cultures and diverse values, both conventional and deviant, coexist. Children growing up in the street culture often find that adults who have adopted a deviant lifestyle are the most financially successful people in the neighborhood: the gambler, the pimp,

transitional neighborhoods Areas undergoing a shift in population and structure, usually from middle-class residential to lower-class mixed use.

or the drug dealer. Required to choose between conventional and deviant lifestyles, many inner-city kids see the value in opting for the latter. They join with other like-minded youths and form law-violating gangs and cliques. The development of teenage law-violating groups is an essential element of youthful misbehavior in lower-class areas. The values that inner-city youths adopt are often in conflict with existing middle-class norms, which demand strict obedience to the legal code. Consequently, a value conflict occurs that sets the delinquent youth and his peer group even further apart from conventional society. The result is a more solid embrace of deviant goals and behavior. To justify their choice of goals, these youths seek support by recruiting new members and passing on the delinquent tradition.

Shaw and McKay's statistical analysis confirmed their theoretical suspicions. Even though crime rates changed, they found that the highest rates were always in Zones I and II (central city and a transitional area). The areas with the highest crime rates retained high rates even when their ethnic composition changed (in the areas Shaw and McKay examined, from German and Irish to Italian and Polish).[43]

The Legacy of Shaw and McKay Social disorganization concepts articulated by Shaw and McKay have remained a prominent fixture of criminological scholarship and thinking for more than 75 years. While cultural and social conditions have changed and American society today is much more heterogeneous and mobile than during Shaw and McKay's time, the most important elements of their findings still hold up:[44]

- Crime rates are sensitive to the destructive social forces operating in lower-class urban neighborhoods.
- Environmental factors, rather than individual differences, are the root cause of crime.
- Crime is a constant fixture in distressed areas regardless of racial or ethnic makeup.
- The weakening of social control is the primary cause of criminal behavior.
- Community values, norms, and cohesiveness affect individual behavior choices.

Shaw and McKay's formulation of social disorganization provides a valuable contribution to our understanding of the causes of criminal behavior. By introducing a new variable—the ecology of the city—to the study of crime, these pioneering criminologists paved the way for a focus on the social influences of criminal and delinquent behavior.

The Social Ecology School

LO5 Differentiate between the various elements of ecological theory

More than 30 years ago, a group of criminologists began to reexamine ecological conditions that support criminality.[45] Contemporary social ecologists developed a "purer" form of structural theory that emphasizes the association of community deterioration and economic decline to criminality, but places less emphasis on the value and norm conflict that lay at the core of Shaw and McKay's vision. According to this more contemporary view, living in deteriorated, crime-ridden neighborhoods exerts a powerful influence over behavior that is strong enough to neutralize the positive effects of a supportive family and close social ties. If individual or family status influences criminality and violence, it is because of the nature of the communities in which disadvantaged persons and families reside and not the strength of family relationships themselves.[46] In the following sections, some of the more recent social ecological research is discussed in detail.

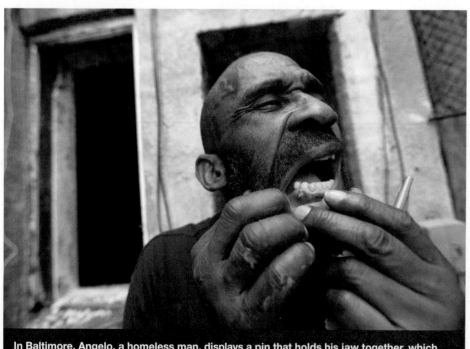

In Baltimore, Angelo, a homeless man, displays a pin that holds his jaw together, which he said he received after being beaten and robbed while sleeping in a vacant row house, seen behind him. A census of Baltimore's homeless population counted more than 4,000 homeless people. Some choose to find shelter in the city's estimated 16,000 vacant or abandoned buildings. According to social structure theory, crime rates are highest in these disorganized neighborhoods, where social control is weak and attenuated.

Community Deterioration Social ecologists have focused their attention on the association between crime rates and community deterioration: disorder, poverty, alienation, disassociation, and fear of crime.[47] They find that neighborhoods with a high percentage of deserted houses and apartments experience high crime rates; abandoned buildings serve as a "magnet for crime."[48] Areas in which houses are in poor repair, boarded up, and burned out, and whose owners are best described as "slumlords," are also the location of the highest violence rates and gun crime.[49] These are neighborhoods in which retail establishments often go bankrupt, are abandoned, and deteriorate physically.[50]

Poverty Concentration William Julius Wilson describes how working- and middle-class families flee inner-city poverty areas, resulting in a poverty **concentration effect** in which the most disadvantaged population is consolidated in the most disorganized urban neighborhoods. Poverty concentration has been associated with income and wealth disparities, nonexistent employment opportunities, inferior housing patterns, and unequal access to health care.[51] Urban areas marked by concentrated poverty become isolated and insulated from the social mainstream and more prone to criminal activity, violence, and homicide.[52]

How does neighborhood poverty concentration produce high crime rates? White families are more likely to leave an area when they perceive that the surrounding neighborhoods have become predominantly minority.[53] As the working and middle classes move out to the suburbs, they take with them their financial and institutional resources and support, undermining the community's level of informal social control.[54] People left behind are socially isolated and have even a tougher time managing urban decay and conflict and/or controlling youth gangs and groups; after all, the most successful people in the community have left for "greener pastures."[55] Businesses are disinclined to locate in poverty areas; banks become reluctant to lend money for new housing or businesses.[56] The resulting deterioration in social capital in high-poverty areas reduces community social control, opening the door forever to expanding community crime rates.[57]

Chronic Unemployment The association between unemployment and crime is still unsettled: aggregate crime rates and aggregate unemployment rates seem weakly related. In other words, crime rates sometimes rise during periods of economic prosperity and fall during periods of economic decline.[58] Yet, as Shaw and McKay claimed, neighborhoods that experience chronic unemployment also encounter social disorganization and crime.[59] How can these divergent trends be explained?

One possibility is that even though short-term national economic trends may have little effect on crime, chronic *unemployment* may have a more significant impact on conditions at the community or neighborhood level; Even in times of economic prosperity, some neighborhoods maintain stubbornly high unemployment rates.[60]

How does job loss lead to crime? Unemployment destabilizes households, and unstable families are the ones most likely to produce children who put a premium on violence and aggression as a means of dealing with limited opportunity. Conflict may also occur when people of the same age cohort compete for relatively scant resources.[61]

Limited employment opportunities also reduce the stabilizing influence of parents and other adults, who may have once been able to counteract the allure of youth gangs. Sociologist Elijah Anderson's analysis of Philadelphia neighborhood life found that "old heads" (i.e., respected neighborhood residents) who at one time played an important role in socializing youth have been displaced by younger street hustlers and drug dealers. While the old heads complain that these newcomers may not have earned or worked for their fortune in the "old-fashioned way," the old heads also admire and envy these kids whose gold chains and luxury cars advertise their wealth amid poverty.[62] The old heads may admire the fruits of crime, but they disdain the violent manner in which they were acquired.

Community Fear People feel safe in neighborhoods that are orderly and in repair.[63] In contrast, those living in neighborhoods that suffer social and physical **incivilities**—rowdy youth, trash and litter, graffiti, abandoned storefronts, burned-out buildings, littered lots, strangers, drunks, vagabonds, loiterers, prostitutes, noise, congestion, angry words, dirt, and stench—are much more likely to be fearful. Put another way, disorder breeds fear.[64]

In neighborhoods where people help one another, residents are less likely to fear crime and be afraid of becoming a crime victim.[65] When people feel distant from one another, disconnected from others in the community, they are more likely to view their environment as a dangerous place.[66] Not surprisingly, people living in areas with especially high crime rates are the ones most likely to experience fear.[67]

People who live in public housing projects, who come into daily contact with civil disorder, are not surprisingly the ones most likely to see their community as disorderly and dangerous.[68] People become afraid when they are approached by someone in the neighborhood selling drugs. They may fear that their children will also be approached and will be seduced into the drug life.[69] Residents who have already been victimized, or know someone else who has, are more fearful of the future than those who have escaped crime.

concentration effect Working- and middle-class families flee inner-city poverty areas, resulting in the most disadvantaged population being consolidated in the most disorganized urban neighborhoods.

incivilities Rude and uncivil behavior; behavior that indicates little caring for the feelings of others.

The presence of such incivilities, especially when accompanied by relatively high crime rates, helps convince residents that their neighborhood is dangerous; becoming a crime victim seems inevitable.[70] Eventually they become emotionally numb, and as their exposure to crime increases, they experience indifference to the suffering of others.[71]

Fear can become contagious. People tell others when they have been victimized, spreading the word that the neighborhood is getting dangerous and that the chances of future victimization are high.[72] They dread leaving their homes at night and withdraw from community life.

When people live in areas where the death rates are high and life expectancies are short, they may alter their behavior out of fear. They may feel, "Why plan for the future when there is a significant likelihood that I may never see it?" In such areas, young boys and girls may psychologically assimilate by taking risks and discounting the future. Teenage birthrates soar and so do violence rates.[73] For these children, the inevitability of death skews their perspective of how they live their lives.

When fear grips a neighborhood, business conditions begin to deteriorate, population mobility increases, and a "criminal element" begins to drift into the area.[74] In essence, the existence of fear incites more crime, increasing the chances of victimization, producing even more fear, in a never-ending loop.[75] Fear is often associated with other community-level factors:

- *Race and fear.* Fear of crime is also bound up in anxiety over racial and ethnic conflicts. Residents experience the most fear in areas undergoing rapid and unexpected racial and age-composition changes, especially when they are out of proportion to the rest of the city.[76]

CONNECTIONS

Remember that in Chapter 3 we discussed the fact that some people may be "victim prone" and fated to suffer repeated victimization over the life course.

Ask Yourself ...

Fear of repeat victimization may be both instinctual and accurate. Some people are victim prone and those who live in dangerous areas may be at risk to repeat victimization. Do you take precautions to protect yourself from crime? Is it something you think about often, that's always on your mind?

siege mentality Residents who become so suspicious of authority that they consider the outside world to be the enemy out to destroy the neighborhood.

Minority group members often experience greater levels of fear than European Americans, especially when they believe they have fewer resources to address ongoing social problems.[77]

- *Gangs and fear.* Gangs flourish in deteriorated neighborhoods with high levels of poverty, lack of investment, high unemployment rates, and population turnover.[78] Unlike any other crime, however, gang activity is frequently undertaken out in the open, on the public ways, and in full view of the rest of the community.[79] Brazen criminal activity undermines community solidarity because it signals that the police can't do anything to curb gang activity. The fact that gangs are willing to openly engage in drug sales and other types of criminal activity shows their confidence to control or intimidate their neighborhoods. The police and the community alike become hopeless about their ability to restore community stability, producing greater levels of community fear.

- *Mistrust and fear.* People who report living in neighborhoods with high levels of crime and civil disorder become suspicious and mistrusting.[80] They develop a sense of powerlessness, which amplifies the effect of neighborhood disorder and increases levels of mistrust. Some residents become so suspicious of authority that they develop a **siege mentality**: they believe there are forces in the outside world set out to destroy the neighborhood. Elijah Anderson found that residents in the African American neighborhoods he studied believed in the existence of a secret plan to eradicate the population by such strategies as permanent unemployment, police brutality, imprisonment, drug distribution, and AIDS.[81] White officials and political leaders were believed to have hatched this conspiracy, and it was demonstrated by the lax law enforcement efforts in poor areas. Residents felt that police cared little about black-on-black crime because it helped reduce the population. Rumors abounded that federal government agencies, such as the CIA, controlled the drug trade and used profits to fund illegal overseas operations. This siege mentality results in mistrust of critical social institutions, including business, government, and schools. Government officials seem arrogant and haughty. Residents become self-conscious, worried about garnering any respect, and are particularly attuned to anyone who disrespects them. Considering this feeling of mistrust, when police ignore crime in poor areas or, conversely, when they are violent and corrupt, anger flares, and people take to the streets and react in violent ways.[82]

Community Change In our postmodern society, the urban areas undergoing rapid structural changes in racial and economic composition also seem to experience the greatest change in crime rates. In contrast, stable neighborhoods, even those with a high rate of poverty, experience relatively low crime rates and have the strength to restrict substance abuse and criminal activity.[83]

Recent studies recognize that change, not stability, is the hallmark of inner-city areas. A neighborhood's residents, wealth, density, and purpose are constantly evolving. Even disorganized neighborhoods acquire new identifying features. Some may become multiracial, while others become racially homogeneous. Some areas become stable and family oriented, while in others, mobile, never-married people predominate.[84]

As areas decline, some residents flee to safer, more stable localities. Those who cannot leave because they cannot afford to live in more affluent communities face an increased risk of victimization. Those who can move to more affluent neighborhoods find that their lifestyles and life chances improve immediately and continue to do so over their life span.[85] Take for instance the Gautreaux Assisted Housing Program, a major initiative ordered by the courts in 1976 to provide a metropolitan-wide remedy for racial discrimination in Chicago's public housing program. The program helped inner-city families relocate to more affluent white suburbs. Research on the effects of the Gautreaux program shows that most families who moved to Chicago's suburbs were still living in those suburbs 10 and even 20 years later. Despite some race-based problems, children's attitudes toward school improved and their grades did not drop. Moreover, as children in these Gautreaux families grew up and left home, they moved to neighborhoods that were far safer and more affluent than the inner-city neighborhoods their families had left behind.[86]

High population turnover can have a devastating effect on community culture because it thwarts communication and information flow.[87] In response to this turnover, a culture may develop that dictates standards of dress, language, and behavior to neighborhood youth that are in opposition to those of conventional society. All these factors are likely to produce increased crime rates.

The Cycles of Community Change   During periods of population turnover, communities may undergo changes that undermine their infrastructure. Urban areas seem to have life cycles, which begin with building residential dwellings and are followed by a period of decline, with marked decreases in socioeconomic status and increases in population density. Later stages in this life cycle include changing racial or ethnic makeup, population thinning, and finally, a renewal stage in which obsolete housing is replaced and upgraded (**gentrification**). Areas undergoing such change seem to experience an increase in their crime rates.[88]

As communities go through cycles, neighborhood deterioration precedes increasing rates of crime and delinquency.[89] Neighborhoods most at risk for high crime rate increases contain large numbers of racial minorities, single-parent families and unrelated people living together, have gone from having owner-occupied to renter-occupied units, and have an economic base that has lost semiskilled and

CONNECTIONS

As you may recall, Chapter 2 discussed the racial threat hypothesis, a phenomenon in which white citizens feel threatened by the competition posed by a greater proportion of African Americans in a community and call for more police protection aimed at controlling the minority population. Have you encountered this form of racial conflict in your own community? Are white residents still threatened by the presence of minorities or are we evolving into a more racially tolerant nation?

unskilled jobs (indicating a growing residue of discouraged workers who are no longer seeking employment).[90] These ecological disruptions strain existing social control mechanisms and inhibit their ability to control crime and delinquency.

Collective Efficacy

LO6   Discuss the association between collective efficacy and crime

Cohesive communities, whether urban or rural, with high levels of social control and social integration, where people know one another and develop interpersonal ties, may also develop **collective efficacy**: mutual trust, a willingness to intervene in the supervision of children, and the maintenance of public order.[91] It is the cohesion among neighborhood residents combined with shared expectations for informal social control of public space that promotes collective efficacy.[92] Residents in these areas are able to enjoy a better life because the fruits of cohesiveness can be better education, health care, and housing opportunities.[93]

In disorganized areas, where the population is transient, interpersonal relationships remain superficial and nonsupportive. Residents find that the social support they need to live a conventional life is absent or lacking.[94] In contrast, as the number of people who have a stake in the community (i.e., they are homeowners) increases, crime rates drop.[95] These more cohesive neighborhoods report less disorder than less-unified communities.[96]

gentrification   A residential renewal stage in which obsolete housing is replaced and upgraded; areas undergoing such change seem to experience an increase in their crime rates.

collective efficacy   Social control exerted by cohesive communities, based on mutual trust, including intervention in the supervision of children and maintenance of public order.

When community social control efforts are blunted, efforts at social control are weak and attenuated, crime rates increase, further diminishing neighborhood cohesiveness.[97] There are actually three forms of collective efficacy: informal, institutional, and public social control.

Informal Social Control   Some elements of collective efficacy operate on the primary or private level and involve peers, families, and relatives. These sources exert informal control by either awarding or withholding approval, respect, and admiration. Informal control mechanisms include direct criticism, ridicule, ostracism, desertion, or physical punishment.[98] Because they already have a propensity to commit crime without informal social controls, some people will be unable to avoid entanglements in anti-social behaviors.[99]

The most important wielder of informal social control is the family, which may keep at-risk kids in check through such mechanisms as corporal punishment, withholding privileges, or ridiculing lazy or disrespectful behavior. The importance of the family to apply informal social control takes on greater importance in neighborhoods with few social ties among adults and limited collective efficacy. In these areas, parents cannot call upon neighborhood resources to take up the burden of controlling children and face the challenge of providing adequate supervision.[100]

The family is not the only force of informal social control. In some neighborhoods, people are committed to preserving their immediate environment by confronting destabilizing forces such as teen gangs.[101] By helping neighbors become more resilient and self-confident, adults in these areas provide the external support systems that enable youth to desist from crime. Residents teach one another that they have moral and social obligations to their fellow citizens; children learn to be sensitive to the rights of others and to respect differences.

In some areas, neighborhood associations and self-help groups form.[102] The threat of skyrocketing violence rates may draw people together to help each other out. While criminologists believe that crime rates are lower in cohesive neighborhoods, it is also possible that an escalating crime rate may bring people closer together to fight a common problem.[103] Some neighbors may get involved in informal social control through surveillance practices, for example, by keeping an eye out for intruders when their neighbors go out of town. Informal surveillance has been found to reduce the levels of some crimes such as street robberies; however, if robbery rates remain high, surveillance may be terminated because people become fearful for their safety.[104]

Institutional Social Control   Social institutions such as schools and churches cannot work effectively in a climate of alienation and mistrust. Unsupervised peer groups and gangs, which flourish in disorganized areas, disrupt the influence of those neighborhood control agents that do exist.[105]

People who reside in these neighborhoods find that involvement with conventional social institutions, such as schools and afternoon programs, is often attenuated or blocked.[106] Children are at risk for recruitment into gangs and law-violating groups when there is a lack of effective public services. Gangs become an attractive alternative when adolescents have little to do after school and must rely on out-of-home care rather than more structured school-based programs.[107] As a result, crime may flourish and neighborhood fear increases, conditions that decrease a community's cohesion and thwart the ability of its institutions to exert social control over its residents.[108]

To combat these influences, communities that have collective efficacy attempt to utilize their local institutions to control crime. Sources of institutional social control include businesses, stores, schools, churches, and social service and volunteer organizations. When these institutions are effective, crime rates decline.[109]

Some institutions, such as recreation centers for teens, have been found to lower crime rates because they exert a positive effect; others, such as taverns and bars, can help destabilize neighborhoods and increase the rate of violent crimes such as rape and robbery.[110]

Public Social Control   Stable neighborhoods are also able to arrange for external sources of social control. If they can draw on outside help and secure external resources—a process referred to as public social control—they are better able to reduce the effects of disorganization and maintain lower levels of crime and victimization.[111] For example, recent research shows that community organizations in low-income Bronx, New York, neighborhoods that were able to develop ties with the larger community experienced a decrease in crime. Property crime was reduced when local community organizations are able to promote the well-being of local families and children.[112]

Racial differences in crime and violence rates may be explained in part by the ability of citizens in affluent, predominantly white neighborhoods to use their economic resources, and the political power they bring, to their own advantage. They demand and receive a level of protection in their communities that is not enjoyed in less affluent minority communities.[113]

The level of policing, one of the primary sources of public social control, may vary from neighborhood to neighborhood. The more efficient and honest police are the more effective they are at reducing crime.[114] The police presence is typically greatest when community organizations and local leaders have sufficient political clout to get funding for additional law enforcement personnel. An effective police presence sends a message that the area will not tolerate deviant behavior. Because they can respond vigorously to crime, the police prevent criminal groups from gaining a toehold in the neighborhood.[115] Criminals and drug dealers avoid such areas and relocate to easier and more appealing targets.[116] In contrast, crime rates are highest in areas where police are mistrusted because they engage in misconduct, such as use of excessive force, or because they are seemingly indifferent to neighborhood problems.[117]

In more disorganized areas, the absence of political powerbrokers limits access to external funding and protection.[118] Without outside funding, a neighborhood may lack the ability to get back on its feet.[119] In these areas, there are fewer police, and those that do patrol the area are less motivated and their resources are stretched tighter. These communities cannot mount an effective social control effort because as neighborhood disadvantage increases, the level of informal social control decreases.[120]

The government can also reduce crime by providing economic support through publicly funded social assistance and welfare programs. Though welfare is often criticized by conservative politicians as being a government handout, there is evidence of a significant association between the amount of welfare money people receive and lowered crime rates.[121] Government assistance may help people improve their social status by providing them with the financial resources to clothe, feed, and educate their children while at the same time reducing stress, frustration, and anger. Using government subsidies to reduce crime is controversial and not all research has found that it actually works as advertised.[122]

People living in disorganized areas may also be able to draw on resources from their neighbors in more affluent surrounding communities, helping to keep crime rates down.[123] This phenomenon may explain, in part, why violence rates are high in poor African American neighborhoods cut off from outside areas for support.[124]

The Effect of Collective Efficacy   In areas where collective efficacy remains high, children are less likely to become involved with deviant peers and engage in problem behaviors.[125] In these more stable areas, kids are able to use their wits to avoid violent confrontations and to feel safe in their own neighborhood, a concept referred to as **street efficacy**.[126] This association is important because adolescents living in communities with high levels of efficacy are less likely to resort to violence themselves or to associate with delinquent peers.[127]

In contrast, adolescents who live in neighborhoods with concentrated disadvantage and low collective efficacy begin to lose confidence in their ability to avoid violence. They perceive, and rightly so, that the community cannot provide the level of social control needed to neutralize or make up for what individuals lack in personal self-control.[128] The lack of community controls may convince them to take matters in their own hands—for example, joining a gang or carrying a weapon for self-protection.

Collective efficacy has other benefits. When residents are satisfied that their neighborhoods are good places to live, they feel a sense of obligation to maintain order themselves and are more willing to work hard to encourage informal social control. In areas where social institutions and processes—such as police protection—are working adequately, residents are willing to intervene personally to help control unruly children and uncivil adults.[129]

Concept Summary 6.1 sets out the features of social disorganization theory.

To read a famous *Atlantic* magazine article titled "Broken Windows," which discusses the concept of community deterioration and crime, go to http://www.theatlantic.com/magazine/archive/1982/03/broken-windows/304465/.

street efficacy   A concept in which more cohesive communities with high levels of social control and social integration foster the ability for kids to use their wits to avoid violent confrontations and to feel safe in their own neighborhood. Adolescents with high levels of street efficacy are less likely to resort to violence themselves or to associate with delinquent peers.

SOCIAL DISORGANIZATION THEORIES

6.1

Theory	Major Premise	Strengths	Research Focus
Shaw and McKay's concentric zones theory	Crime is a product of transitional neighborhoods that manifest social disorganization and value conflict.	Identifies why crime rates are highest in slum areas. Points out the factors that produce crime. Suggests programs to help reduce crime.	Poverty; disorganization; gangs; neighborhood change; community context of crime.
Social ecology theory	The conflicts and problems of urban social life and communities, including fear, unemployment, deterioration, and siege mentality, influence crime rates.	Accounts for urban crime rates and trends. Identifies community-level factors that produce high crime rates.	Social control; fear; collective efficacy; unemployment.

concept summary

STRAIN THEORIES

 LO7 Articulate what is meant by the concepts of strain and anomie

As a group, strain theorists believe that most people share similar values and goals. They want to earn money, have a nice home, drive a great car, and wear stylish clothes. They also want to care for their families and educate their children. Unfortunately, the ability to achieve these personal goals is stratified by socioeconomic class. While the affluent may live out the American Dream, the poor are shut out from achieving their goals. Because they can't always get what they want, they begin to feel frustrated and angry, a condition that is referred to as strain.

Strain is related to criminal motivation. People who feel economically and socially humiliated may perceive the right to humiliate others in return.[130] Psychologists warn that under these circumstances those who consider themselves "losers" begin to fear and envy "winners" who are doing very well at their expense. If they fail to take risky aggressive tactics, they are surely going to lose out in social competition and have little chance of future success.[131] These generalized feelings of **relative deprivation** are precursors to high crime rates.[132]

According to the strain view, sharp divisions between the rich and poor create an atmosphere of envy and mistrust that may lead to violence and aggression.[133] People who feel deprived because of their race or economic class standing eventually develop a sense of injustice and discontent. The less fortunate begin to distrust the society that has nurtured social inequality and obstructed their chances of progressing by legitimate means. The constant frustration that results from these feelings of inadequacy produces pent-up aggression and hostility and, eventually, leads to violence and crime. The effect of inequality may be greatest when the impoverished population believes they are becoming less able to compete in a society where the balance of economic

Poverty
Relative deprivation
Feelings of inadequacy
Siege mentality

▽

Maintenance of conventional rules and norms
Despite adversity, people remain loyal to conventional values and rules of dominant middle-class culture.

▽

Strain
People who desire conventional success but lack means and opportunity will experience strain and frustration.

▽

Formation of gangs and groups
People form law-violating groups to seek alternative means of achieving success.

▽

Crime and delinquency
People engage in antisocial acts to achieve success and relieve their feelings of strain.

▽

Criminal careers
Feelings of strain may endure, sustaining criminal careers.

FIGURE 6.6 The Basic Components of Strain Theory
SOURCE: © Cengage Learning®

and social power is shifting further toward the already affluent. Under these conditions, the likelihood that the poor will choose illegitimate life-enhancing activities increases.[134] The basic components of strain theory are set out in Figure 6.6.

The Concept of Anomie

The roots of strain theories can be traced to Émile Durkheim's notion of **anomie** (from the Greek *a nomos*, "without norms"). According to Durkheim, an anomic society is one in which rules of behavior (i.e., values, customs, and norms) have broken down or become inoperative during periods of rapid social change or social crisis such as war or famine. Anomie is most likely to occur in societies that are moving from a preindustrial society, which is held together by traditions, shared values, and unquestioned beliefs (i.e., **mechanical solidarity**) to a postindustrial social system, which is highly developed and dependent upon the division of labor. In this modern society, people are connected by their interdependent needs for one another's services and production (i.e., **organic solidarity**). The shift

---

relative deprivation The condition that exists when people of wealth and poverty live in close proximity to one another. Some criminologists attribute crime rate differentials to relative deprivation.

anomie According to Durkheim, an anomic society is one in which rules of behavior (i.e., values, customs, and norms) have broken down or become inoperative during periods of rapid social change or social crisis.

mechanical solidarity A characteristic of a preindustrial society, which is held together by traditions, shared values, and unquestioned beliefs.

organic solidarity Postindustrial social systems, which are highly developed and dependent upon the division of labor; people are connected by their interdependent needs for one another's services and production.

in traditions and values creates social turmoil. Established norms begin to erode and lose meaning. If a division occurs between what the population expects and what the economic and productive forces of society can realistically deliver, a crisis situation develops that can manifest itself in normlessness or anomie. This condition can be found in modern day Russia as it shifts from a Communist system to a free enterprise system without the social support and guarantees the population has come to expect.[135]

Anomie undermines society's social control function. Every society works to limit people's goals and desires. If a society becomes anomic, it can no longer establish and maintain control over its population's wants and desires. Because people find it difficult to control their appetites, their demands become unlimited. Under these circumstances, obedience to legal codes may be strained, and alternative behavior choices, such as crimes, may be inevitable.

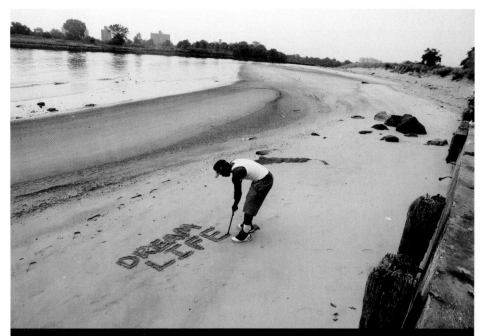

Strain can be caused by the inability to achieve aspirations through legitimate means. Take the residents of the Coney Island neighborhood at the southern point of New York City, best known for its legendary amusement park. The park reached its peak in popularity in the early 1900s and has been in slow decline ever since. Recently, there has been a push to regenerate the amusement park in Coney Island and the city government has put over $100 million into modernizing the boardwalk and rides. Although the situation has improved some in recent decades, drugs, gangs, prostitution, violence, and a high unemployment rate are all still prevalent in Coney Island and people are afraid to walk the streets at night. Many people who have grown up here feel as if they have been forgotten.

Emily Berl/Redux

Contemporary strain theories come in two distinct formulations:

- *Structural strain.* Using a sociological lens, structural strain suggests that economic and social sources of strain shape collective human behavior.
- *Individual strain.* Using a psychological reference, individual strain theories suggest that individual life experiences cause some people to suffer pain and misery, feelings that are then translated into antisocial behaviors.

Below, three popular strain theories are discussed in some detail. Two, anomie theory and American Dream theory, are structural, while the third, general strain theory, relies more on a social psychological framework.

Merton's Theory of Anomie

LO8 Compare and contrast between the different elements in Merton's theory of anomie

Durkheim's ideas were applied to criminology by sociologist Robert Merton in his **theory of anomie**.[136] Merton used a modified version of the concept of anomie to fit social, economic, and cultural conditions found in modern U.S.

society.[137] He found that two elements of culture interact to produce potentially anomic conditions: culturally defined goals and socially approved means for obtaining them. Contemporary society stresses the goals of acquiring wealth, success, and power. Socially permissible means include hard work, education, and thrift.

In the United States, Merton argued, legitimate means to acquire wealth are stratified across class and status lines. Those with little formal education and few economic resources soon find that they are denied the ability to legally acquire wealth—the preeminent success symbol. When socially mandated goals are uniform throughout society and access to legitimate means is bound by class and status, the resulting strain produces anomie among those who are locked out of the legitimate opportunity structure. Consequently, they may develop criminal or delinquent solutions to the problem of attaining goals.

theory of anomie A modified version of the concept of anomie developed by Merton to fit social, economic, and cultural conditions found in modern U.S. society. He found that two elements of culture interact to produce potentially anomic conditions: culturally defined goals and socially approved means for obtaining them.

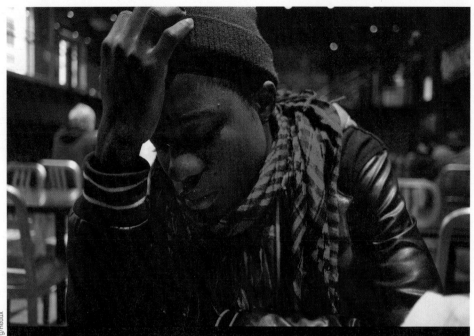

Elbert Chu/Do1Thing/Redux

Strain can hit people on a personal, individual level. After leaving a homeless shelter for youth, Miguel Martinez, 19, prepared himself to report to high school in Brooklyn. "Nobody knows I'm in a shelter—they would all look down on me." His dream is to work someday at Apple or Sephora.

Social Adaptations   Merton argued that each person has his or her own concept of the goals of society and the means at his or her disposal for their attainment. Here is a brief description of each of these modes of adaptation to the association of goals and means:

- *Conformity.* Conformity occurs when individuals embrace conventional social goals and also have the means of attainment at their disposal. The conformist desires wealth and success and can obtain them through education and a high paying job. In a balanced, stable society, this is the most common social adaptation. If a majority of its people did not practice conformity, the society would cease to exist.
- *Innovation.* Innovation occurs when an individual accepts the goals of society but rejects or is incapable of attaining them through legitimate means. Many people desire material goods and luxuries but lack the financial ability to attain them. The resulting conflict forces them to adopt innovative solutions to their dilemma: they steal, sell drugs, or extort money. Of the five adaptations, innovation is most closely associated with criminal behavior.

  If successful, innovation can have serious, long-term social consequences. Criminal success helps convince otherwise law-abiding people that innovative means work better and faster than conventional ones. The prosperous drug dealer's expensive car and flashy clothes give out the message that crime pays. Merton claims, "The process thus enlarges the extent of anomie within the system, so that others, who did not respond in the form of

deviant behavior to the relatively slight anomie which they first obtained, come to do so as anomie is spread and is intensified."[138] This explains why crime is initiated and sustained in certain low-income ecological areas.

- *Ritualism.* Ritualists have gained the tools to accumulate wealth—for example, they are educated and informed—but reject established cultural goals of contemporary society. These are people who enjoy the routine of work without having the ambition to climb to the top of their profession; they are not risk takers. Some may enjoy being midlevel government bureaucrats. They are the professors who want to get tenure but do not strive to become chairperson of the department. Some ritualists gain pleasure from practicing traditional ceremonies regardless of whether they have a real purpose or goal. The rules and customs in religious orders, clubs, and college fraternities are appealing to ritualists. Ritualists should have the lowest level of criminal behavior because they have abandoned the success goal, which is at the root of criminal activity.
- *Retreatism.* Retreatists reject both the goals and the means of society. Merton suggests that people who adjust in this fashion are "in the society but not of it." Included in this category are "psychotics, psychoneurotics, chronic autists, pariahs, outcasts, vagrants, vagabonds, tramps, chronic drunkards, and drug addicts." Because such people are morally or otherwise incapable of using both legitimate and illegitimate means, they attempt to escape their lack of success by withdrawing, either mentally or physically.
- *Rebellion.* Rebellion involves substituting an alternative set of goals and means for conventional ones. Revolutionaries who wish to promote radical change in the existing social structure and who call for alternative lifestyles, goals, and beliefs are engaging in rebellion. Rebellion may be a reaction against a corrupt and hated government or an effort to create alternate opportunities and lifestyles within the existing system.

Evaluation of Anomie Theory   According to anomie theory, social inequality leads to perceptions of anomie. To resolve the goals–means conflict and relieve their sense of strain, some people innovate by stealing or extorting money,

198   PART TWO   Theories of Crime Causation

A police lieutenant swings his baton at Occupy Wall Street activists in New York. Hundreds of activists with a variety of causes spread out over New York City on International Workers Day, or May Day, with Occupy Wall Street members leading a charge against financial institutions. One woman, Cecily McMillan, 25, a graduate student at the New School and a volunteer labor organizer, was sentenced to three months in prison for assaulting a police officer with her elbow, which she claimed was an accident. Ironically, some of the billionaire Wall Street execs she and her colleagues were protesting were involved in large-scale insider trading scandals, but still remain free to pursue their exotic lifestyles.

AP Images

social success. Juveniles may be more interested in immediate goals, such as having an active social life or being a good athlete, than in long-term "ideal" achievements, such as monetary success. Achieving these goals is not a matter of social class alone; other factors, including athletic ability, intelligence, personality, and family life, can either hinder or assist goal attainment.[140] Anomie theory also assumes that all people share the same goals and values, which is false.[141]

Some contemporary theories are grounded on Merton's visionary concepts. Some of these are macro-level theories that hold that the success goal integrated within American society influences the nature and extent of the aggregate crime rate. There are also individual micro-level versions of the theory, which focus on how an individual is affected by feelings of alienation and strain.

others retreat into drugs and alcohol, others rebel by joining revolutionary groups, and still others get involved in ritualistic behavior by joining a religious cult.

Merton's view of anomie has been one of the most enduring and influential sociological theories of criminality. By linking deviant behavior to the success goals that control social behavior, anomie theory attempts to pinpoint the cause of the conflict that produces personal frustration and consequent criminality. By acknowledging that society unfairly distributes the legitimate means to achieving success, anomie theory helps explain the existence of high-crime areas and the apparent predominance of delinquent and criminal behavior among the lower class. By suggesting that social conditions, not individual personalities, produce crime, Merton greatly influenced the direction taken to reduce and control criminality during the latter half of the twentieth century.

A number of questions are left unanswered by anomie theory.[139] Merton does not explain why people choose to commit certain types of crime. For example, why does one anomic person become a mugger and another deal drugs? Anomie may be used to explain differences in crime rates, but it cannot explain why most young criminals desist from crime as adults. Does this mean that perceptions of anomie dwindle with age? Is anomie short-lived?

Critics have also suggested that people pursue a number of different goals, including educational, athletic, and

Institutional Anomie Theory

An important addition to the strain literature is the book *Crime and the American Dream*, by Steven Messner and Richard Rosenfeld.[142] Their macro-level version of anomie theory views antisocial behavior as a function of cultural and institutional influences in U.S. society, a model they refer to as **institutional anomie theory**. Messner and Rosenfeld agree with Merton's view that the success goal is pervasive in American culture. They refer to this as the American Dream, a term they employ as both a goal and a process. As a goal, the **American Dream** involves accumulating material goods and wealth via open individual competition. As a process, it involves both being socialized to pursue material success and believing that prosperity is an achievable goal in American culture. In the United States, the capitalist system encourages innovation in pursuit of monetary rewards.

institutional anomie theory The view that anomie pervades U.S. culture because the drive for material wealth dominates and undermines social and community values.

American Dream The goal of accumulating material goods and wealth through individual competition; the process of being socialized to pursue material success and to believe it is achievable.

Businesspeople such as Mitt Romney, Bill Gates, Jeff Bezos, Warren Buffett, Mark Zuckerberg, and Donald Trump are admired as pundits, authorities and leaders; they are often considered as possible (or actual, in Romney's case) presidential candidates.

Anomic conditions occur because the desire to succeed at any cost drives people apart, weakens the collective sense of community, fosters ambition, and restricts desires to achieve anything that is not material wealth. Achieving a "good name" and respect is not sufficient. Capitalist culture "exerts pressures toward crime by encouraging an anomic cultural environment, an environment in which people are encouraged to adopt an 'anything goes' mentality in the pursuit of personal goals … the anomic pressures inherent in the American Dream are nourished and sustained by an institutional balance of power dominated by the economy."[143]

What is distinct about American society, according to Messner and Rosenfeld, and what most likely determines the exceedingly high national crime rate, is that anomic conditions have been allowed to "develop to such an extraordinary degree."[144] There do not seem to be any alternatives that would serve the same purpose or strive for the same goal.

Impact of Anomie Why does anomie pervade American culture? According to Messner and Rosenfeld, it is because capitalist culture promotes intense pressures for economic success. Prosocial, noneconomic institutions that might otherwise control the exaggerated emphasis on financial success, such as religious or charitable institutions, have been rendered powerless or obsolete. As a result, the value structure of society is dominated by economic realities that weaken institutional social control. In other words, people are so interested in making money that their behavior cannot be controlled by the needs of family or the restraints of morality.

There are three reasons social institutions have been undermined. First, noneconomic functions and roles have been devalued. Performance in other institutional settings— the family, school, or community—is assigned a lower priority than the goal of financial success. Few students go to college to study the classics; most want to major in a field with good job prospects. Second, when conflicts emerge, noneconomic roles become subordinate to and must accommodate economic roles. The schedules, routines, and demands of the workplace take priority over those of the home, the school, the community, and other aspects of social life. A parent given the opportunity for a promotion thinks nothing of uprooting his family and moving them to another part of the country. And third, economic language, standards, and norms penetrate into noneconomic realms. Economic terms become part of the common vernacular.

general strain theory (GST) According to Agnew, the view that multiple sources of strain interact with an individual's emotional traits and responses to produce criminality.

People want to get to the "bottom line"; spouses view themselves as "partners" who "manage" the household. Retired people say they want to "downsize" their household; we "outsource" home repairs instead of doing them ourselves. Corporate leaders run for public office promising to "run the country like a business." People join social clubs to make connections and "network," not to make close friends.

According to Messner and Rosenfeld, the relatively high U.S. crime rates can be explained by the interrelationship between culture and institutions. The dominance of the American Dream mythology ensures that many people will develop wishes and desires for material goods that cannot be satisfied by legitimate means. People are willing to do anything to get ahead, from cheating on tests to get higher grades to engaging in corporate fraud and tax evasion.[145] Those who cannot succeed become willing to risk everything, including a prison sentence.

The American Dream mythos may have a different effect on people depending on their place in the social structure. In their analysis of survey data, Stephen Cernkovich and his associates found that the American Dream mythology had a greater effect on whites than African Americans. Cernkovich reasons that whites may have greater expectations of material success than African Americans, whose aspirations have been tempered by a long history of racial and economic deprivation. When whites experience strain, they are more apt to react with anger and antisocial behavior.[146]

At the institutional level, the dominance of economic concerns weakens the informal social control exerted by the family, church, and school. These institutions have lost their ability to regulate behavior and have instead become a conduit for promoting material success. Parents push their kids to succeed at any cost; schools encourage kids to get into the best colleges; religious institutions promote their wealth and power.[147] Crime rates may rise even in a healthy economy because national prosperity heightens the attractiveness of monetary rewards, encouraging people to gain financial success by any means possible, including illegal ones. Meanwhile, the importance of social institutions as a means of exerting social control is reduced. In this "culture of competition," self-interest prevails and generates amorality, acceptance of inequality, and disdain for the less fortunate.[148]

The Messner-Rosenfeld version of anomie strain may be a blueprint for crime-reduction strategies: if citizens are provided with an economic safety net, they may be able to resist the influence of economic deprivation and commit less crime. Nations that provide such resources—welfare, pension benefits, health care—have significantly lower crime rates.[149] In contrast, crime and violence rates are highest in nations that experience high levels of income inequality.[150]

General Strain Theory

Sociologist Robert Agnew's **general strain theory (GST)** helps identify the social-psychological, individual-level influences that produce strain. Whereas structural, macro-level strain theories explain how interclass socioeconomic differences produce strain and anomie in the lower class, Agnew sees strain as an individual phenomenon. People of any class can feel stress and strain and are then more likely to commit crimes. Agnew therefore offers a more general explanation of criminal activity: it can occur among all elements of society if they experience stress-producing events.[151] If members of the lower class commit more crime, it's because strain is a product of a lower-class lifestyle. Kids growing up poor in a gang-infested community are bound to experience more strain than their wealthier peers being raised in affluent suburban neighborhoods. According to Agnew, the greater the intensity and frequency of strain experiences, the greater their impact and the more likely they are to cause criminality. Each type of strain will increase the likelihood of experiencing such negative emotions as disappointment, depression, fear, and, most important, anger. Anger increases perceptions of being wronged and produces a desire for revenge, energizes individuals to take action, and lowers inhibitions. Violence and aggression seem justified if you have been wronged and are righteously angry.

Because it produces these emotions, strain can be considered a predisposing factor for criminality when it is chronic and repetitive and creates a hostile, suspicious, and aggressive attitude. Individual strain episodes may serve as a situational event or trigger that produces crime, such as when a particularly stressful event ignites a violent reaction. Strain may predispose people toward antisocial behaviors rather than cause them to commit a specific act to relieve strain. So the person who feels strain because of financial need may be as likely to beat up a rival as he is to rob a liquor store.[152]

LO9 Clarify the concept of negative affective states

Causes of Strain Agnew suggests that criminality is the direct result of **negative affective states**—the anger, frustration, and adverse emotions that emerge in the wake of negative and destructive social relationships. He finds that negative affective states are produced by a variety of sources of strain (Figure 6.7):

- *Failure to achieve positively valued goals.* This category of strain, similar to what Merton speaks of in his theory of anomie, is a result of the disjunction between aspirations and expectations. This type of strain occurs when people aspire for wealth and fame, but, lacking financial and educational resources, assume that such goals are impossible to achieve. These people, racked by despair, who feel few opportunities for success, are at risk for crime.[153]

  The failure to achieve is relative. Some very successful people may consider themselves failures. When people compare themselves to peers who seem to be doing a lot better financially or socially (such as making more money or getting better grades), even those doing relatively well feel strain. For example, when a high school senior is accepted at a good college but not a "prestige school" like some of her friends, she will feel strain. Perhaps she is not being treated fairly because the "playing field" is tilted against her; "other kids have connections,"

negative affective states According to Agnew, anger, depression, disappointment, fear, and other adverse emotions that derive from strain.

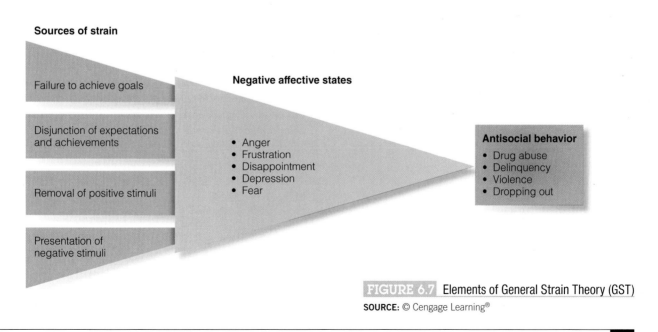

FIGURE 6.7 Elements of General Strain Theory (GST)

SOURCE: © Cengage Learning®

she may say. Perceiving inequity may result in adverse reactions, ranging from running away from its source to lowering the benefits of others through physical attacks or vandalizing their property. Strain then can also be produced when there is a disjunction between expectations and achievements.

- *Removal of positively valued stimuli.* Strain may occur because of the actual or anticipated removal or loss of a positively valued stimulus from the individual. Divorce, romantic breakup, the loss of a friend who moves away, and the death of a loved one can all produce strain.[154] The loss of positive stimuli may lead to criminality when a person tries to prevent the loss, retrieve what has been lost, obtain substitutes, or seek revenge against those responsible for the loss.[155]

  The effect of removal of positive stimuli may be class bound. Middle-class people may be less able to cope with the removal of positive stimuli. When you are expected to succeed because of your class position, failure may be harder to swallow; those who have limited opportunities and lower expectations may be able to take failure in stride.[156]

- *Presentation of negative stimuli.* Strain is also produced by the application of negative or noxious stimuli. Included within this category are painful social interactions such as child abuse and neglect.[157] Stressful life events ranging from unemployment to crime victimization can produce strain that may develop into angry emotionality and subsequent antisocial behaviors.[158] Nor is the effect of negative stimuli a one-shot deal: victims forced to continually interact with the source of negative stimuli (the school yard bully, the abusive parent, the demanding boss) may find that the cumulative effects of strain are overwhelming; negative affective states experienced in childhood can follow a person to the grave.[159]

Sources of Strain

There are a variety of sources of strain. Sometimes it can be a particular individual who is causing problems, such as a peer group rival. When individuals identify a target to blame for their problems, they are more likely to respond with retaliatory action (for example, "Joe stole my wife away by lying about me, so I beat him up!"). Sometimes the source of strain is difficult to pinpoint (for example, "I feel depressed because of the way the world is going"); this type of ambiguous strain is unlikely to produce an aggressive response.

Social Sources of Strain People may begin to feel strain because of their membership in a peer or social group. The relationship may be reciprocal. People who report feelings of stress and anger are more likely to interact with others who are similarly stressed out.[160] Peer group membership has its benefits, such as friendship, companionship, and support, but such groups also force members into behavior patterns (such as using drugs) that can be the source of unwelcome stress. Feelings of strain and being overwhelmed may become magnified as individuals attempt to comply with peer group demands. People may, for example, get involved in an unwanted shoplifting spree to pay for drugs, creating even more stress in their lives.[161] Experiments show that people who perceive strain because they are being treated unfairly report (1) high levels of situational anger that lead to (2) higher levels of theft from an employer.[162] People who live in strain-producing social conditions are more likely to cope with their negative emotions through crime.[163]

Adolescent Sources of Strain Crime peaks during late adolescence because this is a period of social stress caused by the weakening of parental supervision and the development of relationships with a diverse peer group. Because many families are unstable, kids going through the trauma of family breakup and frequent changes in family structure find themselves feeling a high degree of strain. Some may react by becoming involved in precocious sexuality or by turning to substance abuse to mask the strain.[164] Adolescence is also a period during which hormone levels peak, and the behavior moderating aspects of the brain have not fully developed—two factors that make adolescents susceptible to environmental sources of strain.[165]

As they mature, children's expectations increase; some find that they are unable to meet academic and social demands. Adolescents are very concerned about their standing with peers. Those deficient in these areas may find they are social outcasts, another source of strain. While positive peer influence may help adolescents cope with stress, those who turn for help and guidance from peers who themselves are involved in criminality place themselves at risk to crime.[166]

Community Sources of Strain The GST generally focuses on individual-level sources of strain, yet there are distinct ecological variations in the crime rate. Some regions, cities, and neighborhoods are more crime prone than others. Can ecological differences produce "negative affective states" in large segments of the population, which account for these differences? Agnew suggests that there are, in fact, community-level factors, such as blocked opportunities and lack of social support, that produce feelings of strain. According to Agnew, communities contribute to strain in several ways:

- They influence the goals people pursue and the ability people have to meet these goals.
- They influence feelings of relative deprivation and exposure to aversive stimuli, including family conflict, incivility, and economic deprivation.
- They influence the likelihood that angry, strain-filled individuals will interact with one another.

Consequently, not only does GST predict deviance on an individual level, but it can also account for community-level differences in the crime rate.

Coping with Strain

Not all people who experience strain fall into a life of crime and eventually resort to criminality. Some are able to marshal their emotional, mental, and behavioral resources to cope with the anger and frustration produced by strain. Personal temperament, high self-esteem, and a strong self-image underpin the ability to cope.[167] In contrast, people who are impulsive and lack attachments to others are less able to cope than those who are bonded to others and maintain higher levels of self-control.[168] Those high in negative emotionality and low in constraint will be more likely to react to strain with antisocial behaviors.[169] In contrast, those people who can call on family, friends, and social institutions for help and support are better able to cope with strain.[170]

Some defenses are cognitive; individuals may be able to rationalize frustrating circumstances. Not getting the career they desire is "just not that important"; they may be poor, but the "next guy is worse off"; and if things didn't work out, then they "got what they deserved." Others seek behavioral solutions: they run away from adverse conditions or seek revenge against those who caused the strain. Others will try to regain emotional equilibrium with techniques ranging from physical exercise to drug abuse. Some may change their daily routine in order to avoid the negative influences that are causing emotional duress.[171]

Strain and Criminal Careers While some people can effectively cope with strain, others cannot and may turn to antisocial acts to help them relieve the pressures produced by negative affective states. Although it may be socially disapproved, criminality can provide relief and satisfaction for someone living an otherwise stress-filled life. Who is most likely to use crime to cope with strain? GST recognizes that certain people have traits that may make them particularly sensitive to strain.[172] These include an explosive temperament, being overly sensitive or emotional, low tolerance for adversity, and poor problem-solving skills.[173]

Agnew created the concept of storylines to help explain how people deal with the stressors of everyday life. This concept is discussed in the Criminology in Action feature.

CONNECTIONS

Explaining continuity and change in offending rates over the life course has become an important goal of criminologists. Analysis of latent trait and life course theories in Chapter 9 provides some recent thinking on this topic.

Evaluating GST

Agnew's work is important because it both clarifies the concept of strain and directs future research agendas. The model has been shown to predict crime and deviance within a number of subject, racial, gender, and age groups and in different cultures and nations.[174] It also addresses the dynamic nature of criminal behavior: levels of strain vary over the life course and so do crime rates. As levels of strain increase, so does involvement in antisocial activities; as strain levels decrease, so do individual crime rates. Feelings of strain then appear to play a key role in offending continuity and change.[175]

One of the biggest question marks about GST is its ability to adequately explain gender differences in the crime rate. Females experience as much or more strain, frustration, and anger as males, but their crime rate is much lower. Is it possible that there are gender differences either (a) in the relationship between strain and criminality or (b) in the ability to cope with the effects of strain? Not all sources of strain produce the anger envisioned by Agnew.[176] Although females may experience more strain, males may be more deeply affected by interpersonal stress.[177]

There is evidence that stress influences both males and females equally; however, the degree to which it leads to criminal behavior is much higher among males than females.[178] When presented with similar types of strain, males and females respond with a different constellation of negative emotions. Females may be socialized to internalize stress, blaming themselves for their problems; males may take the same type of strain and relieve it by striking out at others and deflecting criticism with aggression.[179] Consequently, males may resort to criminality in the face of stressors of any magnitude, but only extreme levels of strain produce violent reactions from women.[180] Males may also seek out their peers when they are faced with strain, whereas females are less inclined to confide in others. Male bonding with peers may actually increase their involvement with deviant behavior, a risk that is avoided by females. More effort is certainly needed to understand the cross-gender impact of strain.[181]

These issues aside, general strain theory has proven to be an enduring vision of the cause of criminality. Researchers have continued to show that people who perceive strain are the ones most likely to engage in delinquent activity.[182] Concept Summary 6.2 sets out the features of strain theory.

To read more about the work of Émile Durkheim, go to **http://durkheim.uchicago.edu/Biography.html.**
Do you agree with Durkheim that crime is "normal"?

Criminologist Robert Agnew has identified a concept—storylines—to help explain why people commit crimes. He finds that when criminals are asked why they offend, they typically tell a story explaining why they engaged in crime. These stories describe the stressful events and conditions leading up to the crime and how they dealt with the pressure and strain. Very often it is some unusual or unplanned event that led them to feel strain and resort to criminal actions to solve their problems: they were insulted by a rival and sought revenge; they lost money gambling and, needing to pay off their debt, had to commit a burglary; some guy was hitting on their girl so they were forced to give them a beatdown. A storyline is a temporally limited, interrelated set of events and conditions that increases the likelihood that individuals will engage in a crime or a series of related crimes.

Storylines begin with a particular event; that is, "something happens" that is upsetting. This event affects the characteristics of the individual, leads to increased feelings of strain, and alters their associations and interactions. The feeling was temporary; they may claim "that's not really like me." They turn into a new person—jealous, angry, desperate, violent—that is out of character. The storyline ends when some event restores the individual's normal level of functioning, ending the temporary drama in their lives.

What are some typical stories that are told?

- *A Desperate Need for Money.* Offenders often report that they engage in crime during those periods when something has happened that creates a temporary but desperate need for money, and the individual believes that there are no good legitimate options for obtaining such money. Usually cited for this turn of events are unexpected expenses, poor budgeting between paydays, temporary employment problems, the temporary loss of other sources of financial support, demands that debts be repaid, gambling losses, drug binges, or the pressure to pay legal fines or fees. So this storyline might go: "I knew the Knicks were going to beat the Celtics, so I borrowed $500 for a bet, and then they lost on a lucky shot. I had to pay the loan back so I stole my brother-in-law's plasma TV and sold it on the street."

- *An Unresolved Dispute.* This storyline begins when someone does or says something that the individual does not like, or challenges and/or threatens a core identity value or status. The individual experiences one or more negative emotions, such as anger and humiliation, and then finds someone to blame for this negative treatment. This type of storyline often has a romantic twist: "I thought someone was hitting on my girl, because she was acting very strange. I thought she was trying to hook up with someone and I was really upset. Then I saw this guy with her. I was afraid she was going to be unfaithful, so I hit him in the face with a pipe."

- *A Brief but Close Involvement with a Criminal Other(s).* Individuals often develop close associations with criminal others over long periods of time, but sometimes the associations are more fleeting—lasting only hours, days, or weeks. This storyline can have a number of elements. The individual gets involved with another individual or group who entices them into committing a crime they would never have committed on their own. Success in a crime might lead to invitations for other crimes. Using this storyline, a person might say, "I was in a bar drinking when these guys I met told me that I could get some great weed for only $100 an ounce. I usually don't do things like that, but the price seemed so good I couldn't pass it up."

- *A Brief, Tempting Opportunity for Crime.* Individuals may develop or encounter tempting opportunities for crime that last from several hours to weeks. Being tempted means that the cost of crime is perceived as being low while the benefits are high and that this advantaged circumstance will persist for some time. This storyline might be, "I know this guy who is working as a security guard in an electronics store. He will sell me video games for $10 each that I know I can peddle on the street for $30. He can get me 50 games next week. Why pass up an easy $1,000? And besides, I can't get in trouble because I didn't really take the stuff myself."

Of course, individuals may experience more than one storyline at a time, each one contributing to or influencing another: a kid runs away from home, creating a desperate need for money; this gets him into disputes with other kids on the street, putting him in temporary contact with antisocial peers, and creates tempting opportunities for crime.

Agnew believes that storylines are the key to understanding the immediate cause of crime. The ebb and flow of storylines, partly a function of luck and chance, help explain why some people commit crime, then stop, only to start again. They also help us understand the context of crime, why it occurs in some situations and not others. A person may commit a violent act when he or she is in the midst of a domestic crisis, but resolve the same situation peacefully at another point in his or her life.

Critical Thinking

1. What storylines do college students use when they cheat on tests? Smoke pot? Get drunk at a frat party? Are they similar to Agnew's vision?
2. If people use storylines to get involved in crime, are there ones that prevent or inhibit illegal activities?

SOURCE: Robert Agnew, "Storylines as a Neglected Cause of Crime," *Journal of Research in Crime and Delinquency* 43 (2006): 119–147.

Theory	Major Premise	Strengths	Research Focus
Anomie theory	People who adopt the goals of society but lack the means to attain them seek alternatives, such as crime.	Points out how competition for success creates conflict and crime. Suggests that social conditions and not personality can account for crime. Explains high lower-class crime rates.	Frustration; anomie; effects of failure to achieve goals.
Institutional anomie theory	The desire to accumulate wealth and material goods pervades all aspects of American life.	Explains why crime rates are so high in American culture.	Frustration; effects of materialism.
General strain theory	Strain has a variety of sources. Strain causes crime in the absence of adequate coping mechanisms.	Identifies the complexities of strain in modern society. Expands on anomie theory. Shows the influence of social events on behavior over the life course. Explains middle-class crimes.	Strain; inequality; negative affective states; influence of negative and positive stimuli.

concept summary

CULTURAL DEVIANCE THEORIES

LO10 Differentiate between the different forms of cultural deviance theory

The third branch of social structure theory combines the effects of social disorganization and strain to explain how people living in deteriorated neighborhoods react to social isolation and economic deprivation. Because their lifestyle is draining, frustrating, and dispiriting, members of the lower class create an independent **subculture** with its own set of rules and values. Middle-class culture stresses hard work, delayed gratification, formal education, and being cautious; the lower-class subculture stresses excitement, toughness, risk taking, fearlessness, immediate gratification, and "street smarts." The lower-class subculture is an attractive alternative because the urban poor find that it is impossible to meet the behavioral demands of middle-class society.

Unfortunately, subcultural norms often clash with conventional values. People who have close personal ties to the neighborhood, especially when they are to deviant networks such as gangs and criminal groups, may find that community norms interfere with their personal desire for neighborhood improvement. So when the police are trying to solve a gang-related killing, neighbors may find that their loyalty to the gang boy and his family outweighs their desire to create a more stable crime-free community by giving information to the police.

Conduct Norms

The concept that the lower class develops a unique culture in response to strain can be traced to Thorsten Sellin's classic 1938 work, *Culture Conflict and Crime*, a theoretical attempt to link cultural adaptation to criminality.[183] Sellin's main premise is that criminal law is an expression of the rules of the dominant culture. The content of the law, therefore, may create a clash between conventional, middle-class rules and splinter groups, such as ethnic and racial minorities who are excluded from the social mainstream. These groups maintain their own set of **conduct norms**—rules governing the day-to-day living conditions within these subcultures.[184] Conduct norms can be found in almost any culture and are not the property of any particular group, culture, or political structure.

Complicating matters is the fact that most of us belong to several social groups. In a complex society, the number of groups people belong to—family, peer, occupational, and religious—is quite large. "A conflict of norms is said to exist when more or less divergent rules of conduct govern the specific life situation in which a person may find himself."[185] According to Sellin, **culture conflict** occurs when the rules expressed in the criminal law clash with the demands of group conduct norms. To make his point, Sellin

subcultures Groups that are loosely part of the dominant culture but maintain a unique set of values, beliefs, and traditions.

conduct norms Behaviors expected of social group members. If group norms conflict with those of the general culture, members of the group may find themselves described as outcasts or criminals.

culture conflict According to Sellin, a condition brought about when the rules and norms of an individual's subcultural affiliation conflict with the role demands of conventional society.

cited the case of a Sicilian father in New Jersey who killed the 16-year-old boy who seduced his daughter and then expressed surprise at being arrested. He claimed that he had "merely defended his family honor in a traditional way."[186]

Focal Concerns

In his classic 1958 paper, "Lower Class Culture as a Generating Milieu of Gang Delinquency," Walter Miller identified the unique value system that defines lower-class culture.[187] Conformance to these **focal concerns** dominates life among the lower class. According to Miller, clinging to lower-class focal concerns promotes illegal or violent behavior. Toughness may mean displaying fighting prowess; street smarts may lead to drug deals; excitement may result in drinking, gambling, or drug abuse. Focal concerns do not necessarily represent a rebellion against middle-class values; rather, these values have evolved specifically to fit conditions in lower-class areas. The major lower-class focal concerns are set out in Exhibit 6.1.[188]

It is this adherence to the prevailing cultural demands of lower-class society that causes urban crime. Research, in fact, shows that members of the lower class value toughness and want to show they are courageous in the face of provocation.[189] A reputation for toughness helps them acquire social power while at the same time insulating them from becoming victims. Violence is also seen as a means to acquire the accouterments of wealth (nice clothes, flashy cars, or access to clubs), control or humiliate another person, defy authority, settle drug-related "business" disputes, attain retribution, satisfy the need for thrills or risk taking, and respond to challenges to one's manhood.[190]

To some criminologists, the influence of lower-class focal concerns and culture seems as relevant today as when first identified by Miller more than 50 years ago. The Race, Culture, Gender, and Criminology feature "The Code of the Streets" discusses a recent version of the concept of cultural deviance.

Theory of Delinquent Subcultures

Albert Cohen first articulated the theory of delinquent subcultures in his classic 1955 book *Delinquent Boys*.[191] Cohen's central position was that delinquent behavior of lower-class youths is actually a protest against the norms and values of middle-class U.S. culture. Because social conditions make them incapable of achieving success legitimately, lower-class youths experience a form of culture conflict that Cohen

focal concerns According to Miller, the value orientations of lower-class cultures; features include the needs for excitement, trouble, smartness, and personal autonomy.

status frustration A form of culture conflict experienced by lower-class youths because social conditions prevent them from achieving success as defined by the larger society.

EXHIBIT 6.1
Miller's Lower-Class Focal Concerns

Trouble

In lower-class communities, people are evaluated by their actual or potential involvement in making trouble. Getting into trouble includes such behavior as fighting, drinking, and sexual misconduct. Dealing with trouble can confer prestige—for example, when a man establishes a reputation for being able to handle himself well in a fight. Not being able to handle trouble, and having to pay the consequences, can make a person look foolish and incompetent.

Toughness

Lower-class males want local recognition of their physical and spiritual toughness. They refuse to be sentimental or soft and instead value physical strength, fighting ability, and athletic skill. Those who cannot meet these standards risk getting a reputation for being weak, inept, and effeminate.

Smartness

Smartness involves maintaining an image of being streetwise and savvy, using street smarts, and having the ability to outfox and out-con an opponent. Though formal education is not admired, knowing essential survival techniques, such as having money without actually working, conning, and outsmarting the law, is a requirement.

Excitement

Excitement involves the ongoing search for fun and stimulation to enliven an otherwise drab existence. The search for excitement may lead to gambling, fighting, getting drunk, and sexual adventures. In between, the lower-class citizen may simply "hang out" and "be cool."

Fate

Lower-class citizens believe their lives are in the hands of strong spiritual forces that guide their destinies. Getting lucky, finding good fortune, and hitting the jackpot are all slum dwellers' daily dreams.

Autonomy

Being independent of authority figures, such as the police, teachers, and parents, is required. Losing control is an unacceptable weakness, incompatible with toughness.

SOURCE: Walter Miller, "Lower-Class Culture as a Generating Milieu of Gang Delinquency," *Journal of Social Issues* 14 (1958): 5–19.

labels **status frustration**.[192] As a result, many of them join together in gangs and engage in behavior that is "nonutilitarian, malicious, and negativistic."[193]

Cohen viewed the delinquent gang as a separate subculture, possessing a value system directly opposed to that of the larger society. He describes the subculture as one that "takes its norms from the larger culture, but turns them upside down. The delinquent's conduct is right by the standards of his subculture precisely because it is wrong by the norms of the larger culture."[194]

THE CODE OF THE STREETS

a widely cited view of the interrelationship of culture and behavior is Elijah Anderson's concept of the "code of the streets." He sees that life circumstances are tough for the "ghetto poor"—lack of jobs that pay a living wage, stigma of race, fallout from rampant drug use and drug trafficking, and alienation and lack of hope for the future. Living in such an environment places young people at special risk of crime and deviant behavior.

There are two cultural forces running through the neighborhood that shape their reactions. *Decent values* are taught by families committed to middle-class values and representing mainstream goals and standards of behavior. Though they may be better off financially than some of their street-oriented neighbors, they are generally "working poor." They value hard work and self-reliance and are willing to sacrifice for their families; they harbor hopes for a better future for their children. Most go to church and take a strong interest in education. Some see their difficult situation as a test from God and derive great support from their faith and from the church community.

In opposition, *street values* are born in the despair of inner-city life and are in opposition to those of mainstream society. The street culture has developed what Anderson calls a code of the streets, a set of informal rules setting down both proper attitudes and ways to respond if challenged. If the rules are violated, there are penalties and sometimes violent retribution.

At the heart of the code is the issue of respect—loosely defined as being "treated right." The code demands that disrespect be punished or hard-won respect will be lost. With the right amount of respect, a person can avoid being bothered in public. If he is bothered, not only may he be in physical danger, but he has been disgraced or "dissed" (disrespected). Some forms of

dissing, such as maintaining eye contact for too long, may seem pretty mild. But to street kids who live by the code, these actions become serious indications of the other person's intentions and a warning of imminent physical confrontation.

These two orientations—decent and street—socially organize the community. Their coexistence means that kids who are brought up in decent homes must be able to successfully navigate the demands of the street culture. Even in decent families, parents recognize that the code must be obeyed or at the very least negotiated; it cannot simply be ignored.

The Respect Game

Young men in poor inner-city neighborhoods build their self-image on the foundation of respect. Having "juice" (as respect is sometimes called on the street) means that they can take care of themselves even if it means resorting to violence. For street youth, losing respect on the street can be damaging and dangerous. Once they have demonstrated that they can be insulted, beaten up, or stolen from, they become an easy target. Kids from decent families may be able to keep their self-respect by getting good grades or a scholarship. Street kids do not have that luxury. With nothing to fall back on, they cannot walk away from an insult. They must retaliate with violence.

One method of preventing attacks is to go on the offensive. Aggressive, violence-prone people are not seen as easy prey. Robbers do not get robbed, and street fighters are not the favorite targets of bullies. A youth who communicates an image of not being afraid to die and not being afraid to kill has given himself a sense of power on the street.

Testing the Theory

Anderson's work has been well received by the criminological community. A number of researchers have found that the "code of the streets" does in fact

exist and that Anderson's observations are in fact valid. Jeffery Fagan found that the street code's rules for getting and maintaining respect through aggressive behavior forced many "decent" youths to situationally adopt a tough demeanor and perhaps behave violently in order to survive an otherwise hostile and possibly dangerous environment. Similarly, Eric Stewart and Ronald Simons find that adolescents living in urban neighborhoods are often forced to accept the street code even if it violates their own personal values and attitudes. Failure to do so threatens their life and well-being. In another recent study Kristy Matsuda and her associates found that kids who join a gang also increase their street code–related attitudes and emotions. Those whose loyalty to the code of the streets is the greatest also experience the greatest frequency of violent offending. In sum, the weight of the evidence supports the validity of Anderson's groundbreaking research.

Critical Thinking

1. Does the code of the street, as described by Anderson, apply in the neighborhood in which you were raised? That is, is it universal?
2. Is there a form of "respect game" being played out on college campuses? If so, what is the substitute for violence?

SOURCES: Elijah Anderson, *Code of the Street: Decency, Violence, and the Moral Life of the Inner City* (New York: Norton, 2000); Elijah Anderson, "Violence and the Inner-City Street Code," in *Violence and Children in the Inner City,* ed. Joan McCord (New York: Cambridge University Press, 1998), pp. 1–30; Elijah Anderson, "The Code of the Streets," *Atlantic Monthly* 273 (May 1994): 80–94; Eric Stewart and Ronald Simons, "Race, Code of the Street, and Violent Delinquency: A Multilevel Investigation of Neighborhood Street Culture and Individual Norms of Violence," *Criminology* 482 (2010): 569–606; Eric Stewart and Ronald Simons, "Structure and Culture in African American Adolescent Violence: A Partial Test of the 'Code of the Street' Thesis," *Justice Quarterly* 23 (2006): 1–33; Jeffrey Fagan, "Adolescent Violence: A View from the Street," NIJ Research Preview (Washington, DC: National Institute of Justice, 1998).

Cultural deviance theory maintains that gang activity is a function of lack of opportunity that leads to an alternative lifestyle, often with tragic results. Here, a fight breaks out near mourners lining up before the funeral of Hadiya Pendleton, who was fatally shot on January 29, 2013, in what police say was a case of mistaken identity in a gang turf war. Pendleton, 15 and a sophomore at Martin Luther King Jr. College Prep, was shot as she and her friends shielded themselves from rain under a canopy in a Chicago park. She had performed with her school band eight days earlier at President Barack Obama's inauguration.

John Gress/Reuters/Landov

teaching children the necessary techniques for entering the dominant middle-class culture. The consequences of this deprivation include developmental handicaps, poor speech and communication skills, and inability to delay gratification.

Middle-Class Measuring Rods   One significant handicap that lower-class children face is the inability to positively impress authority figures, such as teachers, employers, or supervisors. Cohen calls the standards set by these authority figures **middle-class measuring rods**. The conflict and frustration lower-class youths experience when they fail to meet these standards is a primary cause of delinquency. For example, the fact that a lower-class student is deemed by those in power to be substandard or below the average of what is expected can have an important impact on his or her future life chances. A school record may be reviewed by juvenile court authorities and by the military. Because a military record can influence whether or not someone is qualified for certain jobs, it is quite influential.[195] Negative evaluations become part of a permanent file that follows an individual for the rest of his or her life. When he or she wants to improve, evidence of prior failures is used to discourage advancement.

According to Cohen, the development of the delinquent subculture is a consequence of socialization practices found in the ghetto or inner-city environment. These children lack the basic skills necessary to achieve social and economic success in the demanding U.S. society. They also lack the proper education and therefore do not have the skills upon which to build a knowledge or socialization foundation. He suggests that lower-class parents are incapable of

The Formation of Deviant Subcultures   Cohen believes lower-class boys who suffer rejection by middle-class decision makers usually elect to join one of three existing subcultures: the corner boy, the college boy, or the delinquent boy. The **corner boy** role is the most common response to middle-class rejection. The corner boy is not a chronic delinquent, but may be a truant who engages in petty or status offenses, such as precocious sex and recreational drug abuse. His main loyalty is to his peer group, on which he depends for support, motivation, and interest. His values, therefore, are those of the group with which he is in close personal contact. The corner boy, well aware of his failure to achieve the standards of the American Dream, retreats into the comforting world of his lower-class peers and eventually becomes a stable member of his neighborhood, holding a menial job, marrying, and remaining in the community.

The **college boy** embraces the cultural and social values of the middle class. Rather than scorning middle-class

middle-class measuring rods   According to Cohen, the standards by which teachers and other representatives of state authority evaluate lower-class youths. Because they cannot live up to middle-class standards, lower-class youths are bound for failure, which gives rise to frustration and anger at conventional society.

corner boy   According to Cohen, a role in the lower-class culture in which young men remain in their birth neighborhood, acquire families and menial jobs, and adjust to the demands of their environment.

college boy   A disadvantaged youth who embraces the cultural and social values of the middle class and actively strives to be successful by those standards. This type of youth is embarking on an almost hopeless path because he is ill-equipped academically, socially, and linguistically to achieve the rewards of middle-class life.

measuring rods, he actively strives to be successful by those standards. Cohen views this type of youth as one who is embarking on an almost hopeless path, since he is ill-equipped academically, socially, and linguistically to achieve the rewards of middle-class life.

The **delinquent boy** adopts a set of norms and principles in direct opposition to middle-class values. He engages in short-run hedonism, living for today and letting "tomorrow take care of itself."[196] Delinquent boys strive for group autonomy. They resist efforts by family, school, or other sources of authority to control their behavior. They may join a gang because it is perceived as autonomous, independent, and the focus of "attraction, loyalty, and solidarity."[197] Frustrated by their inability to succeed, these boys resort to a process Cohen calls **reaction formation**. Symptoms of reaction formation include overly intense responses that seem disproportionate to the stimuli that trigger them. For the delinquent boy, this takes the form of irrational, malicious, and unaccountable hostility to the enemy, which in this case are "the norms of respectable middle-class society."[198] Reaction formation causes delinquent boys to overreact to any perceived threat or slight. They sneer at the college boy's attempts at assimilation and scorn the corner boy's passivity. The delinquent boy is willing to take risks, violate the law, and flout middle-class conventions.

Cohen's work helps explain the factors that promote and sustain a delinquent subculture. By introducing the concepts of status frustration and middle-class measuring rods, Cohen makes it clear that social forces and not individual traits promote and sustain a delinquent career. By introducing the corner boy, college boy, delinquent boy triad, he helps explain why many lower-class youth fail to become chronic offenders: there is more than one social path open to indigent youth.[199] His work is a skillful integration of strain and social disorganization theories and has become an enduring element of the criminological literature.

Theory of Differential Opportunity

In their classic work *Delinquency and Opportunity*, written more than 50 years ago, Richard Cloward and Lloyd Ohlin combined strain and social disorganization principles into a portrayal of a gang-sustaining criminal subculture.[200] Cloward and Ohlin agreed with Cohen and found that independent delinquent subcultures exist within society. They consider a delinquent subculture to be one in which certain forms of delinquent activity are essential requirements for performing the dominant roles supported by the subculture.[201]

Youth gangs are an important part of the delinquent subculture. Although not all illegal acts are committed by gang youth, they are the source of the most serious, sustained, and costly criminal behaviors. Delinquent gangs spring up in disorganized areas where youths lack the opportunity to gain success through conventional means. True to strain theory principles, Cloward and Ohlin portray inner-city kids as individuals who want to conform to middle-class values but lack the means to do so.[202]

Differential Opportunities The centerpiece of the Cloward and Ohlin theory is the concept of **differential opportunity**, which states that people in all strata of society share the same success goals but that those in the lower class have limited means of achieving them. People who perceive themselves as failures within conventional society will seek alternative or innovative ways to gain success. People who conclude that there is little hope for advancement by legitimate means may join with like-minded peers to form a gang. Gang members provide the emotional support to handle the shame, fear, or guilt they may develop while engaging in illegal acts. Delinquent subcultures then reward these acts that conventional society would punish. The youth who is considered a failure at school and is only qualified for a menial job at a minimum wage can earn thousands of dollars plus the respect of his or her peers by joining a gang and engaging in drug deals or armed robberies.

Cloward and Ohlin recognize that the opportunity for both successful conventional and criminal careers is limited. In stable areas, adolescents may be recruited by professional criminals, drug traffickers, or organized crime groups. Unstable areas, however, cannot support flourishing criminal opportunities. In these socially disorganized neighborhoods, adult role models are absent, and young criminals have few opportunities to join established gangs or to learn the fine points of professional crime. Cloward and Ohlin's most important finding, then, is that all opportunities for success, both illegal and conventional, are closed for the most truly disadvantaged youth.

Because of differential opportunity, kids are likely to join one of three types of gangs:

- *Criminal gangs.* Criminal gangs exist in stable lower-class areas in which close connections among adolescent, young adult, and adult offenders create an environment for successful criminal enterprise.[203] Youths are recruited into established criminal gangs that provide a

---

delinquent boy A youth who adopts a set of norms and principles in direct opposition to middle-class values, engaging in short-run hedonism, living for today and letting tomorrow take care of itself.

reaction formation According to Cohen, rejecting goals and standards that seem impossible to achieve. Because a boy cannot hope to get into college, for example, he considers higher education a waste of time.

differential opportunity The view that lower-class youths, whose legitimate opportunities are limited, join gangs and pursue criminal careers as alternative means to achieve universal success goals.

training ground for a successful criminal career. Gang membership provides a learning experience in which the knowledge and skills needed for success in crime are acquired. During this "apprenticeship stage," older, more experienced members of the criminal subculture hold youthful "trainees" on tight reins, limiting activities that might jeopardize the gang's profits (for example, engaging in nonfunctional, irrational violence). Over time, new recruits learn the techniques and attitudes of the criminal world and how to "cooperate successfully with others in criminal enterprises."[204] To become a fully accepted member of the criminal gang, novices must prove themselves reliable and dependable in their contacts with their criminal associates.

- *Conflict gangs.* Conflict gangs develop in communities unable to provide either legitimate or illegitimate opportunities. These highly disorganized areas are marked by transient residents and physical deterioration. Crime in this area is "individualistic, unorganized, petty, poorly paid, and unprotected."[205] There are no successful adult criminal role models from whom youths can learn criminal skills. When such severe limitations on both criminal and conventional opportunities intensify frustrations of the young, violence is used as a means of gaining status. The image of the conflict gang member is the swaggering, tough adolescent who fights with weapons to win respect from rivals and engages in unpredictable and destructive assaults on people and property. Conflict gang members must be ready to fight to protect their own and their gang's integrity and honor. By doing so, they acquire a "rep," which provides them with a means for gaining admiration from their peers and consequently helps them develop their own self-image. Conflict gangs, according to Cloward and Ohlin, "represent a way of securing access to the scarce resources for adolescent pleasure and opportunity in underprivileged areas."[206]

- *Retreatist gangs.* Retreatists are double failures, unable to gain success through legitimate means and unwilling to do so through illegal ones. Some retreatists have tried crime or violence but are too clumsy, weak, or scared to be accepted in criminal or violent gangs. They then retreat into a role on the fringe of society. Members of the retreatist subculture constantly search for ways of getting high—alcohol, pot, heroin, unusual sexual experiences, music. They

are always "cool," detached from relationships with the conventional world. To feed their habit, retreatists develop a "hustle"—pimping, conning, selling drugs, and committing petty crimes. Personal status in the retreatist subculture is derived from peer approval.

Evaluating Social Structure Theories

The social structure approach has significantly influenced both criminological theory and crime-prevention strategies. Its core concepts seem to be valid in view of the relatively high crime and delinquency rates and gang activity occurring in the deteriorated inner-city areas of the nation's largest cities.[207] The public's image of the disorganized inner city includes roaming bands of violent teenage gangs, drug users, prostitutes, muggers, and similar frightening examples of criminality. All of these are present today in inner-city areas.

Critics of the approach charge that we cannot be sure that it is lower-class culture itself that promotes crime and not some other force operating in society. They deny that residence in urban areas alone is sufficient to cause people to violate the law.[208] It is possible, they counter, that lower-class crime rates may be an artifact of bias in the criminal justice system. Numerous studies indicate that police use extensive discretion when arresting people and that social status is one factor that influences their decisions.[209] It is possible that adolescents in middle-class neighborhoods commit criminal acts that never show up in official statistics, whereas people in lower-class areas face a far greater chance of arrest and court adjudication.[210] In addition, police are more aggressive in lower-class areas and residents are more likely to be arrested and prosecuted for acts that would be

The Native Mob is one of the largest and most violent American Indian gangs in the United States, most active in Minnesota and Wisconsin but also in Michigan, North Dakota, and South Dakota. It is made up of mostly American Indian men and boys, and started in Minneapolis in the 1990s as members fought for turf to deal drugs. The Native Mob is also active in prison. In all, the Native Mob has about 200 members, with a structure that includes monthly meetings where members are encouraged to assault or kill enemies or anyone who shows disrespect. Three of the gang members, Arthur Francis Cree, William Earl Morris, and Wakinyon Wakan McArthur, are shown here. Authorities said McArthur would direct other members to carry out beatings, shootings, and other violent acts to intimidate rivals.

CULTURAL DEVIANCE THEORIES

Theory	Major Premise	Strengths	Research Focus
Miller's focal concern theory	Citizens who obey the street rules of lower-class life (focal concerns) find themselves in conflict with the dominant culture.	Identifies the core values of lower-class culture and shows their association to crime.	Cultural norms; focal concerns.
Cohen's theory of delinquent gangs	Status frustration of lower-class boys, created by their failure to achieve middle-class success, causes them to join gangs.	Shows how the conditions of lower-class life produce crime. Explains violence and destructive acts. Identifies conflict of lower class with middle class.	Gangs; culture conflict; middle-class measuring rods; reaction formation.
Cloward and Ohlin's theory of opportunity	Blockage of conventional opportunities causes lower-class youths to join criminal, conflict, or retreatist gangs.	Shows that even illegal opportunities are structured in society. Indicates why people become involved in a particular type of criminal activity. Presents a way of preventing crime.	Gangs; cultural norms; culture conflict; effects of blocked opportunity.

treated informally (for example, a warning) in middle-class suburbs. After all, police and prosecutors are members of the middle and upper classes themselves, so it's not surprising that they exhibit class and racial bias.[211]

Even if the higher crime rates recorded in lower-class areas are valid, it is still true that most members of the lower class are not criminals. The discovery of the chronic offender indicates that a significant majority of people living in lower-class environments are not criminals and that a relatively small proportion of the population commits most crimes. If social forces alone could be used to explain crime, how can we account for the vast number of urban poor who remain honest and law abiding? Given these circumstances, law violators must be motivated by some individual mental, physical, or social process or trait.[212]

It is also questionable whether a distinct lower-class culture actually exists. Several researchers have found that gang members and other delinquent youths seem to value middle-class concepts, such as sharing, earning money, and respecting the law, as highly as middle-class youths. Criminologists contend that lower-class youths also value education as highly as middle-class students do.[213] Public opinion polls can also be used as evidence that a majority of lower-class citizens maintain middle-class values. National surveys find that people in the lowest income brackets want tougher drug laws, more police protection, and greater control over criminal offenders.[214] These opinions seem similar to conventional middle-class values rather than representative of an independent, deviant subculture. While this evidence contradicts some of the central ideas of social structure theory, the discovery of stable patterns of lower-class crime, the high crime rates found in disorganized inner-city areas, and the rise of teenage gangs and groups support a close association between crime rates and social class position.

Concept Summary 6.3 sets out the features of cultural deviance theories.

PUBLIC POLICY IMPLICATIONS OF SOCIAL STRUCTURE THEORY

Social structure theory has had a significant influence on public policy. If the cause of criminality is viewed as a schism between lower-class individuals and conventional goals, norms, and rules, it seems logical that alternatives to criminal behavior can be provided by giving inner-city dwellers opportunities to share in the rewards of conventional society. One approach is to give indigent people direct financial aid through welfare programs that assist needy families. Although welfare has been curtailed through the Federal Welfare Reform Act of 1996, research shows that crime rates decrease when families receive supplemental income through public assistance payments.[215]

There are also efforts to reduce crime by improving the community structure in high-crime inner-city areas. Crime-prevention efforts based on social structure precepts can be traced back to the Chicago Area Project, supervised by Clifford R. Shaw. This program attempted to organize existing community structures to develop social stability in otherwise disorganized lower-class neighborhoods. The project sponsored recreation programs for children in the neighborhoods, including summer camping. It campaigned for community improvements in such areas as education, sanitation, traffic safety, physical conservation, and law enforcement. Project members also worked with police and court agencies to supervise and treat gang youth and adult offenders. In a 25-year assessment of the project, Solomon Kobrin found that it was successful in demonstrating the feasibility of creating youth welfare organizations in high-delinquency areas.[216] Kobrin also discovered that the project made a distinct contribution to ending the isolation of urban males from the mainstream of society.

Social structure concepts, especially Cloward and Ohlin's views, were a critical ingredient in the Kennedy and Johnson administrations' "War on Poverty," begun in the early 1960s. Rather than organizing existing community structures, as Shaw's Chicago Area Project had done, this later effort called for an all-out attack on the crime-producing structures of inner-city areas. War on Poverty programs included the Job Corps, VISTA (the urban Peace Corps), Head Start and Upward Bound (educational enrichment programs), Neighborhood Legal Services, and the largest community organizing effort, the Community Action Program. War on Poverty programs were sweeping efforts to change the social structure of the inner-city area. They sought to reduce crime by developing a sense of community pride and solidarity in poverty areas and by providing educational and job opportunities for crime-prone youths. Some War on Poverty programs—Head Start, Neighborhood Legal Services, and the Community Action Program—have continued to help people.

Operation Weed and Seed was a recent example of a structural theory–based crime-reduction strategy. Its aim was to prevent, control, and reduce violent crime, drug abuse, and gang activity in targeted high-crime neighborhoods across the country. Weed and Seed sites ranged in size from several neighborhood blocks to 15 square miles.[217] The strategy involved a two-pronged approach. First, law enforcement agencies and prosecutors cooperated in "weeding out" criminals who participated in violent crime and drug abuse, and attempted to prevent their return to the targeted area. Then agencies began "seeding," which brought human services to the area, encompassing prevention, intervention, treatment, and neighborhood revitalization. A community-oriented policing component bridged weeding and seeding strategies. Officers obtained helpful information from area residents for weeding efforts when they aided residents in obtaining information about community revitalization and seeding resources. Though federal funding for Operation Weed and Seed has ended, Weed and Seed was an example of a modern-day crime-control approach that relied on changing neighborhood structure to reduce crime rates. It also illustrates the difficulty of sustaining community-level crime prevention programs that are dependent on funding from federal sources, which are often subject to budgetary and political considerations.

AN ETHICAL DILEMMA

REDUCING POVERTY, CRIME, AND DRUG ABUSE IN AN URBAN NEIGHBORHOOD

You have just been appointed as a presidential adviser on urban problems. The president informs you that he wants to initiate a demonstration project in a major city aimed at showing that the government can do something to reduce poverty, crime, and drug abuse. The area he has chosen for development is a large inner-city neighborhood with more than a hundred thousand residents. The neighborhood suffers from disorganized community structure, poverty, and hopelessness. Predatory delinquent gangs run free and terrorize local merchants and citizens.

The school system has failed to provide opportunities and education experiences sufficient to dampen enthusiasm for gang recruitment. Stores, homes, and public buildings are deteriorated and decayed. Commercial enterprise has fled the area, and civil servants are reluctant to enter the neighborhood. There is an uneasy truce among the various ethnic and racial groups that populate the area. Residents feel that little can be done to bring the neighborhood back to life. You are faced with suggesting an urban redevelopment program that can revitalize the area and eventually bring down the crime rate. You can bring any element of the public and private sector to bear on this rather overwhelming problem—including the military! You can also ask private industry to help in the struggle, promising them tax breaks for their participation. But before you even begin to create the program you have to ask yourself these basic questions:

Does living and growing up in such an area contribute to high crime and delinquency rates? Is poverty a cause of crime or merely an excuse used to rationalize crime and drug use? Do deviant places create deviant people, or vice versa? After all, when middle-class yuppies move into a poor area and gentrify it, crime rates eventually go down and property values go up. Is it ethical to ask the government to help revitalize communities? Why should my tax money go to increasing the real estate values in another neighborhood owned by another person? Is that fair and just? Answer these questions in a memo to the president!

LO1 Discuss the history of sociological criminology

The application of sociological concepts to criminology can be traced to the works of pioneering sociologists L. A. J. (Adolphe) Quetelet, who used data and statistics in performing research on criminal activity, and (David) Émile Durkheim, who defined crime as a normal and necessary social event. These perspectives have been extremely influential on modern criminology. The primacy of sociological positivism as the intellectual basis of criminology was secured by research begun by the sociology department at the University of Chicago, which pioneered research on the social ecology of the city. Regardless of their race, religion, or ethnicity, the everyday behavior of people was controlled by the social and ecological climate in which they dwelled. According the Chicago School views, criminal behavior is not then a function of personal traits or choice but is linked to environmental conditions that fail to provide residents with proper human relations and development.

LO2 Clarify the association between social structure and crime

According to social structure theory, the root cause of crime can be traced directly to the socioeconomic disadvantages that have become embedded in American society. People in the United States live in a stratified society; social strata are created by the unequal distribution of wealth, power, and prestige. The crushing lifestyle of lower-class areas produces a culture of poverty that is passed from one generation to the next and is stained by apathy, cynicism, helplessness, and mistrust of social institutions. Lower-class people are driven to desperate measures, such as crime and substance abuse, to cope with their economic plight. Aggravating this dynamic is the constant media bombardment linking material possessions to self-worth.

LO3 Identify examples of the elements of social disorganization theory

Crime occurs in disorganized areas where institutions of social control, such as the family, commercial establishments, and schools, have broken down and can no longer perform their expected or stated functions. Indicators of social disorganization include high unemployment and school dropout rates, deteriorated housing, low income levels, and large numbers of single-parent households. Residents in these areas experience conflict and despair, and, as a result, antisocial behavior flourishes.

LO4 Explain the views of Shaw and McKay

Shaw and McKay explained crime and delinquency within the context of the changing urban environment and ecological development of the city. Poverty-ridden transitional neighborhoods suffered high rates of population turnover and were incapable of inducing residents to remain and defend the neighborhoods against criminal groups. The values that slum youths adopt often conflict with existing middle-class norms, which demand strict obedience to the legal code. Consequently, a value conflict further separates the delinquent youth and his or her peer group from conventional society; the result is a more solid embrace of deviant goals and behavior.

LO5 Differentiate between the various elements of ecological theory

Crime rates and the need for police services are associated with community deterioration: disorder, poverty, alienation, disassociation, and fear of crime. In larger cities, neighborhoods with a high percentage of deserted houses and apartments experience high crime rates. In disorganized neighborhoods that suffer social and physical incivilities that cause fear, as fear increases, quality of life deteriorates. People who live in neighborhoods that experience high levels of crime and civil disorder become suspicious and mistrusting and may develop a "siege mentality." As areas decline, residents flee to safer, more stable localities. Transitional neighborhoods have very high crime rates.

LO6 Discuss the association between collective efficacy and crime

Cohesive communities develop collective efficacy: mutual trust, a willingness to intervene in the supervision of children, and the maintenance of public order. Some elements of collective efficacy operate on the primary, or private, level and involve peers, families, and relatives. Communities that have collective efficacy attempt to use their local institutions to control crime. Stable neighborhoods are also able to arrange for external sources of social control, such as more police on patrol, that further reduce crime rates.

LO7 Articulate what is meant by the concepts of strain and anomie

Anomie is a condition that occurs because while social and economic goals are common to people in all economic strata, the ability to obtain these goals is class dependent. Most people in the United States desire wealth, material possessions, power, prestige, and other life comforts. Anomie occurs among members of the lower class who are unable to achieve these symbols of success through conventional means. Consequently, they feel anger, frustration, and resentment, referred to collectively as strain.

LO8 Compare and contrast between the different elements in Merton's theory of anomie

Merton argues that in the United States legitimate means to acquire wealth are stratified across class and status lines. Some people have inadequate means of attaining success; others who have the means reject societal goals. To resolve the goals–means conflict and relieve their sense of strain, some people innovate by stealing or extorting money; others retreat into drugs and alcohol; some rebel by joining revolutionary groups; and still others get involved in ritualistic behavior by joining a religious cult.

LO9 Clarify the concept of negative affective states

Agnew suggests that criminality is the direct result of negative affective states—the anger, frustration, and adverse emotions that emerge in the wake of destructive social relationships. He finds that negative affective states are produced by a variety of sources of strain, including the failure to achieve success, application of negative stimuli, and removal of positive stimuli.

LO10 Differentiate between the different forms of cultural deviance theory

Cultural deviance theory combines elements of both strain and social disorganization theories. A unique lower-class culture has developed in disorganized neighborhoods. These independent subcultures maintain unique values and beliefs that conflict with conventional social norms. Criminal behavior is an expression of conformity to lower-class subcultural values and traditions, not a rebellion from conventional society. Subcultural values are handed down from one generation to the next.

CRITICAL THINKING QUESTIONS

1. Is there a "transition" area in your town or city? Does the crime rate remain constant in this neighborhood regardless of the racial, ethnic, or cultural composition of its residents?
2. Do you believe a distinct lower-class culture exists? Do you know anyone who has the focal concerns Miller talks about? Did you experience elements of these focal concerns while you were in high school? Will forms of communication such as the Internet reduce cultural differences and create a more homogenous society, or are subcultures resistant to such influences?
3. Do you agree with Agnew that there is more than one cause of strain? If so, are there other sources of strain that he did not consider?
4. How would a structural theorist explain the presence of middle-class crime?
5. How would biosocial theories explain the high levels of violent crime in lower-class areas?

KEY TERMS

socially disorganized (182)
stratified society (183)
underclass (183)
culture of poverty (183)
at-risk (183)
social structure theory (187)
social disorganization theory (187)
strain theory (187)
strain (187)
cultural deviance theory (188)

transitional neighborhoods (189)
concentration effect (191)
incivilities (191)
siege mentality (192)
gentrification (193)
collective efficacy (193)
street efficacy (195)
relative deprivation (196)
anomie (196)
mechanical solidarity (196)

organic solidarity (196)
theory of anomie (197)
institutional anomie theory (199)
American Dream (199)
general strain theory (GST) (200)
negative affective states (201)
subcultures (205)
conduct norms (205)
culture conflict (205)

focal concerns (206)
status frustration (206)
middle-class measuring rods (208)
corner boy (208)
college boy (208)
delinquent boy (209)
reaction formation (209)
differential opportunity (209)

NOTES

1. U.S. Department of Justice, "MS-13 Members Convicted in Atlanta for Murders and Attempted Murders," July 16, 2013, http:// www.justice.gov/opa/pr/2013/ July/13- crm-794.html (accessed May 2014).
2. Arian Campo-Flores, "The Most Dangerous Gang in the United States," *Newsweek*, March 28, 2006; Ricardo Pollack, "Gang Life Tempts Salvador Teens," BBC News, http://
news.bbc.co.uk/2/hi/americas/4201183.stm (accessed April 2014).
3. FBI, "The MS-13 Threat, A National Assessment," January 14, 2008, http://www.fbi .gov/page2/jan08/ms13_011408.html (accessed April 2014).
4. Arlen Egley, Jr., and James Howell, *Highlights of the 2011 National Youth Gang Survey* (Washington, DC: Office of Juvenile Justice
and Delinquency Prevention, 2013), http:// www.ojjdp.gov/pubs/242884.pdf (accessed May 2014).
5. Steven Messner and Richard Rosenfeld, *Crime and the American Dream* (Belmont, CA: Wadsworth, 1994), p. 11.
6. Gregory M. Zimmerman, "Impulsivity, Offending, and the Neighborhood: Investigating the Person–Context Nexus," *Journal of*

Quantitative Criminology, published online June 3, 2010.

7. See, generally, Robert Nisbet, *The Sociology of Émile Durkheim* (New York: Oxford University Press, 1974).

8. L. A. J. Quetelet, *A Treatise on Man and the Development of His Faculties* (Gainesville, FL: Scholars' Facsimiles and Reprints, 1969), pp. 82–96.

9. Ibid., p. 85.

10. Émile Durkheim, *Rules of the Sociological Method*, reprinted., trans. W. D. Halls (New York: Free Press, 1982).

11. Émile Durkheim, *The Division of Labor in Society*, reprint ed. (New York: Free Press, 1997).

12. Robert E. Park, "The City: Suggestions for the Investigation of Human Behavior in the City Environment," *American Journal of Sociology* 20 (1915): 579–583.

13. Harvey Zorbaugh, *The Gold Coast and the Slum* (Chicago: University of Chicago Press, 1929); Frederick Thrasher, *The Gang* (Chicago: University of Chicago Press, 1927); Louis Wirth, *The Ghetto* (Chicago: University of Chicago Press, 1928).

14. Robert Park, Ernest Burgess, and Roderic McKenzie, *The City* (Chicago: University of Chicago Press, 1925).

15. Ibid.

16. Robert Frank, "U.S. Millionaire Count Hits All-Time High: 400 Richest Americans Now Worth $2 Trillion," CNBC, September 16, 2013, http://www.cnbc.com/id/101491613 (accessed April 2014).

17. U.S. Census Bureau, *Poverty Thresholds by Size of Family and Number of Children, 2013*.

18. Oscar Lewis, "The Culture of Poverty," *Scientific American* 215 (1966): 19–25.

19. Gunnar Myrdal, *The Challenge of World Poverty* (New York: Vintage Books, 1970).

20. James Ainsworth-Darnell and Douglas Downey, "Assessing the Oppositional Culture Explanation for Racial/Ethnic Differences in School Performances," *American Sociological Review* 63 (1998): 536–553.

21. Barbara Warner, "The Role of Attenuated Culture in Social Disorganization Theory," *Criminology* 41 (2003): 73–97.

22. Yasemin Özkan, Eda Purutçuoğlu, and Şengül Hablemitoğlu, "Interpersonal Impact of the Poverty on Children," *International Journal of Academic Research* 2 (2010): 172–179.

23. Gary Evans, Nancy Wells, and Annie Moch, "Housing and Mental Health: A Review of the Evidence and a Methodological and Conceptual Critique," *Journal of Social Issues* 59 (2003): 475–501.

24. U.S. Census Bureau, *Poverty Thresholds by Size of Family and Number of Children, 2013*.

25. Ibid.

26. Maria Velez, Lauren Krivo, and Ruth Peterson, "Structural Inequality and Homicide: An Assessment of the Black-White Gap in Killings," *Criminology* 41 (2003): 645–672.

27. Karen Parker and Matthew Pruitt, "Poverty, Poverty Concentration, and Homicide," *Social Science Quarterly* 81 (2000): 555–582.

28. Michael Leiber and Joseph Johnson, "Being Young and Black: What Are Their Effects on Juvenile Justice Decision Making?" *Crime and Delinquency* 54 (2008): 560–581.

29. Pew Foundation, *One in 100: Behind Bars in America 2008*, http://www.pewstates.org/uploadedFiles/PCS_Assets/2008/one%20in%20100.pdf (accessed April 2014).

30. John Hagan, Carla Shedd, and Monique Payne, "Race, Ethnicity, and Youth Perceptions of Criminal Injustice," *American Sociological Review* 70 (2005): 381–407.

31. John Hipp, "Spreading the Wealth: The Effect of the Distribution of Income and Race/Ethnicity Across Households and Neighborhoods on City Crime Trajectories," *Criminology* 49 (2011): 631–665; Julie A. Phillips, "White, Black, and Latino Homicide Rates: Why the Difference?" *Social Problems* 49 (2002): 349–374.

32. Justin Patchin, Beth Huebner, John McCluskey, Sean Varano, and Timothy Bynum, "Exposure to Community Violence and Childhood Delinquency," *Crime and Delinquency* 52 (2006): 307–332.

33. David Brownfield, "Social Class and Violent Behavior," *Criminology* 24 (1986): 421–438.

34. See Charles Tittle and Robert Meier, "Specifying the SES/Delinquency Relationship," *Criminology* 28 (1990): 271–295, at 293.

35. See Ruth Kornhauser, *Social Sources of Delinquency* (Chicago: University of Chicago Press, 1978), p. 75.

36. Kerryn E. Bell, "Gender and Gangs: A Quantitative Comparison," *Crime and Delinquency* 55 (2009): 363–387.

37. Arlen Egley and James Howell, *Highlights of the 2011 National Youth Gang Survey* (Washington, DC: Office of Juvenile Justice and Delinquency Prevention, 2012), http://www.ojjdp.gov/pubs/242884.pdf (accessed April 2014).

38. Jonathan Crane, "The Epidemic Theory of Ghettos and Neighborhood Effects on Dropping Out and Teenage Childbearing," *American Journal of Sociology* 96 (1991): 1226–1259; see also Rodrick Wallace, "Expanding Coupled Shock Fronts of Urban Decay and Criminal Behavior: How U.S. Cities Are Becoming 'Hollowed Out,'" *Journal of Quantitative Criminology* 7 (1991): 333–355.

39. Jeffrey Fagan and Garth Davies, "The Natural History of Neighborhood Violence," *Journal of Contemporary Criminal Justice* 20 (2004): 127–147.

40. Clifford R. Shaw and Henry D. McKay, *Juvenile Delinquency and Urban Areas*, rev. ed. (Chicago: University of Chicago Press, 1972).

41. Anthony Platt, *The Child Savers: The Invention of Delinquency* (Chicago: University of Chicago Press, 1968).

42. Shaw and McKay, *Juvenile Delinquency and Urban Areas*, p. 52.

43. Ibid., p. 171.

44. Claire Valier, "Foreigners, Crime and Changing Mobilities," *British Journal of Criminology* 43 (2003): 1–21.

45. For a general review, see James Byrne and Robert Sampson, eds., *The Social Ecology of Crime* (New York: Springer Verlag, 1985).

46. Stacy De Coster, Karen Heimer, and Stacy Wittrock, "Neighborhood Disadvantage, Social Capital, Street Context, and Youth Violence," *Sociological Quarterly* (2006): 723–753.

47. See, generally, Robert J. Bursik, "Social Disorganization and Theories of Crime and Delinquency," *Criminology* 26 (1988): 519–552.

48. William Spelman, "Abandoned Buildings: Magnets for Crime?" *Journal of Criminal Justice* 21 (1993): 481–493.

49. Keith Harries and Andrea Powell, "Juvenile Gun Crime and Social Stress: Baltimore, 1980–1990," *Urban Geography* 15 (1994): 45–63.

50. Ellen Kurtz, Barbara Koons, and Ralph Taylor, "Land Use, Physical Deterioration, Resident-Based Control, and Calls for Service on Urban Streetblocks," *Justice Quarterly* 15 (1998): 121–149.

51. Gregory Squires and Charis Kubrin, "Privileged Places: Race, Uneven Development and the Geography of Opportunity in Urban America," *Urban Studies* 42 (2005): 47–68; Matthew Lee, Michael Maume, and Graham Ousey, "Social Isolation and Lethal Violence Across the Metro/Nonmetro Divide: The Effects of Socioeconomic Disadvantage and Poverty Concentration on Homicide," *Rural Sociology* 68 (2003): 107–131.

52. Lee, Maume, and Ousey, "Social Isolation and Lethal Violence Across the Metro/Nonmetro Divide"; Charis E. Kubrin, "Structural Covariates of Homicide Rates: Does Type of Homicide Matter?" *Journal of Research in Crime and Delinquency* 40 (2003): 139–170; Darrell Steffensmeier and Dana Haynie, "Gender, Structural Disadvantage, and Urban Crime: Do Macrosocial Variables Also Explain Female Offending Rates?" *Criminology* 38 (2000): 403–438.

53. Kyle Crowder and Scott South, "Spatial Dynamics of White Flight: The Effects of Local and Extralocal Racial Conditions on Neighborhood Out-Migration," *American Sociological Review* 73 (2008): 792–812.

54. Paul Jargowsky and Yoonhwan Park, "Cause or Consequence? Suburbanization and Crime in U.S. Metropolitan Areas," *Crime and Delinquency* 55 (2009): 28–50.

55. Edward S. Shihadeh, "Race, Class, and Crime: Reconsidering the Spatial Effects of Social Isolation on Rates of Urban Offending," *Deviant Behavior* 30 (2009): 349–378.

56. Jeffrey Morenoff, Robert Sampson, and Stephen Raudenbush, "Neighborhood Inequality, Collective Efficacy, and the Spatial Dynamics of Urban Violence," *Criminology* 39 (2001): 517–560.

57. Jargowsky and Park, "Cause or Consequence?"

58. Steven Messner, Lawrence Raffalovich, and Richard McMillan, "Economic Deprivation and Changes in Homicide Arrest Rates for White and Black Youths, 1967–1998: A National Time Series Analysis," *Criminology* 39 (2001): 591–614.

59. Steven Messner and Kenneth Tardiff, "Economic Inequality and Levels of Homicide: An Analysis of Urban Neighborhoods," *Criminology* 24 (1986): 297–317.

60. Adam Dobrin, Daniel Lee, and Jamie Price, "Neighborhood Structure Differences Between Homicide Victims and Nonvictims," *Journal of Criminal Justice* 33 (2005): 137–143; G. David Curry and Irving Spergel, "Gang Homicide, Delinquency, and Community," *Criminology* 26 (1988): 381–407; Darrell Steffensmeier and Dana Haynie, "Gender, Structural Disadvantage, and Urban Crime: Do Macrosocial Variables Also Explain Female Offending Rates?" *Criminology* 38 (2000): 403–438; Richard McGahey, "Economic Conditions, Organization, and Urban Crime," in *Communities and Crime*, ed. Albert Reiss and Michael Tonry (Chicago: University of Chicago Press, 1986), pp. 231–270.

61. Scott Menard and Delbert Elliott, "Self-Reported Offending, Maturational Reform, and the Easterlin Hypothesis," *Journal of Quantitative Criminology* 6 (1990): 237–268.

62. Elijah Anderson, *Streetwise: Race, Class, and Change in an Urban Community* (Chicago: University of Chicago Press, 1990), pp. 243–244.

63. Joseph Schafer, Beth Huebner, and Timothy Bynum, "Fear of Crime and Criminal Victimization: Gender-Based Contrasts," *Journal of Criminal Justice* 34 (2006): 285–301.

64. Xu Yili, Mora Fiedler, and Karl Flaming, "Discovering the Impact of Community Policing," *The Journal of Research in Crime and Delinquency* 42 (2005): 147–186.

65. Marc Swatt, Sean Varano, Craig Uchida, and Shellie Solomon, "Fear of Crime, Incivilities, and Collective Efficacy in Four Miami Neighborhoods," *Journal of Criminal Justice* 41 (2013): 1–11; Matthew Lee and Terri Earnest, "Perceived Community Cohesion and Perceived Risk of Victimization: A Cross-National Analysis," *Justice Quarterly* 20 (2003): 131–158.

66. John Hipp, "Micro-Structure in Micro-Neighborhoods: A New Social Distance Measure, and Its Effect on Individual and Aggregated Perceptions of Crime and Disorder," *Social Networks* 32 (2010): 148–159.

67. Michael Hanslmaier, "Crime, Fear and Subjective Well-being: How Victimization and Street Crime Affect Fear and Life Satisfaction," *European Journal of Criminology* 10 (2013): 515–533.

68. Wendy Kilewer, "The Role of Neighborhood Collective Efficacy and Fear of Crime in Socialization of Coping with Violence in Low-Income Communities," *Journal of Community Psychology* 41 (2013): 920–930; Danielle Wallace, "A Test of the Routine Activities and Neighborhood Attachment Explanations for Bias in Disorder Perceptions," *Crime and Delinquency*, first published online December 7, 2011; Michele Roccato, Silvia Russo, and Alessio Vieno, "Perceived Community Disorder Moderates the Relation Between Victimization and Fear of Crime," *Journal of Community Psychology* 39 (2011): 884–888.

69. C. L. Storr, C. Y. Chen, and J. C. Anthony, "'Unequal Opportunity': Neighborhood Disadvantage and the Chance to Buy Illegal Drugs," *Journal of Epidemiology and Community Health* 58 (2004): 231–238.

70. Pamela Wilcox Rountree and Kenneth Land, "Burglary Victimization, Perceptions of Crime Risk, and Routine Activities: A Multi-level Analysis across Seattle Neighborhoods and Census Tracts," *Journal of Research in Crime and Delinquency* 33 (1996): 147–180.

71. Tim Phillips and Philip Smith, "Emotional and Behavioural Responses to Everyday Incivility," *Journal of Sociology* 40 (2004): 378–399.

72. Wesley Skogan, "Fear of Crime and Neighborhood Change," in *Communities and Crime*, ed. Albert Reiss and Michael Tonry (Chicago: University of Chicago Press, 1986), pp. 191–232.

73. Margo Wilson and Martin Daly, "Life Expectancy, Economic Inequality, Homicide, and Reproductive Timing in Chicago Neighborhoods," *British Journal of Medicine* 314 (1997): 1271–1274.

74. Skogan, "Fear of Crime and Neighborhood Change."

75. Ibid.

76. Ralph Taylor and Jeanette Covington, "Community Structural Change and Fear of Crime," *Social Problems* 40 (1993): 374–392; Ted Chiricos, Michael Hogan, and Marc Gertz, "Racial Composition of Neighborhood and Fear of Crime," *Criminology* 35 (1997): 107–131.

77. Jodi Lane and James Meeker, "Social Disorganization Perceptions, Fear of Gang Crime, and Behavioral Precautions Among Whites, Latinos, and Vietnamese," *Journal of Criminal Justice* 32 (2004): 49–62.

78. Curry and Spergel, "Gang Homicide, Delinquency, and Community."

79. Lawrence Rosenthal, "Gang Loitering and Race," *Journal of Criminal Law and Criminology* 91 (2000): 99–160.

80. Catherine E. Ross, John Mirowsky, and Shana Pribesh, "Powerlessness and the Amplification of Threat: Neighborhood Disadvantage, Disorder, and Mistrust," *American Sociological Review* 66 (2001): 568–580.

81. Anderson, Streetwise: Race, Class, and Change in an Urban Community, p. 245.

82. William Terrill and Michael Reisig, "Neighborhood Context and Police Use of Force," *Journal of Research in Crime and Delinquency* 40 (2003): 291–321.

83. Bridget Freisthler, Elizabeth Lascala, Paul Gruenewald, and Andrew Treno, "An Examination of Drug Activity: Effects of Neighborhood Social Organization on the Development of Drug Distribution Systems," *Substance Use and Misuse* 40 (2005): 671–686.

84. Finn-Aage Esbensen and David Huizinga, "Community Structure and Drug Use: From a Social Disorganization Perspective," *Justice Quarterly* 7 (1990): 691–709.

85. Micere Keels, Greg Duncan, Stefanie Deluca, Ruby Mendenhall, and James Rosenbaum, "Fifteen Years Later: Can Residential Mobility Programs Provide a Long-Term Escape from Neighborhood Segregation, Crime, and Poverty?" *Demography* 42 (2005): 51–72.

86. Greg J. Duncan, "New Lessons from the Gautreaux and Moving to Opportunity Residential Mobility Programs," University of California, Irvine, http://merage.uci.edu/ResearchAndCenters/CRE/Resources/Documents/Duncan.pdf (accessed May 2014).

87. Wesley Skogan, *Disorder and Decline: Crime and the Spiral of Decay in American Neighborhoods* (New York: Free Press, 1990), pp. 15–35.

88. Yan Lee, "Gentrification and Crime: Identification Using the 1994 Northridge Earthquake in Los Angeles," *Journal of Urban Affairs* 32 (2010): 549–577.

89. Leo Scheurman and Solomon Kobrin, "Community Careers in Crime," in *Communities and Crime*, ed. Albert Reiss and Michael Tonry (Chicago: University of Chicago Press, 1986), pp. 67–100.

90. Ibid.

91. Jeffrey Michael Cancino, "The Utility of Social Capital and Collective Efficacy: Social Control Policy in Nonmetropolitan Settings," *Criminal Justice Policy Review* 16 (2005): 287–318; Chris Gibson, Jihong Zhao, Nicholas Lovrich, and Michael Gaffney, "Social Integration, Individual Perceptions of Collective

Efficacy, and Fear of Crime in Three Cities," *Justice Quarterly* 19 (2002): 537–564.

92. Robert J. Sampson and Stephen W. Raudenbush, *Disorder in Urban Neighborhoods: Does It Lead to Crime?* (Washington, DC: National Institute of Justice, 2001).

93. Andrea Altschuler, Carol Somkin, and Nancy Adler, "Local Services and Amenities, Neighborhood Social Capital, and Health," *Social Science and Medicine* 59 (2004): 1219–1230.

94. Kelly Socia and Janet Stamatel, "Neighborhood Characteristics and the Social Control of Registered Sex Offenders," *Crime and Delinquency* 58 (2012): 565–587.

95. M. R. Lindblad, K. R. Manturuk, and R. G. Quercia, "Sense of Community and Informal Social Control Among Lower Income Households: The Role of Homeownership and Collective Efficacy in Reducing Subjective Neighborhood Crime and Disorder," *American Journal of Community Psychology* 51 (2013): 123–139.

96. Rebecca Wickes, John R. Hipp, Renee Zahnow, and Lorraine Mazerolle, "'Seeing' Minorities and Perceptions of Disorder: Explicating the Mediating and Moderating Mechanisms of Social Cohesion," *Criminology* 51 (2013): 519–560.

97. Robert Sampson, Jeffrey Morenoff, and Felton Earls, "Beyond Social Capital: Spatial Dynamics of Collective Efficacy for Children," *American Sociological Review* 64 (1999): 633–660.

98. Donald Black, "Social Control as a Dependent Variable," in *Toward a General Theory of Social Control*, ed. D. Black (Orlando: Academic Press, 1990).

99. Shayne Jones and Donald R. Lynam, "In the Eye of the Impulsive Beholder: The Interaction Between Impulsivity and Perceived Informal Social Control on Offending," *Criminal Justice and Behavior* 36 (2009): 307–321.

100. Jennifer Beyers, John Bates, Gregory Pettit, and Kenneth Dodge, "Neighborhood Structure, Parenting Processes, and the Development of Youths' Externalizing Behaviors: A Multilevel Analysis," *American Journal of Community Psychology* 31 (2003): 35–53.

101. Ralph Taylor, "Social Order and Disorder of Street Blocks and Neighborhoods: Ecology, Microecology, and the Systemic Model of Social Disorganization," *Journal of Research in Crime and Delinquency* 34 (1997): 113–155.

102. April Pattavina, James Byrne, and Luis Garcia, "An Examination of Citizen Involvement in Crime Prevention in High-Risk versus Low- to Moderate-Risk Neighborhoods," *Crime and Delinquency* 52 (2006): 203–231.

103. Steven Messner, Eric Baumer, and Richard Rosenfeld, "Dimensions of Social Capital

and Rates of Criminal Homicide," *American Sociological Review* 69 (2004): 882–905.

104. Paul Bellair, "Informal Surveillance and Street Crime: A Complex Relationship," *Criminology* 38 (2000): 137–170.

105. Skogan, *Disorder and Decline*.

106. Robert Sampson and W. Byron Groves, "Community Structure and Crime: Testing Social Disorganization Theory," *American Journal of Sociology* 94 (1989): 774–802; Denise Gottfredson, Richard McNeill, and Gary Gottfredson, "Social Area Influences on Delinquency: A Multilevel Analysis," *Journal of Research in Crime and Delinquency* 28 (1991): 197–206.

107. Jodi Eileen Morris, Rebekah Levine Coley, and Daphne Hernandez, "Out-of-School Care and Problem Behavior Trajectories Among Low-Income Adolescents: Individual, Family, and Neighborhood," *Child Development* 75 (2004): 948–965.

108. Ruth Triplett, Randy Gainey, and Ivan Sun, "Institutional Strength, Social Control, and Neighborhood Crime Rates," *Theoretical Criminology* 7 (2003): 439–467; Fred Markowitz, Paul Bellair, Allen Liska, and Jianhong Liu, "Extending Social Disorganization Theory: Modeling the Relationships Between Cohesion, Disorder, and Fear," *Criminology* 39 (2001): 293–320.

109. George Capowich, "The Conditioning Effects of Neighborhood Ecology on Burglary Victimization," *Criminal Justice and Behavior* 30 (2003): 39–62.

110. Ruth Peterson, Lauren Krivo, and Mark Harris, "Disadvantage and Neighborhood Violent Crime: Do Local Institutions Matter?" *Journal of Research in Crime and Delinquency* 37 (2000): 31–63.

111. Maria Velez, "The Role of Public Social Control in Urban Neighborhoods: A Multi-Level Analysis of Victimization Risk," *Criminology* 39 (2001): 837–864.

112. Lee Ann Slocum, Andres Rengifo, Tiffany Choi, and Christopher Herrmann, "The Elusive Relationship Between Community Organizations and Crime: An Assessment Across Disadvantaged Areas of the South Bronx," *Criminology* 51 (2013): 167–216.

113. Velez, Krivo, and Peterson, "Structural Inequality and Homicide."

114. Tammy Rinehart Kochel, "Robustness of Collective Efficacy on Crime in a Developing Nation: Association with Crime Reduction Compared to Police Services," *Journal of Crime and Justice* 36 (2013): 334–352.

115. David Klinger, "Negotiating Order in Patrol Work: An Ecological Theory of Police Response to Deviance," *Criminology* 35 (1997): 277–306.

116. Rodney Stark, "Deviant Places: A Theory of the Ecology of Crime," *Criminology* 25 (1987): 893–911.

117. Robert Kane, "Compromised Police Legitimacy as a Predictor of Violent Crime in Structurally Disadvantaged Communities," *Criminology* 43 (2005): 469–498.

118. Robert Sampson, "Neighborhood and Community," *New Economy* 11 (2004): 106–113.

119. Robert Bursik and Harold Grasmick, "Economic Deprivation and Neighborhood Crime Rates, 1960–1980," *Law and Society Review* 27 (1993): 263–278.

120. Delbert Elliott, William Julius Wilson, David Huizinga, Robert Sampson, Amanda Elliott, and Bruce Rankin, "The Effects of Neighborhood Disadvantage on Adolescent Development," *Journal of Research in Crime and Delinquency* 33 (1996): 389–426.

121. James DeFronzo, "Welfare and Homicide," *Journal of Research in Crime and Delinquency* 34 (1997): 395–406.

122. John Worrall, "Reconsidering the Relationship Between Welfare Spending and Serious Crime: A Panel Data Analysis with Implications for Social Support Theory," *Justice Quarterly* 22 (2005): 364–391.

123. Sampson, Morenoff, and Earls, "Beyond Social Capital."

124. Thomas McNulty, "Assessing the Race–Violence Relationship at the Macro Level: The Assumption of Racial Invariance and the Problem of Restricted Distribution," *Criminology* 39 (2001): 467–490.

125. Keri Burchfield and Eric Silver, "Collective Efficacy and Crime in Los Angeles Neighborhoods: Implications for the Latino Paradox," *Sociological Inquiry* 83 (2013): 154–176.

126. Patrick Sharkey, "Navigating Dangerous Streets: The Sources and Consequences of Street Efficacy," *American Sociological Review* 71 (2006): 826–846.

127. Sampson, Morenoff, and Earls, "Beyond Social Capital."

128. Per-Olof H. Wikström and Kyle Treiber, "The Role of Self-Control in Crime Causation" *European Journal of Criminology* 4 (2007): 237–264.

129. Eric Silver and Lisa Miller, "Sources of Informal Social Control in Chicago Neighborhoods," *Criminology* 42 (2004): 551–585.

130. John Braithwaite, "Poverty Power, White-Collar Crime, and the Paradoxes of Criminological Theory," *Australian and New Zealand Journal of Criminology* 24 (1991): 40–58.

131. Wilson and Daly, "Life Expectancy, Economic Inequality, Homicide, and Reproductive Timing in Chicago Neighborhoods."

132. Judith Blau and Peter Blau, "The Cost of Inequality: Metropolitan Structure and Violent Crime," *American Sociological Review* 147 (1982): 114–129.

133. P. M. Krueger, S. A. Huie, R. G. Rogers, and R. A. Hummer, "Neighborhoods and Homicide Mortality: An Analysis of Race/Ethnic Differences," *Journal of Epidemiology and Community Health* 58 (2004): 223–230.

134. Gary LaFree and Kriss Drass, "The Effect of Changes in Intraracial Income Inequality and Educational Attainment on Changes in Arrest Rates for African Americans and Whites, 1957 to 1990," *American Sociological Review* 61 (1996): 614–634; Taylor and Covington, "Neighborhood Changes in Ecology and Violence," p. 582; Richard Block, "Community Environment and Violent Crime," *Criminology* 17 (1979): 46–57; Robert Sampson, "Structural Sources of Variation in Race-Age-Specific Rates of Offending Across Major U.S. Cities," *Criminology* 23 (1985): 647–673; Richard Rosenfeld, "Urban Crime Rates: Effects of Inequality, Welfare Dependency, Region and Race," in *The Social Ecology of Crime*, ed. James Byrne and Robert Sampson (New York: Springer Verlag, 1985), pp. 116–130.

135. Sang-Weon Kim and William Pridemore, "Poverty, Socioeconomic Change, Institutional Anomie, and Homicide," *Social Science Quarterly* 86 (2005): 1377–1398.

136. Robert Merton, *Social Theory and Social Structure*, enlarged ed. (New York: Free Press, 1968).

137. For an analysis, see Richard Hilbert, "Durkheim and Merton on Anomie: An Unexplored Contrast in Its Derivatives," *Social Problems* 36 (1989): 242–256.

138. Ibid., p. 243.

139. Albert Cohen, "The Sociology of the Deviant Act: Anomie Theory and Beyond," *American Sociological Review* 30 (1965): 5–14.

140. Robert Agnew, "The Contribution of Social Psychological Strain Theory to the Explanation of Crime and Delinquency," in *Advances in Criminological Theory*, Vol. 6, *The Legacy of Anomie*, ed. Freda Adler and William Laufer (New Brunswick, NJ: Transaction Press, 1995), pp. 111–122.

141. These criticisms are articulated in Messner and Rosenfeld, *Crime and the American Dream*, p. 60.

142. Ibid.

143. Ibid., p. 61.

144. Steven Messner and Richard Rosenfeld, "An Institutional-Anomie Theory of the Social Distribution of Crime," paper presented at the annual meeting of the American Society of Criminology, Phoenix, November 1993.

145. Lisa Mufti, "Advancing Institutional Anomie Theory," *International Journal of Offender Therapy and Comparative Criminology* 50 (2006): 630–653.

146. Stephen Cernkovich, Peggy Giordano, and Jennifer Rudolph, "Race, Crime, and the American Dream," *Journal of Research in Crime and Delinquency* 37 (2000): 131–170.

147. Jon Gunnar Bernburg, "Anomie, Social Change, and Crime: A Theoretical Examination of Institutional-Anomie Theory," *British Journal of Criminology* 42 (2002): 729–743.

148. John Hagan, Gerd Hefler, Gabriele Classen, Klaus Boehnke, and Hans Merkens, "Subterranean Sources of Subcultural Delinquency Beyond the American Dream," *Criminology* 36 (1998): 309–340.

149. Jukka Savolainen, "Inequality, Welfare State and Homicide: Further Support for the Institutional Anomie Theory," *Criminology* 38 (2000): 1021–1042.

150. Kate Pickett, Jessica Mokherjee, and Richard Wilkinson, "Adolescent Birth Rates, Total Homicides, and Income Inequality in Rich Countries," *American Journal of Public Health* 95 (2005): 1181–1183.

151. Robert Agnew, "Foundation for a General Strain Theory of Crime and Delinquency," *Criminology* 30 (1992): 47–87.

152. Stacy De Coster and Lisa Kort-Butler, "How General Is General Strain Theory?" *Journal of Research in Crime and Delinquency* 43 (2006): 297–325.

153. Stephen Baron, "Street Youth, Strain Theory, and Crime," *Journal of Criminal Justice* 34 (2006): 209–223.

154. Matthew Larson and Gary Sweeten, "Breaking Up Is Hard to Do: Romantic Dissolution, Offending, and Substance Use During the Transition to Adulthood," *Criminology* 50 (2012): 605–636.

155. Cesar Rebellon, "Reconsidering the Broken Homes/Delinquency Relationship and Exploring Its Mediating Mechanism(s)," *Criminology* 40 (2002): 103–135.

156. G. Roger Jarjoura, "The Conditional Effect of Social Class on the Dropout–Delinquency Relationship," *Journal of Research in Crime and Delinquency* 33 (1996): 232–255.

157. Stephen Watts and Thomas McNulty, "Childhood Abuse and Criminal Behavior: Testing a General Strain Theory Model," *Journal of Interpersonal Violence* 28 (2013): 3023–3040.

158. Robert Agnew, "Experienced, Vicarious, and Anticipated Strain: An Exploratory Study on Physical Victimization and Delinquency," *Justice Quarterly* 19 (2002): 603–633; Carter Hay and Michelle Evans, "Violent Victimization and Involvement in Delinquency: Examining Predictions from General Strain Theory," *Journal of Criminal Justice* 34 (2006): 261–274.

159. Susan Sharp, Mitchell Peck, and Jennifer Hartsfield, "Childhood Adversity and Substance Use of Women Prisoners: A General Strain Theory Approach," *Journal of Criminal Justice* 40 (2012): 202–211.

160. Paul Mazerolle, Velmer Burton, Francis Cullen, T. David Evans, and Gary Payne, "Strain, Anger, and Delinquent Adaptations Specifying General Strain Theory," *Journal of Criminal Justice* 28 (2000): 89–101; Paul Mazerolle and Alex Piquero, "Violent Responses to Strain: An Examination of Conditioning Influences," *Violence and Victimization* 12 (1997): 323–345.

161. George E. Capowich, Paul Mazerolle, and Alex Piquero, "General Strain Theory, Situational Anger, and Social Networks: An Assessment of Conditioning Influences," *Journal of Criminal Justice* 29 (2001): 445–461.

162. Cesar Rebellon, Nicole Leeper Piquero, Alex Piquero, and Sherod Thaxton, "Do Frustrated Economic Expectations and Objective Economic Inequity Promote Crime? A Randomized Experiment Testing Agnew's General Strain Theory," *European Journal of Criminology* 6 (2009): 47–71.

163. Joanne Kaufman, Cesar Rebellon, Sherod Thaxton, and Robert Agnew, "A General Strain Theory of Racial Differences in Criminal Offending," *Australian and New Zealand Journal of Criminology* 41 (2008): 421–437.

164. Lawrence Wu, "Effects of Family Instability, Income, and Income Instability on the Risk of Premarital Birth," *American Sociological Review* 61 (1996): 386–406.

165. Anthony Walsh, "Behavior Genetics and Anomie/Strain Theory," *Criminology* 38 (2000): 1075–1108.

166. John Hoffman, "A Life-Course Perspective on Stress, Delinquency, and Young Adult Crime," *American Journal of Criminal Justice* 35 (2010): 105–120.

167. Ravinder Barn and Jo-Pei Tan, "Foster Youth and Crime: Employing General Strain Theory to Promote Understanding," *Journal of Criminal Justice* 40 (2012): 212–220.

168. Hay and Evans, "Violent Victimization and Involvement in Delinquency: Examining Predictions from General Strain Theory."

169. Robert Agnew, Timothy Brezina, John Paul Wright, and Francis T. Cullen, "Strain, Personality Traits, and Delinquency: Extending General Strain Theory," *Criminology* 40 (2002): 43–71.

170. Wan-Ning Bao, Ain Haas, and Yijun Pi, "Life Strain, Coping, and Delinquency in the People's Republic of China," *International Journal of Offender Therapy and Comparative Criminology* 51 (2007): 9–24.

171. Fawn T. Ngo and Raymond Paternoster, "Toward an Understanding of the Emotional and Behavioral Reactions to Stalking: A Partial Test of General Strain Theory," *Crime and Delinquency*, first published on November 7, 2013.

172. Robert Agnew, "When Criminal Coping Is Likely: An Extension of General Strain Theory," *Deviant Behavior* 34 (2013): 653–670.

173. Agnew, Brezina, Wright, and Cullen, "Strain, Personality Traits, and Delinquency"; Robert Agnew, "Stability and Change in Crime over the Life Course: A Strain Theory Explanation," in *Advances in Criminological Theory*, Vol. 7, *Developmental Theories of Crime and Delinquency*, ed. Terence Thornberry (New Brunswick, NJ: Transaction Books, 1995), pp. 113–137.

174. Ekaterina Botchkovar and Lisa Broidy, "Accumulated Strain, Negative Emotions, and Crime: A Test of General Strain Theory in Russia," *Crime and Delinquency* 59 (2013): 837–860; Michael Ostrowsky and Steven Messner, "Explaining Crime for a Young Adult Population: An Application of General Strain Theory," *Journal of Criminal Justice* 33 (2005): 463–476.

175. Lee Ann Slocum, Sally Simpson, and Douglas Smith, "Strained Lives and Crime: Examining Intra-Individual Variation in Strain and Offending in a Sample of Incarcerated Women," *Criminology* 43 (2005): 1067–1110.

176. Lisa Broidy, "A Test of General Strain Theory," *Criminology* 39 (2001): 9–36.

177. Robert Agnew and Timothy Brezina, "Relational Problems with Peers, Gender and Delinquency," *Youth and Society* 29 (1997): 84–111.

178. John Hoffmann and S. Susan Su, "The Conditional Effects of Stress on Delinquency and Drug Use: A Strain Theory in Assessment of Sex Differences," *Journal of Research in Crime and Delinquency* 34 (1997): 46–78.

179. Lisa Broidy and Robert Agnew, "Gender and Crime: A General Strain Theory Perspective," *Journal of Research in Crime and Delinquency* 34 (1997): 275–306.

180. Robbin Ogle, Daniel Maier-Katkin, and Thomas Bernard, "A Theory of Homicidal Behavior Among Women," *Criminology* 33 (1995): 173–193.

181. Nicole Leeper Piquero and Miriam Sealock, "Gender and General Strain Theory: A Preliminary Test of Broidy and Agnew's Gender/GST Hypothesis," *Justice Quarterly* 21 (2004): 125–158.

182. Teresa LaGrange and Robert Silverman, "Investigating the Interdependence of Strain and Self-Control," *Canadian Journal of Criminology and Criminal Justice* 45 (2003): 431–464.

183. Thorsten Sellin, *Culture Conflict and Crime*, Bulletin No. 41 (New York: Social Science Research Council, 1938).

184. Ibid., p. 22.

185. Ibid., p. 29.

186. Ibid., p. 68.

187. Walter Miller, "Lower-Class Culture as a Generating Milieu of Gang Delinquency," *Journal of Social Issues* 14 (1958): 5–19.

188. Ibid., pp. 14–17.

189. Fred Markowitz and Richard Felson, "Social-Demographic Attitudes and Violence," *Criminology* 36 (1998): 117–138.

190. Jeffrey Fagan, *Adolescent Violence: A View from the Street*, NIJ Research Preview (Washington, DC: National Institute of Justice, 1998).

191. Albert Cohen, *Delinquent Boys* (New York: Free Press, 1955).

192. Ibid., p. 25.

193. Ibid., p. 28.

194. Ibid.

195. Clarence Schrag, *Crime and Justice American Style* (Washington, DC: U.S. Government Printing Office, 1971), p. 74.

196. Cohen, *Delinquent Boys*, p. 30.

197. Ibid., p. 31.

198. Ibid., p. 133.

199. J. Johnstone, "Social Class, Social Areas, and Delinquency," *Sociology and Social Research* 63 (1978): 49–72; Joseph Harry, "Social Class and Delinquency: One More Time," *Sociological Quarterly* 15 (1974): 294–301.

200. Richard Cloward and Lloyd Ohlin, *Delinquency and Opportunity* (New York: Free Press, 1960).

201. Ibid., p. 7.

202. Ibid., p. 85.

203. Ibid., p. 171.

204. Ibid., p. 23.

205. Ibid., p. 73.

206. Ibid., p. 24.

207. Finn-Aage Esbensen and David Huizinga, "Gangs, Drugs and Delinquency in a Survey of Urban Youth," *Criminology* 31 (1993): 565–587.

208. For a general criticism, see Kornhauser, *Social Sources of Delinquency*.

209. Robert Sampson, "Effects of Socioeconomic Context of Official Reaction to Juvenile Delinquency," *American Sociological Review* 51 (1986): 876–885.

210. Jeffrey Fagan, Ellen Slaughter, and Eliot Hartstone, "Blind Justice? The Impact of Race on the Juvenile Justice Process," *Crime and Delinquency* 33 (1987): 224–258; Merry Morash, "Establishment of a Juvenile Police Record," *Criminology* 22 (1984): 97–113.

211. Charles Tittle, "Social Class and Criminal Behavior: A Critique of the Theoretical Foundations," *Social Forces* 62 (1983): 334–358.

212. James Q. Wilson and Richard Herrnstein, *Crime and Human Nature* (New York: Simon & Schuster, 1985).

213. Kenneth Polk and F. Lynn Richmond, "Those Who Fail," in *Schools and Delinquency*, ed. Kenneth Polk and Walter Schafer (Englewood Cliffs, NJ: Prentice Hall, 1974), p. 67.

214. Kathleen Maguire and Ann Pastore, *Sourcebook of Criminal Justice Statistics, 1996* (Washington, DC: U.S. Government Printing Office, 1996), pp. 150–166.

215. James DeFronzo, "Welfare and Burglary," *Crime and Delinquency* 42 (1996): 223–230.

216. Solomon Kobrin, "The Chicago Area Project—25-Year Assessment," *Annals of the American Academy of Political and Social Science* 322 (1959): 20–29.

217. Community Capacity Development Office website: http://www.ojp.usdoj.gov/ccdo/nonflash.html (accessed May 2014).

learning objectives

LO1 Analyze the associations among socialization, social process, and crime

LO2 Assess the effect of families and education on crime

LO3 Discuss the link between peers and delinquency

LO4 Explain how personal beliefs impact on criminality

LO5 Compare and contrast among social learning, control, and reaction theory

LO6 Explain the different forms social learning theory has taken

LO7 List the principles of Hirschi's social bond theory

LO8 Summarize the basic elements of social reaction or labeling theory

LO9 Discuss the research that underpins the labeling approach

LO10 Describe the efforts to link social process theory to crime prevention efforts

7

SOCIAL PROCESS THEORIES: SOCIALIZATION AND SOCIETY

On June 15, 2013, Ethan Couch, a 16-year-old Texas boy, killed four people while driving drunk. It seems that Couch and seven friends had been drinking for hours before the crash, and some of them were caught on a surveillance video stealing two cases of beer from a nearby Walmart. At around 11:45 P.M., the intoxicated teens were in a Ford F350 pickup going 70 mph (30 over the speed limit) when Couch swerved off the road and into a stalled SUV on the roadside, throwing the owner and three Good Samaritans who were trying to help her get the car going 60 yards in the air. They were killed on impact. Couch was three times over the legal alcohol limit when he slammed into the victims.

What was unusual about the case was that Couch was sentenced to a decade of probation even though prosecutors had sought a maximum sentence of 20 years. One reason for the light sentence was that during his trial, a defense psychologist testified that Couch suffered from "affluenza"—in other words, on the night of the crash he did not understand the consequences of his actions because of his advantaged upbringing. His parents had taught him that wealth buys privilege and he could do anything he wanted without consequences because they were wealthy. If that were true, the state helped fuel those feelings further. Couch was supposed to go to a rehab clinic that would have cost his family approximately $500,000 annually. Instead, he was sent to a state facility which requires the family to only pay $1,100 per month for a $750 per day facility, leaving taxpayers to pay the remaining bill for his therapy. The facility offers a 90-day treatment program that includes horseback riding, mixed martial arts, massage, cookery classes, a swimming pool, basketball, and six acres of land.[1]

The Couch case illustrates the fact that the way we are brought up or socialized can have long-term influence over behavior. If we are to believe the defense, Couch was brought up to believe that his wealth shielded him from responsibility for his actions, freeing him to engage in deviant and criminal behaviors. And the state reinforced these values by granting him a lenient sentence and subsidizing his rehabilitation costs. Who could blame him if he walked away believing that his parents were correct? According to the victims' families, he showed no remorse for killing four innocent people. Lawsuits are pending.

ere we can see how social processes influence both the definition of what is to be considered a crime and who is to be considered a criminal. How people are socialized and how they are perceived by others are critical determinants of a person's status and behavior. And as the Couch case illustrates, agents of the justice system who hold legal power are often swayed by a person's life story. In most instances, the suspect's background includes growing up in a home with poor or absent drug-abusing parents or being sexually assaulted as a child. Such hardships often mitigate guilt and can result in a reduced sentence. In this instance, being raised in affluence was considered a determining factor in a young man's behavior choices.

In this chapter, we will review those theories that associate socialization and criminal behaviors. We begin with an analysis of the elements of socialization.

SOCIALIZATION AND CRIME

 LO1 Analyze the associations among socialization, social process, and crime

The Couch case shows how socialization and social processes can influence both crime and criminality. Why people commit crime and who is to be considered a criminal are social constructs: people are not born criminals, they are made that way; bad acts become crime when they are defined as such through a social process.

This notion of crime and criminality became popular during the 1930s and 1940s: a group of sociologists began to link social-psychological interactions to criminological behavior. **Sociological social psychology** (also known as psychological sociology) is the study of human interactions and relationships that emphasizes such issues as group dynamics and socialization.

According to this school of thought, an individual's relationship to important social processes, such as education, family life, and peer relations, is the key to understanding human behavior. Poverty and social

sociological social psychology The study of human interactions and relationships, emphasizing such issues as group dynamics and socialization.

socialization The interactions people have with various organizations, institutions, and processes of society.

social process or socialization theory The view that criminality is a function of people's interactions with various organizations, institutions, and processes in society.

disorganization alone are not sufficient to cause criminal activity because, after all, the great majority of people living in the most deteriorated areas do not become criminal offenders. More than 46 million Americans live below the poverty line. Even if we were to assume that all criminals come from the lower class—which they do not—it is evident that the great majority of the most indigent Americans do not commit criminal acts even though they may have a great economic incentive. Relatively few adolescents living in the most deteriorated areas become persistent offenders; most kids who do commit crime desist when they reach adulthood despite the continuing pressure of poverty and social decay.

Some other force, then, must be at work to explain why the majority of at-risk individuals do not become persistent criminal offenders and to explain why some who have no economic or social reason to commit crime do so anyway. According to social process theorists, that missing ingredient is **socialization**—the interactions people have with various organizations, institutions, and processes of society. Most people are influenced by their family relationships, peer group associations, educational experiences, and interactions with authority figures, including teachers, employers, and agents of the justice system. If these relationships are positive and supportive, people are able to function effectively within society; if these relationships are dysfunctional and destructive, conventional success may be impossible, and criminal solutions may become a feasible alternative. Taken together, this view of crime is referred to as **social process or socialization theory**.[2] Criminologists have long studied the critical elements of socialization to determine how they contribute to a burgeoning criminal career. Prominent among these elements are the family, the peer group, and the school.

Family Relations

LO2 Assess the effect of families and education on crime

For some time, family relationships have been considered a major determinant of criminal behavior.[3] In fact, there is abundant evidence that parenting factors, such as the ability to communicate and to provide proper discipline, may play a critical role in determining whether people misbehave as children and even later as adults.

Youths who grow up in households characterized by conflict and tension, and where there is a lack of familial love and support, are susceptible to the crime-promoting forces in the environment.[4] Adolescents who live in this type of environment develop poor emotional well-being, externalizing problems, and antisocial behavior.[5]

Even those children living in so-called high-crime areas will be better able to resist the temptations of the streets if they receive fair discipline, care, and support from parents who provide them with strong, positive

INFLUENCES ON FAMILY FUNCTIONING

criminology in action

rand Conger is one of the nation's leading experts on family life. For the past two decades, he has been involved with four major community studies that have examined the influence of economic stress on families, children, and adolescents. In sum, these studies involve almost 1,500 families and over 4,000 individual family members who represent a diverse cross-section of society. The extensive information that has been collected on all of these families over time includes reports by family members, videotaped discussions in the home, and data from schools and other community agencies.

One thing that Conger and his associates have learned is that in all of these different types of families, economic stress appears to have a harmful effect on parents and children. According to his Family Stress Model of economic hardship, such factors as low income and income loss increase parents' sadness, pessimism about the future, anger, despair, and withdrawal from other family members. Economic stress has this impact on parents' social-emotional functioning through the daily pressures it creates for them, such as being unable to pay bills or acquire basic necessities such as adequate food, housing, clothing, and medical care. As parents become more emotionally distressed, they tend to interact with one another and their children in a more irritable and less supportive fashion. These patterns of behavior increase instability in the marriage and also disrupt effective parenting practices, such as monitoring children's activities

and using consistent and appropriate disciplinary strategies. Marital instability and disrupted parenting, in turn, increase children's risk of suffering developmental problems, such as depressed mood, substance abuse, and engaging in delinquent behaviors. These economic stress processes also decrease children's ability to function in a competent manner in school and with peers.

The findings also show, however, that parents who remain supportive of one another, and who demonstrate effective problem-solving skills in spite of hardship, can disrupt this negative process and shield their children and themselves from these adverse consequences of economic stress. These parenting skills can be taught and used by human service professionals to assist families experiencing economic pressure or similar stresses in their lives.

Considerable evidence shows that low socioeconomic status (SES) is associated with poorer physical health, emotional well-being, and cognitive functioning for both children and adults. SES also appears to be an important predictor of problem behaviors in childhood and adolescence, such as delinquency, aggression, conduct problems at school, and other externalizing behaviors.

Furthermore, research has linked child and adolescent problem behavior to adverse outcomes later in life, including dropping out of school, forgoing post-secondary education, long-term unemployment in adulthood, and time spent in correctional facilities. Consistent with

the social causation perspective, researchers found a significant relation between Generation 1 (G1) SES and family stress, predicted Generation 2 (G2) problem behavior and family stress.

Finally, G1 adult SES predicted both material and emotional investments in the G2 child. In turn, emotional investments predicted G2 problem behavior, as did material investments. In sum, this research indicates that parents who are suffering economic stress, a common condition today, produce children who will also suffer from stress and relationship problems.

Critical Thinking

To help deal with these problems, Conger advocates support for social policies that adequately aid families during stressful times as they recover from downturns in the economy. He also advocates educating parents about effective strategies for managing the economic, emotional, and family relationship challenges they will face when hardship occurs. What would you add to the mix to improve family functioning in America?

SOURCES: "Evaluation of the Interactionist Model of Socioeconomic Status and Problem Behavior: A Developmental Cascade Across Generations," Center for Poverty Research at UC Davis, http://poverty.ucdavis.edu/research-paper/evaluation-interactionist-model-socioeconomic-status-and-problem-behavior (accessed April 2014); Rand Conger and Katherine Conger, "Understanding the Processes Through Which Economic Hardship Influences Families and Children," in *Handbook of Families and Poverty*, ed. D. Russell Crane and Tim B. Heaton (Thousand Oaks, CA: Sage Publications, 2008), pp. 64–81.

role models. Nonetheless, living in a disadvantaged neighborhood places terrific strain on family functioning, especially in single-parent families that experience social isolation from relatives, friends, and neighbors. Children who are raised within such distressed families are at risk for delinquency.[6]

The relationship between family structure and crime is critical when the high rates of divorce and single parents are considered. Today more than 30 percent of children live in single-family homes.[7] Family disruption or change can have a long-lasting impact on children. Research conducted in both the United States and abroad shows that children raised in homes with one or both parents absent may be prone to antisocial behavior.[8] It is not surprising that the number of single-parent households in the population is significantly related to arrest rates.[9]

The Effects of Divorce Why is the effect of divorce or separation so devastating? Even if single mothers (or fathers) can make up for the loss of a second parent, it is difficult to do so and the chances of failure increase. Single parents may find it difficult to provide adequate supervision, exposing kids to the negative effects of antisocial peers.[10] Single moms and dads are more likely to work outside the home, leaving kids alone after school, thereby reducing hours of parental supervision. Of course, most kids growing up in single-parent homes do not become delinquents or criminals, and most go on to live highly productive lives.[11] Nonetheless, the strain created by family breakup can take a lifelong toll on children's emotional lives and make them vulnerable to the crime-producing forces in the environment.[12] The Criminology in Action feature on page 223 reviews research on the factors that disrupt family life.

The association between crime and divorce may be due to economic factors. Because their incomes may decrease substantially in the aftermath of marital breakup, some divorced mothers are forced to move to residences in deteriorated neighborhoods that may place children at risk of crime and drug abuse. In poor neighborhoods, single parents cannot call upon neighborhood resources to take up the burden of controlling children, and, as a result, a greater burden is placed on families to provide adequate supervision.[13] Some groups (i.e., Hispanics, Asians) have been raised in cultures where divorce is rare and parents have less experience in developing child-rearing practices that buffer the effects of family breakup on adolescent problem behavior.[14]

When a mother remarries, it does not seem to mitigate the effects of divorce on youth. Children living with a stepparent exhibit as many problems as youth in single-parent families and considerably more problems than those who are living with both biological parents.[15]

Family Deviance A number of studies have found that parental deviance has a powerful influence on children's future behavior. When parents drink, take drugs, and commit crimes, the effects can be both devastating and long term. If they get arrested and wind up in prison, the effects of parental misbehavior are enhanced.[16] The effect is intergenerational: the children of deviant parents produce delinquent children themselves.[17]

Some of the most important data on the influence of parental deviance were gathered by British criminologist David Farrington, whose longitudinal research data were gathered in the long-term Cambridge Study in Delinquent Development (CSDD). Some of the most important results include:

- A significant number of delinquent youths have criminal fathers. About 8 percent of the sons of noncriminal

fathers became chronic offenders, compared to 37 percent of youths with criminal fathers.[18]
- School yard bullying may be both inter- and intragenerational. Bullies have children who bully others, and these "second-generation bullies" grow up to become the parents of children who are also bullies.[19] Thus, one family may have a grandfather, father, and son who are or were school yard bullies.[20]
- Kids whose parents go to prison are much more likely to be at risk for delinquency than children of nonincarcerated parents.[21]

Parental Efficacy While poor parenting and parental deviance may increase exposure to criminality, children raised by parents who have excellent parenting skills, who are supportive and can effectively control their children in a noncoercive fashion, are more insulated from crime-producing forces in society.[22] Effective parenting can help neutralize the effect of both individual (e.g., emotional problems) and social (e.g., delinquent peers) forces that promote delinquent behaviors.[23] Even kids who are at risk to delinquency because of personality problems or neurological syndromes, such as ADHD, have a much better prognosis if they receive effective, supportive parenting.[24]

Research shows that antisocial behavior will be reduced if parents provide the type of structure that integrates children into families, while giving them the ability to assert their individuality and regulate their own behavior—a phenomenon referred to as **parental efficacy**.[25] In some cultures, emotional support from the mother is critical, whereas in others the father's support remains the key factor.[26]

Numerous studies have uncovered links between the quality of family life and delinquency. Children who feel inhibited with their parents and refuse to discuss important issues with them are more likely to engage in deviant activities. Kids who report having troubled home lives also exhibit lower levels of self-esteem and are more prone to antisocial behaviors.[27] One reason for poor communication is parents who rely on authoritarian disciplinary practices, holding a "my way or the highway" orientation. Telling kids that "as long as you live in my house you will obey my rules" does little to improve communications and may instead produce kids who are rebellious and crime prone.[28]

Child Maltreatment There is also a suspected link between crime and child abuse, neglect, and sexual abuse.[29] Numerous studies conducted in the United States and abroad show that there is a significant association between child maltreatment and serious self-reported and official delinquency, even when taking into account gender, race, and class.[30] The more often a child is physically disciplined and the harsher the discipline, the more likely they will engage in antisocial behaviors.[31] Children, both males and females, black or white, who experience abuse, neglect, or sexual abuse are believed to be more crime prone and suffer from other social problems such as depression, suicide

parental efficacy Parenting that is supportive, effective, and noncoercive.

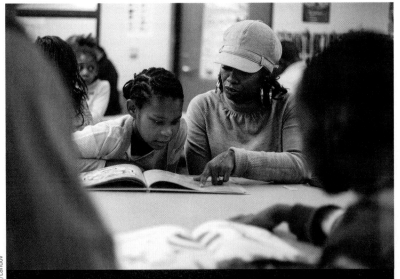

Tonya Stewart listens to her daughter, Laila Thomas, 9, as she reads at Heavenrich Elementary in Saginaw, Michigan. Heavenrich invited parents to come to the school and eat breakfast with their children. After breakfast, parents took their children to the school library to read together.

attempts, substance abuse, and self-injurious behaviors.[32] Nor does the abuse have to be direct: children who observe the physical abuse of a sibling are more likely to externalize misbehavior themselves.[33]

The effects of abuse are felt well beyond childhood. Kids who were abused are less likely to graduate from high school, hold a job, and be happily married; they are more likely to suffer juvenile and adult arrests.[34] Thus the seeds of adult dysfunction are planted early in childhood.[35]

The Chicken or the Egg?   Which comes first, bad parents or bad kids? Does poor parenting cause delinquency or do delinquents undermine their parents' supervisory abilities? According to David Huh and his colleagues, bad kids create bad parents. They found little evidence that poor parenting is a direct cause of children's misbehavior problems but instead discovered that a child's problem behaviors undermine parenting effectiveness. *Increases* in adolescent behavior problems, such as substance abuse, result in a *decrease* in parental control and support.[36] While not everyone agrees with that turn of events, others support Huh's view that parental control weakens *after* kids get involved in delinquency and not before.[37] Parents actually tend to stick by their kids, even when their children are chronic troublemakers; parents do not give up easily on their troubled teens.[38]

Educational Experience

The educational process and adolescent achievement in school have been linked to criminality. Studies show that children who do poorly in school, lack educational motivation, and feel alienated are the most likely to engage in criminal acts.[39] Children who fail in school have been found to offend more frequently than those who are successful in school. These children commit more serious and violent offenses and persist in their offending into adulthood.[40]

Schools contribute to criminality when they label problem youths and set them apart from conventional society. One way in which schools perpetuate this stigmatization is the "track system," which identifies some students as college bound and others as academic underachievers or potential dropouts.[41] Those children placed in tracks labeled advanced placement, college prep, or honors will develop positive self-images and achievement motivation, whereas those assigned to lower level or general courses of study may believe academic achievement is closed to someone of their limited skills.

Dropping Out   Another significant educational problem is that many students leave high school without gaining a diploma. Each year, approximately 1.2 million students fail to graduate from high school.

When surveyed, most dropouts say they left either because they did not like school or because they wanted to get a job. Kids who grow up fast, who are involved in drug abuse or other risky behaviors, may drop out of school in order to pursue an adult lifestyle.[42] Other risk factors include low academic achievement, poor problem-solving ability, low self-esteem, dissatisfaction with school, and being too old for their grade level.[43] Some dropouts could not get along with teachers and had been expelled or were under suspension. Almost half of all female dropouts left school because they were pregnant or had already given birth.

The research on the effect of dropping out is a mixed bag. Some research findings indicate that school dropouts face a significant chance of entering a criminal career, but other efforts using sophisticated methodological tools have failed to find a dropout effect.[44] If there is a "dropout effect," it is because those who leave school early already have a long history of poor school performance and antisocial behaviors.[45] In other words, poor school performance predicts both dropping out and antisocial activity. Even if dropping out is not directly related to crime, it reduces earnings and dampens future life achievements.

Peer Relations and Crime

LO3   Discuss the link between peers and delinquency

Psychologists have long recognized that the peer group has a powerful effect on human conduct and can have a dramatic influence on decision making and behavior choices.[46] Peers guide each other and help each other learn to share and cooperate, to cope with aggressive impulses, and to

Neil Barris/MLive.com/Landov

discuss feelings they would not dare bring up at home. Youths can compare their own experiences with peers and learn that others have similar concerns and problems.[47] It is not surprising, then, that peer influence on criminal behavior appears to be a universal norm.[48] Kids who hang out with delinquent friends, who spend time socializing with them without parental supervision, and who admire and want to emulate them are the ones most likely to increase involvement in antisocial behaviors.[49]

The more antisocial the peer group, the more likely its members will engage in delinquency; nondelinquent friends will help moderate delinquency.[50] One study found that kids involved in delinquency are five times more likely than nonoffenders to associate with delinquent peers.[51] Peer relations may be more important than parental nurturance in the development of long-term behavior.[52] Even children born into high-risk families—such as those with single teen mothers—can avoid delinquency if their friends refrain from drug use and criminality.[53]

While there is agreement that the association between peers and criminality exists, there is some debate over the path of the relationship:

- Delinquent friends cause law-abiding youth to get in trouble. Kids who fall in with a bad crowd are at risk for delinquency.[54] For girls, a "bad crowd" usually means teenage boys![55]
- Antisocial youths seek out and join up with like-minded friends; deviant peers sustain and amplify delinquent careers.[56] Those who choose aggressive or violent friends are more likely to begin engaging in antisocial behavior themselves and suffer psychological deficits.[57]
- As children move through their life course, antisocial friends help youths maintain delinquent careers and obstruct the aging-out process.[58] In stable friendships, the more accepted popular partner exerts greater influence over the less accepted partner. If the more popular friend continually engages in delinquency and alcohol use, the less popular "follower" will also.[59] In contrast, noncriminal friends moderate criminality.[60]
- Troubled kids choose delinquent peers out of necessity rather than desire. The social baggage they cart around prevents them from developing associations with conventional peers. Because they are impulsive, they may join cliques whose members are dangerous and get them into trouble.[61] The most at-risk kids may choose older peers, perhaps because they believe these older, tougher friends can provide some level of protection; their choices may backfire when their more mature companions enmesh them in a deviant subculture.[62] Older peers do not cause

straight kids to go bad, but they amplify the likelihood of a troubled kid getting further involved in antisocial behaviors.[63] The fear of punishment is diminished among kids who hang with delinquent friends, and loyalty to delinquent peers may outweigh the fear of punishment.[64]

Religion and Belief

LO4 Explain how personal beliefs impact on criminality

Logic would dictate that people who hold high moral values and beliefs, who have learned to distinguish right from wrong, and who regularly attend religious services should also eschew crime and other antisocial behaviors.[65] Religion binds people together and forces them to confront the consequences of their behavior. Having high moral beliefs may enhance the deterrent effect of punishment by convincing even motivated offenders not to risk apprehension and punishment.[66] Committing crimes would violate the principles of all organized religions.

More than 40 years ago in a now classic study, Travis Hirschi and Rodney Stark found that, contrary to expectations, the association between religious attendance and belief

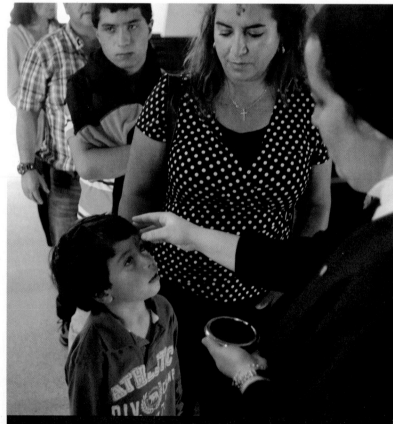

Santiago Cena, of Colombia, receives ashes from Sister Ileana Aponte on Ash Wednesday at Our Lady of Charity Catholic Church in Miami. Do you believe that young Santiago's religious experiences will help shield him from delinquency as he matures?

AP Images/Alan Diaz

and delinquent behavior patterns is negligible and insignificant.[67] Since the publication of their milestone study, there have been numerous research efforts to review the influence of religion on misbehavior, and a majority have reached an opposite conclusion: maintaining religious beliefs and attending religious services significantly helps reduce crime.[68] Richard Petts used data from a national survey and found that adolescents residing within two-parent families are less likely to become delinquent and that supportive parenting practices reduce the likelihood of their becoming delinquent even further. However, whether they reside in single-parent or two-parent families, kids who are involved in religion are less likely to engage in delinquency. Religion enhances the effect of parental affection in two-parent homes and also helps kids living in single-parent homes resist the influence of deviant peers. Petts found that religious participation helps reduce deviant behavior involvement throughout the life course, from adolescence until marriage.[69]

Socialization and Crime

LO5 Compare and contrast among social learning, control, and reaction theory

To many criminologists these elements of social process, social interaction, and socialization are the chief determinants of criminal behavior. While a person's place in the social structure may contribute to crime, environment alone is not enough to explain criminality. People living in even the most deteriorated urban areas can successfully resist inducements to crime if they have a positive self-image, learn moral values, and have the support of their parents, peers, teachers, and neighbors. The girl with a positive self-image who is chosen for a college scholarship has the warm, loving support of her parents and is viewed by friends and neighbors as someone who is "going places." She is less likely to adopt a criminal way of life than another adolescent who is abused at home, lives with criminal parents, and whose bond to her school and peer group is shattered because she is labeled a troublemaker.[70] The boy who has learned criminal behavior from his parents and siblings and then joins a neighborhood gang is much more likely to become an adult criminal than his next-door neighbor who idolizes his hard-working, deeply religious parents. It is socialization, not the social structure, that determines life chances. The more social problems encountered during the socialization process, the greater the likelihood that youths will encounter difficulties and obstacles as they mature, such as being unemployed or becoming a teenage mother.

Theorists who believe that an individual's socialization determines the likelihood of criminality adopt the social process approach to human behavior. The social process approach has several independent branches (Figure 7.1):

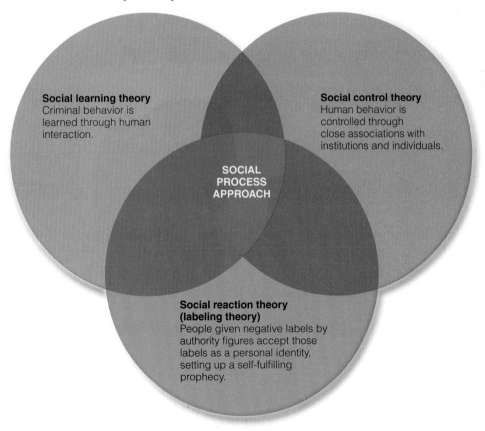

Social learning theory
Criminal behavior is learned through human interaction.

Social control theory
Human behavior is controlled through close associations with institutions and individuals.

SOCIAL PROCESS APPROACH

Social reaction theory (labeling theory)
People given negative labels by authority figures accept those labels as a personal identity, setting up a self-fulfilling prophecy.

FIGURE 7.1 The Social Processes that Control Human Behavior

SOURCE: © Cengage Learning®

- **Social learning theory** suggests that people learn the techniques and attitudes of crime from close and intimate relationships with criminal peers; crime is a learned behavior.
- **Social control theory** maintains that everyone has the potential to become a criminal, but that most people are controlled by their bonds to society. Crime occurs when the forces that bind people to society are weakened or broken.
- **Social reaction theory (labeling theory)** says people become criminals when significant members of society label them as such, and they accept those labels as a personal identity.

Put another way, social learning theory assumes people are born good and learn to be bad; social control theory assumes people are born bad and must be controlled in order to be good; social reaction theory assumes that, whether good or bad, people are controlled by the reactions of others. Each of these independent branches will be discussed separately.

social learning theory The view that human behavior is modeled through observation of human social interactions, either directly from observing those who are close and from intimate contact, or indirectly through the media. Interactions that are rewarded are copied, while those that are punished are avoided.

social control theory The view that people commit crime when the forces that bind them to society are weakened or broken.

social reaction theory (labeling theory) The view that people become criminals when significant members of society label them as such and they accept those labels as a personal identity.

To learn about the Institute for Child and Family Health, whose goal is to stimulate and coordinate the cross-disciplinary work required to make progress on the most difficult child and family policy issues facing the United States, go to **http://www.icfhinc.org/**.

Make a list of all the social process factors that you believe influence a child's future behavior. Can positive socialization overcome the social forces present in disorganized neighborhoods?

SOCIAL LEARNING THEORY

LO6 Explain the different forms social learning theory has taken

Social learning theorists believe crime is a product of learning the norms, values, and behaviors associated with criminal activity. Social learning can involve the actual techniques of crime—how to hot-wire a car or roll a joint—as well as the psychological aspects of criminality—how to deal with the guilt or shame associated with illegal activities. This section briefly reviews the three most prominent forms of social learning theory: differential association theory, differential reinforcement theory, and neutralization theory.

Differential Association Theory

One of the most prominent social learning theories is Edwin H. Sutherland's **differential association theory**. Often considered the preeminent U.S. criminologist, Sutherland first put forth his theory in his 1939 text, *Principles of Criminology*.[71] The final version of the theory appeared in 1947. When Sutherland died in 1950, Donald Cressey, his long-time associate, continued his work. Cressey was so successful in explaining and popularizing his mentor's efforts that differential association remains one of the most enduring explanations of criminal behavior.

Sutherland's research on white-collar crime, professional theft, and intelligence led him to dispute the notion that crime was a function of the inadequacy of people in the lower classes.[72] To Sutherland, criminality stemmed neither from individual traits nor from socioeconomic position; instead, he believed it to be a function of a learning process that could affect any individual in any culture. Acquiring a behavior is a social learning process, not a political or legal process. Skills and motives conducive to crime are learned as a result of contacts with procrime values, attitudes, and definitions and other patterns of criminal behavior.

Principles of Differential Association The basic principles of differential association are explained as follows:[73]

- *Criminal behavior is learned.* This statement differentiates Sutherland's theory from prior attempts to classify criminal behavior as an inherent characteristic of criminals. By suggesting that delinquent and criminal behavior is learned, Sutherland implied that it can be classified in the same manner as any other learned behavior, such as writing, painting, or reading.
- *Learning is a by-product of interaction.* Criminal behavior is learned as a by-product of interacting with others. Sutherland believed individuals do not start violating the law simply by living in a criminogenic environment or by manifesting personal characteristics, such as low IQ or family problems, associated with criminality.

People—family, friends, peers—have the greatest influence on their deviant behavior and attitude development. Relationships with these influential individuals color and control the way people interpret everyday events. For example, research shows that children who grow up in homes where parents abuse alcohol are more likely to view drinking as being socially and physically beneficial.[74] The intimacy of these associations far outweighs the importance of any other form of communication, such as movies or television. Even on those rare occasions when violent motion pictures seem to provoke mass criminal episodes, these outbreaks can be more readily explained as a reaction to peer group pressure than as a reaction to the films themselves.

- *Criminal techniques are learned.* Learning criminal behavior involves acquiring the techniques of committing the crime, which are sometimes very complicated and sometimes very simple. This requires learning the specific direction of motives, drives, rationalizations, and attitudes. Some kids may meet and associate with criminal "mentors" who teach them how to be successful criminals and gain the greatest benefits from their criminal activities.[75] They learn the proper way to pick a lock, shoplift, and obtain and use narcotics. In addition, novice criminals learn to use the proper terminology for their acts and then acquire "proper" reactions to law violations. For example, getting high on marijuana and learning the proper way to smoke a joint are behavior patterns usually acquired from more experienced companions. Moreover, criminals must learn how to react properly to their illegal acts, such as when to defend them, rationalize them, or show remorse for them.
- *Perceptions of the legal code influence motives and drives.* The specific direction of motives and drives is learned from perceptions of various aspects of the legal code as being favorable or unfavorable. The reaction to social rules and laws is not uniform across society, and people constantly come into contact with others who maintain different views on the utility of obeying the legal code. Some people they admire may openly disdain or flout the law or ignore its substance. People experience what Sutherland calls *culture conflict* when they are exposed to different and opposing attitudes toward what is right and wrong, moral and immoral. The conflict of social attitudes and cultural norms is the basis for the concept of differential association.
- *Differential associations may vary in frequency, duration, priority, and intensity.* Whether a person learns to obey the law or to disregard it is influenced by the quality

differential association theory According to Sutherland, the principle that criminal acts are related to a person's exposure to an excess amount of antisocial attitudes and values.

of social interactions. Those of lasting *duration* have greater influence than those that are brief. Similarly, *frequent* contacts have greater effect than rare and haphazard contacts. Sutherland did not specify what he meant by *priority*, but Cressey and others have interpreted the term to mean the age of children when they first encounter definitions of criminality. Contacts made early in life probably have a greater and more far-reaching influence than those developed later on. Finally, *intensity* is generally interpreted to mean the importance and prestige attributed to the individual or groups from whom the definitions are learned. For example, the influence of a father, mother, or trusted friend far outweighs the effect of more socially distant figures.

■ *The process of learning criminal behavior by association with criminal and anticriminal patterns involves all of the mechanisms involved in any other learning process.* This suggests that learning criminal behavior patterns is similar to learning nearly all other patterns and is not a matter of mere imitation.

■ *Criminal behavior is an expression of general needs and values, but it is not excused by those general needs and values because noncriminal behavior is also an expression of those same needs and values.* This principle suggests that the motives for criminal behavior cannot logically be the same as those for conventional behavior. Sutherland rules out such motives as desire to accumulate money or social status, personal frustration, or low self-concept as causes of crime because they are just as likely to produce noncriminal behavior, such as getting a better education or working harder on a job. It is only the learning of deviant norms through contact with an excess of definitions favorable toward criminality that produces illegal behavior.

A person becomes a criminal when he or she perceives more favorable than unfavorable consequences to violating the law. According to Sutherland's theory, individuals become law violators when they are in contact with people, groups, or events that produce an excess of definitions favorable toward criminality and are isolated from counteracting forces. A definition favorable toward criminality occurs, for example, when a person is exposed to friends sneaking into a theater to avoid paying for a ticket or talking about the virtues of getting high on drugs. A definition unfavorable toward crime occurs when friends or parents demonstrate their disapproval of crime. Neutral behavior, such as reading a book, is neither positive nor negative with respect to law violation. Neutral behavior, such as helping parents around the house, is important; when a child is occupied with activities, it prevents him or her from being in contact with those involved in criminal behaviors.[76]

In sum, differential association theory holds that people learn criminal attitudes and behavior while in their adolescence from close and trusted friends and/or relatives. A criminal career develops if learned antisocial values and behaviors are not at least matched or exceeded by conventional attitudes

and behaviors. Criminal behavior, then, is learned in a process that is similar to learning any other human behavior.

Testing Differential Association Theory Numerous research efforts have supported the core principles of differential association. These generally show a correlation between (a) having deviant parents and friends, (b) holding deviant attitudes, and (c) committing deviant acts. Taken as a whole, the research shows that the relationship between crime and measures of differential association are quite strong.[77] Among the most important findings are:

■ Crime appears to be intergenerational. Kids whose parents are deviant and criminal are more likely to become criminals themselves and eventually to produce criminal children. This supports the contention that children learn from deviant parents.[78]

■ The more deviant an adolescent's social network and network of affiliations, including parents, peers, and romantic partners, the more likely that adolescent is to engage in antisocial behavior.[79] This finding supports the hypothesis that children learn criminal attitudes from exposure to deviant others, rather than crime being a function of inherited criminal traits.[80]

■ People who report having attitudes that support deviant behavior are also likely to engage in deviant behavior.[81] As people mature, having delinquent friends who support criminal attitudes and behavior is strongly related to developing criminal careers. Association with deviant peers has been found to sustain the deviant attitudes.[82]

■ The influence of deviant friends is highly supportive of delinquency, regardless of race and/or class.[83] One reason is that within peer groups, high-status leaders will influence and legitimize deviant behavior. In other words, if one of your friends whom you look up to drinks and smokes, it makes it a lot easier for you to engage in those behaviors yourself and to believe they are appropriate.[84]

■ Romantic partners who engage in antisocial activities may influence their partner's behavior, which suggests that partners learn from one another.[85] Adolescents with deviant romantic partners are more delinquent than those youths with more prosocial partners, regardless of friends' and parents' behavior.[86]

■ Kids who associate and presumably learn from deviant peers are more likely to get involved in delinquency.[87] Deviant peers keep kids in criminal careers.[88]

■ Differential association is multicultural. Scales measuring differential association have been significantly correlated with criminal behaviors among samples taken in other nations and cultures.[89]

Differential association also seems especially relevant in trying to explain the onset of substance abuse and a career in the drug trade. This requires learning proper techniques and attitudes from an experienced user or dealer.[90] In his interview study of low-level drug dealers, Kenneth Tunnell found that many novices were tutored by a more experienced criminal dealer who helped them make connections with buyers and sellers. One told him:

> I had a friend of mine who was an older guy, and he introduced me to selling marijuana to make a few dollars. I started selling a little and made a few dollars. For a young guy to be making a hundred dollars or so, it was a lot of money. So I got kind of tied up in that aspect of selling drugs.[91]

Tunnell found that making connections is an important part of the dealer's world. Adolescent drug users are likely to have intimate relationships with a peer friendship network that supports their substance abuse and teaches them how to deal within the drug world.[92]

Differential association may also be used to explain the gender difference in the crime rate. Males are more likely to socialize with deviant peers than females and, when they do, are more deeply influenced by peer relations.[93] Females are shielded by their unique moral sense, which makes caring about people and avoiding social harm a top priority. Males, in contrast, have a more cavalier attitude toward others and are more interested in their own self-interests. They are therefore more susceptible to the influence of deviant peers.[94]

Analysis of Differential Association Theory   There have been a number of important critiques of the theory. According to the *cultural deviance critique*, differential association is invalid because it suggests that criminals are people "properly" socialized into a deviant subculture; that is, they are taught criminal norms by significant others. Supporters counter that differential association also recognizes that individuals can embrace criminality because they have been improperly socialized into the normative culture.[95]

Differential association theory also fails to explain why one youth who is exposed to delinquent definitions eventually succumbs to them, while another, living under the same conditions, is able to avoid criminal entanglements. It also fails to account for the origin of delinquent definitions: How did the first "teacher" learn delinquent attitudes and definitions in order to pass them on? Who taught the teacher?

Differential association theory assumes that youths learn about crime and then commit criminal acts, but it is also possible that experienced delinquents and criminals seek out like-minded peers after they engage in antisocial acts and that the internalization of deviant attitudes follows, rather than precedes, criminality ("birds of a feather flock together").[96] Research on gang boys shows that they are involved in high rates of criminality before they join gangs, indicating that the group experience facilitates their antisocial behavior rather than playing a role in its creation.[97]

Despite these criticisms, differential association theory maintains an important place in the study of criminal behavior. For one thing, it provides a consistent explanation of all types of delinquent and criminal behavior. Unlike social structure theories, it is not limited to the explanation of a single facet of antisocial activity, such as lower-class gang activity. The theory can also account for the extensive delinquent behavior found even in middle- and upper-class areas, where youths may be exposed to a variety of prodelinquent definitions from such sources as overly opportunistic parents and friends. The theory appears flexible and able to explain current trends in crime and is not bound by those that existed when the theory was first created. For example, Sameer Hinduja and Jason Ingram found that adolescents who pirate music off the Internet are influenced by both personal friends and also online friends they meet in chat rooms and so on. Internet music piracy is not a crime that Sutherland had in mind when he first proposed the theory more than 70 years ago.[98]

Edwin H. Sutherland served as the 29th president of the American Sociological Society. His presidential address, "White-Collar Criminality," was delivered at the organization's annual meeting in Philadelphia in December 1939. Read this groundbreaking document at http://cooley .libarts.wsu.edu/criminology/Documents/sutherland.pdf.
According to Sutherland, all crimes are learned, even white-collar offenses. Do you agree?

James Wesley Robinson (right), and his son Zachary Robinson wait for their initial court appearance in Salt Lake City Third District Court, March 13, 2014. Robinson, 50, was charged with operation of a clandestine laboratory, possession of a controlled substance with intent to distribute, and possession or use of a controlled substance. His two sons, Alexander, 21, and Zachary, 18, were charged with similar violations. They were accused of manufacturing the marijuana by-product called "Dab" or "Shatter," a concentrated, caramel-like substance produced from raw pot.

AP Images/Al Hartmann/Salt Lake Tribune

Differential Reinforcement Theory

Differential reinforcement theory is another attempt to explain crime as a type of learned behavior. First proposed by Ronald Akers in collaboration with Robert Burgess in 1966, it is a version of the social learning view that employs both differential association concepts along with elements of psychological learning theory.

According to Akers, the same process is involved in learning both deviant and conventional behavior. People learn to be neither "all deviant" nor "all conforming," but rather strike a balance between the two opposing poles of behavior. This balance is usually stable, but it can undergo revision over time.[99]

A number of learning processes shape behavior. **Direct conditioning**, also called **differential reinforcement**, occurs when behavior is reinforced by being either rewarded or punished while interacting with others. When behavior is punished, this is referred to as **negative reinforcement**. This type of reinforcement can be distributed either by using negative stimuli (punishment) or by loss of a positive

reward. Whether deviant or criminal behavior has been initiated or persists depends on the degree to which it has been rewarded or punished and the rewards or punishments attached to its alternatives.

According to Akers, people learn to evaluate their own behavior through their interactions with significant others and groups in their lives. These groups control sources and patterns of reinforcement, define behavior as right or wrong, and provide behaviors that can be modeled through observational learning. The more individuals learn to define their behavior as good or at least as justified, rather than as undesirable, the more likely they are to engage in it. Adolescents who join a drug-abusing peer group whose members value drugs and alcohol, encourage their use, and provide opportunities to observe people abusing substances will be encouraged, through this social learning experience, to use drugs themselves.

Akers's theory posits that the principal influence on behavior comes from "those groups that control individuals' major sources of reinforcement and punishment and expose them to behavioral models and normative definitions."[100] The important groups are the ones with which a person is in differential association—peer and friendship groups, schools, churches, and similar institutions. Within the context of these critical groups, according to Akers, "deviant behavior can be expected to the extent that it has been differentially reinforced over alternative behavior ... and is defined as desirable or justified."[101] Once people are indoctrinated into crime, their behavior can be reinforced by being exposed to deviant behavior models—associating with deviant peers—without being subject to negative reinforcements for their antisocial acts. The deviant behavior, originally executed by imitating someone else's behavior, is sustained by social support. For example, kids who engage in computer crime and computer hacking may find their behavior reinforced by peers who are playing the same game.[102]

It is possible that differential reinforcements help establish criminal careers and are a key factor in explaining persistent criminality.

Testing Differential Reinforcement The principles of differential reinforcement have been subject to empirical review by Akers and other criminologists.[103] In an important test of his theory, Akers and his associates surveyed 3,065 male and female adolescents on drug- and alcohol-related activities and their perception of variables related to social learning and differential reinforcement. Items in the scale included the respondents' perceptions of esteemed peers' attitudes toward drug and alcohol abuse, the number of people they admired who actually used controlled substances, and whether people they admired would reward or punish them for substance abuse. Akers found a strong association between drug and alcohol abuse and social learning variables: those who believed they would be rewarded for deviance by those they respect were the ones most likely to engage in deviant behavior.[104] Akers's efforts

---

differential reinforcement theory An attempt to explain crime as a type of learned behavior. First proposed by Akers in collaboration with Burgess in 1966, it is a version of the social learning view that employs differential association concepts as well as elements of psychological learning theory.

direct conditioning Behavior is reinforced by being either rewarded or punished while interacting with others; also called differential reinforcement.

differential reinforcement Behavior is reinforced by being either rewarded or punished while interacting with others; also called direct conditioning.

negative reinforcement Using either negative stimuli (punishment) or loss of reward (negative punishment) to curtail unwanted behaviors.

have been supported by research showing that kids whose deviant behavior (such as smoking pot) is reinforced by significant others (such as parents or peers) are more likely to accelerate their rates of deviance.[105]

Akers also found that the learning–deviant behavior link is not static. The learning experience continues within a deviant group as behavior is both influenced by and exerts influence over group processes. For example, adolescents may learn to smoke because their friends are smoking and, therefore, approve of this behavior. Over time, smoking influences friendships and peer group memberships as smokers seek out one another for companionship and support.[106]

Differential reinforcement theory is an important perspective that endeavors to determine the cause of criminal activity. It considers how the content of socialization conditions crime. Because not all socialization is positive, it accounts for the fact that negative social reinforcements and experiences can produce criminal results. This concurs with research that demonstrates that parental deviance is related to adolescent antisocial behavior.[107] Parents may reinforce their children's deviant behavior by supplying negative social reinforcements. Akers's work also fits well with rational choice theory because they both suggest that people learn the techniques and attitudes necessary to commit crime. Criminal knowledge is gained through experience. After considering the outcome of their past experiences, potential offenders decide which criminal acts will be profitable and which are dangerous and should be avoided.[108] Integrating these perspectives, people make rational choices about crime because they have learned to balance risks against the potential for criminal gain.

Neutralization Theory

Neutralization theory is identified with the writings of David Matza and his associate Gresham Sykes.[109] They view the process of becoming a criminal as a learning experience in which potential delinquents and criminals master techniques that enable them to counterbalance or neutralize conventional values and drift back and forth between illegitimate and conventional behavior. One reason this is possible is the subterranean value structure of American society. **Subterranean values** are morally tinged influences that have become entrenched in the culture but are publicly condemned. They exist side by side with conventional values and while condemned in public may be admired or practiced in private. Examples include viewing pornographic films, drinking alcohol to excess, and gambling on sporting events. In American culture, it is common to hold both subterranean and conventional values; few people are "all good" or "all bad."

Matza argues that even the most committed criminals and delinquents are not involved in criminality all the time; they also attend schools, family functions, and religious services. Their behavior can be conceived as falling along a continuum between total freedom and total restraint. This process, which he calls **drift**, refers to the movement from one extreme of behavior to another, resulting in behavior that is sometimes unconventional, free, or deviant and at other times constrained and sober.[110] Learning techniques of neutralization enables a person to temporarily "drift away" from conventional behavior and get involved in more subterranean values and behaviors, including crime and drug abuse.[111]

Sykes and Matza base their theoretical model on these observations:[112]

- *Criminals sometimes voice a sense of guilt over their illegal acts.* If a stable criminal value system existed in opposition to generally held values and rules, it would be unlikely that criminals would exhibit any remorse for their acts, other than regret at being apprehended.
- *Offenders frequently respect and admire honest, law-abiding people.* Really honest people are often revered, and if for some reason such people are accused of misbehavior, the criminal is quick to defend their integrity. Those admired may include sports figures, priests and other clergy, parents, teachers, and neighbors.
- *Criminals draw a line between those whom they can victimize and those whom they cannot.* Members of similar ethnic groups, churches, or neighborhoods are often off limits. This practice implies that criminals are aware of the wrongfulness of their acts.
- *Criminals are not immune to the demands of conformity.* Most criminals frequently participate in many of the same social functions as law-abiding people—for example, in school, church, and family activities.

Because of these factors, Sykes and Matza conclude that criminality is the result of the neutralization of accepted social values through the learning of a standard set of techniques that allow people to counteract the moral dilemmas posed by illegal behavior.[113]

Techniques of Neutralization Sykes and Matza suggest that people develop a distinct set of justifications for their law-violating behavior (Figure 7.2). These neutralization techniques enable them to temporarily drift away from

neutralization theory Neutralization theory holds that offenders adhere to conventional values while "drifting" into periods of illegal behavior. In order to drift, people must first overcome (neutralize) legal and moral values.

subterranean values Morally tinged influences that have become entrenched in the culture but are publicly condemned. They exist side by side with conventional values and while condemned in public may be admired or practiced in private.

drift According to Matza, the view that youths move in and out of delinquency and that their lifestyles can embrace both conventional and deviant values.

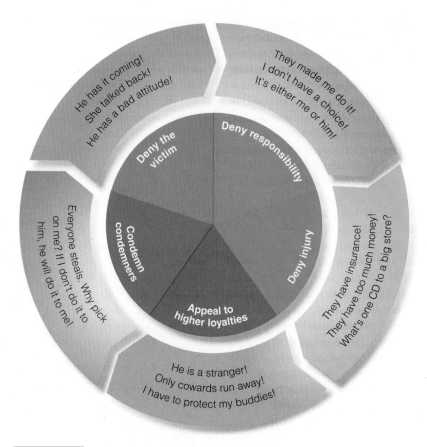

FIGURE 7.2 Techniques of Neutralization

SOURCE: © Cengage Learning®

the rules of the normative society and participate in subterranean behaviors. These techniques of neutralization include the following patterns:

- *Deny responsibility.* Young offenders sometimes claim their unlawful acts were simply not their fault. Criminal acts resulted from forces beyond their control or were accidents.
- *Deny injury.* By denying the wrongfulness of an act, criminals are able to neutralize illegal behavior. For example, stealing is viewed as borrowing; vandalism is considered mischief that has gotten out of hand. Delinquents may find that their parents and friends support their denial of injury. In fact, they may claim that the behavior was merely a prank, helping affirm the offender's perception that crime can be socially acceptable. Since no one was "really hurt" the act was not "really a crime."
- *Deny the victim.* Criminals sometimes neutralize wrongdoing by maintaining that the victim of crime "had it coming." Vandalism may be directed against a disliked teacher or neighbor; homosexuals may be beaten up by a gang because their behavior is considered offensive. Denying the victim may also take the form of ignoring the rights of an absent or unknown victim—for example, stealing from the unseen owner of a department store. It becomes morally acceptable for the criminal

to commit such crimes as vandalism when the victims, because of their absence, cannot be sympathized with or respected.

- *Condemn condemners.* An offender views the world as a corrupt place with a dog-eat-dog code. Because police and judges are on the take, teachers show favoritism, and parents take out their frustrations on their kids, it is ironic and unfair for these authorities to condemn his or her misconduct. By shifting the blame to others, criminals are able to repress the feeling that their own acts are wrong.
- *Appeal to higher loyalties.* Novice criminals often argue that they are caught in the dilemma of being loyal to their own peer group while at the same time attempting to abide by the rules of the larger society. The needs of the group take precedence over the rules of society because the demands of the former are immediate and localized.

In sum, the theory of neutralization presupposes a condition that allows people to neutralize unconventional norms and values by using such slogans as "I didn't mean to do it," "I didn't really hurt anybody," "They had it coming to them," "Everybody's picking on me," and "I didn't do it for myself." These excuses allow people to drift into criminal modes of behavior.

Testing Neutralization Theory   Attempts have been made to verify the assumptions of neutralization theory empirically, but the results have been inconclusive.[114] One area of research has been directed at determining whether there really is a need for law violators to neutralize moral constraints. The thinking behind this research is this: if criminals hold values *in opposition* to accepted social norms, then there is really no need to neutralize. So far, the evidence is mixed. Some studies show that law violators approve of criminal behavior, such as theft and violence, and still others find evidence that even though they may be active participants themselves, criminals voice disapproval of illegal behavior.[115] Some studies indicate that law violators approve of social values such as honesty and fairness; others come to the opposite conclusion.[116]

In addition to youthful delinquent behaviors, the adoption of neutralization techniques has also been used to explain the onset of white-collar crime.[117] Businessmen may find it easier to cut corners by claiming that "the government exaggerates dangers to the consumer" (denial of injury) or the "markets are generally safe so the corporate producers should not have to take blame for the few injuries that occur" (denial of responsibility) or "the bottom line is all that matters" (appeal to higher loyalty). The need to get ahead in the corporate world may help them neutralize the moral constraints that their parents may have taught them in adolescence, such as play fair, don't cheat, take responsibility.

The theory of neutralization, then, is a major contribution to the literature of crime and delinquency. It can account for the aging-out process: youths can forgo criminal behavior as adults because they never really rejected the morality of normative society. It helps explain the behavior of the occasional or nonchronic delinquent, who is able to successfully age out of crime. Because teens are not committed to criminality, as they mature they simply drift back into conventional behavior patterns. While they are young, justifications and excuses neutralize guilt and enable individuals to continue to feel good about themselves.[118] In contrast, people who remain criminals as adults may be using newly learned techniques to neutralize the wrongfulness of their actions and avoid guilt. For example, psychotherapists accused of sexually exploiting their clients blame the victim for "seducing them"; some claim there was little injury caused by the sexual encounter; others seek scapegoats to blame for their actions.[119]

Are Learning Theories Valid?

Learning theories make a significant contribution to our understanding of the onset of criminal behavior. Nonetheless, the general learning model has been subject to some criticism. One complaint is that learning theorists fail to account for the origin of criminal definitions. How did the first "teacher" learn criminal techniques and definitions? Who came up with the original neutralization technique?

And, as the Criminology in Action feature suggests, hardcore offenders feel little need to neutralize moral restraints—they may not have any!

Learning theories also imply that people systematically learn techniques that enable them to be active and successful criminals, but they fail to adequately explain spontaneous and wanton acts of violence and damage and other expressive crimes that appear to have little utility or purpose. Principles of differential association can easily explain shoplifting, but is it possible that a random shooting is caused by excessive deviant definitions? It is estimated that about 70 percent of all arrestees were under the influence of drugs and alcohol when they committed their crime. Do "crack heads" pause to neutralize their moral inhibitions before mugging a victim? Do drug-involved kids stop to consider what they have "learned" about moral values?[120]

Little evidence exists substantiating that people learn the techniques that enable them to become criminals before they actually commit criminal acts. It is equally plausible that people who are already deviant seek out others with similar lifestyles. Early onset of deviant behavior is now considered a key determinant of criminal careers. It is difficult to see how extremely young adolescents had the opportunity to learn criminal behavior and attitudes within a peer group setting.

Despite these criticisms, learning theories maintain an important place in the study of delinquent and criminal behavior. Unlike social structure theories, these theories are not limited to the explanation of a single facet of antisocial activity—for example, lower-class gang activity; they may be used to explain criminality across all class structures. Even corporate executives may be exposed to a variety of procriminal definitions and learn to neutralize moral constraints.

SOCIAL CONTROL THEORY

Social control theories maintain that all people have the potential to violate the law and that modern society presents many opportunities for illegal activity. Criminal activities, such as drug abuse and car theft, are often exciting pastimes that hold the promise of immediate reward and gratification.

Considering the attractions of crime, the question control theorists pose is: why do people obey the rules of society? A choice theorist would respond that it is the fear of punishment; structural theorists would say that obedience is a function of having access to legitimate opportunities; learning theorists would explain that obedience is acquired through contact with law-abiding parents and peers. In contrast, social control theorists argue that people obey the law because behavior and passions are being controlled by internal and external forces. Because they have been properly socialized, most people have developed a strong moral sense, which renders them incapable of hurting others and

WHEN BEING GOOD IS BAD

In their neutralization theory, Sykes and Matza claim that neutralizations provide offenders with a means of preserving a noncriminal self-concept even as they engage in crime and deviance. Sykes and Matza's vision assumes that most criminals believe in conventional norms and values and must use neutralizations in order to shield themselves from the shame attached to criminal activity. Recent research by criminologist Volkan Topalli finds that Sykes and Matza may have ignored the influential street culture that exists in highly disadvantaged neighborhoods. Using data gleaned from 191 in-depth interviews with active criminals in St. Louis, Missouri, Topalli finds that street criminals living in disorganized, gang-ridden neighborhoods "disrespect authority, lionize honor and violence, and place individual needs above those of all others." Rather than having to neutralize conventional values in order to engage in deviant ones, these offenders do not experience guilt that requires neutralizations; they are "guilt free." There is no need for them to "drift" into criminality, Topalli finds, because their allegiance to nonconventional values and lack of guilt perpetually leave them in a state of openness to crime.

Rather than being contrite or ashamed, the offenders Topalli interviewed took great pride in their criminal activities and abilities. Bacca, a street robber who attacked a long-time neighbor without provocation, exemplified such sentiments:

Actually I felt proud of myself just for robbing him, just for doing what I did I felt proud of myself. I didn't feel like I did anything wrong, I didn't feel like I lost a friend 'cause the friends I do have … are lost, they're dead. I feel like I don't have anything to lose. I wanted to do just what I wanted to do.

Topalli refers to streetwise offenders such as Bacca as "hardcores," who experience no guilt for their actions and operate with little or no regard for the law. They have little contact with agents of formal social control or conventional norms because their crimes are not directed toward conventional society—they rob drug dealers. Most hardcores maintain no permanent home, staying in various residences as their whim dictates. Their lifestyles are almost entirely dominated by the street ethics of violence, self-sufficiency, and opportunism. Obsessed with a constant need for cash, drugs, and alcohol in order to "keep the party going" on the one hand, and limited by self-defeating and reckless spending habits on the other, they often engage in violent crime to bankroll their street life activities. They do not have to neutralize conventional values, because they have none.

Rather than neutralizing conventional values, hardcore criminals often have to neutralize deviant values: they are expected to be "bad" and have to explain good behavior. Even if they themselves are the victims of crime, they can never help police or even talk to them, a practice defined as snitching and universally despised and discouraged. Smokedog, a carjacker and drug dealer, described the anticipated guilt of colluding with the police in this way, "You know I ain't never told on nobody and I ain't never gonna tell on nobody 'cause I would feel funny in the world if I told on somebody. You know, I would feel funny, I would have regrets about what I did."

Street criminals are also expected to seek vengeance if they are the target of theft or violence. If they don't, their self-image is damaged, and they look weak and ineffective. If they decide against vengeance, they must neutralize their decision by convincing themselves that they are being merciful, respecting direct appeals by their target's family and friends. T-dog, a young drug dealer and car thief, told Topalli how he neutralized the decision not to seek revenge by allowing his uncle to "calm him down." The older man, a robber and drug dealer himself, intervened before T-dog could leave his house armed with two 9mm automatics: "That's basically what he told me, 'Calm down.' He took both my guns and gave me a little .22 to carry when I'm out to put me back on my feet. Gave me an ounce of crack and a pound of weed. That's what made me let it go." In other cases, offenders claimed the target was just not worth the effort, reserving their vengeance for those who were worthy opponents.

Do these findings indicate that neutralization theory is invalid? Topalli concludes that the strength of the theory is its emphasis on cognitive processes that occur prior to offending. He suggests that neutralization theory's current emphasis on a conventional cultural value orientation must be expanded to accommodate the values of the street culture.

Critical Thinking

1. Are there deviant norms and values that you have to neutralize in order to engage in conventional behaviors? What neutralizations have you come up with in order to save face when your friends wanted to engage in some forms of deviance but you decided not to take the risk?
2. Do you agree with Topalli that kids in disorganized neighborhoods shun conventional values? Or do you agree with Sykes and Matza that everyone shares conventional norms and values?

SOURCE: Volkan Topalli, "When Being Good Is Bad: An Expansion of Neutralization Theory," *Criminology* 43 (2005): 797–836.

violating social norms. They develop a **commitment to conformity**, which requires that they obey the rules of society.[121] Properly socialized people believe that getting caught at criminal activity will hurt a dearly loved parent or jeopardize their chance at a college scholarship, or perhaps they feel that their job will be forfeited if they get in trouble with the law. In other words, people's behavior, including criminal activity, is controlled by their attachment and commitment to conventional institutions, individuals, and processes. On the other hand, those who have not been properly socialized, who lack a commitment to others or themselves, are free to violate the law and engage in deviant behavior. Those who are "uncommitted" are not deterred by the threat of legal punishments because they have little to lose.[122]

Self-Concept and Crime

Early versions of control theory speculated that control was a product of social interactions. Maladaptive social relations produced weak self-concept and poor self-esteem, rendering kids at risk to crime. In contrast, youths who felt good about themselves and maintained a positive attitude were able to resist the temptations of the streets. As early as 1951, sociologist Albert Reiss described how delinquents had weak egos.[123] Scott Briar and Irving Piliavin noted that youths who believe criminal activity will damage their self-image and their relationships with others will be most likely to conform to social rules; they have a commitment to conformity. In contrast, those less concerned about their social standing are free to violate the law.[124] In his **containment theory**, pioneering control theorist Walter Reckless argued that a strong self-image insulates a youth from the pressures and pulls of criminogenic influences in the environment.[125] In a series of studies conducted within the school setting, Reckless and his colleagues found that nondelinquent youths are able to maintain a positive self-image in the face of environmental pressures toward delinquency.[126]

It is Travis Hirschi's vision of social control, articulated in his highly influential 1969 book *Causes of Delinquency* that remains the dominant version of the theory.[127]

Hirschi's Social Bond Theory

 LO7 List the principles of Hirschi's social bond theory

In his insightful work, Hirschi links the onset of criminality to the weakening of the ties that bind people to society. He assumes that all individuals are potential law violators, but they are kept under control because they fear that illegal behavior will damage their relationships with friends, parents, neighbors, teachers, and employers. Without these social ties or bonds, and in the absence of sensitivity to and interest in others, a person is free to commit criminal acts. Hirschi does not view society as containing competing subcultures with unique value systems. Most people

CONNECTIONS

Though his work has achieved a prominent place in criminological literature, Hirschi, along with Michael Gottfredson, has restructured his concept of control by integrating biosocial, psychological, and rational choice theory ideas into a "General Theory of Crime." This theory of self-control is discussed more fully in Chapter 9.

are aware of the prevailing moral and legal codes. He suggests, however, that in all elements of society people vary in how they respond to conventional social rules and values. Among all ethnic, religious, racial, and social groups, people whose bond to society is weak may fall prey to criminogenic behavior patterns.

Elements of the Social Bond Hirschi argues that the **social bond** a person maintains with society is divided into four main elements: attachment, commitment, involvement, and belief (Figure 7.3).

- *Attachment.* Attachment refers to a person's sensitivity to and interest in others.[128] Without a sense of attachment, psychologists believe a person becomes a psychopath and loses the ability to relate coherently to the world. The acceptance of social norms and the development of a social conscience depend on attachment to and caring for other human beings. Hirschi views parents, peers, and schools as the important social institutions with which a person should maintain ties. Attachment to parents is the most important. Even if a family is shattered by divorce or separation, a child must retain a strong attachment to one or both parents. Without this attachment, it is unlikely that feelings of respect for others in authority will develop.

- *Commitment.* Commitment involves the time, energy, and effort expended in conventional lines of action, such as getting an education and saving money for the future. If people build a strong commitment to conventional society, they will be less likely to engage in acts that will jeopardize their hard-won position. Conversely,

commitment to conformity A strong personal investment in conventional institutions, individuals, and processes that prevents people from engaging in behavior that might jeopardize their reputation and achievements.

containment theory The idea that a strong self-image insulates a youth from the pressures and pulls of criminogenic influences in the environment.

social bond Ties a person has to the institutions and processes of society. According to Hirschi, elements of the social bond include commitment, attachment, involvement, and belief.

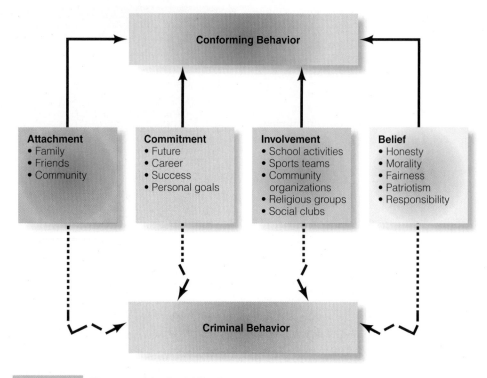

FIGURE 7.3 Elements of the Social Bond

SOURCE: © Cengage Learning®

the lack of commitment to conventional values may foreshadow a condition in which risk-taking behavior, such as crime, becomes a reasonable behavior alternative. The association may be reciprocal. Kids who drink and engage in deviant behavior are more likely to fail in school; kids who fail in school are more likely to later drink and engage in deviant behavior.[129]

- *Involvement.* Heavy involvement in conventional activities leaves little time for illegal behavior. When people become involved in school, recreation, and family, Hirschi believes, it insulates them from the potential lure of criminal behavior, whereas idleness enhances it.
- *Belief.* People who live in the same social setting often share common moral beliefs; they may adhere to such values as sharing, sensitivity to the rights of others, and admiration for the legal code. If these beliefs are absent or weakened, individuals are more likely to participate in antisocial or illegal acts.

Hirschi further suggests that the interrelationship of social bond elements controls subsequent behavior. People who feel kinship with and sensitivity to parents and friends should be more likely to adopt and work toward legitimate goals or gain skills that help them avoid antisocial or dangerous behaviors. Girls, for example, who have higher levels of bonding to parents and develop good social skills in adolescence are less likely to experience dating violence as young adults. The reason: a close bond to parents reduces early adolescent alcohol use, a factor that shields girls from victimization.[130]

Testing Social Bond Theory   One of Hirschi's most significant contributions was his attempt to test the principal hypotheses of social bond theory. He administered a detailed self-report survey to a sample of more than 4,000 junior and senior high school students in Contra Costa County, California.[131] In a detailed analysis of the data, Hirschi found considerable evidence to support the control theory model. Among Hirschi's more important findings are the following:

- Youths who were strongly attached to their parents were less likely to commit criminal acts.
- Commitment to conventional values, such as striving to get a good education and refusing to drink alcohol and "cruise around," was indicative of conventional behavior.
- Youths involved in conventional activity, such as homework, were less likely to engage in criminal behavior.
- Youths involved in unconventional behavior, such as smoking and drinking, were more delinquency prone.
- Youths who maintained weak and distant relationships with people tended toward delinquency.
- Those who shunned unconventional acts were attached to their peers.
- Delinquents and nondelinquents shared similar beliefs about society.

Supporting Research   Hirschi's data lent important support to the validity of control theory. Even when the statistical significance of his findings was less than he expected, the direction of his research data was notably consistent.

Only in very rare instances did his findings contradict the theory's most critical assumptions.

Hirschi's version of social control theory has been corroborated by numerous research studies, in the United States and abroad, showing that delinquent youth often feel detached from society.[132] Their relationships within the family, peer group, and school often appear strained, indicative of a weakened social bond and lack of attachment to significant others.[133] In contrast, strong positive attachments help control delinquency.[134]

- *Attachment.* Research indicates that, as Hirschi predicts, kids who are attached to their families, friends, and school are less likely to get involved in a deviant peer group and consequently less likely to engage in criminal activities.[135] In contrast, family detachment—including intrafamily conflict, abuse of children, and lack of affection, supervision, and family pride—are predictive of delinquent conduct.[136] Attachment to education is equally important. Youths who are detached from the educational experience are at risk of criminality; those who are committed to school are less likely to engage in delinquent acts.[137] Detachment and alienation from school may be even more predictive of delinquency than school failure and/or educational underachievement.[138]
- *Belief.* There is support for Hirschi's view that holding positive beliefs is inversely related to criminality. Children who are involved in religious activities and hold conventional religious beliefs are less likely to become involved in substance abuse.[139] Kids who live in areas marked by strong religious values and who hold strong religious beliefs themselves are less likely to engage in delinquent activities than adolescents who do not hold such beliefs or who live in less devout communities.[140]
- *Commitment.* As predicted by Hirschi, kids who are committed to future success and achievement are less likely to become involved in delinquent behaviors than those who lack such commitment.[141]
- *Involvement.* Research shows that youths who are involved in conventional leisure activities, such as supervised social activities and noncompetitive sports, are less likely to engage in delinquency than those who are involved in unconventional leisure activities and unsupervised, peer-oriented social pursuits.[142] One study found that students who engage in a significant amount of extracurricular activities from 8th grade through 12th grade are more likely to experience high academic achievement and prosocial behaviors extending into young adulthood.[143]

Cross-national surveys have also supported the general findings of Hirschi's control theory.[144] For example, one study of Canadian youth found that perception of parental attachment was the strongest predictor of delinquent or law-abiding behavior. Teens who are attached to their parents may develop the social skills that equip them both to maintain harmonious social ties and to escape life stresses such as school failure.[145]

Opposing Views A great deal of scholarly research has been conducted to corroborate social control theory by replicating Hirschi's original survey techniques.[146] There has been significant empirical support for Hirschi's work, but there are also those who question some or all of its elements. Here are some elements that have come under criticism and need further study:

- *Friendship.* One significant criticism concerns Hirschi's contention that delinquents are detached loners whose bond to their family and friends has been broken. Some critics have questioned whether delinquents (a) do have strained relations with family and peers and (b) may be influenced by close relationships with deviant peers and family members. A number of research efforts do show that delinquents maintain relationships with deviant peers and are influenced by members of their deviant peer group.[147] Delinquents, however, may not be "lone wolves" whose only personal relationships are exploitive; their friendship patterns seem quite close to those of conventional youth.[148] In fact, some types of offenders, such as drug abusers, may maintain even more intimate relations with their peers than nonabusers.[149] Hirschi would counter that what appears to be a close friendship is really a relationship of convenience and that "birds of a feather flock together" only when it suits their criminal activities. His view is supported by research conducted by criminologists Lisa Stolzenberg and Stewart D'Alessio, who found that most juvenile offenses are committed by individuals acting alone and that group offending, when it does occur, is incidental and of little importance to explaining the onset of delinquency.[150]

- *Not all elements of the bond are equal.* Hirschi makes little distinction between the importance of each element of the social bond, yet research evidence suggests that there may be differences. Some adolescents who report high levels of "involvement," which Hirschi suggests should reduce delinquency, are involved in criminal behavior. As kids get involved in behaviors outside the home, it is possible that parental control weakens, and youths have greater opportunity to commit crime.[151] When asked, children report that concepts such as "involvement" and "belief" have relatively little influence over behavior patterns."[152]

- *Deviant involvement.* Adolescents who report high levels of involvement, which Hirschi suggests should reduce delinquency, actually report high levels of criminal behavior. Typically, these are kids who are involved in activities outside the home without parental supervision.[153] Kids who spend a lot of time hanging out with their friends, unsupervised by parents and/or other authority figures, and who own cars that give them the mobility to get into even more trouble are the ones most likely to get involved in antisocial acts such as drinking and taking drugs.[154] This is especially true of dating relationships: kids who date, especially if they have multiple partners, are the ones who are likely to get into trouble and engage in delinquent acts.[155] It is possible that although involvement is important, it depends on the behavior in which a person is involved!

- *Deviant peers and parents.* Hirschi's conclusion that any form of social attachment is beneficial, even to deviant peers and parents, has also been disputed. Rather than deter delinquency attachment to deviant peers, it may support and nurture antisocial behavior. In a now classic study, criminologist Michael Hindelang found that attachment to delinquent peers escalated rather than restricted criminality.[156] In a similar fashion, a number of research efforts have found that youths attached to drug-abusing parents are more likely to become drug users themselves.[157] Attachment to deviant family members, peers, and associates may help motivate youths to commit crime and facilitate their antisocial acts.[158]

- *Restricted in scope.* There is some question as to whether the theory can explain all modes of criminality (as Hirschi maintains) or is restricted to particular groups or forms of criminality. Control variables seem better able to explain minor delinquency (such as alcohol and

According to labeling theory, perceptions guide behavior. Would you want to invite this guy to lunch with your family? He is The Scary Guy (his real name) and he spends his time teaching students and adults about what they can do to change the world by taking responsibility for their own behavior. His mission is to eliminate hate, violence, and prejudice worldwide. He is shown here hammering home his message at Valencia Middle School in Tucson, Arizona. What do you think of him now?

marijuana abuse) than more serious criminal acts and associations (such as the association between child abuse and violence).[159] Research efforts have found control variables are more predictive of female than male behavior.[160] Perhaps girls are more deeply influenced by the quality of their bond to society.

- *Crime and social bonds.* It is possible that Hirschi miscalculated the direction of the relationship between criminality and a weakened social bond.[161] Social bond theory projects that a weakened bond leads to delinquency, but it is possible that the chain of events may flow in the opposite direction: kids who break the law find that their bond to parents, schools, and society eventually becomes weak and attenuated.[162]

Despite these criticisms, the weight of existing empirical evidence supports control theory, and it has emerged as one of the preeminent theories in criminology. For many criminologists, it is perhaps the most important way of understanding the onset of youthful misbehavior.

SOCIAL REACTION THEORY

LO8 Summarize the basic elements of social reaction or labeling theory

Social reaction theory, commonly called labeling theory (the two terms are used interchangeably here), explains how criminal careers form based on destructive social interactions and encounters. Its roots are found in the symbolic interaction theory of sociologists Charles Horton Cooley and George Herbert Mead, and later, Herbert Blumer.[163] Symbolic interaction theory holds that people communicate via symbols—gestures, signs, words, or images—that stand for or represent something else. For example, a gold band on your ring finger conveys many meanings: married, stable, sexually off limits, conventional.

People interpret symbolic gestures from others and incorporate them in their self-image. When a teacher puts an A on your paper, it tells you that you are an excellent student, and the symbol pumps up your self-image. Symbols are used by others to let people know how well they are doing and whether they are liked or appreciated. Wearing a Rolex and driving a Mercedes is a symbolic way of letting people know that you are quite successful. Designer clothes display their symbol to let people know that the wearer has both taste and income. How people view reality then depends on the content of the messages and situations they encounter, the subjective interpretation of these interactions, and how they shape future behavior.

There is no objective reality. When someone takes another person's life, it could be self-defense or cold-blooded murder, depending on how people interpret the act. The difference between a forcible rape and a consensual sexual encounter often rests on whom the members of a jury believe and how they interpret the events that took place. The difference between an excusable act and a criminal one is often subject to change and modification. The police officer who punches a suspect may, depending on how people interpret the incident, get a medal for subduing a dangerous criminal or can be suspended for police brutality.

Because interpretation changes over time, so do the meanings of concepts and symbols. Acts such as performing an abortion, using marijuana, possessing a handgun, and gambling have been legal at some times and places and illegal at others.

Defining Crime and Deviance

Labeling theorists use an interactionist definition of crime. In a defining statement, sociologist Kai Erickson argues, "Deviance is not a property inherent in certain forms of behavior, it is a property conferred upon those forms by the audience which directly or indirectly witnesses them."[164] Crime and deviance, therefore, are defined by the social audience's reaction to people and their behavior and the subsequent effects of that reaction; they are not defined by the moral content of the illegal act itself.[165]

In another famous statement, Howard Becker sums up the importance of the audience's reaction:

Social groups create deviance by making rules whose infractions constitute deviance, and by applying those rules to particular people and labeling them as outsiders. From this point of view, deviance is not a quality of the act a person commits, but rather a consequence of the application by others of rules and sanctions to an "offender." The deviant is one to whom the label has successfully been applied; deviant behavior is behavior that people so label.[166]

In its purest form, social reaction theory argues that such crimes as murder, rape, and assault are only bad or evil because people label them as such. After all, the difference between an excusable act and a criminal one is often a matter of legal definition, which changes from place to place and from year to year.

Becker refers to people who create rules as *moral entrepreneurs*. An example of a moral entrepreneur today might be members of an ultra-orthodox religious group who target the gay lifestyle and mount a campaign to prevent gays from adopting children or conducting same-sex marriages.[167]

Interaction and Interpretation Social reaction theory picks up on these concepts of *interaction* and *interpretation*.[168] Throughout their lives, people are given a variety of symbolic labels and ways to interact with others. These labels represent behavior and attitude characteristics; labels help define not just one trait but the whole person. People labeled insane are also assumed to be dangerous, dishonest, unstable, violent, strange, and otherwise unsound. Valued labels, including smart, honest, and hard working, suggest overall competence. These labels can improve self-image and social standing. Research shows that people who are labeled with one positive trait, such as being physically attractive, are assumed to maintain other traits, such as being intelligent and competent.[169] In contrast, negative labels—including troublemaker, mentally ill, and stupid—help stigmatize the recipients of these labels and reduce their self-image. Those who have accepted these labels are more prone to engage in deviant behaviors than those whose self-image has not been so tarnished.[170] Though a label may be a function of rumor, innuendo, or unfounded suspicion, its adverse impact can be immense.

Patrick Corrigan notes that labeling and **stigma** can harm and diminish both the public and private self. Some groups bear public stigma, and being labeled as part of a stigmatized group "robs people of social opportunities."[171] Public stigma occurs when there is prejudice about a group that stigmatizes members (i.e., sex workers, mental patients) and helps exclude them from social opportunities, including

symbolic interaction theory The sociological view that people communicate through symbols. People interpret symbolic communication and incorporate it within their personality. A person's view of reality, then, depends on his or her interpretation of symbolic gestures.

stigma An enduring label that taints a person's identity and changes him or her in the eyes of others.

housing and work. In contrast, self-stigma occurs when negative social attitudes are internalized, subsequently harming a person's self-esteem and inducing shame.

Labeling Effects and Consequences

Depending on the visibility of the label and the manner and severity with which it is applied, a person will have an increasing commitment to a deviant career. They may be watched and become the leading suspect when a similar crime occurs. Labeled people may find themselves turning to others similarly stigmatized for support and companionship. Isolated from conventional society, they may identify themselves as members of an outcast group and become locked into a deviant career.

Negative labeling can be quite damaging to a person's well-being. Kids who perceive that they have been negatively labeled by significant others are at risk of adopting a deviant self-concept. They may seek out deviant friends and join deviant groups and gangs.[172] If their deviant activities land them in court, the official label increases the risk of their later dropping out of high school. Rather than deterring crime, court intervention increases the likelihood of future criminality.[173] The effects of this stigma become permanent, locking people out of jobs and conventional careers.[174]

Labeling, however, is rarely a one-way street; what some people are quick to reject, others are quite willing to defend. For example, when they learn that their child has been in trouble at school or in the community, some parents are willing to join in and condemn their kid as a "troublemaker," thereby helping to add to the label's impact and further damage their child's self-image; this process is referred to as **reflected appraisals**.[175] In contrast, when parents stick by kids, the effect of negative labels bestowed by others can be neutralized, helping to ward off the damaging effects of labeling.[176]

Joining Deviant Cliques   When people are labeled as deviant, they may join up with similarly outcast delinquent peers who facilitate their behavior.[177] Eventually, antisocial behavior becomes habitual and automatic.[178] The desire to join deviant cliques and groups may stem from a self-rejecting attitude ("at times, I think I am no good at all"), which eventually results in a weakened commitment to conventional values and behaviors. In turn, these people may acquire motives to deviate from social norms. Facilitating this attitude and value transformation is the bond social

outcasts form with similarly labeled peers in the form of a deviant subculture.[179]

Membership in a deviant subculture often involves conforming to group norms that conflict with those of conventional society. Deviant behaviors that defy conventional values can serve a number of different purposes. Some acts are designed to show contempt for the source of the negative labels. Other acts are planned to distance the transgressor from further contact with the source of criticism (for example, an adolescent runs away from critical parents).[180]

Damaged Identity   People who are given deviant labels and become notorious public figures suffer damaged identities. Their bad behavior can even be captured by cell phone cameras and show up on the Internet almost instantly. People engaging in sexual impropriety find their image online, their career in tatters. Take the case of Anthony Weiner, the former U.S. representative who served New York's 9th congressional district from January 1999 until June 2011 and was a rising political star until his "sexting" forced his resignation. Damaged identities follow people around and may never go away. A damaged identity provokes some people into repeating their antisocial behaviors, creating new labels and amplifying old ones.[181]

Once their identity has been damaged, the target may reassess their own self-image: "If everyone says I am a deviant, it must be true."[182] Although labels may not have caused them to initiate antisocial behaviors, once applied, they increase the likelihood of persistent offending.

As Anthony Weiner found, damaged identities are hard to shake. They follow you around and limit conventional opportunities, such as educational attainment and employment.[183] Weiner tried a political comeback, running for New York City mayor in 2013, but his past was too hard to overcome and his bid failed badly.

Retrospective Reading   After someone is labeled because of some unusual or inexplicable act, people begin to reconstruct the culprit's identity so that the act and the label become understandable (e.g., "we always knew there was something wrong with that boy"). It is not unusual for the media to lead the way and interview boyhood friends of an assassin or serial killer. On news programs we can hear them report that the suspect was withdrawn, suspicious, and negativistic as a youth, expressing violent thoughts and ideation, a loner, troubled, and so on. Yet, until now no one was suspicious and nothing was done. This is referred to as **retrospective reading**, a process in which the past of the labeled person is reviewed and reevaluated to fit his or her current status. By conducting a retrospective reading, we can now understand what prompted his current behavior; therefore, the label must be accurate.[184]

Dramatization of Evil   Labels become the basis of personal identity. As the negative feedback of law enforcement agencies, parents, friends, teachers, and other figures amplifies

reflected appraisals When parents are alienated from their children, their negative labeling reduces their children's self-image and increases delinquency.

retrospective reading The reassessment of a person's past to fit a current generalized label.

the force of the original label, stigmatized offenders may begin to reevaluate their own identities. If they are not really evil or bad, they may ask themselves, why is everyone making such a fuss? Frank Tannenbaum, a social reaction theory pioneer, referred to this process as the **dramatization of evil**. With respect to the consequences of labeling delinquent behavior, Tannenbaum stated:

> The process of making the criminal, therefore, is a process of tagging, defining, identifying, making conscious and self-conscious; it becomes a way of stimulating, suggesting and evoking the very traits that are complained of. If the theory of relation of response to stimulus has any meaning, the entire process of dealing with the young delinquent is mischievous insofar as it identifies him to himself or to the environment as a delinquent person. The person becomes the thing he is described as being.[185]

Primary and Secondary Deviance

One of the best-known views of the labeling process is Edwin Lemert's concept of primary deviance and secondary deviance.[186] According to Lemert, **primary deviance** involves norm violations or crimes that have very little influence on the actor and can be quickly forgotten. For example, a college student takes a "five-finger discount" at the campus bookstore. He successfully steals a textbook, uses it to get an A in a course, goes on to graduate, is admitted into law school, and later becomes a famous judge. Because his shoplifting goes unnoticed, it is a relatively unimportant event that has little bearing on his future life.

In contrast, **secondary deviance** occurs when a deviant event comes to the attention of significant others or social control agents who apply a negative label. The newly labeled offender then reorganizes his or her behavior and personality around the consequences of the deviant act. The shoplifting student is caught by a security guard and expelled from college. With his law school dreams dashed and his future cloudy, his options are limited; people who know him say he "lacks character," and he begins to share their opinion. He eventually becomes a drug dealer and winds up in prison (Figure 7.4).

Secondary deviance involves resocialization into a deviant role. The labeled person is transformed into one who, according to Lemert, "employs his behavior or a role based upon it as a means of defense, attack, or adjustment to the overt and covert problems created by the consequent social reaction to him."[187] Secondary deviance produces a deviance amplification effect. Offenders feel isolated from the mainstream of society and become firmly locked within their deviant role. They may seek out others similarly labeled to form deviant subcultures or groups. Ever more firmly enmeshed in their deviant role, they are locked into an escalating cycle of deviance, apprehension, more powerful labels, and identity transformation. Lemert's concept of secondary deviance expresses the core of social reaction theory:

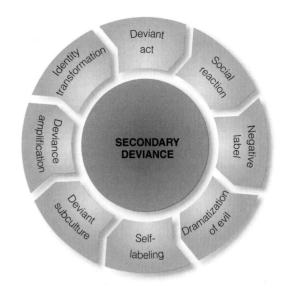

FIGURE 7.4 The Process of Creating Secondary Deviance

SOURCE: © Cengage Learning®

deviance is a process in which one's identity is transformed. Efforts to control the offenders, whether by treatment or punishment, simply help lock them in their deviant role.

Research on Social Reaction Theory

LO9 Discuss research that underpins the labeling approach

Research on social reaction theory can be classified into two distinct categories. The first focuses on the characteristics of offenders who are chosen for labels. The theory maintains that these offenders should be relatively powerless people who are unable to defend themselves against the negative labeling. The second type of research attempts to discover the effects of being labeled. Labeling theorists predict that people who are negatively labeled should view themselves as deviant and commit increasing amounts of criminal behavior.

dramatization of evil As the negative feedback of law enforcement agencies, parents, friends, teachers, and other figures amplifies the force of the original label, stigmatized offenders may begin to reevaluate their own identities. The person becomes the thing he is described as being.

primary deviance According to Lemert, deviant acts that do not help redefine the self-image and public image of the offender.

secondary deviance According to Lemert, accepting deviant labels as a personal identity. Acts become secondary when they form a basis for self-concept, as when a drug experimenter becomes an addict.

Who Gets Labeled? Differential Enforcement

An important principle of social reaction theory is that the law is differentially applied, benefiting those who hold economic and social power and penalizing the powerless. From the police officer's decision on whom to arrest to the prosecutor's decisions on whom to charge and for how many and what kind of charges, to the court's decision on whom to release or on whom to permit bail, to the grand jury's decision on indictment, to the judge's decision on the length of the sentence, discretion works to the detriment of minorities, including African Americans, Latinos, Asian Americans, and Native Americans.[188]

The term *racial profiling* has been used to signify that police suspicion is often directed at minority group males. Minorities and the poor are more likely to be prosecuted for criminal offenses and to receive harsher punishments when convicted.[189] Judges may sympathize with white defendants and help them avoid criminal labels, especially if they seem to come from "good families," whereas minority defendants are not afforded that luxury.[190]

This evidence is used to support the labeling concept that personal characteristics and social interactions are more important variables in developing criminal careers than merely violating the law. Social reaction theorists argue that the content of the law reflects power relationships in society.

Labeling Effects   If during the self-stigma process a devalued status is conferred by an authority figure—police officer, judge—the negative label may cause permanent harm. A negative label given by agents of the justice system—delinquent, criminal—may affect treatment at home, at work, at school, and in other social situations. Children may find that their parents consider them a bad influence on younger brothers and sisters. School officials may limit them to classes reserved for people with behavioral problems. Likewise, when adults are labeled as criminal, ex-con, or drug addict, they may find their eligibility for employment severely restricted. Furthermore, if the label is bestowed as the result of conviction for a criminal offense, the labeled person may be subjected to official sanctions ranging from a mild reprimand to incarceration.

Considerable evidence indicates social sanctions lead to self-labeling and deviance amplification.[191] Children negatively labeled by their parents routinely suffer a variety of problems, including antisocial behavior and school failure.[192] This process has been observed in the United States and abroad, indicating that the labeling process is universal, especially in nations in which a brush with the law brings personal dishonor, such as China and Japan.[193]

Empirical evidence supports the view that labeling plays a significant role in persistent offending.[194] Although labels may not cause adolescents to initiate criminal behaviors, those that do are significantly more likely to continue offending if they believe their parents and peers view them in a negative light; they now have a "damaged identity."[195] Maintaining a damaged identity after official labeling may, along with other negative social reactions from society, produce a "cumulative disadvantage," which provokes some adolescents into repeating their antisocial behaviors.[196]

There is also evidence that people who are involved with official labeling agencies such as the police are the ones most likely to engage in future deviant and criminal behaviors, especially if they are the most vulnerable, at-risk adolescents.[197] Using data collected from middle-school students in seven cities to examine the deviance amplification process, Stephanie Ann Wiley and her associates compared youth with no police contact, those who were stopped by police, and those who were arrested; the latter group reported higher levels of future delinquency.[198] Those with weak social bonds and delinquent peers are the ones most likely to be effected by the negative consequences of police contact. Arrest may amplify a person's "cumulative disadvantage" and trigger exclusionary processes that limit conventional opportunities, such as educational attainment and employment.[199]

Is Labeling Theory Valid?

Labeling theory has been the subject of academic debate in criminological circles. Those who criticize it point to its inability to specify the conditions that must exist before an act or individual is labeled deviant—that is, why some people are labeled and others remain "secret deviants."[200] There are also questions about whether stigma produces crime. Labeling often comes after, rather than before, chronic offending.[201] Getting labeled by the justice system and having an enduring criminal record may have little effect on people who have been burdened with social and emotional problems since birth.[202]

While these criticisms are telling, there has been significant research showing that, as the theory predicts, people who suffer official labels are prone to a delinquent and criminal way of life. For example, recent research by Emily Restivo and Mark Lanier found that official labeling may lead to an increased delinquent self-identity, decreased prosocial expectations, and an increased association with delinquent peers, which then lead to an increased likelihood of engaging in subsequent delinquency. Restivo and Lanier conclude that the labeling process creates a new damaged identity for the individual that places them in the company of other damaged people. The result is they are expected to fail and their association with delinquent peers helps make sure that happens.[203]

In a now classic work, criminologists Raymond Paternoster and Leeann Iovanni have identified features of the labeling perspective that are important contributions to the study of criminality:[204]

- The labeling perspective identifies the role played by social control agents in the process of crime causation. Criminal behavior cannot be fully understood if the agencies and individuals empowered to control and treat it are neglected.
- Labeling theory recognizes that criminality is not a disease or pathological behavior. It focuses attention on the social interactions and reactions that shape individuals and their behavior.

- Labeling theory distinguishes between criminal acts (primary deviance) and criminal careers (secondary deviance) and shows that these concepts must be interpreted and treated differently.

Labeling theory is also important because of its focus on interaction as well as the situations surrounding the crime. Rather than viewing the criminal as a robot-like creature whose actions are predetermined, it recognizes that crime is often the result of complex interactions and processes. The decision to commit crime involves actions of a variety of people, including peers, the victim, the police, and other key characters. Labels may expedite crime because they guide the actions of all parties involved in these criminal interactions. Actions deemed innocent when performed by one person are considered provocative when someone who has been labeled as deviant engages in them. Similarly, labeled people may be quick to judge, take offense, or misinterpret behavior of others because of past experience.

Labeling theory is also supported by research showing that convicted criminals who are placed in treatment programs aimed at reconfiguring their self-image may be able to develop revamped identities and desist from crime. Some are able to go through "redemption rituals" in which they are able to cast off their damaged identities and develop new ones. As a result, they develop an improved self-concept, which reflects the positive reinforcement they receive while in treatment.[205]

EVALUATING SOCIAL PROCESS THEORIES

The branches of social process theory—social learning, social control, and social reaction—are compatible because they suggest that criminal behavior is part of the socialization process. When interactions with critically important social institutions and processes—the family, schools, justice system, peer groups, employers, and neighbors—are troubled and disturbed, people may turn to criminal solutions for their problems.

Though there is some disagreement about the relative importance of those influences and the form they take, there seems to be little question that social interactions shape the behavior, beliefs, values, and self-image of the offender. People who have learned deviant social values, find themselves detached from conventional social relationships, or are the subject of stigma and labels from significant others will be the most

SOCIAL PROCESS THEORIES 7.1
concept summary

Theory	Major Premise	Strengths	Research Focus
SOCIAL LEARNING THEORIES			
Differential association theory	People learn to commit crime from exposure to antisocial definitions.	Explains onset of criminality. Explains the presence of crime in all elements of social structure. Explains why some people in high-crime areas refrain from criminality. Can apply to adults and juveniles.	Measuring definitions toward crime; influence of deviant peers and parents.
Differential reinforcement theory	Criminal behavior depends on the person's experiences with rewards for conventional behaviors and punishment for deviant ones. Being rewarded for deviance leads to crime.	Adds psychological learning theory principles to differential association. Links sociological and psychological principles.	The cause of criminal activity; how the content of socialization conditions crime.
Neutralization theory	Youths learn ways of neutralizing moral restraints and periodically drift in and out of criminal behavior patterns.	Explains why many delinquents do not become adult criminals. Explains why youthful law violators can participate in conventional behavior.	Identifying the neutralizations people use to commit crime without jeopardizing their cherished beliefs and values.
SOCIAL CONTROL THEORY			
Hirschi's control theory	A person's bond to society prevents him or her from violating social rules. If the bond weakens, the person is free to commit crime.	Explains the onset of crime; can apply to both middle- and lower-class crime. Explains its theoretical constructs adequately so they can be measured. Has been empirically tested.	Measuring the association between commitment, attachment, involvement, belief, and crime.
SOCIAL REACTION THEORY			
Labeling theory	People enter into law-violating careers when they are labeled for their acts and organize their personalities around the labels.	Explains the role of society in creating deviance. Explains why some juvenile offenders do not become adult criminals. Develops concepts of criminal careers.	Determining whether self-concept is related to crime. Showing how the differential application of labels produces crime; measuring the effect of stigma.

likely to fall prey to criminal behavior. These negative influences can affect people in all walks of life, beginning in their youth and continuing through their majority. The major strength of the social process view is the vast body of empirical data showing that delinquents and criminals are people who grew up in dysfunctional families, who had troubled childhoods, and who failed at school, at work, and in marriage. Prison data show that these characteristics are typical of inmates.

Although persuasive, these theories do not always account for the patterns and fluctuations in the crime rate. If social process theories are valid, for example, people in the West and South must be socialized differently from those in the Midwest and New England because these latter regions have much lower crime rates. How can the fact that crime rates are lower in October than in July be explained if crime is a function of learning or control? How can social processes explain why criminals escalate their activity or why they desist from crime as they age? Once a social bond is broken, how can it be "reattached"? Once crime is "learned," how can it be "unlearned"?

Concept Summary 7.1 sets out the premises, strengths, and research focus of social process theories.

PUBLIC POLICY IMPLICATIONS OF SOCIAL PROCESS THEORY

LO10 Describe the efforts to link social process theory to crime prevention efforts

Social process theories have had a major influence on policy making since the 1950s. Learning theories have greatly influenced the way criminal offenders are dealt with and treated. The effect of these theories has mainly been felt by young offenders, who are viewed as being more salvageable than "hardened" criminals. If people become criminal by learning definitions and attitudes toward criminality, advocates of the social learning approach argue that they can "unlearn" them by being exposed to definitions toward conventional behavior. It is common today for residential and nonresidential programs to offer treatment programs that teach offenders about the harmfulness of drugs, how to forgo delinquent behavior, and how to stay in school. If learning did not affect behavior, such exercises would be futile.

Control theories have also influenced criminal justice and other public policy. Programs have been developed to increase people's commitment to conventional lines of action.

diversion programs Programs of rehabilitation that remove offenders from the normal channels of the criminal justice system, thus avoiding the stigma of a criminal label.

Some work at creating and strengthening bonds early in life before the onset of criminality. The educational system has been the scene of numerous programs designed to improve basic skills and create an atmosphere in which youths will develop a bond to their schools. The most famous of these efforts is the Head Start program. Today, Head Start is administered by the Head Start Bureau; the Administration on Children, Youth, and Families (ACFY); the Administration for Children and Families (ACF); and the Department of Health and Human Services (DHHS). It receives annual funding of almost $7 billion, enrolls close to 1 million children, and provides support to more than 1,600 individual programs.[206]

Control theories have focused on the family and have played a key role in putting into operation programs designed to strengthen the bond between parent and child. Others attempt to repair bonds that have been broken and frayed. Examples of this approach are the career, work furlough, and educational opportunity programs being developed in the nation's prisons. These programs are designed to help inmates maintain a stake in society so they will be less willing to resort to criminal activity on their release.

Labeling theorists caution against too much intervention. Rather than ask social agencies to attempt to rehabilitate people having problems with the law, they argue, "less is better." Put another way, the more institutions try to "help" people, the more these people will be stigmatized and labeled. For example, a special education program designed to help problem readers may cause them to label themselves and others as slow or stupid. Similarly, a mental health rehabilitation program created with the best intentions may cause clients to be labeled as crazy or dangerous.

Diversion programs are designed to remove both juvenile and adult offenders from the normal channels of the criminal justice process by placing them in programs designed for rehabilitation. A college student whose drunken driving causes injury to a pedestrian may, before a trial occurs, be placed for six months in an alcohol treatment program. If he successfully completes the program, charges against him will be dismissed; he avoids the stigma of a criminal label.

Another label-avoiding innovation that has gained popularity is restitution. Rather than face the stigma of a formal trial, an offender is asked to either pay back the victim of the crime for any loss incurred or do some useful work in the community in lieu of receiving a court-ordered sentence.

There are efforts to reduce labeling and stigma if someone has been charged, convicted, and even sent to prison. Some important ones are discussed in the Policy and Practice in Criminology feature.

Despite their good intentions, stigma-reducing programs have not met with great success. Critics charge that they substitute one kind of stigma for another—for instance, attending a mental health program in place of a criminal trial. In addition, diversion and restitution programs usually screen out violent offenders and repeat offenders. Finally, there is little hard evidence that the recidivism rate of people placed in alternative programs is less than that of people sent to traditional programs.

SECOND CHANCE FOR EX-OFFENDERS ACT

I am writing this letter . . . out of desperation and to tell you a little about the struggles of reentering society as a convicted felon. I have worked hard to turn my life around. I have remained clean for nearly eight years, I am succeeding in college, and I continue to share my story in schools, treatment facilities, and correctional institutions, yet I have nothing to show for it. . . . I have had numerous interviews and sent out more than 200 résumés for jobs for which I am more than qualified. I have had denial after denial because of my felony. I do understand that you are not responsible for the choices that have brought me to this point. Furthermore, I recognize that if I was not abiding by the law, if I was not clean, and if I was not focusing my efforts toward a successful future, I would have no claim to make.

So writes Jay, a man convicted of involuntary vehicular manslaughter and sentenced to 38 months in state prison nine years before. He is not alone: a criminal label can haunt people for the rest of their life, well beyond their offending years and despite the fact that they have stayed "clean" for quite some time.

Many people with records suffer stigma that prevents them from getting jobs. A recent study shows that nearly one-third of American adults have been arrested by age 23. This record will keep many people from obtaining employment, even if they have paid their dues, are qualified for the job, and are unlikely to reoffend.

Criminal records run the gamut from one-time arrests where charges are dropped to lengthy, serious, and violent criminal histories. Many people who have been arrested—and, therefore, technically have a criminal record that shows up on a background check—were never convicted of a crime. This is true not only among those charged with minor crimes

but also for many individuals arrested for serious offenses.

The impact of having a criminal record is most often felt among African Americans, who may already experience racial discrimination in the labor market and are more likely than whites to have a criminal record. Research shows that a criminal record reduces the likelihood of a job callback or offer by approximately 50 percent. This criminal record "penalty" is substantially greater for African Americans than for white applicants. Latinos suffer similar penalties in the employment market.

In addition to these significant and often overlapping challenges, an extra set of punishments, or "collateral consequences," is imposed on individuals as a direct result of their criminal convictions. These legal restrictions create barriers to jobs, housing, benefits, and voting. More than 80 percent of the statutes that place restrictions on people convicted of crime operate as denial of employment opportunities. Although some of these consequences serve important public safety purposes, others may be antiquated and create unnecessary barriers to legitimate work opportunities. A commonly cited example is that in some states formerly incarcerated people who were trained as barbers cannot hold those jobs after release because state laws prohibit felons from practicing the trade, presumably because their access to sharp objects makes them a threat to the public. Regardless of the legal restrictions, the majority of employers indicate they would "probably" or "definitely" not be willing to hire an applicant with a criminal record. There is frequent use of blanket "no-hire" policies among major corporations. Employers do not want to hire individuals who might commit future crimes and who may be a risk to their employees' and customers' safety. The assumption, of course, is that a prior record signals higher odds that the individual will commit more crimes in the future.

States are taking steps to help the situation by passing laws allowing people to erase (expunge) or seal low-level

offenses after a number of years have gone by without reoffending; three states have passed laws to limit the liability of employers that hire people with criminal records.

There are also efforts afoot to reduce the stigma of a stay in prison. New York Congressman Charles Rangel has proposed the Second Chance for Ex-Offenders Act of 2011, a bill that would expunge the record of any felon who (a) hadn't been convicted of a violent crime, (b) served a full sentence and completed all court-ordered requirements, (c) had been free of alcohol or drug dependency for at least a year, (d) received a high school diploma or its equivalent, and (e) completed a year of community service. So far the bill has not gotten much support in Congress, but it may eventually gain traction and serve as a means of helping former inmates avoid stigma and successfully reintegrate back into society.

Critical Thinking

1. Should records be expunged within a certain time frame if a person does not reoffend? Or should knowledge of a prior criminal record be available since an employer or neighbor has a right to know about the background of people they are considering hiring?

2. Does the stigma of a criminal label serve a deterrent purpose? Are people less willing to commit a criminal act because they know that the record will follow them around forever? Would people be more willing to break the law if they knew their record would eventually be expunged?

SOURCES: H.R. 2065 (112th): Second Chance for Ex-Offenders Act of 2011, https://www.govtrack.us/congress/bills/112/hr2065 (accessed April 2014); Amy Solomon, "In Search of a Job: Criminal Records as Barriers to Employment," *NIJ Journal* 270 (2012), http://www.nij.gov/journals/270/pages/criminal-records.aspx (accessed April 2014).

LO1 Analyze the associations among socialization, social process, and crime

Social process theories view criminality as a function of people's interaction with various organizations, institutions, and processes in society. People in all walks of life have the potential to become criminals if they maintain destructive social relationships. Improper socialization is a key component of crime. Social learning theory stresses that people learn how to commit crimes and suggests that people learn criminal behaviors much as they learn conventional behavior. Social control theory analyzes the failure of society to control criminal tendencies. Social reaction (labeling) theory maintains that negative labels produce criminal careers.

LO2 Assess the effect of families and education on crime

Kids growing up in troubled families are crime prone. Parental efficacy reduces crime. Divorce can strain families. School failure is linked to delinquency. Dropping out may influence later criminality. School violence and conflict are also problems.

LO3 Discuss the link between peers and delinquency

Delinquent peers sustain individual offending patterns. Delinquent friends may help kids neutralize the fear of punishment. The greater the exposure to delinquent peers, the greater the likelihood of criminal behavior.

LO4 Explain how personal beliefs impact on criminality

People with high moral standards can resist crime. Church attendance is related to low crime rates: the more people attend religious services, the less likely they will engage in antisocial behaviors.

LO5 Compare and contrast among social learning, control, and reaction theories

According to social learning theory, people learn the techniques and attitudes to support crime from close and intimate relationships with criminal peers; crime is a learned behavior. Social control theory maintains that people are controlled by their bonds to society. Crime occurs when the forces that bind people to society are weakened or broken. At its core, social reaction theory (labeling theory) holds that a criminal career is sustained by social labels and stigma; when significant members of society label them as deviants and criminals, people accept those labels as a personal identity.

LO6 Explain the different forms social learning theory has taken

Differential association theory was formulated by Edwin Sutherland. It holds that criminality is a result of a person's perceiving an excess of definitions in favor of crime. Gresham Sykes and David Matza created the theory of neutralization, which stresses that youths learn mental techniques that enable them to overcome societal values and drift into delinquency. Ronald Akers has posed a behavioral version of social learning called differential reinforcement theory.

LO7 List the principles of Hirschi's social bond theory

Control theory maintains that all people have the potential to become criminals, but their bonds to conventional society prevent them from violating the law. This view suggests that a person's self-concept aids his or her commitment to conventional action. Travis Hirschi's social bond theory describes the social bond as containing elements of attachment, commitment, involvement, and belief. Weakened bonds allow youths to behave antisocially.

LO8 Summarize the basic elements of social reaction or labeling theory

Social reaction or labeling theory holds that criminality is promoted by becoming negatively labeled by significant others. Such labels as "criminal," "ex-con," and "junkie" isolate people from society and lock them into lives of crime. Crime and criminality are social constructs. One person may be labeled deviant, while another finds their behavior excused. Criminality is in the eye of the beholder.

LO9 Discuss the research that underpins the labeling approach

Labels create expectations that the labeled person will act in a certain way; labeled people are always watched and suspected. Eventually these people begin to accept their labels as personal identities, locking them further into lives of crime and deviance. People begin to view themselves as others do: troublemaker, drug addict, criminal. Edwin Lemert suggests that people who accept labels are involved in secondary deviance while primary deviants are able to maintain an undamaged identity.

LO10 Describe the efforts to link social process theory to crime prevention efforts

Social process theories have greatly influenced social policy. They have been applied in treatment orientations as well as community action policies. Some programs teach kids conventional attitudes and behaviors. Others are designed to improve the social bond they have with parents and teachers. Another approach is to reduce the stigma of a criminal conviction by creating alternative treatments and expunging the records of criminal offenders.

CRITICAL THINKING QUESTIONS

1. Do negative labels cause crime? Or do people who commit crime become negatively labeled? That is, are labels a cause of crime or a result?

2. Once weakened, can a person's bonds to society become reattached? What social processes might help reattachment?

3. Can you devise a test of Sutherland's differential association theory? How would you go about measuring an excess of definitions favorable toward criminality?

4. Can you think of ways you may have supported your peers' or siblings' antisocial behavior by helping them learn criminal techniques or attitudes?

5. Do you recall neutralizing any guilt you might have felt for committing a criminal or illegal act? Did your neutralizations come before or after you committed the act in question?

KEY TERMS

sociological social psychology (222)

socialization (222)

social process or socialization theory (222)

parental efficacy (224)

social learning theory (228)

social control theory (228)

social reaction theory (labeling theory) (228)

differential association theory (229)

differential reinforcement theory (232)

direct conditioning (232)

differential reinforcement (232)

negative reinforcement (232)

neutralization theory (233)

subterranean values (233)

drift (233)

commitment to conformity (237)

containment theory (237)

social bond (237)

symbolic interaction theory (241)

stigma (241)

reflected appraisals (242)

retrospective reading (242)

dramatization of evil (243)

primary deviance (243)

secondary deviance (243)

diversion programs (246)

NOTES

1. Hunter Stuart, "Ethan Couch, 'Affluenza' Teen, Facing 5 Lawsuits," *Huffington Post*, December 12, 2013, http://www.huffingtonpost.com/2013/12/18/ethan-couch-affluenza-lawsuits-car-crash-texas_n_4461585.html (accessed May 2014); Ramit Plushnick-Masti, "'Affluenza' Isn't a Recognized Diagnosis, Experts Say After 'Brat' Spared from Jail in Drunk Driving Case," *National Post*, December 12, 2013, http://news.nationalpost.com/2013/12/12/affluenza-defence-used-to-protect-teen-driver-who-killed-four-was-never-meant-to-be-used-in-court-expert-says/ (accessed May 2014).

2. Charles Tittle and Robert Meier, "Specifying the SES/Delinquency Relationship," *Criminology* 28 (1990): 271–299, at 274.

3. Sheldon Glueck and Eleanor Glueck, *Unraveling Juvenile Delinquency* (Cambridge, MA: Harvard University Press, 1950); Ashley Weeks, "Predicting Juvenile Delinquency," *American Sociological Review* 8 (1943): 40–46.

4. Diana Formoso, Nancy Gonzales, and Leona Aiken, "Family Conflict and Children's Internalizing and Externalizing Behavior: Protective Factors," *American Journal of Community Psychology* 28 (2000): 175–199.

5. Ming Cui and Rand D. Conger, "Parenting Behavior as Mediator and Moderator of the Association Between Marital Problems and Adolescent Maladjustment," *Journal of Research on Adolescence* 18 (2008): 261–284; James Unnever, Francis Cullen, and Robert Agnew, "Why Is 'Bad' Parenting Criminogenic? Implications from Rival Theories," *Youth Violence and Juvenile Justice* 4 (2006): 3–33.

6. Roslyn Caldwell, Jenna Silverman, Noelle Lefforge, and Clayton Silver, "Adjudicated Mexican-American Adolescents: The Effects of Familial Emotional Support on Self-Esteem, Emotional Well-Being, and Delinquency," *American Journal of Family Therapy* 32 (2004): 55–69.

7. Annie E. Casey Foundation, Kids Count, 2014, http://datacenter.kidscount.org/data/Tables/106-children-in-single-parent-families (accessed May 2014).

8. Andre Sourander, Henrik Elonheimo, Solja Niemelä, Art-Matti Nuutila, Hans Helenius, Lauri Sillanmäki, Jorma Piha, Tuulk Tamminen, Kirsti Kumpulkinen, Irma Moilanen, and Frederik Almovist, "Childhood Predictors of Male Criminality: A Prospective Population-Based Follow-Up Study from Age 8 to Late Adolescence," *Journal of the American Academy of Child and Adolescent Psychiatry* 45 (2006): 578–586.

9. Jukka Savolainen, "Relative Cohort Size and Age-Specific Arrest Rates: A Conditional Interpretation of the Easterlin Effect," *Criminology* 38 (2000): 117–136.

10. Cesar Rebellon, "Reconsidering the Broken Homes/Delinquency Relationship and Exploring Its Mediating Factors," *Criminology* 40 (2002): 103–136.

11. Joongyeup Lee, Hyunseok Jang, and Leana A. Bouffard, "Maternal Employment and Juvenile Delinquency: A Longitudinal Study of Korean Adolescents," *Crime and Delinquency*, first published online December 7, 2011; Thomas Vander Ven and Francis Cullen, "The Impact of Maternal Employment on Serious Youth Crime: Does the Quality of Working Conditions Matter?" *Crime and Delinquency* 50 (2004): 272–292; Thomas Vander Ven, Francis Cullen, Mark Carrozza, and John Paul Wright, "Home Alone: The Impact of Maternal Employment on Delinquency," *Social Problems* 48 (2001): 236–257.

12. Judith Rich Harris, *The Nurture Assumption: Why Children Turn Out the Way They Do* (New York: Free Press, 1998).

13. Jennifer Beyers, John Bates, Gregory Pettit, and Kenneth Dodge, "Neighborhood Structure, Parenting Processes, and the Development of Youths' Externalizing Behaviors: A Multilevel Analysis," *American Journal of Community Psychology* 31 (2003): 35–53.

14. En-Ling Pan and Michael Farrell, "Ethnic Differences in the Effects of Intergenerational Relations on Adolescent Problem Behavior in

U.S. Single-Mother Families," *Journal of Family Issues* 27 (2006): 1137–1158.

15. Paul Amato and Bruce Keith, "Parental Divorce and the Well-Being of Children: A Meta-Analysis," *Psychological Bulletin* 110 (1991): 26–46.

16. Michael Roettger and Raymond Swisher, "Associations of Fathers' History of Incarceration with Sons' Delinquency and Arrest Among Black, White, and Hispanic Males in the United States," *Criminology* 49 (2011): 1109–1148; Marieke van de Rakt, Joseph Murray, and Paul Nieuwbeerta, "The Long-Term Effects of Paternal Imprisonment on Criminal Trajectories of Children, *Journal of Research in Crime and Delinquency* 49 (2012): 81–108.

17. Daniel Shaw, "Advancing Our Understanding of Intergenerational Continuity in Antisocial Behavior," *Journal of Abnormal Child Psychology* 31 (2003): 193–199.

18. Donald J. West and David P. Farrington, eds., "Who Becomes Delinquent?" in *The Delinquent Way of Life* (London: Heinemann, 1977); Donald J. West, *Delinquency: Its Roots, Careers, and Prospects* (Cambridge, MA: Harvard University Press, 1982).

19. David Farrington, "Understanding and Preventing Bullying," in *Crime and Justice*, Vol. 17, ed. Michael Tonry (Chicago: University of Chicago Press, 1993), pp. 381–457.

20. Carolyn Smith and David Farrington, "Continuities in Antisocial Behavior and Parenting Across Three Generations," *Journal of Child Psychology and Psychiatry* 45 (2004): 230–247.

21. Joseph Murray and David Farrington, "Parental Imprisonment: Effects on Boys' Antisocial Behaviour and Delinquency Through the Life-Course," *Journal of Child Psychology and Psychiatry* 46 (2005): 1269–1278.

22. John Paul Wright and Francis Cullen, "Parental Efficacy and Delinquent Behavior: Do Control and Support Matter?" *Criminology* 39 (2001): 677–706.

23. Christopher Sullivan, "Early Adolescent Delinquency: Assessing the Role of Childhood Problems, Family Environment, and Peer Pressure," *Youth Violence and Juvenile Justice* 4 (2006): 291–313.

24. Andrea Chronis, Heather Jones, Benjamin Lahey, Paul Rathouz, William Pelham, Jr., Stephanie Hall Williams, Barbara Baumann, and Heidi Kipp, "Maternal Depression and Early Positive Parenting Predict Future Conduct Problems in Young Children with Attention-Deficit/Hyperactivity Disorder," *Developmental Psychology* 43 (2007): 70–82.

25. Carter Hay, "Parenting, Self-Control, and Delinquency: A Test of Self-Control Theory," *Criminology* 39 (2001): 707–736.

26. Sonia Cota-Robles and Wendy Gamble, "Parent-Adolescent Processes and Reduced Risk for Delinquency: The Effect of Gender for Mexican American Adolescents," *Youth and Society* 37 (2006): 375–392.

27. Robert Vermeiren, Jef Bogaerts, Vladislav Ruchkin, Dirk Deboutte, and Mary Schwab-Stone, "Subtypes of Self-Esteem and Self-Concept in Adolescent Violent and Property Offenders," *Journal of Child Psychology and Psychiatry* 45 (2004): 405–411.

28. Jacinta Bronte-Tinkew, Kristin Moore, and Jennifer Carrano, "The Father-Child Relationship, Parenting Styles, and Adolescent Risk Behaviors in Intact Families," *Journal of Family Issues* 27 (2006): 850–881.

29. Jennifer Lansford, Laura Wager, John Bates, Gregory Pettit, and Kenneth Dodge, "Forms of Spanking and Children's Externalizing Behaviors," *Family Relations* 6 (2012): 224–236.

30. Carolyn Smith and Terence Thornberry, "The Relationship Between Childhood Maltreatment and Adolescent Involvement in Delinquency," *Criminology* 33 (1995): 451–479.

31. Lansford, Wager, Bates, Pettit, and Dodge, "Forms of Spanking and Children's Externalizing Behaviors."

32. Kristi Holsinger and Alexander Holsinger, "Differential Pathways to Violence and Self-Injurious Behavior: African American and White Girls in the Juvenile Justice System," *Journal of Research in Crime and Delinquency* 42 (2005): 211–242; Eric Slade and Lawrence Wissow, "Spanking in Early Childhood and Later Behavior Problems: A Prospective Study of Infants and Young Toddlers," *Pediatrics* 113 (2004): 1321–1330; Fred Rogosch and Dante Cicchetti, "Child Maltreatment and Emergent Personality Organization: Perspectives from the Five-Factor Model," *Journal of Abnormal Child Psychology* 32 (2004): 123–145.

33. Lynette Renner, "Single Types of Family Violence Victimization and Externalizing Behaviors Among Children and Adolescents," *Journal of Family Violence* 27 (2012): 177–186.

34. Maureen A. Allwood and Cathy Spatz Widom, "Child Abuse and Neglect, Developmental Role Attainment, and Adult Arrests," *Journal of Research in Crime and Delinquency* 50 (2013): 551–578.

35. Todd Herrenkohl, Rick Kosterman, David Hawkins, and Alex Mason, "Effects of Growth in Family Conflict in Adolescence on Adult Depressive Symptoms: Mediating and Moderating Effects of Stress and School Bonding," *Journal of Adolescent Health* 44 (2009): 146–152.

36. David Huh, Jennifer Tristan, Emily Wade, and Eric Stice, "Does Problem Behavior Elicit Poor Parenting? A Prospective Study of Adolescent Girls," *Journal of Adolescent Research* 21 (2006): 185–204.

37. Martha Gault-Sherman, "It's a Two-Way Street: The Bidirectional Relationship Between Parenting and Delinquency," *Journal of Youth and Adolescence* 41 (2012): 121–145.

38. Sonja Siennick, "Tough Love? Crime and Parental Assistance in Young Adulthood," *Criminology* 49 (2011): 163–196.

39. *The Forgotten Half: Pathways to Success for America's Youth and Young Families* (Washington, DC: William T. Grant Foundation, 1988); Lee Jussim, "Teacher Expectations: Self-Fulfilling Prophecies, Perceptual Biases, and Accuracy," *Journal of Personality and Social Psychology* 57 (1989): 469–480.

40. Eugene Maguin and Rolf Loeber, "Academic Performance and Delinquency," in *Crime and Justice: A Review of Research*, Vol. 20, ed. Michael Tonry (Chicago: University of Chicago Press, 1996), pp. 145–264.

41. Jeannie Oakes, *Keeping Track, How Schools Structure Inequality* (New Haven, CT: Yale University Press, 1985).

42. Joseph Gasper, *Drugs Use and Delinquency: Causes of Dropping Out of High School?* (El Paso, TX: LFB Scholarly Publishing, 2012).

43. Spencer Rathus, *Voyages in Childhood* (Belmont, CA: Wadsworth, 2004).

44. Gary Sweeten, Shawn D. Bushway, and Raymond Paternoster, "Does Dropping Out of School Mean Dropping into Delinquency?" *Criminology* 47 (2009): 47–91; G. Roger Jarjoura, "Does Dropping Out of School Enhance Delinquent Involvement? Results from a Large-Scale National Probability Sample," *Criminology* 31 (1993): 149–172; Terence Thornberry, Melanie Moore, and R. L. Christenson, "The Effect of Dropping Out of High School on Subsequent Criminal Behavior," *Criminology* 23 (1985): 3–18.

45. Sweeten, Bushway, and Paternoster, "Does Dropping Out of School Mean Dropping into Delinquency?"

46. Irving Janis, *Groupthink: Psychological Studies of Policy Decisions and Fiascoes* (Boston: Houghton Mifflin, 1982).

47. Ibid., p. 463.

48. Olena Antonaccio, Charles Tittle, Ekaterina Botchkovar, and Maria Kranidioti, "The Correlates of Crime and Deviance: Additional Evidence," *Journal of Research in Crime and Delinquency*, first published online April 28, 2010, (accessed April 2014).

49. Jean Marie McGloin, "Delinquency Balance and Time Use: A Research Note," *Journal of Research in Crime and Delinquency* 49 (2012): 109–121.

50. Callie H. Burt and Carter Rees, "Behavioral Heterogeneity in Adolescent Friendship Networks," *Justice Quarterly*, first published online January 3, 2014.

51. Paul Friday, Xin Ren, Elmar Weitekamp, Hans-Jürgen Kerner, and Terrance Taylor, "A Chinese Birth Cohort: Theoretical Implications," *Journal of Research in Crime and Delinquency* 42 (2005): 123–146.

52. Harris, *The Nurture Assumption*.

53. J. C. Barnes and Robert Morris, "Young Mothers, Delinquent Children: Assessing Mediating Factors Among American Youth," *Youth Violence and Juvenile Justice* 10 (2012): 172–189.

54. Kate Keenan, Rolf Loeber, Quanwu Zhang, Magda Stouthamer-Loeber, and Welmoet van Kammen, "The Influence of Deviant Peers on the Development of Boys' Disruptive and Delinquent Behavior: A Temporal Analysis," *Development and Psychopathology* 7 (1995): 715–726.

55. Brett Johnson Solomon, "Other-Sex Friendship Involvement Among Delinquent Adolescent Females," *Youth Violence and Juvenile Justice* 4 (2006): 75–96.

56. Terence Thornberry and Marvin Krohn, "Peers, Drug Use, and Delinquency," in *Handbook of Antisocial Behavior*, ed. David Stoff, James Breiling, and Jack Maser (New York: Wiley, 1997), pp. 218–233; Thomas Dishion, Deborah Capaldi, Kathleen Spracklen, and Fuzhong Li, "Peer Ecology of Male Adolescent Drug Use," *Development and Psychopathology* 7 (1995): 803–824.

57. Sylvie Mrug, Betsy Hoza, and William Bukowski, "Choosing or Being Chosen by Aggressive-Disruptive Peers: Do They Contribute to Children's Externalizing and Internalizing Problems?" *Journal of Abnormal Child Psychology* 32 (2004): 53–66.

58. Mark Warr, "Age, Peers, and Delinquency," *Criminology* 31 (1993): 17–40.

59. Brett Laursen, Christopher Hafen, Margaret Kerr, and Hakin Stattin, "Friend Influence over Adolescent Problem Behaviors as a Function of Relative Peer Acceptance: To Be Liked Is to Be Emulated," *Journal of Abnormal Psychology* 121 (2012): 88–94.

60. Sara R. Battin, Karl G. Hill, Robert D. Abbott, Richard F. Catalano, and J. David Hawkins, "The Contribution of Gang Membership to Delinquency Beyond Delinquent Friends," *Criminology* 36 (1998): 93–116.

61. Stephen W. Baron, "Self-Control, Social Consequences, and Criminal Behavior: Street Youth and the General Theory of Crime," *Journal of Research in Crime and Delinquency* 40 (2003): 403–425.

62. David Harding, "Violence, Older Peers, and the Socialization of Adolescent Boys in Disadvantaged Neighborhoods," *American Sociological Review* 74 (2009): 445–464.

63. Daneen Deptula and Robert Cohen, "Aggressive, Rejected, and Delinquent Children and Adolescents: A Comparison of Their Friendships," *Aggression and Violent Behavior* 9 (2004): 75–104.

64. Shelley Keith Matthews and Robert Agnew, "Extending Deterrence Theory: Do Delinquent Peers Condition the Relationship Between Perceptions of Getting Caught and Offending?" *Journal of Research in Crime and Delinquency* 45 (2008): 91–118.

65. T. David Evans, Francis Cullen, R. Gregory Dunaway, and Velmer Burton, Jr., "Religion and Crime Reexamined: The Impact of Religion, Secular Controls, and Social Ecology on Adult Criminality," *Criminology* 33 (1995): 195–224.

66. Alex R. Piquero, Jeffrey A. Bouffard, Nicole Leeper Piquero, and Jessica M. Craig, "Does Morality Condition the Deterrent Effect of Perceived Certainty Among Incarcerated Felons?" *Crime and Delinquency*, first published online October 20, 2013.

67. Travis Hirschi and Rodney Stark, "Hellfire and Delinquency," *Social Problems* 17 (1969): 202–213.

68. Colin Baier and Bradley Wright, "If You Love Me, Keep My Commandments: A Meta-Analysis of the Effect of Religion on Crime," *Journal of Research in Crime and Delinquency* 38 (2001): 3–21; Byron Johnson, Sung Joon Jang, David Larson, and Spencer De Li, "Does Adolescent Religious Commitment Matter? A Reexamination of the Effects of Religiosity on Delinquency," *Journal of Research in Crime and Delinquency* 38 (2001): 22–44; Sung Joon Jang and Byron Johnson, "Neighborhood Disorder, Individual Religiosity, and Adolescent Use of Illicit Drugs: A Test of Multilevel Hypothesis," *Criminology* 39 (2001): 109–144.

69. Richard Petts, "Family and Religious Characteristics' Influence on Delinquency Trajectories from Adolescence to Young Adulthood," *American Sociological Review* 74 (2009): 465–483.

70. Walter Miller, *Violence by Youth Gangs and Youth Groups as a Crime Problem in Major American Cities* (Washington, DC: U.S. Government Printing Office, 1975).

71. Edwin H. Sutherland, *Principles of Criminology* (Philadelphia: Lippincott, 1939).

72. See, for example, Edwin Sutherland, "White-Collar Criminality," *American Sociological Review* 5 (1940): 2–10.

73. See Edwin Sutherland and Donald Cressey, *Criminology*, 8th ed. (Philadelphia: Lippincott, 1970), pp. 77–79.

74. Sandra Brown, Vicki Creamer, and Barbara Stetson, "Adolescent Alcohol Expectancies in Relation to Personal and Parental Drinking Patterns," *Journal of Abnormal Psychology* 96 (1987): 117–121.

75. Carlo Morselli, Pierre Tremblay, and Bill McCarthy, "Mentors and Criminal Achievement," *Criminology* 44 (2006): 17–43.

76. Ibid.

77. Travis C. Pratt, Francis T. Cullen, Christine S. Sellers, L. Thomas Winfree, Jr., Tamara D. Madensen, Leah E. Daigle, Noelle E. Fearn, and Jacinta M. Gau, "The Empirical Status of Social Learning Theory: A Meta-Analysis" *Informaworld*, November 2009, http://www.tandfonline.com/doi/abs/10.1080/07418820903379610 (accessed April 2014).

78. Daniel Shaw, "Advancing Our Understanding of Intergenerational Continuity in Antisocial Behavior," *Journal of Abnormal Child Psychology* 31 (2003): 193–199.

79. Robert Lonardo, Peggy Giordano, Monica Longmore, and Wendy Manning, "Parents, Friends, and Romantic Partners: Enmeshment in Deviant Networks and Adolescent Delinquency Involvement," *Journal of Youth and Adolescence* 38 (2009): 367–383.

80. Terence P. Thornberry, "The Apple Doesn't Fall Far from the Tree (Or Does It?): Intergenerational Patterns of Antisocial Behavior—The American Society of Criminology 2008 Sutherland Address," *Criminology* 47 (2009): 297–325; Terence Thornberry, Adrienne Freeman-Gallant, Alan Lizotte, Marvin Krohn, and Carolyn Smith, "Linked Lives: The Intergenerational Transmission of Antisocial Behavior," *Journal of Abnormal Child Psychology* 31 (2003): 171–184.

81. Paul Vowell and Jieming Chen, "Predicting Academic Misconduct: A Comparative Test of Four Sociological Explanations," *Sociological Inquiry* 74 (2004): 226–249.

82. Andy Hochstetler, Heith Copes, and Matt DeLisi, "Differential Association in Group and Solo Offending," *Journal of Criminal Justice* 30 (2002): 559–566.

83. Wesley Church II, Tracy Wharton, and Julie Taylor, "An Examination of Differential Association and Social Control Theory: Family Systems and Delinquency," *Youth Violence and Juvenile Justice* 7 (2009): 3–15.

84. Wesley Younts, "Status, Endorsement and the Legitimacy of Deviance," *Social Forces* 87 (2008): 561–590.

85. Dana Haynie, Peggy Giordano, Wendy Manning, and Monica Longmore, "Adolescent Romantic Relationships and Delinquency Involvement," *Criminology* 43 (2005): 177–210.

86. Lonardo et al., "Parents, Friends, and Romantic Partners."

87. Joel Hektner, Gerald August, and George Realmuto, "Effects of Pairing Aggressive and Nonaggressive Children in Strategic Peer Affiliation," *Journal of Abnormal Child Psychology* 31 (2003): 399–412; Matthew Ploeger, "Youth Employment and Delinquency: Reconsidering a Problematic Relationship," *Criminology* 35 (1997): 659–675; William Skinner and Anne Fream, "A Social Learning Theory Analysis of Computer Crime Among College Students," *Journal of Research in Crime and Delinquency* 34 (1997): 495–518; Denise Kandel and Mark Davies, "Friendship Networks, Intimacy, and Illicit Drug Use in Young Adulthood: A Comparison of Two Competing Theories," *Criminology* 29 (1991): 441–467.

88. Warr, "Age, Peers, and Delinquency."

89. Clayton Hartjen and S. Priyadarsini, "Gender, Peers, and Delinquency," *Youth and Society* 34 (2003): 387–414.

90. Denise Kandel and Mark Davies, "Friendship Networks, Intimacy, and Illicit Drug Use in Young Adulthood: A Comparison of Two Competing Theories," *Criminology* 29 (1991): 441–467.

91. Kenneth Tunnell, "Inside the Drug Trade: Trafficking from the Dealer's Perspective," *Qualitative Sociology* 16 (1993): 361–381, at 367.

92. Krohn and Thornberry, "Network Theory," pp. 123–124.

93. Daniel Mears, Matthew Ploeger, and Mark Warr, "Explaining the Gender Gap in Delinquency: Peer Influence and Moral Evaluations of Behavior," *Journal of Research in Crime and Delinquency* 35 (1998): 251–266.

94. Ibid.

95. Ronald Akers, "Is Differential Association/Social Learning Cultural Deviance Theory?" *Criminology* 34 (1996): 229–247; for an opposing view, see Travis Hirschi, "Theory Without Ideas: Reply to Akers," *Criminology* 34 (1996): 249–256.

96. Robert Burgess and Ronald Akers, "A Differential Association–Reinforcement Theory of Criminal Behavior," *Social Problems* 14 (1966): 128–147.

97. Mons Bendixen, Inger Endresen, and Dan Olweus, "Joining and Leaving Gangs: Selection and Facilitation Effects on Self-Reported Antisocial Behaviour in Early Adolescence," *European Journal of Criminology* 3 (2006): 85–114.

98. Sameer Hinduja and Jason Ingram, "Social Learning Theory and Music Piracy: The Differential Role of Online and Offline Peer Influences," *Criminal Justice Studies: A Critical Journal of Crime, Law and Society* 22 (2009): 405–420.

99. Ronald Akers, *Deviant Behavior: A Social Learning Approach*, 2nd ed. (Belmont, CA: Wadsworth, 1977).

100. Ronald Akers, Marvin Krohn, Lonn Lanza-Kaduce, and Marcia Radosevich, "Social Learning and Deviant Behavior: A Specific Test of a General Theory," *American Sociological Review* 44 (1979): 638.

101. Ibid.

102. Robert G. Morris and Ashley G. Blackburn, "Cracking the Code: An Empirical Exploration of Social Learning Theory and Computer Crime," *Journal of Crime and Justice* 32 (2009): 1–34.

103. Marvin Krohn, William Skinner, James Massey, and Ronald Akers, "Social Learning Theory and Adolescent Cigarette Smoking: A Longitudinal Study," *Social Problems* 32 (1985): 455–471.

104. L. Thomas Winfree, Christine Sellers, and Dennis L. Clason, "Social Learning and Adolescent Deviance Abstention: Toward Understanding the Reasons for Initiating, Quitting, and Avoiding Drugs," *Journal of Quantitative Criminology* 9 (1993): 101–125.

105. Jonathan Brauer, "Testing Social Learning Theory Using Reinforcement's Residue: A Multilevel Analysis of Self-Reported Theft and Marijuana Use in the National Youth Survey," *Criminology* 47 (2009): 929–970.

106. Ronald Akers and Gang Lee, "A Longitudinal Test of Social Learning Theory: Adolescent Smoking," *Journal of Drug Issues* 26 (1996): 317–343.

107. Gary Jensen and David Brownfield, "Parents and Drugs," *Criminology* 21 (1983): 543–554.

108. Ronald Akers, "Rational Choice, Deterrence and Social Learning Theory in Criminology: The Path Not Taken," *Journal of Criminal Law and Criminology* 81 (1990): 653–676.

109. Gresham Sykes and David Matza, "Techniques of Neutralization: A Theory of Delinquency," *American Sociological Review* 22 (1957): 664–670; David Matza, *Delinquency and Drift* (New York: Wiley, 1964).

110. Matza, *Delinquency and Drift*, p. 51.

111. Sykes and Matza, "Techniques of Neutralization," pp. 664–670; see also David Matza, "Subterranean Traditions of Youths," *Annals of the American Academy of Political and Social Science* 378 (1961): 116.

112. Sykes and Matza, "Techniques of Neutralization," pp. 664–670.

113. Ibid.

114. Ian Shields and George Whitehall, "Neutralization and Delinquency Among Teenagers," *Criminal Justice and Behavior* 21 (1994): 223–235; Robert A. Ball, "An Empirical Exploration of Neutralization Theory," *Criminologica* 4 (1966): 22–32. See also M. William Minor, "The Neutralization of Criminal Offense," *Criminology* 18 (1980): 103–120; Robert Gordon, James Short, Desmond Cartwright, and Fred Strodtbeck, "Values and Gang Delinquency: A Study of Street Corner Groups," *American Journal of Sociology* 69 (1963): 109–128.

115. Robert Agnew, "The Techniques of Neutralization and Violence," *Criminology* 32 (1994): 555–580; Michael Hindelang, "The Commitment of Delinquents to Their Misdeeds: Do Delinquents Drift?" *Social Problems* 17 (1970): 500–509; Robert Regoli and Eric Poole, "The Commitment of Delinquents to Their Misdeeds: A Reexamination," *Journal of Criminal Justice* 6 (1978): 261–269.

116. Larry Siegel, Spencer Rathus, and Carol Ruppert, "Values and Delinquent Youth: An Empirical Reexamination of Theories of Delinquency," *British Journal of Criminology* 13 (1973): 237–244.

117. Nicole Leeper Piquero, Stephen Tibbetts, and Michael Blankenship, "Examining the Role of Differential Association and Techniques of Neutralization in Explaining Corporate Crime," *Deviant Behavior* 26 (2005): 159–188.

118. John Hamlin, "Misplaced Role of Rational Choice in Neutralization Theory," *Criminology* 26 (1988): 425–438.

119. Mark Pogrebin, Eric Poole, and Amos Martinez, "Accounts of Professional Misdeeds: The Sexual Exploitation of Clients by Psychotherapists," *Deviant Behavior* 13 (1992): 229–252.

120. Eric Wish, *Drug Use Forecasting 1990* (Washington, DC: National Institute of Justice, 1991).

121. Scott Briar and Irving Piliavin, "Delinquency: Situational Inducements and Commitment to Conformity," *Social Problems* 13 (1965–1966): 35–45.

122. Lawrence Sherman and Douglas Smith, with Janell Schmidt and Dennis Rogan, "Crime, Punishment, and Stake in Conformity: Legal and Informal Control of Domestic Violence," *American Sociological Review* 57 (1992): 680–690.

123. Albert Reiss, "Delinquency as the Failure of Personal and Social Controls," *American Sociological Review* 16 (1951): 196–207.

124. Briar and Piliavin, "Delinquency: Situational Inducements and Commitment to Conformity."

125. Walter Reckless, *The Crime Problem* (New York: Appleton-Century-Crofts, 1967), pp. 469–483.

126. Among the many research reports by Reckless and his colleagues are Walter Reckless, Simon Dinitz, and Ellen Murray, "The Good Boy in a High Delinquency Area," *Journal of Criminal Law, Criminology, and Police Science* 48 (1957): 12–26; Frank Scarpitti, Ellen Murray, Simon Dinitz, and Walter Reckless, "The Good Boy in a High Delinquency Area: Four Years Later," *American Sociological Review* 23 (1960): 555–558; Walter Reckless, Simon Dinitz, and Ellen Murray, "Self-Concept as an Insulator Against Delinquency," *American Sociological Review* 21 (1956): 744–746; Walter Reckless and Simon Dinitz, "Pioneering with Self-Concept as a Vulnerability Factor in Delinquency," *Journal of Criminal Law, Criminology, and Police Science* 58 (1967): 515–523; Walter Reckless, Simon Dinitz, and Barbara Kay, "The Self-Component in Potential Delinquency and Potential Non-Delinquency," *American Sociological Review* 22 (1957): 566–570.

127. Travis Hirschi, *Causes of Delinquency* (Berkeley: University of California Press, 1969).

128. Ibid., p. 231.

129. Robert Crosnoe, "The Connection Between Academic Failure and Adolescent Drinking in Secondary School," *Sociology of Education* 79 (2006): 44–60.

130. Carl Maas, Charles Fleming, Todd Herrenkohl, and Richard Catalano, "Childhood Predictors of Teen Dating Violence Victimization," *Violence and Victims* 25 (2010): 131–149.

131. Hirschi, *Causes of Delinquency*, pp. 66–74.

132. Özden Özbay and Yusuf Ziya Özcan, "A Test of Hirschi's Social Bonding Theory," *International Journal of Offender Therapy and Comparative Criminology* 50 (2006): 711–726; Michael Wiatrowski, David Griswold, and Mary K. Roberts, "Social Control Theory and Delinquency," *American Sociological Review* 46 (1981): 525–541.

133. Patricia van Voorhis, Francis Cullen, Richard Mathers, and Connie Chenoweth Garner, "The Impact of Family Structure and Quality on Delinquency: A Comparative Assessment of Structural and Functional Factors," *Criminology* 26 (1988): 235–261.

134. Bobbi Jo Anderson, Malcolm Holmes, and Erik Ostresh, "Male and Female Delinquents' Attachments and Effects of Attachments on Severity of Self-Reported Delinquency," *Criminal Justice and Behavior* 26 (1999): 435–452.

135. Abigail A. Fagan, M. Lee Van Horn, J. David Hawkins, and Thomas Jaki, "Differential Effects of Parental Controls on Adolescent Substance Use: For Whom Is the Family Most Important?" *Journal of Quantitative Criminology* 29 (2013): 347–368; Helen Garnier and Judith Stein, "An 18-Year Model of Family and Peer Effects on Adolescent Drug Use and Delinquency," *Journal of Youth and Adolescence* 31 (2002): 45–56.

136. Van Voorhis et al., "The Impact of Family Structure and Quality on Delinquency."

137. Allison Ann Payne, "A Multilevel Analysis of the Relationships Among Communal School Organization, Student Bonding, and Delinquency," *Journal of Research in Crime and Delinquency* 45 (2008): 429–455.

138. Norman White and Rolf Loeber, "Bullying and Special Education as Predictors of Serious Delinquency," *Journal of Research in Crime and Delinquency* 45 (2008): 380–397.

139. John Cochran and Ronald Akers, "An Exploration of the Variable Effects of Religiosity on Adolescent Marijuana and Alcohol Use," *Journal of Research in Crime and Delinquency* 26 (1989): 198–225.

140. Mark Regnerus and Glen Elder, "Religion and Vulnerability Among Low-Risk Adolescents," *Social Science Research* 32 (2003): 633–658; Mark Regnerus, "Moral Communities and Adolescent Delinquency: Religious Contexts and Community Social Control," *Sociological Quarterly* 44 (2003): 523–554.

141. Michael Cretacci, "Religion and Social Control: An Application of a Modified Social Bond of Violence," *Criminal Justice Review* 28 (2003): 254–277.

142. Robert Agnew and David Peterson, "Leisure and Delinquency," *Social Problems* 36 (1989): 332–348.

143. Jonathan Zaff, Kristin Moore, Angela Romano Papillo, and Stephanie Williams, "Implications of Extracurricular Activity Participation During Adolescence on Positive Outcomes," *Journal of Adolescent Research* 18 (2003): 599–631.

144. Marianne Junger and Ineke Haen Marshall, "The Interethnic Generalizability of Social Control Theory: An Empirical Test," *Journal of Research in Crime and Delinquency* 34 (1997): 79–112; Josine Junger-Tas, "An Empirical Test of Social Control Theory," *Journal of Quantitative Criminology* 8 (1992): 18–29.

145. LaGrange and Silverman, "Perceived Strain and Delinquency Motivation."

146. Kimberly Kempf, "The Empirical Status of Hirschi's Control Theory," in *Advances in Criminological Theory*, ed. Bill Laufer and Freda Adler (New Brunswick, NJ: Transaction Books, 1992).

147. Thomas Vander Ven, Francis Cullen, Mark Carrozza, and John Paul Wright, "Home Alone: The Impact of Maternal Employment on Delinquency," *Social Problems* 48 (2001): 236–257, at 253.

148. Peggy Giordano, Stephen Cernkovich, and M. D. Pugh, "Friendships and Delinquency," *American Journal of Sociology* 91 (1986): 1170–1202.

149. Denise Kandel and Mark Davies, "Friendship Networks, Intimacy, and Illicit Drug Use in Young Adulthood: A Comparison of Two Competing Theories," *Criminology* 29 (1991): 441–467.

150. Lisa Stolzenberg and Stewart D'Alessio, "Co-Offending and the Age–Crime Curve," *Journal of Research in Crime and Delinquency* 45 (2008): 65–86.

151. Velmer Burton, Francis Cullen, T. David Evans, R. Gregory Dunaway, Sesha Kethineni, and Gary Payne, "The Impact of Parental Controls on Delinquency," *Journal of Criminal Justice* 23 (1995): 111–126.

152. Kimberly Kempf Leonard and Scott Decker, "The Theory of Social Control: Does It Apply to the Very Young?" *Journal of Criminal Justice* 22 (1994): 89–105.

153. Burton et al., "The Impact of Parental Controls on Delinquency."

154. Amy Anderson and Lorine Hughes, "Exposure to Situations Conducive to Delinquent Behavior: The Effects of Time Use, Income, and Transportation," *Journal of Research in Crime and Delinquency* 46 (2009): 5–34.

155. Patrick Seffrin, Peggy Giordano, Wendy Manning, and Monica Longmore, "The Influence of Dating Relationships on Friendship Networks, Identity Development, and Delinquency," *Justice Quarterly* 26 (2009): 238–267.

156. Michael Hindelang, "Causes of Delinquency: A Partial Replication and Extension," *Social Problems* 21 (1973): 471–487.

157. Gary Jensen and David Brownfield, "Parents and Drugs," *Criminology* 21 (1983): 543–554; see also M. Wiatrowski, D. Griswold, and M. Roberts, "Social Control Theory and Delinquency," *American Sociological Review* 46 (1981): 525–541.

158. Leslie Samuelson, Timothy Hartnagel, and Harvey Krahn, "Crime and Social Control Among High School Dropouts," *Journal of Crime and Justice* 18 (1990): 129–161.

159. Cesar Rebellon and Karen van Gundy, "Can Control Theory Explain the Link Between Parental Physical Abuse and Delinquency? A Longitudinal Analysis," *Journal of Research in Crime and Delinquency* 42 (2005): 247–274; Marvin Krohn and James Massey, "Social Control and Delinquent Behavior: An Examination of the Elements of the Social Bond," *Sociological Quarterly* 21 (1980): 529–543.

160. Jill Leslie Rosenbaum and James Lasley, "School, Community Context, and Delinquency: Rethinking the Gender Gap," *Justice Quarterly* 7 (1990): 493–513.

161. Robert Agnew, "Social Control Theory and Delinquency: A Longitudinal Test," *Criminology* 23 (1985): 47–61.

162. Alan E. Liska and M. D. Reed, "Ties to Conventional Institutions and Delinquency: Estimating Reciprocal Effects," *American Sociological Review* 50 (1985): 547–560.

163. George Herbert Mead, *Mind, Self and Society* (Chicago: University of Chicago Press, 1934); George Herbert Mead, *The Philosophy of the Act* (Chicago: University of Chicago Press, 1938); Charles Horton Cooley, *Human Nature and the Social Order* (New York: Schocken, 1964, first published 1902); Herbert Blumer, *Symbolic Interactionism: Perspective and Method* (Englewood Cliffs, NJ: Prentice Hall, 1969).

164. Kai Erickson, "Notes on the Sociology of Deviance," *Social Problems* 9 (1962): 397–414.

165. Edwin Schur, *Labeling Deviant Behavior* (New York: Harper & Row, 1972), p. 21.

166. Howard Becker, *Outsiders, Studies in the Sociology of Deviance* (New York: Macmillan, 1963), p. 9.

167. Laurie Goodstein, "The Architect of the 'Gay Conversion' Campaign," *New York Times*, August 13, 1998, p. A10.

168. Bruce Link, Elmer Streuning, Francis Cullen, Patrick Shrout, and Bruce Dohrenwend, "A Modified Labeling Theory Approach to Mental Disorders: An Empirical Assessment," *American Sociological Review* 54 (1989): 400–423.

169. Linda Jackson, John Hunter, and Carole Hodge, "Physical Attractiveness and Intellectual Competence: A Meta-Analytic

Review," *Social Psychology Quarterly* 58 (1995): 108–122.

170. Mike Adams, Craig Robertson, Phyllis Gray-Ray, and Melvin Ray, "Labeling and Delinquency," *Adolescence* 38 (2003): 171–186.

171. Patrick Corrigan, "How Stigma Interferes with Mental Health Care," *American Psychologist* 59 (2004): 614–625, at 614.

172. Jón Gunnar Bernburg, Marvin Krohn, and Craig Rivera, "Official Labeling, Criminal Embeddedness, and Subsequent Delinquency: A Longitudinal Test of Labeling Theory," *Journal of Research in Crime and Delinquency* 43 (2006): 67–88.

173. Lee Michael Johnson, Ronald Simons, and Rand Conger, "Criminal Justice System Involvement and Continuity of Youth Crime," *Youth and Society* 36 (2004): 3–29.

174. Melvin Ray and William Downs, "An Empirical Test of Labeling Theory Using Longitudinal Data," *Journal of Research in Crime and Delinquency* 23 (1986): 169–194.

175. Ross Matsueda, "Reflected Appraisals: Parental Labeling, and Delinquency: Specifying a Symbolic Interactionist Theory," *American Journal of Sociology* 97 (1992): 1577–1611.

176. Dylan Jackson and Carter Hay, "The Conditional Impact of Official Labeling on Subsequent Delinquency: Considering the Attenuating Role of Family Attachment," *Journal of Research in Crime and Delinquency* 50 (2013): 300–322.

177. Bernburg, Krohn, and Rivera, "Official Labeling, Criminal Embeddedness, and Subsequent Delinquency."

178. Heimer and Matsueda, "Role-Taking, Role-Commitment, and Delinquency."

179. See, for example, Howard Kaplan and Hiroshi Fukurai, "Negative Social Sanctions, Self-Rejection, and Drug Use," *Youth and Society* 23 (1992): 275–298; Howard Kaplan and Robert Johnson, "Negative Social Sanctions and Juvenile Delinquency: Effects of Labeling in a Model of Deviant Behavior," *Social Science Quarterly* 72 (1991): 98–122; Howard Kaplan, Robert Johnson, and Carol Bailey, "Deviant Peers and Deviant Behavior: Further Elaboration of a Model," *Social Psychology Quarterly* 30 (1987): 277–284.

180. Howard Kaplan, *Toward a General Theory of Deviance: Contributions from Perspectives on Deviance and Criminality* (College Station: Texas A&M University, n.d.).

181. Sampson and Laub, "A Life-Course Theory of Cumulative Disadvantage and the Stability of Delinquency."

182. Suzanne Ageton and Delbert Elliott, *The Effect of Legal Processing on Self-Concept* (Boulder, CO: Institute of Behavioral Science, 1973).

183. Jón Gunnar Bernburg and Marvin Krohn, "Labeling, Life Chances, and Adult Crime: The Direct and Indirect Effects of Official Intervention in Adolescence on Crime in Early Adulthood," *Criminology* 41 (2003): 1287–1319.

184. John Lofland, *Deviance and Identity* (Englewood Cliffs, NJ: Prentice Hall, 1969).

185. Frank Tannenbaum, *Crime and the Community* (New York: Columbia University Press, 1938), pp. 19–20.

186. Edwin Lemert, *Social Pathology* (New York: McGraw-Hill, 1951).

187. Ibid., p. 75.

188. Bruce Western, *Punishment and Inequality in America* (New York: Russell Sage Foundation, 2006); Sara Steen, Rodney Engen, and Randy Gainey, "Images of Danger and Culpability: Racial Stereotyping, Case Processing, and Criminal Sentencing," *Criminology* 43 (2005): 435–468; Stephanie Bontrager, William Bales, and Ted Chiricos, "Race, Ethnicity, Threat and the Labeling of Convicted Felons," *Criminology* 43 (2005): 589–622.

189. Marjorie Zatz, "Race, Ethnicity and Determinate Sentencing," *Criminology* 22 (1984): 147–171.

190. Christina DeJong and Kenneth Jackson, "Putting Race into Context: Race, Juvenile Justice Processing, and Urbanization," *Justice Quarterly* 15 (1998): 487–504.

191. Howard Kaplan and Robert Johnson, "Negative Social Sanctions and Juvenile Delinquency: Effects of Labeling in a Model of Deviant Behavior," *Social Science Quarterly* 72 (1991): 98–122.

192. Ruth Triplett, "The Conflict Perspective, Symbolic Interactionism, and the Status Characteristics Hypothesis," *Justice Quarterly* 10 (1993): 540–558.

193. Lening Zhang, "Official Offense Status and Self-Esteem Among Chinese Youths," *Journal of Criminal Justice* 31 (2003): 99–105.

194. Charles Tittle, "Two Empirical Regularities (Maybe) in Search of an Explanation: Commentary on the Age/Crime Debate," *Criminology* 26 (1988): 75–85.

195. Robert Sampson and John Laub, "A Life-Course Theory of Cumulative Disadvantage and the Stability of Delinquency," in *Developmental Theories of Crime and Delinquency*, ed. Terence Thornberry (New Brunswick, NJ: Transaction Press, 1997), pp. 133–161; Douglas Smith and Robert Brame, "On the Initiation and Continuation of Delinquency," *Criminology* 4 (1994): 607–630.

196. Sampson and Laub, "A Life-Course Theory of Cumulative Disadvantage and the Stability of Delinquency."

197. Robert Morris and Alex Piquero, "For Whom Do Sanctions Deter and Label?" *Justice Quarterly* 30 (2013): 837–868.

198. Stephanie Ann Wiley, Lee Ann Slocum, and Finn-Aage Esbensen, "The Unintended Consequences of Being Stopped or Arrested: An Exploration of the Labeling Mechanisms Through Which Police Contact Leads to Subsequent Delinquency," *Criminology* 51 (2013): 927–966.

199. Bernburg and Krohn, "Labeling, Life Chances, and Adult Crime."

200. Jack Gibbs, "Conceptions of Deviant Behavior: The Old and the New," *Pacific Sociological Review* 9 (1966): 11–13.

201. Charles Tittle, "Labeling and Crime: An Empirical Evaluation," in *The Labeling of Deviance: Evaluating a Perspective*, ed. Walter Gove (New York: Wiley, 1975), pp. 157–179.

202. Megan Kurlychek, Robert Brame, and Shawn Bushway, "Enduring Risk? Old Criminal Records and Predictions of Future Criminal Involvement," *Crime and Delinquency* 53 (2007): 64–83.

203. Emily Restivo and Mark M. Lanier, "Measuring the Contextual Effects and Mitigating Factors of Labeling Theory," *Justice Quarterly*, first published online January 11, 2013.

204. Raymond Paternoster and Leeann Iovanni, "The Labeling Perspective and Delinquency: An Elaboration of the Theory and an Assessment of the Evidence," *Justice Quarterly* 6 (1989): 358–394.

205. Shadd Maruna, Thomas Lebel, Nick Mitchell, and Michelle Maples, "Pygmalion in the Reintegration Process: Desistance from Crime Through the Looking Glass," *Psychology, Crime, and Law* 10 (2004): 271–281.

206. National Head Start Association, http://www.nhsa.org/ (accessed May 2014); Office of Head Start, http://www.acf.hhs.gov/programs/ohs (accessed May 2014).

CRITICAL CRIMINOLOGY AND RESTORATIVE JUSTICE

In February and March of 2014, the independent nation of Ukraine was in turmoil after days and nights of clashes between antigovernment protesters and police that ended with a vote in parliament to oust President Viktor Yanukovych, a close ally and supporter of Russia and its leader Vladimir Putin. The cause of the rioting was the government's rejection of an accord with the European Union in favor of stronger ties with Russia. With a population of 45 million people, a majority of Ukrainians sought ties with the West, something that was considered unacceptable to the Russian premier. On February 20, 2014, the streets became a battlefield. At least 77 people were killed and hundreds wounded in clashes between protesters and police, including many shot by uniformed snipers. Russia then sent in troops with the pretext that it was necessary to protect Russian citizens. Most were sent to Ukraine's autonomous republic of Crimea where Russia's Black Sea fleet is based at Sevastopol. Pro-Russian forces gradually took control of the Crimean peninsula. Soon the Crimean parliament and the city council of Sevastopol adopted a resolution to show their intention of joining the Russian Federation. A vote was held and 96 percent of those who voted in Crimea supported joining Russia.

On March 17, 2014, the Crimean parliament officially declared its independence from Ukraine and requested to join the Russian Federation; a day later, President Putin declared Crimea a part of Russia.[1]

he Ukrainian conflict is nothing new or unusual. We live in a world rife with political, social, and economic conflict in nearly every corner of the globe. Conflict comes in many forms, occurs at many levels of society, and involves a whole slew of adversaries: workers and bosses, the United States and its overseas enemies, religious zealots and apostates, citizens and police. It occurs within cities, in neighborhoods, and even within the family.

Conflict can be destructive when it leads to war, violence, and death. It can be functional when it results in positive social change, though sometimes it's hard to discern when change is positive. The uprisings referred to as the Arab Spring that occurred in the Middle East between 2010 and 2014 brought political and social change to Egypt, Libya, Tunisia, and Syria, but at the time of this writing Syria and Iraq are in the midst of a civil war while the Egyptian military now control the nation with an iron hand.[2]

Conflict promotes crime by creating a social atmosphere in which the law is a mechanism for controlling dissatisfied, have-not members of society while the wealthy maintain their power. This is why crimes that are the province of the wealthy, such as illegal corporate activities, are sanctioned much more leniently than those, such as burglary, that are considered lower-class activities.

Criminologists who view crime as a function of social conflict and economic rivalry have in the past been known by a number of titles, such as conflict, Marxist, left, or radical criminologists, but today most commonly they are referred to as **critical criminologists** and their field of study as **critical criminology**.

LO1 Define the concept of social conflict and how it shapes behavior

Like their title hints, critical criminologists view themselves as social critics who dig beneath the surface of society to uncover its inequities. They reject the notion that law is designed to maintain a tranquil, fair society and that criminals are malevolent people who wish to trample the rights of others. They believe that the law is an instrument of power, wielded by those who control society in order to maintain their wealth, social position,

critical criminologists Researchers who view crime as a function of the capitalist mode of production and not the social conflict that might occur in any society regardless of its economic system.

critical criminology The view that capitalism produces haves and have-nots, each engaging in a particular branch of criminality. The mode of production shapes social life. Because economic competitiveness is the essence of capitalism, conflict increases and eventually destabilizes social institutions and the individuals within them.

and class advantage. They consider acts of racism, sexism, imperialism, unsafe working conditions, inadequate child care, substandard housing, pollution of the environment, and war-making as a tool of foreign policy to be "true crimes." The crimes of the helpless—burglary, robbery, and assault—are often an expression of rage over unjust social and economic conditions rather than selfish acts of greedy people.[3]

Contemporary critical criminologists try to explain crime within economic and social contexts and to express the connections among social class, crime, and social control.[4] They are concerned with issues such as these:

- The role government plays in creating a crime-producing environment
- The relationship between personal or group power and the shaping of criminal law
- The prevalence of bias in justice system operations
- The relationship between a capitalist, free-enterprise economy and crime rates

Critical criminologists often take the broader view, opposing what they consider to be "real crimes"—racism, sexism, and genocide—rather than focusing on street crimes such as burglary, robbery, and rape.[5] They want to publicize the fact that while conservative, right-wing politicians propose spending cuts for social programs, they are all for military expansion, presumably to control people in third-world countries so that American corporations can flourish abroad. Other elements of the conservative agenda include the buildup of the prison system and passage of draconian criminal laws that threaten civil rights and liberties such as the death penalty and three-strikes laws. Critical criminologists believe they are responsible both for informing the public about the dangers of these developments and promoting social change through their teaching and research.[6]

This chapter reviews the historical development of critical criminology. It covers its principal ideas and then looks at policies that have been embraced by critical thinkers, which focus on peace and restoration rather than punishment and exclusion. Figure 8.1 illustrates the various independent branches of social conflict theory.

THE HISTORICAL DEVELOPMENT OF CRITICAL CRIMINOLOGY

LO2 Discuss the history of critical theory and its roots in Marxist thought

The roots of critical criminology can be traced to the social philosopher Karl Marx (1818–1883), who identified the economic structures in society that control all human relations. Marx's view of society was shaped by the

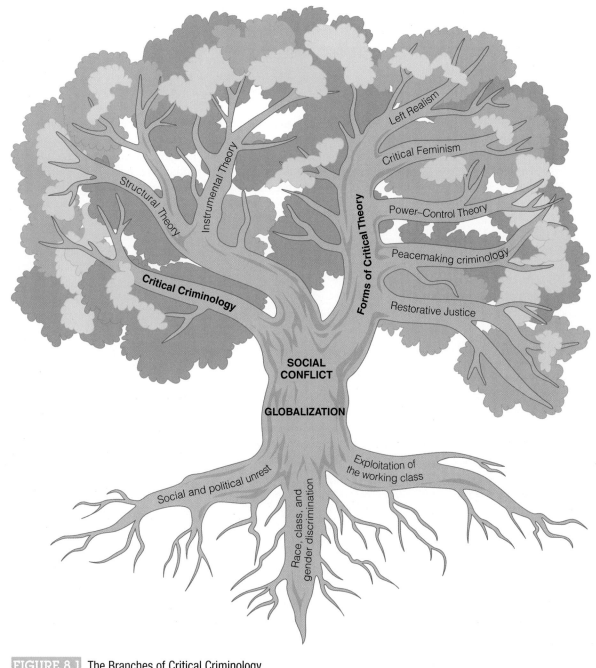

FIGURE 8.1 The Branches of Critical Criminology

SOURCE: © Cengage Learning®

economic trends and structures of that period. He lived in an era of unrestrained capitalist expansion.[7] The tools of the Industrial Revolution had become regular features of society by 1850. Mechanized factories, the use of coal to drive steam engines, and modern transportation all inspired economic development. Production had shifted from cottage industries to large factories. Industrialists could hire workers on their own terms; as a result, conditions in factories were atrocious. Factory owners and the government enforcement agents in their pay ruthlessly suppressed trade unions that promised workers salvation from these atrocities.

Marx's early career as a journalist was interrupted by government suppression of the newspaper where he worked, because of the paper's liberal editorial policy. He then moved to Paris, where he met Friedrich Engels (1820–1895), who would become his friend and economic patron. By 1847, Marx and Engels had joined with a group of primarily German socialist revolutionaries known as the Communist League.

Productive Forces and Productive Relations

In 1848, Marx issued his famous *Communist Manifesto* in which he described the oppressive labor conditions prevalent during the rise of industrial capitalism. The exploitation of the working class, he believed, would eventually lead to class conflict and the end of the capitalist system.

Marx focused his attention on the economic conditions perpetuated by the capitalist system. He stated that its development had turned workers into a dehumanized mass who lived an existence that was at the mercy of their capitalist employers. He wrote of the injustice of young children being sent to work in mines and factories from dawn to dusk. He focused on the people who were being beaten down by a system that demanded obedience and cooperation and offered little in return. These oppressive conditions led Marx to conclude that the character of every civilization is determined by its mode of production—the way its people develop and produce material goods (materialism).

Marx identified the economic structures in society that control all human relations. Production has two components: **productive forces**, which include such things as technology, energy sources, and material resources, and **productive relations**, which are the relationships that exist among the people producing goods and services. The most important relationship in industrial culture is between the owners of the means of production, the **capitalist bourgeoisie**, and the people who do the actual labor, the **proletariat**.

Throughout history, society has been organized this way: master–slave, lord–serf, and now capitalist–proletariat. According to Marx, capitalist society is subject to the development of a rigid class structure with the capitalist bourgeoisie at the top, followed by the working proletariat, who actually produce goods and services, and at the bottom, the fringe, nonproductive members who produce nothing and live, parasitically, off the work of others—the **lumpen proletariat**.

In Marxist theory, the term *class* does not refer to an attribute or characteristic of a person or a group; rather, it denotes position in relation to others. Thus, it is not necessary to have a particular amount of wealth or prestige to be a member of the capitalist class; it is more important to have the power to exploit others economically, legally, and socially. The political and economic philosophy of the dominant class influences all aspects of life. Consciously or unconsciously, artists, writers, and teachers bend their work to the whims of the capitalist system. Thus, the economic system controls all facets of human life. Consequently, people's lives revolve around the means of production.

As Marx said:

> In all forms of society, there is one specific kind of production which predominates over the rest, whose relations thus assign rank and influence to the others. It is a general illumination which bathes all the other colours and modifies their particularity. It is a particular ether which determines the specific gravity of every being which has materialized within it.[8]

Marx believed societies and their structures were not stable and, therefore, could change through slow evolution or sudden violence. If social conflicts are not resolved, they tend to destabilize society, leading to social change.

The ebb and flow of the capitalist business cycle creates social conflicts that contain the seeds of its own destruction. Marx predicted that from its ashes would grow a socialist state in which the workers themselves would own the means of production. In his analysis, Marx used the **dialectic method**, based on the analysis developed by the philosopher Georg Hegel (1770–1831). Hegel argued that for every idea, or **thesis**, there exists an opposing argument, or **antithesis**. Since neither position can ever be truly accepted, the result is a merger of the two ideas, a **synthesis**. Marx adapted this analytic method for his study of class struggle. History, argued Marx, is replete with examples of two opposing forces whose conflict promotes social change. When conditions are bad enough, the oppressed will rise up to fight the owners and eventually replace them. Thus, in the end, the capitalist system will destroy itself.

Communist Manifesto In this document, Marx focused his attention on the economic conditions perpetuated by the capitalist system. He stated that its development had turned workers into a dehumanized mass who lived an existence that was at the mercy of their capitalist employers.

productive forces Technology, energy sources, and material resources.

productive relations The relationships that exist among the people producing goods and services.

capitalist bourgeoisie The owners of the means of production.

proletariat A term used by Marx to refer to the working class members of society who produce goods and services but who do not own the means of production.

lumpen proletariat The fringe members at the bottom of society who produce nothing and live, parasitically, off the work of others.

dialectic method For every idea, or thesis, there exists an opposing argument, or antithesis. Because neither position can ever be truly accepted, the result is a merger of the two ideas, a synthesis. Marx adapted this analytic method for his study of class struggle.

thesis In the philosophy of Hegel, an original idea or thought.

antithesis An opposing argument.

synthesis A merger of two opposing ideas.

Karl Marx and Engels in the printing house of the *Neue Rheinische Zeitung* (a newspaper published in Cologne at the time of the Revolutions of 1848).

Roger Viollet/Getty Images

A Marxist Vision of Crime

Marx did not write a great deal on the subject of crime, but he mentioned it in a variety of passages scattered throughout his writing. He viewed crime as the product of law enforcement policies akin to a labeling process theory.[9] He also saw a connection between criminality and the inequities found in the capitalist system. He reasoned: "There must be something rotten in the very core of a social system which increases in wealth without diminishing its misery, and increases in crime even more rapidly than in numbers."[10]

His collaborator, Friedrich Engels, however, did spend some time on the subject in his work, *The Condition of the Working Class in England in 1844*.[11] Engels portrayed crime as a function of social demoralization—a collapse of people's humanity reflecting a decline in society. Workers, demoralized by capitalist society, are caught up in a process that leads to crime and violence. According to Engels, workers are social outcasts, ignored by the structure of capitalist society and treated as brutes.[12] Left to their own devices, working people commit crime because their choice is a slow death of starvation or a speedy one at the hands of the law. The brutality of the capitalist system, he believed, turns workers into animal-like creatures without a will of their own.

The writings of Karl Marx greatly influenced the development of the view of crime that rested on the concept of social conflict. Even though Marx himself did not write much on the topic of crime, his views on the relationship between the concept of social conflict were first applied to criminology by three distinguished scholars: Willem Bonger, Ralf Dahrendorf, and George Vold. In some instances, their works share the Marxist view that industrial society is wracked by conflict between the proletariat and the bourgeoisie; in other instances, their writings diverge from Marxist dogma. The writing of each of these pioneers is briefly described in Exhibit 8.1.

To read about Marx and his vision, visit **http://plato .stanford.edu/entries/marx/.** Marx is always associated with the Russian revolution, but he actually never traveled there, being born in Germany and living in France and England.

Could a Marxist-style society have benefits if it could be created without the baggage of Russian-style communism— that is, ruthless dictators and thought control?

MARXIST CRITICAL THEORY

Ralf Dahrendorf

Roland Magunia/afp/ddp/Getty Images

famous criminologists

ORIGIN About 1848

FOUNDERS Karl Marx, Willem Bonger, Ralf Dahrendorf, George Vold

MOST IMPORTANT WORKS Friedrich Engels, *The Condition of the Working Class in England in 1844* (1845); Marx and Engels, *The Communist Manifesto* (1848); Bonger, *Criminality and Economic Conditions* (1916); George Rusche and Otto Kircheimer, *Punishment and Social Structure* (1939); Dahrendorf, *Class and Class Conflict in Industrial Society* (1959); Vold, *Theoretical Criminology* (1958)

CORE IDEAS Crime is a function of class struggle. The capitalist system's emphasis on competition and wealth produces an economic and social environment in which crime is inevitable.

MODERN OUTGROWTHS Critical criminology, critical feminist theory, left realism, peacemaking, power–control theory, postmodern theory, restorative justice

EXHIBIT 8.1

Willem Bonger, Ralf Dahrendorf, and George Vold on Crime

Willem Bonger

Bonger believed that society is divided into have and have-not groups, not on the basis of people's innate ability, but because of the system of production that is in force. In every society that is divided into a ruling class and an inferior class, penal law serves the will of the ruling class. Even though criminal laws may appear to protect members of both classes, hardly any act is punished that does not injure the interests of the dominant ruling class. Crimes, then, are considered to be antisocial acts because they are harmful to those who have the power at their command to control society. Under capitalism, the legal system discriminates against the poor by defending the actions of the wealthy. Because the proletariat are deprived of the materials that are monopolized by the bourgeoisie, they are more likely to violate the law.

Ralf Dahrendorf

Dahrendorf argued that modern society is organized into what he called imperatively coordinated associations. These associations comprise two groups: those who possess authority and use it for social domination and those who lack authority and are dominated. Society is a plurality of competing interest groups. He proposed a unified conflict theory of human behavior, which can be summarized as follows:

- Every society is at every point subject to processes of change; social change is everywhere.
- Every society displays at every point dissent and conflict; social conflict is everywhere.
- Every element in a society renders a contribution to its disintegration and change.
- Every society is based on the coercion of some of its members by others.

George Vold

Vold argued that laws are created by politically oriented groups, who seek the government's assistance to help them defend their rights and protect their interests. If a group can marshal enough support, a law will be created to hamper and curb the interests of some opposition group. Every stage of the process—from passing the law to prosecuting the case to developing relationships between inmate and guard, parole agent and parolee—is marked by conflict. Criminal acts are a consequence of direct contact between forces struggling to control society.

SOURCES: Willem Bonger, *Criminality and Economic Conditions*, abridged ed. (Bloomington: Indiana University Press, 1969, first published 1916); Ralf Dahrendorf, *Class and Class Conflict in Industrial Society* (Palo Alto, CA: Stanford University Press, 1959); George Vold, *Theoretical Criminology* (New York: Oxford University Press, 1958).

CREATING A CRITICAL CRIMINOLOGY

The social ferment of the 1960s gave birth to critical criminology. In 1968, a group of British sociologists formed the National Deviancy Conference (NDC). With about 300 members, this organization sponsored several national symposia and dialogues. Members came from all walks of life, but at its core the NDC was a group of academics who were critical of the positivist criminology being taught in British and American universities. More specifically, they rejected the conservative stance of criminologists and their close financial relationship with government funding agencies.

The NDC called attention to ways in which social control might actually cause deviance rather than just respond to antisocial behavior. Many conference members became concerned about the political nature of social control.

In 1973, critical theory was given a powerful academic boost when British scholars Ian Taylor, Paul Walton, and Jock Young published *The New Criminology*.[13] This brilliant, thorough, and well-constructed critique of existing concepts in criminology called for the development of new methods of criminological analysis and critique. *The New Criminology* became the standard resource for scholars critical of both the field of criminology and the existing legal process. Since its publication there has been a tradition for critical criminologists to turn their attention to the field itself, questioning the role criminology plays in supporting the status quo and aiding in the oppression of the poor and powerless.[14]

U.S. scholars were also influenced during the late 1960s and early 1970s by the widespread unrest and social change that shook the world. The war in Vietnam, prison struggles, and the civil rights and feminist movements produced a climate in which criticism of the ruling class seemed a natural byproduct. Mainstream, positivist criminology was criticized as being overtly conservative, pro-government, and antihuman. Critical criminologists scoffed when their fellow scholars used statistical analysis of computerized data to describe criminal and delinquent behavior. Several influential scholars embraced the idea that the social conflict produced by the unequal distribution of power and wealth was at the root cause of crime. William Chambliss and Robert Seidman wrote the well-respected treatise *Law, Order and Power*, which documented how the justice system protects the rich and powerful.[15] Chambliss and Seidman's work showed how control of the political and economic system affects the way criminal justice is administered and that the definitions of crime used in contemporary society favor those who control the justice system.

In another influential work, *The Social Reality of Crime*, Richard Quinney also proclaimed that in contemporary society criminal law represents the interests of those who hold power.[16] Where there is conflict between social groups—the wealthy and the poor—those who hold power will create laws that benefit themselves and keep rivals in check. Law is not an abstract body of rules that represents an absolute moral code; rather, law is an integral part of society, a force that represents a way of life and a method of doing things. Crime is a function of power relations and an inevitable result of social conflict. Criminals are not simply social misfits but people who have come up short in the struggle for success and are seeking alternative means of achieving wealth, status, or even survival.

As a group, these social thinkers began to show how in our postindustrial, capitalist society the economic system invariably produces haves and have-nots.[17] The mode of production shapes social life. Because economic competitiveness is the essence of capitalism, conflict increases and eventually destabilizes both social institutions and social groups.[18]

Contemporary Critical Criminology

LO3 List the core ideas of critical criminology

From these early roots, a robust critical criminology was formed. At first, these alternative forms of criminology were considered Marxist and radical. They have morphed into a critical criminology that is antiestablishment and questioning of the socioeconomic structures that produce crime and criminality.[19]

Today, critical criminologists devote their attention to a number of important themes and concepts. One is the use and misuse of power, or the ability of persons and groups to determine and control the behavior of others and to shape public opinion to meet their personal interests. Because those in power shape the content of the law, it comes as no surprise that their behavior is often exempt from legal sanctions. Those who deserve the most severe sanctions (wealthy white-collar criminals whose crimes cost society millions of dollars) usually receive lenient punishments, while those whose relatively minor crimes are committed out of economic necessity (petty thieves and drug dealers) receive stricter penalties, especially if they are minority group members who lack social and economic power.[20] And once they have done their time, they face a bleak future in a jobless economy in which the poor, minority group members and those with a criminal record are typically un- or under-employed.[21]

Critical criminologists have also been deeply concerned about the current state of the American political system and the creation of what they consider to be an American empire abroad. The wars in Iraq and Afghanistan are viewed as elements of a global policy designed to control the world through the application of military power, tax cuts for the wealthy and less money for social programs. Critical criminologists believe they are responsible for informing the public about the dangers of these developments.[22]

CONNECTIONS

The USA Patriot Act will be discussed further in Chapter 11 within the context of legal efforts to thwart terrorism. While some welcome its provisions that make it easier for the government to monitor people considered dangerous, critical thinkers fear loss of individual freedom at the expense of state power.

HOW CRITICAL CRIMINOLOGISTS DEFINE CRIME

According to critical theorists, crime is a political concept designed to protect the power and position of the upper classes at the expense of the poor. Some, but not all, would include in a list of "real" crimes such acts as violations of human rights due to racism, sexism, and imperialism and other violations of human dignity and physical needs and necessities. Take for instance what Alette Smeulers and Roelof Haveman call supranational crimes: war crimes, crimes against humanity, genocide, and other human rights violations. Smeulers and Haveman believe that these types of crimes should merit more attention by criminologists, and therefore they call for a separate specialization, **supranational criminology**.[23]

The nature of a society controls the direction of its criminality; criminals are not social misfits but products of the society and its economic system.[24] Criminals are not a group of outsiders who can be controlled by increased law enforcement. Criminality, instead, is a function of social and economic organization. To control crime and reduce criminality, societies must remove the social conditions that promote crime.[25]

In our advanced technological society, those with economic and political power control the definition of crime and the manner in which the criminal justice system enforces the law.[26] Consequently, the only crimes available to the poor are the severely sanctioned "street crimes": rape, murder, theft, and mugging. Members of the middle class cheat on their taxes and engage in petty corporate crime (employee theft), acts that generate social disapproval but are rarely punished severely. The wealthy routinely are involved in corporate acts that should be described as crimes but escape sanctions. Regulatory laws control illegal business activities, but these are rarely enforced, and violations are lightly punished. One reason is that an essential feature of capitalism is the need to expand business and create new markets. This goal often conflicts with laws designed to protect the environment and creates clashes with those who seek their enforcement. In our postindustrial society, the need for expansion usually triumphs. For example, corporate spokespeople and their political allies will brand environmentalists as "tree huggers" who stand in the way of jobs and prosperity.[27]

The rich are insulated from street crimes because they live in areas far removed from crime. Those in power use the fear of crime as a tool to maintain their control over society. The poor are controlled through incarceration, and

supranational criminology The study of war crimes, crimes against humanity, and the supranational penal system in which such crimes are prosecuted and tried.

the middle class is diverted from caring about the crimes of the powerful by their fear of the crimes of the powerless.[28] Ironically, they may have more to lose from the economic crimes committed by the rich than from the street crimes of the poor. Stock market swindles and savings and loan scams cost the public billions of dollars but are typically settled with fines and probationary sentences.

Because private ownership of property is the true measure of success in American society (as opposed to, say, being a worthy person), the state becomes an ally of the wealthy in protecting their property interests. As a result, theft-related crimes are often punished more severely than are acts of violence because although the former may be interclass, the latter are typically intraclass.

HOW CRITICAL CRIMINOLOGISTS VIEW THE CAUSE OF CRIME

Critical thinkers believe that the key crime-producing element of modern corporate capitalism is the effort to create **surplus value**—the profits produced by the laboring classes that are accrued by business owners. Once accumulated, surplus value can be either reinvested or used to enrich the owners. To increase the rate of surplus value, workers can be made to toil harder for less pay, be made more efficient, or be replaced by machines or technology. Therefore, economic growth does not benefit all elements of the population, and in the long run it may produce the same effect as a depression or recession.

As the rate of surplus value increases, more people are displaced from productive relationships and the size of the marginal population swells. As corporations downsize to increase profits, high-paying labor and managerial jobs are lost to computer-driven machinery. Displaced workers are forced into service jobs at minimum wage. Many become temporary employees without benefits or a secure position.

As more people are thrust outside the economic mainstream, a condition referred to as **marginalization**, a larger portion of the population is forced to live in areas conducive

surplus value The Marxist view that the laboring classes produce wealth that far exceeds their wages and goes to the capitalist class as profits.

marginalization Displacement of workers, pushing them outside the economic and social mainstream.

dropout factories High schools in which the completion rate is consistently 40 percent or less.

globalization The process of creating transnational markets, politics, and legal systems in an effort to form and sustain a global economy.

to crime. Once people are marginalized, commitment to the system declines creating another crime-producing force: a weakened bond to society.

The government may be quick to respond during periods of economic decline because those in power assume that poverty breed crime and social disorder. When unemployment is increasing, public officials assume the worst and devote greater attention to the criminal justice system, perhaps building new prisons to prepare for the coming "crime wave."[29] Empirical research confirms that economic downturns are indeed linked to both crime rate increases and government activities such as passing anticrime legislation.[30] As the level of surplus value increases, so too do police expenditures, most likely because of the perceived or real need for the state to control those on the economic margin.[31]

 The theory of surplus value can be quite complex. To read more about it, go to **http://www.internationalviewpoint.org/spip.php?article287.** **How do the Internet and web commerce influence the concept of surplus value?**

Failing Social Institutions

Critical thinkers often focus on contemporary social institutions to show how they operate as instruments of class and racial oppression. Critical scholars find that class bias and racial oppression exist from the cradle to the grave. There are significant race-based achievement differences in education, ranging from scores on standardized tests to dropout and high school completion rates. There are high schools, mostly in poverty-stricken inner-city neighborhoods, where the high school completion rate is 40 percent or less; these are referred to as **dropout factories**. There are more than 1,700 of these failing schools in the United States. Although they represent only a small fraction of all public high schools in America, they account for about half of all high school dropouts each year.[32]

One reason for these persistent problems may be linked to differences in discipline meted out in poor and wealthy districts. Research shows that African American children receive more disciplinary infractions than children from other racial categories, despite the fact that their behavior is quite similar. Having a higher percentage of black students in a school translates into a greater use of disciplinary tactics, a factor that may explain why minority students fare less well and are more likely to disengage from school at a younger age than whites.[33] Critical thinkers might suggest that these class- and race-based burdens make crime inevitable.

Globalization

 LO4 Define the concept of globalization and analyze its association with crime

Globalization, which usually refers to the process of creating transnational markets and political and legal systems,

Relatives of garment worker Mohammed Abdullah cry as they pass others looking for missing relatives while collecting his body at a makeshift morgue in a school yard near a building that collapsed April 24, 2013, in Savar, near Dhaka, Bangladesh. The owner of the building, who ignored inspectors' advice to close the structure when cracks appeared in the building a day before the collapse, sits at the nexus of party politics and the powerful $20 billion garment industry that drives the economy of this deeply impoverished nation. Experts say this intersection of politics and business, combined with a minimum wage of $9.50 a week that has made Bangladesh the go-to nation for many of the world's largest clothing brands, has created a predictable danger for factory workers. Government officials, labor activists, manufacturers, and retailers all called for improved safety standards after a November fire in the same suburb, when locked emergency exits trapped hundreds of garment workers inside amid spreading flames and 112 people died. But almost nothing has changed. The Savar catastrophe claimed 1,129 lives, and another 2,500 were injured.

AP Images/Kevin Frayer

has shifted the focus of critical inquiry to a world perspective. Globalization began when large companies decided to establish themselves in foreign markets by adapting their products or services to the local culture. The process took off with the fall of the Soviet Union, which opened new European markets. The development of China into a super industrial power encouraged foreign investors to take advantage of China's huge supply of workers. Capitalists hailed China's entry into the World Trade Organization in 2001 as a significant economic event. However, critical thinkers point out that the economic boom has significant costs. While the average manufacturing wage in China has risen quite a bit, it remains at about $1.75 per hour, less than a tenth of what a worker in the United States earns; many thousands of workers are killed at work each year and millions more disabled.[34]

As the Internet and communication revolution unfolded, companies were able to establish instant communications with their far-flung corporate empires, a technological breakthrough that further aided trade and foreign investments. A series of transnational corporate mergers and takeovers (such as when Ford bought Swedish car maker Volvo

in 1999 and then in 2010 sold Volvo to the Chinese car company Geely) produced ever-larger transnational corporations.

Some experts believe globalization can improve the standard of living in third-world nations by providing jobs and training, but critical theorists question the altruism of multinational corporations. Their motives are exploiting natural resources, avoiding regulation, and taking advantage of desperate workers. When these giant corporations set up a factory in a developing nation, it is not to help the local population but to get around environmental laws and take advantage of needy workers who may be forced to labor in substandard conditions. In some instances, transnational companies take advantage of national unrest and calamity in order to engage in profiteering. For example, recent examinations of illegal mineral expropriation in the Democratic Republic of the Congo (DRC) highlight the role that transnational corporations and international marketplaces played in the theft of Congolese gold. While these companies did not directly encourage the conflict or the massive human rights violations and crimes against humanity committed in the region, they were simply taking advantage of existing disorder and violence in order to make a huge profit.[35]

Globalization has replaced imperialism and colonization as a new form of economic domination and oppression and now presents, according to critical thinkers, a threat to the world economy:

- Growing global dominance and the reach of the free-market capitalist system, which disproportionately benefits wealthy and powerful organizations and individuals
- Increasing vulnerability of indigenous people with a traditional way of life to the forces of globalized capitalism
- Growing influence and impact of international financial institutions (such as the World Bank) and the related relative decline of power of local or state-based institutions
- Nondemocratic operation of international financial institutions[36]

Globalization may have a profound influence on class relations. Workers in the United States may be replaced in high-paying manufacturing jobs not by machines but by foreign workers. Instant communication via the Internet and global communications, a development that Marx could not have foreseen, will speed the effect immeasurably. Globalization will have a profound effect both on the economy and eventually on crime rates.

Alleged drug traffickers are shown to the media at a police station in Yopal, Colombia. Colombian police said they dismantled the private army of a paramilitary warlord, Carlos Mario Jimenez, alias "Macaco," by arresting 147 people believed to be protecting a major cocaine smuggling ring.

Globalization and Crime Globalization may be responsible for unrest in financial systems and in so doing has created a fertile ground for contemporary enterprise crimes. By expanding the reach of both criminal and noncriminal organizations, globalization also increases the vulnerability of indigenous people with a traditional way of life.[37] With money and power to spare, criminal enterprise groups can recruit new members, bribe government officials, and even fund private armies. International organized crime has globalized its activities for the same reasons legitimate multinational corporations have expanded around the world: new markets bring new sources of profits. As international crime expert Louise Shelley puts it:

> Just as multinational corporations establish branches around the world to take advantage of attractive labor or raw material markets, so do illicit businesses. Furthermore, international businesses, both legitimate and illicit, also establish facilities worldwide for production, marketing, and distribution needs. Illicit enterprises are able to expand geographically to take advantage of these new economic circumstances thanks to the communications and international transportation revolution.[38]

Shelley argues that two elements of globalization encourage criminality: one technological, the other cultural. Technological advances such as efficient and widespread commercial airline traffic, improvements in telecommunica-

tions (ranging from global cell phone connectivity to the Internet), and the growth of international trade have all aided the growth in illicit transnational activities. These changes have facilitated the cross-border movement of goods and people, conditions exploited by criminals who now use Internet chat rooms to plan their activities. On a cultural level, globalization brings with it an ideology of free markets and free trade. The cultural shift means less intervention and regulation, conditions exploited by crime groups to cross unpatrolled borders and to expand their activities to new regions of the world. Transnational crime groups freely exploit this new freedom to travel to regions where they cannot be extradited, base their operations in countries with ineffective or corrupt law enforcement, and launder their money in countries with bank secrecy or few effective controls. Globalization has allowed both individual offenders and criminal gangs to gain tremendous operational benefits while reducing risks of apprehension and punishment.

State-Organized Crime

LO5 Explain the concept of state-organized crime

While mainstream criminologists focus on the crimes of the poor and powerless, critical criminologists focus their attention on the law violations of the powerful. One area of concern is referred to as **state-organized crime**—acts defined by law as criminal and committed by state officials, elected or appointed, in pursuit of their jobs as government representatives. Their actions, or in some cases failure to act, amount to a violation of the criminal law they are bound by oath or duty to uphold.

Among the most controversial claims made by critical criminologists are those linking the United States to state-organized crime and violence. Those who study state-organized crime argue that these antisocial behaviors arise from efforts to either maintain governmental power or to uphold the race, class, and gender advantages of those who support the government. In industrial society, the state will do everything to protect the property rights of the wealthy while opposing the real interests of the poor. They might even go to war to support the capitalist classes who need the wealth and resources of other nations. The desire for natural resources such as rubber, oil, and metals was one of the primary reasons for Japan's invasion of China and other Eastern nations that sparked their entry into World War II. Fifty years later, the United States was accused by many media commentators and political pundits of invading Iraq in order to secure its oil for American use.[39]

state-organized crime Acts defined by law as criminal and committed by state officials, either elected or appointed, in pursuit of their jobs as government representatives.

There are a number of categories of state-organized crime and these are set out in some detail below.[40]

Illegal Domestic Surveillance In 2013, a leak of documents stolen from the National Security Agency (NSA) by contract employee Edward Snowden set off an international firestorm. Among other things, Snowden's documents revealed that the NSA had programs that gave it access to a vast quantity of emails, chat logs, and other data directly from Internet companies, including Google, Facebook, and Apple. Snowden revealed that the NSA was collecting millions of email and instant messaging contact lists, searching email content, and tracking and mapping the location of cell phones. The NSA was shown to be secretly tapping into Yahoo and Google data centers to collect information from "hundreds of millions" of account holders worldwide by monitoring undersea cables.[41]

Before fleeing to Russia, Edward Snowden's illegal copying and dissemination of NSA documents showed that the U.S. government was engaging in a wide range of domestic and foreign surveillance activities. Among other things, without a warrant the agency was collecting and analyzing the content of communications of foreigners talking to persons inside the United States. They were able to collect data and information off of fiber optic cables used by the communication industry. Was this a crime? The government was quick to point out that the programs were designed to combat terrorism and protect U.S. citizens. While the NSA programs disturbed many people in the United States and abroad, their actions would only be considered criminal if government agents listen in on telephone conversations or intercept emails without proper approval in order to stifle dissent and monitor political opponents.

The dangers of illegal surveillance by government agencies have become magnified because technology now allows snoopers wide latitude to intercept messages and to enter computers through the Internet without being detected. In addition, closed-circuit TV cameras are now routinely used by metropolitan police agencies. Many cities, including Washington, New York, Chicago, and Los Angeles, have installed significant numbers of police-operated cameras trained on public spaces. While ostensibly used to deter crime, once these surveillance facilities are put in place, police departments can use them to record the faces of political demonstrators, to record what people are reading, and to store their photographs on computer databases

Defend Freedom of Speech

Standing outside the U.S. Consulate General in Hong Kong, a supporter holds a picture of Edward Snowden. To some, Snowden is a patriot who blew the whistle on illegal government practices. To others, he is a traitor who leaked top-secret information about U.S. surveillance programs and violated a position of trust. Snowden is currently living in an unknown location in Russia. Are you concerned that the federal government may be reading your emails and listening in on your cell phone calls? Or is this the price we have to pay for being at war with terrorist forces bent on destroying the United States?

without knowledge or permission. This capability worries both civil libertarians as well as critical criminologists.[42]

Human Rights Violations Some governments, such as Iran, routinely deny their citizens basic civil rights, holding them without trial and using "disappearances" and summary executions to rid themselves of political dissidents. After students rioted against governmental controls in 1999, more than 70 simply disappeared, another 1,200 to 1,400 were detained, and dozens were killed when security forces broke up demonstrations.[43] Similar violent actions to break up demonstrations took place in June 2009 in the wake of the disputed election that returned President Mahmoud

Ahmadinejad to power. Accusations that governments under siege routinely arrest dissidents and hold them without trial have become routine.

Another state-organized crime involves the operation of the correctional systems in nations that are notorious for depriving detainees of basic necessities and routinely using hard labor and torture to punish political dissidents. The CIA has made use of their brutal regimes to soften up terror suspects for interrogation and sent suspected terror suspects to secret prisons abroad, without trial or indictment. There they can be subject to harsh interrogation tactics forbidden in the United States.[44]

Other human rights violations are directed against migrant laborers. For example, thousands of South Asian migrant workers are now working on a $27 billion island development outside the city of Abu Dhabi in the United Arab Emirates. The workers obtain the visas needed to work in the UAE by paying hefty fees to "labor-supply agencies"; many workers sell their homes or land or borrow money at high rates of interest to pay the agencies' fees. Upon arrival in the UAE, the indebted workers—many of whom are illiterate—are required to sign contracts with the construction companies on much worse terms than they had been promised back home, ensuring that their debts can never be paid off. In the worst cases, they are subjected to what may be considered forced labor or virtual slavery.[45] Investigations reveal that migrant laborers building New York University's Abu Dhabi campus on the island may be suffering even worse mistreatment.

- Companies are withholding the passports of migrant workers, keeping them trapped at the work site.
- Dozens of workers were deported for striking over pay and conditions.
- Workers decorating the university live in squalid conditions, with 10 men to a room and no free health care.[46]

State-Corporate Crime This type of state-organized crime is committed by individuals who abuse their state authority or who fail to exercise it when working with people and organizations in the private sector. For example, a state environmental agency may fail to enforce laws, resulting in the pollution of public waterways. State-corporate crime is particularly alarming, considering that regulatory law aimed at controlling private corporations is being scaled back while globalization has made corporations worldwide entities both in production and in advancing the consumption of their products.[47]

State Violence Sometimes nations engage in violence to maintain their power over dissident groups. Army or police officers form death squads—armed vigilante groups that kill suspected political opponents or other undesirables. These groups commit assassinations and kidnappings using extremely violent methods to intimidate the population and deter political activity against the government. For example, on January 24, 2009, Manoel Mattos, human rights activist and vice president of the workers' party in the state of Pernambuco, Brazil, was shot in his own home by intruders. Mattos had received repeated death threats as a result of his work denouncing killings and abuses by death-squads across northeast Brazil. Despite the threats, federal police had recently withdrawn the protection he was receiving, allegedly because they felt it was no longer necessary.[48]

While the use of death squads is common in third-world countries, police violence and use of deadly force are not uncommon in Western industrialized nations. In some nations, such as during the civil war in the Russian province of Chechnya, almost all political detainees are subjected to torture, including electric shocks, burnings, and severe beating with boots, sticks, plastic bottles filled with water or sand, and heavy rubber-coated cables. The rest are subject to psychological pressure, such as threats or imitation of sexual abuse or execution, as well as threats to harm their relatives.[49]

State-Organized Crime and War Critical criminologists go as far to link state-organized crime to attacks on other nations, and they do not exempt the United States from blame. In his book *Mass Deception*, criminologist Scott Bonn argues that the George W. Bush administration manufactured public support for war with Iraq by falsely claiming that its leader, Saddam Hussein, was involved in the terrorist attacks of 9/11 and that Iraq possessed weapons of mass destruction. Bonn explains that the war was a function of a "moral panic" engineered by the Bush administration with the support of the U.S. news media.[50] According to Bonn, the Bush administration initiated a campaign to convince the U.S. public and the world that Iraq (a) was involved in the attacks of 9/11, (b) possessed weapons of mass destruction (WMD), and (c) represented a grave and growing threat to U.S. security. Bonn believes that the war in Iraq amounts to state-organized crime.

The United States is not alone in getting involved in large-scale conflicts. In addition to its Ukrainian crisis Russia has not hesitated to send troops to control local populations when they desire independence. Its two wars against breakaway province Chechnya went on from the mid-1990s until 2009, when with massive firepower they crushed the separatist rebel groups; hundreds of thousands died during the conflict. Enraged by terrorist attacks by Chechen fighters who attacked targets in the homeland, the Russians created death squads made up of elite Russian special forces commandos who would stop at nothing to find, torture, and kill enemy combatants. Intelligence was often extracted by breaking limbs with a hammer, administering electric shocks, and forcing men to perform sexual acts on each other. The bodies were either buried in unmarked pits or pulverized. The scenes would occasionally be filmed and circulated among enemy combatants as a form of psychological warfare.[51]

INSTRUMENTAL VS. STRUCTURAL THEORY

LO6 Compare and contrast structural and instrumental theory

Not all critical thinkers share a similar view of society and its control by the means of production. **Instrumental theorists** view criminal law and the criminal justice system solely as instruments for controlling the poor, have-not members of society. They view the state as the tool of capitalists. In contrast, **structural theorists** believe that the law is not the exclusive domain of the rich; rather, it is used to maintain the long-term interests of the capitalist system and to control members of any class who threaten its existence.

Instrumental Theory

According to the instrumental view, the law and justice system serve the powerful and rich and enable them to impose their morality and standards of behavior on the entire society. Those who wield economic power are able to extend their self-serving definition of illegal or criminal behavior to encompass those who might threaten the status quo or interfere with their quest for ever-increasing profits.[52] The concentration of economic assets in the nation's largest industrial firms translates into the political power needed to control tax laws to limit the firms' tax liabilities.[53] Some have the economic clout to hire top attorneys to defend them against antitrust actions, making them almost immune to regulation.

The poor, according to this branch of critical theory, may or may not commit more crimes than the rich, but they certainly are arrested and punished more often. Under the capitalist system, the poor are driven to crime because a natural frustration exists in a society in which affluence is well publicized but unattainable. When class conflict becomes unbearable, frustration can spill out in riots and urban unrest, Because of class conflict, a deep-rooted hostility is generated among members of the lower class toward a social order they are not allowed to shape and whose benefits are unobtainable.[54]

Instrumental theorists consider it essential to **demystify** law and justice—that is, to unmask its true purpose. Criminological theories that focus on family structure, intelligence, peer relations, and school performance keep the lower classes servile by showing why they are more criminal, less intelligent, and more prone to school failure and family problems than the middle class. Demystification involves identifying the destructive intent of capitalist inspired and funded criminology. Instrumental theory's goal for criminology is to show how capitalist law preserves ruling-class power.[55]

Structural Theory

Structural theorists disagree with the view that the relationship between law and capitalism is unidirectional, always working for the rich and against the poor.[56] If law and jus-

tice were purely instruments of the wealthy, why would laws controlling corporate crimes, such as price-fixing, false advertising, and illegal restraint of trade, have been created and enforced?

To a structuralist, the law is designed to keep the system operating efficiently, and anyone, worker or owner, who rocks the boat is targeted for sanction. For example, antitrust legislation is designed to prevent any single capitalist from dominating the system. If the free enterprise system is to function, no single person can become too powerful at the expense of the economic system as a whole. Structuralists would regard the efforts of the U.S. government to break up Microsoft as an example of a conservative government using its clout to keep the system on an even keel. The long prison sentences given to corporate executives who engage in insider trading are a warning to capitalists that they must play by the rules.

RESEARCH ON CRITICAL CRIMINOLOGY

Among the most important research carried out by critical criminologists are studies aimed at determining whether the criminal justice system operates as an instrument of class oppression or as a fair, even-handed social control agency.

Critical researchers have found disturbing evidence that at every stage of justice, criminal members of powerless, disenfranchised groups are treated less favorably than the wealthy and powerful.[57] Those convicted of crime tend to receive stricter sentences if their personal characteristics (single, young, urban, male) show them to be members of the "dangerous classes."[58] Research has found that jurisdictions with significant levels of economic disparity are also the most likely to have large numbers of people killed by police officers. Police may act more forcefully in areas where class conflict creates the perception that extreme forms of social control are needed to maintain order.[59]

Race and Justice

Critical research also shows that racial bias is present in the justice system, beginning with police contact and continuing through arrest, prosecution, and sentencing. As the numbers of racial and ethnic minorities in the population

instrumental theory The view that criminal law and the criminal justice system are capitalist instruments for controlling the lower class.

structural theory The view that criminal law and the criminal justice system are means of defending and preserving the capitalist system.

demystify To unmask the true purpose of law, justice, or other social institutions.

increase, so too do calls for harsher punishments. As you may recall (Chapter 2), the *racial threat hypothesis* states that as the number of minority group members in the community increases, law enforcement agents become more punitive.[60] There are cries for more "law and order" even when crime rates are declining. As a result, charges of racial profiling have become common. Police are more likely to use racial profiling to stop black motorists as they travel further into the boundaries of predominantly white neighborhoods: black motorists driving in an all-white neighborhood set up a red flag because they are "out of place."[61] All too often these unwarranted stops lead to equally unfair arrests.[62] Police brutality complaints are highest in minority neighborhoods, especially those that experience relative deprivation (African American residents earn significantly less money than the European American majority).[63]

Racine County Wisconsin Sheriff's Deputy Ed Drewitz tickets a motorist stopped for speeding on I-94 near Racine. The officer's laser speed measuring device clocked the motorist at 80 mph. Drewitz said he cannot tell a driver's gender or racial characteristics or the car's license plate as he clocks speeders, sometimes at a distance of 1,600 feet. Despite his disclaimer, racial profiling remains a hot button issue in the United States. Do you think that such practices still exist? Or has awareness of racial inequality actually changed the way officers use their discretion to stop, search, investigate, and arrest?

AP Images/Mark Hertzberg/*Journal Times*

African American defendants are more likely to be prosecuted under habitual offender statutes if they commit crimes where there is a greater likelihood of a white victim—for example, larceny and burglary—than if they commit violent crimes that are largely intraracial; where there is a perceived "racial threat," punishment is enhanced.[64] After conviction, criminal courts also are more likely to dole out harsh punishments to members of powerless, disenfranchised groups.[65] Unemployed racial minorities may be perceived as "social dynamite" who present a real threat to society and must be controlled and incapacitated.[66] States with a substantial minority population have a much higher imprisonment rate than those with predominantly white populations.[67] Critical analysis also shows that despite legal controls the use of the death penalty seems to be skewed against racial minorities.[68]

Taken in sum, critical criminologists claim that these and other studies underpin the foundations of their view: social institutions are designed to favor the rich and powerful and to oppress those who lack economic power and social standing.

CRITIQUE OF CRITICAL CRIMINOLOGY

LO7 Analyze critical criminology and discuss criticisms of the theory

Critical criminology has been sharply criticized by some members of the criminological mainstream, who charge that its contribution has been "hot air, heat, but no real light."[69] In turn, critical thinkers have accused mainstream criminologists of being culprits in developing state control over individual lives and selling out their ideals for the chance to receive government funding.

Mainstream criminologists have also attacked the substance of critical thought. Some argue that critical theory simply rehashes the old tradition of helping the underdog, in which the poor steal from the rich to survive.[70] In reality, most theft is for luxury, not survival. While the wealthy do commit their share of illegal acts, these are nonviolent and leave no permanent injuries.[71] People do not live in fear of corrupt businessmen and stock traders; they fear muggers and rapists.

Other critics suggest that critical theorists unfairly neglect the capitalist system's efforts to regulate itself—for example, by instituting antitrust regulations and putting violators in jail. Similarly, they ignore efforts to institute social reforms aimed at helping the poor.[72] There seems to be no logic in condemning a system that helps the poor and empowers them to take on corporate interests in a court of law. Even inherently conservative institutions such as police departments have made attempts at self-regulation when they become aware of class- and race-based inequality such as the use of racial profiling in making traffic stops.[73]

Some argue that critical thinkers refuse to address the problems and conflicts that exist in socialist countries, such as the gulags and purges of the Soviet Union under Stalin. Similarly, they fail to explain why some highly capitalist countries, such as Japan, have extremely low crime rates. Critical criminologists are too quick to blame capitalism for every human vice without adequate explanation or regard for other social and environmental factors.[74] In so doing, they ignore objective reality and refuse to acknowledge that members of the lower classes tend to victimize one another. They ignore the plight of the lower classes, who must live in crime-ridden neighborhoods, while condemning the capitalist system from the security of the "ivory tower."

ALTERNATIVE VIEWS OF CRITICAL THEORY

Critical criminologists are exploring avenues of inquiry that fall outside the traditional models of critical thinking and analysis. The following sections discuss in detail some of these alternative views of the critical approach to crime.

Left Realism

 LO8 Assess the concept of left realism

Some critical scholars are now addressing the need for the left wing to respond to the increasing power of right-wing conservatives. They are troubled by the emergence of a strict "law and order" philosophy, which has as its centerpiece a policy of punishing juveniles severely in adult court. At the same time, they find the focus of most left-wing scholarship—the abuse of power by the ruling elite—too narrow. It is wrong, they argue, to ignore inner-city gang crime and violence, which often target indigent people.[75] The approach of **left realism** is most often connected to the writings of British scholars John Lea and Jock Young. In their well-respected 1984 work *What Is to Be Done About Law and Order?*, they reject the utopian views of idealists who portray street criminals as revolutionaries.[76] They take the more "realistic" approach that street criminals prey on the poor and disenfranchised, thus making the poor doubly abused, first by the capitalist system and then by members of their own class.

Lea and Young's view of crime causation borrows from conventional sociological theory and closely resembles the relative deprivation approach, which posits that experiencing

poverty in the midst of plenty creates discontent and breeds crime. As they put it, "The equation is simple: relative deprivation equals discontent; discontent plus lack of political solution equals crime."[77]

In *Crime in Context: A Critical Criminology of Market Societies*, Ian Taylor recognizes that anyone who expects an instant socialist revolution to take place is simply engaging in wishful thinking.[78] He uses data from both Europe and North America to show that the world is currently in the midst of multiple crises that are shaping all human interaction, including criminality. These crises include lack of job creation, social inequality, social fear, political incompetence and failure, gender conflict, and family and parenting issues. These crises have led to a society in which the government seems incapable of creating positive social change: people have become more fearful and isolated from one another and some are excluded from the mainstream because of racism and discrimination; manufacturing jobs have been exported overseas to nations that pay extremely low wages; and fiscal constraints inhibit the possibility of reform. These problems often fall squarely on the shoulders of young black men, who suffer from exclusion and poverty and who now feel the economic burden created by the erosion of manufacturing jobs due to the globalization of the economy. In response, they engage in a form of hypermasculinity, which helps increase their crime rates.[79]

Crime Protection   Left realists argue that crime victims in all classes need and deserve protection; crime control reflects community needs. They do not view police and the courts as inherently evil tools of capitalism whose tough tactics alienate the lower classes. In fact, they recognize that these institutions offer life-saving public services. The left realists wish, however, that police would reduce their use of force and increase their sensitivity to the public.[80] They want the police to be more responsive to community needs, end racial profiling, and improve efforts at self-regulation and enforcement through citizen review boards and other control mechanisms.

Preemptive deterrence is an approach in which community organization efforts eliminate or reduce crime before police involvement becomes necessary. The reasoning behind this approach is that if the number of marginalized youths (those who feel they are not part of society and have nothing to lose by committing crime) could be reduced, then delinquency rates would decline.[81]

---

left realism An approach that views crime as a function of relative deprivation under capitalism and that favors pragmatic, community-based crime prevention and control.

preemptive deterrence Efforts to prevent crime through community organization and youth involvement.

LEFT REALISM AND TERRORISM

criminology in action

left realists typically have focused their attention on street crime and how it affects its targets: lower-class citizens are forced to live in dangerous neighborhoods and communities. Left realist Jennifer Gibbs uses a different lens and applies the basic concepts to explain the motivation for terrorist activity.

Gibbs finds four key elements of left realism that should, if valid, underpin terrorist involvement:

- People are recruited into terrorist organizations because of relative deprivation.
- Terrorist organizations are subcultures that provide peer support.
- Victims/targets are selected based on opportunity/routine activities.
- "Get tough" policies that create a police state may backfire.

Gibbs finds evidence to support the first proposition: terrorists are drawn not from extremely poor populations but from those who realize they have fallen behind other groups. Absolute deprivation (e.g., the inability to provide basic necessities) is not the cause of terrorism; relative deprivation (e.g., being less well off than one's peers) seems to carry more weight, an association predicted by left realism. Feelings of deprivation are exacerbated by new technology. Advancements like the Internet make communication easier and people can see how much better off others are, increasing the perception of relative deprivation.

Second, left realist theory argues that men who experience stress as a result of relative deprivation and do not have socially appropriate coping mechanisms turn to similarly situated peers who provide support; they often form subcultures. Likewise, terrorist group members seek peer support with like-minded people, forming subcultures supportive of these values or ideology. In today's postmodern world, technology has created the opportunity for virtual peer groups and subcultures. Peer support does not necessarily need to be face to face within

This undated photo released by the U.S. Attorney's office in Pittsburgh shows Emerson Begolly, of Redbank Township, Pennsylvania. Begolly, whom authorities called a "homegrown, radical extremist," was sentenced July 16, 2013, to eight and a half years in prison for using the Internet to promote terrorist attacks against American military and civilian targets. Read more at http://www.huffingtonpost.com/2013/07/16/emerson-begolly-found-guilty_n_3605876.html.

AP Images/U.S. Attorney's Office/File

groups but can exist in blogs and chat rooms. Those adhering to a particular ideology may find peer support in written communications such as listservs, magazines, and other media.

Gibbs finds weaker support for the role of opportunity in terrorist activities because they tend to be planned rather than spontaneous events. However, there is some evidence that opportunity plays a role in choosing victims: targeting businesses and citizens is easier than targeting government entities or military installations or personnel. Other reasons may include having the "biggest bang for the buck" by targeting businesses—symbolic of capitalism—or civilians, whose deaths generate widespread attention.

The final proposition of left realist theory addressed by Gibbs is that "get tough" policies will not reduce terror. Left realism focuses on noncoercive approaches that can be applied to terrorism. Get-tough policies alienate people and legitimate terrorist organizations. The "war" on terror legitimized groups

like al-Qaeda, attracting more terrorism instead of decreasing it. Also, the military response to terrorism is not a deterrent. Military "solutions," in particular, lead to retaliation, generating a cycle of violence because they tend to be reactive rather than proactive. They provide short-term solutions that fail to address the underlying causes that lead to terrorism in the first place. Instead, left realism theory directs policy toward minimal official response and maximizing informal social control. With terrorism, attempting to address the underlying grievances may be helpful.

Critical Thinking

Do you agree that the way to fight terror is to address the underlying grievances? Sounds good, but is it truly possible in a world with shifting conflicts and myriad points of view? Can we ever satisfy a terrorist? And would we even if we knew how?

SOURCE: Jennifer Gibbs, "Looking at Terrorism Through Left Realist Lenses," *Crime, Law and Social Change* 54 (2010): 171–185.

Although implementing a socialist economy might help eliminate the crime problem, left realists recognize that something must be done to control crime under the existing capitalist system. To develop crime control policies, left realists not only welcome critical ideas but also build on the work of strain theorists, social ecologists, and other mainstream views. Community-based efforts seem to hold the greatest promise of crime control.

Left Realism and Incarceration

Left realists also decry the use of mass incarceration as a crime control device, fearing that it has racial overtones. In *The New Jim Crow: Mass Incarceration in the Age of Colorblindness* (2010), legal scholar Michelle Alexander notes that the number of people in prison has skyrocketed in the past 30 years; there are now more African Americans behind bars than there were slaves at the time of the Civil War. This system of mass incarceration now works as a tightly networked system of laws, policies, customs, and institutions that operate collectively to ensure racial subordination.[82] In a sense, the Jim Crow laws, which worked to segregate minorities and prevented them from voting, have been replaced by the War on Drugs, which has placed millions behind bars and restricted their civil rights upon release; existing laws prevent convicted felons from gaining employment, education, housing, obtaining loans, and voting.

Surprisingly, this left realist perspective may be gaining traction even in the nation's most conservative states (including Texas), which have begun to reduce their prison expenditures while funding treatment, reentry, and alternatives to incarceration programs. In part this policy shift corresponds to a change in public opinion: as crime rates have declined and state budgets are in crisis, the public demands low-cost alternatives to the "lock 'em up" policies that have been predominant for the past few decades. It's possible that a more realistic vision of punishment may be on the horizon.[83]

In the Criminology in Action feature, a left realist focuses on the onset of terrorist activity.

Left realism has been criticized by critical thinkers as legitimizing the existing power structure: by supporting existing definitions of law and justice, it suggests that the "deviant" and not the capitalist system causes society's problems. Critics question whether left realists advocate the very institutions that "currently imprison us and our patterns of thought and action."[84] In rebuttal, left realists say that it is unrealistic to speak of a socialist state lacking a police force or a system of laws and justice. They believe the criminal code does, in fact, represent public opinion.

Critical Feminist Theory: Gendered Criminology

LO9 Articulate the central themes of critical feminism and gendered criminology

Like so many theories in criminology, most of the efforts of critical theorists have been devoted to explaining male

criminality.[85] To remedy this theoretical lapse, a number of feminist writers have attempted to explain the cause of crime, gender differences in crime rates, and the exploitation of female victims from a critical perspective.

Critical feminism views gender inequality as stemming from the unequal power of men and women in a capitalist society, which leads to the exploitation of women by fathers and husbands. Under this system, women are considered a commodity worth possessing, like land or money.[86] Some of the most important issues focused upon by critical feminist criminologists include the unique role of women in policing and corrections, fields that have traditionally been dominated by men. Another important area of study is the role of masculinity in creating the gender gap in serious crime. There is also concern with the role of media in "demonizing" girls and women of color.[87]

Queer Criminology

As part of their interest in gender roles and crime, critical scholars are also focusing attention on the treatment of the lesbian, gay, bisexual, transgender, and queer (LGBTQ) population by society in general and the justice system in particular. Among the issues being studied is how damaging stereotypes and representations of people as sexual deviants developed.[88] They claim that mainstream criminologists have either ignored or portrayed LGBTQ people in a negative light. Areas of interest include defining deviance, crimes against LGBTQ people, and gaining equality before the law.[89]

Gender Differences in Society

The origin of gender differences can be traced to the development of private property and male domination of the laws of inheritance, which led to male control over property and power.[90] A patriarchal system developed in which men's work was valued and women's work was devalued. As capitalism prevailed, the division of labor by gender made women responsible for the unpaid maintenance and reproduction of the current and future labor force, which was derisively called "domestic work." Although this unpaid work done by women is crucial and profitable for capitalists, who reap these free benefits, such labor is exploitative and oppressive for women.[91] Even when women gained the right to work for pay, they were exploited as cheap labor. The dual exploitation of women within the household and in the labor market means that women produce far greater surplus value for capitalists than men.

Patriarchy, or male supremacy, has been and continues to be supported by capitalists. This system sustains female

critical feminism Scholars, both male and female, who focus on the effects of gender inequality and the unequal power of men and women in a capitalist society.

patriarchy A society in which men dominate public, social, economic, and political affairs.

A member of the Oakland (California) Police Department arrests a teen charged with solicitation, as part of a sting operation in hopes of getting the women to talk about their pimps. Once viewed as criminals and dispatched to juvenile centers, sexually exploited teens are increasingly seen as victims of child abuse, with the focus on evaluation and counseling.

oppression at home and in the workplace.[92] Although the number of traditional patriarchal families is in steep decline, in those that still exist, a wife's economic dependence ties men more securely to wage-earning jobs, further serving the interests of capitalists by undermining potential rebellion against the system.

Patriarchy and Crime   Critical feminists link criminal behavior patterns to the gender conflict created by the economic and social struggles common in postindustrial societies. In *Capitalism, Patriarchy, and Crime*, James Messerschmidt argues that capitalist society is marked by both patriarchy and class conflict. Capitalists control the labor of workers, and men control women both economically and biologically.[93] This "double marginality" explains why females in a capitalist society commit fewer crimes than males. Because they are isolated in the family, they have fewer opportunities to engage in elite deviance (white-collar and economic crimes). Although powerful females as well as males will commit white-collar crimes, the female crime rate is restricted because of the patriarchal nature of the capitalist system.[94] Women are also denied access to male-dominated street crimes.

Because capitalism renders lower-class women powerless, they are forced to commit less serious, nonviolent, self-destructive crimes, such as abusing drugs. Recent efforts of the capitalist classes to undermine the social support of the poor has hit women particularly hard. The end of welfare, concentration on welfare fraud, and cutbacks to social services have all directly and uniquely affected women.[95]

Powerlessness also increases the likelihood that women will become targets of violent acts.[96] When lower-class males are shut out of the economic opportunity structure, they try to build their self-image through acts of machismo; such acts may involve violent abuse of women. This type of reaction accounts for a significant percentage of female victims who are attacked by a spouse or intimate partner. It is not surprising to find that incarcerated female offenders report higher rates of mental health problems than incarcerated men and that there is a strong association between suffering intimate partner violence, mental health issues, and involvement with the justice system.[97]

According to this view, female victimization should decline as women's place in society is elevated, and they are able to obtain more power at home, in the workplace, and in government. Empirical research seems to support this view. A 2004 cross-national study of educational and occupational status of women shows that in nations where the status of women is generally high, sexual violence rates are significantly lower than in nations where women do not enjoy similar educational and occupational opportunities.[98] Women's victimization rates decline as they are empowered socially, economically, and legally.[99]

In *Masculinities and Crime*, Messerschmidt expands on these themes.[100] He suggests that in every culture males try to emulate "ideal" masculine behaviors. In Western culture, this means being authoritative, in charge, combative, and controlling. Failure to adopt these roles leaves men feeling effeminate and unmanly. Their struggle to dominate women in order to prove their manliness is called "doing gender." Crime is a vehicle for men to "do gender" because it separates them from the weak and allows them to demonstrate physical bravery. Violence directed toward women is an especially economical way to demonstrate manhood. Would a weak, effeminate male ever attack a woman?

Feminist writers have supported this view by maintaining that in contemporary society men achieve masculinity at the expense of women. In the best-case scenario, men must convince others that in no way are they feminine or have female qualities. For example, they are sloppy and don't cook or do housework because these are "female" activities. More ominously, men may work at excluding, hurting, denigrating, exploiting, or otherwise abusing women. Even in all-male groups, men often prove their manhood by treating the weakest member of the group as "woman-like" and abusing him accordingly. Men need to defend themselves at all costs from being contaminated with femininity, and these efforts begin in children's playgroups and continue into adulthood and marriage.[101]

Exploitation and Criminality Critical feminists also focus on the social forces that shape women's lives and experiences to explain female criminality.[102] They attempt to show how the sexual victimization of girls is a function of male socialization because so many young males learn to be aggressive and to exploit women. Males seek out same-sex peer groups for social support; these groups encourage members to exploit and sexually abuse women. On college campuses, peers encourage sexual violence against women who are considered "teasers," "bar pickups," or "loose women." These derogatory labels allow the males to justify their actions; a code of secrecy then protects the aggressors from retribution.[103]

According to the critical feminist view, exploitation triggers the onset of female criminal and deviant behavior. When young female victims run away and abuse substances, they may be reacting to abuse they have suffered at home or at school. Their attempts at survival are labeled as deviant or delinquent behavior.[104] When the exploited girl finds herself in the arms of the justice system her problems may just be beginning. While boys who get in trouble may be considered "overzealous" youth or kids who just went too far, young girls who get in trouble are seen as in opposition and a threat to acceptable images of femininity; their behavior is considered even more unusual and dangerous than male delinquency.[105]

Power–Control Theory

John Hagan and his associates have created a critical feminist model that uses gender differences to explain the onset of criminality.[106] Hagan's view is that crime and delinquency rates are a function of two factors: class position (power) and family functions (control).[107] The link between these two variables is that, within the family, parents reproduce the power relationships they hold in the workplace; a position of dominance at work is equated with control in the household. As a result, parents' work experiences and class position influence the criminality of children.[108]

In **paternalistic families**, fathers assume the traditional role of breadwinners, while mothers tend to have menial jobs or remain at home to supervise domestic matters. Within the paternalistic home, mothers are expected to control the behavior of their daughters while granting greater freedom to sons. In such a home, the parent–daughter relationship can be viewed as a preparation for the "cult of domesticity," which makes girls' involvement in delinquency unlikely, whereas boys are freer to deviate because they are not subject to maternal control. Girls growing up in patriarchal families are socialized to fear legal sanctions more than are males; consequently, boys in these families exhibit more delinquent behavior than their sisters. The result is that boys not only engage in more antisocial behaviors but have greater access to legitimate adult behaviors, such as working at part-time jobs or possessing their own transportation. In contrast, without these legitimate behavioral outlets, girls who are unhappy or dissatisfied with their status are forced to seek out risky **role exit behaviors**, including such desperate measures as running away and contemplating suicide.

In **egalitarian families**—those in which the husband and wife share similar positions of power at home and in the workplace—daughters gain a kind of freedom that reflects reduced parental control. These families produce daughters whose law-violating behavior mirrors their brothers'. In an egalitarian family, girls may have greater opportunity to engage in legitimate adult status behaviors and less need to enact deviant role exits.[109]

Ironically, Hagan believes that these relationships also occur in female-headed households with absent fathers. Hagan and his associates found that when fathers and mothers hold equally valued managerial positions, the similarity between the rates of their daughters' and sons' delinquency is greatest. By implication, middle-class girls are the most likely to violate the law because they are less closely controlled than their lower-class counterparts. In homes in which both parents hold positions of power, girls are more likely to have the same expectations of career success as their brothers. Consequently, siblings of both sexes will be socialized to take risks and engage in other behavior related to delinquency.

Evaluating Power–Control This **power–control theory** has received a great deal of attention in the criminological community because it encourages a new approach to the study of criminality, one that includes gender differences, class position, and the structure of the family. Empirical analysis of its premises has generally been supportive. Brenda Sims Blackwell's research supports a key element of power–control theory: females in paternalistic households have learned to fear legal sanctions more than have their brothers.[110]

Not all research is as supportive.[111] Some critics have questioned its core assumption that power and control variables can explain crime. More specifically, critics fail to

---

paternalistic families Traditional family model in which fathers assume the role of breadwinners, while mothers tend to have menial jobs or remain at home to supervise domestic matters.

role exit behaviors In order to escape from a stifling life in male-dominated families, girls may try to break away by running away and or even attempting suicide.

egalitarian families Families in which spouses share similar positions of power at home and in the workplace.

power–control theory The view that gender differences in crime are a function of economic power (class position, one-earner versus two-earner families) and parental control (paternalistic versus egalitarian families).

replicate the finding that upper-class girls are more likely to deviate than their lower-class peers or that class and power interact to produce delinquency.[112] Some researchers have found few gender-based supervision and behavior differences in worker-, manager-, or owner-dominated households.[113] Research indicates that single-mother families may be different from two-parent egalitarian families, though Hagan's theory equates the two.[114]

It is possible that the concept of family employed by Hagan may have to be reconsidered. Power–control theorists should consider the multitude of power and control relationships that are emerging in postmodern society: blended families, families where mothers hold managerial positions and fathers are blue-collar workers, and so forth.[115]

Finally, power and control may interact with other personal traits, such as personality and self-control, to shape behavior.[116] Further research is needed to determine whether power–control can have an independent influence on behavior and can explain gender differences in the crime rate.

Peacemaking Criminology

LO10 Explain peacemaking criminology and restorative justice

To members of the **peacemaking** movement, the main purpose of criminology is to promote a peaceful, just society. Rather than standing on empirical analysis of data, peacemaking draws its inspiration from religious and philosophical teachings ranging from Quakerism to Zen.[117] For example, rather than seeing socioeconomic status as a "variable" that is correlated with crime, as do mainstream criminologists, peacemakers view poverty as a source of suffering—almost a crime in and of itself. Poverty enervates people, makes them suffer, and becomes a master status that subjects them to lives filled with suffering. From a peacemaking perspective, a key avenue for preventing crime is, in the short run, diminishing the suffering poverty causes and, in the long run, embracing social policies that reduce the prevalence of economic suffering in contemporary society.[118]

Peacemakers view the efforts of the state to punish and control as crime-encouraging rather than crime-discouraging. These views were first articulated in a series of books with an anarchist theme written by criminologists Larry Tifft and Dennis Sullivan in the 1980s.[119] Tifft argues, "The violent punishing acts of the state and its controlling professions are of the same genre as the violent acts of individuals. In each instance these acts reflect an attempt to monopolize human interaction."[120]

Sullivan stresses the futility of correcting and punishing criminals in the context of our conflict-ridden society: "The reality we must grasp is that we live in a culture of severed relationships, where every available institution provides a form of banishment but no place or means for people to become connected, to be responsible to and for each other."[121] Sullivan suggests that mutual aid rather than coercive punishment is the key to a harmonious society. In *Restorative Justice*, Sullivan and Tifft reaffirm their belief that society must seek humanitarian forms of justice without resorting to brutal punishments:

> By allowing feelings of vengeance or retribution to narrow our focus on the harmful event and the person responsible for it—as others might focus solely on a sin committed and the "sinner"—we tell ourselves we are taking steps to free ourselves from the effects of the harm or the sin in question. But, in fact, we are putting ourselves in a servile position with respect to life, human growth, and the further enjoyment of relationships with others.[122]

peacemaking An approach that considers punitive crime control strategies to be counterproductive and favors the use of humanistic conflict resolution to prevent and control crime.

ALTERNATIVE FORMS OF CRITICAL CRIMINOLOGY

8.1 concept summary

Theory	Major Premise	Strengths	Research Focus
Left realism	Crime is a function of relative deprivation; criminals prey on the poor.	Represents a compromise between conflict and traditional criminology	Deterrence; protection
Critical feminist theory	The capitalist system creates patriarchy, which oppresses women.	Explains gender bias, violence against women, and repression	Gender inequality; oppression; patriarchy
Power–control theory	Girls are controlled more closely than boys in traditional male-dominated households. There is gender equity in contemporary egalitarian homes.	Explains gender differences in the crime rate as a function of class and gender conflict	Power and control; gender differences; domesticity
Peacemaking criminology	Peace and humanism can reduce crime; conflict resolution strategies can work.	Offers a new approach to crime control through mediation	Punishment; nonviolence; mediation

Today, advocates of the peacemaking movement, such as Harold Pepinsky and Richard Quinney, try to find humanist solutions to crime and other social problems.[123] Rather than punishment and prison, they advocate such policies as mediation and conflict resolution.[124]

Concept Summary 8.1 summarizes the various emerging forms of critical criminology.

CRITICAL THEORY AND PUBLIC POLICY

At the core of all the varying branches of social conflict theory is the fact that conflict causes crime. If conflict and competition in society could somehow be reduced, it is possible that crime rates would fall. Some critical theorists believe this goal can only be accomplished by thoroughly reordering society so that capitalism is destroyed and a socialist state is created. Others call for a more "practical" application of conflict principles. Nowhere has this been more successful than in applying peacemaking principles in the criminal justice system.

Rather than punish law violators harshly and make them outcasts of society, peacemakers look for ways to bring them back to the community. This peacemaking movement has adopted nonviolent methods and applied them to what is known as **restorative justice**. Springing both from academia and justice system personnel, the restorative approach relies on nonpunitive strategies for crime prevention and control.[125] The next sections discuss the foundation and principles of restorative justice.

The Concept of Restorative Justice

The term *restorative justice* is often hard to define because it encompasses a variety of programs and practices. According to a leading restorative justice scholar, Howard Zehr, restorative justice requires that society address victims' harms and needs, hold offenders accountable to put right those harms, and involve victims, offenders, and communities in the process of healing. Zehr maintains that the core value of the restoration process can be translated into respect for all, even those who are different from us, even those who seem to be our enemies. At its core, Zehr argues, restorative justice is a set of principles, a philosophy, an alternate set of guiding questions that provide an alternative framework for thinking about wrongdoing.[126] Restorative justice would reject concepts such as "punishment," "deterrence," and "incarceration" and embrace "apology," "rehabilitation," "reparation," "healing," "restoration," and "reintegration."

Restorative justice has grown out of a belief that the traditional justice system has done little to involve the community in the process of dealing with crime and wrongdoing. What has developed is a system of coercive punishments, administered by bureaucrats, that are inherently harmful

AN ETHICAL DILEMMA

IS IT A BRIBE?

A student wants to discuss a personal matter. It seems that a few weeks ago she was at a party when she was sexually assaulted by a fellow student. The attack was quite traumatic, and she suffered both physical and emotional injury. The police were called and the boy charged with rape. Now that a few weeks have passed, she has been contacted by a local program that bills itself as a restorative treatment program. It seems that her attacker is now a client and wants to engage in some form of reconciliation. At an arranged meeting, he professes his regret for the attack and wishes to make amends. He and the program director have worked out a schedule in which the victim will be compensated for her pain and suffering in the amount of $5,000 in exchange for her agreeing to a recommendation to the prosecutor that the case be treated informally rather than going to trial. She doesn't know what to do: she needs the money, having missed work after the attack, but at the same time is concerned that people will think she has accepted a bribe to withdraw the charges.

Write a paper describing the advice you would give to the student in this situation. How would you suggest that she respond to the program director? Do you consider the payment a bribe or restitution for an evil deed? Can restorative justice be used in a crime such as rape?

thinking like a criminologist

to offenders and reduce the likelihood offenders will ever become productive members of society. This system relies on punishment, stigma, and disgrace. In his controversial book *The Executed God: The Way of the Cross in Lockdown America*, theology professor Mark Lewis Taylor discusses the similarities between this contemporary, coercive justice system and that which existed in imperial Rome when Jesus and many of his followers were executed because they were an inspiration to the poor and slave populations. They represented a threat to the ruling Roman power structure. So, too, is our modern justice system designed to keep the downtrodden in their place. Taylor suggests that there should be a movement to reduce such coercive elements of justice as police brutality and the death penalty before our "lockdown society" becomes the model used around the globe.[127]

restorative justice Using humanistic, nonpunitive strategies to right wrongs and restore social harmony.

Advocates of restorative justice argue that rather than today's lockdown mentality, what is needed is a justice policy that repairs the harm caused by crime and that includes all parties who have suffered from that harm: the victim, the community, and the offender. They have made an ongoing effort to reduce the conflict created by the criminal justice system when it hands out harsh punishments to offenders, many of whom are powerless social outcasts. Based on the principle of reducing social harm, restorative justice advocates argue that the old methods of punishment are a failure: after all, upwards of two-thirds of all prison inmates recidivate soon after their release. And tragically, not all inmates are released. Some are given life sentences for relatively minor crimes under three-strikes laws, which mandate such a sentence for a third conviction; some are given sentences of life with no parole, which are in essence death sentences.[128]

Reintegrative Shaming

One of the key foundations of the restoration movement is contained in John Braithwaite's influential book *Crime, Shame, and Reintegration*.[129] Braithwaite's vision rests on the concept of **shame**: the feeling we get when we don't meet the standards we have set for ourselves or that significant others have set for us. Shame can lead people to believe that they are defective, that there is something wrong with them. Braithwaite notes that countries such as Japan in which conviction for crimes brings an inordinate amount of shame have extremely low crime rates. In Japan, criminal prosecution proceeds only when the normal process of public apology, compensation, and the victim's forgiveness breaks down.

Shame is a powerful tool of informal social control. Citizens in cultures in which crime is not shameful, such as the United States, do not internalize an abhorrence for crime because when they are punished, they view themselves as mere victims of the justice system. Their punishment comes at the hands of neutral strangers, such as police and judges, who are being paid to act. In contrast, shaming relies on the victim's participation.[130]

Braithwaite divides the concept of shame into two distinct types. The most common form of shaming typically involves stigmatization, an ongoing process of degradation in which the offender is branded as an evil person and cast out of society. Shaming can occur at a school disciplinary

shame The feeling we get when we don't meet the standards we have set for ourselves or that significant others have set for us.

reintegrative shaming A method of correction that encourages offenders to confront their misdeeds, experience shame because of the harm they caused, and then be reincluded in society.

hearing or a criminal court trial. Bestowing stigma and degradation may have a general deterrent effect: it makes people afraid of social rejection and public humiliation. As a specific deterrent, stigma is doomed to failure; people who suffer humiliation at the hands of the justice system "reject their rejectors" by joining a deviant subculture of like-minded people who collectively resist social control. Despite these dangers, there has been an ongoing effort to brand offenders and make their shame both public and permanent. For example, most states have passed sex offender registry and notification laws that make public the names of those convicted of sex offenses and warn neighbors of their presence in the community.[131]

But the fear of shame can backfire or be neutralized. When shame is managed well, people acknowledge they made mistakes and suffered disappointments, and try to work out what can be done to make things right; this is referred to as shame management. However, in some cases, to avoid the pain of shaming, people engage in improper shame management, a psychological process in which they deny shame by shifting the blame of their actions to their target or to others.[132] They may blame others, get angry, and take out their frustrations on those whom they can dominate. Improper shame management of this sort has been linked to antisocial acts ranging from school yard bullying to tax evasion.[133]

Massive levels of improper shame management may occur on a societal scale during periods of social upheaval. Because of this, some nations that previously have had low crime rates may experience a surge of antisocial behavior during periods of war and revolution. Rape, an act which may have been unthinkable to most men, suddenly becomes commonplace because of the emergence of narcissistic pride, feeling dominant and arrogant, and developing a sense of superiority over others, in this case your enemy. This sense of hubris fosters aggressive actions and allows combatants to rape women whom they perceive as belonging to an enemy group.[134]

Braithwaite argues that crime control can be better achieved through a policy of **reintegrative shaming**. Here disapproval is extended to the offenders' evil deeds, while at the same time they are cast as respected people who can be reaccepted by society. A critical element of reintegrative shaming occurs when the offenders begin to understand and recognize their wrongdoing and shame themselves. To be reintegrative, shaming must be brief and controlled and then followed by ceremonies of forgiveness, apology, and repentance.

To prevent crime, Braithwaite charges, society must encourage reintegrative shaming. For example, the women's movement can reduce domestic violence by mounting a crusade to shame spouse abusers. Similarly, parents who use reintegrative shaming techniques in their childrearing practices may improve parent–child relationships and ultimately reduce the delinquent involvement of their children.[135] Because informal social controls may have a greater impact than legal or formal ones, it may not be surprising that the fear of personal shame can have a greater deterrent effect than the fear of legal sanctions. It may also be applied to produce specific deterrence. Offenders can meet with victims so that the offenders can experience shame. Family members and peers can be present to help the offender reintegrate. Such efforts can humanize a system of justice that today relies on repression rather than forgiveness as the basis of specific deterrence.

The Process of Restoration

The restoration process begins by redefining crime in terms of a conflict among the offender, the victim, and affected constituencies (families, schools, workplaces, and so forth). Therefore, it is vitally important that the resolution take place within the context in which the conflict originally occurred rather than being transferred to a specialized institution that has no social connection to the community or group from which the conflict originated. In other words, most conflicts are better settled in the community than in a court.

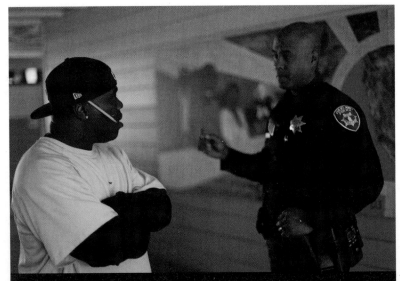

Eric Butler, the coordinator of the restorative justice program at Ralph J. Bunche High School, speaks with Officer Mark Douglas, whose beat for the Oakland Police Department is the school, where he screens students as they enter. Restorative justice, which encourages young people to develop empathy for one another, is increasingly offered in schools seeking an alternative to "zero tolerance" policies.

Jim Wilson/New York Times/Redux

By maintaining "ownership" or jurisdiction over the conflict, the community is able to express its shared outrage about the offense. Shared community outrage is directly communicated to the offender. The victim is also given a chance to voice his or her story, and the offender can directly communicate his or her need for social reintegration and treatment. All restoration programs involve an understanding among all the parties involved in a criminal act: the victim, the offender, and community. Although processes differ in structure and style, they generally include these elements:

- The offender is asked to recognize that he or she caused injury to personal and social relations along with a determination and acceptance of responsibility (ideally accompanied by a statement of remorse). Only then can the offender be restored as a productive member of the community.
- Restoration involves turning the justice system into a "healing" process rather than being a distributor of retribution and revenge.
- Reconciliation is a big part of the restorative approach. Most people involved in offender–victim relationships actually know one another or were related in some way before the criminal incident took place. Instead of treating one of the involved parties as a victim deserving of sympathy and the other as a criminal deserving of punishment, it is more productive to address the issues that produced conflict between these people.[136]
- The effectiveness of justice ultimately depends on the stake a person has in the community (or a particular social group). If a person does not value his or her membership in the group, the person will be unlikely to accept responsibility, show remorse, or repair the injuries

caused by his or her actions. In contrast, people who have a stake in the community and its principle institutions, such as work, home, and school, find that their involvement enhances their personal and familial well-being.[137]

- The offender must make a commitment to both material (monetary) restitution and symbolic reparation (an apology). A determination must also be made of community support and assistance for both victim and offender.

The intended result of the process is to repair injuries suffered by the victim and the community while ensuring reintegration of the offender.

Restoration Programs Negotiation, mediation, consensus-building, and peacemaking have been part of the dispute resolution process in European and Asian communities for centuries.[138] Native American and First Nations (native Canadian) people have long used the type of community participation in the adjudication process (for example, sentencing circles, sentencing panels, elders panels) that restorative justice advocates are now embracing.[139]

In some Native American communities, people accused of breaking the law meet with community members, victims (if any), village elders, and agents of the justice system in a **sentencing circle**. Each member of the circle expresses

sentencing circle A peacemaking technique in which offenders, victims, and other community members are brought together in an effort to formulate a sanction that addresses the needs of all.

his or her feelings about the act that was committed and raises questions or concerns. The accused can express regret about his or her actions and a desire to change the harmful behavior. People may suggest ways the offender can make things up to the community and those he or she harmed. A treatment program, such as Alcoholics Anonymous, can be suggested, if appropriate.

Restorative justice is now being embraced on many levels within our society and the justice system:

- *Community.* Communities that isolate people and have few mechanisms for interpersonal interaction encourage and sustain crime. Those that implement forms of community dialogue to identify problems and plan tactics for their elimination, guided by restorative justice practices and principles, may create a climate in which violent crime is less likely to occur.[140]
- *Schools.* Some schools have embraced restorative justice practices to deal with students who are involved in drug and alcohol abuse without having to resort to more punitive measures such as expulsion. Schools in Minnesota, Colorado, and elsewhere are now trying to involve students in "relational rehabilitation" programs that strive to improve individuals' relationships with key figures in the community who may have been harmed by their actions.[141]
- *Police.* Restorative justice has also been implemented by police when crime is first encountered. The new community policing models are an attempt to bring restorative concepts into law enforcement. Restorative justice relies on the fact that criminal justice policymakers need to listen and respond to the needs of those who are to be affected by their actions, and community policing relies on policies established with input and exchanges between officers and citizens.[142]
- *Courts.* Restorative programs in the courts typically involve diverting the formal court process. These programs encourage meeting and reconciling the conflicts between offenders and victims via victim advocacy, mediation programs, and sentencing circles, in which crime victims and their families are brought together with offenders and their families in an effort to formulate a sanction that addresses the needs of each party. Victims are given a chance to voice their stories, and offenders can help compensate them financially or provide some service (for example, fixing damaged property).[143] The goal is to enable offenders to appreciate the damage they have caused, to make amends, and to be reintegrated back into society.

Restoration programs are being used in court systems around the world. One example is the justice system in Australia, which makes use of a conferencing process to divert offenders from the justice system.[144] This offers offenders the opportunity to attend a conference to discuss and resolve their offense instead of being charged and appearing in court. (Those who deny guilt are not offered conferencing.) The con-ference, normally lasting one to two hours, is attended by the victims and their supporters, the defendant and his or her supporters, and other concerned parties. The conference coordinator focuses the discussion on condemning the act without condemning the character of the actor. Offenders are asked to tell their side of the story, what happened, how they have felt about the crime, and what they think should be done. The victims and others are asked to describe the physical, financial, and emotional consequences of the crime. This discussion may lead the offenders, their families, and their friends to experience the shame of the act, prompting an apology to the victim. A plan of action is developed and signed by key participants. The plan may include the offender paying compensation to the victim, doing work for the victim or the community, or similar solutions. It is the responsibility of the conference participants to determine the outcomes that are most appropriate for these particular victims and these particular offenders. All eight states and territories in Australia have used the conference model at some time or another. Research indicates the conferencing approach is well received by young offenders who believe the outcomes are fair, but it remains to be seen whether it can reduce future crime rates.[145]

Reconciliation Restoration has also been used as a national policy to heal internal rifts. For example, after 50 years of oppressive white rule in South Africa, the race-dividing apartheid policy was abolished in the early 1990s, and in 1994 Nelson Mandela, leader of the African National Congress (ANC), was elected president.[146] Some black leaders wanted revenge for the political murders carried out during the apartheid era, but Mandela established the Truth and Reconciliation Commission. Rather than seeking vengeance for the crimes, this government agency investigated the atrocities with the mandate of granting amnesty to those individuals who confessed their roles in the violence and could prove that their actions served some political motive rather than being based on personal factors such as greed or jealousy.

Supporters of the commission believed that this approach would help heal the nation's wounds and prevent years of racial and ethnic strife. Mandela, who had been unjustly jailed for 27 years by the regime, had reason to desire vengeance. Yet, he wanted to move the country forward after the truth of what happened in the past had been established. Though many South Africans, including some ANC members, believed that the commission was too lenient, Mandela's attempts at reconciliation prevailed. The commission was a model of restoration over revenge.

In sum, restoration can be or has been used at the following stages of justice:

- As a form of final warning to young offenders
- As a tool for school officials
- As a method of handling complaints to police
- As a diversion from prosecution
- As a presentencing, postconviction add-on to the sentencing process

VICTIM OFFENDER RECONCILIATION IN DENVER, COLORADO

The Victim Offender Reconciliation Program (VORP) of Denver began in 1993 in response to a summer of violence in the metro Denver area. VORP has collaborated with the justice system to provide restorative justice processes for the community as a way of addressing issues overlooked in a more traditional, adversarial justice system. VORP has been a catalyst for long-term answers to crime. Each system has its role and provides part of the solution to the problem of administering justice. The VORP program, steeped in diverse cultural roots, gives an opportunity for reconciling and restoring relationships between victims, offenders, and the community.

Programs are conducted by trained volunteers in restorative justice, mediation, facilitation, cultural competency, and communication. Currently VORP offers victim–offender mediation, community group conferencing, peace circles, and a reparative panel as restorative justice tools. As needed, VORP staff and facilitators also work one on one with victims and offenders of crime.

VORP has three principal aims in furthering its mission:

- Reduce recidivism
- Restore and strengthen community relationships
- Empower victims and the community

The RESTORE Program

One of the Denver VORP programs is designed to help kids who have gotten into trouble by shoplifting from a local store. When a youth is referred by juvenile court, a RESTORE intake form is completed. The youth and a parent or guardian attend two RESTORE sessions and complete a contract, as described below.

Part 1. During this session, the youth and his/her parents listen to speakers discuss the impact of shoplifting on the merchant community, as well as the community-at-large. They also hear other youth speak about how shoplifting has affected them, their peers, and their families.

Part 2. The youth and his/her parents meet in smaller groups to talk about the shoplifting incidents they were involved in and how they have been affected by this incident. This group also includes other juvenile shoplifters, their parents, community members, a peer representative, and a merchant representative, and is facilitated by RESTORE volunteers.

Part 3. When the group sessions are complete, each youth (with his/her parent or guardian) reviews and signs a contract to repair the harm to the victim, the community, their family, and themselves, including community service. They sign up for a contract completion date and time to return to the RESTORE council.

The youth returns in one or two months to present his or her completed contract results and projects, including verification of community service and other contract items. By participating in the RESTORE program, youths can:

- Learn more about shoplifting and how it affects victims and the community
- Repair the harm done by the incident in a meaningful way
- Make choices about the consequences for their actions
- Have their theft charge dismissed upon successful completion of the program

The RESTORE program uses the principles of restorative justice to reintegrate young offenders back into the community. It is an example of turning theory into action.

Critical Thinking

1. Could you design a program for recreational drug users using the RESTORE model?
2. Do you believe restorative justice programs can work or are they a method for kids who commit crime to avoid legal responsibility?

SOURCE: Victim Offender Reconciliation Program of Denver, http://www.denvervorp.org (accessed April 2014).

- As a supplement to a community sentence (probation)
- As a preparation for release from long-term imprisonment[147]

The Policy and Practice in Criminology feature reviews a successful restorative justice program.

The Challenge of Restorative Justice

Restorative justice holds great promise, but there are also some concerns:

- Is it a political movement or a treatment process? Restorative justice is viewed as an extremely liberal alternative, and its advocates often warn of the uneven exercise of state power. Some view it as a social movement rather than a method of rehabilitation.[148] Can it survive in a culture that is becoming increasingly conservative and focused on security rather than personal freedom?
- Restorative justice programs must be wary of the cultural and social differences that can be found throughout our heterogeneous society. What may be considered "restorative" in one subculture may be considered insulting and damaging in another.[149]
- There is still no single definition of what constitutes restorative justice.[150] Consequently, many diverse

programs that call themselves restorative-oriented pursue objectives that seem remote from the restorative ideal.

■ Restorative justice programs face the difficult task of balancing the needs of offenders with those of their victims. If programs focus solely on victims' needs, they may risk ignoring the offenders' needs and increase the likelihood of reoffending. Declan Roache, a lecturer in law at the London School of Economics, makes the argument that the seductive promise of restorative justice may blind admirers to the benefits of traditional methods and prevent them from understanding or appreciating some of the pitfalls of restoration. There is danger, he warns, in a process that is essentially informal, without lawyers, and with little or no oversight on the outcome. The restoration process gives participants unchecked power without the benefit of procedural safeguards.[151]

■ Benefits may only work in the short term while ignoring long-term treatment needs. Sharon Levrant and her colleagues suggest that restorative justice programs that feature short-term interactions with victims fail to help offenders learn prosocial ways of behaving. Restorative justice advocates may falsely assume that relatively brief interludes of public shaming will change deeply rooted criminal predispositions.[152]

These are a few of the obstacles that restorative justice programs must overcome to be successful and productive. Yet because the method holds so much promise, criminologists are conducting numerous demonstration projects to find the most effective means of returning the ownership of justice to the people and the community.[153]

SUMMARY

LO1 Define the concept of social conflict and how it shapes behavior

Social conflict theorists view crime as a function of the conflict that exists in society. Conflict theorists suggest that crime in any society is caused by class conflict. Laws are created by those in power to protect their own rights and serve their own interests.

LO2 Discuss the history of critical theory and its roots in Marxist thought

Marx's view of society was shaped by the economic trends and structures of that period. He lived in an era of unrestrained capitalist expansion. During this period owners ruthlessly suppressed workers. The economic system was biased against the poor and designed to protect the wealthy. A view developed that social and political oppression produce crime. Crime would disappear if equality rather than discrimination was the norm.

LO3 List the core ideas of critical criminology

Critical criminology views the competitive nature of the capitalist system as a major cause of crime. The poor commit crimes because of their frustration, anger, and need. The wealthy engage in illegal acts because they are used to competition and because they must do so to maintain their positions in society. Critical scholars have attempted to show that the law is designed to protect the wealthy and powerful and to control the poor, "have-not" members of society.

LO4 Define the concept of globalization and analyze its association with crime

Globalization is a product of the cyber age that allows mega corporations to operate around the world with instant communication and rapid travel. It also allows criminal groups to operate on a global scale and to pick up new recruits from oppressed workers who are being exploited by international capitalists.

LO5 Explain the concept of state-organized crime

State-organized crimes involve a violation of citizen trust. They are acts defined by law as criminal and committed by state officials in pursuit of their jobs as government representatives. Some state-organized crimes are committed by individuals who abuse their state authority, or fail to exercise it, when working with people and organizations in the private sector. State-corporate crime involves the deviant activities by which the privileged classes strive to maintain or increase their power.

LO6 Compare and contrast structural and instrumental theory

Critical theorists subscribe to either instrumental theory or structural theory. Instrumental theorists hold that those in authority wield their power to control society and keep the lower classes in check. Structural theorists believe that the justice system is designed to maintain the status quo and is used to punish the wealthy, as well as members of the lower classes, when they break the rules governing capitalism.

LO7 Analyze critical criminology and discuss criticisms of the theory

Critical criminology has been criticized by traditional criminologists. Some critics suggest that critical criminologists make fundamental errors in their concepts of ownership and class interest. Other critics suggest that critical theorists unfairly neglect the capitalist system's efforts to regulate itself—for example, by instituting antitrust regulations and putting white-collar criminals behind bars. Others question whether socialist and communist nations are any more crime free than capitalist countries.

LO8 Assess the concept of left realism

Left realism sees crime as a function of relative deprivation under capitalism and views the justice system as necessary to protect the lower classes until a socialist society can be developed, which will end crime.

LO9 Articulate the central themes of critical feminism and gendered criminology

Critical feminist writers draw attention to the influence of patriarchal society on crime. They assess how capitalism has created gender conflict and the exploitation of women. They also look at how the concept of masculinity is related to crime, especially the victimization of women. According to power–control theory, gender differences in the crime rate can be explained by the structure of the family in a capitalist society.

LO10 Explain peacemaking criminology and restorative justice

Peacemaking criminology brings a call for humanism to criminology. The restorative justice model holds that reconciliation rather than retribution should be applied to prevent and control crime. Restoration programs are now being used around the United States in schools, justice agencies, and community forums. They employ mediation, sentencing circles, and other techniques.

CRITICAL THINKING QUESTIONS

1. How would a conservative reply to a call for more restorative justice? How would a restorative justice advocate respond to a conservative call for more prisons?

2. Considering recent changes in American culture, how would a power–control theorist explain recent drops in the U.S. crime rate? Can it be linked to changes in the structure of the American family?

3. Is conflict inevitable in all cultures? If not, what can be done to reduce the level of conflict in our own society?

4. If Marx were alive today, what would he think about the prosperity enjoyed by the working class in industrial societies? Might he alter his vision of the capitalist system?

5. Has religious conflict replaced class conflict as the most important issue facing modern society? Can anything be done to heal the rifts between people of different faiths?

KEY TERMS

critical criminologists (258)
critical criminology (258)
communist manifesto (260)
productive forces (260)
productive relations (260)
capitalist bourgeoisie (260)
proletariat (260)
lumpen proletariat (260)
dialectic method (260)

thesis (260)
antithesis (260)
synthesis (260)
supranational
    criminology (263)
surplus value (264)
marginalization (264)
dropout factories (264)
globalization (264)

state-organized crime (266)
instrumental theory (269)
structural theory (269)
demystify (269)
left realism (271)
preemptive deterrence (271)
critical feminism (273)
patriarchy (273)
paternalistic families (275)

role exit behaviors (275)
egalitarian families (275)
power–control
    theory (275)
peacemaking (276)
restorative justice (277)
shame (278)
reintegrative shaming (278)
sentencing circle (279)

NOTES

1. BBC News, "Why Is Ukraine in Turmoil?" February 22, 2014, http://www.bbc.com/news/world-europe-25182823 (accessed April 2014).

2. Emad El-Din Shahin, "Brutality, Torture, Rape: Egypt's Crisis Will Continue until Military Rule Is Dismantled," *The Guardian*, March 5, 2014, http://www.theguardian.com/commentisfree/2014/mar/06/brutality-torture-rape-egypt-military-rule (accessed April 2014).

3. Michael Lynch and W. Byron Groves, *A Primer in Radical Criminology*, 2nd ed. (Albany, NY: Harrow & Heston, 1989), pp. 32–33.

4. Michael Lynch, "Rediscovering Criminology: Lessons from the Marxist Tradition," in *Marxist Sociology: Surveys of Contemporary Theory and Research*, ed. Donald McQuarie and Patrick McGuire (New York: General Hall, 1994).

5. Andrew Woolford, "Making Genocide Unthinkable: Three Guidelines for a Critical Criminology of Genocide," *Critical Criminology* 14 (2006): 87–106.

6. Tony Platt and Cecilia O'Leary, "Patriot Acts," *Social Justice* 30 (2003): 5–21.

7. See, generally, Karl Marx and Friedrich Engels, *Capital: A Critique of Political Economy*, trans. E. Aveling (Chicago: Charles

Kern, 1906); Karl Marx, *Selected Writings in Sociology and Social Philosophy*, trans. P. B. Bottomore (New York: McGraw-Hill, 1956). For a general discussion of Marxist thought, see Lynch and Groves, *A Primer in Radical Criminology*, pp. 6–26.

8. Karl Marx, Grundrisse: Introduction to the Critique of Political Economy, trans. Martin Nicolaus (New York: Vintage, 1973), pp. 106–107.

9. Lynch, "Rediscovering Criminology."

10. Karl Marx, "Population, Crime and Pauperism," in *Karl Marx and Friedrich Engels, Ireland and the Irish Question* (Moscow: Progress, 1859, reprinted 1971), p. 92.

11. Friedrich Engels, *The Condition of the Working Class in England in 1844* (London: Allen & Unwin, 1950).
12. Lynch, "Rediscovering Criminology," p. 5.
13. Ian Taylor, Paul Walton, and Jock Young, *The New Criminology: For a Social Theory of Deviance* (London: Routledge & Kegan Paul, 1973).
14. Biko Agozino, "Imperialism, Crime and Criminology: Towards the Decolonisation of Criminology," *Crime, Law, and Social Change* 41 (2004): 343–358.
15. William Chambliss and Robert Seidman, *Law, Order and Power* (Reading, MA: Addison-Wesley, 1971), p. 503.
16. Richard Quinney, *The Social Reality of Crime* (Boston: Little, Brown, 1970).
17. This section borrows heavily from Richard Sparks, "A Critique of Marxist Criminology," in *Crime and Justice*, Vol. 2, ed. Norval Morris and Michael Tonry (Chicago: University of Chicago Press, 1980), pp. 159–208.
18. Barbara Sims, "Crime, Punishment, and the American Dream: Toward a Marxist Integration," *Journal of Research in Crime and Delinquency* 34 (1997): 5–24.
19. Gregg Barak, "Revisionist History, Visionary Criminology, and Needs-Based Justice," *Contemporary Justice Review* 6 (2003): 217–225.
20. John Braithwaite, "Retributivism, Punishment, and Privilege," in *Punishment and Privilege*, ed. W. Byron Groves and Graeme Newman (Albany, NY: Harrow & Heston, 1986), pp. 55–66.
21. Michael Hallett, "Reentry to What? Theorizing Prisoner Reentry in the Jobless Future," *Critical Criminology* 20 (2012): 213–228.
22. Tony Platt and Cecilia O'Leary, "Patriot Acts," *Social Justice* 30 (2003): 5–21.
23. Alette Smeulers and Roelof Haveman, eds., *Supranational Criminology: Towards a Criminology of International Crimes* (Belgium: Intersentia, 2008).
24. Ibid., p. 4.
25. Lynch and Groves, *A Primer in Radical Criminology*, p. 7.
26. Jeffery Reiman, *The Rich Get Richer and the Poor Get Prison* (New York: Wiley, 1984), pp. 43–44.
27. Rob White, "Environmental Harm and the Political Economy of Consumption," *Social Justice* 29 (2002): 82–102.
28. Sims, "Crime, Punishment, and the American Dream."
29. Steven Box, *Recession, Crime, and Unemployment* (London: Macmillan, 1987).
30. David Barlow, Melissa Hickman-Barlow, and W. Wesley Johnson, "The Political Economy of Criminal Justice Policy: A Time-Series Analysis of Economic Conditions, Crime, and Federal Criminal Justice Legislation, 1948–1987," *Justice Quarterly* 13 (1996): 223–241.
31. Mahesh Nalla, Michael Lynch, and Michael Leiber, "Determinants of Police Growth in Phoenix, 1950–1988," *Justice Quarterly* 14 (1997): 144–163.
32. America's Promise Alliance, "Building a GradNation: Progress and Challenge in Ending the High School Dropout Epidemic," November 30, 2010, http://www.americaspromise.org/Our-Work/Grad-Nation/Building-a-Grad-Nation.aspx (accessed April 2014).
33. Michael Rocques and Raymond Paternoster, "Understanding the Antecedents of the 'School-to-Jail' Link: The Relationship Between Race and School Discipline," *Journal of Criminal Law and Criminology* 101 (2011): 633–665.
34. Bureau of Labor Statistics, Manufacturing in China, 2012, http://www.bls.gov/ilc/china.htm#data_tables (accessed April 2014).
35. Dawn L. Rothe, Jeffrey Ian Ross, Christopher W. Mullins, David Friedrichs, Raymond Michalowski, Gregg Barak, David Kauzlarich, and Ronald C. Kramer, "That Was Then, This Is Now, What About Tomorrow? Future Directions in State Crime Studies," *Critical Criminology* 17 (2009): 3–13.
36. David Friedrichs and Jessica Friedrichs, "The World Bank and Crimes of Globalization: A Case Study," *Social Justice* 29 (2002): 13–36.
37. David Friedrichs and Jessica Friedrichs, "The World Bank and Crimes of Globalization: A Case Study," *Social Justice* 29 (2002): 13–36.
38. Louise Shelley, "The Globalization of Crime and Terrorism," State Department's Bureau of International Information Programs (IIP), 2006, http://iipdigital.usembassy.gov/st/english/publication/2008/06/20080608103639xjyrrep4.218692e-02.html (accessed April 2014).
39. Greg Palast, "Secret US Plan for Iraqi Oil, BBC News," March 17, 2005, http://news.bbc.co.uk/1/hi/programmes/newsnight/4354269.stm (accessed April 2014).
40. Jeffrey Ian Ross, *The Dynamics of Political Crime* (Thousand Oaks, CA: Sage, 2003).
41. Charlie Savage and Mark Mazzetti, "Cryptic Overtures and a Clandestine Meeting Gave Birth to a Blockbuster Story," *New York Times*, June 10, 2013, http://www.nytimes.com/2013/06/11/us/how-edward-j-snowden-orchestrated-a-blockbuster-story.html (accessed April 2014).
42. American Civil Liberties Union, "What's Wrong with Public Video Surveillance? The Four Problems with Public Video Surveillance," http://www.aclu.org/technology-and-liberty/whats-wrong-public-video-surveillance (accessed April 2014).
43. BBC News, "Six Days That Shook Iran," July 11, 2000, http://news.bbc.co.uk/2/hi/middle_east/828696.stm (accessed April 2014).
44. MSNBC News, "Bush Acknowledges Secret CIA Prisons," September 6, 2006, http://www.msnbc.msn.com/id/14689359/ (accessed April 2014); American Civil Liberties Union, "FBI Inquiry Details Abuses Reported by Agents at Guantanamo," January 3, 2007, http://www.aclu.org/safefree/torture/27816prs20070103.html (accessed April 2014).
45. Human Rights Watch, "UAE: Exploited Workers Building 'Island of Happiness,'" May 19, 2009, http://www.hrw.org/en/news/2009/05/18/uae-exploited-workers-building-island-happiness (accessed April 2014).
46. David Batty, "Conditions for Abu Dhabi's Migrant Workers 'Shame the West,'" *Guardian Observer*, December 21, 2013, http://www.theguardian.com/world/2013/dec/22/abu-dhabi-migrant-workers-conditions-shame-west (accessed May 2014).
47. Ross, *The Dynamics of Political Crime*.
48. Amnesty International, "Brazil: One More Human Rights Defender Lost to the Scourge of 'Death-Squads,'" January 26, 2009, http://www.amnesty.org/en/for-media/press-releases/brazil-one-more-human-rights-defender-lost-scourge-death-squads-20090126 (accessed April 2014).
49. Human Rights Watch, "Chechnya: Research Shows Widespread and Systematic Use of Torture," http://hrw.org/english/docs/2006/11/13/russia14557_txt.htm (accessed April 2014).
50. Scott A. Bonn, *Mass Deception: Moral Panic and the U.S. War on Iraq* (Piscataway, NJ: Rutgers University Press, 2010).
51. Andrew Osborn, "Russia Uses Death Squads and Torture in Chechnya, says Amnesty," *The Independent*, June 24, 2004, http://www.independent.co.uk/news/world/europe/russia-uses-death-squads-and-torture-in-chechnya-says-amnesty-6166786.html (accessed May 2014).
52. Gresham Sykes, "The Rise of Critical Criminology," *Journal of Criminal Law and Criminology* 65 (1974): 211–229.
53. David Jacobs, "Corporate Economic Power and the State: A Longitudinal Assessment of Two Explanations," *American Journal of Sociology* 93 (1988): 852–881.
54. Richard Quinney, "Crime Control in Capitalist Society," in *Critical Criminology*, ed. Ian Taylor, Paul Walton, and Jock Young (London: Routledge & Kegan Paul, 1975), p. 199.
55. Ibid.
56. John Hagan, *Structural Criminology* (New Brunswick, NJ: Rutgers University Press, 1989), pp. 110–119.
57. Darrell Steffensmeier and Stephen Demuth, "Ethnicity and Judges' Sentencing Decisions: Hispanic-Black-White Comparisons," *Criminology* 39 (2001): 145–178; Alan Lizotte,

"Extra-Legal Factors in Chicago's Criminal Courts: Testing the Conflict Model of Criminal Justice," *Social Problems* 25 (1978): 564–580.

58. Terance Miethe and Charles Moore, "Racial Differences in Criminal Processing: The Consequences of Model Selection on Conclusions about Differential Treatment," *Sociological Quarterly* 27 (1987): 217–237.

59. David Jacobs and David Britt, "Inequality and Police Use of Deadly Force: An Empirical Assessment of a Conflict Hypothesis," *Social Problems* 26 (1979): 403–412.

60. Graham Ousey and James Unnever, "Racial-Ethnic Threat, Out-Group Intolerance, and Support for Punishing Criminals: A Cross-National Study," *Criminology* 50 (2012): 565–603.

61. Albert Meehan and Michael Ponder, "Race and Place: The Ecology of Racial Profiling African American Motorists," *Justice Quarterly* 29 (2002): 399–431.

62. Tammy Rinehart Kochel, David Wilson, and Stephen Mastrofski, "Effect of Suspect Race on Officers' Arrest Decisions," *Criminology* 49 (2011): 473–512.

63. Malcolm Homes, "Minority Threat and Police Brutality: Determinants of Civil Rights Criminal Complaints in U.S. Municipalities," *Criminology* 38 (2000): 343–368.

64. Charles Crawford, Ted Chiricos, and Gary Kleck, "Race, Racial Threat, and Sentencing of Habitual Offenders," *Criminology* 36 (1998): 481–511.

65. Steffensmeier and Demuth, "Ethnicity and Judges' Sentencing Decisions"; Alan Lizotte, "Extra-Legal Factors in Chicago's Criminal Courts: Testing the Conflict Model of Criminal Justice," *Social Problems* 25 (1978): 564–580.

66. Tracy Nobiling, Cassia Spohn, and Miriam DeLone, "A Tale of Two Counties: Unemployment and Sentence Severity," *Justice Quarterly* 15 (1998): 459–485.

67. David Greenberg and Valerie West, "State Prison Populations and Their Growth, 1971–1991," *Criminology* 39 (2001): 615–654.

68. Michael Lenza, David Keys, and Teresa Guess, "The Prevailing Injustices in the Application of the Missouri Death Penalty (1978 to 1996)," *Social Justice* 32 (2005): 151–166.

69. Jack Gibbs, "An Incorrigible Positivist," *Criminologist* 12 (1987): 2–3.

70. Jackson Toby, "The New Criminology Is the Old Sentimentality," *Criminology* 16 (1979): 513–526.

71. Richard Sparks, "A Critique of Marxist Criminology," in *Crime and Justice*, Vol. 2, ed. Norval Morris and Michael Tonry (Chicago: University of Chicago Press, 1980), pp. 159–208.

72. Carl Klockars, "The Contemporary Crises of Marxist Criminology," in *Radical Criminology: The Coming Crisis*, ed. J. Inciardi (Beverly Hills, CA: Sage, 1980), pp. 92–123.

73. Matthew Petrocelli, Alex Piquero, and Michael Smith, "Conflict Theory and Racial Profiling: An Empirical Analysis of Police Traffic Stop Data," *Journal of Criminal Justice* 31 (2003): 1–10.

74. Ibid.

75. Anthony Platt, "Criminology in the 1980s: Progressive Alternatives to 'Law and Order,'" *Crime and Social Justice* 21–22 (1985): 191–199.

76. John Lea and Jock Young, *What Is to Be Done About Law and Order?* (Harmondsworth, England: Penguin, 1984).

77. Ibid., p. 88.

78. Ian Taylor, *Crime in Context: A Critical Criminology of Market Societies* (Boulder, CO: Westview Press, 1999).

79. Ibid., pp. 30–31.

80. Richard Kinsey, John Lea, and Jock Young, *Losing the Fight Against Crime* (London: Blackwell, 1986).

81. Martin Schwartz and Walter DeKeseredy, *Contemporary Criminology* (Belmont, CA: Wadsworth, 1993), p. 249.

82. Michelle Alexander, *The New Jim Crow: Mass Incarceration in the Age of Colorblindness* (New York: New Press, 2010), p. 2.

83. Michael Jacobson and Lynn Chancer, "From Left Realism to Mass Incarceration: The Need for Pragmatic Vision in Criminal Justice Policy," *Crime, Law and Social Change* 55 (2011): 187–196.

84. Martin D. Schwartz and Walter S. DeKeseredy, "Left Realist Criminology: Strengths, Weaknesses and the Feminist Critique," *Crime, Law, and Social Change* 15 (1991): 51–72.

85. For a general review of this issue, see Kathleen Daly and Meda Chesney-Lind, "Feminism and Criminology," *Justice Quarterly* 5 (1988): 497–538; Douglas Smith and Raymond Paternoster, "The Gender Gap in Theories of Deviance: Issues and Evidence," *Journal of Research in Crime and Delinquency* 24 (1987): 140–172; and Pat Carlen, "Women, Crime, Feminism, and Realism," *Social Justice* 17 (1990): 106–123.

86. Herman Schwendinger and Julia Schwendinger, *Rape and Inequality* (Newbury Park, CA: Sage, 1983).

87. Meda Chesney-Lind and Merry Morash, "Transformative Feminist Criminology: A Critical Re-thinking of a Discipline" *Critical Criminology* 21 (2013): 287–304.

88. Jordan Blair Woods, "Queer Contestations and the Future of a Critical 'Queer' Criminology," *Critical Criminology* 22 (2014): 5–19.

89. Matthew Ball, "What's Queer About Queer Criminology?" in *Handbook of LGBT Communities, Crime, and Justice*, ed. Dana Peterson and Vanessa Panfil (New York: Springer Science + Business Media, 2014), pp. 531–555.

90. Daly and Chesney-Lind, "Feminism and Criminology."

91. Janet Saltzman Chafetz, "Feminist Theory and Sociology: Underutilized Contributions for Mainstream Theory," *Annual Review of Sociology* 23 (1997): 97–121.

92. Janet Saltzman Chafetz, "Feminist Theory and Sociology: Underutilized Contributions for Mainstream Theory," *Annual Review of Sociology* 23 (1997): 97–121.

93. James Messerschmidt, *Capitalism, Patriarchy, and Crime* (Totowa, NJ: Rowman & Littlefield, 1986); for a critique of this work, see Herman Schwendinger and Julia Schwendinger, "The World According to James Messerschmidt," *Social Justice* 15 (1988): 123–145.

94. Kathleen Daly, "Gender and Varieties of White-Collar Crime," *Criminology* 27 (1989): 769–793.

95. Gillian Balfour, "Re-imagining a Feminist Criminology," *Canadian Journal of Criminology and Criminal Justice* 48 (2006): 735–752.

96. Jane Roberts Chapman, "Violence Against Women as a Violation of Human Rights," *Social Justice* 17 (1990): 54–71.

97. Shannon Lynch, April Fritch, and Nicole Heath, "Looking Beneath the Surface: The Nature of Incarcerated Women's Experiences of Interpersonal Violence, Treatment Needs, and Mental Health," *Feminist Criminology* 7 (2012): 381–400.

98. Carrie Yodanis, "Gender Inequality, Violence Against Women, and Fear," *Journal of Interpersonal Violence* 19 (2004): 655–675.

99. Victoria Titterington, "A Retrospective Investigation of Gender Inequality and Female Homicide Victimization," *Sociological Spectrum* 26 (2006): 205–236.

100. James Messerschmidt, *Masculinities and Crime: Critique and Reconceptualization of Theory* (Lanham, MD: Rowman & Littlefield, 1993).

101. Angela P. Harris, "Gender, Violence, Race, and Criminal Justice," *Stanford Law Review* 52 (2000): 777–810.

102. Suzie Dod Thomas and Nancy Stein, "Criminality, Imprisonment, and Women's Rights in the 1990s," *Social Justice* 17 (1990): 1–5.

103. Walter DeKeseredy and Martin Schwartz, "Male Peer Support and Woman Abuse: An Expansion of DeKeseredy's Model," *Sociological Spectrum* 13 (1993): 393–413.

104. Daly and Chesney-Lind, "Feminism and Criminology." See also Drew Humphries and Susan Caringella-MacDonald, "Murdered

Mothers, Missing Wives: Reconsidering Female Victimization," *Social Justice* 17 (1990): 71–78.

105. Kjersti Ericsson and Nina Jon, "Gendered Social Control: 'A Virtuous Girl' and 'a Proper Boy,'" *Journal of Scandinavian Studies in Criminology and Crime Prevention* 9 (2006): 126–141.

106. Hagan, *Structural Criminology*.

107. John Hagan, A. R. Gillis, and John Simpson, "The Class Structure and Delinquency: Toward a Power-Control Theory of Common Delinquent Behavior," *American Journal of Sociology* 90 (1985): 1151–1178; John Hagan, John Simpson, and A. R. Gillis, "Class in the Household: A Power-Control Theory of Gender and Delinquency," *American Journal of Sociology* 92 (1987): 788–816.

108. John Hagan, Bill McCarthy, and Holly Foster, "A Gendered Theory of Delinquency and Despair in the Life Course," *Acta Sociologica* 45 (2002): 37–47.

109. Brenda Sims Blackwell, Christine Sellers, and Sheila Schlaupitz, "A Power-Control Theory of Vulnerability to Crime and Adolescent Role Exits—Revisited," *Canadian Review of Sociology and Anthropology* 39 (2002): 199–219.

110. Brenda Sims Blackwell, "Perceived Sanction Threats, Gender, and Crime: A Test and Elaboration of Power-Control Theory," *Criminology* 38 (2000): 439–488.

111. Christopher Uggen, "Class, Gender, and Arrest: An Intergenerational Analysis of Workplace Power and Control," *Criminology* 38 (2001): 835–862.

112. Gary Jensen and Kevin Thompson, "What's Class Got to Do with It? A Further Examination of Power-Control Theory," *American Journal of Sociology* 95 (1990): 1009–1023. For some critical research, see Simon Singer and Murray Levine, "Power-Control Theory, Gender and Delinquency: A Partial Replication with Additional Evidence on the Effects of Peers," *Criminology* 26 (1988): 627–648.

113. Kevin Thompson, "Gender and Adolescent Drinking Problems: The Effects of Occupational Structure," *Social Problems* 36 (1989): 30–38.

114. Kristin Mack and Michael Leiber, "Race, Gender, Single-Mother Households, and Delinquency: A Further Test of Power-Control Theory," *Youth and Society* 37 (2005): 115–144.

115. See, generally, Uggen, "Class, Gender, and Arrest."

116. Brenda Sims Blackwell and Alex Piquero, "On the Relationships Between Gender,

Power Control, Self-Control, and Crime," *Journal of Criminal Justice* 33 (2005): 1–17.

117. Liz Walz, "One Blood," *Contemporary Justice Review* 6 (2003): 25–36.

118. John F. Wozniak, "Poverty and Peacemaking Criminology: Beyond Mainstream Criminology," *Critical Criminology* 16 (2008): 209–223.

119. See, for example, Dennis Sullivan and Larry Tifft, *Restorative Justice: Healing the Foundations of Our Everyday Lives* (Monsey, NY: Willow Tree Press, 2005); Dennis Sullivan, *The Mask of Love: Corrections in America, Toward a Mutual Aid Alternative* (Port Washington, NY: Kennikat Press, 1980).

120. Larry Tifft, "Foreword," in Sullivan, *The Mask of Love*, p. 6.

121. Sullivan, *The Mask of Love*, p. 141.

122. Sullivan and Tifft, *Restorative Justice*.

123. Richard Quinney, "The Way of Peace: On Crime, Suffering, and Service," in *Criminology as Peacemaking*, ed. Harold Pepinsky and Richard Quinney (Bloomington: Indiana University Press, 1991), pp. 8–9.

124. For a review of Quinney's ideas, see Kevin B. Anderson, "Richard Quinney's Journey: The Marxist Dimension," *Crime and Delinquency* 48 (2002): 232–242.

125. Kathleen Daly and Russ Immarigeon, "The Past, Present and Future of Restorative Justice: Some Critical Reflections," *Contemporary Justice Review* 1 (1998): 21–45.

126. Howard Zehr, *The Little Book of Restorative Justice* (Intercourse, PA: Good Books, 2002): 1–10.

127. Mark Lewis Taylor, *The Executed God: The Way of the Cross in Lockdown America* (Minneapolis: Fortress Press, 2001).

128. Alfred Villaume, "'Life Without Parole' and 'Virtual Life Sentences': Death Sentences by Any Other Name," *Contemporary Justice Review* 8 (2005): 265–277.

129. John Braithwaite, *Crime, Shame, and Reintegration* (Melbourne, Australia: Cambridge University Press, 1989).

130. Ibid., p. 81.

131. Anthony Petrosino and Carolyn Petrosino, "The Public Safety Potential of Megan's Law in Massachusetts: An Assessment from a Sample of Criminal Sexual Psychopaths," *Crime and Delinquency* 45 (1999): 140–158.

132. Eliza Ahmed, Nathan Harris, John Braithwaite, and Valerie Braithwaite, *Shame Management Through Reintegration* (Cambridge, England: Cambridge University Press, 2001).

133. Eliza Ahmed, "'What, Me Ashamed?' Shame Management and School Bullying," *Journal*

of Research in Crime and Delinquency 41 (2004): 269–294.

134. John Braithwaite, "Rape, Shame and Pride," *Journal of Scandinavian Studies in Criminology and Crime Prevention* 7 (2006): 2–16.

135. Carter Hay, "An Exploratory Test of Braithwaite's Reintegrative Shaming Theory," *Journal of Research in Crime and Delinquency* 38 (2001): 132–153.

136. Gene Stephens, "The Future of Policing: From a War Model to a Peace Model," in *The Past, Present and Future of American Criminal Justice*, ed. Brendan Maguire and Polly Radosh (Dix Hills, NY: General Hall, 1996), pp. 77–93.

137. Rick Shifley, "The Organization of Work as a Factor in Social Well-Being," *Contemporary Justice Review* 6 (2003): 105–126.

138. Kay Pranis, "Peacemaking Circles: Restorative Justice in Practice Allows Victims and Offenders to Begin Repairing the Harm," *Corrections Today* 59 (1997): 74–78.

139. Carol LaPrairie, "The 'New' Justice: Some Implications for Aboriginal Communities," *Canadian Journal of Criminology* 40 (1998): 61–79.

140. Diane Schaefer, "A Disembodied Community Collaborates in a Homicide: Can Empathy Transform a Failing Justice System?" *Contemporary Justice Review* 6 (2003): 133–143.

141. David R. Karp and Beau Breslin, "Restorative Justice in School Communities," *Youth and Society* 33 (2001): 249–272.

142. Paul Jesilow and Deborah Parsons, "Community Policing as Peacemaking," *Policing and Society* 10 (2000): 163–183.

143. Gordon Bazemore and Curt Taylor Griffiths, "Conferences, Circles, Boards, and Mediations: The 'New Wave' of Community Justice Decision Making," *Federal Probation* 61 (1997): 25–37.

144. Heather Strang, "Restorative Justice Programs in Australia," http://www.criminologyresearchcouncil.gov.au/reports/strang/report.pdf (accessed April 2014).

145. Hennessey Hayes, Tara Renae McGee, Helen Punter, and Michael John Cerruto, "Agreements in Restorative Justice Conferences: Exploring the Implications of Agreements for Post-conference Offending Behaviour," *British Journal of Criminology* 54 (2014): 109–127.

146. John W. De Gruchy, *Reconciliation: Restoring Justice* (Minneapolis: Fortress, 2002).

147. Lawrence W Sherman and Heather Strang, *Restorative Justice: The Evidence* (London: Smith Institute, 2007).

148. John Braithwaite, "Setting Standards for Restorative Justice," *British Journal of Criminology* 42 (2002): 563–577.

149. David Altschuler, "Community Justice Initiatives: Issues and Challenges in the U.S. Context," *Federal Probation* 65 (2001): 28–33.

150. Lois Presser and Patricia van Voorhis, "Values and Evaluation: Assessing Processes and Outcomes of Restorative Justice Programs," *Crime and Delinquency* 48 (2002): 162–189.

151. Declan Roche, *Accountability in Restorative Justice* (Clarendon Studies in Criminology) (London: Oxford University Press, 2004).

152. Sharon Levrant, Francis Cullen, Betsy Fulton, and John Wozniak, "Reconsidering Restorative Justice: The Corruption of Benevolence Revisited?" *Crime* and *Delinquency* 45 (1999): 3–28.

153. Edward Gumz, "American Social Work, Corrections and Restorative Justice: An Appraisal," *International Journal of Offender Therapy and Comparative Criminology* 48 (2004): 449–460.

Steven Hayes

Joshua Komisarjevsky

learning objectives

LO1 Discuss the history of developmental theory

LO2 Compare and contrast life course, latent trait, and trajectory theories

LO3 List the principles of the life course theory

LO4 Describe examples of problem behaviors that cluster together

LO5 Explain why age of onset is an important factor in crime

LO6 Outline the basic principles of Sampson and Laub's age-graded theory

LO7 Interpret the terms *propensity* and *latent trait*

LO8 Discuss Wilson and Herrnstein's views on crime and human nature

LO9 Explain the basic principles of the General Theory of Crime

LO10 Recognize that there are a variety of criminal trajectories

DEVELOPMENTAL THEORIES: LIFE COURSE, LATENT TRAIT, AND TRAJECTORY

few crimes are as horrific as the murder of Jennifer, Michaela, and Hayley Petit during a home invasion in the leafy suburb of Cheshire, Connecticut. The crime began on July 23, 2007, when career criminals Steven Hayes and Joshua Komisarjevsky spotted the Petits at a grocery store, followed them home, burst into the Petits' home, beat and tied up the Dr. William Petit Jr., raped and assaulted Mrs. Jennifer Petit and her 11-year-old daughter Michaela, and tied up and terrorized 17-year-old Hayley Petit. They forced Mrs. Petit to go to a local bank to withdraw funds when they considered the household haul insufficient. Mrs. Petit was able to inform a bank employee who then called local police. William Petit was able to free himself, escape, and call to a neighbor for help. While police surrounded the home, the pair strangled Mrs. Petit before setting the house on fire with the two girls tied to their beds, causing their death by smoke inhalation. The crime was so gruesome that some jurors had to be treated for PTSD.

During the trial defense lawyers presented evidence in an effort to spare Hayes and Komisarjevsky the death penalty. Komisarjevsky was portrayed as a damaged person who was sexually abused as a child, suffered mood

disorders and head injuries, abused drugs, and cut himself with glass, knives and razors. His evangelical Christian adoptive parents denied him proper care, relying instead on religion.

Dr. Eric Goldsmith, a psychiatrist who interviewed Hayes for about 37 hours on eight occasions, noted that Hayes had a troubled and abusive upbringing, was sexually abused by a teenage babysitter when he was 10 or 11, and had developed a sexual fetish that caused him to associate an object—a woman's old sneaker—with sexual arousal; he said Hayes sought out women who shared his fetish. Hayes claimed that he had killed 17 women in the Northeast and also committed date rapes.

Despite defense efforts Hayes was convicted of the murders and sentenced to death; Komisarjevsky was also found guilty and sentenced to death on January 27, 2012.[1]

Komisarjevsky's family issued a statement: "From the very beginning, we have spoken out about the horror of the crime and taken the position that whatever verdict the jury reached was the right verdict. With today's jury decision, our view is the same. The crime was monstrous and beyond comprehension. There are no excuses."

areer criminals such as Hayes and Komisarjevsky defy what is commonly known about criminal behavior: they do not age out of crime as do most youthful offenders, but persist into their adulthood. Nor do they get involved in a single crime and then forgo illegal activity; they have a long history of antisocial behavior, continually planning and getting involved in criminal acts of greater seriousness until they are captured and imprisoned. Criminologists have struggled to understand the factors that explain the onset and continuation of a criminal career. Rather than look at a single factor, such as poverty or low intelligence, and suggest that people who maintain this trait are predisposed to crime, those who engage in **developmental criminology** attempt to provide a more global vision of a criminal career encompassing its onset, continuation, and termination. This chapter reviews the most important issues in developmental criminology, and discusses major concepts and theories in some detail.

FOUNDATIONS OF DEVELOPMENTAL THEORY

LO1 Discuss the history of developmental theory

During the twentieth century, some criminologists began to integrate sociological, psychological, and economic elements into more complex developmental views of crime causation. Hans Eysenck published *Crime and Personality* in 1964 and proclaimed that antisocial behavior was linked to psychological conditions that were a product of heredity.[2] His controversial theory integrated social, biological, and psychological factors, a vision that upset the sociologists who controlled the field at that time.[3]

However, it is Sheldon (1896–1980) and Eleanor (1898–1972) Glueck who are today considered founders of the developmental branch of criminological theory. While at Harvard University in the 1930s, they conducted research on the careers of known criminals to determine the factors that predicted persistent offending, making extensive use of interviews and records in their elaborate comparisons of criminals and noncriminals.

The Gluecks' research focused on early onset of delinquency as a harbinger of a criminal career: "[T]he deeper the roots of childhood maladjustment, the smaller the chance of adult adjustment."[4] They also noted the stability of offending careers: children who are antisocial early in life are the most likely to continue their offending careers into adulthood.

In a series of longitudinal research studies, the Gluecks followed the careers of known delinquents to determine the characteristics that predicted persistent offending.[5] The Gluecks identified a number of personal and social factors related to persistent offending, the most important of which was family relations. This factor was considered in terms of quality of discipline and emotional ties with parents. The adolescent raised in a large, single-parent family of limited economic means and educational achievement was the most vulnerable to delinquency. Not restricting their analysis to social variables, the Gluecks measured such biological and psychological traits as body type, intelligence, and personality, and found that physical and mental factors also played a role in determining behavior. Children with low intelligence, who had a background of mental disease, and who had a powerful ("mesomorph") physique were the most likely to become persistent offenders.

Integrating biological, social, and psychological elements, the Gluecks' research suggested that the initiation and continuity of a criminal career was a developmental process influenced by both internal and external situations, conditions, and circumstances. While impressive, their research was heavily criticized by sociologists such as Edwin Sutherland who wanted to keep criminology within the field of sociology and feared or disparaged efforts to integrate biological or psychological concepts into the field.[6] The Glueck legacy was the basis of a series of papers by criminologists Robert Sampson and John Laub, who used modern statistical techniques to reanalyze the Gluecks' carefully drawn empirical measurements. Their findings, published in a series of books and articles, fueled the popularity of what is now referred to as the developmental approach.[7]

CONNECTIONS

Social process theories lay the foundation for assuming that peer, family, educational, and other interactions, which vary over the life course, influence behaviors. See the first few sections of Chapter 7 for a review of these issues. As you may recall from Chapter 2, a great deal of research has been conducted on the relationship of age and crime and the activities of chronic offenders. This scholarship has prompted interest in the life cycle of crime.

developmental criminology A view of criminal behavior that places emphasis on the changes people go through over the life course. It presents a criminal career as a dynamic process involving onset, continuity, persistence, acceleration, and eventual desistance from criminal behavior, controlled by individual level traits and conditions.

MULTIFACTOR/INTEGRATED THEORY

ORIGIN About 1930

FOUNDERS Sheldon and Eleanor Glueck; Hans Eysenck

MOST IMPORTANT WORKS Sheldon and Eleanor Glueck: *Five Hundred Delinquent Women* (1934); *Later Criminal Careers* (1937); *Criminal Careers in Retrospect* (1943); *Unraveling Juvenile Delinquency* (1950); Eysenck, *Crime and Personality*

CORE IDEAS Crime is a function of environmental, socialization, physical, and psychological factors. Each makes an independent contribution to shaping and directing behavior patterns. Deficits in these areas of human development increase the risk of crime. People at risk for crime can resist antisocial behaviors if these traits and conditions can be strengthened.

MODERN OUTGROWTHS
Developmental theory, life course theory, propensity/latent trait theory, trajectory theory

Hans Eysenck

© Daily Mail/Rex/Alamy

Criminal Career Research

The Philadelphia cohort research by Marvin Wolfgang and his associates was another milestone prompting interest in explaining criminal career development.[8] As you may recall (Chapter 2), Wolfgang found that while many offenders commit a single criminal act and desist from crime, a small group of chronic offenders engage in frequent and repeated criminal activity and continue to do so across their life span. Wolfgang's research focused attention on criminal careers. Criminologists were now asking this fundamental question: what prompts one person to engage in persistent criminal activity while another, who on the surface suffers the same life circumstances, finds a way to steer clear of crime and travel along a more conventional path?

A 1990 review paper by Rolf Loeber and Marc LeBlanc was another important event that generated interest in developmental theory. In this landmark work, Loeber and LeBlanc proposed that criminologists should devote time and effort to understanding some basic questions about the evolution of criminal careers: Why do people begin committing antisocial acts? Why do some stop while others continue? Why do some escalate the severity of their criminality (that is, go from shoplifting to drug dealing to armed robbery) while others deescalate and commit less serious crimes as they mature? If some terminate their criminal activity, what, if anything, causes them to begin again? Why do some criminals specialize in certain types of crime, whereas others are generalists engaging in a variety of antisocial behavior? According to Loeber and LeBlanc's developmental view, criminologists must pay attention to how a criminal career unfolds, how it begins, why it is sustained, and how it comes to an end.[9]

Life Course, Latent Traits, and Trajectories

LO2 Compare and contrast life course, latent trait, and trajectory theories

These scholarly advances created enormous excitement among criminologists and focused their attention on criminal career research. As research on criminal careers has evolved, three distinct viewpoints have taken shape: life course view, latent trait view, and trajectory view. **Life course theories** see criminality as a dynamic process, influenced by a multitude of individual characteristics, traits, and social experiences. As people travel through the life course, they are constantly bombarded by changing perceptions and experiences, and as a result their behavior will change directions, sometimes for the better and sometimes for the worse (Figure 9.1). In contrast, **latent trait theories** hold that human development is controlled by a stable propensity or "master trait," present at birth or soon after. As people mature from childhood, to adolescence to adulthood, this trait is always there, directing their behavior and shaping life events. Because this master trait is enduring and unchanging, the ebb and flow of criminal behavior are

---

life course theories Theoretical views studying changes in criminal offending patterns over a person's entire life.

latent trait theories Theoretical views that criminal behavior is controlled by a master trait, present at birth or soon after, that remains stable and unchanging throughout a person's lifetime.

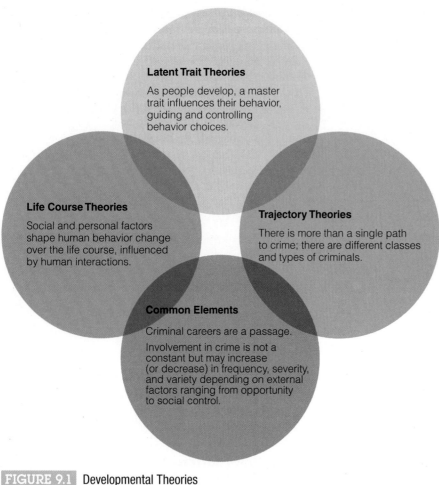

Latent Trait Theories

As people develop, a master trait influences their behavior, guiding and controlling behavior choices.

Life Course Theories

Social and personal factors shape human behavior change over the life course, influenced by human interactions.

Trajectory Theories

There is more than a single path to crime; there are different classes and types of criminals.

Common Elements

Criminal careers are a passage.

Involvement in crime is not a constant but may increase (or decrease) in frequency, severity, and variety depending on external factors ranging from opportunity to social control.

FIGURE 9.1 Developmental Theories

SOURCE: © Cengage Learning®

directed by the impact of external forces such as interpersonal interactions and criminal opportunity.

A third view, **trajectory theory**, suggests there are multiple trajectories in a criminal career. According to this approach, there are numerous subgroups within a population that follow distinctively different criminal career trajectories. Some people may begin involvement in antisocial activities in childhood and adolescence and demonstrate a precocious propensity for crime, while others begin later and are influenced by a different set of life circumstances.

trajectory theory A view of criminal career formation that holds there are multiple paths to crime.

population heterogeneity The view that the propensity of an individual to participate in antisocial behavior is a relatively stable trait, unchanging over his or her life course.

state dependence The propensity to commit crime profoundly and permanently disrupts normal socialization. Early rule breaking strengthens criminal motivation and increases the probability of future rule breaking.

This view suggests that there are different types and classes of offenders and each must be studied independently.[10]

Each of these positions is discussed in detail in the following sections.

Population Heterogeneity vs. State Dependence

Are people truly different, or are we more or less all the same but shaped by our different experiences? This question is the core issue separating the various branches of developmental theory.

The concept of **population heterogeneity** assumes that the propensity of an individual to participate in antisocial and/or criminal behaviors is a relatively stable trait, unchanging over his or her life course. Within a given population people maintain a variety of personal traits: some are hotheaded, violent, and inclined to commit crime, while others remain reasoning, unruffled, and presumably law abiding. According to this view, individual differences remain stable and are not affected by their environment or alterations in their life circumstance.[11] Because people affect their environment and not vice versa, the best predictor of future behavior is past behavior: people who are criminally active in their childhood should remain so in their adulthood, no matter what happens to them in the meantime. Propensity theorists embrace this concept because it suggests that the cause of misbehavior remains the same as people traverse the life course.

In contrast, the concept of **state dependence** suggests that people change and develop as they mature; life events have a significant influence on future behavior. Life course and trajectory theorists embrace this concept because it can explain continuity and desistance from crime: while positive experiences can help the troubled person adjust and conform, damaging encounters and events have the potential to increase future criminal involvement. Even kids who are at risk for crime can avoid a criminal way of life if they encounter people who help, nurture, and support them in their adolescence and adulthood. If past antisocial behavior influences future offending, it's not because they have a similar cause, but because offending disrupts prosocial bonds and informal mechanisms of social control.[12]

LIFE COURSE FUNDAMENTALS

LO3 List the principles of the life course theory

According to the life course view, even as toddlers people begin relationships and behaviors that will determine their adult life course. At first they must learn to conform to social rules and function effectively in society. Later they are expected to begin to think about careers, leave their parental homes, find permanent relationships, and eventually marry and begin their own families.[13] These transitions are expected to take place in order—beginning with finishing school, then entering the workforce, getting married, and having children.

Some individuals, however, are incapable of maturing in a reasonable and timely fashion because of family, environmental, or personal problems.[14] In some cases, transitions can occur too early—an adolescent girl who engages in precocious sex gets pregnant and is forced to drop out of high school. In other cases, transitions may occur too late—a teenage male falls in with the wrong crowd, goes to prison, and finds it difficult to break into the job market upon release; he puts off getting married because of his diminished economic circumstances. Sometimes interruption of one transition can harm another. A teenager who has family problems may find that her educational and career development is upset or that she suffers from psychological impairments.[15]

Kids who get in trouble early may find it difficult to shake the criminal way of life as they mature. Those who join gangs are more likely to get involved in antisocial behavior after they leave the gang than before they joined; gang membership creates long-term disruptions.[16] One reason is that joining a gang can lead to educational underachievement, a factor routinely associated with career criminality. Youths who join gangs are 30 percent less likely to graduate from high school and 58 percent less likely to earn a four-year degree than youths of similar background who do not become gang members.[17] But even those who have been in trouble throughout their adolescence may manage to find stable work and maintain intact marriages as adults; these life events help them desist from crime. In contrast, less fortunate adolescents who develop arrest records and get involved with the wrong crowd may find themselves at risk for delinquency and later adult criminal careers.[18]

Disruption Promotes Criminality

Because the shift from one stage of life to another can be a bumpy ride, the propensity to commit crimes is neither stable nor constant: it is a developmental process. A positive life experience may help some criminals desist from crime, whereas a negative one may cause them to resume their activities. Criminal careers are said to be developmental because people are constantly being influenced by the behavior of those around them, and they, in turn, influence others' behavior. A youth's antisocial behavior may turn his more conventional friends against him; their rejection solidifies and escalates his antisocial behavior.[19]

Disruptions in life's major transitions can be destructive and ultimately can promote criminality. Those who are already at risk because of socioeconomic problems or family dysfunction are the most susceptible to these awkward transitions. Criminality, according to this view, cannot be attributed to a single cause, nor does it represent a single underlying tendency.[20] People are influenced by different factors as they mature. Consequently, a factor that may have an important influence at one stage of life (such as delinquent peers) may have little influence later on.[21]

These negative life events can become cumulative: as people acquire more personal deficits, the chances of acquiring additional ones increases.[22] The cumulative impact of these disruptions sustains criminality from childhood into adulthood.[23]

Changing Life Influences

Life course theories also recognize that as people mature, the factors that influence their behavior change.[24] As people make important life transitions—from child to adolescent, from adolescent to adult, from unwed to married—the nature of social interactions changes.[25]

At first, family relations may be most influential; it comes as no shock to life course theorists when research shows that criminality runs in families and that having criminal relatives is a significant predictor of future misbehaviors.[26] In later adolescence, school and peer relations predominate; in adulthood, vocational achievement and marital relations may be the most critical influences. Some antisocial children who are in trouble throughout their adolescence may manage to find stable work and maintain intact marriages as adults; these life events help them desist from crime. In contrast, less fortunate adolescents who develop arrest records and get involved with the wrong crowd may find themselves limited to menial jobs and at risk for criminal careers. However, even the ability to change wilts with age as people become embedded in a criminal lifestyle. What may help a person resist a life of crime while they are still in their teens (e.g., school achievement and positive family relations) may have little impact once they reach their twenties.[27]

LIFE COURSE CONCEPTS

A view of crime has emerged that incorporates personal change and growth. The factors that produce crime and delinquency at one point in the life cycle may not be relevant at another; as people mature, the social, physical, and environmental influences on their behavior are transformed. People may show a propensity to offend early in their lives, but the nature and frequency of their activities are often affected by forces beyond their control, which elevate and sustain their criminal activity.[28]

The next sections review some of the more important concepts associated with the life course view and discuss some prominent life course theories.

Problem Behavior Syndrome

LO4 Describe examples of problem behaviors that cluster together

Most criminological theories portray crime as the outcome of social problems. Learning theorists view a troubled home life and deviant friends as precursors of criminality; structural theorists maintain that acquiring deviant cultural values leads to criminality. In contrast, the developmental view is that criminality may best be understood as one of many social problems faced by at-risk youth, a view called **problem behavior syndrome (PBS)**. According to this view, crime is one among a group of interrelated antisocial behaviors that cluster together and typically involve family dysfunction, sexual and physical abuse, substance abuse, smoking, precocious sexuality and early pregnancy, educational underachievement, suicide attempts, sensation seeking, and unemployment.[29] People who suffer from one of these conditions typically exhibit many symptoms of the rest.[30] All varieties of criminal behavior, including violence, theft, and drug offenses, may be part of a generalized PBS, indicating that all forms of antisocial behavior have similar developmental patterns (Exhibit 9.1).[31]

Many examples support the existence of PBS:[32]

- Adolescents with a history of gang involvement are more likely to have been expelled from school, be binge drinkers, test positively for marijuana, have been in three or more fights in the past six months, have non-monogamous partners, and test positive for sexually transmitted diseases.[33]
- Kids who gamble and take risks at an early age also take drugs and commit crimes.[34]
- People who exhibit one serious social problem such as drug abuse typically exhibit many others.[35]

Those who suffer from PBS are prone to more difficulties than the general population.[36] They find themselves with

a range of personal dilemmas ranging from drug abuse to being accident prone, requiring more health care and hospitalization, becoming teenage parents, or having mental health problems.[37] PBS has been linked to individual-level personality problems (such as impulsiveness, rebelliousness, and low ego), family problems (such as intrafamily conflict and parental mental disorder), substance abuse, and educational failure.[38] Research shows that social problems such as drug abuse, low income, aggression, single parenthood, residence in isolated urban areas, lack of family support or resources, racism, and prolonged exposure to poverty are all interrelated.[39] Considering the types of problems that cluster together (e.g., mental illness, drug abuse, hospitalization), it is not surprising that people who have a long and varied criminal career are more likely to die early and have greater than average mortality rates. Criminal conduct has been found to increase the chances of premature death due to both natural and unnatural causes, including deaths from accidents, homicide, and suicide. The more crime a person commits, the more likely he or she is to suffer premature death.[40]

In sum, problem behavior syndrome portrays crime as a type of social problem rather than the product of other social problems.[41] People involved in crime may fall prey to other social problems, ranging from poverty to premature death.[42]

Offense Specialization/Generalization

Some offenders are specialists, limiting their criminal activities to a cluster of crime such as theft offenses, including burglary and larceny, or violent offenses such as assault and rape.[43] Others are generalists who engage in a variety of criminal activities such as drug abuse, burglary, and/or rape, depending on the opportunity to commit crime and the likelihood of success.[44] There is an ongoing debate over generalization/specialization: some criminologists believe that most criminals are generalists, while others have found evidence that more serious offenders tend to specialize in a

---

EXHIBIT 9.1

Problem Behaviors

Social
- Family dysfunction
- Unemployment
- Educational underachievement
- School misconduct

Personal
- Substance abuse
- Suicide attempts
- Early sexuality
- Sensation seeking
- Early parenthood

- Accident prone
- Medical problems
- Mental disease
- Anxiety
- Eating disorders (bulimia, anorexia)

Environmental
- High-crime area
- Disorganized area
- Racism
- Exposure to poverty

SOURCE: © Cengage Learning®

---

problem behavior syndrome (PBS) A cluster of antisocial behaviors that may include family dysfunction, substance abuse, smoking, precocious sexuality and early pregnancy, educational underachievement, suicide attempts, sensation seeking, and unemployment, as well as crime.

narrower range of antisocial activities.[45] The answer may lie in between these two positions; there is evidence for specialization, but it is neither overwhelming nor universal.[46] Some offenders may specialize in the short term but engage in a wider variety of offenses when presented with opportunities to commit crime.[47]

Age of Onset

LO5 Explain why age of onset is an important factor in crime

Most life course theories assume that the seeds of a criminal career are planted early in life and that early onset of deviance strongly predicts later and more serious criminality.[48] Children who will later become the most serious delinquents begin their deviant careers at a very early (preschool) age, and the earlier the onset of criminality, the more frequent, varied, and sustained the criminal career.[49] If children are aggressive and antisocial during their public school years, they are much more likely to be troublesome and exhibit aggressive behavior in adulthood.[50]

Early-onset criminals seem to be more involved in aggressive acts ranging from cruelty to animals to peer-directed violence.[51] In contrast, late starters are more likely to be involved in nonviolent crimes such as theft.[52] Recent research by Daniel Nagin and Richard Tremblay shows that late-onset physical aggression is the exception, not the rule, and that the peak frequency of physical aggression occurs during early childhood and generally declines thereafter.[53]

Why is early onset so important? Starting early in delinquent behavior creates a downward spiral in a young person's life.[54] Thereafter tension may begin to develop with parents and other family members, emotional bonds to conventional peers become weakened and frayed, and opportunities to pursue conventional activities like sports dry up and wither away. Replacing them are closer involvement with more deviant peers and involvement in a delinquent way of life.[55] As they emerge into adulthood, persisters report less emotional support, lower job satisfaction, distant peer relationships, and more psychiatric problems than those who desist.[56]

The Cause of Early Onset   What causes some kids to begin offending at an early age? Among the suspected root causes are poor parental discipline and monitoring, inadequate emotional support, distant peer relationships, and psychological issues and problems.[57] These influences may follow kids into their adulthood, helping them shift from one form of deviant life styles to another.[58] The psychic scars of childhood are hard to erase.[59]

Children who are improperly socialized by unskilled parents are the most likely to rebel by wandering the streets with deviant peers.[60] Parental influences may be replaced: in middle childhood, social rejection by conventional peers and academic failure sustains antisocial behavior; in later adolescence, commitment to a deviant peer group creates a training ground for crime. While the youngest and most serious offenders may persist in their criminal activity into late adolescence and even adulthood, others are able to age out of crime or desist.

Persistence and Desistance   Life course theorists are particularly interested in why one person persists in crime and develops a criminal career, while another is able to reduce his or her criminal involvement and eventually desist. How can at-risk kids who have engaged in crime become law-abiding adults? Is desistance a biological phenomenon (i.e., the aging process takes its toll) or an experiential one (i.e., as people mature they take on adult responsibilities that pull them away from law-violating peers)?

One possible answer to this question comes from the data gathered by the Cambridge Study in Delinquent Development, a longitudinal study led by criminologist David Farrington that has followed the offending careers of 411 London boys born in 1953.[61] Farrington suggests that life experiences shape the direction and flow of behavior choices and that factors that predict crime at one point in the life course may not be the ones that foretell criminality. As they mature, former delinquents are able to desist if they enter adult worlds of work and marriage and relocate to a more hospitable environment in the suburbs. Not that this transition is easy: desisters tended to live in unkempt homes and have large debts and low-paying jobs. They were also more likely to remain single, live alone, and experience social isolation. So while these people may have avoided a life of crime, they did not avoid social problems all together.

Gender and Desistance   As they mature, both males and females who have early experiences with antisocial behavior are the ones most likely to persist throughout their life course. Like boys, early-onset girls continue to experience difficulties—increased drug and alcohol use, poor school adjustment, mental health problems, poor sexual health, psychiatric problems, higher rates of mortality, criminal behavior, insufficient parenting skills, relationship dysfunction, lower performance in academic and occupational environments, involvement with social service assistance, and adjustment problems—as they enter young adulthood and beyond.[62]

There are also some distinct gender differences. For males, the path runs from early onset in childhood to later problems at work and involvement with substance abuse. For females, the path seems somewhat different: early antisocial behavior leads to relationship problems, depression, a tendency to commit suicide, and poor health in adulthood.[63] Males seem to be more deeply influenced by an early history of childhood aggression: males who exhibited chronic physical aggression during the elementary school years exhibit the risk of continued physical violence and delinquency during adolescence. There is less evidence of a linkage between childhood physical aggression and adult aggression among females.[64]

High-priced call girl, drug abuser, identity thief—Audrey Atlas, 45 (at the time of the photo), of Laguna Hills, California, has been all of these. Now the mother of four, on parole and sober after doing stints at four prisons, she wants to give hope to other troubled women who think there is no hope. For now, at least, she is beating the odds. Shown here, a dinner/meeting at Pastor Lisa Cram's house; Pastor Cram specializes in counseling women. What could cause a chronic offender such as Atlas to turn her life around and step off the criminal path?

© ZUMA Press/Newscom

integrated theories Models of crime causation that weave social and individual variables into a complex explanatory chain.

age-graded theory A developmental theory that posits that (a) individual traits and childhood experiences are important to understand the onset of delinquent and criminal behavior; (b) experiences in young adulthood and beyond can redirect criminal trajectories or paths; (c) serious problems in adolescence undermine life chances; (d) positive life experiences and relationships can help a person knife off from a criminal career path; (e) positive life experiences such as gaining employment, getting married, or joining the military create informal social control mechanisms that limit criminal behavior opportunities; (f) former criminals may choose to desist from crime because they find more conventional paths more beneficial and rewarding.

THEORIES OF THE CRIMINAL LIFE COURSE

A number of systematic theories have been formulated that account for onset, continuance, and desistance from crime. As a group they integrate societal level variables such as measures of social control, social learning, and structural models. It is not uncommon for life course theories to interconnect *personal factors* such as personality and intelligence, *social factors* such as income and neighborhood, *socialization factors* such as marriage and military service, *cognitive factors* such as information processing and attention/perception, and *situational factors* such as criminal opportunity, effective guardianship, and apprehension risk into complex multifactor explanations of human behavior. In this sense they are **integrated theories** because they incorporate social, personal, and developmental factors into complex explanations of human behavior. They do not focus on the relatively simple question—why do people commit crime?—but on more complex issues: Why do some offenders persist in criminal careers while others desist from or alter their criminal activity as they mature?[65] Why do some people continually escalate their criminal involvement, whereas others slow down and turn their lives around? Are all criminals similar in their offending patterns, or are there different types of offenders and paths to offending? Life course theorists want to know not only why people enter a criminal way of life, but why, once they do, they are able to alter the trajectory of their criminal involvement. One of the more important life course theories, Sampson and Laub's **age-graded theory**, is set out below in some detail. Exhibit 9.2 outlines the principles of some other important life course theories.

Sampson and Laub: Age-Graded Theory

LO6 Outline the basic principles of Sampson and Laub's age-graded theory

Most theories focus on why people get involved in crime. In an important 1993 work, *Crime in the Making*, Robert Sampson and John Laub instead focus on whether there are trails back to conformity. In formulating their *Age-Graded Theory of Informal Social Control* (Figure 9.2). Laub and Sampson relied on the data originally collected by the Gluecks more than 50 years before. Using modern statistical analysis, Laub and Sampson relied on these data to formulate a life course/developmental view of crime.[66] Some of the principles of age-graded theory are listed below:

- Individual traits and childhood experiences are important to understand the onset of delinquent and criminal behavior. But these alone cannot explain the continuity of crime into adulthood.
- Experiences in young adulthood and beyond can redirect criminal transitions. In some cases people can be turned in a positive direction, while in others negative life experiences can be harmful and injurious.

EXHIBIT 9.2

Principal Life Course Theories

Name Social Development Model (SDM)

Principal Theorists J. David Hawkins, Richard Catalano

Major Premise Community-level risk factors make some people susceptible to antisocial behaviors. Preexisting risk factors are either reinforced or neutralized by socialization. To control the risk of antisocial behavior, a child must maintain prosocial bonds. Over the life course, involvement in prosocial or antisocial behavior determines the quality of attachments. Commitment and attachment to conventional institutions, activities, and beliefs insulate youths from the criminogenic influences in their environment. The prosocial path inhibits deviance by strengthening bonds to prosocial others and activities. Without the proper level of bonding, adolescents can succumb to the influence of deviant others.

Name Interactional Theory

Principal Theorists Terence Thornberry, Marvin Krohn, Alan Lizotte, Margaret Farnworth

Major Premise The onset of crime can be traced to a deterioration of the social bond during adolescence, marked by

weakened attachment to parents, commitment to school, and belief in conventional values. The cause of crime and delinquency is bidirectional: weak bonds lead kids to develop friendships with deviant peers and get involved in delinquency. Frequent delinquency involvement further weakens bonds and makes it difficult to reestablish conventional ones. Delinquency-promoting factors tend to reinforce one another and sustain a chronic criminal career. Kids who go through stressful life events such as a family financial crisis are more likely to later get involved in antisocial behaviors and vice versa. Criminality is a developmental process that takes on different meaning and form as a person matures. During early adolescence, attachment to the family is critical; by mid-adolescence, the influence of the family is replaced by friends, school, and youth culture; by adulthood, a person's behavioral choices are shaped by his or her place in conventional society and his or her own nuclear family. Although crime is influenced by these social forces, it also influences these processes and associations. Therefore, crime and social processes are interactional.

SOURCES: Terence Thornberry, "Toward an Interactional Theory of Delinquency," *Criminology* 25 (1987): 863–891; Richard Catalano and J. David Hawkins, "The Social Development Model: A Theory of Antisocial Behavior," in *Delinquency and Crime: Current Theories*, ed. J. David Hawkins (New York: Cambridge University Press, 1996), pp. 149–197.

- Repeat negative experiences create a condition called cumulative disadvantage. Serious problems in adolescence undermine life chances and reduce employability and social relations. People who increase their cumulative disadvantage risk continue offending.
- Positive life experiences and relationships can help a person become reattached to society and allow him or her to *knife off* from a criminal career path.
- Positive life experiences such as gaining employment, getting married, or joining the military create informal social control mechanisms that limit criminal behavior opportunities. These elements of informal social control are called *turning points in crime*.
- Two critical elements of informal social control/turning points are marriage and career. Adolescents who are at risk for crime can live conventional lives if they can find good jobs, achieve successful military careers, or enter into a successful marriage. Turning points may be serendipitous and unexpected: success may hinge on a lucky break; someone takes a chance on them; they win the lottery.
- Another vital feature that helps people desist from crime is "human agency" or the purposeful execution of choice and free will. Former delinquents may choose to go straight and develop a new sense of self and an identity. They can choose to desist from crime and become family men and hard workers.[67]
- While some people persist in crime simply because they find it lucrative or perhaps because it serves as an outlet

for their frustrations, others choose not to participate because as human beings they find other, more conventional paths more beneficial and rewarding. Human choice cannot be left out of the equation.

Trajectories, Transitions, and Turning Points One of Laub and Sampson's most important contributions is identifying the life events that enable adult offenders to desist from crime. According to them, trajectories are long-term patterns in life, while transitions are "short-term events embedded in trajectories."[68] Both transitions and trajectories can have a positive or negative connotation. A positive transition, for example, might include graduating from college and getting a good job; a negative trajectory might be joining a gang.

A major concept in the Sampson and Laub theory is that criminal careers are a dynamic process in which an important life event can (a) produce a transition in the life course, and (b) change the direction of a person's life course trajectory; they refer to these as **turning points**. Two critical turning points are marriage and career. Adolescents who are at risk for crime can live conventional lives if they can find good jobs or achieve successful careers. Even those

turning points According to Laub and Sampson, the life events that alter the development of a criminal career.

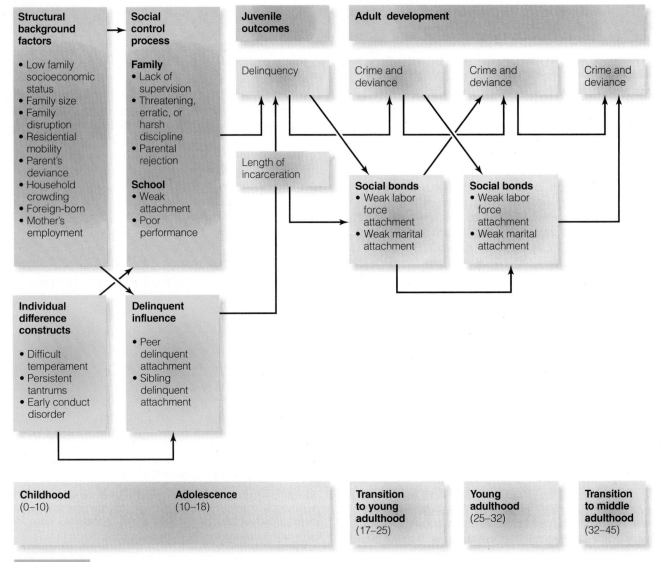

FIGURE 9.2 Sampson and Laub's Age-Graded Theory

SOURCE: Reprinted by permission of the publisher from Robert Sampson and John Laub, *Crime in the Making: Pathways and Turning Points Through Life* (Cambridge, MA: Harvard University Press, Copyright © 1993 by the President and Fellows of Harvard College), pp. 244–245. All rights reserved.

who have been in trouble with the law may turn from crime if employers are willing to give them a chance despite their records.

Cumulative Disadvantage According to age-graded theory, some people experience repeated and varied social problems that weigh down their life chances. Nor do their

cumulative disadvantage A condition in which repeated negative experiences in adolescence undermine life chances and reduce employability and social relations. People who increase their cumulative disadvantage risk continued offending.

social problems simply go away as they mature; they linger and vex people throughout their lives. Miscues accumulated in childhood hurt people further down the life path—for example, kids who get arrested are less likely to find jobs as adults.[69] People who acquire this **cumulative disadvantage** are more likely to commit criminal acts and become crime victims themselves.[70] When faced with personal crisis, they lack the social supports that can help them reject deviant solutions to their problems and instead maintain a conventional behavior trajectory.

Acquiring disadvantage begins at an early age. Adolescents whose parents have a criminal record, were convicted of crime, and suffered incarceration are more likely to become law violators themselves.[71] Parental incarceration erases social capital and escalates cumulative disadvantage: it reduces family income, gives kids the opportunity to gain antisocial peers, and subjects them to negative labels and stigma.[72] That is not their only problem: people who accumulate disadvantages are also more likely to become the target of criminal victimization.[73]

Social Capital Social scientists recognize that people build **social capital**—positive relations with individuals and institutions that are life sustaining. Laub and Sampson view the development of social capital as essential for desistance. In the same manner that building financial capital improves the chances for personal success, building social capital supports conventional behavior and inhibits deviant behavior. A successful marriage creates social capital when it improves a person's stature, creates feelings of self-worth, and encourages people to trust the individual. A successful career inhibits crime by creating a stake in conformity; why commit crime when you are doing well at your job? The relationship is reciprocal. If people are chosen to be employees, they return the favor by doing the best job possible; if they are chosen as spouses, they blossom into devoted partners. In contrast, people who fail to accumulate social capital are more prone to commit criminal acts.[74]

The fact that social capital influences the trajectory of a criminal career underscores the life course view that events that occur in later adolescence and adulthood do in fact influence behavior choices. Life events that occur in adulthood can help either terminate or sustain deviant careers.

Testing Age-Graded Theory There have been a number of research efforts that support the basic assumptions of age-graded theory:

- Empirical research now shows that, as predicted by Sampson and Laub, people change over the life course and that the factors that predict crime in adolescence, such as a weak bond to parents, may have less of an impact on adult crime when other factors, such as marriage and family, take on greater importance.[75]
- Criminality appears to be dynamic and is affected both by the erosion of informal social control and by interaction with antisocial influences. Accumulating deviant peers helps sustain criminality: the more deviant friends one accumulates over time, the more likely one is to maintain a criminal career.[76]
- As levels of cumulative disadvantage increase, crime-resisting elements of social life are impaired. Adolescents who are convicted of crime at an early age are more likely to develop antisocial attitudes later in life. They later develop low educational achievement, declining occupational status, and unstable employment records.[77] People who get involved with the justice system as adolescents may find that their career paths are blocked well into adulthood.[78] The relationship is reciprocal: men who are unemployed or underemployed report higher criminal participation rates than employed men.[79]
- Criminal career trajectories can be reversed if life conditions improve and they gain social capital.[80] First,

communities that can provide social capital opportunities such as a stable work environment that creates job prospects have lower rates of crime and victimization than areas that lack the ability to improve life chances.[81] Second, kids whose life circumstances improve because their parents escape poverty and move to these more attractive environments find that they can knife off from criminal trajectories.[82] Relocating may place them in better educational environments where they can have a positive high school experience, facilitated by occupationally oriented course work, small class size, and positive peer climates; having a positive school experience has been shown to be one of the most important factors that helps people knife off from crime.[83]

- Gaining social capital helps with behavior reversal.[84] As predicted by Laub and Sampson, those who enter the military, serve overseas, and receive veterans' benefits enhance their occupational status (social capital) while reducing criminal involvement.[85] Similarly, people who are fortunate enough to obtain high-quality jobs are likely to reduce their criminal activities even if they had a prior history of offending.[86]

The Marriage Factor

Age-graded theory places a lot of emphasis on the stability brought about by romantic relationships. People headed toward a life of crime can knife off that path if they meet the right mate, fall in love, and get married.[87] Even unstable marriages appear to reduce conviction frequency, at least while they last.[88] The marriage benefit is intergenerational: children who grow up in two-parent families are more likely to later have happy marriages themselves than children who are the product of divorced or never-married parents. If people with marital problems are more crime prone, their children will also suffer a greater long-term risk of marital failure and antisocial activity.[89]

Sometimes it is tough to get married and stay married when life circumstances are chaotic, especially when people are in trouble with the law. Kids who get involved with police during adolescence are also the ones most likely to experience financial hardship during young adulthood, which, in turn, decreases the odds of entering into a stable marriage.[90] However, for those people who can form a stable relationship despite having prior police contact, the effects can be dramatic. When Elaine Eggleston Doherty and Margaret Ensminger analyzed the relationship between marriage and official arrest they found strong evidence of a marriage effect: men experienced a reduction in offending between 21 percent and 36 percent when in a state of marriage.[91]

social capital Positive relations with individuals and institutions that are life sustaining.

Why Does Marriage Work? Why does domestic bliss help people desist from crime? Marriage both transforms people and reduces their opportunity to commit crimes. It helps cut off a person's past, provides new relationships, creates new levels of supervision, and helps the former offender develop structured routines focused on family life. Happy marriages are life sustaining, and marital quality can even improve over time (as people work less and have fewer parental responsibilities). Spending time in marital and family activities also reduces exposure to deviant peers, which in turn reduces the opportunity to become involved in criminal activities.[92] As Mark Warr states:

> For many individuals, it seems, marriage marks a transition from heavy peer involvement to a preoccupation with one's spouse. That transition is likely to reduce interaction with former friends and accomplices and

thereby reduce the opportunities as well as the motivation to engage in crime.[93]

Researchers Alex Piquero, John MacDonald, and Karen Parker tracked 524 men in their late teens and early 20s for seven years after they were paroled from the California Youth Authority during the 1970s and 1980s. They found that former offenders were far less likely to return to crime if they settled down into the routines of a solid marriage. People who get married are more likely to have nine-to-five jobs, come home for dinner, take care of children if they have them, watch television, go to bed, and repeat that cycle over and over again. Single people have a lot of free time to do what they want, especially if they are not employed. There's something about crossing the line of getting married that helps these men stay away from crime.[94]

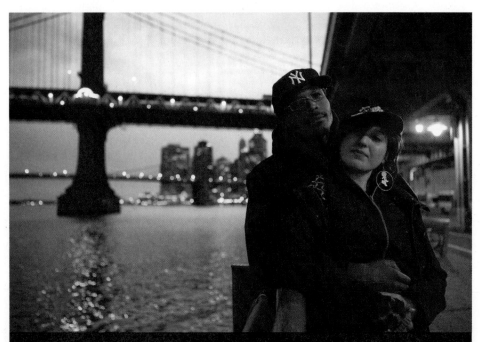

Homeless youth Griffin Kinard and Melissa Castillo are in love. Griffin, 21, has been a poet and writer for the past five years. Photographed under the FDR expressway on the Lower East Side, this is a neighborhood he called home when living in an East Village residential program. Born in Brooklyn, Griffin spent his childhood and teenage years in a series of state institutions—residence programs for at-risk youths such as Children's Village in Dobbs Ferry, New York, and Green Chimneys in Brewster, New York. During the last four years before aging out of the system, he found himself back in New York City, finishing high school while living in a Salvation Army group home for boys, the East Village Residency. A seven-month stint in jail was followed by his 21st birthday—and a new commitment to writing. He is a senior writer at *Represent Magazine*, a bimonthly publication for and by youth in foster care by the nonprofit Youth Communication (http://www.youthcomm.org). Griffin stays at his older sister's home in Harlem most nights, with occasional stints in drop-in shelters when the siblings argue. For the past five months, Melissa Castillo, 20, and Griffin have been a couple. Herself recovering from a history of institutionalization in group homes and psychiatric programs, Melissa for the first time in her life feels like she can love and trust somebody, and she also appreciates the help and guidance Griffin's sister Salina can provide. The young couple fantasizes about getting married and getting a place of their own. Do you agree with Sampson and Laub that if they marry, it would it help them live a more conventional lifestyle? Or can there be obstacles that Laub and Sampson did not foresee?

Katja Heinemann/Do1 Thing.org/Redux

What Happens When It Ends? However, things don't always work out as planned and many relationships end in a breakup: an estimated 40 to 50 percent of first marriages, 67 percent of second marriages, and 74 percent of third marriages end in divorce. And while a happy marriage can reduce crime, separation and divorce seem to have an opposite effect. Both men and women have a greater likelihood of arrest when divorced (or legally separated) compared with when they were married.[95]

Recently, Bianca Bersani and Elaine Eggleston Doherty evaluated the divorce effect with a sample of 3,000 people.[96] They found that the detrimental effects of divorce are long lasting and not related to the immediate turmoil that ended the marriage. The length of marriage had a big effect on its aftermath: the detrimental effects of divorce seem to be most pronounced for longer marriages, prompting an immediate increase in offending. In contrast, offending rates are statistically similar during and after marriage married and when divorced among those people involved in short marriages, especially if they dissolve prior to the first anniversary. However, among the short-marriage group, offending rates are significantly higher when married compared with when single. It's possible, they speculate, that "bad marriages," those that are doomed to quickly fail, are criminogenic and may increase rather than decrease antisocial behaviors—or conversely, the most anti-social people enter quickly into doomed marriages. In either event, not all marriages are the same, but those who can find the right mate and stick with them for the duration are also the people most likely to live happier, crime-free lives.

Age-Graded Theory Validity

Despite the theory's popularity and importance, a number of issues remain to be proved scientifically. One is the causal ordering of the associations. For example, age-graded theory assumes that people who get married reduce their criminal activity. It is also possible that people who are aging out of crime, who want to end their criminal way of life, are ready to get married and settle down. Recent research by Torkild Hovde Lyngstad and Torbjørn Skard-hamar, conducted in Norway, finds that men significantly reduce their criminal involvements before they get married, and once married actually increase their involvement in illegal behavior.[97] Further research is needed on the time order of this important association.

Probably the most important issue that must be addressed is whether the relationships that underpin age-graded theory are still valid today. Laub and Sampson's theory relies heavily on the Glueck data collected more than 50 years ago. The Glueck sample lived in a world that was quite different from contemporary society: they did not watch violent video games or TV shows; they used alcohol but were not part of a drug culture; marriage was the norm and the divorce rate was much lower; globalization and wide-scale job loss were not issues. It is possible that getting involved in the drug culture has a much more damaging effect today than when the Gluecks collected their data.[98] Similarly, joining the military may have a significantly different meaning and produce different effects today than it did for the men in the Glueck sample.[99] An important research task, then, is to determine whether the theory's basic premises are still valid considering these structural changes in society.

To answer some of these questions, Laub and Sampson contacted the surviving members of the Glueck cohort. Some of their findings are discussed in the Criminology in Action feature, on the next page, "Shared Beginnings, Divergent Lives."

 To read an assessment of age-graded theory by Sampson, Laub, and Gary Sweeten, go to **http://books .google.com/books?id=_ojaQpx60uUC&pg=PA313.**

PROPENSITY/LATENT TRAIT THEORIES

LO7 Interpret the terms *propensity* and *latent trait*

In a critical 1990 article, David Rowe, D. Wayne Osgood, and W. Alan Nicewander proposed the concept of latent traits to explain the flow of crime over the life cycle. Their model assumes that a number of people in the population have a personal attribute or characteristic that controls their inclination or **propensity** to commit crimes.[100] This disposition, or **latent trait**, may be either present at birth or established early in life, and it can remain stable over time. Suspected latent traits include defective intelligence, damaged or impulsive personality, genetic abnormalities, the physical-chemical functioning of the brain, and environmental influences on brain function such as drugs, chemicals, and injuries.[101] Some of these master traits are inflexible, stable, and unchanging throughout a person's lifetime; others can be altered, influenced, or changed by experiences and interactions (Exhibit 9.3).

Regardless of gender or environment, those who possess one or more of these latent traits may be at risk to crime and in danger of becoming career criminals; those who lack the propensity to commit crime have a much lower risk.[102] Because the propensity to commit crime is stable over the life course, people who are antisocial during adolescence are the most likely to develop criminal careers. This view is contrary to the life course/state dependence view that life events influence behavior and that what drives people in adolescence may have little influence in adulthood.

EXHIBIT 9.3

Two Types of Latent Traits

Constant Latent Trait	Evolving Latent Trait
Inflexible	Flexible
Unchanging	Varying
Influenced by psychological and biological traits and conditions	Influenced by human interaction, personal relationships, contact, and associations

SOURCE: © Cengage Learning®

propensity An inclination or tendency to behave in a particular way.

latent trait A stable feature, characteristic, property, or condition, present at birth or soon after, that makes some people crime prone over the life course.

SHARED BEGINNINGS, DIVERGENT LIVES

Why are some delinquents destined to become persistent criminals as adults? John Laub and Robert Sampson have conducted a follow-up to their reanalysis of Sheldon Glueck and Eleanor Glueck's study that matched 500 delinquent boys with 500 nondelinquents. The individuals in the original sample were reinterviewed by the Gluecks at ages 25 and 32. Sampson and Laub located and interviewed the survivors of the delinquent sample, the oldest 70 years old and the youngest 62.

Persistence and Desistance

Laub and Sampson find that delinquency and other forms of antisocial conduct in childhood are strongly related to adult delinquency and drug and alcohol abuse. Former delinquents also suffer consequences in other areas of social life, such as school, work, and family life. For example, delinquents are far less likely to finish high school than are nondelinquents and subsequently are more likely to be unemployed, receive welfare, and experience separation or divorce as adults.

In their latest research, Laub and Sampson address one of the key questions posed by life course theories: is it possible for former delinquents to turn their lives around as adults? They find that most antisocial children do not remain antisocial as adults. For example, of men in the study cohort who survived to age 50, 24 percent had no arrests for delinquent acts of violence and property after age 17 (6 percent had no arrests for total delinquency); 48 percent had no arrests for predatory delinquency after age 25 (19 percent for total delinquency); 60 percent had no arrests for predatory delinquency after age 31 (33 percent for total delinquency); and 79 percent had no arrests for predatory delinquency after age 40 (57 percent for total delinquency). They conclude that desistance from delinquency is the norm and that most, if not all, serious delinquents desist from delinquency.

Why Do Delinquents Desist?

Laub and Sampson's earlier research indicated that building social capital through marriage and jobs was a key component of desistance from delinquency.

However, in this new round of research, Laub and Sampson were able to find out more about long-term desistance by interviewing 52 men as they approached age 70. The follow-up showed a dramatic drop in criminal activity as the men aged. Between the ages of 17 and 24, 84 percent of the subjects had committed violent crimes; in their 30s and 40s, that number dropped to 14 percent; it fell to just 3 percent as the men reached their 60s and 70s. Property crimes and alcohol- and drug-related crimes also showed significant decreases. They found that men who desisted from crime were rooted in structural routines and had strong social ties to family and community. Drawing on the men's own words, they found that one important element for "going straight" is the "knifing off" of individuals from their immediate environment and offering the men a new script for the future. Joining the military can provide this knifing-off effect, as does marriage or changing one's residence. One former delinquent (age 69) told them:

> I'd say the turning point was, number one, the Army. You get into an outfit, you had a sense of belonging, you made your friends. I think I

How Can the Aging Out Process Be Explained?

Because latent traits are stable, people who are antisocial during adolescence are the most likely to persist in crime. The positive association between past and future criminality detected in the cohort studies of career criminals reflects the presence of this underlying stable criminal propensity. That is, if an impulsive personality contributes to delinquency in childhood, it should also cause the same people to offend as adults because personality traits remain stable over the life span. According to the concept of population heterogeneity, people are born with the propensity to commit crime and this propensity will disrupt normal socialization. Disruptions in socialization thereafter increase the risk of prolonged antisocial behavior. In this view, early rule breaking increases the probability of future rule breaking because it weakens inhibitions to crime and strengthens criminal

motivation. In other words, once kids get a taste of antisocial behavior, they like it and want to continue down a deviant path.[103]

How then can a latent trait theorist explain the fact that many people commit less crime as they mature? It's possible that the decline in criminal activity may not be a valid indicator of real behavioral change. Why does this illusion exist? Whereas the propensity to commit crime is stable, the opportunity to commit crime fluctuates over time. People may appear to age out of crime as they mature and develop simply because there are fewer opportunities to commit crimes and greater inducements to remain straight. They may marry, have children, and obtain jobs. The former delinquents' newfound adult responsibilities leave them little time to hang with their friends, abuse substances, and get into scrapes with the law. So while their propensity to commit crime remains stable, their opportunity to commit crime has changed.

became a pretty good judge of character. In the Army, you met some good ones, you met some foul balls. Then I met the wife. I'd say probably that would be the turning point. Got married, then naturally, kids come. So now you got to get a better job, you got to make more money. And that's how I got to the Navy Yard and tried to improve myself.

Former delinquents who went straight were able to put structure into their lives. Structure often led the men to disassociate from delinquent peers, reducing the opportunity to get into trouble. Getting married, for example, may limit the number of nights men can "hang with the guys." As one wife of a former delinquent said, "It is not how many beers you have, it's who you drink with." Even multiple offenders who did time in prison were able to desist with the help of a stabilizing marriage.

Former delinquents who can turn their life around, who have acquired a degree of maturity by taking on family and work responsibilities, and who have forged new commitments are the ones most likely to make a fresh start and find new direction and meaning in life. It seems that men who desisted changed their identity as well, and this, in turn, affected their outlook and sense of maturity and responsibility. The ability to change did not reflect delinquency "specialty": violent offenders followed the same path as property offenders.

While many former delinquents desisted from delinquency, they still faced the risk of an early and untimely death. Thirteen percent (N=62) of the delinquent as compared to only 6 percent (N=28) of the nondelinquent subjects died unnatural deaths such as violence, cirrhosis of the liver caused by alcoholism, poor self-care, suicide, and so on. By age 65, 29 percent (N=139) of the delinquent and 21 percent (N=95) of the nondelinquent subjects had died from natural causes. Frequent delinquent involvement in adolescence and alcohol abuse were the strongest predictors of an early and unnatural death. So while many troubled youth are able to reform, their early excesses may haunt them across their life span.

Policy Implications

Laub and Sampson find that social problems—delinquency, substance abuse, violence, dropping out, teen pregnancy—often share common risk characteristics. Intervention strategies, therefore, should consider a broad array of antisocial, criminal, and deviant behaviors and not limit the focus to just one subgroup or delinquency type. Because criminality and other social problems are linked, early prevention efforts that reduce delinquency will probably also reduce alcohol abuse, drunk driving, drug abuse, sexual promiscuity, and family violence. The best way to achieve these goals is through four significant life-changing events: marriage, joining the military, getting a job, and changing one's environment or neighborhood. What appears to be important about these processes is that they all involve, to varying degrees, the following items: a knifing off of the past from the present, new situations that provide both supervision and monitoring as well as new opportunities of social support and growth, and new situations that provide the opportunity for transforming identity. Prevention of delinquency must be a policy at all times and at all stages of life.

Critical Thinking

1. Do you believe that the factors that influenced the men in the original Glueck sample are still relevant for change? For example, considering the high current divorce rate, is marriage still a stabilizing force?

2. Recent reports show that male U.S. veterans are twice as likely to die by suicide than people with no military service, and are more likely to kill themselves with a gun than others who commit suicide. Considering this recent finding, do you agree with Laub and Sampson that military service might be beneficial and help troubled kids turn their lives around?

SOURCES: John Laub and Robert Sampson, *Shared Beginnings, Divergent Lives: Delinquent Boys to Age 70* (Cambridge, MA: Harvard University Press, 2003); John Laub and Robert Sampson, "Understanding Desistance from Delinquency," in *Delinquency and Justice: An Annual Review of Research,* Vol. 28, ed. Michael Tonry (Chicago: University of Chicago Press, 2001), pp. 1–71; John Laub and George Vaillant, "Delinquency and Mortality: A 50-Year Follow-Up Study of 1,000 Delinquent and Non-delinquent Boys," *American Journal of Psychiatry* 157 (2000): 96–102.

To understand this concept of stable criminal propensity better, assume that intelligence as measured by IQ tests is a latent trait associated with crime. Intelligence remains unvarying and unchanging over the life course, but crime rates decline with age. How can latent trait theory explain this phenomenon? Teenagers have more opportunity to commit crime than adults, so at every level of intelligence, adolescent crime rates will be higher. As they mature, however, teens with both high and low IQs will commit less crime because their adult responsibilities provide them with fewer criminal opportunities. They may get married and raise a family, get a job, and buy a home. And like most people, as they age they lose strength and vigor, qualities necessary to commit crime. Though their IQ remains stable and their propensity to commit crime is unchanged, their living environment and physical condition have undergone radical change. Even if they wanted to engage in criminal activities, the former delinquents may lack the opportunity and energy to do so.

Crime and Human Nature

LO8 Discuss Wilson and Herrnstein's views on crime and human nature

Latent trait theorists were encouraged when two prominent social scientists, James Q. Wilson and Richard Herrnstein, published *Crime and Human Nature* in 1985 and suggested that personal traits—such as genetic makeup, intelligence, and body build—may outweigh the importance of social variables as predictors of criminal activity.[104]

According to Wilson and Herrnstein, all human behavior, including criminality, is determined by its perceived consequences. A criminal incident occurs when an individual chooses criminal over conventional behavior (referred to as *noncrime*) after weighing the potential gains and losses of each: "The larger the ratio of net rewards of crime to the net rewards of noncrime, the greater the tendency to commit the crime."[105]

EXHIBIT 9.4

Some Important Latent Trait Theories

Name Integrated Cognitive Antisocial Potential (ICAP) Theory

Principal Theorist David Farrington

Latent Trait Antisocial potential

Major Premise People maintain a range of *antisocial potential* (AP), the potential to commit antisocial acts. AP can be viewed as both a long- and short-term phenomenon. Those with high levels of long-term AP are at risk for offending over the life course; those with low AP levels live more conventional lives. Though AP levels are fairly consistent over time, they peak in the teenage years because of the effects of maturational factors—such as increase in peer influence and decrease in family influence—that directly affect crime rates. Long-term AP can be reduced by life-changing events such as marriage. There is also short-term AP when immediate life events may increase a personal antisocial potential so that, in the immediate moment, people may advance their location on the AP continuum. For example, a person with a relatively low long-term AP may suffer a temporary amplification if he is bored, angry, drunk, or frustrated. According to the ICAP theory, the commission of offenses and other types of antisocial acts depends on the interaction between the individual (with his immediate level of AP) and the social environment (especially criminal opportunities and victims).

Name Differential Coercion Theory

Principal Theorist Mark Colvin

Latent Trait Perceptions of coercion

Major Premise Perceptions of coercion begin early in life when children experience punitive forms of discipline—both physical attacks and psychological coercion, including negative commands, critical remarks, teasing, humiliation, whining, yelling, and threats. Through these destructive family interchanges, coercion becomes ingrained and guides reactions to adverse situations that arise in both family and nonfamily settings.

There are two sources of coercion: interpersonal and impersonal. Interpersonal coercion is direct, involving the use or threat of force and intimidation from parents, peers, and significant others. Impersonal coercion involves pressures beyond individual control, such as economic and social pressure caused by unemployment, poverty, or competition among businesses or other groups. High levels of coercion produce criminality, especially when the episodes of coercive behavior are inconsistent and random, because this teaches people that they cannot control their lives. Chronic offenders grew up in homes where parents used erratic control and applied it in an inconsistent fashion.

Name Control Balance Theory

Principal Theorist Charles Tittle

Latent Trait Control/balance

Major Premise The concept of control has two distinct elements: the amount of control one is subject to by others and the amount of control one can exercise over others. Conformity results when these two elements are in balance; control imbalances produce deviant and criminal behaviors.

Those people who sense a deficit of control turn to three types of behavior to restore balance:

- *Predation* involves direct forms of physical violence, such as robbery, sexual assault, or other forms of assault.
- *Defiance* challenges control mechanisms but stops short of physical harm: for example, vandalism, curfew violations, and unconventional sex.
- *Submission* involves passive obedience to the demands of others, such as submitting to physical or sexual abuse without response.

An excess of control can result in crimes of (a) *exploitation*, which involves using others to commit crimes, such as contract killers or drug runners, (b) *plunder*, which involves using power without regard for others, such as committing a hate crime or polluting the environment, or (c) *decadence*, which involves spur of the moment, irrational acts such as child molesting.

SOURCES: David P. Farrington, "Developmental and Life-Course Criminology: Key Theoretical and Empirical Issues," Sutherland Award address presented at the annual meeting of the American Society of Criminology, Chicago, November 2002, revised March 2003; Charles Tittle, *Control Balance: Toward a General Theory of Deviance* (Boulder, CO: Westview Press, 1995); Mark Colvin, *Crime and Coercion: An Integrated Theory of Chronic Criminality* (New York: Palgrave Press, 2000).

Wilson and Herrnstein's model assumes that both biological and psychological traits influence the crime–noncrime choice. They see a close link between a person's decision to choose crime and such biosocial factors as low intelligence, mesomorphic body type, genetic influences (parental criminality), and possessing an autonomic nervous system that

General Theory of Crime (GTC) According to Gottfredson and Hirschi, a developmental theory that modifies social control theory by integrating concepts from biosocial, psychological, routine activities, and rational choice theories.

responds too quickly to stimuli. Psychological traits, such as an impulsive or extroverted personality or generalized hostility, also determine the potential to commit crime.

In their focus on the association between these constitutional and psychological factors and crime, Wilson and Herrnstein seem to be suggesting the existence of an elusive latent trait that predisposes people to commit crime.[106] Their vision helped inspire other criminologists to identify the elusive latent trait that causes criminal behavior. The most prominent latent trait theory is Gottfredson and Hirschi's **General Theory of Crime (GTC)**. Exhibit 9.4 discusses some other important contributions to the latent trait model.

General Theory of Crime

LO9 Explain the basic principles of the General Theory of Crime

In their important work *A General Theory of Crime*, Michael Gottfredson and Travis Hirschi link the propensity to commit crime to two latent traits: an impulsive personality and a lack of self-control.[107]

Gottfredson and Hirschi attribute the tendency to commit crimes to a person's level of **self-control**. People with limited self-control tend to be impulsive; they are insensitive to other people's feelings, physical (rather than mental), risk takers, shortsighted, and nonverbal.[108] They have a here-and-now orientation and refuse to work for distant goals; they lack diligence, tenacity, and persistence. People lacking self-control tend to be adventuresome, active, and self-centered. As they mature, they often have unstable marriages, jobs, and friendships.[109] They are less likely to feel shame if they engage in deviant acts and are more likely to find them pleasurable.[110] They are also more likely to engage in dangerous behaviors such as drinking, smoking, and reckless driving; all of these behaviors are associated with criminality (see Exhibit 9.5 for a list of factors that indicate low self-control).[111]

Because those with low self-control enjoy risky, exciting, or thrilling behaviors with immediate gratification, they are more likely to enjoy criminal acts, which require stealth, agility, speed, and power, than conventional acts, which demand long-term study and cognitive and verbal skills. As Gottfredson and Hirschi put it, they derive satisfaction from "money without work, sex without courtship, revenge without court delays."[112] Many of these individuals who have a propensity for committing crime also engage in other risky, impulsive behaviors such as smoking, drinking, gambling, and illicit sexuality.[113] Although these acts are not illegal, they too provide immediate, short-term gratification.

What Causes Impulsivity? Gottfredson and Hirschi trace the root cause of poor self-control to inadequate childrearing practices that begin soon after birth and can influence neural development. Parents who refuse or are

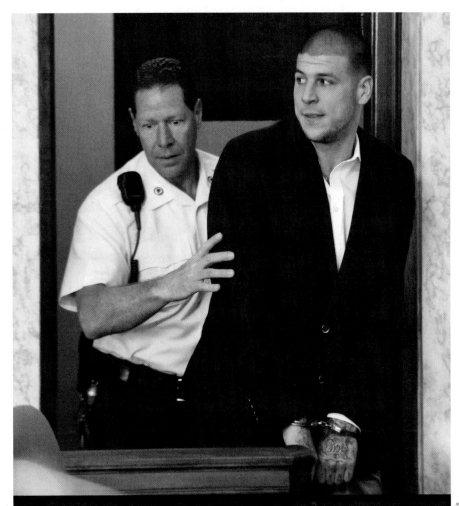

Former New England Patriots NFL football player Aaron Hernandez is led into court in Attleboro, Massachusetts, August 22, 2013, to face murder charges. What would motivate such a successful athlete, who had recently signed a long-term multimillion-dollar contract to commit a heinous crime? Can we simply say he was impulsive and lacked self-control? Or must there be other forces at work here?

AP Images/Josh Reynolds

EXHIBIT 9.5

The Elements of Impulsivity: Signs that a Person Has Low Self-Control

- Insensitive
- Physical
- Shortsighted
- Nonverbal
- Here-and-now orientation
- Unstable social relations
- Enjoys deviant behaviors
- Risk-taker
- Refuses to work for distant goals

- Lacks diligence
- Lacks tenacity
- Adventuresome
- Self-centered
- Shameless
- Imprudent
- Lacks cognitive and verbal skills
- Enjoys danger and excitement

SOURCE: © Cengage Learning®

self-control A strong moral sense that renders a person incapable of hurting others or violating social norms.

CONNECTIONS

In his original version of control theory, discussed in Chapter 7, Hirschi focused on the social controls that attach people to conventional society and insulate them from criminality. In this newer work, he concentrates on self-control as a stabilizing force. The two views are connected, however, because both social control (or social bonds) and self-control are acquired through early experiences with effective parenting.

unable to monitor a child's behavior, to recognize deviant behavior when it occurs, and to punish that behavior will produce children who lack self-control. Children who are not attached to their parents, who are poorly supervised, and whose parents are criminal or deviant themselves are the most likely to develop poor self-control.[114] Even in disadvantaged communities, children whose parents provide adequate and supportive discipline are the ones most likely to develop self-control.[115]

The association between poor parenting and children's antisocial behavior may be both reciprocal and intergenerational. Kids who have low self-control may strain parental attachments and the ability of parents to control children. Parents who themselves have low self-control are the ones most likely to use damaging and inappropriate supervision and punishment mechanisms. Impulsive kids grow up to become poor parents who themselves use improper discipline, producing yet another generation of impulsive kids who lack self-control.[116]

Low self-control may also have a biological basis. Measures of neuropsychological deficits, birth complications, and low birth weight have all been found to have significant direct or indirect effects on levels of self-control.[117] Recent research shows that children who suffer anoxia (oxygen starvation) during birth are the ones most likely to lack self-control later in life, suggesting that impulsivity may have a biological basis.[118] When Kevin Beaver and his associates examined impulsive personality and self-control in twin pairs, they discovered evidence that these traits may be inherited rather than developed. That might explain the stability of these latent traits over the life course.[119]

Crime Rate Variations If individual differences are stable over the life course, why do crime rates vary? Why do people commit less crime as they age? Why are some regions more crime prone than others? Why are some groups more crime prone than others? Does that mean there are between-group differences in self-control? If male crime rates are higher than female rates, does that mean men are more impulsive and lacking in self-control? How does the GTC address these issues?

Gottfredson and Hirschi remind us that criminal propensity and criminal acts are separate concepts (Figure 9.3). On the one hand, criminal acts, such as robberies or burglaries, are illegal events or deeds that offenders engage in when they perceive them to be advantageous. Burglaries are typically committed by young males looking for cash, liquor, and entertainment; the crime provides "easy, short-term gratification."[120] Crime is rational and predictable: people commit crime when it promises rewards with minimal threat of pain; the threat of punishment can deter crime. If targets are well guarded, crime rates diminish. Only the truly irrational offender would dare to strike under those circumstances.

On the other hand, while criminal offenders are people predisposed to commit crimes, they are not robots who commit crime without restraint; their days are also filled with conventional behaviors, such as going to school, parties, concerts, and church. But given the same set of criminal opportunities, such as having a lot of free time for mischief and living in a neighborhood with unguarded homes containing valuable merchandise, crime-prone people have a

Criminal Offender

Impulsive personality
- Physical
- Insensitive
- Risk-taking
- Short-sighted
- Nonverbal

Low self-control
- Poor parenting
- Deviant parents
- Lack of supervision
- Active
- Self-centered

Weakening of social bonds
- Attachment
- Commitment
- Involvement
- Belief

Criminal Opportunity
- Presence of gangs
- Lack of supervision
- Lack of guardianship
- Suitable targets

Criminal/Deviant Act
- Delinquency
- Smoking
- Drinking
- Underage sex
- Crime

FIGURE 9.3 Gottfredson and Hirschi's General Theory of Crime much higher probability of violating the law than do non-criminals. The propensity to commit crimes remains stable throughout a person's life. Change in the frequency of criminal activity is purely a function of change in criminal opportunity.

If we accept this provision of the GTC, then both criminal propensity and criminal opportunity must be considered to explain criminal participation. So if males and females are equally impulsive but their crime rates vary, the explanation is that males have more opportunity to commit crime. Young teenage girls may be more closely monitored by their parents and therefore lack the freedom to offend. Girls are also socialized to have more self-control than boys: although females get angry as often as males, many have been taught to blame themselves for such feelings. Females are socialized to fear that anger will harm relationships; males are encouraged to react with "moral outrage," blaming others for their discomfort.[121]

Opportunity can also be used to explain ecological variation in the crime rate. How does the GTC explain the fact that crime rates are higher in the summer than the winter? The number of impulsive people lacking in self-control is no higher in August than it is in December. Gottfredson and Hirschi would argue that seasonal differences are explained by opportunity: during the summer kids are out of school and have more opportunity to commit crime. Similarly, if crime rates are higher in Los Angeles than Minneapolis, it is because either there are more criminal opportunities in this western city, or because the fast-paced life of L.A. attracts more impulsive people than the laid-back Midwest.

To read an article by Bruce J. Arneklev, Lori Elis, and Sandra Medlicott that tests the General Theory of Crime, go to http://wcr.sonoma.edu/v07n3/41 .arneklev/arneklev.pdf.

Self-Control and Crime   Gottfredson and Hirschi claim that the principles of **self-control theory** can explain all varieties of criminal behavior and all the social and behavioral correlates of crime. That is, such widely disparate crimes as burglary, robbery, embezzlement, drug dealing, murder, rape, and insider trading all stem from a deficiency of self-control. Likewise, gender, racial, and ecological differences in crime rates can be explained by discrepancies in self-control.

Unlike other theoretical models that explain only narrow segments of criminal behavior (i.e., teenage gang formation), Gottfredson and Hirschi argue that self-control applies equally to all crimes, ranging from murder to corporate theft. White-collar crime rates remain low, they claim, because people who lack self-control rarely attain the positions necessary to commit those crimes. However, the relatively few white-collar criminals have relatively less self-control than their law-abiding peers.

Empirical Support for GTC   Since the publication of *A General Theory of Crime*, numerous researchers have attempted to test the validity of Gottfredson and Hirschi's theoretical views.[122] The general consensus of this research is that people with low self-control and poor impulse control are the most likely to engage in serious crime.[123]

One approach has been to identify indicators of impulsiveness and self-control to determine whether these factors correlate with measures of criminal activity. As a group they suggest that the lower a person's self-control, the more likely they are to engage in antisocial behaviors.[124] Kids with low self-control are the ones most likely to fall in with a bad crowd, and once they do so their impulsivity makes them vulnerable to antisocial peer influence.[125] It is not surprising that career criminals have been shown to have significantly lower levels of self-control than non-offenders, and that the lower the level of a person's self-control, the greater his or her chance of becoming a career criminal.[126] Some studies have found self-control to be the strongest predictor of career criminality, exceeding the impact of age, race, ethnicity, gender, socioeconomic status, mental illness, attention deficit hyperactivity disorder diagnosis, and trauma experience.[127]

Analyzing the General Theory of Crime   By integrating the concepts of socialization and criminality, Gottfredson and Hirschi help explain why some people who lack self-control can escape criminality, and, conversely, why some people who have self-control might not escape. People who are at risk because they have impulsive personalities may forgo criminal careers because there are no criminal opportunities that satisfy their impulsive needs; instead, they may find other outlets for their impulsive personalities. In contrast, if the opportunity is strong enough, even people with relatively strong self-control may be tempted to violate the law; the incentives to commit crime may overwhelm self-control.

Integrating criminal propensity and criminal opportunity can explain why some children enter into chronic offending while others living in similar environments are able to resist criminal activity. It can also help us understand why the corporate executive with a spotless record gets caught up in business fraud. Even a successful executive may find self-control inadequate if the potential for illegal gain is large. The driven executive, accustomed to both academic and financial success, may find that the fear of failure can neutralize his or her self-control. During tough economic times, the impulsive manager who fears dismissal may be tempted to circumvent the law to improve the bottom line.[128]

self-control theory According to Gottfredson and Hirschi, the view that the cause of delinquent behavior is an impulsive personality. Kids who are impulsive may find that their bond to society is weak.

Shown here from a scene of *In the Blood*, Danny Trejo (left) was a child drug addict and criminal, in and out of jail for 11 years. While serving time in San Quentin, he won the light-weight and welterweight boxing titles. Imprisoned for armed robbery and drug offenses, he successfully completed a 12-step rehabilitation program that changed his life. While speaking at a Cocaine Anonymous meeting in 1985, Trejo met a young man who later called him for support. Trejo went to meet him at what turned out to be the set of *Runaway Train* (1985). Trejo was immediately offered a role as a convict extra, probably because of his tough tattooed appearance. Also on the set was a screenwriter who did time with Trejo in San Quentin. Remembering Trejo's boxing skills, the screenwriter offered him $350 per day to train the actors for a boxing match. Director Andrey Konchalovskiy saw Trejo training Eric Roberts and immediately offered him a featured role as Roberts's opponent in the film. Trejo has subsequently appeared in many other films, including *Con Air* and *Machete*, usually as a tough criminal or villain. Does Trejo's story indicate that a person can turn their life around if they get a break and can seize the opportunity? Does this contradict the General Theory of Crime?

Questions Remaining about the GTC Although the General Theory seems persuasive, several questions and criticisms remain unanswered. One of the most important issues is the assumption that criminal propensity does not change. Research shows that changing life circumstances, such as starting and leaving school, becoming a member of an antisocial peer group, abusing substances and then getting straight, and starting or ending personal relationships all influence the frequency of offending.[129] In addition, critics argue that the theory is tautological or involves circular reasoning: How do we know when people are impulsive? When they commit crimes! Are all criminals impulsive? Of course, or else they would not have broken the law![130] Gottfredson and Hirschi counter by saying that impulsivity is not itself a propensity to commit crime but a condition that inhibits people from appreciating the long-term consequences of their behavior. Consequently, if given the opportunity, they are more likely to indulge in criminal acts than their nonimpulsive counterparts.[131] According to Gottfredson and Hirschi, impulsivity and criminality are neither identical nor equivalent. Some impulsive people may channel their reckless energies into noncriminal activity, such as trading on the commodities markets or real estate speculation, and make a legitimate fortune for their efforts. Others, more impulsive, may bend the rules for their own benefit.

In addition to these basic issues, numerous studies have attempted to explain or address environmental and individual level differences in the crime rate and determine whether the GTC can explain why they occur:

- *Environmental differences.* The GTC fails to address ecological patterns in the crime rate. If crime rates are higher in Los Angeles than in Albany, New York, can it be assumed that residents of Los Angeles are more impulsive than residents of Albany? There is little evidence of regional differences in impulsivity or self-control. Can these differences be explained solely by variation in criminal opportunity? Gottfredson and Hirschi might counter that crime rate differences may reflect criminal opportunity: one area may have more effective law enforcement, more draconian laws, and higher levels of guardianship. In their view, opportunity is controlled by economy and culture. Environments may interact with personality to shape behaviors, a condition not foreseen by the GTC.[132] Take what criminologist Gregory Zimmerman found when he examined how environment and personality interact. In high-crime neighborhoods, being impulsive and lacking self-control is not associated with criminal behavior. In contrast, in low-crime, safer areas, impulsive kids are the ones most likely to commit criminal acts. How can this environmental effect be explained? In disadvantaged neighborhoods, crime is omnipresent, maintaining low self-control means relatively little. In contrast, in safer, low-crime areas, most kids conform and it's only the most impulsive ones, the few bad apples, who risk engaging in criminal acts. In stable neighborhoods, where legitimate opportunity abounds, only the most reckless kids are foolish enough to commit crime.[133] In sum, environment may influence criminal decision making, an observation that contradicts the GTC.

© Francisco Roman/Anchor Bay Films/courtesy Everett Collection

■ *Racial and gender differences.* Although distinct gender differences in the crime rate exist, there is little evidence that males are more impulsive than females (although females and males differ in many other personality traits).[134] Some research efforts have found gender differences in the association between self-control and crime; the theory predicts no such difference should occur.[135]

Looking at this relationship from another perspective, males who persist in crime exhibit characteristics that are different than female persisters. Women seem to be influenced by their place of residence, childhood and recent abuses, living with a criminal partner, selling drugs, stress, depression, fearfulness, their romantic relationships, their children, and whether they have suicidal thoughts. In contrast, men are more likely to persist because of their criminal peer associations, carrying weapons, alcohol abuse, and aggressive feelings. Impulsivity alone may not be able to explain why males and females persist or desist.[136]

Similarly, Gottfredson and Hirschi explain racial differences in the crime rate as a failure of childrearing practices in the African American community.[137] In so doing, they overlook issues of institutional racism, poverty, and relative deprivation, which have been shown to have a significant impact on crime rate differentials.

■ *Socialization differences.* A number of research efforts show that the quality of peer relations either enhances or controls criminal behavior and that these influences vary over time.[138] As children mature, peer influence continues to grow. Research shows that kids who lack self-control also have trouble maintaining relationships with law-abiding peers. They may either choose or be forced to seek out friends who are similarly limited in their ability to maintain self-control.[139] Similarly, as they mature they may seek out romantic relationships with law-violating boyfriends or girlfriends, and these entanglements enhance the likelihood that they will get further involved in crime (girls seem more deeply influenced by their delinquent boyfriends than boys by their delinquent girlfriends).[140] This finding contradicts the GTC, which suggests the influence of friends should be stable and unchanging and that a relationship established later in life (making deviant friends) should not influence criminal propensity. Gottfredson and Hirschi might counter that it should come as no surprise that impulsive kids, lacking in self-control, seek out peers with similar personality characteristics.

Gottfredson and Hirschi propose that children either develop self-control by the end of early childhood or fail to develop it at all. Research shows, however, that some kids who are predisposed toward delinquency may find their life circumstances improved and their involvement with antisocial behavior diminished if they are exposed to positive and effective parenting that appears later in life.[141] Parenting can influence self-control in later adolescence and kids who receive improved parenting may improve their self-control much later in the life course than predicted by the GTC.[142]

■ *Personality differences.* Not all people have similar personalities and not all criminals are impulsive.[143] The personality is too complex to suggest that only a single element can account for antisocial behavior. There is too much variety in personality traits, ranging from psychopathy to decision-making style to say that a single element is responsible for all crimes.[144]

Despite this evidence, Gottfredson and Hirschi assume that criminals all share certain personality traits: they are impatient or "present-oriented"; they choose to commit crime because the rewards can be enjoyed immediately while the costs or punishments are delayed. However, Steven Levitt and Sudhir Alladi Venkatesh found that many young gang boys are willing to wait years to "rise through the ranks" before becoming gang leaders and earning high wages. Their stay in the gang is fueled by the promises of future compensation, a fact that contradicts the GTC.[145] This finding contradicts Gottfredson and Hirschi's vision of an impulsive criminal who lives for today without worrying about tomorrow.

From the above, it is easy to gauge interest in the GTC. And while there has been criticism, it remains one of the most important criminological theories of the past few decades. Although questions remain, the strength of the GTC lies in its scope and breadth: it attempts to explain all forms of crime and deviance, from lower-class gang delinquency to sexual harassment in the business community. By integrating concepts of criminal choice, criminal opportunity, socialization, and personality, Gottfredson and Hirschi make a plausible argument that all deviant behaviors may originate at the same source. Continued efforts are needed to test the GTC and establish the validity of its core concepts. It remains one of the key developments of modern criminological theory.

TRAJECTORY THEORY

LO10 Recognize that there are a variety of criminal trajectories

Trajectory theory is a third developmental approach that combines elements of propensity and life course theory. The basic premise is that there is more than one path to crime and more than one class of offender; there are different *trajectories* in a criminal career. Because all people are different, no single model of criminality can hope to describe every person's journey through life. Some people are social and have a large peer group, while others are loners who make decisions on their own.[146] Factors that predict offending in males may have little influence on females; there are significant gender differences in offending careers.[147] Criminal trajectories may also vary according to offending specialty: people who commit violent crimes maintain a unique set of personality traits and problem behaviors that separate them from nonviolent property and drug offenders.[148] There are also differences in the onset of criminal careers: some people begin at an early age and later become adult offenders, while others begin their violent careers in adulthood, having escaped and/or avoided crime as juveniles.[149]

One reason that all these different trajectories exist may be that some of the specific causes of crime such as mental disease and personality disorders progress differently, affecting some people in early adolescence while affecting others later in life.[150] As external influences shift and change so too do offending trajectories. For example, as parents change their parenting style, their children alter their antisocial behavior involvement.[151] In sum, people offend at a different pace, commit different kinds of crimes, and are influenced by different external forces.[152]

Because propensity theories disregard social influences during the life span, and life course theories maintain that social events seem to affect all people equally, they both miss the fact that there are different classes and types of offenders. Consequently, criminologists have sought to identify different paths or trajectories to crime.[153] Some important concepts contained within this model will be discussed in some detail.

Early, Late, and Non-Starters

Not all persistent offenders begin at an early age. Some are precocious, beginning their criminal careers early and persisting into adulthood.[154] Those who begin offending at an early age may engage in more age-appropriate crimes as they mature—the violent adolescent school yard bully may mature into the abusive husband in adulthood—but they remain violent over the life course.[155]

Others stay out of trouble in early adolescence and do not violate the law until later in early adulthood. Some offenders may peak their criminal activity during adolescence, whereas others persist into adulthood. Some people maximize their offending rates at a relatively early age and then reduce their antisocial activity; others persist into their 20s. Some are high-rate offenders, whereas others offend at relatively low rates.[156] Some may suffer from mental disease, for example, psychosis, that onsets later in adolescence and results in non-starters suddenly beginning an offending career.[157]

There are even different classes of chronic offenders. Some chronic offenders can be classified as high-rate, whereas others offend at relatively low frequencies but are persistent in their criminal activities, never really stopping.[158] Each of these categories of offenders presents unique problems, and represent serious social and economic cost differentials over the life course. Recent research by Alex Piquero, Wesley Jennings, and David Farrington found that the cost of high-rate chronic offending is nearly two and a half to ten times greater than the cost of high adolescence–peaked offending, very low-rate chronic offending, and low adolescence–peaked offending, respectively. Their research, conducted in England, estimates that a male high-rate chronic offender on average would impose an annual cost of $29 per U.K. citizen or a lifetime cost of $1,185 per U.K. citizen! The average and total costs of crime were significantly different across offending trajectories, with high-rate chronics imposing the most financial burden. Adopting prevention and intervention strategies aimed at reducing the number of high-rate chronics and/or speeding up their eventual desistance will offer many savings to the public and perhaps turn those negative costs into positive contributions.[159]

In sum, there are different paths to crime. Both life course and latent trait theories maintain that most persistent offenders are early starters, beginning their delinquent careers in their adolescence and persisting into adulthood. In contrast, trajectory theories hold that people begin their offending careers at different points of their lives and follow different offending trajectories. Those who engage in repeated and sustained involvement with the law in early adolescence are the ones most likely to continue to violate the law late into their adulthood.[160]

However, not all chronic offenders begin early in life. Some are "late bloomers" who stay out of trouble until relatively late in adolescence.[161] Researchers Sarah Bacon, Raymond Paternoster, and Robert Brame found that late bloomers are actually the teens most likely to get involved in serious adult offending.[162] Because late bloomers combine psychopathology with risk-taking behavior and poor social skills, their behavior becomes increasingly violent over time.[163] So while these late starters may start slow, they eventually catch up later in their adolescence.

Abstainers   There is also a group of abstainers or non-offenders. Despite the fact that most of their peers engage in a wide variety of antisocial activities, these people never break the law; their conventional behavior makes them deviant because offending is the norm!

Why do some people refrain from antisocial activity of any sort? Who are these folks who never ever shoplifted, smoked pot, got drunk, or had a fight? According to social psychologist Terrie Moffitt, abstainers are social introverts as teens, whose unpopularity shielded them from group pressure to commit delinquent acts.[164] Other experts disagree, suggesting that conformity may be related more to close parental monitoring and involvement with prosocial peer groups than it is to being unpopular. Kids who do not learn delinquent behaviors from role models are the ones most likely to be abstainers.[165] Still another explanation may be biological: abstainers maintain a genetic code that insulates them from criminality-producing factors in the environment.[166] Not surprisingly, abstainers are more likely than other youth to become successful, well-adjusted adults.[167]

Jordan Belfort, the financier convicted of fraud and the author of the book *The Wolf of Wall Street*, arrives for the premiere of the film adaptation of his book with his wife, Nadine, in New York, December 17, 2013. Belfort, played by Leonardo DiCaprio in the film, is a late starter to crime, not a typical trajectory but certainly not unique.

Pathways to Crime

Trajectory theory recognizes that criminals may travel more than a single road. Some may specialize in violence and extortion; some may be involved in theft and fraud; others may engage in a variety of criminal acts.[168] Each type of specialist may be unique: kids who commit violent crimes may be different from nonviolent property and drug offenders.[169] But even among these violent offenders, there may be distinct career paths. Some start out as violent kids whose violent behavior declines with age and who eventually desist. Another group are *escalators* whose severity of violence increases over time. Escalators are more likely to live in racially mixed communities, experience racism, and have less parental involvement than people who avoid or decrease their violent behaviors.[170] A study by Georgia Zara and David Farrington identified still another group of violent kids: late-onset escalators. These youths began their violent careers relatively late in their adolescence after suffering a variety of psychological and social disturbances

earlier in childhood, including high anxiety. Zara and Farrington conclude that childhood risk factors may predict this late-onset group of violent young adults.[171]

Some of the most important research on delinquent paths or trajectories has been conducted by Rolf Loeber and his associates. Using data from a longitudinal study of Pittsburgh youth, Loeber has identified three distinct paths to a criminal career (Figure 9.4):[172]

- The **authority conflict pathway** begins at an early age with stubborn behavior. This leads to defiance (doing things one's own way, disobedience) and then to authority avoidance (staying out late, truancy, running away).
- The **covert pathway** begins with minor, underhanded behavior (lying, shoplifting) that leads to property damage (setting nuisance fires, damaging property). This behavior eventually escalates to more serious forms of criminality, ranging from joyriding, pocket picking, larceny, and fencing to passing bad checks, using stolen credit cards, stealing cars, dealing drugs, and breaking and entering.
- The **overt pathway** escalates to aggressive acts beginning with aggression (annoying others, bullying), leading to physical (and gang) fighting, and then to violence (attacking someone, forced theft).

The Loeber research indicates that each of these paths may lead to a sustained deviant career. Some people enter two and even three paths simultaneously: they are stubborn, lie to teachers and parents, are bullies, and commit petty thefts. Those taking more than one path are the most likely to become persistent offenders as they mature.

Although some persistent offenders may specialize in one type of behavior, others engage in varied criminal acts and antisocial behaviors as they mature. As adolescents, they cheat on tests, bully kids in the school yard, take drugs, commit burglary, steal a car, and then shoplift from a store. Later as adults, some specialize in a particular criminal activity such as drug trafficking, while others are involved in an assortment of deviant acts—selling drugs, committing robberies, and getting involved in break-ins—when the situation arises and the opportunities are present.[173] There may be a multitude of criminal career subgroupings (for example, prostitutes, drug dealers), each with its own distinctive career path.

authority conflict pathway The path to a criminal career that begins with early stubborn behavior and defiance of parents.

covert pathway A path to a criminal career that begins with minor underhanded behavior and progresses to fire starting and theft.

overt pathway Pathway to a criminal career that begins with minor aggression, leads to physical fighting, and eventually escalates to violent crime.

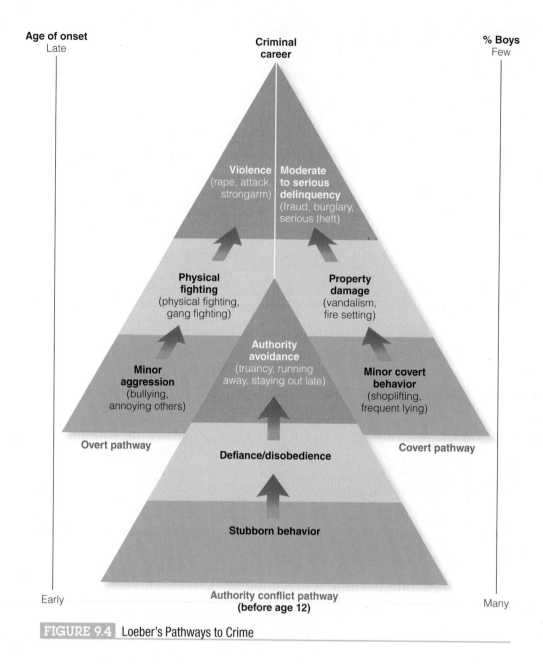

Age of onset
Late

Criminal career

% Boys
Few

Violence
(rape, attack, strongarm)

Moderate to serious delinquency
(fraud, burglary, serious theft)

Physical fighting
(physical fighting, gang fighting)

Property damage
(vandalism, fire setting)

Minor aggression
(bullying, annoying others)

Authority avoidance
(truancy, running away, staying out late)

Minor covert behavior
(shoplifting, frequent lying)

Overt pathway

Covert pathway

Defiance/disobedience

Stubborn behavior

Early

Authority conflict pathway
(before age 12)

Many

FIGURE 9.4 Loeber's Pathways to Crime

Adolescent-Limited Offenders vs. Life Course Persisters

According to psychologist Terrie Moffitt, most young offenders follow one of two paths. **Adolescent-limited offenders** may be considered "typical teenagers" who get into minor scrapes and engage in what might be considered rebellious teenage behavior with their friends.[174] As they reach their mid-teens, adolescent-limited delinquents begin to mimic the antisocial behavior of more troubled teens, only to reduce the frequency of their offending as they mature to around age 18.[175] So while it may be cool for some kids to swagger around and get into trouble during their teenage years, they are ready to settle down and assume more conventional roles as they enter young adulthood.

The second path is the one taken by a small group of **life course persisters** who begin their offending career at a very early age and continue to offend well into adulthood.[176] Moffitt finds that the seeds of life course persistence are planted early in life and may combine the effects of abnormal traits, such as neurological deficits, with severe family dysfunction. Life course persisters are

adolescent-limited offenders Offender who follows the most common criminal trajectory, in which antisocial behavior peaks in adolescence and then diminishes.

life course persisters One of the small group of offenders whose criminal career continues well into adulthood.

AN ETHICAL DILEMMA

THE XBOX KILLERS

In the hot summer months of 2004, Troy Victorino and friends Robert Cannon, Jerome Hunter, and Michael Salas were illegally squatting in a Deltona, Florida, home and using it as a "party house." The owners, who were spending the summer in Maine, asked their granddaughter, Erin Belanger, to check up on the property. When she saw what was going on she called the police in order to get the squatters removed from the premises. Victorino (who was in jail on an unrelated matter at the time his friends were evicted) left behind an Xbox game system and some clothes, and Belanger took possession of these items. Once he was released from jail on bond, Victorino, feeling disrespected because the police had been called and his stuff confiscated, threatened Belanger and slashed the tires on her car. He warned her that unless she returned the items, he was going to come back and beat her with a baseball bat while she was sleeping. It was not an idle threat. On August 6, 2004, in what is now known either as the *Xbox murders* or the *Deltona massacre*, Victorino, Cannon, Hunter, and Salas armed themselves with aluminum bats, put on all-black clothing, covered their faces with scarves, kicked in the front door, and attacked Belanger and her roommates as they slept. All six victims, including Erin Belanger, were beaten and stabbed beyond recognition. All six died.

The perpetrators of the deadly attack left a trail of clues that resulted in their quick arrest and indictment on murder charges. It was a pretty sad bunch; they all seemed to have lived troubled lives. Michael Salas was abused even before his birth by his mother, who used drugs during her pregnancy, traded food stamps for cocaine, and left her three sons alone for long periods during the winter. Child protective services found cigarette burns on the boys' bodies. Salas's father died of AIDS when Salas was 9. Hunter is a clinically depressed, mentally ill man whose parents were both committed to mental hospitals at the time of the massacre. As early as age 3, Hunter conversed with his identical twin brother Jeremy, who died from pneumonia at 6 months old. But it was Victorino, a 6-foot-6, 300-pound career criminal, who most outraged the public. He had spent 8 of the last 11 years before the killings serving prison sentences for a variety of crimes, including auto theft, battery, arson, burglary, and theft. In 1996, he beat a man so severely that doctors needed 15 titanium plates to rebuild the victim's face. Not surprisingly, Victorino also had a long history of physical and sexual abuse that began at the time he was 2 years old. He suffered from neurological impairment that resulted in poor impulse control and the inability to manage his violent temper.

The Xbox killers followed a classic developmental path: early abuse and problems in childhood leading to a long and sustained criminal career. These killers did not age out of crime but persisted and escalated their criminal involvement until it culminated in unspeakable tragedy.

Despite their personal problems, on August 2, 2006, Victorino and Hunter were sentenced to death by lethal injection, and Cannon and Salas to life in prison without the possibility of parole. Victorino and Hunter remain on death row at the Florida State Prison in Starke because the average length of incarceration of a Florida inmate prior to execution is more than 10 years.

Recently the governor has been asked to review the sentence in light of the troubled histories of Victorino and Hunter. Would if be ethical to execute someone who has had a horrendous upbringing? Anti–death penalty groups have asked him to consider commuting the sentences to life in prison considering their childhood traumas. He has asked for your opinion on the matter. Write a memo stating whether you believe that developmental factors should mitigate their culpability in the case. Would it be fair to execute someone who commits a similar crime but had a relatively problem-free childhood?

thinking like a criminologist

---

more likely to manifest abnormal personal traits such as low verbal ability, impaired reasoning skills, limited learning ability, and weak spatial and memory functions than adolescent-limited offenders.[177] Individual traits rather than environment seem to have the greatest influence on life course persistence.[178]

It is not surprising, then, that many life course persisters display elements of problem behavior syndrome, including mental health problems, psychiatric pathologies, limited school achievement, ADHD, and health issues.[179] It is not surprising, then, that life course persisters display social and personal dysfunctions, including lower than average verbal ability, reasoning skills, learning ability, and school achievement nor that they offend more frequently and engage in a greater variety of antisocial acts and mani-

fest significantly more mental health problems, including psychiatric pathologies, than adolescent-limited offenders.[180] Persisters are more likely to manifest traits such as low verbal ability and hyperactivity; they display a negative or impulsive personality and seem particularly impaired on spatial and memory functions.[181] Individual traits rather than environment seem to have the greatest influence on life course persistence.[182]

Supporting research shows that the persistence patterns predicted by Moffitt are valid and accurate.[183] There may also be a genetic basis to life course persistence; some recent research links it to neurological deficiencies.[184] Life course persisters may be aggressive as part of a strategy to increase their reproductive options, a view that jibes with the sociobiology view discussed in Chapter 5.[185]

EVALUATING DEVELOPMENTAL THEORIES

Although the differences among the views presented in this chapter may seem irreconcilable, they in fact share some common ground. They indicate that a criminal career must be understood as a passage along which people travel, that it has a beginning and an end, and that events and life circumstances influence the journey. The factors that affect a criminal career may include structural factors, such as income and status; socialization factors, such as family and peer relations; biological factors, such as size and strength; psychological factors, including intelligence and personality; and opportunity factors, such as free time, inadequate police protection, and a supply of easily stolen merchandise.

Life course theories emphasize the influence of changing interpersonal and structural factors (that is, people change along with the world they live in). Latent trait theories place more emphasis on the fact that behavior is linked less to personal change and more to changes in the surrounding world. Trajectory theories find that there are different classes of offenders who may change at different points of their criminal career.

These perspectives differ in their view of human development. Do people constantly change, as life course theories suggest, or are they stable, constant, and changeless, as the latent trait view indicates? Are the factors that produce criminality different at each stage of life, as the life course view suggests, or does a master trait—such as control balance, self-control, or coercion—steer the course of human behavior? Is there a single path to crime or are there different paths and different trajectories?

It is also possible that these positions are not mutually exclusive, and each may make a notable contribution to understanding the onset and continuity of a criminal career. In other words, stable individual characteristics—latent traits—may interact with or modify the effects of life course–varying social factors to increase their effect and shape the direction of criminal careers.[186] Is it possible that people take different paths to crime because they have different levels of criminal propensity? Needless to say, measuring these effects is quite complex and relies on sophisticated research techniques. One research effort by Bradley Entner Wright and his associates found evidence supporting both latent trait and life course theories.[187] Their research, conducted with subjects in New Zealand, indicates that low self-control in childhood predicts disrupted social bonds and criminal offending later in life, a finding that supports latent trait theory. They also found that maintaining positive social bonds helps reduce criminality and that maintaining prosocial bonds could even counteract the effect of low self-control. Latent traits are an important influence on crime, but their findings indicate that social relationships that form later in life appear to influence criminal behavior "above and beyond" individuals' preexisting characteristics.[188] This finding may reflect the fact that there are different classes of criminals: a less serious group who are influenced by life events, and a more chronic group whose latent traits insulate them from any positive prosocial relationships; this finding supports trajectory theory concepts.[189]

Concept Summary 9.1 sets out the most important life course, latent trait, and trajectory theories.

PUBLIC POLICY IMPLICATIONS OF DEVELOPMENTAL THEORY

There have been a number of policy initiatives based on premises of developmental theory. These typically feature multisystemic treatment efforts designed to provide at-risk kids with personal, social, educational, and family services. For example, one program found that an intervention that promotes academic success, social competence, and educational enhancement during the elementary grades can reduce risky sexual practices and their accompanying health consequences in early adulthood.[190]

Other programs are now employing multidimensional strategies and are aimed at targeting children in preschool through the early elementary grades in order to alter the direction of their life course. Many of the most successful programs focus on strengthening children's social-emotional competence and positive coping skills and suppressing the development of antisocial, aggressive behavior.[191] Research evaluations indicate that the most promising multicomponent crime and substance abuse prevention programs for youths, especially those at high risk, are aimed at improving their developmental skills. They may include a school component, an after-school component, and a parent-involvement component. All of these components have the common goal of increasing protective factors and decreasing risk factors in the areas of the family, the community, the school, and the individual.[192] The Boys and Girls Clubs and School Collaborations' Substance Abuse Prevention Program includes a school component called SMART (Skills Mastery and Resistance Training) Teachers, an after-school component called SMART Kids, and a parent-involvement component called SMART Parents. Each component is designed to reduce specific risk factors in the children's school, family, community, and personal environments.[193]

Another successful program, Fast Track, is designed to prevent serious antisocial behavior and related adolescent problems in high-risk children entering first grade. The intervention is guided by a developmental approach that

Theory	Major Premise	Strengths	Research Focus
LIFE COURSE THEORIES	As people go through the life course, social and personal traits undergo change and influence behavior.	Explains why some at-risk children desist from crime.	Identify critical moments in a person's life course that produce crime.
Interactional Theory	Criminals go through lifestyle changes during their offending career. Crime influences lifestyle and changing lifestyle influences crime.	Combines sociological and psychological theories.	Identify crime-producing interpersonal interactions and their reciprocal effects.
Social Development Model	Community and personal factors interact to strengthen or weaken social bonds.	Shows that crime and other aspects of social life are interactive and developmental.	Measure the relationship between community interaction, personal development, and crime.
Age-Graded Theory	As people mature, the factors that influence their propensity to commit crime change. In childhood, family factors are critical; in adulthood, marital and job factors are key.	Shows how crime is a developmental process that shifts in direction over the life course.	Identify critical points in the life course that produce crime. Analyze the association between social capital and crime.
LATENT TRAIT THEORIES	A master trait controls human development.	Explains the continuity of crime and chronic offending.	Identify master trait that produces crime.
Integrated Cognitive Antisocial Potential (ICAP) Theory	People with antisocial potential (AP) are at risk to commit antisocial acts. AP can be viewed as both a long- and short-term phenomenon.	Identifies different types of criminal propensities and shows how they may influence behavior in both the short and long term.	Identify the components of long- and short-term AP.
General Theory of Crime	Crime and criminality are separate concepts. People choose to commit crime when they lack self-control. People lacking self-control will seize criminal opportunities.	Integrates choice and social control concepts. Identifies the difference between crime and criminality.	Measure associations among impulsivity, low self-control, and criminal behaviors.
Differential Coercion Theory	Individuals exposed to coercive environments develop social-psychological deficits that enhance their probability of engaging in criminal behavior.	Explains why a feeling of coercion is a master trait that determines behavior.	Measuring the sources of coercion.
Control Balance Theory	A person's "control ratio" influences his or her behavior.	Explains how the ability to control one's environment is a master trait.	Measuring control balance and imbalance.
TRAJECTORY THEORY	There is more than one pathway to crime.	Explains the existence of different types and classes of criminals.	Measuring different criminal paths.
Life Course Persistent/ Adolescent Limited	People begin their criminal activities at different points in their lives.	Explains why most adolescent misbehavior is limited to youthful misadventures.	Measuring the starting and stopping points of criminal activity.

suggests that antisocial behavior is the product of the interaction of multiple social and psychological influences:

- Residence in low-income, high-crime communities places stressors and influences on children and families that

increase their risk levels. In these areas, families characterized by marital conflict and instability make consistent and effective parenting difficult to achieve, particularly with children who are impulsive and of difficult temperament.

- Children of high-risk families usually enter the education process poorly prepared for its social, emotional, and cognitive demands. Their parents often are unprepared to relate effectively with school staff, and a poor home–school bond often aggravates the child's adjustment problems. They may be grouped with other children who are similarly unprepared. This peer group may be negatively influenced by disruptive classroom contexts and punitive teachers.

- Over time, aggressive and disruptive children are rejected by families and peers and tend to receive less support from teachers. All of these processes increase the risk of antisocial behaviors, in a process that begins in elementary school and lasts throughout adolescence. During this period, peer influences, academic difficulties, and dysfunctional personal identity development can contribute to serious conduct problems and related risky behaviors.

Compared with children in the control group, children in the intervention group displayed significantly less aggressive behavior at home, in the classroom, and on the playground. By the end of the third grade, 37 percent of the intervention group had become free of conduct problems, in contrast with 27 percent of the control group. By the end of elementary school, 33 percent of the intervention group had a developmental trajectory of decreasing conduct problems, as compared with 27 percent of the control group. Furthermore, placement in special education by the end of elementary school was about one-fourth lower in the intervention group than in the control group.

Group differences continued through adolescence. Court records indicate that by eighth grade, 38 percent of the intervention group boys had been arrested, in contrast with 42 percent of the control group. Finally, psychiatric interviews after ninth grade indicate that the Fast Track intervention has reduced serious conduct disorder by over a third, from 27 percent to 17 percent. These effects generalized across gender and ethnic groups and across the wide range of child and family characteristics measured by Fast Track.

SUMMARY

LO1 Discuss the history of developmental theory

The foundation of this theory is Sheldon and Eleanor Glueck's integration of biological, psychological, and social factors. Later the Glueck data was rediscovered by criminologists Robert Sampson and John Laub. The Philadelphia cohort research by Marvin Wolfgang and his associates investigated criminal career development. Rolf Loeber and Marc LeBlanc proposed that criminologists should devote time and effort to understanding basic questions about the evolution of criminal careers.

LO2 Compare and contrast life course, latent trait, and trajectory theories

Life course theorists view criminality as a dynamic process influenced by a multitude of individual characteristics, traits, and social experiences. Life course theories look at such issues as the onset of crime, the escalation of offenses, the persistence of crime, and desistance from crime. Latent trait theorists believe that human development is controlled by a "master trait" that guides human development and gives some people an increased propensity to commit crime. Trajectory theory holds that there are multiple pathways to crime.

LO3 List the principles of the life course theory

At an early age, people begin relationships and behaviors that will determine their adult life course. Some individuals are incapable of maturing in a reasonable and timely fashion. A positive life experience may help some criminals desist from crime for a while, but a negative experience may cause them to resume their criminal activities. As people mature, the factors that influence their behavior change. The social, physical, and environmental influences on their behavior are transformed.

LO4 Describe examples of problem behaviors that cluster together

Crime is one of a group of interrelated antisocial behaviors that cluster together. Problem behaviors typically involve family dysfunction, sexual and physical abuse, substance abuse, smoking, precocious sexuality and early pregnancy, educational underachievement, suicide attempts, sensation seeking, and unemployment. People who suffer from one of these conditions typically exhibit many symptoms of the rest.

LO5 Discuss why age of onset is an important factor in crime

Early onset of antisocial behavior predicts later and more serious criminality. Adolescent offenders whose criminal behavior persists into adulthood are likely to have begun their deviant careers at a very early (preschool) age. Early-onset kids tend to have poor parental discipline and monitoring, inadequate emotional support, distant peer relationships, and psychological issues and problems.

LO6 Outline the basic principles of Sampson and Laub's age-graded theory

Sampson and Laub find that the maintenance of a criminal career can be affected by events that occur later in life. They recognize the role of social capital and its influence on the trajectory of a criminal career. When faced with personal crisis, offenders lack the social supports that can help them reject criminal solutions. Sampson and Laub view criminal careers as a dynamic process in which important life events can change the direction of a person's life course trajectory; these key events are called turning points.

LO7 Interpret the terms *propensity* and *latent trait*

A propensity or latent trait is a personal attribute or characteristic that controls the inclination to commit crimes. It is a stable feature, characteristic, property, or condition, present at birth or soon after, that makes some people crime prone over the life course. Suspected latent traits include defective intelligence, damaged or impulsive personality, genetic abnormalities, the physical-chemical functioning of the brain, and environmental influences on brain function, such as drugs, chemicals, and injuries.

LO8 Discuss Wilson and Herrnstein's views on crime and human nature

According to Wilson and Herrnstein, all human behavior, including criminality, is determined by its perceived consequences. A criminal incident occurs when an individual chooses criminal over conventional behavior. Wilson and Herrnstein assume that both biological and psychological traits influence the choice between crime and noncrime. Wilson and

Herrnstein suggest the existence of an elusive latent trait that predisposes people to committing crime.

LO9 Explain the basic principles of the General Theory of Crime

Gottfredson and Hirschi link the propensity to commit crime to an impulsive personality and a lack of self-control. People with limited self-control tend to be impulsive; they are insensitive to other people's feelings, predisposed toward physical (rather than mental) activities and solutions, risk takers, short-sighted, and nonverbal. Because those with low self-control enjoy risky, exciting, or thrilling behaviors with immediate gratification, they are more likely to enjoy criminal acts. Gottfredson and Hirschi trace the root cause of poor self-control to inadequate child-rearing practices.

LO10 Recognize that there are a variety of criminal trajectories

There are different pathways to crime and different types of criminals. Some career criminals may specialize in violence and extortion; some may be involved in theft and fraud; some may engage in a variety of criminal acts. Some offenders begin their careers early in life, whereas others are late bloomers who begin committing crime at about the time when most people desist.

CRITICAL THINKING QUESTIONS

1. Do you consider yourself to have social capital? If so, what form does it take?
2. Someone you know gets a perfect score on the SAT. What personal, family, and social characteristics do you think this individual has? Another person becomes a serial killer. Without knowing this person, describe their personal, family, and social characteristics. If bad behavior is explained by multiple problems, is good behavior explained by multiple strengths?
3. Do you believe it is a latent trait that makes a person crime prone, or is crime a function of environment and socialization?
4. Do you agree with Loeber's multiple pathways model? Do you know people who have traveled down those paths?
5. Do people really change, or do they stay the same but appear to be different because their life circumstances have changed?

KEY TERMS

developmental criminology (290)
life course theories (291)
latent trait theories (291)
trajectory theory (292)
population heterogeneity (292)
state dependence (292)

problem behavior syndrome (PBS) (294)
integrated theories (296)
age-graded theory (296)
turning points (297)
cumulative disadvantage (298)
social capital (299)

propensity (301)
latent trait (301)
General Theory of Crime (GTC) (304)
self-control (305)
self-control theory (307)
authority conflict pathway (311)

covert pathway (311)
overt pathway (311)
adolescent-limited offenders (312)
life course persisters (312)

1. David Gardner. "'Things Got Out of control': Chilling Confession of Connecticut Massacre 'Killer'," *Daily Mail*, September 23, 2010; Alaine Griffin, "Judge Sentences Komisarjevsky to Death," Courant.com, January 27, 2012, http://www.courant.com/community/cheshire/cheshire-home-invasion/hc-komisarjevsky-sentenced-0128-20120127,0,1199254.story (accessed April 2014).

2. Hans Eysenck, *Crime and Personality* (London: Methuen, 1964).

3. Nicole Hahn Rafter, "H. J. Eysenck in Fagin's Kitchen: The Return to Biological Theory in 20th-Century Criminology," *History of the Human Sciences* 19 (2006): 37–56.

4. Sheldon Glueck and Eleanor Glueck, *Unraveling Juvenile Delinquency* (Cambridge: Harvard University Press, 1950), p. 48.

5. See, generally, Sheldon Glueck and Eleanor Glueck, *500 Criminal Careers* (New York: Knopf, 1930); Glueck and Glueck, *One Thousand Juvenile Delinquents* (Cambridge, MA: Harvard University Press, 1934); Glueck and Glueck, *Predicting Delinquency and Crime* (Cambridge, MA: Harvard University Press, 1967), pp. 82–83; Glueck and Glueck, *Unraveling Juvenile Delinquency* (Cambridge, MA: Harvard University Press, 1950).

6. John Laub and Robert Sampson, "The Sutherland-Glueck Debate: On the Sociology of Criminological Knowledge," *American Journal of Sociology* 96 (1991): 1402–1440.

7. See, generally, Laub and Sampson, "The Sutherland–Glueck Debate"; John Laub and Robert Sampson, "Unraveling Families and Delinquency: A Reanalysis of the Gluecks' Data," *Criminology* 26 (1988): 355–380.

8. Marvin E. Wolfgang, Robert M. Figlio, and Thorsten Sellin, *Delinquency in a Birth Cohort* (Chicago: University of Chicago Press, 1972).

9. Rolf Loeber and Marc LeBlanc, "Toward a Developmental Criminology," in *Crime and Justice*, Vol. 12, ed. Norval Morris and Michael Tonry (Chicago: University of Chicago Press, 1990), pp. 375–473; Loeber and LeBlanc, "Developmental Criminology Updated," in *Crime and Justice*, Vol. 23, ed. Michael Tonry (Chicago: University of Chicago Press, 1998), pp. 115–198.

10. Alex Piquero, "Taking Stock of Developmental Trajectories of Criminal Activity over the Life Course," in *The Long View of Crime: A Synthesis of Longitudinal Research*, ed. Akiva Liberman (New York: Springer, 2008), pp. 23–78.

11. Shawn Bushway, Robert Brame, and Raymond Paternoster, "Assessing Stability and Change in Criminal Offending: A Comparison of Random Effects, Semiparametric, and Fixed Effects Modeling Strategies," *Journal of Quantitative Criminology* 15 (1999): 23–61.

12. Sarah Bacon, Raymond Paternoster, and Robert Brame, "Understanding the Relationship Between Onset Age and Subsequent Offending During Adolescence," *Journal of Youth and Adolescence* 38 (2009): 301–311.

13. Marvin Krohn, Alan Lizotte, and Cynthia Perez, "The Interrelationship Between Substance Use and Precocious Transitions to Adult Sexuality," *Journal of Health and Social Behavior* 38 (1997): 87–103, at 88.

14. Jennifer M. Beyers and Rolf Loeber, "Untangling Developmental Relations Between Depressed Mood and Delinquency in Male Adolescents," *Journal of Abnormal Child Psychology* 31 (2003): 247–266.

15. Stephanie Milan and Ellen Pinderhughes, "Family Instability and Child Maladjustment Trajectories During Elementary School," *Journal of Abnormal Child Psychology* 34 (2006): 43–56.

16. Chris Melde and Finn-Aage Esbensen, "The Relative Impact of Gang Status Transitions: Identifying the Mechanisms of Change in Delinquency," *Journal of Research in Crime and Delinquency*, first published on October 30, 2013.

17. David C. Pyrooz, "From Colors and Guns to Caps and Gowns? The Effects of Gang Membership on Educational Attainment," *Journal of Research in Crime and Delinquency*, first published online April 29, 2013.

18. Lara DePadilla, Molly Perkins, Kirk Elifson, and Claire Sterk, "Adult Criminal Involvement: A Cross-Sectional Inquiry into Correlates and Mechanisms over the Life Course," *Criminal Justice Review* 37 (2012): 110–126.

19. Bradley Entner Wright, Avshalom Caspi, Terrie Moffitt, and Phil Silva, "The Effects of Social Ties on Crime Vary by Criminal Propensity: A Life-Course Model of Interdependence," *Criminology* 39 (2001): 321–352.

20. Joan McCord, "Family Relationships, Juvenile Delinquency, and Adult Criminality," *Criminology* 29 (1991): 397–417.

21. Paul Mazerolle, "Delinquent Definitions and Participation Age: Assessing the Invariance Hypothesis," *Studies on Crime and Crime Prevention* 6 (1997): 151–168.

22. Peggy Giordano, Stephen Cernkovich, and Jennifer Rudolph, "Gender, Delinquency, and Desistance: Toward a Theory of Cognitive Transformation?" *American Journal of Sociology* 107 (2002): 990–1064.

23. John Hagan and Holly Foster, "S/He's a Rebel: Toward a Sequential Stress Theory of Delinquency and Gendered Pathways to Disadvantage in Emerging Adulthood," *Social Forces* 82 (2003): 53–86.

24. G. R. Patterson, Barbara DeBaryshe, and Elizabeth Ramsey, "A Developmental Perspective on Antisocial Behavior," *American Psychologist* 44 (1989): 329–335.

25. Robert Sampson and John Laub, "Crime and Deviance in the Life Course," *American Review of Sociology* 18 (1992): 63–84.

26. David Farrington, Darrick Jolliffe, Rolf Loeber, Magda Stouthamer-Loeber, and Larry Kalb, "The Concentration of Offenders in Families, and Family Criminality in the Prediction of Boys' Delinquency," *Journal of Adolescence* 24 (2001): 579–596.

27. Shawn D. Bushway, Marvin D. Krohn, Alan J. Lizotte, Matthew D. Phillips, and Nicole M. Schmidt, "Are Risky Youth Less Protectable as They Age? The Dynamics of Protection During Adolescence and Young Adulthood," *Justice Quarterly* 30 (2013): 84–116.

28. Raymond Paternoster, Charles Dean, Alex Piquero, Paul Mazerolle, and Robert Brame, "Generality, Continuity, and Change in Offending," *Journal of Quantitative Criminology* 13 (1997): 231–266.

29. Magda Stouthamer-Loeber and Evelyn Wei, "The Precursors of Young Fatherhood and Its Effect on Delinquency of Teenage Males," *Journal of Adolescent Health* 22 (1998): 56–65.

30. Richard Miech, Avshalom Caspi, Terrie Moffitt, Bradley Entner Wright, and Phil Silva, "Low Socioeconomic Status and Mental Disorders: A Longitudinal Study of Selection and Causation During Young Adulthood," *American Journal of Sociology* 104 (1999): 1096–1131.

31. Deborah Capaldi and Gerald Patterson, "Can Violent Offenders Be Distinguished from Frequent Offenders? Prediction from Childhood to Adolescence," *Journal of Research in Crime and Delinquency* 33 (1996): 206–231.

32. For an analysis of more than 30 studies, see Mark Lipsey and James Derzon, "Predictors of Violent or Serious Delinquency in Adolescence and Early Adulthood: A Synthesis of Longitudinal Research," in *Serious and Violent Juvenile Offenders: Risk Factors and Successful Interventions*, ed. Rolf Loeber and David Farrington (Thousand Oaks, CA: Sage, 1998).

33. Gina Wingood, Ralph DiClemente, Rick Crosby, Kathy Harrington, Susan Davies, and Edward Hook III, "Gang Involvement and the Health of African American Female Adolescents," *Pediatrics* 110 (2002): 57.

34. David Husted, Nathan Shapira, and Martin Lazoritz, "Adolescent Gambling, Substance Use, and Other Delinquent Behavior," *Psychiatric Times* 20 (2003): 52–55.

35. Krohn, Lizotte, and Perez, "The Interrelationship Between Substance Use and Precocious Transitions to Adult Sexuality," p. 88; Jessor, "Risk Behavior in Adolescence."

36. Terence Thornberry, Carolyn Smith, and Gregory Howard, "Risk Factors for Teenage Fatherhood," *Journal of Marriage and the Family* 59 (1997): 505–522; Todd Miller, Timothy Smith, Charles Turner, Margarita

Guijarro, and Amanda Hallet, "A Meta-Analytic Review of Research on Hostility and Physical Health," *Psychological Bulletin* 119 (1996): 322–348; Marianne Junger, "Accidents and Crime," in *The Generality of Deviance*, ed. T. Hirschi and M. Gottfredson (New Brunswick, NJ: Transaction Books, 1993).

37. James Marquart, Victoria Brewer, Patricia Simon, and Edward Morse, "Lifestyle Factors Among Female Prisoners with Histories of Psychiatric Treatment," *Journal of Criminal Justice* 29 (2001): 319–328; Rolf Loeber, David Farrington, Magda Stouthamer-Loeber, Terrie Moffitt, Avshalom Caspi, and Don Lynam, "Male Mental Health Problems, Psychopathy, and Personality Traits: Key Findings from the First 14 Years of the Pittsburgh Youth Study," *Clinical Child and Family Psychology Review* 4 (2002): 273–297.

38. Robert Johnson, S. Susan Su, Dean Gerstein, Hee-Choon Shin, and John Hoffman, "Parental Influences on Deviant Behavior in Early Adolescence: A Logistic Response Analysis of Age and Gender-Differentiated Effects," *Journal of Quantitative Criminology* 11 (1995): 167–192; Judith Brooks, Martin Whiteman, and Patricia Cohen, "Stage of Drug Use, Aggression, and Theft/Vandalism," in *Drugs, Crime and Other Deviant Adaptations: Longitudinal Studies*, ed. Howard Kaplan (New York: Plenum Press, 1995), pp. 83–96.

39. Helene Raskin White, Peter Tice, Rolf Loeber, and Magda Stouthamer-Loeber, "Illegal Acts Committed by Adolescents Under the Influence of Alcohol and Drugs," *Journal of Research in Crime and Delinquency* 39 (2002): 131–153; Candace Kruttschnitt, Jane McLeod, and Maude Dornfeld, "The Economic Environment of Child Abuse," *Social Problems* 41 (1994): 299–312.

40. Paul Nieuwbeerta and Alex Piquero, "Mortality Rates and Causes of Death of Convicted Dutch Criminals 25 Years Later," *Journal of Research in Crime and Delinquency* 45 (2008): 256–286.

41. David Fergusson, L. John Horwood, and Elizabeth Ridder, "Show Me the Child at Seven II: Childhood Intelligence and Later Outcomes in Adolescence and Young Adulthood," *Journal of Child Psychology and Psychiatry and Allied Disciplines* 46 (2005): 850–859.

42. Krysia Mossakowski, "Dissecting the Influence of Race, Ethnicity, and Socioeconomic Status on Mental Health in Young Adulthood," *Research on Aging* 30 (2008): 649–671.

43. Jacqueline Schneider, "The Link Between Shoplifting and Burglary: The Booster Burglar," *British Journal of Criminology* 45 (2005): 395–401.

44. Glenn Deane, Richard Felson, and David Armstrong, "An Examination of Offense Specialization Using Marginal Logit Models," *Criminology* 43 (2005): 955–988.

45. Christopher Sullivan, Jean Marie McGloin, Travis Pratt, and Alex Piquero, "Rethinking the 'Norm' of Offender Generality: Investigating Specialization in the Short-Term," *Criminology* 44 (2006): 199–233.

46. Christopher Sullivan, Jean Marie McGloin, James Ray, and Michael Caudy, "Detecting Specialization in Offending: Comparing Analytic Approaches," *Journal of Quantitative Criminology* 25 (2009): 419–441.

47. Jean Marie McGloin, Christopher J. Sullivan, and Alex R. Piquero, "Aggregating to Versatility? Transitions Among Offender Types in the Short Term," *British Journal of Criminology* 49 (2009): 243–264.

48. Alex R. Piquero and He Len Chung, "On the Relationships Between Gender, Early Onset, and the Seriousness of Offending," *Journal of Criminal Justice* 29 (2001): 189–206.

49. David Nurco, Timothy Kinlock, and Mitchell Balter, "The Severity of Preaddiction Criminal Behavior Among Urban, Male Narcotic Addicts and Two Nonaddicted Control Groups," *Journal of Research in Crime and Delinquency* 30 (1993): 293–316.

50. Hanno Petras, Nicholas Alongo, Sharon Lambert, Sandra Barrueco, Cindy Schaeffer, Howard Chilcoat, and Sheppard Kellam, "The Utility of Elementary School TOCA-R Scores in Identifying Later Criminal Court Violence Among Adolescent Females," *Journal of the American Academy of Child and Adolescent Psychiatry* 44 (2005): 790–797.

51. W. Alex Mason, Rick Kosterman, J. David Hawkins, Todd Herrenkohl, Liliana Lengua, and Elizabeth McCauley, "Predicting Depression, Social Phobia, and Violence in Early Adulthood from Childhood Behavior Problems," *Journal of the American Academy of Child and Adolescent Psychiatry* 43 (2004): 307–315.

52. Dawn Jeglum Bartusch, Donald Lynam, Terrie Moffitt, and Phil Silva, "Is Age Important? Testing a General versus a Developmental Theory of Antisocial Behavior," *Criminology* 35 (1997): 13–48.

53. Daniel Nagin and Richard Tremblay, "What Has Been Learned from Group-Based Trajectory Modeling? Examples from Physical Aggression and Other Problem Behaviors," *Annals of the American Academy of Political and Social Science* 602 (2005): 82–117.

54. Mason et al., "Predicting Depression, Social Phobia, and Violence in Early Adulthood from Childhood Behavior Problems"; Ronald Prinz and Suzanne Kerns, "Early Substance Use by Juvenile Offenders," *Child Psychiatry and Human Development* 33 (2003): 263–268.

55. Bacon, Paternoster, and Brame, "Understanding the Relationship Between Onset Age and Subsequent Offending During Adolescence."

56. Glenn Clingempeel and Scott Henggeler, "Aggressive Juvenile Offenders Transitioning into Emerging Adulthood: Factors Discriminating Persistors and Desistors," *American Journal of Orthopsychiatry* 73 (2003): 310–323.

57. Mary Campa, Catherine Bradshaw, John Eckenrode, and David Zielinski, "Patterns of Problem Behavior in Relation to Thriving and Precocious Behavior in Late Adolescence," *Journal of Youth and Adolescence* 37 (2008): 627–640.

58. Kristin Carbone-Lopez and Jody Miller, "Precocious Role Entry as a Mediating Factor in Women's Methamphetamine Use: Implications for Life-Course and Pathways Research," *Criminology* 50 (2012): 187–220.

59. David Gadd and Stephen Farrall, "Criminal Careers, Desistance and Subjectivity: Interpreting Men's Narratives of Change," *Theoretical Criminology* 8 (2004): 123–156.

60. G. R. Patterson, L. Crosby, and S. Vuchinich, "Predicting Risk for Early Police Arrest," *Journal of Quantitative Criminology* 8 (1992): 335–355.

61. David Farrington, "Key Results from the First Forty Years of the Cambridge Study in Delinquent Development," in *Taking Stock of Delinquency: An Overview of Findings from Contemporary Longitudinal Studies*, ed. Terence Thornberry and Marvin Krohn (New York: Kluwer, 2002), pp. 137–185; David Farrington, "The Development of Offending and Anti-Social Behavior from Childhood: Key Findings from the Cambridge Study of Delinquent Development," *Journal of Child Psychology and Psychiatry* 36 (1995): 2–36; David Farrington, Understanding and Preventing Youth Crime (London: Joseph Rowntree Foundation, 1996).

62. Holly Hartwig and Jane Myers, "A Different Approach: Applying a Wellness Paradigm to Adolescent Female Delinquents and Offenders," *Journal of Mental Health Counseling* 25 (2003): 57–76.

63. Terrie Moffitt, Avshalom Caspi, Michael Rutter, and Phil Silva, *Sex Differences in Antisocial Behavior: Conduct Disorder, Delinquency, and Violence in the Dunedin Longitudinal Study* (London: Cambridge University Press, 2001).

64. Lisa Broidy, Richard Tremblay, Bobby Brame, David Fergusson, John Horwood, Robert Laird, Terrie Moffitt, Daniel Nagin, John Bates, Kenneth Dodge, Rolf Loeber, Donald Lynam, Gregory Pettit, and Frank Vitaro, "Developmental Trajectories of Childhood Disruptive Behaviors and Adolescent Delinquency: A Six-Site, Cross-National Study," *Developmental Psychology* 39 (2003): 222–245.

65. Stephen Farrall and Benjamin Bowling, "Structuration, Human Development, and Desistance from Crime," *British Journal of Criminology* 39 (1999): 253–268.

66. Robert Sampson and John Laub, *Crime in the Making: Pathways and Turning Points Through Life* (Cambridge, MA: Harvard University Press, 1993).

67. Robert Sampson and John Laub, "A Life-Course View of the Development of Crime," *Annals of the American Academy of Political and Social Science* 602 (2005): 12–45.

68. John Laub, Robert J. Sampson, and Gary Sweeten, "Assessing Sampson and Laub's Life-Course Theory of Crime," in *Taking Stock: The Status of Criminological Theory, Vol. 15, Advances in Criminological Theory*, ed. Francis T. Cullen, John Paul Wright, and Kristie R. Blevins (New Brunswick, NJ: Transaction, 2006), p. 314.

69. Joseph Murray, Rolf Loeber, and Dustin Pardini, "Parental Involvement in the Criminal Justice System and the Development of Youth Theft, Marijuana Use, Depression, and Poor Academic Performance," *Criminology* 50 (2012): 255–302; Michael Roettger and Raymond Swisher, "Associations of Fathers' History of Incarceration with Sons' Criminality and Arrest Among Black, White, and Hispanic Males in the United States," *Criminology* 49 (2011): 1109–1148; Joan Reid, "Exploratory Review of Route-Specific, Gendered, and Age-Graded Dynamics of Exploitation: Applying Life Course Theory to Victimization in Sex Trafficking in North America," *Aggression and Violent Behavior* 17 (2012): 257–271.

70. Daniel Nagin and Raymond Paternoster, "Personal Capital and Social Control: The Deterrence Implications of a Theory of Criminal Offending," *Criminology* 32 (1994): 581–606.

71. Roettger and Swisher, "Associations of Fathers' History of Incarceration with Sons' Criminality and Arrest Among Black, White, and Hispanic Males in the United States."

72. Murray, Loeber, and Pardini, "Parental Involvement in the Criminal Justice System and the Development of Youth Theft, Marijuana Use, Depression, and Poor Academic Performance."

73. Reid, "Exploratory Review of Route-Specific, Gendered, and Age-Graded Dynamics of Exploitation."

74. Nagin and Paternoster, "Personal Capital and Social Control."

75. Leonore M. J. Simon, "Social Bond and Criminal Record History of Acquaintance and Stranger Violent Offenders," *Journal of Crime and Justice* 22 (1999): 131–146.

76. Raymond Paternoster and Robert Brame, "Multiple Routes to Delinquency? A Test of Developmental and General Theories of Crime," *Criminology* 35 (1997): 49–84.

77. Spencer De Li, "Legal Sanctions and Youths' Status Achievement: A Longitudinal Study," *Justice Quarterly* 16 (1999): 377–401.

78. Shawn Bushway, "The Impact of an Arrest on the Job Stability of Young White American Men," *Journal of Research on Crime and Delinquency* 35 (1999): 454–479.

79. Mark Collins and Don Weatherburn, "Unemployment and the Dynamics of Offender Populations," *Journal of Quantitative Criminology* 11 (1995): 231–245.

80. Robert Hoge, D. A. Andrews, and Alan Leschied, "An Investigation of Risk and Protective Factors in a Sample of Youthful Offenders," *Journal of Child Psychology and Psychiatry* 37 (1996): 419–424.

81. Matthew Moore and Nicholas Recker, "Social Capital, Type of Crime, and Social Control," *Crime and Delinquency*, first published November 15, 2013.

82. David S. Kirk, "Residential Change as a Turning Point in the Life Course of Crime: Desistance or Temporary Cessation?" *Criminology* 50 (2012): 329–358.

83. Richard Arum and Irenee Beattie, "High School Experience and the Risk of Adult Incarceration," *Criminology* 37 (1999): 515–540.

84. Ross Macmillan, Barbara J. McMorris, and Candace Kruttschnitt, "Linked Lives: Stability and Change in Maternal Circumstances and Trajectories of Antisocial Behavior in Children," *Child Development* 75 (2004): 205–220.

85. Robert Sampson and John Laub, "Socioeconomic Achievement in the Life Course of Disadvantaged Men: Military Service as a Turning Point, circa 1940–1965," *American Sociological Review* 61 (1996): 347–367.

86. Christopher Uggen, "Ex-Offenders and the Conformist Alternative: A Job Quality Model of Work and Crime," *Social Problems* 46 (1999): 127–151.

87. Ronald L. Simons and Ashley B. Barr, "Shifting Perspectives: Cognitive Changes Mediate the Impact of Romantic Relationships on Desistance from Crime," *Justice Quarterly*, first published online July 20, 2012.

88. Marieke Van Schellen, Robert Apel, and Paul Nieuwbeerta, "'Because You're Mine, I Walk the Line'? Marriage, Spousal Criminality, and Criminal Offending over the Life Course," *Journal of Quantitative Criminology*, first published online April 9, 2012.

89. Pamela Webster, Terri Orbuch, and James House, "Effects of Childhood Family Background on Adult Marital Quality and Perceived Stability," *American Journal of Sociology* 101 (1995): 404–432.

90. Nicole M. Schmidt, Giza Lopes, Marvin D. Krohn, and Alan J. Lizotte, "Getting Caught and Getting Hitched: An Assessment of the Relationship Between Police Intervention, Life Chances, and Romantic Unions," *Justice Quarterly*, first published online January 3, 2014.

91. Elaine Eggleston Doherty and Margaret E. Ensminger, "Marriage and Offending Among a Cohort of Disadvantaged African Americans," *Journal of Research in Crime and Delinquency* 50 (2013): 104–131.

92. Mark Warr, "Life-Course Transitions and Desistance from Crime," *Criminology* 36 (1998): 183–216.

93. Ibid.

94. Alex Piquero, John MacDonald, and Karen Parker, "Race, Local Life Circumstances, and Criminal Activity over the Life-Course," *Social Science Quarterly* 83 (2002): 654–671.

95. Matthew Larson and Gary Sweeten, "Breaking Up Is Hard to Do: Romantic Dissolution, Offending, and Substance Use During the Transition to Adulthood," *Criminology* 50 (2012): 605–636.

96. Bianca Bersani and Elaine Eggleston Doherty, "When the Ties that Bind Unwind: Examining the Enduring and Situational Processes of Change Behind the Marriage Effect, *Criminology* 51 (2013): 399–433.

97. Torkild Hovde Lyngstad and Torbjørn Skardhamar, "Changes in Criminal Offending Around the Time of Marriage," *Journal of Research in Crime and Delinquency* 50 (2013): 608–615.

98. Ryan Schroeder, Peggy Giordano, and Stephen Cernkovich, "Drug Use and Desistance Processes," *Criminology* 45 (2007): 191–222.

99. James Ridde et al., "Millennium Cohort: The 2001–2003 Baseline Prevalence of Mental Disorders in the U.S. Military," *Journal of Clinical Epidemiology* 60 (2007): 192–201.

100. David Rowe, D. Wayne Osgood, and W. Alan Nicewander, "A Latent Trait Approach to Unifying Criminal Careers," *Criminology* 28 (1990): 237–270.

101. Lee Ellis, "Neurohormonal Bases of Varying Tendencies to Learn Delinquent and Criminal Behavior," in *Behavioral Approaches to Crime and Delinquency*, ed. E. Morris and C. Braukmann (New York: Plenum, 1988), pp. 499–518.

102. David Rowe, Alexander Vazsonyi, and Daniel Flannery, "Sex Differences in Crime: Do Means and Within-Sex Variation Have Similar Causes?" *Journal of Research in Crime and Delinquency* 32 (1995): 84–100.

103. Bacon, Paternoster, and Brame, "Understanding the Relationship Between Onset Age and Subsequent Offending During Adolescence."

104. James Q. Wilson and Richard Herrnstein, *Crime and Human Nature* (New York: Simon & Schuster, 1985).

105. Ibid., p. 44.

106. Ibid., p. 171.

107. Michael Gottfredson and Travis Hirschi, *A General Theory of Crime* (Stanford, CA: Stanford University Press, 1990).

108. Ibid., p. 90.
109. Ibid., p. 89.
110. Alex Piquero and Stephen Tibbetts, "Specifying the Direct and Indirect Effects of Low Self-Control and Situational Factors in Offenders' Decision Making: Toward a More Complete Model of Rational Offending," *Justice Quarterly* 13 (1996): 481–508.
111. David Forde and Leslie Kennedy, "Risky Lifestyles, Routine Activities, and the General Theory of Crime," *Justice Quarterly* 14 (1997): 265–294.
112. Gottfredson and Hirschi, *A General Theory of Crime*, p. 112.
113. Ibid.
114. Ryan Meldrum, Jacob Young, Carter Hay, and Jamie Flexon, "Does Self-Control Influence Maternal Attachment? A Reciprocal Effects Analysis from Early Childhood Through Middle Adolescence," *Journal of Quantitative Criminology*, first published online March 24, 2012; Jeffrey Bouffard and Stephen Rice, "The Influence of the Social Bond on Self-Control at the Moment of Decision: Testing Hirschi's Redefinition of Self-Control," *American Journal of Criminal Justice* 36 (2011): 138–157.
115. Chris Gibson, Christopher Sullivan, Shayne Jones, and Alex Piquero, "'Does It Take a Village?' Assessing Neighborhood Influences on Children's Self-Control," *Journal of Research in Crime and Criminality* 47 (2010): 31–62.
116. Meldrum et al., "Does Self-Control Influence Maternal Attachment?"; Stacey Nofziger, "The 'Cause' of Low Self-Control: The Influence of Maternal Self-Control," *Journal of Research in Crime and Criminality* 45 (2008): 191–224.
117. Marie Ratchford and Kevin Beaver, "Neuropsychological Deficits, Low Self-Control, and Delinquent Involvement: Toward a Biosocial Explanation of Delinquency," *Criminal Justice and Behavior* 36 (2009): 147–162.
118. Kevin Beaver and John Paul Wright, "Evaluating the Effects of Birth Complications on Low-Control in a Sample of Twins," *International Journal of Offender Therapy and Comparative Criminology* 49 (2005): 450–472.
119. Kevin M. Beaver, J. Eagle Shutt, Brian Boutwell, Marie Ratchford, Kathleen Roberts, and J. C. Barnes, "Genetic and Environmental Influences on Levels of Self-Control and Delinquent Peer Affiliation: Results from a Longitudinal Sample of Adolescent Twins," *Criminal Justice and Behavior* 36 (2009): 41–60.
120. Gottfredson and Hirschi, *A General Theory of Crime*, p. 27.
121. For a review of this issue, see Anne Campbell, *Men, Women, and Aggression* (New York: Basic Books, 1993).
122. David Brownfield and Ann Marie Sorenson, "Self-Control and Juvenile Delinquency: Theoretical Issues and an Empirical Assessment of Selected Elements of a General Theory of Crime," *Deviant Behavior* 14 (1993): 243–264; Harold Grasmick, Charles Tittle, Robert Bursik, and Bruce Arneklev, "Testing the Core Empirical Implications of Gottfredson and Hirschi's General Theory of Crime," *Journal of Research in Crime and Delinquency* 30 (1993): 5–29.
123. Daniel Nagin and Greg Pogarsky, "Time and Punishment: Delayed Consequences and Criminal Behavior," *Journal of Quantitative Criminology* 20 (2004): 295–317.
124. Michael Reisig, Scott Wolfe, and Travis Pratt, "Low Self-Control and the Religiosity-Crime Relationship," *Criminal Justice and Behavior* 39 (2012): 1172–1191; Michael Reisig, Scott Wolfe, and Kristy Holtfreter, "Legal Cynicism, Legitimacy, and Criminal Offending: The Non-Confounding Effect of Low Self-Control," *Criminal Justice and Behavior* 38 (2011): 1170–1184. Norman White and Rolf Loeber, "Bullying and Special Education as Predictors of Serious Delinquency," *Journal of Research in Crime and Delinquency* 45 (2008): 380–397; Christopher Sullivan, Jean Marie McGloin, Travis Pratt, and Alex Piquero, "Rethinking the 'Norm' of Offender Generality: Investigating Specialization in the Short-Term," *Criminology* 44 (2006): 199–233.
125. Kyle Thomas and Jean Marie McGloin, "A Dual-Systems Approach for Understanding Differential Susceptibility to Processes of Peer Influence," *Criminology* 51 (2013): 435–474.
126. Matt Delisi and Michael Vaughn, "The Gottfredson-Hirschi Critiques Revisited: Reconciling Self-Control Theory, Criminal Careers, and Career Criminals," *International Journal of Offender Therapy and Comparative Criminology* 52 (2008): 520–537.
127. Ibid.
128. Michael Benson and Elizabeth Moore, "Are White-Collar and Common Offenders the Same? An Empirical and Theoretical Critique of a Recently Proposed General Theory of Crime," *Journal of Research in Crime and Delinquency* 29 (1992): 251–272.
129. Kyle Thomas, "On the Relationship Between Peer Isolation and Offending Specialization: The Role of Peers in Promoting Versatile Offending" *Crime and Delinquency*, first published online September 11, 2013; Charles R. Tittle and Harold G. Grasmick, "Criminal Behavior and Age: A Test of Three Provocative Hypotheses," *Journal of Criminal Law and Criminology* 88 (1997): 309–342.
130. Ronald Akers, "Self-Control as a General Theory of Crime," *Journal of Quantitative Criminology* 7 (1991): 201–211.
131. Gottfredson and Hirschi, *A General Theory of Crime*, p. 88.
132. Chris Gibson, "An Investigation of Neighborhood Disadvantage, Low Self-Control, and Violent Victimization Among Youth," *Youth Violence and Juvenile Justice* 10 (2012): 41–63.
133. Gregory Zimmerman, "Impulsivity, Offending, and the Neighborhood: Investigating the Person–Context Nexus," *Journal of Quantitative Criminology* 26 (2010): 301–332.
134. Alan Feingold, "Gender Differences in Personality: A Meta Analysis," *Psychological Bulletin* 116 (1994): 429–456.
135. Charles Tittle, David Ward, and Harold Grasmick, "Gender, Age, and Crime/Deviance: A Challenge to Self-Control Theory," *Journal of Research in Crime and Delinquency* 40 (2003): 426–453.
136. Brent Benda, "Gender Differences in Life-Course Theory of Recidivism: A Survival Analysis," *International Journal of Offender Therapy and Comparative Criminology* 49 (2005): 325–342.
137. Gottfredson and Hirschi, *A General Theory of Crime*, p. 153.
138. Delbert Elliott and Scott Menard, "Delinquent Friends and Delinquent Behavior: Temporal and Developmental Patterns," in *Crime and Delinquency: Current Theories*, ed. J. David Hawkins (Cambridge: Cambridge University Press, 1996).
139. Jean Marie McGloin and Lauren O'Neill Shermer, "Self-Control and Deviant Peer Network Structure," *Journal of Research in Crime and Delinquency* 46 (2009): 35–72.
140. Dana Haynie, Peggy Giordano, Wendy Manning, and Monica Longmore, "Adolescent Romantic Relationships and Delinquency Involvement," *Criminology* 43 (2005): 177–210.
141. Callie Harbin Burt, Ronald Simons, and Leslie Simons, "A Longitudinal Test of the Effects of Parenting and the Stability of Self-Control: Negative Evidence for the General Theory of Crime," *Criminology* 44 (2006): 353–396.
142. Carter Hay and Walter Forrest, "The Development of Self-Control: Examining Self-Control Theory's Stability Thesis," *Criminology* 44 (2006): 739–774.
143. Jean-Louis Van Gelder and Reinout E. De Vries, "Traits and States: Integrating Personality and Affect into a Model of Criminal Decision Making," *Criminology* 50 (2012): 637–371.
144. Michael Courey and Paul-Philippe Pare, "A Closer Look at the Relationship Between Low Self-Control and Delinquency: The Effects of Identity Styles," *Crime and Delinquency*, first published online September 16, 2013.

145. Steven Levitt and Sudhir Alladi Venkatesh, "An Economic Analysis of a Drug-Selling Gang's Finances," *Quarterly Journal of Economics* 13 (2000): 755–789.

146. George Higgins, Melissa Ricketts, Catherine Marcum, and Margaret Mahoney, "Primary Socialization Theory: An Exploratory Study of Delinquent Trajectories," *Criminal Justice Studies* 23 (2010): 133–146.

147. Nicole Leeper Piquero and Terrie Moffitt, "Can Childhood Factors Predict Workplace Deviance?" *Justice Quarterly*, first published online February 21, 2012; Yao Zheng and H. Harrington Cleveland, "Identifying Gender-Specific Developmental Trajectories of Nonviolent and Violent Delinquency from Adolescence to Young Adulthood," *Journal of Adolescence* 36 (2013): 371–381.

148. Donald Lynam, Alex Piquero, and Terrie Moffitt, "Specialization and the Propensity to Violence: Support from Self-Reports but Not Official Records," *Journal of Contemporary Criminal Justice* 20 (2004): 215–228.

149. Stacy Tzoumakis, Patrick Lussier, Marc Le Blanc, and Garth Davies, "Onset, Offending Trajectories, and Crime Specialization in Violence," *Youth Violence and Juvenile Justice* 11 (2013): 143–164.

150. Selma Salihovic, Metin Özdemir, and Margaret Kerr, "Trajectories of Adolescent Psychopathic Traits," *Journal of Psychopathology and Behavioral Assessment* 36 (2014): 47–59.

151. Ryan Schroeder and Thomas Mowen, "Parenting Style Transitions and Delinquency," *Youth and Society* 46 (2014): 228–254.

152. Alex Piquero, Robert Brame, Paul Mazerolle, and Rudy Haapanen, "Crime in Emerging Adulthood," *Criminology* 40 (2002): 137–170.

153. Wesley Jennings and Jennifer Reingle, "On the Number and Shape of Developmental/Life-Course Violence, Aggression, and Delinquency Trajectories: A State-of-the-Art Review," *Journal of Criminal Justice* 40 (2012): 472–489.

154. Ick-Joong Chung, Karl G. Hill, J. David Hawkins, Lewayne Gilchrist, and Daniel Nagin, "Childhood Predictors of Offense Trajectories," *Journal of Research in Crime and Delinquency* 39 (2002): 60–91.

155. Alex Piquero, Delphine Theobald, and David Farrington, "The Overlap Between Offending Trajectories, Criminal Violence, and Intimate Partner Violence," *International Journal of Offender Therapy and Comparative Criminology* 58 (2014): 286–302.

156. Amy D'Unger, Kenneth Land, Patricia McCall, and Daniel Nagin, "How Many Latent Classes of Delinquent/Criminal Careers? Results from Mixed Poisson Regression Analyses," *American Journal of Sociology* 103 (1998): 1593–1630.

157. Josanne D. M. van Dongen, Nicole M. L. Buck, and Hjalmar J. C. van Marle, "First Offenders with Psychosis: Justification of a Third Type Within the Early/Late Start Offender Typology," *Crime and Delinquency*, first published online October 28, 2013.

158. Ibid.

159. Alex Piquero, Wesley Jennings, and David Farrington, "The Monetary Costs of Crime to Middle Adulthood: Findings from the Cambridge Study in Delinquent Development," *Journal of Research in Crime and Delinquency* 50 (2013): 53–74.

160. Alex Piquero, David Farrington, Daniel Nagin, and Terrie Moffitt, "Trajectories of Offending and Their Relation to Life Failure in Late Middle Age: Findings from the Cambridge Study in Delinquent Development," *Journal of Research in Crime and Delinquency* 47 (2010): 151–173.

161. Chung et al., "Childhood Predictors of Offense Trajectories."

162. Bacon, Paternoster, and Brame, "Understanding the Relationship Between Onset Age and Subsequent Offending During Adolescence."

163. Victor van der Geest, Arjan Blokland, and Catrien Bijleveld, "Delinquent Development in a Sample of High-Risk Youth: Shape, Content, and Predictors of Delinquent Trajectories from Age 12 to 32," *Journal of Research in Crime and Delinquency* 46 (2009): 111–143.

164. Terrie Moffitt, "A Review of Research on the Taxonomy of Life-Course Persistent versus Adolescence-Limited Antisocial Behavior," in *Taking Stock: The Status of Criminological Theory*, Vol. 15, ed. F. T. Cullen, J. P. Wright, and K. R. Blevins (New Brunswick, NJ: Transaction Publications, 2006), pp. 277–311.

165. Matthew Johnson and Scott Menard, "A Longitudinal Study of Delinquency Abstention: Differences Between Life-Course Abstainers and Offenders from Adolescence into Adulthood," *Youth Violence and Juvenile Justice* 10 (2012): 278–291; Xiaojin Chen and Michele Adam, "Are Teen Delinquency Abstainers Social Introverts? A Test of Moffitt's Theory," *Journal of Research in Crime and Delinquency* 47 (2010): 439–468.

166. J. C. Barnes, Kevin Beaver, and Brian Boutwell, "Examining the Genetic Underpinnings to Moffitt's Developmental Taxonomy: A Behavioral Genetic Analysis," *Criminology* 49 (2011): 923–954.

167. Jennifer Gatewood Owens and Lee Ann Slocum, "Abstainers in Adolescence and Adulthood: Exploring the Correlates of Abstention Using Moffitt's Developmental Taxonomy," *Crime and Delinquency*, published online February 7, 2012.

168. Margit Wiesner and Ranier Silbereisen, "Trajectories of Delinquent Behaviour in Adolescence and Their Covariates: Relations with Initial and Time-Averaged Factors," *Journal of Adolescence* 26 (2003): 753–771.

169. Lynam, Piquero, and Moffitt, "Specialization and the Propensity to Violence."

170. Jennifer Reingle, Wesley Jennings, and Mildred Maldonado-Molina, "Risk and Protective Factors for Trajectories of Violent Criminality Among a Nationally Representative Sample of Early Adolescents," *Youth Violence and Juvenile Justice*, first published online February 16, 2012.

171. Georgia Zara and David Farrington, "Childhood and Adolescent Predictors of Late Onset Criminal Careers," *Journal of Youth and Adolescence* 38 (2009): 287–300.

172. Rolf Loeber, Phen Wung, Kate Keenan, Bruce Giroux, Magda Stouthamer-Loeber, Wemoet van Kammen, and Barbara Maughan, "Developmental Pathways in Disruptive Behavior," *Development and Psychopathology* (1993): 12–48.

173. Sheila Royo Maxwell and Christopher Maxwell, "Examining the 'Criminal Careers' of Prostitutes Within the Nexus of Drug Use, Drug Selling, and Other Illicit Activities," *Criminology* 38 (2000): 787–809.

174. Alex Piquero and Timothy Brezina, "Testing Moffitt's Account of Adolescent-Limited Delinquency," *Criminology* 39 (2001): 353–370.

175. Terrie Moffitt, "Adolescence-Limited and Life-Course Persistent Antisocial Behavior: A Developmental Taxonomy," *Psychological Review* 100 (1993): 674–701.

176. Terrie Moffitt, "Natural Histories of Delinquency" in *Cross-National Longitudinal Research on Human Development and Criminal Behavior*, ed. Elmar Weitekamp and Hans-Jurgen Kerner (Dordrecht, Netherlands: Kluwer, 1994), pp. 3–65.

177. Adrian Raine, Rolf Loeber, Magda Stouthamer-Loeber, Terrie Moffitt, Avshalom Caspi, and Don Lynam, "Neurocognitive Impairments in Boys on the Life-Course Persistent Antisocial Path," *Journal of Abnormal Psychology* 114 (2005): 38–49.

178. Per-Olof Wikstrom and Rolf Loeber, "Do Disadvantaged Neighborhoods Cause Well-Adjusted Children to Become Adolescent Delinquents? A Study of Male Juvenile Serious Offending, Individual Risk and Protective Factors, and Neighborhood Context," *Criminology* 38 (2000): 1109–1142.

179. Alex Piquero, Leah Daigle, Chris Gibson, Nicole Leeper Piquero, and Stephen Tibbetts, "Are Life-Course-Persistent

Offenders at Risk for Adverse Health Outcomes?" *Journal of Research in Crime and Delinquency* 44 (2007): 185–207.

180. Robert Vermeiren, "Psychopathology and Criminality in Adolescents: A Descriptive and Developmental Perspective," *Clinical Psychology Review* 23 (2003): 277–318; Paul Mazerolle, Robert Brame, Ray Paternoster, Alex Piquero, and Charles Dean, "Onset Age, Persistence, and Offending Versatility: Comparisons Across Sex," *Criminology* 38 (2000): 1143–1172.

181. Raine et al., "Neurocognitive Impairments in Boys on the Life-Course Persistent Antisocial Path."

182. Wikstrom and Loeber, "Do Disadvantaged Neighborhoods Cause Well-Adjusted Children to Become Adolescent Delinquents?"

183. Andrea Donker, Wilma Smeenk, Peter van der Laan, and Frank Verhulst, "Individual Stability of Antisocial Behavior from Childhood to Adulthood: Testing the Stability Postulate of Moffitt's Developmental Theory," *Criminology* 41 (2003): 593–609.

184. J. C. Barnes, Kevin Beaver, and Brian Boutwell, "Examining the Genetic Underpinnings to Moffitt's Developmental Taxonomy: A Behavioral Genetic Analysis," *Criminology* 49 (2011): 923–954.

185. Brian Boutwell, J. C. Barnes, Raelynn Deaton, and Kevin Beaver, "On the Evolutionary Origins of Life-Course Persistent Offending: A Theoretical Scaffold for Moffitt's Developmental Taxonomy," *Journal of Theoretical Biology* 322 (2013): 72–80.

186. Graham Ousey and Pamela Wilcox, "The Interaction of Antisocial Propensity and Life-Course Varying Predictors of Delinquent Behavior: Differences by Method of Estimation and Implications for Theory," *Criminology* 45 (2007): 313–354.

187. Bradley Entner Wright, Avshalom Caspi, Terrie Moffitt, and Phil Silva, "Low Self-Control, Social Bonds, and Crime: Social Causation, Social Selection, or Both?" *Criminology* 37 (1999): 479–514.

188. Ibid., p. 504.

189. Stephen Cernkovich and Peggy Giordano, "Stability and Change in Antisocial Behavior: The Transition from Adolescence to Early Adulthood," *Criminology* 39 (2001): 371–410.

190. Heather Lonczk, Robert Abbott, J. David Hawkins, Rick Kosterman, and Richard Catalano, "Effects of the Seattle Social Development Project on Sexual Behavior, Pregnancy, Birth, and Sexually Transmitted Disease Outcomes by Age 21 Years," *Archive of Pediatrics and Adolescent Medicine* 156 (2002): 438–447.

191. Kathleen Bodisch Lynch, Susan Rose Geller, and Melinda G. Schmidt, "Multi-Year Evaluation of the Effectiveness of a Resilience-Based Prevention Program for Young Children," *Journal of Primary Prevention* 24 (2004): 335–353.

192. This section leans on Thomas Tatchell, Phillip Waite, Renny Tatchell, Lynne Durrant, and Dale Bond, "Substance Abuse Prevention in Sixth Grade: The Effect of a Prevention Program on Adolescents' Risk and Protective Factors," *American Journal of Health Studies* 19 (2004): 54–61.

193. Nancy Tobler and Howard Stratton, "Effectiveness of School Based Drug Prevention Programs: A Meta-Analysis of the Research," *Journal of Primary Prevention* 18 (1997): 71–128.

PART
THREE

CRIME TYPOLOGIES

Criminologists group criminal offenders and criminal behaviors into categories or typologies so they may be more easily studied and understood. Are there common traits or characteristics that link offenders together and make them distinct from nonoffenders? Are there common areas between seemingly different acts such as murder and rape?

In this section, we focus on crime typologies. They are clustered into six groups: violent crime (Chapter 10), political crime and terrorism (Chapter 11), property crimes involving common theft offenses and arson (Chapter 12), enterprise crimes involving white-collar, green, and transnational organized criminals (Chapter 13), public order crimes, such as prostitution and drug abuse (Chapter 14), and cybercrimes (Chapter 15). This format groups criminal behaviors by their focus: bringing physical harm to others, misappropriating other people's property, violating laws designed to protect public morals, and using technology to commit crime.

Typologies can be useful in classifying large numbers of criminal offenses or offenders into easily understood categories. This text has grouped offenses and offenders on the basis of their legal definitions and their collective goals, objectives, and consequences.

learning objectives

LO1 Differentiate among the various causes of violent crime

LO2 Articulate the stages in Athens's violentization process

LO3 Discuss the history of rape and the different types of rape and rapists

LO4 Assess the legal issues in rape prosecution

LO5 Compare and contrast the different degrees of murder

LO6 Assess stranger and acquaintance homicide

LO7 Analyze the differences among serial killing, mass murder, and spree killing

LO8 Discuss the root causes of child abuse

LO9 Discuss the crime of robbery and why it is a rational crime

LO10 Describe emerging forms of violence such as stalking, hate crimes, and workplace violence

INTERPERSONAL VIOLENCE

In 2014, the trial of South African athlete Oscar Pistorius made headlines around the world. Pistorius, a double-amputee known as the "Blade Runner" for his scythe-like prosthetic legs, was a Paralympics champion who began competing in able-bodied events. At the 2011 World Championships in Athletics, Pistorius became the first amputee to win a track medal at an international competition. At the 2012 Summer Olympics, Pistorius became the first double leg amputee to participate in the Olympics, making him world famous. Then on February 14, 2013, he was charged with the murder of his beautiful model girlfriend, Reeva Steenkamp. According to all reports, Steenkamp was killed in the bathroom of his Pretoria home when Pistorius shot four times through the closed door. But why the shooting occurred was the key and only issue in the case. According to Pistorius, he was awakened by a noise, heard the bathroom window open, believed an intruder had broken into the house, and shot to defend himself and Reeva before realizing he had made a terrible mistake. His story was disputed by prosecutors, who argued that Pistorius fought with Steenkamp for some unknown reasons and then shot her in anger when she took refuge in the bathroom. Their case was supported by neighbors who testified they heard screams and then shots being fired. The defense rebutted that the neighbors who thought they heard a woman's screams were mistaken: the screams were actually Pistorius, who became frenzied when he realized his mistake. The prosecution also brought witnesses who said that Pistorius had a hot temper, routinely carried guns, and on more than one occasion shot them off in anger.[1]

On September 12, 2014, Pistorius was found guilty of culpable homicide, which means killing someone without intent but through recklessness or negligence. The trial judge ruled that his actions were not those of a reasonable person, who might have first checked where his girlfriend was, or even fired a warning shot.

he Pistorius case illustrates the toll violent crime takes on society in the United States and around the world. It can divide a community, damage reputations, and cause lifelong harm. It tells people that no matter where they go, they may encounter violent acts—at a movie theater, a public park, or even in their own bathroom. Nor is violence committed solely by gang boys and drug dealers. As the Pistorius case sadly shows, you can also be attacked by your own wealthy boyfriend! Millions of violent crimes occur each year. Some are **expressive violence**—acts that vent rage, anger, or frustration—and some are **instrumental violence**—acts designed to improve the financial or social position of the criminal, for example, through an armed robbery or murder for hire. Media accounts of interpersonal violence cause people to live in fear, staying home at night in order to avoid dangerous neighborhoods. Violent crimes can bring disorder to whole communities, disrupting services, driving down real estate values, and destabilizing surrounding areas.[2]

This chapter explores the concept of violence in some depth. First, it reviews the suggested causes of violent crime. Then it focuses on specific types of interpersonal violence—rape, homicide, assault, robbery, and newly recognized types of interpersonal violence such as stalking and workplace violence.

THE CAUSES OF VIOLENCE

LO1 Differentiate among the various causes of violent crime

What sets off a violent person? Criminologists have a variety of views on this subject. Some believe that violence is a function of human traits and makeup. Others point to improper socialization and upbringing. Violent behavior may be culturally determined and relate to dysfunctional social values. The various sources of violence are set out in Figure 10.1.

Psychological/Biological Abnormality

On March 13, 1996, an ex-Scout leader named Thomas Hamilton took four automatic handguns into the primary school of the peaceful Scottish town of Dunblane and slaughtered 16 kindergarten children and their teacher before taking his

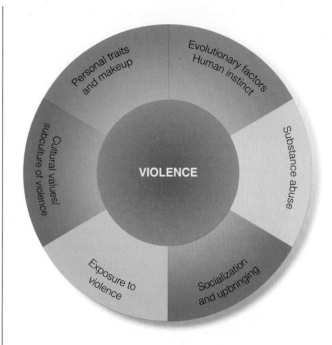

FIGURE 10.1 Sources of Violence

own life. This horrific crime shocked the British Isles into implementing strict controls on all guns.[3] Many of those in the school who were spared, such as tennis star Andy Murray, bear lifelong psychic scars from the tragedy.[4] Bizarre outbursts such as Hamilton's support a link between violence and some sort of mental or biological abnormality.

People who are involved in violent episodes may be suffering from severe mental abnormalities.[5] In a classic work, psychologist Dorothy Otnow Lewis showed that kids who kill may be suffering from multiple symptoms of psychological abnormality: neurological impairment (e.g., abnormal EEGs, multiple psychomotor impairments, and severe seizures), low intelligence, and psychotic symptoms such as paranoia, illogical thinking, and hallucinations.[6] In her book *Guilty by Reason of Insanity*, Lewis found that death row inmates have a history of mental impairment and intellectual dysfunction.[7]

Lewis's research is not unique. Abnormal personality structures, including such traits as depression, impulsivity, aggression, dishonesty, pathological lying, lack of remorse, borderline personality syndrome, and psychopathology, have all been associated with various forms of violence.[8] It comes as no surprise to psychologists that many murderers kill themselves shortly after committing their crime.[9]

There is also evidence that personality disturbance is linked to some physical trait or characteristic. Neuroscientists claim to have found differences in both the limbic system and the prefrontal cortex of the brain that separates aggressive, violent people from the more level-headed and reasonable. According to this view, if some defect or injury impairs communication between the limbic system and the frontal cortex, a person might not be entirely able to moderate his or her emotional reactions.[10] People convicted of murder have in fact been shown to suffer signs of neurological impairment (such as abnormal electroencephalograms (EEGs), multiple psychomotor impairments, and severe seizures), low intelligence as measured on standard IQ tests, psychotic close relatives, mental impairment and intellectual dysfunction, animal cruelty, and psychotic symptoms such as paranoia, illogical thinking, and hallucinations.[11]

If there is a connection between psychological instability and violence, does the availability of mental health treatment help reduce violence rates? A recent international survey found that there is in fact a significant relationship between mental health treatment opportunities and global crime rate trends and that a significant drop in the violence rate may be due to expanded mental health treatment.[12]

Human Instinct

Some anthropologists trace the roots of violence back to our prehistory, when our ancestors lived in social groups and fought for dominance. The earliest humans would not hesitate to retaliate violently against aggressors, and it was common for family, tribe, or clan members to protect one another if they were attacked.[13] According to Harvard psychologist Steven Pinker, the remains of earliest humans indicate that a significant number were the victims of violence rather than dying from natural causes. High violence rates began to decline when our hunter-gatherer ancestors began to settle into agricultural civilizations, which Pinker calls the pacification process.[14] Still, about 15 percent of the earliest tribal bands died violently, compared to about 3 percent of the citizens of the original organized states or empires, when rulers implemented forces to protect the population from harm.

The fact that our ancient ancestors were so violent seems to suggest that violence is instinctual and part of the human condition. Sigmund Freud believed that human behavior is shaped by two instinctual drives: *eros*, the life instinct, which drives people toward self-fulfillment and enjoyment, and *thanatos*, the death instinct, which produces self-destruction. Thanatos can be expressed externally (e.g., violence and sadism) or internally (e.g., suicide, alcoholism, or other self-destructive habits).[15]

In his celebrated book *On Aggression*, anthropologist Konrad Lorenz argued that aggressive energy is produced by inbred instincts that are independent of environmental forces.[16] In the animal kingdom, aggression usually serves a productive purpose—for example, it leads members of grazing species such as zebras and antelopes to spread out over available territory to ensure an ample food supply and the survival of the fittest. Lorenz found that humans possess some of the same aggressive instincts as animals. But within lower species, aggression is rarely fatal; when a conflict occurs, the winner is determined through a test of skill or endurance. This inhibition against killing members of their own species protects animals from self-extinction. Humans, lacking this inhibition against fatal violence, are capable of killing their own kind in war or as a result of interpersonal conflicts such as those arising over finding suitable mates.[17] Lorenz feared that as technology develops and more lethal weapons are produced, the extinction of the human species becomes a significant possibility.

To learn more about Konrad Lorenz, who won the Nobel Prize in Medicine in 1973, go to **http://www.kl .ac.at/Institution/lorenz.htm.**

Do you think humans are aggressive by nature? If not, why have we been so violent since the beginning of time? Why are we constantly involved in war and conquest?

Social Interaction In his recent book *Violence: A Microsociological Theory*, sociologist Randall Collins proposes a theory of violence that seems diametrically opposed to Lorenz: humans are inherently passive and violence is a function of social interaction. Collins argues that most humans shirk from violent encounters and even those who talk aggressively are fearful and tense during violent encounters. Humans typically resort to violence only when they have overwhelming superiority over their opponents in terms of arms and numbers. While the thought of violence makes most people weak and scared, a supportive audience helps it become more palatable. Whether it's gang boys acting in a group or terrorists being supported by their leaders, violence is more of a group process than an individual choice.

Collins finds that the myth that humans enjoy bloodshed is perpetuated by media depictions of violence. Take for instance the barroom brawl shown in numerous films. A fight breaks out in a bar and soon everyone joins in, joyously punching each other and breaking up the premises. When the crowd doesn't join in, they generally will make a space for the individuals to fight, cheering and shouting encouragement. Fights are drawn out with two evenly matched opponents punching each other for long periods of combat. While normative in the movies, Collins points out that these events never actually happen in real life. When a fight does break out, most patrons typically back away to a safe distance and watch, shrinking away as far as possible. Rather than shouting encouragement, onlookers tend to withdraw vocally as well as physically. And rather than drawn-out brawls, fights are over quickly, typically with a single punch. Most brawlers are willing to quit without a clear-cut victory as soon as a few punches are launched. When there is a group brawl, it's because sides had been chosen beforehand based on social and political views or even sports team loyalty. In these instances, the "free-for-all" that may look chaotic and unstructured to outsiders is actually carefully organized. Prior organization, group identity, and support, Collins finds, are what enables individuals to overcome their own pervasive fear of violence and confrontation; if it were not well organized, wide-participation group fighting would not be possible.[18]

AP Images/*Denver Post*, Andy Cross, Pool, File

Shooting suspect James Holmes appears in court in Centennial, Colorado. Holmes killed 12 people and wounded dozens more at an Aurora, Colorado, movie theater in 2012. His lawyers claimed he was "in the throes of a psychotic episode" at the time. Does the frequency of mass killings by psychologically impaired criminals seem to be increasing? Or is this trend merely a function of the availability of high-powered weapons that make their violent outbursts ever more lethal?

- *Economic compulsive behavior.* Drug users resort to violence to obtain the financial resources to support their habit. Studies conducted in the United States and Europe show that addicts commit hundreds of crimes each year.[27]

- *Systemic link.* Violence escalates when drug-dealing gangs flex their muscle to dominate territory and drive out rivals. Those involved in the sale of illicit drugs in urban street markets face an elevated risk for serious victimization. Despite their fierce image, drug dealers are not immune to violence from robbers who realize they carry a lot of cash and cannot call the police when they are victimized. Only those dealers who are very active in the drug market and willing to use violence to protect their turf are immune from violent victimization; there are actually less aggressive dealers who are fair game for armed robbers.[28]

Substance Abuse

Substance abuse has been associated with violence on both the individual and social levels: substance abusers have higher rates of violence than nonabusers; neighborhoods with high levels of substance abuse have higher violence rates when compared to areas with low use rates.[19] A direct association has been found between community levels of crack cocaine and heroin use and the incidence of street robberies.[20] High use areas may also face social disorganization, poverty, and unemployment, factors that further escalate violence rates.[21]

The link between substance abuse and violence appears in three different formats:[22]

- *Psychopharmacological relationship.* Violence may be the direct consequence of ingesting mood-altering substances. High doses of drugs such as PCP and amphetamines and binge drinking can produce violent, aggressive behavior and are associated with violent crime rates.[23] Heavy drinking reduces cognitive ability, information processing skills, and the ability to process and react to verbal and nonverbal behavior. As a result, miscommunication becomes more likely and the capacity for rational dialogue is compromised.[24] It is not surprising that males involved in sexual assaults often claim that they were drinking and misunderstood their victims' intentions.[25] Drinking becomes particularly dangerous when abusers have access to firearms; guns and alcohol do not mix well.[26]

Socialization and Upbringing

Another view is that improper socialization and upbringing are responsible for the onset of violent acts. Absent or deviant parents, inconsistent discipline, physical abuse, and lack of supervision have all been linked to persistent violent offending.[29]

Although infants demonstrate individual temperaments, who they become may have a lot to do with how they are treated during their early years. Some children are harder to soothe than others; in some cases, difficult infant temperament has been associated with later aggression and behavioral problems.[30] Parents who fail to set adequate limits or to use proper, consistent discipline reinforce a child's coercive behavior.[31] The effects of inadequate parenting and early rejection may affect violent behavior throughout life.[32]

There are also indications that children who are subject to even minimal amounts of physical punishment may be more likely one day to use violence themselves.[33] Sociologist Murray Straus reviewed the concept of discipline in a series of surveys and found a powerful relationship between exposure to physical punishment and later aggression.[34] We now know that the more often a child is physically disciplined and the harsher the punishment, the more likely they will later engage in antisocial behaviors.[35] The effect of physical punishment may be mediated or neutralized to some extent if parents also provide support, warmth, and care. When kids experience physical punishment in the absence of parental involvement, they feel angry and unjustly treated and are more willing to defy their parents and engage in antisocial behavior.[36]

The Cycle of Violence   In a series of research studies, criminologist Cathy Widom identified a cycle of violence, in which physical abuse by parents or caregivers is a direct cause of subsequent violent behavior among youth.[37] Kids who were abused are then likely to grow up to be abusers themselves, creating a never-ending cycle of abuse and violence.

Since Widom's pioneering efforts, there has been a significant amount of research supporting the cycle of violence concept, showing that people who suffer abuse in childhood and adolescence are more likely to get involved in violent behavior as teens and adults.[38] Not surprisingly, abused kids are also more likely to experience involvement with the juvenile justice system.[39] People who have been abused are 59 percent more likely to be arrested as a juvenile, 28 percent more likely to be arrested as an adult, and 30 percent more likely to commit violent crime as the nonabused; as many as two-thirds of the people in treatment for drug abuse reported being abused or neglected as children.[40]

The effects of abuse appear to be long term: exposure in early life provides a foundation for violent and antisocial behavior in late adolescence and adulthood.[41] The more often and severe the abuse, the more likely a child will later engage in crime.[42] Samples of convicted murderers reveal a high percentage of seriously abused youth.[43]

There are also distinct class and gender patterns in the abuse–crime association. Lower-class children are more likely to be mistreated than those in the upper and middle classes; abused boys are at greater risk to commit crime than are girls. Children suffering sexual abuse have a greater chance of getting involved in crime and substance abuse than those who are physically abused.[44]

Ironically, while lower-class youth suffer abuse more than their upper- and middle-class peers, it seems to have less effect. One reason: abuse and violence may be more common in lower-class neighborhoods, more culturally accepted, and therefore may have less of an effect on its targets, who view themselves and their upbringing as normative.[45]

Not all abused children become violent criminals. Many do not, and many violent youths come from what appear to be model homes. Although many studies have supported the validity of the cycle of violence concept, others find the association weak and insignificant.[46] More research is needed to clarify this very important association.

LO2   Articulate the stages in Athens's violentization process

The Violentization Process   Lonnie Athens, a well-known criminologist who links violence to early experiences with child abuse, has coined the phrase **violentization process** to describe how abused kids are turned into aggressive adults.[47] The stages of this process are described in Exhibit 10.1.

EXHIBIT 10.1
Stages in the Violentization Process

1. *Brutalization stage.* During this phase of the violentization process, a young victim develops a belligerent, angry demeanor as a result of being mistreated by abusive parents or caretakers. Brutalization can be broader than parental physical or sexual abuse and can result from violent coaching by peers, neighbors, and schoolmates. Although most brutalization occurs early in life, some people can be brutalized as they mature. There are a number of facets in the brutalization stage:

   - *Violent subjugation.* A person is coerced into compliance by physical or verbal force. Coercive violence ends at submission, but retaliatory violence continues regardless of submission, with the goal of gaining long-term submission.
   - *Personal horrification.* An individual is exposed to violence directed at someone else close to them, leading to inner conflict and guilt associated with their helplessness to do anything about the abuse.
   - *Violent coaching.* A brutalizer, through ridicule, threats, or coercion, advises the brutalized individuals to depend only on themselves, encourages defensiveness, and insists that they have a personal responsibility to commit violence.

2. *Belligerency stage.* During this stage, the target of brutalization begins to understand their dilemma. At first they may wonder, "Why can't I stop this violence and brutalization?" Then they begin a cognitive process in which they conclude that sometimes violence is a necessary evil in the world. They think, "Why have I not done anything to stop being the target of violent outbursts?". They then conclude that resorting to violence is sometimes necessary in this world.

3. *Violent performance stage.* Brutalized youth may become belligerent and angry. When confronted at home, school, or on the street, these belligerent youth respond with violent performances of angry, hostile behavior. The success of their violent confrontations provides them with a sense of power and achievement.

4. *Virulency stage.* The emerging criminal develops a violent identity that makes them feared; they enjoy intimidating others. Filled with feelings of power, the brutalized person believes they can perform even more impressive violent feats in the future. They believe they are now invincible. This process takes violent youths full circle from being the victims of aggression to being its initiators; they are now the same person they grew up despising, ready to begin the process with their own children.

SOURCE: Lonnie Athens, *The Creation of Dangerous Violent Criminals* (Urbana: University of Illinois Press, 1992), pp. 27–80.

violentization process According to Lonnie Athens, the process by which abused children are turned into aggressive adults. This process takes violent youths full circle from being the victims of aggression to its initiators; they are now the same person they grew up despising, ready to begin the process with their own children.

Athens recognizes that abuse alone is not a sufficient condition to cause someone to become a dangerous violent criminal. One must complete the full cycle of the violentization process—brutalization, belligerence, violent performances, and virulency—to become socialized into violence. Many brutalized children do not go on to become violent criminals, and some later reject the fact that they were abused as youths and redefine their early years as normative.

Exposure to Violence

People who are constantly exposed to violence in the environment may adopt violent methods themselves.[48] Children living in areas marked by extreme violence may eventually become desensitized to the persistent brutality.[49] Much of the difference in violent crime rates between whites and racial minorities can be explained by the fact that the latter are often forced to live in high-crime neighborhoods, which increases their risk of exposure to violence.[50] Areas where people have little confidence in the police and are therefore reluctant to call for help—a condition common in the minority community—may also experience higher levels of violent behavior.[51]

Social scientist Felton Earls and his associates conducted the Project on Human Development in Chicago Neighborhoods, a government-funded longitudinal study of pathways to violence among 7,000 Chicago area people in 80 randomly selected neighborhoods.[52] Interviews with youths aged 9 to 15 show that large numbers of these children have been victims of or witnesses to violence and that many carry weapons. Between 30 and 40 percent of the children who reported exposure to violence also displayed significant violent behavior themselves. Earls finds that young teens who witness gun violence are more than twice as likely as nonwitnesses to commit violent crime themselves in the following years.[53] Even a single exposure to firearm violence doubles the chance that a young person will later engage in violent behavior.

Children living in these conditions become **crusted over**: they do not let people inside nor do they express their feelings. They exploit others and in turn are exploited by those older and stronger; as a result, they develop a sense of hopelessness.

crusted over Children who have been victims of or witnesses to violence and do not let people inside, nor do they express their feelings. They exploit others and in turn are exploited by those older and stronger; as a result, they develop a sense of hopelessness.

subculture of violence Norms and customs that, in contrast to society's dominant value system, legitimize and expect the use of violence to resolve social conflicts.

disputatiousness Behavior within culturally defined conflict situations in which an individual who has been offended by a negative outcome in a dispute seeks reparations through violent means.

They find that parents and teachers focus on their failures and problems, not their achievements. Consequently, they are vulnerable to the lure of delinquent gangs and groups.[54]

Cultural Values: Subculture of Violence

Violence may be the product of cultural beliefs, values, and behaviors that develop in poor and disorganized neighborhoods.[55] In a classic work, criminologists Marvin Wolfgang and Franco Ferracuti formulated the famous concept that some areas contain an independent **subculture of violence**.[56]

The subculture of violence's norms are separate from society's central, dominant value system. In this subculture, a potent theme of violence influences lifestyles, the socialization process, and interpersonal relationships. Even though the subculture's members share some of the dominant culture's values, they expect that violence will be used to solve social conflicts and dilemmas. In some cultural subgroups, then, violence has become legitimized by custom and norms. It is considered appropriate behavior within culturally defined conflict situations in which an individual who has been offended by a negative outcome in a dispute seeks reparations through violent means—a concept referred to as **disputatiousness**.[57]

There is evidence that a subculture of violence may be found in areas that experience concentrated poverty and social disorganization.[58] Though most people abhor violence, income inequality and racial disparity may help instill a sense of hopelessness that nourishes pro-violence norms and values.[59] In these areas people are more likely to carry weapons and use them in assaults and robberies. Victims are aware of these tactics and are less likely to fight back forcibly when attacked.[60] However, when pressed to the limit even passive victims may eventually fight back. When Charis Kubrin and Ronald Weitzer studied homicide in St. Louis, Missouri, they discovered that a certain type of killing referred to as *cultural retaliatory homicide* is common in neighborhoods that suffer economic disadvantage. In these areas, residents resolve interpersonal conflicts informally—without calling the police—even if it means killing their opponent; neighbors understand and support their violent methods.[61] Because police and other agencies of formal social control are viewed as weak and devalued, understaffed and/or corrupt, people are willing to take matters into their own hands and violence rates increase accordingly.[62]

The Gang Subculture Empirical evidence shows that violence rates are highest in urban areas where subcultural values support teenage gangs whose members typically embrace the use of violence.[63] Gang boys are more likely to own guns and other weapons than nongang members. They are also more likely to have peers who are gun owners and are more likely to carry guns outside the home.[64]

While many boys are predisposed toward violence before joining a gang, research shows that once in gangs their violent behavior quickly escalates; after they leave, it significantly

According to the subculture of violence concept, violence is a normal response to conflict in some communities. In this August 13, 2013, photo, police officers take a report from a woman who had her phone stolen in the Brownsville section in the Brooklyn borough of New York. Strategies that have dropped crime to record lows across the city haven't taken hold in this Brooklyn neighborhood where the cycle of violence, silence, and retribution seems entrenched. And community activists say a big police presence can't make up for the lack of better schools, more jobs, and better housing.

AP Images/Seth Wenig

declines.[65] A recent study by Andrew Papachristos of gang homicide supports the association between cultural values and violence.[66] Papachristos finds that members do not kill because they are poor, young, or live in a socially disadvantaged neighborhood, but rather because they live in a culture that maintains norms conducive to violent retaliation. When a gang boy kills a rival, murders spread through a process of social contagion as gangs are forced to respond in order to maintain their social status and honor through a display of solidarity. The culture that houses gangs associates honor with hypermasculinity and the use of violence to protect reputation. Because formal social control (i.e., the police) is absent in gang areas, violence is condoned or promoted as an acceptable form of social control. The need to conform to cultural values and to protect the gang's rep is more important than individual thoughts and feelings. While some may link gang violence to "turf wars," disputes that lead to murder are less about a parcel of land than about a gang's status and perceived dominance.

Cultural Values: National Values

Some nations—including Colombia, Brazil, Sri Lanka, Angola, Uganda, and the Philippines—have relatively high violence rates, while others, such as Japan, are relatively nonviolent. There are two possible explanations for this discrepancy. One is that nations with high violence rates embrace value structures that support violence, while those that have a

strong communitarian spirit and an emphasis on forgiveness and restorative justice have low violence rates.[67]

The other view is that nations with high violence rates also have negative structural factors such as a high level of poverty, income inequality, illiteracy, and alcohol consumption, and it is these components, rather than a regional culture of violence, that produce high crime rates.[68]

Does the United States maintain values that promote violence? According to historian David Courtwright, relatively high violence rates in the United States can be traced to a frontier culture that was characterized by racism and preoccupation with personal honor.[69] Westerners drank heavily and frequented saloons and gambling halls, where petty arguments could become lethal because most patrons carried guns and knives. Violent acts often went unpunished because law enforcement agencies were unable or unwilling to take action. The population of the frontier was mostly young bachelors who were sensitive about honor, morally indifferent, heavily armed, and unchecked by adequate law enforcement. Many died from disease, but others succumbed to drink and violence. Smoking, gambling, and heavy drinking became a cultural imperative, and those who were disinclined to indulge were considered social outcasts. Courtwright claims that over time gender ratios equalized as more men brought families to the frontier and children of both sexes were born. Many men died, returned home, or drifted elsewhere. By the mid-twentieth century, America's overall male surplus was disappearing, and a balanced population helped bring down the crime rate, but remnants of the frontier mentality still exist in contemporary American society.

In the Criminology in Action feature on page 335, characteristics of America's national history are related to homicide rates.

RAPE

 LO3 Discuss the history of rape and the different types of rape and rapists

Rape (from the Latin *rapere*, to take by force) is defined in common law as "the carnal knowledge of a female forcibly and against her will."[70] It is one of the most loathed,

criminology in action

In *American Homicide*, social historian Randolph Roth charts changes in the homicide rate in the United States from colonial times to the present. Using a variety of data sources, including court records, newspaper accounts, vital records, and attitudes expressed in diaries and letters, he finds that murder rates are closely correlated with four distinct sociocultural factors: political instability; a loss of government legitimacy; a lack of civility among members of society caused by racial, religious, or political conflict; and a loss of confidence in those who hold power.

Roth argues that the United States has a unique culture and the level of interpersonal violence is much higher than in comparable Western nations. These differences were not always present. During the seventeenth century, murder rates were very high, but by the mid-eighteenth century they declined and the nation was relatively nonhomicidal. After the Revolutionary War, murder rates soared as the newly formed United States struggled to absorb British loyalists. While murder rates remained high in the Georgia–South Carolina backcountry, where the revolution was a genuine civil war, they held steady or fell in the Shenandoah Valley of Virginia, which enjoyed political stability under patriot control throughout the revolution, and where support for

the war effort and the new federal government was stronger than anywhere else in the South.

Murder rates eventually declined and by the early nineteenth century, rates in the North and parts of the South were extremely low. But the homicide rate rose substantially across the United States from the late 1840s through the mid-1870s due to the social conflict that grew up around the slavery issue; at the same time, homicide rates in most other Western nations held steady or fell. The end of the Civil War did not end the bitterness many Southerners felt toward the government and consequently there was a dramatic rise in homicides in the rural South.

Homicide rates rose during the Depression and Prohibition eras in the early twentieth century, but fell during the 1930s when Franklin Roosevelt was elected president and Americans had increased faith in their nation and its leadership. The establishment of government legitimacy through the New Deal, World War II, and the Cold War appeared to have reduced homicide rates through the 1950s; the crisis of government legitimacy in the 1960s and 1970s (especially among African Americans) may have contributed to soaring homicide rates.

In sum, Roth argues that American homicide rates are not related to social factors such as poverty and drug

abuse, unemployment, alcohol, race, or ethnicity, but instead are controlled by the feelings that people have toward their government, the degree to which they identify with members of their own communities, and the opportunities they have to earn respect without resorting to violence. If an individual feels secure in his social standing, it's easier to get over life's disappointments. But for a person who feels alienated from the American Dream, even the smallest insult can provoke a murderous rage. To reduce homicide rates, we must learn to trust one another and the government too.

Critical Thinking

Roth says, "State breakdowns and political crises of legitimacy produce surges in nondomestic homicides; the restoration of order and legitimacy produces declines in homicides." Do you agree that homicides involving strangers are a function of the political and social world in which we live? Or is it more personal and a function of intense and immediate interpersonal conflict? How does a political crisis affect someone who robs a liquor store and shoots the owner?

SOURCE: Randolph Roth, *American Homicide* (Cambridge, MA: Belknap Press of the Harvard University Press, 2009).

---

misunderstood, and frightening crimes. Under traditional common-law definitions, rape involves nonconsensual sexual intercourse that a male performs against a female he is neither married to nor cohabitating with.[71] There are of course other forms of sexual assault, including male on male, female on female, and female on male sexual assaults, but these are not considered within the traditional definition of rape.[72] However, recognizing changing contemporary standards, almost every state and the federal government (as in the Uniform Crime Reports) have now revised their rape statutes, making them gender neutral and including other forms of sexual assault beyond

nonconsensual sexual intercourse.[73] In addition, states now recognize that rape can occur among married couples and people who previously have been sexually intimate.[74] And of course, regardless of what form it takes, rape has long-term effects on the victim's emotional and physical well-being.[75]

History of Rape

Rape has been a recognized crime throughout history. It has been the subject of art, literature, film, and theater. Paintings such as *The Rape of the Sabine Women* by Nicolas Poussin,

A woman who was raped was almost automatically suspected of contributing to her attack.

Rape and War

The link between the military and rape is inescapable. Throughout recorded history, rape has been associated with armies and warfare. Soldiers of conquering armies have considered sexual possession of their enemies' women one of the spoils of war. Among the ancient Greeks, rape was socially acceptable within the rules of warfare. During the Crusades, even knights and pilgrims, ostensibly bound by vows of chivalry and Christian piety, took time to rape as they marched toward Constantinople.

The belief that women are part of the spoils of war has continued. During World War II, the Japanese army forced as many as 200,000 Korean women into frontline brothels, where they were repeatedly raped. In a 1998 Japanese ruling, the surviving Korean women were awarded the equivalent of $2,300 each in compensation.[78] Russian soldiers routinely assaulted German women as they marched to Berlin in 1945. By the end of World War II, millions had been raped, including at least 1.4 million women in East Prussia, Pomerania, and Silesia alone.[79]

The use of rape as a weapon of war did not end with World War II. The systematic rape of Bosnian and Kosovar women by Serbian army officers during the civil war in the former Yugoslavia horrified the world during the 1990s. These crimes seemed particularly atrocious because they appeared to be part of an official policy of genocide: rape was deliberately used to impregnate Bosnian women with Serbian children.

On March 9, 1998, Dragoljub Kunarac, 37, a former Bosnian Serb paramilitary commander, admitted before an international tribunal in the Netherlands that he had raped Muslim women during the Bosnian war in 1992. His confession made him the first person to plead guilty to rape as a war crime.[80] Human rights groups have estimated that more than 30,000 women and young girls were sexually abused in the Balkan fighting.

Though shocking, the war crimes discovered in Bosnia have not deterred conquering armies from using rape as a weapon. In 2004, pro-government militias in the Darfur

Rape has been the subject of books, poems, and paintings. Here is "The Rape of the Sabine Women" by Nicolas Poussin (1594–1665). According to legend, Roman men first acquired wives by abducting them from the neighboring Sabine tribe. In early civilization men staked a claim of ownership on women by forcibly abducting and raping them. This practice led to males' solidification of power and their historical domination of women.

The Rape of the Sabines, c.1637–38 (oil on canvas), Poussin, Nicolas (1594–1665)/Louvre, Paris, France/Giraudon/Bridgeman Images

novels such as *Clarissa* by Samuel Richardson, poems such as *The Rape of Lucrece* by William Shakespeare, and films such as *The Accused* and *The Last House on the Left* have sexual violence as their central theme.

In early civilization rape was common. Men staked a claim of ownership on women by forcibly abducting and raping them. This practice led to males' solidification of power and their historical domination of women.[76] Under Babylonian and Hebraic law, the rape of a virgin was a crime punishable by death. However, if the victim was married, then both she and her attacker were considered equally to blame, and unless her husband intervened, both were put to death.

During the Middle Ages, it was common for ambitious men to abduct and rape wealthy women in an effort to force them into marriage. The practice of "heiress stealing" illustrates how feudal law gave little thought or protection to women and equated them with property.[77] Only in the late fifteenth century, after a monetary economy developed, was forcible sex outlawed. Thereafter, the violation of a virgin caused an economic hardship on her family, who expected a significant dowry for her hand in marriage. However, the law only applied to the wealthy; peasant women and married women were not considered rape victims until well into the sixteenth century. The Christian condemnation of sex during this period was also a denunciation of women as evil, having lust in their hearts, and redeemable only by motherhood.

region of Sudan were accused of using rape and other forms of sexual violence "as a weapon of war" to humiliate black African women and girls as well as the rebels fighting the Sudanese government in Khartoum.[81] In April 2014, the Nigerian terror group Boko Haram kidnapped 276 high school girls with the intent of selling them into sexual slavery, an act that prompted worldwide outrage.[82]

In a provocative article, Eileen Zurbriggen proposes that rape is prevalent during war because military socialization emphasizes elements of hypermasculinity that produce emotions and conditions that support a rape culture: status and achievement; toughness and aggression; restricted emotionality; and power, dominance, and control. She argues that society's need for effective soldiers is the root cause of traditional masculine socialization and that this socialization ensures that rape will be prevalent.[83]

Incidence of Rape

According to the most recent UCR data (2012), about 85,000 rapes or attempted rapes are now being reported to U.S. police each year, a rate of about 30 per 100,000 inhabitants.[84] Like other violent crimes, the rape rate has been in a decade-long decline, and preliminary 2013 data indicate that trend is continuing (down about 10 percent compared to 2012).

While the overwhelming percentage of rape victims are female, thousands of men report being sexually assaulted each year. One significant difference: while women most often are attacked by strangers, almost every male rape involves a friend or acquaintance.[85]

Population density influences the rape rate. Metropolitan areas today have rape rates significantly higher than rural areas; nonetheless, urban areas have experienced a much greater drop in rape reports than rural areas. The police make arrests in slightly more than half of all reported rape offenses. Of the offenders arrested, typically about half are under 25 years of age, and about two-thirds are white. The racial and age pattern of rape arrests has been fairly consistent for some time. Finally, rape is a warm-weather crime—most incidents occur during July and August, with the lowest rates occurring during December, January, and February.

Underreporting Rape   These data must be interpreted with caution because rape is a traditionally underreported crime, and some criminologists estimate that as many as 10 percent of all adult women may have been raped during their lifetime.[86] In one important study, Dean Kilpatrick and his research team surveyed more than 5,000 women across the nation. Their findings indicate that about 20 million women (18 percent) in the United States have been raped. Only 16 percent of all rapes were reported to law enforcement authorities. Underreporting helps explain the discrepancy between NCVS findings and UCR data.[87]

Why is rape, one of the most serious violent crimes, also one of the most underreported? Many victims fail to report rapes because they are embarrassed, believe nothing can be done, or blame themselves. Some victims of sexual assaults may even question whether they have really been raped; research indicates that when the assault involves an acquaintance, such as a boyfriend, and the victim had been drinking or taking drugs, they are unlikely to label their situations as being a "real" rape. Similarly, if the assault involved oral or digital sex it is less likely to be labeled a "real" rape.[88] Women are more likely to report rape when it is committed by a stranger who uses a weapon or causes physical injury, or when the rape occurred in a public place—or if at home, was the result of "home blitz" (in which an attacker broke in or entered without permission).[89] Therefore it is likely that many acquaintance rapes and date rapes go unreported.

There may be many more rape victims than the official data allow.[90] But even if victims fail to acknowledge that their attack was "real" and refuse to report it to the police, the experience can have a long-lasting psychological effect.[91]

Types of Rape and Rapists

Some rapes are planned, others are spontaneous; some focus on a particular victim, whereas others occur almost as an afterthought during the commission of another crime, such as a burglary. Some rapists commit a single crime, whereas others are multiple offenders; some attack alone, and others engage in group or gang rapes.[92] Some use force to attack their target, others prey upon those who are incapacitated by drugs and alcohol.[93] Because there is no single type of rape or rapist, criminologists have attempted to define and categorize the vast variety of rape situations.

Criminologists now recognize that there are numerous motivations for rape and as a result various types of rapists. There are many different typologies of rape and one of the best known is the classic work of psychologist A. Nicholas Groth, an expert on classifying and treating sex offenders. According to Groth, every rape encounter contains at least one of these three elements: anger, power, and sadism.[94] Consequently, rapists can be classified according to one of the three dimensions described in Exhibit 10.2. In treating rape offenders, Groth found that about 55 percent were of the power type; about 40 percent, the anger type; and about 5 percent, the sadistic type.[95]

Gang Rape   Research studies estimate that as many as 25 percent or more of rapes involve multiple offenders.[96] There is generally little difference in the demographic characteristics of single- or multiple-victim rapes. However, women who are attacked by multiple offenders are subject to more violence, such as beatings and the use of weapons, and the rapes are more likely to be completed than

Varieties of Forcible Rape

- *Anger rape.* This rape occurs when sexuality becomes a means of expressing and discharging pent-up anger and rage. The rapist uses far more brutality than would have been necessary if his real objective had been simply to have sex with his victim. His aim is to hurt his victim as much as possible; the sexual aspect of rape may be an afterthought.
- *Power rape.* This type of rape involves an attacker who does not want to harm his victim as much as he wants to possess her sexually. His goal is sexual conquest, and he uses only the amount of force necessary to achieve his objective. The power rapist wants to be in control, to be able to dominate women and have them at his mercy.
- *Sadistic rape.* This type of rape involves both sexuality and aggression. The sadistic rapist is caught up in ritual—he may torment his victim, bind her, or torture her. Victims are usually related, in the rapist's view, to a personal characteristic that he wants to harm or destroy.

SOURCE: A. Nicholas Groth and Jean Birnbaum, *Men Who Rape* (New York: Plenum Press, 1979).

individual rapes. **Gang rape** victims are more likely to resist and face injury than those attacked by single offenders. They are more likely to call police, to seek therapy, and to contemplate suicide. Gang rapes then, as might be expected, are more severe in violence and outcome.

Serial Rape Some rapists are one-time offenders, but others engage in multiple or **serial rapes**. Some serial rapists constantly increase their use of force; others do not. Research by Janet Warren and her associates determined that increasers (about 25 percent of serial rapists) tend to be white males who attack multiple victims who are typically older than the norm. During these attacks, the rapist uses excessive profanity and takes more time than during typical rapes. Increasers have a limited criminal history for other crimes, a fact suggesting that their behavior is focused almost solely on sexual violence.[97]

Some serial rapists commit "blitz rapes," in which they attack their victims without warning, whereas others try to "capture" their victims by striking up a conversation or offering them a ride. Others use personal or professional relationships to gain access to their targets.[98]

Acquaintance Rape **Acquaintance rape** involves someone known to the victim, including family members and friends. Included within acquaintance rapes are the subcategories of **date rape**, which involves a sexual attack during a courting relationship; **statutory rape**, in which the victim is underage; and **marital rape**, which is forcible sex between people who are legally married to each other.[99] It is difficult to estimate the ratio between rapes involving strangers and those in which victim and assailant are in some way

acquainted because women may be more reluctant to report acts involving acquaintances. By some estimates, about 50 percent of rapes involve acquaintances, a number that is not surprising considering the prevalence of negative attitudes toward women and attitudes that support sexual coercion among some groups of young men.[100] Stranger rapes are typically more violent than acquaintance rapes; attackers are more likely to carry a weapon, threaten the victim, and harm her physically. Stranger rapes may also be less likely to be prosecuted than acquaintance rapes because victims may be more reluctant to recount their ordeal at trial if the attack involved a stranger than if their attacker was someone they knew or had been involved with in an earlier relationship.[101]

Date Rape Date rape was first identified as a significant social problem in the 1980s when Mary Koss conducted surveys finding that a significant number of college-age women had been sexually assaulted by a dating partner; about 27 percent of the respondents were the victim of rape or attempted rape. However, only about a quarter of the women considered what had happened to them "real" rape; the majority either blamed themselves or denied they had really been raped.[102] The Koss research helped identify a social problem that all too long had remained below the radar.

There is no single form of date rape. Some occur on first dates, others after a relationship has been developing, and still others occur after the couple has been involved for some time. In long-term or close relationships, the male partner may feel he has invested so much time and money in his partner that he is owed sexual relations or that sexual intimacy is an expression that the involvement is progressing. He may make comparisons to other couples who have dated as long and are sexually active.[103] Some use a variety of strategies to coerce sex, including getting their dates drunk, threatening them with termination of the relationship, threatening to disclose negative information, making them feel guilty, or uttering false promises (i.e., "we'll get engaged") to obtain sex.[104]

gang rape Forcible sex involving multiple attackers.

serial rapes Multiple rapes committed by one person over time.

acquaintance rape Forcible sex in which offender and victim are acquainted with each other.

date rape Forcible sex during a courting relationship.

statutory rape Sexual relations between an underage individual and an adult; though not coerced, an underage partner is considered incapable of giving informed consent.

marital rape Forcible sex between people who are legally married to each other.

The actual incidence of date rape may be even higher than surveys indicate, because many victims blame themselves and do not recognize the incident as a rape, saying, for example, "I should have fought back harder" or "I shouldn't have gotten drunk."[105] Victims tend to have histories of excessive drinking and prior sexuality, conditions which may convince them that their intemperate and/or immoderate behavior contributed to their own victimization.[106] Some victims do not report rapes because they do not view their experience as a real rape, which, they believe, involves a strange man "jumping out of the bushes." Other victims are embarrassed and frightened. Many will tell their friends about their rape but refuse to let authorities know what happened; reporting is most common in the most serious cases, such as when a weapon is used; it is less common when drugs and alcohol are involved.[107]

Rape on Campus   A great deal of date and acquaintance rape is committed on college campuses. One survey of college women found that 15 to 30 percent of all college women are victims of rape or attempted rape; 27 percent of the sample had experienced unwanted sexual contact ranging from kissing and petting to sexual intercourse.[108]

Especially troubling is the underreporting of rape on college campuses, where relatively few victims (less than 20 percent) report the incident to police.[109] One reason may be that many incidents, many of which occur in fraternity houses and dorms, involve the victims' voluntary involvement in drinking or substance abuse before the assault occurred and therefore they hold themselves somewhat responsible for the attack; they may not believe the incident was a "real rape" because they were at fault.[110] Misplaced guilt may also explain why so many college women suffer PTSD and other disorders soon after they were attacked.[111] And when they do report rape and file a lawsuit against the frat house or university, the defense is to blame the victim: if she had not been drinking and taking risks, the attack would never have occurred.[112]

Another reason for the lack of reporting may be that colleges and universities are notorious for trying to sweep sexual assault incidents under the rug to protect the image of a safe environment for young women. For example, Johns Hopkins University was accused of not disclosing an alleged rape at a fraternity house, leading a group of students to file a complaint with the U.S. Department of Education. Amid the pressure, university president Ronald J. Daniels said that the university would immediately begin an independent review of how the case was handled.[113]

Marital Rape   In 1978, Greta Rideout filed rape charges against her husband John. This Oregon case grabbed headlines because it was the first in which a husband was prosecuted for raping his wife while sharing a residence with her. John was acquitted, and the couple briefly reconciled; later, continued violent episodes culminated in divorce and a jail term for John.[114]

Traditionally, a legally married husband could not be charged with raping his wife; this was referred to as the **marital exemption**. The origin of this legal doctrine can be traced to the sixteenth-century pronouncement of Matthew Hale, England's chief justice, who wrote:

> But the husband cannot be guilty of rape committed by himself upon his lawful wife, for by their mutual matrimonial consent and contract the wife hath given up herself in this kind unto the husband which she cannot retract.[115]

However, research indicates that many women are raped each year by their husbands as part of an overall pattern of spousal abuse, and they deserve the protection of the law. Many spousal rapes are accompanied by brutal, sadistic beatings and have little to do with normal sexual interests.[116] Not surprisingly, the marital exemption has undergone significant revision. In 1980, only three states had laws against marital rape; today every state recognizes marital rape as a crime.[117] Piercing the marital exemption is not unique to U.S. courts; more than 100 nations have abolished the marital exemption.[118] However, although marital rape is now recognized, most states do not give wives the same legal protection as they would unmarried couples, and when courts do recognize marital rape, the perpetrators are sanctioned less harshly than are those accused of nonmarital sexual assaults.[119] For example, in 30 states, a husband is exempt from charges of rape when he does not have to use force; because of the marital contract, a wife's consent is assumed unless she overtly refuses her husband's advances. The existence of some spousal exemptions in the majority of states indicates that rape in marriage is still treated as a lesser crime than other forms of rape.[120]

Statutory Rape   The term *statutory rape* refers to sexual relations between an underage minor and an adult. Although the sex is not forced or coerced, the law says that young people are incapable of giving informed consent, so the act is legally considered nonconsensual. Typically a state's law will define an age of consent above which there can be no criminal prosecution for sexual relations. Although each state is different, most evaluate the age differences between the parties to determine whether an offense has taken place. For example, Indiana law mandates prosecution of men aged 21 or older who have consensual sex with girls younger than 14. In some states, defendants can claim they mistakenly assumed their victims were above the age of consent, whereas in others,

marital exemption   The practice in some states of prohibiting the prosecution of husbands for the rape of their wives.

"mistake-of-age" defenses are ignored. An American Bar Association (ABA) survey found that prosecution is often difficult in statutory rape cases because the young victims are reluctant to testify. Often parents have given their blessing to the relationships, and juries are reluctant to convict men involved in consensual sex even with young teenaged girls.[121]

Rape by Deception   Rape by deception occurs when the rapist uses fraud or trickery to convince the victim to engage in sex or impersonates someone with whom the victim has been intimate.[122] In one Massachusetts case, a man was convicted of rape after he allegedly impersonated his brother in order to have sex with his brother's girlfriend in the middle of the night. The conviction was overturned because Massachusetts law does not recognize that sex without force can be considered rape. However, a number of other states recognize rape by deception. In Tennessee, rape is defined to include "sexual penetration ... accomplished by fraud"; in Idaho, sex with a woman is defined as rape when because of his "artifice, pretense, or concealment," the victim believes him to be someone other than who he is.[123]

The Causes of Rape

What factors predispose some men to commit rape? Criminologists' responses to this question are almost as varied as the crime itself. However, most explanations can be grouped into a few consistent categories.

Evolutionary, Biological Factors   One explanation is that rape may be instinctual, developed over the ages as a means of perpetuating the species. In more primitive times, forcible sexual contact may have helped spread genes and maximize offspring. Some believe that these prehistoric drives remain: males still have a natural sexual drive that encourages them to have intimate relations with as many women as possible.[124] The evolutionary view is that the sexual urge corresponds to the unconscious need to preserve the species by spreading one's genes as widely as possible. Men who are sexually aggressive will have a reproductive edge over their more passive peers.[125]

Rape remains a small but still present means of reproduction. From the evolutionary perspective, it makes sense that women at the peak of their fertility would be preferential targets, and rape studies have documented that young, attractive women are most often victimized by rapists.[126] However, in a civilized society rape as a reproductive strategy brings with it significant disadvantages. Many of the potential victims have family members or rival mates to ward off or punish rapists, either legally or personally. Also, in contemporary society, reproductive fitness requires parental investment to ensure the survival of offspring. Evolution favors traits of stability and commitment to family on the part of fathers, and these traits will be passed on to surviving offspring as well.[127]

Male Socialization   Some researchers argue that rape is a function of modern male socialization. Some men have been socialized to be aggressive with women and believe that the use of violence or force is legitimate if their sexual advances are rebuffed—that is, "women like to play hard to get and expect to be forced to have sex." Those men who have been socialized to believe that "no means yes" are more likely to be sexually aggressive.[128] The use of sexual violence is aggravated if pro-force socialization is reinforced by peer group members who share similar values.[129]

Diana Russell, a leading expert on sexual violence, suggests that rape is actually not a deviant act but one that conforms to the qualities regarded as masculine in U.S. society.[130] Russell maintains that from an early age boys are taught to be aggressive, forceful, tough, and dominating. Men are taught to dominate at the same time that they are led to believe that women want to be dominated. Russell describes the **virility mystique**—the belief that males must separate their sexual feelings from needs for love, respect, and affection. She believes men are socialized to be the aggressors and expect to be sexually active with many women; consequently, male virginity and sexual inexperience are shameful. Similarly, sexually aggressive women frighten some men and cause them to doubt their own masculinity. Sexual insecurity may lead some men to commit rape to bolster their self-image and masculine identity.[131]

Feminists suggest that as the nation moves toward gender equality there may be an immediate increase in rape rates because of increased threats to male virility and dominance. However, in the long term, gender equality will reduce rape rates because there will be an improved social climate toward women.[132]

Psychological Abnormality   Another view is that rapists suffer from some type of personality disorder or mental illness. Research shows that a significant percentage of incarcerated rapists exhibit psychotic tendencies, and many others have hostile, sadistic feelings toward women.[133] A high proportion of serial rapists and repeat sexual offenders exhibit psychopathic personality structures.[134] There is evidence linking rape proclivity with **narcissistic personality disorder**, a pattern of traits and behaviors that indicate infatuation and fixation with one's self to the exclusion of all others and the egotistic and ruthless pursuit of one's gratification, dominance, and ambition.[135]

---

virility mystique The belief that males must separate their sexual feelings from needs for love, respect, and affection.

narcissistic personality disorder A condition marked by a persistent pattern of self-importance, need for admiration, lack of empathy, and preoccupation with fantasies of unlimited success, power, brilliance, beauty, or ideal love.

Social Learning This perspective submits that men learn to commit rapes much as they learn any other behavior. For example, sexual aggression may be learned through interaction with peers who articulate attitudes supportive of sexual violence.[136] Nicholas Groth found that 40 percent of the rapists he studied were sexually victimized as adolescents.[137] A growing body of literature links personal sexual trauma with the desire to inflict sexual trauma on others.[138] Watching violent or pornographic films featuring women who are beaten, raped, or tortured has been linked to sexually aggressive behavior in men.[139]

Sexual Motivation Most criminologists believe rape is a violent act that is not sexually motivated. Yet it might be premature to dismiss the sexual motive from all rapes.[140] NCVS data reveal that rape victims tend to be young and that rapists prefer younger, presumably more attractive, victims. Richard Felson and his associates found this effect when they studied the risk of sexual and physical assault in prisons and jails.[141] Felson found that male inmates of all ages tend to sexually assault young men and that the young are sexually assaulted because of their sexual attractiveness rather than because of their vulnerability.

Older rapists tend to harm their victims more than younger rapists. This pattern indicates that older criminals may rape for motives of power and control, whereas younger offenders may be seeking sexual gratification and may therefore be less likely to harm their victims.

Rape and the Law

LO4 Assess the legal issues in rape prosecution

On May 14, 2011, Dominique Strauss-Kahn, the distinguished head of the International Monetary Fund and a leading French politician, was arrested for allegedly raping Nafissatou Diallo, a 32-year-old hotel maid. He claimed the sex was consensual. After a thorough investigation, the case soon began to fall apart. It seems that Diallo had lied on her application for citizenship and mysterious bank deposits were uncovered that may have been linked to criminal activity. She also admitted that she returned to Strauss-Kahn's room and cleaned it before calling the police![142]

Unlike other crime victims, women may find that their claim of sexual assault is greeted with some skepticism by police and court personnel.[143] They will soon discover that they have to prove they did not engage in consensual sex and then develop remorse afterwards. Their background and sexual history may impact on whether charges are filed. Police officers may be hesitant to make arrests and testify in court when the alleged assaults do not yield obvious signs of violence or struggle (presumably showing the victim strenuously resisted the attack). Research shows that people are more likely to "blame the victim" in a case of sexual assault than they are in other common-law crimes such as armed robbery. Victim blaming is exacerbated if a prior relationship existed or if the victim did not fight back because they were intoxicated, factors that have less impact in other crimes.[144] However, police and courts are now becoming more sensitive to the plight of rape victims and are just as likely to investigate acquaintance rapes as they are **aggravated rapes** involving multiple offenders, weapons, and victim injuries.

Proving Rape On March 13, 2006, after a "performance" by strippers at a private residence, three members of Duke University's men's lacrosse team allegedly raped one of the women who had been hired to entertain the team. The three players, David Evans, Reade Seligmann, and Collin Finnerty, were charged with first-degree forcible rape, first-degree sexual offense, and kidnapping. Media outlets had a field day with the case because of its racial overtones: the young woman was African American and the players were white. The case began to unravel because there was a lack of physical evidence, the victim's character was questioned, and there were changes to and inconsistencies in her statement. Then it was revealed that Durham District Attorney Mike Nifong deliberately withheld evidence from the defense that might have cleared the suspects (he later lost his job and was disbarred). The Duke case is especially troubling because it supports the notion that a great many rape accusations are false, making it more difficult to prosecute and gain conviction in those that are valid.[145]

Proving guilt in a rape case is extremely challenging for prosecutors. Although the law does not recognize it, jurors are sometimes swayed by the insinuation that the rape was victim precipitated; thus the blame is shifted from rapist to victim. To get a conviction, prosecutors must establish that the act was forced and violent and that no question of voluntary compliance exists. They may be reluctant to prosecute cases where they have questions about the victim's moral character or if they believe that the victim's demeanor and attitude (i.e., they were dressed provocatively) will turn off the jury and undermine the chance of conviction.[146] Prosecutors may be more willing to bring charges in interracial rape cases because they know that juries are more likely to believe victims and convict defendants in cases involving interracial rape than in intraracial rapes.[147]

As well, there is always fear that a frightened and traumatized victim may identify the wrong man, which happened in the case of Dennis Maher, a Massachusetts man freed after spending more than 19 years in prison for rapes he did not commit. Though three victims provided eyewitness identification at trial, DNA testing proved that Maher could not have been the rapist.[148]

---

aggravated rapes Rape involving multiple offenders, weapons, and victim injuries.

Former Duke lacrosse players Dave Evans, Collin Finnerty, and Reade Seligmann smile during a press conference addressing the dismissal of rape charges that had been leveled against them by a woman hired to entertain at a team party. Despite widespread media attention to the problem of sexual assault on campus, many cases are not investigated thoroughly. Highly publicized incidents involving false accusation and prosecutorial misconduct, such as the Duke case, do not help victims receive the justice they deserve.

Travis Long/mct/Landov

Consent   Rape represents a major legal challenge to the criminal justice system for a number of reasons.[149] One issue involves the concept of **consent**. It is essential to prove that the attack was forced and that the victim did not give voluntary consent to her attacker. In a sense, the burden of proof is on the victim to show that her character is beyond question and that she in no way encouraged, enticed, or misled the accused rapist. On the other hand, some states, such as California and Illinois, now recognize that once given, consent can be withdrawn if a woman changes her mind about sex even after relations have begun. Once she says stop, the act must end or else a rape has occurred.

Proving victim dissent is not a requirement in any other violent crime. For example, robbery victims do not have to prove they did not entice their attackers by flaunting expensive jewelry, yet the defense counsel in a rape case can create reasonable doubt about the woman's credibility. A common defense tactic is to introduce suspicion in the minds of the jury that the woman may have consented to the sexual act and later regretted her decision. Even the appearance of impropriety can undermine a case. When Kobe Bryant was accused of raping a young woman in 2003, the alleged victim was described in the press as being promiscuous, suicidal, mentally ill, a gold digger, on drugs, and so on; she was harassed by Kobe's fans, and three men were actually jailed for making threats.[150] When she refused to testify, the charges were dropped; a civil suit was later settled out of court. Research shows that even when a defendant is found guilty

in a sexual assault case, punishment is significantly reduced if the victim's personal characteristics are viewed as being negative (e.g., transient, hitchhiker, gold digger, or substance abuser).[151] Proving the victim has a good character is not a requirement in any other crime.

Conversely, it is difficult for a prosecuting attorney to establish that a woman's character is so impeccable that the absence of consent is a certainty. Such distinctions are important in rape cases because male jurors may be sympathetic to the accused if the victim is portrayed as unchaste. Referring to the woman as "sexually liberated" or "promiscuous" may be enough to result in exoneration of the accused, even if violence and brutality were used in the attack.[152] When Cassia Spohn and David Holleran studied prosecutors' decisions in rape cases, they found that perception of the victim's character was still a critical factor in their decision to file charges. In cases involving acquaintance rape, prosecutors were reluctant to file charges when the victim's character was questioned—for example, when police reports described the victim as sexually active or engaged in a sexually oriented occupation such as stripper. In cases involving strangers, prosecutors were more likely to take action if a gun or knife was used. Spohn and Holleran state that prosecutors are still influenced by perceptions of what constitutes "real rape" and who are "real victims."[153]

Reform   Because of the difficulty rape victims have in obtaining justice, rape laws have been changing around the country. Efforts for reform include changing the language of statutes, dropping the condition of victim resistance, and changing the requirement of use of force to include the threat of force or injury.[154] A number of states and the federal government have replaced rape laws with the more

> **consent** In prosecuting rape cases, it is essential to prove that the attack was forced and that the victim did not give voluntary consent to her attacker. In a sense, the burden of proof is on the victim to show that her character is beyond question and that she in no way encouraged, enticed, or misled the accused rapist. Proving victim dissent is not a requirement in any other violent crime.

gender-neutral term "crimes of sexual assault."[155] Sexual assault laws outlaw any type of forcible sex, including homosexual rape.[156]

Most states and the federal government have developed **shield laws**, which protect women from being questioned about their sexual history unless it directly bears on the case. In some instances these laws are quite restrictive, whereas in others they grant the trial judge considerable discretion to admit prior sexual conduct in evidence if it is deemed relevant for the defense. In an important 1991 case, *Michigan v. Lucas*, the U.S. Supreme Court upheld the validity of shield laws and ruled that excluding evidence of a prior sexual relationship between the parties did not violate the defendant's right to a fair trial.[157]

In addition to requiring evidence that consent was not given, the common law definition of rape required corroboration that the crime of rape actually took place. This involved the need for independent evidence from police officers, physicians, and witnesses that the accused was actually the person who committed the crime, that sexual penetration took place, and that force was present and consent absent. This requirement shielded rapists from prosecution in cases where the victim delayed reporting the crime or in which physical evidence had been compromised or lost. Corroboration is no longer required except under extraordinary circumstances, such as when the victim is too young to understand the crime, has had a previous sexual relationship with the defendant, or gives a version of events that is improbable and self-contradictory.[158]

The federal government may have given rape victims another source of redress when it passed the Violence Against Women Act in 1994. This statute allows rape victims to sue in federal court on the grounds that sexual violence violates their civil rights; the provisions of the act have so far been upheld by appellate courts.[159]

International Trends Rape reform is not unique to the United States and has become an international movement.[160] A number of nations have made rape a gender-neutral crime. For example, South Africa removed gender from its rape law in 1988, dropping the restriction that perpetrators be male and victims female. The Caribbean nations of Antigua and Barbuda dropped their marital-exclusion clause in 1995, thereafter criminalizing nonconsensual sex between a husband and wife. The kinds of persons and acts subject to and protected by rape laws have expanded dramatically. In Zimbabwe, Article 8 of the 2001 Sexual Offences Act punishes any kind of illegal sexual assault with the same kind of penalties provided by law for rape. With this reform, Zimbabwe greatly increased the range of nonconsensual sexual activities that fall under the umbrella of rape. There has also been an international effort to unify rape laws so that they apply equally to men and women of all classes and statuses. Take rape law in the South American nation of Paraguay. Until 1989, Article 315 of that nation's penal code (*Código Penal*) set harsher penalties for the rape of a married woman (four to eight years in prison) than the rape of an unmarried woman (three to six years), even if the latter were "an honest woman of good name." Why the distinction? It was assumed that the rapist could make things right by marrying his victim if she was an unmarried woman! Today, few codes still include such differential treatments.

To read a report on a victim-oriented approach to dealing with statutory rape, visit **http://ojp.gov/ovc/publications/infores/statutoryrape/trainguide/victimoriented.pdf**.

If it were up to you, would a 17-year-old boy be prosecuted for having sexual relations with his 15-year-old girlfriend? If not, what about a 21-year-old? Or 25-year-old?

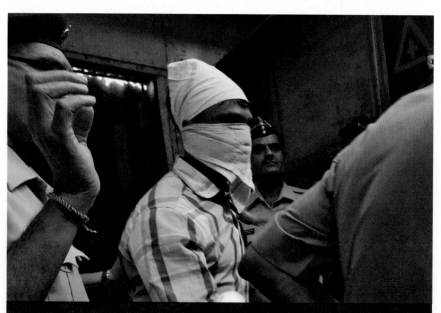
Rape is a worldwide problem, and India has recently experienced a number of outrageous rape cases. Here, police escort one of the five men convicted of raping and terrorizing a photojournalist in Mumbai, India. On March 20, 2014, a Mumbai sessions court convicted all five adults accused in both cases on 13 counts. On April 4, 2014, the court awarded the death penalty to the three repeat offenders; the other two suspects received life imprisonment.

Mansi Thapliyal/Reuters/Landov

shield laws Laws designed to protect rape victims by prohibiting the defense attorney from inquiring about their previous sexual relationships.

MURDER AND HOMICIDE

Murder is defined in common law as "the unlawful killing of a human being with malice aforethought."[161] It is the most serious of all common-law crimes and the only one that can still be punished by death. Western society's abhorrence of murderers is illustrated by the fact that there is no statute of limitations in murder cases. Whereas state laws limit prosecution of other crimes to a fixed period, usually 7 to 10 years, accused killers can be brought to justice at any time after their crimes were committed. In 2012, 72-year-old Jack McCullough was found guilty of killing Maria Ridulph in 1957 when he was 17 years old; 55 years had gone by before the murder was solved.[162] In 2013, Conrado Juarez was arrested in New York City 22 years after killing four-year-old Anjelica Castillo, known as "Baby Hope," whose abused and decomposed body was found in an ice chest by the side of a New York roadway in 1991.[163]

To legally prove that a murder has taken place, most state jurisdictions require prosecutors to show that the accused maliciously intended to kill the victim. "Express or actual malice" is the state of mind assumed to exist when someone kills another person in the absence of any apparent provocation. "Implied or constructive malice" is considered to exist when a death results from negligent or unthinking behavior. In these cases, even though the perpetrator did not wish to kill the victim, the killing resulted from an inherently dangerous act and therefore is considered murder. An unusual example of this concept is the attempted-murder conviction of Ignacio Perea, an AIDS-infected Miami man who kidnapped and raped an 11-year-old boy. Perea was sentenced to up to 25 years in prison when the jury agreed with the prosecutor's contention that the AIDS virus is a deadly weapon.[164]

Degrees of Murder

 LO5 Compare and contrast the different degrees of murder

There are different levels or degrees of homicide.[165] *First-degree murder* is an intentional killing which is deliberate and premeditated.

Premeditation means that the killing was considered beforehand and suggests that it was motivated by more than a simple desire to engage in an act of violence; the murder was planned after careful thought rather than being carried out on impulse. Planning need not be long term and may be an almost instantaneous decision to take another's life. Also, a killing accompanying a felony, such as robbery or rape, usually constitutes first-degree murder (**felony murder**). In some states, statutes have defined murder in the first to include crimes involving multiple deaths, the killing of a child, an agent of the justice system, such as police officer or prison guard, or murder for hire.

Second-degree murder requires the killer to have malice aforethought but not premeditation or **deliberation**. There are three situations that are typically defined as second-degree murder:

- A killing done impulsively without premeditation but with malice aforethought. This occurs when two people get into a heated argument and one pulls out a knife and stabs the victim. The killer did not have an original intent to kill or plan to kill, but they did intend to kill once the argument started or else why did they pull out and use their knife?
- A killing that results from an act intended to cause serious bodily harm. During a fight, someone grabs a baseball bat and hits their opponent, resulting in death. Even though they merely intended to seriously injure and not kill their opponent, their actions caused death.
- Depraved indifference to human life. Someone sets off a bomb and kills a bystander. Though they did not intend to kill a specific person, their wanton disregard of the danger of their actions resulted in death. Any rational person would know that setting off a bomb could cause death.

One of the most famous cases illustrating depraved indifference murder occurred on January 26, 2001, when Diane Whipple, a San Francisco woman, died after two large dogs attacked her in the hallway of her apartment building. One of the dogs' owners/keepers, Robert Noel, was found guilty of manslaughter, and his wife, Marjorie Knoller, was convicted on charges of second-degree murder because they knew that the dogs were highly dangerous but did little or nothing to control their behavior.[166]

Homicide without malice is called **manslaughter**. *Voluntary* or **nonnegligent manslaughter** refers to a killing, typically without a weapon, committed in the heat of passion

---

murder The unlawful killing of a human being (homicide) with malicious intent.

premeditation Consideration of a homicide before it occurs.

felony murder A homicide in the context of another felony, such as robbery or rape; legally defined as first-degree murder.

second-degree murder A homicide with malice but not premeditation or deliberation, as when a desire to inflict serious bodily harm and a wanton disregard for life result in the victim's death.

deliberation Planning a homicide after careful thought, however brief, rather than acting on sudden impulse.

manslaughter A homicide without malice.

nonnegligent manslaughter A homicide committed in the heat of passion or during a sudden quarrel; although intent may be present, malice is not; also called voluntary manslaughter.

or during a sudden quarrel that provoked violence. Death resulting from a misdemeanor is considered voluntary manslaughter: two people get into an argument and exchange blows. One falls, hits his head, and dies. The punch is technically a battery, a misdemeanor, and the resulting death would be considered manslaughter.

Involuntary manslaughter or **negligent manslaughter** refers to a killing that occurs when a person's acts are negligent and without regard for the harm they may cause others. Many involuntary manslaughter cases involve motor vehicle deaths—for example, when a drunk driver kills a pedestrian. While the motorist did not intend to kill anyone, they knew or should have known that drinking and driving was both an illegal act and one that could cause death. Involuntary manslaughter can also be a result of otherwise legal behavior that is performed in a negligent manner: a person leaves a heavy object on her tenth-floor windowsill, it falls and strikes a pedestrian, killing them instantly. A reasonable person should know that an object left by an open window could fall out and strike someone below.

"Born and Alive"   One issue that has received national attention is whether a murder victim can be a fetus that has not yet been delivered; this is referred to as **feticide**. Today about 38 states have some form of fetal homicide laws.[167] In some instances, fetal harm involves a mother whose behavior endangers an unborn child; in other cases, feticide results from the harmful action of a third party.

Some states have prosecuted women for endangering or killing their unborn fetuses by their drug or alcohol abuse. Some of these convictions have been overturned because the law applies only to a "human being who has been born and is alive."[168] However, in *Whitner v. State of South Carolina*, the Supreme Court of South Carolina ruled that a woman could be held liable for actions during pregnancy that could affect her viable fetus.[169] In holding that a fetus is a "viable person," the court opened the door for a potential homicide prosecution if a mother's action resulted in fetal death. As for third-party actions, only 12 states still follow the common-law "born alive" rule: Colorado, Connecticut, Delaware, Hawaii, Montana, New Hampshire, New Jersey, New Mexico, North Carolina, Oregon, Vermont, and Wyoming. In contrast, a number of states have passed legislation creating a separate class of crime that increases criminal penalties when a person causes injury to a woman he or she knows is pregnant, and the injury results in miscarriage or stillbirth. At the federal level, the Unborn Victims of Violence Act of 2004 makes it a separate crime to harm a fetus during an assault on the mother. If the attack causes death or bodily injury to a child who is *in utero* at the time the conduct takes place, the penalty is the same as that for conduct had the injury or death occurred to the unborn child's mother.

There is still a great deal of state-to-state variation in feticide laws. Some make it a separate crime to kill a fetus or commit an act of violence against a pregnant woman. Others have a viability requirement: feticide can only occur if the unborn child could at the time potentially live outside the mother's body.[170]

The Nature and Extent of Murder

It is possible to track U.S. murder rate trends from 1900 to the present with the aid of coroners' reports and UCR data. The murder rate peaked in 1933, a time of high unemployment and lawlessness, and then fell until 1958. Then the homicide rate began to skyrocket, doubling from the mid-1960s to a peak in 1991 when almost 25,000 people were killed in a single year, a rate of about 10 per 100,000 people. The murder rate has since been in a decline. In 2012, there were about 15,000 murders, a rate of about 4.7 per 100,000 population. Preliminary 2013 data show that the decline in the murder rate seems to be continuing.

What else do official crime statistics tell us about murder today? Murder tends to be an urban crime. More than half of homicides occur in cities with a population of 100,000 or more; almost one-quarter of homicides occur in cities with a population of more than 1 million. Why is homicide an urban phenomenon? Large cities experience the greatest rates of structural disadvantage—poverty, joblessness, racial heterogeneity, residential mobility, family disruption, and income inequality—that are linked to high murder rates.[171] Not surprisingly, large cities are much more commonly the site of drug-related killings and gang-related murders, and relatively less likely to be the location of family-related homicides, including murders of intimates.

Murder victims and offenders tend to be males: about 80 percent of homicide victims and nearly 90 percent of offenders are male. Males are more likely to kill others of similar social standing in more public contexts; women kill family members and intimate partners in private locations.[172]

Murder, like rape, tends to be an intraracial crime: about 90 percent of victims are slain by members of their own race. About half of all murder victims are African Americans. Approximately one-third of murder victims and almost half the offenders are under the age of 25.

Some murders involve very young children, a crime referred to as **infanticide** (killing older children is called **filicide**), and others involve senior citizens, referred to as

---

Involuntary manslaughter or **negligent manslaughter** A homicide that occurs as a result of acts that are negligent and without regard for the harm they may cause others, such as driving under the influence of alcohol or drugs; also called involuntary manslaughter.

feticide Endangering or killing an unborn fetus.

infanticide The murder of a very young child.

filicide Murder of an older child.

eldercide.[173] The UCR indicates that about 350 juveniles are murdered each year. The younger the child, the greater the risk for infanticide. At the opposite end of the age spectrum, less than 5 percent of all homicides involve people age 65 or older. Males age 65 or older are more likely than females of the same age to be homicide victims. Although most of the offenders who committed eldercide were age 50 or younger, elderly females were more likely than elderly males to be killed by an elderly offender.[174]

Murderers typically have a long involvement in crime; few people begin a criminal career by killing someone. Research shows that people arrested for homicide are significantly more likely to have been in trouble with the law prior to their arrest than people arrested for other crimes.[175] A recent longitudinal study by David Farrington and his associates found that among the risk predictors for homicide, prior criminal offenses up to age 14 was the most important; 95 percent of offenders had records of violence at the time they committed murder.[176]

Murderous Relations

LO6 Assess stranger and acquaintance homicide

Most murders are expressive—that is, motivated by rage or anger—and they typically involve friends, relatives, and acquaintances. Murderous relations are shaped by gender: males are more likely to kill others of similar social standing in more public contexts, whereas women kill family members and intimate partners in private locations.[177] What other forms do murderous relations take?

Acquaintance Murders Most murders occur among people who are acquainted. Although on the surface the killing might seem senseless, it is often the result of a long-simmering dispute motivated by revenge, dispute resolution, jealousy, drug deals, racial bias, or threats to identity or status.[178] For example, a prior act of violence, motivated by profit or greed, such as when a buyer robs his dealer during a drug transaction, may generate revenge killing.

Intimate Partner Murder Many murders involve husbands and wives, boyfriends and girlfriends, and others involved in romantic relationships. In some jurisdictions, upwards of 40 percent of all murders involve an intimate partner.[179]

Intimate partner murder is a gendered phenomenon. When women commit homicide, the most likely victim is an intimate partner; about 40 percent of all female homicide incidents involve killing a male partner. Less than 10 percent of all murders committed by men involve a female partner. Men who kill romantic partners typically have a long history of violence, while for women, killing their partner may be their first violent offense.[180] This may be the reason that there is a "chivalry effect" in domestic violence murders. In death penalty states such as California the death-sentence rate for single-victim domestic violence murders is significantly lower than the overall death-sentence rate for other kinds of killings. Not surprisingly, when women in these states are found guilty of capital murder, they are far less likely than men to be sentenced to death.[181]

Research also shows most females who kill their mates do so after suffering repeated violent attacks.[182] Women who kill or seriously assault intimate partners are often battered women unable to flee a troubled relationship.[183] Perhaps the number of males killed by their partners has declined because alternatives to abusive relationships, such as shelters for battered women, are becoming more prevalent around the United States. Regions that provide greater social support for battered women and that have passed legislation to protect abuse victims also have lower rates of female-perpetrated homicide.[184] This escape valve may help them avoid retaliation through lethal violence.

Sexually Based Murders Some people kill their mates because they find themselves involved in a love triangle.[185] Interestingly, women who kill out of jealousy aim their aggression at their partners; in contrast, men are more likely to kill their rivals (their mates' suitors). Love triangles tend to become lethal when the offenders believe they have been lied to or betrayed. Lethal violence is more common when (1) the rival initiated the affair, (2) the killer knew the spouse was already in a steady relationship outside the marriage, and (3) the killer was repeatedly lied to or betrayed.[186]

Research indicates that sexually related homicide can take a variety of different forms:[187]

- Domestic disputes involving husbands and wives, men and women, boyfriends and girlfriends, same sex couples, and even on occasion siblings. Sometimes these events are triggered by a partner's unwanted or unexpected pregnancy: homicidal injury is a leading cause of death among pregnant and postpartum women in the United States.[188]
- Love triangles involving former husbands and/or wives and jilted lovers.
- Rape and/or sodomy–oriented assault in which a person intends to commit a rape or sexual assault but uses excessive force to overcome resistance, resulting in the victim's death.
- "Lust murders" that are motivated by obsessive sexual fantasies.
- Vengeance for sexual violence. In these cases, someone exacts vengeance on a sexual violence perpetrator, either on his or her own behalf or on the behalf of a sexual violence victim.

eldercide The murder of a senior citizen.

- Self-defense during sexual violence. In these incidents, sexual violence was taking place and the victim defended herself or himself resulting in the death of the sexual violence perpetrator; or another person intervened to defend the sexual violence victim and this resulted in the death of the sexual violence perpetrator.

The Race, Culture, Gender, and Criminology feature "Honor Killing" discusses one type of sexually based murder: a woman killed by relatives for damaging the family's honor.

Stranger Murders　About 20 percent of all murders involve strangers. Stranger homicides occur most often as felony murders during rapes, robberies, and burglaries, where the perpetrator applied too much force in completing the crime. Others are random acts of urban violence that fuel public fear: a homeowner tells a motorist to move his car because it is blocking the driveway, an argument ensues, and the owner gets a pistol and kills the motorist. Stranger homicides can also result from random gang violence—for example, when a bystander is killed inadvertently in a drive-by shooting. They can also stem from a hate crime (see later in this chapter) directed at a victim merely because of their race, class, gender, and so on. The killing of homeless people by adolescent groups and gangs has also become all too common.[189]

How do these murderous interactions develop between two people who may have had little prior conflict? In a classic study, David Luckenbill examined murder transactions to determine whether particular patterns of behavior are common between the killer and the victim.[190] He found that many homicides follow a sequential pattern. First, the victim makes what the offender considers an offensive move. The offender typically retaliates verbally or physically. An agreement to end things violently is forged with the victim's provocative response. The battle ensues, leaving the victim dead or dying. The offender's escape is shaped by his or her relationship to the victim or by the reaction of the audience, if any.

School Murders　Sadly, violence in schools has become commonplace. There have been a number of mass killings such as the April 20, 1999, shootings at Columbine High School in Colorado, which resulted in the deaths of 15 people, and the Newtown, Connecticut, massacre on

CONNECTIONS

It is possible that men who perceive loss of face aim their aggression at rivals who are competing with them for a suitable partner. Biosocial theory (Chapter 5) suggests that this behavior is motivated by the male's instinctual need to replenish the species and protect his place in the gene pool. Killing a rival would help a spouse maintain control over a potential mother for his children.

December 14, 2012, in which Adam Lanza killed 20 children and 6 staff members. On average, about 25 students are killed each year at school, or on the way to or returning from regular sessions at school, or while the victim was attending or traveling to or from an official school-sponsored event.[191]

Research shows that most shooting incidents occur around the start of the school day, the lunch period, or the end of the school day.[192] In most of the shootings (55 percent), a note, threat, or other action indicating risk for violence occurred before the event. Shooters were also likely to have expressed some form of suicidal behavior and to have been bullied by their peers.[193]

Multiple Murders

 LO7　Analyze the differences among serial killing, mass murder, and spree killing

For 27 years, a killer terrorized Wichita, Kansas. Known as BTK (for Bind, Torture, Kill), he sent taunting letters and packages to the police and the media describing the details of the 10 people he killed during the time period in which the murders took place. Suddenly, in 1991 he went underground and disappeared from view. After 25 years of silence, he renewed his communications with a local news station. His last communication contained a computer disk, which was traced to 59-year-old Dennis Rader after FBI analysis of deleted data on the disk. Rader later confessed to the 10 murders, in an effort to escape the death penalty.

Multiple murderers like Dennis Rader are people who have killed more than one victim. Based on the patterns of their murders, multiple killers are classified into three basic categories—mass murderers, spree killers, and serial killers. Each type of these multiple killers is discussed below.

Serial Murder

Criminologists consider a **serial killer**, such as Dennis Rader, to be a person who kills three or more persons in three or more separate events. In between the murders, the serial killer reverts to his normal lifestyle. Rader worked as a supervisor of the Compliance Department at Park City, Kansas, which put him in charge of animal control, housing problems, zoning, general permit enforcement, and a variety of nuisance cases. A married father of two, he served as a county commissioner, a Cub Scout leader, and a member of Christ Lutheran Church where he had been elected president of the Congregation Council. Rader's biography and personal

serial killer　The killing of a large number of people over time by an offender who seeks to escape detection.

HONOR KILLING

residents of a village on the West Bank in Palestinian territory made their way to an olive tree where the bruised body of Rasha Abu Arra, a young mother of six, was hanging, her veil torn off. She had been killed in the name of honor after rumors spread that she had committed adultery. In recent years, other victims have included a young mother of five who was beaten to death by her father because he suspected she was using her cell phone to talk to a man; a mentally disabled 21-year-old killed by her mother after she was sexually assaulted; and a woman who had divorced an abusive husband and was strangled by her father after being accused of "disgraceful" acts. The number of honor killings in the Palestinian territories has increased significantly: 27 women were killed in 2013 by family members claiming reasons of "honor"— more than double the 13 cases documented in 2012. Unfortunately, honor killings may disguise the fact that the murder was actually committed as a cover for domestic abuse, inheritance disputes, rape, incest, or the desire to punish female independence.

The United Nations estimates that about 5,000 "honor killings" are committed around the world each year. In Pakistan alone, almost 1,000 women and girls were killed in a single year (2011), including 93 minors. Most of the women were killed by husbands or brothers. "Illicit relations" was cited as a reason for 595 cases, and demanding to marry a partner of their choice was noted in 219 cases.

Honor killing and honor crime involve violence against women and girls, including such acts as beating, battering, or killing, by a family member or relative. The attacks are provoked by the belief or perception that an individual's or family's honor has been threatened because of the actual or perceived sexual misconduct of the

female. Honor killings are most common in traditional societies in the Middle East, Southwest Asia, India, China, and Latin America. However, the custom is now being exported around the world: in a crime that outraged Germany, a 24-year-old man, identified as Ahmad-Sobair O., killed his sister Morsal on May 15, 2008. He said he had objected to the pretty schoolgirl's lifestyle, her clothing, and her attempts to distance herself from her family. And Germany is not alone. In 2008, Yaser Abdel Said took his two teenaged daughters for a ride in his taxi cab, under the guise of taking them to get something to eat, then drove them to Irving, Texas, where he allegedly shot both girls to death. The reason: for dating boys against his will.

Honor killing of a woman or girl by her father, brother, or other male relative may occur because of a suspicion that she engaged in sexual activities before or outside marriage and thus has dishonored the family. Even when rape of a woman or girl has occurred this may be seen as a violation of the honor of the family for which the female must be killed. Wives' adultery and daughters' premarital "sexual activity," including rape, are seen as extreme violations of the codes of behavior and thus may result in the death of the female through this so-called honor killing. Honor killing/crime is based on the shame that a loss of control of the woman or girl brings to the family and to the male heads of the family.

According to criminologist Linda Williams, men consider honor killings culturally necessary because any suspicion of sexual activity or suspicion that a girl or a woman was touched by another in a sexual manner is enough to raise questions about the family's honor. Consequently, strict control of women and girls within the home and outside the home is justified. Women are restricted in their activities in the

community, religion, and politics. These institutions, in turn, support the control of females. Williams believes that the existence of honor killing is designed for maintaining male dominance. Submissiveness may be seen as a sign of sexual purity, and a woman's or girl's attempts to assert her rights can be seen as a violation of the family's honor that needs to be redressed. Rules of honor and threats against females who violate such rules reinforce the control of women and have a powerful impact on their lives. Honor killings/crimes serve to keep women and girls from "stepping out of line." The manner in which such behaviors silence women and kill their spirit has led some to label honor killings/crimes more broadly as "femicide."

Critical Thinking

While we may scoff at the idea of honor killings, are there elements of American culture and life that you consider harmful to women yet are still tolerated? What can be done to change them?

SOURCES: Anne-Marie O'Connor, "Honor Killings Rise in Palestinian Territories, Sparking Backlash," *Washington Post*, March 3, 2014, http://www.washingtonpost.com/world/middle_east/honor-killings-rise-in-palestinian-territories-sparking-backlash/2014/03/02/1392d144-940c-11e3-9e13-770265cf4962_story.html (accessed May 2014); Julia Dahl, "'Honor Killing' Under Growing Scrutiny in the U.S.," CBS News, April 5, 2012, http://www.cbsnews.com/news/honor-killing-under-growing-scrutiny-in-the-us/ (accessed May 2014); United Nations, "Impunity for Domestic Violence, 'Honour Killings' Cannot Continue," 2010, http://www.un.org/apps/news/story.asp?NewsID=33971&Cr=violence+against+women&Cr1=#.U2kGNCjLkw (accessed May 2014); Linda M. Williams, "Honor Killings," in *Encyclopedia of Interpersonal Violence*, ed. Claire M. Renzetti and Jeffrey I. Edelson (Thousand Oaks, CA: Sage Publications, 2007); Dan Bilefsky, "How to Avoid Honor Killing in Turkey? Honor Suicide," *New York Times*, July 16, 2006, p. 3; Nadera Shalhoub-Kevorkian, "Reexamining Femicide: Breaking the Silence and Crossing 'Scientific' Borders," *Signs* 28 (2003): 581–608.

life give few clues to his murderous path, which is perhaps why it took more than three decades to track him down.[194]

There is a great deal of fascination with serial killers, and they are frequent subjects for films like *Silence of the Lambs* and TV shows like *Criminal Minds*. They are sometimes portrayed as heroes, as anyone who watched *Dexter* soon found out. They inspire a great many myths and legends, a topic explored in the Criminology in Action feature.

Types of Serial Killers   There are different types of serial killers. Some wander the countryside killing at random; others hide themselves in a single locale and lure victims to their death.[195] Theodore Bundy, convicted killer of three young women and suspected killer of many others, roamed the country in the 1970s, killing as he went. John Wayne Gacy, during the same period, killed more than 30 boys and young men without leaving Chicago.

Some serial killers are sadists who gain satisfaction from torturing and killing.[196] Sadists wish to gain complete control over their victims through humiliation, shame, enslavement, and terror. Dr. Michael Swango, who is suspected of killing between 35 and 60 patients, wrote in his diary of the pleasure he obtained from murder. He wrote of the "sweet, husky, close smell of indoor homicide" and how murders were "the only way I have of reminding myself that I'm still alive."[197]

While Swango obtained pleasure from killing, other health care workers who have committed serial murder rationalize their behavior by thinking they are helping patients end their suffering when they put them to death. Harold Frederick Shipman, Britain's most notorious serial killer, was a general practitioner convicted of 15 murders, most involving elderly patients. After he committed suicide in 2004, further investigation found that he actually killed 218 patients and perhaps even more.[198]

Another type, the psychopathic killer, is motivated by a character disorder that causes an inability to experience shame, guilt, sorrow, or other normal human emotions; these murderers are concerned solely with their own needs and passions.

Serial murder experts James Alan Fox and Jack Levin have developed the following typology of serial killer motivations:

- *Thrill killers* strive for either sexual sadism or dominance. This is the most common form of serial murderer.
- *Mission killers* want to reform the world or have a vision that drives them to kill.
- *Expedience killers* are out for profit or want to protect themselves from a perceived threat.[199]

Female Serial Killers   Female serial killers have been around for quite some time. Locusta, a poisoner, was active in Rome during the first century BCE. Lucretia Patricia Cannon, the first known in the United States, was active between 1802 and 1829 in Delaware.[200]

An estimated 17 percent of serial killers are women, and there are striking differences between male and female killers.[201] Males are much more likely than females to use extreme violence and torture. Whereas males use a "hands-on" approach, including beating, bludgeoning, and strangling their victims, females are more likely to poison or smother their victims. Men track or stalk their victims, but women are much more likely to kill family members and acquaintances. Female serial killers kill those closest to them—husbands, lovers, and other relatives. They also target those who are weak or dependent on them: children and the elderly. In fact, men choose victims whom they can render helpless and women choose victims who are already helpless.[202]

There are also gender-based personality and behavior characteristics. Female killers, somewhat older than their male counterparts, abuse both alcohol and drugs; males are not likely to be substance abusers. Women were diagnosed as having histrionic, manic-depressive, borderline, dissociative, and antisocial personality disorders; men were more often diagnosed as having antisocial personalities. Aileen

Serial killer Dennis Rader, known as the BTK strangler, walks into the El Dorado (Kansas) Correctional Facility with two Sedgwick County sheriff's officers on August 19, 2005. Rader was convicted for killing 10 people over a 30-year span. He is currently serving 10 consecutive life sentences. What drives people like Rader? Are they mentally ill or suffering from some form of personality disorder? Rader was a married man, a member of Christ Lutheran Church where he served as president of the Congregation Council, and a Boy Scout leader. How could he have functioned at such a high level if he was mentally disturbed?

Jeff Tuttle/epa/Landov

Wuornos, executed for killing seven men, was diagnosed with a severe psychopathic personality, which probably arose from her horrific childhood marred by beatings, alcoholism, rape, incest, and prostitution.[203]

Thus, the typical female serial killer is a person who smothers or poisons someone she knows. During childhood she suffered from an abusive relationship in a disrupted family. Female killers' education levels are below average, and if they hold jobs, they are in low-status positions. And because they use stealth and cunning rather than overt brutality, women are more likely to remain at large longer before arousing suspicion. They also remain undetected because they tend to be older and more mature than their male counterparts and, quite possibly, due to the gender biases that underpin the misconception that women cannot be serial murderers.[204]

Why Do Serial Killers Kill? The cause of serial murder eludes criminologists. Such disparate factors as mental illness, sexual frustration, neurological damage, child abuse and neglect, smothering relationships with mothers (David Berkowitz, the notorious Son of Sam, slept in his parents' bed until he was 10), and childhood anxiety are suspected. Most experts view serial killers as sociopaths who from early childhood demonstrate bizarre behavior, such as torturing animals. Some are sadists who enjoy the sexual thrill of murdering and who are both pathological and destructive narcissists.[205]

This behavior extends to the pleasure they reap from killing, their ability to ignore or enjoy their victims' suffering, and their propensity for basking in the media limelight when apprehended for their crimes. Killing provides a way to fill their emotional hunger and reduce their anxiety levels.[206] Wayne Henley, Jr., who along with Dean Corill killed 27 boys in Houston, offered to help prosecutors find the bodies of additional victims so he could break Chicago killer John Wayne Gacy's record of 33 murders.[207]

According to experts Fox and Levin, serial killers enjoy the thrill, the sexual gratification, and the dominance they achieve over the lives of their victims. The serial killer rarely uses a gun because this method is too quick and would deprive him of his greatest pleasure, exulting in his victim's suffering. Levin and Fox dispute the notion that serial killers have some form of biological or psychological problems, such as genetic anomalies or schizophrenia. Even the most sadistic serial murderers are not mentally ill or driven by delusions or hallucinations. Instead, they typically exhibit a sociopathic personality that deprives them of pangs of conscience or guilt to guide their behavior. Serial killers are not insane, they claim, but "more cruel than crazy."[208]

Controlling Serial Killers Serial killers come from diverse backgrounds. To date, law enforcement officials have been at a loss to control random killers who leave few clues, constantly move, and have little connection to their victims.

Catching serial killers is often a matter of luck. To help local law enforcement officials, the FBI has developed a profiling system to identify potential suspects. Because serial killers often use the same patterns in each attack, they leave a signature that might help in their capture.[209]

In addition, the Justice Department's Violent Criminal Apprehension Program (VICAP), a computerized information service, gathers information and matches offense characteristics on violent crimes around the country.[210] This program links crimes to determine if they are the product of a single culprit.

Mass Murders

In contrast to serial killings, **mass murder** involves the killing of four or more victims by one or more assailants within a single event.[211] The murderous incident can last but a few minutes or as long as several hours. Highly organized or institutionalized killings (i.e., war crimes and large-scale acts of political terrorism, as well as certain acts of highly organized crime rings), while atrocious, are not considered mass murder and are motivated by a totally different set of factors.

Mass murderers engage in a single, uncontrollable outburst called "simultaneous killing." Charles Whitman killed 14 people and wounded 30 others from atop the 307-foot tower on the University of Texas campus in August 1966; James Huberty killed 21 people in a McDonald's restaurant in San Ysidro, California, in July 1984; in October 1991, George Hennard killed 22 people in a Killeen, Texas, cafeteria before committing suicide as police closed in; Seung-Hui Cho killed 32 people and wounded 25 at Virginia Tech in April 2007; James Holmes killed 12 people and wounded 70 others in a movie theater in Aurora, Colorado, in July 2012.

Fox and Levin define four types of mass murderers:

- *Revenge killers* seek to get even with individuals or society at large. Their typical target is an estranged wife and "her" children or an employer and "his" employees.
- *Love killers* are motivated by a warped sense of devotion. They are often despondent people who commit suicide and take others, such as a wife and children, with them.
- *Profit killers* are usually trying to cover up a crime, eliminate witnesses, and carry out a criminal conspiracy.
- *Terrorist killers* are trying to send a message. Gang killings tell rivals to watch out; cult killers may actually leave a message behind to warn society about impending doom.[212]

mass murder The killing of a large number of people in a single incident by an offender who typically does not seek concealment or escape.

MYTHS ABOUT SERIAL KILLERS

n his new book *Why We Love Serial Killers: The Curious Appeal of the World's Most Savage Murderers*, criminologist Scott Bonn helps dispel some of the myths that have grown up around serial killers. Some of the most widespread are discussed below.

Myth #1: All Serial Killers Are Men

Reality: This is simply not true, but it is understandable why the public would hold this erroneous belief. As late as 1998, a highly regarded former FBI profiler said, "There are no female serial killers." The news and entertainment media also perpetuate the stereotypes that all serial offenders are male and that women do not engage in horrible acts of violence. In fact, approximately 17 percent of all serial homicides in the United States are committed by women; in contrast, only 10 percent of total murders in the U.S. are committed by women. Therefore, while men commit more serial murders

than women, the female serial killer is not unknown.

Myth #2: All Serial Killers Are Caucasian

Reality: Contrary to popular mythology, not all serial killers are white. Serial killers span all racial and ethnic groups in the United States. The racial diversity of serial killers generally mirrors that of the overall U.S. population. There are well-documented cases of African American, Latino, and Asian American serial killers. African Americans comprise the largest racial minority group among serial killers, representing approximately 20 percent of the total. Significantly, however, only white (and normally, male) serial killers such as Ted Bundy become popular culture icons.

Myth #3: All Serial Killers Are Isolated and Dysfunctional Loners

Reality: Real-life serial killers are not the isolated monsters of fiction. The majority of serial killers are not reclusive, social

misfits who live alone. Frequently, they do not appear to be strange or stand out from the public in any meaningful way. Many serial killers are able to hide out in plain sight for extended periods of time. Those who successfully blend in are typically employed, have families and homes, and outwardly appear to be nonthreatening, normal members of society. In fact, many are highly functioning and appear to be completely normal.

Myth #4: All Serial Murderers Travel Widely and Kill Interstate

Reality: The roaming, homicidal maniac such as Freddy Krueger in the cult film *A Nightmare on Elm Street* is another stereotype that is rarely found in real life. Serial killers typically have a comfort zone—that is, an area that they are intimately familiar with and where they like to stalk and kill their prey. The comfort zone of a serial killer is often defined by an anchor point such as a place of residence or employment. Crime statistics

While it often appears that our society has spawned the mass murder, a recent study by Grant Duwe shows that more than 900 mass killings took place between 1900 and 1999 and that mass killings were nearly as common during the 1920s and 1930s as they are today. More of the earlier incidents involved *familicide* (i.e., killing of one's family) and killers were more likely to be older and more suicidal than they are today. The most significant difference between contemporary mass murders and those in the past: more killers use guns today and more incidents involve drug trafficking.[213]

A recent study by Adam Lankford compared mass murderers who took their own life with those who survived their attack. Lankford found that while only 4 percent of murderers commit suicide, by contrast, 38 percent of mass shooters who attacked in the United States between 1966 and 2010 committed suicide by their own hand, or committed "suicide by cop," so that overall, 48 percent of these offenders died as a result of their attacks. Those mass shooters who died armed themselves with more

weapons, killed more victims, and often struck at different locations (commercial areas) than those who survived their attacks. The suicidal killers tend to engage in profound self-loathing, whereby they feel guilty and ashamed about their inadequacies and weaknesses, including their uncontrolled anger and violent tendencies; they had a vengeful desire to punish themselves and were propelled by more powerful perceptions of personal victimization, social injustice, and general hopelessness than other mass shooters.[214]

Spree Killers   In 2009, Michael McLendon, 28, killed 10 people in rural Alabama before taking his own life. He had a target list that detectives found in his home. After killing seven members of his family, he drove around the county and killed three more people at random.[215] Spree killers like McLendon engage in a rampage of violence taking place over a period of days or weeks. Unlike mass murderers, their killing is not confined to a single outburst, and reveal that serial killers are most likely to commit their first murder very close to their place of residence due to the comfort and familiarity it offers them.

Myth #5: All Serial Killers Are Either Mentally Ill or Evil Geniuses

Reality: The images presented in the news and entertainment media suggest that serial killers either have a debilitating mental illness such as psychosis or they are brilliant but demented geniuses like Dr. Hannibal Lecter. Neither of these two stereotypes is quite accurate. In fact, very few serial killers suffer from any mental illness. Serial killers such as John Wayne Gacy and Dennis Rader may be psychopaths, but they were entirely aware of the illegality of murder while in the process of killing their victims. Their understanding of right and wrong does nothing to impede their crimes, however, because psychopaths have an overwhelming desire and compulsion to kill that causes them to ignore the criminal law with impunity.

There is a popular culture stereotype that serial killers are cunning, criminal geniuses. The reality is that most serial killers who have had their IQ tested score between borderline and above average intelligence. This is very consistent with the general population. Contrary to mythology, it is not high intelligence that makes serial killers successful. Instead, it is obsession, meticulous planning, and a cold-blooded, often psychopathic personality that enable serial killers to operate over long periods of time without detection.

Myth #6: All Serial Killers Must Keep On Killing

Reality: Another common myth is that once serial killers start killing, they cannot stop. Although this claim may seem reasonable, it is inaccurate. There are serial killers who stop murdering altogether before ever being caught.

Myth #7: All Serial Killers Want to Get Caught

Reality: It is popularly believed that serial killers secretly want to get caught. For the vast majority of them, however, this is simply not true. They love the act of killing. Serial killers take satisfaction in their success, particularly at the beginning of their killing careers. The skills and confidence gained through their experience make serial killers very difficult to apprehend. As they continue to operate and avoid capture, serial killers become increasingly emboldened and empowered.

Myth #8: All Serial Killer Victims Are Female

Reality: According to the stereotypical imagery presented in Hollywood films and best-selling novels, male serial killers prey exclusively on female victims. This is not true. Just as not all serial killers are male, not all serial-killer victims are female, although females do represent the majority of victims. The presence of a sexual motive often leads a male serial killer to prey on women, but in reality about 30 percent of victims are men.

Critical Thinking

Why do you think the public is so fascinated by serial killers despite the fact that there are relatively few of them and they commit a very small portion of annual murders? Is it because they represent the dark side of humanity? Or because they represent sex and violence to the extreme, something that has always fascinated the public?

SOURCE: Scott Bonn, *Why We Love Serial Killers: The Curious Appeal of the World's Most Savage Murderers* (New York: Skyhorse Press, 2014).

unlike serial killers, they don't have a "cooling off" period between murders or return to their "normal" identities in between killings.

The most notorious spree killing to date occurred in October 2002, in the Washington, D.C., area.[216] John Lee Malvo, 17, a Jamaican citizen, and his traveling companion John Allen Muhammad, 41, an Army veteran with an expert's rating in marksmanship, went on a rampage that left more than 10 people dead.

Some spree killers target a specific group or class. Joseph Paul Franklin targeted mixed race couples, African Americans, and Jews, committing more than 20 murders in 12 states in an effort to instigate a race war (Franklin also shot and paralyzed *Hustler* publisher Larry Flynt because he published pictures of interracial sex); he was executed on November 20, 2013.[217] Others, like the D.C. snipers Malvo and Muhammed, kill randomly and do not seek out a specific class of victim; their targets included young and old, African Americans and whites, men and women.[218]

ASSAULT AND BATTERY

Although many people mistakenly believe the term *assault and battery* refers to a single act, they are actually two separate crimes. *Battery* requires offensive touching, such as slapping, hitting, or punching a victim. *Assault* requires no actual touching but involves either attempted battery or intentionally frightening the victim by word or deed. Although common law originally intended these twin crimes to be misdemeanors, most jurisdictions now upgrade them to felonies either when a weapon is used or when they occur during the commission of a felony (for example, when a person is assaulted during a robbery). In the UCR, the FBI defines serious assault, or aggravated assault, as "an unlawful attack by one person upon another for the purpose of inflicting severe or aggravated bodily injury"; this definition is similar to the one used in most state jurisdictions.[219]

Under common law, battery required bodily injury, such as broken limbs or wounds. However, under modern law, battery occurs if the victim suffers a temporarily painful blow, even if no injury results. Battery can also involve offensive touching, such as if a man kisses a woman against her will or puts his hands on her body. In some legal jurisdictions, biting someone when infected with AIDS is considered an aggravated assault; some AIDS-infected people have been convicted of aggravated assault for spitting on their victims.[220]

Nature and Extent of Assault

The pattern of criminal assault is similar to that of homicide; one could say that the only difference between the two is that the victim survives.[221] Assaults may be common in our society simply because of common life stresses. Motorists who assault each other have become such a familiar occurrence that the term **road rage** has been coined. There have even been frequent incidents of violent assault among frustrated passengers who lose control while traveling.

Every citizen is bound by the law of assault, even police officers. Excessive use of force can result in criminal charges being filed even if it occurs while police officers are arresting a dangerous felony suspect. Only the minimum amount of force needed to subdue the suspect is allowed by law, and if police use more aggressive tactics than required, they may find themselves the target of criminal charges and civil lawsuits that can run into the millions of dollars.[222]

The FBI records about 760,000 assaults each year, a rate of about 240 per 100,000 inhabitants. Like other violent crimes, the number of assaults has been in decline, down about 20 percent in the past decade. Preliminary 2013 data indicate that the downward trend is continuing.

People arrested for assault and those identified by victims are usually young, male (about 80 percent), and white, although the number of African Americans arrested for assault (about one-third of the total) is disproportionate to their representation in the population. Assault victims tend to be male, but females also face a significant danger. Assault rates are highest in urban areas, during summer, and in southern and western regions. The most common weapons used in assaults are blunt instruments and hands and feet.

The NCVS indicates that only about half of all serious assaults are reported to the police. The NCVS indicates that the number of assault victimizations has been in steep decline, dropping more than 50 percent during the past decade; even weapon-related assaults have dropped sharply.

Assault in the Home

Violent attacks in the home are one of the most frightening types of assault. Criminologists recognize that intrafamily violence is an enduring social problem in the United States and abroad.

The UN's World Health Organization (WHO) found that around the world, women often face the greatest risk for violence in their own homes and in familiar settings. Almost half the women who die due to homicide are killed by their current or former husbands or boyfriends; in some countries about 70 percent of all female deaths are domestic homicides. It is possible that nearly one in four women will experience violence by an intimate partner in their lifetime, and most of these are subjected to multiple acts of violence over extended periods of time. In addition to physical abuse, a third to over half of these cases are accompanied by sexual violence; in some countries, up to one-third of adolescent girls report forced sexual initiation. The WHO report found that the percentage of women assaulted by a spouse or intimate partner varied considerably around the world: less than 3 percent in the United States, Canada, and Australia and up to 38 percent of the married women in the Republic of Korea and 52 percent of Palestinian women on the West Bank and Gaza Strip. In many places, assaults and even murders occur because men believe that their partners have been defiled sexually, either through rape or sex outside of marriage. In some societies, the only way to cleanse the family honor is by killing the offending female. In Alexandria, Egypt, for example, 47 percent of the women who were killed by a relative were murdered after they had been raped.

Child Abuse   One area of intrafamily violence that has received a great deal of media attention is **child abuse**. This term describes any physical or emotional trauma to a child for which no reasonable explanation, such as an accident or ordinary disciplinary practices, can be found.[223] Child abuse can result from actual physical beatings administered to a child by hands, feet, weapons, belts, sticks, burning, and so on. Another form of abuse results from **neglect**—not providing a child with the care and shelter to which he or she is entitled.

The most recent national survey (2012) conducted by the Department of Health and Human Services shows that while child abuse rates are in decline the problem is still significant. Child protective services (CPS) agencies throughout the United States received more than 3.4 million referrals involving approximately 6.3 million children. Of these, 2.1 million reports were considered valid and received a disposition; this amounted to 28 cases per 1,000 children in the national population. Of these cases, 400,000

road rage   A term used to describe motorists who assault each other.

child abuse   Any physical, emotional, or sexual trauma to a child for which no reasonable explanation, such as an accident, can be found. Child abuse can also be a function of neglecting to give proper care and attention to a young child.

neglect   Not providing a child with the care and shelter to which he or she is entitled.

received continuing services after the incident was reported; 150,000 children are taken out of the home each year and put in foster care. About 1,600 children died at the hands of their abusers.[224]

LO8 Discuss the root causes of child abuse

Causes of Child Abuse As Figure 10.2 shows, the great majority of child abuse cases involve parents. Why do parents physically assault their children? Such maltreatment is a highly complex problem with neither a single cause nor a readily available solution. It cuts across ethnic, religious, and socioeconomic lines. Abusive parents cannot be categorized by sex, age, or educational level; they come from all walks of life.[225]

A number of factors have been commonly linked to abuse and neglect:

- Family violence seems to be perpetuated from one generation to another within families. The behavior of abusive parents can often be traced to negative experiences in their own childhood—physical abuse, lack of love, emotional neglect, incest, and so on.
- Blended families, which include children living with an unrelated adult such as a stepparent or another unrelated co-resident, have also been linked to abuse. Children who live with a mother's boyfriend are at much greater risk for abuse than children living with two genetic parents. Some stepparents do not have strong emotional ties to their nongenetic children, nor do they reap emotional benefits from the parent–child relationship.[226]
- Parents may also become abusive if they are isolated from friends, neighbors, or relatives who can help in times of crisis. Potentially abusive parents are often alienated from society; they have carried the concept of the shrinking nuclear family to its most extreme form and are cut off from ties of kinship and contact with other people in the neighborhood.[227]

Sexual Abuse Another aspect of the abuse syndrome is **sexual abuse**—the exploitation of children through rape, incest, and molestation by parents or other adults. It is difficult to estimate the incidence of sexual abuse, but a number of attempts have been made to gauge the extent of the problem. The most recent national survey indicates that about 62,000 cases of sexual abuse were reported. However, these reported cases may vastly undercount the true nature of the problem. In a classic study, Diana Russell's survey of women in the San Francisco area found that 38 percent had experienced intra- or extrafamilial sexual abuse by the time they reached age 18.[228]

Although sexual abuse is still prevalent, the number of reported cases has been in a significant decline, being reduced from about 78,000 reported cases in 2003.[229] This trend must be interpreted with caution. While it is possible that the actual number of cases is truly in decline because of the effectiveness of prevention programs, increased prosecution, and public awareness campaigns, declines might be the result of more cases being overlooked because of (a) increased evidentiary requirements to substantiate cases, (b) increased caseworker caution due to new legal rights for caregivers, and (c) increasing limitations on the types of cases that agencies accept for investigation.[230]

Sexual abuse is of particular concern because children who have been abused experience a long list of symptoms, including fear, post-traumatic stress disorder, behavior problems, sexualized behavior, and poor self-esteem.[231]

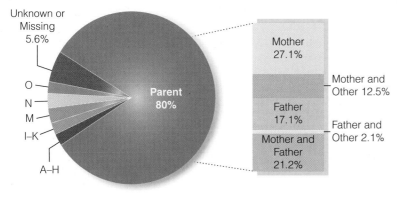

Nonparental

A Daycare staff 1.2%
B Foster parent (female relative) 0.0%
C Foster parent (male relative) 0.1%
D Foster parent (nonrelative) 0.2%
E Foster parent (unknown relationship) 0.0%
F Friend or neighbor 0.4%
G Legal guardian (female) 0.1%
H Legal guardian (male) 0.0%

I More than one nonparental perpetrator 2.3%
J Other professional 0.0%
K Partner of parent (female) 0.1%
L Partner of parent (male) 2.6%
M Relative (female) 2.8%
N Relative (male) 2.0%
O Staff group home 0.0%

FIGURE 10.2 Victims of Child Abuse by Perpetrator Relationship

NOTE: Based on data from 41 states.

SOURCE: U.S. Department of Health and Human Services, Administration for Children and Families, Children's Bureau, *Child Maltreatment 2012* (Washington, DC: U.S. Department of Health and Human Services, 2013), p. 58, Table 4-4, http://www.acf.hhs.gov/sites/default/files/cb/cm2012.pdf (accessed May 2014).

sexual abuse Exploitation of a child through rape, incest, or molestation by a parent or other adult.

Women who were abused as children are also at greater risk to be reabused as adults than those who avoided childhood victimization.[232] The amount of force used during the abuse, its duration, and its frequency are all related to the extent of the long-term effects and the length of time needed for recovery.

Regardless of its cause, child abuse can have devastating long-term effects, ranging from depression to loss of self-esteem.[233] Not surprisingly, a history of childhood sexual and physical abuse among persons with severe mental illness is disproportionately high.[234]

Parental Abuse   Parents are sometimes the target of abuse from their own children. Research conducted by Arina Ulman and Murray Straus found:

- The younger the child, the higher the rate of child-to-parent violence (CPV).
- At all ages, more children were violent to mothers than to fathers.
- Both boys and girls hit mothers more often than fathers.
- At all ages, slightly more boys than girls hit parents.

Ulman and Straus found that child-to-parent violence was associated with some other form of violence by parents, which could either be husband-to-wife, wife-to-husband, corporal punishment of children, or physical abuse. They suggest that if the use of physical punishment could be eliminated or curtailed, then child-to-parent violence would similarly decline.[235]

Spousal Abuse   Spousal abuse has occurred throughout recorded history. Roman men had the legal right to beat their wives for minor acts such as attending public games without permission, drinking wine, or walking outdoors with their faces uncovered.[236] More serious transgressions, such as adultery, were punishable by death. During the later stages of the Roman Empire, the practice of wife beating abated, and by the fourth century, excessive violence on the part of husband or wife was grounds for divorce.[237] During the early Middle Ages, there was a separation of love and marriage.[238] The ideal woman was protected, cherished, and loved from afar. In contrast, the wife, with whom marriage had been arranged by family ties, was guarded jealously and could be punished severely for violating her duties. A husband was expected to beat his wife for "misbehaviors" and might himself be punished by neighbors if he failed to do so.[239]

Through the later Middle Ages and into modern times (from 1400 to 1900), there was little community objection to a man using force against his wife as long as the assault did not exceed certain limits, usually construed as death or disfigurement. By the mid-nineteenth century, severe wife beating fell into disfavor, and accused wife beaters were subject to public ridicule. Nonetheless, limited chastisement was still the rule. By the close of the nineteenth century, England and the United States outlawed wife beating. Yet the long history of husbands' domination of their wives made physical coercion hard to control. Until recent times, the subordinate position of women in the family was believed to give husbands the legal and moral obligation to manage their wives' behavior. Even after World War II, English courts found physical assault a reasonable punishment for a wife who had disobeyed her husband.[240] These ideas form the foundation of men's traditional physical control of women and have led to severe cases of spousal assault.

The Nature and Extent of Spousal Abuse   It is difficult to estimate how widespread spousal abuse is today; however, some statistics indicate the extent of the problem. In their classic study of family violence, Richard Gelles and Murray Straus found that 16 percent of surveyed families had experienced husband–wife assaults.[241] In police departments around the country, 60 to 70 percent of evening calls involve domestic disputes.

Males are also the target of abuse. One recent study of 12,000 male abuse victims serving in the U.S. Army found that abused men were at greater risk for early army discharge and hospitalization than were nonvictims—particularly hospitalizations for depression, alcohol dependence, and mental health problems.[242]

Some of the personal attributes and characteristics of spouse abusers and abusive situations are listed in Exhibit 10.3.

To read more on dating abuse, visit the Harvard School of Public Health website: **http://archive.sph .harvard.edu/press-releases/archives/2001 -releases/press07312001.html.**

Is there something we can do to prevent dating violence? What would you suggest?

Dating Violence

Date rape is not the only form of violence aimed at a boyfriend or girlfriend.[243] A significant portion of all teens have been the target of dating violence, and it is estimated that one high school girl in five may suffer sexual or physical abuse from a boyfriend. Dating violence has been linked to substance abuse, unsafe sex, and eating disorders.[244]

Physical dating violence can involve a wide spectrum of activities—scratching, slapping, pushing, slamming or holding someone against a wall, biting, choking, burning, beating someone up, and assault with a weapon—ranging

EXHIBIT 10.3

Factors that Predict Spousal Abuse

- *Presence of alcohol.* Excessive alcohol use may turn otherwise docile husbands into wife abusers.

- *Access to weapons.* A perpetrator's access to a gun and previous threats with a weapon may lead to abuse.

- *Stepchild in the home.* Having a stepchild living in the home may provoke abuse because the stepparent may have a more limited bond to the child.

- *Estrangement.* This may occur especially in the case of a controlling partner and subsequent involvement with another partner.

- *Hostility toward dependency.* Some husbands who appear docile and passive may resent their dependence on their wives and react with rage and violence; this reaction has been linked to sexual inadequacy.

- *Excessive brooding.* Obsession with a wife's behavior, however trivial, can result in violent assaults.

- *Social learning.* Some males believe society approves of spouse or mate abuse and use these beliefs to justify their violent behavior. Peer support helps shape their attitudes and behaviors.

- *Socioeconomic factors.* Men who fail as providers and are under economic stress may take their frustrations out on their wives.

- *Flashes of anger.* Research shows that a significant amount of family violence results from a sudden burst of anger after a verbal dispute.

- *Military service.* Spousal abuse among men who have served in the military service is extremely high. Those serving in the military are more likely to assault their wives than civilian husbands. The reasons for this phenomenon may be the violence promoted by military training and the close proximity in which military families live to one another.

- *Having been battered children.* Husbands who assault their wives were generally battered as children.

- *Unpredictability.* Batterers are unpredictable, unable to be influenced by their wives, and impossible to prevent from battering once an argument has begun.

SOURCES: Christine Sellers, John Cochran, and Kathryn Branch, "Social Learning Theory and Partner Violence: A Research Note," *Deviant Behavior* 26 (2005) 379–395; Jacquelyn Campbell, Daniel Webster, Jane Koziol-McLain, Carolyn Block, Doris Campbell, Mary Ann Curry, Faye Gary, Nancy Glass, Judith McFarlane, Carolyn Sachs, Phyllis Sharps, Yvonne Ulrich, Susan Wilt, Jennifer Manganello, Xiao Xu, Janet Schollenberger, Victoria Frye, and Kathryn Laughon, "Risk Factors for Femicide in Abusive Relationships: Results from a Multisite Case Control Study," *American Journal of Public Health* 93 (2003): 1089–1097.

from moderate to severe. There is also emotional and psychological abuse, including insulting, criticizing, threatening, humiliating, or berating. An emerging form of emotional abuse is referred to as **relational aggression** in which a partner tries to damage a person's relationship with friends by spreading smears and false rumors or by revealing information or images intended to be private.

ROBBERY

 LO9 Discuss the crime of robbery and why it is a rational crime

In the 1930s, bank robbers had colorful nicknames such as "Pretty Boy" and "Baby Face." We may be returning to that era of colorful bandits: over the past four years, a man whom law enforcement agents have dubbed the "Loan Ranger Bandit" has committed at least a dozen armed robberies of banks and other financial institutions in four different states—and he is so audacious he doesn't bother covering his face. In 2009, the Loan Ranger began robbing banks in Arkansas, Mississippi, Kentucky, and Texas. Police in Tyler, Texas, came up with the moniker "Loan Ranger Bandit" because the robber is known to target financial institutions that make loans, and he wore a Texas Rangers baseball cap in one of his robberies.

In his early robberies, the Loan Ranger would give tellers a demand note and show them a weapon in his waistband. Beginning with the ninth robbery, he began to brandish the weapon. Despite his lack of a disguise, the Loan Ranger Bandit is clever. He picks stand-alone institutions that offer easy access to major roadways—and therefore quick getaways—and he often targets the same banks more than once. He varies his clothing; his outfits have included athletic wear, jeans, and business attire. And he appears very confident in what he is doing. Perhaps he saw the great film *Public Enemies* and heard John Dillinger, played by Johnny Depp, explain to his girlfriend Billie Frechette (Marion Cotillard) why he believed he could never be caught:

> They ain't tough enough, smart enough, or fast enough. I can hit any bank I want, any time. They got to be at every bank, all the time.

The Loan Ranger is a modern day robber in the mold of John Dillinger (though he hasn't shot anyone so far). The common-law definition of robbery (and the one used by the FBI) is "the taking or attempting to take anything of value from the care, custody or control of a person or persons by force or threat of force or violence and/or by putting the victim in fear."[245] A robbery is considered a violent crime because it involves the use of force to obtain money or goods. Robbery is punished severely because the victim's life is put in jeopardy. In fact, the severity of punishment is based on the amount of force used during the crime, not the value of the items taken.

relational aggression Psychological and emotional abuse that involves the spreading of smears, rumors, and private information in order to harm their partner.

The FBI records about 350,000 robberies each year, a rate of about 112 per 100,000 population. As with most other violent crimes, there has been a significant reduction in the robbery rate during the past decade; the robbery rate is down almost 40 percent.

Attempts have been made to classify and explain the nature and dynamics of robbery. One approach is to characterize robberies by type (Exhibit 10.4), and another is to characterize types of robbers based on their specialties (Exhibit 10.5).

As these typologies indicate, the typical armed robber is unlikely to be a professional who carefully studies targets while planning a crime. People walking along the street, convenience stores, and gas stations are much more likely robbery targets than banks or other highly secure environments. Robbers, therefore, seem to be diverted by modest defensive measures, such as having more than one clerk in a store or locating stores in strip malls; they are more likely to try an isolated store.[246]

EXHIBIT 10.4

Types of Robberies

- *Robbery in an open area.* These robberies include street muggings, purse snatchings, and other attacks. Street robberies are the most common type, especially in urban areas, where this type of robbery constitutes about 60 percent of reported totals. Street robbery is most closely associated with mugging or yoking, which refers to grabbing victims from behind and threatening them with a weapon. Street muggers often target unsavory characters such as drug dealers or pimps who carry large amounts of cash, because these victims would find it awkward to report the crime to the police. Most commit their robberies within a short distance from their homes.
- *Commercial robbery.* This type of robbery occurs in businesses ranging from banks to liquor stores. Banks are among the most difficult targets to rob, because they have more personnel and a higher level of security.
- *Robbery on private premises.* This type of robbery involves breaking into people's homes. FBI records indicate that this type of robbery accounts for about 10 percent of all offenses.
- *Robbery after a short, preliminary association.* This type of robbery comes after a chance meeting—in a bar, at a party, or after a sexual encounter.
- *Robbery after a longer association between victim and offender.* An example of this type of robbery would be an intimate acquaintance robbing his paramour and then fleeing the jurisdiction.
- *Carjacking.* This is a completed or attempted theft of a motor vehicle by force or threat of force.

SOURCES: Katie Willis, *Armed Robbery: Who Commits It and Why?* (Canberra: Australian Institute of Criminology, 2006); Patsy Klaus, *Carjackings in the United States, 1992–96* (Washington, DC: Bureau of Justice Statistics, 1999); Peter J. van Koppen and Robert Jansen, "The Road to the Robbery: Travel Patterns in Commercial Robberies," *British Journal of Criminology* 38 (1998): 230–247.

Surveillance video shot of a bank robbery suspect at the Rivertown Credit Union in Alpine Township, Michigan. Like most violent crimes, robbery rates have been in decline.

Handout/Mlive.com/Landov

The Calculating Robber

While many robbers are amateurs, robbery remains a crime of rationality and planning. Marcus Felson describes robbers as foragers, predators who search for victims, preferably close to their homes, where numerous "nutritious" victims are abundant, where the robbers know the territory so that their prey cannot easily escape, and where their victims may be less vigilant because they are on their home turf.[247] Robbers, then, select targets that are *vulnerable, accessible*, and *profitable*.

We can see this element of rationality and planning in the strategies of one type of robber: carjackers, who attack occupied vehicles for the purpose of theft. When Heith Copes, Andy Hochstetler, and Michael Cherbonneau interviewed a sample of carjackers, they were told that to get the

EXHIBIT 10.5

Types of Robbers

- *Professional robbers.* These robbers have a long-term commitment to crime as a source of livelihood. This type of robber plans and organizes crimes prior to committing them and seeks money to support a hedonistic lifestyle. Some professionals are exclusively robbers, whereas others engage in additional types of crimes. Professionals are committed to robbing because it is direct, fast, and profitable. They hold no other steady job and plan three or four "big scores" a year to support themselves. Planning and skill are the trademarks of the professional robber, who usually operates in groups with assigned roles. Professionals usually steal large amounts from commercial establishments. After a score, they may stop for a few weeks until "things cool off."

- *Opportunist robbers.* These robbers steal to obtain small amounts of money when an accessible target presents itself. They are not committed to robbery but will steal from cab drivers, drunks, the elderly, and other vulnerable persons if they need some extra spending money. Opportunists are usually teens and gang members who do not plan their crimes. Although they operate within the milieu of the juvenile gang, they are seldom organized and spend little time discussing weapon use, getaway plans, or other strategies.

- *Addict robbers.* These people steal to support their drug habits. They have a low commitment to robbery because of its danger but a high commitment to theft because it supplies needed funds. The addict is less likely to plan crime or use weapons than the professional robber but is more cautious than the opportunist. Addicts choose targets that present minimal risk; however, when desperate for funds, they are sometimes careless in selecting the victim and executing the crime. They rarely think in terms of the big score; they just want enough money to get their next fix.

- *Alcoholic robbers.* These people steal for reasons related to their excessive consumption of alcohol. Alcoholic robbers steal (a) when, in a disoriented state, they attempt to get some money to buy liquor or (b) when their condition makes them unemployable and they need funds. Alcoholic robbers have no real commitment to robbery as a way of life. They plan their crimes randomly and give little thought to their victim, circumstance, or escape. For that reason, they are the most likely to be caught.

SOURCES: Katie Willis, *Armed Robbery: Who Commits It and Why?* (Canberra: Australian Institute of Criminology, 2006); John Conklin, *Robbery and the Criminal Justice System* (New York: Lippincott, 1972), pp. 1–80.

upper hand, robbers avoid the likelihood of victims fighting back by devoting attention to selecting "proper victims" who are the least likely to resist.[248] Ironically, some steer clear of women drivers, fearing that their victims will panic and start to yell for help, or act erratically, making them difficult to control.

Once a victim has been chosen, carjackers carefully form a line of attack designed to shock the victim into compliance. Some use a blitz method, attacking so rapidly that the target does not have time to respond. Others manipulate their appearance, posing as a street vendor, in order to approach potential victims without causing alarm. Some wait for an opportune moment—for example, lurking in parking lots and approaching inattentive victims as they enter their cars—and demand that they surrender the keys. The research uncovered the fact that carjackers used and reused scripts when committing their crimes. Sticking to their scripts enabled carjackers to reduce the danger and to use their skills and experience to avoid detection. Sticking to the script also prolongs a criminal career. It builds confidence and helps the carjacker act quickly and decisively, analyzing the situation and figuring out what must be done. No matter what the strategy, carjackers seem rational and calculating.

Some robbers target fellow criminals—for example, drug dealers—because they are inviting targets.[249] Although these targets may be dangerous, robbers recognize that people with "dirty hands" are unlikely to call police and get entangled with the law. When Bruce Jacobs interviewed armed robbers, he found that some specialize in targeting drug dealers because they believe that even though their work is hazardous, the rewards outweigh the risks. Drug dealers are plentiful, visible, and accessible, and they carry plenty of cash. Their merchandise is valuable, is easily transported, and can be used by the robber or sold to another. Drug dealers are not particularly popular, so they cannot rely on bystanders to come to their aid. Nor can they call the police and ask them to recover their stolen goods! Of course, drug dealers may be able to "take care of business" themselves, but surprisingly Jacobs found that many choose not to carry a pistol.[250] Drug dealers may be tough and bad, the robbers claim, but *they* are tougher and badder.

Acquaintance Robbery

As Exhibit 10.4 suggests, one type of robber may focus on people they know, a phenomenon referred to as **acquaintance robbery**. This seems puzzling because victims can easily identify their attackers and report them to the police. However, despite this threat, acquaintance robbery may be attractive for a number of rational reasons:[251]

- Victims may be reluctant to report these crimes because they do not want to get involved with the police. They may be involved in crime themselves (drug dealers, for example), or they may fear retaliation if they report the crime. Some victims may be reluctant to gain the label of "rat" or "fink" if they go to the police.

acquaintance robbery Robbers who focus their thefts on people they know.

- Some robberies are motivated by street justice. The robber has a grievance against the victim and settles the dispute by stealing the victim's property. In this instance, robbery may be considered a substitute for an assault: the robber wants retribution and revenge rather than remuneration.[252]
- Because the robber knows the victim personally, the robber has inside information that there will be a "good take." Offenders may target people they know to be carrying a large amount of cash or who just purchased expensive jewelry.
- When a person in desperate need for immediate cash runs out of money, the individual may target people in close proximity simply because they are convenient targets.

When Richard Felson and his associates studied acquaintance robbery, they found that victims were more likely to be injured in acquaintance robberies than in stranger robberies, indicating that revenge rather than reward was the primary motive.[253] Similarly, robberies of family members were more likely to have a bigger payoff than stranger robberies, an indication that the offender was aware that the target had a large amount of cash on hand.

EMERGING FORMS OF INTERPERSONAL VIOLENCE

LO10 Describe emerging forms of violence such as stalking, hate crimes, and workplace violence

Assault, rape, robbery, and murder are traditional forms of interpersonal violence. As more data become available, criminologists have recognized relatively new subcategories within these crime types, such as serial murder and date rape. Additional new categories of interpersonal violence are now receiving attention in criminological

literature; the next sections describe three of these forms of violent crime.

Hate Crimes

Hate crimes usually involve convenient, vulnerable targets who are incapable of fighting back. For example, there have been numerous reported incidents of teenagers attacking vagrants and the homeless in an effort to rid their town or neighborhood of people they consider undesirable.[254] Another group targeted for hate crimes is gay men and women: gay bashing has become common in U.S. cities.

The factors that precipitate hate crimes are listed in Exhibit 10.6.

The Roots of Hate Why do people commit bias crimes? In their book *Hate Crimes*, Jack McDevitt and Jack Levin identify three motivations for hate crimes: **thrill-seeking hate crimes**, **reactive (defensive) hate crimes**, and **mission hate crimes:**

- *Thrill-seeking hate crimes.* In the same way some kids like to get together to shoot hoops, hatemongers join forces to have fun by bashing minorities or destroying property. Inflicting pain on others gives them a sadistic thrill.
- *Reactive (defensive) hate crimes.* Perpetrators of these crimes rationalize their behavior as a defensive stand taken against outsiders whom they believe threaten their community or way of life. A gang of teens that attacks a new family in the neighborhood because they are the "wrong" race is committing a reactive hate crime.
- *Mission hate crimes.* Some disturbed individuals see it as their duty to rid the world of evil. Those on a "mission," such as skinheads, the Ku Klux Klan (KKK), and white supremacist groups, may seek to eliminate people who threaten their religious beliefs because they are members of a different faith or threaten "racial purity" because they are of a different race.[255]

More recent research by McDevitt and Levin with Susan Bennett used data from the Community Disorders

---

hate crimes Acts of violence or intimidation designed to terrorize or frighten people considered undesirable because of their race, religion, ethnic origin, or sexual orientation.

thrill-seeking hate crimes Acts by hatemongers who join forces to have fun by bashing minorities or destroying property; inflicting pain on others gives them a sadistic thrill.

reactive (defensive) hate crimes Perpetrators believe they are taking a defensive stand against outsiders whom they believe threaten their community or way of life.

mission hate crimes Violent crimes committed by disturbed individuals who see it as their duty to rid the world of evil.

EXHIBIT 10.6

Factors that Produce Hate Crimes

- Poor or uncertain economic conditions
- Racial stereotypes in films and on television
- Hate-filled discourse on talk shows or in political advertisements
- The use of racial code language such as "welfare mothers" and "inner-city thugs"
- An individual's personal experiences with members of particular minority groups
- Scapegoating—blaming a minority group for the misfortunes of society as a whole

SOURCE: "A Policymaker's Guide to Hate Crimes," *Bureau of Justice Assistance Monograph* (Washington, DC: Bureau of Justice Assistance, 1997).

Unit (CDU) of the Boston Police Department to uncover a new category of hate crime: **retaliatory hate crimes**. These offenses are committed in response to a hate crime, whether real or perceived; whether the original incident actually occurred is irrelevant. Their more recent research indicates that most hate crimes can be classified as thrill motivated (66 percent) followed by defensive (25 percent) and retaliatory (8 percent). Few cases were mission-oriented offenders.[256]

In his book *The Violence of Hate*, Levin notes that in addition to the traditional hatemongers, hate crimes can be committed by "dabblers"—people who are not committed to hate but drift in and out of active bigotry. They may be young people who get drunk on Saturday night and assault a gay couple or attack an African American man who happens by; they then go back to work or school on Monday. Some are thrill seekers, while others may be reacting to the presence of members of a disliked group in their neighborhood. Levin also notes that some people are "sympathizers": they may not attack African Americans but think nothing of telling jokes with racial themes or agreeing with people who despise gays. Finally, there are "spectators," who may not actively participate in bigotry but who do nothing to stop its course. They may even vote for politicians who are openly bigoted because they agree with their tax policies or some other positions, neglecting to process the fact that their vote empowers prejudice and leads to hate.[257]

Nature and Extent of Hate Crime According to the FBI, about 6,000 hate crime incidents occur each year.[258] And like other violent crimes, the number has been in decline since they peaked at about 8,000 in 2005.

- 55 percent were victims of crimes against persons and 42 percent were victims of crimes against property. The remaining 3 percent were victims of crimes against society (such as drug offenses, gambling, and prostitution).
- 40 percent of the victims of crimes against persons suffered simple assaults, while 38 percent were intimidated and 22 percent were victims of aggravated assault. (Law enforcement also reported 10 murders and 15 rapes as hate crimes.)
- An overwhelming majority—76 percent—of the victims of crimes against property were victimized by acts of destruction, damage, and/or vandalism.
- Of the known offenders, 55 percent were white and 23 percent were black.

In crimes where victims could actually identify the culprits, most victims reported that they were acquainted with their attackers or that their attackers were actually friends, coworkers, neighbors, or relatives. Younger victims were more likely to be victimized by people known to them. Hate crimes can occur in many settings, but most are perpetrated in public settings.

While 6,000 hate-related incidents each year may seem like a lot, many hate crimes go unreported, so that figure may represent only the tip of the iceberg. Defining hate crimes may differ between legal jurisdictions and so may the incentive to enforce hate crime laws. In a recent study, Ryan King and his associates investigated the association between past lynchings (1882 to 1930) and contemporary law enforcement responses to hate crimes in the United States. They found that contemporary hate crime policing and prosecution are less vigorous where lynching was more prevalent prior to 1930, especially in areas that now have large African American populations. That is, past lynching combined with a sizeable black population largely suppresses (a) police compliance with federal hate crime law, (b) police reports of hate crimes that target blacks, and (c) the likelihood of prosecuting a hate crime case. Their conclusion:

A makeshift memorial for Mark Carson, a gay man who was fatally shot in the Greenwich Village neighborhood of New York on May 18, 2013. The suspect in the killing, Elliot Morales, 33, was charged with murder, an act qualified as a hate crime, and with criminal possession of a weapon. Should crimes motivated by hate be punished more harshly than those motivated by greed, vengeance, or jealousy?

Robert Stolarik/*New York Times*/Redux

retaliatory hate crime A hate crime motivated by revenge for another hate crime, either real or imaginary, which may spark further retaliation.

social control of intergroup conflict (i.e., hate-related crime) is in part a function of both current racial threat and a long-held cultural tradition of apathy toward the protection of minorities.[259]

To learn more **about the** FBI's hate crime data collections and to access information on hate crimes, go to **http://www.fbi.gov/about-us/investigate/civilrights/hate_crimes.**

Do you think a crime should be punished more severely if it is based on hate rather than revenge, greed, or anger?

Controlling Hate Crimes   Today, almost every state jurisdiction has enacted some form of legislation designed to combat hate crimes: 45 states have enacted laws against bias-motivated violence and intimidation; 27 states have statutes that specifically mandate the collection of hate crime data.[260]

Some critics argue that it is unfair to punish criminals motivated by hate any more severely than those who commit similar crimes whose motivation is revenge, greed, or anger. There is also the danger that what appears to be a hate crime, because the target is a minority group member, may actually be motivated by some other factor such as vengeance or monetary gain. In November 2004, Aaron McKinney (who is serving a life sentence for killing Matthew Shepard) told *ABC News* correspondent Elizabeth Vargas that he was high on methamphetamine when he killed Shepard, and that his intent was robbery and not hate. His partner, Russell Henderson, claimed that the killing was simply a robbery gone bad: "It was not because me and Aaron had anything against gays."[261]

However, in his important book *Punishing Hate: Bias Crimes Under American Law*, Frederick Lawrence argues that criminals motivated by bias deserve to be punished more severely than those who commit identical crimes for other motives.[262] He suggests that a society dedicated to the equality of all its people must treat bias crimes differently from other crimes and in so doing enhance the punishment of these crimes.[263]

Some criminals choose their victims randomly; others select specific victims, as in crimes of revenge. Bias crimes are different. They are crimes in which (a) distinct identifying characteristics of the victim are critical to the perpetrator's choice of victim, and (b) the individual identity of the victim is irrelevant.[264] Lawrence views a bias crime as one that would not have been committed but for the victim's membership in a particular group.[265] Bias crimes should be punished more severely because the harm caused will exceed that caused by crimes with other motivations:[266]

- Bias crimes are more likely to be violent and involve serious physical injury to the victim.
- Bias crimes will have significant emotional and psychological impact on the victim; they result in a "heightened sense of vulnerability," which causes depression, anxiety, and feelings of helplessness.
- Bias crimes harm not only the victim but also the "target community."
- Bias crimes violate the shared value of equality among citizens and racial and religious harmony in a heterogeneous society.

Recent research by McDevitt and his associates that made use of bias crime records collected by the Boston police supports Lawrence's position. McDevitt found that the victims of bias crime experience more severe post-crime psychological trauma, for a longer period of time, than do victims of similar crimes that are not motivated by hate or bias. Hate crime victims are more likely to suffer intrusive thoughts, feelings of danger, nervousness, and depression at a higher level than other crime victims.[267] Considering the damage caused by bias crimes, it seems appropriate that they be punished more severely than typical common-law crimes.

Legal Controls   Should symbolic acts of hate such as drawing a swastika or burning a cross be banned or are they protected by the free speech clause of the First Amendment? The U.S. Supreme Court helped answer this question in the case of *Virginia v. Black* (2003) when it upheld a Virginia statute that makes it a felony "for any person … with the intent of intimidating any person or group … to burn … a cross on the property of another, a highway or other public place," and specifies that "[a]ny such burning … shall be prima facie evidence of an intent to intimidate a person or group." The Court ruled that cross burning was intertwined with the Ku Klux Klan and its reign of terror throughout the South. The Court has long held that statements in which the speaker intends to communicate intent to commit an act of unlawful violence to a particular individual or group of individuals is not protected free speech and can be criminalized; the speaker need not actually intend to carry out the threat.[268]

Workplace Violence

On August 3, 2010, Omar Thornton, 34, a driver forced to resign after being caught stealing beer from the warehouse where he worked, returned to work and went on a shooting rampage, killing eight people and injuring two before committing suicide.[269]

Sadly, Thornton's violent outburst is not unique. It has become commonplace to read of irate employees or former employees attacking coworkers or sabotaging machinery and production lines. **Workplace violence** is now considered one of the leading causes of occupational injury or

workplace violence Irate employees or former employees attack coworkers or sabotage machinery and production lines; now considered the third leading cause of occupational injury or death.

This black and white image from a surveillance video, provided by Manchester (Connecticut) Police, shows Omar Thornton carrying a lunch box and a handgun as he walks inside Hartford Distributors. Thornton shot 10 coworkers, eight of them fatally, before killing himself at the beer distribution company. Like other forms of mass killings, workplace massacres are facilitated by the easy availability of automatic weapons and handguns.

Creating Workplace Violence

Experts believe that workplace violence is not spontaneous—individuals do not "snap" and suddenly become violent. Instead, the path to violence is taken in small steps, consisting of such behaviors of concern as brooding and odd writings or drawings, which keep building in intensity.[273]

A number of factors precipitate workplace violence. One suspected cause is a management style that appears cold and insensitive to workers. As corporations cut their staffs because of some economic downturn or workers are summarily replaced with cost-effective technology, long-term employees may become irate and irrational; their unexpected layoff can lead to violent reactions. The effect is most pronounced when managers are unsympathetic and nonsupportive; their callous attitude may help trigger workplace violence.

Not all workplace violence is triggered by management-induced injustice. In some incidents coworkers have been killed because they refused romantic relationships with the assailants or reported them for sexual harassment. Others have been killed because they got a job the assailant coveted.

Irate clients and customers have also killed because of poor service or perceived slights. While hospital employees are taught to handle agitated patients, sometimes people whose demands have not been met may turn on these caregivers: health care and social services workers have the highest rate of nonfatal assault injuries. Nurses are three times more likely to experience workplace violence than any other professional group.[274] In one Los Angeles incident, a former patient shot and critically wounded three doctors because his demands for painkillers had gone unheeded.[275] There are a variety of responses to workplace provocations. Some people take out their anger and aggression by attacking their supervisors in an effort to punish the company that dismissed them; this is a form of murder by proxy.[276] Disgruntled employees may also attack family members or friends, misdirecting the rage and frustration caused by their work situation. Others are content with sabotaging company equipment; computer databases are particularly vulnerable to tampering. The aggrieved party may do nothing to rectify the situation; this inaction is

death.[270] It consists of such acts as overt violence causing physical harm, nonfatal assaults with or without weapons, and lethal violence. It may also involve disruptive, aggressive, hostile, or emotionally abusive conduct that interrupts the flow of the workplace and causes employees concern for their personal safety, such as bullying, stalking, and threatening.[271]

Workplace violence can take a number of different forms:

- Violent acts by criminals who have no other connection with the workplace but enter to commit robbery or another crime
- Violence directed at employees by customers, clients, patients, students, inmates, or any others for whom an organization provides services
- Violence against coworkers, supervisors, or managers by a present or former employee
- Violence committed in the workplace by someone who doesn't work there but has a personal relationship with an employee—an abusive spouse or domestic partner[272]

Who engages in workplace violence? The typical offender is a middle-aged white male who faces termination in a worsening economy. The fear of economic ruin is especially strong in agencies such as the U.S. Postal Service, where long-term employees fear job loss because of automation and reorganization. In contrast, younger workers usually kill while committing a robbery or another felony.

referred to as **sufferance**. Over time, the unresolved conflict may be compounded by other events that cause an eventual eruption.

The Extent of Workplace Violence

While a handful of high-profile mass shootings at a workplace have led to increased public awareness of the problem, nonfatal workplace violence is actually a much more common phenomenon: approximately 1.7 million incidents of workplace violence occur each year, with simple and aggravated assaults comprising the largest portion of these events. About 6 percent of workplace violence involve rape, sexual assault, or homicide; about 500 homicides occur in the workplace each year, occurring most often in the aftermath of a robbery. It is estimated that these events cost the American workforce approximately $36 billion dollars per year including lost work time, employee medical benefits, legal expenses, replacing lost employees and retraining new ones, decreased productivity, higher insurance premiums, raised security costs, bad publicity, lost business, and expensive litigation.[277]

Can Workplace Violence Be Controlled?

One approach is to use third parties to mediate disputes. The restorative justice movement (discussed in Chapter 8) advocates the use of mediation to resolve interpersonal disputes. Restorative justice techniques may work particularly well in the workplace, where disputants know one another, and tensions may be simmering over a long period. This may help control the rising tide of workplace violence. Another idea is a human resources approach, with aggressive job retraining and continued medical coverage after layoffs; it is also important to use objective, fair hearings to thwart unfair or biased terminations. Perhaps rigorous screening tests can help identify violence-prone workers so that they can be given anger management training. Most importantly, employers may want to establish policies restricting weapons in the workplace: recent research shows that workplaces where guns were specifically permitted are five to seven times more likely to be the site of a worker homicide than those where all weapons were prohibited.[278]

Stalking

In Wes Craven's popular *Scream* movies, the heroine Sydney (played by Neve Campbell) is pursued by a mysterious adversary who scares her half to death while killing off most of her peer group. Although obviously extreme even by Hollywood standards, the *Scream* movies focus on a recognized form of long-term and repeat victimization: **stalking**.[279] While it is a complex phenomenon, stalking can be defined as a course of conduct directed at a specific person that involves repeated physical or visual proximity, nonconsensual communication, or verbal, written, or implied threats sufficient to cause fear in a reasonable person.[280]

How big a problem is stalking? National studies indicate that stalking is now a routine behavior. The Centers for Disease Control and Prevention recently found that 16 percent of women and 5 percent of men had been stalked during their lifetime and "felt very fearful or believed that they or someone close to them would be harmed or killed as a result of the perpetrator's behavior."[281]

While this research is disturbing, it may actually undercount the problem. The most recent national data indicates that stalkers victimize more than 3 million people each year; while males can be victims, females are nearly three times as likely to be stalked.[282] For example, one study of college-aged women found that 13 percent reported being stalked. Considering that there are more than 6.5 million women attending college in the United States, about 700,000 women are being stalked each year on college campuses alone.[283]

Most victims know their stalker in some way; in about 30 percent of cases, the stalker is a current or former intimate partner. Former partners have leverage over their victim; they can use the information they have about their former partner's friends and family members, where they work, shop, and go for entertainment, to terrorize victims.[284]

Women are most likely to be stalked by an intimate partner—a current spouse, a former spouse, someone they lived with, or even a date. In contrast, men typically are stalked by a stranger or an acquaintance. The typical female victim is stalked because her assailant wants to control her, scare her, or keep her in a relationship. Victims of both genders find that there is a clear relationship between stalking and other emotionally controlling and physically abusive behavior. Some psychologists believe that most stalkers are persons with mental illness who create social and public problems due to their violent behavior.[285]

Stalkers behave in ways that induce fear, but they do not always make overt threats against their victims. Many follow or spy upon their victims, some threaten to kill pets, and others vandalize property. Criminologist Mary Brewster found that stalkers who make verbal threats are the ones most likely to later attack their victims.[286] However, it is not uncommon for stalking to end in violence.

Though stalking is a serious problem, research indicates that many cases are dropped by the courts even though the stalkers often have extensive criminal histories and are frequently the subject of protective orders. A lenient response

sufferance The aggrieved party does nothing to rectify a conflict situation; over time, the unresolved conflict may be compounded by other events that cause an eventual eruption.

stalking A pattern of behavior directed at a specific person that includes repeated physical or visual proximity, unwanted communications, and/or threats sufficient to cause fear in a reasonable person.

may be misplaced considering that there is evidence that stalkers repeat their criminal activity within a short time of the lodging of a stalking charge with police authorities.[287] Victims experience its social and psychological consequences long afterward. About one-third seek psychological treatment, and about one-fifth lose time from work; some never return to work.

Why does stalking stop? Most often because the victim moved away or the police got involved or, in some cases, when the stalker met another love interest.

SUMMARY

LO1 Differentiate among the various causes of violent crime

Violence has become an all-too-common aspect of modern life. Among the various explanations of sources of violent crime are exposure to violence, personal traits and makeup, evolutionary factors and human instincts, cultural values and a subculture of violence, substance abuse, and socialization and upbringing.

LO2 Articulate the stages in Athens's violentization process

According to Lonnie Athens, violence is the product of a full cycle of the violentization process—brutalization, belligerence, violent performances, and virulency—to become socialized into violence. Many brutalized children do not go on to become violent criminals, and some later reject the fact that they were abused as youths and redefine their early years as normative. Only those who are brutalized become violent themselves.

LO3 Discuss the history of rape and the different types of rape and rapists

Rape, the carnal knowledge of a female forcibly and against her will, has been known throughout history, but the view of rape has evolved. Rape has been an instrument of war for thousands of years. There are different types of rapists, including those motivated by anger, power, and sadism. There are numerous forms of rape, including statutory, acquaintance, and date rape.

LO4 Assess the legal issues in rape prosecution

Rape is an extremely difficult charge to prove in court. The victim's lack of consent must be proven; therefore, it almost seems that the victim is on trial. Rape shield laws have been developed to protect victims from having their personal life placed on trial.

LO5 Compare and contrast the different degrees of murder

Murder is defined as killing a human being with malice aforethought. There are different degrees of murder, and punishments vary accordingly. First-degree murder involves malice and premeditation. Second-degree murder requires malice aforethought but not premeditation or deliberation. Voluntary manslaughter refers to a killing, typically without a weapon, committed in the heat of passion or during a sudden quarrel that provoked violence. Although intent may be present, malice is not. Involuntary or negligent manslaughter refers to a killing that occurs when a person's acts are negligent and without regard for the harm they may cause others.

LO6 Assess stranger and acquaintance homicide

One important characteristic of murder is that the victim and criminal often know each other. Murder can be a family affair, the result of a love triangle or relationship gone wrong. Some murders are sexually based. There are also stranger killings that occur during robberies and other crimes. Some occur in schools when shooters kill random students. Stranger murder often involves an interpersonal transaction in which a hostile action by the victim precipitates a murderous relationship. In some instances, it is the victim who initiates the murderous transaction, such as a barroom brawl, and is killed in the aftermath.

LO7 Analyze the differences among serial killing, mass murder, and spree killing

Murder can involve a single victim or be a serial killing, mass murder, or spree killing, which involve multiple victims. The difference between a spree killer and a serial killer is that the latter retains his or her identity and kills secretly. The spree killer abandons his or her normal identity and continues killing until he or she is identified and captured.

LO8 Discuss the root causes of child abuse

A number of factors have been commonly linked to abuse and neglect. Family violence seems to be perpetuated from one generation to another within families. The behavior of abusive parents can often be traced to negative experiences in their own childhood. Blended families, which include children living with an unrelated adult such as a stepparent or another unrelated co-resident, have also been linked to abuse. Parents may also become abusive if they are isolated from friends, neighbors, or relatives who can help in times of crisis.

LO9 Discuss the crime of robbery and why it is a rational crime

The definition of robbery is "the taking or attempting to take anything of value from the care, custody or control of a person or persons by force or threat of force or violence and/or by putting the victim in fear." A robbery is considered a violent crime because it involves the use of force to obtain money or goods. Robbery is punished severely because the victim's life is put in jeopardy. In fact, the severity of punishment is based on the amount of force used during the crime, not the value of the items taken. Robbery that involves people who know each other is acquaintance robbery. Robbers carefully analyze targets and avoid those whom seem dangerous. Robbers therefore appear rational in their choice of crime.

LO10 **Describe emerging forms of violence such as stalking, hate crimes, and workplace violence**

Hate crimes usually involve convenient, vulnerable targets who are incapable of fighting back. People become the target of hate crimes because of their religion, ethnicity, or race, or because they engage in behavior that is considered unacceptable to their attacker, such as being gay. Workplace violence is now considered one of the leading causes of occupational injury or death. It has become commonplace to read of irate employees or former employees attacking coworkers or sabotaging machinery and production lines. Stalking is a course of conduct directed at a specific person that involves repeated physical or visual proximity, nonconsensual communication, or verbal, written, or implied threats sufficient to cause fear in a reasonable person.

CRITICAL THINKING QUESTIONS

1. Should different types of rape receive different legal sanctions? For example, should someone who rapes a stranger be punished more severely than someone who is convicted of marital rape or date rape? If your answer is yes, do you also think that someone who kills a stranger should be more severely punished than someone who kills his wife or girlfriend?

2. Is there a subculture of violence in your home city or town? If so, how would you describe its environment and values?

3. There have been significant changes in rape laws regarding issues such as corroboration and shield laws. What other measures would you take to protect the victims of rape when they are forced to testify in court? Should the names of rape victims be published in the press? Do they deserve more protection than those accused of rape?

4. Should hate crimes be punished more severely than crimes motivated by greed, anger, or revenge? Why should crimes be distinguished by the motivations of the perpetrator? Is hate a more heinous motivation than revenge?

5. Do you believe that murder is an interactive event? If so, does that amount to "blaming the victim"? If there is a murder transaction, should we not consider rape, domestic assault, and so forth as "transactions"?

KEY TERMS

expressive violence (328)
instrumental violence (328)
violentization process (331)
crusted over (332)
subculture of violence (332)
disputatiousness (332)
gang rape (337)
serial rapes (337)
acquaintance rape (337)
date rape (337)
statutory rape (337)
marital rape (337)
marital exemption (338)
virility mystique (339)

narcissistic personality disorder (339)
aggravated rape (340)
consent (341)
shield laws (342)
murder (343)
premeditation (343)
felony murder (343)
second-degree murder (343)
deliberation (343)
manslaughter (343)
nonnegligent manslaughter (343)

involuntary manslaughter or negligent manslaughter (344)
feticide (344)
infanticide (344)
filicide (344)
eldercide (345)
serial killer (346)
mass murder (349)
road rage (352)
child abuse (352)
neglect (352)
sexual abuse (353)
relational aggression (355)

acquaintance robbery (357)
hate crimes (358)
thrill-seeking hate crimes (358)
reactive (defensive) hate crimes (358)
mission hate crimes (358)
retaliatory hate crime (359)
workplace violence (360)
sufferance (362)
stalking (362)

NOTES

1. Anita Powell, "Pistorius Trial Week 2 Features Blood, Tears," Voice of America, March 14, 2014, http://www.voanews.com/content/week-2-of-pistorius-trial-blood-tears-and-vomit/1871130.html (accessed May 2014).

2. George Tita, Tricia Petras, and Robert Greenbaum, "Crime and Residential Choice: A Neighborhood Level Analysis of the Impact of Crime on Housing Prices," *Journal of Quantitative Criminology* 22 (2006): 299–317.

3. Stryker McGuire, "The Dunblane Effect," *Newsweek*, October 28, 1996, p. 46.

4. Benedict Moore-Bridger, "Andy Murray Breaks His Silence on Dunblane School Massacre," *London Evening Standard*, June 24,

2013, http://www.standard.co.uk/news/london/andy-murray-breaks-his-silence-on-dunblane-school-massacre-8671255.html (accessed May 2014).

5. Rokeya Farrooque, Ronnie Stout, and Frederick Ernst, "Heterosexual Intimate Partner Homicide: Review of Ten Years of Clinical Experience," *Journal of Forensic Sciences* 50 (2005): 648–651; Miltos Livaditis, Gkaro Esagian, Christos Kakoulidis, Maria Samakouri, and Nikos Tzavaras, "Matricide by Person with Bipolar Disorder and Dependent Overcompliant Personality," *Journal of Forensic Sciences* 50 (2005): 658–661.

6. Dorothy Otnow Lewis, Ernest Moy, Lori Jackson, Robert Aaronson, Nicholas Restifo, Susan Serra, and Alexander Simos, "Biopsychosocial Characteristics of Children Who Later Murder," *American Journal of Psychiatry* 142 (1985): 1161–1167.

7. Dorothy Otnow Lewis, *Guilty by Reason of Insanity* (New York: Fawcett Columbine, 1998).

8. Richard Rogers, Randall Salekin, Kenneth Sewell, and Keith Cruise, "Prototypical Analysis of Antisocial Personality Disorder," *Criminal Justice and Behavior* 27 (2000): 234–255; Amy Holtzworth-Munroe and Gregory Stuart, "Typologies of Male Batterers: Three Subtypes and the Differences Among Them," *Psychological Bulletin* 116 (1994): 476–497.

9. Katherine van Wormer and Chuk Odiah, "The Psychology of Suicide-Murder and the Death Penalty," *Journal of Criminal Justice* 27 (1999): 361–370.

10. Daniel Strueber, Monika Lueck, and Gerhard Roth, "The Violent Brain," *Scientific American Mind* 17 (2006): 20–27.

11. David P. Farrington, Rolf Loeber, and Mark T. Berg, "Young Men Who Kill: A Prospective Longitudinal Examination from Childhood," *Homicide Studies* 16 (2012): 99–128; Christopher Hensley and Suzanne Tallichet, "Childhood and Adolescent Animal Cruelty Methods and Their Possible Link to Adult Violent Crimes," *Journal of Interpersonal Violence* 24 (2009): 147–158.

12. Dave Marcotte and Sara Markowitz, "A Cure for Crime? Psycho-Pharmaceuticals and Crime Trends," *Journal of Policy Analysis and Management* 30 (2011): 29–56.

13. Christopher Boehm, "Retaliatory Violence in Human Prehistory," *British Journal of Criminology* 51 (2011): 518–534.

14. Steven Pinker, *The Better Angels of Our Nature: Why Violence Has Declined* (New York: Viking, 2011).

15. Sigmund Freud, *Beyond the Pleasure Principle* (London: Inter-Psychoanalytic Press, 1922).

16. Konrad Lorenz, *On Aggression* (New York: Harcourt Brace Jovanovich, 1966).

17. Nigel Barber, "Why Is Violent Crime So Common in the Americas?" *Aggressive Behavior* 32 (2006): 442–450.

18. Randall Collins, *Violence: A Micro-sociological Theory* (Princeton, NJ: Princeton University Press, 2008).

19. William Alex Pridemore and Tony Grubesic, "Alcohol Outlets and Community Levels of Interpersonal Violence: Spatial Density, Outlet Type, and Seriousness of Assault," *Journal of Research in Crime*, first published May 17, 2011; Chris Allen, "The Links Between Heroin, Crack Cocaine, and Crime: Where Does Street Crime Fit In?" *British Journal of Criminology* 45 (2005): 355–372; Arnie Nielsen, Ramiro Martinez, and Matthew Lee, "Alcohol, Ethnicity, and Violence: The Role of Alcohol Availability for Latino and Black Aggravated Assaults and Robberies," *Sociological Quarterly* 46 (2005): 479–502.

20. Allen, "The Links Between Heroin, Crack Cocaine, and Crime."

21. Steven Messner, Glenn Deane, Luc Anselin, and Benjamin Pearson-Nelson, "Locating the Vanguard in Rising and Falling Homicide Rates Across Cities," *Criminology* 43 (2005): 661–696.

22. Paul Goldstein, Henry Brownstein, and Patrick Ryan, "Drug-Related Homicide in New York: 1984–1988," *Crime and Delinquency* 38 (1992): 459–476.

23. Robert Brewer and Monica Swahn, "Binge Drinking and Violence," *JAMA: Journal of the American Medical Association* 294 (2005): 16–20.

24. Tomika Stevens, Kenneth Ruggiero, Dean Kilpatrick, Heidi Resnick, and Benjamin Saunders, "Variables Differentiating Singly and Multiply Victimized Youth: Results from the National Survey of Adolescents and Implications for Secondary Prevention," *Child Maltreatment* 10 (2005): 211–223; James Collins and Pamela Messerschmidt, "Epidemiology of Alcohol-Related Violence," *Alcohol Health and Research World* 17 (1993): 93–100.

25. Antonia Abbey, Tina Zawacki, Philip Buck, Monique Clinton, and Pam McAuslan, "Sexual Assault and Alcohol Consumption: What Do We Know About Their Relationship and What Types of Research Are Still Needed?" *Aggression and Violent Behavior* 9 (2004): 271–303.

26. Scott Phillips, Jacqueline Matusko, and Elizabeth Tomasovic, "Reconsidering the Relationship Between Alcohol and Lethal Violence," *Journal of Interpersonal Violence* 22 (2007): 66–84.

27. Martin Grann and Seena Fazel, "Substance Misuse and Violent Crime: Swedish Population Study," *British Medical Journal* 328 (2004): 1233–1234; Susanne Rogne Gjeruldsen, Bjørn Myrvang, and Stein Opjordsmoen, "Criminality in Drug Addicts: A Follow-Up Study over 25 Years," *European Addiction Research* 10 (2004): 49–56.

28. Bruce Jacobs, *Robbing Drug Dealers: Violence beyond the Law* (New York, NY: Aldine de Gruyter. 2000).

29. Todd Herrenkohl, Bu Huang, Emiko Tajima, and Stephen Whitney, "Examining the Link Between Child Abuse and Youth Violence," *Journal of Interpersonal Violence* 18 (2003): 1189–1208; Pamela Lattimore, Christy Visher, and Richard Linster, "Predicting Rearrest for Violence among Serious Youthful Offenders," *Journal of Research in Crime and Delinquency* 32 (1995): 54–83.

30. Rolf Loeber and Dale Hay, "Key Issues in the Development of Aggression and Violence from Childhood to Early Adulthood," *Annual Review of Psychology* 48 (1997): 371–410.

31. Deborah Capaldi and Gerald Patterson, "Can Violent Offenders Be Distinguished from Frequent Offenders: Prediction from Childhood to Adolescence," *Journal of Research in Crime and Delinquency* 33 (1996): 206–231.

32. Adrian Raine, Patricia Brennan, and Sarnoff Mednick, "Interaction Between Birth Complications and Early Maternal Rejection in Predisposing Individuals to Adult Violence: Specificity to Serious, Early-Onset Violence," *American Journal of Psychiatry* 154 (1997): 1265–1271.

33. Eric Slade and Lawrence Wissow, "Spanking in Early Childhood and Later Behavior Problems: A Prospective Study of Infants and Young Toddlers," *Pediatrics* 113 (2004): 1321–1330.

34. Murray Straus, "Discipline and Deviance: Physical Punishment of Children and Violence and Other Crime in Adulthood," *Social Problems* 38 (1991): 101–123.

35. Jennifer Lansford, Laura Wager, John Bates, Gregory Pettit, and Kenneth Dodge, "Forms of Spanking and Children's Externalizing Behaviors," *Family Relations* 6 (2012): 224–236.

36. Ronald Simons, Chyi-In Wu, Kuei-Hsiu Lin, Leslie Gordon, and Rand Conger, "A Cross-Cultural Examination of the Link Between Corporal Punishment and Adolescent Antisocial Behavior," *Criminology* 38 (2000): 47–79.

37. Cathy Widom, "The Cycle of Violence," *Science* 244 (1989): 160–166; "Understanding Child Maltreatment and Juvenile Delinquency: The Research," Welfare League of America, 2010, http://www.cwla.org/programs/juvenilejustice/ucmjd03.pdf (accessed May 2014).

38. See, for example, Egbert Zavala, "Testing the Link Between Child Maltreatment and Family Violence Among Police Officers," *Crime and Delinquency*, first published online November 22, 2010; Cesar Rebellon and Karen Van Gundy, "Can Control Theory Explain the Link Between Parental Physical Abuse and Delinquency? A Longitudinal Analysis,"

Journal of Research in Crime and Delinquency 42 (2005): 247–274.

39. Wan-Yi Chen, Jennifer Propp, Ellen deLara, and Kenneth Corvo, "Child Neglect and Its Association with Subsequent Juvenile Drug and Alcohol Offense," *Child and Adolescent Social Work Journal* 28 (2011): 273–290.

40. Childhelp, National Child Abuse Statistics, http://www.childhelp.org/pages/statistics (accessed May 2014).

41. Sara Culhane and Heather Taussig, "The Structure of Problem Behavior in a Sample of Maltreated Youths," *Social Work Research* 33 (2009): 70–78.

42. Janet Currie and Erdal Tekin, "Does Child Abuse Cause Crime?" National Bureau of Economic Research, Working Paper No. 12171, 2006, http://www.nber.org/papers/w12171 (accessed May 2014).

43. Dorothy Lewis et al., "Neuropsychiatric, Psychoeducational, and Family Characteristics of 14 Juveniles Condemned to Death in the United States," *American Journal of Psychiatry* 145 (1988): 584–588.

44. Currie and Tekin, "Does Child Abuse Cause Crime?"

45. Emily M. Wright and Abigail A. Fagan, "The Cycle of Violence in Context: Exploring the Moderating Roles of Neighborhood Disadvantage and Cultural Norms," *Criminology* 51 (2013): 217–249.

46. Bruce Rind, Philip Tromovitch, and Robert Bauserman, "A Meta-Analytic Examination of Assumed Properties of Child Sexual Abuse Using College Samples," *Psychological Bulletin* 124 (1998): 22–53.

47. Lonnie Athens, *The Creation of Dangerous Violent Criminals* (Urbana: University of Illinois Press, 1992), pp. 27–80.

48. David Kirk and Margaret Hardy, "The Acute and Enduring Consequences of Exposure to Violence on Youth Mental Health and Aggression," *Justice Quarterly*, first published online November 9, 2012.

49. Eric Stewart, Ronald Simons, and Rand Conger, "Assessing Neighborhood and Social Psychological Influences on Childhood Violence in an African-American Sample," *Criminology* 40 (2002): 801–830.

50. Darrell Steffensmeier, Ben Feldmeyer, Casey T. Harris, and Jeffery T. Ulmer, "Reassessing Trends in Black Violent Crime, 1980–2008: Sorting Out the 'Hispanic Effect' in Uniform Crime Reports Arrests, National Crime Victimization Survey Offender Estimates, and U.S. Prisoner Counts," *Criminology* 49 (2011): 197–251.

51. Barbara Warner, "Robberies with Guns: Neighborhood Factors and the Nature of Crime," *Journal of Criminal Justice* 35 (2007): 39–50.

52. Felton Earls, *Linking Community Factors and Individual Development* (Washington, DC: National Institute of Justice, 1998).

53. Jeffrey B. Bingenheimer, Robert T. Brennan, and Felton J. Earls, "Firearm Violence Exposure and Serious Violent Behavior," *Science* 308 (2005): 1323–1326; "Witnessing Gun Violence Significantly Increases Likelihood that a Child Will Also Commit Violent Crime; Violence May Be Viewed as Infectious Disease," *AScribe Health News Service*, May 26, 2005.

54. Michael Greene, "Chronic Exposure to Violence and Poverty: Interventions that Work for Youth," *Crime and Delinquency* 39 (1993): 106–124.

55. Robert Baller, Luc Anselin, Steven Messner, Glenn Deane, and Darnell Hawkins, "Structural Covariates of U.S. County Homicide Rates Incorporating Spatial Effects," *Criminology* 39 (2001): 561–590.

56. Marvin Wolfgang and Franco Ferracuti, *The Subculture of Violence* (London: Tavistock, 1967).

57. David Luckenbill and Daniel Doyle, "Structural Position and Violence: Developing a Cultural Explanation," *Criminology* 27 (1989): 419–436.

58. Robert Sampson and William Julius Wilson, "Toward a Theory of Race, Crime, and Urban Inequality," in *Crime and Inequality*, ed. John Hagan and Ruth Peterson (Stanford, CA: Stanford University Press, 1995), p. 51.

59. Liqun Cao, Anthony Adams, and Vickie Jensen, "A Test of the Black Subculture of Violence Thesis," *Criminology* 35 (1997): 367–379.

60. Eric Baumer, Julie Horney, Richard Felson, and Janet Lauritsen, "Neighborhood Disadvantage and the Nature of Violence," *Criminology* 41 (2003): 39–71.

61. Charis Kubrin and Ronald Weitzer, "Retaliatory Homicide: Concentrated Disadvantage and Neighborhood Culture," *Social Problems* 50 (2003): 157–180.

62. Robert J. Kane, "Compromised Police Legitimacy as a Predictor of Violent Crime in Structurally Disadvantaged Communities," *Criminology* 43 (2005): 469–499.

63. Steven Messner, "Regional and Racial Effects on the Urban Homicide Rate: The Subculture of Violence Revisited," *American Journal of Sociology* 88 (1983): 997–1007; Steven Messner and Kenneth Tardiff, "Economic Inequality and Levels of Homicide: An Analysis of Urban Neighborhoods," *Criminology* 24 (1986): 297–317.

64. Beth Bjerregaard and Alan Lizotte, "Gun Ownership and Gang Membership," *Journal of Criminal Law and Criminology* 86 (1995): 37–58.

65. Rachel Gordon, Benjamin Lahey, Eriko Kawai, Rolf Loeber, Magda Stouthamer-Loeber, and David Farrington, "Antisocial Behavior and Youth Gang Membership," *Criminology* 42 (2004): 55–88.

66. Andrew Papachristos, "Murder by Structure: Dominance Relations and the Social Structure of Gang Homicide," *American Journal of Sociology* 115 (2009): 74–128.

67. Lonnie Schaible and Lorine Hughes, "Crime, Shame, Reintegration, and Cross-national Homicide: A Partial Test of Reintegrative Shaming Theory," *Sociological Quarterly* 52 (2011): 104–131.

68. Marc Ouimet, "A World of Homicides: The Effect of Economic Development, Income Inequality, and Excess Infant Mortality on the Homicide Rate for 165 Countries in 2010," *Homicide Studies* 16 (2012): 238–258; Don Chon, "Contributing Factors for High Homicide Rate in Latin America: A Critical Test of Neapolitan's Regional Subculture of Violence Thesis," *Journal of Family Violence* 26 (2011): 299–307.

69. David Courtwright, "Violence in America," *American Heritage* 47 (1996): 36–52, at 36; David Courtwright, *Violent Land: Single Men and Social Disorder from the Frontier to the Inner City* (Cambridge, MA: Harvard University Press, 1996).

70. William Green, *Rape* (Lexington, MA: Lexington Books, 1988), p. 5.

71. Susan Randall and Vicki McNickle Rose, "Forcible Rape," in *Major Forms of Crime*, ed. Robert Meyer (Beverly Hills: Sage, 1984), p. 47.

72. Barbara Krah, Renate Scheinberger-Olwig, and Steffen Bieneck, "Men's Reports of Nonconsensual Sexual Interactions with Women: Prevalence and Impact," *Archives of Sexual Behavior* 32 (2003): 165–176.

73. Siegmund Fred Fuchs, "Male Sexual Assault: Issues of Arousal and Consent," *Cleveland State Law Review* 51 (2004): 93–108.

74. Raquel Kennedy Bergen and Paul Bukovec, "Men and Intimate Partner Rape: Characteristics of Men Who Sexually Abuse Their Partner," *Journal of Interpersonal Violence* 21 (2006): 1375–1384.

75. Heidi Zinzow, Heidi Resnick, Ananda Amstadter, Jenna McCauley, Kenneth Ruggiero, and Dean Kilpatrick, "Drug- or Alcohol-Facilitated, Incapacitated, and Forcible Rape in Relationship to Mental Health Among a National Sample of Women," *Journal of Interpersonal Violence* 25 (2010): 2217–2236.

76. Susan Brownmiller, *Against Our Will: Men, Women, and Rape* (New York: Simon & Schuster, 1975).

77. Green, *Rape*, p. 6.

78. Yuri Kageyama, "Court Orders Japan to Pay Sex Slaves," *Boston Globe*, April 28, 1998, p. A2.

79. Anthony Beevor, *Berlin: The Downfall 1945* (New York: Viking Press, 2002).

80. Marlise Simons, "Bosnian Serb Pleads Guilty to Rape Charge Before War Crimes Tribunal," *New York Times*, March 10, 1998, p. 8.

81. Marc Lacey, "Amnesty Says Sudan Militias Use Rape as Weapon," *New York Times*, July 19, 2004, p. A9.

82. Australia News Network, "Boko Claims Responsibility for Kidnapping 276 Students," May 6, 2014, http://www.abc.net.au/news/2014-05-05/boko-haram-claims-responsibility-for-abducting-schoolgirls/5432068 (accessed May 2014).

83. Eileen Zurbriggen, "Rape, War, and the Socialization of Masculinity: Why Our Refusal to Give Up War Ensures that Rape Cannot Be Eradicated," *Psychology of Women Quarterly* 34 (2010): 538–549.

84. FBI, *Crime in the United States, 2012*. Crime data in this chapter come from this source and from preliminary 2013 data, http://www.fbi.gov/about-us/cjis/ucr/crime-in-the-u.s/2012/crime-in-the-u.s.-2012/cius_home (accessed May 2014).

85. Rand, *Criminal Victimization, 2008*, p. 5.

86. Sarah Cook, Christine Gidycz, Mary Koss, and Megan Murphy, "Emerging Issues in the Measurement of Rape Victimization," *Violence Against Women* 17 (2011): 201–218; Bonnie S. Fisher, "The Effects of Survey Question Wording on Rape Estimates: Evidence from a Quasi-Experimental Design," *Violence Against Women* 15 (2009): 133–147.

87. Dean G. Kilpatrick, Heidi S. Resnick, Kenneth J. Ruggiero, Lauren M. Conoscenti, and Jenna McCauley, "Drug-Facilitated, Incapacitated, and Forcible Rape: A National Study," U.S. Department of Justice, 2007, http://www.ncjrs.gov/pdffiles1/nij/grants/219181.pdf (accessed May 2014).

88. Carol Vanzile-Tamsen, Maria Testa, and Jennifer Livingston, "The Impact of Sexual Assault History and Relationship Context on Appraisal of and Responses to Acquaintance Sexual Assault Risk," *Journal of Interpersonal Violence* 20 (2005): 813–822; Arnold Kahn, Jennifer Jackson, Christine Kully, Kelly Badger, and Jessica Halvorsen, "Calling It Rape: Differences in Experiences of Women Who Do or Do Not Label Their Sexual Assault as Rape," *Psychology of Women Quarterly* 27 (2003): 233–242.

89. Jody Clay-Warner and Jennifer McMahon-Howard, "Rape Reporting: 'Classic Rape' and the Behavior of Law," *Violence and Victims* 24 (2009): 723–743.

90. For an analysis of the validity of rape data, see Bonnie S. Fisher, "The Effects of Survey Question Wording on Rape Estimates: Evidence From a Quasi-Experimental Design," *Violence Against Women* 15 (2009): 133–147.

91. Heather Littleton and Craig Henderson, "If She Is Not a Victim, Does That Mean She Was Not Traumatized? Evaluation of Predictors of PTSD Symptomatology Among College Rape Victims," *Violence Against Women* 15 (2009): 148–167.

92. Mark Warr, "Rape, Burglary, and Opportunity," *Journal of Quantitative Criminology* 4 (1988): 275–288.

93. Maria Testa, Jennifer Livingston, and Carol Vanzile-Tamsen, "The Role of Victim and Perpetrator Intoxication on Sexual Assault Outcomes," *Journal of Studies on Alcohol* 65 (2004): 320–329.

94. Nicholas Groth and Jean Birnbaum, *Men Who Rape* (New York: Plenum Press, 1979).

95. For another typology, see Raymond Knight, "Validation of a Typology of Rapists," in *Sex Offender Research and Treatment: State-of-the-Art in North America and Europe*, ed. W. L. Marshall and J. Frenken (Beverly Hills: Sage, 1997), pp. 58–75.

96. Sarah Ullman, "A Comparison of Gang and Individual Rape Incidents," *Violence and Victimization* 14 (1999): 123–134.

97. Janet Warren, Roland Reboussin, Robert Hazlewood, Natalie Gibbs, Susan Trumbetta, and Andrea Cummings, "Crime Scene Analysis and the Escalation of Violence in Serial Rape," *Forensic Science International* (1998): 56–62.

98. James LeBeau, "Patterns of Stranger and Serial Rape Offending Factors Distinguishing Apprehended and At-Large Offenders," *Journal of Criminal Law and Delinquency* 78 (1987): 309–326.

99. Bonnie Fisher, Francis Cullen, and Leah Daigle, "The Discovery of Acquaintance Rape," *Journal of Interpersonal Violence* 20 (2005): 493–500.

100. Leah Adams-Curtis and Gordon Forbes, "College Women's Experiences of Sexual Coercion," *Trauma, Violence and Abuse* 5 (2004): 91–122.

101. Cassia Spohn, Dawn Beichner, and Erika Davis-Frenzel, "Prosecutorial Justifications for Sexual Assault Case Rejection: Guarding the 'Gateway to Justice,'" *Social Problems* 48 (2001): 206–235.

102. Mary Koss, "Hidden Rape: Sexual Aggression and Victimization in a National Sample of Students in Higher Education," in *Rape and Sexual Assault*, Vol. 2, ed. Ann Wolbert Burgess (New York: Garland Publishing, 1988), p. 824.

103. R. Lance Shotland, "A Model of the Causes of Date Rape in Developing and Close Relationships," in *Close Relationships*, ed. C. Hendrick (Newbury Park, CA: Sage, 1989), pp. 247–270.

104. Kimberly Tyler, Danny Hoyt, and Les Whitbeck, "Coercive Sexual Strategies," *Violence and Victims* 13 (1998): 47–63.

105. Julie A. Allison and Lawrence S. Wrightsman, *Rape: The Misunderstood Crime* (Newbury Park, CA: Sage Publications, 1993), p. 64.

106. Amy Buddie and Maria Testa, "Rates and Predictors of Sexual Aggression Among Students and Nonstudents," *Journal of Interpersonal Violence* 20 (2005): 713–725.

107. Bonnie Fisher, Leah Daigle, Francis Cullen, and Michael Turner, "Reporting Sexual Victimization to the Police and Others: Results from a National-Level Study of College Women," *Criminal Justice and Behavior* 30 (2003): 6–39.

108. Alan Gross, Andrea Winslett, Miguel Roberts, and Carol Gohm, "An Examination of Sexual Violence Against College Women," *Violence Against Women* 12 (2006): 288–300.

109. Kate Wolitzky-Taylor, Heidi Resnick, Ananda Amstadter, Jenna McCauley, Kenneth Ruggiero, and Dean Kilpatrick, "Reporting Rape in a National Sample of College Women," *Journal of American College Health* 59 (2011): 582–587.

110. Steven Lawyer, Heidi Resnick, Von Bakanic, Tracy Burkett, and Dean Kilpatrick, "Forcible, Drug-Facilitated, and Incapacitated Rape and Sexual Assault Among Undergraduate Women," *Journal of American College Health* 58 (2010): 453–460.

111. Heidi M. Zinzow, Heidi S. Resnick, Jenna L. McCauley, Ananda B. Amstadter, Kenneth J. Ruggiero, and Dean G. Kilpatrick, "The Role of Rape Tactics in Risk for Posttraumatic Stress Disorder and Major Depression: Results from a National Sample of College Women," *Depression and Anxiety* (27) 2010: 708–715.

112. Caitlin Flanagan, "The Dark Power of Fraternities," *Atlantic Monthly*, February 19, 2014, http://www.theatlantic.com/features/archive/2014/02/the-dark-power-of-fraternities/357580/ (accessed May 2014).

113. Carrie Wells, Erica L. Green, and Justin Fenton, "Johns Hopkins University Under Fire over Not Disclosing Alleged Rape," *Washington Post*, May 7, 2014, http://www.washingtonpost.com/local/johns-hopkins-university-under-fire-over-not-disclosing-alleged-rape/2014/05/03/c86582b4-d305-11e3-8a78-8fe50322a72c_story.html (accessed May 2014).

114. Allison and Wrightsman, *Rape: The Misunderstood Crime*, pp. 85–87.

115. Cited in Diana Russell, "Wife Rape," in *Acquaintance Rape: The Hidden Crime*, ed. A. Parrot and L. Bechhofer (New York: Wiley, 1991), pp. 129–139, at 129.

116. David Finkelhor and K. Yllo, *License to Rape: Sexual Abuse of Wives* (New York: Holt, Rinehart & Winston, 1985).

117. Allison and Wrightsman, *Rape: The Misunderstood Crime*, p. 89.

118. Raquel Kennedy Bergen, with contributions from Elizabeth Barnhill, "Marital Rape: New Research and Directions," National Online Resource Center for Violence Against Women, http://vawnet.org/assoc_

files_vawnet/ar_maritalraperevised
.pdf (accessed May 2014); Associated Press,
"British Court Rejects Precedent, Finds a
Man Guilty of Raping Wife," *Boston Globe*,
March 15, 1991, p. 68.

119. Jill Elaine Hasday, "Contest and Consent: A
Legal History of Marital Rape," *California
Law Review* 88 (2000): 1373–1433.

120. Bergen and Barnhill, "Marital Rape: New
Research and Directions."

121. Sharon Elstein and Roy Davis, *Sexual Rela-
tionships Between Adult Males and Young Teen
Girls: Exploring the Legal and Social Responses*
(Chicago: American Bar Association, 1997).

122. Jed Rubenfeld, "The Riddle of Rape-by-
Deception and the Myth of Sexual Autonomy," *Yale Law Journal* 122 (2013):
1372–1443.

123. Tenn. Codeann. § 39-i3-5O3(a)(4) (2010);
Idaho Codeann. § 18-6101(8) (Supp.
2011).

124. Donald Symons, *The Evolution of Human
Sexuality* (Oxford: Oxford University Press,
1979).

125. Lee Ellis and Anthony Walsh, "Gene-Based
Evolutionary Theories in Criminology,"
Criminology 35 (1997): 229–276.

126. Lawrence Miller "Rape: Sex Crime, Act of
Violence, or Naturalistic Adaptation?"
Aggression and Violent Behavior 19 (2014):
67–81.

127. Ibid.

128. Suzanne Osman, "Predicting Men's Rape
Perceptions Based on the Belief that 'No'
Really Means 'Yes,'" *Journal of Applied Social
Psychology* 33 (2003): 683–692.

129. Martin Schwartz, Walter DeKeseredy, David
Tait, and Shahid Alvi, "Male Peer Support
and a Feminist Routine Activities Theory:
Understanding Sexual Assault on the College Campus," *Justice Quarterly* 18 (2001):
623–650.

130. Diana Russell, *The Politics of Rape* (New
York: Stein and Day, 1975).

131. Diana Russell and Rebecca M. Bolen, *The
Epidemic of Rape and Child Sexual Abuse in
the United States* (Thousand Oaks, CA: Sage,
2000).

132. Rachel Bridges Whaley, "The Paradoxical
Relationship Between Gender Inequality
and Rape: Toward a Refined Theory," *Gender and Society* 15 (2001): 531–555.

133. Paul Gebhard, John Gagnon, Wardell
Pomeroy, and Cornelia Christenson, *Sex
Offenders: An Analysis of Types* (New York:
Harper & Row, 1965), pp. 198–205; Rich-
ard Rada, ed., *Clinical Aspects of the Rapist*
(New York: Grune & Stratton, 1978),
pp. 122–130.

134. Stephen Porter, David Fairweather, Jeff
Drugge, Huues Herve, Angela Birt, and
Douglas Boer, "Profiles of Psychopathy in
Incarcerated Sexual Offenders," *Criminal
Justice and Behavior* 27 (2000): 216–233.

135. Brad Bushman, Angelica Bonacci, Mirjam
van Dijk, and Roy Baumeister, "Narcissism,
Sexual Refusal, and Aggression: Testing a
Narcissistic Reactance Model of Sexual
Coercion," *Journal of Personality and Social
Psychology* 84 (2003): 1027–1040.

136. Schwartz, DeKeseredy, Tait, and Alvi, "Male
Peer Support and a Feminist Routine Activities Theory."

137. Groth and Birnbaum, *Men Who Rape*, p. 101.

138. See, generally, Edward Donnerstein, Daniel
Linz, and Steven Penrod, *The Question of
Pornography* (New York: Free Press, 1987);
Diana Russell, *Sexual Exploitation* (Beverly
Hills: Sage, 1985), pp. 115–116.

139. Neil Malamuth and John Briere, "Sexual
Violence in the Media: Indirect Effects on
Aggression Against Women," *Journal of
Social Issues* 42 (1986): 75–92.

140. Richard Felson and Marvin Krohn, "Motives
for Rape," *Journal of Research in Crime and
Delinquency* 27 (1990): 222–242.

141. Richard Felson, Patrick Cundiff, and Noah
Painter-Davis, "Age and Sexual Assault in
Correctional Facilities: A Blocked Opportunity Approach," *Criminology* 50 (2012):
887–911.

142. CBS News, "DA: Strauss-Kahn Accuser
Cleaned After Encounter," July 1, 2011,
http://www.cbsnews.com/stories/
2011/07/01/national/main20076147.shtml
(accessed May 2014).

143. Laura Monroe, Linda Kinney, Mark Weist,
Denise Spriggs Dafeamekpor, Joyce Dantzler, and Matthew Reynolds, "The Experience of Sexual Assault: Findings from a
Statewide Victim Needs Assessment," *Journal of Interpersonal Violence* 20 (2005):
767–776.

144. Steffen Bieneck and Barbara Krahe, "Blam-
ing the Victim and Exonerating the
Perpetrator in Cases of Rape and Robbery:
Is There a Double Standard?" *Journal of
Interpersonal Violence* 26 (2011):
1785–1797.

145. Susannah Meadows and Evan Thomas, "A
Troubled Spring at Duke: A Lacrosse-Team
Party Spawns Charges of Rape," *Newsweek*,
April 10, 2006, http://www.highbeam.com/
doc/1G1-144103126.html (accessed May
2014); "Duke Lacrosse 'Rape' Accuser
Changes Story Again, Says Seligmann
Didn't Touch Her," Associated Press, January 12, 2007, http://www.foxnews.com/
story/0,2933,243063,00.html (accessed
May 2014); Sal Ruibal, "Rape Allegations
Cast Pall at Duke," *USA Today*, March 29,
2006, http://www.usatoday.com/sports/
college/lacrosse/2006-03-29-duke-
fallout_x.htm (accessed May 2014).

146. Mark Whatley, "The Effect of Participant
Sex, Victim Dress, and Traditional Attitudes
on Causal Judgments for Marital Rape Victims," *Journal of Family Violence* 20 (2005):

191–200; Spohn, Beichner, and Davis-
Frenzel, "Prosecutorial Justifications for
Sexual Assault Case Rejection."

147. Patricia Landwehr, Robert Bothwell, Matthew Jeanmard, Luis Luque, Roy Brown III,
and Marie-Anne Breaux, "Racism in Rape
Trials," *Journal of Social Psychology* 142
(2002): 667–670.

148. "Man Wrongly Convicted of Rape Released
19 Years Later," *Forensic Examiner* (May–
June 2003): 44.

149. Gerald Robin, "Forcible Rape: Institutionalized Sexism in the Criminal Justice System," *Crime and Delinquency* 23 (1977):
136–153.

150. Kirk Johnson, "Prosecutors Drop Kobe Bryant
Rape Case," *New York Times*, September 2,
2004, http://www.nytimes.com/2004/09/02/
national/02kobe.html (accessed May 2014).

151. Rodney Kingsworth, Randall MacIntosh,
and Jennifer Wentworth, "Sexual Assault:
The Role of Prior Relationship and Victim
Characteristics in Case Processing," *Justice
Quarterly* 16 (1999): 276–302.

152. Associated Press, "Jury Stirs Furor by Citing
Dress in Rape Acquittal," *Boston Globe*,
October 6, 1989, p. 12.

153. Cassia Spohn and David Holleran, "Pros-
ecuting Sexual Assault: A Comparison of
Charging Decisions in Sexual Assault Cases
Involving Strangers, Acquaintances, and
Intimate Partners," *Justice Quarterly* 18
(2001): 651–688.

154. Susan Estrich, *Real Rape* (Cambridge, MA:
Harvard University Press, 1987),
pp. 58–59.

155. See, for example, Mich. Comp. Laws
Ann. 750.5200-(1); Florida Statutes
Annotated, Sec. 794.011; see, generally,
Gary LaFree, "Official Reactions to Rape,"
American Sociological Review 45 (1980):
842–854.

156. Martin Schwartz and Todd Clear, "Toward a
New Law on Rape," *Crime and Delinquency*
26 (1980): 129–151.

157. *Michigan v. Lucas* 90–149 (1991); Comment, "The Rape Shield Paradox: Com-
plainant Protection Amidst Oscillating
Trends of State Judicial Interpretation,"
Journal of Criminal Law and Criminology 78
(1987): 644–698.

158. Andrew Karmen, *Crime Victims*
(Pacific Grove, CA: Brooks/Cole, 1990),
p. 252.

159. "Court Upholds Civil Rights Portion of Violence Against Women Act," *Criminal Justice
Newsletter* 28 (1997): 3.

160. This section relies on David John Frank,
Tara Hardinge, and Kassia Wosick-Correa,
"The Global Dimensions of Rape-Law
Reform: A Cross-National Study of Policy
Outcomes," *American Sociological Review* 74
(2009): 272–290.

161. Donald Lunde, *Murder and Madness* (San Francisco: San Francisco Book Company, 1977), p. 3.

162. Clifford Ward, "Former Neighbor Found Guilty of Killing Girl, 7, in 1957," *Chicago Tribune*, September 14, 2012, http://www.chicagotribune.com/news/local/breaking/chi-mccullough-guilty-of-killing-girl-7-in-1957-20120914,0,2995426.story (accessed May 2014).

163. "'Baby Hope' Case: Cousin Confesses to Sexually Assaulting, Killing Toddler Anjelica Castillo More than Two Decades Ago," *New York Daily News*, October 13, 2013, http://www.nydailynews.com/news/crime/relative-arrested-baby-hope-case-article-1.1483690 (accessed May 2014).

164. Lisa Baertlein, "HIV Ruled Deadly Weapon in Rape Case," *Boston Globe*, March 2, 1994, p. 3.

165. The legal principles here come from Wayne LaFave and Austin Scott, *Criminal Law* (St. Paul: West, 1986; updated 1993). The definitions and discussion of legal principles used in this chapter lean heavily on this work.

166. Bob Egelko, "State's Top Court OKs Dog Maul Murder Charge: Judge Ordered to Reconsider Owner's Original Conviction," *San Francisco Chronicle*, June 1, 2007, http://www.sfgate.com/bayarea/article/SAN-FRANCISCO-State-s-top-court-OKs-dog-maul-2557910.php (accessed May 2014); Evelyn Nieves, "Woman Gets 4-Year Term in Fatal Dog Attack," *New York Times*, July 16, 2002, p. 1.

167. The National Conference of State Legislatures, "Fetal Homicide Laws," http://www.ncsl.org/issues-research/health/fetal-homicide-state-laws.aspx (accessed May 2014).

168. Pauline Arrillaga, "Jurors Give Drunk Driver 16 Years in Fetus's Death," *Manchester Union Leader*, October 22, 1996, p. B20.

169. *Whitner v. State of South Carolina*, Supreme Court of South Carolina, Opinion Number 24468, July 15, 1996.

170. The National Conference of State Legislatures, "Fetal Homicide Laws."

171. Dana Haynie and David Armstrong, "Race and Gender-Disaggregated Homicide Offending Rates: Differences and Similarities by Victim-Offender Relations Across Cities," *Homicide Studies* 10 (2006): 3–32.

172. Terance Miethe and Wendy Regoeczi with Kriss Drass, *Rethinking Homicide: Exploring the Structure and Process Underlying Deadly Situations* (Cambridge, MA: Cambridge University Press, 2004).

173. Todd Shackelford, Viviana Weekes-Shackelford, and Shanna Beasley, "An Exploratory Analysis of the Contexts and Circumstances of Filicide-Suicide in Chicago, 1965–1994," *Aggressive Behavior* 31 (2005): 399–406.

174. Ibid.

175. Philip Cook, Jens Ludwig, and Anthony Braga, "Criminal Records of Homicide Offenders," *JAMA: Journal of the American Medical Association* 294 (2005): 598–601.

176. Farrington, Loeber, and Berg, "Young Men Who Kill."

177. Terance Miethe and Wendy Regoeczi with Kriss Drass, *Rethinking Homicide: Exploring the Structure and Process Underlying Deadly Situations* (Cambridge, MA: Cambridge University Press, 2004).

178. Scott Decker, "Deviant Homicide: A New Look at the Role of Motives and Victim–Offender Relationships," *Journal of Research in Crime and Delinquency* 33 (1996): 427–449.

179. Victoria Frye, Vanessa Hosein, Eve Waltermaurer, Shannon Blaney, and Susan Wilt, "Femicide in New York City: 1990 to 1999," *Homicide Studies* 9 (2005): 204–228.

180. Carol E. Jordan, James Clark, Adam Pritchard, and Richard Charnigo, "Lethal and Other Serious Assaults: Disentangling Gender and Context," *Crime and Delinquency* 58 (2012): 425–455.

181. Steven Shatz and Naomi Shatz, "Chivalry Is Not Dead: Murder, Gender, and the Death Penalty," *Berkeley Journal of Gender, Law and Justice* 27 (2012): 64–112.

182. Linda Saltzman and James Mercy, "Assaults Between Intimates: The Range of Relationships Involved," in *Homicide: The Victim/Offender Connection*, ed. Anna Victoria Wilson (Cincinnati: Anderson Publishing, 1993), pp. 65–74.

183. Jordan et al., "Lethal and Other Serious Assaults: Disentangling Gender and Context."

184. Angela Browne and Kirk Williams, "Exploring the Effect of Resource Availability and the Likelihood of Female-Perpetrated Homicides," *Law and Society Review* 23 (1989): 75–94.

185. Richard Felson, "Anger, Aggression, and Violence in Love Triangles," *Violence and Victimization* 12 (1997): 345–363.

186. Ibid., p. 361.

187. Sharon Smith, Kathleen Basile, and Debra Karch, "Sexual Homicide and Sexual Violence–Associated Homicide: Findings from the National Violent Death Reporting System," *Homicide Studies* 15 (2011): 132–153; Vernon J. Geberth, "The Classification of Sex-Related Homicides," http://www.practicalhomicide.com/Research/sexrelatedhomicides.htm (accessed May 2014).

188. Peter Lin and James Gill, "Homicides of Pregnant Women," *American Journal of Forensic Medicine and Pathology* 32 (2011): 161–163.

189. Jeff Gruenewald, "A Comparative Examination of Homicides Perpetrated by Far-Right Extremists," *Homicide Studies* 15 (2011): 177–203.

190. David Luckenbill, "Criminal Homicide as a Situational Transaction," *Social Problems* 25 (1977): 176–186.

191. National Center for Education Statistics, "Violent Deaths at School and Away from School, 2012," http://nces.ed.gov/programs/crimeindicators/crimeindicators2012/ind_01.asp (accessed May 2014)

192. Mark Anderson, Joanne Kaufman, Thomas Simon, Lisa Barrios, Len Paulozzi, George Ryan, Rodney Hammond, William Modzeleski, Thomas Feucht, Lloyd Potter, and the School-Associated Violent Deaths Study Group, "School-Associated Violent Deaths in the United States, 1994–1999," *Journal of the American Medical Association* 286 (2001): 2695–2702.

193. Bryan Vossekuil, Marisa Reddy, Robert Fein, Randy Borum, and William Modzeleski, *Safe School Initiative, An Interim Report on the Prevention of Targeted Violence in Schools* (Washington, DC: United States Secret Service, 2000).

194. "BTK Killer Blames 'Demon' for Murders," *USA Today*, July 7, 2005, http://www.usatoday.com/news/nation/2005-07-07-btk-killings_x.htm (accessed May 2014).

195. Alasdair Goodwill and Laurence Alison, "Sequential Angulation, Spatial Dispersion and Consistency of Distance Attack Patterns from Home in Serial Murder, Rape and Burglary," *Journal of Psychology, Crime and Law* 11 (2005): 161–176.

196. Ronald Holmes and Stephen Holmes, *Murder in America* (Thousand Oaks, CA: Sage, 1994): pp. 13–14.

197. "Killing for Pleasure," Court TV Crime Library, http://www.crimelibrary.com/serial_killers/weird/swango/pleasure_8.html (accessed May 2014).

198. Aneez Esmail, "Physician as Serial Killer—The Shipman Case," *New England Journal of Medicine* 352 (2005): 1483–1844.

199. James Alan Fox and Jack Levin, *Overkill: Mass Murder and Serial Killing Exposed* (New York: Plenum, 1994); James Alan Fox, Jack Levin, and Kenna Quinet, *The Will to Kill: Making Sense of Senseless Murder*, 2nd ed. (Boston: Allyn & Bacon, 2004).

200. Amanda L. Farrell, Robert D. Keppelm and Victoria B. Titterington, "Lethal Ladies: Revisiting What We Know About Female Serial Murderers," *Homicide Studies* 15 (2011): 228–252.

201. Belea Keeney and Kathleen Heide, "Gender Differences in Serial Murderers: A Preliminary Analysis," *Journal of Interpersonal Violence* 9 (1994): 37–56.

202. Farrell, Keppel, and Titterington, "Lethal Ladies: Revisiting What We Know About Female Serial Murderers."

203. Wade Myers, Erik Gooch, and Reid Meloy, "The Role of Psychopathy and Sexuality in a Female Serial Killer," *Journal of Forensic Sciences* 50 (2005): 652–658.

204. Farrell, Keppel, and Titterington, "Lethal Ladies: Revisiting What We Know About Female Serial Murderers." p. 245.

205. Zelda Knight, "Some Thoughts on the Psychological Roots of the Behavior of Serial Killers as Narcissists: An Object Relations Perspective," *Social Behavior and Personality: An International Journal* 34 (2006): 1189–1206.

206. Terry Whitman and Donald Akutagawa, "Riddles in Serial Murder: A Synthesis," *Aggression and Violent Behavior* 9 (2004): 693–703.

207. Holmes and Holmes, *Murder in America*, p. 106.

208. Ibid., p. 17; James Alan Fox and Jack Levin, *Overkill: Mass Murder and Serial Killing Exposed* (New York: Plenum, 1994).

209. Gabrielle Salfati and Alicia Bateman, "Serial Homicide: An Investigation of Behavioural Consistency," *Journal of Investigative Psychology and Offender Profiling* 2 (2005): 121–144.

210. Jennifer Browdy, "VI-CAP System to Be Operational this Summer," *Law Enforcement News*, May 21, 1984, p. 1.

211. James Alan Fox and Jack Levin, "Multiple Homicide: Patterns of Serial and Mass Murder," in *Crime and Justice: An Annual Edition*, Vol. 23, ed. Michael Tonry (Chicago: University of Chicago Press, 1998), pp. 407–455; Fox and Levin, *Overkill: Mass Murder and Serial Killing Exposed*; Fox, Levin, and Quinet, *The Will to Kill*; James Allan Fox and Jack Levin, "A Psycho-Social Analysis of Mass Murder," in *Serial and Mass Murder: Theory, Policy, and Research*, ed. Thomas O'Reilly-Fleming and Steven Egger (Toronto: University of Toronto Press, 1993).

212. James Alan Fox and Jack Levin, "Mass Murder: An Analysis of Extreme Violence," *Journal of Applied Psychoanalytic Studies* 5 (2003): 47–64.

213. Grant Duwe, "The Patterns and Prevalence of Mass Murder in Twentieth-Century America," *Justice Quarterly* 21 (2004): 729–761.

214. Adam Lankford, "Mass Shooters in the USA, 1966–2010: Differences Between Attackers Who Live and Die," *Justice Quarterly*, published online June 20, 2013.

215. Fox News, "Gunman in Alabama Massacre Had Hit List," March 11, 2009, http://www.foxnews.com/story/0,2933,508507,00.html (accessed May 2014).

216. Elissa Gootman, "The Hunt for a Sniper: The Victim; 10th Victim Is Recalled as Motivator on Mission," *New York Times*, October 14, 2002, p. A15; Sarah Kershaw, "The Hunt for a Sniper: The Investigation; Endless Frustration but Little Evidence in Search for Sniper," *New York Times*, October 14, 2002, p. A1.

217. Murderpedia, "Joseph Paul Franklin," http://murderpedia.org/male.F/f/franklin-joseph.htm (accessed May 2014).

218. Francis X. Clines with Christopher Drew, "Prosecutors to Discuss Charges as Rifle Is Tied to Sniper Killings," *New York Times*, October 25, 2002, p. A1.

219. Federal Bureau of Investigation, *Crime in the United States, 2005*.

220. Associated Press, "Woman with HIV Gets 3 Years for Spitting in Face," http://www.11alive.com/news/watercooler/story.aspx?storyid=118948 (accessed May 2014).

221. Keith Harries, "Homicide and Assault: A Comparative Analysis of Attributes in Dallas Neighborhoods, 1981–1985," *Professional Geographer* 41 (1989): 29–38.

222. Kevin Flynn, "Record Payouts in Settlements of Lawsuits Against the New York City Police Are Set for Year," *New York Times*, October 1, 1999, p. 12.

223. See, generally, Ruth S. Kempe and C. Henry Kempe, *Child Abuse* (Cambridge, MA: Harvard University Press, 1978).

224. U.S. Department of Health and Human Services, Administration for Children and Families, Children's Bureau, *Child Maltreatment, 2012* (Washington, DC: U.S. Department of Health and Human Services, 2013), http://www.acf.hhs.gov/sites/default/files/cb/cm2012.pdf#page=11 (accessed May 2014).

225. Wolfner and Gelles, "A Profile of Violence toward Children."

226. Martin Daly and Margo Wilson, "Violence against Stepchildren," *Current Directions in Psychological Science* 5 (1996): 77–81.

227. Ruth Inglis, *Sins of the Fathers: A Study of the Physical and Emotional Abuse of Children* (New York: St. Martin's, 1978), p. 53.

228. Diana Russell, "The Incidence and Prevalence of Intrafamilial and Extrafamilial Sexual Abuse of Female Children," *Child Abuse and Neglect* 7 (1983): 133–146; see also David Finkelhor, *Sexually Victimized Children* (New York: Free Press, 1979), p. 88.

229. Lisa Jones and David Finkelhor, *The Decline in Child Sexual Abuse Cases* (Washington, DC: Office of Juvenile Justice and Delinquency Prevention, 2001); Emily M. Douglas and David Finkelhor, Child Sexual Abuse Fact Sheet, May 2005, Crimes Against Children Research Center, http://www.unh.edu/ccrc/factsheet/pdf/childhood-SexualAbuseFactSheet.pdf (accessed May 2014).

230. Lisa Jones, David Finkelhor, and Kathy Kopie, "Why Is Sexual Abuse Declining? A Survey of State Child Protection Administrators," *Child Abuse and Neglect* 25 (2001): 1139–1141.

231. Eva Jonzon and Frank Lindblad, "Adult Female Victims of Child Sexual Abuse," *Journal of Interpersonal Violence* 20 (2005): 651–666.

232. Jane Siegel and Linda Williams, "Risk Factors for Sexual Victimization of Women," *Violence Against Women* 9 (2003): 902–930.

233. April Chiung-Tao Shen, "Self-Esteem of Young Adults Experiencing Interparental Violence and Child Physical Maltreatment: Parental and Peer Relationships as Mediators," *Journal of Interpersonal Violence* 24 (2009): 770–794.

234. Christina Meade, Trace Kershaw, Nathan Hansen, and Kathleen Sikkema, "Long-Term Correlates of Childhood Abuse Among Adults with Severe Mental Illness: Adult Victimization, Substance Abuse, and HIV Sexual Risk Behavior," *AIDS and Behavior* 13 (2009): 207–216.

235. Arina Ulman and Murray Straus, "Violence by Children Against Mothers in Relation to Violence Between Parents and Corporal Punishment by Parents," *Journal of Comparative Family Studies* 34 (2003): 41–63.

236. R. Emerson Dobash and Russell Dobash, *Violence Against Wives* (New York: Free Press, 1979).

237. Julia O'Faolain and Laura Martines, eds., *Not in God's Image: Women in History* (Glasgow: Fontana/Collins, 1974).

238. Laurence Stone, "The Rise of the Nuclear Family in Modern England: The Patriarchal Stage," in *The Family in History*, ed. Charles Rosenberg (Philadelphia: University of Pennsylvania Press, 1975), p. 53.

239. Dobash and Dobash, *Violence Against Wives*, p. 46.

240. John Braithwaite, "Inequality and Republican Criminology," paper presented at the annual meeting of the American Society of Criminology, San Francisco, November 1991, p. 20.

241. Richard Gelles and Murray Straus, "Violence in the American Family," *Journal of Social Issues* 35 (1979): 15–39.

242. Nicole Bell, "Health and Occupational Consequences of Spouse Abuse Victimization Among Male U.S. Army Soldiers," *Journal of Interpersonal Violence* 24 (2009): 751–769.

243. This section leans heavily on Priscilla Offenhauer and Alice Buchalter, *Teen Dating Violence: A Literature Review and Annotated Bibliography*, April 2011, https://www.ncjrs.gov/pdffiles1/nij/grants/235368.pdf (accessed March 2014).

244. Silverman et al., "Dating Violence Against Adolescent Girls and Associated Substance Abuse, Unhealthy Weight Control, Sexual Risk Behavior, Pregnancy and Suicidality."

245. FBI, *Crime in the United States*, 2012.

246. James Calder and John Bauer, "Convenience Store Robberies: Security Measures and Store Robbery Incidents," *Journal of Criminal Justice* 20 (1992): 553–566.

247. Marcus Felson, *Crime and Nature* (Thousand Oaks, CA: Sage, 2006).

248. Heith Copes, Andy Hochstetler, and Michael Cherbonneau, "Getting the Upper Hand: Scripts for Managing Victim Resistance in Carjackings," *Journal of Research in Crime and Delinquency*, published online May 3, 2011.

249. Elizabeth Ehrhardt Mustaine and Richard Tewksbury, "Predicting Risks of Larceny Theft Victimization: A Routine Activity Analysis Using Refined Lifestyle Measures," *Criminology* 36 (1998): 829–858.

250. Bruce A. Jacobs, *Robbing Drug Dealers: Violence beyond the Law* (Hawthorne, NY: Aldine de Gruyter, 2000).

251. Richard Felson, Eric Baumer, and Steven Messner, "Acquaintance Robbery," *Journal of Research in Crime and Delinquency* 37 (2000): 284–305.

252. Ibid., p. 287.

253. Ibid.

254. "Boy Gets 18 Years in Fatal Park Beating of Transient," *Los Angeles Times*, December 24, 1987, p. 9B.

255. Jack Levin and Jack McDevitt, *Hate Crimes: The Rising Tide of Bigotry and Bloodshed* (New York: Plenum Press, 1993).

256. Jack McDevitt, Jack Levin, and Susan Bennett, "Hate Crime Offenders: An Expanded Typology," *Journal of Social Issues* 58 (2002): 303–318.

257. Jack Levin, *The Violence of Hate, Confronting Racism, Anti-Semitism, and Other Forms of Bigotry* (Boston: Allyn & Bacon, 2002), pp. 29–56.

258. FBI, *Hate Crime Statistics, 2012* (Washington, DC: FBI, 2013), http://www.fbi.gov/news/stories/2013/november/annual-hate-crime-statistics-show-slight-decease/annual-hate-crime-statistics-show-slight-decrease (accessed May 2014).

259. Ryan King, Steven Messner, and Robert Baller, "Contemporary Hate Crimes, Law Enforcement, and the Legacy of Racial Violence," *American Sociological Review* 74 (2009): 291–315.

260. National Gay and Lesbian Task Force, Hate Crime Laws Map, http://www.thetaskforce.org/reports_and_research/hate_crimes_laws (accessed May 2014).

261. Felicia Lee, "Gays Angry Over TV Report on a Murder," *New York Times*, November 26, 2004, p. A3.

262. Frederick M. Lawrence, *Punishing Hate: Bias Crimes Under American Law* (Cambridge, MA: Harvard University Press, 1999).

263. Ibid., p. 3.

264. Ibid., p. 9.

265. Ibid., p. 11.

266. Ibid., pp. 39–42.

267. Jack McDevitt, Jennifer Balboni, Luis Garcia, and Joann Gu, "Consequences for Victims: A Comparison of Bias- and Non-Bias-Motivated Assaults," *American Behavioral Scientist* 45 (2001): 697–714.

268. *Virginia v. Black et al.* No. 01-1107. 2003.

269. Associated Press, "9 Dead in Shooting at Conn. Beer Distributor, Union Official: Gunman Was Employee Who Had Been Caught Stealing" MSNBC.com, August 4, 2010, http://www.msnbc.msn.com/id/38535909/ (accessed May 2014).

270. James Alan Fox and Jack Levin, "Firing Back: The Growing Threat of Workplace Homicide," *Annals* 536 (1994): 16–30.

271. Stephen Romano, Micòl E. Levi-Minzi, Eugene A. Rugala, and Vincent Van Hasselt, "Workplace Violence Prevention Readiness and Response," *FBI Law Enforcement Bulletin*, January 2011, http://www.fbi.gov/stats-services/publications/law-enforcement-bulletin/january2011/workplace_violence_prevention (accessed May 2014).

272. FBI, *Workplace Violence: Issues in Response* (Quantico, VA: National Center for the Analysis of Violent Crime, 2001), http://www.fbi.gov/stats-services/publications/workplace-violence (accessed May 2014).

273. Romano, Levi-Minzi, Rugala, and Van Hasselt, "Workplace Violence Prevention Readiness and Response."

274. Janet R. Cooper, "Response to 'Workplace Violence in Health Care: Recognized but Not Regulated,' by Kathleen M. McPhaul and Jane A. Lipscomb (September 30, 2004)," *Online Journal of Issues in Nursing* 10 (2005): 53–55.

275. Associated Press, "Gunman Wounds 3 Doctors in L.A. Hospital," *Cleveland Plain Dealer*, February 9, 1993, p. 1B.

276. Fox and Levin, "Firing Back," p. 5.

277. Romano, Levi-Minzi, Rugala, and Van Hasselt, "Workplace Violence Prevention Readiness and Response."

278. Dana Loomis, Stephen Marshall, and Myduc Ta, "Employer Policies Toward Guns and the Risk of Homicide in the Workplace," *American Journal of Public Health* 95 (2005): 830–832.

279. The following sections rely heavily on Patricia Tjaden, *The Crime of Stalking: How Big Is the Problem?* (Washington, DC: National Institute of Justice, 1997); see also Robert M. Emerson, Kerry O. Ferris, and Carol Brooks Gardner, "On Being Stalked," *Social Problems* 45 (1998): 289–298.

280. Patrick Kinkade, Ronald Burns, and Angel Ilarraza Fuentes, "Criminalizing Attractions: Perceptions of Stalking and the Stalker," *Crime and Delinquency* 51 (2005): 3–25.

281. Michael Black, Kathleen Basile, Matthew Breiding, Sharon Smith, Mikel Walters, Melissa Merrick, Jieru Chen, and Mark Stevens, *The National Intimate Partner and Sexual Violence Survey (NISVS): 2010 Summary Report* (Atlanta: National Center for Injury Prevention and Control, Centers for Disease Control and Prevention, 2011).

282. Michelle Garcia, "Voices from the Field: Stalking," *NIJ Journal* 266 (2010) http://www.nij.gov/journals/266/pages/stalking.aspx (accessed May 2014).

283. Bonnie Fisher, Francis Cullen, and Michael Turner, "Being Pursued: Stalking Victimization in a National Study of College Women," *Criminology and Public Policy* 1 (2002): 257–309.

284. Garcia, "Voices from the Field: Stalking."

285. Reid Meloy, "Stalking: The State of the Science," *Criminal Behaviour and Mental Health* 17 (2007): 1–7.

286. Mary Brewster, "Stalking by Former Intimates: Verbal Threats and Other Predictors of Physical Violence," *Violence and Victims* 15 (2000): 41–51.

287. Carol Jordan, T. K. Logan, and Robert Walker, "Stalking: An Examination of the Criminal Justice Response," *Journal of Interpersonal Violence* 18 (2003): 148–165.

POССИЯ 24

AP Images/Edward Snowden

POLITICAL CRIME AND TERRORISM

you may recall the case of Edward Snowden (Chapter 8). Born in North Carolina in 1983, Snowden had worked for Booz Allen Hamilton, a provider of management and technology consulting services to the U.S. government.[1] In May 2013, Snowden began collecting top-secret documents regarding NSA domestic surveillance practices and leaking them to the press. Why did he engage in what some people consider treason? He was disturbed that the NSA was engaged in spying on millions of American citizens, a practice he considered an illegal invasion of privacy. When the documents appeared in the press, Snowden was charged under the Espionage Act. He fled to Russia in order to avoid prosecution.

In a series of interviews given in Hong Kong and Russia, Snowden told the press, "I'm willing to sacrifice [my former life] because I can't in good conscience allow the U.S. government to destroy privacy, Internet freedom, and basic liberties for people around the world with this massive surveillance machine they're secretly building." He saw himself as a truth teller, informing the press that the American people have a right to know about government abuses that were being kept hidden. "The secret continuance of these programs represents a far greater danger than their disclosure.... So long as there's broad support amongst a people, it can be argued there's a level of legitimacy even to the most invasive and morally wrong program, as it was an informed and willing decision.... However, programs that are implemented in secret, out of public oversight, lack that legitimacy, and that's a problem. It also represents a dangerous normalization of 'governing in the dark,' where decisions with enormous public impact occur without any public input."[2] Is Snowden a patriot who exposed illegal government practices or a political criminal who engaged in treasonous activity that endangered the national security? Whether he is a political criminal is still a matter of some debate.

olitical crime can be both nonviolent, such as election fraud, and extremely violent, such as a terrorist act designed to undermine the government. It has become an important area of criminological inquiry, and many criminologists who previously paid scant attention to the interaction between political motivation and crime have now made it the focus of intense study.

In this chapter, we will briefly discuss the concept of political crime and some of the forms it takes. We will then go into its most extreme form, terrorism, which now occupies the center stage of both world opinion and government policy. It is important for students of criminology to develop a basic understanding of terrorism's definition, history, and structure, and review the steps being taken to limit or eliminate its occurrence.

POLITICAL CRIME

L01 Define the term *political crime*

The term **political crime** is used to signify illegal acts that are designed to undermine an existing government and threaten its survival.[3] However, unlike other crimes, it is often difficult to decide who is the criminal and who is the victim. Take the series of uprisings that began in 2011 and are known as the "Arab Spring." Some targeted people widely viewed as dictators, such as the popular revolt in February 2011 that toppled the regime of long-term Egyptian ruler Hosni Mubarak. Similar protests broke out in Tunisia,

Yemen, and Libya, where the regime of dictator Muammar Gaddafi was ousted. These revolts were not viewed as terrorist acts but popular political upheavals against hated and evil dictators. The world did not recoil when Gaddafi was apprehended and killed brutally on camera.

When an act becomes a political crime and when an actor is considered a political criminal are often extremely subjective. In highly repressive nations, any form of unsanctioned political activity, including writing a newspaper article critical of the regime, may be considered a political crime, punishable by a prison term or even death. In contrast, people whom some label as terrorists and insurrectionists are viewed by others as freedom fighters and revolutionaries. What would have happened to George Washington and Benjamin Franklin had the British won the Revolutionary War? Would they have been hanged for their political crimes rather than being considered heroes as they are today?

Take for instance the civil war in Syria. In 2011, troops loyal to the ruling party cracked down hard when protests erupted against the government of Bashar al-Assad. The world watched in horror and dismay when state security forces killed hundreds of protesters and arbitrarily arrested thousands, many of whom, including children, were beaten and tortured. The conflict evolved into a full-blown civil war in which more than 100,000 have been killed and chemical weapons used by government forces. At first world leaders denounced the violence: Turkish Prime Minister Recep Tayyip Erdoğan called the crackdown a "barbarity" that is "inhumane" and "cannot be digested."[4] However, as in many political conflicts, things soon became murky: Syrian government officials blamed the violence on "terrorist groups" and "armed gangs." One group that emerged, the Islamic State of Iraq and Syria (ISIS), sent fighters into Iraq with the aim of overthrowing the Iraqi and Syrian government and establishing an Islamic state. The fighting in both Syria and Iraq soon took on sectarian overtones, and Shia and Sunni factions emerged. According to the government, the rebels were really jihadists looking to establish a caliphate based on sharia law; according to the opposition, the rebels were freedom fighters looking to oust an evil dictator and establish democracy.

The Nature of Political Crimes

The political criminal and political crimes may stem from religious or ideological sources. Because their motivations shift between selfish personal needs and selfless, noble, or altruistic desires, political crimes often occupy a gray area between conventional and outlawed behavior. It is easy to condemn interpersonal violent crimes such as rape or murder because their goals are typically selfish and self-centered

---

political crime Illegal acts that are designed to undermine an existing government and threaten its survival. Political crimes can include both violent and nonviolent acts and range in seriousness from dissent, treason, and espionage to violent acts such as terrorism or assassination.

al-Qaeda (Arabic for "the base") An international fundamentalist Islamist organization comprising independent and collaborative cells, whose goal is reducing Western influence upon Islamic affairs. Also spelled al-Qa'ida.

(e.g., revenge or profit). In contrast, political criminals may be motivated by principle, faith or conviction. While it is true that some political crime involves profit (such as selling state secrets for money), most political criminals, including Edward Snowden, do not consider themselves antisocial but instead patriotic and altruistic. They are willing to sacrifice themselves for what they consider to be the greater good. While some concoct elaborate schemes to hide or mask their actions, others are quite brazen, hoping to provoke the government to overreact in their zeal to crack down on dissent. Because state authorities may engage in a range of retaliatory actions that result in human rights violations, even those who support the government may begin to question its activities: maybe the government is corrupt and authoritarian? On the other hand, if the government does nothing, it appears weak and corrupt and unable to protect citizens.

Even those political criminals who profit personally from their misdeeds, such as someone who spies for an enemy nation for financial payoffs, may believe that their acts are motivated by a higher calling than common theft. "My ultimate goal is to weaken or overthrow a corrupt government," they reason, "so selling secrets to the enemy is justified." Political criminals may believe that their acts are criminalized only because the group holding power fears them and wants to curtail their behavior. And while the general public has little objection to laws that control extreme behaviors such as plotting a bloody revolution, they may have questions when a law criminalizes ordinary political dissent or bans political meetings in order to control suspected political criminals.

The Goals of Political Criminals

One survivor of a bombing attack in Iraq told reporters, "There may be a state, there may be a government. But what can that state do? What can they do with all the terrorists? Are they supposed to set up a checkpoint in every house?" In their attack, the bombers succeeded in their efforts to create an atmosphere of intimidation and fear designed to oust the government.[5] Unsettling the populace and reducing faith in the government may be one goal of political criminals; some of the others include:

- *Intimidation.* Some political criminals want to intimidate or threaten an opponent who does not share their political orientation or views.
- *Revolution.* Some political criminals plot to overthrow the existing government and replace it with one that holds views they find more acceptable.
- *Profit.* Another goal of political crime is profit: selling state secrets for personal enrichment or trafficking in stolen arms and munitions.
- *Conviction.* Some political criminals are motivated by altruism; they truly believe their crimes will benefit society and are willing to violate the law and risk punishment in order to achieve what they see as social improvement.

- *Pseudo-conviction.* These political criminals conceal conventional criminal motivations behind a mask of conviction and altruism. They may form a revolutionary movement out of a hidden desire to engage in violence rather than their stated goal of reforming society. The pseudo-convictional criminal is particularly dangerous because they convince followers to join them in their crimes without fully revealing their true motivations.[6]

Becoming a Political Criminal

LO2 Assess the cause of political crime

Why does someone become a political criminal? There is no set pattern or reason; motivations vary widely. Some use political crime as a stepping-stone to public office, while others use it as a method to focus their frustrations. Others hope they can gain respect from their friends and family. Although the motivations for political crime are complex and varied, there does appear to be some regularity in the way ideas are formed. Political crime expert Randy Borum finds that this pattern takes the form of a series of cognitive stages:

- Stage 1: *"It's not right."* An unhappy, dissatisfied individual identifies some type of undesirable event or condition. It could be economic (e.g., poverty, unemployment, poor living conditions), social (e.g., government-imposed restrictions on individual freedoms, lack of order, or morality), or personal ("I am being cheated of what is due me"). While the conditions may vary, those involved perceive the experience as "things are not as they should be."
- Stage 2: *"It's not fair."* The prospective criminal concludes that the undesirable condition is a product of "injustice"—that is, it does not apply to everyone. A government worker may feel his or her low pay scale is "not right" and that corporate workers with less skill are making more money and getting more benefits. At the same time, government workers are portrayed as lazy and corrupt. For those who are deprived, this facilitates feelings of resentment and injustice.
- Stage 3: *"It's your fault."* Someone or some group must be held accountable for the extremist's displeasure. It always helps to identify a potential target. For example, the underpaid worker may become convinced that minorities get all the good jobs while the worker is suffering financially. Extremist groups spread this propaganda to attract recruits. Americans may be portrayed as rich and undeserving by overseas enemies looking to recruit disenfranchised young men and women to become terrorists.
- Stage 4: *"You're evil."* Because good people would not intentionally hurt others, targeted groups are appropriate choices for revenge and/or violence. The disaffected government worker concludes that since his country has

Borum's typology seems similar to the techniques of neutralization discussed in Chapter 7.

Ask Yourself …

Is it possible that terrorists must neutralize feelings of guilt and shame before planting their bombs? Or do their religious and political beliefs negate any need for a psychological process to reduce personal responsibility for violence?

let him down it is only fair to sell state secrets to foreign nations for profit or to join a terrorist group or both. Aggression becomes justifiable when aimed against bad people, particularly those who intentionally cause harm to others. Second, by casting the target as evil, it dehumanizes them and makes justifying aggression even easier. So it's not so bad to rig an election, because the opposing candidates are evil and do not deserve to hold office.[7]

TYPES OF POLITICAL CRIMES

Considering this cognitive thought that produces political crime and terrorism, what are the specific crimes and what form do they take?

Election Fraud

In 2012, Matthew Weaver, a 22-year-old candidate for student council president at California State University San Marcos, hoped to guarantee victory by rigging the election through cyberfraud.[8] Weaver used small electronic devices called key loggers to steal the passwords and identities of nearly 750 fellow students. Then he cast votes for himself—and some of his friends on the ballot—using the stolen names. Those who used the machines were unaware that Weaver could later retrieve every keystroke they made, enabling him to obtain their usernames and passwords and then gain access to all their information. The evidence against

election fraud Illegal interference with the process of an election. Acts of fraud tend to involve affecting vote counts to bring about a desired election outcome, whether by increasing the vote share of the favored candidate, depressing the vote share of the rival candidates, or both. Varieties of election fraud include intimidation, disruption of polling places, distribution of misinformation such as the wrong election date, registration fraud, and vote buying.

Weaver was overwhelming, and he pleaded guilty in March 2013 to identity theft, wire fraud, and unauthorized access of a computer. He received a year in prison for his scheme.

Some political criminals want to shape elections to meet their personal needs (even elections for student council president). In some instances their goal is altruistic: the election of candidates who reflect their personal political views. In others, their actions are motivated by profit: they are paid by a candidate to rig the election. And in some cases, such as Matthew Weaver's, they simply want to get elected!

Whatever the motive, **election fraud** is illegal interference with the political process. Acts of fraud tend to involve affecting vote counts to bring about a desired election outcome, whether by increasing the vote share of the favored candidate, depressing the vote share of the rival candidates, or both.

In some third-world dictatorships, election fraud is the norm, and it is common for the ruling party to announce, after party members counted the votes, that they were returned to office with an overwhelming majority. Sometimes allegations of voter fraud by ruling juntas can have disastrous consequences. Take for instance the parliamentary elections that took place in 2007 in Kenya. When it was announced that President Mwai Kibaki had won the presidential election over opposition candidate Raila Odinga, fighting broke out that tore this African nation apart. More than 1,200 Kenyans were reported killed, thousands more injured, hundreds of thousands made homeless; more than 40,000 houses, farms, and businesses were looted or destroyed.[9] Despite the post-election chaos, Kibaki retained his victory and his power, continuing in office until 2013.

Election fraud, a feature of political life since Roman times, includes a variety of behaviors designed to give a candidate or his/her party an unfair advantage:

- *Intimidation.* Voters can be scared away from the polls through threats or intimidation. Having armed guards posted at polling places may convince people it is dangerous to vote. Lists of registered voters can be obtained and people subjected to threatening calls before the election.
- *Disruption.* Bomb threats can be called into voting places in areas that are known to heavily favor the opposing party, with the goal of suppressing the vote. There can be outright sabotage of polling places, ballots, ballot boxes, and voting machines.
- *Misinformation.* Flyers are sent out to voters registered with the opposition party containing misleading information such as the wrong election date or saying that rules have been changed about who is eligible to vote.
- *Registration fraud.* Political operatives may try to shape the outcome of an election by busing in ineligible voters from other districts. Because many jurisdictions require minimal identification and proof of citizenship, political criminals find it easy to get around residency requirements.

They may provide conspirators with "change of address" forms to allow them to vote in a particular election, when in fact no actual change of address has occurred.

- *Vote buying.* Securing votes by payment or other rewards or the selling of one's vote is an age-old problem that still exists. One popular method is to buy absentee ballots from people who are in need of cash. The fraudulent voter can then ensure that the vote goes their way, an outcome that cannot be guaranteed if the conspirator casts a secret ballot at a polling place.

Most states have created laws to control and punish voter fraud. The federal government has a number of statutes designed to control and/or restrict fraud, including 18 U.S.C. § 594, which provides:

Whoever intimidates, threatens, coerces, or attempts to intimidate, threaten, or coerce, any other person for the purpose of interfering with the right of such other person to vote or to vote as he may choose, or of causing such other person to vote for, or not to vote for, any candidate for the office of President, Vice President, Presidential elector, Member of the Senate, Member of the House of Representatives, Delegate from the District of Columbia, or Resident Commissioner, at any election held solely or in part for the purpose of electing such candidate, shall be fined under this title or imprisoned not more than one year, or both.

Another provision that applies to voting is 18 U.S.C. § 245(b)(1)(A):

Whoever, whether or not acting under color of law, by force or threat of force willfully injures, intimidates or interferes with, or attempts to injure, intimidate or interfere with (1) any person because he is or has been, or in order to intimidate such person or any other person or any class of persons from (A) voting or qualifying to vote, qualifying or campaigning as a candidate for elective office, or qualifying or acting as a poll watcher, or any legally authorized election official, in any primary, special, or general election....

This provision is in the Civil Rights section of Title 18, the federal criminal code, and it protects the right of all citizens to vote and campaign for office.

Abuse of Office/Public Corruption

On August 14, 2013, former Congressman Jesse L. Jackson Jr. was sentenced to 30 months in prison for conspiring to defraud his reelection campaigns by converting $750,000 in campaign funds to pay for personal items and expenses, including high-end appliances and electronics. He filed misleading reports to conceal his illegal activities.[10] Jackson, the son of famed Reverend Jesse Jackson, is but one of many examples of public officials using their office to enrich themselves illegally. Another well-known Illinois politician, Governor Rod Blagojevich is serving a 14-year sentence in federal prison following conviction for corruption and the soliciting of bribes for political appointments, including an attempt to sell the U.S. Senate seat formerly occupied by Barack Obama.

Public corruption involves a breach of public trust and/or abuse of position by government officials and their private sector accomplices. Whether elected, appointed or hired, they are committing a crime if while in office they demand, solicit, accept, or agree to receive anything of value in return for being manipulated in the performance of their official duties. They and their relatives and friends may be the recipients of illegal funds paid for by businesspeople willing to bribe to gain public contracts and other government actions. The victims of public corruption are the general public, who pay for corruption through inflated costs and sometimes higher taxes. The Profile in Crime feature focuses on a recent case of public corruption that made national headlines.

Former Detroit Mayor Kwame Kilpatrick is shown being handcuffed just after being sentenced to one-and-a-half to five years in prison Kilpatrick took cash payments for himself, friends, and relatives in return for political favors and contracts.

AP Images/Paul Sancya

Public corruption is also considered a white-collar crime. We will return to this issue in Chapter 13 when we cover bribery and extortion.

Ask Yourself ...

Should public officials who accept bribes go to prison? After all, they are not really dangerous people. How about requiring that they really do public service: volunteering in the community after their illegal gains are confiscated?

Treason

LO3 Compare and contrast the terms *espionage* and *treason*

Few people can forget the image of John Walker Lindh, the so-called *American Taliban*, when he was captured during the American invasion of Afghanistan. Lindh, who had spent

treason An act of disloyalty to one's nation or state.

his early years in an affluent northern California community, converted to Islam and through a convoluted path wound up first in an al-Qaeda training camp and then fighting with the Taliban on the front lines in Afghanistan. He was captured on November 25, 2001, by Afghan Northern Alliance forces, and questioned by CIA agents. Later that day, there was a violent uprising in the prison in which he was being held and during the attack a CIA agent was killed. Walker escaped only to be recaptured seven days later. At his trial, he apologized for fighting alongside the Taliban, saying, "Had I realized then what I know now ... I never would have joined them." The 21-year-old said Osama bin Laden was against Islam and that he "never understood jihad to mean anti-American or terrorism." (See Exhibit 11.1.) "I understand why so many Americans were angry when I was first discovered in Afghanistan. I realize many still are, but I hope in time that feeling will change." After a plea agreement, John Walker Lindh was sentenced to 20 years in prison.[11] He is expected to be released in 2019.

Lindh's behavior amounts to what is commonly called **treason**, an act of disloyalty to one's nation or state. While the crime of treason is well known and the word "traitor" is a generic term, there have actually been fewer than

profiles in crime

KWAME KILPATRICK: BETRAYING THE PUBLIC'S TRUST

When Kwame Kilpatrick became mayor of Detroit in 2002, he promised to revitalize the city but instead used his position for personal gain. As a result, he was sentenced in 2013 to a 28-year prison term for his role in a wide-ranging racketeering conspiracy that included extortion, bribery, and fraud. Thirty-two other associates were also convicted of crimes in connection with the case, including contractor Bobby Ferguson, a close friend of Kilpatrick, who received a 21-year prison term.

What did the conspirators do to earn such a draconian punishment? Kilpatrick extorted money from people doing business with the city, rigged bids, and took bribes. He illegally appropriated funds from nonprofit civic organizations. For example, Kilpatrick and Ferguson obtained more than $500,000 from the state of Michigan and private donors for nonprofit organizations they controlled. The organizations were supposed to help the community. Instead,

the mayor spent large sums on himself for luxury vacations, spa treatments, and golf clubs. In addition, Kilpatrick coerced contractors to rig the awarding of public contracts to ensure that Ferguson obtained a portion of the revenue from those contracts. Ferguson obtained at least $73 million in revenues from municipal contracts through this scheme, a portion of which he shared with his co-conspirators.

The government used text messages from Kilpatrick, given to them by his cell phone service provider, that discussed bid rigging, bribes, and other criminal activity; Kilpatrick had no idea the messages were being recorded. Federal investigators also found that he was making large cash deposits into his bank accounts, and this amounted to $840,000 more than he earned from his salary as mayor; none of this income was disclosed on his tax returns. The amazing aspect of the case was that the mayor did little to cover his tracks.

He actually would hand an officer on his protective detail an envelope with cash and tell him to take it to the bank and pay his credit card bill. Believing he was above the law, he thought he could get away with repeated and prolonged betrayal of the public trust, but he didn't.

Critical Thinking

Kwame Kilpatrick received more than 20 years in prison for his crimes. Is this excessive considering that he was not a violent person? After all, many people who are convicted of rape, assault, and even murder are given lesser sentences. How should someone like Kilpatrick be punished?

SOURCE: U.S. Attorney's Office, Eastern District of Michigan, "Former Detroit Mayor Kwame Kilpatrick, Contractor Bobby Ferguson, and Bernard Kilpatrick Sentenced on Racketeering, Extortion, Bribery, Fraud, and Tax Charges," press release, October 17, 2013, http://www.justice.gov/usao/mie/news/2013/2013_10_17_kkilpatrick_et_al.html (accessed May 2014).

What Is Jihad?

When John Walker Lindh used the word *jihad*, he made reference to a term that has become all too familiar in contemporary society. Often assumed to mean "holy war," the term is more complex than that simple meaning. According to terror expert Andrew Silke, the term derives from the Arabic for "struggle," and within Islam there are two forms of jihad: the Greater Jihad and the Lesser Jihad. The Greater Jihad refers to a Muslim's personal struggle to live a good and charitable life and adhere to God's commands. In this sense, jihad is a strictly personal and nonviolent phenomenon. The Lesser Jihad refers to violent struggle on behalf of Islam. Jihadists are "those who struggle" and refers to individuals who have volunteered to fight in the Lesser Jihad. The term is used by members of groups such as al-Qaeda to describe themselves and their goals. Jihadists sometimes call themselves *mujahideen*, meaning "holy warriors," and the term is commonly used to refer to Muslims engaged in the Lesser Jihad.

SOURCE: Andrew Silke, "Holy Warriors: Exploring the Psychological Processes of Jihadi Radicalization," *European Journal of Criminology* 5 (2008): 99–123.

40 prosecutions for treason in the entire history of the United States and most have resulted in acquittal. In fact, though his behavior might be considered *treasonous*, Lindh was not actually charged or convicted of treason but was charged with serving in the Taliban army and carrying weapons.

While the Lindh case grabbed headlines, the most famous treason case in U.S. history is still the 1807 trial of former Vice President Aaron Burr, a man best known for killing Secretary of the Treasury Alexander Hamilton in 1804 in a duel over a matter of honor. Burr was accused of hatching a plot to separate the western states from the union. When that plot went awry, he conspired to seize Mexico and set up a puppet government with himself as king! Arrested on charges of treason, he was acquitted when the Federal Court, headed by John Marshall, ruled that to be guilty of treason an overt act must be committed; planning is not enough.[12]

Because treason is considered such a heinous crime, and to deter would-be traitors, many nations apply or have applied the death penalty to those convicted of attempting to overthrow the existing government. Treason was considered particularly loathsome under English common law, and until the nineteenth century it was punishable by being "drawn and quartered," a method of execution that involved hanging the offender, removing their intestines while still living, and finally cutting the offender into four pieces for public display. William Wallace, the Scottish patriot made famous in the film *Braveheart*, was so displayed after his execution.

Acts can be considered treasonous in order to stifle political dissent. In eighteenth-century England, it was considered treasonous to merely criticize the king or his behavior, and not surprisingly, the American colonists feared giving their own central government that much power. Therefore treason is the only crime mentioned in the United States Constitution, which defines treason as levying war against the United States or "in adhering to their Enemies, giving them Aid and Comfort," and requires the testimony of two witnesses or a confession in open court for conviction. The purpose of this was to limit the government's ability to bring charges of treason against opponents and to make it more difficult to prosecute those who are so charged.[13]

Today, the United States Criminal Code codifies treason as "whoever, owing allegiance to the United States, levies war against them or adheres to their enemies, giving them aid and comfort within the United States or elsewhere, is guilty of treason and shall suffer death, or shall be imprisoned not less than five years and fined under this title but not less than $10,000; and shall be incapable of holding any office under the United States."[14] Helping or cooperating with the enemy in a time of war (as Lindh did) would be considered treason; so too would be creating or recruiting a military force to help a foreign nation overthrow the government. After World War II, two women, Iva Ikuko Toguri D'Aquino, a Japanese American born in Los Angeles and known as Tokyo Rose, and Mildred Elizabeth Gillars, born in Portland, Maine, and known as Axis Sally, served prison terms for broadcasting for the Axis powers in an effort to demoralize American troops.

Espionage

Robert Hanssen was a counterintelligence agent for the FBI assigned to detect and identify Russian spies. A former Chicago police officer, Hanssen's assignment required him to have access to sensitive top-secret information. In one of the most shocking cases in U.S. history, Hanssen volunteered to become a paid spy for the KGB during the Cold War and over a period of 15 years received at least $1.4 million in cash and diamonds. He was arrested on February 18, 2001, after leaving a package of classified documents for his Russian handlers under a footbridge in a park outside Washington. During his years as a double agent, Hanssen not only provided more than 6,000 pages of documents to the Soviet Union but also caused the death of two U.S. double agents whose identities were uncovered with the aid of his secret documents. The Hanssen case was the subject of the 2007 film *Breach*, which starred Chris Cooper as the corrupt agent.[15]

Espionage (more commonly called "spying") is the practice of obtaining information about a government,

espionage The practice of obtaining information about a government, organization, or society that is considered secret or confidential without the permission of the holder of the information. Commonly called spying.

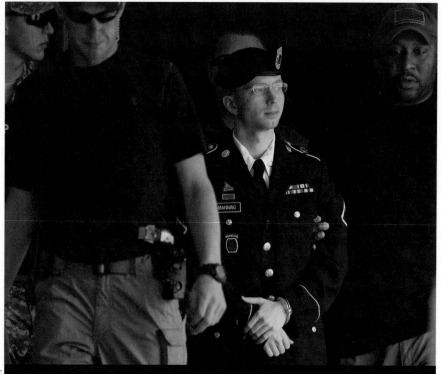

Army Pfc. Bradley Manning is escorted out of a courthouse in Fort Meade, Maryland, on July 30, 2013, after being acquitted of aiding the enemy—the most serious charge he faced—but being convicted of espionage, theft, and other charges, for revealing government secrets to WikiLeaks. Now known as Chelsea Manning, he received a 35-year sentence for his crimes.

during the Cold War at prestigious Cambridge University in England by Russia's foreign intelligence service, the KGB. The five were motivated by the belief that capitalism was corrupt and that the Soviet Union offered a better model for society. After graduation, they secured sensitive government posts that gave them access to valuable intelligence they then passed on to the Soviet Union. Two of the conspirators, Guy Burgess and Donald Maclean, were exposed in 1951 and defected to the Soviet Union before they could be captured; Kim Philby, who had worked as a high-level intelligence agent, defected to Russia in 1963 but not before passing on information that cost hundreds of lives. The last two members of the ring, Anthony Blunt and John Cairncross, went undetected for many years.[17]

While some spies, like the Cambridge Five, are motivated by ideology, others, like FBI agent Robert Hanssen and CIA operative Harold Nicholson, were looking for profit. In 1997, Nicholson was convicted of selling U.S. intelligence to Russia for $180,000 and was sentenced to 23.5 years imprisonment; Nicholson was the highest ranking CIA official ever convicted for spying for a foreign country. Hanssen sold American secrets to Russia for more than $1.4 million in cash and diamonds; he is currently serving a life sentence.[18]

Government employees in a position of trust may offer to misappropriate state secrets for a payoff from a foreign government. One of the most infamous of these cases, that of CIA double agent Aldrich Ames, is set out in the Profiles in Crime feature.

organization, or society that is considered secret or confidential without the permission of the holder of the information. Espionage involves obtaining the information illegally by covertly entering the area where the information is stored, secretly photographing forbidden areas, or subverting through threat or payoff people who know the information and will divulge it through subterfuge.[16]

Espionage is typically associated with spying on potential or actual enemies, by a foreign agent who is working for his or her nation's intelligence service. With the end of the Cold War, the threat of espionage seemed reduced until 2010, when a major Russian spy group was unraveled and 10 people arrested. These were sleeper agents who had spent decades fitting seamlessly in their new environment. Neighbors were shocked to find out that "Richard Murphy" and "Cynthia Murphy" were actually spies named Vladimir Guryev and Lydia Guryev, while "Michael Zottoli" and "Patricia Mills" were in reality Mikhail Kutsik and Natalia Pereverzeva, agents of the Russian Federation. The case was settled when the Russians were exchanged for four American spies being held in Russian prisons.

Not all spies are foreign nationals. There are numerous cases of homegrown spies who are motivated by misguided altruism or belief. Perhaps the most famous international case involved a group of five upper-crust students recruited

Industrial Espionage   The concept of espionage has been extended to spying involving corporations, referred to as industrial espionage. This involves such unethical or illegal activities as bribing employees to reveal trade secrets such as computer codes or product formulas. The traditional methods of industrial espionage include recruiting agents and inserting them into the target company or breaking into an office to take equipment and information. It can also involve surveillance and spying on commercial organizations in order to determine the direction of their new product line or even what bid they intend to make on a government contract. Such knowledge can provide vast profits when it allows a competitor to save large sums on product development or to win an undeserved contract by underbidding.[19]

ALDRICH HAZEN AMES

AP Images/Mark Wilson

Aldrich Hazen Ames was arrested by the FBI in Arlington, Virginia, on espionage charges on February 24, 1994. At the time of his arrest, Ames was a 31-year veteran of the Central Intelligence Agency (CIA) who had been spying for the Russians since 1985. Arrested with him was his wife, Rosario Ames, who had aided and abetted his espionage activities.

Ames was a CIA case officer who spoke Russian and specialized in the Russian intelligence services, including the KGB, the USSR's foreign intelligence service. His initial overseas assignment was in Ankara, Turkey, where he targeted Russian intelligence officers for recruitment. Later, he worked in New York City and Mexico City. On April 16, 1985, while assigned to the CIA's Soviet/East European Division at CIA Headquarters in Langley, Virginia, he secretly volunteered to KGB officers at the USSR Embassy in Washington, D.C. Shortly thereafter, the KGB

paid him $50,000. During the summer of 1985, Ames met several times with a Russian diplomat to whom he passed classified information about CIA and FBI human sources, as well as technical operations targeting the Soviet Union. In December 1985, Ames met with a Moscow-based KGB officer in Bogota, Colombia. In July 1986, Ames was transferred to Rome.

In Rome, Ames continued his meetings with the KGB, including a Russian diplomat assigned to Rome and a Moscow-based KGB officer. At the conclusion of his assignment in Rome, Ames received instructions from the KGB regarding clandestine contacts in the Washington, D.C., area, where he would next be assigned. In the four years after he volunteered, the KGB paid Ames $1.88 million.

Upon his return to Washington, D.C., in 1989, Ames continued to pass classified documents to the KGB, using "dead drops" or prearranged hiding places where he would leave the documents to be picked up later by KGB officers from the USSR Embassy in Washington. In return, the KGB left money and instructions for Ames, usually in other "dead drops."

In the meantime, the CIA and FBI learned that Russian officials who had been recruited by them were being arrested and executed. These human sources had provided critical intelligence information about the USSR, which was used by U.S. policymakers in determining U.S. foreign policy. Following analytical reviews and receipt of information about Ames's unexplained wealth, the FBI opened an investigation in May 1993.

FBI special agents and investigative specialists conducted intensive physical and electronic surveillance of Ames during a 10-month investigation. Searches of Ames's residence revealed documents and other information linking Ames to the Russian foreign intelligence service. On October 13, 1993, investigative specialists observed a chalk mark Ames made on a mailbox confirming to the Russians his intention to meet them in Bogota, Colombia. On November 1, special agents observed him and, separately, his Russian handler in Bogota. When Ames planned foreign travel, including a trip to Moscow, as part of his official duties, a plan to arrest him was approved.

Following guilty pleas by both Ames and his wife on April 28, 1994, Ames was sentenced to incarceration for life without the possibility of parole. Rosario Ames was sentenced on October 20, 1994, to 63 months in prison. Ames also forfeited his assets to the United States, and $547,000 was turned over to the Justice Department's Victims Assistance Fund. Ames is serving his sentence in the federal prison system. Rosario Ames completed her sentence and was released.

Critical Thinking

How can you explain the criminal motivation of someone like Aldrich Ames? Which theory of crime causation would best explain his treasonous behavior?

SOURCE: FBI, "Famous Cases and Criminals: Aldrich Hazen Ames," http://www.fbi.gov/about-us/history/famous-cases/aldrich-hazen-ames/ (accessed May 2014).

Foreign Industrial Espionage In 2014, five Chinese men were indicted for stealing thousands of "sensitive, internal communications" from U.S. companies, including Alcoa, United States Steel Corporation, and Westinghouse.[20] This international hacking case shows that not all corporate espionage is home-grown, and some attacks have been carried out by foreign agents. A report of the National

Counterintelligence Center lists biotechnology, aerospace, telecommunications, computer software, transportation, advanced materials, energy research, defense, and semiconductor companies as the top targets for foreign economic espionage.[21]

Industrial espionage by foreign agents' efforts have hurt the United States by eroding the U.S. military advantage by enabling foreign militaries to acquire sophisticated capabilities that might otherwise have taken years to develop. Such efforts also undercut the U.S. economy by making it possible for foreign firms to gain a competitive economic edge over U.S. companies.

Many foreign agents did not come to the United States specifically to engage in espionage, but when an opportunity arose they jumped on the chance in order to satisfy their desire for profits, for academic or scientific acclaim, or out of a sense of patriotism to their home countries.

A number of factors have combined to facilitate private-sector technology theft. Globalization, while generating major gains for the U.S. economy, has given foreigners unprecedented access to U.S. firms and to sensitive technologies. There has also been a proliferation of devices that have made it easy for private-sector experts to illegally retrieve, store, and transfer massive amounts of information, including trade secrets and proprietary data; such devices are increasingly common in the workplace.

In addition to private citizens conducting espionage, foreign government organizations also mount their own operations, including:

- Targeting U.S. firms for technology that would strengthen their foreign defense capabilities
- Posting personnel at U.S. military bases to collect classified information to bolster military modernization efforts
- Employing commercial firms in the United States in a covert effort to target and acquire U.S. technology
- Recruiting students, professors, scientists, and researchers to engage in technology collection
- Making direct requests for classified, sensitive, or export-controlled information via personal contacts, telephone, email, fax, and other forms of communication
- Forming ventures with U.S. firms in the hope of placing collectors in proximity to sensitive technologies or else establishing foreign research

Foreign companies seek entrée into U.S. firms and other targeted institutions by pursuing business relationships that provide access to sensitive or classified information, technologies, or projects:

state political crime Political crime that arises from the efforts of the state to either maintain governmental power or to uphold the race, class, and gender advantages of those who support the government. It is possible to divide state political crimes into five varieties: (1) political corruption, (2) illegal domestic surveillance, (3) human rights violations, (4) state violence such as torture, illegal imprisonment, police violence and use of deadly force, and (5) state corporate crime committed by individuals who abuse their state authority or who fail to exercise it when working with people and organizations in the private sector.

- *Conferences, conventions, and trade shows.* These public venues offer opportunities for foreign adversaries to gain access to U.S. information and experts in dual-use and sensitive technologies.
- *Official foreign visitors and exploitation of joint research.* Foreign government organizations, including intelligence services, use official visits to U.S. government and cleared defense contractor facilities, as well as joint research projects between foreign and U.S. entities, to target and collect information.
- *Foreign targeting of U.S. visitors overseas.* Whether traveling for business or personal reasons, U.S. travelers overseas—businesspeople, U.S. government employees, and contractors—are routinely targeted by foreign collectors, especially if they are assessed as having access to some sensitive information. Some U.S. allies engage in this practice, as do less friendly powers such as Russia and China. Targeting takes many forms: exploitation of electronic media and devices, surreptitious entry into hotel rooms, aggressive surveillance, and attempts to set up sexual or romantic entanglements.
- *Open source information.* Foreign collectors are aware that much U.S. economic and technological information is available in professional journals, social networking and other public websites, and the media.[22]

Legal Controls   Until 1996, there was no federal statute that explicitly penalized industrial espionage. Recognizing the increasingly important role that intellectual property plays in the well-being of the American economy, Congress enacted the Economic Espionage Act (EEA) of 1996, which criminalizes the theft of trade secrets. The EEA actually contains two separate provisions, one that penalizes foreign agents from stealing American trade secrets and one directed at domestic spying.

Convictions of foreign agents under the Economic Espionage Act have been relatively rare. It was not until 2006 that the first conviction occurred, when two Chinese Nationals, Fei Ye and Ming Zhong, pleaded guilty to stealing secret information from Sun Microsystems and Transmeta Corporation.[23]

State Political Crime

LO4   List the components of state political crime

While some political crimes are committed by people who oppose the state, others are perpetrated by state authorities against the people they are supposed to serve; this is referred to as **state political crime**. Critical criminologists argue that rather than being committed by disaffected people, a great deal of political crime arises from the efforts of the state to either maintain governmental power or to uphold the race, class, and gender advantages of those who support the government. In industrial society, the state will do everything to protect the property rights of the wealthy while opposing the real interests of the poor. They might even go to war to support the capitalist classes who need the wealth and resources of other nations. The desire for natural resources such as rubber, oil, and metals was one of the primary reasons for Japan's invasion of China and other Eastern nations that sparked their entry into World War II.

Using Torture

LO5 Debate the use and misuse of torture

On February 23, 2007, Osama Hassan Mustafa Nasr, an Egyptian cleric, made worldwide headlines when he claimed that he had been kidnapped in Italy by American CIA agents and sent to Egypt for interrogation as part of the CIA's "extraordinary rendition." Nasr claimed, "I was subjected to the worst kind of torture in Egyptian prisons. I have scars of torture all over my body." Italy indicted 26 Americans and five Italian agents accused of seizing him and sending him to Egypt without trial or due process.[24]

Of all state political crimes, the use of **torture** to gain information from suspected political criminals is perhaps the most notorious.

Can the torture of a suspected terrorist determined to destroy the government and harm innocent civilians ever be permissible or is it always an example of state-sponsored political crime? While most people loathe the thought of torturing anyone, some experts argue that torture can sometimes be justified in what they call the **ticking bomb scenario**. Suppose the government found out that a captured terrorist knew the whereabouts of a dangerous explosive device that was set to go off and kill thousands of innocent people. Would it be permissible to engage in the use of torture on this single suspect if it would save the population of a city?

The ticking bomb scenario has appeal. Famed social commentator and legal scholar Alan Dershowitz argues that the "vast majority" of Americans would expect law enforcement agents to use any means necessary to obtain information needed to prevent a terror attack. To protect against abuse, Dershowitz proposes the creation of a "torture warrant" that can only be issued by a judge in cases where (a) there is an absolute need to obtain immediate information in order to save lives and (b) there is probable cause that the suspect has such information and is unwilling to reveal it to law enforcement agents. The suspect would be given immunity from prosecution based on information elicited by the torture; it would only be to save lives. The warrant would limit the torture to nonlethal means, such as sterile needles being inserted beneath the nails to cause excruciating pain without endangering life.[25]

Not everyone agrees with Dershowitz.[26] Opponents of torture believe that even imminent danger does not justify state violence. There is a danger that such state-sponsored violence would become calculated and premeditated;

AN ETHICAL DILEMMA

thinking like a criminologist

TORURE OR NOT?

As a criminologist, your specialty is terrorism, so it comes as no surprise that the director of the CIA asks you to draw up a protocol setting out the rules for the use of torture with suspected terrorists. The reason for his request is that a series of new articles has exposed the agency's practice of sending suspected terrorists to friendly nations that are less squeamish about using torture. Shocking photo evidence of torture from detention facilities at the Guantanamo base in Cuba support these charges. Legal scholars have argued that these tactics violate both international treaties and domestic statutes prohibiting torture. Some maintain that the U.S. Constitution limits the authority of an executive agency like the CIA to act against foreigners abroad and also limits physical coercion by the government under the Fifth Amendment due process and self-incrimination clauses and the Eighth Amendment prohibition against cruel and unusual punishments. Legally, it is impermissible for United States authorities to engage in indefinite detention or torture regardless of the end, the place, or the victim.

Write a memo to the CIA director outlining the protocol you recommend for the use of torture with suspected terrorists. In your document, address when torture should be used, who it should be used on, and what tortures you recommend using. Of course, if you believe the use of torture is always unethical, you could let the director know why you have reached this conclusion.

torturers would have to be trained, ready, and in place for the ticking bomb argument to work. We couldn't be running around looking for torturers with a bomb set to go off, could we? Because torturers would be part of the government bureaucracy, there is no way to ensure that they would only use their skills in certain morally justifiable cases.[27] What happens if a superior officer tells them to torture someone, but they believe the order is unjustified? Should they follow

torture An act that causes severe pain or suffering, whether physical or mental, that is intentionally inflicted on a person for such purposes as obtaining a confession, punishing them for a crime they may have committed, or intimidating or coercing them into a desired action.

ticking bomb scenario A scenario that some experts argue in which torture can perhaps be justified if the government discovers that a captured terrorist knows the whereabouts of a dangerous explosive device that is set to go off and kill thousands of innocent people.

orders or risk a court martial for being disobedient? Furthermore, there is very little empirical evidence suggesting that torture provides any real benefits and much more that suggests it can create serious problems. It can damage civil rights and democratic institutions and cause the general public to have sympathy for the victims of torture no matter their evil intent.[28]

The Waterboarding Controversy Can a bright line be drawn between what is considered torture and what constitutes firm but legal interrogation methods? This issue made headlines when it was revealed in 2007 that the CIA made routine use of the waterboarding technique while interrogating suspected terrorists.[29] Waterboarding involves immobilizing a person on his or her back, with the head inclined downward, and pouring water over the face and into the breathing passages. It produces an immediate gag reflex and an experience akin to drowning; the subject believes his or her death is imminent.

The use of waterboarding is controversial because there seems to be no agreement on whether it is torture or a relatively harmless instrument of interrogation. While official U.S. government policy and government doctrine is vehemently opposed to torture, it has condoned harsh interrogation techniques that combine physical and psychological tactics, including head slapping, waterboarding, and exposure to extreme cold. Waterboarding even became an issue during the 2008 presidential campaign when Senator John McCain, a former prisoner of war who experienced torture firsthand in a North Vietnamese prison camp, told the press, "All I can say is that it was used in the Spanish Inquisition, it was used in Pol Pot's genocide in Cambodia, and there are reports that it is being used against Buddhist monks today. They should know what it is. It is not a complicated procedure. It is torture."[30]

TERRORISM

LO6 Distinguish among terrorists, insurgents, guerillas, and revolutionaries

In September 2012, the U.S. Ambassador to Libya J. Christopher Stevens and three other Americans were killed in an attack on the U.S. consulate in Benghazi. At first it was suspected that the deaths were the result of rioting prompted by an American-produced film that insulted the prophet Muhammad. Later it appeared that the attack was planned, because the attackers used military-grade weapons, including RPGs (rocket-propelled grenades), and knew details of the consulate and a safe

terrorism The illegal use of force against innocent people to achieve a political objective.

house where U.S. personnel fled after the attack began. Some authorities believe the attack was coordinated by elements of the former Gaddafi government while others claim that the raid was planned by a Libyan-based terrorist group with links to al-Qaeda.[31]

The political crime that many people are most concerned with is terrorism, and the remainder of this chapter focuses on the history, nature, and extent of terrorism and the methods being employed for its control. Despite its long history, it is often difficult to precisely define terrorism (from the Latin *terrere*, which means to frighten) and to separate terrorist acts from interpersonal crimes of violence. For example, if a group robs a bank to obtain funds for its revolutionary struggles, should the act be treated as terrorism or as a common bank robbery? In this instance, defining a crime as terrorism depends on the kind of legal response the act evokes from those in power. To be considered **terrorism**, which is a political crime, an act must carry with it the intent to disrupt and change the government and must not be merely a common-law crime committed for greed or egotism.

Because of its complexity, an all-encompassing definition of terrorism is difficult to formulate, although most experts agree that it generally involves the illegal use of force against innocent people to achieve a political objective. According to the U.S. State Department, the term *terrorism* means premeditated, politically motivated violence perpetrated against noncombatant targets by subnational groups or clandestine agents, usually intended to influence an audience. The term *international terrorism* means terrorism involving citizens or the territory of more than one country. A terrorist group is any group practicing, or that has significant subgroups that practice, international terrorism.[32] Exhibit 11.2 sets out a number of definitions of terrorism drafted or used by prominent governmental agencies or organizations.

Terrorism usually involves a type of political crime that emphasizes violence as a mechanism to promote change. Whereas some political criminals sell secrets, spy, and the like, terrorists systematically murder and destroy or threaten such violence to terrorize individuals, groups, communities, or governments into conceding to the terrorists' political demands.[33] Because terrorists lack large armies and formidable weapons, their use of subterfuge, secrecy, and hit-and-run tactics is designed to give them a psychological advantage and the power to neutralize the physical superiority of their opponents.

However, it may be erroneous to assume that all terrorists have political goals. Some may try to bring about what they consider to be social reform—for example, by attacking women wearing fur coats or sabotaging property during a labor dispute. Terrorism must also be distinguished from conventional warfare, because it requires secrecy and clandestine operations to exert social control over large populations.[34] So terrorist activities may be aimed at promoting an ideology other than political change.

EXHIBIT 11.2

Definitions of Terrorism

League of Nations Convention (1937)

All criminal acts directed against a State and intended or calculated to create a state of terror in the minds of particular persons or a group of persons or the general public.

United Nations Resolution Language (1999)

1. *Strongly condemns* all acts, methods and practices of terrorism as criminal and unjustifiable, wherever and by whomsoever committed;

2. *Reiterates* that criminal acts intended or calculated to provoke a state of terror in the general public, a group of persons or particular persons for political purposes are in any circumstance unjustifiable, whatever the considerations of a political, philosophical, ideological, racial, ethnic, religious or other nature that may be invoked to justify them. (GA Res. 51/210, "Measures to Eliminate International Terrorism.")

Short Legal Definition Proposed by A. P. Schmid to United Nations Crime Branch (1992)

Act of Terrorism = Peacetime Equivalent of War Crime

Academic Consensus Definition Used by the United Nations

Terrorism is an anxiety-inspiring method of repeated violent action, employed by (semi-) clandestine individual, group or state actors, for idiosyncratic, criminal or political reasons, whereby—in contrast to assassination—the direct targets of violence are not the main targets. The immediate human victims of violence are generally chosen randomly (targets of opportunity) or selectively (representative or symbolic targets) from a target population, and serve as message generators. Threat- and violence-based communication processes between terrorist (organization), (imperiled) victims, and main targets are used to manipulate the main target (audience[s]), turning it into a target of terror, a target of demands, or a target of attention, depending on whether intimidation, coercion, or propaganda is primarily sought.

United States Department of State

The term "terrorism" means premeditated, politically motivated violence perpetrated against noncombatant targets by subnational groups or clandestine agents, usually intended to influence an audience.

The term "international terrorism" means terrorism involving citizens or the territory of more than one country.

The term "terrorist group" means any group practicing, or that has significant subgroups that practice, international terrorism.

SOURCES: *Patterns of Global Terrorism* (Washington: Department of State) http://www.state.gov/j/ct/rls/pgtrpt/ (accessed June 2014); National Institute of Justice, Terrorism, http://www.nij.gov/topics/crime/terrorism/ (accessed June 2014); Alex Schmid, *Routledge Handbook of Terrorism Research* (London: Routledge, 2013).

Terrorist and Guerilla

The word *terrorist* is often used interchangeably with the word *guerilla*, but the terms are quite different. **Guerilla** comes from the Spanish term meaning "little war," which developed out of the Spanish rebellion against French troops after Napoleon's 1808 invasion of the Iberian Peninsula.[35] Terrorists have an urban focus. Operating in small bands, or cadres, of three to five members, they target the property or persons of their enemy, such as members of the ruling class.[36] However, terrorists may not have political ambitions, and their actions may be aimed at stifling or intimidating other groups who oppose their religious, social, or economic views. For example, terrorists who kill abortion providers in order to promote their "pro-life" agenda are not aiming for regime change. Guerillas, on the other hand, are armed military bands, typically located in rural areas, that attack military, police, and government officials in an effort to destabilize the existing government. Their organizations can grow quite large and eventually take the form of a conventional military force. Some guerilla bands infiltrate urban areas (urban guerillas). For the most part, guerillas are a type of quasi-military organization.

Terrorist and Insurgent

An insurgency is a political movement that may use terror tactics to achieve their goals. **Insurgents** wish to confront the existing government for control of all or a portion of its territory, or force political concessions in sharing political power by competing with the opposition government for popular support.[37] What makes the insurgent unique is that they have the luxury of receiving aid from neighboring

guerilla The term means "little war" and developed out of the Spanish rebellion against French troops after Napoleon's 1808 invasion of the Iberian Peninsula. Guerillas are an informal military band seeking to overthrow the government.

insurgents The typical goal of an insurgency is to confront the existing government for control of all or a portion of its territory, or force political concessions in sharing political power. While terrorists may operate in small bands with a narrow focus, insurgents represent a popular movement and may also seek external support from other nations to bring pressure on the government.

Fighters of the Islamic State in Iraq and Syria (ISIS) are shown leading Iraqi soldiers captured in June 2014. The militant insurgents have carried out mass executions, captured major cities, and created havoc in their ongoing struggle to topple the governments of Syria and Iraq. Their immediate goal is to combine those nations—or at least the Sunni-controlled parts—into a caliphate operating under strict sharia law. Also known as the Islamic State in Iraq and the Levant or the Islamic State in Iraq and al-Sham, the group's ultimate goal is to take over much of the Middle East, including Israel, southern Turkey, Jordan, and Lebanon and remove all Western influence.

AP Images/Militant Website, File

holds control of the land, or between the existing government and local groups over issues of ideology and power. Historically, the American Revolution may be considered an example of a struggle between nationalistic groups and an imperialistic overseas government. Classic examples of ideological rebellions are the French Revolution, which pitted the middle class and urban poor against the aristocracy, and the Russian Revolution of 1917, during which the Czarist government was toppled by the Bolsheviks. More recent ideological revolutions have occurred in China, Cuba, Nicaragua, and Chile, to name but a few.

While some revolutions (such as the American, French, and Russian) rely on armed force, terror activities, and violence, others can be nonviolent, depending on large urban protests and threats. Such was the case when the Shah Mohammad Reza Pahlavi was toppled in Iran in the 1979 revolution that transformed Iran into an Islamic republic under the rule of Ayatollah Ruhollah Khomeini. Similar events unfolded in Egypt in early 2011 in the effort to topple the government of Hosni Mubarak that had been in power for 30 years.

Concept Summary 11.1 describes the components of various types of radical political groups.

A BRIEF HISTORY OF TERRORISM

Acts of terrorism have been known throughout history. The assassination of Julius Caesar on March 15, 44 BCE is considered an act of terrorism. Terrorism became widespread at the end of the Middle Ages, when political leaders were frequently subject to assassination by their enemies.

Religious Roots

The first terrorist activities were committed by members of minority religious groups who engaged in violence to (a) gain the right to practice their own form of religion, (b) establish the supremacy of their own religion over others, or (c) meet the requirements of the bloodthirsty gods they worshipped.[40]

In some instances, a conquered people used force and violence to maintain their right to worship in their own faith.

sympathizers, allowing them to base their insurgency outside the target nation, thereby protecting them from their enemies. For example, Taliban members took shelter in Pakistan when the U.S. military drove them out of Afghanistan. Insurgencies may attract recruits who do not actually live in the disputed area but are sympathetic to the cause. In 2014, insurgents from ISIS (the Islamic State in Iraq and Syria) surged into Iraq from Syria, routed the Iraqi army, and occupied major cities such as Mosul. ISIS is a violent Sunni extremist group that has the goal of creating a caliphate, based on a very conservative Islamic religious code, that spans Sunni-dominated sections of Iraq and Syria. ISIS is made up of Islamic fighters from around the world, highly trained and motivated. They were able to launch their insurgency after organizing outside of Iraq and then filtering through the porous border with Syria where they had played a major role in the ongoing civil war.[38]

Insurgents tend to live isolated and stressful lives and enjoy varying levels of public support.[39] Although insurgents may engage in violence, they also may use nonviolent methods or political tactics. For example, they may set up food distribution centers and schools in areas in which they gain control in order to provide the population with needed services while contrasting their benevolent rule with the government's incompetence and corruption.

Terrorist and Revolutionary

A revolution (from the Latin *revolutio*, "a revolving," and *revolvere*, "turn, roll back") is generally seen as a civil war fought between nationalists and a sovereign power that

	Terrorist	Guerilla	Insurgent	Revolutionary
Description	Groups who engage in premeditated, politically motivated violence perpetrated against noncombatant targets.	Armed groups operating in rural areas who attack the military, the police, and other government officials.	Groups who engage in armed uprising, or revolt against an established civil or political authority.	Engages in civil war against sovereign power that holds control of the land.
Examples	Al-Qaeda, Hamas	Mao's People's Liberation Army, Ho Chi Minh's Viet Cong	Iraqi insurgent groups	American Revolution, French Revolution, Russian Revolution
Goals	Personal, criminal, or political gain or change.	Replace or overthrow existing government.	Win over population by showing government's incompetence. Force government into political concessions and/or power sharing.	Gain independence or oust existing government or monarchy.
Methods	Small, clandestine cells who use systematic violence for purpose of intimidation.	Use unconventional warfare and mobile tactics. May grow large and use tactics similar to conventional military force.	May use violent (bombings and kidnappings) or nonviolent means (food distribution centers and creating schools).	Can use violent armed conflict or nonviolent methods such as Gandhi used in India.

Zealots, Hebrew warrior groups, were active during the Roman occupation of Palestine during the first century CE. A subgroup of the Zealots, the Sciari (literally translated as "daggermen"), were so named after the long curved knives they favored as a weapon to assassinate Romans or their sympathizers. The Zealots carried out their attacks in broad daylight, typically with witnesses around, in order to send a message that the Roman authorities and those Jews who collaborated with them would not be safe. Ironically, this tactic is still being used by contemporary terrorists. The Zealots and Sciari led the revolt in 66 CE against Roman occupation of the Holy Land, during which they occupied the fortress of Masada. Here they held out for more than seven months before engaging in mass suicide rather than surrender to the Roman legions. The revolt ended badly and the Romans destroyed the Jewish temple and sent the population into exile.

Some religious terrorists want to promote the supremacy of their own sect over a rival group. The (Shi'ite) Muslim Order of the Assassins (*assassin* literally means "hashish-eater," a reference to the commonly held belief that gang members engaged in acts of ritual intoxication and smoked hashish just prior to undertaking their missions) was active in Persia, Syria, and Palestine from 1090 to 1272, killing a great number of their enemies, mainly Sunnis whom they considered apostates, but also Christians who were then the rulers of the kingdom of Jerusalem.[41] The Assassins also were prone to stabbing their victims in an effort to spread their vision of Islam, and carried out missions in public places on holy days in order to publicize their cause. Successful assassinations guaranteed them a place in heaven.

Another form of religious terror is inspired by the requirements of belief. Some religious beliefs have focused on violence, the gods demanding the death of nonbelievers. In India, members of the Thugee cult (from which the modern term *thug* was derived) were devoted to Kali, the goddess of death and destruction. The thugs believed each murder prevented Kali's arrival for 1,000 years, thus sparing the nation from her death and destruction. The thugs traveled in gangs of up to 100 with each member having a defined role—some lured unwary travelers, while others strangled the chosen victim. The gang used secret argot and jargon, which only they could understand, and signs so that members could recognize each other even in the most remote parts of India. Cult members may have killed hundreds of thousands of victims over a 300-year span. They would attach themselves to travelers and when the opportunity arose, strangle them with a noose around their necks, steal their money, and bury their bodies. The killings were highly ritualistic and involved religious rites and prayers. By the mid-nineteenth century the British made it a policy to end Thugee activities, hanged nearly 4,000, and all but eradicated the cult. Thugees represented the last serious

zealots The original Zealots were Hebrew warrior groups active during the Roman occupation of Palestine during the first century BCE. Today the term commonly refers to a fanatical or over-idealistic follower of a political or religious cause.

religion-inspired terrorist threat until the emergence of Islamic terrorism in the 1980s.

Political Roots

When rulers had absolute power, terrorist acts were viewed as one of the only means of gaining political rights. At times European states encouraged terrorist acts against their enemies. In the sixteenth century, Queen Elizabeth I empowered her naval leaders, including famed captains John Hawkins and Francis Drake, to attack the Spanish fleet and take prizes. These privateers would have been considered pirates had they not operated with government approval. American privateers attacked the British during the Revolutionary War and the War of 1812 and were considered heroes for their actions against the English navy.

The term *terrorist* first became popular during the French Revolution. Use of the word *terrorism* began in 1793 in reference to the **Reign of Terror** initiated by the revolutionary government during which agents of the Committee of Public Safety and the National Convention were referred to as terrorists. In response, royalists and opponents of the Revolution employed terrorist tactics in resistance to the Revolutionists. The widespread use of the guillotine is an infamous reminder of the revolutionary violence; urban mobs demanded blood, and many government officials and aristocrats were beheaded in gruesome public spectacles. From the fall of the Bastille on July 14, 1789, until July 1794, thousands suspected of counterrevolutionary activity were killed on the guillotine. Here again, the relative nature of political crime is documented: most victims of the French Reign of Terror were revolutionaries who had been denounced by rival factions, whereas thousands of the hated nobility lived in relative tranquility. The end of the terror was signaled by the death of its prime mover, Maximilien Robespierre, on July 28, 1794, as the result of a successful plot to end his rule. He was executed on the same guillotine to which he had sent almost 20,000 people.

In the hundred years following the French Revolution, terrorism continued to be a political tool around the world. Terrorist acts became the preferred method of political action for national groups in the early years of the twentieth century. In Eastern Europe, the Internal Macedonian Revolutionary Organization campaigned against the Turkish government, which controlled its homeland (Macedonia became part of the former Yugoslavia). Similarly, the protest of the Union of Death Society, or Black Hand, against

the Austro-Hungarian Empire's control of Serbia led to the group's assassination of Archduke Franz Ferdinand, which started World War I. Russia was the scene of left-wing revolutionary activity, which killed the czar in 1917 and gave birth to the Marxist state.

After the war ended, the Treaty of Versailles restructured Europe and broke up the Austro-Hungarian Empire. The result was a hodgepodge of new nations controlled by majority ethnic groups. Self-determination was limited to European nations and ethnic groups and denied to others, especially the colonial possessions of the major European powers, creating bitterness and setting the stage for the long conflicts of the anticolonial period. The Irish Republican Army, established around 1916, steadily battled British forces from 1919 to 1923, culminating in the Republic of Ireland gaining independence.

Between the World Wars, right-wing terrorism existed in Germany, Spain, and Italy. One source of tension, according to author Michael Kellogg, was the virulently anti-Communist exiles who fled Russia after the 1917 Revolution (called White Russians) and took up residence in Germany and other Western nations. According to Kellogg, between 1920 and 1923, Adolf Hitler was deeply influenced by the Aufbau (Reconstruction), the émigrés' organization. Members of the Aufbau allied with the Nazis to overthrow the legitimate German government and thwart German communists from seizing power. The White Russians deep-seated anti-Semitism may have inspired Hitler to go public with his campaign to kill the European Jews, prompting both the Holocaust and the invasion of Russia, which spelled the eventual doom of Hitler and National Socialism.[42]

During World War II, resistance to the occupying German troops was common throughout Europe. The Germans considered the resistors to be terrorists, but the rest of the world considers them heroes. Meanwhile, in Palestine, Jewish terrorist groups—the Haganah, Irgun, and Stern Gang, whose leaders included Menachem Begin, who later became Israel's prime minister—waged war against the British to force them to allow Jewish survivors of the Holocaust to settle in their traditional homeland. Today, of course, many of these alleged terrorists are considered freedom fighters who laid down their lives for a just cause.

After the war, Arab nationalists felt that they had been betrayed. Believing they were promised postwar independence, they were doubly disappointed—first when the French and British were given authority over their lands, and then especially when the British allowed Zionist immigration into Palestine in keeping with a promise contained in the Balfour Declaration.

Since the end of World War II, terrorism has accelerated its development into a major component of contemporary conflict. Primarily in use immediately after the war as a subordinate element of anticolonial insurgencies, it expanded beyond that role. In the service of various ideologies and aspirations, terrorism sometimes supplanted other forms of conflict completely. It became a far-reaching weapon capable

Reign of Terror The origin of the term *terrorism*, the French Revolution's Reign of Terror began in 1793 and was initiated by the revolutionary government during which agents of the Committee of Public Safety and the National Convention were referred to as terrorists.

of effects no less global than the intercontinental bomber or missile. It has also proven to be a significant tool of diplomacy and international power for states inclined to use it.

CONTEMPORARY FORMS OF TERRORISM

LO7 List the various forms of terrorism

Today the term *terrorism* encompasses many different behaviors and goals. Some of the more common forms are briefly described here.

Revolutionary Terrorists

Revolutionary terrorists use violence to frighten those in power and their supporters in order to replace the existing government with a regime that holds acceptable political or religious views. Terrorist actions such as kidnapping, assassination, and bombing are designed to draw repressive responses from governments trying to defend themselves. These responses help revolutionaries to expose, through the skilled use of media coverage, the government's inhumane nature. The original reason for the government's harsh response may be lost as the effect of counterterrorist activities is felt by uninvolved people.

Jemaah Islamiyah, an Indonesian terrorist organization aligned with al-Qaeda, is believed to be intent on driving away foreign tourists and ruining the nation's economy so they can usurp the government and set up a pan-Islamic nation in Indonesia and neighboring Malaysia.

Political Terrorists

Political terrorism is directed at people or groups who oppose the terrorists' political ideology or whom the terrorists define as "outsiders" who must be destroyed. Political terrorists may not want to replace the existing government but to shape it so that it accepts the terrorists' views.

Right-Wing Political Groups Domestic terrorists in the United States can be found across the political spectrum. On the right, they tend to be heavily armed groups organized around such themes as white supremacy, anti-abortion, militant tax resistance, and religious revisionism. Identified groups have included, at one time or another, the Aryan Republican Army, the Aryan Nation, the Posse Comitatus, and the Ku Klux Klan. These groups want to shape U.S. government policy over a range of matters, including ending abortion rights, extending the right to bear arms, and eliminating federal taxation. Anti-abortion groups have demonstrated at abortion clinics, attacked clients, bombed offices, and killed doctors who perform abortions. On October 23, 1998, Dr. Barnett Slepian was shot by a sniper and killed in his Buffalo, New York, home; he was one of a growing number of abortion providers believed to be the victims of terrorists who ironically claim to be "pro-life." Although unlikely to topple the government, these individualistic acts of terror are difficult to predict or control. On April 19, 1995, 168 people were killed during the Oklahoma City bombing, the most severe example of political terrorism in the United States so far.

Left-Wing Political Groups During the turmoil of the 1960s, a number of left-wing political groups emerged to challenge the existing power structure. Some, such as the Black Panther Party—founded in 1966 in Oakland, California, by Bobby Seale and Huey Newton—demanded the right to control community schools, police, and public assistance programs. While many of their activities were productive, such as sponsoring breakfast programs and medical clinics in poor neighborhoods, they also began to openly carry rifles and shotguns while patrolling areas where the Oakland police were rumored to be harassing the community's black citizens. The Panthers' confrontational style led to clashes with police, shootings, and arrests. Because its leaders were faced with criminal charges of varying degrees, the Black Panthers steadily eroded.

Another influential 1960s group, the Students for a Democratic Society (SDS) was founded in Chicago in 1962 and was active on college campuses throughout the sixties protesting the United States' involvement in Vietnam. Though the SDS was nonviolent, a splinter group known as the Weathermen utilized terror tactics to achieve their goals. They were involved in a number of bombings at corporation headquarters and federal institutions, though they typically sent out warnings to evacuate the buildings. The group lost influence when on March 6, 1970, a bomb accidentally exploded in one of their safe houses in New York City. The detonations were so powerful that they collapsed the three-story house, killing three members. The Weathermen disbanded in 1977.

Eco-Terrorism Rebecca Rubin lived a quiet life while working as a nanny and helping care for animals. But this seemingly peaceful woman was actually on the lam from federal authorities, having committed numerous crimes when she was an active member of the underground Earth Liberation Front and Animal Liberation Front. Among her various eco-terror activities:

- In November 1997, she freed 400 wild horses from a U.S. Bureau of Land Management corral while the place was set ablaze.
- In 1998, she and others carried gasoline and timing devices for an attempted arson at a ski resort in Vail, Colorado. There they performed reconnaissance for an arson that was intended as a protest against expansion into pristine wilderness.

- Also in 1998, Rubin took part in an attempt to set fire to the headquarters of U.S. Forest Industries in Medford, Oregon, which was eventually burned by others in the group.
- In 2001, she helped release horses from a BLM horse and burro corral at Litchfield, California.

Rubin surrendered to authorities in 2013, pleaded guilty to arson charges, and received a five- to seven-year prison sentence.[43]

Rebecca Rubin is typical of people involved in left-leaning domestic terror groups that are committed to the protection of the environment. Of these groups, the Earth Liberation Front (ELF) is perhaps the best known. Founded in 1992 in Brighton, England, by members of the Earth First! environmental movement, ELF has been active since 1994 throughout the world, including the United States. Operating in secret, ELF cells have conducted a series of actions intent on damaging individuals or corporations that they consider a threat to the environment. On October 19, 1998, ELF members claimed responsibility for fires that were set atop Vail Mountain, a luxurious ski resort in Colorado, claiming that the action was designed to stop the resort from expanding into animal habitats (especially that of the mountain lynx); the fires caused an estimated $12 million in damages. On August 22, 2003, members of ELF claimed responsibility for fires that destroyed about a dozen sport utility vehicles at a Chevrolet dealership in West Covina, California.[44] Fires have also been set in government labs where animal research is conducted. Spikes have been driven into trees to prevent logging in fragile areas. Members have conducted arson attacks on property ranging from a Nike shop in a mall north of Minneapolis to new homes on Long Island, New York. On February 7, 2004, ELF group members targeted construction equipment at a 30-acre development site in Charlottesville, Virginia.[45] On March 2, 2008, ELF is believed to have burned a row of luxury homes in Seattle, causing $7 million in damage. While the multimillion-dollar homes used green technology such as formaldehyde-free materials, energy-efficient appliances, and landscaping that included native plants in their construction, the development had drawn opposition because of fear that septic systems could damage critical wetlands needed to protect an aquifer used by about 20,000 people in the area and could harm streams used by Chinook salmon.[46]

Read more about the Earth Liberation Front by visiting their website at http://earth-liberation-front.com/. **Do you think environmental activists should really be considered terrorists?**

Another group, the Animal Liberation Front (ALF), focuses their efforts on protecting animals from being used as food, in clothing, or as experimental subjects. Their philosophy is that animals are entitled to the moral right to possess their own lives and control their own bodies, while rejecting the view that animals are merely capital goods or property intended for the benefit of humans and can be bought, sold, or killed by humans. ALF members conduct actions against scientists who conduct animal research, vandalizing their homes and cars, attacking labs, and setting animals free. They also conduct actions against animal breeding farms and food processing plants. ALF members have raided turkey farms before Thanksgiving and rabbit farms before Easter. Their activities have had significant impact on the commercial aspects of scientific testing, driving up the price of products, such as drugs, which rely on animal experimentation.[47]

Nationalist Terrorism

Nationalist terrorism promotes the interests of a minority ethnic or religious group that believes it has been persecuted under majority rule and wishes to carve out its own independent homeland.

In the Middle East, terrorist activities have been linked to the Palestinians' desire to wrest their former homeland from Israel. At first, the Palestinian Liberation Organization (PLO), led by Yasser Arafat, directed terrorist activities against Israel. Now the group Hamas is perpetuating the conflict with Israel and is behind a spate of suicide bombings and terrorist attacks designed to elicit a sharp response from Israel and set back any chance for peace in the region. Hundreds on both sides of the conflict have been killed during terrorist attacks and reprisals. In Lebanon, Hezbollah (from the Arabic, meaning "party of God") is a Lebanese Shi'ite Islamist organization founded in 1982 in response to the presence of Israeli forces in southern Lebanon. At inception, its goals were to both drive Israeli troops out of Lebanon and to form a Shi'ite Islamic republic in Lebanon. Taking its inspiration from Iran, Hezbollah members follow a distinct version of Shia ideology developed in Iran and have also received arms and financial support from Iran. Hezbollah is anti-West and anti-Israel and has engaged in a series of terrorist actions including kidnappings, car bombings, and airline hijackings.[48] Recently, Hezbollah has shifted its focus and has become increasingly embroiled in the Syrian civil war, fighting for the Assad regime. Ironically, this shift has alienated some of its Lebanese constituents and prompted deadly reprisals in Beirut from partisans of the predominantly Sunni Muslim Syrian rebels. The U.S. government and its European allies consider Hezbollah a global terrorist threat and a menace to Middle East stability.

The Middle East is not the only source of nationalistic terrorism. The Chinese government has been trying to suppress separatist groups fighting for an independent state in the northwestern province of Xinjiang. The rebels are drawn from the region's Uyghur people, most of whom practice Sufi Islam, speak a Turkic language, and wish to set up a Muslim state called Eastern Turkistan. During the past decade, the Uyghur separatists have organized demonstrations, bombings, and political assassinations.[49] Russia fought a series of protracted wars with Chechen nationalists intent on creating a free Chechen homeland before the uprising was finally crushed in 2009.

Retributive Terrorism

Some terrorist groups are not nationalist, political, or revolutionary organizations. They do not wish to set up their own homeland or topple a government but rather want to impose their social and religious code on others.[50] One prime example is the Boko Haram group operating in Nigeria. It made international news when the group abducted more than 200 schoolgirls attending a Western school, saying it would treat them as slaves and marry them off—a reference to an ancient Islamic belief that women captured in conflict are part of the "war booty."[51] Its followers take to heart a phrase from the Quran that says: "Anyone who is not governed by what Allah has revealed is among the transgressors." Therefore, the group promotes a version of Islam that makes it *haram*, or forbidden, for Muslims to take part in any political or social activity associated with Western society, including voting in elections, wearing shirts and trousers, or receiving a secular education.

Retributive terrorists such as Boko Haram have a number of characteristics that are unique and separate them from guerrillas, revolutionaries, and other terrorists:[52]

- Violence is used as a method of influence, persuasion, or intimidation. The true target of the terrorist act extends far beyond those directly affected by the attack and is designed to lead to some desired behavior on the part of the larger target population or government.
- Victims are usually selected for their maximum propaganda value, usually ensuring a high degree of media coverage. The message is that the target population had better comply with their demands because the terrorists are desperate enough to "do anything." Sometimes this may backfire if the attack results in the death of innocents, especially children, along with the symbolic targets.
- Unconventional military tactics are used, especially secrecy and surprise, as well as targeting civilians, including women and children. Because the goal is to inflict maximum horror, it makes sense to choose targets that contain the largest number of victims from all walks of life. The message: everyone is a target; no one is safe.

How do retributive terror groups use violence to achieve their goals? According to researchers at the Rand Corporation, there are actually four independent views on the topic:

- *Coercion hypothesis.* Terrorists use violence to cause pain, notably casualties, to frighten the opposition and get it to bend to their will (e.g., withdrawing from the Middle East).

- *Damage hypothesis.* Terrorists want to damage the enemy's economy to weaken its ability to intervene in international affairs.
- *Rally hypothesis.* Violence is used to attract the attention of potential recruits and supporters.
- *Franchise hypothesis.* Jihadists use violence to pursue their own, often local, goals and only receive some support and encouragement from international organizations such as al-Qaeda.[53]

RAND researchers have found that the coercion and damage hypotheses are most consistent with prior attack patterns.

Today, retributive terrorists can be categorized into four main groups:

- Al-Qaeda, including the group's strategy, ideology, operations, tactics, finances, changing character, and possible future.
- Terrorist groups that have adopted al-Qaeda's worldview and concept of mass-casualty terrorist attacks, even if the groups are not formally part of al-Qaeda.
- Violent Islamist and non-Islamist terrorist and insurgent groups without known links to al-Qaeda that threaten United States interests, friends, and allies. These include Hezbollah and Hamas, along with insurgencies in Iraq, the Philippines, and other countries.
- The nexus between terrorism and organized crime, including the terrorists and insurgents that use criminal organizations and connections to finance their activities. Such actions also tend to weaken and corrupt political and social institutions.[54]

Al-Qaeda is the paradigm of the new retributive terrorist organization. Rather than fighting for a homeland, its message is a call to take up a cause: there is a war of civilizations in which "Jews and Crusaders" want to destroy Islam and must therefore be defeated. Armed jihad is the individual obligation of every Muslim; terrorism and violence are appropriate methods for defeating even the strongest powers. The end product would be a unified Muslim world, the Caliphate, ruled under Muslim law free of Western influence.

These themes are preached in schools, on the Internet, and disseminated in books, cassette tapes, and pamphlets. Videotapes are distributed in which al-Qaeda's leaders expound on political topics, going as far as calling Western

retributive terrorists Terror groups who refrain from tying specific acts to direct demands for change. They want to instead redirect the balance between what they believe is good and evil. They see their revolution as existing on a spiritual plane; their mission is to exact retribution against sinners.

leaders liars and drunkards. As a result of this media strategy, al-Qaeda's messages have penetrated deeply into Muslim communities around the world, finding a sympathetic response among many Muslims who have a sense of helplessness both in the Arab world and in the Western Muslim diaspora. Al-Qaeda appears to have had an impact by offering a sense of empowerment to young men who feel lost in their adopted cultures.[55]

State-Sponsored Terrorism

State-sponsored terrorism occurs when a repressive government regime forces its citizens into obedience, oppresses minorities, and stifles political dissent. Death squads and the use of government troops to destroy political opposition parties are often associated with political terrorism. Much of what we know about state-sponsored terrorism comes from the efforts of human rights groups such as London-based Amnesty International, whose research shows that tens of thousands of people continue to become victims of security operations that result in disappearances and executions. Political prisoners are now being tortured in about 100 countries, people have disappeared or are being held in secret detention in about 20 countries, and government-sponsored death squads have been operating in more than 35 countries. Countries known for encouraging violent control of dissidents include Brazil, Colombia, Guatemala, Honduras, Peru, Iraq, and Sudan.

State-sponsored terrorism became a world issue when South and Central American dictatorships in the 1970s and 1980s unleashed state violence against political dissidents through forced disappearance, political imprisonment, torture, blacklisting, and massive exile. The region-wide state repression in this period emerged in response to the rise of the 1960s radical movements, which demanded public reforms and programs to help the lower classes in urban areas and agricultural workers in the countryside. Local authoritarian governments, which used repression to take control of radical political groups, were given financial support by the economic elites who dominated Latin American politics and were fearful of a socialist revolution.[56]

As might be expected, governments claim that repressive measures are needed to control terror and revolutionary groups that routinely use violence. Thus the use of terror is sometimes a way of defending the nation against violence, a conundrum that supports the idea that a state is both protective and destructive.[57]

It is sometimes difficult to assess blame for state terror—is it a few rogue government agents who act on their own authority or the government itself? The issue of responsibility for improper acts hit home during the Abu Ghraib scandal in Iraq. Photos beamed around the world embarrassed the United States when they showed military personnel victimizing suspected insurgents. The government's response was to prosecute and imprison the perpetrators. However, some critics, such as criminologist Mark Hamm, suggest that these images constitute the photographic record of a state-sponsored crime.[58] He argues that rather than being the work of a few rogue officers, the sophisticated interrogation practices at Abu Ghraib were designed and executed by the U.S. Central Intelligence Agency and that the torturing of detainees at Abu Ghraib followed directly from decisions made by top government officials to get tough with prisoner interrogations. So while we condemn state-sponsored violence, it is not easy to identify who is truly responsible.

Criminal Terrorism

Sometimes terrorist groups become involved in common-law crimes such as drug dealing and kidnapping, and piracy to support their cause. Illegal activities may on occasion become so profitable that they replace the group's original focus. In some instances, the line between being a terrorist organization with political support and vast resources and an organized criminal group engaging in illicit activities for profit becomes blurred. What appears to be a politically motivated action, such as the kidnapping of a government official for ransom, may turn out to be merely a crime for profit.[59]

In some cases, there has been close cooperation between organized criminal groups and guerillas in which illegal activity is used to fund terror operations. The Revolutionary Armed Forces of Colombia (FARC) imposes a tax on Colombian drug producers, but evidence indicates that the group cooperates with Colombia's top drug barons in running the trade (currently the FARC and the Colombian government are in peace talks which hope to end their long-running guerilla war).

Al-Shabaab, the Somalia-based terror group that became infamous with their 2013 attack on Westgate Mall in Nairobi, Kenya, that resulted in hundreds of casualties and more than 60 deaths, has long been linked to criminal activity. They require a share of the payment of ransoms given to Somalian pirates who launch cross-ocean raids from the al-Shabaab–controlled territory; piracy would be impossible without cooperation from al-Shabaab. The group is also heavily involved in smuggling, slapping taxes on illegal charcoal exports to the Gulf, arms shipments from Yemen, and electronic goods destined for the region.[60]

state-sponsored terrorism Terrorism that occurs when a repressive government regime forces its citizens into obedience, oppresses minorities, and stifles political dissent.

HOW ARE TERROR GROUPS ORGANIZED?

Terror groups tend to be networked or hierarchical. Newer terrorist organizations tend to be formed as **networks**, loosely organized groups located in different parts of a city, state, or country (or worldwide) that share a common theme or purpose, but have a diverse leadership and command structure and are only in intermittent communication with one another. While there may be a variety of antigovernment groups operating in the United States, there is little evidence that they share a single command structure or organizational fabric. These groups have few resources and little experience, so it is critical that they operate under cover and with as little public exposure as possible.

When needed, networked groups can pull factions together for larger-scale operations, such as an attack on a military headquarters, or conversely, they can readily splinter off into smaller groups to avoid detection when a counterterrorism operation is under way. The advent of the Internet has significantly improved communications among networked terror groups.

As terror organizations evolve and expand, they may eventually develop a hierarchical organization with a commander at the top, captains, local area leaders, and so on. Ideological and religious groups tend to gravitate toward this model since a common creed/dogma controls their operations and a singular leader may be needed to define and disseminate group principles and maintain discipline. In a hierarchical model, the leader has the power to increase or decrease levels of violence for political purposes (i.e., they may order their followers to initiate a bombing campaign to influence an election). Schools may be off limits so that the population is not antagonized, or schools may become a target to show that the government cannot protect their children.

Regardless of what organizational structure is used, most groups subdivide their affiliates into **terror cells** for both organizational and security purposes. To enhance security, each cell may be functionally independent so that each member has little knowledge of other cells, their members, locations, and so on. However, individual cell members provide emotional support to one another and maintain loyalty and dedication. Because only the cell leader knows how to communicate with other cells and/or a central command, capture of one cell does not then compromise other group members.

Terror cell formations may be based on location, employment, or family membership. Some are formed on the basis of function: some are fighters, others political organizers. The number of cells and their composition depend on the size of the terrorist group: local or national groups will have fewer cells than international terrorist groups that may operate in several countries, such as the al-Qaeda group.

The various forms that terror groups take are summarized in Concept Summary 11.2

networks When referring to terrorist organizations, networks are loosely organized groups located in different parts of the city, state, or country (or world) that share a common theme or purpose, but have a diverse leadership and command structure and are only in intermittent communication with one another.

terror cells Divisions of terrorist group affiliates, each of which may be functionally independent so that each member has little knowledge of other cells, their members, locations, and so on. The number of cells and their composition depend on the size of the terrorist group. Local or national groups will have fewer cells than international terrorist groups that may operate in several countries, such as the al-Qaeda group.

THE VARIETY OF TERROR GROUPS — 11.2

Revolutionary terrorists	Use violence to frighten those in power and their supporters in order to replace the existing government with a regime that holds acceptable political or religious views.
Political terrorists	Political terrorism is directed at people or groups who oppose the terrorists' political ideology or whom the terrorists define as "outsiders" who must be destroyed.
Eco-terrorism	Political terror groups involved in violent actions to protect the environment.
Nationalist terrorism	Groups whose actions promote the interests of a minority ethnic or religious group that has been persecuted under majority rule and/or wishes to carve out its own independent homeland.
Retributive terrorism	Groups that use violence as a method of influence, persuasion, or intimidation in order to achieve a particular aim or objective.
State-sponsored terrorism	Carried out by a repressive government regime in order to force its citizens into obedience, oppress minorities, and stifle political dissent.
Criminal terrorism	Terrorist groups that become involved in common-law crimes such as drug dealing and kidnapping, even selling nuclear materials.

concept summary

WHAT MOTIVATES THE TERRORIST?

LO8 Explain what motivates the terrorist to commit violent acts

In the aftermath of the September 11, 2001, destruction of the World Trade Center in New York City, many Americans asked themselves the same simple question: Why? What could motivate someone like Osama bin Laden to order the deaths of thousands of innocent people? How could someone who had never been to the United States or suffered personally at its hands develop such lethal hatred? Some experts believed the attacks had a political basis, claiming that bin Laden's anger was fueled by the U.S.'s Middle East policies. Others saw a religious motivation and claimed that Osama was a radical Muslim at war with the liberal religions of the West. Another view was that Osama's rage was fueled by deep-rooted psychological problems.

Who was this man who caused so much death and destruction before his death at the hands of SEAL Team Six? And what motivated him to choose a terrorist path? He came from a wealthy family founded by his father, Mohammed bin Laden, whose industrial empire continued to expand even after his death until it employed more than 40,000 people. So poverty and alienation were certainly not motives.

Osama was a devout Muslim, and his terrorist activity may have been motivated by religious beliefs and anger over the presence of Western influences in the Middle East. In a 1995 interview with a French journalist, bin Laden explained why he chose to join the *mujahideen* fight against the Russians at that time:

> To counter these atheist Russians, the Saudis chose me as their representative in Afghanistan.... I did not fight against the communist threat while forgetting the peril from the West. For us, the idea was not to get involved more than necessary in the fight against the Russians, which was the business of the Americans, but rather to show our solidarity with our Islamist brothers. I discovered that it was not enough to fight in Afghanistan, but that we had to fight on all fronts against communist or Western oppression. The urgent thing was communism, but the next target was America.... This is an open war up to the end, until victory.[61]

It is also possible that bin Laden's motivation was psychological, and his efforts an unconscious attempt to gain his father's approval. "My father was very keen that one of his sons should fight against the enemies of Islam. So I am the one son who is acting according to the wishes of his father." Perhaps this need for acceptance explains bin Laden's religious zeal, which was in excess of anyone else's in his large extended family.

Whether his motivations were psychological, political, or religious—or a combination of all three—is still uncertain. It is likely that we will never truly understand Osama's motivations to attack the West.[62]

Before terrorism can be effectively fought, controlled, and eradicated, it is important to understand something about the kind of people who become terrorists, what motivates their behavior, and how their ideas are formed. Unfortunately, this is not an easy task. Terrorism researchers have generally concluded that there is no single personality trait or behavior pattern that distinguishes the majority of terrorists or sets them apart so they can be easily identified and apprehended. Some seem truly disturbed, whereas many others have not suffered long-term mental illness or displayed sociopathic traits and/or tendencies; if that were so, bizarre or violent behavior in their early childhood would be a giveaway.[63] As such, there have been a number of competing visions of why terrorists engage in criminal activities such as bombings, shootings, and kidnappings to achieve a political end. Four views stand out.

Psychological View

One of the most controversial views of terrorists is that some if not all suffer from psychological deficits, and that the typical terrorist can be described as an emotionally disturbed individual who acts out his or her psychoses within the confines of violent groups. According to this view, terrorist violence is not so much a political instrument as an end in itself; it is the result of compulsion or psychopathology. Terrorists do what they do because of garden variety emotional problems, including but not limited to self-destructive urges and disturbed emotions combined with problems with authority.[64] As terrorism expert Jerrold M. Post puts it, "Political terrorists are driven to commit acts of violence as a consequence of psychological forces, and ... their special psychology is constructed to rationalize acts they are psychologically compelled to commit."[65]

Some terror experts say that the majority of research on terrorists indicates that most are not psychologically abnormal.[66] Even suicide bombers, a group that should show signs of psychological abnormality, exhibit few signs of the mental problems such as depression that are typically found in people who choose to take their own life. Rather than acting disturbed and disoriented, those terrorists willing to die for their cause display a heightened sense of purpose, group allegiance, and task focus.[67] After carefully reviewing existing evidence on the psychological state of terrorists, mental health expert Randy Borum concludes:

- Mental illness is not a critical factor in explaining terrorist behavior. Also, most terrorists are not psychopaths.
- There is no "terrorist personality," nor is there any accurate profile—psychological or otherwise—of the terrorist.
- Histories of childhood abuse and trauma and themes of perceived injustice and humiliation often are prominent in terrorist biographies, but do not really help to explain terrorism.[68]

Alienation View

Another explanation for terrorist activity is that a lack of opportunity creates a sense of alienation that motivates men and women to embrace terrorism.[69] Regions such as South Asia breed terrorists because they house an incendiary mix of strong ethnic identities and diverse religious communities, many of which are concentrated within exclusionary ghettos. Young men and women residing in these areas are motivated to join terror groups when they feel left out of the social and economic mainstream because of their religious or ethnic status.[70] According to this view, terror recruits suffer alienation from friends, family, and society.[71] Many have been raised to hate the groups who are in power and believe that they have been victimized by state authorities whom they view as oppressors.

Terrorism has also become an alternative for people whose religious beliefs alienate them from our postmodern, technological, global society in which foreign influences routinely clash with age-old traditions. They may believe that modern forms of communication, entertainment, and social interaction have brought foreign influences that are corrupting and disrespectful to their traditional way of life. Some may join terror groups whose goal is to eliminate these corrupting external influences—for example, the name of the terrorist group Boko Haram can be translated as "Western education is sin." Alienation can become so powerful that the terrorist may even believe that a suicide mission will help cleanse them of the corruption of the modern world while at the same time scaring off outsiders.

While at first glance terrorists seem alienated from modern society, when Marc Sageman studied members of extremist Islamist groups he found that most tend to be well educated; about 60 percent had some form of higher education. More than 75 percent came from upper- or middle-class backgrounds. When they joined a terror organization, the majority had professional occupations such as doctor or engineer, or semiskilled employment, such as a civil servant; fewer than 25 percent were unemployed or working in unskilled jobs. Surprisingly, Sageman found that almost three-quarters were married and that most had children.[72] These findings suggest that terrorists are not suffering from the social problems usually associated with alienation: poverty, lack of education, and ignorance.

Because some terrorists are motivated by alienation and psychological abnormality it should come as no surprise that they act on their own, without support or contact with others. This type of terrorist is the subject of the Criminology in Action feature.

Family Conflict View   Terrorists report that they are products of dysfunctional families in which the father was absent or, even if present, was a distant and cold figure.[73] Because of this family estrangement, the budding terrorist may have been swayed to join a group or cult by a charismatic leader who serves as an alternative father figure. Some find it in religious schools run by strong leaders who demand strict loyalty from their followers while indoctrinating them in political causes.[74] In this sense, terror groups, similar to what happens in urban street gangs, provide a substitute family–like environment, which can nurture a heretofore emotionally underprivileged youth.

Political View   When people are left out of the political process, having their votes restricted or even losing the right to vote, they may be inclined to join terror groups.[75] Analyzing cross-national data, Laura Dugan and Gary LaFree, of the National Consortium for the Study of Terrorism and Responses to Terrorism, found that most of the risk for political violence lies in those nations that are nearly democracies, which experience three times as many terror attacks as full democracies. Ironically, the most autocratic countries, governed by dictators and without free elections, generally had the lowest average number of attacks. In contrast, **failed states**—those where governments have lost physical control of their own territory, are unable to provide reasonable public services, and cannot interact properly with other states—have extremely high rates of terrorist activity. Dugan and LaFree also found evidence that terrorist attacks against failed states were much more lethal than attacks against other nations. Their finding suggests that nations that provide access to the political process for people holding a wide range of diverse viewpoints create a culture that helps reduce the frustration that could lead to terrorist violence. Those states that cannot maintain order or provide services to its citizens are fertile grounds for terrorists. And while iron-handed dictators may keep terrorism under control in the short term, their long-term prospects are sketchy at best, as recent events in Egypt, Libya, and Syria have shown.

Socialization/Friendship View

Many jihadist recruits were living in foreign countries when they got involved with terrorist organizations. Feeling homesick, they sought out people with similar backgrounds, whom they would often find at mosques.[76] If they appeared to be motivated by religious fervor, it was because they were seeking friends in a foreign land. They moved in together in order to share the rent and also to eat together under strict Muslim dietary laws. The group solidified their beliefs and created a sense of solidarity with like-minded people. If one became committed to terror, others may follow rather than let him down.

---

failed states A nation whose government has lost control of its own territory, is unable to provide public services and protection, and lacks the ability to interact with other states as a full member of the international community.

LONE-ACTOR TERRORISTS

On November 5, 2009, U.S. Major Nidal Malik Hasan attacked fellow soldiers at Fort Hood, leaving 12 dead and 31 wounded. On July 22, 2011, Anders Breivik killed 77 civilians in and around Oslo, Norway. Dzhokhar and Tamerlan Tsarnaev set off bombs at the finish line of the Boston Marathon in 2013, killing 3 and wounding more than 250. These mass killings have drawn attention to so-called lone-actor terrorists who plan and carry out an attack without assistance from others. To find out more about them, Clark McCauley and Sophia Moskalenko conducted research in order to answer the basic question: Why would any individual take this kind of risk and choose to sacrifice themselves for a cause?

They found that lone actors may see themselves as representing some larger group or cause and may have had some experience in a group, organization, or social movement related to this cause. However, it was difficult for them to stay or be part of a group because they tend to suffer from some form of psychological disturbance, are socially isolated, and tend to be loners with few friends.

Many have a military background and have recently suffered some form of serious personal disruption that triggered a violent attack, such as divorce or the death of a partner. For example, Major Hasan had no close relationships and experience with weapons. He had turned to the Quran after the death of his parents and was about to be transferred to Afghanistan. He saw himself discriminated against as a Muslim and viewed the war on terrorism as a war on Islam, thereby developing both personal and political grievances.

Taken together, these results provide a portrait of the typical lone actor as grievance-fueled individual, likely to have weapons experience, who suffers from depression or other mental disorders, and experiences temporary or chronic social isolation. McCauley and Moskalenko call this the *disconnected-disordered* profile.

However, not all lone-actor terrorists fit the disconnected-disordered profile: there are some who are neither loners nor suffer mental disorder, but who nonetheless undertake lone-actor terrorist violence. They may be motivated by some emotionally charged event that sets them off on a destructive path: the political becomes personal. They are radicalized by feelings of moral obligation to right a perceived wrong: a man bombs abortion clinics after a family member loses a child at birth; a woman burns down a factory farm after witnessing the suffering of animals. The Tsarnaev brothers were motivated by their sensitivity to what they perceived as the oppression of Muslims by the West. A note that Dzhokhar Tsarnaev wrote while hiding from authorities on a dry-docked boat said in part: "God has a plan for each person. Mine was to hide in this boat and shed some light on our actions. . . . Stop killing our innocent people and we will stop."

What sets this type of lone terrorist apart is their unusual capacity to care about the suffering of others. Those who fit this *caring-compelled profile* have social relations and are not mentally ill. But they care too much and find that there is a dark side to caring greatly about others. Individuals can kill for love, including love of strangers seen as victimized.

In sum, McCauley and Moskalenko believe that lone-actor terrorists fit one of these two profiles: disconnected-disordered or caring-compelled. They suspect that the caring-compelled profile is less common than the disconnected-disordered profile—not least because self-sacrifice for others is less common than self-interest—but this hypothesis remains to be tested.

Critical Thinking

Does creating such a profile actually help curb terrorism or is it merely an academic exercise? After all, there are many people who share these characteristics who never engage in violence or terrorist acts. What benefit can these profiles have for law enforcement agents hoping to prevent terrorist acts?

SOURCES: Clark McCauley and Sophia Moskalenko, "Two Possible Profiles of Lone-Actor Terrorists," National Consortium for the Study of Terrorism and Responses to Terrorism (START), 2013, http://www.start.umd.edu/publication/two-possible-profiles-lone-actor-terrorists (accessed May 2014); Jeff Gruenewald, Steven Chermak, and Joshua Freilich, "Distinguishing 'Loner' Attacks from Other Domestic Extremist Violence," *Criminology and Public Policy* 12 (2013): 65–91; *Boston Globe*, "Text from Dzhokhar Tsarnaev's Note Written in Watertown Boat," May 22, 2014, http://www.bostonglobe.com/metro/2014/05/22/text-from-dzhokhar-tsarnaev-note-left-watertown-boat/KnRIeqqr95rJQbAbfnj5EP/story.html (accessed June 2014).

Ideological View

Another view is that terrorists hold extreme ideological beliefs that prompt their behavior. They may have developed heightened perceptions of oppressive conditions, believing they are being victimized by some group or government for their beliefs or way of life. Once they conclude that the government will not help people with their beliefs, they decide to resort to violence to encourage change.

Facilitating the use of violence is the ability to divide people based on religious, ethnic, racial, or other cultural criteria, into two categories: those with common interests and beliefs who are avenged through terrorist activities ("us") and those against whom the terrorist activities are to be directed ("them"). Those associated with "us" are viewed as moral, right, good, and strong. Those associated with "them" are seen as immoral, wrong, bad, and weak.[77] Once this division is made, the terrorist can act with impunity to further their ideological beliefs because those harmed have beliefs that make them less than human.

Religious Fanaticism   Some terrorists, like the Tsarnaev brothers, are motivated by extreme religious beliefs, which often coincide with their ideological views. But how can they justify using violence if they are truly religious, since most of the world's religions eschew violence? Islamic terrorists believe that their commitment to God justifies their extreme actions. They regard the actions of people they trust as a testimony to the righteousness of their acts. They trust significant others, and rely on their wisdom, experience, and testimony and accept their expressions of faith. To the terrorist, someone like Osama bin Laden has demonstrated the strength of his faith by living in poverty and giving up a more luxurious and leisurely life in the name of God. When he calls them to jihad, they are likely to follow, even if it means killing those who deny their faith or beliefs. Perceived miracles, such as the defeat of a superpower through faith alone (e.g., the Soviet/Afghan war or the fight against the United States in Iraq), also increase confidence in the righteousness of the cause. Some have mystical experiences during prayers or dreams that demonstrate the existence of God and reinforce faith. In a videotape in the fall of 2001, Osama bin Laden said that he had banned the reporting of dreams of airplanes flying into buildings prior to September 11 for fear of revealing the plot.[78]

Explaining State-Sponsored Terrorism

How can state-sponsored terrorism be explained? After all, these violent acts are not directed at a foreign government or overseas adversaries but against natives of one's own country. In her book *Reigns of Terror*, Patricia Marchak finds that people willing to kill or maim their fellow countrymen are likely to be highly susceptible to unquestioning submission to authority. They are conformists who want to be part of the central group and who are quite willing to be part of a state regime. They are vulnerable to ideology that dehumanizes their targets and can utilize propaganda to distance themselves psychologically from those they are terrorizing.[79] So the Nazis had little trouble recruiting people to carry out horrific acts during the Holocaust because many Germans wanted to be part of the popular social/political movement and were easily indoctrinated by the Nazi propaganda that branded Jews as subhuman. Stalin was able to carry out his reign of terror in Russia because his victims were viewed as state enemies who were trying to undermine the Communist regime. How can these tendencies be neutralized? Marchak sees little benefit to international intervention that results in after-the-fact punishment of the perpetrators, a course of action that was attempted in the former Yugoslavia

after death squads had performed "ethnic cleansing" of undesirables. Instead she argues for a prevention strategy that involves international aid and economic development by industrialized nations to those in the third world that are on the verge of becoming collapsed states, the construction of social welfare systems, and the acceptance of international legal norms and standards of human rights.[80]

EXTENT OF THE TERRORISM THREAT

Osama bin Laden is not the only top al-Qaeda leader who was removed from the battlefield in recent years. Ilyas Kashmiri, one of the most capable terrorist operatives in South Asia, was killed in Pakistan in 2011. Harun Fazul, an architect of the 1998 U.S. Embassy bombings in Kenya and Tanzania, and the foremost member of al-Qaeda in East Africa, was killed in Somalia by the Transitional Federal Government. Atiya Abdul Rahman, al-Qaeda's second-in-command after bin Laden's death and a senior operational commander, was killed in Pakistan. Anwar al-Aulaqi, al-Qaeda in the Arabian Peninsula's chief of external operations, was killed in Yemen. And on November 1, 2013, Hakimullah Mehsud, the leader the Pakistani Taliban, died in a drone strike.[81]

Does the pressure being put on al-Qaeda, the Taliban, and other terror groups through drone attacks and commando raids mean that the end of the global terrorism threat is at hand? Not likely. Terror cells have now dispersed around the world, helping to offset this loss in leadership. When one leader is killed, a new and even more violent one may take command. Upon the death of Mehsud, hard-line commander Mullah Fazlullah was elected the new leader of the Pakistani Taliban and soon promised a wave of terror attacks in revenge for the death of his predecessor. Fazlullah refuses to consider peace talks, opposes educating females, was blamed for ordering the beheading of 17 Pakistani soldiers in a check-post attack in June 2012 and planting a bomb that killed a Pakistani major general—hardly an improvement over the brutal Mehsud.

The most recent data from the National Consortium for the Study of Terrorism and Responses to Terrorism (START) supports the fact that the terrorist danger has not diminished, quite the opposite in fact. START finds that terrorist acts touched 85 countries in 2012, though just three—Pakistan, Iraq, and Afghanistan—suffered more than half the attacks (54 percent) and fatalities (58 percent). The next five most frequently targeted countries were India, Nigeria, Somalia, Yemen, and Thailand. In all more than 8,400 terrorist attacks occurred in a single year, killing more than 15,400 people—an increase in attacks and fatalities over the past decade.[82]

Who were the most active groups? They included the Taliban in Afghanistan, Boko Haram in Nigeria, al-Qaeda in the Arabian Peninsula, Tehrik-i-Taliban Pakistan, al-Qaeda in Iraq, and al-Shabaab in Somalia. These groups are

EXHIBIT 11.3

Current Trends in Terrorism

- The terrorist threat continues to evolve rapidly, with an increasing number of groups around the world—including both al-Qaeda affiliates and other terrorist organizations—posing a threat to the United States, our allies, and our interests.

- As a result of both ongoing worldwide efforts against the organization and senior leadership losses, al-Qaeda's core leadership has been degraded, limiting its ability to conduct attacks and direct its followers. Subsequently, there has been a rise in increasingly aggressive and autonomous al-Qaeda affiliates and like-minded groups in the Middle East and Africa who took advantage of the weak governance and instability in the region to broaden and deepen their operations.

- Al-Qaeda leader Ayman al-Zawahiri experienced difficulty in maintaining influence throughout the organization and was rebuffed in his attempts to mediate a dispute among affiliates operating in Syria. Guidance issued by al-Zawahiri in 2013 for al-Qaeda affiliates to avoid collateral damage was routinely disobeyed, notably in increasingly violent attacks by these affiliates against civilian populations.

- Syria continues to be a major battleground for terrorism on both sides of the conflict and remains a key area of longer-term concern. Thousands of foreign fighters traveled to Syria to join the fight against the Asad regime—with some joining violent extremist groups—while Iran, Hezbollah, and other Shia militias provided a broad range of critical support to the regime. The Syrian conflict also empowered another offshoot, the Islamic State of Iraq and Syria (ISIS), to expand its cross-border operations in Syria, and dramatically increase attacks against Iraqi civilians and government targets in 2013.

- Terrorist violence is increasingly fueled by sectarian motives, marking a worrisome trend, particularly in Syria, but also in Lebanon and Pakistan.

- Terrorist groups engage in a range of criminal activity to raise needed funds, with kidnapping for ransom remaining the most frequent and profitable source of illicit financing. Private donations from the Gulf also remain a major source of funding for Sunni terrorist groups, particularly for those operating in Syria.

- "Lone offender" violent extremists also continue to pose a serious threat.

- Many other terrorist groups not tied to al-Qaeda were responsible for attacks in 2013, including the People's Liberation Party/Front (DHKP/C), which carried out a number of high-profile attacks, including a February 1 suicide plot targeting the U.S. Embassy in Ankara, Turkey.

SOURCE: U.S. State Department, Country Reports on Terrorism, 2013, http://www.state.gov/j/ct/rls/crt/2013/224819.htm (accessed May 2014).

generally considered allied with the central al-Qaeda group. And despite the fact that al-Qaeda was not responsible for a single attack in 2012, its alliance with these groups means that it remains a central player in a network of highly lethal and active terrorist organizations.[83]

The most recent trends in international terror are set out in Exhibit 11.3.

RESPONSE TO TERRORISM

LO9 List examples of the efforts being made to centralize intelligence gathering

After the 9/11 attacks, agencies of the criminal justice system began to focus their attention on combating the threat of terror. Even local police agencies created anti-terror programs designed to protect their communities from the threat of attack. How should the nation best prepare itself

to thwart potential attacks? The National Commission on Terrorist Attacks Upon the United States (also known as the 9/11 Commission), an independent, bipartisan commission, was created in late 2002 and given the mission of preparing an in-depth report of the events leading up to the 9/11 attacks. Part of their goal was to create a comprehensive plan to ensure that no further attacks of that magnitude take place.

To monitor the more than 500 million people who annually cross in and out of America, the commission recommended that a single agency should be created to screen border crossings. They also recommended creation of an investigative agency to monitor all aliens in the United States and to gather intelligence on the way terrorists travel across borders. The commission suggested that people who wanted passports be tagged with biometric measures to make them easily identifiable.

In response to the commission report, a **Director of National Intelligence (DNI)** was created and charged with coordinating data from the nation's primary intelligence-gathering agencies. The DNI serves as the principal intelligence adviser to the president and the statutory intelligence advisor to the National Security Council. On February 17, 2005, President George W. Bush named U.S. Ambassador to Iraq John Negroponte to be the first person to hold the post; he was confirmed on April 21, 2005; the current director is

Director of National Intelligence (DNI) Government official charged with coordinating data from the nation's primary intelligence-gathering agencies.

James R. Clapper, a former Air Force general and director of the Defense Intelligence Agency.

Among the agencies reporting to the DNI is the National Counterterrorism Center (NCTC), which is staffed by terrorism experts from the CIA, FBI, and the Pentagon; the Privacy and Civil Liberties Board; and the National Counterproliferation Center. The NCTC serves as the primary organization in the U.S. government for analyzing and integrating all intelligence possessed or acquired by the government pertaining to terrorism and counterterrorism, excepting purely domestic counterterrorism information.

While the 9/11 Commission report outlines what has already been done, what has not been done, and what needs to be done, agencies of the justice system have begun to respond to the challenge.

Confronting Terrorism with Law Enforcement

Ending the threat of terror is not easy. One reason is the very nature of American society. Because we live in a free and open nation, it is extremely difficult to seal the borders and prevent the entry of terrorist groups. In his book *Nuclear Terrorism*, Graham Allison, an expert on nuclear weapons and national security, describes the almost superhuman effort it would take to seal the nation's borders from nuclear attack considering the thousands of trucks, rail cars, and ships that deliver goods every day. The potential for terrorists to obtain bombs is significant: there are more than 100 nuclear research reactors now in operation around the world, and many are contained in states hostile to the United States, such as Iran and North Korea. Even if terrorists lack the knowledge to build their own bomb, they may be able to purchase an intact device on the black market. Russia alone has thousands of nuclear warheads and material for many thousands of additional weapons; all of these are vulnerable to theft. Terrorists may also be able to buy the knowledge to construct bombs. In one well-known incident, Pakistan's leading nuclear scientist, A. Q. Khan, sold comprehensive "nuclear starter kits" that included advanced centrifuge components, blueprints for nuclear warheads, and uranium samples in quantities sufficient to make a small bomb, and even provided personal consulting services to assist in nuclear development.[84]

Recognizing this problem, law enforcement agencies around the country began to realign their resources to combat future terrorist attacks. In response to 9/11, law enforcement agencies undertook a number of steps: increasing the number of personnel engaged in emergency response planning; updating response plans for chemical, biological, or radiological attacks; and reallocating internal resources or increasing departmental spending to focus on terrorism preparedness.[85] Actions continue to be taken on the federal, state, and local levels.

Federal Law Enforcement

LO10 Describe the efforts by the FBI and DHS to fight terrorism

One of the most significant changes has been a realignment of the Federal Bureau of Investigation (FBI), the federal government's main law enforcement agency. The FBI has announced a reformulation of its priorities, making protecting the United States from terrorist attack its number one commitment. It is now charged with coordinating intelligence collection with the Border Patrol, Secret Service, and the CIA. The FBI must also work with and share intelligence with the National Counterterrorism Center (NCTC). Another initiative has been the creation of Joint Terrorism Task Forces (JTTFs), which are now located in 103 cities nationwide. The JTTFs include more than 4,400 members nationwide, hailing from over 600 state and local agencies and 50 federal agencies (the Department of Homeland Security, the U.S. military, Immigration and Customs Enforcement, and the Transportation Security Administration, to name a few). JTTFs enable a shared intelligence base across many agencies, among other benefits.[86]

Department of Homeland Security (DHS) Soon after the 2001 attack, President George W. Bush proposed the creation of a new cabinet-level agency called the **Department of Homeland Security (DHS)**, which is engaged in:

- Preventing terrorist attacks within the United States
- Reducing America's vulnerability to terrorism
- Minimizing the damage and recovering from attacks that do occur

Rather than start from the ground up, the DHS combined a number of existing agencies into a superagency. Among its components are:

- *Border and transportation security.* The Department of Homeland Security is responsible for securing our nation's borders and transportation systems, which include 350 ports of entry. The department manages who and what enters the country, and works to prevent the entry of terrorists and the instruments of terrorism while simultaneously ensuring the speedy flow of legitimate traffic. The DHS also is in charge of securing territorial waters, including ports and waterways.
- *Emergency preparedness and response.* The department ensures the preparedness of emergency response

Department of Homeland Security (DHS) An agency of the federal government charged with preventing terrorist attacks within the United States, reducing America's vulnerability to terrorism, and minimizing the damage and aiding recovery from attacks that do occur.

professionals, provides the federal government's response, and aids America's recovery from terrorist attacks and natural disasters. The department is responsible for reducing the loss of life and property and protecting institutions from all types of hazards through an emergency management program of preparedness, mitigation, response, and recovery.

- *Chemical, biological, radiological, and nuclear countermeasures.* The department leads the federal government's efforts in preparing for and responding to the full range of terrorist threats involving weapons of mass destruction. To do this, the department sets national policy and establishes guidelines for state and local governments. It directs exercises and drills for federal, state, and local chemical, biological, radiological, and nuclear (CBRN) response teams and plans. The department is assigned to prevent the importation of nuclear weapons and material.

- *Information analysis and infrastructure protection.* The department analyzes information from multiple available sources, including the CIA and FBI, in order to assess the dangers facing the nation. It also analyzes law enforcement and intelligence information.[87]

The DHS has numerous and varied duties. It is responsible for port security and transportation systems and manages airport security with its Transportation Security Administration (TSA). It has its own intelligence section, and it covers every special event in the United States, including political conventions.

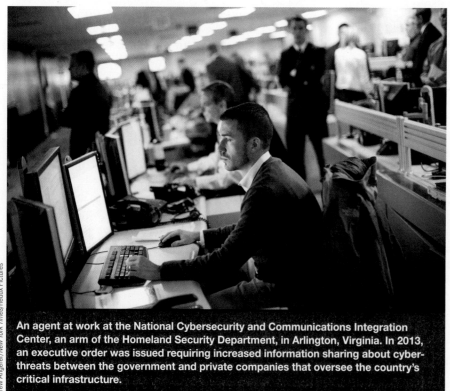

An agent at work at the National Cybersecurity and Communications Integration Center, an arm of the Homeland Security Department, in Arlington, Virginia. In 2013, an executive order was issued requiring increased information sharing about cyberthreats between the government and private companies that oversee the country's critical infrastructure.

Drew Angerer/New York Times/Redux Pictures

State and County Law Enforcement In the wake of the 9/11 attacks, a number of states have beefed up their intelligence-gathering capabilities and aimed them directly at homeland security. For example, Arizona maintains the Arizona Counter Terrorism Information Center (ACTIC), a statewide intelligence system designed to combat terrorism.[88] It consists of two divisions. One is unclassified and draws together personnel from various public safety agencies. The other operates in a secretive manner and is made up of personnel from the FBI's Joint Terrorism Task Force. Its Fusion Center is responsible for sharing information about situations that might affect jurisdictions in the state and combs through diverse informational sources to provide early warning of incidents at the local, regional, and state levels.[89] ACTIC also has an outreach program known as the Community Liaison Program (CLP). Community partners, including religious groups, businesses, and community crime watches, provide intelligence information to ACTIC personnel as the need arises.

Some counties are now engaging in anti-terror and homeland security activities. For example, the Harris County, Texas, Office of Homeland Security & Emergency Management (OHSEM) is responsible for an emergency management plan that prepares for public recovery in the event of natural disasters or human-caused catastrophes or attacks. It works in conjunction with state, federal, and local authorities, including the city of Houston and other municipalities in the surrounding Harris County area when required. If needed, OHSEM activates an Emergency Operations Center to facilitate coordination of all support agencies to provide continuity of services to the public. OHSEM is responsible for advisement, notification, and assembly of services that are in the best interest of the citizens of Harris County. It prepares and distributes information and procedures governing the same.[90]

Local Law Enforcement Federal law enforcement agencies are not alone in responding to the threat of terrorism. And, of course, nowhere is the threat of terrorism being taken more seriously than in New York City, one of the main targets of the 9/11 attacks, which has established a Counterterrorism Bureau.[91] After the 9/11 attacks, the NYPD augmented its anti-terrorism forces from 17 to 125 and assigned them to the operational control of the Counterterrorism Bureau. Teams within the bureau have been trained to examine potential targets in the city and attempt to insulate them from possible attack. Viewed as prime targets are the city's bridges, the Empire State Building, Rockefeller Center, and the United Nations. Bureau detectives are assigned overseas to work with the police in several foreign cities, including cities in Canada and Israel. Detectives have been assigned as liaisons with the FBI and with INTERPOL, in Lyon, France. The city recruits detectives with language skills from Pashtun and Urdu to Arabic, Fujianese, and other dialects. The New York City Police Intelligence Division has been revamped, and agents are examining foreign newspapers and monitoring Internet sites. The department has set up several backup command centers in different parts of the city in case a terror attack puts headquarters out of operation. Backup senior command teams have been created so that if people at the highest levels of the department are killed, individuals will already have been tapped to step into their jobs. For example, the Lower Manhattan Security Initiative (LMSI) is a networked surveillance project designed to detect threats and perform preoperational terrorist surveillance south of Canal Street in lower Manhattan.

The department is also drawing on the expertise of other institutions around the city. For example, medical specialists have been enlisted to monitor daily developments in the city's hospitals to detect any suspicious outbreaks of illness that might reflect a biological attack. And the police are conducting joint drills with the New York Fire Department to avoid the problems in communication and coordination that marked the emergency response on September 11.

Combating Terrorism with the Courts

In April 2009, the U.S. attorney for the Southern District of New York brought federal charges against Haji Juma Khan, an Afghan who allegedly provided the Taliban with funding through his lucrative (and illegal) opium, morphine, and heroin trafficking organization, dubbed the "Khan Organization."[92] In the same month, Wesam al-Delaema pleaded guilty to conspiring to kill U.S. personnel in Iraq.[93] These are but two of the many terrorism-related cases that have been tried in the nation's court system. Prosecutions began to spike right after 9/11 and continue to grow today; there have been more than 800 prosecutions of suspected terrorists in the United States in the last decade.[94] Some notable terrorism prosecutions in recent years are set out in Exhibit 11.4.

EXHIBIT 11.4

Notable Terror Prosecutions

- *Toledo terror cell (Northern District of Ohio).* In June 2008, Mohammad Amawi, Marwan El-Hindi, and Wassim Mazloum were convicted of conspiracy to commit terrorist acts against Americans overseas, including U.S. armed forces in Iraq, and conspiracy to provide material support to terrorists. Amawi and El-Hindi were also convicted of distributing information regarding suicide bomb vests and improvised explosive devices.

- *Christopher Paul (Southern District of Ohio).* In June 2008, Paul pleaded guilty to conspiring with members of a German terrorist cell to use a weapon of mass destruction (explosive devices) against Americans vacationing at foreign tourist resorts and against Americans in the United States, as well as against U.S. embassies, diplomatic premises, and military bases in Europe.

- *Hassan Abujihaad (District of Connecticut).* In March 2008, Abujihaad, a former member of the U.S. Navy, was convicted of providing material support to terrorists and delivering classified information on the movements of a U.S. Navy battle group to Azzam Publications, a London-based organization alleged to have provided material support to persons engaged in terrorism.

- *Mohammed Jabarah (Southern District of New York).* In January 2008, Jabarah was sentenced to life in prison after pleading guilty to terrorism charges stemming from his participation in a plot to bomb U.S. embassies in Singapore and the Philippines. Jabarah trained in al-Qaeda camps in Afghanistan and spent time with Osama bin Laden, to whom he swore an oath of allegiance.

- *California prison plot (Central District of California).* In December 2007, Kevin James, who formed a radical Islamic organization while in California state prison, and two of his recruits, Levar Washington and Gregory Patterson, pleaded guilty to terrorism conspiracy charges, admitting they conspired to attack U.S. military facilities and Jewish facilities in Los Angeles.

- *Jose Padilla and co-defendants (Southern District of Florida).* In August 2007, a federal jury convicted Padilla, Adham Hassoun, and Kifah Jayyousi of conspiracy to murder, kidnap, and maim individuals in a foreign country, conspiracy to provide material support, and providing material support to terrorists. Padilla was sentenced to more than 17 years in prison.

- *Zacarias Moussaoui (Eastern District of Virginia).* In May 2006, Moussaoui was sentenced to six consecutive life terms after pleading guilty in April 2005 to various terrorism violations, admitting that he conspired with al-Qaeda to hijack and crash planes into prominent U.S. buildings as part of the 9/11 attacks.

- *Ahmed Omar Abu Ali (Eastern District of Virginia).* In November 2005, Ali was convicted on all counts of an indictment charging him with, among other violations, providing material support to al-Qaeda, conspiracy to assassinate the U.S. president, conspiracy to commit air piracy, and conspiracy to destroy aircraft. Ali was sentenced to 30 years in prison.[95]

SOURCE: U.S. Justice Department, "Fact Sheet: Justice Department Counter-Terrorism Efforts Since 9/11," http://www.justice.gov/opa/pr/2008/September/08-nsd-807 .html (accessed June 2014).

In addition to the trial courts, the Supreme Court has been involved in terror issues ever since Congress authorized President Bush to use "all necessary and appropriate force" against those responsible for the attacks in New York and Washington, D.C. Yaser Hamdi, an American citizen who had left the United States in his youth, was captured in Afghanistan and detained by military forces at Guantanamo Bay, Cuba, for supposedly aiding the Taliban. He was later moved to a military prison in Norfolk, Virginia, where he filed a writ of *habeas corpus*, arguing that, as a U.S. citizen, he was entitled to challenge the constitutionality of his confinement in federal court. In *Hamdi v. Rumsfeld* (2004), the Supreme Court agreed with his argument, holding in a 6–3 decision that the due process clause of the Fifth Amendment requires that U.S. citizens be given the opportunity to challenge their confinement in this way.[96] The Court also decided in *Rasul v. Bush* (2004) that the federal courts have jurisdiction to hear *habeas corpus* petitions from foreign nationals captured outside the United States.[97]

One year later, the Supreme Court heard a case involving Salim Hamdan, a Yemeni and former driver for Osama bin Laden. He was captured by Afghan warlords and turned over to U.S. forces in 2001. He was then transferred in 2002 to Guantanamo Bay and, in 2003, was slated to be tried for various conspiracy offenses before a military tribunal. He filed a *habeas corpus* petition in the U.S. District Court for the Western District of Washington, claiming that he could not legally be tried by a military tribunal. In a 5–3 decision, the Supreme Court agreed.[98] It held that the military commission at issue violated the Uniform Code of Military Justice and the four Geneva Conventions signed in 1949. Charges against him were subsequently dropped, but Hamdan was later deemed an "unlawful enemy combatant," tried once again before a military tribunal, and convicted. He was sentenced to five-and-a-half years in prison, given credit for time served, and sent back to Yemen. He was not named a combatant before going into his first trial, which is partly why the first military tribunal was illegal.

Shortly after Hamdan's case was decided, Congress passed the Military Commissions Act of 2006, which stripped the federal courts of jurisdiction to hear *habeas corpus* petitions from detainees who have been designated as "enemy combatants." In a 5–4 decision, the Supreme Court held that prisoners (even foreign nationals held at Guantanamo Bay) had the right to *habeas corpus* under the U.S. Constitution and that their arguments could be heard in the federal courts.[99] In effect, the Court held that the Military

Commissions Act of 2006 was an unconstitutional suspension of the right to *habeas corpus*. In October 2009, President Obama signed into law the Military Commissions Act of 2009, which attempted to improve on—and address some of the deficiencies of—the earlier legislation. For example, the law does not permit a U.S. citizen to be tried by a military commission.[100]

As a result of these cases, detainees, enemy combatants, terror suspects, and the like enjoy greater protection now than they did in the past. Indeed, all but a few of them enjoy the same rights as anyone else, whether or not they are U.S. citizens.

Confronting Terrorism with the Law

Soon after the September 11 terrorist attacks, the U.S. government enacted several laws focused on preventing further acts of violence against the United States and creating greater flexibility in the fight to control terror activity. Most importantly, Congress passed the **USA Patriot Act (USAPA)** on October 26, 2001. The bill is over 342 pages long, creates new laws, and makes changes to more than 15 existing statutes. Its aim is to give new powers to domestic law enforcement and international intelligence agencies in an effort to fight terrorism, to expand the definition of terrorist activities, and to alter sanctions for violent terrorism. While it is impossible to discuss every provision of this sweeping legislation here, a few of its more important elements will be examined.

The USA Patriot Act USAPA expands all four traditional tools of surveillance—wiretaps, search warrants, pen/trap orders (installing devices that record phone calls), and subpoenas. The Foreign Intelligence Surveillance Act (FISA), which allows domestic operations by intelligence agencies, is also expanded. USAPA gives greater power to the FBI to check and monitor phone, Internet, and computer records without first needing to demonstrate that they were being used by a suspect or target of a court order.

The government may now serve a single wiretap, or pen/trap order, on any person regardless of whether that person or entity is named in a court order. Prior to this act, telephone companies could be ordered to install pen/trap devices on their networks that would monitor calls coming to a surveillance target and to whom the surveillance target made calls; the USAPA extends this monitoring to the Internet. Law enforcement agencies may now also obtain the email addresses and websites visited by a target, and emails of the people with whom they communicate. It is possible to require that an Internet service provider install a device that records email and other electronic communications on its servers, looking for communications initiated or received by the target of an investigation. Under USAPA, the government does not need to show a court that the information or communication is relevant to a criminal investigation,

USA Patriot Act (USAPA) Legislation giving U.S. law enforcement agencies a freer hand to investigate and apprehend suspected terrorists.

nor does it have to report where it served the order or what information it received.

The act also allows enforcement agencies to monitor cable operators and obtain access to their records and systems. Before the act, a cable company had to give prior notice to the customer, even if that person was a target of an investigation. Information can now be obtained on people with whom the cable subscriber communicates, the content of the person's communications, and the person's subscription records; prior notice is still required if law enforcement agencies want to learn what television programming a subscriber purchases.

The act also expands the definition of "terrorism" and enables the government to monitor more closely those people suspected of "harboring" and giving "material support" to terrorists (Sections 803, 805). It increases the authority of the U.S. attorney general to detain and deport noncitizens with little or no judicial review. The attorney general may certify that he has "reasonable grounds to believe" that a noncitizen endangers national security and is therefore eligible for deportation. The attorney general and secretary of state are also given the authority to designate domestic groups as terrorist organizations and deport any noncitizen who is a member.

Civil Rights and the USA Patriot Act   Although law enforcement agencies may applaud these new laws, civil libertarians are troubled because they view the act as eroding civil rights. Some complain that there are provisions that permit the government to share information from grand jury proceedings and from criminal wiretaps with intelligence agencies. First Amendment protections may be violated because the Patriot Act authority is not limited to true terrorism investigations but covers a much broader range of activity involving reasonable political dissent. Though many critics have called for its repeal, the act has been repeatedly revised and extended. There have been a slew of provisions ensuring that the act does not violate civil rights by limiting its surveillance and wiretap authorizations.[101] The PATRIOT Sunsets Extension Act of 2011 extended provisions of the act concerning roving electronic surveillance orders, requests for the production of business records and other tangible things until June 1, 2015, and amended and extended the Intelligence Reform and Terrorism Prevention Act of 2004, revising the definition of an "agent of a foreign power" to include any non-U.S. person who engages in international terrorism or preparatory activities (the "lone wolf" provision).[102]

Combating Terrorism with Politics

In the long run, it may simply be impossible to defeat terror groups and end terrorism using military, law enforcement, or legal solutions. Using force may play into terrorists' hands and convince them that they are freedom fighters valiantly struggling against a better armed and more ruthless foe. No matter how many terrorists are killed and/or captured, military/deterrence-based solutions may be doomed. Aggressive reprisals will cause terrorist ideology to spread and gain greater acceptance in the underdeveloped world. The resulting anger and alienation will produce more terrorists than can be killed off through violent responses. In contrast, if the terrorist ideology is countered and discredited, the appeal of terror groups such as al-Qaeda will wither and die.

One approach suggested by policy experts is to undermine support for terrorist groups by being benevolent nation-builders giving aid to the nations that house terror groups.[103] This is the approach the United States took after World War II to rebuild Germany and Japan (the Marshall Plan) all the while gaining support for its Cold War struggle against the Soviet Union. According to the Rand Corporation, a nonprofit research group, the following steps are required to defeat jihadist groups such as al-Qaeda:

- Attack the ideological underpinnings of global jihadism
- Sever ideological and other links between terrorist groups
- Strengthen the capabilities of front-line states to counter local jihadist threats

This approach may work because al-Qaeda's goal of toppling "apostate" regimes in Saudi Arabia, Egypt, and Pakistan and creating an ultraorthodox pan-Islamic government spanning the world does not sit well with large groups of Muslims; their monolithic vision has no room for other Muslim sects such as Shi'ites and Sunni moderates. Therefore, political and social appeals may help fracture local support for al-Qaeda. In addition, the United States should seek to deny sanctuaries to terrorist groups and strengthen the capabilities of foreign governments to deal with terrorist threats, but in an advisory capacity by providing intelligence. In his book *Unconquerable Nation*, Brian Michael Jenkins, a noted expert on the topic, identifies the strategic principles he believes are the key to combating terror in contemporary society. These beliefs are summarized in Exhibit 11.5.

To access the websites of two leading government agencies that are involved in anti-terror activity and information gathering, go to:

- The Office of the Director of National Intelligence, **http://www.dni.gov/**
- The National Counterterrorism Center (NCTC), **http://www.nctc.gov/**

Do you believe the threat of terror in the United States has diminished because of governmental efforts? Or is it impossible to stop lone-wolf terrorists who act on their own?

EXHIBIT 11.5
Countering Terror

- *Destroy the jihadist enterprise.* Jihadists have proven to be flexible and resistant and capable of continued action despite sustained military actions. They remain the primary threat to U.S. national security and will continue to be so for the foreseeable future. Therefore, they must be destroyed and their ability to operate damaged.

- *Conserve resources for a long war.* These include blood, treasure, the will of the American people, and the support of needed allies. This means picking future fights carefully, making security measures both effective *and* efficient, maintaining domestic support, avoiding extreme measures that alienate the people, and cultivating rather than bullying other countries.

- *Wage more-effective political warfare.* Political solutions must be pragmatic. We must be ready to compromise. Amnesty should be offered to terrorists who have become disillusioned. Local leaders should be accommodated and deals cut to co-opt enemies.

- *Break the cycle of jihadism.* Jihadism is a cycle beginning with recruitment and ending with death, arrest, or detention. Combating terror must involve neutralizing terror groups' ability to radicalize and indoctrinate potential recruits before the cycle begins and then, at the end of the cycle, deal effectively with terror suspects once they have been captured and detained.

- *Impede recruitment.* Recruitment sites must be identified and made dangerous and therefore unusable. Alternatives to terror must be offered. Former, now disillusioned terrorists can be used to denounce terror and counteract its appeal with potential recruits.

- *Encourage defections and facilitate exits.* Potential defectors must be identified and encouraged to quit through the promise of amnesty, cash, job training, and homes.

- *Persuade detainees to renounce terrorism.* Rehabilitation of known terror suspects may be more important than prosecution and imprisonment.

- *Maintain international cooperation.* International cooperation is a prerequisite to success, a precious commodity not to be squandered by bullying, unreciprocated demands, indifference to local realities, or actions that repel even America's closest friends.

- *Reserve the right to retaliate—a muscular deterrent.* Terror groups and their sponsors should know that any attack using weapons of mass destruction will be met with all-out warfare against any group or government known to be or even suspected of being responsible.

SOURCE: Brian Michael Jenkins, *Unconquerable Nation: Knowing Our Enemy, Strengthening Ourselves* (Santa Monica, CA: Rand Corporation, 2006).

SUMMARY

LO1 Define the term *political crime*

Political crime is used to signify illegal acts that are designed to undermine an existing government and threaten its survival. Political crimes can include both violent and nonviolent acts and range in seriousness from dissent, treason, and espionage to violent acts such as terrorism or assassination.

LO2 Assess the cause of political crime

The political criminal and political crimes may stem from religious or ideological sources. They often occupy a gray area between conventional and outlawed behavior. While common criminals may be motivated by greed, vengeance, or jealousy, political criminals have a somewhat different agenda from common criminals. There is no set pattern or reason why someone becomes a political criminal. Some use political crime as a stepping-stone to public office while others use it as a method to focus their frustrations.

LO3 Compare and contrast the terms *espionage* and *treason*

Helping or cooperating with the enemy in a time of war would be considered treason. Espionage is the practice of obtaining information about a government, organization, or a society that is considered secret or confidential without the permission of the holder of the information. Industrial espionage involves unethical or illegal activities such as bribing employees to reveal trade secrets such as computer codes or product formulas.

LO4 List the components of state political crime

While some political crimes are committed by people who oppose the state, others are perpetrated by state authorities against the people they are supposed to serve. State political crime has five components: political corruption, illegal domestic surveillance, human rights violations, state violence, and state-corporate crime.

LO5 Debate the use and misuse of torture

The use of torture to gain information from suspected political criminals is highly controversial. The use of waterboarding has become a national issue because there seems to be no agreement on whether it is torture or a relatively harmless instrument of interrogation.

LO6 Distinguish among terrorists, insurgents, guerillas, and revolutionaries

Terrorism is generally defined as the illegal use of force against innocent people to achieve a political objective. The term *guerilla* refers to antigovernment forces located in rural areas that attack the military, the police, and government officials. The typical goal of an insurgency is to confront the existing government for control of all or a portion of its territory, or force political concessions in sharing political power. A revolution is generally seen as a civil war fought between nationalists and a sovereign power that holds control of the land, or between the existing government and local groups over issues of ideology and power.

LO7 List the various forms of terrorism

Revolutionary terrorists use violence to frighten those in power and their supporters in order to replace the existing government with a regime that holds acceptable political or religious views. Political terrorism is directed at people or groups who oppose the terrorists' political ideology or whom the terrorists define as "outsiders" who must be destroyed. Nationalist terrorism promotes the interests of a minority ethnic or religious group that believes it has been persecuted under majority rule and wishes to carve out its own independent homeland. Retributive terrorists want to impose their social and religious code on others. State-sponsored terrorism occurs when a repressive government regime forces its citizens into obedience, oppresses minorities, and stifles political dissent. Sometimes terrorist groups become involved in common-law crimes such as drug dealing and kidnapping, even selling nuclear materials.

LO8 Explain what motivates the terrorist to commit violent acts

While not all terrorists suffer from psychological deficits, enough do so that the typical terrorist can be described as an emotionally disturbed individual who acts out his or her psychoses within the confines of violent groups. Another view is that because they are out of the political and social mainstream, young men and women are motivated to join terror groups because they suffer alienation and lack the tools to compete in a post-technological society. Yet another view is that terrorists hold extreme religious and/or ideological beliefs that prompt their behavior.

LO9 List examples of the efforts being made to centralize intelligence gathering

The Director of National Intelligence (DNI) is charged with coordinating data from the nation's primary intelligence-gathering agencies. The National Counterterrorism Center (NCTC) serves as the primary organization in the U.S. government for analyzing and integrating all intelligence possessed or acquired by the government pertaining to terrorism and counterterrorism, excepting purely domestic counterterrorism information.

LO10 Describe the efforts by the FBI and DHS to fight terrorism

The FBI announced a reformulation of its priorities, making protecting the United States from terrorist attack its number one commitment. It is now charged with coordinating intelligence collection with the Border Patrol, Secret Service, and the CIA. The Department of Homeland Security (DHS) is the federal agency responsible for preventing terrorist attacks within the United States, reducing America's vulnerability to terrorism, and minimizing the damage and recovering from attacks that do occur.

CRITICAL THINKING QUESTIONS

1. Would you be willing to give up some of your civil rights in order to aid the war on terror?
2. Should terror suspects arrested in a foreign land be given the same rights and privileges as an American citizen accused of crime?
3. What groups in America might be the breeding ground for terrorist activity in the United States?
4. In light of the 9/11 attack, should acts of terrorism be treated differently from other common-law violent crimes?

Should terrorists be executed for their acts even if no one is killed during their attack?

5. Can the use of torture ever be justified? Is the "ticking bomb" scenario valid?
6. A spy gives plans for a new weapon to the enemy. They build the weapon and use it to kill American soldiers. Is the spy guilty of murder?

political crime (374)

al-Qaeda (Arabic for "the base") (374)

election fraud (376)

treason (378)

espionage (379)

state political crime (382)

torture (383)

ticking bomb scenario (383)

terrorism (384)

guerilla (385)

insurgents (385)

zealots (387)

Reign of Terror (388)

retributive terrorists (391)

state-sponsored terrorism (392)

networks (393)

terror cells (393)

failed state (395)

Director of National Intelligence (DNI) (398)

Department of Homeland Security (DHS) (399)

USA Patriot Act (USAPA) (402)

NOTES

1. Charlie Savage and Mark Mazzetti, "Cryptic Overtures and a Clandestine Meeting Gave Birth to a Blockbuster Story," *New York Times*, June 10, 2013, http://www.nytimes.com/2013/06/11/us/how-edward-j-snowden-orchestrated-a-blockbuster-story.html (accessed June 2014).

2. James Risen, "Snowden Says He Took No Secret Files to Russia," *New York Times*, January 20, 2014, http://www.nytimes.com/2013/10/18/world/snowden-says-he-took-no-secret-files-to-russia.html (accessed June 2014).

3. Jeffrey Ian Ross, *The Dynamics of Political Crime* (Thousand Oaks, CA: Sage, 2003).

4. Human Rights Watch, "UN: Reject Syria's Human Rights Council Candidacy, Country Under Investigation by Rights Body Not Fit to Join," May 6, 2011, http://www.hrw.org/en/news/2011/05/06/un-reject-syria-s-human-rights-council-candidacy (accessed May 2014).

5. Stephen Farrell and Anthony Shadid, "Dozens Killed in Wave of Attacks Across Iraq," *New York Times*, August 25, 2010, http://www.nytimes.com/2010/08/26/world/middleeast/26iraq.html (accessed May 2014).

6. Stephen Schafer, *The Political Criminal, The Problem of Morality and Crime* (New York: Free Press, 1974), pp. 154–157.

7. Randy Borum, "Understanding the Terrorist Mind-Set," *FBI Law Enforcement Bulletin* 72 (2003): 7–10.

8. FBI, "Election Hack: Stealing Votes the Cyber Way," August 5, 2013, http://www.fbi.gov/news/stories/2013/august/election-hack-stealing-votes-the-cyber-way/election-hack-stealing-votes-the-cyber-way (accessed May 2014).

9. Amnesty International, "Kenya: Amnesty International Concerned at Police Killings in Election Protests," December 31, 2007, http://www.amnesty.org/en/for-media/press-releases/kenya-amnesty-international-concerned-police-killings-election-protests- (accessed May 2014).

10. Internal Revenue Service, "Examples of Public Corruption Investigations – Fiscal Year 2013."

11. BBC news, "Profile of John Walker Lindh," January 24, 2002, http://news.bbc.co.uk/2/hi/americas/1779455.stm (accessed May 2014).

12. University of Missouri–Kansas City School of Law, Douglas Linder, "The Treason Trial of Aaron Burr," http://www.law.umkc.edu/faculty/projects/ftrials/burr/burraccount.html (accessed May 2014).

13. John Ziff and Austin Sarat, *Espionage and Treason* (New York: Chelsea House, 1999).

14. United States Criminal Code at 18 U.S.C. § 2381.

15. CNN, "Accused FBI Spy Hanssen Pleads Not Guilty," May 31, 2001, http://edition.cnn.com/2001/LAW/05/31/hanssen.arraignment.02/ (accessed May 2014).

16. David Owen, *Hidden Secrets: The Complete History of Espionage and the Technology Used to Support It* (Ontario, Canada: Firefly Books, 2002).

17. BBC News, "Key Cases in Soviet-UK Espionage," January 23, 2006, http://news.bbc.co.uk/2/hi/europe/4639130.stm (accessed May 2014).

18. Lawrence Schiller, *Into the Mirror: The Life of Master Spy Robert P. Hanssen* (Darby, PA: Diane Publications, 2004).

19. Hedieh Nasheri, *Economic Espionage and Industrial Spying* (Cambridge, England: Cambridge University Press, 2004).

20. Tim Culpan, "China's Clock-Punching Hackers Show Spying as Routine Job," *Bloomberg News*, May 27, 2014, http://www.bloomberg.com/news/2014-05-27/china-s-clock-punching-hackers-show-spying-as-routine-job.html (accessed May 2014).

21. Office of the National Counterintelligence Executive, "Annual Report to Congress on Foreign Economic Collection and Industrial Espionage, 2005," http://www.fas.org/irp/ops/ci/docs/2005.pdf (accessed May 2014).

22. Office of the National Counterintelligence Executive, "Foreign Spies Stealing US Economic Secrets in Cyberspace," 2011, http://www.ncix.gov/publications/reports/fecie_all/Foreign_Economic_Collection_2011.pdf (accessed May 2014).

23. Department of Justice news release, "Two Men Plead Guilty to Stealing Trade Secrets from Silicon Valley Companies to Benefit China," December 14, 2006, http://www.justice.gov/criminal/cybercrime/press-releases/2006/yePlea.htm (accessed May 2014).

24. Nadia Abou El-Magd, "Accuser in Case vs. CIA Agents Tells of Torture: Muslim Cleric Says Egyptians Used Electricity," *Boston Globe*, February 23, 2007, A3.

25. Alan M. Dershowitz, *Shouting Fire: Civil Liberties in a Turbulent Age* (New York: Little, Brown, 2002); Dershowitz, "Want to Torture? Get a Warrant," *San Francisco Chronicle*, January 22, 2002.

26. Human Rights Watch, "The Twisted Logic of Torture," January 2005, http://hrw.org/wr2k5/darfurandabughraib/6.htm (accessed May 2014).

27. Jessica Wolfendale, "Training Torturers: A Critique of the 'Ticking Bomb' Argument," *Social Theory and Practice* 31 (2006): 269–287. Elizabeth Sepper, "The Ties That Bind: How the Constitution Limits the CIA's Actions in the War on Terror," *New York University Law Review* 81 (2006): 1805–1843.

28. Vittorio Bufacchi and Jean Maria Arrigo, "Torture, Terrorism and the State: A Refutation of the Ticking-Bomb Argument," *Journal of Applied Philosophy* 23 (2006): 355–373.

29. Scott Shane, David Johnston, and James Risen, "Secret U.S. Endorsement of Severe Interrogations," *New York Times*, October 4, 2007, http://www.nytimes.com/2007/10/04/washington/04interrogate.html (accessed May 2014).

30. Michael Cooper and Marc Santora, "McCain Rebukes Giuliani on Waterboarding Remark," *New York Times*, October 26, 2007, http://www.nytimes.com/2007/10/26/us/politics/26giuliani.html (accessed May 2014).

31. CNN News, "Benghazi Consulate Attack Fast Facts," http://www.cnn.com/2013/09/10/world/benghazi-consulate-attack-fast-facts/ (accessed May 2014).

32. Title 22 of the United States Code section 2656f (d) (1999).

33. Paul Wilkinson, *Terrorism and the Liberal State* (New York: Wiley, 1977), p. 49.

34. Jack Gibbs, "Conceptualization of Terrorism," *American Sociological Review* 54 (1989): 329–340, at 330.

35. Robert Friedlander, *Terrorism* (Dobbs Ferry, NY: Oceana Publishers, 1979), p. 14.

36. Daniel Georges-Abeyie, "Political Crime and Terrorism," in *Crime and Deviance: A Comparative Perspective*, ed. Graeme Newman (Beverly Hills: Sage, 1980), pp. 313–333.

37. "Differences Between Terrorism and Insurgency," http://www.terrorism-research.com/insurgency/ (accessed May 2014).

38. Tim Arango, Kareem Fahim and Ben Hubbard, "Rebels' Fast Strike in Iraq Was Years in the Making," *New York Times*, June 15, 2014, http://www.nytimes.com/2014/06/15/world/middleeast/rebels-fast-strike-in-iraq-was-years-in-the-making.html (accessed June 2014).

39. Andrew Silke, "Holy Warriors: Exploring the Psychological Processes of Jihadi Radicalization," *European Journal of Criminology* 5 (2008): 99–123.

40. Walter Laqueur, *The New Terrorism: Fanaticism and the Arms of Mass Destruction* (New York: Oxford University Press, 1999).

41. This section relies heavily on Friedlander, *Terrorism*, pp. 8–20.

42. Michael Kellogg. *The Russian Roots of Nazism: White Russians and the Making of National Socialism, 1917–1945* (New York: Cambridge University Press, 2005).

43. Bryan Denson, "Eco-Saboteur Rebecca Rubin Pleads Guilty to Arson, but Won't Give Up Any Names, *The Oregonian*, October 11, 2013, http://www.oregonlive.com/portland/index.ssf/2013/10/eco-saboteur_rebecca_rubin_ple.html (accessed May 2014).

44. Jocelyn Parker, "Vehicles Burn at Dealership: SUV Attacks Turn Violent," *Detroit Free Press*, August 23, 2003, p. 1.

45. "Brutal Elves in the Woods," *The Economist* 359 (2001): 28–30.

46. Steve Miletich, "Hunt Is On: Who Torched the Street of Dreams?" *Seattle Times*, March 4, 2008, http://seattletimes.com/html/snohomishcountynews/2004258337_arson04m.html (accessed May 2014).

47. Fiona Proffitt, "Costs of Animal Rights Terror," *Science* 304 (2004): 1731–1739.

48. Council on Foreign Relations, "Hezbollah," http://www.cfr.org/lebanon/hezbollah-k-hizbollah-hizbullah/p9155 (accessed May 2014).

49. Chung Chien-Peng, "China's War on Terror," *Foreign Affairs* 81 (2002): 8–13.

50. Angel Rabasa, Peter Chalk, Kim Cragin, Sara A. Daly, Heather S. Gregg, Theodore W. Karasik, Kevin A. O'Brien, and William Rosenau, *Beyond al-Qaeda Part 1, The Global Jihadist Movement*, xviii, and *Part 2, The Outer Rings of the Terrorist Universe* (Santa Monica, CA: Rand Corporation, 2006).

51. Farouk Chothia, "Who are Nigeria's Boko Haram Islamists?" BBCNews Africa, May 20, 2014, http://www.bbc.com/news/world-africa-13809501 (accessed May 2014).

52. Lawrence Miller, "The Terrorist Mind: A Psychological and Political Analysis, Part I," *International Journal of Offender Therapy and Comparative Criminology* 50 (2006): 121–138.

53. Martin Libicki, Peter Chalk, and Melanie Sisson, *Exploring Terrorist Targeting Preferences* (Santa Monica, CA: Rand Corporation 2007), http://www.rand.org/pubs/monographs/MG483/ (accessed May 2014).

54. Mark Mazzetti and David Rohde, "Al Qaeda Chiefs Are Seen to Regain Power," *New York Times*, February 19, 2007, p. 1; Sanjeev Gupta, Benedict Clements, Rina Bhattacharya, and Shamit Chakravarti, "Fiscal Consequences of Armed Conflict and Terrorism in Low- and Middle-Income Countries," *European Journal of Political Economy* 20 (2004): 403–421.

55. Ibid.

56. Gabriela Fried, "Piecing Memories Together After State Terror and Policies of Oblivion in Uruguay: The Female Political Prisoner's Testimonial Project (1997–2004)," *Social Identities* 12 (2006): 543–562.

57. Martin Miller, "Ordinary Terrorism in Historical Perspective." *Journal for the Study of Radicalism* 2 (2008): 125–154.

58. Mark Hamm, "'High Crimes and Misdemeanors': George W. Bush and the Sins of Abu Ghraib," *Crime, Media, Culture: An International Journal* 3 (2007): 259–284.

59. Chris Dishman, "Terrorism, Crime, and Transformation," *Studies in Conflict and Terrorism* 24 (2001): 43–56.

60. Richard Lough, "Piracy Ransom Cash Ends Up with Somali Militants," Reuters, July 6, 2011, http://www.reuters.com/article/2011/07/06/somalia-piracy-idUSL-DE7650U320110706 (accessed May 2014).

61. *Frontline*, "Osama bin Laden v. the U.S.: Edicts and Statements," http://www.pbs.org/wgbh/pages/frontline/shows/binladen/who/edicts.html (accessed May 2014).

62. Michael Scott Doran, "Somebody Else's Civil War," *Foreign Affairs* 81 (2002): 22–25; Peter L. Bergen, *Holy War, Inc.: Inside The Secret World of Osama bin Laden* (New York, Free Press, 2001), pp. 41–50; Yonah Alexander and Michael S. Swetnam, *Usama bin Laden's al-Qaida: Profile of a Terrorist Network* (New York: Transnational Publishers, 2001); Michael Kranish and Anthony Shadid, "Bin Laden Zeal for Stature Used Psychology, Religion," *Boston Globe*, November 19, 2001, p. 3; *Frontline*, "Osama bin Laden v. the U.S.: Edicts and Statements."

63. Stephen J. Morgan, *The Mind of a Terrorist Fundamentalist: The Psychology of Terror Cults* (Awe-Struck E-Books, 2001); Martha

Crenshaw, "The Psychology of Terrorism: An Agenda for the 21st Century," *Political Psychology* 21 (2000): 405–420.

64. Andrew Silke, "Courage in Dark Places: Reflections on Terrorist Psychology," *Social Research* 71 (2004): 177–198.

65. Arie Kruglanski and Shira Fishman, "Terrorism: Between 'Syndrome' and 'Tool,'" *Current Directions in Psychological Science* 15 (2006): 45–48.

66. Charles Ruby, "Are Terrorists Mentally Deranged?" *Analyses of Social Issues and Public Policy* 2 (2002): 15–26.

67. David Lester, Bijou Yang, and Mark Lindsay, "Suicide Bombers: Are Psychological Profiles Possible?" *Studies in Conflict and Terrorism* 27 (2004): 283–295.

68. Randy Borum, *Psychology of Terrorism* (Tampa: University of South Florida, 2004), http://www.ncjrs.gov/pdffiles1/nij/grants/208552.pdf (accessed May 2014).

69. Ethan Bueno de Mesquita, "The Quality of Terror," *American Journal of Political Science* 49 (2005): 515–530.

70. Saroj Kumar Rath, *Social Research Reports* 21 (2012): 23–36.

71. Jerrold Post, "When Hatred Is Bred in the Bone: Psycho-cultural Foundations of Contemporary Terrorism," *Political Psychology* 25 (2005): 615–637.

72. Marc Sageman, *Understanding Terror Networks* (Philadelphia: University of Pennsylvania Press, 2004), Ch. 4.

73. This section leans heavily on Anthony Stahelski, "Terrorists Are Made, Not Born: Creating Terrorists Using Social Psychological Conditioning," *Journal of Homeland Security* (March 2004), https://docs.google.com/document/d/1PF1hNe_V0Jc3w3v-zyEct-dq4NOypxWWWMSMu7nmHHXc/ (accessed May 2014).

74. Sageman, *Understanding Terror Networks*, Chapter 4.

75. Seth Schwartz, Curtis Dunkel, and Alan Waterman, "Terrorism: An Identity Theory Perspective," *Studies in Conflict and Terrorism* 32 (2009): 537–559.

76. Ibid.

77. Schwartz, Dunkel, and Waterman, "Terrorism: An Identity Theory Perspective."

78. Sageman, *Understanding Terror Networks*.

79. Patricia Marchak, *Reigns of Terror* (Montreal: McGill-Queen's University Press, 2003).

80. Ibid., pp. 153–155.

81. Daniel Miller, "New Leader of Pakistan Taliban Vows Wave of Terror Attacks to Avenge the Death of His Predecessor," *Daily Mail*, November 8, 2013, http://www.dailymail.co.uk/news/article-2492823/New-leader-Pakistan-Taliban-vows-wave-terror-attacks-avenge-death-predecessor.html (accessed May 2014).

82. National Consortium for the Study of Terrorism and Responses to Terrorism (START), "Despite Fewer Attacks in Western World,

Global Terrorism Increasing," December 19, 2013, http://www.start.umd.edu//news/despite-fewer-attacks-western-world-global-terrorism-increasing (accessed May 2014).

83. William Braniff, "Discussion Point: The State of Al-Qaida, its Affiliates and Associated Groups," House Armed Services Committee Oral Testimony, February 4, 2014, http://www.start.umd.edu/news/discussion-point-state-al-qaida-its-affiliates-and-associated-groups (accessed May 2014).

84. Graham Allison, *Nuclear Terrorism: The Ultimate Preventable Catastrophe* (New York: Times Books, 2004).

85. Rand Corporation, "How Prepared Are State and Local Law Enforcement for Terrorism?" http://www.rand.org/publications/RB/RB9093/ (accessed May 2014).

86. FBI, "Protecting America from Terrorist Attack: Our Joint Terrorism Task Forces," http://www.fbi.gov/about-us/investigate/terrorism/terrorism_jttfs (accessed May 2014).

87. Homeland Security, "Information Sharing," http://www.dhs.gov/topic/information-sharing (accessed May 2014). The section on homeland security relies heavily on "The Department of Homeland Security," http://www.whitehouse.gov/infocus/homeland/ (accessed May 2014).

88. Arizona Department of Public Safety, *Arizona Fusion Center*, http://www.azdps.gov/about/Task_Forces/Fusion/. Also see http://www.azactic.gov/ (sites accessed May 2014.)

89. http://www.azactic.gov/About/Operation/ (accessed May 2014).

90. Harris County Homeland Security and Emergency Management, http://www.hcoem.org (accessed May 2014).

91. NYPD, Counterterrorism Bureau, http://www.nyc.gov/html/nypd/html/administration/counterterrorism_units.shtml (accessed May 2014).

92. U.S. Attorney for the Southern District of New York Press Release No. 09-103, "Afghan Drug Kingpin Charged with Terrorist Financing for Funding Taliban Insurgency," April 21, 2009.

93. Del Quentin Wilbur, "U.S. Judge Sentences Dutch Man to 25 Years for Crimes in Iraq," *Washington Post*, April 17, 2009, A7.

94. Center on Law and Security, New York School of Law, *Terrorist Trial Report Card*.

95. U.S. Justice Department, "Fact Sheet: Justice Department Counter-Terrorism Efforts Since 9/11," http://www.justice.gov/opa/pr/2008/September/08-nsd-807.html (accessed May 2014).

96. *Hamdi v. Rumsfeld*, 542 U.S. 507 (2004).

97. *Rasul v. Bush*, 542 U.S. 466 (2004).

98. *Hamdan v. Rumsfeld*, 548 U.S. 557 (2006).

99. *Boumediene v. Bush*, 553 U.S. 723 (2008).

100. See Section 948c of the Military Commissions Act of 2009, http://www.defense.gov/news/2009%20MCA%20Pub%20%20Law%20111-84.pdf (accessed May 2014).

101. Senator Feingold on the USA Patriot Act, http://epic.org/privacy/terrorism/usapatriot/feingold.html (accessed May 2014).

102. United States Department of Justice, "Uniting and Strengthening America by Providing Appropriate Tools Required to Intercept and Obstruct Terrorism (USA PATRIOT) Act of 2001," https://it.ojp.gov/default.aspx?area=privacy&page=1281 (accessed May 2014).

103. Rabasa et al., *Beyond al-Qaeda* Part 1.

learning objectives

LO1 Discuss the history of theft offenses

LO2 Compare and contrast professional and amateur thieves

LO3 Describe the activities of a professional fence

LO4 Differentiate between petty and grand larceny

LO5 Compare professional and amateur shoplifters

LO6 Explain the concept of embezzlement

LO7 Describe the elements of sexual burglary

LO8 Compare the activities of male and female burglars

LO9 Describe what it takes to be a "good burglar"

LO10 Discuss why people commit arson for profit

PROPERTY CRIME

When it comes to shoplifting, Sameh Khaled Danhach knew how to run a serious and sophisticated operation. Danhach headed up SKD Trading, Inc., and Lifetime Wholesale, Inc., both shell companies located in Houston that allowed him to carry out a large-scale shoplifting scheme. Danhach employed teams who targeted major U.S. retail stores and pharmacies, walking out with stolen products of all kinds, from medicine and baby formula to beauty supplies. Team members received a small percentage of the actual value of the stolen property, always in cash so there'd be no paper trail. The shoplifting team then shipped the merchandise back to Danhach's warehouse using phony accounts with bogus business names, email addresses, and credit cards set up by Danhach. The shipping companies were also victimized—they rarely, if ever, got paid. Once the stolen merchandise was in Danhach's possession, he would have his people remove antitheft devices and store stickers, and then he would ship the goods to various wholesalers, who in some cases sold them right back to the companies from which they had been stolen. Danhach's scheme involved an estimated $10 million worth of products that were swiped *every year* from 2008 to 2012. To make matters worse, many of the goods—compromised by being stored and shipped under improper conditions and some sold past their expiration dates—eventually were resold to unsuspecting consumers.

When law enforcement agents entered Danhach's warehouse with a warrant, they found more than $300,000 worth of stolen over-the-counter medications, shampoos, and baby formula, along with financial ledgers showing that he made more than a million dollars in profit during one six-month period.[1]

While Danhach's scheme was certainly substantial, it is by no means unique. NCVS data tell us that about 20 million theft-related offenses occur each year, and the number and rate have been relatively stable for the past decade.[2]

As a group, theft offenses involve the intentional and unauthorized taking, keeping, or using of another's property. Theft can be accomplished through stealth, deceit, or fraud, but the intent is to misappropriate someone else's property for the thief's personal benefit. The range and scope of U.S. criminal activity motivated by the desire for financial gain are tremendous. Self-report studies show that property crime is widespread among the young in every social class. National surveys of criminal behavior indicate that millions of personal and household thefts occur annually. Though average citizens may be puzzled and enraged by violent crimes, believing them to be both senseless and cruel, they often view economic crimes with a great deal more ambivalence. Society generally disapproves of crimes involving theft and corruption, but the public seems quite tolerant of the "gentleman bandit," even to the point of admiring such figures. They pop up as characters in popular myths and legends—such as the famed English outlaw Robin Hood—and in films such as *Ocean's Eleven* (2001) and *Ocean's Twelve* (2004), and *Ocean's Thirteen* (2007) in which a suave George Clooney and roguish Brad Pitt lead a band of thieves who loot hundreds of millions of dollars from casinos, galleries, and so on (see also *The Italian Job* with Mark Wahlberg or *Inside Man* with Denzel Washington for more films featuring gentlemen bandits).

How can such ambivalence toward thievery be explained? For one thing, if self-report surveys are accurate, national tolerance toward economic criminals may be prompted by the fact that almost every U.S. citizen has at some time been involved in economic crime. Even those among us who would never consider ourselves lawbreakers may have at one time engaged in petty theft as a teen, stolen a textbook from a college bookstore, cheated on our income tax, or pilfered from our place of employment. Consequently, it may be difficult for society to condemn economic criminals without feeling hypocritical.

People may also be somewhat more tolerant of **economic crimes** because they never seem to seriously hurt anyone—banks are insured, large businesses pass along losses to consumers, stolen cars can be easily replaced and, in most cases, are insured. The true pain of economic crime often goes unappreciated. Convicted offenders, especially businesspeople who commit white-collar crimes involving millions of dollars, often are punished rather lightly.

This chapter is the first of two that review the nature and extent of economic crime in the United States. It is divided into two principal sections. The first deals with the concept of professional crime and focuses on different types of professional criminals, including the **fence**, a buyer and seller of stolen merchandise. The chapter then turns to a discussion of common-law theft-related offense such as larceny, burglary, and arson. Chapter 13 covers crimes that involve individuals and organizations involved in criminal enterprise—white-collar, green, and organized crime.

A BRIEF HISTORY OF THEFT

LO1 Discuss the history of theft offenses

Theft is not a phenomenon unique to modern times; the illegal taking of the personal property of another has been known throughout recorded history. The Crusades of the eleventh century inspired peasants and downtrodden noblemen to leave the shelter of their estates to prey on passing pilgrims.[3] Crusaders felt it within their rights to appropriate the possessions of any infidels—Greeks, Jews, or Muslims—they happened to encounter during their travels.

By the thirteenth century, returning pilgrims, not content to live as serfs on feudal estates, gathered in the forests of England and the Continent to poach game that was the rightful property of their lord or king and, when possible, to steal from passing strangers. By the fourteenth century, many such highwaymen and poachers were full-time livestock thieves, stealing great numbers of cattle and sheep.[4] The fifteenth and sixteenth centuries brought hostilities between England and France in what has come to be known as the Hundred Years' War. Foreign mercenary troops fighting for both sides roamed the countryside; loot and pillage were viewed as a rightful part of their pay. As cities developed and a permanent class of propertyless urban poor was established, theft became more professional.[5] By the eighteenth century, three separate groups of property criminals were active: skilled thieves, smugglers, and poachers.

- **Skilled thieves** typically worked in the larger cities, such as London and Paris. This group included pickpockets, forgers, and counterfeiters, who operated freely. They congregated in **flash houses**—public meeting places, often taverns, that served as headquarters for

economic crime An act in violation of the criminal law that is designed to bring financial gain to the offender.

fence A buyer and seller of stolen merchandise.

skilled thieves Thieves who typically work in the larger cities, such as London and Paris. This group includes pickpockets, forgers, and counterfeiters, who operate freely.

flash houses Public meeting places in England, often taverns, that served as headquarters for gangs.

gangs. Here, deals were made, crimes were plotted, and the sale of stolen goods was negotiated.[6]

- **Smugglers** moved freely in sparsely populated areas and transported goods, such as spirits, gems, gold, spices, tea, and coffee, without bothering to pay tax or duty.
- **Poachers** lived in the country and supplemented their diet and income by hunting game such as deer and pheasants that belonged to a landlord.

Professional thieves in the larger cities banded together into gangs to protect themselves, increase the scope of their activities, and help dispose of stolen goods. Jack Wild, perhaps London's most famous thief, perfected the process of buying and selling stolen goods and gave himself the title of Thief-Taker General of Great Britain and Ireland. Before he was hanged, Wild controlled numerous gangs and dealt harshly with any thief who violated his strict code of conduct.[7] During this period, individual theft-related crimes began to be defined by the common law. The most important of these categories are still used today.

Theft in the Nineteenth Century: Train Robbery and Safecracking

In the nineteenth century, two new forms of theft appeared. Train robbery hit the nation hard when, in 1866, $700,000 (the equivalent of more than $9 million in today's currency) was taken from an Adams Express car on the New York, New Haven, and Hartford Railroad; it was the first train robbery on record. Also in 1866, the Reno brothers stole $13,000 in their first train holdup. The four brothers and their gang went on to rob a number of banks and trains in southern Indiana and Illinois before being tracked down by the Pinkerton Detective Agency in 1868 (three of the four brothers were lynched by a gang of vigilantes who attacked the jail where they were being held before trial).[8]

To read about the colorful history of the Pinkerton detectives, go to their website: **http://www.pinkerton .com/history/.**
Would you consider the early Pinkerton detectives bounty hunters?

Train robbery flourished toward the end of the nineteenth century because professional robbers considered trains easy pickings.[9] Law enforcement was decentralized, and robbers could escape over the border to a neighboring state to avoid detection. Security arrangements were minimal, and robbers could stop, board, and loot trains with little fear of capture. As the threat to trains increased, improvements were initiated in an effort to deter would-be robbers:

- Plainclothes officers were placed on trains and rode unobtrusively among the passengers.
- Baggage cars were equipped with ramps and stalls containing fleet horses that could be used to immediately pursue bandits.
- Cars were made with finer precision and strength to make them impregnable.
- Forensic science made it easier to identify robbers, and improved communication made it easier to capture them.

Federal involvement in train protection extended the ability of law enforcement beyond the county or state in which the robbery occurred. As a result of these innovations, the number of train robberies decreased from 29 in 1900 to 7 in 1905; by 1920, train robbers had all but disappeared.[10]

Safecracking Secured boxes and safes have existed for centuries, but it wasn't until early in the twentieth century that use of cast iron became widespread and was used to create solid metal boxes. Safecracking also underwent a dramatic change due to technological changes in the design of safes. In the early 1900s, safes were made of manganese steel because it was resistant to drilling and was fireproof. With the invention and distribution of acetylene torches in the latter part of the nineteenth century, safes constructed of manganese became vulnerable and encouraged safecrackers to commit bold crimes. Safe manufacturers fought back by constructing safes with alternating sheets of copper and steel. The copper diffused heat and made the safe resistant to being torched. In response, safecrackers shifted their approach to attacking safes' locks and locking mechanisms. They developed mechanical devices that either dismantled or destroyed locks. Some burglars developed methods of peeling the laminated layers of the safe apart.

After World War II, safecrackers began using carbide and then diamond drill bits, which tore through metal. Safe manufacturers responded by lining safes with new metals designed to chip or break drill bits. They also developed sophisticated security systems featuring light beams, which would trip an alarm if the beam was interrupted by an intruder. When thieves learned how to neutralize these alarms, motion detectors and ultrasonic systems were implemented, which fill the space with sound waves and set off alarms when they are disturbed. Though these systems can be defeated, it requires expensive electronic gear, which

smugglers Thieves who move freely in sparsely populated areas and transport goods, such as spirits, gems, gold, and spices, without bothering to pay tax or duty.

poachers Early English thieves who typically lived in the country and supplemented their diet and income with game that belonged to a landlord.

most criminals can neither afford nor operate. As a result, the number of safecrackers has declined, and the crime of safecracking is relatively rare.[11]

To read more about Jack Wild and his times, go to the website of the Old Bailey Court in England: http://www.oldbaileyonline.org/. Who would be the contemporary equivalent of Jack Wild? How about Whitey Bulger? Read about him here http://www.biography.com/people/whitey-bulger–328770.

CONTEMPORARY THEFT

LO2 Compare and contrast professional and amateur thieves

Theft is still a popular criminal pastime, and millions of property and theft-related crimes occur each year. Most are committed by **occasional criminals** who do not define themselves by a criminal role or view themselves as committed career criminals; other theft-offenders are in fact skilled **professional criminals**. The following sections review these two orientations toward property crime.

Occasional Thieves

Occasional offenders are not professional criminals; they do not make theft their occupation. Many are school-age youths who are unlikely to enter into a criminal career and whose behavior has been described as drifting between conventional and criminal. Added to the pool of amateur thieves are adults who may occasionally violate the criminal law—shoplifters, pilferers, petty thieves—but whose main source of income comes from conventional means and whose self-identity is not criminal. Added together, their behaviors form the bulk of theft crimes.

occasional criminals Offenders who do not define themselves by a criminal role or view themselves as committed career criminals.

professional criminals Offenders who make a significant portion of their income from crime.

situational inducement Short-term influence on a person's behavior, such as financial problems or peer pressure, that increases risk taking.

When amateurs decide to steal, their decision is spontaneous and based on **situational inducements**, short-term influences on a person's behavior that increase risk taking.[12] They include psychological factors, such as an immediate and unsolvable financial problem, and social factors, such as peer pressure to commit a spontaneous criminal act—taking a car for a drunken joyride or breaking into a store or home.

While members of every layer of the economy may at some time experience a situational inducement, the opportunity to solve economic crisis through criminal activity is structured by class. While the poor are forced to engage in low-profit, high-risk crimes, members of the upper class have the opportunity to engage in the more lucrative business-related crimes of price fixing, bribery, and embezzlement.

Unlike professionals, occasional thieves do not receive informal peer group support for their crimes. In fact, they will deny any connection to a criminal lifestyle and instead view their transgressions as being "out of character." They may see their crimes as being motivated by necessity. When apprehended, they say they were only "borrowing" the car the police caught them with; they were going to pay for the merchandise they stole from the store, they just "forgot" to go through the checkout line. Because of their lack of commitment to a criminal lifestyle, occasional offenders may be the most likely to respond to the general deterrent effect of the law.

Professional Thieves

In contrast to occasional thieves, professional criminals make a significant portion of their income from crime. Professionals do not delude themselves with the belief

Bank robbery is still a common occurrence. A series of photos shows Andrew Maberry, a serial bank robber dubbed the "I-55 Bandit," in (from left) Hurricane, West Virginia, on July 30, 2013; Arnold, Missouri, on July 2, 2013; and Bel Air, Maryland, on June 5, 2013. Maberry, 19, of O'Fallon, Illinois, pleaded guilty to a bank robbery charge in U.S. District Court in St. Louis. He was eventually sentenced to five years in prison.

AP Images/Federal Bureau of Investigation

that their acts are impulsive, one-time efforts, nor do they employ elaborate rationalizations to excuse the harmfulness of their action ("shoplifting doesn't really hurt anyone"). Consequently, professionals pursue their craft with vigor, attempting to learn from older, experienced criminals the techniques that will earn them the most money with the least risk. Though their numbers are relatively few, professionals engage in crimes that produce the greater losses to society and perhaps cause the more significant social harm.

Professional theft traditionally refers to nonviolent forms of criminal behavior that are undertaken with a high degree of skill for monetary gain and that exploit interests tending to maximize financial opportunities and minimize the possibilities of apprehension. The most typical forms include pocket-picking, burglary, shoplifting, forgery and counterfeiting, extortion, sneak theft, and confidence swindling.[13]

Relatively little is known about the career patterns of professional thieves and criminals. From the literature on crime and delinquency, three patterns emerge:

- Youth come under the influence of older, experienced criminals who teach them the trade.
- Juvenile gang members continue their illegal activities at a time when most of their peers have dropped out to marry, raise families, and take conventional jobs.
- Youth sent to prison for minor offenses learn the techniques of crime from more experienced thieves.

In a classic work, *Box Man: A Professional Thief's Journey*, Harry King, a professional thief, relates this story to criminologist William Chambliss about his entry into crime after being placed in a shelter-care home by his recently divorced mother:

It was while I was at this parental school that I learned that some of the kids had been committed there by the court for stealing bikes. They taught me how to steal and where to steal them and where to sell them. Incidentally, some of the "nicer people" were the ones who bought bikes from the kids. They would dismantle the bike and use the parts: the wheels, chains, handlebars, and so forth.[14]

Here we can see how would-be criminals may be encouraged in their illegal activities by so-called honest people who are willing to buy stolen merchandise and gain from criminal enterprise.

There is some debate in the criminological literature over who may be defined as a professional criminal. In his classic works, Edwin Sutherland used the term to refer only to thieves who do not use force or physical violence in their crimes and who live solely by their wits and skill.[15] It is more common today for criminologists to use the term to refer to any criminal who identifies with a criminal subculture, who makes the bulk of his or her living from crime, and who possesses a degree of skill in his or her chosen trade.[16] Thus, one can become a professional safecracker, burglar, car thief, or fence. Some criminologists would

not consider drug addicts who steal to support their habit as professionals; they lack skill and therefore are amateur opportunists rather than professional technicians. However, some professional criminals take drugs without losing their lofty status in the criminal hierarchy.

Becoming a Professional Thief   What we know about the lives of professional criminals has come to us through their journals, diaries, autobiographies, and the first-person accounts they have given to criminologists. The best-known account of professional theft is the life of Chic Conwell, in Edwin Sutherland's classic book *The Professional Thief*.[17] Conwell and Sutherland's concept of professional theft has two critical dimensions.

First, professional thieves engage in limited types of crime, which are described in Exhibit 12.1.[18] Professionals depend solely on their wit and skill. Thieves who use force or commit crimes that require little expertise are not considered worthy of the title "professional." Their areas of activity include "heavy rackets," such as bank robbery, car theft, burglary, and safecracking. You can see that Conwell and Sutherland's criteria for professionalism are weighted heavily toward con games and trickery and give little attention to common street crimes.

 You can read selections from *The Professional Thief* on Google Books: **http://books.google .com/books/about/The_professional_thief .html?id=G9nBxdMR4IAC.**

Do books and stories like this glamorize crime and make it seem daring and appealing?

The second requirement of professional theft is the exclusive use of wits, "front" (a believable demeanor), and talking ability. Manual dexterity and physical force are of little importance. Professional thieves must acquire status in their profession. Status is based on their technical skill,

EXHIBIT 12.1

Sutherland's Typology of Professional Thieves

- Pickpocket (cannon)
- Thief in rackets related to confidence games
- Forger
- Extortionist from those engaging in illegal acts (shakedown artist)
- Confidence game artist (con artist)
- Thief who steals from hotel rooms (hotel prowl)
- Jewel thief who substitutes fake gems for real ones (pennyweighter)
- Shoplifter (booster)
- Sneak thief from stores, banks, and offices (heel)

SOURCE: Chic Conwell, *The Professional Thief*, ed. Edwin Sutherland (Chicago: University of Chicago Press, 1937).

financial standing, connections, power, dress, manners, and wide knowledge base. In their world, "thief" is a title worn with pride. Conwell and Sutherland also argue that professional thieves share common feelings, sentiments, and behaviors. Of these, none is more important than the code of honor of the underworld; even under the threat of the most severe punishment, a professional thief must never inform (squeal) on his or her fellows. Sutherland and Conwell view professional theft as an occupation with much the same internal organization as that characterizing such legitimate professions as advertising, teaching, or police work. They conclude:

> A person can be a professional thief only if he is recognized and received as such by other professional thieves. Professional theft is a group way of life. One can get into the group and remain in it only by the consent of those previously in the group. Recognition as a professional thief by other professional thieves is the absolutely necessary, universal, and definitive characteristic of the professional thief.[19]

The sections below describe two types of professional thieves: fences and cargo thieves.

The Fence

LO3 Describe the activities of a professional fence

Some experts have argued that Sutherland's view of the professional thief may be outdated because modern thieves often work alone, are not part of a criminal subculture, and were not tutored early in their careers by other criminals.[20] However, some important research efforts show that the principles set down by Sutherland still have value for understanding the behavior of one contemporary criminal type—the fence, who earns his or her living solely by buying and reselling stolen merchandise. The fence's critical role in criminal transactions has been recognized since the eighteenth century.[21] They act as middlemen who purchase stolen merchandise—ranging from diamonds to auto hubcaps—and resell them to merchants who market them to legitimate customers.[22]

Much of what we know about fences comes from relatively few in-depth studies of the lives and activities of these specialized professional criminals. Carl Klockars examined the life and times of one successful fence who used the alias Vincent Swaggi. Through 400 hours of listening to and observing Swaggi, Klockars found that this highly professional criminal had developed techniques that made him almost immune to prosecution. During the course of a long and profitable career in crime, Swaggi spent only four months in prison. He stayed in business, in part, because of his sophisticated knowledge of the law of stolen property. To convict someone of receiving stolen goods, the prosecution must prove that the accused was in possession of the goods and knew that they had been stolen. Swaggi had

the skills to make sure that these elements could never be proved. Also helping Swaggi stay out of the law's grasp were the close working associations he maintained with society's upper classes, including influential members of the justice system. Swaggi helped them purchase stolen items at below-cost, bargain prices. He also helped authorities recover stolen goods and therefore remained in their good graces. Klockars's work strongly suggests that fences customarily cheat their thief-clients and at the same time cooperate with the law.

Sam Goodman, a fence interviewed by sociologist Darrell Steffensmeier, lived in a world similar to Vincent Swaggi's. He also purchased stolen goods from a wide variety of thieves and suppliers, including burglars, drug addicts, shoplifters, dockworkers, and truck drivers. According to Goodman, to be successful, a fence must meet the following conditions:

- *Upfront cash.* All deals are cash transactions, so an adequate supply of ready cash must always be on hand.
- *Knowledge of dealing—learning the ropes.* The fence must be schooled in the knowledge of the trade, including developing a "larceny sense"; learning to "buy right" at acceptable prices; being able to "cover one's back" and not get caught; finding out how to make the right contacts; and knowing how to "wheel and deal" and how to create opportunities for profit.
- *Connections with suppliers of stolen goods.* The successful fence must be able to engage in long-term relationships with suppliers of high-value stolen goods who are relatively free of police interference. The warehouse worker who pilfers is a better supplier than the narcotics addict, who is more likely to be apprehended and talk to the police.
- *Connections with buyers.* The successful fence must have continuing access to buyers of stolen merchandise who are inaccessible to the common thief. For example, they must make contacts with local pawnshops and other distributors of secondhand goods and be able to move their material without drawing attention from the authorities.[23]
- *Complicity with law enforcers.* The fence must work out a relationship with law enforcement officials who invariably find out about the fence's operations. Steffensmeier found that to stay in business the fence must either bribe officials with good deals on merchandise and cash payments or act as an informer who helps police recover particularly important merchandise and arrest thieves.

Sam had a strong commitment to crime throughout the course of his life. The height of his personal commitment to crime was during the middle phase of his career when he was a "big, wide-open" fence. Nonetheless, his favorable attitudes toward crime and other criminals endured into the later "moonlighting" phase of his career when he was less involved in crime. At that point, he also developed more positive attitudes toward legitimate people and associations (such as his employees and legitimate antique dealers). Furthermore, the moonlighting phase of his career saw some changes in Sam's self-definition, as reflected in this assessment in the final weeks of his life (p. 375):

> I never cared how the cops saw me but I wanted the public to see me in a different light. Not as a guy who did time, not as a burglar, not even as a fence, but as a businessman. As a good Joe. In that way I knew what I done was wrong.... If they saw me as a crook, that I could handle. But not a [expletive] bum. I wanted the people to respect me as me. As a businessman taking care of business in my shop.

Deviants, even persistent criminals, are seldom deviant in all or even most aspects of their lives. Sam comfortably rubbed shoulders with thieves, gamblers, and quasi-legitimate businessmen but also courted respectability and pledged allegiance to some major normative standards. Sam was unapologetic about his criminal career. While he realized that his behavior may have violated the law, he took pride in the way he conducted himself and did business, as these deathbed comments illustrate:

> I do not feel sad about my life. I did what I thought I had to do at the time. But I would not wish my life on somebody else. I made that very goddamn plain to your students—a life in crime can be a bitch.... I done wrong, pulled some very rank shit. But helped a whole lot of people, too. If somebody needed something, came into my shop, I more or less gave it away. Anyone that worked for me, I dealt with fairly. Got paid a good dollar and helped them out in little ways.[24]

Fences handle a tremendous variety of products, including televisions, cigarettes, stereo equipment, watches, autos, and cameras.[25] In dealing their merchandise, they operate through many legitimate fronts, including art dealers, antique stores, furniture and appliance retailers, remodeling companies, salvage companies, trucking companies, and jewelry stores. In the Internet age, some sell their merchandise online on a variety of merchandising websites.

When deciding what to pay the thief for goods, the fence uses a complex pricing policy: professional thieves who steal high-priced items are usually given the highest amounts—about 30 to 50 percent of the wholesale price. An item valued at $5,000 may be bought for $1,500. However, the amateur thief or drug addict who is not in a good bargaining position may receive only 10 cents on the dollar.

Fencing seems to contain many of the elements of professional theft as described by Sutherland: fences live by their wits, never engage in violence, depend on their skill in negotiating, maintain community standing based on connections and power, and share the sentiments and behaviors of their fellows. The only divergence between Sutherland's thief and the fence is the code of honor; it seems likely that the fence is much more willing to cooperate with authorities than most other professional criminals.

The Occasional Fence Professional fences have attracted the attention of criminologists, but like other forms of theft, fencing is not dominated solely by professional criminals. A significant portion of all fencing is performed by amateur or occasional criminals. Novice burglars, such as juveniles and drug addicts, often find it so difficult to establish relationships with professional fences that they turn instead to nonprofessionals to unload the stolen goods.[26]

One type of occasional fence is the part-timer who, unlike professional fences, has other sources of income. Part-timers are often "legitimate" businesspeople who integrate the stolen merchandise into their regular stock. A rental store manager who buys stolen merchandise and rents it along with his legitimate merchandise is a part-time fence. An added benefit of the illegitimate part of his work is the profit he makes on these stolen items, which is not reported for tax purposes.

Some merchants become actively involved in theft either by specifying the merchandise they want the burglars to steal or by "fingering" victims. Some businesspeople sell merchandise and then describe the customers' homes and vacation plans to known burglars so that they can steal it back!

Associational fences are amateur fences who barter stolen goods for services. These amateurs typically have legitimate professional dealings with known criminals such as bail bond agents, police officers, and attorneys. A lawyer may demand an expensive watch from a client in exchange for legal services. Bartering for stolen merchandise avoids taxes and becomes a transaction in the underground economy.

Neighborhood hustlers buy and sell stolen property as one of the many ways they make a living. They keep some of the booty for themselves and sell the rest in the neighborhood. These dealmakers are familiar figures to neighborhood burglars looking to get some quick cash by selling them stolen merchandise.

Amateur receivers can be complete strangers approached in a public place by someone offering a great deal on valuable commodities. It is unlikely that anyone buying a $2,000 home theater system for $500 cash would not suspect that it may have been stolen. Some amateur receivers make a habit of buying suspect merchandise at reasonable prices from a "trusted friend," establishing an ongoing relationship. This practice encourages crime because the criminals know that there will always be someone to buy their merchandise. In addition to the professional fence, the nonprofessional fence may account for a great deal of criminal receiving. Both professional and amateur thieves have a niche in the crime universe.

Professional Cargo Thieves

Some professionals work in highly organized groups, targeting specific items and employing "specialists" who bring a different set of criminal skills to the table. Take for example professional cargo thieves, whose bases of operations are truck yards, hubs for commercial freight carriers, airports, and port cities. These thieves prey upon the huge fleet of cargo ships, planes, and trucks that bring in a daily array of valuable cargoes. While other thieves target cash and jewels, these professionals make off with frozen shrimp, clothing, and electronic goods. Their criminal activities cost the public billions of dollars each year. Cargo thieves use sophisticated operations with well-organized hierarchies of leadership. They employ specialists who carry out a variety of tasks, including thieves and brokers or fences who help unload the stolen goods on the black market. "Lumpers" physically move the goods and work with drivers in transporting the stolen merchandise from the docks. Gangs usually employ a specialist who is an expert at foiling the antitheft locks on truck trailers. Cargo thieves heist whole truckloads of merchandise—the average freight on a trailer can be valued at up to $3 million.[27]

Criminologists and legal scholars recognize that common theft offenses fall into several categories linked together because they involve the intentional misappropriation of property for personal gain. In fencing, goods are bought from another who is in illegal possession of those goods. In the case of embezzlement, burglary, and larceny, the property is taken through stealth. In other kinds of theft, such as bad checks, fraud, and false pretenses, goods are obtained through deception. Some of the major categories of common theft offenses are discussed in the next sections in some detail.

LARCENY/THEFT

Ten years ago it was called the "Body Snatchers Case." New York City detectives uncovered a scheme being run by a former Manhattan dentist named Michael Mastromarino, who had lost his practice and money because of a substance abuse addiction. Needing capital to maintain his lifestyle, he and three other men set up a body harvesting scheme, looting bones and tissue from more than a thousand corpses sent to a Brooklyn funeral home. The men then sold the body parts to legitimate companies that supplied hospitals around the United States. They forged death certificates to hide the fact that the donors were too old or sick to be used for medical purposes or when relatives refused to donate their loved ones' body parts. Hundreds of people in states as far away as Florida, Nebraska, and Texas received tissue and bone carved from looted corpses. The tissue was used in such procedures as joint and heart-valve replacements, back

surgery, dental implants, and skin grafts; a single harvested body yielded $7,000 in parts. Some patients suffered severe infection, septic shock, and even paralysis due to having received an implant made from infected cadaver tissue from Mastromarino's company. After his arrest, Mastromarino was charged with, among other crimes, grand larceny vis-à-vis his body snatching.[28] He died in prison from bone cancer on July 7, 2013.

The body snatcher's case illustrates the wide variety of schemes that make up the crime of larceny: taking the possessions of another; in this case, the possessions were bodily organs and the victims were dead! Larceny/theft was one of the earliest common-law crimes created by English judges to define acts in which one person took for his or her own use the property of another.[29] According to common law, larceny was defined as "the trespassory taking and carrying away of the personal property of another with intent to steal."[30] Most state jurisdictions have incorporated the common-law crime of larceny in their legal codes. Today, definitions of larceny often include such familiar acts as shoplifting, passing bad checks, and other theft offenses that do not involve using force or threats on the victim (robbery) or forcibly breaking into a person's home or place of work (burglary).

When it was originally construed, larceny involved taking property that was in the possession of the rightful owners. For example, it would have been considered larceny for someone to go secretly into a farmer's field and steal a cow. Thus, the original common-law definition required a "trespass in the taking"; this meant that for an act to be considered larceny, goods must have been taken from the physical possession of the rightful owner. In creating this definition of larceny, English judges were more concerned with people disturbing the peace than they were with thefts. If someone tried to steal property from another's possession, they reasoned that the act could eventually lead to a physical confrontation and possibly the death of one party or the other, thereby disturbing the peace. Consequently, the original definition of larceny did not include crimes in which the thief had come into the possession of the stolen property by trickery or deceit. It was therefore not considered larceny if someone entrusted with another person's property decided to keep it for themselves.

The growth of manufacturing and the development of the free enterprise system required greater protection for private property. The pursuit of commercial enterprise often required that one person's legal property be entrusted to a second party; therefore larceny evolved to include the theft of goods that had come into the thief's possession through legitimate means.

To get around the element of "trespass in the taking," English judges created the concept of **constructive possession**. This legal fiction applied to situations in which persons voluntarily and temporarily gave up custody of their property but still believed the property was legally theirs. If a person gave a jeweler her watch for repair, she would still believe

constructive possession In the crime of larceny, willingly giving up temporary physical possession of property but retaining legal ownership.

she owned the watch even though she had handed it over to the jeweler. Similarly, when a person misplaces his wallet and someone else finds it and keeps it—although identification of the owner can be plainly seen—the concept of constructive possession makes the person who has kept the wallet guilty of larceny.

Larceny Today

LO4 Differentiate between petty and grand larceny

Most U.S. state criminal codes separate larceny into **petit (or petty) larceny** and **grand larceny**. The former involves small amounts of money or property and is punished as a misdemeanor. Grand larceny, involving merchandise of greater value, is a felony punished by a sentence in the state prison. Each state sets its own boundary between grand larceny and petty larceny. For example, in the Virginia Criminal Code the main distinction between petit and grand larceny is the value of the item taken: larceny of an item with a value of $200 or more is considered grand larceny, while taking something with a value of less than $200 is considered petit larceny. In Virginia, how the larceny is committed may affect its definition. For example, while grand larceny generally requires theft of property valued at more than $200, if the money or property is taken directly *from a person*, then anything over $5 is considered grand larceny; taking money or property with a value of less than $5 from a person is petit larceny. Taking a firearm from a home or car is automatically considered grand larceny.[31]

How larceny is categorized can have a significant influence on the level of punishment. Looking at Virginia again as an example, grand larceny is a felony with a specific punishment of not less than one year in prison but not more than 20, or at the discretion of a jury (or judge) trying the case, it can also be punished with a jail sentence of not more than 12 months and/or a fine not to exceed $2,500. In contrast, petit larceny is a class 1 misdemeanor punishable by up to 12 months in jail and/or a fine of up to $2,500.[32] In New York State, the cutoff is $1,000; there are different classes of grand larceny, the most serious being theft over $1,000,000.[33]

The distinction between petit and grand larceny can be especially significant in states such as California that employ three-strikes laws mandating that someone convicted of a third felony be given a life sentence. The difference may not be lost on potential criminals: research by John Worrall shows that larceny rates in California have been significantly lowered since passage of the three-strikes law.[34]

Larceny/theft is probably the most common criminal offense. According to the FBI, about 6 million larcenies are reported to the police annually, a rate of about 2,000 per 100,000 population.[35] Despite the rather large number of annual larcenies, their number and rate have declined by about 20 percent during the past decade. The average value of property taken during larceny/thefts is now about $1,000 per offense. When the average value is applied to the estimated number of larceny/thefts, the loss to victims nationally is about $6 billion. Thefts of motor vehicle parts, accessories, and contents make up the largest portion of reported larcenies, almost 25 percent.

Types of Larceny

There are many different varieties of larceny. Most involve small items of little value. Many of these go unreported, however, especially if the victims were business owners who do not want to take the time to get involved with police. They simply write off the losses as part of doing business. Hotel owners estimate that guests filch millions a year in towels, bathrobes, ashtrays, bedspreads, showerheads, flatware, and even television sets and wall paintings.[36]

Shoplifting

Shoplifting is a very common form of larceny/theft involving the taking of goods from retail stores. Usually shoplifters try to snatch items—jewelry, clothes, records, or appliances—when store personnel are otherwise occupied, hiding the goods on their person.

The "five-finger discount" is not a recent phenomenon and there are cases as early as the seventeenth century. Shoplifting became a common criminal act when London and Paris became mercantile centers in the nineteenth century. Consumers flocked to department stores such as Harrods and Le Bon Marché where they were left to shop on their own without a clerk keeping watch. Goods that were displayed to encourage buying inadvertently encouraged theft.[37] In a famous historical incident, in August 1799, Mrs. Leigh-Perrot, the aunt of author Jane Austen, was arrested for theft, accused of stealing a length of lace from a local store. Though she insisted that it was a mistake, Leigh-Perrot was held in confinement for eight months in the home of the local jailer until her trial, where she was found not guilty. At the time the alleged shoplifting took place, theft of any item worth five shillings or more was punishable by hanging or, as was more likely in her case, deportation to Australia for 14 years.[38]

Extent of Shoplifting Of the 6 million larcenies recorded each year by the UCR about 20 percent or 1.2 million are shoplifting incidents. About 1.2 million people are arrested

---

petit (or petty) larceny Theft of a small amount of money or property, punished as a misdemeanor.

grand larceny Theft of money or property of substantial value, punished as a felony.

shoplifting The taking of goods from retail stores.

for larceny each year and if ratios hold true that means about 240,000 shoplifting arrests occur on an annual basis.

Of course, not every shoplifting incident is reported to police nor is every shoplifter caught by store security staff arrested. Most are handled informally, their name kept on file; many are told never to return to the store. Hayes International, a loss prevention/shrinkage control consulting business, does an annual survey of major retailers around the United States. The 23 major retailers (with 18,900 stores and over $596 billion in retail sales) they surveyed (2012) apprehended over 1.1 million shoplifters and dishonest employees and recovered over $189 million. In addition, 71,095 dishonest employees were apprehended in 2012, up 5.5 percent from 2011; $50 million was recovered from employee apprehensions in 2012, up 7 percent from 2011; one in every 40 employees was apprehended and the value of each of their thefts far outstripped the amount stolen by shoplifters ($715.24 versus $129.12).[39]

Retail security measures add to the already high cost of this crime, all of which is passed on to the consumer. Some studies estimate that about one in every nine shoppers steals from department stores. Moreover, the increasingly popular discount stores, such as Costco, Walmart, and Target, have a minimum of sales help and depend on highly visible merchandise displays to attract purchasers, all of which makes them particularly vulnerable to shoplifters.

LO5 Compare professional and amateur shoplifters

Shoplifters: Amateurs and Professionals In the early 1960s, Mary Owen Cameron conducted a classic study of shoplifting.[40] In her pioneering effort, Cameron found that the majority of shoplifters are amateur pilferers, called **snitches** in thieves' argot. Snitches are usually respectable people who do not conceive of themselves as thieves but are systematic shoplifters who steal merchandise for their own use. Some snitches are simply overcome by an uncontrollable urge to snatch something that attracts them, while others arrive at the store intending to steal. Some adolescents become shoplifters because they have been coerced by older kids into becoming "proxy shoplifters," forced to steal goods with the understanding that if caught their youth will protect them from prosecution.[41]

When caught, they may try to rationalize or neutralize their behavior. When Paul Cromwell and Quint Thurman

interviewed 137 apprehended shoplifters, they found widespread use of techniques of neutralizations—statements such as "I don't know what comes over me. It's like, you know, it's somebody else doing it, not me" (denial of responsibility) or "I like to get nice stuff for my kids, you know. I know it's not O.K., you know what I mean? But I want my kids to dress nice and stuff" (appeal to higher loyalties).[42]

If they are not professionals and want to deny their culpability, why do they steal? Some are impulsive sensation seekers who are driven to shoplift by their psychological need to live on the edge.[43] Others are motivated by rational choice and the desire to get something for nothing. Still another motivation for shoplifting seems to be psychological distress; some amateur shoplifters are looking for a release from anxiety and depression.[44]

Regardless of their motives, snitches are likely to reform if caught because they are not part of a criminal subculture and do not think of themselves as criminals. Cameron reasoned that they are deterred by an initial contact with the law. Getting arrested has a traumatic effect on them, and they will not risk a second offense.

Professional Shoplifters Professional shoplifters such as Sameh Khaled Danhach, whose story was described in the opening vignette, can walk into a department store, fill up a cart with expensive medicines, DVDs, iPods, baby formula, and other high-cost items, and use deceptive techniques to slip past security guards.[45] Hitting several stores in a day and the same store once a month, a professional thief can make between $100,000 and $200,000 a year.

Pros wear or carry devices and implements that help them avoid detection while shoplifting. They place a large open shopping bag obtained from another store, name prominently displayed, on the floor by their feet and casually drop in merchandise. They use a **booster box**, a device with a false bottom that can be opened and shut by the operator.

The boxes are lined with metal or some other substance to prevent security tags from setting off alarms. The box is placed over merchandise, the bottom opened and then closed, capturing the goods. A professional female shoplifter will stroll into a store with a baby carriage accompanied by a friend wearing maternity clothes. Carriages are useful because no one wants to disturb a sleeping baby wrapped in blankets, which of course can also be used to hide stolen merchandise. And who would suspect a visibly pregnant woman, even though the expandable outfit is perfect for stuffing in high-priced merchandise and walking casually out the door.

Pros will later sell the merchandise in their own discount stores, at flea markets, or through online auctions. Some sell to fences who repackage—or "scrub"—the goods and pawn them off on retailers at prices that undercut legitimate distributors. Ironically, some stolen merchandise can actually make its way back onto the shelves of the chain store from which it was stolen.[46] In her pioneering effort, Mary Owen

snitches Amateur shoplifters who do not self-identify as thieves but who systematically steal merchandise for personal use.

booster box Device with a false bottom that can be opened and shut by a professional shoplifter, lined with metal or some other substance to prevent security tags from setting off alarms, placed over merchandise.

Some shoplifters do not rely on stealth and concealment. Nor are their actions impulsive and unplanned. A surveillance video shows Amanda Barnes pulling items on a cart at a Home Depot in Ogden, Utah. Barnes was charged with stealing and pawning more than $20,000 in barbeque grills, vacuums, and other home improvement tools. Barnes, 26, would list items on KSL-TV's classified website, and once a buyer contacted her to purchase an item, she would steal it from local stores.

AP Images/Ogden Police Department

Prevention Strategies Retail stores initiate a number of strategies designed to reduce or eliminate shoplifting. **Target removal strategies** involve putting dummy or disabled goods on display while the real merchandise is kept under lock and key. Audio equipment with missing parts is displayed, and only after items are purchased are the necessary components installed. Some stores sell from a catalogue while keeping merchandise in stockrooms.

Target-hardening strategies involve locking goods in place or having them monitored by electronic systems. Clothing stores may use racks designed to prevent large quantities of garments from being slipped off easily. Store owners may rely on electronic article surveillance (EAS) systems, featuring tags with small electronic sensors that trip sound and light alarms if not removed by employees before the item leaves the store. Security systems now feature source tagging, a process by which manufacturers embed the tag in the packaging or in the product itself. Thieves are hard-pressed to remove or defeat such tags, and retailers save on the time and labor needed to attach the tags at their stores.[48] Situational measures place the most valuable goods in the least vulnerable places, use warning signs to deter potential thieves, and use closed-circuit cameras.

Another approach to shoplifting prevention is to create specialized programs that use methods such as doing community service, paying monetary restitution, writing essays, watching anti-shoplifting videos, writing apology letters, and being placed in individual and/or family counseling. Evaluations indicate that such programs can be successful in reducing recidivism of young shoplifters.[49]

Overzealous Enforcement These methods may control shoplifting, but stores must be wary of becoming

Cameron found that about 10 percent of all shoplifters were professionals, called boosters, or heels. Professional shoplifters steal with the intention of reselling stolen merchandise to pawnshops or fences, usually at half the original price.

Controlling Shoplifting One major problem associated with combating shoplifting is that many customers who observe pilferage are reluctant to report it to security agents. Store employees themselves are often loathe to get involved in apprehending a shoplifter. It is also likely that a store owner's decision to prosecute shoplifters will be based on the value of the goods stolen, the nature of the goods stolen, and the manner in which the theft was realized. Shoplifters who planned their crime by using a concealed apparatus, such as a bag pinned to the inside of their clothing, are more apt to be prosecuted than those who impulsively put merchandise into their pockets.[47] The concealment indicates that the crime was premeditated and not a spur of the moment loss of control.

To encourage the arrest of shoplifters, a number of states have passed *merchant privilege laws* designed to protect retailers and their employers from litigation stemming from improper or false arrests of suspected shoplifters. These laws protect but do not immunize merchants from lawsuits. They typically require that arrests be made on reasonable grounds or probable cause, detention be of short duration, and store employees or security guards conduct themselves in a reasonable fashion.

target-removal strategies Displaying dummy or disabled goods as a means of preventing shoplifting.

target-hardening strategies Making one's home or business crime proof through the use of locks, bars, alarms, and other devices.

overzealous in their enforcement policies. Those falsely accused have won significant judgments in civil actions.[50] In one case, a woman accused of shoplifting at a JCPenney store in Media, Pennsylvania, was awarded $250,000, charging them with false confinement and malicious prosecution after she was mistakenly taken for a shoplifter.[51] In 2013, a Portland, Oregon, woman won a $67,000 judgment from Walgreens after an assistant store manager's accusations that the woman shoplifted makeup prompted a police investigation.[52]

Stores may be liable if security guards use excessive force when subduing a suspected shoplifter. There is also the danger of profiling based on gender, age, or racial and ethnic background, resulting in customers being targeted, detained, and searched for inappropriate reasons.[53] And of course, searching and detaining customers based on stereotyping is legally indefensible: in one case, eight African American plaintiffs sued the Dillard's department store chain, claiming that employees and security workers questioned them while they were shopping in the stores and accused them of stealing merchandise, solely based on their race. In a separate case, Dillard's was ordered to pay a $1.2 million verdict to an African American woman who was detained on suspicion of shoplifting in a store in Overland Park, Kansas.[54]

Bad Checks

Another form of larceny is cashing bad bank checks, knowingly and intentionally drawn on a nonexistent or underfunded bank account, to obtain money or property. In general, for a person to be guilty of passing a bad check, the bank the check is drawn on must refuse payment, and the check casher must fail to make the check good within 10 days after finding out the check was not honored.

More than 60 years ago, Edwin Lemert conducted the best-known study of check forgers.[55] The majority of check forgers—**naive check forgers**—are amateurs who do not believe their actions will hurt anyone. Most naive check forgers come from middle-class backgrounds and have little identification with a criminal subculture. They cash bad checks because of a financial crisis that demands an immediate resolution—perhaps they have lost money at the horse track and have some pressing bills to pay. Lemert refers

to this condition as **closure**. Naive check forgers are often socially isolated people who have been unsuccessful in their personal relationships. They are risk prone when faced with a situation that is unusually stressful for them. The willingness of stores and other commercial establishments to cash checks with a minimum of fuss to promote business encourages the check forger to risk committing a criminal act.

Not all check forgers are amateurs. Lemert found that a few professionals—whom he calls **systematic forgers**—make a substantial living by passing bad checks. However, professionals constitute a relatively small segment of the total population of check forgers. It is difficult to estimate the number of such forgeries committed each year or the amounts involved. Stores and banks may choose not to press charges because the effort to collect the money due them is often not worth their while. It is also difficult to separate the true check forger from the neglectful shopper.

Some of the different techniques used in check fraud schemes, which may cost retail establishment upwards of $1 billion per year, are set out in Exhibit 12.2.

naive check forgers Amateurs who cash bad checks because of some financial crisis but have little identification with a criminal subculture.

closure A term used by Lemert to describe people from a middle-class background who have little identification with a criminal subculture but cash bad checks because of a financial crisis that demands an immediate resolution.

systematic forgers Professionals who make a living by passing bad checks.

Credit Card Theft

In 2013, ten individuals, including Babar Qureshi, Ijaz Butt, and Khawaja Ikram, were indicted in one of the largest credit card fraud schemes in the nation's history. The charges involved a plot to fabricate more than 7,000 false identities to obtain tens of thousands of credit cards and steal more than $200 million. The conspiracy involved a three-step process. First, the defendants would make up a false identity by creating fraudulent identification documents and a fraudulent credit profile with the major credit bureaus. Then they would pump up the credit of the false identity by providing fake information about that identity's creditworthiness to those credit bureaus. Finally, they borrowed or spent as much as they could, based on the phony credit history, but did not repay the debts. The scope of the criminal fraud enterprise required the conspirators to construct an elaborate network of false identities. Across the country, the conspirators maintained more than 1,800 "drop addresses," including houses, apartments, and post office boxes, which they used as the mailing addresses for the false identities.[56]

This ongoing criminal conspiracy is by no means unique nor is the elaborate planning and technical know-how needed to bring it off that unusual. Another similar scam, involving conspirators in Estonia, Ukraine, China, and Belarus, stole 40 million credit and debit card numbers from companies such as Marshall's, T.J.Maxx, BJ's Wholesale Club, OfficeMax, and Barnes and Noble by hacking into their computer systems and installing "sniffer" programs designed to capture credit card numbers, passwords, and account information as they moved through the retailers' card processing networks. The thieves then concealed the data in encrypted computer servers they controlled in the United States and Eastern Europe. Some of the credit and debit card numbers were "cashed out" by encoding the numbers on the magnetic strips of blank cards and using these cards to withdraw tens of thousands of dollars at a time from automatic teller machines (ATMs). A card stolen in Amsterdam could be used to make bogus online purchases in Prague within hours.[57]

The use of stolen credit cards is a major problem in U.S. society. It has been estimated that fraud has been responsible for a billion-dollar loss in the credit card industry. Most credit card abuse is the work of amateurs who acquire stolen cards through theft or mugging and then use them for two or three days. However, professional credit card rings such as those described above are getting into the act. They collect or buy from employees the names and credit card numbers of customers in retail establishments; then they buy plain plastic cards and have the customers' numbers embossed on them. They create fictitious wholesale companies and apply for and receive authorization to accept credit cards from the customers. They then use the phony cards to charge nonexistent purchases on the accounts of the people whose names and card numbers they collected.

One approach is to first obtain the victim's address and card number from a confederate (e.g., a store employee where the victim shops). They may then call the victim, claiming to be from the credit card company, and informing them that their account has been flagged because of suspicious activity. After offering credentials such as a bogus badge ID number, the thief tells them that someone has used the card to purchase a $1,500 television from a local store. When the consumer denies making the purchase, the scammer explains that he is starting a fraud investigation, gives the consumer a "confirmation" number, and asks them for the three-digit security number on the back of the card. The security code allows the thief to make purchases over the Internet or from local merchants.[58]

To combat losses from credit card theft, Congress passed a law in 1971 limiting a person's liability to $50 per stolen card. Some states, such as California, have passed specific statutes making it a misdemeanor to obtain property or services by means of cards that have been stolen, forged, canceled, or revoked, or whose use is for any reason unauthorized.[59]

The problem of credit card misuse is being compounded by thieves who set up bogus Internet sites strictly to trick people into giving them their credit card numbers, which they then use for their own gain. The problem is growing so rapidly that a number of new technologies are aimed at combating credit card number theft over the Internet. One method is to incorporate digital signatures into computer operating systems, which can be accessed with a digital key that comes with each computer. Owners of new systems can present three forms of identification to a notary public and trade a notarized copy of their key for a program that will sign files. The basis of the digital signature is a digital certificate, a small block of data that contains a person's "public key." This certificate is signed, in turn, by a certificate authority. This digital certificate will act like a credit card with a hologram and a photograph and identify the user to the distant website and vice versa.[60]

Auto Theft

Motor vehicle theft is another common larceny offense. Because of its frequency and seriousness, it is treated as a separate category in the Uniform Crime Report (UCR). The FBI now records about 700,000 yearly auto thefts,

CONNECTIONS

Similar frauds are conducted over the Internet. These will be discussed in Chapter 15.

Ask Yourself ...

While some people refuse to give card information online or on the phone, is that actually more risky than handing a waiter your card in a restaurant far from home?

accounting for a total loss of $4 billion. Like other crimes, there has been a significant reduction in motor vehicle theft rates over the past decade, and the number of car thefts has declined more than 40 percent. UCR projections on auto theft are similar to the projections of the National Crime Victim Survey (NCVS), probably because almost every state requires owners to insure their vehicles, and auto theft is one of the most highly reported of all major crimes (75 percent of all auto thefts are reported to police).

Which Cars Are Taken Most?   According to the Highway Loss Data Institute, the rate at which people file insurance claims and the amount of loss per claim is highest for trucks (see Table 12.1).

 To read more about car theft, go to the National Insurance Crime Bureau (NICB) website at **https://www.nicb.org/.**

Has your car ever been stolen? If not, what do you do to prevent that from happening?

According to the National Insurance Crime Bureau (NICB), the 10 most stolen vehicles in the United States in a single year (2012) include the following:

1. Honda Accord   58,596
2. Honda Civic   47,037
3. Ford Pickup (full size)   26,770
4. Chevrolet Pickup (full size) 23,745
5. Toyota Camry   16,251
6. Dodge Caravan   11,799
7. Dodge Pickup (full size) 11,755
8. Acura Integra   9,555
9. Nissan Altima   9,169
10. Nissan Maxima   6,947

Why these models? Many cars are stolen and then stripped for parts. Thieves target vehicles that can bring them the greatest return in the used-part market. The NICB found that older Honda Accords and Civics were by far the most stolen models, led by the 1996 Accord. Accords and Civics account for the first 16 spots on the most stolen list and all are 1990–2000 models. By comparison, newer Hondas are rarely stolen, thanks to improved antitheft technology.[61]

Amateur Auto Thieves   Amateur thieves steal cars for a number of reasons that involve some form of temporary personal use.[62] Among the reasons why an amateur would steal a car include:

- *Joyriding.* Many car thefts are motivated by teenagers' desire to acquire the power, prestige, sexual potency, and recognition associated with an automobile. Joyriders steal cars not for profit or gain but to experience, even briefly, the benefits associated with owning an automobile.
- *Short-term transportation.* Auto theft for short-term transportation is similar to joyriding. It involves the theft of a car simply to go from one place to another. In more serious cases, the thief may drive to another city or state and then steal another car to continue the journey.
- *Long-term transportation.* Thieves who steal cars for long-term transportation intend to keep the cars for their personal use. Usually older than joyriders and from a lower-class background, these auto thieves may repaint and otherwise disguise cars to avoid detection.
- *Profit.* Auto theft for profit is motivated by the hope of monetary gain. Some amateurs hope to sell the entire car, but most are auto strippers who steal batteries, tires, and wheel covers to sell or to reequip their own cars.
- *Commission of another crime.* A few auto thieves steal cars to use in other crimes, such as robberies and thefts. This type of auto thief desires both mobility and anonymity.

Professional Car Thieves   At one time, most auto theft was the work of amateurs, and most cars were taken by relatively affluent, middle-class teenagers looking for excitement.[63] There appears to be a change in this pattern: fewer cars are being taken today, and fewer stolen cars are being recovered. Part of the reason is that there has been an increase in highly organized professionals who resell expensive cars after altering their identification numbers and falsifying their registration papers. Exporting stolen vehicles has become a global problem, and the emergence of capitalism in Eastern Europe has increased the demand for U.S-made cars.

TABLE 12.1

Most Stolen Vehicles in the U.S. by Type of Vehicle and Amount of Loss

Vehicle	Type	Theft per 1,000 Insured Vehicles	Loss Payment per Claim	Theft Loss per Incident
Ford F-250 crew 4WD	Very large pickup	7.0	$7,060	$50
Chevrolet Silverado 1500 crew	Large pickup	6.7	$5,463	$37
Chevrolet Avalanche 1500	Very large SUV	6.1	$6,163	$38
GMC Sierra 1500 crew	Large pickup	6.0	$6,366	$38
Ford F-350 crew 4WD	Very large pickup	5.6	$7,517	$42

SOURCE: Highway Loss Data Institute, http://www.iihs.org/iihs/news/desktopnews/ford-f-250-has-highest-theft-rate-of-any-2010-12-vehicle-cadillac-escalade-drops-to-6th-on-list-after-years-on-top (accessed June 2014).

Many cars are now stolen in order to be sold to chop shops for spare parts. Among the most attractive targets are these parts:

- *Global positioning system.* It now costs approximately $1,500 to replace one on a Toyota Camry. The whole unit for a Honda Odyssey can cost up to $1,200, navigation included.
- *Air conditioning.* Today, the air conditioning compressor for a Toyota Camry costs up to $1,000. One for a Ford goes between $500 and $1,000.
- *Air bags.* These life savers do well in the auto-part seller's market. Air bags go for about $200.
- *Exhaust.* The exhaust system carries emissions from the engine to the atmosphere. An overall exhaust system—including catalytic converter in some vehicles—for a Chevrolet can be had for between $500 and $1,000.[64]

Car Cloning   One new form of professional auto theft is called "cloning." After stealing a luxury car from a mall or parking lot, car thieves later visit a large car dealership in another state and look for a car that's the exact make and model (and even the same color) of the stolen one. The thieves jot down the vehicle identification number (VIN) stamped on the top of the dashboard and drive off. The manufacturer-installed VIN plate on the stolen car is removed and replaced with a homemade counterfeit, similar to the original, only this one bears the VIN of the legitimate vehicle. Phony ownership and registration documents

complete the cloning. At that point, the stolen vehicle can be easily registered with a motor vehicle agency in another state and sold to an unwary buyer. In one Tampa, Florida, case, more than 1,000 cloned cars were sold to buyers in 20 states and several countries, with estimated losses of more than $25 million to consumers, auto insurers, and other victims.

Carjacking   You may have read the awful account of a young attorney, Justin Friedland, shot to death in 2013 by carjackers as he and his wife were Christmas shopping at the Mall at Short Hills in Millburn, New Jersey. Friedland, 30, was killed by four men after they rolled up on him and his wife in the parking deck and the thieves tried to enter his car while his wife in the front seat. Friedland's wife managed to escape the vehicle unharmed, but he tragically was killed.[65] This type of auto theft has become so common that it has its own name, **carjacking**.[66] Carjacking is legally considered a type of robbery because it involves force to steal.[67]

Both victims and offenders in carjackings tend to be young men. Urban residents are more likely to experience carjacking than suburban or rural residents. About half of all carjackings are typically committed by gangs or groups. These crimes are most likely to occur in the evening, in the central city, in an open area, or in a parking garage. This pattern may reflect the fact that carjacking seems to be a crime of opportunity; it is the culmination of the carjacker's personal needs and desires coinciding with the immediate opportunity for gain. This decision is also shaped by the carjacker's participation in urban street culture.[68]

Weapons, most often guns, were used in about three-quarters of all carjacking victimizations.[69] Despite the presence of weapons, victims resist the offender in two-thirds of carjackings, and, not surprisingly, about one-third of victims of completed carjackings and about 20 percent of victims of attempted carjackings are injured. Serious injuries, such as gunshot or knife wounds, broken bones, or internal injuries, occur in about 10 percent of carjackings. More minor injuries, such as bruises and chipped teeth, occurred in about 15 percent of cases.

Carjacking is a particularly scary crime. A surveillance video shows carjacker Ryan Stone, 29, forcing a woman from her car, which he then stole and drove off on March 12, 2014, in Lone Tree, Colorado. Suspected of stealing an SUV with a 4-year-old boy inside, carjacking two other vehicles, and seriously injuring a state trooper, Stone was arrested after police tracked him, and at times chased him, around the Denver area during morning rush hour.

AP Images/Ryan Stone/CBS-4 TV Denver

carjacking Theft of a car by force or threat of force.

Combating Auto Theft Auto theft is a significant target of situational crime prevention efforts. One approach to theft deterrence has been to increase the risks of apprehension. Hotlines offer rewards for information leading to the arrest of car thieves. Another approach has been to place fluorescent decals on windows that indicate that the car is never used between 1 A.M. and 5 A.M.; if police spot a car with the decal being operated during this period, they know it is stolen.[70]

Highly sophisticated tracking and security systems may also be deterring car thieves from stealing newer model cars. OnStar, a car safety device, provides a navigation system that can be used to track and disable stolen vehicles from afar through tracking and remote ignition blocking.[71] The LoJack system involves installing a hidden tracking device in cars that gives off a signal, enabling the police to pinpoint its location.[72] LoJack therefore has the advantage of tracking cars in some places GPS systems are ineffective. LoJack units are tied to a car's vehicle identification number (VIN), so when a car is reported stolen and the VIN is entered into the state police crime computer, it automatically triggers the LoJack unit in the vehicle.

Because car thieves cannot tell that LoJack has been installed, it does not reduce the likelihood that a protected car will be stolen. However, cars installed with LoJack have a much higher recovery rate. There may also be a general deterrent effect: areas with high rates of LoJack use experience significant reductions in their auto theft rates. Ironically, LoJack owners actually accrue a smaller than anticipated reward for their foresight than the general public because they have to pay for installation and maintenance of the device. Those without it actually gain more because they benefit from a lower auto theft rate in their community without paying any additional cost.

Other prevention efforts involve making it more difficult to steal cars. Take the VINshield program. Every vehicle has its own unique vehicle identification number (VIN) located on the dashboard, where it's viewable through the car's windshield and where it can be covered up by thieves. The VINshield program enables owners to etch the VIN number on all the car's windows, making it difficult and expensive to sell the car off for parts.[73]

Publicity campaigns have been directed at encouraging people to lock their cars. Parking lots have been equipped with theft-deterring closed-circuit TV cameras and barriers. Manufacturers have installed more sophisticated steering column locking devices and other security systems that make theft more difficult.

The most effective methods appear to be devices that immobilize a vehicle by cutting off the electrical power needed to start the engine when a theft is detected. However, car thieves with modest resources—just a few hundred dollars in off-the-shelf equipment—and some computer knowledge can crack the codes of millions of car keys and suborn these security systems.[74]

False Pretenses or Fraud

The crime of **false pretenses**, or **fraud**, involves misrepresenting a fact in a way that causes a victim to willingly give his or her property to the wrongdoer, who then keeps it.[75] In 1757, the English Parliament defined false pretenses to cover an area of law left untouched by larceny statutes. The first false pretenses law punished people who "knowingly and designedly by false pretense or pretenses, [obtained] from any person or persons, money, goods, wares or merchandise with intent to cheat or defraud any person or persons of the same."[76]

False pretense differs from traditional larceny because the victims willingly give their possessions to the offender, and the crime does not, as does larceny, involve a "trespass in the taking." An example of false pretenses would be an unscrupulous merchant selling someone a chair by claiming it was an antique, but knowing all the while that it was a cheap copy. Another example would be a phony healer selling a victim a bottle of colored sugar water as an elixir that would cure a disease.

Swindlers have little shame when defrauding people out of their money; they often target the elderly, sick, and infirm. In the aftermath of Hurricane Katrina, in 2005, swindlers used the tragedy to solicit relief funds from charitable and well-meaning victims and then convert the money for their own usage.[77] About 150,000 people are arrested for fraud schemes each year, though that is probably only the tip of the iceberg.[78]

Confidence Games

Some fraudulent schemes involve getting a **mark** (target) interested in some get-rich-quick scheme, which may have illegal overtones; this is known as a **confidence game** or con game. The criminal's hope is that when victims lose their money, they will be either too embarrassed or too afraid to call the police. There are hundreds of varieties of con games, but the most common is called the **pigeon drop**.[79] Here, a package or shopping bag containing money

---

false pretenses (fraud) Misrepresenting a fact in a way that causes a deceived victim to give money or property to the offender.

mark The target of a con man or woman.

confidence game A swindle, usually involving a get-rich-quick scheme, often with illegal overtones, so that the victim will be afraid or embarrassed to call the police.

pigeon drop A con game in which a package or wallet containing money is "found" by a con man or woman, and the victims are bilked out of money they are asked to put up as collateral.

is "found" by a con man or woman. A passing victim is stopped and asked for advice about what to do, since there is no identification. Another "stranger," who is part of the con, approaches and enters the discussion. The three decide to split the money, but first, to make sure everything is legal, one of the swindlers goes off to consult a lawyer. Upon returning, he or she says that the lawyer claims the money can be split up; first, however, each party must prove he or she is financially stable or has the means to reimburse the original owner, should one show up. The victim then is asked to give some good-faith money for the lawyer to hold. Later, when the victim goes to the lawyer's office to pick up a share of the loot, he or she finds the address bogus and the money gone.

Other cons include:

- A self-proclaimed "contractor" offers an unusually low price for an expensive job such as driveway repair and then uses old motor oil rather than asphalt to make the "repairs." The first rain brings disaster. Some cons offer a free home inspection that turns up several expensive repairs. They then offer a cheap rate to fix the problem, but of course the repairs are actually bogus.
- A business office receives a mailing that looks like an invoice with a self-addressed envelope that makes it look like it comes from the phone company (walking fingers on a yellow background). It appears to be a contract for an ad in the Yellow Pages. On the back, in small print, will be written, "By returning this confirmation, you're signing a contract to be an advertiser in the upcoming, and all subsequent, issues." If the invoice is returned, the business soon finds that it has agreed to a long-term contract to advertise in some private publication that is not widely distributed.
- Con artists read the obituary column and then send a surviving spouse bills supposedly owed by the deceased person. Or they deliver an item, such as a Bible, that they say the deceased relative ordered just before he died.
- A con artist, posing as a bank employee, stops a customer as he or she is about to enter the bank. The con man claims to be an investigator who is trying to catch a dishonest teller. He asks the customer to withdraw cash to see if he or she gets the right amount. After the cash is withdrawn, the conman asks that it be turned over to him so he can check the serial numbers and promises to return the cash in a few minutes, gives the customer a receipt, and escapes through a back exit.
- An old musician carrying his violin enters a restaurant and orders an expensive meal. When asked to pay he claims that he left his wallet at home. He begs the owner to be allowed to retrieve his money and leaves his violin as collateral. While he's gone, another man presents himself to the owner as a rare instrument dealer—he has a personal business card. He wants to have a look at the violin he saw in passing, and as soon as it's produced,

he claims it is a valuable antique, perhaps a Stradivarius worth hundreds of thousands of dollars! He asks the owner to give the old violinist his business card as soon as he returns. The old violinist returns and the business owner offers him a thousand dollars for his violin. While the old man seems clueless, he asks for more and they settle on a price of $5,000. He walks out with the money, and when the owner calls the number on the card, ready to resell, he finds out it's a false number. The old man and the "dealer" meet up later, split the cash, and buy another $50 violin. Hence the expression "fiddling around."

Third-Party Fraud In some instances of false pretenses, the "victim" is a third party, such as an insurance company forced to pay for false claims or the people who have to pay higher claims because of the swindle. Cheating on an entrance exam may be considered third-party fraud because the victims are people who took the test honestly and received lower grades. One example of an innovative third-party cheating scheme was instituted by a man named Po Chieng Ma, who conspired to sell answers to the Graduate Management Administration Test (GMAT), the Graduate Record Examinations (GRE), and the Test of English as a Foreign Language (TOEFL) to an estimated 788 customers, each of whom had paid him between $2,000 and $9,000. In the scheme, people were paid to take the multiple-choice tests in Manhattan and then call California, where the same tests were to be given, with the answers. The answers were passed on to Ma, who, taking advantage of the three-hour time difference, carved the answers in code on the sides of pencils, which were then given to his customers. Ma pleaded guilty to conspiracy and obstruction of justice and received a four-year prison term for his efforts. In this case, there were many victims, including the testing service, universities, and the students who lost places in school because those who inflated their scores through the scheme were admitted instead.[80]

Auto Accident Fraud Another common scheme involves fake auto accidents, including the ones described below:

- The "swoop and squat." A driver is stuck in heavy traffic on a busy highway. A confederate cuts off the driver in front, forcing him or her to slam on the brakes, resulting in a rear-end collision. After the "accident," everyone in the damaged car files bogus injury claims with the driver's insurance company. They may even go to crooked physical therapists, chiropractors, lawyers, or auto repair technicians to further exaggerate their claims.
- The drive down. A driver is attempting to merge into a traffic lane. Suddenly, another driver waves her forward, indicating he will allow her to merge. Instead of letting her in, he slams into the car, causing an accident. When the police arrive, the "injured" driver denies ever

motioning, claims serious injury, and files an insurance claim with the victim's company.

- *The sideswipe.* As a driver rounds a corner at a busy intersection with multiple turn lanes, the driver drifts slightly into the next lane. The car in that lane, waiting for such an opportunity, steps on the gas and sideswipes the driver, producing an accident.
- *The t-bone.* A driver is crossing an intersection when a car coming from a side street accelerates and hits the car. When the police arrive, the driver and several planted "witnesses" claim that the driver ran a red light or stop sign.[81]

How common are such fraudulent schemes? Staged accidents cost the insurance industry about $20 billion a year, increasing insurance rates on the average motorist between $100 and $300 extra per car per year.[82]

Embezzlement

LO6 Explain the concept of embezzlement

In 2013, Ephonia M. Green, 44, pleaded guilty to federal embezzlement charges stemming from her plot to steal from her former employer, the Association of American Medical Colleges, a nonprofit corporation. Green, an administrative assistant, was responsible for processing invoices from the association's vendors. Separately, Green owned a bridal shop in Upper Marlboro, Maryland, that conducted business under the name Fabulous Concepts Inc (FCI). Green created and submitted false invoices to the Association of American Medical Colleges in the name of FCI, seeking payment for services that were never provided while keeping hidden from her employer the fact that she would be the actual recipient of the payments. Through this fraudulent scheme, Green embezzled approximately $5.1 million from her employer.[83]

Embezzlement occurs when someone who is trusted with property fraudulently converts it—that is, keeps it for his or her own use or the use of others. It can be distinguished from fraud on the basis of when the criminal intent was formed. Most U.S. courts require that a serious breach of trust must have occurred before a person can be convicted of embezzlement. The mere act of moving property without the owner's consent, or damaging it or using it, is not considered embezzlement. However, using it up, selling it, pledging it, giving it away, or holding it against the owner's will is considered to be embezzlement.

embezzlement A type of larceny that involves taking the possessions of another (fraudulent conversion) that have been placed in the thief's lawful possession for safekeeping, such as a bank teller misappropriating deposits or a stockbroker making off with a customer's account.

Embezzlement is not a recent crime. It was mentioned in early Greek culture when, in his writings, Aristotle alluded to theft by road commissioners and other government officials.[84] It was first codified in law by the English Parliament during the sixteenth century to fill a gap in the larceny law.[85] Until then, to be guilty of theft, a person had to take goods from the physical possession of another (trespass in the taking). However, as explained earlier, this definition did not cover instances in which one person trusted another and willfully gave that person temporary custody of his or her property. Store clerks, bank tellers, brokers, and merchants gain lawful possession but not legal ownership of other people's money.

Although it is impossible to know how many embezzlement incidents occur annually, the 16,000 people arrested for embezzlement in 2012 was probably an extremely small percentage of all embezzlers. There has also been a rash of embezzlement-type crimes around the world, especially in third-world countries where poverty is all too common and the economy is poor and supported by foreign aid and loans. Government officials and businessmen who have their hands on this money are tempted to convert it for their own use—a scenario that is sure to increase the likelihood of embezzlement. For example, some critics have complained that billions were embezzled by unscrupulous businessmen and contractors in the run-up to the Winter Olympics games in Sochi, Russia.[86]

 Want to avoid credit card theft? The Federal Trade Commission has some important tips: **http://www.consumer.ftc.gov/articles/0216-protecting-against-credit-card-fraud.**

Do you think that limiting personal liability on credit cards discourages people from taking special care to protect their cards?

BURGLARY

LO7 Describe the elements of sexual burglary

In common law, the crime of burglary is defined as "the breaking and entering of a dwelling house of another in the nighttime with the intent to commit a felony within."[87] Burglary is considered a much more serious crime than larceny/theft because it often involves entering another's home, a situation in which the threat of harm to occupants is great. Even though the home may be unoccupied at the time of the burglary, the potential for harm to the occupants is so significant that most state jurisdictions punish burglary as a felony.

The legal definition of burglary has undergone considerable change since its common-law origins. When first created by English judges during the late Middle Ages, laws against burglary were designed to protect people whose homes might be set upon by wandering criminals. Including the phrase "breaking and entering" in the definition protected people from unwarranted intrusions; if an invited guest stole something, it would not be considered a burglary. Similarly, the requirement that the crime be committed at nighttime was added because evening was considered the time when honest people might fall prey to criminals.[88]

In more recent times, state jurisdictions have changed the legal requirements of burglary, and most have discarded the necessity of a nighttime forced entry into a dwelling house. Nor does a burglary have to involve theft; the purpose of the crime could be to attack the occupant or damage their property. The Race, Culture, Gender, and Criminology feature covers burglaries that are not motivated by financial needs.

SEXUAL BURGLARY

race, culture, gender, and criminology

Some burglaries have a sexual motivation, while others involve sexual attacks that, though unplanned, occur when the burglar finds the residence unexpectedly occupied. To investigate this type of burglary, Amélie Pedneault, Danielle Harris, and Raymond Knight used a sample of 224 specific incidents of burglary that had evident sexual components. Sexual components were identified through offending behaviors, considering the nature of the property stolen (e.g., underwear) or the nature of the offender's actions (e.g., voyeurism, rape). The 224 burglaries were committed by 104 offenders sent to the Massachusetts Treatment Center for Sexually Dangerous Persons (MTC). The analysis showed that burglaries with a sexual component can be divided into three types.

Fetishistic Noncontact Burglaries

These burglaries typically occur in unoccupied houses and involve fetishistic behavior but no theft, violence, or weapon. This type of sexual burglary is motivated to fulfill a sexual fantasy but involves neither victim contact nor material gain. The covert type involves voyeurism (e.g., breaking and entering to see a woman getting undressed or showering). In contrast, the overt fetishistic burglary is motivated by sexual fantasies and typically involves breaking and entering into homes to steal objects with a sexually arousing value for the burglar (e.g., female underwear

or accessories such as handbags or shoes); neither type involves sexual contact with a victim.

Example: The offender was peeping through a house window at night. He illegally entered a house by forcing the lock and watched the 23-year-old female occupant undress. He then proceeded to steal a suitcase that he filled with the occupant's underwear before leaving.

Versatile Contact Burglaries

These burglaries are characterized by rapes occurring in homes and involving theft, violence, and weapons. An example of this type of burglary is an offender who, while burglarizing a residence he thought was unoccupied, finds a woman at home alone. The characteristics that render a residence at risk for burglary are the same characteristics as those which render the female occupant at greater risk for rape; isolation, easy access, and time were all considerations of the perpetrators of burglaries and rapes in residences.

Example: The offender entered the 20-year-old female victim's apartment by breaking a rear window at 1 A.M. while the victim was sleeping. The offender awoke the victim by leaning on her and threatened her with a knife. The victim struggled with the offender, which resulted in a deep laceration to her hand. The offender pushed the victim to the floor where he vaginally raped her while repeatedly threatening and hitting her. When he was done, the offender

ransacked the apartment and left with money, jewelry, and electronic goods.

Sexually Oriented Contact Burglaries

In this type of sexually oriented burglary, the criminal rapes the victim at home, but these incidents rarely involve theft, violence, or weapons. This "home intruder rapist" uses breaking and entering primarily to gain access to his rape victim. These rapists appeared to be less concerned with the victim and more focused on the residence in their selection. More than half of serial rapists use breaking and entering to access their victim, without giving thought to material gain. These burglaries appear to have been perpetrated with the unique goal of gaining access to a sexual victim (with violence and theft being infrequent).

Example: At 2:30 A.M., the offender illegally entered an apartment occupied by a female and her child. The offender awoke the female occupant and vaginally raped her, forcing her compliance by threatening to harm her child. When he was done, the offender left without stealing anything.

Critical Thinking

Does the fact that burglars seek out specific targets for specific needs indicate that burglary is a rational crime, rather than a spontaneous event committed by occasional criminals?

SOURCE: Amélie Pedneault, Danielle Harris, and Raymond A. Knight, "Toward a Typology of Sexual Burglary: Latent Class Findings," *Journal of Criminal Justice* 40 (2012): 278–284.

It is common for penal codes to recognize different degrees of burglary. Such issues as being armed, whether force was used, and whether the structure was a home or business can affect the level of crime seriousness and consequently the punishment attached to the crime. Typically, the more serious and severely punished burglaries involve a forced entry by an armed burglar into a home; the least serious an unforced entry into a nonresidential structure by an unarmed offender. Several gradations of the offense may be found between these extremes.

The Nature and Extent of Burglary

LO8 Compare the activities of male and female burglars

According to the UCR, about 2 million burglaries occur annually; the NCVS reports that about 3.7 million residential burglaries are either attempted or completed annually. Both data sources report that the number and rate of burglaries have been rather stable, declining less than 5 percent over the past decade.

Most burglaries occur during daylight hours, in residential structures (about two-thirds). The homes most likely to be burglarized are occupied by relatively poor Latino and African American families. Rural owner-occupied and single-family residences have lower burglary rates than urban, renter-occupied, and multiple-family dwellings. Households in the northeast are less likely to experience burglary than households in other regions of the country.

The UCR tells us that most people arrested for burglary are adults (80 percent), white (67 percent), and male (83 percent). While most burglars are male, more than 30,000 women are arrested for burglary annually and that number has been increasing. What motivates female burglars, and how do they differ from males? These are the topics of the Race, Culture, Gender, and Criminology feature "Gender Differences in Burglary."

Residential Burglaries

About 75 percent of all burglaries involve entering a home or residence. Some residential burglars are crude thieves who will smash a window and enter a home or structure with minimal preparation; others plan out a strategy. In urban areas and their immediate suburbs, experienced burglars learn to avoid areas of the city in which most residents are renters and not homeowners, reasoning that renters are less likely to be suitable targets than are more affluent homeowners.[89]

Experienced residential burglars also learn that if they want to operate in daylight they have to be careful of their target choice. If they want to break into a home in an upscale neighborhood during the day, they better choose one that is set back from the street, providing better cover for their forced entry.

Social factors may also condition residential burglary planning. When unemployment rates increase, home guardianship does also because unemployed people are home during the workday protecting their possessions.[90]

Homeowners in affluent neighborhoods have higher employment levels, so daylight burglaries are a safer and more lucrative bet in wealthier communities. After dark, the patterns seem to change—burglars who operate at night may shift their targets to apartments and townhouses closer to home even though the risk of someone being home is greater.[91]

In a classic work, Francis Hoheimer, an experienced professional burglar, described how he learned the "craft of burglary" from a fellow inmate, Oklahoma Smith, when the two were serving time in the Illinois State Penitentiary. Among Smith's recommendations are these:

> Never wear deodorant or shaving lotion; the strange scent might wake someone up. The more people there are in a house, the safer you are. If someone hears you moving around, they will think it's someone else... If they call, answer in a muffled sleepy voice... Never be afraid of dogs, they can sense fear. Most dogs are friendly, snap your finger, they come right to you.[92]

Despite his elaborate preparations, Hoheimer spent many years in confinement.

Repeat Burglary Residential burglars often attack the same target more than once. The reasons burglars like to return to the scene of the crime include the following:

- It takes less effort to burgle a home or apartment known to be a suitable target than an unknown or unsuitable one.
- The burglar is already aware of the target's layout.
- The ease of entry of the target has probably not changed, and escape routes are known.
- The lack of protective measures and the absence of nosy and intrusive neighbors that made the first burglary a success have probably not changed.
- Goods have been observed that could not be taken out the first time.[93]
- Burgled items are often considered indispensable (e.g., flat screen televisions) and therefore are quickly replaced; burglars return to steal these newer replacement goods.[94]

Commercial Burglary

Some burglars prefer to victimize commercial property rather than private homes. Of all business establishments, retail stores are burglars' favorite targets. They display merchandise so that burglars know exactly what to look for, where it can be found, and—because the prices are displayed—how much they can hope to gain in resale to a fence. Burglars can legitimately enter a retail store during

GENDER DIFFERENCES IN BURGLARY

does gender play a role in shaping burglary careers? Are there differences in the way professional male and female burglars approach their craft? Do gender roles influence the burglar lifestyle? To find out, Christopher Mullins and Richard Wright used interviews with 18 active female burglars and 36 males, matched approximately for age. Their findings indicate that significant gender-based differences exist in the way males and females begin and end their offending careers and how they carry out their criminal tasks.

There were similarities in the way most offenders, male or female, were initiated into residential burglary. Burglars of both genders became involved via interaction in intimate groups, such as older friends, family members, or street associates. One told how they got started in burglary:

> [M]e and my brother, we wanted, you know, he came and got me and say he know where a house at to break into. And, uhm, we go there and uh, we just do it . . . me and my brother, he and some more friends.

But there was one key difference between the male and female offenders: the men typically became involved in burglary with male peers; women more often were introduced to crime by their boyfriends. Males are more likely to bring their male peers and family members into their offending networks and resist working with women except their girlfriend or female relative. And when they do include women, they put them in a subservient role, such as a lookout.

Why do they get involved in a burglary career in the first place? Both males and females generally said they got involved in break-ins to finance a party lifestyle centered on drug use and to buy designer clothing and bling-bling jewelry. There were some differences: males reportedly wanted money to pursue sexual conquests; female burglars were far more likely to say that they needed money to buy necessities for their children.

When asked what they were looking for in a prospective residential burglary target, the male and female offenders expressed similar preferences; both wanted to find a dwelling that was (a) unoccupied and (b) contained something of value. Both the men and the women wanted to know something about the people who lived in the residence, be familiar with their day-to-day routine, and have an idea of the target's valuables. Male offenders used their legitimate jobs as home remodelers, cable television installers, or gardeners to scout potential burglary targets. Female burglars who lacked legitimate entry had to rely on information generated by the men in their immediate criminal social network. Some used sexual attraction to gain the victim's confidence and gather information.

Mullins and Wright also found that men preferred to commit residential burglaries by themselves, while women most often worked with others. Males seemed unwilling to trust accomplices and were also unwilling to share the proceeds. Females, on the other hand, reported that they lacked the knowledge or skills needed to break into a dwelling on their own and were therefore more willing to work with a team.

Finally, when asked what it would take to make them stop committing crime, both male and female offenders claimed that a good job that paid well and involved little or no disciplined subordination to authority would be required to get them to give up their careers in crime. Men also claimed they would probably give up burglary once they settled down and started a family. Because they were dependent on male help, female burglars needed to sever their relationships with criminally involved males in order to reduce their offending. Female burglars were also more sensitive than the males to shaming and ostracism at the hands of their relatives and might quit under family pressure.

Mullins and Wright found that residential burglary is a significantly gender-stratified offense; the processes of initiation, commission, and potential desistance are heavily structured by gender. Women have to negotiate the male-dominated world of burglary to accomplish their crimes. Gender, they found, plays a significant role in shaping opportunity (such as initiation) and the events leading up to residential burglaries (for example, information gathering), while playing a lesser but still important role in molding actual offense commission.

Critical Thinking

1. Do the gender differences in burglary reflect the gender differences found in other segments of society?
2. Do you think gender discrimination helps reduce the female crime rate? If gender equality were achieved, would differences in the crime rate narrow?

SOURCE: Christopher Mullins and Richard Wright, "Gender, Social Networks, and Residential Burglary," *Criminology* 41 (2003): 813–839.

race, culture, gender, and criminology

AN ETHICAL DILEMMA

RATIONAL CHOICE

You are a criminology professor at a local college. You are approached by the police chief, who is quite concerned about high burglary rates in some areas of the city. She is a former student of yours and well aware of recent developments in criminological theory. The chief is a strong advocate of rational choice theory and has already instituted a number of programs based on a deterrence/situational crime prevention model of control. The existing police initiatives include these programs:

- The police offer target hardening measures to repeat victims. They install high-tech security equipment in homes so the homes can be monitored on a 24-hour basis. The police plan an advertising campaign to alert would-be offenders that they are on watch at prior target residences.

- A new police initiative identifies repeat burglars in the area and provides intervention designed to supply them with legitimate economic opportunities to reduce their criminal motivation.

- A new school-based program designed to reduce criminal motivation seeks to raise young people's awareness of the dangers of burglary and how it can result in a long prison sentence.

- The police have developed a series of environmental improvements in the target area with a view to minimizing burglary opportunities. These include improved visibility, better access control, and lighting in areas that have relatively high burglary rates. They have also instituted high-visibility police patrols in these areas to deter criminals from committing crimes there.

- A burglary control model house, fitted with low-cost methods of security such as strengthened door/window frames, bolts, locks, and so on, has been built and will be advertised to encourage residents to help themselves avoid burglary.

The chief has asked you to look over these initiatives and write a memo discussing their effectiveness. She wants you to develop a policy plan discussing whether you think there are any possible ethical pitfalls with these initiatives. If you do find problems, she wants you to suggest other policy initiatives that might prove effective in reducing the opportunity to commit burglary and deter potential burglars.

business hours and gain knowledge about what the store contains and where it is stored; they can also check for security alarms and devices. Commercial burglars perceive retail establishments as quick sources of merchandise that can be easily sold.

Other commercial establishments such as service centers, warehouses, and factories are less attractive targets

because it is more difficult to gain legitimate access to plan the theft. The burglar must use a great deal of guile to scope out these places, perhaps posing as a delivery person. In addition, the merchandise is more likely to be used, and it may be more difficult to fence at a premium price.

If burglars choose to attack factories, warehouses, or service centers, the most vulnerable properties are those located far from major thoroughfares and away from pedestrian traffic. Establishments located within three blocks of heavily traveled thoroughfares have been found to be less vulnerable to burglary than those located farther away; commercial establishments in wealthier communities have a higher probability of burglary.[95]

Though alarms have been found to be an effective deterrent to burglary, they are less effective in isolated areas because it takes police longer to respond than on more heavily patrolled thoroughfares, and an alarm is less likely to be heard by a pedestrian who would be able to call for help. Even in the most remote areas, however, burglars are wary of alarms and try to choose targets without elaborate or effective security systems. One study found that the probability of burglary of non-alarmed properties is 4.57 times higher than that of similar property with alarms.[96]

Careers in Burglary

When Debbie Baskin and Ira Sommers evaluated the impact of forensic evidence on criminal case outcomes, they found that despite great technological strides in the collection of forensic evidence only about 12 percent of more than 1,000 burglaries they studied resulted in arrest and 3 percent resulted in a conviction.[97] One reason for this success may be that burglars learn from experience and become good at their trade.

Some criminals make burglary their career and continually develop new and specialized skills to aid their profession. Burglars must learn to spot environmental cues nonprofessionals fail to notice.[98] Whether they operate alone or in groups, experienced burglars like to choose targets in neighborhoods they know so they can make their way home undetected if things go awry.[99] They must learn which targets contain valuables worth stealing and which are most likely to prove to be a dry hole. Research shows that burglary rates for student-occupied apartments are actually much lower than rates for other residences in the same neighborhoods; burglars appear to have learned which apartments to avoid.[100]

There have been a number of important studies of the "burglary career" and these are described below.

LO9 Describe what it takes to be a "good burglar"

The Good Burglar In a now classic study, Neal Shover reviewed the careers of professional burglars and uncovered the existence of a particularly successful type, which he labels the "**good burglar**."[101] Professional burglars use this title to characterize colleagues who have distinguished themselves as burglars. Characteristics of the good burglar include:

- Technical competence
- Maintenance of personal integrity
- Specialization in burglary
- Financial success
- The ability to avoid prison sentences

Shover found that to receive recognition as good burglars novices must develop four key requirements of the trade.

First, they must learn the many skills needed to commit lucrative burglaries. This process may include learning how to gain entry into homes and apartment houses; how to select targets with high potential payoffs; how to choose items with a high resale value; how to open safes properly, without damaging their contents; and how to use the proper equipment, including cutting torches, electric saws, explosives, and metal bars.

Second, the good burglar must be able to team up to form a criminal gang. Choosing trustworthy companions is essential if the obstacles to completing a successful job—police, alarms, and secure safes—are to be overcome.

Third, the good burglar must have inside information. Without knowledge of what awaits them inside, burglars can spend a tremendous amount of time and effort on empty safes and jewelry boxes.

Finally, the good burglar must cultivate fences or buyers for stolen wares. Once the burglar gains access to people who buy and sell stolen goods, he or she must also learn how to successfully sell these goods for a reasonable profit. Evidence of these skills was discovered in a study of more than 200 career burglars in Australia. Burglars reported that they had developed a number of relatively safe methods for disposing of their loot. Some traded stolen goods directly for drugs; others used fences, legitimate businesses, pawnbrokers, and secondhand dealers as trading partners. Surprisingly, many sold their illegal gains to family or friends. Burglars report that disposing of stolen goods was actually low risk and more efficient than expected. One reason was that in many cases fences and shady businesspeople put in a request for particular items, and the ready-made market allowed the stolen merchandise to be disposed of quickly, often in less than one hour. Though the typical markdown was 67 to 75 percent of the price of the goods, most reported that they could still earn a good living, averaging $2,000 per week. Those who benefited most from these transactions were the receivers of stolen property, who make considerable profits and are unlikely to be caught.[102]

According to Shover, a person becomes a good burglar by learning the techniques of the trade from older, more experienced burglars. During this process, the older burglar teaches the novice how to handle such requirements as dealing with defense attorneys, bail bond agents, and other

CONNECTIONS

Shover finds that the process of becoming a professional burglar is similar to the process described in Sutherland's theory of differential association. You can read more about this theory in Chapter 7.

agents of the justice system. Apprentices must be known to have the appropriate character before they are taken under the wing of the old pro. Usually, the opportunity to learn burglary comes as a reward for being a highly respected juvenile gang member, from knowing someone in the neighborhood who has made a living at burglary, or, more often, from having built a reputation for being solid while serving time in prison. Consequently, the opportunity to become a good burglar is not open to everyone.

Burglars on the Job   In an important book titled *Burglars on the Job*, Richard Wright and Scott Decker describe the working conditions of active professional burglars.[103] Most are motivated by the need for cash in order to get high; they want to enjoy the good life, "keeping the party going" without having to work. As Exhibit 12.3 shows, they approach their "job" in a rational workmanlike fashion, but their lives are controlled by their culture and environment. Unskilled and uneducated, urban burglars make the choices they do because there are few conventional opportunities for success. This rationality and cool decision making may help explain why most burglaries go unsolved. Most burglars do not like to travel far from their residence, choosing close-by neighborhoods with single-family homes.[104] However, experienced burglars are more willing to travel to find rich targets. They have access to transportation that enables them to select a wider variety of targets than younger, more inexperienced thieves.[105] They also seem to be sensitive to police anticrime efforts: when police are active and forceful, burglary rates decline. Experienced burglars may locate to safer areas or bide their time and wait for the police to reduce their anticrime initiatives as crime rates decline.[106]

The Burglary "Career Ladder"   Paul Cromwell, James Olson, and D'Aunn Wester Avary interviewed 30 active burglars in Texas and found that burglars go through stages of career development. They begin as young *novices* who learn

good burglar Professional burglars use this title to characterize colleagues who have distinguished themselves as burglars. Characteristics of the good burglar include technical competence, maintenance of personal integrity, specialization in burglary, financial success, and the ability to avoid prison sentences.

According to active burglars:

- Most avoid occupied residences, considering them high-risk targets.
- Most are not deterred by alarms and elaborate locks; in fact, these devices tell them there is something inside worth stealing.
- Some call occupants from a pay phone, and if the phone is still ringing when they arrive, they know no one is home.
- Once entering a residence, anxiety turns to calm as they first turn to the master bedroom for money and drugs. They also search kitchens, believing that some people keep money in a mayonnaise jar.
- Most work in groups, one serving as a lookout while another ransacks the place.
- Some dispose of goods through a professional fence; others try to pawn the goods. Some exchange goods for drugs; some sell them to friends and relatives; and a few keep the stolen items for themselves, especially guns and jewelry.
- Many approach a target masquerading as workmen, such as carpenters or house painters.
- Some stake out residences to learn occupants' routines.
- Tipsters help them select attractive targets.
- Drug dealers are favored targets because they tend to have a lot of cash and drugs, and victims are not going to call the police.
- Targets are often acquaintances.

SOURCE: Richard Wright and Scott Decker, *Burglars on the Job: Streetlife and Residential Break-Ins* (Boston: Northeastern University Press, 1994).

the trade from older, more experienced burglars, frequently siblings or relatives. Novices will continue to get this tutoring as long as they can develop their own markets (fences) for stolen goods. After their education is over, novices enter the *journeyman* stage, characterized by forays in search of lucrative targets and careful planning. At this point, they develop reputations as experienced, reliable criminals. Finally, they become *professional* burglars when they have developed advanced skills and organizational abilities that give them the highest esteem among their peers.

The Texas burglars also displayed evidence of rational decision making. Most seemed to carefully evaluate potential costs and benefits before deciding to commit crime. There is evidence that burglars follow this pattern in their choice of burglary sites. Burglars show a preference for corner houses because they are easily observed and offer the maximum number of escape routes.[107] They look for houses that show evidence of long-term care and wealth. Though people may erect fences and other barriers to deter burglars, these devices may actually attract crime because they are viewed as protecting something worth stealing: if there is nothing valuable inside, why go to so much trouble to secure the premises?[108]

Cromwell, Olson, and Avary also found that many burglars had serious drug habits and that their criminal activity was, in part, aimed at supporting their substance abuse.

ARSON

Arson is the willful and malicious burning of a home, public building, vehicle, or commercial building. Slightly more than 50,000 arsons are now recorded each year, with an average loss of about $12,000. Like other crimes, both the number and cost per arson have been in decline.

Arson has been a common occurrence in America and was even tried as a weapon during the Civil War. In 1864, a small group of Confederate agents attempted to set New York City ablaze by using a liquid called "solidified Greek fire"; the plot failed because they improperly used the chemical.[109]

There are several motives for arson. Adult arsonists may be motivated by severe emotional turmoil. Some psychologists view fire starting as a function of a disturbed personality. Arson, therefore, should be viewed as a mental health problem and not a criminal act.[110] It is alleged that arsonists often experience sexual pleasure from starting fires and then observing their destructive effects. Although some arsonists may be aroused sexually by their activities, there is little evidence that most arsonists are psychosexually motivated.[111] It is equally likely that fires are started by angry people looking for revenge against property owners or by teenagers out to vandalize property. These findings support the claim that arson should be viewed as a mental health problem, not a criminal act, and that it should be treated with counseling and other therapeutic measures rather than severe punishments.[112]

The Juvenile Fire Starter

Juveniles, the most prolific fire starters, may get involved in arson for a variety of reasons as they mature. Juvenile fire setting has long been associated with psychological abnormality, including depression conduct problems, such as disobedience, aggressiveness, anger, hostility, and resentment over parental rejection.[113] According to research by sociologist Wayne Wooden, juvenile arsonists can be classified in one of four categories:

- *The "playing with matches" fire setter.* This is the youngest fire starter, usually between the ages of 4 and 9, who sets fires because parents are careless with matches and lighters. Proper instruction on fire safety can help prevent fires set by these young children.
- *The "crying for help" fire setter.* This type of fire setter is a 7- to 13-year-old who is suffering emotional turmoil. The source of the stress could be family conflict, divorce, death, or abuse. These youngsters have difficulty expressing their feelings of sorrow, rage, or anger

and turn to fire as a means of relieving stress or getting back at their antagonists.

- *The "delinquent" fire setter.* Some youths set fire to school property or surrounding areas to retaliate for some slight experienced at school. These kids may break into the school to vandalize property with friends and later set a fire to cover up their activities.
- *The "severely disturbed" fire setter.* This youngster is obsessed with fires and often dreams about them in "vibrant colors." This is the most disturbed type of juvenile fire setter and the one most likely to set numerous fires with the potential for death and damage.[114]

During the past decade, hundreds of jurisdictions across the nation have established programs to address the growing problem of juvenile fire setting. Housed primarily within the fire service, these programs are designed to identify, evaluate, and treat juvenile fire setters to prevent the recurrence of fire-setting behaviors. A promising approach is the Fire Safe Children and Families effort, which combines a training curriculum for fire-safety educators, a training program for community professionals to identify potential behavior that may lead to arson, and a cognitive-behavioral therapy (CBT) program to treat children who are at risk of becoming juvenile fire starters and their families.[115]

To learn more about the Fire Safe program, go to http://www.firesafe.us/.

Can this really help or are kids who start fires too psychologically damaged to be treated?

Professional Arson

LO10 Discuss why people commit arson for profit

Other arsons are set by professional arsonists who engage in **arson for profit**. People looking to collect insurance money, but who are afraid or unable to set the fire themselves, hire professional arsonists. These professionals have acquired the skills to set fires yet make the cause seem accidental (for example, like an electrical short). Another form is **arson fraud**, which involves a business owner burning his or her property, or hiring someone to do it, to escape financial problems.[116] Over the years, investigators have found that businesspeople are willing to become involved in arson to collect fire insurance or for various other reasons, including but not limited to these:

- Obtaining money during a period of financial crisis
- Getting rid of outdated or slow-moving inventory
- Destroying outmoded machines and technology
- Paying off legal and illegal debt
- Relocating or remodeling a business; for example, when a theme restaurant has not been accepted by customers
- Taking advantage of government funds available for redevelopment
- Applying for government building money, pocketing it without making repairs, and then claiming that fire destroyed the "rehabilitated" building
- Planning bankruptcies to eliminate debts, after the merchandise supposedly destroyed was secretly sold before the fire
- Eliminating business competition by burning out rivals
- Employing extortion schemes that demand that victims pay up or the rest of their holdings will be burned
- Solving labor–management problems; arson may be committed by a disgruntled employee
- Concealing another crime, such as embezzlement

Some recent technological advances may help prove that many alleged arsons were actually accidental fires. There is now evidence of a fire effect called **flashover**. During the course of an ordinary fire, heat and gas at the ceiling of a room can reach 2,000 degrees. This causes clothes and furniture to burst into flame, duplicating the effects of arsonists' gasoline or explosives. It is possible that many suspected arsons are actually the result of flashover.[117]

arson for profit People looking to collect insurance money, but who are afraid or unable to set the fire themselves, hire professional arsonists. These professionals have acquired the skills to set fires, yet make the cause seem accidental.

arson fraud A business owner burns his or her property, or hires someone to do it, to escape financial problems.

flashover An effect in a fire when heat and gas at the ceiling of a room reach 2,000 degrees, and clothes and furniture burst into flame, duplicating the effects of arsonists' gasoline or explosives. It is possible that many suspected arsons are actually the result of flashover.

SUMMARY

LO1 Discuss the history of theft offenses

Common theft offenses include larceny, fraud, and embezzlement. These are common-law crimes, originally defined by English judges. Skilled thieves included pickpockets, forgers, and counterfeiters, who operated freely. Smugglers transported goods, such as spirits, gems, gold, and spices, without paying tax or duty. Poachers supplemented their diet and income with game that belonged to a landlord.

LO2 Compare and contrast professional and amateur thieves

Economic crimes are designed to reap financial rewards for the offender. Opportunistic amateurs commit the majority of economic crimes. Economic crime has also attracted professional criminals. Professionals earn most of their income from crime, view themselves as criminals, and possess skills that aid them in their law-breaking behavior. An example of the professional criminal is the fence who buys and sells stolen merchandise.

LO3 Describe the activities of a professional fence

Fences buy stolen goods and sell them at a profit. Some specialize in jewelry, auto parts, or electronic products, while others are generalists. They may act as middlemen and resell the stolen items to local merchants who market them to legitimate customers, or sell the items themselves in pawn shops or on the Internet. The key to becoming a successful fence is to develop relationships with people on both sides of the law: the criminals who steal, the merchants who sell, and members of the justice system with whom they come into contact.

LO4 Differentiate between petty and grand larceny

Larceny, the most common theft crime, involves taking the legal possessions of another. Petty larceny is typically theft of amounts under a particular amount, ranging from $5 to $1,000 (depending on state law); grand larceny is theft over that amount. Grand larceny is a felony, petty larceny a misdemeanor.

LO5 Compare professional and amateur shoplifters

Some shoplifters are amateurs who steal on the spur of the moment. These snitches are otherwise respectable persons who do not view themselves as thieves but take goods for their own use. Called boosters or heels, professional shoplifters steal with the intention of reselling stolen merchandise to pawnshops or fences, usually at half the original price. Boosters know how to hit stores without being detected, use devices to help them steal, and have partners who can unload merchandise after it is stolen.

LO6 Explain the concept of embezzlement

Embezzlement occurs when a person in a position of trust uses their position to convert or steal property or money from another without their consent. Embezzlement is premeditated, systematic, not spontaneous, and involves long-term schemes that involve small amounts taken over a long period of time.

LO7 Describe the elements of sexual burglary

Fetishistic noncontact burglaries typically occur in unoccupied houses and involve fetishistic behavior but no theft, violence, and weapon. This type of sexual burglary is motivated to fulfill a sexual fantasy but involves neither victim contact nor material gain. Versatile contact burglaries are characterized by rapes occurring in the home and involving theft, violence, and weapons. In sexually oriented contact burglaries, the criminal rapes the victim at home, but these incidents rarely involve theft, violence, or weapons.

LO8 Compare the activities of male and female burglars

Both male and female burglars engage in other forms of theft, such as shoplifting and assault. Males are more likely to steal cars to supplement their income. Female burglars are much more likely to work with a partner, whereas males are more likely to go it alone. Males begin their offending careers at an earlier age than females and are more likely to be repeat and recurrent offenders.

LO9 Describe what it takes to be a "good burglar"

Because burglary involves planning and risk, it attracts professional thieves. The most competent have technical skill and personal integrity, specialize in burglary, are financially successful, and avoid prison sentences. Professional burglars size up the value of a particular crime and balance it against the perceived risks. Many have undergone training in the company of older, more experienced burglars.

LO10 Discuss why people commit arson for profit

Arson is the willful, malicious burning of a home, public building, vehicle, or commercial building. Most arsonists are teenage vandals. Professional arsonists specialize in burning commercial buildings for profit. The owners of commercial buildings may resort to arson to get rid of outdated inventory, to qualify for government redevelopment funds, to collect insurance money, to claim the loss of merchandise already sold, or to eliminate business competition (by burning a building owned by a competitor).

KEY TERMS

economic crime (412)
fence (412)
skilled thieves (412)
flash houses (412)
smugglers (413)
poachers (413)
occasional criminals (414)
professional criminals (414)

situational inducement (414)
constructive possession (418)
petit (or petty) larceny (419)
grand larceny (419)
shoplifting (419)
snitches (420)
booster box (420)
target-removal strategies (421)

target-hardening strategies (421)
naive check forgers (422)
closure (422)
systematic forgers (422)
carjacking (425)
false pretenses (fraud) (426)
mark (426)

confidence game (426)
pigeon drop (426)
embezzlement (428)
good burglar (433)
arson for profit (435)
arson fraud (435)
flashover (435)

CRITICAL THINKING QUESTIONS

1. Differentiate between an occasional and a professional criminal. Which one would be more likely to resort to violence? Which one would be more easily deterred?

2. What crime occurs when a person who owns an antique store sells a client an "original" Tiffany lamp that the seller knows is a fake? Would it still be a crime if the person selling the lamp was not aware that it was a fake? As an antique dealer, should the seller have a duty to determine the authenticity of the products he or she sells?

3. What are the characteristics of good burglars? Can you compare their career path to any other professionals, such as doctors or lawyers? Which theory of criminal behavior best predicts the development of the good burglar?

4. You have been the victim of repeat burglaries. What could you do to reduce the chances of future victimization? (Hint: Buying a gun is not an option!)

NOTES

1. U.S. Attorney's Office, Southern District of Texas, "Foreign National Convicted in Multi-Million-Dollar, Multi-State Criminal Operation," March 04, 2013, http://www.fbi.gov/houston/press-releases/2013/foreign-national-convicted-in-multi-million-dollar-multi-state-criminal-operation (accessed June 2014).

2. Jennifer Truman, Lynn Langton, and Michael Planty, *Criminal Victimization, 2012* (Washington, DC: Bureau of Justice Statistics, 2013), http://www.bjs.gov/content/pub/pdf/cv12.pdf (accessed June 2014).

3. Andrew McCall, *The Medieval Under-world* (London: Hamish Hamilton, 1979), p. 86.

4. Ibid., p. 104.

5. J. J. Tobias, *Crime and Police in England, 1700–1900* (London: Gill and Macmillan, 1979).

6. Ibid., p. 9.

7. Marilyn Walsh, *The Fence* (Westport, CT: Greenwood Press, 1977), pp. 18–25.

8. Don DeNevi, *Western Train Robberies* (Millbrae, CA: Celestial Arts, 1976); Harry Sinclair Drago, *Road Agents and Train Robbers: Half a Century of Western Banditry* (New York: Dodd, Mead, 1973).

9. Neal Shover, *Great Pretenders, Pursuits, and Careers of Persistent Thieves* (Boulder, CO: Westview Press, 1996).

10. Ibid., pp. 50–51.

11. Ibid.

12. John Hepburn, "Occasional Criminals," in *Major Forms of Crime*, ed. Robert Meier (Beverly Hills, CA: Sage, 1984), pp. 73–94.

13. James Inciardi, "Professional Crime," in *Major Forms of Crime*, p. 223.

14. Harry King and William Chambliss, *Box Man: A Professional Thief's Journey* (New York: Harper & Row, 1972), p. 24.

15. Edwin Sutherland, "White-Collar Criminality," *American Sociological Review* 5 (1940): 2–10.

16. Gilbert Geis, "Avocational Crime," in *Handbook of Criminology*, ed. D. Glazer (Chicago: Rand McNally, 1974), p. 284.

17. Chic Conwell, *The Professional Thief*, ed. Edwin Sutherland (Chicago: University of Chicago Press, 1937).

18. Ibid., pp. 197–198.

19. Ibid., p. 212.

20. See, for example, Edwin Lemert, "The Behavior of the Systematic Check Forger," *Social Problems* 6 (1958): 141–148.

21. Cited in Walsh, *The Fence*, p. 1.

22. Carl Klockars, *The Professional Fence* (New York: Free Press, 1976); Darrell Steffensmeier, *The Fence: In the Shadow of Two Worlds* (Totowa, NJ: Rowman and Littlefield, 1986); Walsh, *The Fence*, pp. 25–28.

23. Simon Fass and Janice Francis, "Where Have All the Hot Goods Gone? The Role of Pawnshops," *Journal of Research in Crime and Delinquency* 41 (2004): 156–179.

24. Darrell Steffensmeier and Jeffery Ulmer, *Confessions of a Dying Thief: Understanding Criminal Careers and Illegal Enterprise* (Piscataway, NJ: Transaction-Aldine, 2005), p. 375.

25. Walsh, *The Fence*, p. 34.

26. Paul Cromwell, James Olson, and D'Aunn Avary, "Who Buys Stolen Property? A New Look at Criminal Receiving," *Journal of Crime and Justice* 16 (1993): 75–95.

27. FBI, "Cargo Theft's High Cost: Thieves Stealing Billions Annually," July 26, 2006, http://www.fbi.gov/news/stories/2006/july/cargo_theft072106 (accessed June 2014).

28. Michael Powell and David Segal, "In New York, a Grisly Traffic in Body Parts, Illegal Sales Worry Dead's Kin, Tissue Recipients," *Washington Post*, January 18, 2006, p. A03; William Sherman, "Clients Flee Biz Eyed in Ghoul Probe," *New York Daily News*, October 13, 2005.

29. This section depends heavily on a classic book, Wayne La Fave and Austin Scott, *Handbook on Criminal Law* (St. Paul, MN: West Publishing, 1972).

30. Ibid., p. 622.

31. Virginia Crime Codes, https://leg1.state.va.us/cgi-bin/legp504.exe?000+cod+18.2-95 (accessed June 2014).

32. Ibid.

33. New York Penal Law, http://ypdcrime.com/penal.law/article155.htm (accessed June 2014).

34. John Worrall, "The Effect of Three-Strikes Legislation on Serious Crime in California," *Journal of Criminal Justice* 32 (2004): 283–296.

35. Data in this chapter on crime rates and trends come from FBI, Uniform Crime Reports, *Crime in the United States, 2012*, http://www.fbi.gov/about-us/cjis/ucr/crime-in-the-u.s/2012/crime-in-the-u.s.-2012/property-crime/property-crime (accessed June 2014).

36. Margaret Loftus, "Gone: One TV," *U.S. News and World Report*, July 14, 1997, p. 61.

37. Rachel Shteir, *The Steal: A Cultural History of Shoplifting* (New York: Penguin Press, 2011).

38. Laura Boyle, "The Life and Crimes of Jane Leigh-Perrot," http://www.janeausten.co.uk/the-life-and-crimes-of-jane-leigh-perrot/ (accessed June 2014).

39. Hayes International, Annual Retail Theft Survey, http://hayesinternational.com/news/annual-retail-theft-survey/ (accessed June 2014).

40. Mary Owen Cameron, *The Booster and the Snitch* (New York: Free Press, 1964).

41. Janne Kivivuori, "Crime by Proxy: Coercion and Altruism in Adolescent Shoplifting," *British Journal of Criminology* 47 (2007): 817–833.

42. Paul Cromwell and Quint Thurman, "The Devil Made Me Do It: Use of Neutralizations by Shoplifters," *Deviant Behavior* 24 (2003): 535–550.

43. Ellen Beate Hansen and Gunnar Breivik, "Sensation Seeking as a Predictor of Positive and Negative Risk Behavior Among Adolescents," *Personality and Individual Differences* 30 (2001): 627–640.

44. Yves Lamontagne, Richard Boyer, Celine Hetu, and Celine Lacerte-Lamontagne, "Anxiety, Significant Losses, Depression, and Irrational Beliefs in First-Offense

Shoplifters," *Canadian Journal of Psychiatry* 45 (2000): 64–66.

45. FBI, *Organized Retail Theft: New Initiative to Tackle the Problem* (Washington, DC: Federal Bureau of Investigation, 2007).

46. Ibid.

47. Michael Hindelang, "Decisions of Shoplifting Victims to Invoke the Criminal Justice Process," *Social Problems* 21 (1974): 580–595.

48. Jill Jordan Sieder, "To Catch a Thief, Try This," *U.S. News and World Report*, September 23, 1996, p. 71.

49. Thomas Kelley, Daniel Kennedy, and Robert Homant, "Evaluation of an Individualized Treatment Program for Adolescent Shoplifters," *Adolescence* 38 (2003): 725–733.

50. Shaun Gabbidon and Patricia Patrick, "Characteristics and Outcomes of Shoplifting Cases in the U.S. Involving Allegations of False Arrest," *Security Journal* 18 (2005): 7–18.

51. *Ruditys v. J.C. Penney Co.*, No. 02-4114 (Delaware Co., PA, Ct. C.P. 2003).

52. Helen Jung, "Walgreens Must Pay NE Portland Mother and Son in Case over Shoplifting Accusations, Jury Says," *The Oregonian*, November 20, 2013, http://www.oregonlive.com/portland/index.ssf/2013/11/walgreens_must_pay_ne_portland.html (accessed June 2014).

53. Dean Dabney, Laura Dugan, Volkan Topalli, and Richard Hollinger, "The Impact of Implicit Stereotyping on Offender Profiling: Unexpected Results from an Observational Study of Shoplifting," *Criminal Justice and Behavior* 33 (2006): 646–674.

54. Security Information Watch, "Lawsuit Claims Dillard's Used Racial Profiling to Fight Shoplifting," February 6, 2009, http://www.securityinfowatch.com/press_release/10593712/lawsuit-claims-dillards-used-racial-profiling-to-fight-shoplifting (accessed June 2014).

55. Edwin Lemert, "An Isolation and Closure Theory of Naive Check Forgery," *Journal of Criminal Law, Criminology and Police Science* 44 (1953): 297–298.

56. U. S. Attorney, District of New Jersey, "Ten Indicted in $200 Million International Credit Card Fraud Conspiracy," September 27, 2013, http://www.fbi.gov/newark/press-releases/2013/ten-indicted-in-200-million-international-credit-card-fraud-conspiracy (accessed June 2014).

57. CNN Money.com, "11 Charged in Theft of More than 40M Card Numbers," August 6, 2008, http://money.cnn.com/2008/08/05/news/companies/card_fraud/?postversion=2008080604 (accessed June 2014).

58. Kimberly Palmer, "Beware the Latest Credit Card Scam," *U.S. News and World Report*, May 15, 2008, http://www.usnews.com/blogs/alpha-consumer/2008/05/15/

beware-the-latest-credit-card-scam.html (accessed June 2014).

59. La Fave and Scott, *Handbook on Criminal Law*, p. 672.

60. Peter Wayner, "Bogus Web Sites Troll for Credit Card Numbers," *New York Times*, February 12, 1997, p. A18.

61. National Insurance Crime Bureau, "NICB's *Hot Wheels*: Popular 10 Most Stolen Vehicles List Gets a Makeover," August 20, 2013, https://www.nicb.org/newsroom/news-releases/hot-wheels-2012 (accessed June 2014).

62. Charles McCaghy, Peggy Giordano, and Trudy Knicely Henson, "Auto Theft," *Criminology* 15 (1977): 367–381.

63. Donald Gibbons, *Society, Crime and Criminal Careers* (Englewood Cliffs, NJ: Prentice Hall, 1977), p. 310.

64. All prices here were obtained on eBay, March 2014.

65. Richard Cowen and Chris Harris, "Short Hills Mall Killing Latest Turn in Surge of Carjackings," NewJersey.com, http://www.northjersey.com/news/short-hills-mall-killing-latest-turn-in-surge-of-carjackings-1.682194 (accessed June 2014).

66. Michael Rand, *Carjacking* (Washington, DC: Bureau of Justice Statistics, 1994), p. 1.

67. Patsy Klaus, *Carjacking, 1993–2002* (Washington, DC: Bureau of Justice Statistics, 2004).

68. Bruce Jacobs, Volkan Topalli, and Richard Wright, "Carjacking, Streetlife, and Offender Motivation," *British Journal of Criminology* 43 (2003): 673–688.

69. Klaus, *Carjacking, 1993–2002.*

70. Ronald Clarke and Patricia Harris, "Auto Theft and Its Prevention," in *Crime and Justice: An Annual Review*, ed. N. Morris and M. Tonry (Chicago: University of Chicago Press, 1992).

71. OnStar, https://www.onstar.com/ (accessed June 2014).

72. LoJack, http://www.lojack.com/ (accessed June 2014).

73. VINshield, http://www.vinshield.com/ (accessed June 2014).

74. P. Weiss, "Outsmarting the Electronic Gatekeeper: Code Breakers Beat Security Scheme of Car Locks, Gas Pumps," *Science News* 167 (2005): 86.

75. La Fave and Scott, *Handbook on Criminal Law*, p. 655.

76. 30 Geo. III, C. 24 (1975).

77. Internet Crime Complaint Center, "Fraudulent Sites Capitalizing on Relief Efforts of Hurricane Katrina," http://www.ic3.gov/media/2005/050902.aspx (accessed June 2014).

78. FBI, *Crime in the United States, 2012*, Table 29, http://www.fbi.gov/about-us/cjis/ucr/crime-in-the-u.s/2012/crime-in-the-u.s.-2012/tables/29tabledatadecpdf (accessed June 2014).

79. As described in Charles McCaghy, *Deviant Behavior* (New York: Macmillan, 1976), pp. 230–231.

80. Benjamin Weiser, "4-Year Sentence for Mastermind of Scheme to Cheat on Graduate School Tests," *New York Times*, October 3, 1998, p. 8.

81. FBI, "A Cautionary Tale: Staged Auto Accident Fraud: Don't Let It Happen to You," http://www.fbi.gov/news/stories/2005/february/staged_auto021805 (accessed June 2014).

82. Ibid.

83. U.S. Attorney's Office, District of Columbia, "Former Employee Pleads Guilty to Embezzling More Than $5.1 Million from Non-Profit Money Stolen over Eight-Year Period; Non-Profit Alerted Authorities upon Discovery of the Scheme," November 25, 2013, http://www.fbi.gov/washingtondc/press-releases/2013/former-employee-pleads-guilty-to-embezzling-more-than-5.1-million-from-non-profit (accessed June 2014).

84. Jerome Hall, *Theft, Law and Society* (Indianapolis: Bobbs-Merrill, 1952), p. 36.

85. La Fave and Scott, *Handbook on Criminal Law*, p. 644.

86. Radio Free Europe, "Nemtsov Alleges Billions Embezzled from Sochi Olympics," May 30, 2013, http://www.rferl.org/content/russia-nemtsov-sochi-billions-embezzled/25002191.html (accessed June 2014).

87. La Fave and Scott, *Handbook on Criminal Law*, p. 708.

88. E. Blackstone, *Commentaries on the Laws of England* (London: 1769), p. 224.

89. Elizabeth Groff and Nancy La Vigne, "Mapping an Opportunity Surface of Residential Burglary," *Journal of Research in Crime and Delinquency* 38 (2001): 257–278.

90. Stewart D'Alessio, David Eitle, and Lisa Stolzenberg, "Unemployment, Guardianship, and Weekday Residential Burglary," *Justice Quarterly* 29 (2012): 919–932.

91. Timothy Coupe and Laurence Blake, "Daylight and Darkness Targeting Strategies and the Risks of Being Seen at Residential Burglaries," *Criminology* 44 (2006): 431–464.

92. Frank Hoheimer, *The Home Invaders: Confessions of a Cat Burglar* (Chicago: Chicago Review, 1975).

93. Graham Farrell, Coretta Phillips, and Ken Pease, "Like Taking Candy: Why Does Repeat Victimization Occur?" *British Journal of Criminology* 35 (1995): 384–399, at 391.

94. Ronald Clarke, Elizabeth Perkins, and Donald Smith, Jr., "Explaining Repeat Residential Burglaries: An Analysis of Property Stolen," in *Repeat Victimization, Crime Prevention Studies*, Vol. 12, ed. Graham Farrell and Ken Pease (Monsey, NY: Criminal Justice Press, 2001), pp. 119–132.

95. Simon Hakim and Yochanan Shachmurove, "Spatial and Temporal Patterns of CommercialBurglaries," *American Journal of Economics and Sociology* 55 (1996): 443–457.

96. Ibid., pp. 443–456.

97. Deborah Baskin and Ira Sommers, "Solving Residential Burglaries in the United States: The Impact of Forensic Evidence on Case Outcomes," *International Journal of Police Science and Management* 13 (2011): 70–86.

98. Richard Wright, Robert Logie, and Scott Decker, "Criminal Expertise and Offender Decision Making: An Experimental Study of the Target Selection Process in Residential Burglary," *Journal of Research in Crime and Delinquency* 32 (1995): 39–53.

99. Wim Bernasco, "Co-Offending and the Choice of Target Areas in Burglary," *Journal of Investigative Psychology and Offender Profiling* 3 (2006): 139–155.

100. Matthew Robinson, "Accessible Targets, but Not Advisable Ones: The Role of 'Accessibility' in Student Apartment Burglary," *Journal of Security Administration* 21 (1998): 28–44.

101. See, generally, Neal Shover, "Structures and Careers in Burglary," *Journal of Criminal Law, Criminology and Police Science* 63 (1972): 540–549.

102. Richard Stevenson, Lubica Forsythe, and Don Weatherburn, "The Stolen Goods Market in New South Wales, Australia: An Analysis of Disposal Avenues and Tactics," *British Journal of Criminology* 41 (2001): 101–118.

103. Richard Wright and Scott Decker, *Burglars on the Job: Streetlife and Residential Break-Ins* (Boston: Northeastern University Press, 1994).

104. Wim Bernasco and Paul Nieuwbeerta, "How Do Residential Burglars Select Target Areas? A New Approach to the Analysis of Criminal Location Choice," *British Journal of Criminology* 45 (2005): 296–315.

105. Brent Snook, "Individual Differences in Distance Travelled by Serial Burglars," *Journal of Investigative Psychology and Offender Profiling* 1 (2004): 53–66.

106. John Worrall, "Does Targeting Minor Offenses Reduce Serious Crime? A Provisional, Affirmative Answer Based on an Analysis of County-Level Data," *Police Quarterly* 9 (2006): 47–72.

107. Paul Cromwell, James Olson, and D'Aunn Wester Avary, *Breaking and Entering: An Ethnographic Analysis of Burglary* (Newbury Park, CA: Sage, 1991), pp. 48–51.

108. See M. Taylor and C. Nee, "The Role of Cues in Simulated Residential Burglary: A Preliminary Investigation," *British Journal of Criminology* 28 (1988): 398–401; Julia MacDonald and Robert Gifford, "Territorial Cues and Defensible Space Theory: The Burglar's Point of View," *Journal of Environmental Psychology* 9 (1989): 193–205.

109. Jane Singer, *The Confederate Dirty War: Arson, Bombings, Assassination and Plots for Chemical and Germ Attacks on the Union* (Jefferson, NC, and London: McFarland & Company, 2005), p. 21.

110. Nancy Webb, George Sakheim, Luz Towns-Miranda, and Charles Wagner, "Collaborative Treatment of Juvenile Firestarters: Assessment and Outreach," *American Journal of Orthopsychiatry* 60 (1990): 305–310.

111. Vernon Quinsey, Terry Chaplin, and Douglas Unfold, "Arsonists and Sexual Arousal to Fire Setting: Correlations Unsupported," *Journal of Behavior Therapy and Experimental Psychiatry* 20 (1989): 203–209.

112. John Taylor, Ian Thorne, Alison Robertson, and Ginny Avery, "Evaluation of a Group Intervention for Convicted Arsonists with Mild and Borderline Intellectual Disabilities," *Criminal Behaviour and Mental Health* 12 (2002): 282–294.

113. Mark Dadds and Jennifer Fraser, "Fire Interest, Fire Setting and Psychopathology in Australian Children: A Normative Study," *Australian and New Zealand Journal of Psychiatry* 40 (2006): 581–586; Pekka Santtila, Helina Haikkanen, Laurence Alison, Laurence Whyte, and Carrie Whyte, "Juvenile Firesetters: Crime Scene Actions and Offender Characteristics," *Legal and Criminological Psychology* 8 (2003): 1–20.

114. Wayne Wooden, "Juvenile Firesetters in Cross-Cultural Perspective: How Should Society Respond?" in *Official Responses to Problem Juveniles: Some International Reflections*, ed. James Hackler (Onati, Spain: Onati Publications, 1991), pp. 339–348.

115. Scott Turner, "Funding Sparks Effort to Cut Juvenile Arson Rate," *George Street Journal* 27 (2003): 1.

116. Leigh Edward Somers, *Economic Crimes* (New York: Clark Boardman, 1984), pp. 158–168.

117. Michael Rogers, "The Fire Next Time," *Newsweek*, November 26, 1990, p. 63.

ENTERPRISE CRIME: WHITE-COLLAR, GREEN, AND TRANSNATIONAL ORGANIZED CRIME

robert Allen Stanford was a financier who lived like a king on the tropical island of Antigua.[1] "Sir Robert" (as he liked to be called after being knighted by the Antiguan prime minister) ran a high-flying investment bank that offered investors high-yielding bank certificates of deposit. In 2008, at the height of his power, he was one of the richest men in the world, worth an estimated $2.2 billion. And he knew how to live the life: he spent $100 million on aircraft, including helicopters and private jets; another $12 million was spent lengthening his yacht by just six feet.[2]

Sir Robert's financial activities soon began to raise eyebrows among American authorities. His promises of lucrative returns on relatively safe certificates of deposit were often more than twice the going rate offered by mainstream banks. Stanford's investment opportunities sounded almost too good to be true and unfortunately for investors, they were. Instead of the safe investments being promised, Stanford secretly used the money in very risky long-term real estate and private equity investments; $2 billion was actually lent to Stanford himself. Antiguan auditors did not examine the bank's portfolio or verify its assets because (according to witnesses) they had received bribes to cover up Stanford's scheme and misinform U.S. regulatory commissions. Stanford withheld these facts from investors, who were told that their money was totally safe thanks to monitoring by a team of more than 20 analysts and yearly audits by Antiguan bank regulators.

Before being seized by the government, Stanford's bank had misappropriated $8.5 billion in assets belonging to 30,000 clients in 131 countries. Stanford was convicted of fraud in 2012 and is currently serving a 110-year prison sentence. He is eligible for release in 2105.

windlers such as Stanford use their position in the marketplace for illegal gains. Their criminal activities are typically ongoing and may involve confederates who provide support and expertise for them; they are rarely spontaneous or opportunistic. Because of their connection to business and commerce, these criminals are committing what are referred to here as **enterprise crimes**.

In this chapter, we divide these crimes of illicit entrepreneurship into three distinct categories: white-collar crime, green crime, and (transnational) organized crime. White-collar crime involves illegal activities of people and institutions whose acknowledged purpose is illegal profit through legitimate business transactions. Green crime involves environmental harm, and the violation of environmental laws and regulations.[3] Organized crime involves illegal activities of people and organizations whose acknowledged purpose is profit through illegitimate business enterprise.

THE CONCEPT OF ENTERPRISE CRIME

LO1 Describe what is meant by the term *enterprise crime*

Enterprise crimes are linked here because in each category offenders twist legal rules to enhance their personal economic position through ongoing illicit and illegal business practices. Because they are so connected, these three broad categories of crime often overlap:

- Corporate execs, in order to increase profits, may engage in environmental crimes.
- Green criminals may disguise their acts through elaborate corporate structures employing corrupt business practices.
- Organized criminals may buy legitimate businesses to launder money.

The Profiles in Crime feature shows the overlap between different elements of enterprise crime.

Business enterprise crimes taint and corrupt the free market system. They mix and match illegal and legal methods and legal and illegal products in all phases of commercial activity. They involve illegal business practices (embezzlement, price-fixing, pollution, dumping, bribery, and so on) to merchandise what are normally legitimate commercial products (securities, medical care, disposing of computer equipment).[4] They can also involve using standard business methods and accounting to market illegal goods (drugs) and services (gambling, money laundering).

The public may not view enterprise crime as particularly dangerous. Nonetheless, hundreds of thousands of occupational deaths occur each year from illegal and unsafe working conditions; illegal pollution annually kills and injures more people than all street crimes combined.[5] So while business crimes typically involve stealth and fraud, they may also include violence and death.

WHITE-COLLAR CRIME

LO2 Define white-collar crime

While we sometimes think of enterprise crimes as a new phenomenon, they have been around for hundreds of years, ever since the Industrial Revolution began. The period between 1750 and 1850 witnessed the widespread and unprecedented emergence of financial offences—such as fraud and embezzlement—frequently perpetrated by respectable middle-class offenders as the banking and commercial systems developed. Not surprisingly, scholars have long recognized that some unscrupulous businesspeople use their position of trust to fleece the public. In 1907, pioneering sociologist Edward Alsworth Ross recognized the phenomenon when he coined the phrase "the criminaloid" to describe the kind of person who hides behind his or her image as a pillar of the community and paragon of virtue to get personal gain through any means necessary.[6]

In the late 1930s, the distinguished criminologist Edwin Sutherland first used the phrase "white-collar crime" to describe the criminal activities of the rich and powerful. He defined white-collar crime as "a crime committed by a person of respectability and high social status in the course of his occupation."[7] As Sutherland saw it, white-collar crime involved conspiracies by members of the wealthy classes to use their position in commerce and industry for personal gain without regard to the law. Often these actions were handled by civil courts because injured parties were more concerned with recovering their losses than with seeing the offenders punished criminally. Consequently, Sutherland believed that the great majority of white-collar criminals did not become the subject of criminological study. Yet the cost of white-collar crime is probably several times greater than all the common law theft crimes (e.g., burglary, larceny) committed each year. In addition, white-collar offenses breed distrust in economic and social institutions, lower public morale, and undermine faith in business and government.[8]

---

enterprise crimes Ongoing illegal activities by an individual or a group of individuals involved in commerce that either violate the laws regulating legitimate business or whose acknowledged purpose is profit through illegitimate commercial enterprise.

CRIMINAL CRIMINAL DEFENSE ATTORNEY

Paul W. Bergrin was once a prominent lawyer who defended the soldiers involved in the Abu Ghraib case and celebrities, including Queen Latifah and other pop stars. Despite his high-profile cases, Bergrin got involved in crime himself. On March 18, 2013, a jury convicted Bergrin on 23 counts, including conspiracy to murder a witness and other racketeering, cocaine, and prostitution offenses, earning him a life sentence in prison.

When Paul Bergrin went on trial in 2013, the list of charges against him made him seem like a gang leader, drug lord, or organized crime boss: running a criminal enterprise, conspiring to murder a federal witness, committing wire fraud, distributing cocaine, and facilitating prostitution, bribery, and other crimes. But Bergrin, who was convicted on 23 criminal counts and sentenced to life in prison, was actually a high-powered lawyer, a former New Jersey state and federal prosecutor turned defense attorney.

How did this turn of events occur? For years, Bergrin and his law firm were highly successful. His client roster included a wide range of people, from celebrities to gang leaders and drug traffickers. Living the life, Bergrin was a man-about-town who wore expensive suits, drove luxury cars, and rarely lost a case. But the FBI placed him under investigation when in 2004 an informant who had damaging information about one of Bergrin's criminal clients was killed. The investigation uncovered evidence that revealed Bergrin was using his law offices as a cover to conduct illegal activities to protect his criminal clients from prosecution and carry on their unlawful pursuits. He was paid handsomely for using his position as a criminal defense attorney to manipulate and disrupt court proceedings on behalf of his clients.

Bergrin's criminal actions included:

- Counseling, intimidating, and sometimes bribing witnesses to offer perjured testimony in favor of his clients or to flee so they wouldn't be available to testify
- Coaching an eight-year-old murder witness to lie on the stand, resulting in the acquittal of one of his clients
- Conspiring with clients to identify, locate, and murder witnesses who would testify against them

- Using his law firm to launder money for clients, associates, and himself and to set up phony corporations or other legal entities to facilitate even more crimes
- Running a drug trafficking operation and a prostitution business for two of his clients while they were in jail

Bergrin recruited others—including his girlfriend (who worked at the law firm), his law partner, and one of his criminal clients—to take part in his racketeering enterprise. All told, eight of the nine individuals charged pleaded guilty and Bergrin received eight 20-year prison terms for drug offenses, one 10-year term for plotting to murder witnesses, and eight 5-year terms on conspiracy, prostitution, drug, and currency reporting counts.

Critical Thinking

The General Theory of Crime suggests that criminals are impulsive people who lack self-control. Is it possible that an attorney who had gone to college and law school and studied for the bar lacked self-control? How would Hirschi and Gottfredson explain the crimes of Paul Bergrin?

SOURCE: FBI, "Attorney-Turned-Racketeer, 'Stunning' Betrayal of the Law," October 31, 2013, http://www.fbi.gov/news/stories/2013/october/attorney-turned-racketeer-a-stunning-betrayal-of-the-law/attorney-turned-racketeer-a-stunning-betrayal-of-the-law (accessed June 2014).

 To read more about the history of white-collar crime and Edwin Sutherland, go to **http://www.heritage.org/research/reports/2004/10/the-sociological-origins-of-white-collar-crime.**

Is there a big difference between a corporate bigwig who scams millions and a low-level employee who pilfers some company supplies? Could their motives be the same?

Although Sutherland's work is considered a milestone in criminological history, his focus was on corporate criminality, including the crimes of the rich and powerful. Contemporary definitions of white-collar crime are typically much broader and include both middle-income Americans and corporate titans who use the marketplace for their criminal activity.[9] Included within recent views of white-collar crime are such acts as income tax evasion, credit card fraud, and bankruptcy fraud. Other white-collar criminals use their positions of trust in business or government to commit crimes. Their activities might include pilfering, soliciting bribes or kickbacks, and embezzlement. Some white-collar criminals set up business for the sole purpose of victimizing the general public. They engage in land swindles (i.e., representing a swamp as a choice building site), securities theft, medical fraud, and so on.

CONNECTIONS

You may recall Sutherland's work on differential association theory, which was set out in Chapter 7. Sutherland argued that crime was a learned behavior. Apply his concepts to white-collar crime.

In addition to acting as individuals, some white-collar criminals become involved in criminal conspiracies designed to improve the market share or profitability of their corporations. This type of white-collar crime, which includes antitrust violations, price fixing, and false advertising, is known as **corporate crime**.

Nature and Extent of White-Collar Crime

 LO3 Compare and contrast the various forms of white-collar crime

It is difficult to estimate the extent and influence of white-collar crime because these crimes are not tallied by either the UCR or NCVS. Some private and quasi-public organizations do conduct surveys on white-collar crime which help determine the extent of the problem. The National White Collar Crime Center is one such agency. Its most recent national survey of more than 2,500 adults tapped into individual experiences with mortgage fraud, credit card fraud, identity theft, unnecessary home or auto repairs, price misrepresentation, and losses occurring due to false stockbroker information, fraudulent business ventures, and Internet scams. The study gives a picture of how widespread white-collar crime is and how many citizens are affected by enterprise crimes:[10]

- Twenty-four percent of households and 17 percent of individuals reported experiencing at least one form of white-collar crime within the previous year.
- White-collar crimes happened at both household and individual levels, most often as a result of credit card fraud, price misrepresentation, and unnecessary object repairs.

corporate crime White-collar crime involving a legal violation by a corporate entity, such as price-fixing, restraint of trade, or hazardous waste dumping.

- More than half (55 percent) of the households surveyed reported at least one external recipient or agency (e.g., credit card company, business or person involved, law enforcement, consumer protection agency, personal attorney).
- Only about 12 percent of the crimes were reported to law enforcement or some other crime control agency.
- The general public views white-collar crimes seriously, considering them more damaging than traditional crimes.[11]

It is not surprising, then, that some estimates of the annual cost of white-collar crime is as high as $660 billion.[12] These losses far outstrip the expense of any other type of crime. Nor is it likely that the full extent of white-collar crime will ever be fully known because many victims (70 percent) are reluctant to report their crime to police, believing that nothing can be done and that getting further involved is pointless.[13]

Beyond the monetary cost, white-collar crime can cause significant economic, social, and personal damage. White-collar crime also destroys confidence, saps the integrity of commercial life, and has the potential for devastating destruction.

 The National Association of Fraud Investigators was established to improve communications and to expand the networking of those in investigation of white-collar crime and related fields, which include but are not limited to law enforcement, insurance investigators, professional investigators, security specialists, bond enforcement agents, attorneys, forensic examiners, tracers/locators, credit card investigators, auto theft investigators, and their international counterparts. Learn more at **http://www.nafraud.com/**

Does a career as a fraud investigator sound interesting? Visit their website to help make up your mind.

White-collar crime today represents a range of behaviors involving individuals acting alone and within the context of a business structure. The victims of white-collar crime can be the general public, the organization that employs the offender, or a competing organization. There have been numerous attempts to create subcategories or typologies of white-collar criminality. The one used here contains seven elements, ranging from an individual using a business enterprise to swindle clients to large-scale corporate enterprises collectively engaging in illegitimate activity.[14]

White-Collar Swindlers

As you may recall (Chapter 12), fraud is a common-law crime in which someone uses trickery and deceit to separate a mark from his money. A common-law swindle occurs when the con artist tells people she just inherited a Picasso from her deceased aunt and then sells it to an unsuspecting purchaser who later discovers it to be a forgery. In contrast, **white-collar swindles** involve a person using his or her institutional or business position to commit fraud and fleece victims over an extended period of time. It would be common-law fraud to sell a forged autograph of Peyton Manning or Tom Brady to someone you just met at a poker game. In contrast, someone who sets up a sports memorabilia business, advertises the sale of sports posters, photos, and other items allegedly signed by famous athletes, and then sells forgeries to unsuspecting clients is engaging in a white-collar swindle. Here, a criminal enterprise was created specifically to engage in illegal activity.

White-collar swindles take many forms, some of which are described in detail below.

Investment Swindles   On March 12, 2009, financier Bernard Madoff pleaded guilty to an 11-count criminal complaint, charged with violations of the antifraud provisions of the Securities Act of 1933, the Securities Exchange Act of 1934, and the Investment Advisers Act of 1940. At his hearing, Madoff admitted that he had swindled thousands of investors in one of the nation's most elaborate financial crimes. On June 29, 2009, Madoff was sentenced to 150 years in prison, a life sentence.

How did Madoff's swindle unfold? He founded the Wall Street firm Bernard L. Madoff Investment Securities LLC in 1960, and it soon became one of Wall Street's largest "specialist" firms, handling the money of celebrities such as Kevin Bacon and Steven Spielberg. Rather than being a Wall Street genius, Madoff was running a giant **Ponzi scheme** (see Exhibit 13.1). Madoff had not actually invested any of the money but instead deposited it in various banks. He used money given to him to pay dividends and interest owed investors, and encouraged people to keep their money in the account and reinvest profit and dividends. Every month investors got a statement showing more and more paper profits. When the stock market melted down in 2007 and people wanted to cash in their stock, Madoff's house of cards fell apart: all the money was gone. Losses amounted to about $18 billion. In the end, Madoff was regarded as the symbol of the greed run amuck that almost destroyed the nation's financial system.

 To read more about Bernard Madoff, go to **http://topics.nytimes.com/top/reference/timestopics/people/m/bernard_l_madoff/.**

Should nondangerous people like Madoff be put in prison at the taxpayers' expense? Or should he be made to do community service after all his wealth has been confiscated?

EXHIBIT 13.1

What Is a Ponzi Scheme?

A Ponzi scheme is an investment swindle that involves the payment of purported returns to existing investors from funds contributed by new investors. Ponzi scheme organizers often solicit new investors by promising to invest funds in opportunities claimed to generate high returns with little or no risk. In many Ponzi schemes, the swindlers focus on attracting new money to make promised payments to earlier-stage investors and to use for personal expenses, instead of engaging in any legitimate investment activity. With little or no legitimate earnings, the schemes require a consistent flow of money from new investors to continue. Ponzi schemes tend to collapse when it becomes difficult to recruit new investors or when a large number of investors ask to cash out.

Why are they called "Ponzi schemes"? The term comes from one Charles Ponzi, who duped thousands of New England residents into investing in a postage stamp speculation scheme back in the 1920s. At a time when the annual interest rate for bank accounts was 5 percent, Ponzi promised investors that he could provide a 50 percent return in just 90 days. Ponzi initially bought a small number of international mail coupons in support of his scheme, but quickly switched to using incoming funds to pay off earlier investors.

SOURCE: U.S. Securities and Exchange Commission, "Ponzi Schemes," http://www.sec.gov/answers/ponzi.htm (accessed June 2014).

Madoff's Ponzi scheme is not unique. There have been numerous swindles in the financial world designed to fraudulently siphon off clients' money, some so great that they have threatened to collapse the world's financial markets (see Exhibit 13.2).

Subprime Mortgage Swindles   A subprime mortgage is a home loan given to borrowers who, because of their income, would not ordinarily qualify for bank loans. Once the subprime loans have been issued, the vendors typically bundle them into large pools and sell them as securities, a process known as **securitization**. Because they carry risk, they typically pay a higher interest rate than normal securities, making them attractive to investors. With this advantage, by

white-collar swindle A crime in which people use an ongoing business enterprise to fraudulently expropriate money from unsuspecting victims.

Ponzi scheme An investment fraud that involves the payment of purported returns to existing investors from funds contributed by new investors.

securitization The process by which vendors take individual subprime loans and bundle them into large pools and sell them as securities.

EXHIBIT 13.2

Financial Swindles

- *The pyramid scheme.* Similar to Ponzi schemes, the money collected from newer victims of the fraud is paid to earlier victims to provide a veneer of legitimacy. In pyramid schemes, however, the victims themselves are induced to recruit further victims through the payment of recruitment commissions.

- *Prime bank investment swindle.* In these schemes, perpetrators claim to have access to a secret trading program endorsed by large financial institutions such as the Federal Reserve Bank, U.S. Treasury Department, World Bank, International Monetary Fund, and so on. Perpetrators often claim the unusually high rates of return and low risk are the result of a worldwide "secret" exchange open only to the world's largest financial institutions. Victims are often drawn into prime bank investment frauds because the criminals use sophisticated terms and legal-looking documents, and claim the investments are insured against loss.

- *Advance fee fraud.* This category of fraud encompasses a broad variety of schemes designed to induce their victims into remitting up-front payments in exchange for the promise of goods, services, and/or prizes. Victims are informed that in order to participate in a promising investment opportunity, they must first pay various taxes and/or fees.

- *Commodities swindle.* These schemes typically involve the deceptive or fraudulent sale of commodity investments. Victims are duped into providing funds for commodities transactions that either never occur or are inconsistent with the original sales pitches. Alternatively, commodities market participants may attempt to illegally manipulate the market for a commodity by such actions as fraudulently reporting price information or cornering the market to artificially increase the price of the targeted commodity.

- *Foreign currency exchange swindle.* These schemes are characterized by the use of false or deceptive sales practices, alleging high rates of return for minimal risk, to induce victims to invest in the foreign currency exchange market. The touted transactions either never occur, are inconsistent with the original sales pitches, or are executed for the sole purpose of generating excessive trading commissions in breach of fiduciary responsibilities to the victim client.

SOURCE: FBI, "Financial Crimes Report to the Public, Fiscal Years 2010–2011," http://www.fbi.gov/stats-services/publications/financial-crimes-report-2010-2011/financial-crimes-report-2010-2011#Financial (accessed June 2014).

2006 subprimes had grown to 20 percent of the mortgage market, up from 2 percent a decade earlier; this means an estimated $1.3 trillion of the total $4.5 trillion total mortgage loans outstanding is subprime.[15]

While subprime mortgages can help first-time home buyers of limited means, they also have been the source of

> To learn more about subprime mortgages and mortgages in general, go to the Mortgage Bankers Association website at **http://www.mortgagebankers.org/**.
> **What would prompt bankers to loan money to people with questionable finances?**

Matthew Taylor, a former trader with the Goldman Sachs Group, Inc., exits federal court in New York on April 3, 2013, after pleading guilty to concealing $8 billion in unauthorized trading, causing the bank to lose $118 million. What theory of crime would best explain Taylor's management fraud?

Scott Eells/Bloomberg/Getty Images

fraud by other borrowers and lenders. First-time home buyers were encouraged to borrow almost the full value of their property without regard to their ability to pay back the loans. Borrowers often provided false information to the mortgage broker and/or lender, enabling them to get loans for which they were not qualified. Some of those involved in mortgage lending—mortgage brokers, lenders, appraisers, underwriters, accountants, real estate agents, settlement attorneys, land developers, investors, builders, bank account representatives, trust account representatives, investment banks, and credit rating agencies—became involved in criminal fraud to cash in on the housing boom and to maintain or increase their current standard of living. Desperate for funds, some subprime lenders, in order to stave off regulators, engaged in false accounting entries and fraudulently inflated assets and revenues. Some manipulated their reported loan portfolio risks and used various accounting schemes to inflate their financial reports. And in some cases, before these subprime lenders' stocks rapidly declined in value, executives with insider information sold their equity positions and profited illegally. In addition to traditional industry conspirators, there have been instances involving various organized criminal groups and gang members in mortgage fraud activity.

Foreclosure Rescue Scams   Not only has the availability of subprime mortgages presented opportunities for people to commit fraud, but it also created scams designed to prey upon people who obtained a mortgage and now cannot make payments. There are a variety of foreclosure rescue scams:

- *Phantom help.* A desperate homeowner is offered help by a supposed "expert" in avoiding foreclosures. They are then saddled with charges for things they could have done on their own, such as calling the bank. The phantom helper promises to help, collects a fee, and never follows through. Soon it's too late to stop the foreclosure from taking place.
- *Bailout.* In this scam, someone offers to bail out the homeowner by taking the house off their hands with the promise that they can stay on as renters and buy the house back once things have been "fixed." The homeowner soon finds out that the promise is false, they can't buy their own house back, and the supposed rescuers get most, if not all, of the equity when it is sold.
- *Bait and switch.* Scammers tell the victim that they are signing documents for a new loan that will solve their problems. In reality, they are signing forged documents that transfer ownership of the home, which the scammers quickly try to sell to a third party at a reduced rate. The victim still owes the bank for the mortgage but no longer owns the home.[16]

Religious Swindles   In 2013, Adriano Sotomayor, a New Jersey man claiming to be a priest, contacted an elderly nun and said she had been named beneficiary of a $2.1 million estate. Sotomayor also told the nun that before receiving her funds, she had to wire money to the company handling the will—a New Jersey–based business called Flex Account—to cover various taxes, processing, and legal fees. Her order, the Sisters of Fatima, thought they could use the money from the will to develop a religious community in Haiti. To get through the legal red tape, the Sisters of Fatima community and their family and friends raised the money and per Sotomayor's instructions wired it to various locations in the Atlantic City area. Many of the transfers went to casinos—Sotomayor was known to be a gambler—and were picked up by individuals working for him. The nun gave the wiring instructions to her acquaintances who were willing to loan her money; they in turn sent their shares to those same places. Sotomayor began telling the nun that there were problems with the will, including a legal challenge by the deceased's son, and additional money was needed to avoid lawsuits. He threatened her with media attention and law enforcement action if she didn't send more money. Of course, there was no money; Sotomayor was really the center of a cruel religious swindle. He was eventually caught, convicted, and sent to prison for 18 years.[17]

Swindlers love to target the religious, taking advantage of their hope. Swindlers take in worshippers of all persuasions: Jews, Baptists, Lutherans, Catholics, Mormons, and Greek Orthodox have all fallen prey to religious swindles. How do religious swindlers operate? Some create fraudulent charitable organizations and convince devout people to contribute to their seemingly worthwhile cause. Some use religious television and radio shows to sell their products. Others place verses from the scriptures on their promotional literature to comfort hesitant investors.

Another particularly cruel swindle is to prey upon couples desperate to adopt children and use religious organizations or local ministries to conduct their scams. In one Indiana case, Victoria Farahan approached the director of a new local adoption ministry and said she could provide healthy newborns from Hospital 31 in Moscow. Couples were provided with pictures of the babies (which turned out to be pictures of Farahan's own children). Because the scam was run through a religious institution, people took it at face value. Before being discovered, Farahan was able to bilk couples out $100,000. She pleaded guilty to two counts of mail fraud and five counts of wire fraud.[18]

White-Collar Chiseling

White-collar **chiseling** involves a business owner regularly cheating customers and clients, or an employee stealing from the organization they work for, by deception or deceit. When chiselers target an individual client, they may overbill them for the services they did receive or charge for something that they never collected. For example, in New York City, some cab drivers routinely overcharge customers by activating a switch that alters the meter, charging passengers out-of-town rates even though the ride has taken place within city limits. Because the schemes are so subtle, the victim may not even realize they have been cheated.[19]

Auto repair shops have long been suspected of overcharging customers for bogus auto repairs that were not required or never performed.[20] When someone brings their car in for repair and are told the brakes are shot, how often do they examine them themselves? And auto repair clients seldom ask to see proof that new high-quality parts were used, making it easy for unscrupulous chiselers to substitute off brands or used parts.

chiseling Crimes that involve using illegal means to cheat an organization, its consumers, or both on a regular basis.

Chiseling the public can also involve other schemes, such as short weighting, intentionally tampering with the accuracy of scales used to weigh products in markets, or adding filler to what is being sold as unadulterated food products. Recently whistleblowers let on that almost 70 percent of ground meat sold in supermarkets contained "**pink slime**," a substance made by gathering waste trimmings, simmering them at low heat so the fat separates easily from the muscle, and spinning the trimmings using a centrifuge to complete the separation. Next, the mixture is sent through pipes where it is sprayed with ammonia gas to kill bacteria—sounds appetizing.[21] While not illegal, a number of businesses (including McDonald's) stopped using pink slime after the story broke.

Professional Chiseling It is not uncommon for professionals to use their positions to chisel clients. Pharmacists have been known to alter prescriptions or substitute low-cost generic drugs for more expensive name brands.[22] In one of the most notorious cases in the nation's history, Kansas City pharmacist Robert R. Courtney was charged with fraud when it was discovered that he had been selling diluted mixtures of the medications Taxol, Gemzar, Paraplatin, and Platinol, which are used to treat a variety of illnesses, including pancreatic and lung cancer, advanced ovarian and breast cancer, and AIDS-related Kaposi's sarcoma. In one instance, Courtney provided a doctor with only 450 milligrams of Gemzar for a prescription that called for 1,900 mg, a transaction that netted him a profit of $779.[23] After he pleaded guilty, Courtney told authorities that his drug dilution activities were not limited to the conduct he admitted to at the time of his guilty plea. His criminal activities had actually begun in 1992 or even earlier, affected the patients of 400 doctors, involved 98,000 prescriptions, and harmed approximately 4,200 patients.[24] There is no telling how many people died or suffered serious medical complications because of Courtney's criminal conduct.

Securities Chiseling Mathew Martoma was an up-and-coming portfolio manager for the hedge fund company SAC Capital, taking millions of dollars each year in bonus money for his stock-picking prowess. But as it turns out, Martoma's success was based not on his investment savvy but on illegally obtained inside information. From 2006 until July 2008, Martoma arranged for dozens of "consultations" with doctors working for pharmaceutical firms in order to get inside information on how drug trials were going. He often engaged in subterfuge to disguise the nature of their communications (e.g., sending emails to schedule meetings or phone calls on bogus topics). Taking full advantage of his financial and personal relationships with them, Martoma and SAC Capital traded aggressively in the stocks, racking up hundreds of millions in profits for the company and himself.[25] Martoma was convicted of two counts of securities fraud, which carries a maximum 20-year term, and one count of conspiracy, which has a maximum 5-year term. He is not alone: in 2012, security executive Matthew Kluger was sent to prison for 12 years as a result of a $37 million scheme, and investment guru Raj Rajaratnam got 11 years for chiseling $72 million.[26]

Why did these executives go to prison? It is against the law for securities to profit from inside business information, referred to as **insider trading**. The information can be used to buy and sell securities, giving the trader an unfair advantage over the general public. As originally conceived, insider trading made it illegal for corporate employees with direct knowledge of market-sensitive information to use that information for their own benefit—for example, by buying stock in a small company that is being taken over by their employer. In recent years, the definition of insider trading has been expanded by federal courts to include employees of financial institutions, such as law or banking firms, who use illegally obtained confidential information on pending corporate actions to purchase stock or give the information to a third party so that party can buy shares in the company. Courts have ruled that such actions are deceptive and violate security trading codes.[27]

Because there is no such thing as making too much money, a great deal of chiseling takes place on the commodities and stock markets, where individuals who are already rich engage in deceptive practices that are prohibited by federal law in order to become even richer.[28] Stockbrokers violate accepted practices when they engage in churning the client's account by repeated, excessive, and unnecessary buying and selling of stock.[29] Other broker fraud includes front running, in which brokers place personal orders ahead of a customer's large order to profit from the market effects of the trade, and bucketing, which is skimming customer trading profits by falsifying trade information.[30]

White-Collar Exploitation

White-collar **exploitation** occurs when an individual abuses their power or position in an organization to extort or coerce people into making payments to them for services to which they are already entitled. If the payments are not made, the services for which the victim is entitled to are withheld.

pink slime A substance made by gathering waste trimmings, cooking them so the fat separates easily from the muscle, and using a centrifuge to complete the separation.

insider trading Illegal buying of stock in a company based on information provided by someone who has a fiduciary interest in the company, such as an employee or an attorney or accountant retained by the firm. Federal laws and the rules of the Securities and Exchange Commission require that all profits from such trading be returned and provide for both fines and a prison sentence.

exploitation Forcing victims to pay for services to which they have a clear right.

In most cases, exploitation occurs when the victim has a clear right to expect a service, and the offender threatens to withhold the service unless an additional payment or bribe is forthcoming. On the local and state levels, exploitation may occur when a government official who holds discretionary power—liquor license board members, food inspectors, fire inspectors—demand extortion money. People who want a license are told that unless they pay the board member he will turn down the request. A fire inspector demands payment for approving an addition to a business or demands that the owner of a restaurant pay him for an operating license to which they are by law entitled. Exploitation involves a threat: "If you don't pay me, I will cause you trouble."

Exploitation can also occur in private industry. Purchasing agents in large companies often demand a piece of the action for awarding contracts to suppliers and distributors. Managing agents in some of New York City's most luxurious buildings have been convicted on charges that they routinely extorted millions of dollars from maintenance contractors and building suppliers, steering repair and maintenance work to particular contractors in exchange for kickbacks totaling millions of dollars.[31]

Exploitation is particularly troubling in the criminal justice system when police officers threaten victims with arrest if they do not make payments or when judges bully defendants, threatening conviction unless they are paid off. Thomas Spargo, a New York State Supreme Court justice, was convicted of extorting money from a lawyer: if extortion money was not paid, cases handled by his law firm and the lawyer's own personal divorce proceeding would be handled in a biased fashion with negative outcomes![32]

White-Collar Influence Peddling

In 2014, a scam was exposed in which corrupt state employees and their accomplices were selling California driver's licenses for cash. A man who owned a driving school let his students know that—for a price—he could guarantee them a license, even if they had already failed the driving test. Often they didn't even have to take the test, thanks to the man's connections at the Department of Motor Vehicles (DMV) office in El Cajon, California. Those willing to pay anywhere from $500 to $2,500 to corrupt DMV employees could get a license with no questions asked. The driving school catered mostly to Middle Eastern immigrants, and soon word of easy licenses in that community spread north to Los Angeles and beyond. People flew in from other states just to take a California driving test. A number of DMV employees who participated in the scam went to prison for up to 18 months.[33]

Sometimes individuals holding important institutional positions sell power, influence, and information to outsiders who have an interest in influencing the activities of the institution or buying information on what the institution may do in the future. In addition to DMV employees

selling licenses to people who do not deserve them, offenses within this category include government employees taking kickbacks from contractors in return for awarding them contracts they could not have won on merit, or outsiders bribing government officials, such as those in the Securities and Exchange Commission, who might sell information about future government activities. A police officer who sells information on future raids or takes a bribe in lieu of handing out a citation or making an arrest is engaging in influence peddling. These schemes can net the culprit significant amounts: one recent case in which a government agent awarded contracts for bribes netted him more than $12 million.[34]

Though they are somewhat similar, **influence peddling** can be distinguished from exploitation. Exploiters force victims to pay for services to which they have a clear right; they are engaging in extortion. In contrast, influence peddlers take bribes to use their positions to grant favors and sell information to which their co-conspirators are not entitled. In sum, in crimes of exploitation, the victim is threatened and forced to pay, whereas the victim of influence peddling is the organization compromised by its employees for their own interests.

Influence Peddling in Government   When Representative Randy "Duke" Cunningham (R-CA) resigned from Congress after confessing to accepting $2.4 million in bribes, including a Rolls-Royce, a yacht, and a nineteenth-century Louis-Philippe commode, he proclaimed: "In my life, I have known great joy and great sorrow. And now I know great shame."[35]

It has become all too common for elected and appointed government officials to be forced to resign or even to be jailed for accepting bribes to use their influence. The Cunningham case is by no means unique. On April 17, 2006, former Illinois Governor George Ryan was convicted of steering government contracts to people who were willing to give him kickbacks and bribes. The prosecution said Ryan and his family got fancy vacations, money, and other items worth at least $167,000, and in return offered special political favors and state business in the dozen years he served in the state's top roles.[36] Ryan's successor Governor Rod Blagojevich was forced to resign after he was overheard in federal wiretaps planning to sell president-elect Obama's open Senate seat to the highest bidder.[37] Blagojevich was subsequently impeached and removed from office on January 29, 2009. In March 2012, Blagojevich began serving a 14-year sentence in federal prison following conviction for corruption, including the soliciting of bribes.

> **influence peddling** Using an institutional position to grant favors and sell information to which their co-conspirators are not entitled.

Influence Peddling in Criminal Justice   Agents of the criminal justice system have also been accused of influence peddling. Police have routinely been accused and convicted of accepting bribes from individuals engaged in illegal activities. Some have been convicted on charges that they have provided protection and given warning of planned raids on brothels, gambling dens, and drug houses. Even customs inspectors have been convicted on charges that they were in the pay of drug cartels for looking the other way as large shipments of illegal substances were brought across the border.[38] Thirty years ago, the Knapp Commission found that police corruption in New York City was pervasive and widespread, ranging from patrol officers accepting small gratuities from local businesspeople to senior officers receiving payoffs in the thousands of dollars from gamblers and narcotics violators.[39] Despite years of effort to eradicate police corruption, instances still abound. In New York City more than 20 officers were alleged to have been patrons of prostitutes working at 335 West 39th Street and a nearby massage parlor; some officers were filmed demanding sex.[40]

Police are not the only justice officials who have been caught in the web of bribery and influence peddling. Sadly, judges have been accused of taking bribes in order to influence their decision making. For example, in 2009, Louisiana judge Wayne G. Cresap was charged with accepting bribes in order to influence his bail decision making. Cresap released defendants on their own recognizance, without requiring cash bail, if their lawyers would later give him a payoff in return![41] While Cresap's actions are troubling, they pale in comparison to what may be the most shocking case of judicial malfeasance on record. In 2009, two Pennsylvania judges, Mark Ciavarella and Michael Conahan, were indicted for accepting $2.6 million in bribes to place juvenile offenders in a privately run youth detention facility. Thousands of kids were put away for minor infractions so that the judges could earn millions in illegal payoffs while the owners of the private corrections facility received millions in state payments; both judges eventually pleaded guilty and received seven-year prison sentences.[42]

Influence Peddling in Business   On August 13, 2010, the Apple manager in charge of selecting Asian suppliers, Paul Shin Devine, was arrested for disclosing confidential information to suppliers in exchange for payments. The information helped the suppliers gain an edge when bidding for Apple's business. Devine had the suppliers send payments to his wife's bank account to avoid attracting attention; unfortunately for him, he neglected to delete incriminating emails.[43]

Influence peddlers use their position in a firm or the government for their own personal benefit. Here, former New York City police commissioner Bernard Kerik leaves his car to enter a New York courthouse. Kerik was indicted by a federal grand jury on charges of conspiracy, tax fraud, and making false statements for concealing the fact that he accepted $255,000 in renovations to his Riverdale, Bronx, apartment from a company seeking to do business with the city of New York and hiding the income from the Internal Revenue Service in order to avoid paying taxes. Prosecutors also charged Kerik with lying while trying to land a cabinet post with the Bush administration and with concealing royalties from his autobiography *The Lost Son*. On November 5, 2009, Kerik pleaded guilty to eight felony tax and false statement charges and was sent to a federal facility in Maryland; he was discharged from federal custody on October 15, 2013, after serving the last five months of his sentence in home confinement.

Politicians and government officials are not the only ones accused of bribery; business has had its share of scandals. People who hold power in a business may force those wishing to work with the company to pay them some form of bribe or gratuity to gain a contract. In the building industry, a purchasing agent may demand a kickback from contractors hoping to gain a service contract. Sometimes influence peddling can benefit both parties. In the record industry, payola is the routine practice of paying radio stations or DJs to play songs. While the recording companies are forced to pay, they also benefit from having their recording artists receive air time they might not otherwise have gotten. Some large companies have been caught in payola scandals; Sony records paid $10 million to the State of New York to settle a claim that its promoters gave gifts to radio station managers to get songs played.[44]

Business-related bribery is not unique to the United States. In some foreign countries, soliciting bribes to do business is a common, even expected, practice. In European countries, such as Italy and France, giving gifts to secure contracts is a routine practice.[45] It is common for foreign officials to solicit bribes to allow American firms to do business in their countries. In 2013, the International Business Machines Corporation (IBM) settled a case and agreed to pay some $10 million over improper gifts to government officials in South Korea and China. That did not end IBM's ordeal: the Department of Justice continues to investigate allegations of illegal activity by a former IBM employee in Poland, Argentina, Bangladesh, and Ukraine.[46] In response to these revelations, Congress passed the Foreign Corrupt Practices Act (FCPA), which makes it a criminal offense to bribe foreign officials or to make other questionable overseas payments. Violations of the FCPA draw strict penalties for both the defendant company and its officers.[47] Moreover, all fines imposed on corporate officers are paid by them, not absorbed by the company. If a domestic company violates the antibribery provisions of the FCPA, it can be fined up to $1 million. Company officers, employees, or stockholders who are convicted of bribery may have to serve a prison sentence of up to five years and pay a $10,000 fine.

White-Collar Embezzlement and Employee Fraud

Another type of white-collar crime involves individuals' use of their positions to embezzle company funds or appropriate company property for themselves. Here the company or organization that employs the criminal, rather than an outsider, is the victim of white-collar crime.

Blue-Collar Pilferage Is nothing sacred? Three employees and a friend allegedly stole moon rocks from a NASA laboratory in Houston. FBI agents arrested them after they tried to sell the contraband to an undercover agent in Orlando, Florida. The would-be seller reportedly asked $2,000 per gram for the rocks initially but later bumped the price to $8,000 per gram.[48] While the theft of moon rocks does not happen very often, systematic theft of company property by employees, or pilferage, is common.[49]

Employee theft is most accurately explained by factors relevant to the work setting, such as job dissatisfaction and the workers' belief that they are being exploited by employers or supervisors; economic problems play a relatively small role in the decision to pilfer. So, although employers attribute employee fraud to economic conditions and declining personal values, workers themselves say they steal because of strain and conflict. The Profiles in Crime feature discusses one instance of employee theft that occurred in Buffalo, New York.

Management Fraud Blue-collar workers are not the only employees who commit corporate theft. Management-level fraud is also quite common. Such acts include converting company assets for personal benefit; fraudulently receiving increases in compensation (such as raises or bonuses); fraudulently increasing personal holdings of company stock; retaining one's present position within the company by manipulating accounts; and concealing unacceptable performance from stockholders.[50]

Management fraud has involved some of the nation's largest companies and richest people. Multibillionaire L. Dennis Kozlowski was imprisoned in 2005 for taking excessive bonuses totaling $430 million, tax evasion, and stealing more than $100 million from his firm Tyco International; he was released on parole in 2014.[51] In an even greater scandal, chief financial officer (CFO) Andrew Fastow, chief executive officer (CEO) Jeffrey Skilling, and chairman and CEO Kenneth Lay of Enron, one of the nation's largest companies, were charged with conspiracy, securities fraud, wire fraud, bank fraud, and making false statements. The three fooled the public into believing that the company was doing great and would reach its profit targets, even though they knew it was losing billions of dollars. People who had invested heavily in Enron lost their life savings when the company collapsed. Fastow was sentenced to six years in prison for his role in the accounting scandal, and Skilling was sentenced to 24 years and four months in prison. CEO Kenneth Lay died of natural causes before he could be sentenced.[52] Why did they do it? Kenneth Lay alone received approximately $300 million from the sale of Enron stock options and restricted stock and made over $217 million in profit; he was also paid more than $19 million in salary and bonuses.

Client Fraud

Client fraud occurs when an organization that either (a) advances credit, (b) provides loans, (c) supports people financially, or (d) reimburses them for services provided to a third party is the target of criminal activity. Victims of client fraud might be an insurance company that pays out on false claims or repays health care providers that put in false claims for bogus charges. Included in this category are insurance fraud, bank fraud, credit card fraud, fraud related to welfare and Medicare programs, and tax evasion.

Health Care Fraud In 2014, Arrey Kingsly Etchi-Banyi was arrested by federal agents investigating health care fraud. He was involved in a scheme that involved fraud, kickbacks, and false billings in the growing field of home care services for Medicaid patients, this time in Washington, D.C. Medicaid provides for personal care aides who help clients in performing activities of daily living, such as getting in and out of bed, bathing, dressing, keeping track of medication, and so forth. In order to be covered for such benefits, the beneficiaries must get a doctor's prescription. Etchi-Banyi and his associates were accused of recruiting and teaming up with Medicaid beneficiaries who faked or exaggerated symptoms so they could sign up for home health care. They then received cash payments of approximately $200 every two weeks to sign timesheets falsely stating that they received home care services. Bills were submitted on behalf of these individuals for services that never were provided, costing D.C. Medicaid millions of dollars.[53]

Crooked health care providers find it lucrative to engage in fraud in obtaining patients and administering their treatment and for patients to try to scam the system for their

TAKE NO QUARTER: THE CASE OF THE PARKING METER THIEF

2011-10-13 11:16:01

A surveillance video shows former parking meter mechanic James Bagarozzo lifting a bag of quarters off the seat of a truck while at work in Buffalo, New York. Bagarozzo is the parking meter mechanic who stole thousands of dollars in quarters from Buffalo parking meters while on the job.

In 2013, James Bagarozzo, 57, of Buffalo, New York, was convicted of stealing $210,000 from the city of Buffalo, sentenced to 30 months in prison, and ordered to pay $210,000 in restitution. In 2003, Bagarozzo began working as a parking meter mechanic for the city. He was responsible for repairing defective parking meter machines but was not authorized to collect any money deposited into the machines. For the next eight years, instead of making necessary repairs, Bagarozzo rigged more than 75 parking meters so that the money inserted into the meters by the public would not drop into collection boxes. Bagarozzo would go to the rigged meters, remove the coins, and store them in bags in his car or in his pants pockets. He then took them to a local bank and told tellers that the coins were from vending machines owned by a friend; bank tellers told authorities that Bagarozzo would deposit between $3,000 and $5,000 a week!

How was he caught? Under a new leader, the city of Buffalo's Department of Parking Enforcement initiated a review of parking meters after noting that new electronic meters were making substantially more money than the old coin-operated ones. Subsequently, video surveillance was conducted that showed Bagarozzo stealing quarters from the meters on a daily basis.

Critical Thinking

In the aftermath of Bagarozzo's arrest, U.S. Attorney William Hochul stated, "This defendant admitted stealing almost a quarter-million dollars that would have gone to the residents of Buffalo. That the defendant operated day in and day out over eight years, committed his crimes while on city time using city vehicles, and utilized his mechanic skills to alter parking meters and make his thefts easier, ranks this as one of the more egregious breaches of honesty, ethics, and the public trust Buffalo has seen." Do you agree?

SOURCE: U.S. Attorney's Office, Western District of New York, "Former City of Buffalo Employee Sentenced for Stealing Hundreds of Thousands of Dollars from Parking Meters," August 16, 2013, http://www.fbi.gov/buffalo/press-releases/2013/former-city-of-buffalo-employee-sentenced-for-stealing-hundreds-of-thousands-of-dollars-from-parking-meters (accessed June 2014).

own benefit. The FBI estimates that health care fraud now costs the nation $80 billion per year.[54] There are numerous health care–related schemes, including:

- Billing for services that were never rendered by using genuine patient information to fabricate entire claims or by adding to claims with charges for procedures or services that did not take place.
- Billing for more expensive services or procedures than were actually provided or performed, commonly known as "upcoding." This practice requires "inflation" of the patient's diagnosis code to a more serious condition consistent with the false procedure code.
- Performing medically unnecessary services solely for the purpose of generating insurance payments. This scheme occurs most often in nerve-conduction and other diagnostic-testing schemes. Some Southern California clinics performed unnecessary, and sometimes harmful, surgeries on patients who had been recruited and paid to have these unnecessary surgeries performed.

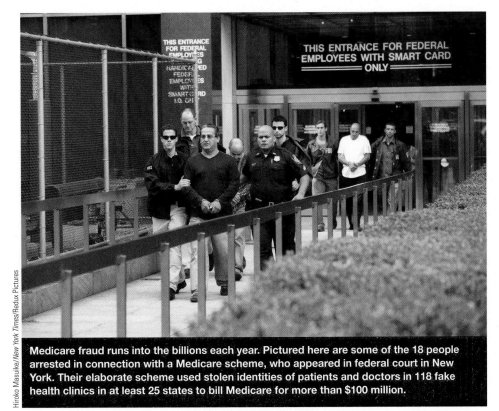

Medicare fraud runs into the billions each year. Pictured here are some of the 18 people arrested in connection with a Medicare scheme, who appeared in federal court in New York. Their elaborate scheme used stolen identities of patients and doctors in 118 fake health clinics in at least 25 states to bill Medicare for more than $100 million.

Hiroko Masuike/New York Times/Redux Pictures

services to federal health care programs are also regulated by federal laws that prohibit kickbacks and self-referrals. The Health Insurance Portability and Accountability Act of 1996 (HIPAA) established health care fraud as an independent federal criminal offense, with the basic crime carrying a federal prison term of up to 10 years in addition to significant financial penalties.[59] HIPAA doubles the prison term to up to 20 years should a perpetrator's fraud result in injury to a patient; if the fraud results in a patient's death, the perpetrator can be sentenced to life in federal prison. It is a crime, punishable by up to five years in prison, to provide anything of value, money or otherwise, directly or indirectly, with the intent to induce a referral of a patient or a health care service. Liability attaches to both parties in the transaction—the entity or individual providing the kickbacks and the individual receiving payment of the referral. The law also prohibits physicians and other health care providers from referring beneficiaries in federal health care programs to clinics or other facilities in which the physician or health care provider has a financial interest. For example, it is illegal for a doctor to refer her patients to a blood-testing lab in which she has an ownership share. These practices—kickbacks and self-referrals—are prohibited under federal law because they would compromise a medical professional's independent judgment. Congress also mandated the establishment of a nationwide Coordinated Fraud and Abuse Control Program to coordinate federal, state, and local law enforcement efforts against health care fraud and to include "the coordination and sharing of data" with private health insurers.

Health care fraud is expected to continue to rise as people live longer and produce a greater demand for Medicare benefits. In the future, the utilization of long- and short-term care facilities such as skilled nursing, assisted living, and hospice services will expand substantially. Additionally, fraudulent billings and medically unnecessary services billed to health care insurers are now prevalent throughout the country and are expected to grow in the future.[60]

Bank Fraud Encompassing such diverse schemes as check kiting, check forgery, false statements on loan applications, sale of stolen checks, bank credit card fraud, unauthorized use of automatic teller machines (ATMs), auto title fraud,

- Misrepresenting noncovered treatments as medically necessary covered treatments for purposes of obtaining insurance payments. This scheme occurs in cosmetic-surgery in which noncovered cosmetic procedures such as nose jobs, tummy tucks, liposuction, or breast augmentations are billed to patients' insurers as deviated-septum repairs, hernia repairs, or lumpectomies.[55]

A central target of medical fraud is the federal Medicaid program. The Office of Inspector General of the U.S. Department of Health and Human Services estimates that 6 percent of all Medicaid payments (more than $12 billion) should not have been paid due to erroneous billing or payment, inadequate provider documentation of services to back up the claims, and/or outright fraud.[56] One reason that thieves found Medicare an inviting target is because it operated under a system that paid providers first and investigated later. The so-called "pay and chase method" gave abusers 90 days lag time to fleece the government out of millions before authorities were aware a crime had been committed.[57]

In addition to individual physicians, some large health care providers and hospitals have been accused of routinely violating the law to obtain millions in illegal payments by overstating expenses to Medicare, filing false claims for reimbursement, billing for unnecessary procedures, and other practices.[58]

The government has attempted to tighten control over the industry in order to restrict the opportunity for physicians to commit fraud. Health care companies providing and illegal transactions with offshore banks, bank fraud can cost billions per year.[61] Among the schemes used to defraud banks are mortgage frauds in which a group of conspirators fraudulently obtain loans on overvalued or nonexistent property. Some of the more common schemes are set out in Exhibit 13.3.[62]

To be found guilty of bank fraud, one must knowingly execute or attempt to execute a scheme to fraudulently obtain money or property from a financial institution. A car dealer would commit bank fraud by securing loans on titles to cars it no longer owned. A real estate owner would be guilty of bank fraud if he or she obtained a false appraisal on a piece of property with the intention of obtaining a bank loan in excess of the property's real worth. Penalties for bank fraud include a maximum fine of $1 million and up to 30 years in prison.

Tax Evasion   Another important aspect of client fraud is tax evasion. Here the victim is the government that is cheated by one of its clients, the errant taxpayer to whom

it extended credit by allowing the taxpayer to delay paying taxes on money he or she had already earned. Tax fraud is a particularly challenging area for criminological study because so many U.S. citizens regularly underreport their income, and it is often difficult to separate honest error from deliberate tax evasion.

The basic law on tax evasion is contained in the U.S. Internal Revenue Code, section 7201, which states:

> Any person who willfully attempts in any manner to evade or defeat any tax imposed by this title or the payment thereof shall, in addition to other penalties provided by law, be guilty of a felony and, upon conviction thereof, shall be fined not more than $100,000 or imprisoned not more than five years, or both, together with the costs of prosecution.

To prove tax fraud, the government must find that the taxpayer either underreported his or her income or did not report taxable income. No minimum dollar amount is stated before fraud exists, but the government can take legal action

---

EXHIBIT 13.3

Some Common Bank Fraud Schemes

- *Fraudulent property flipping*. Property is purchased, falsely appraised at a higher value, and then quickly sold at a higher value than the market. A home worth $200,000 may be appraised for $800,000 or higher and sold to a co-conspirator who gets a mortgage based on a phony appraisal. The new owner quickly defaults on the loan. This type of scheme typically involves one or more of the following: fraudulent appraisals, doctored loan documentation, and/or inflating buyer income. Kickbacks to buyers, investors, property/loan brokers, appraisers, or title company employees are common in this scheme.

- *Silent second*. The buyer of a property borrows the down payment from the seller through the issuance of a nondisclosed second mortgage. The primary lender believes the borrower has invested his own money in the down payment, when in fact it is borrowed. The second mortgage may not be recorded to further conceal its status from the primary lender.

- *Nominee loans/straw buyers*. The identity of the borrower is concealed through the use of a nominee who allows the borrower to use the nominee's name and credit history to apply for a loan.

- *Fictitious/stolen identity*. A fictitious/stolen identity may be used on the loan application. The applicant may be involved in an identity theft scheme: the applicant's name, personal identifying information, and credit history are used without the true person's knowledge.

- *Inflated appraisals*. A corrupt home appraiser acts in collusion with a borrower and provides a misleading appraisal report to the lender. The report inaccurately states an inflated property value.

- *Foreclosure schemes*. The perpetrator identifies homeowners who are at risk of defaulting on loans or whose houses are already in foreclosure. Perpetrators mislead the homeowners into believing that they can save their homes in exchange for a transfer of the deed and up-front fees. The perpetrator profits from these schemes by remortgaging the property or pocketing fees paid by the homeowner.

- *Equity skimming*. An investor may use a straw buyer, false income documents, and false credit reports to obtain a mortgage loan in the straw buyer's name. Subsequent to closing, the straw buyer signs the property over to the investor in a quit claim deed, which relinquishes all rights to the property and provides no guaranty to title. The investor does not make any mortgage payments and rents the property until foreclosure takes place several months later.

- *Air loans*. This is a nonexistent property loan where there is usually no collateral. An example of an air loan would be where a broker invents borrowers and properties, establishes accounts for payments, and maintains custodial accounts for escrows. They may set up an office with a bank of telephones, each one used as the employer, appraiser, credit agency, etc., for verification purposes.

- *Hedge fund fraud*. Hedge funds (HFs) are private investment partnerships that routinely accept only high-wealth clients willing to invest at least hundreds of thousands of dollars. Historically, these high-wealth investors were deemed "financially sophisticated," and, as a result, HFs have been unregulated and are not required to register with any federal or state regulatory agency. More recently, many middle-class investors have been exposed to HFs through ancillary investments such as pensions and endowments. There are about 9,000 HFs currently operating, with over a trillion dollars in assets under management.

SOURCE: FBI, "Common Fraud Schemes," 2014, http://www.fbi.gov/scams-safety/fraud (accessed June 2014).

---

when there is a "substantial underpayment of tax." A second element of tax fraud is "willfulness" on the part of the tax evader. In the major case on this issue, willfulness was defined as a "voluntary, intentional violation of a known legal duty and not the careless disregard for the truth."[63] Finally, to prove tax fraud, the government must show that the taxpayer has purposely attempted to evade or defeat a tax payment. If the offender is guilty of passive neglect, the offense is a misdemeanor. Passive neglect means simply not paying taxes, not reporting income, or not paying taxes when due. On the other hand, affirmative tax evasion, such as keeping double books, making false entries, destroying books or records, concealing assets, or covering up sources of income, constitutes a felony.

Although tax cheating is a serious crime, the great majority of major tax cheats (in some categories, four of five cheaters) are not prosecuted because the IRS lacks the money to enforce the law.[64]

Corporate Crime

Yet another component of white-collar crime involves situations in which powerful institutions or their representatives willfully violate the laws that restrain these institutions from doing social harm or require them to do social good. This is also known as corporate or organizational crime.

Interest in corporate crime first emerged in the early 1900s, when a group of writers, known as muckrakers, targeted the monopolistic business practices of John D. Rockefeller and other corporate business leaders. In a 1907 article, sociologist E. A. Ross described the "criminaloid": a business leader who while enjoying immunity from the law victimized an unsuspecting public.[65] Edwin Sutherland focused theoretical attention on corporate crime when he began his research on the subject in the 1940s; corporate crime was probably what he had in mind when he coined the phrase "white-collar crime."[66]

Corporate crimes are socially injurious acts committed by people who control companies to further their business interests. The target of their crimes can be the general public, the environment, or even company workers. What makes these crimes unique is that the perpetrator is a legal fiction—a corporation—and not an individual. In reality, it is company employees or owners who commit corporate crimes and who ultimately benefit through career advancement or greater profits. For a corporation to be held criminally liable, the employee committing the crime must be acting within the scope of his employment and must have actual or apparent authority to engage in the particular act in question. Actual authority occurs when a corporation knowingly gives authority to an employee; apparent authority is satisfied if a third party, such as a customer, reasonably believes the agent has the authority to perform the act in question. Courts have ruled that actual authority may occur even when the illegal behavior is not condoned by the corporation but is nonetheless within the scope of the employee's authority.[67]

Some of the acts included within corporate crime are price-fixing and illegal restraint of trade, false advertising, and the use of company practices that violate environmental protection statutes. The variety of crimes contained within this category is great, and they cause vast damage. The following subsections examine some of the most important offenses.

Illegal Restraint of Trade and Price-Fixing In 2013, nine Japan-based companies pleaded guilty and were forced to pay a total of more than $740 million in criminal fines for their roles in conspiracies to fix the prices of more than 30 different products sold to U.S. car manufacturers, including Chrysler, Ford, and General Motors, as well as to the U.S. subsidiaries of Honda, Mazda, Mitsubishi, Nissan, Toyota, and Subaru. Executives in the companies attended meetings and communicated by telephone in the United States and Japan to set prices, to conspire to keep bids for merchandise higher than needed, and to control the supply of auto parts sold to the car manufacturers. They took measures to keep their conduct secret by using code names and meeting in remote locations. Afterwards they had further secret communications to monitor and enforce their illegal agreements.[68]

The executives at these auto part supply companies engaged in restraint of trade and price-fixing. A restraint of trade involves a contract or conspiracy designed to stifle competition, create a monopoly, artificially maintain prices, or otherwise interfere with free market competition. The control of restraint of trade violations has its legal basis in the **Sherman Antitrust Act**, which subjects to criminal or civil sanctions any person "who shall make any contract or engage in any combination or conspiracy" in restraint of interstate commerce.[69] The Sherman Act carries maximum penalties of a $100 million criminal fine for corporations and a $1 million criminal fine and 10 years in prison for individuals. The maximum fine may be increased to twice the gain derived from the crime or twice the loss suffered by the victims of the crime, if either of those amounts is greater than the statutory maximum fine.[70] The act outlaws conspiracies between corporations designed to control the marketplace.

In most instances, the act lets the presiding court judge whether corporations have conspired to "unreasonably restrain competition." However, four types of market conditions are considered so inherently anticompetitive that federal courts, through the Sherman Antitrust Act, have

Sherman Antitrust Act Law that subjects to criminal or civil sanctions any person "who shall make any contract or engage in any combination or conspiracy" in restraint of interstate commerce.

defined them as illegal per se, without regard to the facts or circumstances of the case:

- *Division of markets*. Firms divide a region into territories, and each firm agrees not to compete in the others' territories.
- *Tying arrangement*. A corporation requires customers of one of its services to use other services it offers. For example, it would be an illegal restraint of trade if a railroad required that companies doing business with it or supplying it with materials ship all goods they produce on trains owned by the rail line.[71]
- *Group boycott*. An organization or company boycotts retail stores that do not comply with its rules or desires.
- *Price-fixing*. A conspiracy to set and control the price of a necessary commodity is considered an absolute violation of the act.

Deceptive Pricing   Even the largest U.S. corporations commonly use deceptive pricing schemes when they respond to contract solicitations. Deceptive pricing occurs when contractors provide the government or other corporations with incomplete or misleading information on how much it will actually cost to fulfill the contracts on which they are bidding or use mischarges once the contracts are signed. For example, defense contractors have been prosecuted for charging the government for costs incurred on work they are doing for private firms or shifting the costs on fixed-price contracts to ones in which the government reimburses the contractor for all expenses ("cost-plus" contracts).

False Claims Advertising   Executives in even the largest corporations sometimes face stockholders' expectations of ever-increasing company profits that seem to demand that sales be increased at any cost. At times executives respond to this challenge by making claims about their products that cannot be justified by actual performance. However, the line between clever, aggressive sales techniques and fraudulent claims is fine. It is traditional to show a product in its best light, even if that involves resorting to fantasy. It is not fraudulent to show a delivery service vehicle taking off into outer space or to imply that taking one sip of beer will make people feel they have just jumped into a freezer. However, it is illegal to knowingly and purposely advertise a product as possessing qualities that the manufacturer realizes it does not have, such as the ability to cure the common cold, grow hair, or turn senior citizens into rock stars (though some rock stars are senior citizens these days).

In 2003, the U.S. Supreme Court, in the case of *Illinois Ex Rel. Madigan v. Telemarketing Associates*, helped define the line separating illegal claims from those that are artistic hyperbole protected by free speech.[72] Telemarketing Associates, a for-profit fundraising corporation, was retained by a charity to solicit donations to aid Vietnam veterans in the state of Illinois. Though donors were told that a significant portion of the money would go to the vets, the telemarketers actually retained 85 percent of all the money collected. The Illinois attorney general filed a complaint in state court, alleging that such representations were knowingly deceptive and materially false. The telemarketers said they were exercising their First Amendment free speech rights when they made their pitch for money.

The Supreme Court disagreed and found that states may charge fraud when fundraisers make false or misleading representations designed to deceive donors about how their donations will be used. The Court held that it is false and misleading for a solicitor to fool potential donors into believing that a substantial portion of their contributions would fund specific programs or services knowing full well that was not the case.

Worker Safety Violations   Some corporations have endangered the lives of their own workers by maintaining unsafe conditions in their plants and mines. It has been estimated that more than 20 million workers have been exposed to hazardous materials while on the job. Each year about 4 million workers are injured and 4,000 killed on the job. Some industries have been hit particularly hard by complaints and allegations. The control of workers' safety has been the province of the Occupational Safety and Health Administration (OSHA). OSHA sets industry standards for the proper use of such chemicals as benzene, arsenic, lead, and coke. Intentional violation of OSHA standards can result in criminal penalties.

 The National Whistleblowers Center is a nonprofit educational advocacy organization that works for the enforcement of environmental laws, nuclear safety, civil rights, and government and industry accountability through the support and representation of employee whistleblowers. Learn more at **http://www.whistleblowers.org/**.

White-Collar Law Enforcement Systems

Who deals with these crimes and enforces the laws controlling violations of business enterprise law? The Commerce Clause of the U.S. Constitution gives the federal government the authority to regulate white-collar crime. Detection and enforcement are primarily in the hands of administrative departments and agencies, including the FBI, the Internal Revenue Service, the Secret Service, U.S. Customs, the Environmental Protection Agency, and the Securities and Exchange Commission.[73] The decision to pursue criminal rather than civil violations usually is based on the seriousness of the case and the perpetrator's intent, actions to conceal the violation, and prior record. Enforcement generally is reactive (generated by complaints) rather than proactive (involving ongoing investigations or the monitoring of activities). Investigations are carried out by the various federal agencies and the FBI. If criminal prosecution is called for, the case will be handled by attorneys from the criminal, tax, antitrust, and civil rights divisions of the Justice

Department. If insufficient evidence is available to warrant a criminal prosecution, the case will be handled civilly or administratively by some other federal agency. The Federal Trade Commission can issue a cease and desist order in antitrust or merchandising fraud cases.

The number of state-funded technical assistance offices to help local prosecutors has increased significantly; more than 40 states offer such services. On the state and local levels, law enforcement officials have made progress in a number of areas, such as controlling consumer fraud. Nonetheless, while local agencies recognize the seriousness of enterprise-type crimes, they rarely have the funds necessary for effective enforcement.[74]

Local prosecutors pursue white-collar criminals more vigorously if they are part of a team effort involving a network of law enforcement agencies.[75] National surveys of local prosecutors find that many do not consider white-collar crimes particularly serious problems. They are more willing to prosecute cases if the offense causes substantial harm and if other agencies fail to act. Relatively few prosecutors participate in interagency task forces designed to investigate white-collar criminal activity.[76]

Controlling White-Collar Crime

LO4 Discuss efforts to control white-collar crime

In years past, it was rare for a corporate or white-collar criminal to receive a serious criminal penalty.[77] White-collar criminals are often considered nondangerous offenders because they usually are respectable older citizens who have families to support. These "pillars of the community" are not seen in the same light as a teenager who breaks into a drugstore to steal a few dollars. Their public humiliation at being caught is usually deemed punishment enough; a prison sentence seems unnecessarily cruel.

The main reason, according to legal expert Stuart Green, is that perception of white-collar crime is clouded by moral ambiguity. White-collar crimes are typically committed by society's success stories, by the rich and the powerful, and frequently have no visible victim at their root. Both the public and the justice system have had trouble distinguishing criminal fraud from mere lawful exaggeration, tax evasion from "tax avoidance," insider trading from "savvy investing," obstruction of justice from "zealous advocacy," bribery from "horse trading," and extortion from "hard bargaining."[78] Hence, white-collar criminals are treated more leniently than lower-class offenders.

The prevailing wisdom, then, is that many white-collar criminals avoid prosecution, and those who are prosecuted receive lenient punishment. What efforts have been made to bring violators of the public trust to justice? White-collar criminal enforcement typically involves two strategies designed to control organizational deviance: compliance and deterrence.[79]

AN ETHICAL DILEMMA

IMPRISONING THE RICH

You may recall that style guru Martha Stewart was imprisoned as a result of an investigation into an insider trading scheme. The case caused quite a bit of controversy since Martha did not present a danger to society and she was never convicted of insider trading but of the charge of lying to federal investigators. As trial attorney Kevin Mahoney put it:

It is a shameful day. The federal government will imprison a woman for lying to its investigators. Not a lie that stampeded a country into an unnecessary war, that defrauded the country in millions of dollars, or endangered people's lives. The lie was no more than the denial of wrongdoing, a protestation of innocence. Shame on us for permitting our government to terrorize us.

Yet the people who were shocked when décor diva Stewart did time for some vague white-collar offense seem to have no problem with imprisoning a lower-class woman who had been caught possessing drugs. Even though both crimes had no discernible victim, Martha's white-collar crime seemed like the more trivial offense—or did it?

Write an essay that confronts this critical issue: Is it ethical to imprison someone who claims to be innocent when confronted by police? Does that mean a person has to admit guilt or face a prison sentence? What is the purpose of putting someone like Martha Stewart in prison for some trivial white-collar offense? Is she a danger to society? Or even multibillion-dollar swindler Bernard Madoff? Or would it be better, to quote Billy Ray Valentine (Eddie Murphy in the classic 1983 film *Trading Places*), "You know, it occurs to me that the best way you hurt rich people is by turning them into poor people"

Compliance Strategies Compliance strategies aim for law conformity without the necessity of detecting, processing, or penalizing individual violators. At a minimum, they ask for cooperation and self-policing among the business community. Compliance systems attempt to create conformity by giving companies economic incentives to obey the law. They rely on administrative efforts to prevent unwanted conditions before they occur. Compliance systems depend on the threat of economic sanctions or civil penalties to control corporate violators.

One method of compliance is to set up administrative agencies to oversee business activity. The Securities and Exchange Commission regulates Wall Street activities, the Food and Drug Administration regulates drugs, cosmetics, medical devices, meats and other foods, and so on.

The legislation creating these agencies usually spells out the penalties for violating regulatory standards.[80] It is easier and less costly to be in compliance, the theory goes, than to pay costly fines and risk criminal prosecution for repeat violations. Moreover, the federal government bars people and businesses from receiving government contracts if they have engaged in repeated business law violations.

Another compliance approach is to force corporate boards to police themselves and take more oversight responsibility. In the wake of the Enron and WorldCom cases, the federal government enacted the Sarbanes-Oxley (SOX) legislation in 2002 to combat fraud and abuse in publicly traded companies.[81] This law limits the services auditing firms can perform for publicly traded companies in order to make sure accounting firms do not fraudulently collude with corporate officers; it places greater responsibilities on boards to preserve an organization's integrity and reputation, primarily for U.S. publicly traded companies. It also penalizes any attempts to alter or falsify company records in order to delude shareholders:

> Sec. 802(a) Whoever knowingly alters, destroys, mutilates, conceals, covers up, falsifies, or makes a false entry in any record, document, or tangible object with the intent to impede, obstruct, or influence the investigation or proper administration of any matter within the jurisdiction of any department or agency of the United States or any case filed under title 11, or in relation to or contemplation of any such matter or case, shall be fined under this title, imprisoned not more than 20 years, or both.

In sum, compliance strategies attempt to create a marketplace incentive to obey the law. Compliance strategies avoid punishing, stigmatizing, and shaming businesspeople by focusing on the act, rather than the actor, in white-collar crime.[82]

Deterrence Strategies   Some criminologists say that the punishment of white-collar crimes should include a retributive component similar to that used in common-law crimes. White-collar crimes, after all, are immoral activities that have harmed social values and deserve commensurate punishment.[83] Even the largest fines and penalties are no more than a slap on the wrist to multibillion-dollar companies. Corporations can get around economic sanctions by moving their rule-violating activities overseas, where legal controls over injurious corporate activities are lax or nonexistent.[84] They argue that the only way to limit white-collar crime is to deter potential offenders through fear of punishment.

Deterrence strategies involve detecting criminal violations, determining who is responsible, and penalizing the offenders to deter future violations.[85] Deterrence systems are oriented toward apprehending violators and punishing them rather than creating conditions that induce conformity to the law.

Deterrence strategies should work—and they have— because white-collar crime by its nature is a rational act whose perpetrators are extremely sensitive to the threat of criminal sanctions. Perceptions of detection and punishment for white-collar crimes appear to be powerful deterrents to future law violations. Although deterrence strategies may prove effective, federal agencies have traditionally been reluctant to throw corporate executives in jail. The government seeks criminal indictments in corporate violations only in "instances of outrageous conduct of undoubted illegality," such as price-fixing.[86] The government has also been lenient with companies and individuals that cooperate voluntarily after an investigation has begun; leniency is not given as part of a confession or plea arrangement. Those who comply with the leniency policy are charged criminally for the activity reported.[87]

Despite years of neglect, there is growing evidence that white-collar crime deterrence strategies have become normative. This get-tough deterrence approach appears to be affecting all classes of white-collar criminals. Although many people believe affluent corporate executives usually avoid serious punishment, public displeasure with such highly publicized white-collar crimes may be producing a backlash that is resulting in more frequent use of prison sentences.[88] With the Enron scandal depriving so many people of their life savings, the general public has become educated as to the damage caused by white-collar criminals and may now consider white-collar crimes as more serious offenses than common-law theft offenses.[89]

Some commentators now argue that the government may actually be going overboard in its efforts to punish white-collar criminals, especially for crimes that are the result of negligent business practices rather than intentional criminal conspiracy.[90] The U.S. Sentencing Commission has voted to increase penalties for high-dollar fraud and theft offenses.[91] Both fines and penalties have been increasing, and in one case a food company executive was sentenced to serve more than five years in prison for his role in a bid-rigging scheme; it was the longest single prison sentence ever obtained for an antitrust violation.[92]

> Since 1999, Florida's Department of Environmental Protection has fielded a multiagency Strike Force—led by the department's Division of Law Enforcement—to investigate pollutant discharges and the release of hazardous material statewide. Check it out at **http://www.dep.state.fl.us/**

GREEN CRIME

LO5   Explain the concept of green crime

The Federal Environmental Protection Agency requires the proper handling and disposal of hazardous wastes. Before they are released into local sewers and wastewater treatment plants, EPA rules require that toxic chemicals be treated in order to protect rivers, lakes, and streams. This rule was lost on Larkin Baggett, who owned and operated Chemical Consultants, Inc., in North Salt Lake City, Utah, a company that mixed and sold chemical products used in the trucking, construction, and concrete industries. Baggett illegally dumped pollutants onto the ground and into a drain that led to the treatment plant operated by the South Davis Sewer Improvement District in West Bountiful, Utah. The treatment plant had a permit to discharge treated effluent to the Jordan River, which empties into the Great Salt Lake. One of the wastes, nonylphenol, is a powerful organic chemical and heavy-duty industrial cleaner that is toxic to aquatic life. Baggett's actions caused the plant to violate permit limits for acute toxicity 22 times. In 2009, Baggett was sentenced to 20 years in prison for illegally dumping pollutants in violation of the Federal Clean Water and Resource Conservation and Recovery Act and for assaulting federal officers.[93]

Green crime is a type of enterprise crime involving violation of laws protecting the environment. Illegal dumping schemes are just part of the green crime problem. Environmental activists have long called attention to a variety of ecological threats that they feel should be deemed criminal: green crimes involve a wide range of actions and outcomes that harm the environment and that stem from decisions about what is produced, where it is produced, and how it is produced.[94] Global warming, overdevelopment, population growth, and other changes will continue to bring these issues front and center.[95]

Defining Green Crime

There is no single vision to define the concept of green crimes. Three independent views exist:

- *Legalist.* According to the legalist perspective, environmental crimes are violations of existing criminal laws designed to protect people, the environment, or both. This definition would include crimes against workers such as occupational health and safety crimes, as well as laws designed to protect nature and the environment (e.g., Clean Air Act, Clean Water Act).
- *Environmental justice.* According to the environmental justice view, limiting environmental crimes to actual violations of the criminal law is too narrow. A great deal of environmental damage occurs in third-world nations desperate for funds and willing to give mining and oil companies a free hand to develop resources. These nations have meager regulatory laws and therefore allow businesses wide latitude in environmental contamination that would be forbidden in the United States. In addition, environmental justice advocates believe that corporations themselves have attempted to co-opt or manipulate environmental laws, thereby limiting their scope and reach. Executives fear that the environmental movement will force changes in their production practices and place limits on their growth and corporate power. Some try to co-opt green laws by public relations and advertising campaigns that suggest they are doing

everything in their power to respect the environment, thereby reducing the need for government regulation. Criminologists must take a broader view of green crimes than the law allows.
- *Biocentric.* According to the biocentric approach, environmental harm is viewed as any human activity that disrupts a biosystem, destroying plant and animal life. This more radical approach would criminalize any intentional or negligent human activity or manipulation that impacts negatively on the earth's natural resources.[96] Environmental harm, according to this view, is much greater than what is defined by law as environmental crimes. As criminologist Rob White points out, this is because some of the most ecologically destructive activities, such as clear felling of old-growth forests, are quite legal. Environmental crimes are typically oriented toward protecting humans and their property and have a limited interest in the interests of animals and plants.[97] Environmental laws protect animal and fish processing plants that treat nature and wildlife simply and mainly as resources for human exploitation. Human beings are the cause of environmental harm and need to be controlled.

The Harms Perspective Green criminologists typically use what is known as the *harms perspective* when they conceptualize crime and deviance.[98] Accordingly, crime is a social construction that can and should be expanded to include all serious *social harms*, activities that cause any discomfort, present or future, to individuals. Harms may include physical, financial/economic, emotional or psychological, and cultural safety harm. Using the harms perspective, it would be appropriate to sanction toxic waste dumping or air pollution severely because they cause residual harm that will last many years, poisoning the environment and producing diseases such as cancer. However, in many instances this action is punished civilly, not criminally. For example, in 2013, AK Steel Corp. was fined a $1.65 million civil penalty to resolve alleged violations of air pollution laws that occurred at its now-closed coke plant in Ashland, Kentucky. To a billion-dollar corporation, such a fine is a mere slap on the wrist. In the Criminology in Action feature, one enterprise that may fit the harms test, chicken farming, is discussed in some detail.

 The American Humane Association is a champion of animal rights. Learn more at **http://www .americanhumane.org**.
Should people who kill animals be sent to prison? Before you answer, think about hunting, fishing, and bullfighting, not to mention chicken farming.

green crime Acts involving illegal environmental harm that violate environmental laws and regulations.

IS CHICKEN FARMING FOUL?

green criminologists who favor the harms perspective believe that business enterprise that damages people and hurts animals should be a crime. One good example is the chicken farming industry, whose practices, though currently legal, are actually destructive and harmful.

Green criminologists point out that the modern poultry industry began about 50 years ago with the use of artificial incubators and food additives added to chicken feed. These additives stimulated unnatural and rapid growth and also staved off potential diseases that were spread due to the cramped confinement of the indoor farms. Some chemicals made chickens produce more eggs, while different mixtures were used to make chickens grow larger and faster. With the discovery of genetic and chemical manipulation, chickens became a moldable product used to embody what humans need for their own consumption.

The results of these modifications have created a bird that no longer resembles the natural chicken. From 1935 to 1995, the average weight of a broiler chicken increased by 65 percent. The time they took to grow to this size decreased by 60 percent, while their food was decreased by 57 percent. The chicken industry created a product that drove down costs by producing more meat in a shorter amount of time while spending far less on food.

The chicken industry has grown tremendously within the last 50 years. Today, America raises over 9 billion chickens, China 7 billion, and Europe about 6 billion. Some estimate about 50 billion chickens are raised around the world each year.

Of course, there is a price to pay. On average the modern chicken farm houses 30,000 to 40,000 birds. Of these chickens, up to 4 percent will die from sudden death syndrome, a cardiovascular disorder that can be compared to having a heart attack. This syndrome is most often associated with an abnormally fast growth rate. Five percent will develop excess fluid in their body cavities that is caused from growth rates, cold temperatures, and excessive salt in their feed; three out of four will be unable to walk. Other problems include bacterial infections in the bones, internal

Forms of Green Crime

LO6 List the components of green crime

Green crime can take many different forms, ranging from deforestation and illegal logging to violations of worker safety. Below a few of the most damaging forms are set out.

Illegal Logging Illegal logging involves harvesting, processing, and transporting timber or wood products in violation of existing laws and treaties.[99] It is a universal phenomenon, occurring in major timber-producing countries, especially in the third world where enforcement is lax. Logging violations include taking trees in protected areas such as national parks, going over legally prescribed logging quotas, processing logs without acquiring licenses, and exporting logs without paying export duties. By sidestepping the law, loggers can reap greater profits than those generated through legal methods. The situation is serious because illegal logging can have severe environmental and social impact:

- Illegal logging exhausts forests, destroys wildlife, and damages its habitats. Illegal logging in central Africa is destroying the habitats and threatening the survival of populations of the great apes, including gorillas and chimpanzees.
- It causes ruinous damage to the forests, including deforestation and forest degradation worldwide. The destruction of forest cover can cause flash floods and landslides that have killed thousands of people.
- By reducing forest cover, illegal logging impairs the ability of land to absorb carbon emissions.
- Illegal logging costs billions each year in government revenue, impairing the ability of third-world nations to provide needed social services.
- It creates unsustainable economic devastation in the poorest countries. Vietnam, for example, has lost a third of its forest cover; in nearby Cambodia, illegal logging is at least 10 times the size of the legal harvest. These rates of extraction are clearly unsustainable, destroying valuable sources of employment and export revenues for the future.
- The substantial revenues from illegal logging fund national and regional conflict. In Cambodia, for several years, Khmer Rouge insurgents were sustained primarily by revenue from logging areas under their control.[100]

While the scale of illegal logging is difficult to estimate, it is believed that more than half of all logging activities in the most vulnerable forest regions—southeast Asia, central Africa, South America and Russia—may be conducted illegally. Worldwide, estimates suggest that illegal activities may account for over a tenth of the total global timber trade, representing products worth at least $15 billion per year.

Illegal Wildlife Exports The smuggling of wildlife across national borders is a serious matter.[101] Exporters find a bleeding, respiratory disease, and weakened immune systems.

The process of preparing the chicken for consumption is also objectively cruel and harmful to the birds. Chickens are crated and typically travel hundreds of miles with no food or water. Often the chickens already have broken bones and injuries from the journey when they arrive at the processing plant. They are then strung up by their ankles and are moved through a water bath that is electrified in order to stun them. The chicken is then brought to a throat-slitter machine; this cuts the throat to drain blood from the carcass. It is common for the major arteries to be missed and for these cases they have "kill men" whose job it is to slaughter those chickens left alive; they also sometimes miss the arteries, causing severe pain. The birds are then dumped into a scald tank containing water heated to 140 degrees Fahrenheit, which loosens the chicken's feathers so they are easily removed without burning off the chicken skin; scald water may be a source of salmonella. When the birds are beheaded, a high-speed machine cuts the bodies vertically, often nicking the intestines and contaminating the body with feces. After inspection the chickens are dunked in a tank of cold water. In this tank the feces that released from the bowels is mixed with and sits in the water.

Beyond the inhumane treatment of chickens during the factory process, the process can have a devastating effect on the human consumer. It is clear that many birds are sent into the market covered in feces and bacteria. Between 39 and 75 percent of chickens in grocery stores are infected with E. coli, 8 percent contain salmonella, and 70 to 90 percent contain campylobacter, which causes diarrhea, nausea, and vomiting.

Despite these cruel and dangerous practices, chicken farming is legal. Green criminologists believe that the practices constitute a crime, and if changes cannot be made the practice should be abandoned entirely.

Critical Thinking

Is it realistic, considering how much chicken is produced and how critical it is for diets here and abroad, that chicken farming could be halted? Is this just the price that must be paid to feed 7 billion people around the world? Or would it be worth doubling or tripling the price of this food product to make it more humane?

SOURCES: Julie Siegel, "Capitalism and Green Crime: An Examination of Chicken Farming," University of South Florida, 2014; Jonathan Foer, *Eating Animals* (New York, NY: Little, Brown and Company, 2009); Humane Society of America, Cruel Confinement, 2014, http://www.humanesociety.org/issues/confinement_farm/ (accessed June 2014).

lucrative trade in the demand for such illicit wildlife commodities as tiger parts, caviar, elephant ivory, rhino horn, and exotic birds and reptiles. Wildlife contraband may include live pets, hunting trophies, fashion accessories, cultural artifacts, ingredients for traditional medicines, wild meat for human consumption (or bushmeat), and other products. Illegal profits can be immense.

There are numerous problems presented by illegal wildlife exporting. Poachers imperil endangered species and threaten them with extinction. By evading government controls, they create the potential for introducing pests and diseases into formerly unaffected areas.[102] They import non-native species, which could harm the receiving habitats. Florida's Everglades have been overrun with non-native species such as pythons, imported as pets and abandoned in the wild. Illegal wildlife traders range from independent one-person operations that sell a single item to complex multi-ton, commercial-sized consignments shipped all over the world.

Adding all these sources together, the global trade in illegal wildlife is a growing phenomenon and is now estimated to be $7 billion to $10 billion annually. The United States is estimated to purchase nearly 20 percent of all illegal wildlife and wildlife products on the market, perhaps as much as $3 billion annually. The trade is so lucrative because exotic animals and animal parts are enormously expensive, providing an economic incentive that proves irresistible to smugglers in third-world nations.[103] Take the illegal poaching of elephants for their ivory. Poaching levels have increased since 2006; in 2012, poachers killed more than 30,000 African elephants. Why poach? A pair of tusks measuring 92 inches around the outside curve and weighing over 100 pounds each was recently advertised on the Internet for $45,000.[104]

The U.S. Congress has passed numerous laws that regulate and restrict wildlife imports and exports, including the Endangered Species Act of 1973 and the Lacey Act, which protects both plants and wildlife by creating civil and criminal penalties for a wide array of violations. The original act was directed at preserving game and wild birds and prohibiting the introduction of non-native birds and animals into native ecosystems. The act has been amended and in 1981 was changed to include illegal trade in plants, fish, and wildlife both domestically and abroad. The maximum penalty was increased to $10,000 with possible imprisonment for one year. Additionally, the mental state required for a criminal violation was increased to "knowingly and willfully;" civil penalties were expanded to apply to negligent violations.[105]

These laws and others establish authorities and guidelines for wildlife trade inspection at ports of entry, and wildlife crime law enforcement and prosecution. There are international laws restricting the wildlife trade. The United Nations Convention on International Trade in Endangered Species of Wild Fauna and Flora (CITES), serves as the primary vehicle for regulating wildlife trade. Despite these

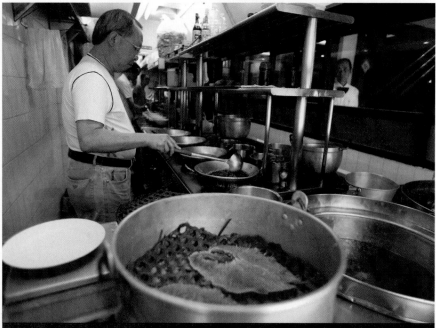

Illegal fishing creates the danger of wiping out whole species of fish. Here, a chef prepares shark fin soup at a restaurant in Bangkok, Thailand, in 2013. Animal rights groups in Thailand launched a campaign against the sale and consumption of shark fin soup, calling on businesses to ban the dish and advising people to refrain from eating the traditional Chinese delicacy. The global demand for shark fin soup has led to a catastrophic decline in shark populations; some species have been reduced by 99 percent since the 1950s due to legal and illegal fishing.

regulators may look the other way because the needs for short-term economic, social, or political gains are given more weight than long-term sustainability. As a result, species of whales, abalone, lobsters, Patagonian toothfish (known in the United States as Chilean sea bass) have become endangered.[106]

Industrial fishing is mainly operated through joint ventures between the government and foreign companies from Japan and Spain. The main commercial species are lobster, crabs, gamba (deep-water shrimp), shrimp, crayfish, and squid. Lobster, shrimp, and gamba are the main exports with key markets in other African states, Hong Kong, Japan, Italy, Spain, Portugal, and the UK.

Illegal Dumping Some green criminals want to skirt local, state, and federal restrictions on dumping dangerous substances in the environment. Rather than pay expensive processing fees they may secretly dispose of hazardous wastes in illegal dump sites. Illegally dumped wastes can either be hazardous or nonhazardous materials that are discarded in an effort to avoid either disposal fees or the time and effort required for proper disposal. Materials dumped ranged from used motor oil to waste from construction sites.

One of the largest and fastest growing problems is the disposal of 7 million tons of obsolete high-tech electronics, called e-waste, such as televisions, computers and computer monitors, laptops, VCRs, and so on. According to research by Carole Gibbs, Edmund McGarrell, and Mark Axelrod, while most e-waste in the United States is disposed of in landfills or is incinerated, the toxic material contained in electronic gear (such as lead) encourages illegal dumping in order to avoid recycling costs.[107] Consequently a considerable amount of e-waste is sent abroad to developing nations for recycling, often in violation of international laws restricting such commerce. All too often, the material overwhelms recycling plants and is instead dumped in local villages near people and water sources. Illegal dump sites have been documented in Nigeria, Ghana, China, the Philippines, Indonesia, Pakistan, and India, and they pose severe threats to both human health and the natural environment.

Illegal Polluting The *Deepwater Horizon* oil rig was built by Hundai Heavy Industries of Korea, owned by the Transocean Drilling Corporation, and leased by BP (formerly British Petroleum) in order to drill a deepwater (5,000 feet below the surface) oil well in the Gulf of Mexico.

controls it has been argued that one way in which to effectively control the movements of creatures across regions is to allow commercial export of wildlife. However, where legalized trade is allowed, experience shows that this opens up opportunities for forging permits and other documentation, as well as for other types of enabling activity. For instance, opening up a legal export trade in captive-bred birds would provide opportunities for laundering wild-caught birds and concealing rare species of similar appearance.

Illegal Fishing Unlicensed and illegal fishing is another billion-dollar green crime. It can take many forms and involve highly different parties, ranging from huge factory ships operating on the high seas that catch thousands of tons of fish on each voyage, to smaller, locally operating ships that confine themselves to national waters. Illegal fishing occurs when these ships sign on to their home nation's rules but then choose to ignore their scope and boundary, or operate in a country's waters without permission or on the high seas without a flag. Because catches are not reported by the fishing vessels, their illegal fishing can have a detrimental effect on species as government regulators have no idea how many are being caught. Stocks become depleted and species endangered.

In addition, illegal fishing techniques, including fishermen using the wrong sized nets or fishing in prohibited areas, can damage fragile marine ecosystems, threatening coral reefs, turtles, and seabirds. In underdeveloped nations,

Rungroj Yongrit/EPA/Landov

The drilling was overseen by Halliburton. On April 20, 2010, an explosion occurred on the rig, killing 11 platform workers and injuring 17 others. Following the sinking of the rig, a leak was discovered at the level of the ocean floor. First estimates of the oil leak were 5,000 barrels a day, but they quickly rose to 60,000.[108] While company officials frantically tried to stem the flow with a variety of failed schemes, millions of barrels of escaping oil created a slick that covered thousands of square miles, devastating wildlife and causing one of the greatest natural disasters in the nation's history. The leak was finally stopped in September 2010. In the November 2012 resolution of the federal charges against it, BP also agreed to plead guilty to 11 felony counts related to the deaths of the 11 workers and paid a $4 billion fine.[109]

This is not the first instance of an illegal act by a major corporation causing major pollution: In 1989, the oil tanker *Exxon Valdez* hit a reef in Prince William Sound and devastated Prudhoe Bay on the coast of Alaska. Exxon Mobil was fined $150 million and paid an additional $100 million as restitution for damage caused to fish, wildlife, and land, and also agreed to pay $900 million in 10 annual installments to civil claimants. In 1994, a jury found that Exxon acted recklessly and awarded victims $5 billion in punitive damages. The U.S. Supreme Court cut the amount to $507.5 million in June 2008, hardly a day's pay for the largest company on earth.[110] While the environmental damage was immense, it pales in comparison to what occurred in India in 1984, an incident discussed in Exhibit 13.4.

Because of these and other environmental crimes, a great deal of attention is now paid to intentional or negligent environmental pollution caused by many large corporations. The numerous allegations in this area involve almost every aspect of U.S. business. Most environmental crime statutes contain overlapping civil, criminal, and administrative penalty provisions, which gives the government latitude in enforcement. Over time, Congress has elevated some violations from misdemeanors to felonies and has increased potential jail sentences and fines for those convicted.[111]

Criminal environmental pollution is defined as the intentional or negligent discharge of a toxic or contaminating substance into the biosystem that is known to have an adverse effect on the natural environment or life. It may involve the ground release of toxic chemicals such as kepone, vinyl chloride, mercury, PCBs, and asbestos. Illegal and/or controlled air pollutants include hydrochlorofluorocarbons (HCFCs), aerosols, asbestos, carbon monoxide, chlorofluorocarbons (CFCs), criteria air pollutants, lead, mercury, methane, nitrogen oxides (NOx), radon, refrigerants, and sulfur oxide (SO_2). Water pollution, defined as the dumping of a substance that degrades or alters the quality of the waters to an extent that is detrimental for use by humans or by an animal or a plant

EXHIBIT 13.4

The Bhopal Incident

In December 1984, in Bhopal, India, thousands of people were affected by a leakage of methyl isocyanate gas and other chemicals from a Union Carbide pesticide plant. About 3,787 were killed outright soon after the leak, but as many as 8,000 may have died from medical complications caused by the chemical. Two years later, the Indian government claimed that almost 600,000 people may have been affected, 200,000 of them being children. Many suffer from long-term and incurable respiratory complaints. The company claimed that the leak was sabotage and they should not be held responsible for what had happened. But there had been previous complaints about safety violations, and there were other leaks that left workers injured or dead. Local authorities in Bhopal had warned the company on several occasions about the potential for accidents.

SOURCE: M. Arun Subramaniam and Ward Morehouse, *The Bhopal Tragedy: What Really Happened and What It Means for American Workers and Communities at Risk* (Washington, DC: Apex Press, 1986).

that is useful to humans. This includes the disposal into rivers, lakes, and streams of:

- Excess fertilizers, herbicides, and insecticides from agricultural lands and residential areas
- Oil, grease, and toxic chemicals from urban runoff and energy production
- Sediment from improperly managed construction sites, crop and forest lands, and eroding streambanks
- Salt from irrigation practices and acid drainage from abandoned mines
- Bacteria and nutrients from livestock, pet wastes, and faulty septic systems

One way to relieve the problems caused by illegal dumping is to pay people to clean up dump sites. In Shelby County, Tennessee, inmates unload tires during the opening day of the city of Memphis tire redemption program on February 27, 2013. A line more than a half-mile long formed so that people could get a jump on the city's offer of paying $1 per tire as a way of cleaning up the illegally dumped tires around the city.

AP Images/*Commercial Appeal*/Mike Brown

Controlling Green Crime

The United States and most other nations have passed laws making it a crime to pollute or damage the environment. Among environmental laws in the United States are included the following:

- *Clean Water Act (1972)*. Establishes and maintains goals and standards for U.S. water quality and purity. It was amended in 1987 to increase controls on toxic pollutants, and in 1990 to more effectively address the hazard of oil spills.
- *Emergency Planning and Community Right-to-Know Act (1986)*. Requires companies to disclose information about toxic chemicals they release into the air and water and dispose of on land.
- *Endangered Species Act (1973)*. Designed to protect and recover endangered and threatened species of fish, wildlife, and plants in the United States and beyond. The law works in part by protecting species' habitats.
- *Oil Pollution Act (1990)*. Enacted in the aftermath of the *Exxon Valdez* oil spill in Alaska's Prince William Sound, this law streamlines federal response to oil spills by requiring oil storage facilities and vessels to prepare spill-response plans and provide for their rapid implementation. The law also increases polluters' liability for cleanup costs and damage to natural resources.

Enforcing these federal laws is the Environmental Protection Agency, which was given full law enforcement authority in 1988. The EPA has successfully prosecuted significant violations across all major environmental statutes, including data fraud cases (for instance, private laboratories submitting false environmental data to state and federal environmental agencies); indiscriminate hazardous waste dumping that resulted in serious injuries and death; industry-wide ocean dumping by cruise ships; oil spills that caused significant damage to waterways, wetlands, and beaches; international smuggling of CFC refrigerants that damage the ozone layer and increase skin cancer risk; and illegal handling of hazardous substances such as pesticides and asbestos that exposed children, the poor, and other especially vulnerable groups to potentially serious illness.[112] Its Criminal Investigation Division (EPA CID) investigates allegations of criminal wrongdoing prohibited by various environmental statutes. Such investigations involve, but are not limited to:

- The illegal disposal of hazardous waste
- The export of hazardous waste without the permission of the receiving country
- The illegal discharge of pollutants to a water of the United States
- The removal and disposal of regulated asbestos-containing materials in a manner inconsistent with the law and regulations
- The illegal importation of certain restricted or regulated chemicals into the United States
- Tampering with a drinking water supply

- Mail fraud
- Wire fraud
- Conspiracy and money laundering relating to environmental criminal activities

There are also local and state law enforcement efforts devoted to controlling green crimes and enforcing state environmental laws. The Environmental Crimes Strike Force in Los Angeles County, California, is considered a model for the control of illegal dumping and pollution. Some of the more common environmental offenses investigated and prosecuted by the task force include:

- The illegal transportation, treatment, storage, or disposal of hazardous waste
- Oil spills
- Fraudulent certification of automobile smog tests[113]

Citizen Groups   There have also been charges that efforts to control green crime are less than successful. One reason is that law enforcement efforts may be stratified by class and race: authorities seem to be less diligent when victims are poor or minority group members or the crimes take place in minority areas. When Michael Lynch and his associates studied petroleum refineries' law violations, they found that those polluting black, Latino, and low-income communities receive smaller fines than those refineries in white and affluent communities. They also found that violations of the Clean Air Act, the Clean Water Act, and/or the Resource Conservation and Recovery Act in minority areas received much smaller fines than the same types of violations occurring in white areas ($108,563 versus $341,590).[114]

Therefore, in addition to state and federal environmental agencies citizen groups have also become active in environmental monitoring and combating green crime. One well-known organization, the Group Against Smog and Pollution (GASP), was founded in 1969 by a group of 43 volunteers concerned about air quality issues in southwestern Pennsylvania. Since its founding, not only has GASP educated the public on questions of pollution, it has also used the courts to achieve its goal of a cleaner environment. GASP has cooperated in a number of cases with the EPA in bringing about enforcement of air quality standards. In each case the court action resulted in substantial fines and/or remedial actions being imposed on the defendant.[115]

Water quality is another concern of community groups. Citizen water-monitoring organizations have worked with environmental enforcement agencies across the United States. Community members help monitor water quality so they can help direct state action as well as identify sources of pollution that impact their communities. Citizen water-monitoring organizations engage in informal surveillance activities that are designed to identify environmental violations, and they can report those violations to authorities.

Have these groups been effective? Michael Lynch and Paul Stretesky found that while potentially effective, citizen-based groups may be skewed by the racial and ethnic makeup of the communities they serve.[116] Communities with fewer economic resources and those with higher concentrations of minority populations receive less official protection and hence a reduced level of environmental justice; these inequities also extend to informal organizations. Equipment to monitor pollution is expensive and not easily available in less well-off areas that actually need it the most.

ORGANIZED AND TRANSNATIONAL ORGANIZED CRIME

Organized crime also involves ongoing criminal enterprise but one whose ultimate purpose is gain through illegitimate means, which can include violence and threat. Organized crime groups may create a structured enterprise system to supply consumers with merchandise and services banned by criminal law but for which a ready market exists: prostitution, pornography, gambling, and narcotics.

Organized crime groups may also use illegitimate means to dominate and control legitimate enterprises. They enter, buy or control legitimate industries such as construction and trash hauling. However, rather than play by the rules, organized crime groups use violence and strong-arm tactics to remove rivals, collect money owed, and intimidate people into cooperation. Their ability to operate freely may be the result of their buying off corrupt officials and using graft, extortion, intimidation, and murder to maintain their operations.[117] The economic impact alone is staggering: it's estimated that global organized crime reaps illegal profits of around $1 trillion per year.[118]

Because of its secrecy, power, and fabulous wealth, a great mystique has grown up about organized crime. Its legendary leaders—Al Capone, Meyer Lansky, Lucky Luciano—have been the subjects of books and films. The famous *Godfather* films popularized and humanized organized crime figures; the media often glamorize organized crime figures.[119] Watching the exploits of Tony Soprano and his family life became a national craze. This section briefly reviews the history of traditional organized crime, its decline, and the rise of its replacement: transnational organized crime groups.

Origins of Organized Crime

LO7 Describe the evolution of organized crime

Organized crime itself is not a recent phenomenon and can be traced as far back as the sixteenth century. In the 1600s, London was terrorized by organized gangs that called themselves Hectors, Bugles, Dead Boys, and other colorful names. In the seventeenth and eighteenth centuries, English gang members wore distinctive belts and pins marked with serpents, animals, stars, and the like. The first mention of youth gangs in America occurred in the late 1780s, when prison reformers noted the presence of gangs of young people hanging out on Philadelphia's street corners. By the 1820s, New York's Bowery and Five Points districts, Boston's North End and Fort Hill, and the outlying Southwark and Moyamensing sections of Philadelphia were the locales of youth gangs with colorful names like the Roach Guards, Chichesters, the Plug Uglies, and the Dead Rabbits.[120]

The Mafia The Mafia originated in Sicily around 1860, and started as a criminal gang employed by wealthy landowners to function as agents of social and land control, keeping peasant workers in line. At the turn of the twentieth century, La Mano Nera (the Black Hand), an offshoot of Sicilian criminal groups, established themselves in northeastern urban centers. Gangsters demanded payments from local businessmen in return for "protection"; those who would not pay were beaten and their shops vandalized. Eventually the Black Hand merged with gangs of Italian heritage to form larger urban-based gangs and groups.

A turning point in the development of organized gangs occurred on January 16, 1919, when the Eighteenth Amendment to the U.S. Constitution was ratified. The new amendment prohibited the sale, manufacture, and transportation of intoxicating liquors. Until then, gangs had remained relatively small and local, but now the national market for controlled substances opened the door to riches. Charles "Lucky" Luciano, who had come to the United States during this era, is credited with helping to create a national syndicate, La Cosa Nostra, with rules and codes that all members were required to follow. When Luciano was deported back to Italy in 1946 for operating a prostitution ring, he became a liaison between the Sicilian Mafia and La Cosa Nostra.[121]

What emerged was a national syndicate, referred to as Cosa Nostra or the Mafia, that was centrally coordinated and whose various component gangs worked cooperatively to settle disputes, dictate policy, and assign territory.[122] Despite efforts at cooperation and control, numerous and bloody gang wars and individual vendettas were common. The power of the Mafia continued to grow. Meyer Lansky (1902–1983) a close associate of Luciano, was involved in a wide range of organized criminal activity from the 1920s to the 1970s. Lansky was especially active in gambling ventures, including the rise of Las Vegas, and led efforts by the mob to build casinos in Cuba before the communist revolution.

The Mafia remains active in the United States. The FBI estimates that the Mafia has approximately 25,000 members total, with 250,000 affiliates worldwide. Most of the members and affiliates in the United States are scattered throughout the major cities in the Northeast, the Midwest, California, and the South. Their largest presence centers around New York, southern New Jersey, and Philadelphia. The families control crime in distinct geographic areas. New

York City, the most important organized crime area, alone contains five families—the Gambino, Columbo (formerly Profaci), Lucchese, Bonanno, and Genovese families—named after their founding "godfathers." In contrast, Chicago contains a single mob organization called the "outfit," which also influences racketeering in such cities as Milwaukee, Kansas City, and Phoenix. The families are believed to be ruled by a "commission" made up of the heads of the five New York families and bosses from Detroit, Buffalo, Chicago, and Philadelphia, which settles personal problems and jurisdictional conflicts and enforces rules that allow members to gain huge profits through the manufacture and sale of illegal goods and services.

The Mafia in Decline

The American Mafia has been in decline. One reason: high-profile criminal prosecutions using up-to-date IT methods for surveillance and evidence collection. For example, Chicago mob boss Frank Calabrese, Sr., was sentenced to life in prison in 2009 for his role in 18 gangland slayings dating back to 1970. His arrest—along with 13 others—meant that the Chicago mob does not have the power and influence it once had in the city. In another high-profile case, James "Whitey" Bulger was arrested and convicted of murder in 2013 after having been on the run for 16 years. Bulger, who once ran Boston's feared Winter Hill Gang, was wanted for his role in 19 murders.

The Mafia leadership is aging. A number of the reigning family heads are quite old, in their 80s and older. A younger generation of mob leaders have stepped in to take control of the families, and they seem to lack the skill and leadership of the older bosses. The code of silence that protected Mafia leaders is now broken regularly by younger members who turn informer rather than face prison terms. When Joe Calabrese was on trial, his own son testified against him in court. In addition, active government enforcement policies have halved what the estimated mob membership was 25 years ago, and a number of the highest-ranking leaders have been imprisoned.

Traditional organized crime has also been hurt by changing values in U.S. society. European American neighborhoods, which were the locus of Mafia power, have been shrinking as families move to the suburbs. Organized crime groups lost their urban-centered political and social base of operations. In addition, success has hurt organized crime families: younger family members are better educated than their forebears and are equipped to seek their fortunes through legitimate enterprise. So while the "traditional

---

transnational organized crime A criminal enterprise that involves the planning and execution of the distribution of illicit materials or services by groups or networks of individuals working in more than one country.

Mafia" is still in business, its power may be eroding and being replaced by transnational crime cartels. Traditional organized families had well-defined turf; transnational gangs respect no boundaries.

The Rise of Transnational Organized Crime

LO8 Be familiar with transnational organized crime

Transnational organized crime (TOC or transnational crime) is a form of organized crime operating across national borders. It involves groups or networks of individuals working in more than one state or even across cultures and nations, to plan and execute illegal business ventures. Cross-national gangs are often large criminal organizations, some with more than 20,000 members.

According to criminologist Jay Albanese, the distinction between these new organizations that operate across borders and the traditional Mafia whose activities were bounded by neighborhood territory is actually not that great. They overlap in terms of the crimes committed, the offenders involved, and how criminal opportunities are exploited for profit. They are, he concludes, manifestations of the same underlying conduct and the same pool of criminal offenders who exploit similar criminal opportunities.[123]

Characteristics of Transnational Organized Crime

A precise description of the characteristics of transnational organized crime is difficult to formulate, but here are some of its general traits:[124]

- Transnational organized crime is a conspiratorial activity, involving the coordination of numerous people in the planning and execution of illegal acts or in the pursuit of a legitimate objective by unlawful means (e.g., threatening a legitimate business to get a stake in it).
- An offense is transnational if:
  - It is committed in more than one state or nation.
  - It is committed in one state or nation but a substantial part of its preparation, planning, direction, or control takes place in another state or nation.
  - It is committed in one state or nation but involves an organized criminal group that engages in criminal activities in more than one state or nation.
  - It is committed in one state of nation but has substantial effects in another state of nation.[125]
- Transnational organized crime involves continuous commitment by primary members, although individuals with specialized skills may be brought in as needed.
- Transnational organized crime is usually structured along hierarchical lines—a chieftain supported by close advisers, lower subordinates, and so on.

- Transnational organized crime has economic gain as its primary goal, although power and status may also be motivating factors. Economic gain is achieved through global supply of illegal goods and services, including drugs, sex slaves, arms, and pornography.
- In addition to providing illegal material such as narcotics, contemporary global syndicates engage in business crimes such as laundering illegal money through legitimate businesses, land fraud, and computer crime.
- Transnational criminal syndicates employ predatory tactics, such as intimidation, violence, and corruption.
- Transnational organized crime groups are quick and effective in controlling and disciplining their members, associates, and victims and will not hesitate to use lethal violence against those who flaunt organizational rules.
- Transnational crime depends heavily on the instruments of the IT age: the Internet, global communications, rapid global transportation systems, universal banking system, and global credit card and payment systems.
- Transnational organized crime groups do not include terror organizations, though there may be overlap. Some terror groups are involved in criminality to fund their political objectives and some have morphed from politically motivated organizations to ones solely involved in for-profit criminal activity. Transnational criminal organizations may aid terror groups with transportation and communication.

Activities of Transnational Organized Crime

What are the main activities of transnational organized crime? The traditional sources of income are derived from providing illicit materials, such as narcotics, and using force to enter into and maximize profits in legitimate businesses. Income is generated from such activities as narcotics distribution, extortion, gambling, pornography, and cargo theft rings. Transnational crime groups are now branching into more exotic activities, set out in Exhibit 13.5.

Because cross-national and transnational gangs are a product of the cyber age, members often use cyberspace to communicate and promote their illicit activities.[126] Gangs typically use the voice and text messaging capabilities of cell phones to conduct drug transactions and prearrange meetings with customers. Prepaid cell phones are used when conducting drug trafficking operations. Internet-based methods, such as social networking sites, encrypted email, and instant messaging, are commonly used by gang members to communicate with one another and with drug customers. Gang members use social networking sites such as YouTube and Facebook as well as personal web pages to communicate and boast about their gang membership and related activities. Some use the Internet to intimidate rival gang members and maintain websites to recruit new members. Gang members flash gang signs and wear gang colors in videos and photos posted on the Web. Sometimes, rivals "spar" on Internet message boards.[127]

Transnational Gangs

Traditional Eurocentric gangs are being replaced by transnational mega-gangs. Some, such as the Crips, Bloods, and MS-13, have expanded from local street gangs to national mega-gangs with thousands of members. For example, the Sureños is an alliance of hundreds of individual Mexican American street gangs that originated in Southern California. Sureños gang members' main sources of income are retail-level distribution of cocaine, heroin, marijuana, and methamphetamine within prison systems and in the community as well as extortion of drug distributors on the streets. Some members have direct links to Mexican drug traffickers, brokering large drug transactions; they are also involved in other criminal activities such

The movie *Captain Phillips*, with Tom Hanks in the lead role, focused attention on piracy off the coast of Africa. Here, on January 23, 2014, suspected Somali pirates captured by the Dutch navy working under NATO command are seen behind bars at the Mombasa Law Courts in the Kenyan coastal city of Mombasa. A Kenyan court sentenced the 24 Somalis to seven years each in prison for attempting to hijack an Iranian merchant vessel, *FV Ariya*, in the Gulf of Oman in October 2010. The men were handed over to Kenyan authorities because Somalia, which is struggling to rebuild after two decades of civil war, was not seen as stable enough to try them properly.

Joseph Okanga/Reuters/Landov

EXHIBIT 13.5

Contemporary Transnational Crimes

- Organized crime groups have become involved in trafficking in cultural property. Antiques, artifacts, and relics stolen through illegal archaeological digs are sold to gangs who then smuggle the goods out of the country and sell them either through legitimate markets such as auctions and the Internet or in underground markets where collectors buy offered goods, no questions asked. Trafficking in cultural property is also becoming an important source for money laundering.

- Maritime piracy (a crime made famous in the 2013 film *Captain Phillips*, with Tom Hanks in the title role) is the specialty of Somali gangs. Pirates from this nation located on the Horn of Africa are now arming themselves with a higher grade of weaponry and basing themselves on "mother ships" from which they can send out smaller attack boats. This system allows them to hijack larger vessels over wider distances, hundreds of miles off the coast. Piracy is also linked to other forms of organized crime, since it requires sophisticated intelligence collection networks and systematic corruption of local officials. Piracy is a key source of income for many in the local communities, who receive funds from ransoms that their own governments fail to provide.

- Organized crime groups are quite active in human trafficking, the acquisition of people by improper means such as force, fraud, or deception, with the aim of exploiting them in such illegal activities as prostitution, sexual exploitation, forced labour, slavery, or similar practices. Every year, thousands of men, women, and children fall into the hands of traffickers in their own countries and abroad. Almost every country in the world is affected by trafficking, whether as a country of origin, transit, or destination for victims.

- Organized crime groups profit from smuggling migrants. Criminals are increasingly providing smuggling services to irregular migrants to evade national border controls, migration regulations, and visa requirements. Most irregular migrants resort to the assistance of profit-seeking smugglers because as border controls have improved in developed nations, migrants are deterred from attempting to illegally cross them themselves and are diverted into the hands of smugglers. Migrant smugglers are becoming more and more organized, establishing professional networks that transcend borders and regions. Nonetheless, thousands of people have lost their lives as a result of the indifferent or even deliberate actions of migrant smugglers.

- The demand for organs has outstripped supply, creating an underground market for illicitly obtained organs. Desperate recipients and donors create an avenue ready for exploitation by international organ trafficking syndicates. Traffickers exploit the desperation of donors to improve the economic situation of themselves and their families, and they exploit the desperation of recipients who may have few other options to improve or prolong their lives. Like other victims of trafficking in persons, those who fall prey to traffickers for the purpose of organ removal may be vulnerable by virtue of poverty. Traffickers may enlist the services of doctors, nurses, ambulance drivers, and health care professionals who are involved in legitimate activities when they are not participating in trafficking in persons for the purpose of organ removal.

SOURCE: United Nations Office on Drugs and Crime, "Emerging Crimes, 2014," https://www.unodc.org/unodc/en/organized-crime/emerging-crimes.html (accessed June 2014).

as assault, carjacking, home invasion, homicide, and robbery. While most members remain in Southern California cities, the gang has spread significantly and can be found throughout much of the United States.[128]

In addition to these home-grown gangs, international gangs based in Asia, Eastern Europe, North, South, and Latin America use the Internet and IT devices to facilitate their operations across nations and continents. Emerging transnational crime syndicates are primarily located in nations whose governments are too weak to present effective opposition. If they believe that the government is poised to interfere with their illegal activities, they will carry out a terror campaign, killing police and other government officials to achieve their goals. Easier international travel, expanded world trade, and financial transactions that cross national borders have enabled them to branch out of local and regional crime to target international victims and develop criminal networks within more prosperous countries and regions.[129] For example, Africa, a continent that has experienced political turmoil, has also seen the rise of transnational gangs. African criminal enterprises in Nigeria, Ghana, and Liberia have developed quickly since the 1980s due to the globalization of the world's economies and the great advances in communications technology. Nigerian criminal enterprises, primarily engaged in drug trafficking and financial frauds, are the most significant of these groups and operate in more than 80 countries. They are infamous for their email-based financial frauds, which cost the United States alone an estimated $1 billion to $2 billion each year.

Some of the most prominent transnational gang clusters are described here in some detail.

Eastern European Gangs

Eastern European gangs trace their origins to countries spanning the Baltics, the Balkans, Central/Eastern Europe, Russia, the Caucasus, and Central Asia. For example, Albanian organized crime activities in the United States include gambling, money laundering, drug trafficking, human smuggling, extortion, violent witness intimidation, robbery, attempted murder, and murder.[130]

Although ethnically based, they work with other ethnic groups when perpetrating crimes. Trading in illegal arms, narcotics, pornography, and prostitution, they operate a multibillion-dollar transnational crime cartel. Balkan organized crime groups have recently expanded into more

Transnational gangs are heavily involved in the drug trade and use intimidation to protect their illegal dealing. Leader of the Gulf drug cartel Jorge Eduardo Costilla Sánchez, aka "El Coss" (second from right), is presented to the media along with his bodyguards at the Mexican Navy's Center for Advanced Naval Studies in Mexico City. One of Mexico's most-wanted men, Costilla, 41, was charged in the United States with drug-trafficking and threatening U.S. law enforcement officials. Does the arrest of leaders such as El Coss spell the end of the cartel, or merely an opening at the top for a new leader to emerge?

money laundering.[132] No area of the world seems immune, especially not the United States. America is the land of opportunity for unloading criminal goods and laundering dirty money.

Russian organized crime is not primarily based on ethnic or family structures. Instead, Russian organized crime is based on economic necessity that was nurtured by the oppressive Soviet regime. Here, a professional criminal class developed in Soviet prisons during the Stalinist period that began in 1924—the era of the gulag. These criminals adopted behaviors, rules, values, and sanctions that bound them together in what was called the thieves' world, led by the elite *vory v zakone*, criminals who lived according to the "thieves' law." This thieves' world, and particularly the *vory*, created and maintained the bonds and climate of trust necessary for carrying out organized crime. The following are some specific characteristics of Russian organized crime in the post-Soviet era:

sophisticated crimes, including real estate fraud. Take for instance Armenian Power (AP), an international organized crime group whose illegal activities allegedly range from bank fraud and identity theft to violent extortion and kidnapping. In one scheme, AP caused more than $2 million in losses when members secretly installed "skimming" devices in cash register credit card swipe machines at Southern California 99 Cents Only stores to steal customer account information and then used it to create counterfeit debit and credit cards to empty accounts. With 200 known members, AP got its start as a neighborhood gang in the 1980s, but has now morphed into a transnational crime group with close ties to other gangs, including the Mexican Mafia. AP's leadership also maintains ties to Armenia and Russia and deals directly with top organized crime figures in those countries, even to the point of using respected organized crime mediators—known as "thieves-in-law"—to settle disputes.[131]

Organized groups prey upon women in the poorest areas of Europe—Romania, Ukraine, Bosnia—and sell them into virtual sexual slavery. Many of these women are transported as prostitutes around the world, some finding themselves in the United States.

Russian Transnational Crime Groups Since the collapse of the Soviet Union in 1991, criminal organizations in Russia and other former Soviet republics such as Ukraine have engaged in a variety of crimes: drugs and arms trafficking, stolen automobiles, trafficking in women and children, and

- Russian criminals make extensive use of the state governmental apparatus to protect and promote their criminal activities. For example, most businesses in Russia—legal, quasi-legal, and illegal—must operate with the protection of a *krysha* (roof). The protection is often provided by police or security officials employed outside their "official" capacities for this purpose. In other cases, officials are "silent partners" in criminal enterprises that they, in turn, protect.
- As Communism collapsed, the privatization of industry resulted in the massive use of state funds for criminal gain. Valuable properties are purchased through insider deals for much less than their true value and then resold for lucrative profits.
- Criminals have been able to directly influence the state's domestic and foreign policy to promote the interests of organized crime, either by attaining public office themselves or by buying public officials.

Beyond these particular features, organized crime in Russia shares other characteristics that are common to organized crime elsewhere in the world:

- Systematic use of violence, including both the threat and use of force
- Hierarchical structure
- Limited or exclusive membership
- Specialization in types of crime and a division of labor
- Military-style discipline, with strict rules and regulations for the organization as a whole

- Possession of high-tech equipment, including military weapons
- Threats, blackmail, and violence used to penetrate business management and assume control of commercial enterprises or, in some instances, to found their own enterprises with money from their criminal activities

As a result of these activities, corruption and organized crime are globalized. Russian organized crime is active in Europe, Africa, Asia, and North and South America. Massive money laundering is now common, which allows Russian and foreign organized crime to flourish. In some cases, it is tied to terrorist funding.

The organized crime threat to Russia's national security is now becoming a global threat. Russian organized crime operates both on its own and in cooperation with foreign groups. The latter cooperation often comes in the form of joint money laundering ventures. Russian criminals have become involved in killings for hire in central and western Europe, Israel, Canada, and the United States.

In the United States, with the exception of extortion and money laundering, Russians have had little or no involvement in some of the more traditional types of organized crime, such as drug trafficking, gambling, and loan sharking. However, thousands of Russian immigrants are believed to be involved in criminal activity, primarily in Russian enclaves in New York City.[133] Russian criminal groups are extensively engaged in a broad array of frauds and scams, including health care fraud, insurance scams, stock frauds, antiquities swindles, forgery, and fuel tax evasion schemes. Russians are believed to be the main purveyors of credit card fraud in the United States. Legitimate businesses, such as the movie business and the textile industry, have become targets of criminals from the former Soviet Union, and they are often used for money laundering and extortion.

Latin American and Mexican Drug Cartels

Transnational crime cartels operate freely in South American nations such as Peru and Colombia. Caribbean nations such as Jamaica, the Dominican Republic, and Haiti are home to drug and gun smuggling gangs. The money from illicit trade strengthens and enlarges the gangs, enabling them to increase their involvement in intraregional and transnational dealing in order to gain more money. Furthermore, drug trafficking has contributed to a sharp increase in the availability and usage of firearms.[134]

However, while island groups flourish, it is the Mexican drug cartels that are now of greatest concern. These transnational gangs have become large-scale suppliers of narcotics, marijuana, and methamphetamines to the United States, and Mexico has become a drug-producing and transit country. In addition, an estimated 90 percent of cocaine entering the United States transits Mexico. Mexican drug gangs routinely use violence, and fighting for control of the border regions has affected U.S. citizens. More than 60 Americans have been kidnapped, and Mexican drug cartel

members have threatened to kill U.S. journalists covering drug violence in the border region. Although Mexican drug cartels, or drug trafficking organizations, have existed for quite some time, they have become more powerful since Colombia was able to crack down on the Cali and Medellín cartels in the 1990s. Mexican drug cartels now dominate the wholesale illicit drug market in the United States. As a result, Mexican cartels are the leading wholesale launderers of drug money from the United States. Mexican and Colombian trafficking organizations annually smuggle an estimated $8 to $25 billion in drug proceeds into Mexico for laundering.

There are numerous drug cartels operating in Mexico, the main ones being Gulf, Tijuana, Sinaloa, Juárez, Millennium, Oaxaca, and Colima. Some are dominant in local regions, while the major gangs—Gulf, Sinaloa, and Juárez—are present throughout all of Mexico. In recent years, new cartels have formed and others have become allies, in a constantly shifting landscape of drug activity. The Tijuana cartel formed an alliance with the Gulf cartel, and several cartels (Sinaloa, Juárez, and Valencia) have also formed an alliance known as "the Federation."

Asian Transnational Crime Groups

Asian-based transnational crime groups are also quite active in such areas as human trafficking, narcotics, and money laundering.[135] Chinese gangs are involved in importing heroin from the neighboring Golden Triangle area and distributing it throughout the country. They are also involved in gambling and prostitution, activities that had all but disappeared under Mao Zedong's Communist regime. The two leading organized crime problems in Cambodia are drug production/trafficking and human trafficking. Drug traffickers also use Cambodia as a transit country and traffic Cambodian women into Thailand for sexual activities. In Taiwan, the number one organized crime problem is *heijin*, the penetration of mobsters into the legitimate business sector and the political arena. Gangs are now heavily involved in the businesses of bid-rigging, waste disposal, construction, cable television networks, telecommunications, stock trading, and entertainment. Further, starting in the mid-1980s, many criminals have successfully run for public office in order to protect themselves from police crackdowns. Taiwan's gangs are involved in gambling, prostitution, loan sharking, debt collection, extortion, and gang violence; kidnapping for ransom is also a serious concern.

Among the best-known Asian crime groups are:

- *Yakuza*. Japanese criminal group. Often involved in multinational criminal activities, including human trafficking, gambling, prostitution, and undermining licit businesses.
- *Fuk Ching*. Chinese organized criminal group in the United States. They have been involved in smuggling, street violence, and human trafficking.

- *Triads.* Underground criminal societies based in Hong Kong. They control secret markets and bus routes and are often involved in money laundering and drug trafficking.
- *Heijin.* Taiwanese gangsters who are often executives in large corporations. They are often involved in white-collar crimes, such as illegal stock trading and bribery, and sometimes run for public office.
- *Jao Pho.* Organized crime group in Thailand. They are often involved in illegal political and business activity.
- *Red Wa.* Gangsters from Thailand. They are involved in manufacturing and trafficking methamphetamine.[136]

Controlling Transnational Crime

LO9 Discuss the characteristics of transnational organized crime

Efforts to combat transnational organized crime are typically in the hands of federal agencies. One approach is to form international working groups to collect intelligence, share information, and plot unified strategies among member nations. The FBI belongs to several international working groups aimed at combating transnational gangs in various parts of the world. For example, to combat the influence and reach of Eurasian organized crime the FBI is involved in the following groups and activities:

- *Eurasian Organized Crime Working Group.* Established in 1994, it meets to discuss and jointly address the transnational aspects of Eurasian organized crime that impact member countries and the international community in general. The member countries are Canada, Great Britain, Germany, France, Italy, Japan, the United States, and Russia.
- *Central European Working Group.* This group is part of a project that brings together the FBI and Central European law enforcement agencies to discuss cooperative investigative matters covering the broad spectrum of Eurasian organized crime. A principal concern is the growing presence of Russian and other Eurasian organized criminals in Central Europe and the United States. The initiative works on practical interaction between the participating agencies to establish lines of communication and working relationships, to develop strategies and tactics to address transnational organized crime matters impacting the region, and to identify potential common targets.
- *Southeast European Cooperative Initiative.* This is an international organization intended to coordinate police and customs regional actions for preventing and combating transborder crime. It is headquartered in Bucharest, Romania, and has 12 fully participating member countries. The United States has been one of 14 countries with observer status since 1998. The initiative's center serves as a clearinghouse for information

and intelligence sharing, allowing the quick exchange of information in a professional and trustworthy environment. The initiative also supports specialized task forces for countering transborder crime such as the trafficking of people, drugs, and cars; smuggling; financial crimes; terrorism; and other serious transborder crimes.

Anti–Organized Crime Laws Congress has passed a number of laws that have made it easier for agencies to bring transnational gangs to justice. One of the first measures aimed directly at organized crime was the Interstate and Foreign Travel or Transportation in Aid of Racketeering Enterprises Act (Travel Act).[137] The Travel Act prohibits travel in interstate commerce or use of interstate facilities with the intent to promote, manage, establish, carry on, or facilitate an unlawful activity; it also prohibits the actual or attempted engagement in these activities.

In 1970, Congress passed the Organized Crime Control Act. Title IX of the act, probably its most effective measure, is the **Racketeer Influenced and Corrupt Organization (RICO) Act**.[138] RICO did not create new categories of crimes but rather new categories of offenses in racketeering activity, which it defined as involvement in two or more acts prohibited by 24 existing federal and 8 state statutes. The offenses listed in RICO include state-defined crimes (such as murder, kidnapping, gambling, arson, robbery, bribery, extortion, and narcotic violations) and federally defined crimes (such as bribery, counterfeiting, transmission of gambling information, prostitution, and mail fraud). RICO is designed to limit patterns of organized criminal activity by prohibiting involvement in acts intended to do the following:

- Derive income from racketeering or the unlawful collection of debts and use or investment of such income
- Acquire through racketeering an interest in or control over any enterprise engaged in interstate or foreign commerce
- Conduct business through a pattern of racketeering
- Conspire to use racketeering as a means of making income, collecting loans, or conducting business

Racketeer Influenced and Corrupt Organization (RICO) Act Federal legislation that enables prosecutors to bring additional criminal or civil charges against people whose multiple criminal acts constitute a conspiracy. RICO features monetary penalties that allow the government to confiscate all profits derived from criminal activities. Originally intended to be used against organized criminals, RICO has also been used against white-collar criminals.

An individual convicted under RICO is subject to 20 years in prison and a $25,000 fine. Additionally, the accused must forfeit to the U.S. government any interest in a business in violation of RICO. These penalties are much more potent than simple conviction and imprisonment.

Why Is It So Difficult to Eradicate Transnational Gangs?   While international cooperation is now common and law enforcement agencies are willing to work together to fight transnational gangs, these criminal organizations are extremely hard to eradicate. The gangs are ready to use violence and well equipped to carry out threats. Take for instance Los Zetas, whose core members are former members of the Mexican military's elite Special Air Mobile Force Group (Grupo Aeromovil de Fuerzas Especiales, or GAFES). Military trained, the Zetas are able to carry out complex operations and use sophisticated weaponry.[139] The Zetas, which began as enforcers for the Gulf cartel's regional domination, are now their rivals, and are considered the most powerful Mexican transnational gang. Their base is Nuevo Laredo, but the criminal organization's sphere of influence extends across Mexico and deep into Central America. Unlike most gangs, which obtain most of their income from narcotics, Los Zetas earns about half their income trafficking in arms, kidnapping, and competing for control of trafficking routes along the eastern half of the U.S.–Mexico border. The cartel is now considered Mexico's most brutal, and they are suspected of kidnapping and killing Central American migrants headed for the border as well as Mexican bus passengers who traveled through their territory.[140]

Even when a gang can be taken out, it is soon replaced as long as money can be made. Take the case of the La Familia Michoacana cartel, which became an independent drug trafficking organization in Mexico and later allied itself with the Gulf cartel. Originated in the 1980s, La Familia was heavily armed and utilized violence to support its narcotics trafficking business, including murders, kidnappings, and assaults in the Michoacan state of Mexico. The killing of its founder and leader Nazario Moreno González in 2011 spelled the end of La Familia. However, that did not spell the end of gang activity in the area. Two of his subordinates, Enrique Plancarte Solís and Servando Gómez Martínez, broke away and formed the Knights Templar gang (Caballeros Templarios). The Knights extort protection money from legitimate businesspeople in Michoacan and tax farmers' crops; they tell restaurant owners what to charge for food and then demand a kickback.

Adding to control problems is the fact that the drug trade is an important source of foreign revenue, and its destruction actually undermines the economies of third-world nations. Even if the government of one nation were willing to cooperate in vigorous drug suppression efforts, suppliers in other nations, eager to cash in on the sellers' market, would be encouraged to turn more acreage over to coca or poppy production. Today, almost every Caribbean country is involved with narcotrafficking, and illicit drug shipments in the region are worth more money than the top five legitimate exports combined. Drug gangs are able to corrupt the political structure and destabilize countries. Drug addiction and violent crime are now common in Jamaica, Puerto Rico, and even small islands like St. Kitts. The corruption of the police and other security forces has reached a crisis point, where an officer can earn the equivalent of half a year's salary by simply looking the other way on a drug deal.[141] There are also indications that the drug syndicates may be planting a higher yield variety of coca and improving refining techniques to replace crops lost to government crackdowns.

The United States has little influence in some key drug-producing areas such as Taliban-held Afghanistan and Myanmar (formerly Burma). War and terrorism also may make gang control strategies problematic. After the United States toppled Afghanistan's Taliban government, the remnants began to grow and sell poppy to support their insurgency; Afghanistan now supplies 90 percent of the world's opium.[142] And while the Colombian guerillas may not be interested in joining or colluding with crime cartels, they finance their war against the government by aiding drug traffickers and "taxing" crops and sales. Considering these problems, it is not surprising that transnational gangs continue to flourish.

THE CAUSES OF ENTERPRISE CRIME

LO10   Explain the causes of enterprise crime

Why do people get involved in risky schemes to use their institutional positions to steal money? Why do people risk going to prison because they pollute the environment? Why do criminal gangs form? Can the same factors that predict other types of criminal offenses also apply to crimes of criminal enterprise? After all, unlike most common-law crimes, enterprise crimes are not committed by impoverished teenagers living in the inner city but by people who are often well-off, highly educated businesspeople. In order to commit an enterprise crime, someone must have already obtained a position of power and trust. This section describes some of the most prominent views of why people commit crimes of criminal enterprise.

Rational Choice: Greed

When Kansas City pharmacist Robert Courtney was asked after his arrest why he substituted improper doses of drugs instead of what doctors had prescribed, he told investigators he cut the drugs' strength "out of greed."[143] Courtney is not alone. One view of enterprise crime is that greedy people rationally choose to take shortcuts to acquire wealth, believing that the potential profits far outweigh future punishments. Most believe they will not get caught; they are far too clever to be detected by mere civil servants who work for government agencies.

Recently criminologists and Neal Shover and Peter Grabosky introduced the concept of "lure" to help explain why some people choose the illegal yet alluring benefits of enterprise crime:[144]

> It may be discomforting to acknowledge, but experience teaches that at any given time there are persons in the larger world that are either bent on breaking the law or are easily tempted to do so…. Tempted individuals possess qualities or experiences that make them more likely than peers who lack these distinctions to weigh illicit exploitation of lure. The size of the pool of the predisposed and tempted waxes and wanes depending upon a variety of other conditions in their worlds. These include the size of the supply of lure, prevailing estimates of the credibility of external oversight, and how extensively effective mechanisms of internal oversight and self-restraint are deployed.[145]

The lure of enterprise crime has diverse sources. When states create loopholes in the law that provide criminal opportunities, someone is bound to take advantage of the error. As the supply of lure expands so too will the number of people willing to risk legal censure to acquire financial benefits. The lure of crime expands in the absence of capable control systems. For example, when financial oversight was absent in the United States economic markets, the crash of 2008 became inevitable.

CONNECTIONS

The rational choice view was first discussed in Chapter 4.

Ask Yourself …

Do you believe it's the most accurate way of explaining enterprise crime? Would the General Theory of Crime, discussed in Chapter 9, be a more appropriate and valid explanation? Think *Wolf of Wall Street*!

Rational Choice: Need

Greed is not the only motivation for enterprise crime; need also plays an important role. Some people turn to crime to fulfill an overwhelming financial or psychological need. Executives may tamper with company books because they feel the need to keep or improve their jobs, satisfy their egos, or support their children. Blue-collar workers may pilfer because they need to keep pace with inflation or buy a new car. People may join a transnational gang, despite the risks, because they can think of no other way to make a living. A lot of people convicted of white-collar crime typically work in lower-echelon positions, and their acts seem motivated more by economic survival than by greed and power.[146] People may engage in green crime such as illegal fishing and hunting out of desperation rather than greed.

Rationalization/Neutralization View

Rationalizing guilt is a common trait of enterprise criminals.[147] What they did was not so bad; what some call crime is merely a "technicality"; the organized crime figure feels tremendous loyalty to his comrades. One offender convicted of price-fixing denied the illegality of his actions: "We did not fix prices. I am telling you that all we did was recover costs."[148] Some white-collar criminals believe that everyone violates business laws, so it is not so bad if they do so themselves.

In his classic research on fraud, Donald Cressey found that the door to solving personal financial problems through criminal means is opened by the rationalizations people develop for white-collar crime: "Some of our most respectable citizens got their start in life by using other people's money temporarily"; "in the real estate business, there is nothing wrong about using deposits before the deal is closed"; "all people steal when they get in a tight spot."[149] Offenders use these and other rationalizations to resolve the conflict they experience over engaging in illegal behavior.

Organized crime figures rationalize their behavior by insisting they are only providing a service that people want, even if it's illegal. Some white-collar offenders feel free to engage in business crime because they can easily rationalize its effects. Some convince themselves that their actions are not really crimes because the acts involved do not resemble street crimes. A banker who uses his position of trust to lend his institution's assets to a company he secretly controls may see himself as a shrewd businessman, not as a criminal. A pharmacist who chisels customers on prescription drugs may rationalize her behavior by telling herself that it does not really hurt anyone. Further, some businesspeople feel justified in committing enterprise crimes because they believe government regulators do not really understand the business world or the problems of competing in the free enterprise system.[150] When asked, enterprise criminals often use techniques of neutralization to defuse guilt: (1) everyone else does it, (2) it's not my fault or responsibility, and (3) no one is hurt except insurance companies and they are wealthy.

California Attorney General Kamala Harris addresses the Domestic Human Trafficking symposium in Los Angeles on April 25, 2014, hoping to bring increased attention to the problem. Human trafficking, sexual servitude, and forced labor bring in more than $30 billion annually, making it the second most profitable criminal enterprise after illegal arms trafficking. The vast majority of those trafficked are women and children, from all milieus of society.

tolerant of employee deviance. New employees learn the attitudes and techniques needed to commit crime from their business peers. Under these circumstances, the attitudes of closest coworkers and the perceived attitudes of executives have a more powerful control over decision making than the attitudes of outsiders—closest friends and business professors—whose more moderate views might have tempered the decision to commit crime.[151]

Those holding the culture view would point to the Enron scandal as a prime example of what happens when people work in organizations in which the cultural values stress profit over fair play, government scrutiny is limited and regulators are viewed as the enemy, and senior members encourage newcomers to believe that "greed is good." One method of controlling enterprise crime, then, is to redirect institutional culture and focus more on values and trust than profit and greed.[152]

Cultural View

According to this view, some organizations promote criminal enterprise in the same way that lower-class culture encourages the development of juvenile gangs and street crime. According to the cultural view, some enterprises cause crime by placing excessive demands on employees while at the same time maintaining a business climate

CONNECTIONS

The view that white-collar crime is a learning process is reminiscent of Edwin Sutherland's description of how gang boys learn the techniques of drug dealing and burglary from older youths through differential association. See Chapter 7 for a description of this process.

Self-Control View

In their General Theory of Crime, Travis Hirschi and Michael Gottfredson suggest that the motives that produce enterprise crimes—quick benefits with minimal effort—are the same as those that produce any other criminal behaviors.[153] Enterprise criminals have low self-control and are inclined to follow momentary impulses without considering the long-term costs of such behavior.[154] Even though bankers and stockbrokers are not a group known for being impulsive, those who commit enterprise crimes are the most impulsive of the bunch. Hirschi and Gottfredson collected data showing that the demographic distribution of white-collar crime is similar to other crimes. For example, gender, race, and age ratios are the same for crimes such as embezzlement and fraud as they are for street crimes such as burglary and robbery.

LO1 Describe what is meant by the term *enterprise crime*

Enterprise crime involves criminal acts that twist the legal rules of commercial enterprise for criminal purposes. They taint the free market system, because they mix and match illegal and legal methods in all phases of commercial activity. They involve illegal business practices to merchandise what are normally legitimate commercial products. They can also involve the use of standard business methods and accounting to market illegal goods.

LO2 Define white-collar crime

Edwin Sutherland first used the phrase "white-collar crime" to describe the criminal activities of the rich and powerful. He defined white-collar crime as "a crime committed by a person of respectability and high social status in the course of his occupation." Included within recent views of white-collar crime are such acts as income tax evasion, credit card fraud, and bankruptcy fraud. Other white-collar criminals use their positions of trust in business or government to commit crimes. Their activities might include pilfering, soliciting bribes or kickbacks, and embezzlement.

LO3 Compare and contrast the various forms of white-collar crime

There are a variety of categories of white-collar crime. White-collar fraud involves using a business enterprise as a front to swindle people. Chiseling involves businesspeople and professionals who use their positions to cheat clients on a regular basis. Embezzlement and employee fraud occur when a person uses a position of trust to steal from an organization. White-collar exploitation occurs when an individual abuses his or her power or position in an organization to coerce people into making payments for services to which they are already entitled. If the payments are not made, the services are withheld. In most cases, exploitation occurs when the victim has a clear right to expect a service, and the offender threatens to withhold the service unless an additional payment or bribe is forthcoming. In contrast, influence peddling occurs when individuals holding important institutional positions sell power, influence, and information to outsiders who have an interest in influencing the activities of the institution or buying information on what the institution may do in the future. Client fraud involves theft from an organization that advances credit, covers losses, or reimburses for services. Corporate, or organizational, crime involves various illegal business practices such as price-fixing, restraint of trade, and false advertising.

LO4 Discuss efforts to control white-collar crime

The government has used various law enforcement strategies to combat white-collar crime. Some involve deterrence, which uses punishment to frighten potential abusers. Others involve economic or compliance strategies, which create economic incentives to obey the law. Most offenders do not view themselves as criminals and therefore do not seem to be deterred by criminal statutes. Although thousands of white-collar criminals are prosecuted each year, their numbers are insignificant compared with the magnitude of the problem. Detection and enforcement are primarily in the hands of administrative departments and agencies, including the FBI, the Internal Revenue Service, the Secret Service, U.S. Customs, the Environmental Protection Agency, and the Securities and Exchange Commission. On the state and local levels, law enforcement officials have made progress in a number of areas, such as controlling consumer fraud. One approach is to ensure compliance with business rules and law by threatening economic sanction. Another is to deter white-collar crime by punishing individual offenders and putting them in prison as a deterrent to other would-be criminals.

LO5 Explain the concept of green crime

Green crimes involve a wide range of actions and outcomes that harm the environment and that stem from decisions about what is produced, where it is produced, and how it is produced. There is more than one perspective on green crime: according to the legalist perspective, environmental crimes are violations of existing criminal laws designed to protect people, the environment, or both. According to the environmental justice (EJ) view, limiting environmental crimes to actual violations of the criminal law is too narrow and should be broader than the law allows. According to the biocentric approach, environmental harm is viewed as any human activity that disrupts a biosystem, destroying plant and animal life.

LO6 List the components of green crime

Green crime can take many different forms, ranging from deforestation and illegal logging to violations of worker safety. Elements of green crime include illegal dumping and pollution, illegal logging, illegal fishing, and the exportation of endangered species.

LO7 Describe the evolution of organized crime

Organized criminals used to be white ethnics—Jews, Italians, and Irish—but today African Americans, Latinos, and other groups have become involved in organized crime activities. The old-line "families" are now more likely to use their criminal wealth and power to buy into legitimate businesses. The most common view of organized crime today is an ethnically diverse group of competing gangs dedicated to extortion or to providing illegal goods and services. Efforts to control organized crime have been stepped up by the federal government, which has used antiracketeering statutes to arrest syndicate leaders.

LO8 Be familiar with transnational organized crime

Organized crime today is transnational. With the aid of the Internet and instant communications, groups are operating on a global scale to traffic drugs and people, to launder money, and to sell arms. Eastern European crime families are active abroad and in the United States. Russian organized crime has become a major problem for law enforcement agencies. Mexican and Latin American groups are quite active in the drug trade; Asian crime families are involved in smuggling and other illegal activities.

LO9 Discuss the characteristics of transnational organized crime

Efforts to combat transnational organized crime are typically in the hands of federal agencies. One approach is to form international working groups to collect intelligence, share information, and plot unified strategies among member nations. The FBI belongs to several international working groups aimed at combating transnational gangs in various parts of the world. While international cooperation is now common and law enforcement agencies are willing to work together to fight transnational gangs, these criminal organizations are extremely hard to eradicate. The gangs are ready to use violence and well equipped to carry out threats.

LO10 Explain the causes of enterprise crime

There are numerous explanations for enterprise crime. Some offenders are motivated by greed; others offend due to personal problems. They use rationalizations to allow their financial needs to be met without compromising their values. Culture theory suggests that some organizations actually encourage employees to cheat or cut corners. The self-control view is that enterprise criminals are like any other law violators: impulsive people who lack self-control.

CRITICAL THINKING QUESTIONS

1. How would you punish a corporate executive whose product killed people if the executive had no knowledge that the product was potentially lethal? What if the executive did know?

2. Is organized crime inevitable as long as immigrant groups seek to become part of the American Dream?

3. Does the media glamorize organized crime? Does it paint an inaccurate picture of noble crime lords fighting to protect their families?

4. Apply traditional theories of criminal behavior to white-collar, green, and organized crime. Which one seems to best predict why someone would engage in these behaviors?

KEY TERMS

enterprise crimes (442)
corporate crime (444)
white-collar swindle (445)
Ponzi scheme (445)
securitization (445)

chiseling (447)
pink slime (448)
insider trading (448)
exploitation (448)
influence peddling (449)

Sherman Antitrust Act (455)
green crime (459)
transnational organized crime (466)

Racketeer Influenced and Corrupt Organizations (RICO) Act (471)

NOTES

1. Clifford Krauss, Phillip L. Zweig, and Julie Creswell, "Texas Firm Accused of $8 Billion Fraud," *New York Times*, February 18, 2009, http://www.nytimes.com/2009/02/18/business/18stanford.html (accessed June 2014).

2. CNBC, "Allen Stanford: Descent from Billionaire to Inmate #35017-183," October 5, 2012, http://www.cnbc.com/id/49276842 (accessed June 2014).

3. Rob White, "Researching Transnational Environmental Harm: Toward an Eco-Global Criminology," *International Journal of Comparative and Applied Criminal Justice* 33 (2009): 229–248.

4. Mark Haller, "Illegal Enterprise: A Theoretical and Historical Interpretation," *Criminology* 28 (1990): 207–235.

5. Nancy Frank and Michael Lynch, *Corporate Crime, Corporate Violence* (Albany, NY: Harrow & Heston, 1992), p. 7.

6. Edward Alsworth Ross, *Sin and Society: An Analysis of Latter-Day Iniquity* (Boston: Houghton Mifflin Company, 1907): 45–71.

7. Edwin Sutherland, *White-Collar Crime: The Uncut Version* (New Haven, CT: Yale University Press, 1983).

8. Edwin Sutherland, "White-Collar Criminality," *American Sociological Review* 5 (1940): 2–10.

9. David Weisburd and Kip Schlegel, "Returning to the Mainstream," in *White-Collar Crime Reconsidered*, eds. Kip Schlegel and David Weisburd (Boston: Northeastern University Press, 1992), pp. 352–365.

10. Rodney Huff, Christian Desilets, and John Kane, 2010 National Public Survey on White Collar Crime, http://www.nw3c.org/docs/publications/2010-national-public-survey-on-white-collar-crime.pdf (accessed June 2014).

11. Ibid

12. Ibid.

13. Natalie Taylor, "Under-Reporting of Crime Against Small Business: Attitudes Towards Police and Reporting Practices," *Policing and Society* 13 (2003): 79–90.

14. The typology used here leans closely on Mark Moore, "Notes Toward a National Strategy to Deal with White-Collar Crime," in *A National Strategy for Containing White-Collar Crime*, eds. Herbert Edelhertz and

Charles Rogovin (Lexington, MA: Lexington Books, 1980), pp. 32–44.

15. Data provided by the Mortgage Bankers Association, http://www.mortgagebankers.org/ (accessed June 2014).

16. Fraud Guides, Mortgage Foreclosure Rescue Scams, http://www.fraudguides.com/mortgage-foreclosure-rescue-scam.asp (accessed June 2014).

17. FBI, "Scamming Nuns: Con Artist Gets His Due," August 27, 2013, http://www.fbi.gov/news/stories/2013/august/con-artist-who-scammed-nuns-gets-his-due (accessed June 2014).

18. FBI, "Empty Promises, Empty Cradles: Adoption Scams Bilk Victims, Break Hearts," August 28, 2006, http://www.fbi.gov/news/stories/2006/august/adoptscams_082806 (accessed June 2014).

19. Bao Ong, "633 Cabbies to Lose Their Licenses," New York Times, May 14, 2010, http://cityroom.blogs.nytimes.com/2010/05/14/633-cabbies-lose-their-licenses/ (accessed June 2014).

20. Federal Trade Commission, "Auto Repair Basics," https://www.consumer.ftc.gov/articles/0211-auto-repair-basics (accessed June 2014).

21. Jim Avila, "70 Percent of Ground Beef at Supermarkets Contains 'Pink Slime'," ABC News, March 7, 2012, http://abcnews.go.com/blogs/headlines/2012/03/70-percent-of-ground-beef-at-supermarkets-contains-pink-slime/ (accessed June 2014).

22. Richard Quinney, "Occupational Structure and Criminal Behavior: Prescription Violation of Retail Pharmacists," Social Problems 11 (1963): 179–185; see also John Braithwaite, Corporate Crime in the Pharmaceutical Industry (London: Routledge and Kegan Paul, 1984).

23. Pam Belluck, "Prosecutors Say Greed Drove Pharmacist to Dilute Drugs," New York Times, August 18, 2001, p. 3.

24. Press release, April 22, 2002, Kansas City Division, Federal Bureau of Investigation.

25. FBI, "Historic Insider Trading Scheme: Stock Manager Busted," February 28, 2014, http://www.fbi.gov/news/stories/2014/february/historic-insider-trading-scheme/historic-insider-trading-scheme (accessed June 2014).

26. Patricia Hurtado, "SAC's Martoma Faces Up to 20 Years at June 10 Sentencing," Bloomberg News, February 8, 2014, http://www.bloomberg.com/news/2014-02-08/sac-capital-s-martoma-faces-up-to-20-years-at-june-10-sentencing.html (accessed June 2014).

27. Carpenter v. United States, 484 U.S. 19 (1987); also see John Boland, "The SEC Trims the First Amendment," Wall Street Journal, December 4, 1986, p. 28.

28. Anish Vashista, David Johnson, and Muhtashem Choudhury, "Securities Fraud," American Criminal Law Review 42 (2005): 877–942.

29. James Armstrong, et al., "Securities Fraud," American Criminal Law Review 33 (1995): 973–1016.

30. Scott McMurray, "Futures Pit Trader Goes to Trial," Wall Street Journal, May 8, 1990, p. C1; Scott McMurray, "Chicago Pits' Dazzling Growth Permitted a Free-for-All Mecca," Wall Street Journal, August 3, 1989, p. A4.

31. Charles V. Bagli, "Kickback Investigation Extends to Middle-Class Buildings in New York," New York Times, October 14, 1998, p. A19.

32. Elizabeth Dwoskin, "Former NY Supreme Court Judge Convicted of Extortion," Village Voice, August 27, 2009, http://blogs.villagevoice.com/runninscared/archives/2009/08/former_ny_supre.php (accessed June 2014).

33. FBI, "A (Driver's) License to Steal: Corruption in a San Diego Motor Vehicle Office," February 25, 2014, http://www.fbi.gov/news/stories/2014/february/corruption-in-a-san-diego-motor-vehicle-office/corruption-in-a-san-diego-motor-vehicle-office (accessed June 2014).

34. FBI, "Cheating in Contracts: A $30 Million Case of Corruption," July 19, 2013, http://www.fbi.gov/news/stories/2013/july/a-30-million-case-of-corruption/a-30-million-case-of-corruption (accessed June 2014).

35. Charles R. Babcock and Jonathan Weisman, "Congressman Admits Taking Bribes, Resigns," Washington Post, November 29, 2005, p. 1.

36. Monica Davey and John O'Neil, "Ex-Governor of Illinois Is Convicted on All Charges," New York Times, April 18, 2006, p. 1.

37. MSNBC: "Feds: Governor Tried to 'Auction' Obama's Seat," December 9, 2008, http://www.msnbc.msn.com/id/28139155/ (accessed June 2014).

38. FBI, "Abuse of Trust: The Case of the Crooked Border Official," June 8, 2009 http://www.fbi.gov/news/stories/2009/june/border060809 (accessed June 2014).

39. The Knapp Commission Report on Police Corruption (New York: George Braziller, 1973), pp. 1–3, 170–182.

40. David Kocieniewski and David M. Halbfinger, "New York's Most Respected Officers Led Precinct Where Sex Scandal Festered," New York Times, July 20, 1998, p. 1.

41. Justice Department News Release, "St. Bernard Parish Judge Wayne Cresap, Two Lawyers Charged in Bribery Scheme," July 1, 2009, http://www.fbi.gov/neworleans/press-releases/2009/no070109a.htm (accessed June 2014).

42. MSNBC, "Pa. Judges Accused of Jailing Kids for Cash: Judges Allegedly Took $2.6 Million in Payoffs to Put Juveniles in Lockups," February 11, 2009, http://www.msnbc.msn.com/id/29142654/ (accessed June 2014).

43. Henry Blodget, "Apple Manager Paul Shin Devine Busted In $1 Million Kickback Scheme," Business Insider, August 15, 2010, http://www.businessinsider.com/apple-manager-paul-shin-devine-busted-in-1-million-kickback-scheme-2010-8 (accessed June 2014).

44. Disclosure of payments to individuals connected with broadcasts, United States Criminal Code, Title 47, Chapter 5, Subchapter V § 508.

45. Marshall Clinard and Peter Yeager, Corporate Crime (New York: Free Press, 1980), p. 67.

46. Alina Selyukh, "U.S. Judge Approves IBM's Foreign Bribery Case Settlement with SEC," Reuters, July 25, 2013, http://www.reuters.com/article/2013/07/25/us-ibm-sec-idUS-BRE96O1FB20130725 (accessed June 2014).

47. PL No. 95-213, 101-104, 91 Stat. 1494.

48. Adrian Cho, "Hey Buddy … Wanna Buy a Moon Rock?" Science Now, July 7, 2002, p. 1.

49. Charles McCaghy, Deviant Behavior (New York: Macmillan, 1976), p. 178.

50. J. Sorenson, H. Grove, and T. Sorenson, "Detecting Management Fraud: The Role of the Independent Auditor," in White-Collar Crime, Theory and Research, eds. G. Geis and E. Stotland (Beverly Hills: Sage, 1980), pp. 221–251.

51. Jason Knott, "Ex-Tyco CEO Dennis Kozlowski Released from Prison," January 17, 2014, http://www.cepro.com/article/ex_tyco_ceo_dennis_kozlowski_released_from_prison/ (accessed June 2014).

52. Bethany McLean and Peter Elkind, The Smartest Guys in the Room: The Amazing Rise and Scandalous Fall of Enron (New York: Penguin, 2003); Kurt Eichenwald, "Ex-Andersen Partner Pleads Guilty in Record-Shredding," New York Times, April 12, 2002, p. C1; John A. Byrne, "At Enron, the Environment Was Ripe for Abuse," BusinessWeek, February 25, 2002, p. 12;. Peter Behr and Carrie Johnson, "Govt. Expands Charges Against Enron Execs," Washington Post, May 1, 2003, p. 1.

53. U.S. Attorney's Office, District of Columbia, "More Than 20 People Arrested Following Investigations into Widespread Health Care Fraud in D.C. Medicaid Program," February 20, 2014, http://www.fbi.gov/washingtondc/press-releases/2014/more-than-20-people-arrested-following-investigations-into-widespread-health-care-fraud-in-d.c.-medicaid-program (accessed June 2014).

54. FBI, "Rooting Out Health Care Fraud Is Central to the Well-Being of Both Our Citizens and the Overall Economy," 2014, http://www.fbi.gov/about-us/investigate/white_collar/health-care-fraud (accessed June 2014).

55. National Health Care Anti-Fraud Association, "The Challenge of Health Care Fraud," 2014, http://www.nhcaa.org/resources/health-care-anti-fraud-resources/the-challenge-of-health-care-fraud.aspx (accessed June 2014).

56. Ibid.

57. U.S. Department of Justice press release, "Three Miami Area Brothers and Physician's Assistant Charged in $110 Million Health Care Fraud Scheme," June 11, 2008, http://www.justice.gov/opa/pr/2008/June/08-crm-526.html (accessed June 2014).

58. U.S. Attorney's Office, Eastern District of Kentucky, "Saint Joseph London Hospital to Pay

$16.5 Million to Settle False Claims Act Allegations of Unnecessary Heart Procedures," January 28, 2014, http://www.fbi.gov/louisville/press-releases/2014/saint-joseph-london-hospital-to-pay-16.5-million-to-settle-false-claims-act-allegations-of-unnecessary-heart-procedures (accessed une 2014).

59. Health Insurance Portability and Accountability Act of 1996 (HIPAA), United States Code, Title 18, Section 1347.

60. FBI, "Common Fraud Schemes," 2014, http://www.fbi.gov/scams-safety/fraud (accessed August 2014).

61. 18 U.S.C. section 1344 (1994).

62. FBI, "Financial Crime Report to the Public 2006," http://www.fbi.gov/stats-services/publications/fcs_report2005/2006 (accessed June 2014).

63. *United States v. Bishop*, 412 U.S. 346 (1973).

64. David Cay Johnston, "Departing Chief Says I.R.S. Is Losing War on Tax Cheats," *New York Times*, November 5, 2002, p. 1.

65. Cited in Frank and Lynch, *Corporate Crime, Corporate Violence*, pp. 12–13.

66. Sutherland, "White-Collar Criminality," pp. 2–10.

67. Joseph S. Hall, "Corporate Criminal Liability," *American Criminal Law Review* 35 (1998): 549–560.

68. U.S. Department of Justice, "Nine Automobile Parts Manufacturers and Two Executives Agree to Plead Guilty to Fixing Prices on Automobile Parts Sold to U.S. Car Manufacturers and Installed in U.S. Cars: Companies Agree to Pay Total of More than $740 Million in Criminal Fines," September 26, 2013, http://www.fbi.gov/news/pressrel/press-releases/nine-automobile-parts-manufacturers-and-two-executives-agree-to-plead-guilty-to-fixing-prices-on-automobile-parts-sold-to-u.s.-car-manufacturers-and-installed-in-u.s.-cars (accessed June 2014).

69. 15 U.S.C. section 1 (1994).

70. 15 U.S.C. § 1 – Trusts, Etc., in Restraint of Trade Illegal; Penalty, http://www.law.cornell.edu/uscode/text/15/1 (accessed June 2014).

71. *Northern Pacific Railways v. United States*, 356 U.S. 1 (1958).

72. *Illinois Ex Rel. Madigan v. Telemarketing Associates, Inc., et al.* No. 01-1806 (2003).

73. This section relies heavily on Daniel Skoler, "White-Collar Crime and the Criminal Justice System: Problems and Challenges," in *A National Strategy for Containing White-Collar Crime*, eds. Edelhertz and Rogovin, pp. 57–76.

74. Ronald Burns, Keith Whitworth, and Carol Thompson, "Assessing Law Enforcement Preparedness to Address Internet Fraud," *Journal of Criminal Justice* 32 (2004): 477–493.

75. Michael Benson, Francis Cullen, and William Maakestad, "Local Prosecutors and Corporate Crime," *Crime and Delinquency* 36 (1990): 356–372.

76. Ibid., pp. 369–370.

77. David Simon and D. Stanley Eitzen, *Elite Deviance* (Boston: Allyn & Bacon, 1982), p. 28.

78. Stuart P. Green, *Lying, Cheating, and Stealing: A Moral Theory of White Collar Crime* (London: Oxford University Press, 2006).

79. This section relies heavily on Albert Reiss, Jr., "Selecting Strategies of Social Control over Organizational Life," in *Enforcing Regulation*, eds. Keith Hawkins and John M. Thomas (Boston: Kluwer Publications, 1984), pp. 25–37.

80. John Braithwaite, "The Limits of Economism in Controlling Harmful Corporate Conduct," *Law and Society Review* 16 (1981–1982): 481–504.

81. Sarbanes-Oxley Act, H.R. 3763-2 (2002).

82. Michael Benson, "Emotions and Adjudication: Status Degradation Among White-Collar Criminals," *Justice Quarterly* 7 (1990): 515–528; John Braithwaite, *Crime, Shame, and Reintegration* (Sydney: Cambridge University Press, 1989).

83. Kip Schlegel, "Desert, Retribution and Corporate Criminality," *Justice Quarterly* 5 (1988): 615–634.

84. Raymond Michalowski and Ronald Kramer, "The Space Between Laws: The Problem of Corporate Crime in a Trans-national Context," *Social Problems* 34 (1987): 34–53.

85. Ibid.

86. Christopher M. Brown and Nikhil S. Singhvi, "Antitrust Violations," *American Criminal Law Review* 35 (1998): 467–501.

87. Howard Adler, "Current Trends in Criminal Antitrust Enforcement," *Business Crimes Bulletin* (April 1996): 1.

88. David Weisburd, Elin Waring, and Stanton Wheeler, "Class, Status, and the Punishment of White-Collar Criminals," *Law and Social Inquiry* 15 (1990): 223–243.

89. Sean Rosenmerkel, "Wrongfulness and Harmfulness as Components of Seriousness of White-Collar Offenses," *Journal of Contemporary Criminal Justice* 17 (2001): 308–328.

90. Mark Cohen, "Environmental Crime and Punishment: Legal/Economic Theory and Empirical Evidence on Enforcement of Federal Environmental Statutes," *Journal of Criminal Law and Criminology* 82 (1992): 1054–1109.

91. Russell Mokhiber, "White Collar Crime Penalties," *Multinational Monitor* 22 (2001): 30.

92. Jonathan Lechter, Daniel Posner, and George Morris, "Antitrust Violations," *American Criminal Law Review* 39 (2002): 225–273.

93. Environmental Protection Agency, "Utah Man Sentenced to 20 Years in Prison for Environmental, Other Crimes," October 14, 2009, http://yosemite.epa.gov/opa/admpress.nsf/3881d73f4d4aaa0b85257359003f5348/a81ecbfea25c31f08525764f00625b5d!OpenDocument (accessed June 2014).

94. Michael J. Lynch and Paul Stretesky, "Green Criminology in the United States," in *Issues in Green Criminology*, ed. Piers Beirne and Nigel South (Portland, OR: Willan, 2008), pp. 248–269, at p. 249.

95. Michael M. O'Hear, "Sentencing the Green-Collar Offender: Punishment, Culpability, and Environmental Crime," *Journal of Criminal Law and Criminology* 95 (2004): 133–276.

96. F. J. W. Herbig and S. J. Joubert, "Criminological Semantics: Conservation Criminology—Vision or Vagary?" *Acta Criminologica* 19 (2006): 88–103.

97. Rob White, "Researching Transnational Environmental Harm: Toward an Eco-Global Criminology," *International Journal of Comparative and Applied Criminal Justice* 33 (2009): 229–248.

98. Paddy Hillyard, Christina Pantazis, Dave Gordon, and Steve Tombs, *Beyond Criminology: Taking Harm Seriously* (London: Pluto Press, 2004).

99. This section relies on Duncan Brack, *Illegal Logging* (London: Chatham House, 2007), http://www.illegal-logging.info/uploads/1_Illegal_logging_bp_07_01.pdf (accessed June 2014).

100. Ibid.

101. This section leans heavily on Liana Sun Wyler and Pervaze A. Sheikh, *International Illegal Trade in Wildlife: Threats and U.S. Policy* (Washington, DC: Congressional Research Service, 2008), http://fpc.state.gov/documents/organization/110404.pdf (accessed June 2014).

102. White, "Researching Transnational Environmental Harm: Toward an Eco-Global Criminology."

103. Liana Sun Wyler and Pervaze A. Sheikh, *International Illegal Trade in Wildlife: Threats and U.S. Policy* (Washington, DC: Congressional Research Service, 2013), http://www.fas.org/sgp/crs/misc/RL34395.pdf (accessed June 2014).

104. Boone Trading Company, 2014, http://www.boonetrading.com/Pg24.html (accessed June 2014).

105. The Lacey Act, 16 U.S.C. §§ 3371–3378.

106. U. R. Sumaila, J. Alder, and H. Keith, "Global Scope and Economics of Illegal Fishing," *Marine Policy* 30 (2006): 696–703.

107. Carole Gibbs, Edmund F. McGarrell, and Mark Axelrod, "Transnational White-collar Crime and Risk : Lessons from the Global Trade in Electronic Waste," *Criminology and Public Policy* 9 (2010): 543–560.

108. Abrahm Lustgarten, *Run to Failure: BP and the Making of the Deepwater Horizon Disaster* (New York: Norton, 2012).

109. Ibid.

110. Bob Egelko, "Punitive Damages Appealed in Valdez Spill: Oil Company Says It Has Been Punished Enough for Accident," *San Francisco Chronicle*, January 28, 2006, http://www.sfgate.com/bayarea/article/SAN-FRANCISCO-Punitive-damages-appealed-in-2523668.php (accessed June 2014).

111. Andrew Oliveira, Christopher Schenck, Christopher Cole, and Nicole Janes, "Environmental Crimes (Annual Survey of White Collar Crime)," *American Criminal Law Review* 42 (2005): 347–380.

112. Environmental Protection Agency, Criminal Investigation Division, http://www2.epa.gov/enforcement/criminal-enforcement (accessed June 2014).

113. Los Angeles County District Attorney's Office, Environmental Crimes/OSHA, 2014, http://da.lacounty.gov/envosha.htm (accessed June 2014).

114. Michael Lynch, Paul Stretesky, and Ronald Burns, "Slippery Business," *Journal of Black Studies* 34 (2004): 421–440.

115. Group Against Smog and Pollution (GASP), http://gasp-pgh.org/ (accessed June 2014).

116. Michael J. Lynch and Paul B. Stretesky, "The Distribution of Water-Monitoring Organizations Across States: Implications for Community Environmental Policing and Social Justice," *Policing: An International Journal of Police Strategies & Management* 36 (2013): 6–26.

117. FBI, Organized Crime Overview, 2013, http://www.fbi.gov/about-us/investigate/organizedcrime/overview (accessed June 2014).

118. Ibid.

119. Frederick Martens and Michele Cunningham-Niederer, "Media Magic, Mafia Mania," *Federal Probation* 49 (1985): 60–68.

120. Christopher Adamson, "Defensive Localism in White and Black: A Comparative History of European-American and African American Youth Gangs," *Ethnic and Racial Studies* 23 (2000): 272–298.

121. FBI, Organized Crime Overview, 2013.

122. Donald Cressey, *Theft of the Nation* (New York: Harper & Row, 1969).

123. Jay Albanese, "Deciphering the Linkages Between Organized Crime and Transnational Crime," *Journal of International Affairs* 66 (2012): 1–16.

124. *Organized Crime Today*, pp. 7–8.

125. James O. Finckenauer and Ko-lin Chin, *Asian Transnational Organized Crime and Its Impact on the United States* (Washington,

DC: National Institute of Justice, 2007), http://www.ncjrs.gov/pdffiles1/nij/214186.pdf (accessed June 2014).

126. Information in this section comes from the National Gang Intelligence Center, "National Gang Threat Assessment, 2009," http://www.fbi.gov/stats-services/publications/national-gang-threat-assessment-2009-pdf (accessed June 2014).

127. Ibid.

128. Ibid.

129. FBI, "African Criminal Enterprises," http://www.fbi.gov/about-us/investigate/organizedcrime/african (accessed June 2014).

130. FBI, "Balkan Criminal Enterprises," http://www.fbi.gov/about-us/investigate/organizedcrime/balkan (accessed June 2014).

131. FBI, "Operation Power Outage: Armenian Organized Crime Group Targeted," March 3, 2011, http://www.fbi.gov/news/stories/2011/march/armenian_030311/ (accessed June 2014).

132. Louise I. Shelley, "Crime and Corruption: Enduring Problems of Post-Soviet Development," *Demokratizatsiya* 11 (2003): 110–114; James O. Finckenauer and Yuri A. Voronin, *The Threat of Russian Organized Crime* (Washington, DC: National Institute of Justice, 2001).

133. Omar Bartos, "Growth of Russian Organized Crime Poses Serious Threat," *CJ International* 11 (1995): 8–9.

134. Bilyana Tsvetkova, "Gangs in the Caribbean," *Harvard International Review*, June 2009, http://hir.harvard.edu/gangs-in-the-caribbean (accessed June 2014).

135. This section leans heavily on Finckenauer and Chin, *Asian Transnational Organized Crime and Its Impact on the United States*.

136. National Institute of Justice, "Major Transnational Organized Crime Groups, 2010," http://www.nij.gov/topics/crime/organized-crime/pages/major-groups.aspx (accessed June 2014).

137. 18 U.S.C. 1952 (1976).

138. Public Law 91-452, Title IX, 84 Stat. 922 (1970) (codified at 18 U.S.C. 1961–68, 1976).

139. William Booth, "Mexican Azteca Gang Leader Arrested in Killings of 3 Tied to U.S.," *Washington Post*, March 30, 2010, http://www.washingtonpost.com/wp-dyn/content/article/2010/03/29/AR2010032903373.html (accessed March 2014).

140. Angela Kocherga, "Zeta Leader Captured in Mexico," KVUE News, July 4, 2011, http://www

kvue.com/story/news/2014/05/20/2272772/ (accessed June 2014).

141. Orlando Patterson, "The Other Losing War," *New York Times*, January 13, 2007.

142. White House press release, "Presidential Determination—Major Drug Transit and Drug Producing Countries for FY 2014," http://www.whitehouse.gov/the-press-office/2013/09/13/presidential-determination-major-drug-transit-and-drug-producing-countri (accessed June 2014).

143. Belluck, "Prosecutors Say Greed Drove Pharmacist to Dilute Drugs," p. 3.

144. See also, Neal Shover and Andrew Hochstetler, *Choosing White-Collar Crime* (England: Cambridge University Press, 2006).

145. Neal Shover and Peter Grabosky, "White-Collar Crime and the Great Recession," *Criminology and Public Policy* 9 (2010): 429–433.

146. Kathleen Daly, "Gender and Varieties of White-Collar Crime," *Criminology* 27 (1989): 769–793.

147. Mandeep Dhami, "White-Collar Prisoners' Perceptions of Audience Reaction," *Deviant Behavior* 28 (2007): 57–77.

148. Edelhertz and Rogovin, eds., *A National Strategy for Containing White-Collar Crime*, Appendix A, pp. 122–123.

149. Donald Cressey, *Other People's Money: A Study of the Social Psychology of Embezzlement* (Glencoe, IL: Free Press, 1973), p. 96.

150. Rhonda Evans and Dianne Porche, "The Nature and Frequency of Medicare/Medicaid Fraud and Neutralization Techniques Among Speech, Occupational, and Physical Therapists," *Deviant Behavior* 26 (2005): 253–271.

151. Nicole Leeper Piquero, Stephen Tibbetts, and Michael Blankenship, "Examining the Role of Differential Association and Techniques of Neutralization in Explaining Corporate Crime," *Deviant Behavior* 26 (2005): 159–188.

152. Tom R. Tyler, "Reducing Corporate Criminality: The Role of Values," *American Criminal Law Review* 51 (2014): 267–292.

153. Travis Hirschi and Michael Gottfredson, "Causes of White-Collar Crime," *Criminology* 25 (1987): 949–974.

154. Michael Gottfredson and Travis Hirschi, *A General Theory of Crime* (Stanford, CA: Stanford University Press, 1990), p. 191.

John Carey/Photolibrary/Getty Images

learning objectives

LO1 Clarify the association between law and morality

LO2 Interpret what is meant by the term *social harm*

LO3 List examples of the activities of moral crusaders

LO4 Describe the various forms of outlawed deviant sexuality

LO5 Summarize the history of prostitution and review what the term means today

LO6 Distinguish between the different types of prostitutes

LO7 Explain what is meant by the terms *obscenity* and *pornography*

LO8 Assess the causes of substance abuse

LO9 Compare and contrast the different methods of drug control

LO10 State the arguments for and against legalizing drugs

PUBLIC ORDER CRIME: SEX AND SUBSTANCE ABUSE

n March 2012, members of a violent Virginia street gang, Underground Gangster Crips (UGC), pleaded guilty to various federal charges related to a sex trafficking conspiracy. The leader of the gang—27-year-old Justin Strom—was sentenced to 40 years in prison, while the sentences handed down for the other four defendants totaled 53 years. The UGC was a branch or "set" of the original Crips gang that originated in Los Angeles in the late 1960s and early 1970s.

To recruit girls into prostitution, Strom and his UGC associates would surf the Net, going to social networking sites, looking for attractive young women. They also recruited vulnerable adolescent girls from schools and bus stops. The gang used phony identities, complimenting girls on their looks, asking to get to know them better, sometimes offering the opportunity to make money.

If the victim expressed interest (and many did, being young and easily flattered by the attention), Strom or one of his associates would ask for a cell phone number to contact her and make plans to meet. After some more flattery about their attractiveness, sometimes hits of illegal drugs and alcohol, and even mandatory sexual "tryouts" with Strom and other gang members, the girls were lured into engaging in commercial sex, often with the help of more senior girls showing them the ropes. The girls might be sent to an apartment complex with instructions to knock on doors looking for potential customers, driven to hotels for prearranged meetings, or taken to Strom's house, where they had sex with paying customers.

Some of the juvenile victims were threatened with violence if they didn't perform as directed, and many were given drugs or alcohol to keep them sedated and compliant. Strom and his associates did not discriminate—their victims were from across the socioeconomic spectrum and represented different ethnic backgrounds.[1]

throughout history, tribes, groups, and nation states have banned or limited behaviors believed to run contrary to social norms, customs, and values. These behaviors, are often referred to as **public order crimes** or **victimless crimes**, although the latter term can be misleading, as the coercive activities of Strom and his fellow gang members suggest.[2] Public order crimes involve acts that interfere with the operations of society and the ability of people to function efficiently. Put another way, whereas common-law crimes such as rape or robbery are banned because they cause **social harm**, other behaviors are outlawed simply because they conflict with social policy, prevailing moral rules, and current public opinion.

Statutes designed to uphold public order usually prohibit the manufacture and distribution of morally questionable goods and services such as erotic material, commercial sex, and mood-altering drugs. They ban acts that people holding political and social power consider morally tinged. Statutes like these are controversial in part because millions of otherwise law-abiding citizens often engage in these outlawed activities and consequently become criminals. They are also controversial because they selectively prohibit desired goods, services, and behaviors; in other words, they outlaw sin and vice. They typically create boundaries rather than bright lines: it's legal to drink at age 21, but it's a crime at age 20, even though 20-year-olds can fight for their country and vote in elections. Such boundaries often create confusion and ambivalence: if an act is immoral and illegal, why is it okay for some people to engage in it but not others?

This chapter first briefly discusses the relationship between law and morality. Next, the chapter addresses public order crimes of a sexual nature: paraphilias, prostitution, and pornography. The chapter concludes by focusing on the abuse of drugs and alcohol.

public order crimes Acts that are considered illegal because they threaten the general well-being of society and challenge its accepted moral principles. Prostitution, drug use, and the sale of pornography are considered public order crimes.

victimless crimes Violations of the criminal law without any identifiable evidence of an individual victim who has suffered damage from the crime.

social harm A view that behaviors harmful to other people and society in general must be controlled. These acts are usually outlawed, but some acts that cause enormous amounts of social harm are perfectly legal, such as the consumption of tobacco and alcohol.

LAW AND MORALITY

 LO1 Clarify the association between law and morality

Legislation of moral issues has continually frustrated lawmakers because many of their constituents see little harm in visiting a prostitute or smoking some pot. When a store is robbed or a child assaulted, it is easy to identify with the victim and condemn the harm done. It is, however, more difficult to sympathize with or even identify the victims of immoral acts, such as pornography or prostitution, where the parties involved may be willing participants. Some porn stars and call girls are paid more for a few days' work than a waitress or a teacher makes in a year. Can we consider them "victims"? People who employ call girls and escorts may be wealthy and powerful men, such as former New York Governor Eliot Spitzer and Louisiana Senator David Vitter, who freely and voluntarily spent their money for sexual services; Vitter later took responsibility for his "sin" and asked voters for forgiveness so he could run for governor.[3] Certainly they were not the "victim" here. If there is no victim, can there be a crime?

To answer this question, we might first consider whether there is actually a victim in so-called "victimless crimes." While some young women voluntarily engage in highly paid sex work, others, such as those recruited by Justin Strom, have been coerced into the sex trade; they are therefore true victims. It is common for young runaways and abandoned children to be coerced into a life on the streets, where they are cruelly treated and held as virtual captives.[4] It has been estimated that women involved in street prostitution are 60 to 100 times more likely to be murdered than the average woman and that most of the killings are the result of a dispute over money rather than being sexually motivated.[5] Clearly prostitution carries with it significant professional risk. Other sexually related offenses, such as pornography, may involve people who voluntarily perform in "adult films." But as critics such as Andrea Dworkin point out, women involved in adult films, far from being highly paid stars, are "dehumanized—turned into objects and commodities."[6]

Even if public order crimes do not actually harm their participants, perhaps society as a whole should be considered the victim of these crimes. Is the community harmed when an adult website goes online or a brothel opens down the street? Does this signal that a neighborhood is in decline? Does it teach children that deviance is both tolerated and profitable? If women are degraded and sexualized in adult sex films, does that send a message that it is acceptable to demean and/or harm women?

Debating Morality

In 2011, rising political star Anthony Weiner was forced to resign from office after compromising photos he "tweeted" to young women were posted online. At first, Weiner denied responsibility, telling the media that his account had been hacked and/or that the pictures had possibly been altered. Finally, he admitted on June 6, 2011, that he had sent sexually explicit text messages and photographs to several women, both before and after he got married.[7] Did Weiner's behavior really cause public harm? After all, he never actually met any of the women with whom he carried on a cyber-relationship. All his victims had to do was disconnect or delete his texts, tweets, and emails.

While some may view Weiner's behavior as odd yet essentially harmless, others considered his "sexting" as immoral and unworthy of a public figure. Was Weiner's sexting grossly immoral or merely an example of those harmless human quirks and eccentricities we all possess in some measure? New York City voters may not be as forgiving as those in Louisiana: when Weiner tried a political comeback in 2013, his campaign for mayor of New York City was shot down when the media found out that he sent women more explicit photos using the alias "Carlos Danger."

The debate over morality has existed for all of recorded history: As the Bible (Genesis 18:20) tells us, God destroyed the "Cities of the Plain" because "The outcry against Sodom and Gomorrah is so great and their sin so grievous."[8] Though Abraham begs God for mercy, his prayers go unanswered because, despite a posse of angels looking for them, ten righteous residents could not be found.

Punishing immorality with legal sanctions continues today (though not fire and brimstone). Acts such as pornography, prostitution, and substance abuse are believed to erode the moral fabric of society and are therefore prohibited and punished. They are crimes, according to the great legal scholar Morris Cohen, because "it is one of the functions of the criminal law to give expression to the collective feeling of revulsion toward certain acts, even when they are not very dangerous."[9] In his classic statement on the function of morality in the law, legal scholar Sir Patrick Devlin states,

> Without shared ideas on politics, morals, and ethics no society can exist…. If men and women try to create a society in which there is no fundamental agreement about good and evil, they will fail; if having based it on common agreement, the agreement goes, the society will disintegrate. For society is not something that is kept together physically; it is held by the invisible bonds of common thought. If the bonds were too far relaxed, the members would drift apart. A common morality is part of the bondage. The bondage is part of the price of society; and mankind, which needs society, must pay its price.[10]

According to this view, so-called victimless crimes are prohibited because one of the functions of criminal law is to express a shared sense of public morality.[11]

Some influential legal scholars have questioned the propriety of legislating morals. H. L. A. Hart states,

> It is fatally easy to confuse the democratic principle that power should be in the hands of the majority with the utterly different claim that the majority, with power in their hands, need respect no limits. Certainly there is a special risk in a democracy that the majority may dictate how all should live.[12]

Hart may be motivated by the fact that defining morality may be an impossible task: Who defines morality? Are we not punishing differences rather than social harm? As U.S. Supreme Court Justice William O. Douglas once so succinctly put it, "What may be trash to me may be prized by others."[13] After all, many of the great works of Western art depict nude males and females, some quite young. Are the paintings of Rubens or the sculpture of Michelangelo obscene?

Sociologist Joseph Gusfield argues that the purpose of outlawing immoral acts is to show the moral superiority of those who condemn the acts over those who partake of them. The legislation of morality "enhances the social status of groups carrying the affirmed culture and degrades groups carrying that which is condemned as deviant."[14] Research indicates that people who define themselves as liberals are also the most tolerant of sexually explicit material. Demographic attributes such as age, educational attainment, and occupational status may also influence views of pornography: the young and better educated tend to be more tolerant than older, less-educated people.[15] Whose views should prevail?

And, if a majority of the population chooses to engage in what might objectively be considered immoral or deviant behavior, would it be fair or just to prohibit or control such behavior or render it criminal? While it's difficult to measure or calculate the visits to porn sites on the Internet, according to Google's DoubleClick Ad Planner, which tracks users across the Web with a cookie, dozens of adult destinations populate the top 500 websites; the largest gets 4.4 billion page views per month, three times more than CNN or ESPN.[16] Should all obscenity and pornography be legalized if so many people are active users and wish to enjoy its content? And if the law tried to define or limit objectionable material, might it not eventually inhibit free speech and political dissent? Not so, according to social commentator Irving Kristol:

> If we start censoring pornography and obscenity, shall we not inevitably end up censoring political opinion? A lot of people seem to think this would be the case—which only shows the power of doctrinaire thinking over reality. We had censorship of pornography and obscenity for 150 years, until almost yesterday, and I am not aware that freedom of opinion in this country was in any way diminished as a consequence of this fact.[17]

Cultural clashes may ensue when behavior that is considered normative in one society is deplored by those living in another. Amnesty International estimates that more than 140 million of the world's females have undergone genital mutilation and there are 3 million girls who now suffer the procedure

Anthony Weiner, a New York City mayoral candidate, fields questions beside his wife, Huma Abedin, in New York, on July 23, 2013. Weiner was forced to end his political career after he got involved in a sexting scandal.

laws banning *superbia* (hubris/pride), *avaritia* (avarice/greed), *luxuria* (extravagance or lust), *invidia* (envy), *gula* (gluttony), *ira* (wrath), and *acedia* (sloth) even though they are considered the "seven deadly sins." Nor is it a crime to ignore the pleas of a drowning child, even though to do so might be considered callous, coldhearted, and unfeeling. (Of course, some people—lifeguards, paramedics, firemen, police, and the parents—have a legal duty to help save the child.)

While the theory of social harm can explain most criminal acts, it cannot explain them all. Some acts that cause enormous amounts of social harm are perfectly legal, while others that many people consider virtually harmless are outlawed and severely punished.

It is now estimated more than 500,000 deaths in the United States each year can be linked to the consumption of tobacco and alcohol, yet these "deadly substances" remain legal to produce and sell. Similarly, sports cars and motorcycles that can accelerate to more than 150 miles per hour are perfectly legal to sell and possess though almost 40,000 people die each year in car accidents, while under 20,000 die from illicit drug overdoses (another 20,000 succumb to prescription drug overdoses).[22] According to the theory of social harm, if more people die each year from alcohol, tobacco, and automobile-related causes than illicit drugs, shouldn't cocaine and heroin be legalized and Corvettes, Johnny Walker, and Marlboros outlawed? But they are not.

each year.[18] Custom and tradition are by far the most frequently cited reasons for mutilation, and it is often carried out in a ritual during which the young woman is initiated into adulthood.[19] The surgery is done to ensure virginity, remove sexual sensation, and render the females suitable for marriage; a girl in these societies cannot be considered an adult unless she has undergone genital mutilation. Critics of this practice, led by American author Alice Walker (*The Color Purple*), consider the procedure mutilation and torture; others argue that this ancient custom should be left to the discretion of the indigenous people who consider it part of their culture. "Torture," counters Walker, "is not culture." Can an outsider define the morality of another culture?[20] Amnesty International and the United Nations have worked to end the practice. Because of outside pressure, the procedure is now forbidden in Senegal, Egypt, Burkina Faso, the Central African Republic, Djibouti, Ghana, Guinea, and Togo. Other countries, among them Uganda, discourage it. In North Africa, the Egyptian Supreme Court upheld a ban on the practice and also ruled it had no place in Islam.[21] Despite these efforts, millions of girls are still subject to female circumcision every day in Africa and the Middle East and in Muslim areas all over the world.

Social Harm

LO2 Interpret what is meant by the term *social harm*

Most societies have long banned or limited behaviors that are believed to run contrary to social norms, customs, and values. Acts that create social harm are made illegal. However, many acts that most of us deem highly immoral and objectionable are not in fact criminal. There are no

CONNECTIONS

In Chapter 13, we discussed the fact that the meat production industry, especially chicken farming, employs practices that are harmful to animals and humans while being perfectly legal.

Ask Yourself ...

What other industries or products that are now legal would you criminalize? Remember that more people die from fast cars, smoking, and drinking than from guns, knives, and poison.

Moral Crusades and Crusaders

LO3 List examples of the activities of moral crusaders

In the early West, vigilance committees were set up in San Francisco and other boom towns to pursue cattle rustlers and stagecoach robbers and to dissuade undesirables from moving in. These **vigilantes** held a strict standard of morality that, when they caught their prey, resulted in sure and swift justice.

The avenging vigilante has remained part of popular culture. Fictional do-gooders who take it on themselves to enforce the law, battle evil, and personally deal with those whom they consider immoral have become enmeshed in the public consciousness. From the Lone Ranger to Spiderman, the righteous vigilante is expected to go on moral crusades without any authorization from legal authorities. Who actually told Spiderman he can destroy half of New York while fighting Dr. Octopus or the Green Goblin? And what about the Justice League? What gives the Martian Manhunter, Wonder Woman, Plastic Man, and their superhero colleagues the right to fight crime in America? (In contrast, the Avengers—Iron Man, Black Widow, Thor, the Hulk, Captain America, and so on—work for the Strategic Homeland Intervention, Enforcement, and Logistics Division [S.H.I.E.L.D.], so at least they operate under the rule of law.) The assumption that it is okay to take matters into your own hands if the cause is right and the target is immoral is not lost on the younger generation. Gang boys sometimes take on the street identity of "Batman" or "Superman" so they can battle their rivals with impunity.

Fictional characters are not the only ones who take it upon themselves to fight for moral decency; members of special interest groups are also ready to do battle.[23] Public order crimes often trace their origin to **moral crusaders** who seek to shape the law toward their own way of thinking; Howard Becker calls them **moral entrepreneurs**. These rule creators, argues Becker, operate with an absolute certainty that their way is right and that any means are justified to get their way: "The crusader is fervent and righteous, often self-righteous."[24] Today's moral crusaders take on such issues as prayer in school, gun ownership, gay marriage, abortion, and the distribution of sexually explicit books and magazines.

During the 1930s, Harry Anslinger, then head of the Federal Bureau of Narcotics, used magazine articles, public appearances, and public testimony to sway public opinion about the dangers of marijuana, which until that time was legal to use and possess.[25] In testimony before the House Ways and Means Committee, considering passage of the Marijuana Tax Act of 1938, Anslinger stated:

In Florida a 21-year-old boy under the influence of this drug killed his parents and his brothers and sisters. The evidence showed that he had smoked marihuana.

In Chicago recently two boys murdered a policeman while under the influence of marihuana. Not long ago we found a 15-year-old boy going insane because, the doctor told the enforcement officers, he thought the boy was smoking marihuana cigarettes. They traced the sale to some man who had been growing marihuana and selling it to these boys all under 15 years of age, on a playground there.[26]

As a result of Anslinger's efforts, a deviant behavior—marijuana use—became a criminal behavior, and previously law-abiding citizens were defined as criminal offenders.

Moral Crusades Today

Moral crusades are sometimes designed to publicize the differences between behaviors that are considered morally acceptable and those that right-thinking people should consider deviant and unacceptable. Today, popular targets of moral crusaders are abortion clinics, pornographers, gun dealers, and despoilers of the environment.

Of course, what is right and moral is often in the eye of the beholder. Take anti-smut campaigns that target books considered too "racy" or controversial to be suitable for a public school library. According to the American Library Association, between 2000 and 2006 the *Harry Potter* series topped the yearly top 10 list of books challenged by critics who demanded their removal from school library shelves. Most of the objections to J. K. Rowling's popular series about a young wizard in England centered on the charge that the books promote Satanism and magic. Currently, the leading targets include *Captain Underpants*, by Dav Pilkey (critics claim that it uses offensive language unsuited for the targeted age group), and *Tango Makes Three*, by Peter Parnell and Justin Richardson, a children's book that tells the story of two male penguins who find an abandoned egg and raise a baby penguin chick (critics claim it glorifies the same-sex lifestyle).[27]

 See the American Library Association's lists of the most frequently challenged books of the twenty-first century at **http://www.ala.org/bbooks/frequentlychallengedbooks/top10**.

Should racy books be banned from libraries, or should parents instruct their children to avoid them if they object to the content?

vigilantes Individuals who go on moral crusades without any authorization from legal authorities. The assumption is that it is okay to take matters into your own hands if the cause is right and the target is immoral.

moral crusaders People who strive to stamp out behavior they find objectionable. Typically, moral crusaders are directed at public order crimes, such as drug abuse or pornography.

moral entrepreneurs Interest groups that attempt to control social life and the legal order in such a way as to promote their own personal set of moral values. People who use their influence to shape the legal process in ways they see fit.

In their efforts to protect society, moral crusaders may themselves sometimes engage in illegal and immoral conduct. Abortion foes have resorted to violence and murder to rid the nation of prochoice health care providers whom they consider immoral, while failing to realize the depravity of their own extreme acts.

The Gay Marriage Crusade   One of the most heated of "moral crusades" has been directed at influencing public acceptance of the gay lifestyle. One group of crusaders is determined to prevent the legalization of gay marriage; their objective is passage of a constitutional amendment declaring that marriage is between one man and one woman. The Defense of Marriage Act in 1996, which defined marriage as a union of one man and one woman for the purposes of federal law, is one of their legal achievements.[28]

Opposing them are groups of activists who have tirelessly campaigned for the civil rights of gay men and women. One of their most important victories occurred in 2003 when the U.S. Supreme Court delivered a historic decision in *Lawrence v. Texas*, which made it impermissible for states to criminalize oral and anal sex and all other forms of intercourse that are not heterosexual under statutes prohibiting sodomy, deviant sexuality, or buggery.[29] The *Lawrence* case involved two gay men who had been arrested in 1998 for having sex in the privacy of their Houston home. In overturning their convictions, the Court said this:

> Although the laws involved … here … do not more than prohibit a particular sexual act, their penalties and purposes have more far-reaching consequences, touching upon the most private human conduct, sexual behavior, and in the most private of places, the home. They seek to control a personal relationship that, whether or not entitled to formal recognition in the law, is within the liberty of persons to choose without being punished as criminals. The liberty protected by the Constitution allows homosexual persons the right to choose to enter upon relationships in the confines of their homes and their own private lives and still retain their dignity as free persons.

As a result of the decision, all sodomy laws in the United States were suddenly unconstitutional and unenforceable; acts that were once a crime were suddenly legalized. The *Lawrence* decision paved the way for states to rethink their marriage laws. In 2003, Massachusetts's highest court ruled that same-sex couples are legally entitled to wed under the state constitution, and that the state may not "deny the protections, benefits, and obligations conferred by civil marriage to two individuals of the same sex who wish to marry."[30] As of this writing, 19 other states and the District of Columbia have followed along. In 2013, in *United States v. Windsor*, the Supreme Court held that Section 3 of Defense of Marriage Act (DOMA) which restricted the U.S. federal interpretation of "marriage" and "spouse" to apply only to heterosexual unions is unconstitutional. Such a restriction,

the Court wrote, "disparage[s] and … injure[s] those whom the State, by its marriage laws, sought to protect in personhood and dignity…. DOMA is unconstitutional as a deprivation of the equal liberty of persons that is protected by the Fifth Amendment."[31]

 To read the Supreme Court's opinion in *United States v. Windsor*, go to **http://www.supremecourt .gov/opinions/12pdf/12-307_6j37.pdf.** **Regardless of your own opinion, should the federal government get involved in issues such as marriage, which is traditionally a state matter?**

Despite these legal changes, the debate over gay marriage rages on. The majority of states still do not sanction gay marriage and about 35 percent of the population say they are in opposition to same-sex unions.[32] Is it fair to prevent one group of loyal taxpaying citizens from engaging in a behavior that is allowed for others? Are there objective standards of morality or should society respect people's differences? After all, opponents charge, polygamy is banned and there are age standards for marriage in every state. If gay marriage is legalized, what about marriage to multiple partners or with underage minors? How far should the law go in curbing human behaviors that do not cause social harm? Who controls the law? And should the law be applied to shape morality?

The public order crimes discussed in this chapter are divided into two broad areas. The first relates to what conventional society considers deviant sexual practices: paraphilias, prostitution, and pornography. The second area concerns the use of substances that have been outlawed or controlled because of the alleged harm they cause: drugs and alcohol.

SEXUALLY RELATED OFFENSES

 LO4   Describe the various forms of outlawed deviant sexuality

In a case that became a media sensation, between 2002 and 2004 Ariel Castro kidnapped Michelle Knight, Amanda Berry, and Georgina "Gina" DeJesus and held them in his house on Seymour Avenue in Cleveland until May 6, 2013, when Berry was able to shout through a locked door and alert her neighbors. The women had been raped and beaten continually. Knight had become pregnant five times and endured a miscarriage brought on by beatings and starvation. Berry had also become pregnant and had a six-year-old daughter by the time of her rescue. After his arrest, Castro pleaded guilty to 937 criminal counts of rape, kidnapping, and aggravated murder and was sentenced to life in prison without the chance of parole plus 1,000 years. Castro hanged himself in his prison cell within a month of his incarceration.[33]

Unfortunately, Castro's dastardly act is not unique. In 2009, Phillip Garrido, a long-time sex offender, was arrested for the kidnapping of Jaycee Lee Dugard, who had been abducted on June 10, 1991, when she was 11 years old and held captive for 18 years, in Antioch, California. Raped repeatedly, Dugard gave birth to daughters in 1994 and 1998. In 2011, Garrido was sentenced to 431 years in prison; his wife received a sentence of 36 to life. In another case, on June 5, 2002, Elizabeth Smart was abducted from her bedroom in Salt Lake City, Utah, and held captive until found nine months later. Elizabeth had been kidnapped by Brian David Mitchell, who was indicted for her kidnapping and sent to a mental health facility after being ruled mentally unfit to stand trial.[34] After six years there he was declared mentally competent, found guilty at trial, and sentenced to life without parole. He is currently being housed in a federal prison in Tucson.

Although these sex-related kidnappings are stunning in their sordidness, they are not rare. Each year thousands of children are abducted by strangers, and hundreds of thousands are subjected to some form of sexual exploitation, including sexual abuse, prostitution, pornography, and molestation.[35]

Because of these alarming statistics and also because some sexual practices are believed to cause social harm, some elements of sexual conduct have been made illegal in the United States and abroad. Below, three of the most common offenses, paraphilias, prostitution, and pornography, are discussed in some detail.

PARAPHILIAS

Paraphilias (Greek *para*, "to the side of" and *philos*, "loving") encompasses bizarre or abnormal sexual practices involving recurrent sexual urges focused on (a) nonhuman objects (such as underwear, shoes, or leather), (b) humiliation or the experience of receiving or giving pain (such as in sadomasochism or bondage), or (c) children or others who cannot grant consent. More than 2,000-year-old Buddhist texts contain references to sexually deviant behaviors among monastic communities, including sexual activity with animals and sexual interest in corpses. Richard von Krafft-Ebing's *Psychopathia Sexualis*, first published in 1887, was the first text to discuss such paraphilias as sadism, bestiality, and incest.[36]

Paraphilias are legal if they are not harmful to others, such as wearing clothes normally worn by the opposite sex (transvestite fetishism) or are engaged in by adults in the privacy of their homes—for example, asphyxiophilia, self-strangulation that restricts the supply of oxygen or blood to the brain in order to increase sexual intensity. However, when paraphilias involve unwilling or underage victims they are considered socially harmful and subject to criminal penalties. And paraphilias that are legal can also be harmful: on June 4, 2009, actor David Carradine (*Kill Bill*) was found dead in a Thailand hotel, the victim of asphyxiophilia gone awry.[37]

Included in this group of outlawed sexual behaviors are these practices:

- *Pedophilia or* paedophilia. A sexual attraction by an adult or late adolescent to prepubescent children, generally age 11 years or younger.

- *Frotteurism.* Rubbing against or touching a nonconsenting person in a crowd, elevator, or other public area.
- *Voyeurism.* Obtaining sexual pleasure from spying on a stranger while he or she disrobes or engages in sexual behavior with another.
- *Exhibitionism.* Deriving sexual pleasure from exposing the genitals to surprise or shock a stranger.
- *Sadomasochism.* Deriving pleasure from receiving pain or inflicting pain on another.

Marvin Fong/*Plain Dealer*/Landov

Ariel Castro was sentenced to prison for life on hundreds of charges including kidnapping, rape, and holding captive Amanda Berry, Gina DeJesus, and Michelle Knight for nearly a decade. Castro committed suicide while in prison.

paraphilias Bizarre or abnormal sexual practices that may involve recurrent sexual urges focused on objects, humiliation, or children.

JOHN EVANDER COUEY AND THE JESSICA LUNSFORD MURDER CASE

Brian LaPate/Pool/Landov

On February 24, 2005, 9-year-old Jessica Lunsford was reported missing from her home. When a child is reported missing, the police typically check on all the known sex offenders in the area, which in this case included John Evander Couey, 46, who was not living at the address where he was registered, a legal violation. Police located Couey and searched his room, not finding anything. Couey had a long list of convictions including burglary, carrying a concealed weapon, disorderly intoxication, driving under the influence, indecent exposure, disorderly conduct, fraud, insufficient funds, and larceny. A habitual drug abuser, in 1991 he had been arrested and charged with "fondling a child under the age of 16."

Nineteen days after Jessica Lunsford was first reported missing, detectives returned to Couey's home and this time found blood on the mattress. Couey had fled but was arrested in Georgia. While in police custody, Couey admitted that he had entered the Lunsford home at around 3 A.M. on February 24, 2005, and found Jessica asleep in her bed. He woke her and ordered her to be quiet. "Don't yell or nothing," he said and

Pedophilia

Between 2002 and 2004, the archdiocese of Boston was shaken by allegations that a significant number of priests had engaged in sexual relations with minor children. The archdiocese eventually turned over the names of nearly 100 priests to prosecutors. As the scandal spread, clergy elsewhere in the United States and abroad resigned amid allegations that they had abused children or failed to stop abuse of which they had knowledge. In Ireland, the Most Reverend Brendan Comiskey, the Bishop of Ferns, offered his resignation to the pope for failing in his efforts to stop abuse in his diocese, and an archbishop in Wales was forced to resign because he had ignored complaints about two priests later convicted of sexually abusing children. Responding to the crisis, Pope John Paul II called a special meeting of American Catholic leaders in April 2002 to create new policies on sex abuse. The pope issued a statement in which he said that there is "no place in the priesthood ... for those who would harm the young." He added that sexual abuse by the clergy was not only an "appalling sin" but a crime, and he noted that "many are offended at the way in which church leaders are perceived to have acted in this matter."[38]

Nowhere did the scandal take on greater proportion than in the Boston area, where Cardinal Bernard Law was forced to step down as leader of the diocese. Numerous churches were closed or sold to help raise money for legal fees and victim compensation. Among the most notorious offenders was Father James Porter, accused of molesting at least 125 children of both sexes over a 30-year period reaching back to the early 1960s. Porter was eventually sentenced to an 18- to 20-year prison term. The church continues to be haunted by charges levied against priests. Fr. Lawrence Murphy, who taught at St. John's School for the Deaf in a suburb of Milwaukee from 1950 through 1974, sexually abused about 200 boys.[39]

 To read the most significant report on the pedophilia crisis in the Catholic Church, prepared by researchers at John Jay College of Criminal Justice, go to **http://www.jjay.cuny.edu/churchstudy/main.asp.**

Should people convicted of child molestation be punished as criminals or considered as mentally ill and be given treatment?

Of all the commonly practiced paraphilias, **pedophilia** is the one that most concerns the general public. While the cause of pedophilia has not been determined, suspected factors brain include abnormal brain structure, social maladaption, and neurological dysfunction. The central processing of sexual stimuli in pedophiles may be controlled by a disturbance in the prefrontal networks of the brain.[40] There is also some evidence that pedophilia is heritable and genetic factors are responsible for the development of pedophilia.[41] Other suspected connections range from cognitive distortions to exposure to pornography.[42]

pedophilia A psychosexual disorder in which an adult has sexual fantasies about or engages in sexual acts with an underage minor child.

told her to follow him back to his sister's house, where he raped her repeatedly and kept her in a closet for three days. When he learned that detectives were searching for him, he panicked and buried her even though she was still alive. He showed investigators the shallow grave where they found Jessica's body inside two tied plastic garbage bags. Her wrists were bound, but she had managed to poke two fingers through the plastic in an attempt to free herself.

Couey was found guilty of murder on March 7, 2007, and a death penalty hearing was held soon after. In closing statements, prosecutor Ric Ridgway called the crime "evil" and asked jurors to remember how Jessica died by suffocating in the hole Couey dug, accompanied only by a stuffed toy she had grabbed as she was being abducted. "She was in pain. In the dark. She was certainly terrified," Ridgway said in his closing statement. "If this is not the person who deserves the death penalty, who does?"

Defense lawyers pleaded for mercy, arguing that Couey deserved no more than a life sentence in prison because of mental retardation and mental illness, neglect as a child, and the effects of alcohol and drug abuse. "No matter what you do, John Couey is going to die in prison," said defense attorney Alan Fanter. "No child should have to die the way Jessica Lunsford did. But justice is not vengeance." The jury did not buy that argument and sentenced Couey to death on March 14, 2007.

In the aftermath of Jessica Lunsford's abduction, Florida passed legislation that requires increased prison sentences, electronic tracking of all convicted sex offenders on probation, and the mandatory use of state databases by all local probation officials so that known sex offenders could not avoid the scrutiny of law enforcement. Can such measures control the behavior of pedophiles such as Couey before they kill their innocent victims?

SOURCES: Court TV Crime Library, Jessica Lunsford, http://www.crimelibrary.com/serial_killers/predators/jessica_lunsford/9.html (accessed June 2014); Curt Anderson, "Death Sentence Endorsed in Lunsford Case," *Washington Post*, March 15, 2007, http://www.washingtonpost.com/wp-dyn/content/article/2007/03/15/AR2007031500518.html (accessed June 2014).

While men are overrepresented in the ranks of sexual predators, women are also involved. One study of more than 100 adult female sex offenders found that 77 percent of the cases involved abuse of their own child, typically with a male intimate partner.[43] One of the most horrific cases of pedophilia involved the kidnapping and death of 9-year-old Jessica Lunsford, which is the subject of the Profiles in Crime feature.

PROSTITUTION

 LO5 Summarize the history of prostitution and review what the term means today

On July 16, 2007, Louisiana's conservative Republican Senator David Vitter apologized to the public after his telephone number showed up in the phone records of Pamela Martin and Associates, the prostitution ring run in the nation's capital by so-called "D.C. Madam" Deborah Jeane Palfrey. "This was a very serious sin in my past for which I am, of course, completely responsible," Vitter said remorsefully. Soon after he issued his statement, Jeanette Maier, a former madam who ran a house of prostitution in New Orleans, claimed Vitter was also a client in her brothel. She told the press: "As far as the girls coming out after seeing David, all they had was nice things to say. It wasn't all about sex. In fact, he just wanted to have somebody listen to him, you know. And I said his wife must not be listening." Vitter continues to serve as senator and plans a run for governor of Louisiana. Frequenting brothels and employing prostitutes is hardly the behavior expected from a married senator known for his strong advocacy of family values; he opposes sex education and abortion and has earmarked money for Christian groups who oppose the teaching of evolution.[44] Senator Vitter was not alone in enjoying the services of the D.C. Madam; also on her call list was Randall L. Tobias, who was forced to step down as deputy secretary of state, and Harlan K. Ullman, the military affairs scholar who created the Pentagon's concept known as "shock and awe."[45]

Prostitution has been known for thousands of years. The term derives from the Latin *prostituere*, which means "to cause to stand in front of." The prostitute is viewed as publicly offering his or her body for sale. The earliest record of prostitution appears in ancient Mesopotamia, where priests engaged in sex to promote fertility in the community. All women were required to do temple duty, and passing strangers were expected to make donations to the temple after enjoying its services.[46]

Modern commercial sex appears to have its roots in ancient Greece, where Solon established licensed brothels in 500 BCE. The earnings of Greek prostitutes helped pay for the temple of Aphrodite. Famous men openly went to prostitutes to enjoy intellectual, aesthetic, and sexual stimulation; prostitutes, however, were prevented from marrying.[47]

During the Middle Ages, although prostitution was a sin under canon law, it was widely practiced and considered a method of protecting "respectable" women who might otherwise be attacked by young men. In 1358, the Grand Council of Venice declared that prostitution was "absolutely indispensable to the world."[48] Some church leaders such as St. Thomas Aquinas condoned prostitution; St. Augustine wrote: "If you expel prostitution from society, you will unsettle everything on account of lusts."[49] Nonetheless, prostitution was officially condemned, and working girls were confined to ply their trade in certain areas of the city and required to wear distinctive outfits so they could be easily recognized. Any official tolerance disappeared after the Reformation. Martin Luther advocated abolishing prostitution on moral grounds, and Lutheran doctrine depicted prostitutes as emissaries of the devil who were sent to destroy the faith.[50]

During the early nineteenth century, prostitution was tied to the rise of English breweries: saloons controlled by the companies employed prostitutes to attract patrons and encourage them to drink. This relationship was repeated in major U.S. cities, such as Chicago, until breweries were forbidden to own the outlets that distributed their product.

Prostitution Today

Prostitution is now defined as granting nonmarital sexual access, established by mutual agreement of the prostitute, their client, and their employer (i.e., pimp) for remuneration. This definition is sexually neutral because prostitutes can be straight or gay and male or female.

Prostitutes are referred to by sociologists as "street-level sex workers" whose activities are similar to any other service industry. These conditions are usually present in a commercial sexual transaction:

- *Activity that has sexual significance for the customer.* This includes the entire range of sexual behavior, from sexual intercourse to exhibitionism, sadomasochism, oral sex, and so on.
- *Economic transaction.* Something of economic value, not necessarily money, is exchanged for the activity.
- *Emotional indifference.* The sexual exchange is simply for economic consideration. Although the participants may know each other, their interaction has nothing to do with affection.[51] Clients believe that the lack of involvement makes hiring a prostitute less of a hassle and less trouble than becoming involved in a romantic relationship.[52]

Sociologist Monica Prasad observed these conditions when she interviewed both men and women about their motivation to employ a prostitute. Although their choice was shaped by sexuality, she found that their decision was also influenced by pressure from friends to try something different and exciting, the wish for a sexual exchange free from obligations, and curiosity about the world of prostitution.

Prasad found that most customers who became "regulars" began to view prostitution merely as a "service occupation."[53]

Incidence of Prostitution

The Uniform Crime Report (UCR) indicates that about 56,000 prostitution arrests are made annually, with the gender ratio about 2 to 1 female to male.[54] The number of arrests for prostitution has declined significantly during the past 20 years; in 1995, the UCR recorded 97,000 arrests for prostitution.

How can this decline in arrests for prostitution be explained? The sexual revolution has liberalized sexuality so that men are less likely to use prostitutes because legitimate alternatives for sexuality are now available. In addition, the prevalence of sexually transmitted diseases has caused many men to avoid visiting prostitutes for fear of irreversible health hazards. While traditional forms of prostitution may be in decline, **ehooking**, that uses the Internet to shield identities and contact clients, may be responsible for a resurgence in sex for hire, especially in times of economic turmoil.[55]

Despite the decline in the arrest rate, a recent survey by the Urban Institute shows that prostitution still flourishes in major cities. The findings are set out in the Race, Culture, Gender, and Criminology feature.

Prostitution in Other Cultures

Prostitution flourishes abroad, and sex trafficking is now an important source of income for transnational criminal syndicates. In some nations such as Hungary, Switzerland, and the Netherlands, prostitution is legal and regulated by the government, while other countries punish prostitution with the death penalty. An example of the former is Germany, which has a flourishing legal sex trade. In 2002, Germany passed a new law removing the prohibition against prostitution and allowed prostitutes to obtain regular work contracts and receive health insurance. In turn, the prostitutes were required to register with the authorities and pay taxes. The city of Cologne made headlines when it introduced a sex tax that brings in more than a million dollars per year. Each prostitute in pays a tax of 150 euros per month, and sex club owners pay three euros per 90 square feet of space in their establishments. Some of the larger German brothels offer senior citizen discounts. Many sex establishments are quite lavish and an estimated 400,000 people work in the German sex trade.[56] In contrast, many Islamic countries, including Iran and Saudi Arabia, punish prostitution with death.

There is also a troubling overseas trade in prostitution in which men from wealthy countries frequent semi-regulated sex areas in needy nations such as Thailand in order to procure young girls forced or sold into prostitution—a phenomenon known as *sex tourism*. In addition to sex tours, there has also been a soaring demand for pornography, strip clubs, lap dancing, escorts, and telephone sex in developing countries.[57] To protect children from sex tourism, the Violent Crime Control and Law Enforcement Act of

prostitution The granting of nonmarital sexual access for remuneration.

ehooking Using the Internet to advertise sexual services and make contact with clients.

THE SEX TRADE IN CONTEMPORARY SOCIETY

race, culture, gender, and criminology

meredith Dank and her colleagues at the Urban Institute conducted a recent study of prostitution in contemporary society, focusing on eight US cities—Atlanta, Dallas, Denver, Kansas City, Miami, Seattle, San Diego, and Washington, D.C. Contemporary prostitution runs the gamut from high-end escort services to high school "sneaker pimps." As a result, the sex trade leaves no demographic unrepresented and circuits almost every major U.S. city. They found that the underground sex economy's worth to these cities was between $40 million and $290 million. Almost all types of commercial sex venues—massage parlors, brothels, escort services, and street- and Internet-based prostitution—existed in some degree.

Pimps

Profiting from this vast enterprise were pimps and traffickers, who took home between $5,000 and $32,833 a week. Most pimps believed that the media portrayals exaggerated their violence; some saw the term "pimp" as derogatory. They told the research team that they rarely used physical abuse for punishment, but instead relied on frequent use of psychological coercion to maintain control over their employees; they rely on their natural capacity for manipulation more than force and violence. No matter how persuasive they are, pimps are rarely the sole reason a man or woman enters the sex trade. Most sex workers had a history of social problems that began long before they met their pimp.

And not all sex workers had pimps. Some solicited protection from friends and acquaintances, some of whom had exposed them to the sex trade at a young age and influenced their decision to participate.

The Internet Is Changing the Sex Trade

Dank and her associates found that prostitution is decreasing on the street, but thriving online. Pimps and sex workers advertise on social media and sites like Backpage.com to attract customers and new employees, and to gauge business opportunities in other cities. An increasing online presence makes it both easier for law enforcement to track activity in the underground sex economy and for an offender to promote and provide access to the trade.

Dank and her colleagues also looked at the distribution of obscene material and found that explicit content involving younger victims is becoming increasingly available and graphic on the Net. Online child pornography communities frequently trade content for free; offenders often consider their participation a "victimless crime."

The Sex Trade Is Low Risk

Pimps, traffickers, and child pornography offenders said that their crimes were low-risk despite some fears of prosecution. Those who got caught for child pornography generally had low technological know-how, and multiple pimp offenders expressed that "no one

actually gets locked up for pimping," despite their own incarcerations.

What can be done to reduce or control the incidence of prostitution?

- Cross-train drug, sex, and weapons trade investigators to better understand circuits and overlaps
- Continue using federal and local partnerships to disrupt travel circuits and identify pimps
- Offer law enforcement training for both victim and offender interview techniques, including identifying signs of psychological manipulation
- Increase awareness among school officials and the general public about the realities of sex trafficking to deter victimization and entry
- Consistently enforce the laws for offenders to diminish low-risk perception
- Impose more fines for ad host websites

Critical Thinking

Rather than control or eliminate prostitution, might we be better off to legalize and regulate it? After all, it's the world's oldest profession, and it seems unlikely that it can be eliminated. What are the drawbacks to legalization?

SOURCE: Meredith Dank, Bilal Khan, P. Mitchell Downey, Cybele Kotonias, Debbie Mayer, Colleen Owens, Laura Pacifici, and Lilly Yu, *Estimating the Size and Structure of the Underground Commercial Sex Economy in Eight Major US Cities* (Washington, DC: Urban Institute, 2014), http://www.urban.org/publications/413047.html (accessed June 2014).

1994 included a provision, referred to as the Child Sexual Abuse Prevention Act, which made it a criminal offense to travel abroad for the purpose of engaging in sexual activity with a minor.[58] Despite these efforts, prosecuting sex tourists is often tricky due to the difficulty of gathering evidence of crimes that were committed in other countries and that involve minor children.[59]

Types of Prostitutes

 LO6 Distinguish between the different types of prostitutes

Several different types of prostitutes operate in the United States. As you will see, each group operates in a particular venue.

Streetwalkers Prostitutes who work the streets in plain sight of police, citizens, and customers are referred to as *hustlers, hookers,* or *streetwalkers*. Although glamorized by the Julia Roberts character in the film *Pretty Woman* (who winds up with a billionaire played by Richard Gere), streetwalkers are considered the least attractive, lowest paid, most vulnerable men and women in the profession. They are most likely to be impoverished members of ethnic or racial minorities. Many are young runaways who gravitate to major cities to find a new, exciting life and escape from sexual and physical abuse at home.[60] In the United States and abroad, streetwalkers tend to be younger than other prostitutes, start working at a younger age, and have less education. More use money from sex work for drugs and use drugs at work; they are more likely than other prostitutes to be the targets of extreme forms of violence.[61]

Streetwalkers wear bright clothing, makeup, and jewelry to attract customers, and they take their customers to hotels. The term "hooker," however, is not derived from the ability of streetwalkers to hook clients on their charms. It actually stems from the popular name given women who followed Union General "Fighting Joe" Hooker's army during the Civil War.[62] Because streetwalkers must openly display their occupation, they are likely to be involved with the police.

Research shows that there are a variety of working styles among women involved in street-based prostitution. Some are controlled by pimps who demand and receive a major share of their earnings. Others are independent entrepreneurs interested in building stable groups of steady clients. Another group might manipulate and exploit their customers and may engage in theft and blackmail.[63]

The street life is very dangerous. Teela Sanders's research on the everyday life of British sex workers found that street-level sex workers use rational decision making and learning experiences to reduce the risk of violent victimization. Experienced sex workers are able to come up with protective strategies that help them manage the risk of the profession. Most do not randomly accept all clients and eliminate those they consider dangerous or threatening. They also develop methods to deal with the emotional strain of the work as well as techniques to maintain their privacy and keep their "occupation" hidden from family and neighbors.[64]

brothel A house of prostitution, typically run by a madam who sets prices and handles "business" arrangements.

madam A woman who employs prostitutes, supervises their behavior, and receives a fee for her services.

call girls Prostitutes who make dates via the phone and then service customers in hotel rooms or apartments. Call girls typically have a steady clientele who are repeat customers.

Bar Girls B-girls, as they are also called, spend their time in bars, drinking and waiting to be picked up by customers. Although alcoholism may be a problem, B-girls usually work out an arrangement with the bartender so they are served diluted drinks or water colored with dye or tea, for which the customer is charged an exorbitant price. In some bars, the B-girl is given a credit for each drink she gets the customer to buy. It is common to find B-girls in towns with military bases and large transient populations.[65]

Brothel Prostitutes Also called bordellos, cathouses, sporting houses, and houses of ill repute, **brothels** flourished in the nineteenth and early twentieth centuries. They were large establishments, usually run by madams, that housed several prostitutes. A **madam** is a woman who employs prostitutes, supervises their behavior, and receives a fee for her services; her cut is usually 40 to 60 percent of the prostitute's earnings. The madam's role may include recruiting women into prostitution and socializing them in the trade.[66]

Brothels declined in importance following World War II. The closing of the last brothel in Texas is chronicled in the play and movie *The Best Little Whorehouse in Texas*. Today the most well-known brothels exist in Nevada, where prostitution is legal outside large population centers (one, the Mustang Ranch, has an official website that sells souvenirs!). Despite their decline, some madams and their brothels have achieved national prominence.

Call Girls The aristocrats of prostitution are **call girls**. Some charge customers thousands per night and net hundreds of thousands per year. Some gain clients through employment in escort services, and others develop independent customer lists. Many call girls come from middle-class backgrounds and service upper-class customers. Attempting to dispel the notion that their service is simply sex for money, they concentrate on making their clients feel important and attractive. Working exclusively via telephone "dates," call girls get their clients by word of mouth or by making arrangements with bellhops, cab drivers, and so on. They either entertain clients in their own apartments or visit clients' hotels and apartments. Upon retiring, a call girl can sell her "date book" listing client names and sexual preferences for thousands of dollars. Despite the lucrative nature of their business, call girls suffer considerable risk by being alone and unprotected with strangers. They often request the business cards of their clients to make sure they are dealing with "upstanding citizens."

Ehooking The technological revolution has begun to alter the world of prostitution. Instead of working with a cell phone, cyberprostitutes set up personal websites or put listings on Web boards, such as "Adult Friendfinder," that carry personals. They may use loaded phrases such as "looking for generous older man" in their self-descriptions. When contacted, they ask to exchange emails, chat online,

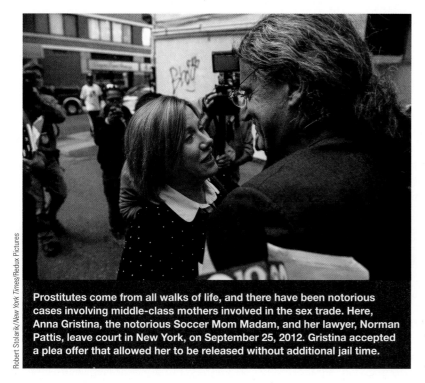

Prostitutes come from all walks of life, and there have been notorious cases involving middle-class mothers involved in the sex trade. Here, Anna Gristina, the notorious Soccer Mom Madam, and her lawyer, Norman Pattis, leave court in New York, on September 25, 2012. Gristina accepted a plea offer that allowed her to be released without additional jail time.

or make voice calls with prospective clients. They may even exchange pictures. This allows them to select whom they want to be with and avoid clients who may be threatening or dangerous. Some cyberprostitution rings offer customers the opportunity to choose women from their Internet page and then have them flown in from around the country.

Escort Services/Call House   Some escort services are fronts for prostitution rings. Both male and female sex workers can be sent out after the client calls an ad in the yellow pages. Las Vegas has more than 400 listings for adult services in the yellow pages; New York City lists more than 100. While most escort agencies deny that they are involved in prostitution and claim that their employees never provide sexual services, very few are exclusively involved in "social companionship." The Internet makes it easy to find escort services for travelers: a recent Google search found more than 5 million listings under "adult escort services."

A relatively new phenomenon, call houses, combines elements of the brothel and call girl rings. A madam receives a call from a prospective customer, and if she finds the client acceptable, she arranges a meeting between the caller and a prostitute in her service. The madam maintains a list of prostitutes who are on call rather than living together in a house. The call house insulates the madam from arrest because she never meets the client or receives direct payment.[67]

Circuit Travelers   Prostitutes known as circuit travelers move around in groups of two or three to lumber, labor, and agricultural camps. They ask the foremen for permission to ply their trade, service the whole crew in an evening, and then move on. Some circuit travelers seek clients at truck stops and rest areas. Sometimes young girls are forced to become circuit travelers by unscrupulous pimps who force them to work as prostitutes in agricultural migrant camps.[68]

Skeezers   Surveys conducted in New York and Chicago have found that a significant portion of female prostitutes have substance abuse problems, and more than half claim that prostitution is how they support their drug habits; on the street, women who barter drugs for sex are called **skeezers**. Not all drug-addicted prostitutes barter sex for drugs, but those who do report more frequent drug abuse and sexual activity than other prostitutes.[69] In a recent study, Jessica Edwards, Carolyn Halpern, and Wendee Wechsberg looked into factors that distinguish female crack cocaine users who become skeezers and found that they were more likely to be homeless and unemployed, and suffered more psychological distress than crack users who steered clear of the sex trade.[70] Other research studies found that skeezers were less likely to have a main sexual partner, and had lower self-esteem, greater depression and anxiety, poorer decision-making confidence, more hostility, less social conformity, greater risk-taking behaviors, and more problems growing up, compared to drug users who refrain from trading sex.[71]

Massage Parlors/Photo Studios   Some "working girls" are based in massage parlors and photo studios. Although it is unusual for a masseuse to offer all the services of prostitution, oral sex and manual stimulation are common. Most localities have attempted to limit commercial sex in massage parlors by passing ordinances specifying that the masseuse keep certain parts of her body covered and limiting the areas of the body that can be massaged. Some photo studios allow customers to put body paint on models before the photo sessions start.

Who Becomes a Prostitute?

At 38, Lt. Cmdr. Rebecca Dickinson had risen from the enlisted ranks in the navy to its officer corps. She started her navy career in 1986 as an aviation electronics technician,

skeezers Prostitutes who trade sex for drugs, usually crack.

attended Auburn University and the Naval Supply Corps School. After becoming a commissioned officer, Dickinson served on the support ship *Camden*, the supply ship *Santa Barbara*, and the cruiser *Bunker Hill*. She was assigned to the Naval Academy where she helped teach a leadership course. But faced with money and marital problems, Dickinson contacted the D.C. Madam Deborah Jeane Palfrey (whose client list included Senator David Vitter) and worked as a prostitute for some of the richest and most powerful men in Washington. When asked why she did it, she replied, "I needed the money, yes, I did." This desperate Navy officer, whose career was destroyed in the scandal, was paid $130 for a 90-minute session.[72]

Why do people like Lt. Cmdr. Dickinson turn to prostitution? She was a successful career officer (she was earning over $75,000 per year from the navy) motivated by an immediate financial need. However, her history is certainly not the norm: it is more common for male and female street-level sex workers to come from troubled homes marked by extreme conflict and hostility.[73] Many had experienced sexual trauma at an early age.[74] Future prostitutes were initiated into sex by family members at ages as young as 10 to 12 years; they have long histories of sexual exploitation and abuse.[75]

Sexual abuse is not the only social problem that is a forerunner to prostitution. Young women involved in prostitution also have extensive histories of substance abuse, health problems, posttraumatic stress disorder (PTSD), social stigmatization, and isolation. Often having little family support, they turn to equally troubled peers for survival: self-medicating with drugs and alcohol and self-mutilation are the norm.[76] One survey of street-level sex workers in Phoenix, Arizona, found that women engaging in prostitution have limited educational backgrounds; most did not complete high school.[77] Girls who get into "the life" report conflict with school authorities, poor grades, and an overly regimented school experience; a significant portion have long histories of drug abuse.[78] Young girls who frequently use drugs and begin using at an early age are most at risk for prostitution to support their habits.[79]

Once they get into the life, personal danger begins to escalate. Girls who may be directed toward prostitution because of childhood sexual abuse are also likely to become revictimized as adults.[80] When sociologist Jolanda Sallmann interviewed women with histories of prostitution in the Midwest, she discovered that they were hurt when people labeled and depersonalized them as "whores" or "hookers."[81] Despite their sensitivity, their lives were chaotic. The majority had suffered physical and/or sexual violence. One woman showed Sallmann the scar across her neck where her pimp literally slit her throat years earlier. Another woman told how she was kidnapped and raped by a client at knifepoint while she was still a juvenile. Despite being told that she "was gonna die," she survived the incident.

So why do women remain on the street? Even when street prostitutes try to go straight, they often return to prostitution because their limited education and lack of skills make finding employment very difficult. Without a means to support themselves and their children, they may think staying on the streets is less risky than leaving prostitution. Most self-identified themselves as struggling with a substance use problem throughout most or all of their involvement in prostitution, typically involving crack cocaine, cocaine, and/or heroin.

Considering the linkage between substance abuse and prostitution, it's not surprising that the threat of HIV and STDs is also a daily worry. Recent research directed at the health risks faced by prostitutes found that many suffer from blood-borne viral infections, sexually transmitted diseases, and mental health symptoms. Prostitution was associated with use of emergency care in women and use of inpatient mental health services for men.[82] While some take precautions, such as using or making their clients use condoms, many forego protection if their pimps and brothel owners forbid it or clients refuse to cooperate.[83] Their continuous exposure to danger and violence, both as victims and as witnesses, leads many to self-medication with illegal drugs. Prostitutes then find themselves in a vicious cycle of violence, substance abuse, and AIDS risk.[84]

Child Prostitution Child prostitution is not a recent development. For example, it was routine for poor young girls to serve as prostitutes in nineteenth-century England.[85] In contemporary society, child prostitution has been linked to sexual trauma experienced at an early age.[86] Many have long histories of sexual exploitation and abuse.[87] The early experiences with sex help teach them that their bodies have value and that sexual encounters can be used to obtain affection, power, or money. Each year in the United States, thousands of children are subjected to some form of sexual exploitation, which often begins with sexual assaults by relatives and acquaintances, such as a teacher, coach, or a neighbor. Abusers are nearly always men, many married with children.

Once they flee an abusive situation at home, kids are vulnerable to life on the streets. Some get hooked up in the sex trade, starting as strippers and lap dancers and drifting into prostitution and pornography. They remain in the trade because they have lost hope and are resigned to their fate.[88] Some meet pimps who quickly turn them to a life of prostitution and beat them if they do not make their daily financial quotas. Others who fled to the streets exchange sex for money, food, and shelter. Some have been traded between prostitution rings, and others are shipped from city to city and even trafficked overseas as prostitutes.

One danger of child prostitution is that it leaves permanent damage. The women Jolanda Sallmann interviewed shared stories of feeling permanently altered by their prostitution and substance use. Although the majority of participants were no longer using substances or exchanging sex, they could not escape their past lives. As one, B.T., explained:

> *B.T.:* The damage is done.
>
> *Interviewer:* And what do you think the damage is?
>
> *B.T.:* My spirit, my health. Um, my mind, because it's never going to leave me. I'm, you know, even when I'm not selling my body, I was still a prostitute. Before in the past, you know.
>
> *Interviewer:* What does that mean?
>
> *B.T.:* Like once a prostitute always a prostitute. I sold my body. For a long time.
>
> *Interviewer:* So you feel that that is something that doesn't leave you?
>
> *B.T.:* It doesn't go away.[89]

Controlling Prostitution

In the late nineteenth and early twentieth centuries, efforts were made to regulate prostitution in the United States through medical supervision and the licensing and zoning of brothels in districts outside residential neighborhoods.[90] After World War I, prostitution became associated with disease, and the desire to protect young servicemen from harm helped to end almost all experiments with legalization in the United States.[91] Some reformers attempted to paint pimps and procurers as immigrants who used their foreign ways to snare unsuspecting American girls into prostitution. Such fears prompted passage of the federal Mann Act (1925), which prohibited bringing women into the country or transporting them across state lines for the purposes of prostitution. Often called the "white slave act," it carried a $5,000 fine, five years in prison, or both.[92]

Today, prostitution is considered a misdemeanor, punishable by a fine or a short jail sentence. Most states punish both people engaging in prostitution and those who hire people for sexual activities. Take the Minnesota statute for example:

> Subd. 3. *Engaging in, hiring, or agreeing to hire an adult to engage in prostitution; penalties.* Whoever intentionally does any of the following may be sentenced to imprisonment for not more than 90 days or to payment of a fine of not more than $1,000, or both:
>
> (1) engages in prostitution with an individual 18 years of age or above; or
>
> (2) hires or offers or agrees to hire an individual 18 years of age or above to engage in sexual penetration or sexual contact. Except as otherwise provided in subdivision 4, a person who is convicted of violating clause (1) or (2) while acting as a patron must, at a minimum, be sentenced to pay a fine of at least $500.[93]

In practice, clients (known generically as johns) are rarely arrested, though some studies show that an arrest can deter future involvement.[94] Most law enforcement is uneven and

aims at confining illegal activities to particular areas in the city.[95] Some local police agencies concerned about prostitution have used high-visibility patrols to discourage prostitutes and their customers, undercover work to arrest prostitutes and drug dealers, and collaboration with hotel and motel owners to identify and arrest pimps and drug dealers.[96] One novel approach is "john schools," described in Exhibit 14.1, attended by clients who desire to avoid a criminal label.

Legalize Prostitution?

While most research depicts prostitutes as troubled women who have lived troubled lives, there may be a trend for some young women to enter the sex trade as a rational choice based on economic need. Changing sexual mores help reduce or eliminate the stigma attached to prostitution. There is even evidence that students turn to prostitution to help pay tuition bills.[97] One recent research study conducted in Australia found that the sex industry has become attractive to college students as a way to supplement their income during a time of reduced government aid and increasing educational costs. They view sex work as a "normal" form of employment for students seeking to obtain a higher education.[98] If this more liberal attitude toward prostitution becomes normative, should the practice become legal?

In some countries, especially in the Muslim world, prostitution carries the death penalty. In others, such as Holland, prostitutes pay taxes and belong to a union. Other countries, such as Australia, allow adults to engage in prostitution but regulate their activities, such as requiring that they must get timely health checkups. Still other countries, such as Brazil, allow women to become prostitutes but criminalize earning money from the work of prostitutes—that is, serving as a pimp. In the United States, prostitution is illegal in all states, though brothels are legal in a number of counties in Nevada (but not in Las Vegas or Reno).

Some feminists have staked out conflicting views of prostitution. One position is that women must become emancipated from male oppression and reach sexual equality. The *sexual equality view* considers the prostitute a victim of male dominance. In patriarchal societies, male power is predicated on female subjugation, and prostitution is a clear example of this gender exploitation.[99] In contrast, for some feminists, the fight for equality depends on controlling all attempts by men or women to impose their will on women. The *free choice view* is that prostitution, if freely chosen, expresses women's equality and is not a symptom of subjugation.

Advocates of both positions argue that the penalties for prostitution should be reduced (decriminalized); neither side advocates outright legalization. Decriminalization would relieve already desperate women of the additional burden of severe legal punishment. In contrast, legalization might be coupled with regulation by male-dominated justice agencies. For example, required medical examinations would mean increased governmental control over women's bodies.

Both positions have had significant influence around the world. In Sweden, feminists have succeeded in getting legislation passed that severely restricts prostitution and criminalizes any effort to buy sexual activities.[100] In contrast, Holland legalized brothels in 2001 but ordered that they be run under a strict set of guidelines.[101]

Should prostitution be legalized? In her book *Brothel*, Alexa Albert, a Harvard-trained physician who interviewed young women working at a legal brothel in Nevada, makes

AN ETHICAL DILEMMA

LEGALIZE PROSTITUTION

Those in favor of legalizing prostitution claim that removing criminal penalties would actually create safer working conditions and remove the stigma of working in the sex trade. Those who oppose legalization fear it would cause an expansion of the sex trade, which is ultimately harmful to participants, morally suspect, and ethically unacceptable.

Considering the well-known dangers the sex trade presents, can you devise an ethically acceptable plan that incorporates the best of both worlds: regulating the industry but discouraging its expansion?

a compelling case for legalization. She found that the women remained HIV-free and felt safer working in a secure environment than alone on city streets. Despite long hours and rules that gave too much profit to the owners, the women actually took pride in their work. In addition to the added security, most earned between $300 and $1,500 per day.[102]

Not all experts agree. Roger Matthews, a British criminologist, opposes legalizing prostitution. It is foolish, he claims, to view prostitution as "sex work" that should be either legalized and/or tolerated and regulated. An example is Holland's "tolerance zones," where women can engage in prostitution without fear of arrest. After studying street prostitution for more than two decades, Matthews finds that women on the street are extremely desperate, damaged, and disorganized and are at frequent risk for beatings, rape, and other forms of violence. Prostitution is, he concludes, the world's most dangerous occupation. His solution is to treat the women forced into prostitution as victims and the men who purchase their services as the criminals. He applauds Sweden's decision to make buying sexual services a crime, thus criminalizing the johns rather than the women in prostitution. Matthews believes that, sadly, when governments legalize prostitution, it leads to a massive expansion of the trade, both legal and illegal.[103]

OBSCENITY AND PORNOGRAPHY

LO7 Explain what is meant by the terms *obscenity* and *pornography*

Pornography derives from the Greek *porne*, meaning "prostitute," and *graphein*, meaning "to write." Pornography refers to the explicit portrayal of sexual subject matter in media, books, photographs, and magazines for the purpose of sexual arousal. Although material depicting pornography is typically legal, protected by the First Amendment's provision limiting governmental control of speech, most criminal codes prohibit its production, display, and sale when it crosses the line and is considered *obscene*. The term **obscenity**, derived from the Latin *caenum*, for "filth," is defined by Webster's dictionary as "deeply offensive to morality or decency … designed to incite to lust or depravity."[104]

The problem of controlling pornography centers on this definition of obscenity. Police and law enforcement officials can legally seize only material that is judged obscene. But who, critics ask, is to judge what is obscene? At one time, such novels as *Tropic of Cancer* by Henry Miller, *Ulysses* by James Joyce, and *Lady Chatterley's Lover* by D. H. Lawrence were prohibited because they were considered obscene; today they are considered works of great literary value. Thus, what is obscene today may be considered socially acceptable at a future time. After all, *Playboy* and other adult magazines, sold openly on most college campuses, display nude models in all kinds of sexually explicit poses. Though at one time they were considered "racy"; today they are relatively tame and you can buy shares on the New York Stock Exchange.

Allowing individual judgments on what is obscene makes the Constitution's guarantee of free speech unworkable. Could not anti-obscenity statutes also be used to control political and social dissent? The uncertainty surrounding this issue is illustrated by Supreme Court Justice Potter Stewart's famous 1964 statement on how he defined obscenity: "I know it when I see it." Because of this legal and moral ambiguity, a global pornography industry is becoming increasingly mainstream, currently generating many billions per year in revenue.[105] Nonetheless, while adult material has gone mainstream, courts still hold that the First Amendment was not intended to protect indecency and therefore material considered offensive and obscene can be controlled by the rule of law.[106] Most of this concern involves children and underage minors.

Child Pornography

The use of children in pornography is the most controversial and reprehensible aspect of the business. Each year more than a million children are believed to be used in pornography or prostitution, many of them runaways whose plight is exploited by adults.[107] Sexual exploitation by child pornography rings can devastate victims, causing them physical problems ranging from headaches and loss of appetite to genital soreness, vomiting, and urinary tract infections, and psychological problems including mood swings, withdrawal, edginess, and nervousness. In cases of extreme, prolonged victimization, children may lock on to the sex group's behavior and become prone to further victimization or even become victimizers themselves.

Child pornography has become widespread on the Internet. In his book, *Beyond Tolerance: Child Pornography on the Internet*, sociologist Philip Jenkins argues that activists are focused on stamping out Internet pornography but that they have not focused on its most dangerous form, kiddie porn, which sometimes involves pictures of 4- and 5-year-old girls in sexual encounters.

When an effort is made to target pedophilic websites, investigators often go in the wrong direction, failing to recognize that most sites are short-lived entities whose addresses are passed around to users. Jenkins suggests that kiddie porn is best combated by more effective law enforcement: instead of focusing on users, efforts should be directed against suppliers. He also suggests that newsgroups and bulletin boards that advertise and discuss kiddie porn be criminalized.[108]

Does Pornography Cause Violence?

An issue critical to the debate over pornography is whether viewing it produces sexual violence or assaultive behavior. This debate was given added attention when serial killer Ted Bundy claimed his murderous rampage was fueled by reading pornography.

The evidence is mixed. Some studies indicate that viewing sexually explicit material actually has little effect on sexual violence. When Neil Malamuth, Tamara Addison, and Mary Koss surveyed 2,972 male college students, they discovered that frequent use of pornography was not related to sexual aggression. There were only relatively minor differences in sexual aggression between men who report using pornography very frequently when compared to those who said they rarely used it at all. However, men who were both at high risk for sexual aggression and who were very frequent users of pornography were much more likely to engage in sexual aggression than their counterparts who consume pornography less frequently. Put simply, if a person has relatively aggressive sexual inclinations resulting from various personal and cultural factors, exposure to pornography may activate and reinforce associated coercive tendencies and behaviors. But even high levels of exposure to pornography do not turn nonaggressive men into sexual predators.[109]

How might we account for this surprisingly modest association?[110] It is possible that viewing erotic material may act as a safety valve for those whose impulses might otherwise lead them to violence. Convicted rapists and sex offenders report less exposure to pornography than a control group of nonoffenders.[111] Viewing prurient material may have the

obscenity According to current legal theory, sexually explicit material that lacks a serious purpose and appeals solely to the prurient interest of the viewer. While nudity per se is not usually considered obscene, open sexual behavior, masturbation, and exhibition of the genitals is banned in most communities.

unintended side effect of satisfying erotic impulses that otherwise might result in more sexually aggressive behavior.

While the pornography–violence link seems modest, there is more evidence that people who are predisposed to violence and exposed to material that portrays violence, sadism, and women enjoying being raped and degraded are also likely to be sexually aggressive toward female victims.[112] Individuals who are already predisposed to sexually offend may become aroused by pornography exposure and have a greater willingness to undertake sexual coercion.[113] For example, men who engage in domestic violence also tend to watch pornography and those who do are more controlling and violent.[114]

Laboratory experiments conducted by a number of leading authorities have found that men exposed to violent pornography are more likely to act aggressively and hold aggressive attitudes toward women.[115] James Fox and Jack Levin find it common for serial killers to collect and watch violent pornography. Some make their own "snuff" films starring their victims.[116] Research indicates that nations that consume the highest levels of pornography also have extremely high rape rates.[117] However, it is still not certain if such material drives people to sexual violence or whether people predisposed to sexual violence are drawn to pornography with a violent theme. A recent study by Michael Bourke and Andres Hernandez compared a group of men who had been convicted of possessing kiddie porn but had no known history with "hands-on" sexual abuse, with a second group of child

pornographers who also had been convicted of sexual offending. The goal was to determine whether the former group of offenders were "merely" collectors of child pornography who presented no actual physical risk to children. They found that the Internet offenders were significantly likely to have sexually abused a child via a hands-on contact even though they had not been caught or convicted and that they were likely to have offended against multiple victims.[118] While this research doesn't prove that viewing child pornography is a per se cause of child molesting, it does indicate there is a high correlation between viewing and acting out, regardless of whether the behavior has been detected or remains hidden.

CONNECTIONS

Chapter 5 discusses the effects of media on violence. As you may recall, while there is some evidence that people exposed to violent media will become violent themselves, the association is still being debated.

Pornography and the Law

All states and the federal government prohibit the sale and production of pornographic material. Under existing federal law, trafficking in obscenity (18 U.S.C. Sec. 1462, 1464, 1466), child pornography (18 U.S.C. Sec. 2252), harassment (18 U.S.C. Sec. 875(c)), illegal solicitation or luring of minors (18 U.S.C. Sec. 2423(b)), and threatening to injure someone (18 U.S.C. Sec. 875(c)) are all felonies punished by long prison sentences.

While these laws are designed to control obscene material, the First Amendment of the U.S. Constitution protects free speech and prohibits police agencies from limiting the public's right of free expression. This legal protection has sent the government along a torturous road in the attempt to define when material is criminally obscene and eligible for legal control. For example, the Supreme Court held in the twin cases of *Roth v. United States* and *Alberts v. California* that the First Amendment protects all "ideas with even the slightest redeeming social importance—unorthodox ideas, controversial ideas, even ideas hateful to the prevailing climate of opinion, but implicit in the history of the First Amendment is the rejection of obscenity as utterly without redeeming social importance."[119] In the 1966 case of *Memoirs v. Massachusetts*, the Supreme Court again required that for a work to be considered obscene it must be shown to be "utterly without redeeming

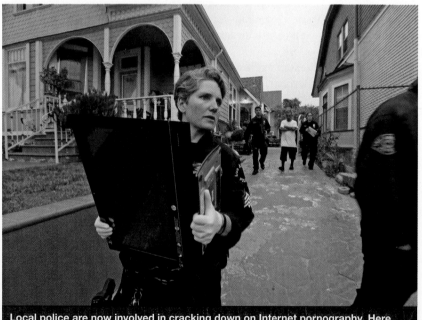

Local police are now involved in cracking down on Internet pornography. Here, Detective Shannon Geaney, with the Los Angeles Police Department Internet Crimes Against Children Task Force, carries a suspect's personal computer after law enforcement agents with a search warrant arrived at the home of Alvaro Rosas, a man considered to be California's most active trader of child pornography. Investigators found on Rosas's computer hard drive at least 1,000 videos and 200 photos with file titles that referred to children, including mention of toddlers, 4-year-olds, and preteen hardcore.

AP Images/Damian Dovarganes

social value."[120] These decisions left unclear how obscenity is defined. If a highly erotic movie tells a "moral tale," must it be judged legal even if 95 percent of its content is objectionable? Adult porn films made after the *Roth* decision alleged that they were educational so they could not be said to lack redeeming social importance. Many state obscenity cases were appealed to federal courts so judges could decide whether the films totally lacked redeeming social importance. To rectify the situation, the Supreme Court redefined its concept of obscenity in the case of *Miller v. California*:

> The basic guidelines for the trier of fact must be (a) whether the average person applying contemporary community standards would find that the work taken as a whole appeals to the prurient interest; (b) whether the work depicts or describes, in a patently offensive way, sexual conduct specifically defined by the applicable state law; and (c) whether the work, taken as a whole, lacks serious literary, artistic, political or scientific value.[121]

To convict a person of obscenity under the *Miller* doctrine, the state or local jurisdiction must specifically define obscene conduct in its statute, and the pornographer must engage in that behavior. The Court gave some examples of what is considered obscene: "patently offensive representations or descriptions of masturbation, excretory functions and lewd exhibition of the genitals." In subsequent cases, the Court overruled convictions for "offensive" or "immoral" behavior; these are not considered obscene. The *Miller* doctrine has been criticized for not spelling out how community standards are to be determined. Obviously, a plebiscite cannot be held to determine the community's attitude for every trial concerning the sale of pornography. Works that are considered obscene in Omaha might be considered routine in New York, but how can we be sure? To resolve this dilemma, the Supreme Court articulated in *Pope v. Illinois* a reasonableness doctrine: a work is not obscene if a reasonable person applying objective standards would find that the material in question has at least some social value:[122]

> The ideas that a work represents need not obtain majority approval to merit protection, and the value of that work does not vary from community to community based on the degree of local acceptance it has won. The proper inquiry is not whether an ordinary member of any given community would find serious value in the allegedly obscene material, but whether a reasonable person would find such value in the material, taken as a whole.[123]

The Law and Child Pornography   Because the use of children in pornography is considered so serious, kiddie porn is usually a separate legal category that involves either the creation or reproduction of materials depicting minors engaged in actual or simulated sexual activity ("sexual exploitation of minors") or the publication or distribution of obscene, indecent, or harmful materials to minors.[124]

Computer-generated images and other high-tech innovations now make it possible for pornographers to create and distribute virtual images of a child engaging in sexual activity that is almost impossible to distinguish from an actual child. Fearing the proliferation of kiddie porn over the Internet, Congress enacted the Child Pornography Prevention Act of 1996 (CPPA) that outlawed sexually related material that used or *appeared to use* children under 18 engaging in sexual conduct. In *Ashcroft v. The Free Speech Coalition*, the Supreme Court struck down sections of the CPPA relating to virtual kiddie porn: sexually related material in which an actual child appears is illegal, but possessing "virtual" pornography is legal. The Court reasoned that real children are not harmed with a virtual child.

In response to the Court's decision, Congress passed the PROTECT Act of 2003 (Prosecutorial Remedies and Other Tools to End the Exploitation of Children), which outlawed virtual kiddie porn that makes it almost impossible to distinguish the difference between a real child and a morphed or created image.[125] The Supreme Court reviewed this law in a 2008 case, *United States v. Williams*, which concerned Michael Williams, who was convicted in federal district court of "pandering" (promoting) child pornography under the PROTECT Act. At trial, the district court held that the government can legitimately outlaw the pandering of material as child pornography, even if the images are computer generated, if they were being offered to someone who *thought they were buying images of real children*. The Court noted that offers to engage in illegal transactions are excluded from First Amendment protection, so that the "speech" of an individual claiming to be in possession of child pornography is therefore not protected by the First Amendment. The Court also stated that the law did not violate due process because its requirements were clear and could be understood by courts, juries, and potential violators.[126] In sum, someone who offers to sell child pornography can be found guilty of a crime even if the images they are selling are fake or computer generated. It is the intent to sell that is the crime; no real images are necessary to be convicted.

Controlling Pornography

Sex for profit predates Western civilization. Considering its longevity, there seems to be little evidence that it can be controlled or eliminated by legal means alone. In 1986, the Attorney General's Commission on Pornography advocated a strict law enforcement policy to control obscenity, directing that "the prosecution of obscene materials that portray sexual violence be treated as a matter of special urgency."[127] Since then, there has been a concerted effort by the federal government to prosecute the distribution of obscenity. Law enforcement has been so fervent that industry members have filed suit claiming they are the victims of a "moral crusade" by right-wing zealots.[128]

Although politically appealing, controlling sex for profit is difficult because of the public's desire to purchase sexually related material and services. Law enforcement crusades may not necessarily obtain the desired effect. A get-tough policy could make sex-related goods and services scarce, driving up prices and making their sale even more desirable and profitable. Going after national distributors may help decentralize the adult movie and photo business and encourage local rings to expand their activities, for example, by making and marketing videos as well as still photos or distributing them through computer networks.

An alternative approach has been to restrict the sale of pornography within acceptable boundaries. Some municipal governments have tolerated or even established adult entertainment zones in which obscene material can be openly sold.[129] While these efforts are applauded, the Internet has become a favored method of delivering adult material and one that defies easy regulation since distribution can be international in scope.

The topic of Internet porn will be discussed once more in Chapter 15 as a type of cybercrime.

SUBSTANCE ABUSE

On February 2, 2014, the Academy Award–winning actor Philip Seymour Hoffman was found dead in his Manhattan apartment of what the medical examiner's office ruled was an accidental overdose of "acute mixed drug intoxication, including heroin, cocaine, benzodiazepines, and amphetamines.[130] His death followed that of other stars, including Heath Ledger, who also died in his New York apartment in 2008, a victim of an accidental overdose of six drugs—painkillers and sedatives—namely hydrocodone, diazepam, temazepam, alprazolam, doxylamine (more commonly called Vicodin, Valium, Xanax, Restoril, Unisom), and Oxycodone.[131]

CONNECTIONS

The debate over dangerous prescription drug use has been intensified because they are now easily obtained on the Web. Many suppliers do not require prescriptions. For more on this issue, see the discussion in Chapter 15 on obtaining dangerous drugs via the Internet.

The death of these two great actors is a stark reminder of the dangers of substance abuse, a social problem that spans every segment of society. Large urban areas are beset by drug-dealing gangs, drug users who engage in crime to support their habits, and alcohol-related violence. Rural areas are important staging centers for the shipment of drugs across the country and are often the production sites for synthetic drugs and marijuana farming.[132]

Despite the scope of the drug problem, some still view it as another type of victimless public order crime. There is great debate over the legalization of drugs and the control of alcohol. Some consider drug use a private matter and drug control another example of government intrusion into people's private lives. Furthermore, legalization could reduce the profit of selling illegal substances and drive suppliers out of the market.[133] Others see these substances as dangerous, believing that the criminal activity of users makes the term "victimless" nonsensical. Still another position is that the possession and use of all drugs and alcohol should be legalized but that the sale and distribution of drugs should be heavily penalized. This would punish those profiting from drugs and would enable users to be helped without fear of criminal punishment.

When Did Drug Use Begin?

The use of chemical substances to change reality and to provide stimulation, relief, or relaxation has gone on for thousands of years. The opium poppy was first cultivated more than 5,000 years ago and was used by the Persians, Sumerians, Assyrians, Babylonians, and Egyptians. Users discovered the bliss that could be achieved by smoking the extract derived from crushing the seed pods; the poppy yielded a pleasurable, peaceful feeling throughout the body. Known as the Hul Gil or "plant of joy," its use spread quickly around the Fertile Crescent.[134] The ancient Greeks knew and understood the problem of drug use. At the time of the Crusades, the Arabs were using marijuana. In the Western Hemisphere, natives of Mexico and South America chewed coca leaves and used "magic mushrooms" in their religious ceremonies.[135] Drug use was also accepted in Europe well into the twentieth century. Recently uncovered pharmacy records circa 1900 to 1920 showed sales of cocaine and heroin solutions to members of the British royal family; records from 1912 show that Winston Churchill, then a member of Parliament, was sold a cocaine solution while staying in Scotland.[136]

In the early years of the United States, opium and its derivatives were easily obtained. Opium-based drugs were used in various patent medicine cure-alls. Morphine was used extensively to relieve the pain of wounded soldiers in the Civil War. By the turn of the twentieth century, an estimated 1 million U.S. citizens were opiate users.[137]

Several factors precipitated the current stringent U.S. drug laws. The rural religious creeds of the nineteenth century—especially those of the Methodists, Presbyterians, and Baptists—emphasized individual human toil and self-sufficiency while designating the use of intoxicating substances as an unwholesome surrender to the evils of urban morality. Religious leaders were thoroughly opposed to the use and sale of narcotics. The medical literature of the late 1800s began to designate the use of morphine and opium as a vice, a habit, an appetite, and a disease. Nineteenth- and early twentieth-century police literature described drug users as habitual criminals. Moral crusaders in the nineteenth century defined drug use as evil and directed that local and national entities should outlaw the sale and possession of drugs. Some well-publicized research efforts categorized drug use as highly dangerous.[138] Drug use was also associated with the foreign immigrants recruited to work in factories and mines; they brought with them their national drug habits. Early antidrug legislation appears to be tied to prejudice against immigrating ethnic minorities.[139]

After the Spanish-American War of 1898, the United States inherited Spain's opium monopoly in the Philippines. Concern over this international situation, along with the domestic issues just outlined, led the U.S. government to participate in the First International Drug Conference, held in Shanghai in 1908, and a second one at The Hague in 1912. Participants in these two conferences were asked to strongly oppose free trade in drugs. The international pressure, coupled with a growing national concern, led to the passage of the antidrug laws discussed here.

Alcohol and Its Prohibition

The history of alcohol and the law in the United States has also been controversial and dramatic. At the turn of the century, a drive was mustered to prohibit the sale of alcohol. This **temperance movement** was fueled by the belief that the purity of the U.S. agrarian culture was being destroyed by the growth of the city. Urbanism was viewed as a threat to the lifestyle of the majority of the nation's population, then living on farms and in villages. The forces behind the temperance movement were such lobbying groups as the Anti-Saloon League led by Carrie Nation, the Women's Christian Temperance Union, and the Protestant clergy of the Baptist, Methodist, and Congregationalist faiths.[140] They viewed the growing city, filled with newly arriving Irish, Italian, and Eastern European immigrants, as centers of degradation and wickedness. The propensity of these ethnic people to drink heavily was viewed as the main force behind their degenerate lifestyle. The eventual prohibition of the sale of alcoholic beverages brought about by ratification of the Eighteenth Amendment in 1919 was viewed as a triumph of the morality of middle- and upper-class Americans over the threat posed to their culture by the "new Americans."[141]

Prohibition failed. It was enforced by the Volstead Act, which defined intoxicating beverages as those containing one-half of 1 percent, or more, alcohol.[142] What doomed Prohibition? One factor was the use of organized crime to supply illicit liquor. Also, the law made it illegal only to sell alcohol, not to purchase it; this cut into the law's deterrent capability. Finally, despite the work of Eliot Ness and his "Untouchables," law enforcement agencies were inadequate to control illegal alcohol sales, and some officials were bribed and corrupted by bootleggers.[143] Eventually, in 1933, the Twenty-First Amendment to the Constitution repealed Prohibition, signaling the end of the "noble experiment."

How Much Drug Use Is There Today?

How extensive is the use of illegal drugs today? One main source, the National Survey on Drug Use and Health (NSDUH) conducted by the U.S. Department of Health and Human Services, contacts more than 67,000 people in order to obtain information on nine categories of illicit drug use: use of marijuana, cocaine, heroin, hallucinogens (LSD, PCP, peyote,

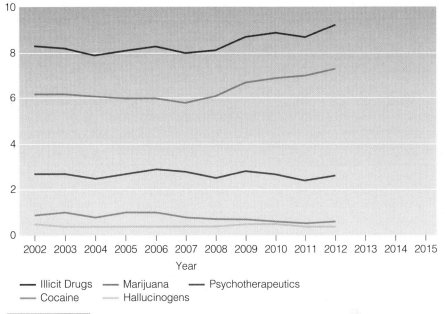

Percent Using in Past Month

FIGURE 14.1 Trends in Illicit Drug Use

SOURCE: Results from the 2012 National Survey on Drug Use and Health: Summary of National Findings (2013), http://www.samhsa.gov/data/NSDUH/2012SummNatFindDetTables/NationalFindings/NSDUHresults2012.htm#fig2.1 (accessed June 2014).

mescaline, psilocybin mushrooms, and "Ecstasy" [MDMA]), inhalants (nitrous oxide, amyl nitrite, cleaning fluids, gasoline, spray paint, other aerosol sprays, and glue), as well as the non-medical use of prescription-type pain relievers, tranquilizers, stimulants, and sedatives. What does the most recent (2012) tell us about substance abuse in the United States?

- An estimated 24 million Americans aged 12 or older were current (past month) illicit drug users. This means that about 9 percent of the population aged 12 or older use illegal drugs on a routine basis.
- While drug use has stabilized, it is now higher than it was a decade ago.
- Marijuana was the most commonly used illicit drug, with 19 million or 79 percent of all current illicit drug users.
- There were 1.6 million current cocaine users aged 12 or older, comprising 0.6 percent of the population.
- There are almost 700,000 heroin users in the U.S. Heroin usage has been rising significantly during the past decade.
- More than 1 million people have recently used hallucinogens, a number that has been stable for a decade.

As Figure 14.1 shows, drug use has increased over the past decade (2002–2012), but almost the entire increase is reflected in the use of marijuana.

temperance movement An effort to prohibit the sale of liquor in the United States that resulted in the passage of the Eighteenth Amendment to the Constitution in 1919, which prohibited the sale of alcoholic beverages.

Monitoring the Future   Another way of measuring drug use trends is to survey large populations of the nation's youth, a group known for indulging in illegal drug and alcohol abuse. The most important source of data is the annual Monitoring the Future (MTF) survey conducted by the Institute for Social Research at the University of Michigan.

Chapter 2 used data from the Monitoring the Future study to track self-reported delinquent behavior. The MTF is an ongoing study of the behaviors, attitudes, and values of American secondary school students, college students, and young adults. About 50,000 8th, 10th, and 12th grade students are surveyed (12th graders since 1975, and 8th and 10th graders since 1991).

Using self-report data from a large sample of 8th, 10th, and 12th graders, the MTF study has been tracking drug use among high school students. As Figure 14.2 shows, the MTF surveys found that drug use peaked in 1981 (66 percent of seniors reported using drugs) before a long and gradual decline to 41 percent in 1992—the low point. After 1992 the proportion of youth who used some illegal substance rose considerably, reaching a recent high point of 55 percent in 1999, when it began another decline. In 2013, the proportions of students indicating any use of an illicit drug in the prior 12 months are 15 percent of 8th graders, 32 percent of 10th graders, and 40 percent of seniors.

By the time they finished high school, half of America's high school seniors will have tried an illicit drug, and 4 in 10 have used it in just the past year. Like the National Survey, MTF finds that marijuana is by far the most prevalent of the many illicitly used drugs. On a positive note, high school students continue to reduce cigarette smoking and have shunned designer drugs such as "bath salts" (whose effect is similar to amphetamines) and synthetic marijuana.

Alcohol Abuse

Alcohol abuse is another significant national problem.[144] According to the latest data gathered by the National Institute on Alcohol Abuse and Alcoholism, almost 90 percent of people aged 18 or older report that they drank alcohol at some point in their lifetime; 71 percent report that they drank in the past year; 56 percent reported that they drank in the past month. While imbibing is not a significant problem per se, binge drinking (having five or more alcoholic drinks on the same occasion) can be, and 25 percent of all people surveyed reported that they engage in binge drinking; 7 percent reported that they binged at least once a week. An estimated 17 million Americans have an alcohol disorder; each year in the United States nearly 80,000 people die from alcohol-related causes.

Costs of Substance Abuse

Considering how many people indulge in illicit drug and alcohol abuse, it should not be surprising that the costs of drug and alcohol abuse are quite significant. The National

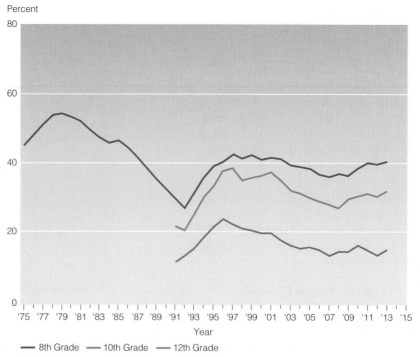

FIGURE 14.2   Trends in Annual Prevalence of an Illicit Drug Use Index

SOURCE: University of Michigan, Michigan News, "American Teens More Cautious about Using Synthetic Drugs," Fig. 3, http://www.monitoringthefuture.org//pressreleases/13drugpr_complete.pdf (accessed June 2014).

TABLE 14.1

Costs of Drug and Alcohol Abuse

	Health Care	Overall
Tobacco	$96 billion	$193 billion
Alcohol	$30 billion	$235 billion
Illicit drugs	$11 billion	$193 billion

SOURCE: National Institute on Drug Abuse, 2014, http://www.drugabuse.gov/related-topics/trends-statistics (accessed June 2014).

Institute on Drug Abuse estimates that health and other costs directly related to substance abuse are now $600 billion per year (see Table 14.1).

In addition to these, enforcement costs add additional billions. Recent research compiled by the Cato Institute, a Washington, D.C., think tank, estimates that legalizing drugs would save roughly $41 billion per year in government enforcement expenditure. State and local governments could save about $25 billion per year; $16 billion would accrue to the federal government.[145]

What Causes Substance Abuse?

LO8 Assess the causes of substance abuse

What causes people to abuse substances? Although there are many different views on the causes of drug use, most can be characterized as seeing the onset of an addictive career as being either an environmental or a personal matter.

Subcultural View Those who view drug abuse as having an environmental basis concentrate on lower-class addiction. Because a disproportionate number of drug abusers are poor, the onset of drug use can be tied to such factors as racial prejudice, devalued identities, low self-esteem, poor socioeconomic status, and the high level of mistrust, negativism, and defiance found in impoverished areas. Residents feel trapped in a cycle of violence, drug abuse, and despair.[146] Youths in these disorganized areas may join peers to learn the techniques of drug use and receive social support for their habit. Research shows that peer influence is a significant predictor of drug careers that actually grow stronger as people mature.[147] Drug use splits some communities into distinct groups of relatively affluent abstainers and desperately poor abusers.[148]

Psychological View There is evidence linking substance abuse to psychological deficits such as impaired cognitive functioning, personality disturbance, and emotional problems that can strike people in any economic class.[149]

Research on the psychological characteristics of drug abusers does in fact reveal the presence of a significant degree of personal pathology. Studies have found that addicts suffer personality disorders characterized by low frustration tolerance, anxiety, and fantasies of omnipotence. Many addicts exhibit psychopathic or sociopathic behavior characteristics, forming what is called an addiction-prone personality.[150] Statistics from the most recent National Survey on Drug Use and Health support this hypothesis: more than 8 million adults in the United States have both a mental and substance use disorder.[151] However, only 8 percent of people receive treatment for both conditions, and 54 percent receive no treatment at all.[152]

What is the connection between psychological disorder and drug abuse? Drugs may help people deal with unconscious needs and impulses and relieve dependence and depression. People may turn to drug abuse as a form of self-medication in order to reduce the emotional turmoil of adolescence, deal with troubling impulses, or cope with traumatic life experiences such as institutional child abuse (kids who were sexually or physically abused in foster care, mental institutions, juvenile detention centers, day care centers, etc.).[153] Survivors of sexual assault and physical abuse in the home have also been known to turn to drug and alcohol abuse as a coping mechanism.[154] Depressed people may use drugs as an alternative to more radical solutions to their pain such as suicide.[155] Kids who are self-conscious about their body image or who have poor self-esteem may turn to drugs to ease psychological turmoil.[156]

The Criminology in Action feature looks at the substance abuse involvement of people with severe mental disorders.

Genetic Factors Research shows that substance abuse may have a genetic basis.[157] For example, a number of studies comparing alcoholism among identical twins and fraternal twins have found that the degree of concordance (both siblings behaving identically) is twice as high among the identical twin groups.[158]

Taken as a group, studies of the genetic basis of substance abuse suggest that people whose parents were alcoholic or drug dependent have a greater chance of developing a problem than the children of nonabusers, and this relationship occurs regardless of parenting style or the quality of the parent–child relationship.[159] However, not all children of abusing parents become drug dependent themselves, suggesting that even if drug abuse is heritable, environment and socialization must play some role in the onset of abuse.[160]

Social Learning Social psychologists suggest that drug abuse may also result from observing parental drug use. Parental drug abuse begins to have a damaging effect on children as young as 2 years old, especially when parents manifest drug-related personality problems such as depression or poor impulse control.[161] Children whose parents abuse drugs are more likely to have persistent abuse problems than the children of nonabusers.[162]

People who learn that drugs provide pleasurable sensations may be the most likely to experiment with illegal substances; a habit may develop if the user experiences lower

SUBSTANCE ABUSE AND PSYCHOSIS

most estimates suggest that people diagnosed with mood or anxiety disorders are about twice as likely as the general population to also suffer from a substance use disorder. Studies exploring the link between substance use disorders and other mental illnesses have typically not included people with severe psychotic illnesses.

In a recent study, 9,142 people diagnosed with schizophrenia, schizoaffective disorder, or bipolar disorder with psychotic features were matched with 10,195 controls according to geographic region. Mental disorder diagnoses were confirmed using the Diagnostic Interview for Psychosis and Affective Disorder (DI-PAD), and the controls were screened to verify the absence of schizophrenia or bipolar disorder in themselves or close family members. The DI-PAD was also used for all participants to determine substance use rates.

Compared to the controls, people with severe mental illness were about 4 times more likely to be heavy alcohol users (four or more drinks per day), 3.5 times more likely to use marijuana regularly (21 times per year), and 4.6 times more likely to use other drugs at least 10 times in their lives. The greatest differences were seen with tobacco, with patients with severe mental illness 5 times more likely to be daily smokers. This is of concern because smoking is the leading cause of preventable death in the United States. The association between mental issues and substance abuse was constant when controlling for gender, age, and race.

Previous research has shown that people with schizophrenia have a shorter life expectancy than the general population, and chronic cigarette smoking has been suggested as a major contributing factor to higher morbidity and mortality from malignancy as well as cardiovascular

and respiratory diseases. These new findings indicate that the rates of substance use in people with severe psychosis may be underestimated, highlighting the need to improve the understanding of the association between substance use and psychotic disorders so that both conditions can be treated effectively.

Critical Thinking

What is the connection between psychosis and substance abuse? Is it possible that people with severe mental disorders use drugs and alcohol to self-medicate and relieve their symptoms? What other reasons might there be for the connection?

SOURCE: Sarah M. Hartz, Carlos N. Pato, Helena Medeiros, Patricia Cavazos-Rehg, Janet L. Sobell, James A. Knowles, Laura Bierut, and Michele T. Pato, "Comorbidity of Severe Psychotic Disorders with Measures of Substance Use," *JAMA Psychiatry* 71 (2014): 248–254.

---

anxiety, fear, and tension levels.[163] Having a history of family drug and alcohol abuse has been found to be a characteristic of violent teenage sexual abusers.[164] Heroin abusers report an unhappy childhood that included harsh physical punishment and parental neglect and rejection.[165]

Problem Behavior Syndrome (PBS) For many people, substance abuse is just one of many problem behaviors.[166] Longitudinal studies show that drug abusers are maladjusted, alienated, and emotionally distressed and that drug use is only one among many social problems.[167] Having a deviant lifestyle begins early in life and is punctuated with criminal relationships, family history of substance abuse, educational failure, and alienation. Crack cocaine use has been linked to sexual abuse as children and social isolation as adults.[168] There is robust support for the interconnection of problem drinking and drug abuse in adolescence and delinquency, precocious sexual behavior, school failure, running away, homelessness, family conflict, and other similar social problems.[169] In adulthood, people who manifest substance abuse problems also exhibit a wide variety of other social and legal problems.[170]

Rational Choice Not all people who abuse drugs do so because of personal pathology. Some may use drugs and alcohol because they want to enjoy their effects: get high, relax, improve creativity, escape reality, and increase sexual responsiveness. Claire Sterk-Elifson's research on middle-class drug-abusing women shows that most were introduced by friends in the context of "just having some fun."[171]

Substance abuse, then, may be a function of the rational but mistaken belief that drugs can benefit the user. The decision to use drugs involves evaluations of personal consequences (such as addiction, disease, and legal punishment) and the expected benefits of drug use (such as peer approval, positive affective states, heightened awareness, and relaxation). Adolescents may begin using drugs because they believe their peers expect them to do so.[172]

Is There a Drug Gateway?

Some experts believe that, regardless of its cause, most people fall into drug abuse slowly, beginning with alcohol and then following with marijuana and more serious drugs as the need for a more powerful high intensifies. A number of research efforts have confirmed this **gateway model**. In a now classic study, James Inciardi, Ruth Horowitz, and Anne Pottieger found a clear pattern of adult involvement in adolescent drug abuse. Kids on crack started their careers with early experimentation with alcohol at age 7, began getting drunk at age 8, had alcohol with an adult present by age 9, and became regular drinkers by the time they were 11 years old.[173] Drinking with an adult present, presumably a parent, was a significant precursor of future substance abuse and delinquency. "Adults who gave children alcohol," they argue, "were also giving them a head start in a delinquent career."[174]

Other research efforts support this view when they find that the most serious drug users have a history of recreational drug and alcohol abuse.[175] Kids who begin using alcohol and other drugs become involved in increasing levels of deviant behavior as they mature.[176] One analysis by Cesar Rebellon and Karen Van Gundy found evidence that marijuana users are up to five times more likely to escalate their drug abuse and try cocaine and heroin than nonusers.[177] In sum, while most marijuana smokers do not become hard drug users, some do, and the risk of using dangerous substances may be increased by first engaging in recreational drugs.

The drug gateway vision is popular, but not all research efforts find that users progress to ever-more potent drugs, and some show that, surprisingly, many hard-core drug abusers never actually smoked pot or used alcohol.[178] And although many American youths have tried marijuana, few actually progress to crack or heroin abuse.[179]

Types of Drug Users and Abusers

The general public often groups all drug users together without recognizing that there are many varieties, ranging from adolescent recreational drug users to adults who run large smuggling operations.[180]

Adolescents Who Distribute Small Amounts of Drugs
Some dealers began their involvement in the drug trade by using and distributing small amounts of drugs; they do not commit any other serious criminal acts. Some start out as "stash dealers" who sell drugs to maintain a consistent access to drugs for their own consumption; their customers are almost always personal acquaintances, including friends and relatives.[181] They are insulated from the legal system because their activities rarely result in apprehension and sanction.

Adolescents Who Frequently Sell Drugs
A small number of adolescents, most often multiple-drug users or heroin or cocaine users, are high-rate dealers who bridge the gap between adult drug distributors and the adolescent user. Frequent dealers often have adults who "front" for them—that is, loan them drugs to sell without upfront cash. The teenagers then distribute the drugs to friends and acquaintances, returning most of the proceeds to the supplier while keeping a commission for themselves. Frequent dealers are more likely to sell drugs in public and can be seen in known drug user hangouts in parks, schools, or other public places. Deals are irregular, so the chances of apprehension are slight.

Teenage Drug Dealers Who Commit Other Delinquent Acts
A more serious type of drug-involved youth comprises those who use and distribute multiple substances and also commit both property and violent crimes; many are gang members.[182] Although these youngsters make up about 2 percent of the teenage population, they commit 40 percent of the robberies and assaults and about 60 percent of all teenage felony thefts and drug sales.

These youths are frequently hired by older dealers to act as street-level drug runners. Each member of a crew of three to twelve boys will handle small quantities of drugs, perhaps three bags of heroin, which are received on consignment and sold on the street; the supplier receives 50 to 70 percent of the drug's street value. The crew members also act as lookouts, recruiters, and guards. Between drug sales, the young dealers commit robberies, burglaries, and other thefts.[183]

Adolescents Who Cycle In and Out of the Justice System
Some drug-involved youths are failures at both dealing and crime. They do not have the savvy to join gangs or groups and instead begin committing unplanned, opportunistic crimes that increase their chances of arrest. They are heavy drug users, which both increases apprehension risk and decreases their value for organized drug distribution networks. Drug-involved "losers" can earn a living steering customers to a seller in a "copping" area, "touting" drug availability for a dealer, or acting as a lookout. However, they are not considered trustworthy or deft enough to handle drugs or money. They may bungle other criminal acts, which solidifies their reputation as undesirable.

Drug-Involved Youth Who Continue to Commit Crimes as Adults
Although about two-thirds of substance-abusing youths continue to use drugs after they reach adulthood, about half desist from other criminal activities. Those who persist in both substance abuse and crime as adults exhibit a wide variety of social and developmental problems. Some evidence also exists that these drug-using persisters have low nonverbal IQs and poor physical coordination.

Outwardly Respectable Adults Who Are Top-Level Dealers
A few outwardly respectable adult dealers sell large quantities of drugs to support themselves in

gateway model An explanation of drug abuse that posits that users begin with a more benign drug (alcohol or marijuana) and progress to more potent drugs.

high-class lifestyles. These dealers are often indistinguishable from other young professionals. Upscale dealers seem to drift into dealing from many different walks of life. Some begin as campus dealers who seem just like other students.[184] Frequently they are drawn from professions and occupations that are unstable, have irregular working hours, and accept drug abuse. Some use their business skills and drug profits to get into legitimate enterprises or illegal scams. Others drop out of the drug trade because they are the victims of violent crime committed by competitors or disgruntled customers; a few wind up in jail or prison.

Smugglers Smugglers import drugs into the United States. They are generally men, middle-aged or older, who have strong organizational skills, established connections, capital to invest, and a willingness to take large business risks. Smugglers are a loosely organized, competitive group of individual entrepreneurs. There is a constant flow in and out of the business as some sources become the target of law enforcement activities, new drug sources become available, older smugglers become dealers, and former dealers become smugglers.

Adult Predatory Drug Users Who Are Frequently Arrested Many users who begin abusing substances in early adolescence continue in drugs and crime in their adulthood. Getting arrested, doing time, using multiple drugs, and committing predatory crimes are a way of life for them. They have few skills, did poorly in school, and have long criminal records. The threat of conviction and punishment has little effect on their criminal activities. These "losers" have friends and relatives involved in drugs and crime. They specialize in robberies, burglaries, thefts, and drug sales. They filter in and out of the justice system and begin committing crimes as soon as they are released. In some populations, at least one-third of adult males are involved in drug trafficking and other criminal acts well into their adulthood.[185]

If they make a "big score," perhaps through a successful drug deal, they may significantly increase their drug use. Their increased narcotics consumption then destabilizes their lifestyle, destroying family and career ties. When their finances dry up, they may become *street junkies*, people whose traditional lifestyle has been destroyed, who turn to petty crime to maintain an adequate supply of drugs. Cut off from a stable source of quality heroin, not knowing from where their next fixes or the money to pay for them will come, looking for any opportunity to make a buck, getting sick or "jonesing," being pathetically unkempt and unable to maintain even the most primitive routines of health or hygiene, street junkies live a very difficult existence. Because they are unreliable and likely to become police informants, street junkies pay the highest prices for the poorest quality heroin; lack of availability increases their need to commit habit-supporting crimes.[186]

Adult Predatory Drug Users Who Are Rarely Arrested Some drug users are "winners." They commit hundreds of crimes each year but are rarely arrested. On the streets, they are known for their calculated violence. Their crimes are carefully planned and coordinated. They often work with partners and use lookouts to carry out the parts of their crimes that have the highest risk of apprehension. These "winners" are more likely to use recreational drugs, such as coke and pot, than the more addicting heroin or opiates. Some become high-frequency users and risk apprehension and punishment. But for the lucky few, their criminal careers can stretch for up to 15 years without interruption by the justice system. These users are sometimes referred to as *stabilized junkies* who have learned the skills needed to purchase and process larger amounts of heroin. Their addiction enables them to maintain normal lifestyles, although they may turn to drug dealing to create contacts with drug suppliers. They are employable, but earning legitimate income does little to reduce their drug use or dealing activities.[187]

Less Predatory Drug-Involved Adult Offenders Most adult drug users are petty criminals who avoid violent crime. These occasional users are people just beginning their addiction, who use small amounts of narcotics, and whose habit can be supported by income from conventional jobs; narcotics have relatively little influence on their lifestyles.[188] They are typically high school graduates and have regular employment that supports their drug use. They usually commit petty thefts or pass bad checks. They stay on the periphery of the drug trade by engaging in such acts as helping addicts shoot up, bagging drugs for dealers, operating shooting galleries, renting needles and syringes, and selling small amounts of drugs. These petty criminal drug users do not have the stomach for a life of hard crime and drug dealing. They violate the law in proportion to the amount and cost of the drugs they are using. Pot smokers have a significantly lower frequency of theft violations than daily heroin users, whose habit is considerably more costly.

Outwardly Respectable Adults Who Are Frequent Users Some drug users continue their activities into their adulthood, while others may initiate drug use as part of a new lifestyle developed in adulthood. These users may be successful college graduates who become caught up in the club scene in major cities and get involved in recreational drug use. Surveys of urban young adults find that almost 40 percent report usage of at least one club drug.[189]

Another element of the outwardly respectable adult drug abuser uses illegal substances to enhance their professional careers. The sports world has been rocked with stories of famed athletes who have admitted taking performance-enhancing drugs. Recent research shows that professional ballet dancers, a group not usually suspected to be drug involved, routinely use banned substances to improve performance.[190]

The number of outwardly respectable drug users is expected to rise as the aging baby boomers, who grew up in the drug culture, both live longer and continue to use banned substances. Evidence shows that this group, who may amount to 70 million people by 2030, will continue to use illegal substances in amounts unheard of for people of their age and lifestyle.[191]

Drug-Involved Female Offenders Women who are drug-involved offenders constitute a separate type of substance abuser. Although women are far less likely than men to use addictive drugs, research conducted by the National Center on Addiction and Substance Abuse (CASA) at Columbia University found that 15 million girls and women use illicit drugs or abuse controlled prescription drugs, 32 million smoke cigarettes, and 6 million are alcohol abusers and alcoholics. Substance abuse is nondiscriminatory and affects all women—rich, poor, young, old, urban, rural, professional and homemaker.[192]

Though infrequently violent criminals, women who abuse substances are more likely to get involved in prostitution and low-level drug dealing; a few become top-level dealers. Many are pregnant or are already mothers, and because they share needles, they are at high risk of contracting AIDS and passing the HIV virus to their newborn children. They maintain a high risk of victimization. One study of 171 women using crack cocaine found that since initiating crack use, 62 percent of the women reported suffering a physical attack and 32 percent suffered rape; more than half were forced to seek medical care for their injuries.[193]

Drugs and Crime

One of the main reasons for the criminalization of particular substances is the assumed association between drug abuse and crime. People who use illicit drugs are more likely to engage in criminal activity; people involved in criminal activity are more likely to use drugs. While drug use does not turn people violent, it does increase the frequency of criminal activity.[194] Substance abuse appears to be an important precipitating factor in a variety of criminal acts, especially income-generating crimes such as burglary.[195]

Numerous self-report studies have examined the criminal activity of drug users. As a group, they show that people who take drugs also have extensive involvement in crime.[196] Youths who abuse alcohol are also the most likely to engage in violence during their life course; violent adolescents report histories of alcohol abuse; adults with long histories of drinking are also more likely to report violent offending patterns.[197]

Arrestee Data ADAM II is a federal data collection program that shows drug use patterns among arrestees in five U.S. cities: Atlanta, Chicago, Denver, New York, and Sacramento. In each of these areas, data are collected from adult male arrestees, through voluntary interviews and drug tests, within 48 hours of arrest. The sample of almost 2,000 people was drawn from all adult males arrested, not just those arrested on drug charges.

What do the data show about the association between drug use and crime? Marijuana remained the drug most often detected in arrestees, ranging from 37 percent of arrestees testing positive in Atlanta to 58 percent testing positive in Chicago. In three of the five sites, over half of the adult male arrestees tested positive for marijuana. While cocaine and crack remain highly associated with arrest, they continued to show a significant decline in use everywhere. The percentage of arrestees testing positive for cocaine has declined significantly: in 2000, 50 percent of arrestees tested positive in Chicago, declining to about 19 percent today; in New York, 52 percent of arrestees tested positive for cocaine and crack in 2000, today about 25 percent.

Heroin abuse dipped significantly (about 50 percent decline) in New York and Chicago since 2000 but has risen in the other three jurisdictions. Methamphetamine was a significant problem in Sacramento (40 percent testing positive) and Denver (13 percent testing positive). These data show that a high percentage of arrestees test positively for illicit drugs and that there are significant regional differences and trends in drug use. Despite these variations and trends, the drug–crime connection is strongly supported by the ADAM data.[198]

Correctional Surveys Another indication of a drug–crime connection is found in correctional surveys that disclose that many convicted criminals are lifelong substance abusers.[199] The most recent surveys show that the drug use rate among parolees is double that of the general population. Similarly, about 24 percent of adults on probation reported drug abuse, more than double the rate than the general population.[200]

Researchers at CASA found that approximately 85 percent of current inmates could benefit from drug abuse treatment. CASA estimates that 1.5 million of the current 2.3 million prison inmates meet the clinical criteria for substance abuse or addiction. Another 458,000 inmates have a history of substance abuse and either:

- Were under the influence of alcohol or other drugs at the time of their crime
- Committed their offense to get money to buy drugs
- Were incarcerated for an alcohol or drug law violations

The CASA study also found that alcohol and drugs are significant factors in the commission of many crimes. Alcohol and drugs are involved in the following:

- 78 percent of violent crimes
- 83 percent of property crimes
- 77 percent weapon offenses
- 77 percent of probation or parole violations[201]

These data seem to show a powerful connection between drug abuse, crime, and punishment.

Is There a Drug–Crime Connection? It is of course possible that most criminals are not actually drug users but that police are more likely to apprehend muddle-headed substance abusers than clear-thinking abstainers. A second, and probably more plausible, interpretation is that most criminals are in fact substance abusers.

Although the drug–crime connection is powerful, the true relationship is still uncertain because many users have had a history of criminal activity before the onset of their substance abuse. It is possible that:

- Chronic criminal offenders begin to abuse drugs and alcohol *after* they have engaged in crime; that is, crime causes drug abuse.
- Substance abusers turn to a life of crime to support their habits; that is, the economics of drug abuse causes crime. Employed drug users don't commit crime, only those who need money to support their habits.
- Drug use and crime co-occur in individuals; that is, both crime and drug abuse are caused by some other common factor. For example, risk takers may abuse drugs and also commit crime.[202] Individuals with psychotic behavioral disorders may use drugs to self-medicate and are also prone to crime. Psychosis may bring on both drug abuse and criminality; particularly those who also abuse drugs and alcohol tend to engage in higher levels of violence than individuals with other forms of mental illness.[203]
- Drug users engage in activities that involve them with peers who encourage them to commit crime or support their criminal activity.[204] Kids who join gangs are more likely later to abuse substances and commit crime.
- Drug abusers face social problems that lead them to crime. They are more likely to drop out of school, be underemployed, engage in premarital sex, and become unmarried parents.[205] Social problems and not drug use are the cause of crime.

Considering these scenarios, it is still impossible to make a definitive statement such as "drugs cause crime."[206]

In sum, while there is no conclusive evidence that taking drugs turns otherwise law-abiding citizens into criminals, there are indications that people who commit crime also use drugs significantly more than the average citizen. As addiction levels increase, so too do the frequency and seriousness of criminality. Even if the crime rate of drug users were actually half that reported in the research literature, users would be responsible for a significant portion of the total criminal activity in the United States.

Drugs and the Law

The federal government first initiated legal action to curtail the use of some drugs early in the twentieth century. In 1906, the Pure Food and Drug Act required manufacturers to list the amounts of habit-forming drugs in products on the labels but did not restrict their use. However, the act prohibited the importation and sale of opiates except for medicinal purposes. In 1914, the Harrison Narcotics Tax Act restricted importation, manufacture, sale, and dispensing of narcotics. It defined *narcotic* as any drug that induces sleep and relieves pain, such as heroin, morphine, and opium. The act was revised in 1922 to allow importation of opium and coca (cocaine) leaves for qualified medical practitioners. The Marihuana Tax Act of 1937 required registration and payment of a tax by all who imported, sold, or manufactured marijuana. Because marijuana was classified as a narcotic, those registering would also be subject to criminal penalty.

In later years, other federal laws were passed to clarify existing drug statutes and revise penalties. For example, the Boggs Act of 1951 provided mandatory sentences for violating federal drug laws. The Durham-Humphrey Act of 1951 made it illegal to dispense barbiturates and amphetamines without a prescription. The Narcotic Control Act of 1956 increased penalties for drug offenders. In 1965, the Drug Abuse Control Act set up stringent guidelines for the legal use and sale of mood-modifying drugs, such as barbiturates, amphetamines, LSD, and any other "dangerous drugs," except narcotics prescribed by doctors and pharmacists. Illegal possession was punished as a misdemeanor and manufacture or sale as a felony. In 1970, the Comprehensive Drug Abuse Prevention and Control Act set up unified categories of illegal drugs and associated penalties with their sale, manufacture, or possession. The law gave the U.S. attorney general discretion to decide in which category to place any new drug.

Since then, various federal laws have attempted to increase penalties imposed on drug smugglers and limit the manufacture and sale of newly developed substances. For example, the 1984 Controlled Substances Act set new, stringent penalties for drug dealers and created five categories of narcotic and non-narcotic substances subject to federal laws.[207] The Anti-Drug Abuse Act of 1986 again set new standards for minimum and maximum sentences for drug offenders, increased penalties for most offenses, and created a new drug penalty classification for large-scale offenses (such as trafficking in more than 1 kilogram of heroin), for which the penalty for a first offense was 10 years to life in prison.[208] With President George H. W. Bush's endorsement, Congress passed the Anti-Drug Abuse Act of 1988, which created a coordinated national drug policy under a "drug czar," set treatment and prevention priorities, and, symbolizing the government's hard-line stance against drug dealing, imposed the death penalty for drug-related killings.[209]

For the most part, state laws mirror federal statutes. Some states now apply extremely heavy penalties for selling or distributing dangerous drugs, involving long prison sentences of up to 25 years. The main disconnect is in the sale and possession of marijuana, which a number of states have either legalized or decriminalized. In response, the federal government pledged not to enforce laws restricting marijuana in these states.[210]

Drug Control Strategies

 LO9 Compare and contrast the different methods of drug control

Substance abuse remains a major social problem in the United States. Politicians looking for a safe campaign issue can take advantage of the public's fear of drug addiction by calling for a war on drugs even when drug usage is stable or in decline. Can these efforts pay off? Can illegal drug use be eliminated or controlled?

A number of different drug control strategies have been tried with varying degrees of success. Some aim to deter drug use by stopping the flow of drugs into the country, apprehending and punishing dealers, and cracking down on street-level drug deals. Others focus on preventing drug use by educating potential users to the dangers of substance abuse (convincing them to "say no to drugs") and by organizing community groups to work with the at-risk population in their area. Still another approach is to treat known users so they can control their addictions. Some of these efforts are discussed here.

Source Control One approach to drug control is to deter the sale and importation of drugs through the systematic apprehension of large-volume drug dealers, coupled with the enforcement of strict drug laws that carry heavy penalties. This approach is designed to capture and punish known international drug dealers and deter those who are considering entering the drug trade. A major effort has been made to cut off supplies of drugs by destroying overseas crops and arresting members of drug cartels in Central and South America, Asia, and the Middle East, where many drugs are grown and manufactured. The federal government has been in the vanguard of encouraging exporting nations to step up efforts to destroy drug crops and prosecute dealers. Translating words into deeds is a formidable task. Drug lords are willing and able to fight back through intimidation, violence, and corruption when necessary.

Transnational gangs (see Chapter 13) are actively involved in the drug trade and are immune from prosecution because they are active in areas where the United States has little influence.[211] War and terrorism make source control strategies problematic. Similarly, cocaine production is surging in Peru's remote tropical valleys, helping to make it a contender to surpass Colombia as the world's largest exporter of cocaine. One reason is that the antigovernment Shining Path guerrillas are competing with outside groups from Mexico and Colombia to control the cocaine trade. Despite government efforts, Peruvian traffickers export almost 300 tons of cocaine each year.[212]

Interdiction Strategies Law enforcement efforts have also been directed at intercepting drug supplies as they enter the country. Border patrols and military personnel using sophisticated hardware have been involved in massive interdiction efforts; many impressive multimillion-dollar seizures have been made. Government sources indicate that cocaine movement into the United States has declined significantly in the past few years. One reason: more than 500 metric tons of cocaine are now being seized by law enforcement agents each year.[213]

While law enforcement efforts are impressive, U.S. borders are so vast and unprotected that total interdiction is impossible. Drug importers have dug cross-border tunnels to evade detection, use go-fast boats and constantly changing transshipment points, use an army of "drug mules" to trans-ship narcotics, and may be bribing border guards to look the other way when drug shipments pass through their checkpoints.[214]

If all importation were shut down, homegrown marijuana and laboratory-made drugs, such as "ice," LSD, and PCP, could become the drugs of choice. Even now, their easy availability and relatively low cost are increasing their popularity among the at-risk population.

On February 22, 2014, Joaquin "El Chapo" Guzman, the head of Mexico's Sinaloa cartel, is shown being escorted to a helicopter in Mexico City following his capture in the beach resort town of Mazatlan. Despite such captures, drug cartels flourish, making billions each year. Would legalization cut down on their profits and power? Or is that the wrong way to reduce drug crime?

AP Images/Eduardo Verdugo

Law Enforcement Strategies Local, state, and federal law enforcement agencies have been actively fighting against drugs. One approach is to direct efforts at large-scale drug rings. The long-term consequence has been to decentralize drug dealing and has encouraged new groups to become major suppliers. Asian, Latin American, and Jamaican groups, motorcycle clubs, and local gangs, such as the Crips and Bloods, are all now involved in large-scale dealing. Colombian syndicates have established cocaine distribution centers on every continent, and Mexican organizations are responsible for large methamphetamine shipments to U.S., Russian, Turkish, Italian, Nigerian, Chinese, Lebanese, and Pakistani heroin trafficking syndicates, which are now competing for dominance.

Police can also target, intimidate, and arrest street-level dealers and users in an effort to make drug use so much of a hassle that consumption is cut back and the crime rate reduced. Some departments use reverse stings, in which undercover agents pose as dealers to arrest users who approach them for a buy.

In terms of weight and availability, there is still no commodity more lucrative than illegal drugs. They cost relatively little to produce and provide large profit margins to dealers and traffickers. It is difficult for law enforcement agencies to counteract the inducement of drug profits. When large-scale drug busts are made, supplies become scarce and market values increase, encouraging more people to enter the drug trade. There are also suspicions that a displacement effect occurs: stepped-up efforts to curb drug dealing in one area or city simply encourage dealers to seek out friendlier territory.[215]

Punishment Strategies Even if law enforcement efforts cannot produce a general deterrent effect, the courts may achieve the required result by severely punishing known drug dealers and traffickers. A number of initiatives have made the prosecution and punishment of drug offenders a top priority. State prosecutors have expanded their investigations into drug importation and distribution and created special prosecutors to focus on drug dealers. Once convicted, drug dealers can get very long sentences.

However, these efforts often have their downside. Defense attorneys consider delay tactics to be sound legal maneuvering in drug-related cases. Courts are so backlogged that prosecutors are anxious to plea bargain. The consequence of this legal maneuvering is that about 25 percent of people convicted on federal drug charges are granted probation or some other form of community release. Even so, prisons have become jammed with inmates, many of whom were involved in drug-related cases. Many drug offenders sent to prison do not serve their entire sentences because they are released in an effort to relieve prison overcrowding. The mean sentence for drug trafficking is 55 months, but the actual time served is 24 months or about half of the original sentence.[216]

It is unlikely that the public would approve of a drug control strategy that locks up large numbers of traffickers; research indicates that the public already believes drug trafficking penalties are too harsh (while supporting the level of punishment for other crimes).[217] And some critics are disturbed because punishment strategies seem to have a disproportionate effect on minority group members and the impoverished. Some have gone as far as suggesting that government agencies are either ignoring or covering up the toll harsh drug penalties have on society's disadvantaged because it is politically expedient to be a tough defender of the nation's moral climate.[218]

Community Strategies Another type of drug control effort relies on the involvement of local community groups to lead the fight against drugs. Representatives of various local government agencies, churches, civic organizations, and similar institutions are being brought together to create drug prevention and awareness programs.

Citizen-sponsored programs attempt to restore a sense of community in drug-infested areas, reduce fear, and promote conventional norms and values.[219] These efforts can be classified into one of four distinct categories:[220]

- *Law enforcement-type efforts.* These may include block watches, cooperative police–community efforts, and citizen patrols. Some of these citizen groups are nonconfrontational: they simply observe or photograph dealers, write down their license plate numbers, and then notify police. On occasion, telephone hotlines have been set up to take anonymous tips on drug activity. Other groups engage in confrontational tactics that may even include citizens' arrests. Area residents have gone as far as contracting with private security firms to conduct neighborhood patrols.
- *Using the civil justice system to harass offenders.* Landlords have been sued for owning properties that house drug dealers, and neighborhood groups have scrutinized drug houses for building code violations. Information acquired from these various sources is turned over to local authorities, such as police and housing agencies, for more formal action.
- *Community-based treatment efforts.* Some of these programs utilize citizen volunteers who participate in self-help support programs. Some, such as Narcotics Anonymous or Cocaine Anonymous, have more than 1,000 chapters nationally. Other programs provide youths with martial arts training, dancing, and social events as an alternative to the drug life.
- *Enhancing the quality of life, improving interpersonal relationships, and upgrading the neighborhood's physical environment.* Activities might include the creation of drug-free school zones (which encourage police to keep drug dealers away from the vicinity of schools) and consciousness-raising efforts such as demonstrations and marches to publicize the drug problem and build solidarity among participants.

These community crime prevention efforts seem appealing, but there is little conclusive evidence that they are an effective drug control strategy. Some surveys indicate that most residents do not participate in programs. There is also evidence that community programs work better in stable, middle-income areas than in those that are crime ridden and disorganized.[221] Although these findings are discouraging, some studies do find that on occasion deteriorated areas can sustain successful antidrug programs.[222] Future evaluations of community control efforts should determine whether they can work in the most economically depressed areas.

Education Strategies   According to this view, substance abuse would decline if kids could be taught about the dangers of drug use. The most widely known drug education program, Drug Abuse Resistance Education (D.A.R.E.), is an elementary school course designed to give students the skills for resisting peer pressure to experiment with tobacco, drugs, and alcohol. Dennis Rosenbaum and his associates found that it had only a marginal impact on student drug use and attitudes.[223] A longitudinal study by psychologist Donald Lynam and his colleagues found that D.A.R.E. had no effect on students' drug use at any time.[224] These evaluations caused D.A.R.E. to revise its curriculum and it is now aimed at older students and relies more on having them question their assumptions about drug use than on listening to lectures on the subject.

Drug-Testing Strategies   Drug testing of students, private employees, government workers, and criminal offenders is believed to deter substance abuse. In the workplace, employees are tested to enhance on-the-job safety and productivity. In some industries, such as mining and transportation, drug testing is considered essential because abuse can pose a threat to the public.[225] Mandatory drug-testing programs in government and industry have become routine. The federal government requires employee testing in regulated industries such as nuclear energy and defense contracting. About 4 million transportation workers are subject to testing.

Drug testing is also part of the federal government's Drug-Free Workplace Program, which has the goal of improving productivity and safety. Employees most likely to be tested include presidential appointees, law enforcement officers, and people in positions of national security.

Criminal defendants are now routinely tested at all stages of the justice system, from arrest to parole. The goal is to reduce criminal behavior by detecting current users and curbing their abuse. Can such programs reduce criminal activity? Two evaluations of pretrial drug-testing programs found little evidence that monitoring defendants' drug use influenced their behavior.[226]

Schools have adopted drug testing of students and there is some evidence that random tests can reduce drug use among youth. Those who favor student testing believe it may also help improve the learning environment in schools by diminishing the culture of drugs without sacrificing school morale.[227]

Drug Treatment Strategies   A number of approaches are taken to treat known users, getting them clean of drugs and alcohol, and thereby reducing the at-risk population. One approach rests on the assumption that each user is an individual and successful treatment must be geared to the using patterns and personality of the individual offenders in order to build a sense of self.[228] Some programs have placed abusers in regimens of outdoor activities and wilderness training to create self-reliance and a sense of accomplishment.[229] Others focus on problem-solving skills, helping former and current addicts deal with their real-world issues.[230] Providing supportive housing for formerly homeless drug addicts may also lead to better access to medical care, food, and job opportunities—all of which result in lower levels of addiction.[231]

More intensive efforts use group therapy approaches relying on group leaders who have been substance abusers; through such sessions users get the skills and support to help them reject social pressure to use drugs. These programs are based on the Alcoholics Anonymous approach, which holds that users must find within themselves the strength to stay clean and that peer support from those who understand their experiences can help them achieve a drug-free life.

Some detoxification efforts use medical procedures to wean patients from the more addicting drugs to others, such as methadone, that can be more easily regulated. Methadone is a drug similar to heroin, and addicts can be treated at clinics where they receive methadone under controlled conditions. However, methadone programs have been undermined because some users sell their methadone on the black market and others supplement their dosages with illegally obtained heroin. Other programs utilize drugs such as Naxalone, which counter the effects of narcotics and ease the trauma of withdrawal.[232] Others, such as Naltrexone, are used in conjunction with counseling and social support to help people who have already terminated their substance abuse and help them avoid drinking or using drugs. Naltrexone works by blocking the effects of heroin or other opioids at their receptor sites. Medications have also been developed to ease withdrawal symptoms and help the transition to a drug-free life. Other therapeutic programs attempt to deal with the psychological causes of drug use. Hypnosis, aversion therapy (getting users to associate drugs with unpleasant sensations, such as nausea), counseling, biofeedback, and other techniques are often used.

Some treatment programs are delivered on an outpatient basis while others rely on residential care. Which approach is better is still being debated. A stay in a residential program may stigmatize people as addicts and while in treatment they may be introduced to other users with whom they will associate after release. Users do not often enter these programs voluntarily and have little motivation to change.[233]

The best treatment for drug use may be a continuum of care that includes a customized treatment

EXHIBIT 14.2

Effective Treatment Approaches

Medications

Medications can be used to help with different aspects of the treatment process.

- *Withdrawal.* Medications offer help in suppressing withdrawal symptoms during detoxification. Patients who go through medically assisted withdrawal but do not receive any further treatment show drug abuse patterns similar to those who were never treated.
- *Treatment.* Medications can be used to help reestablish normal brain function and to prevent relapse and diminish cravings. Medications are now available for treating opioids (heroin, morphine), tobacco (nicotine), and alcohol addiction; other are being developed for treating stimulant (cocaine, methamphetamine) and cannabis (marijuana) addiction. A significant problem: many addicts are polydrug users, requiring multiple medications.

Behavioral Treatments

Behavioral treatments help patients engage in the treatment process, modify their attitudes and behaviors related to drug abuse, and increase healthy life skills. These treatments can also enhance the effectiveness of medications and help people stay in treatment longer. Outpatient behavioral treatment encompasses a wide variety of programs for patients who visit a clinic at regular intervals. Most of the programs involve individual or group drug counseling. Some programs also offer other forms of behavioral treatment such as:

- *Cognitive-behavioral therapy*, which seeks to help patients recognize, avoid, and cope with the situations in which they are most likely to abuse drugs

- *Multidimensional family therapy*, which was developed for adolescents with drug abuse problems—as well as their families—and addresses a range of influences on their drug abuse patterns and is designed to improve overall family functioning
- *Motivational interviewing*, which capitalizes on the readiness of individuals to change their behavior and enter treatment
- *Motivational incentives* (contingency management), which uses positive reinforcement to encourage abstinence from drugs

Residential treatment programs can also be very effective, especially for those with more severe problems.

- *Therapeutic communities* (TCs) are highly structured programs in which patients remain at a residence, typically for 6 to 12 months. TCs differ from other treatment approaches principally in their use of the community—treatment staff and those in recovery—as a key agent of change to influence patient attitudes, perceptions, and behaviors associated with drug use.
- Patients in TCs may include those with relatively long histories of drug addiction, involvement in serious criminal activities, and seriously impaired social functioning. TCs are now also being designed to accommodate the needs of women who are pregnant or have children. The focus of the TC is on the resocialization of the patient to a drug-free, crime-free lifestyle.

SOURCE: National Institute on Drug Abuse, "DrugFacts: Treatment Approaches for Drug Addiction," http://www.drugabuse.gov/publications/drugfacts/treatment-approaches-drug-addiction (accessed June 2014).

regimen—addressing all aspects of an individual's life, including medical and mental health services—and follow–up options (e.g., community- or family-based recovery support systems) that can be crucial to a person's success in achieving and maintaining a drug-free lifestyle.[234] Exhibit 14.2 covers the most commonly used and relevant treatment strategies. However, relatively few drug-dependent people actually receive the treatment efforts they so desperately need. Many people who need treatment are unaware or in denial. And even those who could be helped soon learn that there are simply more users who need treatment than there are beds in treatment facilities. Many facilities are restricted to users whose health insurance will pay for short-term residential care; when their insurance coverage ends, patients are often released, even though their treatment is incomplete.

Supporters of treatment argue that many addicts are helped by intensive inpatient and outpatient treatment. As one District of Columbia program shows, clients who complete treatment programs are less likely to use drugs than those who drop out.[235] Although such data support treatment strategies, it is also possible that completers are motivated individuals who would have stopped using drugs even if they had not been treated.

In order to aid in dispensing treatment, state jurisdictions have developed specialized drug courts. These are described in the Policy and Practice in Criminology feature.

Employment Programs There have been a number of efforts to provide vocational rehabilitation for drug abusers. One approach is the supported work program, which typically involves job-site training, ongoing assessment, and job-site intervention. Rather than teach work skills in a classroom, support programs rely on helping drug abusers deal with real work settings. Other programs that have merit provide training to overcome the barriers to employment and improve work skills, including help with motivation, education, experience, the job market, job-seeking skills, and personal issues.[236]

DRUG COURTS

the mission of drug courts is to stop the abuse of alcohol and other drugs and related criminal activity by offenders. Drug courts handle cases involving drug-addicted offenders through an extensive supervision and treatment program. In exchange for successful completion of the program, the court may dismiss the original charge, reduce or set aside a sentence, offer some lesser penalty, or offer a combination of these. The aim is to place nonviolent first offenders into intensive treatment programs rather than in jail or prison.

The drug court movement began in 1989, when the Dade County (Miami) Circuit Court developed an intensive, community-based treatment, rehabilitation, and supervision program for felony drug defendants designed to reduce recidivism rates. There are now more than 2,000 drug courts in operation with hundreds more being planned or developed.

Drug court diverts nonviolent, substance abusing offenders from prison and jail into treatment. By increasing direct supervision of offenders, coordinating public resources, and expediting case processing, drug courts can help break the cycle of criminal behavior, alcohol and drug use, and incarceration. The most recent research indicates that drug court reduces crime by lowering rearrest and conviction rates, improving substance abuse treatment outcomes, and reuniting families, and also produces measurable cost benefits.

Drug courts address the overlap between the public health threats of drug abuse and crime: crimes are often drug related; drug abusers are frequently involved with the criminal justice system. Drug courts provide an ideal setting to address these problems by linking the justice system with health services and drug treatment providers while easing the burden on the already overtaxed correctional system.

Are Drug Courts Effective?

The U.S. government has a great deal of confidence in drug courts and points to the most recent research on programs around the nation, which taken in sum confirms that drug courts are successful. There are numerous success stories. One study of nine adult drug courts in California reported that rearrest rates over a four-year period were 29 percent for drug court clients (and only 17 percent for those completing the program) as compared to 41 percent for similar drug offenders who did not participate in a drug court program. Another study of four adult drug courts in Massachusetts found that drug court participants were 13 percent less likely to be rearrested, 34 percent less likely to be reconvicted, and 24 percent less likely to be reincarcerated than probationers who had been carefully matched to the drug court participants. These evidence-based evaluations support the utility of the drug court concept.

Not Everyone Agrees

While this research is reassuring, drug courts have been criticized by the influential Drug Policy Alliance, a nonprofit organization dedicated to reforming the nation's drug laws. According to the Alliance, drug courts often "cherry pick" people expected to do well anyway, many of whom are in drug court because of a petty drug law violation, including marijuana. As a result, drug courts do not typically divert people from lengthy prison terms. Because they focus on low-level offenses, even positive results for individual participants translate into little public safety benefit to the community. Treatment in the community, whether voluntary or probation-supervised, often produces better results. The Alliance also finds that drug courts leave many people worse off than if they had received drug treatment outside the criminal justice system, had been left alone, or even had been conventionally sentenced. The successes represent only some of those who pass through drug courts and only a tiny fraction of people arrested. One reason is that drug court participants spend more days in jail *while in drug court* than if they had been conventionally sentenced, but participants deemed "failures" may actually face longer sentences than those who did not enter drug court in the first place (often because they lost the opportunity to plead to a lesser charge). The participants, they conclude, who stand the best chance of succeeding in drug courts are those without a drug problem, while those struggling with compulsive drug use are more likely to end up incarcerated.

Critical Thinking

1. Are drug courts inherently coercive? Should drug users be forced to go into treatment?
2. Are drug treatment programs doomed to failure because there are so many different types of drug abusers, with entirely different motivations?

SOURCES: C. West Huddleston III, Douglas Marlowe, and Rachel Casebolt, *Painting the Current Picture: A National Report Card on Drug Courts and Other Problem-Solving Court Programs in the United States* (Washington, DC: National Drug Court Institute, Bureau of Justice Assistance, 2008), http://www.ndci.org/sites/default/files/ndci/PCPII1_web%5B1%5D.pdf (accessed June 2014); Drug Policy Alliance, "Drug Courts Are Not the Answer: Toward a Health-Centered Approach to Drug Use," 2011, http://www.drugpolicy.org/sites/default/files/Drug%20Courts%20Are%20Not%20the%20Answer_Final2.pdf (accessed June 2014).

policy and practice in criminology

Control Strategy	Main Focus	Problems/Issues
Source control	Destroy overseas crops and drug labs	Drug profits hard to resist; drug crops in hostile nations are off limits
Interdiction	Seal borders; arrest drug couriers	Extensive U.S. borders hard to control
Law enforcement	Police investigation and arrest of dealers	New dealers are recruited to replace those in prison
Punishment	Deter dealers with harsh punishments	Crowded prisons promote bargain justice
Community programs	Help community members deal with drug problems on the local level	Relies on community cohesion and efficacy
Drug education	Teach kids about the harm of taking drugs	Evaluations do not show programs are effective
Drug testing	Threaten employees with drug tests to deter use	Evaluations do not show drug testing is effective; people cheat on tests
Treatment	Use of therapy to get people off drugs	Expensive, requires motivation; clients associate with other users
Employment	Provide jobs as an alternative to drugs	Requires that former addicts become steady employees
Legalization	Decriminalize or legalize drugs	Political hot potato; danger of creating more users

Does providing work experiences help reduce drug use? In one of the most comprehensive studies of this issue, Christopher Uggen and Sarah Shannon interviewed young adults leaving drug treatment to find out whether receiving employment helps reduce their substance abuse levels. They found that while finding employment did not actually reduce their dependence on cocaine and/or heroin, it did correlate favorably on reducing their involvement in crime. The rate of robbery and burglary arrests fell by approximately 46 percent for the users who found meaningful work. The implication is that drugs themselves are not a cause of crime; rather, it's the lack of income experienced by most users that accounts for their involvement in criminal activity.[237]

Concept Summary 14.1 summarizes the various drug control efforts.

Drug Legalization

LO10 State the arguments for and against legalizing drugs

In terms of weight and availability, there is still no commodity more lucrative than illegal drugs. They cost relatively little to produce and provide large profit margins to dealers and traffickers. At the current average street price of $170 per gram in the United States, a metric ton of pure cocaine is worth more than $150 million; cutting it and reducing purity can double or triple the value.[238] With that kind of profit to be made, can any strategy, whether it be treatment or punishment oriented, reduce the lure of drug trafficking? The futility of drug control efforts is illustrated by the fact that despite massive long-term efforts the price of illegal narcotics such as crack cocaine and heroin has drifted downward as supplies become more plentiful. Considering these problems, some commentators have called for the legalization or decriminalization of restricted drugs.

Despite the massive effort to control drugs through prevention, deterrence, education, and treatment strategies, the fight against substance abuse is always difficult. There are enormous profits involved in the drug trade, and few treatment efforts have been successful. There is no uniform method of drug control; some use enforcement and punishment and others rely on treatment and rehabilitation. While the former approach requires drug users to be secretive and discreet in order to avoid detection, the latter demands openness and receptivity to treatment.[239] Some experts believe that the only effective way to deal with the drug problem is through legalization of most drugs and decriminalization of drug offenses. Legalization is warranted because the use of mood-altering substances is customary in almost all human societies; people have always wanted—and will find ways of obtaining—psychoactive drugs.[240]

The Drug Policy Alliance, a national organization dedicated to ending the war against drugs, cites a number of reasons why the drug war should end and drugs decriminalized:

- Since the war on drugs began, the Supreme Court has sent a consistent message that when it comes to fighting drug crime, privacy and personal liberties take a back seat. In most drug-related cases brought before the Court, the majority has favored scaling back constitutional protections, clearing the way for drug policies that infringe on our rights to free speech, religious expression, and protection from unreasonable searches. Police now routinely search individuals without cause, raid homes on flimsy evidence, and engage in racial profiling. Employers, schools, and hospitals may conduct suspicionless drug testing.

- Public health problems like HIV and hepatitis C are all exacerbated by draconian laws that keep users in hiding and restrict their access to clean needles. And when they get caught and go to prison their families suffer: children of inmates are at risk of educational failure, joblessness, addiction, and delinquency. People suffering from cancer, AIDS, and other debilitating illnesses are regularly denied access to their medicine or even arrested and prosecuted for using medical marijuana.

- Policies that exclude and discriminate against people with a conviction are numerous and varied and have effectively created a permanent second-class status for millions of Americans. Given the systemic racism inherent in the drug war, these lifelong exclusions inequitably affect individuals and communities of color. For example, a drug arrest can result in even a legal resident's deportation.

- A drug arrest can result in denying child custody, voting rights, employment, business loans, trade licensing, student aid, and even public housing and other public assistance. Relative to the crime being committed, the punishments for drug law violations are unjustifiably harsh and cause more harm than the drug itself.

- The drug war creates racial discrimination by law enforcement and disproportionate drug war misery suffered by communities of color. Although rates of drug use and selling are comparable across racial lines, people of color are far more likely to be stopped, searched, arrested, prosecuted, convicted, and incarcerated for drug law violations than are whites. The mass criminalization of people of color, particularly young African American men, is as profound a system of racial control as the Jim Crow laws were in this country until the mid-1960s.

- The drug war is responsible for hundreds of billions of wasted tax dollars and misallocated government spending, as well as devastating human costs that far outweigh the damage caused by drugs alone. The war on drugs has also driven the drug trade underground, creating a violent illicit market that is responsible for far too many lost lives and broken communities. Organized crime, gangs, and drug cartels have the most to gain financially from prohibition, and these profits can easily be funneled into arms smuggling, violence, and corruption. The devastation wrought by Mexican cartels in

particular has made it far too costly to continue with a failed prohibition strategy.

The DPA is not the only organization to note the expense created by the so-called war on drugs. According to Cato Institute researchers Jeffrey Miron and Katherine Waldock, drug control is now costing $40 billion a year. Not only would legalization save the government enforcement money, it would yield tax revenue of $46.7 billion annually, assuming legal drugs were taxed at rates comparable to those on alcohol and tobacco. Approximately $8.7 billion of this revenue would result from legalization of marijuana and $38 billion from legalization of other drugs.[241]

If drugs were legalized, the argument goes, price and distribution could be controlled by the government. This would reduce addicts' cash requirements, so crime rates would drop because users would no longer need the same cash flow to support their habits. Drug-related deaths would decline because government control would reduce needle sharing and the spread of AIDS. Legalization would also destroy the drug-importing cartels and gangs. Because drugs would be bought and sold openly, the government would reap a tax windfall both from taxes on the sale of drugs and from income taxes paid by drug dealers on profits that have been part of the hidden economy. Of course, drug distribution would be regulated, like alcohol, keeping drugs away from adolescents, public servants such as police and airline pilots, and known felons.

The Consequences of Legalization Critics claim the legalization approach might have the short-term effect of reducing the crime rate, but it might also have grave social consequences. Legalization would increase the nation's rate of drug usage, creating an even larger group of nonproductive, drug-dependent people who must be cared for by the rest of society.[242] If drugs were legalized and freely available, drug users might significantly increase their daily intake. In countries like Iran and Thailand, where drugs are cheap and readily available, the rate of narcotics use is quite high. Historically, the availability of cheap narcotics has preceded drug-use epidemics, as was the case when British and American merchants sold opium in nineteenth-century China. Furthermore, if the government tried to raise money by taxing legal drugs, as it now does with liquor and cigarettes, that might encourage drug smuggling to avoid tax payments, creating a black market supply chain; these "illegal" drugs might then fall into the hands of adolescents.

There are also health concerns. Because women may become dependent on cocaine or heroin if legalized, the number of drug-dependent babies could begin to match or exceed the number delivered with fetal alcohol syndrome.[243] Drunk-driving fatalities, which today number about 12,000 per year, might be matched by deaths due to driving under the influence of pot or crack. And although distribution would be regulated, it is likely that adolescents would have the same opportunity to obtain potent drugs as they now have to obtain alcoholic beverages.

Decriminalization or legalization of controlled substances is unlikely in the near term, but further study is warranted. What effect would a policy of partial decriminalization (for example, legalizing small amounts of marijuana) have on drug use rates? Would a get-tough policy help to "widen the net" of the justice system and actually deepen some youths' involvement in substance abuse? Can society provide alternatives to drugs that will reduce teenage drug dependency?[244] The answers to these questions have proven elusive.

SUMMARY

LO1 Clarify the association between law and morality

Public order crimes are acts considered illegal because they conflict with social policy, accepted moral rules, and public opinion. There is usually great debate over public order crimes. Some charge that they are not really crimes at all and that it is foolish to legislate morality. Others view such morally tinged acts as prostitution, gambling, and drug abuse as harmful and therefore subject to public control.

LO2 Interpret what is meant by the term *social harm*

According to the theory of social harm, acts become crimes when they cause injury and produce harm to others. However, some dangerous activities are not considered crimes and others that do not appear harmful are criminalized. For example, it is legal to sell cigarettes and alcohol though they may be more dangerous than illicit drugs. Sports cars are legal though more people are killed in traffic accidents than from drug overdoses.

LO3 List examples of the activities of moral crusaders

Moral crusaders seek to shape the law toward their own way of thinking. These moral entrepreneurs go on moral crusades to take on such issues as prayer in school, gun ownership, abortion, and the distribution of sexually explicit books and magazines. One group of crusaders is determined to prevent the legalization of gay marriage; their objective is passage of a constitutional amendment declaring that marriage is between one man and one woman. Opposing them are groups of activists who have tirelessly campaigned for the civil rights of gay men and women.

LO4 Describe the various forms of outlawed deviant sexuality

Outlawed sexual behavior, known as paraphilias, include such acts as: frotteurism, rubbing against or touching a nonconsenting person in a crowd, elevator, or other public area; voyeurism, obtaining sexual pleasure from spying on a stranger while he or she disrobes or engages in sexual behavior with another; exhibitionism, deriving sexual pleasure from exposing the genitals to surprise or shock a stranger; sadomasochism, deriving pleasure from receiving pain or inflicting pain on another; and pedophilia, attaining sexual pleasure through sexual activity with prepubescent children.

LO5 Summarize the history of prostitution and 0review what the term means today

Prostitution has been known for thousands of years. The earliest record of prostitution appears in ancient Mesopotamia, where priests engaged in sex to promote fertility in the community. Modern commercial sex appears to have its roots in ancient Greece. Today, prostitution can be defined as granting nonmarital sexual access, established by mutual agreement of the prostitutes, their clients, and their employers, for remuneration.

LO6 Distinguish between the different types of prostitutes

Prostitutes who work the streets in plain sight of police, citizens, and customers are referred to as hustlers, hookers, or streetwalkers. B-girls spend their time in bars, drinking and waiting to be picked up by customers. Brothel prostitutes live in a house with a madam who employs them, supervises their behavior, and receives a fee for her services. Call girls work via telephone "dates," get their clients by word of mouth or by making arrangements with bellhops, cab drivers, and so on. Some escort services are fronts for prostitution rings. Prostitutes known as circuit travelers move around in groups of two or three to lumber, labor, and agricultural camps. Prostitutes set up personal websites or put listings on web boards that carry personals.

LO7 Explain what is meant by the terms *obscenity* and *pornography*

Pornography involves the production, distribution, and sale of sexually explicit material intended to sexually excite paying customers. The depiction of sex and nudity is not illegal, but it does violate the law when it is judged obscene. "Obscenity" is a legal term that today is defined as material offensive to community standards. Legally, something is considered obscene if the average person applying contemporary community standards would find that the work taken as a whole appeals to the prurient interest; that the work depicts or describes prohibited sexual conduct; and whether the work, taken as a whole, lacks serious literary, artistic, political, or scientific value. Thus, each local jurisdiction must decide what pornographic material is obscene. A growing problem is the exploitation of children in obscene materials (kiddie porn), which has been expanded through the Internet.

LO8 Assess the causes of substance abuse

The onset of drug use can be tied to such factors as racial prejudice, devalued identities, low self-esteem, poor socio-economic status, and the high level of mistrust, negativism, and defiance found in impoverished areas. Some experts have linked substance abuse to psychological deficits such as impaired cognitive functioning, personality disturbance, and emotional problems. Substance abuse may have a genetic basis. Social psychologists suggest that drug abuse may also result from observing parental drug use. Substance abuse may be just one of many social problem behaviors. Some may use drugs and alcohol because they want to enjoy their effects: get high, relax, improve creativity, escape reality, and increase sexual responsiveness.

LO9 Compare and contrast the different methods of drug control

A number of different drug control strategies have been tried, with varying degrees of success. Some aim to deter drug use by stopping the flow of drugs into the country, apprehending and punishing dealers, and cracking down on street-level drug deals. Others focus on preventing drug use by educating potential users to the dangers of substance abuse (convincing them to "say no to drugs") and by organizing community groups to work with the at-risk population in their area. Still another approach is to treat known users so they can control their addictions.

LO10 State the arguments for and against legalizing drugs

Drugs should be legalized because the money spent on control could be used on education and economic development. People have always wanted, and will find ways of obtaining, psychoactive drugs. The drug war causes many health problems like HIV and hepatitis C because users are in hiding and thus their access to clean needles is restricted. Children of addicts are at risk of educational failure, joblessness, addiction, and delinquency. People suffering from cancer, AIDS, and other debilitating illnesses are arrested and prosecuted for using medical marijuana. Banning drugs creates networks of manufacturers and distributors, many of whom use violence as part of their standard operating procedures. If drugs were legalized, price and distribution could be controlled by the government. Those who oppose legalization fear that it will lead to much more widespread use of dangerous drugs, leading to drug smuggling to avoid tax payments. There are also health concerns. The number of drug-dependent babies could begin to match or exceed the number delivered with fetal alcohol syndrome.

KEY TERMS

public order crimes (482)	moral entrepreneurs (485)	brothel (492)	obscenity (497)
victimless crimes (482)	paraphilias (487)	madam (492)	temperance movement (501)
social harm (482)	pedophilia (488)	call girls (492)	gateway model (505)
vigilantes (485)	prostitution (490)	skeezers (493)	
moral crusaders (485)	ehooking (490)	pornography (496)	

CRITICAL THINKING QUESTIONS

1. Under what circumstances, if any, might the legalization or decriminalization of drugs be beneficial to society?

2. Do you consider alcohol a drug? Should greater control be placed on the sale of alcohol?

3. Do TV shows and films glorify drug usage and encourage youths to enter the drug trade? Should all images on TV of drugs and alcohol be banned?

4. Is prostitution really a crime? Should a man or woman have the right to sell sexual favors if they so choose?

5. Do you believe there should be greater controls placed on the distribution of sexually explicit material on the Internet? Would you approve of the online sale of sexually

explicit photos of children if they were artificial images created by computer animation?

6. Which statement is more accurate? (a) Sexually aggressive men are drawn to pornography because it reinforces their preexisting hostile orientation to sexuality. (b) Reading or watching pornography can make men become sexually aggressive.

7. Are there objective standards of morality? Does the existing criminal code reflect contemporary national moral standards? Or are laws banning sexual behaviors and substance abuse the product of a relatively few "moral entrepreneurs" who seek to control other people's behaviors?

1. FBI, "Teen Prostitution: Gang Used Social Media Sites to Identify Potential Victims," September 14, 2012, http://www.fbi.gov/news/stories/2012/september/teen-prostitution/teen-prostitution (accessed June 2014).

2. Huffington Post, "Emperors Club: All About Eliot Spitzer's Alleged Prostitution Ring," March 10, 2008, http://www.huffingtonpost.com/2008/03/10/emperors-club-all-about-_n_90768.html (accessed June 2014); Edwin Schur, *Crimes Without Victims* (Englewood Cliffs, NJ: Prentice Hall, 1965).

3. Eric Ostermeier, "David Vitter Launches Historic Gubernatorial Bid in Louisiana," Smart Politics, January 24, 2014, http://blog.lib.umn.edu/cspg/smartpolitics/2014/01/david_vitter_launches_historic.php (accessed June 2014).

4. Jennifer Williard, *Juvenile Prostitution* (Washington, DC: National Victim Resource Center, 1991).

5. C. Gabrielle Salfati, Alison James, and Lynn Ferguson, "Prostitute Homicides: A Descriptive Study," *Journal of Interpersonal Violence* 23 (2008): 505–543.

6. Andrea Dworkin, quoted in "Where Do We Stand on Pornography," *Ms.* (January–February 1994): 34.

7. Raymond Hernandez, "Weiner Resigns in Chaotic Final Scene," *New York Times*, June 16, 2011, http://www.nytimes.com/2011/06/17/nyregion/anthony-d-weiner-tells-friends-he-will-resign.html (accessed June 2014).

8. The Bible, No. 02-102, June 26, Genesis 18:20.

9. Morris Cohen, "Moral Aspects of the Criminal Law," *Yale Law Journal* 49 (1940): 1017.

10. Sir Patrick Devlin, *The Enforcement of Morals* (New York: Oxford University Press, 1959), p. 20.

11. See Joel Feinberg, *Social Philosophy* (Englewood Cliffs, NJ: Prentice Hall, 1973), Ch. 2, 3.

12. H. L. A. Hart, "Immorality and Treason," *Listener* 62 (1959): 163.

13. *United States v. 12 200-ft Reels of Super 8mm Film*, 413 U.S. 123 (1973) at 137.

14. Joseph Gusfield, "On Legislating Morals: The Symbolic Process of Designating Deviancy," *California Law Review* 56 (1968): 58–59.

15. John Franks, "The Evaluation of Community Standards," *Journal of Social Psychology* 139 (1999): 253–255.

16. Sebastian Anthony, "Just How Big Are Porn Sites?" ExtremeTech, April 4, 2012, http://www.extremetech.com/computing/123929-just-how-big-are-porn-sites (accessed June 2014).

17. Irving Kristol, "Liberal Censorship and the Common Culture," *Society* 36 (September 1999): 5.

18. Amnesty International, "15 Facts on Sex, Pregnancy, Marriage and Violence," March 6, 2014, http://www.amnesty.org/en/news/sex-pregnancy-marriage-and-violence-15-facts-2014-03-06 (accessed June 2014).

19. Barbara Crossette, "Senegal Bans Cutting of Genitals of Girls," *New York Times*, January 18, 1999, p. A11.

20. David Kaplan, "Is It Torture or Tradition?" *Newsweek* (December 20, 1993): 124.

21. Crossette, "Senegal Bans Cutting of Genitals of Girls."

22. Centers for Disease Control and Prevention, "Prescription Drug Overdose in the United States: Fact Sheet," http://www.cdc.gov/homeandrecreationalsafety/overdose/facts.html (accessed June 2014).

23. Howard Becker, *Outsiders* (New York: Macmillan, 1963), pp. 13–14.

24. Ibid.

25. Edward Brecher, *Licit and Illicit Drugs* (Boston: Little, Brown, 1972), pp. 413–416.

26. Hearings on H.R. 6385, April 27, 28, 29, 30, and May 4, 1937, http://www.hempfarm.org/Papers/Hearing_Transcript_1.html (accessed June 2014).

27. *American Library Association,* "Top Ten Most Frequently Challenged Books of 2012," http://www.ala.org/bbooks/frequentlychallengedbooks/top10 (accessed June 2014).

28. US Code, Title 1 § 7. Definition of "marriage" and "spouse."

29. *Lawrence et al. v. Texas*, No. 02-102, June 26, 2003.

30. *Hillary Goodridge et al. vs. Department of Public Health and Another*, SJC-08860, November 18, 2003.

31. *United States v. Windsor*, 570 U.S. ___ (2013).

32. Peyton M. Craighill and Scott Clement, "Support for Same-Sex Marriage Hits New High; Half Say Constitution Guarantees Right," *Washington Post*, March 5, 2014, http://www.washingtonpost.com/politics/support-for-same-sex-marriage-hits-new-high-half-say-constitution-guarantees-right/2014/03/04/f737e87e-a3e5-11e3-a5fa-55f0c77bf39c_story.html (accessed June 2014).

33. Lateef Mungin and Dave Alsup, "Cleveland Kidnapper Ariel Castro Dead: Commits Suicide in Prison," CNN, September 4, 2013, http://www.cnn.com/2013/09/04/justice/ariel-castro-cleveland-kidnapper-death/ (accessed June 2014).

34. David Gardner, "I Feel Guilty: Girl Held for 18 Years 'Bonded with Kidnapper,'" *London Evening Standard*, August 28, 2009, http://www.standard.co.uk/news/i-feel-guilty-girl-held-for-18-years-bonded-with-kidnapper-6745223.html (accessed June 2014).

35. Richard Estes and Neil Alan Weiner, *The Commercial Sexual Exploitation of Children in the U.S., Canada, and Mexico* (Philadelphia: University of Pennsylvania Press, 2001).

36. W. P. de Silva, "Sexual Variations," *British Medical Journal* 318 (1999): 654–655.

37. Associated Press, "David Carradine Found Dead in Thailand Hotel," *Today*, June 4, 2009, http://www.today.com/id/31103217#.U6MIgyhwz74 (accessed June 2014).

38. *Boston Globe* archives, "The Boston Area's First Predator Priest Case," http://www.boston.com/globe/spotlight/abuse/extras/porter_archive.htm (accessed June 2014).

39. CNN, "Archbishop: Mistakes Made in Priest Sex Abuse Case," March 31, 2010, http://www.cnn.com/2010/US/03/31/wisconsin.church.abuse/ (accessed June 2014).

40. Boris Schiffer, Thomas Paul, Elke Gizewski, Michael Forsting, Norbert Leygraf, Manfred Schedlowski, and Tillmann H.C. Kruger, "Functional Brain Correlates of Heterosexual Paedophilia" *NeuroImage* 41 (2008): 80–91.

41. Michael Allan and Randolph Grace, "Psychometric Assessment of Dynamic Risk Factors for Child Molesters," *Sexual Abuse: A Journal of Research* 19 (2007): 347–367.

42. For an analysis of this issue, see Theresa Gannon, and Devon Polaschek, "Cognitive Distortions in Child Molesters: A Re-Examination of Key Theories and Research," *Clinical Psychology Review* 26 (2006): 1000–1019.

43. Miriam Catrien and Jan Hendriks, "Women Don't Do Such Things! Characteristics of Female Sex Offenders and Offender Types," *Sexual Abuse: A Journal of Research and Treatment* 22 (2010): 135–156.

44. Fox News, "Louisiana Senator David Vitter Apologizes Again for Connection to D.C. Madam Scandal," July 16, 2007, http://www.foxnews.com/story/2007/07/17/louisiana-senator-david-vitter-apologizes-again-for-connection-to-dc-madam/ (accessed June 2014).

45. Ginger Thompson and Philip Shenon, "Navy Officer Describes Working as a Prostitute," *New York Times*, April 12, 2008, http://www.nytimes.com/2008/04/12/us/12officer.html (accessed June 2014).

46. See generally V. Bullogh, *Sexual Variance in Society and History* (Chicago: University of Chicago Press, 1958), pp. 143–144.

47. Spencer Rathus, *Human Sexuality* (New York: Holt, Rinehart & Winston, 1983), p. 463.

48. Jeffery Richards, *Sex, Dissidence and Damnation: Minority Groups in the Middle Ages* (New York: Routledge, 1994). p. 125.

49. Ibid., p. 118.

50. Annette Jolin, "On the Backs of Working Prostitutes: Feminist Theory and Prostitution Policy," *Crime and Delinquency* 40 (1994): 60–83.

51. Charles McCaghy, *Deviant Behavior* (New York: Macmillan, 1976), pp. 348–349.

52. Marian Pitts, Anthony Smith, Jeffrey Grierson, Mary O'Brien, and Sebastian Misson, "Who Pays for Sex and Why? An Analysis of Social and Motivational Factors Associated with Male Clients of Sex Workers," *Archives of Sexual Behavior* 33 (2004): 353–358.

53. Monica Prasad, "The Morality of Market Exchange: Love, Money, and Contractual Justice," *Sociological Perspectives* 42 (1999): 181–187.

54. FBI, "Crime in the United States, 2012," Table 33, http://www.fbi.gov/about-us/cjis/ucr/crime-in-the-u.s/2012/crime-in-the-u.s.-2012/tables/33tabledatadecoverviewpdf (accessed June 2014).

55. Scott Shuger, "Hookers.com, How E-Commerce Is Transforming the Oldest Profession," *Slate*, http://www.slate.com/articles/briefing/articles/2000/01/hookerscom.html (accessed June 2014).

56. Mark Landler, "World Cup Brings Little Pleasure to German Brothels," *New York Times*, July 3, 2006, http://www.nytimes.com/2006/07/03/world/europe/03berlin.html (accessed June 2014).

57. Elizabeth Bernstein, "The Meaning of the Purchase: Desire, Demand, and the Commerce of Sex," *Ethnography* 2 (2001): 389–420.

58. 18 U.S.C. [section] 2423(b) (2000).

59. Sara K. Andrews, "U.S. Domestic Prosecution of the American International Sex Tourist: Efforts to Protect Children from Sexual Exploitation," *Journal of Criminal Law and Criminology* 94 (2004): 415–453.

60. Mark-David Janus, Barbara Scanlon, and Virginia Price, "Youth Prostitution," in *Child Pornography and Sex Rings*, ed. Ann Wolbert Burgess (Lexington, MA: Lexington Books, 1989), pp. 127–146.

61. Teela Sanders and Rosie Campbell, "Designing Out Vulnerability, Building in Respect: Violence, Safety and Sex Work Policy," *British Journal of Sociology* 58 (2007): 1–19.

62. Charles Winick and Paul Kinsie, *The Lively Commerce* (Chicago: Quadrangle Books, 1971), p. 58.

63. Celia Baker, "Women in Street-based Prostitution: A Typology of Their Work Styles," *Qualitative Social Work* 8 (2009): 27–44.

64. Teela Sanders, *Sex Work: A Risky Business* (Devon, England: Willan Publishing, 2005).

65. Winick and Kinsie, *The Lively Commerce*, pp. 172–173.

66. Paul Goldstein, "Occupational Mobility in the World of Prostitution: Becoming a Madam," *Deviant Behavior* 4 (1983): 267–279.

67. Ibid., pp. 267–270.

68. Mireya Navarro, "Group Forced Illegal Aliens into Prostitution, U.S. Says," *New York Times*, April 24, 1998, p. A10.

69. Paul Goldstein, Lawrence Ouellet, and Michael Fendrich, "From Bag Brides to Skeezers: A Historical Perspective on Sex-for-Drugs Behavior," *Journal of Psychoactive Drugs* 24 (1992): 349–361.

70. Jessica Edwards, Carolyn Halpern, and Wendee Wechsberg, "Correlates of Exchanging Sex for Drugs or Money Among Women Who Use Crack Cocaine," *AIDS Education and Prevention* 18 (2006): 420–429.

71. Jan Risser, Sandra Timpson, Sheryl McCurdy, Michael Ross, and Mark Williams, "Psychological Correlates of Trading Sex for Money Among African American Crack Cocaine Smokers," *American Journal of Drug and Alcohol Abuse* 32 (2006): 645–653.

72. Thompson and Shenon, "Navy Officer Describes Working as a Prostitute."

73. Alyson Brown and David Barrett, *Knowledge of Evil: Child Prostitution and Child Sexual Abuse in Twentieth Century England* (Devon, England: Willan, 2002).

74. Jocelyn Brown, Patricia Cohen, Henian Chen, Elizabeth Smailes, and Jeffrey Johnson, "Sexual Trajectories of Abused and Neglected Youths," *Journal of Developmental and Behavioral Pediatrics* 25 (2004): 77–83.

75. Gerald Hotaling and David Finkelhor, *The Sexual Exploitation of Missing Children* (Washington, DC: U.S. Department of Justice, 1988).

76. Tammy Heilemann, and Janaki Santhiveeran, "How Do Female Adolescents Cope and Survive the Hardships of Prostitution? A Content Analysis of Existing Literature," *Journal of Ethnic and Cultural Diversity in Social Work* 20 (2011): 57–76.

77. Lisa Kramer and Ellen Berg, "A Survival Analysis of Timing of Entry into Prostitution: The Differential Impact of Race, Educational Level, and Childhood/Adolescent Risk Factors," *Sociological Inquiry* 73 (2003): 511–529.

78. John Potterat, Richard Rothenberg, Stephen Muth, William Darrow, and Lynanne Phillips-Plummer, "Pathways to Prostitution: The Chronology of Sexual and Drug Abuse Milestones," *Journal of Sex Research* 35 (1998): 333–342.

79. Sheila Royo Maxwell and Christopher Maxwell, "Examining the 'Criminal Careers' of Prostitutes Within the Nexus of Drug Use, Drug Selling, and Other Illicit Activities," *Criminology* 38 (2000): 787–809.

80. Michael Miner, Jill Flitter, and Beatrice Robinson, "Association of Sexual Revictimization with Sexuality and Psychological Function," *Journal of Interpersonal Violence* 21 (2006): 503–524.

81. Jolanda Sallmann, "Living with Stigma: Women's Experiences of Prostitution and Substance Use," *Afillia Journal of Women and Social Work* 25 (2010): 146–159.

82. Mandi Burnette, Emma Lucas, Mark Ilgen, Susan Frayne, Julia Mayo, and Julie Weitlauf, "Prevalence and Health Correlates of Prostitution Among Patients Entering Treatment for Substance Use Disorders," *Archives of General Psychiatry* 65 (2008): 337–344.

83. Michael Rekart, "Sex-Work Harm Reduction," *The Lancet* 366 (2005): 2123–2134.

84. Nancy Romero-Daza, Margaret Weeks, and Merrill Singer, "Nobody Gives a Damn if I Live or Die: Violence, Drugs, and Street-Level Prostitution in Inner-City Hartford, Connecticut," *Medical Anthropology* 22 (2003): 233–259.

85. Brown and Barrett, *Knowledge of Evil: Child Prostitution and Child Sexual Abuse in Twentieth Century England.*

86. Brown et al., "Sexual Trajectories of Abused and Neglected Youths."

87. Hotaling and Finkelhor, *The Sexual Exploitation of Missing Children.*

88. Shu-ling Hwang and Olwen Bedford, "Juveniles' Motivations for Remaining in Prostitution," *Psychology of Women Quarterly* 28 (2004): 136–137.

89. Sallmann, "Living with Stigma: Women's Experiences of Prostitution and Substance Use," 153.

90. Barbara G. Brents and Kathryn Hausbeck, "State-Sanctioned Sex: Negotiating Formal and Informal Regulatory Practices in Nevada Brothels," *Sociological Perspectives* 44 (2001): 307–335.

91. Ibid.

92. Mara Keire, "The Vice Trust: A Reinterpretation of the White Slavery Scare in the United States, 1907–1917," *Journal of Social History* 35 (2001): 5–42.

93. Minnesota Statute 609.324, "Other Prostitution Crimes; Patrons, Prostitutes, and Individuals Housing Individuals Engaged in Prostitution; Penalties," https://www.revisor.mn.gov/statutes/?id=609.324 (accessed June 2014).

94. Devon Brewer, John Potterat, Stephen Muth, John Roberts, Jr., Jonathan Dudek, and Donald Woodhouse, *Clients of Prostitute Women: Deterrence, Prevalence, Characteristics, and Violence* (Washington, DC: National Institute of Justice, 2007), http://www.ncjrs.gov/pdffiles1/nij/grants/218253.pdf (accessed June 2014).

95. Ronald Weitzer, "The Politics of Prostitution in America," in *Sex for Sale*, ed. Ronald Weitzer (New York: Routledge, 2000): 159–180.

96. Sherry Plaster Carter, Stanley Carter, and Andrew Dannenberg, "Zoning Out Crime and Improving Community Health in Sarasota, Florida: Crime Prevention Through Environmental Design," *American Journal of Public Health* 93 (2003): 1442–1445.

97. Ron Roberts, Sandra Bergström, and David La Rooy, "UK Students and Sex Work: Current Knowledge and Research Issues," *Journal of Community and Applied Social Psychology* 17 (2007): 141–146.

98. Sarah Lantz, "Students Working in the Melbourne Sex Industry: Education, Human Capital and the Changing Patterns of the Youth Labour Market," *Journal of Youth Studies* 8 (2005): 385–401.

99. Andrea Dworkin, *Pornography* (New York: Dutton, 1989).

100. Arthur Gould, "The Criminalisation of Buying Sex: The Politics of Prostitution in Sweden," *Journal of Social Policy* 30 (2001): 437–438.

101. Suzanne Daley, "New Rights for Dutch Prostitutes, but No Gain," *New York Times*, August 12, 2001, p. A4.

102. Alexa Albert, *Brothel: Mustang Ranch and Its Women* (New York: Random House, 2001).

103. Roger Matthews, *Prostitution, Politics and Policy* (London, Routledge-Cavendish, 2008).

104. *Merriam-Webster Dictionary* (New York: Pocket Books, 1974), p. 484.

105. Neil Malamuth, Tamara Addison, and Mary Koss, "Pornography and Sexual Aggression: Are There Reliable Effects and Can We Understand Them?" *Annual Review of Sex Research* 11 (2000): 26–94.

106. Lynn Morgan, "Indecency, Pornography, and the Protection of Children," *Georgetown Journal of Gender and the Law* 7 (2006): 701–721.

107. Albert Belanger et al., "Typology of Sex Rings Exploiting Children," in *Child Pornography and Sex Rings*, ed. Ann Wolbert Burgess (Lexington, MA: Lexington Books, 1984), pp. 51–81.

108. Philip Jenkins, *Beyond Tolerance: Child Pornography Online* (New York: New York University Press, 2001).

109. Malamuth, Addison, and Koss, "Pornography and Sexual Aggression."

110. Berl Kutchinsky, "The Effect of Easy Availability of Pornography on the Incidence of Sex Crimes," *Journal of Social Issues* 29 (1973): 95–112.

111. Michael Goldstein, "Exposure to Erotic Stimuli and Sexual Deviance," *Journal of Social Issues* 29 (1973): 197–219.

112. Joetta Carr and Karen VanDeusen, "Risk Factors for Male Sexual Aggression on College Campuses," *Journal of Family Violence* 19 (2004): 279–289; see Edward Donnerstein, Daniel Linz, and Steven Penrod, *The Question of Pornography* (New York: Free Press, 1987).

113. Michael Seto, Alexandra Maric, and Howard Barbaree, "The Role of Pornography in the Etiology of Sexual Aggression," *Aggression and Violent Behaviour* 6 (2001): 35–53.

114. Catherine Simmons and Peter Shannon Collier-Tenison, "Linking Male Use of the Sex Industry to Controlling Behaviors in Violent Relationships: An Exploratory Analysis," *Violence Against Women* 14 (2008): 406–417.

115. Edward Donnerstein, "Pornography and Violence Against Women," *Annals of the New York Academy of Science* 347 (1980): 277–288; E. Donnerstein and J. Hallam, "Facilitating Effects of Erotica on Aggression Against Women," *Journal of Personality and Social Psychology* 36 (1977): 1270–1277.

116. James Alan Fox and Jack Levin, "Multiple Homicide: Patterns of Serial and Mass Murder," in *Crime and Justice: An Annual Edition*, vol. 23, ed. Michael Tonry (Chicago: University of Chicago Press, 1998): 418–419.

117. John Court, "Sex and Violence: A Ripple Effect," *Pornography and Aggression*, ed. Neil Malamuth and Edward Donnerstein (Orlando: Academic Press, 1984).

118. Michael Andres Hernandez, "The 'Butner Study' Redux: A Report of the Incidence of Hands-on Child Victimization by Child Pornography Offenders," *Journal of Family Violence* 24 (2009): 183–191.

119. *Roth v. United States*, 354 U.S. 476 (1957).

120. *A Book Named "John Cleland's Memoirs of a Woman of Pleasure" v. Attorney General of Massachusetts* 383 U.S. 413 (1966).

121. *Miller v. California*, 413 U.S. 15 (1973).

122. *Pope v. Illinois*, 481 U.S. 497 (1987).

123. Ibid.

124. "State Laws on Obscenity, Child Pornography, and Harassment," http://www.lorenavedon.com/laws.htm (accessed June 2014).

125. "The Prosecutorial Remedies and Other Tools to End the Exploitation of Children," 18 U.S.C. 1466A (2003).

126. *United States v. Williams*, 553 U.S. 285 (2008).

127. *Pornography Commission*, pp. 376–377.

128. Bob Cohn, "The Trials of Adam and Eve," *Newsweek* (January 7, 1991): 48.

129. 427 U.S. 50 (1976).

130. Skynews, "Philip Seymour Hoffman Died from Drugs Mix," February 28, 2014, http://news.sky.com/story/1219150/philip-seymour-hoffman-died-from-drugs-mix (accessed June 2014).

131. CNN, "Ledger's Death Caused by Accidental Overdose," February 8, 2008, http://www.cnn.com/2008/SHOWBIZ/Movies/02/06/heath.ledger/ (accessed June 2014).

132. Ralph Weisheit, "Studying Drugs in Rural Areas: Notes from the Field," *Journal of Research in Crime and Delinquency* 30 (1993): 213–232.

133. Arnold Trebach, *The Heroin Solution* (New Haven, CN: Yale University Press, 1982).

134. James Inciardi, *The War on Drugs* (Palo Alto, CA: Mayfield, 1986), p. 2.

135. See generally David Pittman, "Drug Addiction and Crime," in *Handbook of Criminology*, ed. D. Glazer (Chicago: Rand McNally, 1974), pp. 209–232; Board of Directors, National Council on Crime and Delinquency, "Drug Addiction: A Medical, Not a Law Enforcement, Problem," *Crime and Delinquency* 20 (1974): 4–9.

136. Associated Press, "Records Detail Royals' Turn-of-Century Drug Use," *Boston Globe*, August 29, 1993, p. 13.

137. See Brecher, *Licit and Illicit Drugs*.

138. James Inciardi, *Reflections on Crime* (New York: Holt, Rinehart & Winston, 1978), p. 15.

139. William Bates and Betty Crowther, "Drug Abuse," in *Deviants: Voluntary Actors in a Hostile World*, ed. E. Sagarin and F. Montanino (New York: Foresman and Co., 1977), p. 269.

140. Inciardi, *Reflections on Crime*, pp. 8–10. See also A. Greeley, William McCready, and Gary Theisen, *Ethnic Drinking Subcultures* (New York: Praeger, 1980).

141. Joseph Gusfield, *Symbolic Crusade* (Urbana: University of Illinois Press, 1963), Ch. 3.

142. McCaghy, *Deviant Behavior*, p. 280.

143. Ibid.

144. The National Institute on Alcohol Abuse and Alcoholism (NIAAA), "Alcohol Facts and Statistics," http://www.niaaa.nih.gov/alcohol-health/overview-alcohol-consumption/alcohol-facts-and-statistics (accessed June 2014).

145. Jeffrey Miron and Katherine Waldock, "The Budgetary Impact of Ending Drug Prohibition," Cato Institute (Washington, DC: Cato Institute, 2010), http://www.cato.org/sites/cato.org/files/pubs/pdf/DrugProhibitionWP.pdf (accessed June 2014).

146. Susan James, Janice Johnson, and Chitra Raghavan, "I Couldn't Go Anywhere," *Violence Against Women* 10 (2004): 991–1015.

147. Marvin Krohn, Alan Lizotte, Terence Thornberry, Carolyn Smith, and David McDowall, "Reciprocal Causal Relationships Among Drug Use, Peers, and Beliefs: A Five-Wave Panel Model," *Journal of Drug Issues* 26 (1996): 205–428.

148. Kellie Barr, Michael Farrell, Grace Barnes, and John Welte, "Race, Class, and Gender Differences in Substance Abuse: Evidence of Middle-Class/Underclass Polarization Among Black Males," *Social Problems* 40 (1993): 314–326.

149. Peter Giancola, "Constructive Thinking, Antisocial Behavior, and Drug Use in Adolescent Boys with and without a Family History of a Substance Use Disorder," *Personality and Individual Differences* 35 (2003): 1315–1331.

150. Jerome J. Platt, *Heroin Addiction and Theory, Research and Treatment: The Addict the Treatment Process and Social Control* (Melbourne, FL: Krieser Publishing, 1995), p. 127.

151. The Substance Abuse and Mental Health Services Administration (SAMHSA), Results from the 2012 National Survey on Drug Use and Health (NSDUH), 2013, http://www.samhsa.gov/data/NSDUH/2012 SummNatFindDetTables/ (accessed June 2014).

152. Ibid.

153. Alan Carr, Barbara Dooley, Mark Fitzpatrick, Edel Flanagan, Roisin Flanagan-Howard, Kevin Tierney, Megan White, and Margaret Egan, "Adult Adjustment of Survivors of Institutional Child Abuse in Ireland," *Child Abuse and Neglect* 34 (2010): 477–489.

154. Daniel Smith, Joanne Davis, and Adrienne Fricker-Elhai, "How Does Trauma Beget Trauma? Cognitions About Risk in Women with Abuse Histories," *Child Maltreatment* 9 (2004): 292–302.

155. Sean Kidd, "The Walls Were Closing In, and We Were Trapped," *Youth and Society* 36 (2004): 30–55.

156. David Black, Steve Sussman, Jennifer Unger, Pallay Pokhrel, and Ping Sun, "Gender Differences in Body Consciousness and Substance Use Among High-Risk Adolescents," *Substance Use and Misuse* 45 (2010): 1623–1635.

157. Tracy Hampton, "Genes Harbor Clues to Addiction, Recovery," *Journal of the American Medical Association* 292 (2004): 321–323.

158. D. W. Goodwin, "Alcoholism and Genetics," *Archives of General Psychiatry* 42 (1985): 171–174.

159. Martha Vungkhanching, Kenneth Sher, Kristina Jackson, and Gilbert Parra, "Relation of Attachment Style to Family History of Alcoholism and Alcohol Use Disorders in Early Adulthood," *Drug and Alcohol Dependence* 75 (2004): 47–54.

160. For a thorough review of this issue, see John Petraitis, Brian Flay, and Todd Miller, "Reviewing Theories of Adolescent Substance Use: Organizing Pieces in the Puzzle," *Psychological Bulletin* 117 (1995): 67–86.

161. Judith Brooks and Li-Jung Tseng, "Influences of Parental Drug Use, Personality, and Child Rearing on the Toddler's Anger and Negativity," *Genetic, Social and General Psychology Monographs* 122 (1996): 107–128.

162. Thomas Ashby Wills, Donato Vaccaro, Grace McNamara, and A. Elizabeth Hirky, "Escalated Substance Use: A Longitudinal Grouping Analysis from Early to Middle Adolescence," *Journal of Abnormal Psychology* 105 (1996): 166–180.

163. Denise Kandel and Mark Davies, "Friendship Networks, Intimacy, and Illicit Drug Use in Young Adulthood: A Comparison of Two Competing Theories," *Criminology* 29 (1991): 441–471.

164. J. S. Mio, G. Nanjundappa, D. E. Verlur, and M. D. DeRios, "Drug Abuse and the Adolescent Sex Offender: A Preliminary Analysis," *Journal of Psychoactive Drugs* 18 (1986): 65–72.

165. D. Baer and J. Corrado, "Heroin Addict Relationships with Parents During Childhood and Early Adolescent Years," *Journal of Genetic Psychology* 124 (1974): 99–103.

166. Chie Noyori-Corbett and Sung Seek Moon, "Multifaceted Reality of Juvenile Delinquency: An Empirical Analysis of Structural Theories and Literature," *Child and Adolescent Social Work Journal* 27 (2010): 245–268.

167. John Wallace and Jerald Bachman, "Explaining Racial/Ethnic Differences in Adolescent Drug Use: The Impact of Background and Lifestyle," *Social Problems* 38 (1991): 333–357.

168. Amy Young, Carol Boyd, and Amy Hubbell, "Social Isolation and Sexual Abuse Among Women Who Smoke Crack," *Journal of Psychosocial Nursing* 39 (2001): 16–19.

169. Xiaojin Chen, Kimberly Tyler, Les Whitbeck, and Dan Hoyt, "Early Sexual Abuse, Street Adversity, and Drug Use Among Female Homeless and Runaway Adolescents in the Midwest," *Journal of Drug Issues* 34 (2004): 1–20.

170. Michael Hallstone, "Types of Crimes Committed by Repeat DUI Offenders," *Criminal Justice Studies* 27 (2014): 159–171.

171. Claire Sterk-Elifson, "Just for Fun? Cocaine Use Among Middle-Class Women," *Journal of Drug Issues* 26 (1996): 63–76, at 69.

172. Icek Ajzen, *Attitudes, Personality and Behavior* (Homewood, IL: Dorsey Press, 1988).

173. James Inciardi, Ruth Horowitz, and Anne Pottieger, *Street Kids, Street Drugs, Street Crime: An Examination of Drug Use and Serious Delinquency in Miami* (Belmont, CA: Wadsworth, 1993), p. 43.

174. Ibid.

175. Cesar Rebellon and Karen Van Gundy, "Can Social Psychological Delinquency Theory Explain the Link Between Marijuana and Other Illicit Drug Use? A Longitudinal Analysis of the Gateway Hypothesis," *Journal of Drug Issues*, Summer 36 (2006): 515–539; Mary Ellen Mackesy-Amiti, Michael Fendrich, and Paul Goldstein, "Sequence of Drug Use Among Serious Drug Users: Typical vs. Atypical Progression," *Drug and Alcohol Dependence* 45 (1997): 185–196.

176. Bu Huang, Helene White, Rick Kosterman, Richard Catalano, and J. David Hawkins, "Developmental Associations Between Alcohol and Interpersonal Aggression During Adolescence," *Journal of Research in Crime and Delinquency* 38 (2001): 64–83.

177. Rebellon and Van Gundy, "Can Social Psychological Delinquency Theory Explain the Link Between Marijuana and Other Illicit Drug Use? A Longitudinal Analysis of the Gateway Hypothesis."

178. Andrew Golub and Bruce Johnson, "The Multiple Paths Through Alcohol, Tobacco and Marijuana to Hard Drug Use Among Arrestees," paper presented at the annual meeting of the American Society of Criminology, San Diego, November 1997.

179. Andrew Golub and Bruce D. Johnson, *The Rise of Marijuana as the Drug of Choice Among Youthful Adult Arrestees* (Washington, DC: National Institute of Justice, 2001).

180. These lifestyles are described in Marcia Chaiken and Bruce Johnson, *Characteristics of Different Types of Drug-Involved Offenders* (Washington, DC: National Institute of Justice, 1988).

181. Kenneth Tunnell, "Inside the Drug Trade: Trafficking from the Dealer's Perspective," *Qualitative Sociology* 16 (1993): 361–381.

182. Lening Zhang, John Welte, and William Wieczorek, "Youth Gangs, Drug Use and Delinquency," *Journal of Criminal Justice* 27 (1999): 101–109.

183. Carolyn Rebecca Block, Antigone Christakos, Ayad Jacob, and Roger Przybylski, *Street Gangs and Crime* (Chicago: Illinois Criminal Justice Information Authority, 1996).

184. Richard Tewksbury and Elizabeth Ehrhardt Mustaine, "Lifestyle of the Wheelers and Dealers: Drug Dealing Among American College Students," *Journal of Crime and Justice* 21 (1998): 37.

185. Hilary Saner, Robert MacCoun, and Peter Reuter, "On the Ubiquity of Drug Selling Among Youthful Offenders in Washington, D.C., 1985–1991: Age, Period, or Cohort

Effect?" *Journal of Quantitative Criminology* 11 (1995): 362–373.

186. Charles Faupel and Carl Klockars, "Drugs–Crime Connections: Elaborations from the Life Histories of Hard-Core Heroin Addicts," *Social Problems* 34 (1987): 54–68.

187. Charles Faupel, "Heroin Use, Crime and Unemployment Status," *Journal of Drug Issues* 18 (1988): 467–479.

188. Faupel and Klockars, "Drugs–Crime Connections."

189. Jeffrey T. Parsons, Perry N. Halkitis, and David S. Bimbi, "Club Drug Use Among Young Adults Frequenting Dance Clubs and Other Social Venues in New York City," *Journal of Child and Adolescent Substance Abuse* 15 (2006): 1–14.

190. Damir Sekulic, Mia Peric, and Jelena Rodek, "Substance Use and Misuse Among Professional Ballet Dancers," *Substance Use and Misuse* 45 (2010): 1420–1430.

191. David Duncan, Thomas Nicholson, John White, Dana Burr Bradley, and John Bonaguro, "The Baby Boomer Effect: Changing Patterns of Substance Abuse Among Adults Ages 55 and Older," *Journal of Aging and Social Policy* 22 (2010): 237–248.

192. The National Center on Addiction and Substance Abuse (CASA), *Women Under the Influence* (Baltimore: The Johns Hopkins University Press, 2006).

193. Russel Falck, Jichuan Wang, and Robert Carlson, "The Epidemiology of Physical Attack and Rape Among Crack-Using Women," *Violence and Victims* 16 (2001): 79–89.

194. Benjamin Nordstrom, and Charles Dackis, "Drugs and Crime," *Journal of Psychiatry and Law* 39 (2011): 663–687.

195. Denise Gottfredson, "Substance Use, Drug Treatment, and Crime: An Examination of Intra-Individual Variation in a Drug Court Population," *Journal of Drug Issues* 38 (2008): 601–630.

196. Ibid.

197. Huang et al., "Developmental Associations Between Alcohol and Interpersonal Aggression During Adolescence."

198. Office of National Drug Control Policy, "Fact Sheet: The 2012 Arrestee Drug Abuse Monitoring Program II," May 23, 2013, http://www.whitehouse.gov/sites/default/files/ondcp/Fact_Sheets/adamfactsheet_for_web.pdf (accessed June 2014).

199. Jerome Cartier, David Farabee, and Michael Prendergast, "Methamphetamine Use, Self-Reported Violent Crime, and Recidivism Among Offenders in California Who Abuse Substances," *Journal of Interpersonal Violence* 21 (2006): 435–445.

200. Bureau of Justice Statistics, "Drugs and Crime Facts," http://bjs.ojp.usdoj.gov/content/dcf/duc.cfm (accessed June 2014).

201. The National Center on Addiction and Substance Abuse (CASA), "Behind Bars II: Substance Abuse and America's Prison Population," February 2010, http://www.casacolumbia.org/addiction-research/reports/substance-abuse-prison-system-2010 (accessed June 2014).

202. Evelyn Wei, Rolf Loeber, and Helene White, "Teasing Apart the Developmental Associations Between Alcohol and Marijuana Use and Violence," *Journal of Contemporary Criminal Justice* 20 (2004): 166–183.

203. Matt Vogel, "Mental Illness and Criminal Behavior," *Sociology Compass* 8 (2014): 337–347.

204. Susan Martin, Christopher Maxwell, Helene White, and Yan Zhang, "Trends in Alcohol Use, Cocaine Use, and Crime," *Journal of Drug Issues* 34 (2004): 333–360.

205. Marvin Krohn, Alan Lizotte, and Cynthia Perez, "The Interrelationship Between Substance Use and Precocious Transitions to Adult Sexuality," *Journal of Health and Social Behavior* 38 (1997): 87–103, at 88.

206. Arielle Baskin-Sommers and Ira Sommers, "Methamphetamine Use and Violence Among Young Adults," *Journal of Criminal Justice* 34 (2006): 661–674.

207. Controlled Substance Act, 21 U.S.C. 848 (1984).

208. Anti-Drug Abuse Act of 1986, PL 99-570, U.S.C. 841 (1986).

209. Anti-Drug Abuse Act of 1988, PL 100-690; 21 U.S.C. 1501; Subtitle A—Death Penalty, Sec. 7001, Amending the Controlled Substances Abuse Act, 21 U.S.C. 848.

210. Huffington Post, "Eric Holder Says DOJ Will Let Washington, Colorado Marijuana Laws Go into Effect," September 3, 2103, http://www.huffingtonpost.com/2013/08/29/eric-holder-marijuana-washington-colorado-doj_n_3837034.html (accessed June 2014).

211. George Rengert, *The Geography of Illegal Drugs* (Boulder, CO: Westview Press, 1996), p. 2.

212. Simon Romero, "Coca Production Makes a Comeback in Peru," *New York Times*, June 13, 2010, http://www.nytimes.com/2010/06/14/world/americas/14peru.html (accessed June 2014).

213. Office of National Drug Control Policy, "Cocaine Smuggling in 2011," http://www.whitehouse.gov/sites/default/files/ondcp/cocaine_smuggling_in_2011_english.pdf (accessed June 2014).

214. CNN, "Official: Mexican Cartels Use Money, Sex to Bribe U.S. Border Agents,"

June 9, 2011, http://www.cnn.com/2011/US/06/09/mexico.border.corruption/ (accessed June 2014).

215. Mark Moore, *Drug Trafficking* (Washington, DC: National Institute of Justice, 1988).

216. Matthew Durose and Patrick Langan, *Felony Sentences in State Courts, 2002* (Washington, DC: Bureau of Justice Statistics, 2004).

217. Peter Rossi, Richard Berk, and Alec Campbell, "Just Punishments: Guideline Sentences and Normative Consensus," *Journal of Quantitative Criminology* 13 (1997): 267–283.

218. Michael Welch, Russell Wolff, and Nicole Bryan, "Recontextualizing the War on Drugs: A Content Analysis of NIJ Publications and Their Neglect of Race and Class," *Justice Quarterly* 15 (1998): 719–742.

219. Robert Davis, Arthur Lurigio, and Dennis Rosenbaum, eds., *Drugs and the Community* (Springfield, IL: Charles C Thomas, 1993), pp. xii–xv.

220. Saul Weingart, "A Typology of Community Responses to Drugs," in Davis, Lurigio, and Rosenbaum, *Drugs and the Community*, pp. 85–105.

221. Davis, Lurigio, and Rosenbaum, *Drugs and the Community*, pp. xii–xiii.

222. Marianne Zawitz, *Drugs, Crime and the Justice System* (Washington, DC: Bureau of Justice Statistics, 1992), pp. 109–112.

223. Dennis Rosenbaum, Robert Flewelling, Susan Bailey, Chris Ringwalt, and Deanna Wilkinson, "Cops in the Classroom: A Longitudinal Evaluation of Drug Abuse Resistance Education (D.A.R.E.)," *Journal of Research in Crime and Delinquency* 31 (1994): 3–31.

224. Donald R. Lynam, Rich Milich, Rick Zimmerman, Scott Novak, T. K. Logan, Catherine Martin, Carl Leukefeld, and Richard Clayton, "Project D.A.R.E.: No Effects at 10-Year Follow-Up," *Journal of Consulting and Clinical Psychology* 67 (1999): 590–593.

225. Ibid., pp. 115–122.

226. John Goldkamp and Peter Jones, "Pretrial Drug-Testing Experiments in Milwaukee and Prince George's County: The Context of Implementation," *Journal of Research in Crime and Delinquency* 29 (1992): 430–465; Chester Britt, Michael Gottfredson, and John Goldkamp, "Drug Testing and Pretrial Misconduct: An Experiment on the Specific Deterrent Effects of Drug Monitoring Defendants on Pretrial Release," *Journal of Research in Crime and Delinquency* 29 (1992): 62–78.

227. Joseph R. McKinney, "The Effectiveness and Legality of Random Student Drug Testing

Programs Revisited," *West's Education Law Reporter* 196 (2006); "Effectiveness of Random Student Drug-Testing Programs, 2005," http://www.studentdrugtesting .org/2005%20McKinney%20survey%20 results.pdf (accessed June 2014).

228. Katherine Theall, Kirk Elifson, Claire Sterk, and Eric Stewart, "Criminality Among Female Drug Users Following an HIV Risk-Reduction Intervention," *Journal of Interpersonal Violence* 22 (2007): 85–107.

229. See generally Peter Greenwood and Franklin Zimring, *One More Chance* (Santa Monica, CA: Rand, 1985).

230. Daniel Rosen, Jennifer Morse, and Charles Reynolds, "Adapting Problem-Solving Therapy for Depressed Older Adults in Methadone Maintenance Treatment," *Journal of Substance Abuse Treatment* 40 (2011): 132–141.

231. Audrey Hickert and Mary Jane Taylor, "Supportive Housing for Addicted, Incarcerated Homeless Adults," *Journal of Social Service Research* 37 (2011): 136–151.

232. Tracy Beswick, David Best, Jenny Bearn, Michael Gossop, Sian Rees, and John Strang, "The Effectiveness of Combined Naloxone/ Lofexidine in Opiate Detoxification: Results from a Double-Blind Randomized and Placebo-Controlled Trial," *American Journal on Addictions* 12 (2003): 295–306.

233. Eli Ginzberg, Howard Berliner, and Miriam Ostrow, *Young People at Risk: Is Prevention Possible?* (Boulder, CO: Westview Press, 1988), p. 99.

234. National Institute on Drug Abuse, "InfoFacts: Treatment Approaches for Drug Addiction," http://www.drugabuse.gov/ publications/drugfacts/treatment- approaches-drug-addiction (accessed June 2014).

235. National Evaluation Data and Technical Assistance Center, *The District of Columbia's Drug Treatment Initiative (DCI)* (Washington, DC: author, February 1998).

236. Celia Lo, "Sociodemographic Factors, Drug Abuse, and Other Crimes: How They Vary Among Male and Female Arrestees," *Journal of Criminal Justice* 32 (2004): 399–409.

237. Christopher Uggen and Sarah Shannon, "Productive Addicts and Harm Reduction: How Work Reduces Crime but Not Drug Use," *Social Problems* 61 (2014): 105–130.

238. United Nations Office on Drugs and Crime, "Cocaine Retail Prices," http://www.unodc .org/unodc/secured/wdr/Cocaine_Heroin_ Prices.pdf (accessed June 2014).

239. Barry Goetz, "Pre-Arrest/Booking Drug Control Strategies: Diversion to Treatment, Harm Reduction and Police Involvement," *Contemporary Drug Problems* 33 (2006): 473–520.

240. Ethan Nadelmann, "An End to Marijuana Prohibition," *National Review*, July 12, 2004; Peter Andreas and Ethan Nadelmann, *Policing the Globe: Criminalization and Crime Control in International Relations* (London: Oxford University Press, 2006).

241. Miron and Waldock, "The Budgetary Impact of Ending Drug Prohibition."

242. David Courtwright, "Should We Legalize Drugs? History Answers No," *American Heritage* (February–March 1993): 43–56.

243. James Inciardi and Duane McBride, "Legalizing Drugs: A Gormless, Naive Idea," *Criminologist* 15 (1990): 1–4.

244. Kathryn Ann Farr, "Revitalizing the Drug Decriminalization Debate," *Crime and Delinquency* 36 (1990): 223–237.

CRIMES OF THE NEW MILLENNIUM: CYBERCRIME

americans have become very familiar with a previously unknown website called WikiLeaks, an international organization that publishes classified and secret documents that are submitted by unnamed and anonymous sources. Launched in 2006 and run by Julian Assange, an Australian who emigrated to Sweden, WikiLeaks has supporters around the globe. A few years ago the site began to post videos and documents that had been illegally appropriated from U.S. diplomatic and military computers by unknown hackers. For example, one video showed a 2007 incident in which Iraqi civilians and journalists were killed by U.S. forces. It also leaked more than 76,000 classified war documents from Afghanistan, including U.S. State Department cables. In the aftermath of the leaks, Army Specialist Bradley Manning, 22, was arrested after an informant told federal authorities that he had overheard him bragging about giving WikiLeaks a video of a helicopter assault in Iraq plus more than 260,000 classified U.S. diplomatic cables taken from government computers. Both the U.S. and foreign governments were embarrassed when the confidential cables hit the Net.[1]

Wanted on a series of charges stemming from an alleged sexual assault in Sweden and threatened with extradition to the United States to face charges of espionage, Assange was granted asylum by the government of Ecuador and is currently residing in their London embassy. Bradley Manning (now known as Chelsea Elizabeth Manning) was convicted under the espionage act and sentenced to up to 35 years in prison.

To check out the WikiLeaks site, go to **https://wikileaks.org/.**

just a few years ago, complex, global incidents involving leaking classified documents could not have been contemplated, let alone transacted. Innovation brings change and with it new opportunities to commit crime.

The technological revolution has provided new tools to misappropriate funds, damage property, sell illicit material, or conduct warfare, espionage, and terror. It has created **cybercrime**, a new breed of offenses that can be singular or ongoing, but typically involve the theft and/or destruction of information, resources, or funds utilizing computers, computer networks, and the Internet.

DEVELOPMENT OF CYBERCRIME

 LO1 Discuss the evolution of cybercrime

The widespread use of computers and the Internet ushered in the age of **information technology (IT)** and made it an intricate part of daily life in most industrialized societies. IT involves computer networking, the Internet, and

CONNECTIONS

In Chapter 11, the Edward Joseph Snowden case was discussed in some detail. As you may recall, he is an American computer professional and former contractor for the National Security Agency (NSA) who also disclosed thousands of classified documents to several media outlets and then fled to Russia.

Ask Yourself ...

Are people like Manning and Snowden traitors? Or patriots who risk everything to expose governmental abuse of power?

cybercrime The use of modern technology for criminal purposes.

information technology (IT) All forms of technology used to create, store, retrieve, and exchange data in all its various forms, including electronic, voice, and still image.

globalization The process of creating transnational markets, politics, and legal systems in an effort to form and sustain a global economy.

advanced communications. It is the key to the economic system and will become even more important as major industries continue to shift their manufacturing plants to areas of the world where production is much cheaper. IT is responsible for the **globalization** phenomenon, the process of creating transnational markets, politics, and legal systems—in other words, creating a global economy. The Internet coupled with ever more powerful computers is now the chosen medium to provide a wide range of global services, ranging from entertainment and communication to research and education.

The cyberage has also generated an enormous amount of revenue. Total spending on IT and telecommunications is forecasted to grow by more than 6 percent each year. Worldwide enterprise IT spending is forecast to reach $2.5 trillion in 2015.[2] More than 2 billion people are using email, sending 90 trillion messages per year. Social media sites like Facebook and Twitter are expanding exponentially and are now approaching 1 billion users.[3] Magnifying the importance of the Internet is the fact that many critical infrastructure functions are now being conducted online, ranging from banking to control of shipping on the Mississippi River.

 To read an article on the implications of the IT revolution, go to the Brookings Institute website: **http://www.brookings.edu/research/reports/2003/02/labormarkets-sommers.**

According to Christopher Donner and his associates, cybercrime has gone through three stages of development:

- The first generation of cybercrime involved deviant acts characterized by the illegal exploitation of mainframe computers and operating systems. These behaviors involved crimes that were in existence before the creation of computers and the Internet, but technological innovations provided another method of commission. They were designed for financial gain or destruction of restricted information.
- The second generation of cybercrime used computer networks and is considered hybrid crime. It involves criminality that was already in existence but has expanded and adapted through the use of the Internet. Hacking and cracking are common forms of this generation, as they were a product of early "phone phreakers." (Phone phreakers dialed around the telephone network to understand how the phone system worked, using their knowledge to make illegal phone calls, wiretap telephones, or steal telephone company equipment.) These crimes were created prior to the creation of the Internet but could now be performed in a different and more criminally effective manner. Using the Internet made cybercrime more difficult to detect and rendered cybercriminals more immune from prosecution.

- The third generation of cybercrime is identified by the nature of distribution and was solely developed by the creation of the Internet. These crimes would not exist if not for the Internet, as that is the only place they can occur. Dissemination of malware, such as viruses or Trojan horses, is an example of this generation of cybercrime.[4]

CONTEMPORARY CYBERCRIME

LO2 Compare and contrast cybertheft, cybervandalism, and cyberwar

The vast network of mobile and stationary computer networks has become a target for illegal activities and enterprise. Criminals are becoming more technologically sophisticated, routinely using the Internet to carry out their criminal conspiracies. Some cybercriminals use modern technology to sell illegal goods and services, or conversely, to illegally appropriate legitimate products and services. **Cybertheft** schemes range from illegal copying of copyrighted material to using technology to commit traditional theft-based offenses such as larceny and fraud.

Another type of cybercriminal is motivated less by profit and more by the urge to commit **cybervandalism** or technological destruction. They aim their malicious attacks at disrupting, defacing, and destroying technology that they find offensive.

A third type of cybercrime, **cyberwar**, is political, involving spying, espionage, and even **cyberterrorism**, acts aimed at undermining the social, economic, and political system of an enemy nation by destroying its electronic infrastructure and disrupting its economy.

In sum, some cybercriminals are high-tech thieves while others are high-tech vandals; the property they destroy is electronic rather than physical. And some use the Internet to plot and carry out terrorist activities, going as far as to wage cyberwar (see Concept Summary 15.1).

This new array of crimes presents a compelling challenge for the justice system and law enforcement community because (a) it is rapidly evolving with new schemes being created daily, (b) it is difficult to detect through traditional law enforcement channels, and (c) its control demands that agents of the justice system develop technical skills that match those of the perpetrators.[5] It may even be possible that the recent crime drop is a result of cybercrime replacing traditional street crime. Instead of robbing a bank at gunpoint, a new group of contemporary thieves finds it easier to hack into accounts and transfer funds to offshore banks. Instead of shoplifting from a brick and mortar store, the contemporary cyberthief devises clever schemes to steal from etailers. And instead of limiting their criminal escapades to the local population, transnational gang members now find a whole world of opportunity.

Cybercrimes also present a significant challenge for criminologists because they defy long-held assumptions about the cause of crime. How can we say that crime is a function of social forces, the social environment, or the social structure, when these contemporary criminals are typically highly educated and technologically sophisticated people who commit their crimes in places far removed from their victims? By their very nature, cybercrimes demand a

cybertheft Use of computer networks for criminal profits. Illegal copyright infringement, identity theft, and Internet securities fraud are examples of cybertheft.

cybervandalism Malicious attacks aimed at disrupting, defacing, and destroying technology.

cyberwar Using cyberspace for acts of war, including spying and disrupting an enemy's computer network.

cyberterrorism Internet attacks against an enemy nation's technological infrastructure.

TYPES OF CYBERCRIME

15.1

concept summary

Crime	Definition	Examples
Cybertheft	Use of cyberspace to distribute illegal goods and services or to defraud people for quick profits	Illegal copyright infringement, identity theft, Internet securities fraud, warez
Cybervandalism	Use of cyberspace for revenge, destruction, and to achieve a malicious intent	Website defacement, worms, viruses, cyberstalking, cyberbullying
Cyberwarfare	An effort by enemy forces to disrupt the intersection where the virtual electronic reality of computers meets the physical world	Logic bombs used to disrupt or destroy "secure" systems or networks, Internet used to communicate covertly with agents around the world

CONNECTIONS

Chapter 13 reviewed the concept of enterprise crime and its motivations, and Chapter 14 covered public order crimes. Cybercrime can be viewed as a type of enterprise crime employing sophisticated technology to achieve illegal profits. It can also involve public order crimes such as the online purchase and sale of pornography and controlled substances. The Internet now enables these previously localized crimes to be conducted on a global scale.

Ask Yourself ...

Which theories of crime do you believe best explain cybercrimes? Are cybercriminals impulsive people who lack self-control? If so, how did they attain the technological expertise to devise intricate Internet theft schemes or hack into the computers of financial institutions?

high degree of self-control and planning, something a truly impulsive or mentally unstable person would have difficulty achieving. As cybercrime expert Majid Yar explains, it may be that "considerable theoretical innovation" will be required before criminologists can fully understand this phenomenon.[6]

CYBERTHEFT: CYBERCRIMES FOR PROFIT

In 2014, Russian national Aleksandr Andreevich Panin pleaded guilty to a conspiracy charge associated with his role as the primary developer and distributor of malicious software, malware specifically designed to facilitate online theft from financial institutions. SpyEye infected more than 1.4 million computers and had the ability to detect and copy information stored on those computers and using it to transfer money out of victims' bank accounts and into accounts controlled by criminals. What made this case unusual was that rather than using SpyEye himself, Panin sold the "product" online in criminal forums. He actually advertised the features of the program, bragging that it could be used to obtain credit card information. His 150 "clients" paid him up to $8,500 for the program and then used it to infect victims' computers. The program collected large amounts of financial and personal information and sent it back to servers under the control of the criminals. They were then able to hack into bank accounts, withdraw stolen funds, create bogus credit cards, and so on. Things were going well until one of Panin's clients turned out to be an FBI agent.[7]

It is ironic that technological breakthroughs since the dawn of the Industrial Revolution—such as telephones and automobiles—not only brought with them dramatic improvements for society but also created new opportunities for criminal wrongdoing: criminals use the telephone to place bets or threaten victims; cars can be stolen and sold for big profits.[8] The same pattern is now occurring during the IT revolution. The computer and Internet provide opportunities for socially beneficial endeavors—such as education, research, commerce, and entertainment—while at the same time serving as a tool to facilitate illegal activity. Computer-based technology allows criminals to operate in a more efficient and effective manner. Cyberthieves now have the luxury of remaining anonymous, living in any part of the world, conducting their business during the day or in the evening, working alone or in a group, while at the same time reaching a much wider number of potential victims than ever before. No longer is the con artist or criminal entrepreneur limited to fleecing victims in a particular geographic locale; the whole world can be his or her target. The advent of these international cybercrimes necessitates novel approaches to law enforcement. Take the case of Aleksandr Panin, the SpyEye program developer. He lived in Russia, beyond the reach of American law. However, he made the mistake of traveling to the Dominican Republic for a vacation, where he was detained by local police. He was then put on a plane to Atlanta, where he was taken into custody by federal agents.

The technology revolution has opened novel methods for cybertheft that heretofore were nonexistent, ranging from the unlawful distribution of computer software to Internet security fraud. Cyberthieves conspire to use cyberspace to either distribute illegal goods and services or to defraud people for quick profits. Some of the most common methods are discussed here.

Computer Fraud

 List some examples of computer fraud

Jason Schrum was employed by Axis Worldwide Supply Chain & Logistics, Inc., a company that provides services related to international and interstate shipping and logistics, including shipping large materials used in construction projects. Schrum was a transportation manager for Axis and an administrator for their computer system until his termination over a dispute. He then went to work for a competitor of Axis. Despite the fact that he no longer was an employee of Axis or had authorized access to their computer systems, one night Schrum accessed the Axis computer system and carried out numerous actions, including deleting customer shipment records and manipulating shipping rate tables, costing the company thousands to repair and correct. After he was caught, Schrum pleaded guilty to one felony count of computer fraud.[9]

Jason Schrum's crime falls under the general category of computer fraud—not a unique offense, but rather a common-law crime committed using contemporary technology. Many computer crimes are prosecuted under such traditional criminal statutes as larceny or fraud. However, not all computer crimes fall under common-law statutes, because the property stolen may be intangible (electronic and/or magnetic impulse). Some of these crimes are listed in Exhibit 15.1. These are but a few of the most common examples, and the list is as long as the imagination of the criminal mind.

There are a number of recent trends in computer frauds. Internal attacks are now outgrowing external attacks at the world's largest financial institutions. According to one global security survey, about 60 percent of U.S. companies report being hit by computer network attacks in the past year, and as Figure 15.1 shows, most of these were by employees.[10]

Theft from ATMs

Automatic teller machines (ATMs) attract the attention of cybercriminals looking for easy profits.[11] Rather than robbing an ATM user at gunpoint, the cybercriminal relies on stealth and technological skill to commit the crime. Take for instance the case of two brothers from Bulgaria who were charged with attempting to defraud two banks

EXHIBIT 15.1

Examples of Computer Fraud

- *Theft of information.* The unauthorized obtaining of information from a computer (hacking), including software that is copied for profit.
- *The "salami" slice.* With this type of fraud, the perpetrator carefully skims small sums from the balances of a large number of accounts in order to bypass internal controls and escape detection.
- *Software theft.* The comparative ease of making copies of computer software has led to a huge illegal market, depriving authors of very significant revenues.
- *Manipulation of accounts/banking systems.* Similar to a "salami" slice but on a much larger and usually more complex scale. Sometimes perpetrated as a "one-off kamikaze" fraud.
- *Corporate espionage.* Trade secrets are stolen by a company's competitors, which can be either domestic or foreign. The goal is to increase the rival company's (or nation's) competitive edge in the global marketplace.

SOURCES: Australian Institute of Criminology, "Nine Types of Computer Crime," http://www.crime.hku.hk/cybercrime.htm; Cross Domain Solutions, "Cyber Crime," http://www.crossdomainsolutions.com/cyber-crime/ (sites accessed June 2014).

Top Security Threats

Which of the following possible sources of breaches or espionage pose the greatest threat to your organization in 2012?

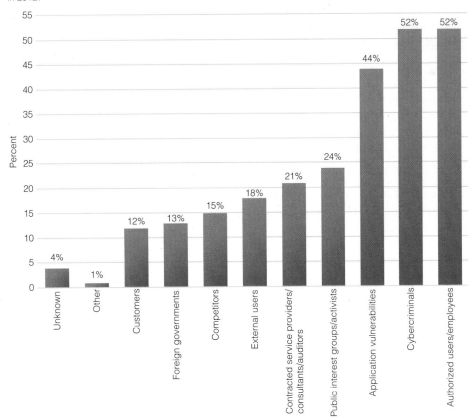

FIGURE 15.1 Computer Security Threats Against US Companies

SOURCE: *InformationWeek,* "Global Security Survey 2012," July 2013, http://reports.informationweek.com/abstract/21/8815/security/research-2012-strategic-security-survey.html (accessed June 2014).

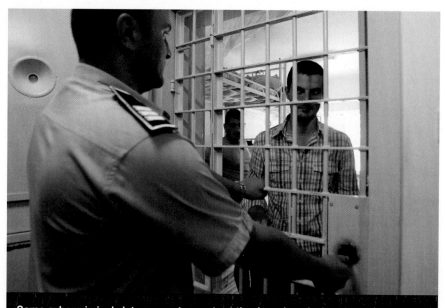

Some cybercriminals later go on to create anti-cybercrime devices. Their specialized knowledge can come in handy to law enforcement. On May 15, 2013, a prison guard opens the fenced door leading to the cell of Valentin Boanta at the Vaslui penitentiary, northeast of Bucharest, Romania. Boanta has created a device which he says could make the world's ATMs impregnable, even to tech-savvy criminals like himself. Boanta says his Secure Revolving System (SRS) can be installed in any ATM. It allows the bank card to be inserted longer side first and then rotates it to prevent skimmers being able to lock on to the magnetic data strip. The system returns the card to its user with a reverse rotation. Boanta, 33, is six months into a five-year sentence for supplying gadgets to an organized crime gang used to conceal ATM skimmers, which can copy data from an unsuspecting ATM user's card so a clone card can be created.

Bogdan Cristel/Reuters/Landov

of more than $1 million by engaging in **ATM skimming**: placing an electronic device on an ATM that scoops information from a bank card's magnetic strip whenever a customer uses the machine. Skimmers can then create their own bank cards and steal from customer accounts.[12] ATM skimming now costs U.S. banks hundreds of millions of dollars annually.

The devices planted on ATMs are usually undetectable because they blend right into the ATM's physical structure. Some cybercriminals attach a phony keypad on top of the real keypad which records every keystroke as customers punch in their PINs. These skimming devices are installed for short periods of time—usually just a few hours—so they're often attached to an ATM by nothing more than double-sided tape. They are then removed by the criminals, who download the stolen account information and encode it onto blank cards. The cards are used to make withdrawals

ATM skimming Using an electronic device or camera that copies information from a bank card's magnetic strip whenever a customer uses an ATM, by photographing their key strokes.

from victims' accounts at other ATMs. Some cyberthieves use a realistic-looking card reader placed over the factory-installed card reader. When customers insert their ATM card into the phony reader, their account info is swiped and stored on a small attached laptop sent wirelessly to the criminals waiting nearby.

Skimmers can also make use of a hidden camera, installed on or near an ATM, to record customers' entry of their PINs into the ATM's keypad.

Distributing Illicit or Illegal Services and Material

LO4 Assess how the Internet can facilitate the sale of illegal materials

The Internet has become a prime source for the delivery of illicit or legally prohibited material. Included within this market are distribution of pornography and obscene material, including kiddie porn, and the distribution of dangerous drugs.

Distributing Obscenity In March 2008, 22 people, including 12 Americans, were charged with participating in an international child pornography ring. Investigators confiscated more than 400,000 pictures, video files, and other images showing children engaged in sexual behavior. Some of the child victims were as young as 5 years old; many displayed innocent characteristics such as wearing their hair in pigtails. The ring was begun in Australia and recruited pornographers all over the world, including England, Canada, and Germany.

Though the ring was first discovered and infiltrated in 2006, it took more than two years to get indictments because of its technical sophistication, which included the use of encryption, background checks, and other security measures. One of the men indicted, 54-year-old Raymond Roy of San Juan Capistrano, California, posted videos of Thai children "to give everyone something to do for an afternoon." Another posting made on July 10, 2007, stated, "This one may offend here, so a word of caution, these girls are heavily drugged. Not much action to speak of, the girls are (sic) to (expletive deleted) up to move, or resist. Three girls, the first one being the youngest, around 8 or 9 yo." ("Yo" stands for "years old.")

The 12 men were charged with engaging in a child exploitation enterprise; illegally posting notices seeking to receive, exchange, and distribute child porn across state lines; and obstruction of justice. Several also were charged with producing the pornography—meaning they had contact with the children who were exploited.[13]

The IT revolution has revitalized the porn industry. The Internet is an ideal venue for selling and distributing obscene material; the computer is an ideal device for storage and viewing. It is difficult to estimate the vast number of websites featuring sexual content, including nude photos, videos, live sex acts, and webcam strip sessions among other forms of "adult entertainment."[14]

While there is no conclusive data on the extent of Internet porn sites, some experts claim that about 5 percent of the top million websites, more than 40,000, are sex related and about 15 percent of all searches are for "adult" content.[15] That would mean that adult sites get billions of hits each year. The single most popular adult site in the world is Live-Jasmin.com, a webcam site which gets around 32 million visitors a month, or almost 2.5 percent of all Internet users.[16] But these data may undercount the actual number of adult sites: a search in Google on the word "porn" returned over 80 million pages, and "xxx" returned more than 128 million web pages. People are often directed to these sites through "porn-napping" and "typosquatted" websites. Porn-nappers buy expired domain names of existing sites and then try to sell adult material to people who stumble on them while surfing. Typosquat websites are those where a pornographer has deliberately registered names with typos so that people surfing the Net are directed to pornography sites if they misspell a word or put in the wrong keystroke—for example, typing in teltubbies.com instead of teletubbies.[17]

How do adult sites operate today? There are a number of different schemes in operation:[18]

- A large firm sells annual subscriptions in exchange for unlimited access to content.
- Password services charge an annual fee to deliver access to hundreds of small sites, which share the subscription revenues.
- Large firms provide free content to smaller affiliate sites. The affiliates post the free content and then try to channel visitors to the large sites, which give the smaller sites a percentage of the fees paid by those who sign up.
- Webmasters forward traffic to another porn site in return for a small per-consumer fee. In many cases, the consumer is sent to the other sites involuntarily, which is known in the industry as *mousetrapping*. Web surfers who try to close out a window after visiting an adult site are sent to anotherweb page automatically. This can repeat dozens of times, causing users to panic and restart their computers in order to escape.
- Adult sites cater to niche audiences looking for specific kinds of adult content. While some sites cater to legal sexually related material, others cross the legal border by peddling access to obscene material or even kiddie porn.

Prosecuting Internet Pornography Despite some successful prosecutions, it has been difficult to control Internet pornography. One reason is that offenders can be scattered around the world, making identification and arrest difficult. There needs to be significant law enforcement agency cooperation to gather evidence and locate suspects. Take for instance the recent Lost Boy case, which resulted in lengthy prison sentences for the principals involved. The Lost Boy online bulletin board was dedicated to men who have a sexual interest in young boys and was established to provide a forum to trade child pornography. Law enforcement authorities in the United States were made aware of the bulletin board after receiving information from Eurojust, the judicial cooperation arm of the European Union. Eurojust had obtained information from Norwegian and Italian authorities indicating that a North Hollywood, California, man was communicating with an Italian national about child pornography and how to engage in child sex tourism in Romania. Investigation revealed that Lost Boy had 35 members, 16 of whom were U.S. nationals. Other members of the network were located in countries around the world, including Belgium, Brazil, Canada, France, Germany, New Zealand, and the United Kingdom. To shield themselves from prosecution, the Lost Boy network had developed a thorough vetting process for new members, who were required to post child pornography to join the organization. Once accepted, members were required to continue posting child pornography to remain in good standing and to avoid removal from the board. Lost Boy members advised each other on techniques to evade detection by law enforcement, which included using screen names to mask identities and encrypting computer data. European law enforcement, the Brazilian Federal Police, and other agencies identified child molestation suspects in South America, Europe, and New Zealand. Three suspects in Romania, one in France, and another in Brazil have been charged, and offenders have been convicted in Norway and the United Kingdom. Law enforcement efforts have also identified dozens of child victims located in Norway, Romania, Brazil, and other nations.[19] The Lost Boy case illustrates the difficulty of controlling Internet pornography. Getting evidence sufficient for prosecution involved the cooperation of law enforcement agencies from around the world and the arrests of people in multiple countries, a very expensive and time-consuming activity. And while this prosecution was successful many other kiddie porn distributors are able to go free.

Distributing Dangerous Drugs

In 2013, Michael Arnold was sentenced to five years in prison for his role as the organizer and leader of the Pitcairn Internet pharmacy. From 2003 through 2007, Pitcairn sold more than 14 million doses of Schedule III and IV controlled substances, earning over $69 million in its four years of operation using websites such as ezdietpills.net, pillsavings.com, and doctorrefill.net. Arnold laundered Pitcairn's illegal proceeds through accounts in at least eight different countries, including Switzerland, Liechtenstein, the Netherlands, Canada, Panama, the Bahamas, St. Kitts and Nevis, and Curaçao.[20]

The Arnold case, in addition to many others, shows how the Internet has become a prime purveyor of prescription drugs, some of which can be quite dangerous when they are used to excess or fall into the hands of minors. Surveys by the National Center on Addiction and Substance Abuse at Columbia University found that despite a recent decline in the number of websites advertising or selling controlled prescription drugs such as Oxycontin, Valium, Xanax, Vicodin, Ritalin, and Adderall, 85 percent of websites that sold such drugs did not require a prescription. They uncovered a total of 365 websites that advertised or sold controlled prescription drugs. Only 2 of the 365 sites were certified by the National Association of Boards of Pharmacy as Verified Internet Pharmacy Practice Sites.[21] Relatively few required that the patient provide a prescription from his or her doctor, and of those that did, about half only required that an original prescription be provided. This allowed prescriptions to be faxed, giving buyers the opportunity for multiple purchases with a single script. The report also found sites selling online "medical consultations," where doctors see many patients a day to fill or refill prescriptions for controlled drugs without regard for the standards of medical practice.

Children are especially at risk, and more than 2 million kids are feared to be abusing an illegally obtained prescription drug. More teens have abused these drugs than many other illegal drugs, including Ecstasy, cocaine, crack, and methamphetamine. With access to a credit card, they

denial-of-service attack Extorting money from an Internet service user by threatening to prevent the user from having access to the service.

can order opioid-based drugs (e.g., codeine, Demerol, Oxycontin, Percocet, and Darvon), depressants (e.g., Xanax, Librium, and Valium), and stimulants (e.g., Adderall, Dexedrine, and Ritalin).

Denial-of-Service Attack

In March 2013, in an attack that was called DarkSeoul, malware designed to destroy data in the hard drives of tens of thousands of PCs and servers was launched at targeted financial institutions and media firms in South Korea, with the payload set to activate at the same time. At the same time the malware was triggered, the website of the Korean network provider LG U+ was defaced and the networks of other targeted organizations started going down. Some experts believed the attacks were instituted by North Korea to disrupt South Korea economically, but others concluded that the attacks were meant to conceal financial gain and that plans for DarkSeoul may have been put in motion as far back as 2011 in order to conceal the wiring of fraudulent funds from victims' accounts. The attackers, it seems, were attempting to create a diversion in order to cash out as many compromised accounts as possible before operations were ground to a halt by security systems.[22]

DarkSeoul is an example of a **denial-of-service attack**, a type of cybercrime that can take on many forms. Examples include:

- Attempts to flood a computer network, thereby preventing legitimate network traffic
- Attempts to disrupt connections within a computer network, thereby preventing access to a service
- Attempts to prevent a particular individual from accessing a service
- Attempts to disrupt service to a specific system or person

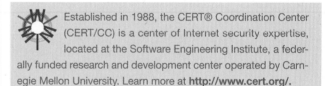

Established in 1988, the CERT® Coordination Center (CERT/CC) is a center of Internet security expertise, located at the Software Engineering Institute, a federally funded research and development center operated by Carnegie Mellon University. Learn more at **http://www.cert.org/**.

A denial-of-service attack may involve threatening or actually flooding an Internet site with millions of bogus messages or orders so that the services will be tied up and unable to perform as promised. Unless the site operator pays extortion, the attackers threaten to keep up the interference until real consumers become frustrated and abandon the site. Even so-called respectable businesspeople have been accused of launching denial-of-service attacks against rival business interests.[23]

Online gambling casinos—a multibillion-dollar a year industry—have proven particularly vulnerable to attack. Hundreds of attacks have been launched against online casinos located in Costa Rica, the Caribbean, and Great

Britain. If the attack coincides with a big sporting event such as the Super Bowl, the casinos may give in and make payments rather than lose revenue and fray customer relations.[24] Another vulnerable target is online gaming sites. In 2014, massive attacks disrupted service on games such as Blizzard's Battle.net, Riot Games' League of Legends, and the Origin service run by Electronic Arts.[25]

Illegal Copyright Infringement

LO5 Distinguish between the different forms of stealing intellectual property

Groups of individuals have been working together to illegally obtain software and then "crack" or "rip" its copyright protections, before posting it on the Internet for other members of the group to use; this is called **warez**.

Frequently, these new pirated copies reach the Internet days or weeks before the legitimate product is commercially available. The government has actively pursued members of the warez community, and some have been charged and convicted under the Computer Fraud and Abuse Act (CFAA), which criminalizes accessing computer systems without authorization to obtain information,[26] and the Digital Millennium Copyright Act (DMCA), which makes it a crime to circumvent antipiracy measures built into most commercial software and also outlaws the manufacture, sale, or distribution of code-cracking devices used to illegally copy software.[27]

File Sharing Another form of illegal copyright infringement involves file-sharing programs that allow Internet users to download music and other copyrighted material without paying the artists and record producers their rightful royalties. Theft through the illegal reproduction and distribution of movies, software, games, and music is estimated to cost U.S. industries more than $20 billion worldwide each year.

Although some students routinely share files and download music, criminal copyright infringement represents a serious economic threat. The United States Criminal Code provides penalties for a first-time offender of five years incarceration and a fine of $250,000.[28] Other provisions provide for the forfeiture and destruction of infringing copies and all equipment used to make the copies.[29]

On June 27, 2005, copyright protection of music and other types of entertainment distributed via the Internet was upheld by the Supreme Court in the case of *MGM Studios, Inc. v. Grokster*, 125 S. Ct. 2764 (2005). The Court unanimously held that software distributors such as Grokster could be sued for inducing copyright infringement if they market file-sharing software that might induce people to illegally copy protected material even if that software could also be used for legitimate purposes. Justice Souter wrote:

We hold that one who distributes a device with the object of promoting its use to infringe copyright, as shown by the clear expression or other affirmative steps taken to foster infringement, is liable for the resulting acts of infringement by third parties.

As a result of the opinion, on November 7, 2005, Grokster announced that it would suspend its file-sharing service; it was also forced to pay $50 million to the music and recording industries.

Internet Securities Fraud

Fifteen-year-old Jonathan Lebed was charged with securities fraud by the SEC after he repeatedly bought low-cost, thinly traded stocks and then spread hundreds of false and misleading messages concerning them—generally baseless price predictions. After their values were artificially inflated, Lebed sold the securities at an inflated price. His smallest one-day gain was $12,000, and one day he made $74,000. Lebed agreed to findings of fraud but later questioned whether he had done anything wrong; he was forced to hand over his illicit gains, plus interest, which came to $285,000.[30]

Though he might not agree, young Lebed's actions are considered Internet fraud because they involve using the Internet to intentionally manipulate the securities marketplace for profit. There are three major types of Internet securities fraud today:

- *Market manipulation*. Stock market manipulation occurs when an individual tries to control the price of stock by interfering with the natural forces of supply and demand. There are two principal forms of this crime: the "pump and dump" and the "cybersmear." In a pump and dump scheme, erroneous and deceptive information is posted online to get unsuspecting investors interested in a stock while those spreading the information sell previously purchased stock at an inflated price. The cybersmear is a reverse pump and dump: negative information is spread online about a stock, driving down its price and enabling people to buy it at an artificially low price before rebuttals by the company's officers reinflate the price.[31]
- *Fraudulent offerings of securities*. Some cybercriminals create websites specifically designed to fraudulently sell securities. To make the offerings look more attractive than they are, assets may be inflated, expected returns overstated, and risks understated. In these schemes, investors are promised abnormally high profits on their investments. No investment is actually made. Early investors are paid returns with the investment money received from the later investors. The system

> **warez** A term computer hackers and software pirates use to describe a game or application that is made available for use on the Internet in violation of its copyright protection.

Hanjuan Jin enters the federal courthouse in Chicago before being sentenced to four years in prison for stealing trade secrets from Motorola. Jin, who worked as a software engineer for Motorola for nine years, was stopped during a random security search at Chicago's O'Hare International Airport before she could board a flight to China. Prosecutors say she was carrying $31,000 and hundreds of confidential Motorola documents, many stored on a laptop, four external hard drives, thumb drives, and other devices. Among the secrets she carried were descriptions of a walkie-talkie type feature on Motorola cell phones that would have benefited the Chinese military.

no money was actually invested, the dividends were paid from new investments, and most of the cash was siphoned off by the schemers.

- *Illegal touting.* This crime occurs when individuals make securities recommendations and fail to disclose that they are being paid to disseminate their favorable opinions. Section 17(b) of the Securities Act of 1933 requires that paid touters disclose the nature, source, and amount of their compensation. If those who tout stocks fail to disclose their relationship with the company, information misleads investors into believing that the speaker is objective and credible rather than bought and paid for.

Identity Theft

LO6 Define the terms *identity theft* and *phishing*

Identity theft occurs when a person uses the Internet to steal someone's identity and/or impersonate the victim to open a new credit card account or conduct some other financial transaction. It is a type of cybercrime that has grown at surprising rates over the past few years.[33]

Identity theft can destroy a person's life by manipulating credit records or stealing from their bank accounts. Identity thieves use a variety of techniques to steal information. They may fill out change of address cards at the post office and obtain people's credit card bills and bank statements. They may then call the credit card issuer and, pretending to be the victim, ask for a change in address on the account. They can then charge numerous items over the Internet and have the merchandise sent to the new address. It may take months for the victim to realize the fraud because the victim is not getting bills from the credit card company.

What are the most common goals of credit card thieves? One survey found that opening new lines of credit remains the most frequently occurring use for a victim's identity, followed by using personal information to make charges on stolen credit cards and debit cards, obtaining utilities, applying for bogus personal loans and business loans, and check fraud (personal information is used to access an existing account via theft or the creation of false checks).[34]

Some identity theft schemes are extremely elaborate. In one scam, 19 people were indicted on charges that they had created an organization called Shadowcrew to provide stolen credit card numbers and identity documents through an online marketplace. The stolen account numbers were contributed by approved "vendors" who had been granted permission to sell on the Shadowcrew site after being vetted through a complex review process. Shadowcrew members allegedly trafficked in at least 1.5 million stolen credit card numbers and caused total losses in excess of $4 million.[35]

usually collapses, and the later investors do not receive dividends and lose their initial investment. For example, the Tri-West Investment Company solicited investments in "prime bank notes."[32] Visitors to their website were promised an annualized rate of return of 120 percent plus return of their principal at the end of a year, as well as substantial referral fees of 15 percent on all referred investments. The website, which contained alleged testimonials describing instant wealth from early investors, also told visitors that their investments were "guaranteed." Investors contributed $60 million in funds to Tri-West, and some "dividends" were paid. However,

identity theft Using the Internet to steal someone's identity and/or impersonate the victim in order to conduct illicit transactions such as committing fraud using the victim's name and identity.

While this scheme highlights the seriousness and extent of the problem, relatively little is known about the extent of identity theft and further research is required to better understand this growing cybercrime.[36]

Phishing Some identity thieves create false emails or websites (there are now more than 40,000 in operation) that look legitimate but are designed to gain illegal access to a victim's personal information; this is known as **phishing** (also known as *carding* and *spoofing*).[37]

Some phishers send out emails that look like they come from a credit card company or online store telling victims there is a problem with their account credit or balance. To fix the problem and update their account, they are asked to submit their name, address, phone numbers, personal information, credit card account numbers, and Social Security number (SSN). Or the email may direct them to a phony website that purports to be a legitimate company or business enterprise. Once victims access the website, they are asked to provide personal information or financial account information so the problem can be fixed. Some phishing schemes involve job offers. Once the unsuspecting victims fill out the "application," answering personal questions and including their Social Security number, the phisher has them in his or her grasp. Another variation of this crime is **spear-phishing**, where cybercriminals target specific victims, sending them emails that contain accurate information about their lives, friends, and activities that was obtained from social networking sites, blogs, or other websites. Personal information makes the message seem legitimate and increases the chances the victims will open the email or go to a tainted website by clicking on a link where malware harvests details such as the victims' usernames and passwords, bank account details, credit card numbers, and other personal information. The criminals can also gain access to private networks and cause disruptions or steal intellectual property and trade secrets.[38] One ingenious scam is referred to as *reshipping* and is discussed in Exhibit 15.2.

Once phishers have a victim's personal information, they can do three things. They can gain access to preexisting accounts, banking, credit cards, and buy things using those accounts. Phishers can use the information to open brand new banking accounts and credit cards without the victim's knowledge. Finally, the phishers can implant viruses into their software that forwards the phishing email to other recipients once one person responds to the original email, thereby luring more potential victims into their net. Some common phishing scams are listed in Exhibit 15.3.

Phishing emails and websites have become even more of a problem now that cybercriminals can easily copy brand names, logos, and corporate personnel insignia directly into the email. The look is so authentic that victims believe the email comes from the advertised company. Most phishers send out spam emails to a large number of recipients knowing that some of those recipients will have accounts with the company they are impersonating.

Money Mules Once phishers get your personal and financial information through deception and trickery, how do they profit from their account access? One way is to divert money electronically from bank accounts in order to buy high-end merchandise such as precious stones and expensive watches from jewelry stores.[39] The phishers contact these jewelry stores, tell them what they'd like to buy, and promise they will wire the money the next day. A **money mule** goes to the

phishing Sometimes called carding or brand spoofing, phishing is a scam where the perpetrator sends out emails appearing to come from legitimate web enterprises such as eBay, Amazon, and PayPal in an effort to get the recipient to reveal personal and financial information.

spear-phishing Targeting specific victims, sending them emails that contain accurate information about their lives obtained from social networking sites, and asking them to open an email attachment where malware harvests details such as the victims' usernames and passwords, bank account details, credit card numbers, and other personal information.

money mule Someone who collects and transfers money or goods acquired illegally and then transfers them to a third party.

EXHIBIT 15.3

Common Phishing Scams

- *Account verification scams.* Individuals purchase domain names that are similar to those of legitimate companies, such as *Amazon.Accounts.net*. The real company is Amazon, but it does not have *Accounts* in its domain name. These con artists then send out millions of emails asking consumers to verify account information and Social Security numbers. The victim is directed to a bogus website by clicking the legitimate-looking address.

- *Sign-in rosters.* There are some companies and governmental agencies (colleges, EDD, state-sponsored programs) that ask you to put your name and SSN on a sign-in roster. Identity thieves may sign up toward the end of a page so that they can copy and collect personal identifying information.

- *"Help move money from my country," aka Nigerian 419 scam.* A bogus email is sent from an alleged representative of a foreign government asking the victim to help move money from one account to another. Some forms include requests to help a dying woman or free a political prisoner. Some claim that the victim has been the recipient of a legacy or a winning lottery ticket. Nigerian money offers now account for about 12 percent of the scam offers.

- *Canadian/Netherlands lottery.* Originating from the Netherlands and other foreign countries, these scams usually ask for money to hold the prize until the victim can collect in person.

- *"Free credit report."* Almost all "free credit report" emails are scams. Either the person is trying to find out the victim's Social Security number or the victim is billed for services later on.

- *"You have won a free gift."* The victims receive an email about a free gift or prize. They just have to send their credit card info to take care of shipping and handling. Responding may result in hundreds of spams or telemarketing calls.

- *Email chain letters/pyramid schemes.* Victims are sent an official looking email requesting cooperation by sending a report to five friends or relatives. Those who respond are then contacted for money in order to keep the chain going.

- *"Find out everything on anyone."* This email is trying to solicit money by offering a CD or program that victims can use to find out personal information on another person. However, the information is actually in the public domain and can be easily accessed without the program.

- *Job advertisement scams.* Phishers spoofing legitimate Internet job websites (for instance spoofing Monster.com) contact a victim promising a high-paying job. They solicit personal information, including Social Security numbers.

- *VISA/MasterCard scam.* A VISA or MasterCard "employee" sends an email asking to confirm unusual spending activity and asks the victim for the code on the back of his or her credit card.

SOURCE: Identity Theft Resource Center (ITRC), "Scams and Consumer Alerts," http://www.idtheftcenter.org (accessed June 2014).

store to pick up the merchandise and either gives the items to the organizers of the scheme or converts them to cash and uses money transfer services to launder the funds.

In many cases, these money mules are willing participants in the criminal scheme. But increasingly, as part of this scheme, they are unsuspecting people hired via "work-at-home" advertisements who end up laundering some of the funds stolen from bank accounts. The criminals email prospective candidates claiming to have seen their résumés on job websites and offer them a job. The hired employees are provided long and seemingly legitimate work contracts and actual websites to log into for instructions. They're instructed to either open a bank account or use their own bank account in order to receive funds via wire and transactions from numerous banks and then use money transfer services to send the money overseas.

Vishing Voice over Internet Protocol (VoIP) is a technology that allows people to make voice calls using a broadband Internet connection instead of a regular (or analog) phone line.[40] Some VoIP services only allow subscribers to call other people using the same service, but others allow you to call anyone who has a telephone number—including local, long distance, mobile, and international numbers. Also, while some VoIP services only work over a computer or a special VoIP phone, others allow traditional phone hookups connected to a VoIP adapter. Cyberthieves have already employed this technology in identity theft schemes.

In one version, the victim receives an email that gives him or her a number to call. Those who call this "customer service" number (a VoIP account, not a real financial institution) are led through a series of voice-prompted menus that ask for account numbers, passwords, and other critical information. In another version, the victim is contacted over the phone instead of by email. The call is either a live person or a recorded message directing the victim to take action to protect a personal account. The visher may have collected some personal information, including account or credit card numbers, which can create a false sense of security for the victim.[41]

A complex phishing scheme is set out in the Profiles in Crime feature.

Combating Phishing and Identity Theft To meet the increasing threat of phishing and identity theft, Congress passed the Identity Theft and Assumption Deterrence Act of 1998 (Identity Theft Act) to make it a federal crime when anyone:

Knowingly transfers or uses, without lawful authority, a means of identification of another person with the intent

OPERATION PHISH PHRY

The FBI called it Operation Phish Phry, a play on words for the popular cyber-crime of phishing, fraudulently collecting personal information from victims that can be used to defraud financial institutions by creating dummy accounts or bogus credit cards. However, this Phish Phry was not a "mom and pop" scam, but an international conspiracy involving more than 50 people in the United States and Egypt. An elaborate global conspiracy designed to steal identities by targeting U.S.-based financial institutions, Phish Phry victimized account holders by fraudulently using their personal financial information. Egypt-based hackers obtained bank account numbers and related personal identification information from bank customers by sending email messages that appeared to be official correspondence from banks or credit card vendors. The bank customers were directed to fake web-sites purporting to be linked to financial institutions, where the customers were asked to enter their account numbers, passwords, and other information. Because the websites appeared to be legitimate—complete with bank logos and legal disclaimers—the customers did not realize that the websites did not belong to legitimate financial institutions.

Armed with the bank account information, members of the conspiracy hacked into accounts at two banks. Once they accessed the accounts, the Egyptians communicated via text messages, telephone calls, and Internet chat groups with co-conspirators in the United States. Through these communications, members of the criminal ring coordinated the illicit online transfer of funds from compromised accounts to newly created fraudulent accounts. In the United States, conspirators directed associates to recruit "runners" who set up bank accounts where the funds stolen from the compromised accounts could be transferred and withdrawn. A portion of the illegally obtained funds were then transferred via wire services to individuals operating in Egypt who had originally provided the bank account information obtained via phishing.

After the case was blown open by American and Egyptian law enforcement agents, the conspirators were charged with a variety of crimes, including conspiracy to commit wire fraud and bank fraud; aggravated identity theft; conspiracy to commit computer fraud, specifically unauthorized access to protected computers in connection with fraudulent bank transfers; and domestic and international money laundering.

SOURCE: FBI press release, "One Hundred Linked to International Computer Hacking Ring Charged by United States and Egypt in Operation Phish Phry," October 7, 2009.

---

to commit, or to aid or abet, any unlawful activity that constitutes a violation of Federal law, or that constitutes a felony under any applicable State or local law.[42]

Violations of the act are investigated by federal investigative agencies such as the U.S. Secret Service, the FBI, and the U.S. Postal Inspection Service. In 2004, the Identity Theft Penalty Enhancement Act was signed into law; the act increases existing penalties for the crime of identity theft, establishes aggravated identity theft as a criminal offense, and establishes mandatory penalties for aggravated identity theft. According to this law, anyone who knowingly "transfers, possesses, or uses, without lawful authority" someone else's identification will be sentenced to an extra prison term of two years with no possibility of probation. Committing identity fraud while engaged in crimes associated with terrorism—such as aircraft destruction, arson, airport violence, or kidnapping top government officials—will receive a mandatory sentence enhancement of five years.[43]

Etailing Fraud

New fraud schemes are evolving to reflect the fact that billions of dollars in goods are sold on the Internet each year. **Etailing fraud** can involve both illegally buying and selling merchandise on the Net.

Not only do etail frauds involve selling merchandise, they can also involve buyer fraud. One scam involves purchasing top of the line electronic equipment over the Net and then purchasing a second, similar looking but cheaper model of the same brand. The cheaper item is then returned to the etailer after switching bar codes and boxes with the more expensive unit. Because etail return processing centers don't always check returned goods closely, they may send a refund for the value of the higher priced model.

In another tactic, called *shoplisting*, a person obtains a legitimate receipt from a store either by buying it from a customer or finding it in the trash and then returns to the store and, casually shopping, picks up an identical product. He then takes the product and receipt to the returns departments and attempts to return it for cash, store credit, or a gift card, which the thief then sells on the Internet at a discount for quick cash. Not surprisingly, the underground market for receipts has been growing, as stores have liberalized return policies.[44] Some of the most common fraud schemes are included in Exhibit 15.4. Before you say, "How could anyone fall for this stuff?" remember that more than

etailing fraud Illegally buying and/or selling merchandise on the Internet.

EXHIBIT 15.4

Common Internet Fraud Schemes

Auto Auction Fraud

This is an Internet auction fraud involving the sale of automobiles. Many of the listings are for vehicles located outside the United States. In most cases the criminal attempts to sell vehicles they do not own. Criminals create attractive deals by advertising vehicles at prices below book value and claim that they must sell the vehicle because they are moving or being relocated for work. Due to the pending move, the criminals often refuse to meet with potential buyers or allow vehicle inspections and ultimately try to rush the sale. In an attempt to make the deal appear legitimate, the criminal often instructs victims to send full or partial payments to third-party agents via wire transfers and to fax their payment receipt to the seller as proof of payment. Once payment is made, the criminal pockets the money and the victim never receives the vehicle.

Hitman Scam

The victim receives an email from a member of an organization such as the "Ishmael Ghost Islamic Group." The emailer claims to have been sent to assassinate the victim and the victim's family members. The emailer asserts that the reason for the impending assassination resulted from an alleged offense, by the victim, against a member of the emailer's gang. In a bizarre twist, however, the emailer reveals that upon obtaining the victim's information, another member of the gang (purported to know a member of the victim's extended family) pleaded for the victim's pardon. The emailer alleges that an agreement was reached with the pleading gang member to allow the victim pardon from assassination if the victim takes some action such as sending $800 to a receiver in the United Kingdom for the migration of Islamic expatriates from the United States. Victims of this email are typically instructed to send the money via Western Union or Money Gram to a receiver in the United Kingdom. The emailer often gives the victim 72 hours to send the money or else pay with his/her life.

Economic Stimulus Scam

Another popular scam involves unsolicited calls regarding fraudulent "government stimulus money." The Internet Crime Complaint Center (IC3) received numerous complaints from victims receiving unsolicited telephone calls with a recorded message. The recorded voice message reportedly sounds very much like President Barack Obama discussing alleged government funds available for those who apply. Victims are warned that the offer is only available for a limited time and are instructed to visit certain websites to receive their money. These sites require victims to enter personal identifying information after which they are directed to a second page to receive notification of eligibility. Upon completion of an online application and payment of small fees, victims are guaranteed to receive a large sum of stimulus money, but they never do.

Pet Scams

A self-proclaimed breeder posts an online ad (along with a cute picture or even a streaming video) offering to sell a pet. The breeder asks the buyer to send in money, plus a little extra for delivery costs. But the buyer never gets the pet; the scam artist simply takes the money and runs.

Secret Shoppers and Funds Transfer Scams

Individuals are hired via the Web to rate experiences while shopping or dining. They are paid by check and asked to wire a percentage of the money to a third party. The check they had been sent bounces, and they are out the money they sent to the other party. As part of the scam, the fraudsters often use real logos from legitimate companies.

Adoption and Charity Fraud

A person is sent an email that tugs on his or her heartstrings, asking for a pressing donation to a charity and often using the subject header, "Urgent Assistance Is Needed." The name of a real charity is generally used, but the information provided sends the money to a con artist. One set of scams used the name of a legitimate British adoption agency to ask for money for orphaned or abandoned children.

Romance Fraud

A person encounters someone in an online dating or social networking site who lives far away or in another country. That person strikes up a relationship with him or her and then wants to meet, but needs money to cover travel expenses. Typically, that's just the beginning—the person may claim to have been taken ill or injured during the journey and ask for money to pay the hospital expenses.

Child Pornography Scareware

Malware is transmitted when computer users visit an infected website that is designed to "scare" the victim. The victim's computer locks up and displays a warning that the user has violated U.S. federal law. Child pornography is either embedded in a banner image that appears on the victim's screen or is revealed via an automatic browser redirecting them to a child pornography website. The scareware is used as an extortion technique by threatening prosecution for visiting or viewing these images. The victim is also informed that they have been recorded using audio, video, and other devices. The only way to unlock the computer is to pay the fine, usually between $300 and $5,000.

SOURCES: FBI, "Internet Crime Report 2013," http://www.ic3.gov/media/annualreport/2013_IC3Report.pdf; FBI, "Internet Crime Report 2008 and 2009," http://www.ic3.gov/media/annualreport/2009_IC3Report.pdf; "Internet Crime Report: The Top Scams of 2007," http://www.fbi.gov/page2/april08/ic3_report040308.html (sites accessed June 2014).

200,000 people file complaints with the government's Internet fraud center each year and these scams create more than $240 million in losses each year.[45]

CYBERVANDALISM: CYBERCRIME WITH MALICIOUS INTENT

LO7 Describe the different types of cybervandalism

In 2012, computers around the nation were attacked by the Reveton virus used by hackers in conjunction with Citadel malware—a software delivery platform that can disseminate various kinds of computer viruses. Unlike many other viruses—which activate when users open a file or attachment—Reveton is a drive-by virus that installs itself when users go to a compromised website; once infected, the victim's computer immediately locks. In the case of the Reveton virus, the infected computer's monitor displayed an official-looking screen with an FBI logo stating there had been a violation of federal law: illegal use of downloaded media, underage porn viewing, or computer-use negligence. It listed fines and penalties for each, and directed victims to pay $200 via a MoneyPak order. Victims were told if the demands were not met, criminal charges would be filed and the computer would remain locked on that screen. Some variants of Reveton can even turn on computer webcams and display the victim's picture on the frozen screen. Unfortunately for victims, the virus is difficult to resolve and may require professional attention. Even if victims are able to unfreeze their computer, the malware may still operate in the background and gather personal information such as usernames, passwords, and credit card numbers through embedded keystroke logging programs.[46]

Some cybercriminals may not be motivated by greed or profit but by the desire for revenge and destruction, to achieve a malicious intent (such as a denial-of-service attack launched in retaliation for some slight), to hurt and embarrass someone they are angry at, or simply to hurt people because they enjoy being destructive. They do not profit from their crimes other than to enjoy the havoc and harm they inflict on others; they are vandals in cyberspace.

Cybervandalism ranges from sending destructive viruses and worms to stalking or bullying people using cyberspace as a medium. Cybervandals may want to damage or deface websites or even, as Exhibit 15.5 reveals, pull a virtual fire alarm!

Cybervandals are motivated more by malice than greed:

- Some cybervandals target computers and networks seeking revenge for some perceived wrong.
- Some desire to exhibit their technical prowess and superiority.
- Some want to highlight the vulnerability of computer security systems. Some desire to spy on other people's

private financial and personal information (computer voyeurism).
- Some are mean-spirited bullies who want to harm others socially rather than physically.
- Some want to destroy computer security because they believe in a philosophy of open access to all systems and programs.[47]

What forms does cybervandalism take?

Worms, Viruses, Trojan Horses, Logic Bombs, and Spam

The most typical use of cyberspace for destructive intent comes in the sending or implanting of disruptive programs, called viruses, worms, Trojan horses, logic bombs, and spam.

EXHIBIT 15.5

Swatting

Cybervandals have developed a form of "entertainment" called "swatting": calling 911 and faking an emergency that draws a response from law enforcement—usually a SWAT team. The callers often tell tales of hostages about to be executed or bombs about to go off. The community is placed in danger as responders rush to the scene, taking them away from real emergencies. And the officers are placed in danger as unsuspecting residents may try to defend themselves. In one case, a swatter in Washington State was charged with pretending to be calling from the home of a California couple, saying he had just shot and murdered someone. A local SWAT team arrived on the scene, and the husband, who had been asleep in his home with his wife and two young children, heard something and went outside to investigate—after first stopping in the kitchen to pick up a knife. What he found was a group of SWAT assault rifles aimed directly at him. Fortunately, the situation didn't escalate, and no one was injured.

Swatters have become more sophisticated in their targets and use of technology. Consider the following Texas case. Five swatters in several states targeted people who were using online telephone party chat lines (or their family or friends). The swatters found personal details on the victims by accessing telecommunication company information stored on protected computers. Then, by manipulating computer and phone equipment, they called 911 operators around the country. By using "spoofing technology," the swatters even made it look like the calls were actually coming from the victims! The five swatters called 911 lines in more than 60 cities nationwide, impacting more than 100 victims, causing a disruption of services for telecommunications providers and emergency responders, and resulting in up to $250,000 in losses. "Swats" that the group committed included using bomb threats at sporting events, causing the events to be delayed; claiming that hotel visitors were armed and dangerous, causing an evacuation of the entire hotel; and making threats against public parks and officials.

SOURCE: FBI, "Don't Make the Call: The New Phenomenon of 'Swatting'," http://www.fbi.gov/page2/feb08/swatting020408.html (accessed June 2014).

Viruses and Worms Viruses are a type of malicious software program (also called **malware**) that disrupts or destroys existing programs and networks, causing them to perform the task for which the virus was designed.[48] The virus is then spread from one computer to another when a user sends out an infected file through email, a network, or a disk. **Computer worms** are similar to viruses but use computer networks or the Internet to self-replicate and send themselves to other users, generally via email, without the aid of the operator.

Trojan Horses Some hackers introduce a **Trojan horse** program into a computer system. The Trojan horse looks like a benign application but contains illicit codes that can damage the system operations. Sometimes hackers with a sense of irony will install a Trojan horse and claim that it is an antivirus program. When it is opened, it spreads viruses in the computer system. Though Trojan horses do not replicate themselves like viruses, they can be just as destructive.

Logic Bombs A fourth type of destructive attack that can be launched on a computer system is the **logic bomb**, a program that is secretly attached to a computer system, monitors the network's work output, and waits for a particular signal such as a date to appear. Also called a *slag code*, it is a type of delayed-action virus that may be set off when a program user makes certain input that sets it in motion. A logic bomb may cause a variety of problems ranging from displaying or printing a spurious message to deleting or corrupting data. For example, William Shea was convicted of placing malicious computer code on the network of Bay Area Credit Services, of San Jose, California, that caused the deletion and modification of financial records and disruption of the proper functioning of the company's computer network.[49] Shea's bomb affected more than 50,000 debtor accounts and caused the company more than $100,000 in damages. Shea, a disgruntled former employee, still had administrative level access to and familiarity with the company's computer systems, including the database server. Company officials did not know when he left the company that he had placed malicious code on the computer network that was set to modify and delete data at the end of the month.

Spam An unsolicited advertisement or promotional material, spam typically comes in the form of an unwanted email message; spammers use electronic communications to send unsolicited messages in bulk. While email is the most common form of spam, it can also be sent via instant messaging, online newsgroup, and texting, among other media.

Spam can simply be in the form of an unwanted and unwelcome advertisement. For example, it may advertise sexually explicit websites and get into the hands of minors. A more dangerous and malicious form of spam contains a Trojan horse disguised as an email attachment advertising some commodity such as free software or an electronic game. If the recipient downloads or opens the attachment, a virus may be launched that corrupts the victim's computer. The Trojan horse may also be designed to capture important data from the victim's hard drive and send it back to the hacker's email address.

Sending spam can become a crime and even lead to a prison sentence when it causes serious harm to a computer or network.

Website Defacement

Cybervandals may aim their attention at the websites of their victims. **Website defacement** is a type of cybervandalism that occurs when a computer hacker intrudes on another person's website by inserting or substituting codes that expose visitors to the site to misleading or provocative information. Defacement can range from installing humorous graffiti to sabotaging or corrupting the site. In some instances, defacement efforts are not easily apparent or noticeable—for example, when they are designed to give misinformation by substituting or replacing authorized text on a company's web page. The false information may mislead customers and frustrate their efforts to utilize the site or make it difficult for people using search engines to find the site as they surf the Net.

Almost all defacement attacks are designed to vandalize web pages rather than bring profit or gain to the intruders (though some defacers may eventually extort money from their targets). Some defacers are simply trying to impress the hacking community with their skills. Others may target a corporation when they oppose its business practices and policies (such as oil companies, tobacco companies, or

---

malware A malicious software program intended to damage or disable computers and computer systems.

computer worms Programs that attack computer networks (or the Internet) by self-replicating and sending themselves to other users, generally via email, without the aid of the operator.

Trojan horse A computer program that looks like a benign application but contains illicit codes that can damage the system operations. Though Trojan horses do not replicate themselves like viruses, they can be just as destructive.

logic bomb A program that is secretly attached to a computer system, monitors the network's work output, and waits for a particular signal such as a date to appear. Also called a slag code, it is a type of delayed-action virus that may be set off when a program user makes certain input that sets it in motion. A logic bomb may cause a variety of problems ranging from displaying or printing a spurious message to deleting or corrupting data.

website defacement A type of cybervandalism that occurs when a computer hacker intrudes on another person's website by inserting or substituting codes that expose visitors to the site to misleading or provocative information. Defacement can range from installing humorous graffiti to sabotaging or corrupting the site.

defense contractors). Some defacement has political goals such as disrupting the website of a rival political party or fund-raising group.

Content analysis of web page defacements indicates that about 70 percent are pranks instituted by hackers, while the rest have a political motive. Defacers are typically members of an extensive social network who are eager to demonstrate their reasons for hacking and often leave calling cards, greetings, and taunts on web pages.[50]

Website defacement is a significant and major threat to online businesses and government agencies. It can harm the credibility and reputation of the organization and demonstrate that its security measures are inadequate. As a result, clients lose trust and may be reluctant to share information such as credit card numbers and personal information. An etailer may lose business if potential clients believe the site is not secure. Financial institutions, such as web-based banks and brokerage houses, are particularly vulnerable because they rely on security and credibility to protect their clients' accounts.[51]

Cyberstalking

In 2012, a scandal rocked the nation when General David Petraeus, head of the Central Intelligence Agency, was forced to resign when word came out that he had a long-term extramarital affair with his biographer, Paula Broadwell. The affair was uncovered when Jill Kelley, a Florida socialite, asked a friend in the FBI to investigate a series of harassing emails she had received from an unknown person.[52] The FBI traced the emails to Broadwell, and found that she was also exchanging intimate messages with an email account belonging to Petraeus. The head of the CIA was brought down because his former girlfriend was cyberstalking a rival!

Cyberstalking refers to the use of the Internet, email, or other electronic communication devices to stalk another person. Traditional stalking involves repeated harassing or threatening behavior, such as following a person, appearing at a person's home or place of business, making harassing phone calls, leaving written messages or objects, or vandalizing a person's property. In the Internet age, stalkers can pursue victims through online chat rooms. Pedophiles can use the Internet to establish a relationship with the child, and later make contact for the purpose of engaging in criminal sexual activities. Research by Janis Wolak and her colleagues found that publicity about online "predators" who prey on naive children using trickery and violence is largely inaccurate. Today, Internet predators are more likely to meet, develop relationships with at-risk adolescents, and beguile underage teenagers, rather than use coercion and violence.[53] The Profiles in Crime feature discusses a particularly vicious cyberpredator, Christopher Gunn.

> **cyberstalking** Use of the Internet, email, or other electronic communications devices to stalk another person. Some cyberstalkers pursue minors through online chat rooms; others harass their victims electronically.

CHRISTOPHER GUNN, CYBERSTALKER

profiles in crime

In 2011, Christopher Gunn pleaded guilty to producing child pornography in connection with an online sextortion scheme that spanned the globe. Over a period of more than two years, Gunn repeatedly used computers, chat rooms, and other social media outlets to threaten hundreds of young girls ages 9 to 16 located throughout the United States and internationally and coerce them into sending him sexually suggestive photos. The first scheme—dubbed "The New Kid Ruse"—involved contacting the victims over Facebook and pretending to be a new kid in town looking for friends. Once he had gained their trust through chatting, Gunn would ask the girls a series of personal questions, such as their sexual histories, intimate details about their bodies, and so on. If they divulged that personal information, Gunn would then ask the girls to send him a topless photo. If they refused, he would threaten to email their intimate conversation to the school principal or post it on Facebook for everyone to see. The second scheme—dubbed "The Justin Bieber Ruse"—involved pretending to be pop star Justin Bieber, contacting young girls via video chat services, such as Omegle and Skype, and offering them free concert tickets, backstage passes, or some other fan-related benefits if they would agree to send him a webcam transmission or a photo of themselves with their breasts exposed.

For those who complied, Gunn continued sending further demands and more threatening communications. If any of his demands were not met, Gunn would threaten to withhold the benefits he had promised the girls and/or to injure the girls' reputations by publishing their compromising images and videos over the Internet. More than 10 girls were forced to send him sexually suggestive photos. For his acts, Gunn received a 35-year prison term.

Gunn may have been looking to achieve sexual gratification and a sense of power over his victims. Yet his criminal plot could not have been launched without the use of the Internet, access to social media, and employing aliases to try to avoid detection.

SOURCE: U.S. Attorney's Office, Middle District of Alabama, "Montgomery Man Pleads Guilty to Massive Online Sextortion Plot," August 23, 2012, http://www.justice.gov/usao/alm/press/2012/2012_08_23_gunn.html (accessed June 2014).

Not all cyberstalkers are sexual predators. Some send repeated threatening or harassing messages via email and use programs to send messages at regular or random intervals without being physically present at a computer terminal. A cyberstalker may trick other people into harassing or threatening a victim by impersonating the victim on Internet bulletin boards or chat rooms, posting messages that are provocative, such as "I want to have sex." The stalker then posts the victim's name, phone number, or email address hoping that other chat participants will stalk or hassle the victim without the stalker's personal involvement.

Cyberbullying

LO8 Articulate the extent of cyberbullying and the damage it causes people

Experts define bullying among children as repeated negative acts committed by one or more children against another. These negative acts may be physical or verbal in nature— for example, hitting or kicking, teasing or taunting—or they may involve indirect actions such as manipulating friendships or purposely excluding other children from activities. Implicit in this definition is an imbalance in real or perceived power between the bully and the victim. It may come as no surprise, then, that lesbian, gay, bisexual, and transgender (LGBT) students are subject to a disproportionate amount of bullying:

- Eight in ten LGBT students have been verbally harassed at school.
- Four in ten have been physically harassed at school.
- Six in ten have felt unsafe at school.
- One in five have been the victim of a physical assault at school.[54]

Studies of bullying suggest that there are short- and long-term consequences for both the perpetrators and the victims of bullying. Students who are chronic victims of bullying experience more physical and psychological problems than their peers who are not harassed by other children, and they tend not to grow out of the role of victim. Young people mistreated by peers may not want to be in school and may thereby miss out on the benefits of school connectedness as well as educational advancement. Longitudinal studies have found that victims of bullying in early grades also reported being bullied several years later.[55] Chronically victimized students may, as adults, be at increased risk for depression, poor self-esteem, and other mental health problems, including schizophrenia.[56]

While bullying is a problem that remains to be solved, it has now morphed from the physical to the virtual. Because of the creation of cyberspace, physical distance is no longer

cyberbullying Willful and repeated harm inflicted through the medium of electronic text.

a barrier to the frequency and depth of harm doled out by a bully to his or her victim.[57] **Cyberbullying** is defined as willful and repeated harm inflicted through the medium of electronic text. Like their real-world counterparts, cyberbullies are malicious aggressors who seek implicit or explicit pleasure or profit through the mistreatment of other individuals. Although power in traditional bullying might be physical (stature) or social (competency or popularity), online power may simply stem from Net proficiency. Cyberbullies are able to navigate the Net and utilize technology in a way that puts them in a position of power relative to their victim. There are two major formats that bullies can employ to harass their victims: (1) a cyberbully can use a computer and send harassing emails or instant messages, post obscene, insulting, and slanderous messages to online bulletin boards or social networking sites, or develop websites to promote and disseminate defamatory content; (2) a cyberbully can use a cell phone to send harassing text messages to the victim.[58] In the Criminology in Action feature, a unique form of cyberbullying, catfishing, is discussed in some detail.

How common is cyberbullying? Sameer Hinduja and Justin Patchin, leading experts on cyberbullying, have conducted yearly surveys using large samples of high school youth.[59] Their most recent effort (see Figure 15.2) finds that about 35 percent of the high school and middle school students they surveyed report having been the target of some form of Internet harassment. Over the last decade, Hinduja and Patchin have conducted eight different surveys with nearly 15,000 middle school and high school students in nine different studies from over 80 different schools throughout the United States. On average, about 25 percent of the students said they have been the victim of cyberbullying at some point in their lifetime and about 16 percent of the students admitted that they have cyberbullied others at least once (see Figure 15.3). Among Hinduja and Patchin's most important findings include:

- Adolescent girls are just as likely, if not more likely, than boys to experience cyberbullying (as a victim and offender).
- Cyberbullying is related to low self-esteem, suicidal ideation, anger, frustration, and a variety of other emotional and psychological problems.
- Cyberbullying is related to other issues in the real world, including school problems, antisocial behavior, and substance use.
- Traditional bullying is still more common than cyberbullying.
- Traditional bullying and cyberbullying are closely related: those who are bullied at school are bullied online and those who bully at school bully online.

Hinduja and Patchin's research is supported by other survey results. According to data compiled by the National Center for Education Statistics, about 13 percent of all students report being bullied annually.[60] Older students are more often targets: primary schools reported lower

Lifetime Cyberbullying Victimization Rates

Eight Different Studies 2007–2014

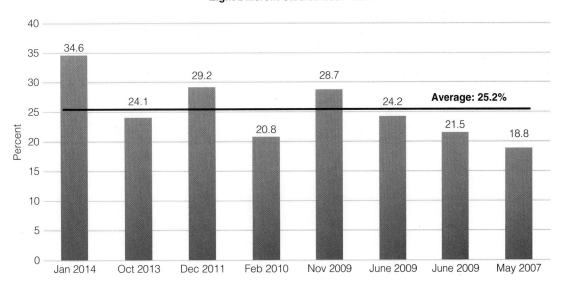

FIGURE 15.2 Lifetime Cyberbullying Victimization Rates

SOURCE: Justin W. Patchin and Sameer Hinduja, Cyberbullying Research Center, http://cyberbullying.us/blog/wp-content/uploads/2013/07/Cyberbullying_Victimization_2007-2014.jpg (accessed June 2014).

Lifetime Cyberbullying Offending Rates

Eight Different Studies 2007–2014

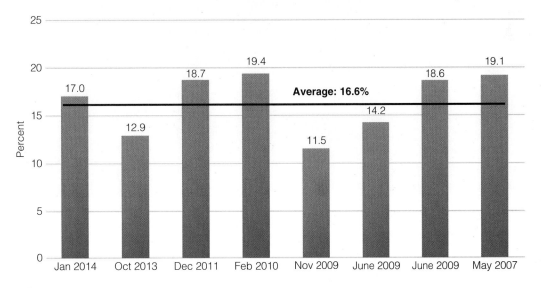

FIGURE 15.3 Lifetime Cyberbullying Offending Rates

SOURCE: Justin W. Patchin and Sameer Hinduja, Cyberbullying Research Center, http://cyberbullying.us/blog/wp-content/uploads/2013/07/Cyberbullying_Offending_2007-2014.jpg (accessed June 2014).

CATFISHING

AP Photo/Disney-ABC, Lorenzo Bevilaqua

Notre Dame linebacker Manti Te'o was drawn into a catfishing scheme that helped make the public aware of this type of cyberhoax. Here, he is shown speaking with talk show host Katie Couric during an interview in New York. Te'o told Couric that he briefly lied about his online girlfriend, Lennay Kekua, after discovering she didn't exist, while maintaining that he had no part in creating the hoax.

Some cyberbullies want to stalk victims, and some stalkers want to bully their targets. Take the practice that has become known as *catfishing*, a term that refers to the practice of setting up a fictitious online profile, most often for the purpose of luring another into a fraudu-

lent romantic relationship. According to the Urban Dictionary, a catfish is "someone who pretends to be someone they're not using Facebook or other social media to create false identities, particularly to pursue deceptive online romances." So, to "catfish someone" is to set up a fake social media profile with

the goal of duping that person into falling for the false persona.

While catfishing has been around awhile, it became a topic of public interest when 13-year-old Megan Meier began an online relationship with a boy she knew as Josh Evans. For almost a month, Megan corresponded with this boy exclusively online because he said he didn't have a phone and was homeschooled. One day Megan received a message from Josh on her MySpace profile saying, "I don't know if I want to be friends with you any longer because I hear you're not nice to your friends." This was followed by bulletins being posted through MySpace calling Megan "fat" and a "slut." After seeing the messages, Megan became distraught and ran up into her room. A few minutes later, Megan's mother Tina found her daughter hanging in her bedroom closet. Though Tina rushed her to the hospital, Megan died the next day.

percentages of cyberbullying among students (2 percent) than middle schools (19 percent) or high schools (18 percent). As Figure 15.4 shows, of those students who say they were cyberbullied, about 28 percent said it occurred frequently and about 3 percent reported that it occurred every day; 26 percent reported the bullying to an adult.

Cyberspying

Spyware is a type of software that gathers personal information, including web browser histories, emails, and online purchases. Once information is gathered, it is auto-

matically transmitted to those who installed the software either directly on the computer or when the victim opened an attachment. In some instances, the computer operator gives consent to the spying, which is legal. For example, an employee agrees to have their computer monitored by their employer to make sure they are not Web surfing during business hours.

Parents can legally install the software on their minor child's computer if they are the owner of the machine. If their child is a legal adult, they must obtain consent. The FlexiSPY Corporation of Wilmington, Delaware, offers software to capture every Facebook message, email, text, and

Six weeks after their daughter's death, the Meier family learned that the boy with whom Megan had been corresponding never existed. Josh Evans (and his online profile) was created by Lori Drew, a neighbor and the mother of one of Megan's friends. She created the profile as a way to spy on what Megan was saying about her daughter. Drew was charged with violations of the Computer Fraud and Abuse Act (CFAA), though her conviction was later overturned.

Catfishing also created national headlines when former Notre Dame and current NFL football star Manti Te'o was the target of a catfish. Te'o developed an online relationship with someone he knew as Lennay Kekua. It is difficult to know how deep the relationship was, but he did refer to her as his "girlfriend" and mentioned repeatedly that he loved her. Te'o amassed a wide following when it was learned that his grandmother and girlfriend (Kekua) died on the same day early in the 2012 football season. While his grandmother did in fact die on that day, his girlfriend did not and media investigations revealed that she had never existed in the first place. Kekua was a fictitious online persona created by a friend of Te'o's. In a statement to the press, Te'o maintained that he was a target: "To realize that I was the victim of what was apparently someone's sick joke and constant lies was, and is, painful and humiliating."

Unlike Lori Drew, some catfishers do not escape punishment. Anthony Stancl impersonated two girls ("Kayla" and "Emily") on Facebook. He befriended and formed online romantic relationships with a number of boys in his high school (again, while posing and interacting as these two girls). He then convinced at least 31 of those boys to send him nude pictures or videos of themselves. Communicating through Facebook, Stancl tried to convince more than half to meet with a male friend and let him perform sexual acts on them. If they refused, "she" told them that the pictures and videos would be released for all to see. Seven boys actually submitted and allowed Stancl to perform sex acts on them or they performed sex acts on him. He took numerous pictures of these encounters with his cell phone, and the police eventually found over 300 nude images of male teens on his computer. He was charged with five counts of child enticement, two counts of second-degree sexual assault of a child, two counts of third-degree sexual assault, possession of child pornography, and repeated sexual assault of the same child, and received a 15-year sentence in prison.

Seeking Revenge

Some catfishing victims don't take kindly to being misled and seek vengeance on their deceivers. Take for instance Brian Curtis Hile, a Michigan man who became involved in an Internet-only relationship that lasted two years. Hile exchanged explicit photos and romantic communications with someone he believed to be a woman. When he learned that "she" was actually a man living in South Africa, Hile became enraged and vowed to find the man who deceived him—and the woman whose images played a role in the deception. Since South Africa was too far, Hile traveled to San Diego intending to kill the woman whose photos were part of the deception. But unknown to him she had played no part in the schemes and her photos has actually been stolen from her online account. Using his computer skills, Hile compiled detailed personal information about the woman and her live-in boyfriend as well as their extended family and friends. Fortunately, Hile's family sensed that he was planning something and alerted authorities, which eventually led to Hile's detention in San Diego—about a mile from the woman's residence and in possession of her address, telephone numbers, and information such as her favorite restaurant. He also had duct tape, zip ties, and a to-do list that included obtaining a knife and chloroform. The cyberbullied victim had turned into a stalker with revenge on his mind. Hile was sentenced to five years in federal prison for his attempted retaliation against his stalker.

SOURCES: Justin Patchin, "Catfishing as a Form of Cyberbullying," Cyberbullying Research Center, http://cyberbullying.us/catfishing-as-a-form-of-cyberbullying/ (accessed June 2014); FBI, "Cyber Stalker: A Cautionary Tale About Online Romance and Revenge," December 23, 2013, http://www.fbi.gov/news/stories/2013/december/cautionary-tale-of-online-romance-and-revenge/cautionary-tale-of-online-romance-and-revenge (accessed June 2014); Fox News, "Missouri Woman Indicted in MySpace Cyber-Bullying Case that Ended in Teen's Suicide," May 15, 2008, http://www.foxnews.com/printer_friendly_story/0,3566,356056,00.html (accessed June 2014).

photo sent from a phone, as well as record phone calls. They also promote the ability to catch cheating spouses by monitoring their cell phone so that the purchaser "will know for sure what your partner is really feeling, saying and doing when you are not there. FlexiSPY will let you read all their cell phone messages … and let you know their location at any time, and even let you listen to their cell phone conversations as they happen. It's easy to install and is completely hidden so they will never know." These services are legal only if the person installing the software also owns the device or was given consent by the owner, a warning that the FlexiSPY makes clear on their website.[61]

The most well-known case of criminal spyware involved Carlos Enrique Perez-Melara, the creator and marketer of a spyware program called Loverspy, who was indicted by a federal grand jury and charged with such crimes as manufacturing a surreptitious interception device, sending a surreptitious interception device, and advertising a surreptitious interception device.[62]

Loverspy was a computer program designed and marketed by Perez-Melara for people to use to spy on others. Prospective purchasers, after paying $89 through a website based in Texas, were electronically redirected to Perez-Melara's computers in San Diego. Purchasers would then

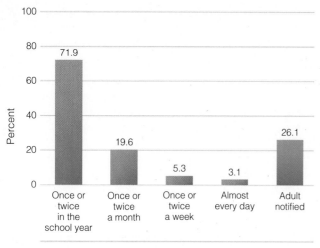

FIGURE 15.4 Frequency of Cyberbullying Among Students Who Report Being Bullied Online

SOURCE: National Center for Education Statistics, *Indicators of School Crime and Safety, 2012*, http://nces.ed.gov/pubs2013/2013036.pdf (accessed June 2014).

select an electronic greeting card to send to up to five different victims' email addresses. Unbeknownst to the victims, once the email greeting card was opened, Loverspy secretly installed itself on their computer and recorded all their activities, including emails sent and received, websites visited, and passwords entered. Loverspy also gave the purchaser the ability to remotely control the victim's computer, including accessing, changing, and deleting files, and turning on web-enabled cameras. Over 1,000 purchasers from the United States and elsewhere purchased Loverspy and used it against more than 2,000 victims.[63]

Perez-Melara was indicted for engaging in **cyberspying**, illegally using the Internet to gather information considered private and confidential. He fled the country and still remains at large.

Cyberspies have a variety of motivations. Some are people involved in marital disputes who may want to seize the emails of their

estranged spouse. Business rivals might hire disgruntled former employees, consultants, or outside contractors to steal information from their competitors. These commercial cyberspies target upcoming bids, customer lists, product designs, software source code, voicemail messages, and confidential email messages.[64] Some of the commercial spying is conducted by foreign competitors who seek to appropriate trade secrets in order to gain a business advantage.[65]

Cyberspying by the Government While spyware to monitor Internet messages and traffic by spouses, children, employees and so on has become common, spying by government agencies on U.S. citizens remains quite controversial.

In Chapter 11, Edward Snowden's effort to warn the public about the NSA's domestic spying program was discussed within the context of espionage. This effort, known in official government circles as the "President's Surveillance Program," was first implemented by President George W. Bush shortly after the attacks on September 11, 2001. To carry out the cyberspying, the government convinced the major telecommunications companies to hand over the "call detail records" of their customers, including names, street addresses, and other personal information. In addition, the government received records of calls they made—across town or across the country—to family members, co-workers, business contacts, and others.

Carlos Enrique Perez-Melara has made it to the FBI's "Most Wanted" list for his involvement in manufacturing spyware that was used to intercept the private communications of thousands of victims. As part of the scheme, Perez-Melara ran a website offering customers a way to "catch a cheating lover" by sending spyware masquerading as an electronic greeting card. Victims who opened the greeting card would unwittingly install a program on their computers that collected keystrokes and other incoming and outgoing electronic communications. The program would periodically send email messages back to the purchasers of the service containing the acquired communications, including the victims' passwords, lists of visited websites, intercepted email messages, and keystroke logs.

cyberspying Illegally using the Internet to gather information that is considered private and confidential.

The telecommunications companies also allowed the NSA to install communications surveillance equipment that gave the NSA access to large streams of domestic and international communications in real time—what amounted to at least 1.7 billion emails a day. The NSA could then datamine and analyze this traffic for suspicious keywords, patterns, and connections. The surveillance was undertaken without a warrant which some legal scholars claim was in violation of federal law and the Constitution.[66]

THE COSTS OF CYBERCRIME

How common are cybercrimes, and how costly are cybercrimes to American businesses and the general public? The Internet has become a vast engine for illegal profits and criminal entrepreneurs. An accurate accounting of cybercrime will probably never be made because so many offenses go unreported, but there is little doubt that its incidence is growing rapidly.

Though thousands of breaches occur each year, most are not reported to local, state, or federal authorities. Some cybercrime goes unreported because it involves low-visibility acts—such as copying computer software in violation of copyright laws—that simply never get detected.[67] Some businesses choose not to report cybercrime because they fear revealing the weaknesses in their network security systems. However, the information that is available indicates that the profit in cybercrime is vast and continually growing.[68]

Losses due to vishing, phishing, and identity theft are now in the billions of dollars and rising with the continuing growth of ecommerce. One example of the breadth of the loss can be found in a new audit of the Internal Revenue Service (IRS) that found the agency paid refunds to criminals who filed false tax returns, in some cases on behalf of people who had died. In all, the IRS is expected to lose as much as $21 billion in revenue between 2012 and 2017 due to identity theft.[69]

COMBATING CYBERCRIME

LO9 Discuss efforts to control cybercrime

The proliferation of cybercrime and its cost to the economy have created the need for new laws and enforcement processes specifically aimed at controlling its emerging formulations. Because technology evolves so rapidly, the enforcement challenges are particularly vexing. There are numerous organizations set up to provide training and support for law enforcement agents. In addition, new federal

AN ETHICAL DILEMMA

BIG BROTHER IS WATCHING YOU

The president's national security advisor approaches you with a problem. It seems that a tracking device has been developed that can be implanted under the skin that will allow people to be constantly monitored. Implanted at birth, the data surveillance device could potentially cover *everyone*, with a record of every transaction and activity they engage in entered into databases monitored by powerful search engines that would keep them under constant surveillance. The surveillance device would enable the government to keep tabs on their whereabouts as well as monitoring biological activities such as brain waves, heart rate, and so on. The benefits are immense. Once a person becomes a suspect in a crime or is believed to be part of a terrorist cell, he or she can be easily monitored from a distance without danger to any government agent. The suspect cannot hide or escape detection. Physical readings could be made to determine if the suspect is under stress, using banned substances, and so on.

The director wants you to write a paper for the NSA expressing your opinion on this device. You begin by reading what the American Civil Liberties Union has to say: "The United States is at risk of turning into a full-fledged surveillance society. The tremendous explosion in surveillance-enabling technologies, combined with the ongoing weakening in legal restraints that protect our privacy, mean that we are drifting toward a surveillance society. The good news is that it can be stopped. Unfortunately, right now the big picture is grim." Is it worthwhile considering the threats faced by America from terrorists and criminals or, as the ACLU suggests, would it be unethical because it violates the personal privacy and freedom of people before they have broken any law?

and state laws have been aimed at particular areas of high-tech crimes.

Congress has treated computer-related crime as a distinct federal offense since the passage of the Counterfeit Access Device and Computer Fraud and Abuse Law in 1984.[70] The 1984 act protected classified U.S. defense and foreign relations information, financial institution and consumer reporting agency files, and access to computers operated for the government. The act was supplemented in 1996 by the National Information Infrastructure Protection Act (NIIPA), which significantly broadens the scope of the law.[71]

Because cybercrime is relatively new, existing laws sometimes are inadequate to address the problem. Therefore new legislation has been drafted to protect the public from the cybercriminal. For example, before October 30, 1998, when the Identity Theft and Assumption Act of 1998 became law, there was no federal statute that made identity theft a crime. Today, federal prosecutors are making substantial use of the statute and are actively prosecuting cases of identity theft.[72]

In the wake of the 9/11 attacks, the NIIPA has been amended by sections of the USA Patriot Act to make it easier to enforce laws against crimes by terrorists and other organized enemies against the nation's computer systems. Subsection 1030(a)(5)(A)(i) of the act criminalizes knowingly causing the transmission of a program, code, or command, and as a result, intentionally causing damage to a protected computer. This section applies regardless of whether the user had authorization to access the protected computer; company insiders and authorized users can be culpable for intentional damage to a protected computer. The act also prohibits intentional access without authorization that results in damage but does not require intent to damage; the attacker can merely be negligent or reckless.

In addition to these main acts, computer-related crimes can also be charged under at least 40 different federal statutes. These include the Copyright Act and Digital Millennium Copyright Act, the National Stolen Property Act, the mail and wire fraud statutes, the Electronic Communications Privacy Act, the Communications Decency Act of 1996, the Child Online Protection Act, the Child Pornography Prevention Act of 1996, and the Internet False Identification Prevention Act of 2000.[73] Movie pirates who use the Internet to sell illegally copied films have led the federal government to create the Family Entertainment and Copyright Act of 2005. One part of that statute, known as the ART Act (Artists' Rights and Theft Prevention Act of 2005), criminalizes the use of recording equipment to make copies of films while in movie theaters. The statute also makes it illegal to make a copy of a work in production and put it on the Internet so it will be accessible to members of the public when the individual making the copy knew or should have known the work was intended for commercial distribution.[74]

International Treaties

Because cybercrime is essentially global, international cooperation is required for its control. The Convention on Cybercrime, ratified by the U.S. Senate in August 2006, is the first international treaty that addresses the definition and enforcement of cybercrime. Now signed by 43 nations, it focuses on improving investigative techniques and increasing cooperation among nations. The convention includes a list of crimes that each signatory state must incorporate into its own law, including such cyber offenses as hacking, distribution of child pornography, and protection of intellectual property rights. It also allows law enforcement agencies new powers, including the ability to require that an Internet service provider monitor a person's online viewing and search choices in real time. The convention also requires signatory states to cooperate whenever possible in the investigations and prosecution of cybercriminals. The vision is that a common legal framework will eliminate jurisdictional hurdles to facilitate the law enforcement of borderless cybercrimes.[75]

Carrying out this mandate may be difficult to achieve given the legal rights afforded U.S. citizens that may not be realized by residents of other nations. For example, First Amendment protections that restrict the definition of pornography and obscenity in this country may not apply overseas. It is not surprising that watchdog institutions such as the ACLU have condemned the treaty and campaigned against U.S. participation.[76]

Cybercrime Enforcement Agencies

To enforce these laws, the federal government is now operating a number of organizations to control cyberfraud. One approach is to create working groups that coordinate the activities of numerous agencies involved in investigating cybercrime. For example, the Interagency Telemarketing and Internet Fraud Working Group brings together representatives of numerous U.S. attorneys' offices, the FBI, the Secret Service, the Postal Inspection Service, the Federal Trade Commission, the Securities and Exchange Commission, and other law enforcement and regulatory agencies to share information about trends and patterns in Internet fraud schemes.[77]

Specialized enforcement agencies have been created. The Internet Fraud Complaint Center, based in Fairmont, West Virginia, is run by the FBI and the National White Collar Crime Center. It brings together about 1,000 state and local law enforcement officials and regulators. Its goal is to analyze fraud-related complaints in order to find distinct patterns, develop information on particular cases, and send investigative packages to law enforcement authorities in the jurisdiction that appears likely to have the greatest investigative interest in the matter. The center now receives more than 200,000 complaints each year, including auction fraud, nondelivery, and credit/debit card fraud, as well as nonfraudulent complaints such as computer intrusions, spam/unsolicited email, and child pornography.[78] Law enforcement has made remarkable strides in dealing with identity theft as a crime problem over the last several years.

The Secret Service maintains Electronic Crimes Task Forces (ECTFs), which focus on identifying and locating international cybercriminals connected to cyber intrusions, bank fraud, data breaches, and other computer-related crimes. One of the most successful of these efforts is the New York–New Jersey Electronic Crimes Task Force (NYECTF), a partnership between the U.S. Secret Service and a host of other public safety agencies and private corporations. The task force consists of more than 250 individual members representing federal, state, and local law enforcement, the private sector, and computer science specialists from 18 different universities. Since 1995, the task force has charged more than 1,000 individuals with electronic crime losses, exceeding $1 billion. It has trained more than 60,000 law enforcement personnel, prosecutors, and private

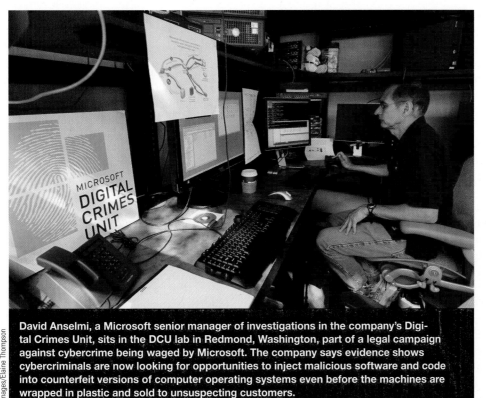

David Anselmi, a Microsoft senior manager of investigations in the company's Digital Crimes Unit, sits in the DCU lab in Redmond, Washington, part of a legal campaign against cybercrime being waged by Microsoft. The company says evidence shows cybercriminals are now looking for opportunities to inject malicious software and code into counterfeit versions of computer operating systems even before the machines are wrapped in plastic and sold to unsuspecting customers.

AP Images/Elaine Thompson

command systems and compromising air defenses. Instead of blowing up air defense radar systems and giving up the element of surprise before hitting targets, in the age of cyberwar the computers controlling the air defense are put out of action.

Cyberespionage

Intelligence agencies are now able to penetrate computer networks of an enemy nation's most sensitive military bases, defense contractors, and aerospace companies in order to steal important data or to damage their infrastructure. In one well-known **cyberespionage** case, Chinese agents were able to penetrate computers, enter hidden sections of a hard drive, zip up as many files as possible, and transmit the data to way stations in South Korea, Hong Kong, and Taiwan before sending them to mainland China. The spy ring, known as Titan Rain, compromised networks ranging from the Redstone Arsenal military base to NASA and the World Bank; the U.S. Army's flight-planning software was also electronically stolen. Hundreds of Defense Department computer systems have been penetrated, and similar attacks have been launched against classified systems in Britain, Canada, Australia, and New Zealand.[80]

Cyber Attacks In addition to espionage and the theft of military intelligence, cyberwar can also involve attacks on an enemy's defense industry, compromising their ability to wage war. As a response to such a cyber attack that occurred on November 23, 2010, Iran was forced to shut down its main uranium enrichment plant at Natanz for seven days after it was targeted by the Stuxnet computer worm. Experts believe that Stuxnet was specifically designed to attack systems at the plant that control the speed at which the enrichment centrifuges spin. The source of the attack remains unknown, but suspects include the United States and Israel security agencies.[81]

Cyberwar can also involve attacks designed to compromise an enemy's command and control structure by

industry representatives in cybercrime prevention. Its success has prompted similar electronic crime task forces to be set up in Boston, Miami, Charlotte, Chicago, Las Vegas, San Francisco, Los Angeles, and Washington, D.C.[79]

CYBERWAR: POLITICALLY MOTIVATED CYBERCRIME

LO10 Define the concepts of cyberwarfare and cyberterrorism

It is now generally accepted and understood that the developed world is totally dependent upon electronic communication and data storage for its survival. The protection of the key critical technological infrastructure of a nation has been raised in priority so that it is now considered by many countries alongside the other traditional aspects of national defense.

It is routine for defense agencies around the world to employ units to conduct cyber attacks on enemy nations. Cyberwar enables the forces of one nation-state to penetrate another nation's computers or networks for the purposes of causing damage or disruption. Computer systems may be compromised so that vital war material is misdirected or even destroyed. Attacks are facilitated by destroying

> **cyberespionage** Efforts by intelligence agencies to penetrate computer networks of an enemy nation in order to steal important data.

hacking into computer systems to disrupt missile targeting systems, rendering them ineffective during attacks. For example, according to cyberwar experts Richard Clarke and Rob Knake, in September 2007, Israeli cyberunits "blinded" Syrian antiaircraft installations guarding a secret nuclear plant that was being constructed for Syria by North Korea. While the exact methodology remains classified, Syrian defense computers that controlled their missile defenses were reprogrammed so that the attacking Israeli aircraft did not show up on radar screens. Israel was able to penetrate a sophisticated defense system without losing an aircraft.[82]

Clarke and Knake also tell how U.S. cyberwar agents infiltrated the Iraqi "closed-loop" private, secure military network before the start of the second Gulf War. The agents sent email to thousands of Iraqi military officers on the Iraqi Defense Ministry email system telling them they would not be harmed if they left their tanks and weapons parked on the side of the road and went home; many did just that.

The United States and Israel are not alone in perfecting cyberwar capability. The Chinese government has established an online warfare team to beef up the defense capabilities of the People's Liberation Army (PLA). The 30-man cyberwar unit, or "cyber blue team," operates under the Guangzhou military region—one of seven across China—and has conducted synchronized Internet exercises with different military units.[83]

Cyberterrorism

Cyberterrorism can be seen as an effort by covert forces to disrupt the intersection where the virtual electronic reality of computers meets the physical world.[84] Cyberspace is a handy battlefield for the terrorist because an attack can strike directly at a target that bombs won't affect: the economy. Because technological change plays a significant role in the development of critical infrastructures, they are particularly vulnerable to attack. And because of rapid technological change, and the interdependence of systems, it is difficult to defend against efforts to disrupt services.[85]

Cyberterrorists have many advantages. There are no borders of legal control, making it difficult for prosecutors to apply laws to some crimes. Criminals can operate from countries where cyber laws barely exist, making them almost untouchable. Cyberterrorists can also use the Internet and hacking tools to gather information on targets.[86] There is no loss of life and no need to infiltrate enemy territory. Terrorists can commit crimes from anyplace in the world, and the costs are minimal. Nor do terror organizations lack for skilled labor to mount cyber attacks. There are a growing number of highly skilled computer experts in developing countries who are available at reasonable costs. Cyberterrorism may result in a battered economy in which the government is forced to spend more on the military and cut back on social programs and education. These outcomes can weaken the terrorists' target and undermine its resolve to continue to resist.

Recruitment and Fund Raising   Terrorist organizations are now using cyberspace in a number of different operational areas. They use the Internet to recruit new members and disseminate information. For example, Islamic militant organizations use the Internet to broadcast anti-Western slogans and information. An organization's charter and political philosophy can be displayed on its website, which can also be used to solicit funds.

Terrorist groups have used the Internet to raise funds to buy arms and carry out operations.[87] One method of funding is through fraudulent charitable organizations claiming to support a particular cause such as disaster relief or food services. Charitable organizations in the United States raise more than $130 billion per year. Using bogus charities to raise money is particularly attractive to cyberterrorists because they face far less scrutiny from the government than for-profit corporations and individuals. They may also qualify for financial assistance from government-sponsored grant programs. One such bogus group, Holy Land Foundation for Relief and Development (HLFRD) provided more than $12 million to the terrorist group Hamas; in total, HLFRD raised more than $57 million but only reported $36.2 million to the IRS.[88]

Bogus companies have also been used by terrorist groups to receive and distribute money. These shell companies may engage in legitimate activities to establish a positive reputation in the business community but produce bills for nonexistent products that are "paid" by another party with profits from illegal activities, such as insurance fraud or identity theft.[89] If a shell company generates revenues, funds can be distributed by altering financial statements to hide profits and then depositing the profits in accounts that are used directly or indirectly to support terrorist activities.[90]

Cyberterror Attacks   Cyberspace can be used by terrorist groups to remain connected and communicate covertly with agents around the world. Networks are a cost-effective tool for planning and striking.[91] They enable terror groups to plan and carry out a variety of Internet-related attacks. Here are some possible scenarios:

- Logic bombs are implanted in an enemy's computer. They can go undetected for years until they are instructed through the Internet to overwhelm a computer system.
- Programs are used to allow terrorists to enter "secure" systems and disrupt or destroy the network.
- Using conventional weapons, terrorists overload a network's electrical system, thereby threatening computer security.[92]
- The computer system of a corporation whose welfare is vital to national security—such as Boeing or Raytheon—is breached and disrupted.

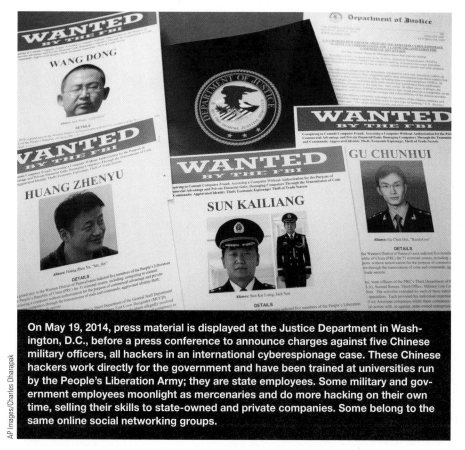

On May 19, 2014, press material is displayed at the Justice Department in Washington, D.C., before a press conference to announce charges against five Chinese military officers, all hackers in an international cyberespionage case. These Chinese hackers work directly for the government and have been trained at universities run by the People's Liberation Army; they are state employees. Some military and government employees moonlight as mercenaries and do more hacking on their own time, selling their skills to state-owned and private companies. Some belong to the same online social networking groups.

AP Images/Charles Dharapak

- Internet-based systems used to manage basic infrastructure needs—such as an oil pipeline's flow or water levels in dams—are attacked and disrupted, posing a danger of loss of life and interruption of services.

One attack method is to release a *botnet* or software robot, also known as a zombie or drone, that allows an unauthorized user to remotely take control of a host computer without the victim's knowledge or permission.[93] Infected computers can be used to launch denial-of-service attacks, send spam and spyware, or commit cyber extortion. In one attack, a global telecommunications company with a business unit in Central America experienced several unusual problems, including multiple network outages—some lasting up to six hours—which disrupted businesses and national connectivity, and took automated teller machines offline for extended periods of time. A botnet-based distributed denial-of-service attack had crippled the country's infrastructure.[94] The Center for Strategic and International Studies has uncovered cyberterror attacks on the National Security Agency, the Pentagon, and a nuclear weapons laboratory; operations were disrupted at all of these sites.[95]

Financial System Attacks In ever-increasing numbers people are spending and investing their money electronically, using online banking, credit card payment, and online brokerage services. The banking/financial system transacts billions of dollars each day through a complex network of institutions and systems. Efficient and secure electronic functioning is required if people are willing to conduct credit and debit card purchases, money transfers, and stock trading. A cyber attack can disrupt these transactions and interfere with the nation's economic well-being.[96]

The financial service sector is a prime target and has been victimized by information warfare. For example, in 2013, a massive cyber attack was directed at some of the nation's largest banks, including JPMorgan Chase, Bank of America, and Citigroup, by a hacker group calling itself Izz ad-Din al-Qassam Cyber Fighters. What made this different was that the traffic came from data centers around the world that had been infected with a sophisticated form of malware designed to evade detection by antivirus solutions. The bank attackers used those infected servers to simultaneously fire traffic at each banking site until it slowed or collapsed. The purpose of the attack: to punish the American financial system in retaliation for a film insulting to Moslems.[97]

Combating Cyberwar

There are a number of government agencies assigned with the task of countering cyberwar and cyberterror. The military has formed the United States Cyber Command (USCYBERCOM), a division that "plans, coordinates, integrates, synchronizes and conducts activities to: direct the operations and defense of specified Department of Defense information networks and; prepare to, and when directed, conduct full spectrum military cyberspace operations in order to enable actions in all domains, ensure US/Allied freedom of action in cyberspace and deny the same to our adversaries."[98] USCYBERCOM ties together the cyberwarfare arms of the various service branches.

The National Security Agency/Central Security Service (NSA/CSS) encompasses both Signals Intelligence (SIGINT) and Information Assurance (IA) products. The Information Assurance mission is to prevent foreign adversaries from gaining access to sensitive or classified national security information. The Signals Intelligence mission collects, processes, and disseminates intelligence information from foreign signals for intelligence and counterintelligence purposes and to support military operations.[99]

LO1 Discuss the evolution of cybercrime

Cybercrime is a new breed of offenses that involve the theft and/or destruction of information, resources, or funds utilizing computers, computer networks, and the Internet. Cybercrime presents a challenge for the justice system because it is rapidly evolving, it is difficult to detect through traditional law enforcement channels, and its control demands that agents of the justice system develop technical skills that match those of the perpetrators. Cybercrime has grown because information technology (IT) has become part of daily life in most industrialized societies.

LO2 Compare and contrast cybertheft, cybervandalism, and cyberwarfare

Some cybercrimes use modern technology to accumulate goods and services (cybertheft). Cybervandalism involves malicious attacks aimed at disrupting, defacing, and destroying technology that the attackers find offensive. Cyberwarfare is aimed at undermining the social, economic, and political system of an enemy nation by destroying its electronic infrastructure and disrupting its economy. A significant aspect of modern cyberwarfare is the use of the Internet by terrorists to plan operations, raise funds, and attack computer networks.

LO3 List some examples of computer fraud

Computer fraud involves compromising a computer system in order to steal property or use the system for personal gain. Theft from an ATM machine (a type of computer), reprogramming a computer to send funds illegally, illegally obtaining information from a computer, manipulating accounts, and corporate espionage would all be considered computer frauds.

LO4 Assess how the Internet can facilitate the sale of illegal materials

The Internet has become an important source for selling and distributing obscene material. While some sites cater to legal sexually related material, others cross the legal border by peddling access to obscene material or even kiddie porn. It is unlikely that any law enforcement efforts will put a dent in the Internet porn industry. It is also possible to obtain drugs via the Net without a prescription or with bogus prescriptions.

LO5 Distinguish between the different forms of stealing intellectual property

Warez refers to illegally obtained software acquired by groups of individuals who work together to then "crack" or "rip" its copyright protections before posting it on the Internet for other members of the group to use. Another type of illegal copyright infringement involves file-sharing programs that allow Internet users to download music and other copyrighted material without paying the artists and record producers their rightful royalties.

LO6 Define the terms *identity theft* and *phishing*

Identity theft occurs when a person uses the Internet to steal someone's identity and/or impersonate the victim to open a new credit card account or conduct some other financial transaction. Identity theft can destroy a person's life by manipulating credit records or stealing from their bank accounts. Phishing involves the creation of false emails and/or websites that look legitimate but are designed to gain illegal access to a victim's personal information. Vishing is a form of phishing utilizing Internet phone protocols.

LO7 Describe the different types of cybervandalism

Cybervandalism ranges from sending destructive viruses and worms to hacker attacks designed to destroy important computer networks. A computer virus is one type of malicious software program that disrupts or destroys existing programs and networks, causing them to perform the task for which the virus was designed. Computer worms are similar to viruses but use computer networks or the Internet to self-replicate and send themselves to other users, generally via email, without the aid of the operator. A Trojan horse looks like a benign application but contains illicit codes that can damage the system operations. A logic bomb is a program that is secretly attached to a computer system, monitors the network's work output, and waits for a particular signal such as a date to appear.

LO8 Articulate the extent of cyberbullying and the damage it causes people

Cyberbullying is defined as the willful and repeated harm inflicted through the medium of electronic text. Cyberbullies are malicious aggressors who seek implicit or explicit pleasure or profit through the mistreatment of other individuals. About 35 percent of the high school and junior high school students surveyed report having been the target of some form of Internet harassment. Adolescent girls are just as likely, if not more likely, than boys to experience cyberbullying (as a victim and offender). Victims of bullying suffer long-term consequences and mental health issues. There have been well-known cases where kids who were cyberbullied have taken their own lives.

LO9 Discuss efforts to control cybercrime

The growth of cybercrime and its cost to the economy have created the need for new laws and enforcement processes specifically aimed at controlling its new and emerging formulations. Congress has treated computer-related crime as a distinct federal offense since passage of the Counterfeit Access Device and Computer Fraud and Abuse Law in 1984. Because cybercrime is relatively new, existing laws sometimes are inadequate to address the problem. Therefore new legislation has been drafted to protect the public from this new breed of criminal. Specialized enforcement agencies have been created to crack down on cybercriminals.

Define the concepts of cyberwarfare and cyberterrorism

Cyberwar enables the forces of one nation-state to penetrate another nation's defense networks for the purposes of causing damage or disruption. Computer systems may be compromised so that vital war material is misdirected or even destroyed. Attacks are facilitated by destroying command systems and compromising air defenses. Cyberterrorism can be viewed as an effort by covert forces to disrupt the intersection where the virtual electronic reality of computers meets the physical world. Some experts question the existence of cyberterrorism, going so far as to claim that not a single case of cyberterrorism has yet been recorded, that cybervandals and hackers are regularly mistaken for terrorists, and cyber defenses are more robust than is commonly supposed.

CRITICAL THINKING QUESTIONS

1. Which theories of criminal behavior best explain the actions of cybercriminals, and which ones do you believe fail to explain cybercrime?

2. How would you punish a web page defacer who placed an antiwar message on a government site? Prison? Fine?

3. What guidelines would you recommend for the use of IT in law enforcement?

4. Are we creating a "Big Brother" society and is the loss of personal privacy worth the price of safety?

5. How can cyberbullies be convinced of their harmfulness of their acts? Would it be ethical to create a web page mocking them as punishment?

KEY TERMS

cybercrime (526)
information technology (IT) (526)
globalization (526)
cybertheft (527)
cybervandalism (527)
cyberwar (527)

cyberterrorism (527)
ATM skimming (530)
denial-of-service attack (533)
warez (533)
identity theft (534)
phishing (535)
spear-fishing (535)

money mule (535)
etailing fraud (537)
malware (540)
computer worms (540)
Trojan horse (540)
logic bomb (540)
website defacement (540)

cyberstalking (541)
cyberbullying (542)
cyberspying (546)
cyberespionage (549)

NOTES

1. John F. Burns and Ravi Somaiya, "WikiLeaks Founder on the Run, Trailed by Notoriety," *New York Times*, October 23, 2010, http://www.nytimes.com/2010/10/24/world/24assange.html (accessed June 2014).

2. Gartner, Inc., "Forecast Alert: IT Spending, Worldwide, 2008–2015, 4Q11 Update," https://www.gartner.com/doc/1886414 (accessed June 2014).

3. Internet World Stats, http://www.internetworldstats.com/stats.htm (accessed June 2014).

4. Christopher M. Donner, Catherine Marcum, Wesley Jennings, George E. Higgins, and Jerry Banfield, "Low Self-Control and **Cybercrime**: Exploring the Utility of the General Theory of Crime Beyond Digital Piracy," *Computers in Human Behavior* 34 (2014): 165–172.

5. "Statement of Michael A. Vatis, Director, National Infrastructure Protection Center, Federal Bureau of Investigation, on Cybercrime Before the Senate Judiciary Committee, Criminal Justice Oversight Subcommittee and House Judiciary Committee, Crime Subcommittee," February 29, 2000.

6. Majid Yar, *Cybercrime and Society* (Thousand Oaks, CA: Sage Publications, 2006), p. 19.

7. FBI, "Botnet Bust: SpyEye Malware Mastermind Pleads Guilty," January 28, 2014, http://www.fbi.gov/news/stories/2014/january/spyeye-malware-mastermind-pleads-guilty/ (accessed June 2014).

8. The President's Working Group on Unlawful Conduct on the Internet, "The Electronic Frontier: The Challenge of Unlawful Conduct Involving the Use of the Internet,"

2000, http://www.politechbot.com/docs/unlawfulconduct.txt (accessed June 2014).

9. U.S. Attorney's Office Eastern District of Missouri, "Jefferson County Man Pleads Guilty to Computer Fraud," February 8, 2012, http://www.fbi.gov/stlouis/press-releases/2012/jefferson-county-man-pleads-guilty-to-computer-fraud (accessed June 2014).

10. *InformationWeek*, "Global Security Survey 2012," July 2013, http://reports.informationweek.com/abstract/21/8815/security/research-2012-strategic-security-survey.html (accessed June 2014).

11. Brian Krebs, "Thieves Planted Malware to Hack ATMs," Krebs on Security, May 30, 2014, http://krebsonsecurity.com/tag/atm-skimmer/ (accessed June 2014).

12. FBI, "Taking a Trip to the ATM? Beware of 'Skimmers,'" July 14, 2011, http://www.fbi.gov/news/stories/2011/july/atm_071411 (accessed June 2014).

13. Associated Press, "International Child Porn Ring Uncovered," Goldstein Report, 2008, http://goldsteinreport.com/article.php?article=4145 (accessed June 2014).

14. Andreas Philaretou, "Sexuality and the Internet," *Journal of Sex Research* 42 (2005): 180–181.

15. Julie Ruvolo, "How Much of the Internet Is Actually for Porn, *Forbes*, September 7, 2011, http://www.forbes.com/sites/julieruvolo/2011/09/07/how-much-of-the-internet-is-actually-for-porn/ (accessed June 2014).

16. Ibid.

17. Marie-Helen Maras, *Computer Forensics: Cybercriminals, Laws, and Evidence* (Sudbury, MA: Jones and Bartlett, 2011).

18. Jeordan Legon, "Sex Sells, Especially to Web Surfers: Internet Porn a Booming, Billion-Dollar Industry," CNN, December 11, 2003, http://www.cnn.com/2003/TECH/internet/12/10/porn.business/ (accessed June 2014).

19. FBI, "Three Individuals Sentenced to Prison for Participating in International Child Pornography Ring," March 9, 2012, http://www.fbi.gov/losangeles/press-releases/2012/three-individuals-sentenced-to-prison-for-participating-in-international-child-pornography-ring (accessed June 2014).

20. U.S. Attorney's Office, Northern District of California, "Nine Sentenced for Illegally Distributing Controlled Substances over the Internet," March 27, 2013, http://www.justice.gov/usao/can/news/2013/2013_03_27_nine.sentenced.press.html (accessed June 2014).

21. National Center on Addiction and Substance Abuse at Columbia University, "'You've Got Drugs!' V: Prescription Drug Pushers on the Internet," 2008, http://www.casacolumbia.org/addiction-research/reports/youve-got-drugs-perscription-drug-pushers-internet-2008 (accessed June 2014).

22. Cisco Systems, Annual Security Report, 2014, https://www.cisco.com/web/offer/gist_ty2_asset/Cisco_2014_ASR.pdf (accessed June 2014).

23. Saul Hansell, "U.S. Tally in Online-Crime Sweep: 150 Charged," *New York Times*, August 27, 2004, p. C1.

24. Stephen Baker and Brian Grow, "Gambling Sites, This Is a Holdup," *BusinessWeek*, August 9, 2004, pp. 60–62.

25. John Callaham, "Steam and Other Online Gaming Services Hit by DDoS Attacks," January 3, 2014, http://www.neowin.net/news/steam-and-other-online-gaming-services-hit-by-ddos-attacks (accessed June 2014).

26. The Computer Fraud and Abuse Act (CFAA), 18 U.S.C. §1030 (1998).

27. The Digital Millennium Copyright Act, Public Law 105-304 (1998).

28. Title 18, United States Code, Section 2319.

29. Title 17, United States Code, Section 506.

30. This section is based on Richard Walker and David M. Levine, "'You've Got Jail': Current Trends in Civil and Criminal Enforcement of Internet Securities Fraud," *American Criminal Law Review* 38 (2001): 405–430.

31. Jim Wolf, "Internet Scams Targeted in Sweep: A 10-Day Crackdown Leads to 62 Arrests and 88 Indictments," *Boston Globe*, May 22, 2001, p. A2.

32. U.S. Department of Justice, "Alleged Leaders of $60 Million Internet Scam Indicted on Fraud and Money Laundering Charges: Massive Internet Investment Fraud Case Involves 15,000 Investors from 60 Countries," January 3, 2003.

33. These sections rely on APWG, "Phishing Activity Trends Report, Q1 2014," http://www.apwg.org/apwg-news-center/ (accessed June 2014).

34. Linda Foley, Karen Barney, and Jay Foley, "Identity Theft: The Aftermath 2009," Identity Theft Resource Center (ITRC), https://www.allclearid.com/themes/allclearid/docs/Aftermath_2009_20100520.pdf (accessed June 2014).

35. U.S. Department of Justice, "Nineteen Individuals Indicted in Internet 'Carding' Conspiracy," October 28, 2004.

36. Michael White and Christopher Fisher, "Assessing Our Knowledge of Identity Theft: The Challenges to Effective Prevention and Control Efforts," *Criminal Justice Policy Review* 19 (2008): 3–24.

37. APWG, "Phishing Activity Trends Report, Q1 2014."

38. FBI, "Cyber Criminals Continue to Use Spear-Phishing Attacks to Compromise Computer Networks," June 25, 2013, http://www.fbi.gov/scams-safety/e-scams (accessed June 2014).

39. FBI, "Malware Targets Bank Accounts: 'Gameover' Delivered via Phishing E-Mails," January 6, 2012, http://www.fbi.gov/news/stories/2012/january/malware_010612/malware_010612 (accessed June 2014).

40. Federal Communications Commission, "Voice over Internet Protocol," http://www.fcc.gov/voip/ (accessed June 2014).

41. FBI, "Something Vishy," February 23, 2007, http://www.fbi.gov/news/stories/2007/february/vishing_022307/ (accessed June 2014).

42. Identity Theft and Assumption Deterrence Act, as amended by Public Law 105-318, 112 Stat. 3007 (October 30, 1998).

43. Public Law 108-275 (2004).

44. Elizabeth Woyke and Dan Beucke, "Many Not-So-Happy Returns," *BusinessWeek*, August 15, 2005, p. 10.

45. FBI, "Internet Crime Report: 2012," http://www.ic3.gov/media/annualreport/2012_IC3Report.pdf (accessed June 2014).

46. FBI, "New Internet Scam: 'Ransomware' Locks Computers, Demands Payment," August 9, 2012, http://www.fbi.gov/news/stories/2012/august/new-internet-scam/ (accessed June 2014); FBI, "Five Domestic Defendants Linked to International Computer Hacking Ring Guilty of Federal Fraud Charges: 46 People Charged in Operation 'Phish Phry' Have Now Been Convicted," http://www.fbi.gov/losangeles/press-releases/2011/la032511.htm (accessed June 2014).

47. Anne Branscomb, "Rogue Computer Programs and Computer Rogues: Tailoring Punishment to Fit the Crime," *Rutgers Computer and Technology Law Journal* 16 (1990): 24–26.

48. Heather Jacobson and Rebecca Green, "Computer Crimes," *American Criminal Law Review* 39 (2002): 272–326.

49. U.S. Department of Justice, Northern District of California, "Federal Jury Convicts Former Technology Manager of Computer Hacking Offense: Defendant Found Guilty of Placing Computer 'Time Bomb' on Employer's Network Following Employment Dispute," September 8, 2005.

50. Hyung-jin Woo, Yeora Kim, and Joseph Dominick, "Hackers: Militants or Merry Pranksters? A Content Analysis of Defaced Web Pages," *Media Psychology* 6 (2004): 63–82.

51. Yona Hollander, "Prevent Web Page Defacement," *Internet Security Advisor* 2 (2000): 1–4.

52. Peter Foster, "David Petraeus Scandal: Jill Kelley Issues Legal Letters," *The Telegraph*, November 28, 2012, http://www.telegraph.co.uk/news/worldnews/northamerica/usa/9709972/David-Petraeus-scandal-Jill-Kelley-issues-legal-letters.html (accessed June 2014).

53. Janis Wolak, David Finkelhor, Kimberly Mitchell, and Michele Ybarra, "Online 'Predators' and Their Victims: Myths, Realities, and Implications for Prevention and Treatment," *American Psychologist* 63 (2008): 111–128.

54. Centers for Disease Control and Prevention, "Lesbian, Gay, Bisexual and Transgender Health," http://www.cdc.gov/lgbthealth/youth.htm (accessed June 2014).

55. Jane Ireland and Rachel Monaghan, "Behaviors Indicative of Bullying Among Young and Juvenile Male Offenders: A Study of Perpetrator and Victim Characteristics," *Aggressive Behavior* 32 (2006): 172–180.

56. Dan Olweus, "A Useful Evaluation Design, and Effects of the Olweus Bullying Prevention Program," *Psychology, Crime and Law* 11 (2005): 389–402.

57. This section leans heavily on Justin Patchin and Sameer Hinduja, "Bullies Move Beyond the Schoolyard: A Preliminary Look at Cyberbullying," *Youth Violence and Juvenile Justice* 4 (2006): 148–169.

58. Sameer Hinduja and Justin Patchin, "Cyberbullying: An Exploratory Analysis of Factors Related to Offending and Victimization," *Deviant Behavior* 29 (2008): 129–156.

59. Data in this section come from Sameer Hinduja and Justin Patchin, Cyberbullying Research Center, 2014, http://cyberbullying.us/cyberbullying-research-2013-update/ (accessed June 2014).

60. National Center for Education Statistics, "Indicators of School Crime and Safety: 2012," http://nces.ed.gov/pubsearch/pubsinfo.asp?pubid=2013036 (accessed June 2014).

61. FlexiSPY, Inc., http://www.flexispy.com/en/catch-cheating-spouse-cell-phone.htm (accessed June 2014).

62. Manufacturing a Surreptitious Interception Device, Title 18, United States Code, Section 2512(1)(b); Advertising a Surreptitious Interception Device, Title 18, United States Code, Section 2512(1)(c)(i).

63. U.S. Department of Justice, Southern District of California, "Creator and Four Users of Loverspy Spyware Program Indicted," http://www.justice.gov/criminal/cybercrime/press-releases/2005/perezIndict.htm (accessed June 2014).

64. Tom Yager, "Cyberspying: No Longer a Crime for Geeks Only," *InfoWorld* 22 (2000): 62.

65. Nathan Vardi, "Chinese Take Out," *Forbes* 176 (2005).

66. CBS News, "NSA Surveillance Exposed," http://www.cbsnews.com/feature/nsa-surveillance-exposed/ (accessed June 2014).

67. Clyde Wilson, "Software Piracy: Uncovering Mutiny on the Cyberseas," *Trial* 32 (1996): 24–31.

68. Deloitte, "2006 Global Security Survey," http://www.deloitte.com/view/en_MK/mk/industries/financialservices/42b88e6bc220e110VgnVCM100000ba42f00aRCRD.htm (accessed June 2014).

69. Jeremy Kirk, "Identity Theft May Cost IRS $21 Billion over Next Five Years," *PC World*, August 3, 2012, http://www.pcworld.idg.com.au/article/432584/identity_theft_may_cost_irs_21_billion_over_next_five_years/ (accessed June 2014).

70. Public Law 98-473, Title H, Chapter XXI, [sections] 2102(a), 98 Stat. 1837, 2190 (1984).

71. Public Law 104-294, Title II, [sections] 201, 110 Stat. 3488, 3491–3494 (1996).

72. Heather Jacobson and Rebecca Green, "Computer Crime," *American Criminal Law Review* 39 (2002): 273–326; Identity Theft and Assumption Act of 1998 (18 U.S.C. S 1028(a)(7)).

73. Comprehensive Crime Control Act of 1984, PL 98-473, 2101–03, 98 Stat. 1837, 2190 (1984), Adding 18 USC 1030 (1984); Counterfeit Active Device and Computer Fraud and Abuse Act, Amended by PL 99-474, 100 Stat. 1213 (1986), Codified at 18 U.S.C. 1030 (Supp. V 1987); Computer Abuse Amendments Act 18 U.S.C. Section 1030 (1994); Copyright Infringement Act 17 U.S.C. Section 506(a) 1994; Electronic Communications Privacy Act of 1986 18 U.S.C. 2510–2520 (1988 and Supp. II 1990).

74. Family Entertainment and Copyright Act of 2005, Title 18 United States Code Section 2319B.

75. Council of Europe Convention on Cybercrime, CETS No. 185, http://conventions.coe.int/Treaty/Commun/QueVoulezVous.asp?NT=185&CL=ENG (accessed June 2014).

76. ACLU Memo on the Council of Europe Convention on Cybercrime, June 16, 2004, https://www.aclu.org/technology-and-liberty/aclu-memo-council-europe-convention-cybercrime (accessed June 2014).

77. Bruce Swartz, Deputy Assistant General, Criminal Division, Justice Department, "Internet Fraud Testimony Before the House Energy and Commerce Committee," May 23, 2001.

78. IC3 Annual Internet Fraud Report 2006, http://www.ic3.gov/media/annualreport/2006_IC3Report.pdf (accessed June 2014).

79. "Statement of Mr. Bob Weaver, Deputy Special Agent in Charge, New York Field Office, United States Secret Service, Before the House Financial Services Committee Subcommittee on Financial Institutions and Consumer Credit and the Subcommittee on Oversight and Investigations," U.S. House of Representatives, April 3, 2003, http://www.iwar.org.uk/ecoespionage/resources/fraud/040303bw.pdf (accessed June 2014).

80. Bradley Graham, "Hackers Attack Via Chinese Web Sites," *Washington Post*, August 25, 2005, http://www.washingtonpost.com/wp-dyn/content/article/2005/08/24/AR2005082402318.html (accessed June 2014).

81. Ken Timmerman, "Computer Worm Shuts Down Iranian Centrifuge Plant," Newsmax.com, November 29, 2010, http://www.newsmax.com/KenTimmerman/iaea-stuxnet-computer-worm/2010/11/29/id/378288 (accessed June 2014).

82. Richard A. Clarke and Rob Knake, *Cyber War: The Next Threat to National Security and What to Do About It* (New York: HarperCollins, 2012).

83. Eileen Yu, "China Dispatches Online Army," ZDNet, May 7, 2011, http://www.zdnet.com/china-dispatches-online-army-2062300502/

84. Barry C. Collin, "The Future of CyberTerrorism: Where the Physical and Virtual Worlds Converge," http://www.crime-research.org/library/Cyberter.htm (accessed June 2014).

85. Tomas Hellström, "Critical Infrastructure and Systemic Vulnerability: Towards a Planning Framework," *Safety Science* 45 (2007): 415–430.

86. Mathieu Gorge, "Cyberterrorism: Hype or Reality?" *Computer Fraud and Security* 2 (2007): 9–12.

87. This section leans heavily on John Kane and April Wall, "Identifying the Links Between White-Collar Crime and Terrorism," National White Collar Crime Center, 2004, http://www.ncjrs.gov/pdffiles1/nij/grants/209520.pdf (accessed June 2014).

88. *United States v. Holy Land Foundation for Relief and Development*, http://scholar.google.com/scholar_case?case=4324794569509460028 (accessed June 2014).

89. Kane and Wall, "Identifying the Links Between White-Collar Crime and Terrorism."

90. Loretta Napoleoni, *Modern Jihad: Tracing the Dollars Behind the Terror Networks* (Sterling, VA: Pluto Press, 2003).

91. Michael Whine, "Cyberspace—A New Medium for Communication, Command, and Control by Extremists," http://www.tandfonline.com/doi/abs/10.1080/105761099265748#.U6t-JoShwz75 (accessed June 2014).

92. Yael Shahar, "Information Warfare," IWS: The Information Warfare Site, http://www.iwar.org.uk/cyberterror/resources/CIT.htm (accessed June 2014).

93. Frank Hayes, "Botnet Threat," *Computerworld* 40 (2006): 50.

94. Gale Reference Team, "McAfee Reports Botnets Threaten National Security," *Computer Security Update*, December 1, 2006, pp. 2–4.

95. Daniel Benjamin, *America and the World in the Age of Terrorism* (Washington, DC: CSIS Press, 2005), pp. 1–216.

96. General Accounting Office, "Critical Infrastructure Protection: Efforts of the Financial Services Sector to Address Cyber Threats."

97. Nicole Perlroth, "U.S. Banks Again Hit by Wave of Cyberattacks," *New York Times*, January 4, 2013, http://bits.blogs.nytimes.com/2013/01/04/u-s-banks-again-hit-by-wave-of-cyberattacks/ (accessed June 2014).

98. U.S. Army Cyber Command, http://www.arcyber.army.mil/org-uscc.html (accessed June 2014).

99. National Security Agency, http://www.nsa.gov/ (accessed June 2014).

GLOSSARY

acquaintance rape Forcible sex in which offender and victim are acquainted with each other.

acquaintance robbery Robbers who focus their thefts on people they know.

active precipitation The view that the source of many criminal incidents is the aggressive or provocative behavior of victims.

adolescent-limited offender Offender who follows the most common criminal trajectory, in which antisocial behavior peaks in adolescence and then diminishes.

age-graded theory A developmental theory that posits that (a) individual traits and childhood experiences are important to understand the onset of delinquent and criminal behavior; (b) experiences in young adulthood and beyond can redirect criminal trajectories or paths; (c) serious problems in adolescence undermine life chances; (d) positive life experiences and relationships can help a person knife off from a criminal career path; (e) positive life experiences such as gaining employment, getting married, or joining the military create informal social control mechanisms that limit criminal behavior opportunities; (f) former criminals may choose to desist from crime because they find more conventional paths more beneficial and rewarding.

aggravated rape Rape involving multiple offenders, weapons, and victim injuries.

aging out The process by which individuals reduce the frequency of their offending behavior as they age. It is also known as spontaneous remission, because people are believed to spontaneously reduce the rate of their criminal behavior as they mature. Aging out is thought to occur among all groups of offenders.

alexithymia A deficit in emotional cognition that prevents people from being aware of their feelings or being able to understand or talk about their thoughts and emotions; they seem robotic and emotionally dead.

al-Qaeda (Arabic for "the base") An international fundamentalist Islamist organization comprising independent and collaborative cells, whose goal is reducing Western influence upon Islamic affairs. Also spelled al-Qa'ida.

American Dream The goal of accumulating material goods and wealth through individual competition; the process of being socialized to pursue material success and to believe it is achievable.

anal stage In Freud's schema, the second and third years of life, when the focus of sexual attention is on the elimination of bodily wastes.

androgens Male sex hormones.

anomie According to Durkheim, an anomic society is one in which rules of behavior (i.e., values, customs, and norms) have broken down or become inoperative during periods of rapid social change or social crisis.

antithesis An opposing argument.

arousal theory A view of crime suggesting that people who have a high arousal level seek powerful stimuli in their environment to maintain an optimal level of arousal. These stimuli are often associated with violence and aggression. Sociopaths may need greater than average stimulation to bring them up to comfortable levels of living; this need explains their criminal tendencies.

arson for profit People looking to collect insurance money, but who are afraid or unable to set the fire themselves, hire professional arsonists. These professionals have acquired the skills to set fires, yet make the cause seem accidental.

arson fraud A business owner burns his or her property, or hires someone to do it, to escape financial problems.

atavistic anomalies According to Lombroso, the physical characteristics that distinguish born criminals from the general population and are throwbacks to animals or primitive people.

ATM skimming Using an electronic device or camera on an ATM that copies information from a bank card's magnetic strip whenever a customer uses the machine or photographs their key strokes.

at-risk Children and adults who lack the education and skills needed to be effectively in demand in modern society.

attachment theory The belief that the ability to form attachments—that is, emotionally bond to another person—has important lasting psychological implications that follow people across the life span.

attention deficit hyperactivity disorder (ADHD) A psychological disorder in which a child shows developmentally inappropriate impulsivity, hyperactivity, and lack of attention.

authority conflict pathway The path to a criminal career that begins with early stubborn behavior and defiance of parents.

behaviorism The branch of psychology concerned with the study of observable behavior rather than unconscious motives. It focuses on the relationship between particular stimuli and people's responses to them.

behavior modeling Process of learning behavior (notably aggression) by observing others. Aggressive models may be parents, criminals in the neighborhood, or characters on television or in video games and movies.

biological determinism A belief that criminogenic traits can be acquired through indirect heredity from a degenerate family whose members suffered from such ills as insanity, syphilis, and alcoholism, or through direct heredity—being related to a family of criminals.

biophobia A view held by sociologists that no serious consideration should be given to biological factors when attempting to understand human nature.

biosocial theory An approach to criminology that focuses on the interaction between biological and social factors as they relate to crime.

bipolar disorder An emotional disturbance in which moods alternate between periods of wild elation and deep depression.

blameworthy Basing punishment solely on whether a person is responsible for wrongdoing and deserving of censure or blame.

booster box Device with a false bottom that can be open and shut by a professional shoplifter, lined with metal or some other substance to prevent security tags from setting off alarms, placed over merchandise.

boosters Professional shoplifters who steal with the intention of reselling stolen merchandise.

brothel A house of prostitution, typically run by a madam who sets prices and handles "business" arrangements.

California Personality Inventory (CPI) A frequently administered personality test used to distinguish deviant groups from nondeviant groups.

call girls Prostitutes who make dates via the phone and then service customers in hotel rooms or apartments. Call girls typically have a steady clientele who are repeat customers.

capable guardians Effective deterrents to crime, such as police or watchful neighbors.

capitalist bourgeoisie The owners of the means of production.

career criminal A person who repeatedly violates the law and organizes his or her lifestyle around criminality.

carjacking Theft of a car by force or threat of force.

cerebral allergies A physical condition that causes brain malfunction due to exposure to some environmental or biochemical irritant.

chemical restraints or chemical straitjackets Antipsychotic drugs such as Haldol, Stelazine, Prolixin, and Risperdal, which help control levels of neurotransmitters (such as serotonin/dopamine), that are used to treat violence-prone people.

child abuse Any physical, emotional, or sexual trauma to a child for which no reasonable explanation, such as an accident, can be found. Child abuse can also be a function of neglecting to give proper care and attention to a young child.

chiseling Crimes that involve using illegal means to cheat an organization, its consumers, or both on a regular basis.

chivalry hypothesis The idea that low female crime and delinquency rates are a reflection of the leniency with which police treat female offenders.

chronic offender According to Wolfgang, a delinquent offender who is arrested five or more times before he or she is 18 stands a good chance of becoming an adult criminal; such offenders are responsible for more than half of all serious crimes.

chronic victimization Those who have been crime victims maintain a significantly higher chance of future victimization than people who have remained nonvictims. Most repeat victimizations occur soon after a previous crime has occurred, suggesting that repeat victims share some personal characteristic that makes them a magnet for predators.

civil law The set of rules governing relations between private parties, including both individuals and organizations (such as business enterprises and/or corporations). The civil law is used to resolve, control, and shape such personal interactions as contracts, wills and trusts, property ownership, and commerce.

classical criminology Eighteenth-century social thinkers believed that criminals choose to commit crime and that crime can be controlled by judicious punishment.

cleared crimes Crimes are cleared in two ways: when at least one person is arrested, charged, and turned over to the court for prosecution; or by exceptional means, when some element beyond police control precludes the physical arrest of an offender (for example, the offender leaves the country).

closure A term used by Lemert to describe people from a middle-class background who have little identification with a criminal subculture but cash bad checks because of a financial crisis that demands an immediate resolution.

cognitive theory The study of the perception of reality and of the mental processes required to understand the world in which we live.

cohort A sample of subjects whose behavior is followed over a period of time.

collective efficacy Social control exerted by cohesive communities, based on mutual trust, including intervention in the supervision of children and maintenance of public order.

college boy A disadvantaged youth who embraces the cultural and social values of the middle class and actively strives to be successful by those standards. This type of youth is embarking on an almost hopeless path because he is ill-equipped academically, socially, and linguistically to achieve the rewards of middle-class life.

commitment to conformity A strong personal investment in conventional institutions, individuals, and processes that prevents people from engaging in behavior that might jeopardize their reputation and achievements.

common law Early English law, developed by judges, that incorporated Anglo-Saxon tribal custom, feudal rules and practices, and the everyday rules of behavior of local villages. Common law became the standardized law of the land in England and eventually formed the basis of the criminal law in the United States.

Communist Manifesto In this document, Marx focused his attention on the economic conditions perpetuated by the capitalist system. He stated that its development had turned workers into a dehumanized mass who lived an existence that was at the mercy of their capitalist employers.

computer worms Programs that attack computer networks (or the Internet) by self-replicating and sending themselves to other users, generally via email, without the aid of the operator.

concentration effect Working- and middle-class families flee inner-city poverty areas, resulting in the most disadvantaged population being consolidated in the most disorganized urban neighborhoods.

conduct disorders A pattern of repetitive behavior in which the rights of others or social norms are violated.

conduct norms Behaviors expected of social group members. If group norms conflict with those of the general culture, members of the group may find themselves described as outcasts or criminals.

confidence game A swindle, usually involving a get-rich-quick scheme, often with illegal overtones, so that the victim will be afraid or embarrassed to call the police.

conflict view The view that human behavior is shaped by interpersonal conflict and that those who maintain social power will use it to further their own needs.

conscience One of two parts of the superego; it distinguishes between what is right and wrong.

consensus view The belief that the majority of citizens in a society share common ideals and work toward a common good and that crimes are acts that are outlawed because they conflict with the rules of the majority and are harmful to society.

consent In prosecuting rape cases, it is essential to prove that the attack was forced and that the victim did not give voluntary consent to her attacker. In a sense, the burden of proof is on the victim to show that her character is beyond question and that she in no way encouraged, enticed, or misled the accused rapist. Proving victim dissent is not a requirement in any other violent crime.

constructive possession In the crime of larceny, willingly giving up temporary physical possession of property but retaining legal ownership.

contagion effect Genetic predispositions and early experiences make some people, including twins, susceptible to deviant behavior, which is transmitted by the presence of antisocial siblings in the household.

containment theory The idea that a strong self-image insulates a youth from the pressures and pulls of criminogenic influences in the environment.

continuity of crime The view that crime begins early in life and continues throughout the life course. Thus, the best predictor of future criminality is past criminality.

corner boy According to Cohen, a role in the lower-class culture in which young men remain in their birth neighborhood, acquire families and menial jobs, and adjust to the demands of their environment.

corporate crime White-collar crime involving a legal violation by a corporate entity, such as price-fixing, restraint of trade, or hazardous waste dumping.

covert pathway A path to a criminal career that begins with minor underhanded behavior and progresses to fire starting and theft.

crackdowns The concentration of police resources on particular problem areas, such as street-level drug dealing, to eradicate or displace criminal activity.

crime discouragers Discouragers can be grouped into three categories: guardians, who monitor targets (such as store security guards); handlers, who monitor potential offenders (such as parole officers and parents); and managers, who monitor places (such as homeowners and doorway attendants).

crime typology The study of criminal behavior involving research on the links between different types of crime and criminals. Because people often disagree about types of crimes and criminal motivation, no standard exists within the field. Some typologies focus on the criminal, suggesting the existence of offender groups, such as professional criminals, psychotic criminals, occasional criminals, and so on. Others focus on the crimes, clustering them into categories such as property crimes, sex crimes, and so on.

criminal anthropology Early efforts to discover a biological basis of crime through measurement of physical and mental processes.

criminality A personal trait of the individual as distinct from a "crime," which is an event.

criminal justice The field of study that focuses on law enforcement, the legal system, corrections, and other agencies of justice involved in the apprehension, prosecution, defense, sentencing, incarceration, and supervision of those suspected of or charged with criminal offenses.

criminologists Researchers who use scientific methods to study the nature, extent, cause, and control of criminal behavior.

criminology The scientific study of the nature, extent, cause, and control of criminal behavior.

crisis intervention Emergency counseling for crime victims.

critical criminologists Researchers who view crime as a function of the capitalist mode of production and not the social conflict that might occur in any society regardless of its economic system.

critical criminology The view that capitalism produces haves and have-nots, each engaging in a particular branch of criminality. The mode of production shapes social life. Because economic competitiveness is the essence of capitalism, conflict increases and eventually destabilizes social institutions and the individuals within them.

critical feminism Scholars, both male and female, who focus on the effects of gender inequality and the unequal power of men and women in a capitalist society.

cross-sectional survey Survey data derived from all age, race, gender, and income segments of the population measured simultaneously. Because people from every age group are represented, age-specific crime rates can be determined. Proponents believe this is a sufficient substitute for the more expensive longitudinal approach that follows a group of subjects over time to measure crime rate changes.

crusted over Children who have been victims of or witnesses to violence and do not let people inside, nor do they express their feelings. They exploit others and in turn are exploited by those older and stronger; as a result, they develop a sense of hopelessness.

cultural deviance theory Branch of social structure theory that sees strain and social disorganization together resulting in a unique lower-class culture that conflicts with conventional social norms.

culture conflict According to Sellin, a condition brought about when the rules and norms of an individual's subcultural affiliation conflict with the role demands of conventional society.

culture of poverty The view that people in the lower class of society form a separate culture with its own values and norms that are in conflict with conventional society; the culture is self-maintaining and ongoing.

cumulative disadvantage A condition in which repeated negative experiences in adolescence undermine life chances and reduce employability and social relations. People who increase their cumulative disadvantage risk continued offending.

cyberbullying Willful and repeated harm inflicted through the medium of electronic text.

cybercrime The use of modern technology for criminal purposes.

cyberespionage Efforts by intelligence agencies to penetrate computer networks of an enemy nation in order to steal important data.

cyberspying Illegally using the Internet to gather information that is considered private and confidential.

cyberstalking Use of the Internet, email, or other electronic communications devices to stalk another person. Some cyberstalkers pursue minors through online chat rooms; others harass their victims electronically.

cyberterrorism Internet attacks against an enemy nation's technological infrastructure.

cybertheft Use of computer networks for criminal profits. Illegal copyright infringement, identity theft, and Internet securities fraud are examples of cybertheft.

cybervandalism Malicious attacks aimed at disrupting, defacing, and destroying technology.

cyberwar Using cyberspace for acts of war, including spying and disrupting an enemy's computer network.

cycle of violence The idea that victims of crime, especially childhood abuse, are more likely to commit crimes themselves.

date rape Forcible sex during a courting relationship.

defective intelligence Traits such as feeblemindedness, epilepsy, insanity, and defective social instinct, which Goring believed had a significant relationship to criminal behavior.

defensible space The principle that crime prevention can be achieved through modifying the physical environment to reduce the opportunity individuals have to commit crime.

deliberation Planning a homicide after careful thought, however brief, rather than acting on sudden impulse.

delinquent boy A youth who adopts a set of norms and principles in direct opposition to middle-class values, engaging in short-run hedonism, living for today and letting tomorrow take care of itself.

demystify To unmask the true purpose of law, justice, or other social institutions.

denial-of-service attack Extorting money from an Internet service user by threatening to prevent the user from having access to the service.

Department of Homeland Security (DHS) An agency of the federal government charged with preventing terrorist attacks within the United States, reducing America's vulnerability to terrorism, and minimizing the damage and aiding recovery from attacks that do occur.

deterrence theory The view that if the probability of arrest, conviction, and sanctioning increases, crime rates should decline.

developmental criminology A view of criminal behavior that places emphasis on the changes people go through over the life course. It presents a criminal career as a dynamic process involving onset, continuity, persistence, acceleration, and eventual desistance from criminal behavior, controlled by individual level traits and conditions.

deviant behavior Behavior that departs from the social norm.

deviant place theory People become victims because they reside in socially disorganized, high-crime areas where they have the greatest risk of coming into contact with criminal offenders.

dialectic method For every idea, or thesis, there exists an opposing argument, or antithesis. Because neither position can ever be truly accepted, the result is a merger of the two ideas, a synthesis. Marx adapted this analytic method for his study of class struggle.

differential association theory According to Sutherland, the principle that criminal acts are related to a person's exposure to an excess amount of antisocial attitudes and values.

differential opportunity The view that lower-class youths, whose legitimate opportunities are limited, join gangs and pursue criminal careers as alternative means to achieve universal success goals.

differential reinforcement Behavior is reinforced by being either rewarded or punished while interacting with others; also called direct conditioning.

differential reinforcement theory An attempt to explain crime as a type of learned behavior. First proposed by Akers in collaboration with Burgess in 1966, it is a version of the social learning view that employs differential association concepts as well as elements of psychological learning theory.

differential susceptibility model The belief that there is an indirect association between traits and crime.

diffusion of benefits Efforts to prevent one crime help prevent another; in other instances, crime control efforts in one locale reduce crime in another area.

direct conditioning Behavior is reinforced by being either rewarded or punished while interacting with others; also called differential reinforcement.

Director of National Intelligence (DNI) Government official charged with coordinating data from the nation's primary intelligence-gathering agencies.

discouragement Crime control efforts targeting a particular locale help reduce crime in surrounding areas and populations.

disorders Any type of psychological problems (formerly labeled neuroses or psychoses), such as anxiety disorders, mood disorders, and conduct disorders.

displacement A program that helps lower crime rates at specific locations or neighborhoods may be redirecting offenders to alternative targets.

disputatiousness Behavior within culturally defined conflict situations in which an individual who has been offended by a negative outcome in a dispute seeks reparations through violent means.

diversion programs Programs of rehabilitation that remove offenders from the normal channels of the criminal justice system, thus avoiding the stigma of a criminal label.

dramatization of evil As the negative feedback of law enforcement agencies, parents, friends, teachers, and other figures amplifies the force of the original label, stigmatized offenders may begin to reevaluate their own identities. The person becomes the thing he is described as being.

drift According to Matza, the view that youths move in and out of delinquency and that their lifestyles can embrace both conventional and deviant values.

dropout factories High schools in which the completion rate is consistently 40 percent or less.

early onset A term that refers to the assumption that a criminal career begins early in life and that people who are deviant at a very young age are the ones most likely to persist in crime.

economic crime An act in violation of the criminal law that is designed to bring financial gain to the offender.

edgework The excitement or exhilaration of successfully executing illegal activities in dangerous situations.

egalitarian families Families in which spouses share similar positions of power at home and in the workplace.

ego The part of the personality, developed in early childhood, that helps control the id and keep people's actions within the boundaries of social convention.

ego ideal Part of the superego; directs the individual into morally acceptable and responsible behaviors, which may not be pleasurable.

ehooking Using the Internet to advertise sexual services and make contact with clients.

elder abuse A disturbing form of domestic violence by children and other relatives with whom elderly people live.

eldercide The murder of a senior citizen.

election fraud Illegal interference with the process of an election. Acts of fraud tend to involve affecting vote counts to bring about a desired election outcome, whether by increasing the vote share of the favored candidate, depressing the vote share of the rival candidates, or both. Varieties of election fraud include intimidation, disruption of polling places, distribution of misinformation such as the wrong election date, registration fraud, and vote buying.

Electra complex A stage of development when girls begin to have sexual feelings for their fathers.

electroencephalograph (EEG) A device that can record the electronic impulses given off by the brain, commonly called brain waves.

embezzlement A type of larceny that involves taking the possessions of another (fraudulent conversion) that have been placed in the thief's lawful possession for safekeeping, such as a bank teller misappropriating deposits or a stockbroker making off with a customer's account.

Enlightenment A philosophical, intellectual, and cultural movement of the seventeenth and eighteenth centuries that stressed reason, logic, criticism, education, and freedom of thought over dogma and superstition.

enterprise crimes Ongoing illegal activities by an individual or a group of individuals involved in commerce that either violate the laws regulating legitimate business or whose acknowledged purpose is profit through illegitimate commercial enterprise.

eros The instinct to preserve and create life, a basic human drive present at birth.

espionage The practice of obtaining information about a government, organization, or society that is considered secret or confidential without the permission of the holder of the information. Commonly called spying.

etailing fraud Illegally buying and/or selling merchandise on the Internet.

exploitation Forcing victims to pay for services to which they have a clear right.

expressive crimes Crimes that have no purpose except to accomplish the behavior at hand, such as shooting someone.

expressive violence Violence that is designed not for profit or gain but to vent rage, anger, or frustration.

failed state A nation whose government has lost control of its own territory, is unable to provide public services and protection, and lacks the ability to interact with other states as a full member of the international community.

false pretenses (fraud) Misrepresenting a fact in a way that causes a deceived victim to give money or property to the offender.

felony A serious offense, such as rape, murder, robbery, or burglary, that is punishable by a prison sentence or, in the case of first-degree murder, by capital punishment.

felony murder A homicide in the context of another felony, such as robbery or rape; legally defined as first-degree murder.

fence A buyer and seller of stolen merchandise.

feticide Endangering or killing an unborn fetus.

filicide Murder of an older child.

fixated An adult who exhibits behavior traits characteristic of those encountered during infantile sexual development.

flash houses Public meeting places in England, often taverns, that served as headquarters for gangs.

flashover An effect in a fire when heat and gas at the ceiling of a room reach 2,000 degrees, and clothes and furniture burst into flame, duplicating the effects of arsonists' gasoline or explosives. It is possible that many suspected arsons are actually the result of flashover.

focal concerns According to Miller, the value orientations of lower-class cultures; features include the needs for excitement, trouble, smartness, and personal autonomy.

gang rape Forcible sex involving multiple attackers.

gateway model An explanation of drug abuse that posits that users begin with a more benign drug (alcohol or marijuana) and progress to more potent drugs.

general deterrence A crime control policy that depends on the fear of criminal penalties. General deterrence measures, such as long prison sentences for violent crimes, are aimed at convincing the potential law violator that the pains associated with crime outweigh its benefits.

general strain theory (GST) According to Agnew, the view that multiple sources of strain interact with an individual's emotional traits and responses to produce criminality.

General Theory of Crime (GTC) According to Gottfredson and Hirschi, a developmental theory that modifies social control theory by integrating concepts from biosocial, psychological, routine activities, and rational choice theories.

gentrification A residential renewal stage in which obsolete housing is replaced and upgraded; areas undergoing such change seem to experience an increase in their crime rates.

globalization The process of creating transnational markets, politics, and legal systems in an effort to form and sustain a global economy.

good burglar Professional burglars use this title to characterize colleagues who have distinguished themselves as burglars. Characteristics of the good burglar include technical competence, maintenance of personal integrity, specialization in burglary, financial success, and the ability to avoid prison sentences.

grand larceny Theft of money or property of substantial value, punished as a felony.

green crime Acts involving illegal environmental harm that violate environmental laws and regulations.

guerilla The term means "little war" and developed out of the Spanish rebellion against French troops after Napoleon's 1808 invasion of the Iberian Peninsula. Guerillas are an informal military band seeking to overthrow the government.

hate crimes Acts of violence or intimidation designed to terrorize or frighten people considered undesirable because of their race, religion, ethnic origin, or sexual orientation.

humanistic psychology A branch of psychology that stresses self-awareness and "getting in touch with feelings."

hypoglycemia A condition that occurs when glucose (sugar) levels in the blood fall below the necessary level for normal and efficient brain functioning.

id The primitive part of people's mental makeup, present at birth, that represents unconscious biological drives for food, sex, and other life-sustaining necessities. The id seeks instant gratification without concern for the rights of others.

identity crisis A psychological state, identified by Erikson, in which youth face inner turmoil and uncertainty about life roles.

identity theft Using the Internet to steal someone's identity and/or impersonate the victim in order to conduct illicit transactions such as committing fraud using the victim's name and identity.

incapacitation effect The idea that keeping offenders in confinement will eliminate the risk of their committing further offenses.

incivilities Rude and uncivil behavior; behavior that indicates little caring for the feelings of others.

index crimes The eight crimes that, because of their seriousness and frequency, the FBI reports the incidence of in the annual Uniform Crime Report. Index crimes include murder, rape, assault, robbery, burglary, arson, larceny, and motor vehicle theft.

individual vulnerability model Assumes there is a direct link between traits and crime; some people are vulnerable to crime from birth.

infanticide The murder of a very young child.

inferiority complex People who have feelings of inferiority and compensate for them with a drive for superiority.

influence peddling Using an institutional position to grant favors and sell information to which their co-conspirators are not entitled.

informal sanctions Disapproval, stigma, or anger directed toward an offender by significant others (parents, peers, neighbors, teachers), resulting in shame, embarrassment, and loss of respect.

information processing A branch of cognitive psychology that focuses on the way people process, store, encode, retrieve, and manipulate information to make decisions and solve problems.

information technology (IT) All forms of technology used to create, store, retrieve, and exchange data in all its various forms, including electronic, voice, and still image.

inheritance school Advocates of this view trace the activities of several generations of families believed to have an especially large number of criminal members.

insider trading Illegal buying of stock in a company based on information provided by someone who has a fiduciary interest in the company, such as an employee or an attorney or accountant retained by the firm. Federal laws and the rules of the Securities and Exchange Commission require that all profits from such trading be returned and provide for both fines and a prison sentence.

institutional anomie theory The view that anomie pervades U.S. culture because the drive for material wealth dominates and undermines social and community values.

instrumental crimes Offenses designed to improve the financial or social position of the criminal.

instrumental theory The view that criminal law and the criminal justice system are capitalist instruments for controlling the lower class.

instrumental violence Violence used in an attempt to improve the financial or social position of the criminal.

insurgents The typical goal of an insurgency is to confront the existing government for control of all or a portion of its territory, or force political concessions in sharing political power. While terrorists may operate in small bands with a narrow focus, insurgents represent a popular movement and may also seek external support from other nations to bring pressure on the government.

integrated theories Models of crime causation that weave social and individual variables into a complex explanatory chain.

intelligence A person's ability to reason, think abstractly, understand complex ideas, learn from experience, and discover solutions to complex problems.

interactionist view The view that one's perception of reality is significantly influenced by one's interpretations of the reactions of others to similar events and stimuli.

involuntary manslaughter or negligent manslaughter A homicide that occurs as a result of acts that are negligent and without regard for the harm they may cause others, such as driving under the influence of alcohol or drugs.

just desert The philosophy of justice that asserts that those who violate the rights of others deserve to be punished. The severity of punishment should be commensurate with the seriousness of the crime.

justice The quality of being fair under the law. Justice is defined by the relationship that exists between the individual and the state; justice demands that the state treats every person as equally as possible without regard to their gender, religion, race, or any other personal status.

latency A developmental stage that begins at age 6. During this period, feelings of sexuality are repressed until the genital stage begins at puberty; this marks the beginning of adult sexuality.

latent delinquency A psychological predisposition to commit antisocial acts because of an id-dominated personality that renders an individual incapable of controlling impulsive, pleasure-seeking drives.

latent trait A stable feature, characteristic, property, or condition, present at birth or soon after, that makes some people crime prone over the life course.

latent trait theories Theoretical views that criminal behavior is controlled by a master trait, present at birth or soon after, that remains stable and unchanging throughout a person's lifetime.

learning disability (LD) A disorder in one or more of the basic psychological processes involved in understanding or using spoken or written languages.

left realism An approach that views crime as a function of relative deprivation under capitalism and that favors pragmatic, community-based crime prevention and control.

liberal feminist theory Theory suggesting that the traditionally lower crime rate for women can be explained by their second-class economic and social position. As women's social roles have changed and their lifestyles have become more like those of men, it is believed that their crime rates will converge.

life course persisters One of the small group of offenders whose criminal career continues well into adulthood.

life course theories Theoretical views studying changes in criminal offending patterns over a person's entire life.

lifestyle theory People may become crime victims because their lifestyle increases their exposure to criminal offenders.

logic bomb A program that is secretly attached to a computer system, monitors the network's work output, and waits for a particular signal such as a date to appear. Also called a slag code, it is a type of delayed action virus that may be set off when a program user makes certain input that sets it in motion. A logic bomb may cause a variety of problems ranging from displaying or printing a spurious message to deleting or corrupting data.

lumpen proletariat The fringe members at the bottom of society who produce nothing and live, parasitically, off the work of others.

madam A woman who employs prostitutes, supervises their behavior, and receives a fee for her services.

mala in se Acts that are outlawed because they violate basic moral values, such as rape, murder, assault, and robbery.

mala prohibitum Acts that are outlawed because they clash with current norms and public opinion, such as tax, traffic, and drug laws.

malware A malicious software program.

manslaughter A homicide without malice.

marginal deterrence The concept that a penalty for a crime may prompt commission of a marginally more severe crime because that crime receives the same magnitude of punishment as the original one.

marginalization Displacement of workers, pushing them outside the economic and social mainstream.

marital exemption The practice in some states of prohibiting the prosecution of husbands for the rape of their wives.

marital rape Forcible sex between people who are legally married to each other.

mark The target of a con man or woman.

masculinity hypothesis The view that women who commit crimes have biological and psychological traits similar to those of men.

mass murder The killing of a large number of people in a single incident by an offender who typically does not seek concealment or escape.

mechanical solidarity A characteristic of a preindustrial society, which is held together by traditions, shared values, and unquestioned beliefs.

meta-analysis A research technique that uses the grouped data from several different studies.

middle-class measuring rods According to Cohen, the standards by which teachers and other representatives of state authority evaluate lower-class youths. Because they cannot live up to middle-class standards, lower-class youths are bound for failure, which gives rise to frustration and anger at conventional society.

minimal brain dysfunction (MBD) An abruptly appearing, maladaptive behavior that interrupts an individual's lifestyle and life flow. In its most serious form, MBD has been linked to serious antisocial acts, an imbalance in the urge-control mechanisms of the brain, and chemical abnormality.

Minnesota Multiphasic Personality Inventory (MMPI) A widely used psychological test that has subscales designed to measure many different personality traits, including psychopathic deviation (Pd scale), schizophrenia (Sc scale), and hypomania (Ma scale).

misdemeanor A minor or petty crime, typically punished by a fine, community sentence, or a jail term.

mission hate crimes Violent crimes committed by disturbed individuals who see it as their duty to rid the world of evil.

money mule Someone who collects money or goods acquired illegally and then transfers them to a third party.

moral crusaders People who strive to stamp out behavior they find objectionable. Typically, moral crusaders are directed at public order crimes, such as drug abuse or pornography.

moral development The way people morally represent and reason about the world.

moral entrepreneurs Interest groups that attempt to control social life and the legal order in such a way as to promote their own personal set of moral values. People who use their influence to shape the legal process in ways they see fit.

motivated offenders The potential offenders in a population. According to rational choice theory, crime rates will vary according to the number of motivated offenders.

Multidimensional Personality Questionnaire (MPQ) A test that allows researchers to assess such personality traits as control, aggression, alienation, and well-being. Evaluations using this scale indicate that adolescent offenders who are crime prone maintain negative emotionality, a tendency to experience aversive affective states such as anger, anxiety, and irritability.

murder The unlawful killing of a human being (homicide) with malicious intent.

naive check forgers Amateurs who cash bad checks because of some financial crisis but have little identification with a criminal subculture.

narcissistic personality disorder A condition marked by a persistent pattern of self-importance, need for admiration, lack of empathy, and preoccupation with fantasies of unlimited success, power, brilliance, beauty, or ideal love.

National Crime Victimization Survey (NCVS) The ongoing victimization study conducted jointly by the Justice Department and the U.S. Census Bureau that surveys victims about their experiences with law violation.

National Incident-Based Reporting System (NIBRS) A program that requires local police agencies to provide a brief account of each incident and arrest within 22 crime patterns, including incident, victim, and offender information.

nature theory The view that intelligence is largely determined genetically and that low intelligence is linked to criminal behavior.

negative affective states According to Agnew, anger, depression, disappointment, fear, and other adverse emotions that derive from strain.

negative reinforcement Using either negative stimuli (punishment) or loss of reward (negative punishment) to curtail unwanted behaviors.

neglect Not providing a child with the care and shelter to which he or she is entitled.

negligent manslaughter A homicide that occurs as a result of acts that are negligent and without regard for the harm they may cause others, such as driving under the influence of alcohol or drugs; also called involuntary manslaughter.

neocortex A part of the human brain; the left side of the neocortex controls sympathetic feelings toward others.

networks When referring to terrorist organizations, networks are loosely organized groups located in different parts of the city, state, or country (or world) that share a common theme or purpose, but have a diverse leadership and command structure and are only in intermittent communication with one another.

neuroallergies Allergies that affect the nervous system and cause the allergic person to produce enzymes that attack wholesome foods as if they were dangerous to the body. They may also cause swelling of the brain and produce sensitivity in the central nervous system—conditions that are linked to mental, emotional, and behavioral problems.

neurophysiology The study of brain activity.

neutralization theory Neutralization theory holds that offenders adhere to conventional values while "drifting" into periods of illegal behavior. In order to drift, people must first overcome (neutralize) legal and moral values.

nonnegligent manslaughter A homicide committed in the heat of passion or during a sudden quarrel; although intent may be present, malice is not; also called voluntary manslaughter.

nurture theory The view that intelligence is not inherited but is largely a product of environment. Low IQ scores do not cause crime but may result from the same environmental factors.

obscenity According to current legal theory, sexually explicit material that lacks a serious purpose and appeals solely to the prurient interest of the viewer. While nudity per se is not usually considered obscene, open sexual behavior, masturbation, and exhibition of the genitals is banned in most communities.

obsessive-compulsive disorder An extreme preoccupation with certain thoughts and compulsive performance of certain behaviors.

occasional criminals Offenders who do not define themselves by a criminal role or view themselves as committed career criminals.

Oedipus complex A stage of development when males begin to have sexual feelings for their mothers.

offender-specific crime The idea that offenders evaluate their skills, motives, needs, and fears before deciding to commit crime.

offense-specific crime The idea that offenders react selectively to the characteristics of particular crimes.

oral stage In Freud's schema, the first year of life, when a child attains pleasure by sucking and biting.

organic solidarity Postindustrial social systems, which are highly developed and dependent upon the division of labor; people are connected by their interdependent needs for one another's services and production.

overt pathway Pathway to a criminal career that begins with minor aggression, leads to physical fighting, and eventually escalates to violent crime.

paraphilias Bizarre or abnormal sexual practices that may involve recurrent sexual urges focused on objects, humiliation, or children.

parental efficacy Parenting that is supportive, effective, and noncoercive.

Part I crimes Another term for index crimes; eight categories of serious, frequent crimes.

Part II crimes All crimes other than index and minor traffic offenses. The FBI records annual arrest information for Part II offenses.

passive precipitation The view that some people become victims because of personal and social characteristics that make them attractive targets for predatory criminals.

paternalistic families Traditional family model in which fathers assume the role of breadwinners, while mothers tend to have menial jobs or remain at home to supervise domestic matters.

patriarchy A society in which men dominate public, social, economic, and political affairs.

peacemaking An approach that considers punitive crime control strategies to be counterproductive and favors the use of humanistic conflict resolution to prevent and control crime.

pedophilia A psychosexual disorder in which an adult has sexual fantasies about or engages in sexual acts with an underage minor child.

perceptual deterrence The theory that the perceived certainty, severity, and celerity of punishment are inversely related to the decisions by would-be offenders to commit crime, regardless of the actual likelihood of being apprehended and punished. People who believe they will be punished will be deterred even if the actual likelihood of punishment is insignificant.

permeable neighborhoods Areas with a greater than usual number of access streets from traffic arteries into the neighborhood.

persistence The idea that those who started their delinquent careers early and who committed serious violent crimes throughout adolescence are the most likely to persist as adults.

personality The reasonably stable patterns of behavior, including thoughts and emotions, that distinguish one person from another.

petit (petty) larceny Theft of a small amount of money or property, punished as a misdemeanor.

phallic stage In Freud's schema, the third year, when children focus their attention on their genitals.

phishing Sometimes called carding or brand spoofing, phishing is a scam where the perpetrator sends out emails appearing to come from legitimate web enterprises such as eBay, Amazon, and PayPal in an effort to get the recipient to reveal personal and financial information.

pigeon drop A con game in which a package or wallet containing money is "found" by a con man or woman, and the victims are bilked out of money they are asked to put up as collateral.

pink slime A substance made by gathering waste trimmings, cooking them so the fat separates easily from the muscle, and using a centrifuge to complete the separation.

pleasure principle According to Freud, a theory in which id-dominated people are driven to increase their personal pleasure without regard to consequences.

poachers Early English thieves who typically lived in the country and supplemented their diet and income with game that belonged to a landlord.

political crime Illegal acts that are designed to undermine an existing government and threaten its survival. Political crimes can include both violent and nonviolent acts and range in seriousness from dissent, treason, and espionage to violent acts such as terrorism or assassination.

Ponzi scheme An investment fraud that involves the payment of purported returns to existing investors from funds contributed by new investors.

population All people who share a particular personal characteristic, such as all high school students or all police officers.

population heterogeneity The view that the propensity of an individual to participate in antisocial behavior is a relatively stable trait, unchanging over his or her life course.

pornography Sexually explicit books, magazines, films, or tapes intended to provide sexual titillation and excitement for paying customers.

positivism The branch of social science that uses the scientific method of the natural sciences and suggests that human behavior is a product of social, biological, psychological, or economic forces.

posttraumatic stress disorder (PTSD) Psychological reaction to a highly stressful event; symptoms may include depression, anxiety, flashbacks, and recurring nightmares.

power–control theory The view that gender differences in crime are a function of economic power (class position, one-earner versus two-earner families) and parental control (paternalistic versus egalitarian families).

preemptive deterrence Efforts to prevent crime through community organization and youth involvement.

premeditation Consideration of a homicide before it occurs.

premenstrual syndrome (PMS) The stereotype that several days prior to and during menstruation females are beset by irritability and poor judgment as a result of hormonal changes.

primary deviance According to Lemert, deviant acts that do not help redefine the self-image and public image of the offender.

primary prevention programs Treatment programs that seek to correct or remedy personal problems before they manifest themselves as crime.

problem behavior syndrome (PBS) A cluster of antisocial behaviors that may include family dysfunction, substance abuse, smoking, precocious sexuality and early pregnancy, educational underachievement, suicide attempts, sensation seeking, and unemployment, as well as crime.

procedural criminal laws Those laws that set out the basic rules of practice in the criminal justice system. Some elements of the law of criminal procedure are the rules of evidence, the law of arrest, the law of search and seizure, questions of appeal, jury selection, and the right to counsel.

productive forces Technology, energy sources, and material resources.

productive relations The relationships that exist among the people producing goods and services.

professional criminals Offenders who make a significant portion of their income from crime.

proletariat A term used by Marx to refer to the working class members of society who produce goods and services but who do not own the means of production.

propensity An inclination or tendency to behave in a particular way.

prostitution The granting of nonmarital sexual access for remuneration.

psychoanalytic or psychodynamic perspective Branch of psychology holding that the human personality is controlled by unconscious mental processes developed early in childhood.

psychopath People who have an antisocial personality that is a product of a defect or aberration within themselves.

psychopathic personality A personality characterized by a lack of warmth and feeling, inappropriate behavior responses, and an inability to learn from experience. Some psychologists view psychopathy as a result of childhood trauma; others see it as a result of biological abnormality.

psychosis A mental state in which the perception of reality is distorted. People experiencing psychosis hallucinate, have paranoid or delusional beliefs, change personality, exhibit disorganized thinking, and engage in unusual or bizarre behavior.

public (or administrative) law The branch of law that deals with the government and its relationships with individuals or other governments. It governs the administration and regulation of city, county, state, and federal government agencies.

public order crimes Acts that are considered illegal because they threaten the general well-being of society and challenge its accepted moral principles. Prostitution, drug use, and the sale of pornography are considered public order crimes.

racial profiling Selecting suspects on the basis of their ethnic or racial background.

racial threat hypothesis The belief that as the percentage of minorities in the population increases, so too does the amount of social control that police direct at minority group members.

Racketeer Influenced and Corrupt Organizations (RICO) Act Federal legislation that enables prosecutors to bring additional criminal or civil charges against people whose multiple criminal acts constitute a conspiracy. RICO features monetary penalties that allow the government to confiscate all profits derived from criminal activities. Originally intended to be used against organized criminals, RICO has also been used against white-collar criminals.

rational choice theory The view that crime is a function of a decision-making process in which the potential offender weighs the potential costs and benefits of an illegal act.

reaction formation According to Cohen, rejecting goals and standards that seem impossible to achieve. Because a boy cannot hope to get into college, for example, he considers higher education a waste of time.

reactive (defensive) hate crimes Perpetrators believe they are taking a defensive stand against outsiders whom they believe threaten their community or way of life.

reality principle According to Freud, the ability to learn about the consequences of one's actions through experience.

reasoning criminals According to the rational choice approach, law-violating behavior occurs when an offender decides to risk breaking the law after considering both personal factors (such as the need for money, revenge, thrills, and entertainment) and situational factors (how well a target is protected and the efficiency of the local police force).

reciprocal altruism According to sociobiology, acts that are outwardly designed to help others but that have at their core benefits to the self.

reflected appraisals When parents are alienated from their children, their negative labeling reduces their children's self-image and increases delinquency.

Reign of Terror The origin of the term *terrorism*, the French Revolution's Reign of Terror began in 1793 and was initiated by the revolutionary government during which agents of the Committee of Public Safety and the National Convention were referred to as terrorists.

reintegrative shaming A method of correction that encourages offenders to confront their misdeeds, experience shame because of the harm they caused, and then be reincluded in society.

relational aggression Psychological and emotional abuse that involves the spreading of smears, rumors, and private information in order to harm their partner.

relative deprivation The condition that exists when people of wealth and poverty live in close proximity to one another. Some criminologists attribute crime rate differentials to relative deprivation.

restitution agreements Conditions of probation in which the offenders repay society or the victims of crime for the trouble the offenders caused. Monetary restitution involves a direct payment to the victim as a form of compensation. Community service restitution may be used in victimless crimes and involves work in the community in lieu of more severe criminal penalties.

restorative justice Using humanistic, nonpunitive strategies to right wrongs and restore social harmony.

restrictive deterrence Convincing criminals that committing a serious crime is too risky and that other less-dangerous crimes or actions might be a better choice.

retaliatory hate crime A hate crime motivated by revenge for another hate crime, either real or imaginary, which may spark further retaliation.

retributive terrorists Terror groups who refrain from tying specific acts to direct demands for change. They want to instead redirect the balance between what they believe is good and evil. They see their revolution as existing on a spiritual plane; their mission is to exact retribution against sinners.

retrospective cohort study A study that uses an intact cohort of known offenders and looks back into their early life experiences by checking their educational, family, police, and hospital records.

retrospective reading The reassessment of a person's past to fit a current generalized label.

road rage A term used to describe motorists who assault each other.

role exit behaviors In order to escape from a stifling life in male-dominated families, girls may try to break away by running away and or even attempting suicide.

routine activities theory The view that the volume and distribution of predatory crime are closely related to the interaction of suitable targets, motivated offenders, and capable guardians.

sadistic personality disorder A repeat pattern of cruel and demeaning behavior. People suffering from this type of extreme personality disturbance seem prone to engage in serious violent attacks, including homicides motivated by sexual sadism.

sampling Selecting a limited number of people for study as representative of a larger group.

schizophrenia A type of psychosis often marked by bizarre behavior, hallucinations, loss of thought control, and inappropriate emotional responses. Schizophrenic types include catatonic, which characteristically involves impairment of motor activity; paranoid, which is characterized by delusions of persecution; and hebephrenic, which is characterized by immature behavior and giddiness.

scientific method Using verifiable principles and procedures for the systematic acquisition of knowledge; typically involves formulating a problem, creating a hypothesis, and collecting data through observation and experiment to verify the hypothesis.

secondary deviance According to Lemert, accepting deviant labels as a personal identity. Acts become secondary when they form a basis for self-concept, as when a drug experimenter becomes an addict.

secondary prevention programs Treatment programs aimed at helping offenders after they have been identified.

second-degree murder A homicide with malice but not premeditation or deliberation, as when a desire to inflict serious bodily harm and a wanton disregard for life result in the victim's death.

securitization The process by which vendors take individual subprime loans and bundle them into large pools and sell them as securities.

self-control A strong moral sense that renders a person incapable of hurting others or violating social norms.

self-control theory According to Gottfredson and Hirschi, the view that the cause of delinquent behavior is an impulsive personality. Kids who are impulsive may find that their bond to society is weak.

self-report survey A research approach that requires subjects to reveal their own participation in delinquent or criminal acts.

sentencing circle A peacemaking technique in which offenders, victims, and other community members are brought together in an effort to formulate a sanction that addresses the needs of all.

serial killer The killing of a large number of people over time by an offender who seeks to escape detection.

serial rape Multiple rapes committed by one person over time.

sexual abuse Exploitation of a child through rape, incest, or molestation by a parent or other adult.

shame The feeling we get when we don't meet the standards we have set for ourselves or that significant others have set for us.

Sherman Antitrust Act Law that subjects to criminal or civil sanctions any person "who shall make any contract or engage in any combination or conspiracy" in restraint of interstate commerce.

shield laws Laws designed to protect rape victims by prohibiting the defense attorney from inquiring about their previous sexual relationships.

shoplifting The taking of goods from retail stores.

siege mentality Residents who become so suspicious of authority that they consider the outside world to be the enemy out to destroy the neighborhood.

situational crime prevention A method of crime prevention that stresses tactics and strategies to eliminate or reduce particular crimes in narrow settings, such as reducing burglaries in a housing project by increasing lighting and installing security alarms.

situational inducement Short-term influence on a person's behavior, such as financial problems or peer pressure, that increases risk taking.

skeezers Prostitutes who trade sex for drugs, usually crack.

skilled thieves Thieves who typically work in the larger cities, such as London and Paris. This group includes pickpockets, forgers, and counterfeiters, who operate freely.

smugglers Thieves who move freely in sparsely populated areas and transport goods, such as spirits, gems, gold, and spices, without bothering to pay tax or duty.

snitches Amateur shoplifters who do not self-identify as thieves but who systematically steal merchandise for personal use.

social bond Ties a person has to the institutions and processes of society. According to Hirschi, elements of the social bond include commitment, attachment, involvement, and belief.

social capital Positive relations with individuals and institutions that are life sustaining.

social control theory The view that people commit crime when the forces that bind them to society are weakened or broken.

social disorganization theory Branch of social structure theory that focuses on the breakdown of institutions such as the family, school, and employment in inner-city neighborhoods.

social harm A view that behaviors harmful to other people and society in general must be controlled. These acts are usually outlawed, but some acts that cause enormous amounts of social harm are perfectly legal, such as the consumption of tobacco and alcohol.

socialization The interactions people have with various organizations, institutions, and processes of society.

social learning theory The view that human behavior is modeled through observation of human social interactions, either directly from observing those who are close and from intimate contact or indirectly through the media. Interactions that are rewarded are copied, while those that are punished are avoided.

socially disorganized Communities where social institutions are incapable of functioning as expected and as a result their ability to create social control is nullified.

social process or socialization theory The view that criminality is a function of people's interactions with various organizations, institutions, and processes in society.

social reaction theory (labeling theory) The view that people become criminals when significant members of society label them as such and they accept those labels as a personal identity.

social structure theory The view that disadvantaged economic class position is a primary cause of crime.

sociobiology The scientific study of the determinants of social behavior, based on the view that such behavior is influenced by both the individual's genetic makeup and interactions with the environment.

sociological social psychology The study of human interactions and relationships, emphasizing such issues as group dynamics and socialization.

sociopath Personality disorder characterized by superficial charm and glibness, a lack of empathy for others, amoral conduct, and lack of shame, guilt, or remorse for antisocial behavior. The term may be used interchangeably with psychopath, but both terms have been replaced by antisocial behavior disorder.

somatotype A system developed for categorizing people on the basis of their body build.

spear-phishing Targeting specific victims, sending them emails that contain accurate information about their lives obtained from social networking sites, and asking them to open an email attachment where malware harvests details such as the victims' usernames and passwords, bank account details, credit card numbers, and other personal information.

specific deterrence The view that if experienced punishment is severe enough, convicted offenders will be deterred from repeating their criminal activity.

stalking A pattern of behavior directed at a specific person that includes repeated physical or visual proximity, unwanted communications, and/or threats sufficient to cause fear in a reasonable person.

stalking statutes Laws that prohibit "the willful, malicious, and repeated following and harassing of another person."

state dependence The propensity to commit crime profoundly and permanently disrupts normal socialization. Early rule breaking strengthens criminal motivation and increases the probability of future rule breaking.

state-organized crime Acts defined by law as criminal and committed by state officials, either elected or appointed, in pursuit of their jobs as government representatives.

state political crime Political crime that arises from the efforts of the state to either maintain governmental power or to uphold the race, class, and gender advantages of those who support the government. It is possible to divide state political crimes into five varieties: (1) political corruption, (2) illegal domestic surveillance, (3) human rights violations, (4) state violence such as torture, illegal imprisonment, police violence and use of deadly force, and (5) state corporate crime committed by individuals who abuse their state authority or who fail to exercise it when working with people and organizations in the private sector.

state-sponsored terrorism Terrorism that occurs when a repressive government regime forces its citizens into obedience, oppresses minorities, and stifles political dissent.

status frustration A form of culture conflict experienced by lower-class youths because social conditions prevent them from achieving success as defined by the larger society.

statutory rape Sexual relations between an underage individual and an adult; though not coerced, an underage partner is considered incapable of giving informed consent.

stigma An enduring label that taints a person's identity and changes him or her in the eyes of others.

strain The emotional turmoil and conflict caused when people believe they cannot achieve their desires and goals through legitimate means. Members of the lower class might feel strain because they are denied access to adequate educational opportunities and social support.

strain theory Branch of social structure theory that sees crime as a function of the conflict between people's goals and the means available to obtain them.

stratified society Grouping according to social strata or levels. American society is considered stratified on the basis of economic class and wealth.

street efficacy A concept in which more cohesive communities with high levels of social control and social integration foster the ability for kids to use their wits to avoid violent confrontations and to feel safe in their own neighborhood. Adolescents with high levels of street efficacy are less likely to resort to violence themselves or to associate with delinquent peers.

structural theory The view that criminal law and the criminal justice system are means of defending and preserving the capitalist system.

subculture of violence Norms and customs that, in contrast to society's dominant value system, legitimate and expect the use of violence to resolve social conflicts.

subcultures Groups that are loosely part of the dominant culture but maintain a unique set of values, beliefs, and traditions.

substantive criminal law The branch of the law that defines crimes and their punishment. It involves such issues as the mental and physical elements of crime, crime categories, and criminal defenses.

subterranean values Morally tinged influences that have become entrenched in the culture but are publicly condemned. They exist side by side with conventional values and while condemned in public may be admired or practiced in private.

sufferance The aggrieved party does nothing to rectify a conflict situation; over time, the unresolved conflict may be compounded by other events that cause an eventual eruption.

suitable target According to routine activities theory, a target for crime that is relatively valuable, easily transportable, and not capably guarded.

superego Incorporation within the personality of the moral standards and values of parents, community, and significant others.

supranational criminology The study of war crimes, crimes against humanity, and the supranational penal system in which such crimes are prosecuted and tried.

surplus value The Marxist view that the laboring classes produce wealth that far exceeds their wages and goes to the capitalist class as profits.

symbolic interaction theory The sociological view that people communicate through symbols. People interpret symbolic communication and incorporate it within their personality. A person's view of reality, then, depends on his or her interpretation of symbolic gestures.

synthesis A merger of two opposing ideas.

systematic forgers Professionals who make a living by passing bad checks.

systematic review A research technique that involves collecting the findings from previously conducted studies, appraising and synthesizing the evidence, and using the collective evidence to address a particular scientific question.

target hardening Making one's home or business crime proof through the use of locks, bars, alarms, and other devices.

target-removal strategies Displaying dummy or disabled goods as a means of preventing shoplifting.

temperance movement An effort to prohibit the sale of liquor in the United States that resulted in the passage of the Eighteenth Amendment to the Constitution in 1919, which prohibited the sale of alcoholic beverages.

terror cells Divisions of terrorist group affiliates, each of which may be functionally independent so that each member has little knowledge of other cells, their members, locations, and so on. The number of cells and their composition depend on the size of the terrorist group. Local or national groups will have fewer cells than international terrorist groups that may operate in several countries, such as the al-Qaeda group.

terrorism The illegal use of force against innocent people to achieve a political objective.

tertiary prevention programs Crime control and prevention programs that may be a requirement of a probation order, part of a diversionary sentence, or aftercare at the end of a prison sentence.

testosterone The principal male steroid hormone. Testosterone levels decline during the life cycle and may explain why violence rates diminish over time.

thanatos According to Freud, the instinctual drive toward aggression and violence.

theory of anomie A modified version of the concept of anomie developed by Merton to fit social, economic, and cultural conditions found in modern U.S. society. He found that two elements of culture interact to produce potentially anomic conditions: culturally defined goals and socially approved means for obtaining them.

thesis In the philosophy of Hegel, an original idea or thought.

thrill-seeking hate crimes Acts by hatemongers who join forces to have fun by bashing minorities or destroying property; inflicting pain on others gives them a sadistic thrill.

ticking bomb scenario A scenario that some experts argue in which torture can perhaps be justified if the government discovers that a captured terrorist knows the whereabouts of a dangerous explosive device that is set to go off and kill thousands of innocent people.

tipping point The minimum amount of expected punishment necessary to produce a significant reduction in crime rates.

torture An act that causes severe pain or suffering, whether physical or mental, that is intentionally inflicted on a person for such purposes as obtaining a confession, punishing them for a crime they may have committed, or intimidating or coercing them into a desired action.

trait theory The view that criminality is a product of abnormal biological and/or psychological traits.

trajectory theory A view of criminal career formation that holds there are multiple paths to crime.

transitional neighborhood Areas undergoing a shift in population and structure, usually from middle-class residential to lower-class mixed use.

transnational organized crime A criminal enterprise that involves the planning and execution of the distribution of illicit materials or services by groups or networks of individuals working in more than one country.

treason An act of disloyalty to one's nation or state.

Trojan horse A computer program that looks like a benign application but contains illicit codes that can damage the system operations. Though Trojan horses do not replicate themselves like viruses, they can be just as destructive.

turning points According to Laub and Sampson, the life events that alter the development of a criminal career.

underclass The lowest social stratum in any country, whose members lack the education and skills needed to function successfully in modern society.

Uniform Crime Report (UCR) Large database, compiled by the Federal Bureau of Investigation, of crimes reported and arrests made each year throughout the United States.

USA Patriot Act (USAPA) Legislation giving U.S. law enforcement agencies a freer hand to investigate and apprehend suspected terrorists.

victim compensation The victim ordinarily receives compensation from the state to pay for damages associated with the crime. Rarely are two compensation schemes alike, however, and many state programs suffer from lack of both adequate funding and proper organization within the criminal justice system. Compensation may be made for medical bills, loss of wages, loss of future earnings, and counseling. In the case of death, the victim's survivors can receive burial expenses and aid for loss of support.

victimization by the justice system While the crime is still fresh in their minds, victims may find that the police interrogation following the crime is handled callously, with innuendos or insinuations that they were somehow at fault. Victims have difficulty learning what is going on in the case; property is often kept for a long time as evidence and may never be returned. Some rape victims report that the treatment they receive from legal, medical, and mental health services is so destructive that they cannot help but feel "re-raped."

victimless crimes Violations of the criminal law without any identifiable evidence of an individual victim who has suffered damage from the crime.

victimologists People who study the victim's role in criminal transactions.

victim precipitation theory The idea that the victim's behavior was the spark that ignited the subsequent offense, as when the victim abused the offender verbally or physically.

victim-witness assistance programs Government programs that help crime victims and witnesses; may include compensation, court services, and/or crisis intervention.

vigilantes Individuals who go on moral crusades without any authorization from legal authorities. The assumption is that it is okay to take matters into your own hands if the cause is right and the target is immoral.

violentization process According to Lonnie Athens, the process by which abused children are turned into aggressive adults. This process takes violent youths full circle from being the victims of aggression to its initiators; they are now the same person they grew up despising, ready to begin the process with their own children.

virility mystique The belief that males must separate their sexual feelings from needs for love, respect, and affection.

warez A term computer hackers and software pirates use to describe a game or application that is made available for use on the Internet in violation of its copyright protection.

website defacement A type of cybervandalism that occurs when a computer hacker intrudes on another person's website by inserting or substituting codes that expose visitors to the site to misleading or provocative information. Defacement can range from installing humorous graffiti to sabotaging or corrupting the site.

white-collar swindle A crime in which people use an ongoing business enterprise to fraudulently expropriate money from unsuspecting victims.

workplace violence Irate employees or former employees attack coworkers or sabotage machinery and production lines; now considered the third leading cause of occupational injury or death.

zealots The original Zealots were Hebrew warrior groups active during the Roman occupation of Palestine during the first century BCE. Today the term commonly refers to a fanatical or over-idealistic follower of a political or religious cause.

CASE INDEX

NAME INDEX

Bachman, Jerald, 60nn21, 22; 521n167
Bacon, Kevin, 445
Bacon, Sarah, 310; 318n12; 319n55; 320n103; 322n162
Badger, Kelly, 367n88
Baer, D., 521n165
Baer, Judith, 175n239
Baertlein, Lisa, 369n164
Bagarozzo, James, 452
Baggett, Larkin, 459
Baier, Colin, 251n68
Bailey, Carol, 254n179
Bailey, Susan, 522n223
Bakanic, Von, 367n110
Baker, Celia, 519n63
Balboni, Jennifer, 371n267
Baldus, David, 115
Bales, William, 254n188
Balfour, Gillian, 285n95
Bali, J.P., 169n39
Ball, Matthew, 285n89
Ball, Robert A., 252n114
Ballard, Danny, 175n240; 176n278
Baller, Robert, 366n55; 371n259
Balter, Mitchell, 319n49
Bandura, Albert, 155; 174n215
Banfield, Jerry, 553n4
Banich, Marie T., 171n109
Bao, Win-Ning, 218n170
Barak, Gregg, 284nn19, 35
Barbaree, Howard, 520n113
Barber, Nigel, 329; 365n17
Bardo, Robert John, 19
Barendregt, Marko, 174n204
Barker, Gareth, 171n108
Barkley, Russell, 172n120
Barlow, David, 284n30
Barn, Ravinder, 218n167
Barnes, Grace, 521n148
Barnes, J.C., 169n21; 173n177; 176n268; 251n53; 321n119; 322n166; 323nn184, 185
Barney, Karen, 554n34
Barnhill, Elizabeth, 367n118; 368n120
Baron, R.A., 61n51
Baron, Stephen W., 218n153; 251n60
Barr, Ashley B., 320n87
Barr, Dana, 170n78
Barr, Kellie, 521n148
Barr, Robert, 126n128
Barrett, Angelina, 169n41
Barrett, David, 519nn73, 85
Barrios, Lisa, 369n192
Barrueco, Sandra, 319n50
Bartels, Jared, 176n269
Bartos, Omar, 479n133
Bartusch, Dawn Jeglum, 319n52
Basile, Kathleen, 369n187; 371n281
Baskin, Deborah, 432; 439n97
Baskin-Sommers, Arielle, 522n206
Bateman, Alicia, 370n209
Bates, John, 217n100; 249n13; 250nn29, 31; 319n64; 365n35
Bates, William, 520n139

Battin, Sara R., 251n60
Batty, David, 284n46
Bauer, John, 371n246
Baumann, Barbara, 250n24
Baumeister, Roy, 127n159; 368n135
Baumer, Eric, 60n9; 63n130; 125n56; 217n103; 366n60; 371nn251–253
Baumhover, Lorin, 127n143
Bauserman, Robert, 366n46
Bayer, Ronald, 124n12
Bayley, David, 127n145
Bazemore, Gordon, 286n143
Beach, Steven R.H., 169n24; 172nn131, 141
Beal, Morgan, 75; 90n82
Bearn, Jenny, 523n232
Beasley, Shanna, 369nn173, 184
Beattie, Irenee, 320n83
Beauchaine, Theodore, 169n29
Beauregard, Eric, 89n39
Beaver, Kevin M., 88n32; 163; 171n95; 172nn142–144; 173nn177–179; 175nn237, 249; 176nn268, 269; 306; 321nn117–119; 322n166; 323nn184, 185
Beccaria, Cesare, 97; 98; 114; 122
Bechara, Etelvino J.H., 170n79
Bechhofer, L., 367n115
Beck, Allen, 128n180
Becker, Howard, 13; 24n18; 228; 241; 253n166; 485; 518nn23, 24
Becker, Jill, 170n58
Bedford, Olwen, 519n88
Beech, Anthony, 175n236
Beever, Anthony, 366n79
Begin, Menachem, 388
Begolly, Emerson, 272
Beichner, Dawn, 367n101
Beirne, Piers, 478n94
Belanger, Albert, 520n107
Belanger, Erin, 313
Belfort, Jordan, 311
Bell, Kerryn E., 215n36
Bell, Nicole, 370n242
Bell, Paul, 61n53
Bellair, Paul, 90n100; 104; 125n65; 217nn103, 108
Bellinger, David C., 170n79
Beloof, Douglas E., 91n140
Belsky, Jay, 169n23
Bendixen, Mons, 252n97
Benjamin, Daniel, 555n95
Bennett, Susan, 358; 371n256
Bennett, Trevor, 105; 125n81
Benson, Michael, 321n128; 478nn75, 76, 82
Bentham, Jeremy, 97; 98; 124nn4–6
Berg, Ellen, 519n77
Bergen, Peter L., 407n62
Bergen, Raquel Kennedy, 366nn74, 118; 368n120
Berger, Mark T., 365n11
Bergrin, Paul, 443
Bergstrom, Sandra, 520n97

Berk, Richard, 117; 522n217
Berkowitz, David ("Son of Sam"), 153; 349
Berliner, Howard, 523n233
Bernard, Thomas J., 174n196; 219n180
Bernasco, Wim, 124n38; 125n88; 439n99
Bernburg, Jon Gunnar, 218n147; 254nn172, 177, 183, 199
Berner, Wolfgang, 171n94; 175nn252, 253
Bernstein, Elizabeth, 519n57
Berry, Amanda, 486
Bersani, Bianca E., 45; 300; 320n96
Best, Connie, 90n118
Best, David, 523n232
Beswick, Tracy, 523n232
Beurs, Edwin, 174n204
Beutel, Ann, 62n89
Beyers, Jennifer M., 174n204; 217n100; 249n13; 318n14
Bezos, Jeff, 200
Bhattacharya, Rina, 407nn54, 55
Bieber, Justin, 541
Bieneck, Steffen, 366n72; 368n144
Bierut, Laura, 504
Biesecker, Gretchen, 171n85
Bihrle, Susan, 171n92
Bijleveld, Catrien, 322n163
Bilefsky, Dan, 347
Bimbi, David S., 522n189
bin Laden, Mohammed, 394
bin Laden, Osama, 378; 394; 397; 401
Bingenheimer, Jeffrey B., 366n53
Binsfield, Peter, 96
Birkbeck, Christopher, 124n34; 125n96
Birmaher, Boris, 174n197
Birnbaum, Jean, 337; 367n94; 368n137
Birt, Angela, 368n134
Bistolaki, E., 172n132
Bjerregaard, Beth, 60n25; 366n64
Black, David, 521n156
Black, Donald, 172n123; 217n98
Black, Michael, 371n281
Blackburn, Ashley G., 252n102
Blackstone, E., 438n88
Blackwell, Brenda Sims, 275; 286nn109, 110, 116
Blagojevich, Rod, 378; 449
Blair, James, 162; 163; 175n250
Blair, Karina, 163
Blais, Etienne, 126n135
Blake, Laurence, 90n108; 438n91
Blalock, Hurbert, Jr., 62n104
Blaney, Shannon, 369n179
Blankenship, Michael, 252n117; 479n151
Blau, Judith, 61n66; 217n132
Blau, Peter, 61n66; 217n132
Blevins, Claire, 117
Blevins, Kristie R., 320n68; 322n164
Blickle, Gerhard, 175n251
Block, Carolyn, 355; 521n183
Block, Richard, 61n66; 218n134
Blokland, Arjan A.J., 128n197; 322n163
Blumer, Herbert, 24n17; 241; 253n163
Blumstein, Alfred, 45; 60n31; 128n196
Blunt, Anthony, 380

Canela-Cacho, Jose, 128*n*196
Canfield, Richard L., 170*n*77; 171*n*86
Cannon, Lucretia Patricia, 348
Cannon, Robert, 313
Cantor, David, 91*n*149
Cao, Liqun, 366*n*59
Capaldi, Deborah, 251*n*56; 318*n*31; 365*n*31
Caplan, Joel, 83; 91*n*139; 128*n*198
Capone, Al, 465
Capowich, George E., 217*n*109; 218*n*161
Carano, Gina, 308
Carbone-Lopez, Kristin, 89*n*52; 319*n*58
Cardoso, Maria R.A., 170*n*79
Carey, Gregory, 172*n*140; 173*n*160
Caringella-MacDonald, Susan, 285*n*104
Carlen, Pat, 285*n*85
Carlson, Robert, 522*n*193
Carr, Alan, 521*n*153
Carr, Joetta, 520*n*112
Carradine, David, 487
Carrano, Jennifer, 250*n*28
Carrien, Miriam, 518*n*43
Carrington, Frank, 85; 91*n*157
Carroll, Douglas, 176*n*276
Carrozza, Mark, 249*n*11; 253*n*147
Carson, Ann, 124*n*16
Carson, D., 172*n*121
Carson, Jennifer Varriale, 127*n*138
Carter, Lisa, 170*n*44
Carter, Sherry Plaster, 520*n*96
Carter, Stanley, 520*n*96
Cartier, Jerome, 522*n*199
Cartwright, Desmond, 252*n*114
Casebolt, Rachel, 513
Caspi, Avshalom, 173*nn*156, 183; 174*n*191;
    175*n*258; 318*nn*19, 30; 319*nn*37, 63;
    322*n*177; 323*nn*187, 188
Cassity, James "Doug," 95; 96
Castillo, Anjelica ("Baby Hope"), 343
Castillo, Melissa, 300
Castro, Ariel, 486
Catalano, Richard F., 251*n*60; 253*n*130;
    297; 323*n*190; 521*n*176
Cauce, Mari, 90*n*81
Caudy, Michael S., 319*n*46
Cauffman, Elizabeth, 62*n*92; 89*n*44;
    174*n*208; 175*n*225
Cavanagh, Marsha D., 170*n*83
Cavazos-Rehg, Patricia, 504
Cecil, Joe, 25*n*43
Cederblad, Marianne, 176*n*279
Cena, Santiago, 226
Cernkovich, Stephen, 60*n*24; 200;
    218*n*146; 253*n*148; 318*n*22; 320*n*98;
    323*n*189
Cerruto, Michael John, 286*n*145
Chafetz, Janet Saltzman, 285*nn*91, 92
Chaiken, Marcia, 521*n*180
Chakravarti, Shamit, 407*nn*54, 55
Chalk, Peter, 407*nn*50, 53
Chambliss, William, 262; 284*n*15; 415;
    437*n*14
Chamlin, Mitchell, 126*n*136

Chan, Raymond, 171*n*107
Chan, Tony, 169*n*27
Chancer, Lynn, 285*n*83
Chaplin, Terry, 439*n*111
Chapman, Jane Roberts, 285*n*96
Chappell, Duncan, 60*n*8
Charlebois, P., 63*n*148
Charnigo, Richard, 369*n*180
Chayet, Ellen, 128*n*183
Chen, C.Y., 216*n*69
Chen, Frances, 172*n*136
Chen, Henlan, 519*n*74
Chen, Jieming, 251*n*81
Chen, Jieru, 371*n*281
Chen, Wan-Yi, 366*n*39
Chen, Xiaojin, 322*n*165; 521*n*169
Cheng, Zhongqi, 169*n*35
Chepke, Lindsey, 117
Cherbonneau, Michael, 356; 371*n*248
Chermak, Steven, 62*n*113; 396
Chesney-Lind, Meda, 285*nn*85, 87, 90, 104
Cheuk, D.K.L., 169*n*34
Chien-Peng, Chung, 407*n*49
Chilcoat, Howard, 319*n*50
Chin, Ko-lin, 479*nn*125, 135
Chiricos, Theodore, 61*n*71; 127*nn*156,
    170; 216*n*76; 254*n*188; 285*n*64
Cho, Adrian, 477*n*48
Cho, Seung-Hui, 349
Choi, Tiffany, 217*n*112
Chon, Don, 366*n*68
Christakos, Antigone, 521*n*183
Christenson, Cornelia, 368*n*133
Christenson, R.L., 250*n*44
Christodoulou, G., 172*n*132
Chronis, Andrea, 250*n*24
Chung, He Len, 319*n*48
Chung, Ick-Joong, 322*nn*154, 161
Church, II, Wesley, 251*n*83
Churchill, Winston, 500
Ciavarella, Mark, 450
Cicchetti, Dante, 250*n*32
Cirillo, Kathleen, 175*nn*240, 243; 176*n*278
Clapper, James R., 399
Clark-Daniels, Carolyn, 127*n*143
Clark, James, 369*n*180
Clark, Richard D., 127*n*160
Clarke, Gregory N., 174*n*200
Clarke, Richard A., 550; 555*n*82
Clarke, Ronald V., 91*n*147; 108; 124*nn*18,
    35; 126*nn*104, 105, 107, 109, 111,
    121, 125; 438*n*70; 438*n*94
Clarke-Stewart, K. Alison, 169*n*27
Clason, Dennis L., 252*n*104
Classen, Gabriele, 218*n*148
Clay-Warner, Jody, 367*n*89
Clayton, Richard, 522*nn*224, 225
Clear, Todd, 368*n*156
Clements, Benedict, 407*nn*54, 55
Cleveland, H. Harrington, 175*n*261; 322*n*147
Clinard, Marshall, 477*n*45
Clingempeel, Glenn, 319*nn*56, 57
Clinton, Monique, 365*n*25

Clooney, George, 412
Close, Billy, 62*n*100
Cloward, Richard, 209; 212; 219*nn*200–206
Cochran, John, 124*n*25; 125*n*97; 253*n*139;
    355
Cochran, Joshua, 176*n*275
Coes, Heith, 251*n*82
Cohen, Albert, 206; 208; 209; 218*nn*139;
    219*nn*191–194, 196–198
Cohen, Jacqueline, 24*n*7; 60*n*31; 90*n*88;
    125*n*63; 127*n*151; 128*n*196
Cohen, Lawrence, 76; 77; 90*nn*101, 112;
    173*n*165
Cohen, Mark, 478*n*90
Cohen, Morris, 483; 518*n*9
Cohen, Patricia, 319*n*38; 519*n*74
Cohen, Robert, 90*n*91; 251*n*63
Cohen-Bendahan, Celina, 170*n*61
Cohen-Kettenis, Peggy, 170*n*61
Cohn, Ellen, 46; 61*nn*50, 54, 56
Colby, Reggy, 47
Cole, Christopher, 479*n*111
Cole, David, 198*n*201
Coletti, Patrick, 171*n*92
Coley, Rebekah Levine, 217*n*107
Collier, Sean, 3
Collier-Tenison, Peter Shannon, 520*n*114
Collins, James, 365*n*24
Collins, Mark, 320*n*79
Collins, Randall, 329; 365*n*18
Colvin, Mark, 304
Colwell, Brian, 175*n*240; 176*n*278
Colwell, Lori, 60*n*20
Comer, James, 63*n*118
Comiskey, Brendan, 488
Comstock, George, 157
Comte, Auguste, 132
Conahan, Michael, 450
Conger, Katherine, 223
Conger, Rand D., 223; 249*n*5; 254*n*173;
    365*n*36; 366*n*49
Conklin, John, 170*n*70; 357
Connolly, Eric J., 176*n*268
Connolly, Jennifer, 157
Conoscenti, Lauren M., 367*n*87
Conwell, Chic, 415; 416; 437*nn*17–19
Cook, Philip, 126*n*124; 369*n*175
Cook, Sarah, 367*n*86
Cooley, Charles Horton, 13; 241; 253*n*163
Coomer, Brandi Wilson, 60*n*30
Cooper, Alison, 169*n*41
Cooper, Cary, 61*n*55; 170*n*62
Cooper, Chris, 379
Cooper, Janet R., 371*n*274
Copes, Heith, 356; 371*n*248
Cordella, Peter, 172*n*135
Corill, Dean, 349
Cornish, Derek, 124*nn*18, 35; 126*n*107
Corrado, J., 521*n*165
Corrigan, Patrick, 241; 254*n*171
Cortese, Samuele, 169*n*31
Corvo, Kenneth, 366*n*39
Cory-Slechta, Deborah A., 171*n*86

Costanzo, Michael, 125n60
Costello, Jane, 174n209
Cota-Robles, Sonia, 250n26
Cotillard, Marion, 355
Couch, Ethan, 221; 222
Couey, John Evander, 488; 489
Coupe, Richard Timothy, 90n108
Coupe, Timothy, 438n91
Courey, Michael, 321n144
Couric, Katie, 544
Court, John, 520n117
Courtney, Robert R., 448; 472–473
Courtwright, David, 333; 366n69; 523n242
Covington, Jeanette, 216n76; 218n134
Cox, Louis, 99; 124n11
Cragin, Kim, 407n50
Craig, Jessica M., 251n66
Craig, Wendy, 157
Crane, D. Russell, 223
Crane, Jonathan, 215n38
Craven, Wes, 362
Crawford, Charles, 285n64
Creamer, Vicki, 251n74
Cree, Arthur Francis, 210
Cresap, Wayne G., 450
Cressey, Donald, 4; 11–12; 24nn3, 15; 229;
    230; 251n73; 473; 479nn122, 149
Cretacci, Michael, 253n141
Crews, F.T., 169n30
Crinella, Francis, 169n27
Croisdale, Tim, 63n144
Cromwell, Paul, 125nn58, 59, 75; 420;
    433; 434; 437n26; 437n42; 439n107
Crosby, L., 319n60
Crosby, Rick, 318n33
Crosnoe, Robert, 252n129
Crouch, Ben, 128n195
Crow, Matthew, 53; 62n111
Crowder, Kyle, 215n53
Crowe, R.R., 173n164
Crowley, Thomas, 171n109
Crowther, Betty, 520n139
Cruise, Keith, 365n8
Crumpler, Debbie, 169n41
Cruz, Miguel Esteban, 106
Cui, Ming, 249n5
Culhane, Sara, 366n41
Cullen, Francis T., 61n75; 62n89; 89nn38,
    68; 90nn80, 85, 86; 125n79; 136;
    169n19; 174n206; 218nn160, 169;
    219n173; 249nn5, 11; 250n22;
    251nn65, 77; 253nn133, 147, 151,
    168; 287n152; 320n68; 322n164;
    367nn99, 107; 371n283; 478nn75, 76
Cummings, Andrea, 367n97
Cundiff, Patrick, 368n141
Cunningham, Randy "Duke," 449
Cunningham-Niederer, Michele, 479n119
Currie, Janet, 366nn42, 44
Curry, G. David, 216nn60, 78
Curry, Mary Ann, 355
Cuvelier, Steven, 125n79
Czaja, Ronald, 60n27

D

da Silva, W.P., 518n36
Dabney, Dean, 438n53
Dackis, Charles, 522n194
Dadds, Mark, 439n113
Dafeamekpor, Denise Spriggs, 368n143
Dahl, Julia, 347
Dahrendorf, Ralf, 261; 262
Daigle, Leah E., 89nn38, 68; 251n77;
    322n179; 367nn99, 107
Daily, Martin, 89n75
DaLalla, David, 172n140
Dalen, Lindy, 169n41
D'Alessio, Stewart, 61n78; 240; 253n150;
    438n90
Dalton, Katharina, 139; 170n67
Dalwani, Manish S., 171n109
Daly, Kathleen, 285nn85, 90, 94, 104;
    286n125; 479n146
Daly, Martin, 148; 173nn168, 174–176;
    216n73; 217n131; 370n226
Daly, Sara A., 407n50
Danhach, Sameh Khaled, 411; 420
Daniels, R. Steven, 127n143
Daniels, Ronald J., 338
Dank, Meredith, 491
Dann, Robert, 114; 115
Dannefer, Dale, 62n97
Dannenberg, Andrew, 520n96
Dantzler, Joyce, 368n143
D'Aquino, Iva Ikuko Toguri ("Tokyo Rose"),
    379
Darrow, William, 519n78
Darwin, Charles, 132
Das, Shaymal, 170n56
Davidson, Laura, 61n74
Davies, Garth, 215n39; 322n149
Davies, Mark, 251n87; 252n90; 253n149;
    521n163
Davies, Susan, 318n33
Davies-Netley, Sally, 88n18
Davis, Joanne, 521n154
Davis, John, 169n27
Davis, Robert C., 88n29; 91n148; 91nn122,
    138, 148; 522nn219–221
Davis, Roy, 368n121
Davis-Frenzel, Erika, 367n101
Davison, Elizabeth, 125n87
Dawes, Chris, 172n134
De Coster, Stacy, 215n46; 218n152
De Gruchy, John W., 286n146
De Li, Spencer, 251n68; 320n77
De Vries, Reinout E., 321n143
Dean, Charles, 117; 318n28
Deane, Glenn, 60n7; 319n44; 365n21;
    366n55
Deaton, Raelynn, 173n177; 323n185
DeBaryshe, Barbara, 318n24
Deboutte, Dirk, 250n27
Decker, Scott, 125n90; 253n152; 369n178;
    433; 434; 439nn98, 103
Deeley, Quentin, 163
DeFronzo, James, 217n121; 219n215

DeHart, Erica, 89n37
DeJesus, Georgina "Gina," 484
Dejong, Christina, 128bn177, 181, 184;
    254n190
DeKeseredy, Walter, 285nn81, 84, 103;
    368nn129, 136
DeLamatre, Mary, 90n88
Delaney, Kathleen, 20
deLara, Ellen, 366n39
DeLisi, Matt, 171n95; 172nn142, 143;
    175nn226, 237, 249; 251n82;
    321nn126, 127
DeLone, Miriam, 285n66
Deluca, Stefanie, 216n85
Demuth, Stephen, 53; 62nn112, 114;
    284n56; 285n65
DeNevi, Don, 437n8
Dengate, Sue, 169n32
Denney, Robert, 90n93
Denno, Deborah, 171nn85, 91, 97;
    173nn180, 181
Densley, James A., 105; 125n80
DePadilla, Lara., 318n18
Depp, Johnny, 355
Deptula, Daneen, 90n91; 251n63
DeRios, M.D., 521n164
Dershowitz, Alan M., 383; 406n25
Derzon, James, 318n32
Desai, Manisha, 171n87
Desilets, Christian, 476nn10–12
Deutsch, Joseph, 125n62
Devine, Paul Shin, 450
Devlin, Sir Patrick, 518n10
Dhami, Mandeep, 479n147
Diallo, Nafissatou, 340
DiCaprio, Leonardo, 13
Dickerson, Andre, Jr., 106
Dickinson, Rebecca, 493–494
DiClemente, Ralph, 318n33
Dieckman, Duane, 127n146
Dietz, Tracy, 89n58
Dillinger, John, 355
Dinitz, Simon, 252n126
Dishion, Thomas, 251n56
Dishman, Chris, 407n59
Dobash, R. Emerson, 370nn236, 239
Dobash, Russell, 370nn236, 239
Dobrin, Adam, 89n38; 90n88; 216n60
Dodge, K.A., 175n222
Dodge, Kenneth, 217n100; 249n13;
    250nn29, 31; 319n64; 365n35
Doerner, Jill, 53; 62n112
Doherty, Elaine Eggleston, 299; 300;
    320nn91, 96
Dohrenwend, Bruce, 253n168
Dollar, Cindy Brooks, 45
Dolling, Dieter, 127n140
Dominick, Joseph, 554n50
Donker, Andrea, 323n183
Donner, Christopher M., 526; 553n4
Donnerstein, Edward, 368n138; 520nn112,
    115, 117
Donohue, John J., 45

Finckenauer, James, 25n44; 479nn125, 132, 135
Finkelhor, David, 73; 88n12; 89nn53, 55, 66; 367n116; 370nn228–230; 519nn75, 87; 554n53
Finn, Peter, 91nn124, 142, 143; 495
Finnerty, Collin, 340; 341
Fischer, Mariellen, 172n120
Fishbein, Diana, 139; 170nn46, 70, 71, 98
Fisher, Bonnie S., 75; 89nn50, 68, 69; 90nn78–80, 85, 86; 367nn90, 99, 107; 371n283
Fisher, Christopher, 554n36
Fishman, Shira, 407n65
Fitzpatrick, Mark, 521n153
Flaherty, Austin, 91n144
Flaherty, Sara, 91n144
Flaming, Karl, 216n64
Flanagan, Caitlin, 367n112
Flanagan, Edel, 521n153
Flanagan-Howard, Roisin, 521n153
Flannery, Daniel, 62n95; 320n102
Flay, Brian, 125n78; 521n160
Fleming, Charles, 253n130
Fletcher, Jason, 144; 172n122
Fletcher, Kenneth, 172n120
Flewelling, Robert, 63n124; 522n223
Flexon, Jamie, 321n114
Flitter, Jill Klotz, 88n20; 519n80
Flygare, Chris, 493
Flynt, Larry, 351
Fogel, C.A., 171n90
Foglia, Wanda, 127nn170, 171
Foley, Jay, 554n34
Foley, Linda, 554n34
Fong, Grace, 171n103
Forbes, Gordon, 367n100
Forde, David, 321n111
Formby, William, 127n143
Formoso, Diana, 249n4
Fornango, Robert, 45; 60n31; 61n71
Forrest, Walter, 321n142
Forsting, Michael, 518n40
Forsythe, Lubica, 439n102
Foster, Holly, 286n108; 318n23
Fowler, Tom, 172n141
Fox, James Alan, 348; 349; 369n199; 370nn208, 211, 212; 371nn270, 276; 498; 520n116
Fox, Kristan, 62n110
Francis, Janice, 437n23
Frank, David John, 368n160
Frank, Nancy, 476n5; 478n65
Frank, Robert, 215n16
Franks, John, 483; 518n15
Franz Ferdinand (Archduke), 388
Frase, Richard, 122; 128nn207, 208
Fraser, Jennifer, 439n113
Frayne, Susan, 519n82
Frazee, Sharon Glave, 125n87
Fream, Anne, 251n87
Frederick, Tyler, 88n31
Freeman, Naomi J., 126n123
Freeman-Gallant, Adrienne, 173n151; 251n80

Freisthler, Bridget, 216n83
Frellich, Joshua, 396
French, Michael T., 66; 88n6
Freng, Adrienne, 62n107
Frenken, J., 367n95
Freud, Sigmund, 133; 150; 152; 329; 365n15
Frey, William, 63n129
Fricker-Elhai, Adrienne, 521n154
Friday, Paul, 250n51
Fried, Gabriela, 407n56
Friedland, Justin, 425
Friedlander, Laura, 156; 157
Friedlander, Robert, 407nn35, 41
Friedrichs, David, 284nn35–37
Friedrichs, Jessica, 284nn36, 37
Frisell, Thomas, 173n146
Fritch, April, 285n97
Fritsch, Eric, 126n113
Frost, S.S., 169n40
Frye, Victoria, 355; 369n179
Fu, Chao, 115
Fuchs, Siegmund Fred, 366n73
Fuentes, Angel Ilarraza, 371n280
Fukurai, Hiroshi, 254n179
Fulton, Betsy, 287n152
Fyfe, James, 127n148

G

Gabbidon, Shaun, 438n50
Gacy, John Wayne, 348; 349; 351
Gadd, David, 319n59
Gaddafi, Muammar, 374
Gaffney, Michael, 216n91
Gagnon, C., 63n148
Gagnon, John, 368n133
Gainey, Randy, 217n108; 254n188
Gajewski, Francis, 127n152
Gale, Nathan, 125n60
Gall, Franz Joseph, 133; 134
Gamble, Wendy, 250n26
Gannon, Theresa, 518n42
Gans, Bryon, 112
Garcia, Luis, 217n102; 371n267
Garcia, Michelle, 371nn282, 284
Gardner, Carol Brooks, 371n279
Gardner, David, 318n1
Garfinkel, Robin, 170n78
Garner, Connie Chenoweth, 253n133
Garnier, Helen, 253n135
Garofalo, James, 90n95; 91n141; 168n10
Garofalo, Raffaele, 134; 135
Garrido, Phillip, 487
Gartner, Rosemary, 90n77
Gary, Faye, 355
Gasper, Joseph, 250n42
Gates, Bill, 200
Gatzke-Kopp, Lisa M., 169n29
Gau, Jacinta M.., 251n77
Gault-Sherman, Martha, 250n37
Gaylor, Rita, 174n204
Ge, Xiaojia, 61n77
Geaney, Shannon, 498
Geberth, Vernon J., 369n187

Gebhard, Paul, 368n133
Geis, Gilbert, 60n8; 437n16
Geller, Susan Rose, 323n191
Gelles, Richard, 354; 370nn225, 241
George, David, 171n103
Georges-Abeyie, Daniel, 407n36
Gerstein, Dean, 319n38
Gertz, Marc, 46; 61n60; 125n84; 216n76
Gialopsos, Brooke Miller, 89n62
Giancola, Peter, 521n149
Gibbons, Donald, 175n245; 438n63
Gibbons, Frederick X., 169n24; 172nn131, 141
Gibbs, Carole, 462; 478n107
Gibbs, Jack, 127n156; 254n200; 285n69; 407n34
Gibbs, Jennifer, 272
Gibbs, John, 62n89; 125n77
Gibbs, Natalie, 367n97
Gibson, Chris, 88n32; 172n143; 216n91; 321nn115, 132
Gidycz, Christine, 367n86
Gifford, Robert, 439n108
Giffords, Gabrielle, 116
Gilchrist, Lewayne, 322n154
Gill, James, 369n188
Gillars, Mildred Elizabeth ("Axis Sally"), 379
Gillis, A.R., 286n107
Gillman, Matthew W., 171n88
Ginzberg, Eli, 523n233
Giordano, Peggy, 60n24; 218n146; 251nn79, 85; 253nn148, 155; 318n22; 320n98; 321n140; 323n189; 438n62
Giroux, Bruce, 322n172
Gizewski, Elke, 518n40
Gjeruldsen, Susanne Rogne, 365n27
Glass, Laura, 176n269
Glass, Nancy, 355
Glaze, Lauren, 128n189
Glazer, D., 520n135
Glueck, Eleanor, 161; 175n246; 249n3; 290; 291; 296; 302; 316; 318n4
Glueck, Sheldon, 161; 175n246; 249n3; 290; 291; 296; 302; 316; 318n4
Goddard, Henry H., 135; 164; 168n12
Goetz, Barry, 523n239
Goffman, Alice, 52–53
Gohm, Carol, 367n108
Gold, Martin, 62n95
Golding, Jean, 169n27
Goldkamp, John, 127n148; 522n226
Goldsmith, Eric, 289
Goldstein, Michael, 520n111
Goldstein, Paul, 365n22; 519nn66, 67, 69; 521n175
Golinelli, Daniela, 124n16
Golub, Andrew, 521nn178, 179
Gonzales, Nancy, 249n4
González, Nazario Moreno, 472
Gooch, Erik, 370n203
Gooch, Teresa, 60n38
Goodman, Robert, 174n199
Goodman, Sam, 416

Hayes, Steven, 289; 290
Haynie, Dana, 173*n*155; 215*n*52; 216*n*60; 251*n*85; 321*n*140; 369*n*171
Hayslett-McCall, Karen L., 174*n*196
Hazlewood, Robert, 367*n*97
He, J., 169*n*30
Heald, F.P., 171*n*111
Healy, William, 164; 175*n*260
Heath, Nicole, 285*n*97
Heaton, Tim B., 223
Hecker, Jeffrey, 175*n*232
Hefler, Gerd, 218*n*148
Hegel, Georg, 2260
Heide, Kathleen, 369*n*201
Heimer, Karen, 125*n*96; 215*n*46; 254*n*178
Hektner, Joel, 251*n*87
Helenius, Hans, 249*n*8
Hellemann, Tammy, 519*n*76
Hellstrom, Tomas, 555*n*85
Henderson, Charles R., Jr., 171*n*86
Henderson, Craig, 88*n*10; 367*n*91
Henderson, Russell, 360
Hendriks, Jan, 518*n*43
Henggeler, Scott, 174*n*219; 319*nn*56, 57
Henigsberg, Neven, 88*n*11
Henley, Wayne, Jr., 349
Hennard, George, 349
Hennessy, James, 171*nn*93, 102
Hennigan, Karen, 127*n*138
Henry II (King of England), 15
Hensley, Christopher, 365*n*11
Henson, Trudy Knicely, 438*n*62
Hepburn, John, 437*n*12
Herba, Catherine, 171*n*108
Herberman, Erinn, 128*n*189
Herbig, E.J., 478*n*96
Hermann, Dieter, 127*n*140
Hernandez, Aaron, 305
Hernandez, Andres, 498
Hernandez, Daphne, 217*n*107
Hernandez, Michael Andres, 520*n*118
Herrenkohl, Todd I., 89*n*42; 250*n*35; 253*n*130; 319*n*51; 365*n*29
Herrmann, Christopher, 217*n*112
Herrnstein, Richard, 22; 25*n*42; 61*nn*81, 82; 128*n*175; 164; 176*nn*267, 272; 219*n*212; 303; 304; 316; 320*nn*104–106
Herve, Huues, 368*n*134
Hetu, Celine, 437*n*44
Hibbeln, Joseph, 169*n*27
Hickert, Audrey, 523*n*231
Hickey, Eric, 125*n*92
Hickey, J., 174*n*218
Hickman-Barlow, Melissa, 284*n*30
Hidaym, Virginia, 174*n*211
Higgins, George E., 175*n*237; 322*n*146; 553*n*4
Hilbert, Richard, 218*nn*137, 138
Hile, Brian Curtis, 545
Hill, Andreas, 171*n*94; 175*nn*252, 253
Hill, D., 170*n*47
Hill, Karl G., 251*n*60; 322*n*154
Hillyard, Paddy, 478*n*98

Hinckley, John, 156
Hindelang, Michael, 25*n*41; 62*n*95; 164; 175*n*256; 176*nn*264, 265; 240; 253*n*156; 438*n*47
Hinduja, Sameer, 231; 252*n*98; 542; 543; 554*n*57; 555*nn*58, 59
Hinshaw, Stephen, 172*n*124
Hipp, John R., 61*n*67; 62*n*105; 215*n*30; 216*n*66; 217*n*96
Hippchen, Leonard, 169*nn*25, 26; 170*n*73
Hirky, A. Elizabeth, 521*n*162
Hirschel, J. David, 117
Hirschi, Travis, 25*n*41; 48; 60*n*16; 61*n*76; 90*n*95; 107; 124*n*36; 125*n*99; 164; 176*nn*264, 265; 226; 228; 237–240; 248; 251*n*67; 252*nn*95, 127, 128; 253*n*131; 304–309; 316; 319*n*36; 320*n*107; 321*nn*108, 109, 112, 113, 120, 131, 137; 474; 479*nn*153, 154
Hitler, Adolf, 388
Ho, Ching-hua, 174*n*203
Hobbes, Thomas, 97
Hobbs, David, 16
Hochstetler, Andrew, 90*n*110; 124*n*23; 251*n*82; 356; 371*n*248; 479*n*144
Hodge, Carole, 253*n*169
Hoek, Hans, 174*n*204
Hoepner, Lori, 170*n*78
Hoffman, Harry, 168*n*2
Hoffman, John, 218*n*166; 219*n*178; 319*n*38
Hoffman, Philip Seymour, 105; 500
Hogan, Michael, 216*n*76
Hoge, Robert, 320*n*80
Hogg, J., 176*nn*273, 274
Hoheimer, Francis, 430
Hoheimer, Frank, 438*n*92
Holand, Ashleigh, 172*n*143
Holcomb, Jefferson, 62*n*114
Holland, A.J., 172*n*121
Hollander, Yona, 554*n*51
Holleran, David, 341; 368*n*153
Hollinger, Richard, 438*n*53
Holmes, James, 330; 349
Holmes, Malcolm, 62*n*107; 253*n*134
Holmes, Oliver Wendell, 17; 25*n*26
Holmes, Ronald, 369*n*196; 370*nn*207, 208
Holmes, Stephen, 369*n*196; 370*nn*207, 208
Holmqvist, Rolf, 163
Holsinger, Alexander, 127*n*149; 250*n*32
Holsinger, Kristi, 250*n*32
Holtfreter, Kristy, 321*n*124
Holtzworth-Munroe, Amy, 365*n*8
Homant, Robert, 438*n*49
Homel, Ross, 126*n*107
Homes, Malcolm, 285*n*63
Hommer, Daniel, 171*n*103
Hong, Rachelle, 91*n*137
Hook, Edward, III, 318*n*33
Hooker, "Fighting Joe," 492
Hooton, Earnest, 134
Hope, Tim, 89*n*63
Horney, Julie, 60*n*28; 170*n*69; 366*n*60

Horowitz, Ruth, 505; 521*nn*173, 174
Horwood, L. John, 319*nn*41, 64
Hosein, Vanessa, 369*n*179
Hoskin, Anthony, 60*n*7
Hotaling, Gerald, 519*nn*75, 87
Hough, Richard, 88*n*18
House, James, 320*n*89
Howard, C. VyVyan, 169*n*40
Howard, Gregory, 125*n*89; 318*n*36
Howell, James, 63*n*147; 90*n*90; 125*n*89; 215*n*37
Hoyt, Dan, 90*n*81; 367*n*104; 521*n*169
Hoza, Betsy, 90*n*92; 251*n*57
Hrabac, Pero, 88*n*11
Hribal, Alex, 159
Hu, Howard, 171*n*88
Huang, Bo, 89*n*42; 365*n*29; 521*n*176; 522*n*197
Hubbell, Amy, 521*n*168
Huberty, James, 349
Huddleston, III, C. West, 513
Huebner, Beth, 215*n*32; 216*n*63
Huff, Rodney, 476*nn*10–12
Hughes, Lorine, 45; 253*n*154; 366*n*67
Huh, David, 225; 250*n*36
Huie, S.A., 218*n*133
Huizinga, David, 62*n*97; 117; 124*n*28; 216*n*84; 217*n*121; 219*n*207
Hummer, R.A., 218*n*133
Humphries, Drew, 285*n*104
Hunt, Dana, 495
Hunter, Denis, 25*n*32
Hunter, Jerome, 313
Hunter, John, 253*n*169
Hureau, David M., 126*n*127
Hurlburt, Michael, 88*n*18
Hurley, Jimmy, 88*n*9
Hurley, Robert S., 175*n*240; 176*n*278
Husted, David, 318*n*34
Hutchison, Ira, 117
Hwang, Shu-ling, 519*n*88
Hyde, Janet Shibley, 62*n*89

I

Ikram, Khawaja, 423
Ilgen, Mark, 519*n*82
Ilonen, Noora, 88*n*13
Immarigeon, Russ, 286*n*125
Inciardi, James, 437*n*13; 505; 520*nn*134, 138, 140; 521*nn*173, 174; 523*n*243
Inglis, Ruth, 370*n*227
Ingram, Jason, 231; 252*n*98
Innes, Christopher, 89*n*70
Iovanni, Leeann, 244; 254*n*204
Ireland, Jane, 554*n*55
Ireland, Timothy, 89*n*40
Irwin, John, 124*n*17

J

Jackson, Dylan, 254*nn*176
Jackson, Jennifer, 367*n*88
Jackson, Jesse L., Jr., 377
Jackson, Kenneth, 254*n*190
Jackson, Kristina, 521*n*159

Jackson, Linda, 253n169
Jackson, Lori, 365n6
Jackson, Michael, 105
Jackson, Patrick, 60n10
Jackson, Shelley, 72
Jacob, Ayad, 521n183
Jacobs, Bruce A., 103; 104; 115; 124nn49–53; 125n68; 125nn54, 55; 127n164; 128n187; 169n21; 365n28; 371n250; 438n67
Jacobs, David, 62n108; 63n122; 284n53; 285n59
Jacobs, K.J., 170n75
Jacobson, Heather, 554n48; 555n72
Jacobson, Michael, 285n83
Jacoby, Kristen, 24n12
Jaffe, Pater, 91n133
Jaffee, Sara, 173n156
Jaki, Thomas, 253n135
Jalbert, Sarah Kuck, 495
James, Alison, 518n5
James, J.E., 169n40
James, Kevin, 401
James, Susan, 520n146
James, William, 157
Janes, Nicole, 479n111
Jang, Hyunseok, 249n10
Jang, Sung Joon, 251n68
Janis, Irving, 250nn46, 47
Jansen, Robert, 125n86; 356
Janus, Mark-David, 519n60
Jargowsky, Paul, 215n54; 216n57
Jarjoura, G. Roger, 218n156; 250n44
Jayyousi, Kifah, 401
Jeanmard, Matthew, 368n147
Jeffery, C. Ray, 108; 126n102
Jenkins, Brian Michael, 403; 404
Jenkins, Philip, 497; 520n108
Jennings, J. Richard, 172n136
Jennings, Wesley, 8; 310; 322nn153, 159, 160, 170; 553n4
Jensen, Gary, 62n95; 90n84; 252n107; 253n157; 286n112
Jensen, Vickie, 366n59
Jesilow, Paul, 286n142
Jimenez, Carlos Mario ("Macaco"), 266
Jin, Hanjuan, 530
Joe, Karen Ann, 103; 124n48
John Paul II (Pope), 488
Johnson, Bruce, 521nn178–180
Johnson, Byron, 251n68
Johnson, Dawn, 88n23
Johnson, Holly, 173n175
Johnson, Janice, 520n146
Johnson, Jeffrey, 519n74
Johnson, Joseph, 215n28
Johnson, Kathrine, 53; 62n111
Johnson, Kirk, 368n150
Johnson, L. Clark, 128n185
Johnson, Lee Michael, 254n173
Johnson, Matthew, 322n165
Johnson, Norman, 174n205
Johnson, Robert, 254nn179, 191; 319n38
Johnson, W. Wesley, 284n30

Johnson, Wendell, 88n33
Johnston, Lloyd, 60nn21, 22, 44
Johnstone, J., 219n199
Jolin, Annette, 518n50
Jolliffe, Darrick, 318n26
Jon, Nina, 286n105
Jones, Alice, 171n108
Jones, Donald, 147; 173nn162, 163
Jones, Heather, 250n24
Jones, Lisa, 370nn229, 230
Jones, Marshall, 147; 173nn162, 163
Jones, Peter, 63n142; 522n226
Jones, Shayne, 217n99; 321n115
Jonzon, Eva, 370n231
Jordan, Carol E., 369nn180, 183; 371n287
Jordan, Lamar, 89n56
Jorgensen, Jenel S., 174n200
Jorgensen, P.J., 169n31
Joubert, S.J., 478n96
Joyce, James, 497
Juarez, Conrado, 343
Julius Caesar, 386
Junger, Marianne, 253n144; 319n36
Junger-Tas, Josine, 253n144
Jusko, Todd A., 171n86
Jussim, Lee, 250n39

K

Kageyama, Yuri, 366n78
Kahler, Christopher, 88n23
Kahn, Arnold, 367n88
Kakoulidis, Christis, 365n5
Kalb, Larry, 318n26
Kaloupek, Danny, 89n43
Kaluala-Heino, Riittakerttu, 174n201
Kandel, Denise, 251n87; 252n90; 253n149; 521n163
Kandel, Elizabeth, 171n90
Kane, John, 476nn10–12; 555nn87, 89
Kane, Robert J., 217n117; 366n62
Kanka, Maureen, 85
Kanka, Megan, 8; 19; 85; 86
Kanka, Richard, 85
Kaplan, Howard, 254nn179, 180, 191; 319n38
Karasik, Teodore W., 407n50
Karch, Debra, 369n187
Karmaus, Wilfried, 170n83
Karmen, Andrew, 31; 91n135
Karp, David R., 286n141
Kashmiri, Ilyas, 397
Kassin, Saul, 60n20
Kasza, Kristen, 169n28
Kates, Don, 125n66
Katz, Jack, 102
Kauffman, K., 174n218
Kaufman, Jeanne, 88n16
Kaufman, Joanne, 63n120; 218n163; 369n192
Kauzlarich, David, 284n35
Kawai, Eriko, 366n65
Kay, Barbara, 252n126
Kaysen, Debra, 62n93; 90n87
Kazemian, Lila, 60n29; 63n143

Keckler, Charles N.W., 127n163
Keeler, Gordon, 174n209
Keels, Micere, 216n85
Keen, Bradley, 62n108
Keenan, Kate, 251n54; 322n172
Keeney, Belea, 369n201
Keilitz, Ingo, 172n116
Keire, Mara, 519n92
Keith, Bruce, 250n15
Keith, H., 478n106
Kekua, Lennay, 544; 545
Kelley, Jill, 541
Kelley, Thomas, 438n49
Kelling, George, 127n146
Kellogg, Michael, 388; 407n42
Kelly, Kathryn, 173n187
Kemp, Jana, 89n51
Kempe, C. Henry, 370n223
Kempe, Ruth S., 370n223
Kemper, Rick, 126n105
Kempf, Kimberly, 253n146
Kempf-Leonard, Kimberly, 56–57; 61n84; 63nn146, 147; 128n178
Kennedy, Daniel, 438n49
Kennedy, Leslie, 91n146; 321n111
Kenney, T.J., 171n111
Keppel, Robert D., 369nn200, 202; 370n204
Kerbs, Jodi, 174n204
Kerich, Michael, 171n103
Kerik, Bernard, 450
Kerner, Hans-Jürgen, 250n51; 322n176
Kerns, Suzanne, 319n54
Kerr, Margaret, 251n59; 322n150
Kershaw, Trace, 370n234
Kessler, Daniel, 113; 127n154
Kethineni, Seshi, 253n151
Kevorkian, Jack, 19
Keys, David, 285n68
Khan, A.Q., 399
Khan, Bilal, 491
Khan, Haji Juma, 401
Khomeini, Ayatollah Ruhollah, 386
Kibaki, Mwai, 376
Kidd, Sean, 521n155
Kilewer, Wendy, 216n68
Kilias, Martin, 45
Killip, Steve, 91n133
Kilpatrick, Dean, 88nn12, 25; 90n118; 336; 365n24; 366n75; 367nn87, 109–111
Kilpatrick, Kwame, 377; 378
Kim, D., 169n30
Kim, Julia Yun Soo, 60n26
Kim, KiDeuk, 127n162
Kim, Min Jung, 89n42
Kim, Sang-Weon, 218n135
Kim, Yeora, 554n50
Kinard, Griffin, 300
King, Harry, 415; 437n14
King, Ryan, 61n83; 107; 125n95; 359; 371n259
Kingery, Paul M., 175n240; 176n278

Lengua, Liliana, 319n51
Lenza, Michael, 285n68
Leo, Richard, 60n20
Leonard, Kimberly Kempf, 253n152
Leopold, Nathan, 38
Leschied, Alan, 320n80
Lester, David, 407n67
Letourneau, Elizabeth, 8
Leukefeld, Carl, 522nn224, 225
Levenson, Jill, 8; 126n112
Levi-Minzi, Micol E., 371nn271, 273, 277
Levin, Jack, 348; 349; 358; 359; 369n199;
    370nn208, 211, 212; 371nn255–257,
    270; 498; 520n116
Levin, Steven D., 127n154
Levine, David M., 554n30
Levine, Murray, 286n112
Levitt, Steven D., 42; 45; 61n48; 113; 116;
    119; 128nn173, 191; 309; 322n145
Levrant, Sharon, 287n152
Levy, Diane, 169n35
Lewis, Dorothy Otnow, 328; 365nn6, 7;
    366n43
Lewis, John, 60n28
Lewis, Oscar, 183; 215n18
Lewis, S.A., 171n101
Leygraf, Norbert, 518n40
Li, Fuzhong, 251n56
Libicki, Martin, 407n53
Lichtenstein, Paul, 173n146
Lin, Kuei-Hsiu, 365n36
Lin, Peter, 369n188
Lind, Bronwyn, 90n109
Lindblad, Frank, 370n231
Lindblad, M.R., 217n95
Lindgren, Scott, 170n45
Lindh, John Walker, 39; 378
Lindner, Douglas, 406n12
Lindsay, Mark, 407n67
Lindsay, W.R., 172n121
Link, Bruce, 174n206; 253n168
Linster, Richard, 365n29
Linz, Daniel, 368n138
Lipps, Thomas, 65
Lipscomb, Jane A., 371n274
Lipsey, Mark, 318n32
Lipton, D., 175n235
Liska, Allen, 90n100; 217n108; 253n162
Listokin, Yair, 127n161
Littleton, Heather, 88n10; 367n91
Liu, Jianhong, 169n42; 217n108
Liu, Xinhua, 169n35
Livaditis, Miltos, 365n5
Livingston, Jennifer, 367nn88, 93
Lizotte, Alan, 90nn91, 150; 125n89;
    173n151; 251n80; 285n65; 297;
    318nn13, 27, 35; 320n90; 366n64;
    520n147; 522n205
Lo, Celia, 523n236
Lochman, J.E., 175n233
Locusta, 348
Loeber, Rolf, 63n148; 90nn88, 89; 169n28;
    172n136; 174nn197, 204; 175n238;
    250n40; 251n54; 253n138; 291; 311;

312; 316; 318nn9, 14, 26, 32; 319nn39,
    64; 320nn69, 72; 321n124; 322nn172,
    177, 178; 323n182; 365nn11, 30;
    366n65; 369n176; 522n202
Lofland, John, 254n184
Logan, T.K., 371n287; 522nn224, 225
Logie, Robert, 439n98
Logio, Kim, 88n14
Lok, Kris, 169n41
Lolacono, Nancy J., 169n35
Lombroso, Cesare, 49; 62n85; 133; 134;
    149; 166; 168n7
Lonardo, Robert, 251nn79, 86
Loncar, Mladen, 88n11
Lonczk, Heather, 323n190
Longmore, Monica, 251nn79, 85; 253n155;
    321n140
Loomis, Dana, 371n278
Lopes, Giza, 320n90
Lorenz, Konrad, 329; 365n16
Loughner, Jared, 116
Loughran, Thomas, 127nn141, 142
Loveless, Peggy, 172n123
Lovell, David, 128n185
Lovrich, Nicholas, 216n91
Lowenstein, George, 127n168
Lu, Chunmeng, 90n85
Lucas, Emma, 519n82
Luciano, Lucky, 465
Luckenbill, David, 346; 366n57; 369n190
Ludwig, Jens, 126n124; 369n175
Luebbers, Stefan, 174n214
Lueck, Monika, 365n10
Lui, Kung-Jong, 91n151
Lunde, Donald, 369n161
Lunsford, Jessica, 488–489
Luque, Luis, 368n147
Lurigio, Arthur J., 88nn5, 29; 91n148;
    127n166; 522nn219–221
Lussier, Patrick, 322n149
Lustgarten, Abrahm, 478nn108, 109
Luther, Martin, 490
Luukkaala, Tiina, 174n201
Luzaich, Lisa, 20
Lyght, C.E., 172n130
Lykken, David, 127n167; 168n5; 175n248
Lynam, Donald R., 171n90; 173n183;
    175n227; 176n266; 217n99; 319nn37,
    52, 64; 322nn148, 169, 177; 511;
    522nn224, 225
Lynch, James, 91n149; 198n200
Lynch, Kathleen Bodisch, 323n191
Lynch, Michael, 170n81; 173n171;
    274n12; 283nn3, 4, 7, 9; 284nn12, 25,
    31; 464–465; 476n5; 478nn65, 94;
    479nn114, 116
Lynch, Shannon, 285n97
Lyngstad, Torkild Hovde, 301; 320n97
Lyon, Matthew, Sarah, 25n36
Lysiak, Matthew, 168n1

M

Ma, Po Chieng, 427
Maakestad, William, 478nn75, 76

Maas, Carl, 253n130
Maberry, Andrew, 414
MacCoun, Robert, 522n185
MacDonald, John, 61n69; 89n38; 300
MacDonald, Julia, 439n108
Mace, David E., 174n200
Machalek, Richard, 173n165
Machon, Ricardo, 171n90
MacIntosh, Randall, 368n151
Mack, Kristin, 286n114
Mackesy-Amiti, Mary Ellen, 521n175
Maclean, Donald, 380
MacMillan, Ross, 61n83; 320n84
Madan, Anjana, 156; 157
Maddan, Sean, 126n122
Madensen, Tamara D., 125n71; 251n77
Madoff, Bernard, 445
Maercker, Andreas, 89n45; 91n132
Maguin, Eugene, 250n40
Maguire, Brendan, 286n136
Maguire, Kathleen, 60n43; 219n214
Maher, Dennis, 340
Mahoney, Kevin, 457
Mahoney, Margaret, 322n146
Maier, Jeanette, 489
Maier-Katkin, Daniel, 219n180
Makarios, Matthew, 128n193
Malamuth, Neil, 368n139; 497; 520nn105,
    109, 117
Maldonado-Molina, Mildred, 322n170
Mallory, W.A., 172n116
Mallouk, Mohammed, 43
Malvo, John Lee, 351
Mancini, Christina, 89n39
Mandela, Nelson, 280
Manganello, Jennifer, 355
Mannheim, Hermann, 173n185
Manning, Bradley (Chelsea Elizabeth
    Manning), 380; 525
Manning, Wendy, 251nn79, 85; 253n155;
    321n140
Manski, C.F., 115
Manturuk, K.R., 217n95
Maples, Michelle, 254n205
Maras, Marie-Helen, 554n17
Marchak, Patricia, 397; 407nn79, 80
Marchbanks, Polly, 91n151
Marcotte, Dave, 365n12
Marcum, Catherine, 322n146; 553n4
Maric, Alexandra, 520n113
Marini, Margaret Mooney, 62n89
Markianos, M., 172n132
Markowitz, Fred, 217n108; 219n189
Markowitz, Sara, 365n12
Marlowe, Douglas, 513
Marquart, James, 125n79; 128n195;
    319n37
Marques, Antonio F., 170n79
Marshall, Ineke Haen, 253n144
Marshall, John, 379
Marshall, Paul, 170n74
Marshall, Stephen, 371n278
Marshall, W.L., 367n95
Martel, Michelle, 170n83

O'Malley, Patrick, 60*nn*21, 44
Opjordsmoen, Stein, 365*n*27
Opler, Mark, 171*n*87
Oranen, Mikko, 88*n*13
Orbach, Yael, 82
Orbuch, Terri, 320*n*89
O'Reilly-Fleming, Thomas, 370*n*211
Orlebeke, Jacob, 170*n*61
Ormrod, Richard, 88*n*12; 89*n*55
Orobio de Castro, Bram, 175*n*231
Orth, Ulrich, 89*n*45; 91*n*132
Osborn, Andrew, 284*n*51
Osborn, Denise, 89*n*63
Osgood, D. Wayne, 60*n*22; 62*n*88; 89*n*48; 124*n*37; 170*nn*53, 55; 301; 320*n*100
Osman, Suzanne, 368*n*128
Ostermann, Michael, 128*n*198; 174*n*207
Ostresh, Erik, 253*n*134
Ostrow, Miriam, 523*n*233
Ostrowsky, Michael, 219*n*174
Ouellet, Lawrence, 519*n*69
Ouimet, Marc, 366*n*68
Ouimette, Paige Crosby, 174*n*190
Ousey, Graham C., 89*n*69; 215*nn*51, 52; 285*n*60; 323*n*186
Owen, David, 406*n*16
Owen, Michael, 172*n*141
Owens, Colleen, 491
Owens, Elizabeth, 172*n*124
Owens, Jennifer Gatewood, 322*n*166
Ozdemir, Metin, 322*n*150
Ozkan, Yasemin, 215*n*22
Øzbay, Øzden, 253*n*132
Øzcan, Yusuf Ziya, 253*n*132

P

Pacifici, Laura, 491
Padilla, Jose, 401
Pahlavi, Mohammad Reza, 386
Paige, Karen, 170*n*71
Painter-Davis, Noah, 368*n*141
Palast, Greg, 284*n*39
Palfrey, Deborah Jeane ("D.C. Madam"), 489; 494
Pallone, Nathaniel, 171*nn*93, 102
Palloni, Alberto, 24*n*2
Pan, En-Ling, 249*n*14
Panin, Aleksandr Andreevich, 528
Pantazis, Christina, 478*n*98
Papachristos, Andrew, 126*n*127; 333; 366*n*66
Papillo, Romano, 253*n*143
Paqette, Mark, 5
Paradis, Emily, 88*n*22
Pardini, Dustin, 172*n*136; 320*nn*69, 72
Pare, Paul-Philippe, 321*n*144
Park, Robert E., 180; 182; 188; 215*nn*12, 14, 15
Park, Yoonhwan, 215*n*54; 216*n*57
Parker, Jocelyn, 407*n*44
Parker, Karen, 45; 63*n*121; 215*n*27; 300; 320*n*94
Parker, Robert Nash, 61*n*62
Parnell, Peter, 485

Parra, Gilbert, 521*n*159
Parrot, A., 367*n*115
Parsons, Deborah, 286*n*142
Parsons, Jeffrey T., 522*n*189
Parsons, Patrick J., 171*n*86
Parsons, Rehtaeh, 65
Parvez, Faruque, 169*n*35
Paschall, Mallie, 63*n*124
Pastore, Ann, 60*n*43; 219*n*214
Patchin, Justin, 215*n*32; 542; 543; 545; 554*n*57; 555*nn*58, 59
Pate, Tony, 127*n*146
Paternoster, Raymond, 10; 61*n*70; 88*n*27; 127*nn*157, 162, 168, 170; 128*n*184; 218*n*170; 244; 250*nn*44, 45; 254*n*204; 284*n*33; 285*n*85; 310; 318*nn*11, 12, 28; 319*n*55; 320*nn*70, 74, 76, 103; 322*n*162
Patil, Sujata, 24*n*12
Pato, Carlos N., 504
Pato, Michele T., 504
Patrick, Patricia, 438*n*50
Pattavina, April, 217*n*102
Patterson, Gerald, 318*n*31; 365*n*31
Patterson, G.R., 318*n*24; 319*n*60
Pattison, Philippa, 175*n*236
Paul, Christopher, 401
Paul, Thomas, 518*n*40
Paulozzi, Len, 369*n*192
Pauwels, Lieven, 124*n*38
Pawitan, Yudi, 173*n*146
Payne, Allison Ann, 253*n*137
Payne, Gary, 218*n*160; 253*n*151
Pearson-Nelson, Benjamin, 365*n*21
Pease, Ken, 89*n*67; 126*n*128; 438*nn*93, 94
Peck, Mitchell, 218*n*159
Pedneault, Amélie, 429
Peete, Thomas, 127*n*158
Pelham, Molina, Jr., 172*n*120
Pelham, William, Jr., 250*n*24
Peltonen, Kirsi, 88*n*13
Pendleton, Hadiya, 208
Penrod, Steven, 368*n*138; 520*n*112
Pepinsky, Harold, 277; 286*n*123
Pepler, Debra, 157
Pepper, J.V., 115
Perea, Ignacio, 343
Perera, Frederica, 170*n*78
Pereverzeva, Natalia, 380
Perez, Cynthia, 318*nn*13, 35; 522*n*205
Perez-Melara, Enrique, 545–546
Peric, Mia, 522*n*190
Perkins, Elizabeth, 438*n*94
Perkins, Molly, 318*n*18
Persico, Nicola, 62*n*101
Peterson, David, 253*n*142
Peterson, Ruth, 63*n*117; 215*n*26; 217*nn*110, 113
Petit, Hayley, 289
Petit, Jennifer, 289
Petit, Michaela, 289
Petit, William, 289
Petraitis, John, 125*n*78; 521*n*160
Petras, Hanno, 319*n*50

Petras, Tricia, 364*n*2
Petraus, David, 541
Petrocelli, Matthew, 285*nn*73, 74
Petrosino, Anthony, 25*n*44; 286*n*131
Petrosino, Carolyn, 286*n*131
Petrossian, Gohar A., 126*n*105
Pettit, Gregory, 217*n*100; 249*n*13; 250*nn*29, 31; 319*n*64; 365*n*35
Petts, Richard, 227; 251*n*69
Pezzin, Liliana, 124*n*44
Philaretou, Andreas, 554*n*14
Philby, Kim, 380
Philibert, Robert A., 169*n*24; 172*nn*131, 141
Philip, Michael, 62*n*116
Phillips, Coretta, 89*n*67; 438*n*93
Phillips, Julie A., 63*n*127; 215*n*30
Phillips, Matthew D., 318*n*27
Phillips, Monte, 171*n*103
Phillips, Scott, 365*n*26
Phillips, Susan, 174*n*209
Phillips, Tim, 216*n*71
Phillips-Plummer, Lynanne, 519*n*78
Pi, Yijun, 218*n*170
Piaget, Jean, 157; 174*n*216
Pickett, Kate, 169*n*28; 218*n*148
Piehl, Anne Morrison, 63*n*134
Pietz, Christina, 90*n*93
Piha, Jorma, 249*n*8
Pihl, Robert, 171*n*91
Piipsa, Minna, 88*n*13
Piliavin, Irving, 237; 252*nn*121, 124
Pilkey, Dav, 485
Pinderhughes, Ellen, 318*n*15
Pinel, Philippe, 133
Pinker, Steven, 329; 365*n*14
Pipe, Margaret-Ellen, 82
Piquero, Alex R., 89*n*38; 127*n*141; 128*nn*172, 184, 188; 170*n*59; 174*n*208; 175*n*225; 218*nn*160–162; 251*n*66; 254*n*197; 285*nn*73, 74; 286*n*116; 300; 310; 318*nn*10, 28; 319*nn*40, 45, 47, 48; 320*n*94; 321*nn*110, 115, 124; 322*nn*148, 152, 155, 159, 160; 322*nn*169, 174, 179
Piquero, Nicole Leeper, 218*n*162; 219*n*181; 251*n*66; 252*n*117; 322*nn*147, 179; 479*n*151
Pistorius, Oscar, 327
Pitt, Brad, 412
Pittman, David, 520*n*135
Pitts, Marian, 519*n*52
Planells-Struse, Simón, 61*n*57
Planty, Michael, 60*nn*6, 42; 88*n*4; 89*n*49; 437*n*2
Platt, Alyssa, 117
Platt, Anthony, 215*n*41; 283*n*6; 284*n*22; 285*n*75
Platt, Jerome J., 521*n*150
Ploeger, Matthew, 62*n*91; 251*n*87; 252*nn*93, 94
Plomin, Robert, 173*n*161; 175*n*250
Plushnick-Masti, Ramit, 249*n*1
Podboy, J.W., 172*n*116
Podolsky, E., 170*n*48

Pogarsky, Greg, 126n132; 127nn139, 153, 162; 128n188; 321n123
Pogrebin, Mark, 252n119
Pokhrel, Pallav, 521n156
Polaschek, Devon, 518n42
Polge, A., 169n39
Polk, Kenneth, 219n213
Pollack, Otto, 62n86
Pomeroy, Wardell, 368n133
Ponder, Michael, 285n61
Ponischil, Kristina, 68
Ponzi, Charles, 445
Poole, Eric, 252nn115, 119
Popkin, Susan, 88n33
Porche, Dianne, 479n150
Porteous, Lucy, 169n41
Porter, James, 488
Porter, Stephen, 368n134
Portnoy, Jill, 172n136
Posner, Daniel, 478n92
Post, Charles, 172n115
Post, Jerrold M., 394; 407n71
Pott, Audrie, 65
Potter, Lloyd, 369n192
Potterat, John, 519nn78, 94
Pottieger, Anne, 505; 521nn173, 174
Poussin, Nicolas, 334
Powell, Andrea, 215n48
Pradai-Prat, D., 169n39
Pranis, Kay, 286n138
Prasad, Monica, 490; 519n53
Pratt, Travis C., 89n44; 175n224; 251n77; 319n45; 321n124
Prendergast, Michael, 522n199
Presser, Lois, 287n150
Pribesh, Shana, 216n80
Price, Jamie, 216n60
Price, Virginia, 519n60
Pridemore, William, 218n135; 365n19
Prince, Emily, 169n41
Prinz, Ronald, 169n38; 319n54
Pritchard, Adam, 369n180
Priyadarsini, S., 252n89
Proctor, Keith, 126n119
Proffitt, Fiona, 407n47
Prom-Wormley, Elizabeth, 172n134
Propp, Jennifer, 366n39
Proulx, Jean, 125n94
Pruitt, B.E., 175n240; 176n278
Pruitt, Matthew, 215n27
Prunella, Jill, 171n104
Przybylski, Roger, 521n183
Pugh, M.D., 253n148
Pugh, Meredith, 60n24
Pullmann, Michael, 174n204
Punter, Helen, 286n145
Purutçuoglu, Eda, 215n22
Putin, Vladimir, 257
Pyrooz, David C., 318n17

Q

Quercia, R.G., 217n95
Quetelet, L.A.J. (Adolphe), 181; 213; 215nn8, 9

Quinet, Kenna Davis, 89n61; 369n199; 370n211
Quinney, Richard, 262; 277; 284nn16, 54, 55; 286n123; 477n22
Quinsey, Vernon, 439n111
Qureshi, Babar, 43

R

Raaijmakers, Quinten, 174n221
Rabasa, Angel, 407n50; 408n103
Rabideau-Stevens, Debr, 81
Rada, Richard, 368n133
Radelet, Michael, 115
Rader, Dennis, 346; 348; 351
Radosevich, Marcia, 62n96; 252nn100, 101
Radosh, Polly, 286n136
Raffalovich, Lawrence, 61n68; 90n113; 216n58
Rafter, Nicole Hahn, 168nn3, 4, 8, 9; 318n3
Raghavan, Chitra, 520n146
Rahman, Atiya Abdul, 397
Raine, Adrian, 138; 141; 145; 166; 169nn26, 42; 171nn92, 96, 105, 106, 114; 172nn136–138; 173n182; 175nn223, 241; 322n177; 323n181; 365n32
Raitt, F.E., 170n68
Raley, R. Kelly, 63n126
Ramsey, Elizabeth, 318n24
Ramsey, Susan, 88n23
Rand, Michael R., 367n85; 438n66
Randall, Susan, 366n71
Range, Lillian, 88n18
Rangel, Charles, 247
Rankin, Bruce, 217n120
Rankin, Joseph, 60n19
Rapin, J., 169n39
Rapp, Geoffrey, 115
Rappley, Marsha D., 170n83
Ratchford, Marie, 321nn117, 119
Ratcliffe, Jerry, 60n40; 126n130
Rath, Saroj Kumar, 407n70
Rathouz, Paul, 250n24
Rathus, Spencer, 175n256; 250n43; 252n116; 518n47
Raudenbush, Stephen W., 216n56; 217n92
Rauh, Virginia, 170n78
Rawlings, Robert, 171n103
Ray, James V., 319n46
Ray, Melvin, 254nn170, 173
Raymond, Kristen M., 171n109
Reagan, Ronald, 78; 156
Realmuto, George, 251n87
Rebellon, Cesar, 218nn155, 162, 163; 249n10; 253n159; 365n38; 505; 521nn175, 177
Reboussin, Roland, 367n97
Reckdenwald, Amy, 89n39
Recker, Nicholas, 320n81
Reckless, Walter, 180; 252nn125, 126
Redd, Troy, 112
Reddy, Marisa, 369n193
Reed, Elizabeth, 90n87

Reed, M.D., 253n162
Rees, Carter, 250n50
Rees, Sian, 523n232
Regenerus, Mark, 253n140
Regoeczi, Wendy, 369nn172, 177
Regoli, Robert, 252n115
Reid, Joan, 320nn69, 73
Reiman, Jeffrey, 284n26
Reingle, Jennifer, 322nn153, 170
Reisig, Michael, 216n82; 321n124
Reiss, Albert, 125n70; 175n242; 176n277; 216nn60, 89, 90; 237; 252n123; 478
Reitzel, Deborah, 91n133
Rekart, Michael, 519n83
Remy, Nicholas, 96
Ren, Xin, 250n51
Rengert, George, 91n149; 124n33; 125nn57, 60, 76; 128n172; 522n211
Rengifo, Andres, 45; 217n112
Renner, Lynette, 250n33
Rennison, Callie Marie, 60n18; 108; 126n108
Reno brothers, 413
Renzetti, Claire M., 347
Resick, Patricia, 62n93; 90n117; 91n119
Resnick, Heidi, 88n25; 365n24; 366n75; 367nn87, 109–111
Restifo, Nicholas, 365n6
Restivo, Emily, 244; 254n203
Reuter, Peter, 522n185
Reyna-Ozuna, Jairo, 179
Reynolds, B.J., 171n111
Reynolds, Charles, 523n230
Reynolds, Kimber, 118
Reynolds, Matthew, 368n143
Reynolds, Mike, 118
Reynolds, Morgan, 124n18
Rheingold, Alyssa, 88n25
Rhodes, William, 495
Rice, Frances, 172n141
Rice, Stephen, 321n114
Rich, Karen, 91n129
Rich, William, 172n116
Rich-Edwards, Janet W., 171n88
Richards, Jeffery, 518nn48, 49
Richards, Maryse, 90nn94, 96
Richardson, Alexandra, 169n36
Richardson, Deborah, 90n105
Richardson, Justin, 485
Richardson, Samuel, 334
Richman, Kimberly, 60n20
Richmond, F. Lynn, 219n213
Richmond, Ma'lik, 65
Richter, Linda, 124n20
Ricketts, Melissa, 322n146
Ridde, James, 320n99
Ridder, Elizabeth, 319n41
Riddle, David, 169n38
Rideout, Greta, 338
Rideout, John, 338
Ridulph, Maria, 343
Riess, Julie, 171n85
Riggs, Shelley, 174n195
Rijsdijk, Fruhling, 173n156

Schrag, Clarence, 60n41; 219n195
Schreck, Christopher, 89n48; 90n79
Schroeder, Ryan, 320n98; 322n151
Schrum, Jason, 528
Schulenberg, John, 60n44
Schumacher, Michael, 56; 63n141
Schur, Edwin, 253n165
Schutt, Russell, 62n97
Schwab-Stone, Mary, 250n27
Schwartz, Joseph A., 163; 176n268
Schwartz, Martin D., 285nn81, 84, 103;
    368nn129, 136, 156
Schwartz, Seth, 407nn75–77
Schwendinger, Herman, 60n36; 285nn86, 93
Schwendinger, Julia, 60n36; 285nn86, 93
Scott, Austin, 369n165; 437nn29, 30;
    438nn59, 75, 85, 87
Scott, Peter, 168n6
Seale, Bobby, 389
Sealock, Miriam, 62n99; 219n181
Seeley, John R., 174n200
Seffrin, Patrick, 91n129; 253n155
Segal, Nancy, 173n157
Seguin, Jean, 171n91
Seidman, Robert, 262; 284n15
Sekulic, Damir, 522n190
Seligmann, Reade, 340; 341
Sellars, James, 25n32
Sellers, Christine S., 251n77; 252n104;
    286n109; 355
Sellers, Courtenay, 174n212
Sellin, Thorsten, 55; 59; 63n136; 205;
    219nn183–186; 318n8
Selyukh, Alina, 477n46
Semple, W.E., 171n102
Sengul Hablemitoglu, 215n22
Sepper, Elizabeth, 406n27
Serra, Susan, 365n6
Seto, Michael, 520n113
Sewell, Kenneth, 365n8
Shachmurove, Yochanan, 438n95; 439n96
Shackelford, Todd, 369nn173, 174
Shah, Saleem, 169n25
Shahar, Yael, 555n92
Shahin, Emad El-Din, 283n1
Shakespeare, William, 335
Shalhoub-Kevorkian, Nadra, 347
Shane, Jon, 174n212
Shannon, Lyle, 63n139
Shannon, Sarah, 523n237
Shapira, Nathan, 318n34
Sharkey, Patrick, 217n126
Sharp, Susan, 218n159
Sharps, Phyllis, 355
Shatz, Naomi, 369n181
Shatz, Steven, 369n181
Shaughnessy, Rita, 172n125
Shaw, Clifford R., 180; 188; 189; 190; 191;
    211; 213; 215nn40, 42, 43
Shaw, Daniel, 250n17; 251n78
Shea, William, 540
Sheikh, Pervaze A., 478nn101, 103
Sheldon, William, 135; 169n14
Shelley, Louise, 266; 284n38; 479n132

Shelly, Peggy, 125n77
Shen, April Chiung-Tao, 370n233
Shen, Ce, 174n212
Shepard, Mathew, 360
Shepherd, Joanna, 115
Sheppard, David, 90n91
Sher, Kenneth, 521n159
Sherman, Lawrence W., 113; 117;
    127n150; 252n122; 286n147
Shermer, Lauren O'Neill, 321n139
Sherrer, Margaret, 174n212
Shevlin, Mark, 88n15
Shields, Ian, 252n114
Shifley, Rick, 286n137
Shihadeh, Edward S., 216n55
Shin, Hee-Choon, 319n38
Shipley, Bernard, 128n180
Shipman, Harold Frederick, 348
Shively, Michael, 495
Short, James, 61n64; 252n114
Short, Tamsin B.R., 174n214
Shotland, R. Lance, 367n103
Shover, Neal, 124n47; 432–433; 437nn9–11;
    439n101; 473; 479nn144, 145
Showers, Carolin, 62n89
Shrout, Patrick, 253n168
Shteir, Rachel, 437n37
Shum, David, 171n107
Shutt, J. Eagle, 321n119
Sieder, Jill Jordan, 438n48
Siegel, Jane, 88n19; 370n232
Siegel, Julie, 461
Siegel, Larry, 60n8; 172n135; 175n256;
    252n116
Sieleni, Bruce, 172n123
Sieler, DeDe, 174n204
Siennick, Sonja, 250n38
Sigfusdottir, I.D., 169n40
Sikkema, Kathleen, 370n234
Silbereisen, Ranier, 322n166
Silberman, Matthew, 127n156
Silke, Andrew, 379; 407nn39, 64
Sillanmaki, Lauri, 249n8
Silva, Manori, 170n77
Silva, Phil, 63n149; 171n90; 173n183;
    174n191; 175n258; 318nn19, 30;
    319nn52, 63; 323nn187, 188
Silver, Clayton, 249n6
Silver, Eric, 174n210; 217nn125, 129
Silverman, Eli B., 31; 60n11
Silverman, Jenna, 249n6
Silverman, Robert, 253n145
Simister, John, 61n55; 170n62
Simmons, Catherine, 520n114
Simon, David, 478n77
Simon, Leonore, 60n23; 172n119; 320n75
Simon, Patricia, 319n37
Simon, Rita James, 24n9; 62n94
Simon, Thomas, 369n192
Simons, Leslie, 321n141
Simons, Marlise, 366n80
Simons, Ronald, 147; 169n24; 172nn131,
    141; 173n167; 207; 254n173; 320n87;
    321n141; 365n36; 366n49

Simos, Alexander, 365n6
Simpson, John, 286n107
Simpson, M.K., 176nn273, 274
Simpson, Murray, 176nn273, 274
Simpson, Sally, 62n99; 219n175
Sims, Barbara, 284nn18, 28
Singer, Jane, 439n109
Singer, Merrill, 519n84
Singer, Simon, 286n112
Singh, Piyusha, 127n151
Singhvi, Nikhil S., 478n86
Sisson, Melanie, 407n53
Sitren, Alicia, 128n176
Skardhamar, Torbjørn, 301; 320n97
Skilling, Jeffrey, 451
Skinner, William, 251n87; 252n103
Skogan, Wesley, 216nn72, 74, 75, 87;
    217n105
Skoler, Daniel, 478n73
Skondras, M., 172n132
Slade, Eric, 250n32; 365n33
Slaughter, Ellen, 219n210
Slavkovich, Vesna, 169n35
Slawson, John, 176n262
Slepian, Barnett, 389
Sloan, Frank, 117
Sloan, John, 90n85
Slocum, Lee Ann, 217n112; 219n175;
    254n198; 322n166
Smailes, Elizabeth, 519n74
Small, Albion, 182
Smallbone, Stephen, 125n93
Smallish, Lori, 172n120
Smart, Elizabeth, 487
Smeenk, Wilma, 323n183
Smeulers, Alette, 263; 284nn23, 24
Smit, Paul, 60n45
Smith, Anthony, 519n52
Smith, Barbara, 91n138
Smith, Brad, 62n107
Smith, Carolyn, 173nn151, 152; 250nn20,
    30; 251n80; 318n36; 520n147
Smith, Daniel, 88n12; 521n154
Smith, Donald, Jr., 438n94
Smith, Douglas, 61nn65, 74; 219n175;
    252n122; 254n195; 285n85
Smith, M. Dwayne, 61n63
Smith, Michael, 285nn73, 74
Smith, Oklahoma, 430
Smith, Philip, 216n71
Smith, Sharon, 369n187; 371n281
Smith, Timothy, 318n36
Smith, William, 125n87
Smolej, Mirka, 24n6; 88n26; 89n36
Snedker, Karen, 89n34
Snell, Tracy, 198n203
Snodgrass, G. Matthew, 128n182
Snook, Brent, 439n105
Snowden, Edward, 267; 373; 374; 526;
    546
Snyder, Thomas D., 89n51
Sobell, Janet L., 504
Socia, Kelly, 8; 217n94
Socrates, 182

Thomas, Kyle J., 10; 321nn125, 129
Thomas, Laila, 225
Thomas, Melvin, 63n123
Thomas, Stuart, 174n214
Thomas, Suzie Dod, 285n102
Thomas, W.I., 13; 182
Thomlinson, R. Paul, 90n93
Thompson, Carol, 478n74
Thompson, Kevin, 286nn112, 113
Thompson, Martie, 174n203
Thompson, Melissa, 102; 124nn30, 42, 45
Thornberry, Terence, 60n25; 62n98;
    63n145; 173n151; 250nn30, 44;
    251nn56, 80; 252n92; 254n195; 297;
    318n36; 319n61; 520n147
Thorne, Ian, 439n112
Thornton, Omar, 360; 361
Thrasher, Frederic, 180; 182
Thurman, Quint, 420; 437n42
Tibbetts, Stephen, 252n117; 321n110;
    322n179; 479n151
Tice, Peter, 319n39
Tierney, Kevin, 521n153
Tierney, Laura, 495
Tifft, Larry, 276; 286nn119, 120, 122
Tillyer, Marie Skubak, 73; 89nn41, 50, 62;
    90n78; 125n71
Timmendequas, Jesse, 85; 86
Timpson, Sandra, 519n71
Tita, George, 90n88; 364n2
Titchener, Edward, 157
Titterington, Victoria B., 89n54; 285n99;
    369nn200, 202; 370n204
Tittle, Charles, 61n65; 127n144; 215n34;
    219n211; 249n2; 250n48; 254nn194,
    201; 304; 321nn122, 129, 135
Tjaden, Patricia, 371n279
Tobias, J.J., 437nn5, 6
Tobias, Randall L., 489
Tobin, Kimberly, 125n89
Tobin, Michael, 171n85
Tobin, Terri, 116; 117
Tobler, Nancy, 323n193
Toby, Jackson, 285n70
Toch, Hans, 174n215
Todd, Petra, 62n101
Tomaskovic-Devey, Donald, 60n27
Tomasovic, Elizabeth, 365n26
Tombs, Steve, 478n98
Tompson, Lisa, 61n49
Tonry, Michael, 91n147; 124n15; 125n70;
    126n128; 169n25; 171n89; 173nn150,
    168, 169; 216nn60, 89, 90; 250n40;
    284n17; 285n71; 303; 318n9;
    370n211; 520n116
Topalli, Volkan, 236; 438nn53, 67
Towns-Miranda, Luz, 439n110
Tracy, Paul, 56–57; 61n84; 62n98;
    63nn146, 147; 128n178
Travis, Lawrence, 128n193
Trebach, Arnold, 520n133
Treiber, Kyle, 217n128
Trejo, Danny, 308
Tremblay, Pierre, 251nn75, 76

Tremblay, Richard, 63n148; 124n43;
    171n91; 295; 319nn53, 64
Treno, Andrew, 216n83
Trickett, Alan, 89n63
Triplett, Ruth, 217n108; 254n192
Tristan, Jennifer, 250n36
Tromovitch, Philip, 366n46
Truman, Jennifer, 60nn6, 42; 88n4;
    89nn49, 51; 437n2
Trumbetta, Susan, 367n97
Trump, Donald, 200
Tsarnaev, Dzhokhar, 2; 3; 396; 397
Tsarnaev, Tamerlan, 2; 3; 396; 397
Tseng, Li-Jung, 521n161
Tsvetkova, Bilyana, 479n134
Tuch, Steven, 62n115
Tunnell, Kenneth, 125n64; 230; 231;
    251n87; 252n91; 521n181
Turanovic, Jillian J., 89n44
Turic, Darko, 172n141
Turner, Alezandria, 174n213
Turner, Charles, 318n36
Turner, Heather, 88n12; 89nn53, 55
Turner, Michael, 90n80; 86; 127n149;
    172n143; 367n107; 371n283
Turner, Scott, 439n115
Turpin-Petrosino, Carolyn, 25n44
Tyler, Kimberly, 75; 90n82; 367n104;
    521n169
Tyler, Tom R., 479n152
Tzavaras, Nikos, 365n5
Tzoumakis, Stacy, 322n149

U

Uchida, Craig, 216n65
Uggen, Christopher, 102; 124nn30, 42, 45;
    286nn111, 115; 320n86; 523n237
Ullman, Harlan K., 489
Ullman, Sarah, 367n96
Ulman, Arina, 354; 370n235
Ulmer, Jeffrey T., 366n50; 437n24
Ulrich, Yvonne, 355
Umhau, John, 171n103
Unfold, Douglas, 439n111
Unger, Jennifer, 521n156
Unnever, James, 249n5; 285n60
Urban, Lynn, 176n269

V

Vaccaro, Donato, 521n162
Vaillant, George, 303
Valiente, Carlos, 172n139
Valier, Claire, 215n44
van de Rakt, Marieke, 250n16
van den Bergle, Pierre, 169n15
Van den Bree, Marianne, 172n141
van Den Haag, Ernest, 127n165
van den Oord, Edwin, 175n261
van der Geest, Victor, 322n163
van der Laan, Peter, 323n183
van der Staak, Cees, 169n37
van Dijk, Jan, 60n45
van Dijk, Mirjam, 368n135
van Dongen, Josanne D.M., 322nn157, 148

van Dusen, Katherine Teilmann, 63n138
van Geen, Alexander, 169n35
Van Gelder, Jean-Louis, 321n143
van Goozen, Stephanie, 170nn44, 61
van Gundy, Karen, 253n159; 365n38; 505;
    521nn175,; 177
Van Hasselt, Vincent, 371nn271, 273, 277
van Hoof, Anne, 174n221
Van Horn, M. Lee, 253n135
van Kammen, Wemoet, 251n54; 322n172
van Kesteren, John, 60n45
van Koppen, J., 356
van Koppen, Peter, 125n86
van Marle, Hjalmar J.C., 322n157;
    322nn157, 158
Van Schellen, Marieke, 320n88
Van Voorhis, Patricia, 253nn133, 136;
    287n150
van Wormer, Katherine, 365n9
Vander Ven, Thomas, 171n91; 253n147
VanDeusen, Karen, 520n112
Vanzile-Tamsen, Carol, 367nn88, 93
Varano, Sean, 215n32; 216n65
Vardi, Nathan, 555n65
Vargas, Elizabeth, 360
Vashista, Anish, 477n28
Vásquez, Bob Edward, 126n122
Vaughn, Michael, 172n143; 175bn237,
    249; 321nn126, 127
Vazsonyi, Alexander, 62n95; 320n102
Veach-White, Ernie, 174n204
Velez, Maria, 215n26; 217nn111, 113
Venables, Peter, 169n42; 172n138;
    175n223
Veneziano, Carol, 174n220
Veneziano, Louis, 174n220
Venkatesh, Sudhir Alladi, 116; 128n173;
    309; 322n145
Verhulst, Frank, 323n183
Verlur, D.E., 521n164
Vermeiren, Robert, 250n27; 323n180
Vermeule, Adrian, 121; 198n204
Veronen, Lois, 90n118
Veysey, Bonita, 174n212
Victor, Timothy, 25n43
Viding, Essi, 171n108; 175n250
Vieno, Alessio, 216n68
Villaume, Alfred, 286n128
Villemez, Wayne, 61n65
Vinkers, David, 174n204
Virkkunen, Matti, 170n50; 171n90
Visher, Christy, 365n29
Vitaro, Frank, 319n64
Vitter, David, 482; 489; 494
Vogel, Matt, 522n203
Volavka, Jan, 169n25; 170n65; 171n101;
    174n205
Vold, George, 261; 262
Von, Judith, 90n118
von Hentig, Hans, 9; 24n13; 89n71
von Hirsch, Andrew, 22; 121; 198nn205,
    206
Voronin, Yuri A., 479n132
Voss, Harwin, 62n96

Vossekuil, Bryan, 369n193
Vowell, Paul, 251n81
Vuchinich, S., 319n60
Vungkhanching, Martha, 521n159

W

Wade, Emily, 250n36
Wadsworth, Tim, 45
Wager, Laura, 250nn29, 31; 365n35
Wagner, Charles, 439n110
Wagner, H. Ryan, 174n211
Wahlberg, Mark, 412
Waite, Phillip, 323n192
Wakschlag, Lauren, 169n28
Waldo, Gordon, 127nn156, 170
Waldock, Katherine, 515; 520n145;
    523n241
Walker, Alice, 484
Walker, Jeffery T., 126n122
Walker, Richard, 554n30
Walker, Robert, 371n287
Wall, April, 555nn87, 89
Wallace, Danielle, 216n68
Wallace, Harry, 127n159
Wallace, John, 521n167
Wallace, Rodrick, 215n38
Wallace, William, 379
Wallerstedt, John, 128n194
Walsh, Anthony, 169n22; 170nn57, 60;
    218n165; 368n125
Walsh, Marilyn, 437nn7, 21, 25
Waltermaurer, Eve, 369n179
Walters, Glenn, 173n166; 175n226
Walters, Mikel, 371n281
Walton, Paul, 262; 284nn13, 54, 55
Walz, Liz, 286n117
Wang, Jichuan, 522n193
Wang, Morgan, 61n52
Wanson, Jeffrey, 174n211
Ward, Clifford, 369n162
Ward, David A., 124n19; 175n230;
    321n135
Ward, Tony, 175nn229, 236
Waring, Elin, 127n152; 128n183; 478n88
Warner, Barbara, 60n30; 215n21; 366n51
Warner, David, 89nn59, 60
Warner, John O., 169n41
Warr, Mark, 62n91; 251n58; 252nn88, 93,
    94; 300; 320nn92, 93; 367n92
Warren, Janet, 337; 367n97
Washington, Denzel, 412
Wasilchick, John, 124n33; 125n57
Wasserman, Gail, 169n35
Waterman, Alan, 407nn75–77
Watts, Stephen, 218n157
Weatherburn, Don, 90n109; 320n79;
    439n102
Weaver, John, 24n21
Weaver, Matthew, 376
Webb, Barry, 126n109
Webb, Nancy, 439n110
Weber, Eugen, 124n3
Webster, Cheryl Marie, 127n155
Webster, Daniel, 355

Webster, Pamela, 320n89
Wechsberg, Wendee, 493; 519n70
Weekes-Shackelford, Viviana, 369nn173,
    174
Weeks, Margaret, 519n84
Weerman, Frank, 124n38
Wei, Evelyn, 318n29; 522n202
Weihe, P., 169n31
Weiner, Anthony, 242; 482–483; 484
Weiner, Neil Alan, 518n35
Weingart, Saul, 522n220
Weis, Joseph, 175n256
Weisburd, David, 109; 126nn116, 125, 126;
    127n152; 128n183; 476n9; 478n88
Weiser, Benjamin, 438n80
Weisheit, Ralph, 520n132
Weiss, Alexander, 62n113
Weiss, P., 438n74
Weist, Mark, 368n143
Weitekamp, Elmar, 250n51; 322n176
Weitlauf, Julie, 519n82
Weitzer, Ronald, 62n115; 89n47; 332;
    366n61; 519n95
Welch, Michael, 127n158; 522n218
Welchans, Sarah, 25n35
Wells, Carrie, 367n113
Wells, L. Edward, 60n19
Wells, Nancy, 215n23
Wellsmith, Melanie, 90nn103, 114; 124n26
Welsh, Brandon C., 38; 60n37; 90n107;
    126nn120, 131; 166; 175n241
Welte, John, 521nn148, 182
Wenk, Ernst, 61n77
Wentworth, Jennifer, 368n151
Wermink, Hilde, 128n197
West, Donald J., 63n140; 173nn147, 148;
    250n18
West, Valerie, 285n67
Western, Bruce, 254n188
Westmoreland, Patricia, 144; 172n123
Whaley, Rachel Bridges, 368n132
Wharton, Tracy, 251n83
Whatley, Mark, 368n146
Wheeler, J.R., 172n121
Wheeler, Kristin, 495
Wheeler, Stanton, 478n88
Whipple, Diane, 343
Whitbeck, Les, 367n104; 521n169
Whitcomb, Debra, 91n131
White, Garland, 125nn72, 73
White, Helene Raskin, 319n39; 521n176;
    522n202, 204
White, Jennifer, 63n149
White, John, 522n191
White, Megan, 521n153
White, Michael, 127n148; 554n36
White, Norman, 253n138; 321n124
White, Rob, 284n27; 459; 476n3;
    478nn97, 102
Whitehall, George, 252n114
Whitehead, Ralph, 170n78
Whiteman, Martin, 319n38
Whitman, Charles, 349
Whitman, Terry, 370n206

Whitney, Stephen, 365n29
Whittinger, Naureen, 172n141
Whitworth, Keith, 478n74
Whyatt, Robin, 170n78
Whyte, Carrie, 439n113
Whyte, Laurence, 439n113
Whyte, William F., 38; 60n35
Wiatrowski, Michael, 253nn132, 158
Wickes, Rebecca, 62n105; 217n96
Widom, Cathy Spatz, 88n16; 89nn39, 40;
    331; 365n37
Wieczorek, William, 521n182
Wiederman, Michael, 88n18
Wiesner, Margit, 322n166
Wikstrom, Per-Olof H., 217n128; 322n178;
    323n182
Wilcox, Pamela, 89nn50, 62, 69; 90n78;
    125n71; 216n70; 323n186
Wilczak, Andrew, 89nn59, 60
Wild, Jack, 413
Wiley, Stephanie Ann, 244; 254n198
Wilkenson, Paul, 406n33
Wilkinson, Deanna, 522n223
Wilkinson, Richard, 218n148
Williams, Cathy, 169n27
Williams, Dominic P., 169n40
Williams, Kirk, 369n184
Williams, Linda, 88n19; 347; 370n232
Williams, Marian, 62n114
Williams, Mark, 175n223; 519n71
Williams, Stephanie, 250n24; 253n143
Williams, Wendol, 171n103
Williard, Jennifer, 518n4
Willis, Katie, 356; 357
Wills, Thomas Ashby, 521n162
Wilson, Anna Victoria, 369n182
Wilson, Bradley, 115
Wilson, Clyde, 555n67
Wilson, David, 285n62
Wilson, Edmund O., 135; 166; 169n18
Wilson, James Q., 60n32; 61nn81, 82; 99;
    122; 124n25; 124nn13, 14; 125n97;
    128n175; 138; 170n51; 219n212; 303;
    304; 316; 320nn104–106
Wilson, Margo, 89n75; 148; 173nn168,
    174–176; 216n73; 217n131; 370n226
Wilson, William Julius, 76; 90n100; 186;
    191; 217n120; 366n58
Wilt, Susan, 355; 369n179
Winehouse, Amy, 105
Winfree, L. Thomas, Jr., 251n77; 252n104
Wingood, Gina, 318n33
Winick, Charles, 519nn62, 65
Winslett, Andrea, 367n108
Wirth, Louis, 182; 215n13
Wish, Eric, 252n120
Wislar, Joseph S., 60n26
Wissow, Lawrence, 250n32; 365n33
Wittebrood, Karin, 89n61; 90n106
Wittrock, Stacy, 215n46
Wolak, Janis, 541; 554n53
Wolfe, Barbara, 144; 172n122
Wolfe, Scott, 321n124
Wolfendale, Jessica, 406n27

Braveheart (movie), 379
Breach (movie), 379
Breaking and entering, as Part I crime, 29
Bribery. *See* Influence peddling
Brothel (Albert), 496
Brothels, 492, 516
Brutalization stage, violentization process, 331
Bullying, 224
  See also Cyberbullying
Bureau of Justice Statistics, website, 28
Burglars, rational choice and, 105
Burglars on the Job (Wright and Decker), 433
Burglary, 17, 428–434
  burglar characteristics, 432–433
  burglary "career ladder," 433–434
  clearance rate, 30
  commercial burglary, 430, 432
  gender differences in, 431, 436
  "good burglars," 433, 436
  nature and extent of, 430
  as Part I crime, 29
  repeat burglary, 430
  residential burglaries, 430
  sexual burglary, 428–430, 436
Business, influence peddling in, 450
Business-related bribery, 450–451

C

Cab drivers, chiseling by, 447
Caballeros templarios (gang), 472
California
  crime discouragers, 109
  immigration and crime trends, 55
  medical marijuana statute, 21
  rape statute, 20
  sexual predator law, 19
California Personality Inventory (CPI), 163
Call girls, 492
Call houses, 493
Cambodia, 460, 470
Cambridge Five (spies), 380
Cambridge Study in Delinquent
    Development (CSDD), 146, 295
Canadian lottery (cybertheft), 536
Capable guardians, 76
Capital punishment
  constitutional limits on, 16
  crime rate and, 114–115
  cruel and unusual punishment, 16
  deterrence effect of, 114–115, 121
  DNA evidence and, 9
Capitalism, Patriarchy, and Crime
    (Messerschmidt), 274
Capitalist bourgeoisie, 260
Capitalist class, 260
Capitalist system
  essential feature of, 263
  Marx on, 260
Captain Phillips (movie), 467, 468
Captain Underpants (Pilkey), 485
Car cloning, 425
Carding, 535

Career criminals, 55–56
Caregiver stress view, of elder abuse, 72
Cargo thieves, 417–418
Carjacking, 356–357, 425
Cartographic school of criminology, 181
CASA. *See* National Center on Addiction
    and Substance Abuse
Casa Nostra (criminal group), 465
"Castle doctrine," 84
CATCH Program, 39
Catfishing (cybercrime), 544–545
Catholic Church, pedophilia, 488
CCTV. *See* Closed-circuit television
CD. *See* Conduct disorder
Celerity of punishment, 114
Central European Working Group, 471
Cerebral allergies, 140
CERT® Coordination Center (CERT/CC), 533
Certainty of punishment, 112–113
CFAA. *See* Computer Fraud and Abuse Act
Charity fraud, 538
Cheater theory, 148
Check fraud, 422
Check kiting, 422
Chemical restraints, 145
Chemical straitjackets, 145
Chemicals, biosocial theory and, 137–138
Chicago
  Chicago Area Project, 211–212
  concentric zones map, 189–190
  Gautreaux Assisted Housing Program, 193
  mob organizations, 466
  Project on Human Development in
      Chicago Neighborhoods, 332
Chicago Area Project, 211–212
Chicago School, 182, 188–189, 213
Chicken farming, 461–462
Child abuse, 224–225, 352–353
  causes of, 353, 363
  cycle of violence, 331
  helping victims, 81
  international trends, 42
  interview techniques for sexual abuse
      victims, 82
  statistics, 352–353
  victims by perpetrator
      relationship, 353
  violentization process, 331–332
Child molesters, rational choice and, 107
Child Online Protection Act, 438
Child pornography, 497, 499
Child Pornography Prevention Act (1996), 548
Child pornography scareware, 538
Child poverty, 183–184
Child prostitution, 494–495
Child Protection Act (1990), 83
Child Sexual Abuse Prevention Act, 491
Child-to-parent violence, 354
Children
  child pornography, 497, 499
  child prostitution, 494–495

continuity of crime, 57
crimes against, international trends, 42
"crusted over," 332
cyberbullying, 542–544, 546
delinquency, age of onset, 295–296, 310, 316
fire starters, 434–435
gender and cognitive differences, 50
illegally obtained prescription drugs, 532, 552
labeling, 242–244
murder of, 344
pedophilia, 487–488, 541
poverty of, 183–184
socialization of, 50
testimony by, 81
victimization in childhood, 67
as witnesses, 81
youthful offenders and chronicity, 35, 57, 310
  See also Child abuse
China
  cyber attacks by, 550
  dumping, illegal, 462
  globalization of, 265
  Uyghur separatists, 390–391
Chinese gangs, 470
Chiseling, 447–448, 475
Chivalry hypothesis, 49
Chlorpyrifos, 140
Chronic offenders, 35, 55–56, 163, 310
CIA. *See* U.S. Central Intelligence Agency
Circuit travelers, 493, 516
Citadel malware, 539
CITES. *See* Convention on International
    Trade in Endangered Species of Wild
    Fauna and Flora
Citizen groups, to control green crime, 464–465
Civil law, 15, 23
Civil rights, USA Patriot Act, 403
Clarissa (Richardson), 334
Class. *See* Social class
Classical criminology, 97–98
Clean Water Act (1972), 464
Clearance rate, 30
Cleared crimes, 30
Client fraud, 451–455, 475
Climate, crime patterns and, 43
Cloning (car cloning), 425
Closed account fraud, 422
Closed-circuit television (CCTV), for crime
    prevention, 110
Closure, 422
"Co-offending" hypothesis, 48
Cocaine, 501, 532
Code of Hammurabi, 14
"Code of the streets," 207
Coercion hypothesis, terrorism, 391
Cognitive-behavioral therapy,
    drug use, 512
Cognitive deficits, 160
Cognitive processing, 158
Cognitive theory, 150, 156–160, 167

severity of punishment and, 113
speed (celerity) of punishment and, 114
General strain theory (GST), 200–203, 205
coping with, 203
elements of, 201
evaluating, 203
sources of strain, 202
A General Theory of Crime (Gottfredson and
Hirschi), 307
General Theory of Crime (GTC), 304–309,
315, 317
analysis of, 307–309
crime rate variations and, 306–307
impulsivity and, 305–306
self-control, 305, 307
summary of, 306
Genetics
adoption studies, 147
biosocial theory and, 146–147, 149
crime and, 146–147, 167
evaluating genetic research, 147
psychopathic personality and, 163, 167
sibling effects, 146
of substance abuse, 503
twin studies, 146–147
Genital mutilation, 483–484
Gentrification, 193
The Ghetto (Wirth), 182
Global positioning system (GPS), vehicle
theft for, 425
Globalization
crime and, 266
critical criminologists and, 264–266, 282
defined, 264, 526
state-corporate crime, 268
Glucose metabolism, behavior and, 138
Godfather (movies), 465
The Gold Coast and the Slum (Zorbaugh),
182
Good burglar, 433, 436
Government
cyberspying by, 546–547
influence peddling in, 449
tax evasion, 454–455
GPS. *See* Global positioning system
Grand larceny, 419, 436
Greater Jihad, 379
Greed
enterprise crime and, 472–473
general deterrence and, 116
Green crime, 458–465, 475
citizen groups to control, 464–465
controlling, 464
defined, 459, 475
dumping, illegal, 462
fishing, illegal, 462
harms perspective, 459
logging, illegal, 460
polluting, illegal, 459, 462–463
wildlife exports, illegal, 460–462
Grokster case, 533
Group Against Smog and Pollution (GASP),
464

Group boycott, 456
GST. *See* General strain theory
GTC. *See* General Theory of Crime
Guardianship
criminality and, 101
victimization and, 77
Guerillas, terrorism compared, 385, 387,
405
Guilt
Middle Ages determination of, 14
in rape cases, 340
Guilty by Reason of Insanity (Lewis), 328
Gun availability, trends in crime and, 44,
46
Guns
for self-protection, 84
trends in crime and, 44

H

Hacking, 381, 526
Hallucinogens, 501
Hamas (terror group), 390
Hammurabi, Code of, 14
Handguns. *See* Guns
Harms perspective, 459
Harrison Narcotics Tax Act (1914), 508
Harry Potter (J. K. Rowling), 485
Hate, rational choice theory and, 107
Hate crimes, 107, 358–360, 364
controlling, 360
legal control of, 360
nature and extent of, 359–360
Hate Crimes (McDevitt and Levin), 358
Hazardous waste, illegal dumping, 462
Head injuries, behavior and, 144–145
Head Start programs, 246
Health care fraud, 451–453
Health Insurance Portability and
Accountability Act of 1996 (HIPAA),
453
Hedge fund fraud, 454
Heels, 421, 436
Heijin (gangsters), 470, 471
Heroin, 501, 507
Hezbollah (terror group), 390
"Hierarchy rule," 32
HIPAA. *See* Health Insurance Portability
and Accountability Act of 1996
Hirschi's social bond theory, 237–240, 245,
248
Hispanic Americans. *See* Race and ethnicity
Hitman scam, 538
HLFRD. *See* Holy Land Foundation for
Relief and Development
Holland, prostitution in, 496
Holy Land Foundation for Relief and
Development (HLFRD) (bogus
organization), 551
Homes
burglary of, 430
foreclosure rescue scams, 447, 454
Homicide
cultural retaliatory homicide, 332

international trends, 42
nature of, 9
as Part I crime, 29
rational choice and, 106
See also Capital punishment; Murder
Homicide (Daly and Wilson), 148
Homosexual rape, 341
Hong Kong, triads (criminal societies),
471
Honor-based killings, 45
Honor killing, 347
Hookers, 492, 516
Hormones, behavior and, 138–139, 167
Hot spots of crime, 77
Human development
perceptions, shaping, 159
psychosexual stages, 151
Human instinct, violence and, 329
Human nature, crime and, 303–304
Human rights violations, 267–268
Human trafficking, 468, 470
Humanistic psychology, 157
Humiliation, crime deterrence and, 113
Hundred Years' War, 412
Husband-wife assault, 354
Hustlers, 492, 516
Hypoglycemia, behavior and, 138
Hypotheses, 8–9

I

ICAP theory. *See* Integrated cognitive
antisocial potential (ICAP) theory
Id, 150
Idaho Crime Victims Compensation
Program (ICVC), 80
Identity assumption, check fraud, 422
Identity crisis, 151–152
Identity theft, 20, 454, 534–537, 552
Identity Theft and Assumption Act (1998),
536–537, 547–548
Illegal domestic surveillance, 267, 374,
525, 546–547
Immigration, trends in crime and, 42, 44,
55
Impulsivity
General Theory of Crime, 305–306
of victims, 74
Incapacitation effect, 118–120, 123
Incarceration
crime rate and, 118–119
left realism and, 273
See also Prisons
Incivilities, 191
Index crimes, 28–29
India, 397
dumping, illegal, 462
Thugee cult, 387
Indirect association, neurological deficits,
141
Indirect heredity, 134
Individual strain, 197
Individual vulnerability model, 136
Industrial espionage, 380

Infanticide, 344
Inferiority complex, 151
Influence peddling, 449–451, 475
Informal sanctions, 113
Informal social control, 194
Information Assurance (IA) products, 551
Information processing, 157, 158–159
Information technology (IT), 526
    See also Cybercrime
Inheritance school, 135
Innovation, 198
Inside Man (movie), 412
Insider trading, 448
Instability, 161
Instinct, violence and, 329
Institutional anomie theory, 199–200, 205
Institutional social control, 194
Instrumental crimes, 46
Instrumental theory, 269, 282
Instrumental violence, 328
Insurgents
    defined, 385
    terrorism compared, 385–386, 387, 405
Integrated cognitive antisocial potential
    (ICAP) theory, 304, 315
Integrated theories, 296
Intellectual development theory, 157–158
Intellectual property, cybertheft, 533, 552
Intelligence, crime and, 164–165, 167
Intelligence quotient (IQ), 164
Intelligence Reform and Terrorism
    Prevention Act (2004), 403
Intent. *See* Criminal intent
Intentional torts, 16
Interaction, social reaction theory, 241
Interactional theory, 297, 315
Interactionist view of crime, 13–14, 23
Interactive cause, neurological deficits, 141
Interagency Telemarketing and Internet
    Fraud Working Group, 438
Internal Macedonian Revolutionary
    Organization, 388
Internal Revenue Service (IRS), 547
International crime trends, 41–42
International treaties, cybercrime, 548
Internet, 526
    ehooking, 490, 492–493
    porn sites, 483, 531–532, 551
    sex trade and, 491
    terrorist recruitment and fund raising
        using, 550–551
    website defacement, 540–541
    See also Cybercrime
Internet False Identification Prevention Act
    (2000), 548
Internet fraud, economic stimulus scam,
    538
Internet Fraud Complaint Center, 548
Internet pharmacies, 532
Internet pornography, 483, 531–532, 552
Internet predators, 541
Internet securities fraud, 534
Interpersonal violence, 327–364
    assault and battery, 351–355

causes of, 328–333
emerging forms of, 358–363
hate crimes, 107, 358–360, 364
murder, 17, 343–351
rape, 333–342, 363
robbery, 355–358, 363
stalking, 19, 362–363, 364
workplace violence, 360–362, 364
    See also Assault
Interpretation, social reaction theory, 241
Interstate and Foreign Travel or
    Transportation in Aid of Racketeering
    Enterprises Act, 471
Interview research, 37–38
Interview techniques, for child victims of
    sexual abuse, 82
Intimate partner murder, 345
Intimate partner violence (IPV), 67–68, 71
Intimidation
    in election fraud, 376
    political crime for, 375
Introverts, 161
Investment swindles, 445
Involuntary manslaughter, 344
Involvement, crime and, 238, 239
IQ. *See* Intelligence quotient
Iran, 386, 397, 399, 490, 515
Iraq, 386, 401, 550
Iraq War, 268
ISIS (Islamic State in Iraq and Syria), 386
Israel, cyber attacks by, 550
IT. *See* Information technology
The Italian Job (movie), 412

J
Jacob Wetterling Act (1994), 19
Jao Pho (crime group), 471
Japan, Yakuza (criminal group), 471
Jemaah Islamiyah (terrorist organization),
    389
Jihadists, 378, 379, 395
Jim Crow laws, 273
Job advertisement scams, 536
"Johns," 495
Joint Terrorism Task Forces (JTTFs), 399
"Jonesing," 506
Joyriding, 424
Judicial rulings, 16, 23
Just desert policies, 121–122
Justice
    defined, 5
    effectiveness of, 279
    environmental justice, 459
    just desert, 12–122
    race and ethnicity and, 269–270
    restorative justice, 277, 280, 281–282
Justice for All Act (2004), 79
Justice policy, trends in crime and, 45
Justification defense, 19
Juvenile fire starters, 434–435

K
Kenya, 376, 392
Key loggers, 376

Kickbacks, 453
Kids Count (project), 184
Knights Templar (gang), 472
Ku Klux Klan, 360, 389

L
La Familia Michoacana cartel, 472
Labeling, 241
    dramatization of evil, 242–243
    effects of, 244
    negative labeling, 242
    retrospective reading, 242
    social reaction theory, 242–243
Labeling theory, 227, 228, 240–245, 248
    public policy implications of, 246
    summary of, 245
    validity of, 244–245
Lacey Act, 461
Lady Chatterley's Lover (Lawrence), 497
Larceny
    clearance rate, 30
    in common law, 15
    as Part I crime, 29
Larceny/fraud, con artists, 427
Larceny/theft, 418–428
    embezzlement, 428, 436, 451, 475
    grand larceny, 419, 436
    petty larceny, 17, 419, 436
    shoplifting, 105, 414, 419–422
    See also Fraud
The Last House on the Left (movie), 335
Late-onset escalators, 311
Latency, 151
Latent delinquency, 152
Latent trait, 301, 302, 318
Latent trait theories, 291, 292, 301–309,
    315, 316, 317
    aging out, 302–303
    control balance theory, 304, 315
    crime and human nature, 303–304
    differential coercion theory, 304, 315
    General Theory of Crime (GTC),
        304–309, 315, 317
    integrated cognitive antisocial potential
        (ICAP) theory, 304, 315
Latin American drug cartels, 470, 472
Latino Americans. *See* Race and ethnicity
Law, Order and Power (Chambliss and
    Seidman), 262
Law(s)
    categories of, 15–16, 23
    drugs and, 408
    effectiveness of, 9
    history of, 14–15
    morality and, 482–486, 516
    obscenity and pornography, 498–499
    rape, 340
    sociology of, 7, 11
    See also Civil law; Common Law;
        Criminal law
Lead ingestion, behavior and, 140–141, 167
Learning
    choosing crime, 103
    of criminal behavior, 229, 230

Multifactor/integrated theory, 291
Multiple murders, 346
Murder, 17, 343–351
  acquaintance murders, 74, 345, 363
  assault and battery, 17, 351–355
  clearance rate, 30
  degrees of murder, 343–346, 363
  homicide rate in U.S., 334
  mass murders, 349–351, 363
  as Part I crime, 29
  rational choice theory and, 106
  by relative or acquaintance, 74
  season and climate and, 43
  serial murder, 346, 348–349, 350, 363
  spree killers, 350–351, 363
  of strangers, 346, 363
  See also Capital punishment; Homicide
Music industry, file sharing case, 533
Muslim Order of the Assassins, 387
Myanmar, 472

N

NACP. *See* National Advocate Credentialing
    Program
Naive check forgers, 422
Naltrexone, 511
Narcissistic personality disorder, 339
Narcotic Control Act (1956), 508
National Advocate Credentialing Program
    (NACP), 68
National Center for Educational Statistics,
    70
National Center for Victims of Crime, 69
National Center on Addiction and
    Substance Abuse (CASA), 507
National Consortium for the Study of
    Terrorism and Responses to Terrorism
    (START), 397
National Counterterrorism Center (NCTC),
    399, 405
National Crime Victimization Survey
    (NCVS), 33–34, 58
  advantages and disadvantages, 34
  evaluation, 36
  methodology, 33–34
  results from, 41, 66, 69–70, 340
National Deviancy Conference (NDC), 262
National Incident-Based Reporting System
    (NIBRS), 32, 55
National Information Infrastructure
    Protection Act (NIIPA) (1996), 547
National Institute of Justice, 21
National Institute of Mental Health, 21
National Mental Health Association
    (NMHA), 154
National Organization for Victim
    Assistance, 68
National Science Foundation, 21
National Security Agency/Central Security
    Service (NSA/CSS), 551
National Stolen Property Act, 548
National Survey on Drug Use and Health
    (NSDUH), 501
Nationalist terrorism, 390–391, 393

Native Americans, sentencing circle,
    279–280
Native Mob (gang), 210
Nature vs. nurture, 164
Naxalone, 511
NCTC. *See* National Counterterrorism
    Center
NCVS. *See* National Crime Victimization
    Survey
NDC. *See* National Deviancy Conference
Necessity, 19
Need, general deterrence and, 116
Negative affective states, 201, 214
Negative labeling, 242
Negative reinforcement, 232
Neglect, 352, 353
Negligence, criminal intent and, 18
Negligent manslaughter, 344
Negligent torts, 16
Neighborhood hustlers, 417
Neighborhoods. *See* Community
Neocortex, 139
Netherlands, prostitution in, 496
Netherlands lottery (cybertheft), 536
Networks, 393
Neuroallergies, 140
Neurological impairment, measuring, 142
Neurophysiological conditions
  crime and, 141–145, 149
  psychopathic personality, 163, 167
Neurophysiology, 141
Neurotransmitters, 145
Neutralization, techniques of, 233–234
Neutralization theory, 233–235, 236, 245,
    420, 473
The New Criminology (Taylor, Walton, and
    Young), 262
New Jersey Victims of Crime Compensation
    Office, 80
*The New Jim Crow: Mass Incarceration in the
    Age of Colorblindness* (Alexander), 273
The New Synthesis (Wilson), 166
New York City
  Counterterrorism Bureau, 400–401
  police corruption in, 450
New York-New Jersey Electronic Crimes
    Task Force (NYECTF), 548
Newton massacre, 346
NIBRS. *See* National Incident-Based
    Reporting System
Nigeria, 37, 462
Boko Haram (terrorist group), 336, 391,
    395, 397
Nigerian letter scam, 536
NIIPA. *See* National Information
    Infrastructure Protection Act
9/11 attacks, 400
9/11 Commission, 398, 399
NMHA. *See* National Mental Health
    Association
"No frills" prisons, 121
Nominee loans, 454
Nonnegligent manslaughter
  clearance rate, 30

defined, 343–344
  as Part I crime, 29
North Korea
  denial-of-service attacks by, 532–533
  nuclear capability of, 399
NSA/CSS. *See* National Security Agency/
    Central Security Service
Nuclear Terrorism (Allison), 399
Nurture vs. nature, 164

O

Obitiatry, 19
Obscenity
  defined, 497, 516
  illegal Internet distribution, 530–531,
    552
  laws, 498–499
  sociology of law and, 7
  See also Pornography
Observational and interview research,
    37–38
Obsessive-compulsive disorder (OCD), 68
Occasional criminals, 414, 435
Occasional fences, 417
Occasional thieves, 414
Occupational Safety and Health
    Administration (OSHA), 456
Ocean's Eleven/Twelve/Thirteen (movies),
    412
ODD. *See* Oppositional defiant disorder
Oedipus complex, 151
Offender-specific crime, 101
Offenders
  adolescent-limited offenders, 312–313
  life course persisters, 312–313
  psychodynamic model of, 152
  reconciliation, 83, 279, 280–281
  Victim Offender Reconciliation Program
    (VORP), 83, 281
Offense-specific crime, 101
Office for Victims of Crime (OVC), 75
Office of Homeland Security & Emergency
    Management (OHSEM), 400
Office on National Drug Control Policy
    (ONDCP), 6
Oil Pollution Act (1990), 464
Oil spills, 462–463
Oklahoma City bombing, 18, 389
Omnibus Victim and Witness Protection
    Act, 79
On Aggression (Lorenz), 329
Online gambling casinos, denial-of-service
    attacks on, 533
Operation Phish Phry, 537
Operation Weed and Seed, 212
Opiates, 500
Opioids, 532
Opium, 501
Oppositional defiant disorder (ODD), 153
Oral stage, 151
Organ trafficking, 468
Organic solidarity, 196, 197
Organizational crime. *See* Corporate crime
Organized crime, 465–472

defined, 99
drug dealers and dealing, 102–103, 105
drug use and, 102, 103
excitement and thrills and, 102
general deterrence, 111–116, 120, 123
hate and, 107
history of, 96–99, 122
homicide and, 106
just desert policies, 121–122
on offense and offender, 100–101
public policy implications of, 121–122
rape and, 107
robbery and, 104, 106
sex offenders and, 107
situational deterrence, 107–111, 120, 123
substance abuse and, 504
target of crimes, choosing, 104
theft and, 104–105
time and place of crime, choosing, 104
type of crime, choosing, 104
violence and, 105–106
Rationality, general deterrence and, 116
Reaction formation, 209
Reactive aggression, 143
Reactive hate crimes, 358
Reality principle, 151
Reasoning criminals, 100
Rebellion, 198
Recidivism, 56–57
See also Chronic offenders
Reciprocal altruism, 136
Recklessness, criminal intent and, 18
Reconciliation, 279, 280–281
Reconciliation programs, 83
Recording industry, file sharing case, 533
Red Wa (crime group), 471
Reflected appraisals, 242
Registering sex offenders. *See* Sex offender registration
Registration fraud, in election fraud, 376
Reign of Terror (France), 388
Reigns of Terror (Marchak), 397
Reintegrative shaming, 278–279
Relational aggression, 355
Relationship stress, 67–68
Relative deprivation, 54, 196
Religion, 226–227, 248
Religious fanaticism, terrorism and, 397
Religious swindles, 447
Repeat burglary, 430
Repeat victimization, 73, 87
Reporting practices, 31, 35
Research
  brain research, 143
  cohort research, 36–37
  on crime discouragers, 109
  crime typology, 9, 11
  on criminal behavior systems, 9, 11
  on critical criminology, 269–270
  ethics of, 21–22
  experimental research, 37
  observational and interview research, 37–38

on personality, 162–163
relevant issues, 7
on social control theory, 238–239
on social reaction theory, 243
on terrorism, 9
Reshipping scheme, 535
Residential burglaries, 430
Respect, 207
Responsibility, neutralization and, 234
Restitution, 246
  criminal law providing, 17
  programs for, 83
Restoration
  criminal law providing, 17
  programs for, 279–280
  reintegrative shaming, 278
  restorative justice, 277, 280, 281–282
Restorative justice, 277, 280, 281–282
Restorative Justice (Sullivan and Tifft), 276
Restraint of trade, 455
Restrictive deterrence, 115
Retaliatory hate crimes, 359
Retreatism, 198
Retreatist gangs, 210
Retributive terrorism, 391–392, 393
Retrospective cohort study, 37
Retrospective reading, 242
Revenge, 17, 69
Revenge killers, 349
Reveton virus, 539
Revolution, political crime for, 375
Revolutionaries, terrorists compared, 386, 387, 405
Revolutionary Armed Forces of Colombia (FARC), 392
Revolutionary terrorists, 389, 393
Rich, crime and, 263
RICO Act. *See* Racketeer Influenced and Corrupt Organization Act
Right-wing political groups, 389
Ritualism, 198
Road rage, 352
Robbers
  planning by, 356–357
  types of, 357
Robbery, 355–358, 363
  of acquaintances, 357–358
  carjacking, 356–357
  clearance rate, 30
  commercial robbery, 356
  defined, 41
  gender of victim and, 71
  as Part I crime, 29
  planning of, 356–357
  rational choice theory and, 104, 106, 363–364
  season and climate and, 43
  statistics, 356
  types of robbery, 356
Rochester Youth Development Study (RYDS), 146
Role exit behaviors, 275
Roman Empire, spousal abuse in, 354
Romance fraud, 538

Routine activities, 77, 79, 103
Routine activities theory, of victimization, 76–77, 79, 103
Rushton's theory of race and evolution, 148
Russia, 399
Russian transnational crime groups, 469–470
RYDS. *See* Rochester Youth Development Study

S

Sadistic personality disorder, 161
Sadistic rape, 336, 337
Sadomasochism, 487
Safecracking, 413–414
Salami cyberfraud, 529
Same-sex marriage, 486
Sampling, 32
Sandy Hook school shooting, 16, 70, 131, 132, 136
Sarbanes-Oxley Act, 458
Saudi Arabia, 490
Scareware, 538
Schizophrenia, 153
School
  bullying in, 224
  dropping out, 225, 264
  failing schools, 264
  "track system," 225
  victimization and, 70, 110
  See also Education
School crime, 70
School failure rationale, 143
Schools
  cyberbullying , 542–544, 546
  murders in, 346
  restoration programs, 280
Sciari (group), 387
Scientific method, 4, 132, 133
Scream (movies), 362
SDM. *See* Social developments model
Season, crime patterns and, 43
Second Chance for Ex-Offenders Act (2011), 247
Second-degree murder, 343
Secondary deviance, 243
Secondary prevention programs, 165
Secret shopper scams, 538
Securities
  chiseling, 448
  hedge fund fraud, 454
Securities Act (1933), 534
Securities and Exchange Commission, 457–458
Securities fraud, online, 534
Securitization, 445
Security breaches
  against U.S. companies, 529
  See also Cybercrime
Sedition, 18
Seductions of Crime (Katz), 102
"Seeding," 212
Self-concept, crime and, 237
Self-control, General Theory of Crime, 305, 307

Self-control theory, 307
Self-defense, 19
Self-protection for victims, 84–85
Self-referrals, medical fraud, 453
Self-report surveys, 34–36, 41
Self-reporting, 35–36, 41
Self-stigma process, 242, 244
Sentencing circle, 279–280
Serial killers, 346, 348–349, 350–351
    choosing target, 106
Serial murder, 346, 348–349, 350, 363
Serial rape, 337
Serial rapists, 107
SES. *See* Socioeconomic structure
"Severely disturbed" fire setter, 438
Severity of punishment, 113
Sex establishments, taxes on in Europe,
    490
Sex offender registration, 8, 19–20, 85, 110
Sex offenders, rational choice and, 107
Sex-related kidnappings, 486–487
Sex tourism, 490
Sex trade, 490, 491
"Sexting" scandal, 242
Sexual abuse, 353–354
    crime and, 331
    interview techniques for abused children,
        82
    prostitution and, 494
Sexual assault
    gender of victim and, 71
    by relative or acquaintance, 74
    repeat victimization, 73, 87
    self-defense during, 346
    stress following, 67
    victimization risk, 75
    See also Rape
Sexual burglary, 428–430, 436
Sexual equality view, of prostitution, 496
Sexual predator law, California, 19
Sexual predators, 486–489, 541–542
Sexual slavery, 469
Sexually based murder, 345
Sexually oriented contact burglary, 429
Sexually related offenses, 481, 482, 486–
    500, 516
    paraphilias, 487–489
    pedophilia, 487–488, 541
    prostitution, 489–496
    sex-related kidnappings, 486–487
    See also Pornography; Rape; Sexual abuse
Shadowcrew (identity theft ring), 534–535
Shame
    as crime deterrent, 113
    increasing, crime prevention with, 110
    reintegrative shaming, 278
Sherman Antitrust Act, 455–456
Shield laws, 342
Shi'ite Muslim Order of the Assassins, 387
Shoplifters, boosters, 105, 421, 436
Shoplifting, 105, 414, 419–422
    amateurs, 420, 436
    booster box, 420
    controlling, 421

extent of, 419–420
    merchant privilege laws, 421
    overzealous enforcement of, 421–422
    pilferers, 414, 420
    prevention strategies, 421
    professional shoplifters, 420–421, 436
    "proxy shoplifters," 420
    snitches, 420
    target hardening strategies, 84, 421
    target removal strategies, 421
Shoplisting, 537–539
Siblings
    behavior traits and, 146
    See also Twin studies
Sideswipe auto accident fraud, 428
Siege mentality, 192
Sign-in rosters (cybertheft), 536
Signals Intelligence (SIGINT) products, 551
Sildenafil, behavior and, 138
Silent second, white-collar crime, 454
Simultaneous killing, 349
Single-family homes, 223
Single photon emission computed
    tomography (SPECT), 142
Situational crime prevention, 107–111,
    120, 123
    costs and benefits, 110–111
    methods, 107–110
Situational inducements, 414
Skeezers, 493
Skilled thieves, 412
Skimmers, 530
Slag code, 540
SMART (Skills Mastery and Resistance
    Training) Teachers, 314
Smartness, as focal concern, 206
Smoking, biosocial theory and, 137
Smugglers, 413, 435, 506
Smuggling migrants, 468
Snitches, 420
Social adaptations, 198
Social and cultural change, trends in crime
    and, 45
Social bond
    defined, 237
    elements of, 237–238
Social bond theory, 237–240
Social bonds, crime and, 240
Social capital, 299
Social class, trends in crime and, 44–47, 58
Social conflict, 258, 282
Social conflict theory, branches of, 259
Social control, 11, 188
    anomie and, 197
    informal social control, 194
    institutional social control, 194
    public social control, 194–195
    reintegrative shaming, 278
Social control theory, 17, 227, 228, 235,
    237–240, 248
    Hirschi's social bond theory, 237–240,
        245, 248
    opposing views, 239–240
    public policies and, 246

research on, 238–239
    self-concept and crime, 237
    summary of, 245
Social developments model (SDM), 297, 315
Social disorganization theory, 187,
    188–190, 213
    concentric zones, 189–190, 195
    elements of, 188
    foundations of, 188–189
    transitional neighborhoods, 189
Social ecology, of victims and victimization,
    69–70, 86
Social ecology school, 190–195, 213
    chronic unemployment, 191
    collective efficacy, 193–195
    community change and, 193
    community deterioration, 191
    community fear, 191
    poverty concentration, 191
Social exchange view, of elder abuse, 72
Social forces, 7
Social harm, 12, 459, 482, 484
Social interaction, violence and, 329
Social learning theory, 8, 155–156, 227,
    228, 229–235, 248
    differential association theory, 229,
        230–231, 245
    differential reinforcement theory,
        232–233, 245
    neutralization theory, 233–235, 236,
        245, 420, 473
    substance abuse and, 503
    summary of, 245
    Sutherland on, 229
    validity of, 235
Social learning view, of elder abuse, 72
Social media, 526
Social order, criminal law and, 17
Social positivism, 181
Social process theories, 222, 227, 228, 290
    evaluating, 245–246
    labeling theory, 227, 228, 240–245
    public policy implications, 246
    social control theory, 17, 227, 228, 235,
        237–240, 245, 248
    social learning theory, 8, 155–156, 227,
        228, 229–235, 245, 248
    social reaction theory, 227, 228,
        240–245, 248
    summary of, 245
Social reaction theory, 227, 228, 240–245,
    248
    research on, 243
    summary of, 245
    validity of, 244–245
The Social Reality of Crime (Quinney), 262
Social status, victimization and, 71–72
Social structure theories, 185–213
    cultural deviance theories, 188,
        205–211, 214
    evaluating, 210–211
    public policy implications of, 211–212
    social disorganization theory, 187,
        188–190, 213

Timeline of Criminological Theories

ORIGIN — Classical Theory
- Beccaria — *On Crimes and Punishment* (1764)
- Kant — *Philosophy of Law* (1887)
- Brockway — *The American Reformatory* (1910)
- Mabbott — *Punishment* (1939)

CONTEMPORARY THEORY — (Rational) Choice Theory (p.101)
- Bentham — *Moral Calculus* (1789)
- Bentham — *The Rationale of Punishment* (1830)

ORIGIN — Positivist Theory
- Gall — *Cranioscopy/Phrenology* (1800)
- Lombroso — *Criminal Man* (1863)
- Garofalo — *Criminology* (1885)
- Kretschmer — *Physique and Character* (1921)
- Hooton — *American Criminal* (1939)

CONTEMPORARY THEORY — Biosocial Theory (p.144)
- Dugdale — *The Jukes* (1877)
- Ferri — *Criminal Sociology* (1884)
- Goring — *The English Convict* (1913)

ORIGIN — Positivist Theory
- Maudsley — *Pathology of Mind* (1867)
- Tarde — *Penal Philosophy* (1912)
- Freud — *General Introduction to Psychoanalysis* (1920)

CONTEMPORARY THEORY — Psychological Trait Theory (p.150)
- Pinel — *Treatise on Insanity* (1800)
- Healy — *The Individual Delinquent* (1915)

ORIGIN — Marxist Theory
- Marx — *Communist Manifesto* (1848)
- Bonger — *Criminality and Economic Conditions* (1916)
- Rusche & Kircheimer — *Punishment and Social Structure* (1939)

CONTEMPORARY THEORY — Critical Criminology (p.258)

ORIGIN — Sociological Theory
- Quetelet — *The Propensity of Crime* (1831)
- Durkheim — *The Division of Labor in Society* (1893)
- Park, Burgess, & McKenzie — *The City* (1925)
- Merton — *Social Structure and Anomi* (1938)

CONTEMPORARY THEORY — Social Structure Theory (p.211)
- Shaw et al. (1925) *Delinquency Areas*
- Thrasher — *The Gang* (1926)
- Sellin — *Culture, Conflict and Crime* (1938)

ORIGIN — Sociological Theory
- Mead — *The Psychology of Punitive Justice* (1917)
- Sutherland — *Principles of Criminology* (1939)

CONTEMPORARY THEORY — Socialization Theory (p.229)
- Sutherland — *Criminology* (1924)
- Sutherland — *The Professional Thief* (1937)

ORIGIN — Multifactor/Integrated Theory
- Glueck & Glueck — *500 Criminal Careers* (1930)

CONTEMPORARY THEORY — Life Course Theory (p.293)

ORIGIN — Multifactor/Integrated Theory

CONTEMPORARY THEORY — Latent Trait Theory (p.301)

Timeline axis: 1775 · 1800 · 1825 · 1850 · 1875 · 1900 · 1925 · 1939

Andenaes
General Preventive Effects of Punishment (1966)

Martinson
What Works (1974)

Cohen & Felson
Routine Activities (1979)

Clarke
Situational Crime Prevention (1992)

Packer
The Limits of Criminal Sanction (1968)

Newman
Defensible Space (1973)

J. Q. Wilson
Thinking About Crime (1975)

Katz
Seductions of Crime (1988)

Montagu
Man and Aggression (1968)

Jeffery
Crime Prevention (1971)

E. O. Wilson
Sociobiology (1975)

Mednick & Volavka
Biology and Crime (1980)

Rowe
The Limits of Family Influence (1995)

Harris
The Nurture Assumption (1

Sheldon
Varieties of Delinquent Youth (1949)

Dalton
The Premenstrual Syndrome (1971)

Ellis
Evolutionary Sociobiology (1989)

Friedlander
Psychoanalytic Approach to Delinquency (1947)

Eysenck
Crime and Personality (1964)

Bandura
Aggression (1973)

Hirschi & Hindelang
Intelligence and Delinquency (1977)

Henggeler
Delinquency in Adolescence (1989)

Moffitt
Neuropsychology of Crime (1992)

Wilson & Daly
Evolutionary Psychology (1997)

Murray & Herrnstein
The Bell Curve (1994)

Vold
Theoretical Criminology (1958)

Chambliss & Seidman
Law, Order and Power (1971)

Lea & Young
Left Realism (1984)

Hagan
Structural Criminology (1989)

Braithwaite
Crime, Shame, and Reintegration (1989)

Zehr & Mika
Fundamental Concepts Restorative Justice (1

Dahrendorf
Class and Class Conflict in Industrial Society (1959)

Taylor, Walton, & Young
The New Criminology (1973)

Daly & Chesney-Lind
Feminist Theory (1988)

Quinney & Pepinsky
Criminology as Peacemaking (1991)

Barak & Henry
An Integrative-Constitu. Theory of Crime (199

Cloward & Ohlin
Delinquency and Opportunity (1960)

Kornhauser
Social Sources of Delinquency (1978)

Wilson
The Truly Disadvantaged (1987)

Agnew
General Strain Theory (1992)

Courtwright
Violent Land (1996)

Anderson
Code of the Street (1999)

Lewis
The Culture of Poverty (1966)

Blau & Blau
The Cost of Inequality (1982)

Messner & Rosenfeld
Crime and the American Dream (1994)

LaFree
Losing Legitimacy (1998)

Lemert
Social Pathology (1951)

Hirschi
Causes of Delinquency (1969)

Schur
Labeling Deviant Behavior (1972)

Akers
Deviant Behavior (1977)

Kaplan
General Theory of Deviance (1992)

Akers
Social Learning and Social Structure (199

Becker
Outsiders (1963)

Heimer & Matsueda
Differential Social Control (1994)

Glueck & Glueck
Unraveling Juvenile Delinquency (1950)

West & Farrington
Delinquent Way of Life (1977)

Thornberry
Interactional Theory (1987)

Sampson & Laub
Crime in the Making (1993)

Loeber
Pathways to Delinquency (1998)

Weis
Social Development Theory (1981)

Moffitt
Adolescence-Limited and Life-Course Persistent Antisocial Behavior (1995)

Hathaway & Monachesi
Analyzing and Predicting Juvenile Delinquency with the MMPI (1953)

Wolfgang, Figlio, & Sellin
Delinquency in Birth Cohorts (1972)

Wilson & Herrnstein
Crime and Human Nature (1985)

Tittle
Control Balance: Toward a General Theory of Deviance (1995)

Eysenck
Crime and Personality (1964)

Gottfredson & Hirschi
General Theory of Crime (1990)

| 1947 | 1969 | 1975 | 1980 | 1991 | 1995 | 1997 | 1998 |